Formulas

1. *CPU time* = Instruction count × Clock cycles per instruction × Clock cycle time (page 32)

2. *Amdahl's Law:* $\text{Speedup}_{overall} = \dfrac{\text{Execution time}_{old}}{\text{Execution time}_{new}} = \dfrac{1}{(1 - \text{Fraction}_{enhanced}) + \dfrac{\text{Fraction}_{enhanced}}{\text{Speedup}_{enhanced}}}$ (page 30)

3. *Average memory-access time* = Hit time + Miss rate × Miss penalty (page 384)

4. *Means*—arithmetic (AM), weighted arithmetic (WAM), harmonic (HM), and weighted harmonic (WHM):

$$AM = \frac{1}{n} \sum_{i=1}^{n} \text{Time}_i \qquad WAM = \sum_{i=1}^{n} \text{Weight}_i \times \text{Time}_i \qquad HM = \frac{n}{\displaystyle\sum_{i=1}^{n} \frac{1}{\text{Rate}_i}} \qquad WHM = \frac{1}{\displaystyle\sum_{i=1}^{n} \frac{\text{Weight}_i}{\text{Rate}_i}}$$

where Time_i is the execution time for the *i*th program of a total of *n* in the workload, Weight_i is the weighting of the *i*th program in the workload, and Rate_i is a function of $1/\text{Time}_i$ (pages 25–26)

5. *Cost of integrated circuit* = $\dfrac{\text{Cost of die} + \text{Cost of testing die} + \text{Cost of packaging and final test}}{\text{Final test yield}}$ (page 10)

6. *Die yield* = $\text{Wafer yield} \times \left(1 + \dfrac{\text{Defects per unit area} \times \text{Die area}}{\alpha}\right)^{-\alpha}$

where Wafer yield accounts for wafers that are so bad they need not be tested and α corresponds to the number of masking levels critical to die yield (usually $\alpha = 3.0$, page 12)

7. *Speedup from pipelining* = $\dfrac{1}{1 + \text{Pipeline stall cycles per instruction}} \times \dfrac{\text{Clock cycle unpipelined}}{\text{Clock cycle pipelined}}$

$= \dfrac{1}{1 + \text{Pipeline stall cycles per instruction}} \times \text{Pipeline depth}$

where Pipeline stall cycles account for clock cycles lost due to pipeline hazards (page 141)

8. *Little's Law:* Mean number of tasks in system = Arrival rate × Mean response time assuming the system is in equilibrium (page 508)

Rules of Thumb

1. *Amdahl/Case Rule:* A balanced computer system needs about 1 MB of main memory capacity and 1 megabit per second of I/O bandwidth per MIPS of CPU performance.

2. *90/10 Locality Rule:* A program executes about 90% of its instructions in 10% of its code (page 38).

3. *DRAM-Growth Rule:* Density increases by about 60% per year, quadrupling in three years (page 7).

4. *Disk-Growth Rule:* Density increases by about 50% per year, quadrupling in just over three years (page 7).

5. *Address-Consumption Rule:* The memory needed by the average program grows by about a factor of 1.5 to 2 per year; thus, it consumes between 1/2 and 1 address bit per year (page 6).

6. *85/60 Branch-Taken Rule:* About 85% of backward-going branches are taken while about 60% of forward-going branches are taken (page 166).

7. *2:1 Cache Rule:* The miss rate of a direct-mapped cache of size *N* is about the same as a two-way set-associative cache of size *N*/2 (page 396).

Computer
Architecture
A
Quantitative
Approach

Second Edition

Computer Architecture
A
Quantitative Approach

Second Edition

David A. Patterson
UNIVERSITY OF CALIFORNIA AT BERKELEY

John L. Hennessy
STANFORD UNIVERSITY

With a Contribution by
David Goldberg
Xerox Palo Alto Research Center

MORGAN KAUFMANN PUBLISHERS, INC.
SAN FRANCISCO, CALIFORNIA

Sponsoring Editor Bruce M. Spatz
Production Manager Yonie Overton
Production Editor Julie Pabst
Text Design Gary Head, with second edition
     modifications by Ross Carron Design
Cover Art Direction David Lance Goines
Cover Design Ross Carron Design

Illustration Illustrious, Inc.
Copyeditors Ken DellaPenta, Gary Morris,
     Sharilyn Hovind, Jessie Wood
Proofreader Jeff Van Bueren
Composition Nancy Logan
Printer Courier Corporation

Morgan Kaufmann Publishers, Inc.
Editorial and Sales Office
340 Pine Street, Sixth Floor
San Francisco, CA 94104-3205 USA
Telephone: 415 / 392-2665, *Facsimile:* 415 / 982-2665, *Internet:* mkp@mkp.com
Order toll free: 800 / 745-7323

Published 1990. Second Edition 1996
Printed in the United States of America
03 02 01 00   10 9 8 7 6

ADVICE, PRAISE, & ERRORS: Any correspondence related to this publication or intended for the authors should be addressed to the Editorial and Sales Office of Morgan Kaufmann Publishers, Inc., Dept. P&H APE. Information regarding error sightings is encouraged. Any error sightings that are accepted for correction in subsequent printings will be rewarded by the authors with a payment of $1.00 (U.S.) per correction upon availability of the new printing. Electronic mail can be sent to arc2bugs@mkp.com. (Please include your full name and permanent mailing address.)

INSTRUCTOR SUPPORT: For information on classroom software and other instructor materials available to adopters, please contact the Editorial and Sales Office of Morgan Kaufmann Publishers, Inc. (415 / 392-2665) or visit our web site at http://www.mkp.com.

Library of Congress Cataloging-in-Publication Data
Patterson, David A.
     Computer architecture: a quantitative approach / David A. Patterson, John L. Hennessy; with a contribution by David Goldberg.
     —2nd ed.
         p. cm.
     Includes bibliographical references and index.
     ISBN 1-55860-329-8 (cloth). —ISBN 1-55860-372-7 (paper)
     1. Computer architecture. I. Hennessy, John L. II. Goldberg, David. III. Title.
     QA76.9.A73P377   1995
     004.2'2—dc20   95-37027
                                                           CIP

To Andrea, Linda, and our four sons

Foreword

by C. Gordon Bell

Once again, I am honored and delighted to write the foreword to what is now the second edition of this landmark book.

With this edition, which is actually a whole new book, my 1990 prediction that *Computer Architecture: A Quantitative Approach* would be the standard reference for computer systems analysis and design is reaffirmed. In the interim between editions, the authors wrote and published *Computer Organization and Design: The Hardware/Software Interface* to serve as the introductory foundation for this book.

In the two three-year generations of Moore's Law since the first edition of *Computer Architecture*, the number of transistors per chip has increased by a factor of 16 and circuit speed has more than quadrupled. Disk densities have increased at similar rates of 60% per year. However, main memory and disk access times have not improved at comparable rates. These order-of-magnitude changes in technology have initiated numerous changes in instruction set and system architecture, which have driven the revision of this text around the theme of increased parallelism.

Of course, many of the technological changes we are speaking of were spurred on by advances in hardware. Since the first edition, we have seen the need for a two- or three-level cache and memory hierarchy to match processing speeds; the adoption of hardwired, pipelined instruction level parallelism in architectures; the universal adoption of the shared bus multiprocessor, or "multi," to replace the use of many uniprocessors; a significant decrease in the use of vector processors; the use of parallel disks or redundant arrays of inexpensive disks (RAID)—previously covered in only two pages; and the prevalence of interconnected computers for performance and reliability.

In addition to these hardware-induced changes, the new text reflects a conceptual change: The notion of a unique computer architecture for size and class has been replaced by a comparison and description of various Alpha, MIPS, SPARC, PowerPC, and PA-RISC microprocessors that can be combined to scale a range of applications. Gone from this edition are the VAX and IBM 360 architectures, known as a minicomputer and mainframe, respectively. Instead, the Intel 80x86, or PC architecture, is described in its own appendix, because after all it is the reference architecture that all others compete with in PCs, workstations, various multiprocessors, and networks.

Thus, the material herein is required *understanding* for anyone working with architecture or hardware, including architects, chip and computer system engineers, and compiler and operating system engineers. It would prove beneficial to

3.10   Fallacies and Pitfalls   209
3.11   Concluding Remarks   211
3.12   Historical Perspective and References   212
       Exercises   214

4   **Advanced Pipelining and Instruction-Level Parallelism**

4.1   Instruction-Level Parallelism: Concepts and Challenges   221
4.2   Overcoming Data Hazards with Dynamic Scheduling   240
4.3   Reducing Branch Penalties with Dynamic Hardware Prediction   262
4.4   Taking Advantage of More ILP with Multiple Issue   278
4.5   Compiler Support for Exploiting ILP   289
4.6   Hardware Support for Extracting More Parallelism   299
4.7   Studies of ILP   318
4.8   Putting It All Together: The PowerPC 620   335
4.9   Fallacies and Pitfalls   349
4.10   Concluding Remarks   352
4.11   Historical Perspective and References   354
       Exercises   362

5   **Memory-Hierarchy Design**

5.1   Introduction   373
5.2   The ABCs of Caches   375
5.3   Reducing Cache Misses   390
5.4   Reducing Cache Miss Penalty   411
5.5   Reducing Hit Time   422
5.6   Main Memory   427
5.7   Virtual Memory   439
5.8   Protection and Examples of Virtual Memory   447
5.9   Crosscutting Issues in the Design of Memory Hierarchies   457
5.10   Putting It All Together: The Alpha AXP 21064 Memory Hierarchy   461
5.11   Fallacies and Pitfalls   466
5.12   Concluding Remarks   471
5.13   Historical Perspective and References   472
       Exercises   476

6   **Storage Systems**

6.1   Introduction   485
6.2   Types of Storage Devices   486
6.3   Buses—Connecting I/O Devices to CPU/Memory   496
6.4   I/O Performance Measures   504
6.5   Reliability, Availability, and RAID   521
6.6   Crosscutting Issues: Interfacing to an Operating System   525
6.7   Designing an I/O System   528
6.8   Putting It All Together: UNIX File System Performance   539
6.9   Fallacies and Pitfalls   548
6.10   Concluding Remarks   553
6.11   Historical Perspective and References   553
       Exercises   557

7   **Interconnection Networks**

7.1   Introduction   563
7.2   A Simple Network   565
7.3   Connecting the Interconnection Network to the Computer   573

7.4   Interconnection Network Media   576
7.5   Connecting More Than Two Computers   579
7.6   Practical Issues for Commercial Interconnection Networks   597
7.7   Examples of Interconnection Networks   601
7.8   Crosscutting Issues for Interconnection Networks   605
7.9   Internetworking   608
7.10   Putting It All Together: An ATM Network of Workstations   613
7.11   Fallacies and Pitfalls   622
7.12   Concluding Remarks   625
7.13   Historical Perspective and References   626
        Exercises   629

8 Multiprocessors

8.1   Introduction   635
8.2   Characteristics of Application Domains   647
8.3   Centralized Shared-Memory Architectures   654
8.4   Distributed Shared-Memory Architectures   677
8.5   Synchronization   694
8.6   Models of Memory Consistency   708
8.7   Crosscutting Issues   721
8.8   Putting It All Together: The SGI Challenge Multiprocessor   728
8.9   Fallacies and Pitfalls   734
8.10   Concluding Remarks   740
8.11   Historical Perspective and References   745
        Exercises   755

Appendix A: Computer Arithmetic

by DAVID GOLDBERG
Xerox Palo Alto Research Center

A.1   Introduction   A-1
A.2   Basic Techniques of Integer Arithmetic   A-2
A.3   Floating Point   A-13
A.4   Floating-Point Multiplication   A-17
A.5   Floating-Point Addition   A-22
A.6   Division and Remainder   A-28
A.7   More on Floating-Point Arithmetic   A-34
A.8   Speeding Up Integer Addition   A-38
A.9   Speeding Up Integer Multiplication and Division   A-46
A.10   Putting It All Together   A-61
A.11   Fallacies and Pitfalls   A-65
A.12   Historical Perspective and References   A-66
        Exercises   A-72

Appendix B: Vector Processors

B.1   Why Vector Processors?   B-1
B.2   Basic Vector Architecture   B-3
B.3   Two Real-World Issues: Vector Length and Stride   B-15
B.4   Effectiveness of Compiler Vectorization   B-22
B.5   Enhancing Vector Performance   B-23
B.6   Putting It All Together: Performance of Vector Processors   B-29
B.7   Fallacies and Pitfalls   B-35

B.8   Concluding Remarks   B-37
B.9   Historical Perspective and References   B-38
       Exercises   B-43

Appendix C: Survey of RISC Architectures

C.1   Introduction   C-1
C.2   Addressing Modes and Instruction Formats   C-3
C.3   Instructions: The DLX Subset   C-5
C.4   Instructions: Common Extensions to DLX   C-9
C.5   Instructions Unique to MIPS   C-13
C.6   Instructions Unique to SPARC   C-15
C.7   Instructions Unique to PowerPC   C-18
C.8   Instructions Unique to PA-RISC   C-19
C.9   Concluding Remarks   C-22
C.10   References   C-25

Appendix D: An Alternative to RISC: The Intel 80x86

D.1   Introduction   D-1
D.2   80x86 Registers and Data Addressing Modes   D-2
D.3   80x86 Integer Operations   D-6
D.4   80x86 Floating-Point Operations   D-9
D.5   80x86 Instruction Encoding   D-11
D.6   Putting It All Together: Measurements of Instruction Set Usage D-15
D.7   Concluding Remarks   D-22
D.8   Historical Perspective and References   D-23

Appendix E: Implementing Coherence Protocols

E.1   Implementation Issues for the Snooping Coherence Protocol   E-1
E.2   Implementation Issues in the Distributed Directory Protocol   E-6
       Exercises   E-12

References   R-1

Index   I-1

Preface

I started in 1962 to write a single book with this sequence of chapters, but soon found that it was more important to treat the subjects in depth rather than to skim over them lightly. The resulting length has meant that each chapter by itself contains enough to publish the series in separate volumes...

Donald Knuth, *The Art of Computer Programming,*
Preface to Volume 1 (of 7) (1968)

Why We Wrote This Book

This quote from Donald Knuth has never been truer, at least, not for us! Although this is officially the second edition of *Computer Architecture: A Quantitative Approach,* it is really our third book in a series that began with the first edition, continued with *Computer Organization and Design: The Hardware/Software Interface,* and brings us now to this book, one that we have largely written from scratch. Since a major goal of our efforts has been to present concepts in the context of the most recent machines, there was remarkably little from the first edition that could be preserved intact.

This said, we once again offer an enthusiastic welcome to anyone who came along with us the first time, as well as to those who are joining us now. Either way, we can promise the same quantitative approach to, and analysis of, real machines.

As with the first edition, our goal has been to describe the basic principles underlying what will be tomorrow's technological developments. For readers who are new to our series with this book, we hope to demonstrate what we stated about computer architecture in our preface to the first edition: It is not a dreary science of paper machines that will never work. No! It's a discipline of keen intellectual interest, requiring the balance of marketplace forces to cost/performance, leading to glorious failures and some notable successes.

Our primary objective in writing our first book was to change the way people learn and think about computer architecture. We feel this goal is still valid and important. The field is changing daily and must be studied with real examples and measurements on real machines, rather than simply as a collection of definitions and designs that will never need to be realized.

We have strived to produce a new edition that will continue to be as relevant for professional engineers and architects as it is for those involved in advanced computer architecture and design courses. As much as its predecessor, this edition aims to demystify computer architecture through an emphasis on cost/performance tradeoffs and good engineering design. We believe that the field has continued to mature and move toward the rigorous quantitative foundation of long-established scientific and engineering disciplines. Our greatest satisfaction derives from the fact that the principles described in our first edition in 1990 could be applied successfully to help predict the landscape of computing technology that exists today. We hope that our new book will allow readers to apply the fundamentals for similar results as we look forward to the coming decades.

This Edition

The second edition of *Computer Architecture: A Quantitative Approach* should have been easy to write. After all, our approach hasn't changed and we sought to continue our focus on the basic principles of computer design. Unfortunately for our task as authors, though the principles haven't changed, the examples that are relevant today and the conclusions that may be drawn have changed a great deal.

Consequently, we started with a careful evaluation of the first edition content from some very helpful readers who are gratefully acknowledged in the section that follows. We also thought carefully about what we would need to do to fulfill the book's original objectives, given the current state of computing. Being pragmatists, we started with a selective view of what would need to be revised, but there was no way to avoid the fact that everything needed to be reexamined. In the end we can offer you something that is virtually new.

We created fresh drafts, we condensed, we rewrote, we revised, and we eliminated less essential discussions. We enlarged the discussion of the topics we feel are the most exciting and valuable new ideas of computer engineering and science, and we reduced the coverage of other topics. In addition, we benefited from the help of another beta class-testing.

Despite these efforts or perhaps because of them, the second edition was actually harder to write than the first. We blame our workload on society's hunger for faster computers. The microprocessors being shipped today are the most sophisticated computers ever built, and feeding an expectation of doubled performance every 18 months has meant introducing new and extremely sophisticated implementation techniques.

Perhaps most important, we did not want to produce a new edition unless we were certain that it could meet the standard of contribution that we set for ourselves in our first book. In the final cut, the basic concepts and approach remain, but they are now viewed with the added perspective of several years of progress in the field.

Topic Selection and Organization

As before, we have taken a conservative approach to topic selection, for there are many more interesting ideas in the field than can reasonably be covered in a treatment of basic principles. We have steered away from a comprehensive survey of every architecture a reader might encounter. Instead, our presentation focuses on core concepts likely to be found in any new machine. The key criterion remains that of selecting ideas that have been examined and utilized successfully enough to permit their discussion in quantitative terms.

Again, our hope is that the design principles and quantitative data in this book will delimit discussions of architecture styles to terms like *faster* and *cheaper,* in contrast to previous debates.

Our first dilemma in determining the new topic selections was that topics requiring only a few pages in the first edition have since exploded in their importance. Secondly, topics that we excluded previously have matured to a point where they can be discussed based on our quantitative criteria and their success in the marketplace.

As a final filter, we evaluated the extent of introductory material necessary for this presentation independent of our decision making for the first edition. Again, our reviewers and readers were immensely helpful. To the extent that readers felt certain discussions were less necessary, we eliminated them in favor of new material. For example, many of our readers learned the basics of our approach in the first edition or from *Computer Organization and Design: The Hardware/Software Interface.*

Our intent has always been to focus on material that is not available in equivalent form from other sources, so we continue to emphasize advanced content wherever possible. With the availability at this writing of a complete introduction in *Computer Organization and Design,* the focus on advanced topics was somewhat easier to maintain than in our first book.

An Overview of the Content

In keeping with our focus on advanced topics, we consolidated the first five chapters of our earlier edition into two. The basic content of the first edition Chapters 1 (Fundamentals of Computer Design) and 2 (Performance and Cost) are introduced in the opening chapter, Fundamentals of Computer Design. These ideas work better together than they did in isolation.

The two chapters on instruction sets from the previous edition are now presented in our second chapter, Instruction Set Principles and Examples, and its companion piece, Appendix D, An Alternative to RISC: The Intel 80x86. We rewrote this material to show how program measurements led to the design of our generic RISC machine, DLX. Because of the dominance of the 80x86 design, we no longer cover the VAX or IBM 360 instruction sets. The 80x86 appendix represents increased coverage and can form the basis of a careful study of this architecture and other computers of its class.

This de-emphasis on the history of instruction sets follows the continuing evolution of the content of computer architecture courses. In the 1950s and 1960s, course content consisted primarily of computer arithmetic. In the 1970s and early 1980s, it was largely instruction set design. Today, it is largely high-performance processor implementation, memory hierarchy, input/output, and multiprocessors.

packaging, power, and cooling. Optimizing the design requires familiarity with a very wide range of technologies, from compilers and operating systems to logic design and packaging.

In the past, the term *computer architecture* often referred only to instruction set design. Other aspects of computer design were called *implementation,* often insinuating that implementation is uninteresting or less challenging. The authors believe this view is not only incorrect, but is even responsible for mistakes in the design of new instruction sets. The architect's or designer's job is much more than instruction set design, and the technical hurdles in the other aspects of the project are certainly as challenging as those encountered in doing instruction set design. This is particularly true at the present when the differences among instruction sets are small (see Appendix C).

In this book the term *instruction set architecture* refers to the actual programmer-visible instruction set. The instruction set architecture serves as the boundary between the software and hardware, and that topic is the focus of Chapter 2. The implementation of a machine has two components: organization and hardware. The term *organization* includes the high-level aspects of a computer's design, such as the memory system, the bus structure, and the internal CPU (central processing unit—where arithmetic, logic, branching, and data transfer are implemented) design. For example, two machines with the same instruction set architecture but different organizations are the SPARCstation-2 and SPARCstation-20. *Hardware* is used to refer to the specifics of a machine. This would include the detailed logic design and the packaging technology of the machine. Often a line of machines contains machines with identical instruction set architectures and nearly identical organizations, but they differ in the detailed hardware implementation. For example, two versions of the Silicon Graphics Indy differ in clock rate and in detailed cache structure. In this book the word *architecture* is intended to cover all three aspects of computer design—instruction set architecture, organization, and hardware.

Computer architects must design a computer to meet functional requirements as well as price and performance goals. Often, they also have to determine what the functional requirements are, and this can be a major task. The requirements may be specific features, inspired by the market. Application software often drives the choice of certain functional requirements by determining how the machine will be used. If a large body of software exists for a certain instruction set architecture, the architect may decide that a new machine should implement an existing instruction set. The presence of a large market for a particular class of applications might encourage the designers to incorporate requirements that would make the machine competitive in that market. Figure 1.2 summarizes some requirements that need to be considered in designing a new machine. Many of these requirements and features will be examined in depth in later chapters.

Once a set of functional requirements has been established, the architect must try to optimize the design. Which design choices are optimal depends, of course, on the choice of metrics. The most common metrics involve cost and perfor-

Functional requirements	Typical features required or supported
Application area	Target of computer
General purpose	Balanced performance for a range of tasks (Ch 2,3,4,5)
Scientific	High-performance floating point (App A,B)
Commercial	Support for COBOL (decimal arithmetic); support for databases and transaction processing (Ch 2,7)
Level of software compatibility	Determines amount of existing software for machine
At programming language	Most flexible for designer; need new compiler (Ch 2,8)
Object code or binary compatible	Instruction set architecture is completely defined—little flexibility—but no investment needed in software or porting programs
Operating system requirements	Necessary features to support chosen OS (Ch 5,7)
Size of address space	Very important feature (Ch 5); may limit applications
Memory management	Required for modern OS; may be paged or segmented (Ch 5)
Protection	Different OS and application needs: page vs. segment protection (Ch 5)
Standards	Certain standards may be required by marketplace
Floating point	Format and arithmetic: IEEE, DEC, IBM (App A)
I/O bus	For I/O devices: VME, SCSI, Fiberchannel (Ch 7)
Operating systems	UNIX, DOS, or vendor proprietary
Networks	Support required for different networks: Ethernet, ATM (Ch 6)
Programming languages	Languages (ANSI C, Fortran 77, ANSI COBOL) affect instruction set (Ch 2)

FIGURE 1.2   Summary of some of the most important functional requirements an architect faces. The left-hand column describes the class of requirement, while the right-hand column gives examples of specific features that might be needed. The right-hand column also contains references to chapters and appendices that deal with the specific issues.

mance. Given some application domain, the architect can try to quantify the performance of the machine by a set of programs that are chosen to represent that application domain. Other measurable requirements may be important in some markets; reliability and fault tolerance are often crucial in transaction processing environments. Throughout this text we will focus on optimizing machine cost/performance.

In choosing between two designs, one factor that an architect must consider is design complexity. Complex designs take longer to complete, prolonging time to market. This means a design that takes longer will need to have higher performance to be competitive. The architect must be constantly aware of the impact of his design choices on the design time for both hardware and software.

In addition to performance, cost is the other key parameter in optimizing cost/performance. In addition to cost, designers must be aware of important trends in both the implementation technology and the use of computers. Such trends not only impact future cost, but also determine the longevity of an architecture. The next two sections discuss technology and cost trends.

1.3 | Technology and Computer Usage Trends

If an instruction set architecture is to be successful, it must be designed to survive changes in hardware technology, software technology, and application characteristics. The designer must be especially aware of trends in computer usage and in computer technology. After all, a successful new instruction set architecture may last decades—the core of the IBM mainframe has been in use since 1964. An architect must plan for technology changes that can increase the lifetime of a successful machine.

Trends in Computer Usage

The design of a computer is fundamentally affected both by how it will be used and by the characteristics of the underlying implementation technology. Changes in usage or in implementation technology affect the computer design in different ways, from motivating changes in the instruction set to shifting the payoff from important techniques such as pipelining or caching.

Trends in software technology and how programs will use the machine have a long-term impact on the instruction set architecture. One of the most important software trends is the increasing amount of memory used by programs and their data. The amount of memory needed by the average program has grown by a factor of 1.5 to 2 per year! This translates to a consumption of address bits at a rate of approximately 1/2 bit to 1 bit per year. This rapid rate of growth is driven both by the needs of programs as well as by the improvements in DRAM technology that continually improve the cost per bit. Underestimating address-space growth is often the major reason why an instruction set architecture must be abandoned. (For further discussion, see Chapter 5 on memory hierarchy.)

Another important software trend in the past 20 years has been the replacement of assembly language by high-level languages. This trend has resulted in a larger role for compilers, forcing compiler writers and architects to work together closely to build a competitive machine. Compilers have become the primary interface between user and machine.

In addition to this interface role, compiler technology has steadily improved, taking on newer functions and increasing the efficiency with which a program can be run on a machine. This improvement in compiler technology has included traditional optimizations, which we discuss in Chapter 2, as well as transformations aimed at improving pipeline behavior (Chapters 3 and 4) and memory system behavior (Chapter 5). How to balance the responsibility for efficient execution in modern processors between the compiler and the hardware continues to be one of the hottest architecture debates of the 1990s. Improvements in compiler technology played a major role in making vector machines (Appendix B) successful. The development of compiler technology for parallel machines is likely to have a large impact in the future.

Trends in Implementation Technology

To plan for the evolution of a machine, the designer must be especially aware of rapidly occurring changes in implementation technology. Three implementation technologies, which change at a dramatic pace, are critical to modern implementations:

- *Integrated circuit logic technology*—Transistor density increases by about 50% per year, quadrupling in just over three years. Increases in die size are less predictable, ranging from 10% to 25% per year. The combined effect is a growth rate in transistor count on a chip of between 60% and 80% per year. Device speed increases nearly as fast; however, metal technology used for wiring does not improve, causing cycle times to improve at a slower rate. We discuss this further in the next section.

- *Semiconductor DRAM*—Density increases by just under 60% per year, quadrupling in three years. Cycle time has improved very slowly, decreasing by about one-third in 10 years. Bandwidth per chip increases as the latency decreases. In addition, changes to the DRAM interface have also improved the bandwidth; these are discussed in Chapter 5. In the past, DRAM (dynamic random-access memory) technology has improved faster than logic technology. This difference has occurred because of reductions in the number of transistors per DRAM cell and the creation of specialized technology for DRAMs. As the improvement from these sources diminishes, the density growth in logic technology and memory technology should become comparable.

- *Magnetic disk technology*—Recently, disk density has been improving by about 50% per year, almost quadrupling in three years. Prior to 1990, density increased by about 25% per year, doubling in three years. It appears that disk technology will continue the faster density growth rate for some time to come. Access time has improved by one-third in 10 years. This technology is central to Chapter 6.

These rapidly changing technologies impact the design of a microprocessor that may, with speed and technology enhancements, have a lifetime of five or more years. Even within the span of a single product cycle (two years of design and two years of production), key technologies, such as DRAM, change sufficiently that the designer must plan for these changes. Indeed, designers often design for the next technology, knowing that when a product begins shipping in volume that next technology may be the most cost-effective or may have performance advantages. Traditionally, cost has decreased very closely to the rate at which density increases.

These technology changes are not continuous but often occur in discrete steps. For example, DRAM sizes are always increased by factors of four because of the basic design structure. Thus, rather than doubling every 18 months, DRAM technology quadruples every three years. This stepwise change in technology leads to

Distribution of Cost in a System: An Example

To put the costs of silicon in perspective, Figure 1.6 shows the approximate cost breakdown for a color desktop machine in the late 1990s. While costs for units like DRAMs will surely drop over time from those in Figure 1.6, costs for units whose prices have already been cut, like displays and cabinets, will change very little. Furthermore, we can expect that future machines will have larger memories and disks, meaning that prices drop more slowly than the technology improvement.

The processor subsystem accounts for only 6% of the overall cost. Although in a mid-range or high-end design this number would be larger, the overall breakdown across major subsystems is likely to be similar.

System	Subsystem	Fraction of total
Cabinet	Sheet metal, plastic	1%
	Power supply, fans	2%
	Cables, nuts, bolts	1%
	Shipping box, manuals	0%
	Subtotal	**4%**
Processor board	Processor	6%
	DRAM (64 MB)	36%
	Video system	14%
	I/O system	3%
	Printed circuit board	1%
	Subtotal	**60%**
I/O devices	Keyboard and mouse	1%
	Monitor	22%
	Hard disk (1 GB)	7%
	DAT drive	6%
	Subtotal	**36%**

FIGURE 1.6   Estimated distribution of costs of the components in a low-end, late 1990s color desktop workstation assuming 100,000 units. Notice that the largest single item is memory! Costs for a high-end PC would be similar, except that the amount of memory might be 16–32 MB rather than 64 MB. This chart is based on data from Andy Bechtolsheim of Sun Microsystems, Inc. Touma [1993] discusses workstation costs and pricing.

Cost Versus Price—Why They Differ and By How Much

Costs of components may confine a designer's desires, but they are still far from representing what the customer must pay. But why should a computer architecture book contain pricing information? Cost goes through a number of changes before it becomes price, and the computer designer should understand how a design decision will affect the potential selling price. For example, changing cost by $1000 may change price by $3000 to $4000. Without understanding the relationship of cost to price the computer designer may not understand the impact on price of adding, deleting, or replacing components. The relationship between price and volume can increase the impact of changes in cost, especially at the low end of the market. Typically, fewer computers are sold as the price increases. Furthermore, as volume decreases, costs rise, leading to further increases in price. Thus, small changes in cost can have a larger than obvious impact. The relationship between cost and price is a complex one with entire books written on the subject. The purpose of this section is to give you a simple introduction to what factors determine price and typical ranges for these factors.

The categories that make up price can be shown either as a tax on cost or as a percentage of the price. We will look at the information both ways. These differences between price and cost also depend on where in the computer marketplace a company is selling. To show these differences, Figures 1.7 and 1.8 on page 16 show how the difference between cost of materials and list price is decomposed, with the price increasing from left to right as we add each type of overhead.

Direct costs refer to the costs directly related to making a product. These include labor costs, purchasing components, scrap (the leftover from yield), and warranty, which covers the costs of systems that fail at the customer's site during the warranty period. Direct cost typically adds 20% to 40% to component cost. Service or maintenance costs are not included because the customer typically pays those costs, although a warranty allowance may be included here or in gross margin, discussed next.

The next addition is called the *gross margin*, the company's overhead that cannot be billed directly to one product. This can be thought of as indirect cost. It includes the company's research and development (R&D), marketing, sales, manufacturing equipment maintenance, building rental, cost of financing, pretax profits, and taxes. When the component costs are added to the direct cost and gross margin, we reach the *average selling price*—ASP in the language of MBAs—the money that comes directly to the company for each product sold. The gross margin is typically 20% to 55% of the average selling price, depending on the uniqueness of the product. Manufacturers of low-end PCs generally have lower gross margins for several reasons. First, their R&D expenses are lower. Second, their cost of sales is lower, since they use indirect distribution (by mail, phone order, or retail store) rather than salespeople. Third, because their products are less unique, competition is more intense, thus forcing lower prices and often lower profits, which in turn lead to a lower gross margin.

List price and average selling price are not the same. One reason for this is that companies offer volume discounts, lowering the average selling price. Also, if the product is to be sold in retail stores, as personal computers are, stores want to keep 40% to 50% of the list price for themselves. Thus, depending on the distribution system, the average selling price is typically 50% to 75% of the list price.

1.5 | Measuring and Reporting Performance

When we say one computer is faster than another, what do we mean? The computer user may say a computer is faster when a program runs in less time, while the computer center manager may say a computer is faster when it completes more jobs in an hour. The computer user is interested in reducing *response time*—the time between the start and the completion of an event—also referred to as *execution time*. The manager of a large data processing center may be interested in increasing *throughput*—the total amount of work done in a given time.

In comparing design alternatives, we often want to relate the performance of two different machines, say X and Y. The phrase "X is faster than Y" is used here to mean that the response time or execution time is lower on X than on Y for the given task. In particular, "X is *n* times faster than Y" will mean

$$\frac{\text{Execution time}_Y}{\text{Execution time}_X} = n$$

Since execution time is the reciprocal of performance, the following relationship holds:

$$n = \frac{\text{Execution time}_Y}{\text{Execution time}_X} = \frac{\dfrac{1}{\text{Performance}_Y}}{\dfrac{1}{\text{Performance}_X}} = \frac{\text{Performance}_X}{\text{Performance}_Y}$$

The phrase "the throughput of X is 1.3 times higher than Y" signifies here that the number of tasks completed per unit time on machine X is 1.3 times the number completed on Y.

Because performance and execution time are reciprocals, increasing performance decreases execution time. To help avoid confusion between the terms *increasing* and *decreasing,* we usually say "improve performance" or "improve execution time" when we mean *increase* performance and *decrease* execution time.

Whether we are interested in throughput or response time, the key measurement is time: The computer that performs the same amount of work in the least time is the fastest. The difference is whether we measure one task (response time) or many tasks (throughput). Unfortunately, time is not always the metric quoted in comparing the performance of computers. A number of popular measures have been adopted in the quest for a easily understood, universal measure of computer performance, with the result that a few innocent terms have been shanghaied from their well-defined environment and forced into a service for which they were never intended. The authors' position is that the only consistent and reliable measure of performance is the execution time of real programs, and that all proposed alternatives to time as the metric or to real programs as the items measured have eventually led to misleading claims or even mistakes in computer design. The dangers of a few popular alternatives are shown in *Fallacies and Pitfalls*, section 1.8.

Measuring Performance

Even execution time can be defined in different ways depending on what we count. The most straightforward definition of time is called *wall-clock time*, *response time*, or *elapsed time*, which is the latency to complete a task, including disk accesses, memory accesses, input/output activities, operating system over-head—everything. With multiprogramming the CPU works on another program while waiting for I/O and may not necessarily minimize the elapsed time of one program. Hence we need a term to take this activity into account. *CPU time* recognizes this distinction and means the time the CPU is computing, *not* including the time waiting for I/O or running other programs. (Clearly the response time seen by the user is the elapsed time of the program, not the CPU time.) CPU time can be further divided into the CPU time spent in the program, called *user CPU time*, and the CPU time spent in the operating system performing tasks requested by the program, called *system CPU time*.

These distinctions are reflected in the UNIX time command, which returns four measurements when applied to an executing program:

90.7u 12.9s 2:39 65%

User CPU time is 90.7 seconds, system CPU time is 12.9 seconds, elapsed time is 2 minutes and 39 seconds (159 seconds), and the percentage of elapsed time that is CPU time is (90.7 + 12.9)/159 or 65%. More than a third of the elapsed time in this example was spent waiting for I/O or running other programs or both. Many measurements ignore system CPU time because of the inaccuracy of operating systems' self-measurement (the above inaccurate measurement came from UNIX) and the inequity of including system CPU time when comparing performance between machines with differing system codes. On the other hand, system code on some machines is user code on others, and no program runs without some operating system running on the hardware, so a case can be made for using the sum of user CPU time and system CPU time.

In the present discussion, a distinction is maintained between performance based on elapsed time and that based on CPU time. The term *system performance* is used to refer to elapsed time on an *unloaded* system, while *CPU performance* refers to *user* CPU time on an unloaded system. We will concentrate on CPU performance in this chapter.

Choosing Programs to Evaluate Performance

Dhrystone does not use floating point. Typical programs don't ...

Rick Richardson, *Clarification of Dhrystone* (1988)

This program is the result of extensive research to determine the instruction mix of a typical Fortran program. The results of this program on different machines should give a good indication of which machine performs better under a typical load of Fortran programs. The statements are purposely arranged to defeat optimizations by the compiler.

H. J. Curnow and B. A. Wichmann [1976], Comments in the Whetstone Benchmark

A computer user who runs the same programs day in and day out would be the perfect candidate to evaluate a new computer. To evaluate a new system the user would simply compare the execution time of her *workload*—the mixture of programs and operating system commands that users run on a machine. Few are in this happy situation, however. Most must rely on other methods to evaluate machines and often other evaluators, hoping that these methods will predict performance for their usage of the new machine. There are four levels of programs used in such circumstances, listed below in decreasing order of accuracy of prediction.

1. *Real programs*—While the buyer may not know what fraction of time is spent on these programs, she knows that some users will run them to solve real problems. Examples are compilers for C, text-processing software like TeX, and CAD tools like Spice. Real programs have input, output, and options that a user can select when running the program.

2. *Kernels*—Several attempts have been made to extract small, key pieces from real programs and use them to evaluate performance. Livermore Loops and Linpack are the best known examples. Unlike real programs, no user would run kernel programs, for they exist solely to evaluate performance. Kernels are best used to isolate performance of individual features of a machine to explain the reasons for differences in performance of real programs.

3. *Toy benchmarks*—Toy benchmarks are typically between 10 and 100 lines of code and produce a result the user already knows before running the toy program. Programs like Sieve of Eratosthenes, Puzzle, and Quicksort are popular because they are small, easy to type, and run on almost any computer. The best use of such programs is beginning programming assignments.

4. *Synthetic benchmarks*—Similar in philosophy to kernels, synthetic benchmarks try to match the average frequency of operations and operands of a large set of programs. Whetstone and Dhrystone are the most popular synthetic benchmarks.

A description of these benchmarks and some of their flaws appears in section 1.8 on page 44. No user runs synthetic benchmarks, because they don't compute anything a user could want. Synthetic benchmarks are, in fact, even further removed from reality because kernel code is extracted from real programs, while synthetic code is created artificially to match an average execution profile. Synthetic benchmarks are not even *pieces* of real programs, while kernels might be.

Because computer companies thrive or go bust depending on price/performance of their products relative to others in the marketplace, tremendous resources are available to improve performance of programs widely used in evaluating machines. Such pressures can skew hardware and software engineering efforts to add optimizations that improve performance of synthetic programs, toy programs, kernels, and even real programs. The advantage of the last of these is that adding such optimizations is more difficult in real programs, though not impossible. This fact has caused some benchmark providers to specify the rules under which compilers must operate, as we will see shortly.

Benchmark Suites

Recently, it has become popular to put together collections of benchmarks to try to measure the performance of processors with a variety of applications. Of course, such suites are only as good as the constituent individual benchmarks. Nonetheless, a key advantage of such suites is that the weakness of any one benchmark is lessened by the presence of the other benchmarks. This is especially true if the methods used for summarizing the performance of the benchmark suite reflect the time to run the entire suite, as opposed to rewarding performance increases on programs that may be defeated by targeted optimizations. In the remainder of this section, we discuss the strengths and weaknesses of different methods for summarizing performance.

Benchmark suites are made of collections of programs, some of which may be kernels, but many of which are typically real programs. Figure 1.9 describes the programs in the popular SPEC92 benchmark suite used to characterize performance in the workstation and server markets. The programs in SPEC92 vary from collections of kernels (nasa7) to small, program fragments (tomcatv, ora, alvinn, swm256) to applications of varying size (spice2g6, gcc, compress). We will see data on many of these programs throughout this text. In the next subsection, we show how a SPEC92 report describes the machine, compiler, and OS configuration, while in section 1.8 we describe some of the pitfalls that have occurred in attempting to develop the benchmark suite and to prevent the benchmark circumvention that makes the results not useful for comparing performance among machines.

Benchmark	Source	Lines of code	Description
espresso	C	13,500	Minimizes Boolean functions.
li	C	7,413	A lisp interpreter written in C that solves the 8-queens problem.
eqntott	C	3,376	Translates a Boolean equation into a truth table.
compress	C	1,503	Performs data compression on a 1-MB file using Lempel-Ziv coding.
sc	C	8,116	Performs computations within a UNIX spreadsheet.
gcc	C	83,589	Consists of the GNU C compiler converting preprocessed files into optimized Sun-3 machine code.
spice2g6	FORTRAN	18,476	Circuit simulation package that simulates a small circuit.
doduc	FORTRAN	5,334	A Monte Carlo simulation of a nuclear reactor component.
mdljdp2	FORTRAN	4,458	A chemical application that solves equations of motion for a model of 500 atoms. This is similar to modeling a structure of liquid argon.
wave5	FORTRAN	7,628	A two-dimensional electromagnetic particle-in-cell simulation used to study various plasma phenomena. Solves equations of motion on a mesh involving 500,000 particles on 50,000 grid points for 5 time steps.
tomcatv	FORTRAN	195	A mesh generation program, which is highly vectorizable.
ora	FORTRAN	535	Traces rays through optical systems of spherical and plane surfaces.
mdljsp2	FORTRAN	3,885	Same as mdljdp2, but single precision.
alvinn	C	272	Simulates training of a neural network. Uses single precision.
ear	C	4,483	An inner ear model that filters and detects various sounds and generates speech signals. Uses single precision.
swm256	FORTRAN	487	A shallow water model that solves shallow water equations using finite difference equations with a 256×256 grid. Uses single precision.
su2cor	FORTRAN	2,514	Computes masses of elementary particles from Quark-Gluon theory.
hydro2d	FORTRAN	4,461	An astrophysics application program that solves hydrodynamical Navier Stokes equations to compute galactical jets.
nasa7	FORTRAN	1,204	Seven kernels do matrix manipulation, FFTs, Gaussian elimination, vortices creation.
fpppp	FORTRAN	2,718	A quantum chemistry application program used to calculate two electron integral derivatives.

FIGURE 1.9   The programs in the SPEC92 benchmark suites. The top six entries are the integer-oriented programs, from which the SPECint92 performance is computed. The bottom 14 are the floating-point-oriented benchmarks from which the SPECfp92 performance is computed. The floating-point programs use double precision unless stated otherwise. The amount of nonuser CPU activity varies from none (for most of the FP benchmarks) to significant (for programs like gcc and compress). In the performance measurements in this text, we use the five integer benchmarks (excluding sc) and five FP benchmarks: doduc, mdljdp2, ear, hydro2d, and su2cor.

Reporting Performance Results

The guiding principle of reporting performance measurements should be *reproducibility*—list everything another experimenter would need to duplicate the results. Compare descriptions of computer performance found in refereed scientific journals to descriptions of car performance found in magazines sold at supermarkets. Car magazines, in addition to supplying 20 performance metrics, list all optional equipment on the test car, the types of tires used in the performance test, and the date the test was made. Computer journals may have only seconds of execution labeled by the name of the program and the name and model of the computer—spice takes 187 seconds on an IBM RS/6000 Powerstation 590. Left to the reader's imagination are program input, version of the program, version of compiler, optimizing level of compiled code, version of operating system, amount of main memory, number and types of disks, version of the CPU—all of which make a difference in performance. In other words, car magazines have enough information about performance measurements to allow readers to duplicate results or to question the options selected for measurements, but computer journals often do not!

A SPEC benchmark report requires a fairly complete description of the machine, the compiler flags, as well as the publication of both the baseline and optimized results. As an example, Figure 1.10 shows portions of the SPECfp92 report for an IBM RS/6000 Powerstation 590. In addition to hardware, software, and baseline tuning parameter descriptions, a SPEC report contains the actual performance times, shown both in tabular form and as a graph.

The importance of performance on the SPEC benchmarks motivated vendors to add many benchmark-specific flags when compiling SPEC programs; these flags often caused transformations that would be illegal on many programs or would slow down performance on others. To restrict this process and increase the significance of the SPEC results, the SPEC organization created a *baseline performance* measurement in addition to the optimized performance measurement. Baseline performance restricts the vendor to one compiler and one set of flags for all the programs in the same language (C or FORTRAN). Figure 1.10 shows the parameters for the baseline performance; in section 1.8, *Fallacies and Pitfalls,* we'll see the tuning parameters for the optimized performance runs on this machine.

Comparing and Summarizing Performance

Comparing performance of computers is rarely a dull event, especially when the designers are involved. Charges and countercharges fly across the Internet; one is accused of underhanded tactics and the other of misleading statements. Since careers sometimes depend on the results of such performance comparisons, it is understandable that the truth is occasionally stretched. But more frequently discrepancies can be explained by differing assumptions or lack of information.

Hardware		Software	
Model number	Powerstation 590	O/S and version	AIX version 3.2.5
CPU	66.67 MHz POWER2	Compilers and version	C SET++ for AIX C/C++ version 2.1 XL FORTRAN/6000 version 3.1
FPU	Integrated	Other software	See below
Number of CPUs	1	File system type	AIX/JFS
Primary cache	32KBI+256KBD off chip	System state	Single user
Secondary cache	None		
Other cache	None		
Memory	128 MB		
Disk subsystem	2x2.0 GB		
Other hardware	None		

SPECbase_fp92 tuning parameters/notes/summary of changes:

FORTRAN flags: -O3 -qarch=pwrx -qhsflt -qnofold -bnso -BI:/lib/syscalss.exp

C flags: -O3 -qarch=pwrx -Q -qtune=pwrx -qhssngl -bnso -bI:/lib/syscalls.exp

FIGURE 1.10   The machine, software, and baseline tuning parameters for the SPECfp92 report on an IBM RS/6000 Powerstation 590. SPECfp92 means that this is the report for the floating-point (FP) benchmarks in the 1992 release (the earlier release was renamed SPEC89) The top part of the table describes the hardware and software. The bottom describes the compiler and options used for the baseline measurements, which must use one compiler and one set of flags for all the benchmarks in the same language. The tuning parameters and flags for the tuned SPEC92 performance are given in Figure 1.18 on page 49. Data from SPEC [1994].

We would like to think that if we could just agree on the programs, the experimental environments, and the definition of *faster,* then misunderstandings would be avoided, leaving the networks free for scholarly discourse. Unfortunately, that's not the reality. Once we agree on the basics, battles are then fought over what is the fair way to summarize relative performance of a collection of programs. For example, two articles on summarizing performance in the same journal took opposing points of view. Figure 1.11, taken from one of the articles, is an example of the confusion that can arise.

	Computer A	Computer B	Computer C
Program P1 (secs)	1	10	20
Program P2 (secs)	1000	100	20
Total time (secs)	1001	110	40

FIGURE 1.11   Execution times of two programs on three machines. Data from Figure I of Smith [1988].

Using our definition of faster than, the following statements hold:

A is 10 times faster than B for program P1.

B is 10 times faster than A for program P2.

A is 20 times faster than C for program P1.

C is 50 times faster than A for program P2.

B is 2 times faster than C for program P1.

C is 5 times faster than B for program P2.

Taken individually, any one of these statements may be of use. Collectively, however, they present a confusing picture—the relative performance of computers A, B, and C is unclear.

Total Execution Time: A Consistent Summary Measure

The simplest approach to summarizing relative performance is to use total execution time of the two programs. Thus

B is 9.1 times faster than A for programs P1 and P2.

C is 25 times faster than A for programs P1 and P2.

C is 2.75 times faster than B for programs P1 and P2.

This summary tracks execution time, our final measure of performance. If the workload consisted of running programs P1 and P2 an equal number of times, the statements above would predict the relative execution times for the workload on each machine.

An average of the execution times that tracks total execution time is the *arithmetic mean*

$$\frac{1}{n} \sum_{i-1}^{n} \text{Time}_i$$

where Time_i is the execution time for the ith program of a total of n in the workload. If performance is expressed as a rate, then the average that tracks total execution time is the *harmonic mean*

$$\frac{n}{\sum_{i=1}^{n} \frac{1}{\text{Rate}_i}}$$

where Rate_i is a function of $1/\text{Time}_i$, the execution time for the ith of n programs in the workload.

Weighted Execution Time

The question arises: What is the proper mixture of programs for the workload? Are programs P1 and P2 in fact run equally in the workload as assumed by the arithmetic mean? If not, then there are two approaches that have been tried for summarizing performance. The first approach when given an unequal mix of programs in the workload is to assign a weighting factor w_i to each program to indicate the relative frequency of the program in that workload. If, for example, 20% of the tasks in the workload were program P1 and 80% of the tasks in the workload were program P2, then the weighting factors would be 0.2 and 0.8. (Weighting factors add up to 1.) By summing the products of weighting factors and execution times, a clear picture of performance of the workload is obtained. This is called the *weighted arithmetic mean*:

$$\sum_{i=1}^{n} \text{Weight}_i \times \text{Time}_i$$

where Weight_i is the frequency of the ith program in the workload and Time_i is the execution time of that program. Figure 1.12 shows the data from Figure 1.11 with three different weightings, each proportional to the execution time of a workload with a given mix. The *weighted harmonic mean* of rates will show the same relative performance as the weighted arithmetic means of execution times. The definition is

$$\frac{1}{\displaystyle\sum_{i=1}^{n} \frac{\text{Weight}_i}{\text{Rate}_i}}$$

	A	**B**	**C**	**W(1)**	**W(2)**	**W(3)**
Program P1 (secs)	1.00	10.00	20.00	0.50	0.909	0.999
Program P2 (secs)	1000.00	100.00	20.00	0.50	0.091	0.001
Arithmetic mean:W(1)	500.50	55.00	20.00			
Arithmetic mean:W(2)	91.91	18.19	20.00			
Arithmetic mean:W(3)	2.00	10.09	20.00			

FIGURE 1.12   Weighted arithmetic mean execution times using three weightings. W(1) equally weights the programs, resulting in a mean (row 3) that is the same as the unweighted arithmetic mean. W(2) makes the mix of programs inversely proportional to the execution times on machine B; row 4 shows the arithmetic mean for that weighting. W(3) weights the programs in inverse proportion to the execution times of the two programs on machine A; the arithmetic mean is given in the last row. The net effect of the second and third weightings is to "normalize" the weightings to the execution times of programs running on that machine, so that the running time will be spent evenly between each program for that machine. For a set of n programs each taking Time_i on one machine, the equal-time weightings on that machine are

$$w_i = \frac{1}{\text{Time}_i \times \displaystyle\sum_{j=1}^{n}\left(\frac{1}{\text{Time}_j}\right)} \quad.$$

Normalized Execution Time and the Pros and Cons of Geometric Means

A second approach to unequal mixture of programs in the workload is to normalize execution times to a reference machine and then take the average of the normalized execution times. This is the approach used by the SPEC benchmarks, where a base time on a VAX-11/780 is used for reference. This measurement gives a warm fuzzy feeling, because it suggests that performance of new programs can be predicted by simply multiplying this number times its performance on the reference machine.

Average normalized execution time can be expressed as either an arithmetic or *geometric* mean. The formula for the geometric mean is

$$\sqrt[n]{\prod_{i=1}^{n} \text{Execution time ratio}_i}$$

where Execution time ratio$_i$ is the execution time, normalized to the reference machine, for the ith program of a total of n in the workload. Geometric means also have a nice property for two samples X_i and Y_i:

$$\frac{\text{Geometric mean}(X_i)}{\text{Geometric mean}(Y_i)} = \text{Geometric mean}\left(\frac{X_i}{Y_i}\right)$$

As a result, taking either the ratio of the means or the mean of the ratios yields the same result. In contrast to arithmetic means, geometric means of normalized execution times are consistent no matter which machine is the reference. Hence, the arithmetic mean should *not* be used to average normalized execution times. Figure 1.13 shows some variations using both arithmetic and geometric means of normalized times.

	Normalized to A			Normalized to B			Normalized to C		
	A	**B**	**C**	**A**	**B**	**C**	**A**	**B**	**C**
Program P1	1.0	10.0	20.0	0.1	1.0	2.0	0.05	0.5	1.0
Program P2	1.0	0.1	0.02	10.0	1.0	0.2	50.0	5.0	1.0
Arithmetic mean	1.0	5.05	10.01	5.05	1.0	1.1	25.03	2.75	1.0
Geometric mean	1.0	1.0	0.63	1.0	1.0	0.63	1.58	1.58	1.0
Total time	1.0	0.11	0.04	9.1	1.0	0.36	25.03	2.75	1.0

FIGURE 1.13   Execution times from Figure 1.11 normalized to each machine. The arithmetic mean performance varies depending on which is the reference machine—in column 2, B's execution time is five times longer than A's, while the reverse is true in column 4. In column 3, C is slowest, but in column 9, C is fastest. The geometric means are consistent independent of normalization—A and B have the same performance, and the execution time of C is 0.63 of A or B (1/1.58 is 0.63). Unfortunately, the total execution time of A is 10 times longer than that of B, and B in turn is about 3 times longer than C. As a point of interest, the relationship between the means of the same set of numbers is always harmonic mean ≤ geometric mean ≤ arithmetic mean.

Because the weightings in weighted arithmetic means are set proportionate to execution times on a given machine, as in Figure 1.12, they are influenced not only by frequency of use in the workload, but also by the peculiarities of a particular machine and the size of program input. The geometric mean of normalized execution times, on the other hand, is independent of the running times of the individual programs, and it doesn't matter which machine is used to normalize. If a situation arose in comparative performance evaluation where the programs were fixed but the inputs were not, then competitors could rig the results of weighted arithmetic means by making their best performing benchmark have the largest input and therefore dominate execution time. In such a situation the geometric mean would be less misleading than the arithmetic mean.

The strong drawback to geometric means of normalized execution times is that they violate our fundamental principle of performance measurement—they do not predict execution time. The geometric means from Figure 1.13 suggest that for programs P1 and P2 the performance of machines A and B is the same, yet this would only be true for a workload that ran program P1 100 times for every occurrence of program P2 (see Figure 1.12 on page 26). The total execution time for such a workload suggests that machines A and B are about 50% faster than machine C, in contrast to the geometric mean, which says machine C is faster than A and B! In general there is *no workload* for three or more machines that will match the performance predicted by the geometric means of normalized execution times. Our original reason for examining geometric means of normalized performance was to avoid giving equal emphasis to the programs in our workload, but is this solution an improvement?

An additional drawback of using geometric mean as a method for summarizing performance for a benchmark suite (as SPEC92 does) is that it encourages hardware and software designers to focus their attention on the benchmarks where performance is easiest to improve rather than on the benchmarks that are slowest. For example, if some hardware or software improvement can cut the running time for a benchmark from 2 seconds to 1, the geometric mean will reward those designers with the same overall mark that it would give to designers that improve the running time on another benchmark in the suite from 10,000 seconds to 5000 seconds. Of course, everyone interested in running the second program thinks of the second batch of designers as their heroes and the first group as useless. Small programs are often easier to "crack," obtaining a large but unrepresentative performance improvement, and the use of geometric mean rewards such behavior more than a measure that reflects total running time.

The ideal solution is to measure a real workload and weight the programs according to their frequency of execution. If this can't be done, then normalizing so that equal time is spent on each program on some machine at least makes the relative weightings explicit and will predict execution time of a workload with that mix. The problem above of unspecified inputs is best solved by specifying the inputs when comparing performance. If results must be normalized to a specific machine, first summarize performance with the proper weighted measure and then do the normalizing.

1.6 | Quantitative Principles of Computer Design

Now that we have seen how to define, measure, and summarize performance, we can explore some of the guidelines and principles that are useful in design and analysis of computers. In particular, this section introduces some important observations about designing for performance and cost/performance, as well as two equations that we can use to evaluate design alternatives.

Make the Common Case Fast

Perhaps the most important and pervasive principle of computer design is to make the common case fast: In making a design trade-off, favor the frequent case over the infrequent case. This principle also applies when determining how to spend resources, since the impact on making some occurrence faster is higher if the occurrence is frequent. Improving the frequent event, rather than the rare event, will obviously help performance, too. In addition, the frequent case is often simpler and can be done faster than the infrequent case. For example, when adding two numbers in the CPU, we can expect overflow to be a rare circumstance and can therefore improve performance by optimizing the more common case of no overflow. This may slow down the case when overflow occurs, but if that is rare, then overall performance will be improved by optimizing for the normal case.

We will see many cases of this principle throughout this text. In applying this simple principle, we have to decide what the frequent case is and how much performance can be improved by making that case faster. A fundamental law, called *Amdahl's Law*, can be used to quantify this principle.

Amdahl's Law

The performance gain that can be obtained by improving some portion of a computer can be calculated using Amdahl's Law. Amdahl's Law states that the performance improvement to be gained from using some faster mode of execution is limited by the fraction of the time the faster mode can be used.

Amdahl's Law defines the *speedup* that can be gained by using a particular feature. What is speedup? Suppose that we can make an enhancement to a machine that will improve performance when it is used. Speedup is the ratio

$$\text{Speedup} = \frac{\text{Performance for entire task using the enhancement when possible}}{\text{Performance for entire task without using the enhancement}}$$

Alternatively,

$$\text{Speedup} = \frac{\text{Execution time for entire task without using the enhancement}}{\text{Execution time for entire task using the enhancement when possible}}$$

Speedup tells us how much faster a task will run using the machine with the enhancement as opposed to the original machine.

Amdahl's Law gives us a quick way to find the speedup from some enhancement, which depends on two factors:

1. *The fraction of the computation time in the original machine that can be converted to take advantage of the enhancement*—For example, if 20 seconds of the execution time of a program that takes 60 seconds in total can use an enhancement, the fraction is 20/60. This value, which we will call $\text{Fraction}_{\text{enhanced}}$, is always less than or equal to 1.

2. *The improvement gained by the enhanced execution mode; that is, how much faster the task would run if the enhanced mode were used for the entire program*—This value is the time of the original mode over the time of the enhanced mode: If the enhanced mode takes 2 seconds for some portion of the program that can completely use the mode, while the original mode took 5 seconds for the same portion, the improvement is 5/2. We will call this value, which is always greater than 1, $\text{Speedup}_{\text{enhanced}}$.

The execution time using the original machine with the enhanced mode will be the time spent using the unenhanced portion of the machine plus the time spent using the enhancement:

$$\text{Execution time}_{\text{new}} = \text{Execution time}_{\text{old}} \times \left((1 - \text{Fraction}_{\text{enhanced}}) + \frac{\text{Fraction}_{\text{enhanced}}}{\text{Speedup}_{\text{enhanced}}} \right)$$

The overall speedup is the ratio of the execution times:

$$\text{Speedup}_{\text{overall}} = \frac{\text{Execution time}_{\text{old}}}{\text{Execution time}_{\text{new}}} = \frac{1}{(1 - \text{Fraction}_{\text{enhanced}}) + \dfrac{\text{Fraction}_{\text{enhanced}}}{\text{Speedup}_{\text{enhanced}}}}$$

EXAMPLE   Suppose that we are considering an enhancement that runs 10 times faster than the original machine but is only usable 40% of the time. What is the overall speedup gained by incorporating the enhancement?

ANSWER $\text{Fraction}_{\text{enhanced}} = 0.4$

$\text{Speedup}_{\text{enhanced}} = 10$

$$\text{Speedup}_{\text{overall}} = \frac{1}{0.6 + \dfrac{0.4}{10}} = \frac{1}{0.64} \approx 1.56$$

■

Amdahl's Law expresses the law of diminishing returns: The incremental improvement in speedup gained by an additional improvement in the performance of just a portion of the computation diminishes as improvements are added. An important corollary of Amdahl's Law is that if an enhancement is only usable for a fraction of a task, we can't speed up the task by more than the reciprocal of 1 minus that fraction.

A common mistake in applying Amdahl's Law is to confuse "fraction of time converted to use an enhancement" and "fraction of time after enhancement is in use." If, instead of measuring the time that we *could use* the enhancement in a computation, we measure the time *after* the enhancement is in use, the results will be incorrect! (Try Exercise 1.2 to see how wrong.)

Amdahl's Law can serve as a guide to how much an enhancement will improve performance and how to distribute resources to improve cost/performance. The goal, clearly, is to spend resources proportional to where time is spent. We can also use Amdahl's Law to compare two design alternatives, as the following Example shows.

EXAMPLE   Implementations of floating-point (FP) square root vary significantly in performance. Suppose FP square root (FPSQR) is responsible for 20% of the execution time of a critical benchmark on a machine. One proposal is to add FPSQR hardware that will speed up this operation by a factor of 10. The other alternative is just to try to make all FP instructions run faster; FP instructions are responsible for a total of 50% of the execution time. The design team believes that they can make all FP instructions run two times faster with the same effort as required for the fast square root. Compare these two design alternatives.

ANSWER   We can compare these two alternatives by comparing the speedups:

$$\text{Speedup}_{\text{FPSQR}} = \cfrac{1}{(1-0.2) + \cfrac{0.2}{10}} = \frac{1}{0.82} = 1.22$$

$$\text{Speedup}_{\text{FP}} = \cfrac{1}{(1-0.5) + \cfrac{0.5}{2.0}} = \frac{1}{0.75} = 1.33$$

Improving the performance of the FP operations overall is better because of the higher frequency.   ∎

In the above Example, we needed to know the time consumed by the new and improved FP operations; often it is difficult to measure these times directly. In the next section, we will see another way of doing such comparisons based on the use of an equation that decomposes the CPU execution time into three separate components. If we know how an alternative affects these three components, we can determine its overall performance effect. Furthermore, it is often possible to build simulators that measure these components before the hardware is actually designed.

The CPU Performance Equation

Most computers are constructed using a clock running at a constant rate. These discrete time events are called *ticks*, *clock ticks*, *clock periods*, *clocks*, *cycles*, or *clock cycles*. Computer designers refer to the time of a clock period by its duration (e.g., 2 ns) or by its rate (e.g., 500 MHz). CPU time for a program can then be expressed two ways:

$$\text{CPU time} = \text{CPU clock cycles for a program} \times \text{Clock cycle time}$$

or

$$\text{CPU time} = \frac{\text{CPU clock cycles for a program}}{\text{Clock rate}}$$

In addition to the number of clock cycles needed to execute a program, we can also count the number of instructions executed—the *instruction path length* or *instruction count* (IC). If we know the number of clock cycles and the instruction count we can calculate the average number of *clock cycles per instruction* (CPI):

$$\text{CPI} = \frac{\text{CPU clock cycles for a program}}{\text{IC}}$$

This CPU figure of merit provides insight into different styles of instruction sets and implementations, and we will use it extensively in the next four chapters.

By transposing instruction count in the above formula, clock cycles can be defined as $\text{IC} \times \text{CPI}$. This allows us to use CPI in the execution time formula:

$$\text{CPU time} = \text{IC} \times \text{CPI} \times \text{Clock cycle time}$$

or

$$\text{CPU time} = \frac{\text{IC} \times \text{CPI}}{\text{Clock rate}}$$

Expanding the first formula into the units of measure shows how the pieces fit together:

$$\frac{\text{Instructions}}{\text{Program}} \times \frac{\text{Clock cycles}}{\text{Instruction}} \times \frac{\text{Seconds}}{\text{Clock cycle}} = \frac{\text{Seconds}}{\text{Program}} = \text{CPU time}$$

As this formula demonstrates, CPU performance is dependent upon three characteristics: clock cycle (or rate), clock cycles per instruction, and instruction count. Furthermore, CPU time is *equally* dependent on these three characteristics: A 10% improvement in any one of them leads to a 10% improvement in CPU time.

Unfortunately, it is difficult to change one parameter in complete isolation from others because the basic technologies involved in changing each characteristic are also interdependent:

- *Clock cycle time*—Hardware technology and organization

- *CPI*—Organization and instruction set architecture

- *Instruction count*—Instruction set architecture and compiler technology

Luckily, many potential performance improvement techniques primarily improve one component of CPU performance with small or predictable impacts on the other two.

Sometimes it is useful in designing the CPU to calculate the number of total CPU clock cycles as

$$\text{CPU clock cycles} = \sum_{i=1}^{n} \text{CPI}_i \times \text{IC}_i$$

where IC_i represents number of times instruction i is executed in a program and CPI_i represents the average number of clock cycles for instruction i. This form can be used to express CPU time as

$$\text{CPU time} = \left(\sum_{i=1}^{n} \text{CPI}_i \times \text{IC}_i \right) \times \text{Clock cycle time}$$

and overall CPI as

$$\text{CPI} = \frac{\sum_{i=1}^{n} \text{CPI}_i \times \text{IC}_i}{\text{Instruction count}} = \sum_{i=1}^{n} \text{CPI}_i \times \left(\frac{\text{IC}_i}{\text{Instruction count}} \right)$$

The latter form of the CPI calculation multiplies each individual CPI_i by the fraction of occurrences of that instruction in a program. CPI_i should be measured and not just calculated from a table in the back of a reference manual since it must include cache misses and any other memory system inefficiencies.

Consider our earlier example, here modified to use measurements of the frequency of the instructions and of the instruction CPI values, which, in practice, are easier to obtain.

EXAMPLE   Suppose we have made the following measurements:

Frequency of FP operations = 25%
Average CPI of FP operations = 4.0
Average CPI of other instructions = 1.33
Frequency of FPSQR= 2%
CPI of FPSQR = 20

Assume that the two design alternatives are to reduce the CPI of FPSQR to 2 or to reduce the average CPI of all FP operations to 2. Compare these two design alternatives using the CPU performance equation.

ANSWER   First, observe that only the CPI changes; the clock rate and instruction count remain identical. We start by finding the original CPI with neither enhancement:

$$CPI_{original} = \sum_{i=1}^{n} CPI_i \times \left(\frac{IC_i}{Instruction\ count}\right)$$
$$= (4 \times 25\%) + (1.33 \times 75\%) = 2.0$$

We can compute the CPI for the enhanced FPSQR by subtracting the cycles saved from the original CPI:

$$CPI_{with\ new\ FPSQR} = CPI_{original} - 2\% \times (CPI_{old\ FPSQR} - CPI_{of\ new\ FPSQR\ only})$$
$$= 2.0 - 2\% \times (20 - 2) = 1.64$$

We can compute the CPI for the enhancement of all FP instructions the same way or by summing the FP and non-FP CPIs. Using the latter gives us

$$CPI_{new\ FP} = (75\% \times 1.33) + (25\% \times 2.0) = 1.5$$

Since the CPI of the overall FP enhancement is lower, its performance will be better. Specifically, the speedup for the overall FP enhancement is

$$Speedup_{new\ FP} = \frac{CPU\ time_{original}}{CPU\ time_{new\ FP}} = \frac{IC \times Clock\ cycle \times CPI_{original}}{IC \times Clock\ cycle \times CPI_{new\ FP}}$$
$$= \frac{CPI_{original}}{CPI_{new\ FP}} = \frac{2.00}{1.5} = 1.33$$

Happily, this is the same speedup we obtained using Amdahl's Law on page 31. ∎

It is often possible to measure the constituent parts of the CPU performance equation. This is a key advantage for using the CPU performance equation versus Amdahl's Law in the above example. In particular, it may be difficult to measure things such as the fraction of execution time for which a set of instructions is responsible. In practice this would probably be computed by summing the product of the instruction count and the CPI for each of the instructions in the set. Since the starting point is often individual instruction count and CPI measurements, the CPU performance equation is incredibly useful.

Measuring the Components of CPU Performance

To use the CPU performance equation to determine performance, we need measurements of the individual components of the equation. Building and using tools to measure aspects of a design is a large part of a designer's job—at least for designers who base their decisions on quantitative principles!

To determine the clock cycle, we need only determine one number. Of course, this is easy for an existing CPU, but estimating the clock cycle time of a design in progress is very difficult. Low-level tools, called *timing estimators* or *timing verifiers*, are used to analyze the clock cycle time for a completed design. It is much more difficult to estimate the clock cycle time for a design that is not completed, or for an alternative for which no design exists. In practice, designers determine a target cycle time and estimate the impact on cycle time by examining what they believe to be the critical paths in a design. The difficulty is that control, rather than the data path of a processor, often turns out to be the critical path, and control is often the last thing to be done and the hardest to estimate timing for. So, designers rely heavily on estimates and on their experience and then do whatever is needed to try to make their clock cycle target. This sometimes means changing the organization so that the CPI of some instructions increases. Using the CPU performance equation, the impact of this trade-off can be calculated.

The other two components of the CPU performance equation are easier to measure. Measuring the instruction count for a program can be done if we have a compiler for the machine together with tools that measure the instruction set behavior. Of course, compilers for existing instruction set architectures are not a problem, and even changes to the architecture can be explored using modern compiler organizations that provide the ability to retarget the compiler easily. For new instruction sets, developing the compiler early is critical to making intelligent decisions in the design of the instruction set.

Once we have a compiled version of a program that we are interested in measuring, there are two major methods we can apply to obtain instruction count information. In most cases, we want to know not only the total instruction count, but also the frequency of different classes of instructions (called the *instruction mix*). The first way to obtain such data is an instruction set simulator that interprets the instructions. The major drawbacks of this approach are speed (since emulating the instruction set is slow) and the possible need to implement substantial infrastructure, since to handle large programs the simulator will need to provide support for operating system functions. One advantage of an instruction set simulator is that it can measure almost any aspect of instruction set behavior accurately and can also potentially simulate systems programs, such as the operating system. Typical instruction set simulators run from 10 to 1000 times slower than the program might, with the performance depending both on how carefully the simulator is written and on the relationship between the architectures of the simulated machine and host machine.

The alternative approach uses execution-based monitoring. In this approach, the binary program is modified to include *instrumentation code*, such as a counter

Under these assumptions, CPU A, with the shorter clock cycle time, is faster than CPU B, which executes fewer instructions.

If CPU A were only 1.1 times faster, then Clock cycle time$_B$ is $1.10 \times$ Clock cycle time$_A$, and the performance of CPU B is

$$\begin{aligned} \text{CPU time}_B &= \text{IC}_B \times \text{CPI}_B \times \text{Clock cycle time}_B \\ &= 0.8 \times \text{IC}_A \times 1.25 \times (1.10 \times \text{Clock cycle time}_A) \\ &= 1.10 \times \text{IC}_A \times \text{Clock cycle time}_A \end{aligned}$$

With this improvement CPU B, which executes fewer instructions, is now faster.   ∎

Locality of Reference

While Amdahl's Law is a theorem that applies to any system, other important fundamental observations come from properties of programs. The most important program property that we regularly exploit is *locality of reference*: Programs tend to reuse data and instructions they have used recently. A widely held rule of thumb is that a program spends 90% of its execution time in only 10% of the code. An implication of locality is that we can predict with reasonable accuracy what instructions and data a program will use in the near future based on its accesses in the recent past.

To examine locality, 10 application programs in the SPEC92 benchmark suite were measured to determine what percentage of the instructions were responsible for 80% and for 90% of the instructions executed. The data are shown in Figure 1.14.

Locality of reference also applies to data accesses, though not as strongly as to code accesses. Two different types of locality have been observed. *Temporal locality* states that recently accessed items are likely to be accessed in the near future. Figure 1.14 shows one effect of temporal locality. *Spatial locality* says that items whose addresses are near one another tend to be referenced close together in time. We will see these principles applied in the next section.

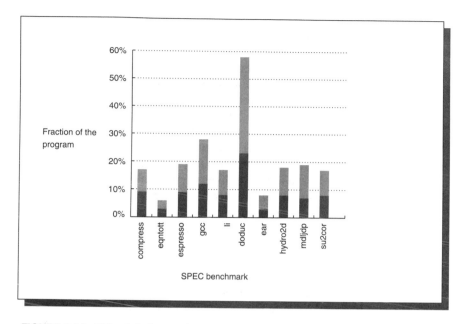

FIGURE 1.14   This plot shows what percentage of the instructions are responsible for 80% and for 90% of the instruction executions. The total bar height indicates the fraction of the instructions that account for 90% of the instruction executions while the dark portion indicates the fraction of the instructions responsible for 80% of the instruction executions. For example, in compress about 9% of the code accounts for 80% of the executed instructions and 16% accounts for 90% of the executed instructions. On average, 90% of the instruction executions comes from 10% of the instructions in the integer programs and 14% of the instructions in the FP programs. The programs are described in more detail in Figure 1.9 on page 22.

1.7 | Putting It All Together: The Concept of Memory Hierarchy

In the *Putting It All Together* sections that appear near the end of every chapter, we show real examples that use the principles in that chapter. In this first chapter, we discuss a key idea in memory systems that will be the sole focus of our attention in Chapter 5.

To begin, let's look at a simple axiom of hardware design: *Smaller is faster.* Smaller pieces of hardware will generally be faster than larger pieces. This simple principle is particularly applicable to memories built from the same technology for two reasons. First, in high-speed machines, signal propagation is a major cause of delay; larger memories have more signal delay and require more levels to decode addresses. Second, in most technologies we can obtain smaller memories that are faster than larger memories. This is primarily because the designer can use more power per memory cell in a smaller design. The fastest memories are generally available in smaller numbers of bits per chip at any point in time, and they cost substantially more per byte.

Performance of Caches: The Basics

Because of locality and the higher speed of smaller memories, a memory hierarchy can substantially improve performance. There are several ways that we can look at the performance of a memory hierarchy and its impact on CPU performance. Let's start with an example that uses Amdahl's Law to compare a system with and without a cache.

EXAMPLE   Suppose a cache is 10 times faster than main memory, and suppose that the cache can be used 90% of the time. How much speedup do we gain by using the cache?

ANSWER   This is a simple application of Amdahl's Law.

$$\text{Speedup} = \frac{1}{(1 - \% \text{ of time cache can be used}) + \dfrac{\% \text{ of time cache can be used}}{\text{Speedup using cache}}}$$

$$\text{Speedup} = \frac{1}{(1 - 0.9) + \dfrac{0.9}{10}}$$

$$\text{Speedup} = \frac{1}{0.19} \approx 5.3$$

Hence, we obtain a speedup from the cache of about 5.3 times.   ■

In practice, we do not normally use Amdahl's Law for evaluating memory hierarchies. Most machines will include a memory hierarchy, and the key issue is really how to design that hierarchy, which depends on more detailed measurements. An alternative method is to expand our CPU execution time equation to account for the number of cycles during which the CPU is stalled waiting for a memory access, which we call the *memory stall cycles*. The performance is then the product of the clock cycle time and the sum of the CPU cycles and the memory stall cycles:

CPU execution time = (CPU clock cycles + Memory stall cycles) × Clock cycle

This equation assumes that the CPU clock cycles include the time to handle a cache hit, and that the CPU is stalled during a cache miss. In Chapter 5, we will analyze memory hierarchies in more detail, examining both these assumptions.

The number of memory stall cycles depends on both the number of misses and the cost per miss, which is called the *miss penalty*:

$$
\begin{aligned}
\text{Memory stall cycles} &= \text{Number of misses} \times \text{Miss penalty} \\
&= \text{IC} \times \text{Misses per instruction} \times \text{Miss penalty} \\
&= \text{IC} \times \text{Memory references per instruction} \times \text{Miss rate} \times \text{Miss penalty}
\end{aligned}
$$

The advantage of the last form is that the components can be easily measured: We already know how to measure IC (instruction count), and measuring the number of memory references per instruction can be done in the same fashion, since each instruction requires an instruction access and we can easily decide if it requires a data access. The component *Miss rate* is simply the fraction of cache accesses that result in a miss (i.e., number of accesses that miss divided by number of accesses). Miss rates are typically measured with cache simulators that take a *trace* of the instruction and data references, simulate the cache behavior to determine which references hit and which miss, and then report the hit and miss totals. The miss rate is one of the most important measures of cache design, but, as we will see in Chapter 5, not the only measure.

EXAMPLE   Assume we have a machine where the CPI is 2.0 when all memory accesses hit in the cache. The only data accesses are loads and stores, and these total 40% of the instructions. If the miss penalty is 25 clock cycles and the miss rate is 2%, how much faster would the machine be if all instructions were cache hits?

ANSWER   First compute the performance for the machine that always hits:

$$
\begin{aligned}
\text{CPU execution time} &= (\text{CPU clock cycles} + \text{Memory stall cycles}) \times \text{Clock cycle} \\
&= (\text{IC} \times \text{CPI} + 0) \times \text{Clock cycle} \\
&= \text{IC} \times 2.0 \times \text{Clock cycle}
\end{aligned}
$$

Now for the machine with the real cache, first we compute memory stall cycles:

$$
\begin{aligned}
\text{Memory stall cycles} &= \text{IC} \times \text{Memory references per instruction} \times \text{Miss rate} \times \text{Miss penalty} \\
&= \text{IC} \times (1 + 0.4) \times 0.02 \times 25 \\
&= \text{IC} \times 0.7
\end{aligned}
$$

where the middle term (1 + 0.4) represents one instruction access and 0.4 data accesses per instruction. The total performance is thus

$$
\begin{aligned}
\text{CPU execution time}_{\text{cache}} &= (\text{IC} \times 2.0 + \text{IC} \times 0.7) \times \text{Clock cycle} \\
&= 2.7 \times \text{IC} \times \text{Clock cycle}
\end{aligned}
$$

The performance ratio is the inverse of the execution times:

of a machine with optional
e clock cycles per floating-
g-point programs using the
routines take less time but
xecutes simpler instructions,
many more that overall exe-

g compilers.

1.8 Fa

The p been made. The compiler
some U) instructions, although it
call su noring systems issues and
exampl clock rate) and 1.57 unopti-
eralizat mized code versus unopti-
sections ree with the ranking of

the load-store machine for

Falla
computer

	Clock cycle count
	1
	2
	2
	2

One alterr
For a given

the load-store machine.

Some find th
and CPI is u
Relating MIP so

$$\frac{500\text{MHz}}{1.57 \times 10^6} = 318.5$$

ode is

Since MIPS is a
the inverse of ex $1C_{unoptimized} \times 1.57 \times (2 \times 10^{-9})$

The good new $3.14 \times 10^{-9} \times IC_{unoptimized}$
tomer, and faster
problem with usin $\frac{1 + 0.21 \times 2 + 0.12 \times 2 + 0.24 \times 2}{1 - (0.43/2)} = 1.7$

- MIPS is depend
  of computers wi are discarded (0.43/2) and the instruc

- MIPS varies betw ng ALU instructions. Thus,

- Most importantly, $\frac{500 \text{ MHz}}{1.73 \times 10^6} = 289.0$

  otimized =

Design

le is

$IC_{unoptimized}) \times 1.73 \times (2 \times 10^{-9})$

$\times IC_{unoptimized}$

imes faster, but its MIPS rating is

■

n fail to give a true picture of per-
e.

asure of performance.

ion floating-point operations
S but always pronounced
lefinition of the acronym:

is in a program
$\times 10^6$

e and on the program.
ormance, it is not appli-
e, have a MFLOPS rat-
ers rarely use floating-

is rather than instruc-
different machines.
mputers would exe-
f floating-point op-
the set of floating-
ple, the Cray C90
square root, sine,
ating changes not
also on the mix-
a program with
am with 100%
oblem in Exer-

S rating for a
ce metric for
tion time for
cution time,
is tempting

to characterize a machine with a single MIPS or MFLOPS rating without naming the program, specifying the I/O, or describing the versions of the OS and compilers.

Fallacy: Synthetic benchmarks predict performance for real programs.

The best known examples of such benchmarks are Whetstone and Dhrystone. These are not real programs and, as such, may not reflect program behavior for factors not measured. Compiler and hardware optimizations can artificially inflate performance of these benchmarks but not of real programs. The other side of the coin is that because these benchmarks are not natural programs, they don't reward optimizations of behaviors that occur in real programs. Here are some examples:

- Optimizing compilers can discard 25% of the Dhrystone code; examples include loops that are only executed once, making the loop overhead instructions unnecessary. To address these problems the authors of the benchmark "require" both optimized and unoptimized code to be reported. In addition, they "forbid" the practice of inline-procedure expansion optimization, since Dhrystone's simple procedure structure allows elimination of all procedure calls at almost no increase in code size.

- Most Whetstone floating-point loops execute small numbers of times or include calls inside the loop. These characteristics are different from many real programs. As a result Whetstone underrewards many loop optimizations and gains little from techniques such as multiple issue (Chapter 4) and vectorization (Appendix B).

- Compilers can optimize a key piece of the Whetstone loop by noting the relationship between square root and exponential, even though this is very unlikely to occur in real programs. For example, one key loop contains the following FORTRAN code:

      X = SQRT(EXP(ALOG(X)/T1))

It could be compiled as if it were

      X = EXP(ALOG(X)/(2×T1))

since

$$\mathrm{SQRT(EXP(X))} \ = \ \sqrt[2]{e^{X}} = e^{X/2} \ = \ \mathrm{EXP(X/2)}$$

It would be surprising if such optimizations were ever invoked except in this synthetic benchmark. (Yet one reviewer of this book found several compilers that performed this optimization!) This single change converts all calls to the square root function in Whetstone into multiplies by 2, surely improving performance— if Whetstone is your measure.

used. Over a long period of time, these changes may make even a well-chosen benchmark obsolete.

Fallacy: Peak performance tracks observed performance.

One definition of peak performance is performance a machine is "guaranteed not to exceed." The gap between peak performance and observed performance is typically a factor of 10 or more in supercomputers. (See Appendix B on vectors for an explanation.) Since the gap is so large, peak performance is not useful in predicting observed performance unless the workload consists of small programs that normally operate close to the peak.

As an example of this fallacy, a small code segment using long vectors ran on the Hitachi S810/20 at 236 MFLOPS and on the Cray X-MP at 115 MFLOPS. Although this suggests the S810 is 2.05 times faster than the X-MP, the X-MP runs a program with more typical vector lengths 1.97 times faster than the S810. These data are shown in Figure 1.19.

Measurement	Cray X-MP	Hitachi S810/20	Performance
A(i)=B(i)*C(i)+D(i)*E(i)(vector length 1000 done 100,000 times)	2.6 secs	1.3 secs	Hitachi 2.05 times faster
Vectorized FFT (vector lengths 64,32,…,2)	3.9 secs	7.7 secs	Cray 1.97 times faster

FIGURE 1.19   Measurements of peak performance and actual performance for the Hitachi S810/20 and the Cray X-MP. Data from pages 18–20 of Lubeck, Moore, and Mendez [1985]. Also see *Fallacies and Pitfalls* in Appendix B.

While the use of peak performance has been rampant in the supercomputer business, its use in the microprocessor business is just as misleading. For example, in 1994 DEC announced a version of the Alpha microprocessor capable of executing 1.2 billion instructions per second at its 300-MHz clock rate.The only way this processor can achieve this performance is for two integer instructions and two floating-point instructions to be executed each clock cycle. This machine has a peak performance that is almost 50 times the peak performance of the fastest microprocessor reported in the first SPEC benchmark report in 1989 (a MIPS M/2000, which had a 25-MHz clock). The overall SPEC92 number of the DEC Alpha processor, however, is only about 15 times higher on integer and 25 times higher on FP. This rate of performance improvement is still spectacular, even if peak performance is not a good indicator.

The authors hope that peak performance can be quarantined to the supercomputer industry and eventually eradicated from that domain. In any case, approaching supercomputer performance is not an excuse for adopting dubious supercomputer marketing habits.

1.9 | Concluding Remarks

This chapter has introduced a number of concepts that we will expand upon as we go through this book. The major ideas in instruction set architecture and the alternatives available will be the primary subjects of Chapter 2. Not only will we see the functional alternatives, we will also examine quantitative data that enable us to understand the trade-offs. The quantitative principle, *Make the common case fast,* will be a guiding light in this next chapter, and the CPU performance equation will be our major tool for examining instruction set alternatives. Chapter 2 concludes with a hypothetical instruction set, called DLX, which is designed on the basis of observations of program behavior that we will make in the chapter.

In Chapter 2, we will include a section, *Crosscutting Issues,* that specifically addresses interactions between topics addressed in different chapters. In that section within Chapter 2, we focus on the interactions between compilers and instruction set design. This *Crosscutting Issues* section will appear in all future chapters, with the exception of Chapter 4 on advanced pipelining. In later chapters, the *Crosscutting Issues* sections describe interactions between instruction sets and implementation techniques.

In Chapters 3 and 4 we turn our attention to pipelining, the most common implementation technique used for making faster processors. Pipelining overlaps the execution of instructions and thus can achieve lower CPIs and/or lower clock cycle times. As in Chapter 2, the CPU performance equation will be our guide in the evaluation of alternatives. Chapter 3 starts with a review of the basics of machine organization and control and moves through the basic ideas in pipelining, including the control of more complex floating-point pipelines. The chapter concludes with an examination and analysis of the R4000. At the end of Chapter 3, you will be able to understand the pipeline design of almost every processor built before 1990. Chapter 4 is an extensive examination of advanced pipelining techniques that attempt to get higher performance by exploiting more overlap among instructions than the simple pipelines in use in the 1980s. This chapter begins with an extensive discussion of basic concepts that will prepare you not only for the wide range of ideas examined in Chapter 4, but also to understand and analyze new techniques that will be introduced in the coming years. Chapter 4 uses examples that span about 20 years, drawing from the first modern supercomputers (the CDC 6600 and IBM 360/91) to the latest processors that first reached the market in 1995. Throughout Chapters 3 and 4, we will repeatedly look at techniques that rely either on clever hardware techniques or on sophisticated compiler technology. These alternatives are an exciting aspect of pipeline design, likely to continue through the decade of the 1990s.

In Chapter 5 we turn to the all-important area of memory system design. The *Putting It All Together* section in this chapter serves as a basic introduction. We will examine a wide range of techniques that conspire to make memory look infinitely large while still being as fast as possible. The simple equations we computer field believe that this term gives too much credit to von Neumann, who wrote up the ideas, and too little to the engineers, Eckert and Mauchly, who worked on the machines. For this reason, this term will not appear in this book.

In 1946, Maurice Wilkes of Cambridge University visited the Moore School to attend the latter part of a series of lectures on developments in electronic computers. When he returned to Cambridge, Wilkes decided to embark on a project to build a stored-program computer named EDSAC, for Electronic Delay Storage Automatic Calculator. The EDSAC became operational in 1949 and was the world's first full-scale, operational, stored-program computer [Wilkes, Wheeler, and Gill 1951; Wilkes 1985, 1995]. (A small prototype called the Mark I, which was built at the University of Manchester and ran in 1948, might be called the first operational stored-program machine.) The EDSAC was an accumulator-based architecture. This style of instruction set architecture remained popular until the early 1970s. (Chapter 2 starts with a brief summary of the EDSAC instruction set.)

In 1947, Eckert and Mauchly applied for a patent on electronic computers. The dean of the Moore School, by demanding the patent be turned over to the university, may have helped Eckert and Mauchly conclude they should leave. Their departure crippled the EDVAC project, which did not become operational until 1952.

Goldstine left to join von Neumann at the Institute for Advanced Study at Princeton in 1946. Together with Arthur Burks, they issued a report based on the 1944 memo [1946]. The paper led to the IAS machine built by Julian Bigelow at Princeton's Institute for Advanced Study. It had a total of 1024 40-bit words and was roughly 10 times faster than ENIAC. The group thought about uses for the machine, published a set of reports, and encouraged visitors. These reports and visitors inspired the development of a number of new computers. The paper by Burks, Goldstine, and von Neumann was incredible for the period. Reading it today, you would never guess this landmark paper was written 50 years ago, as most of the architectural concepts seen in modern computers are discussed there.

Recently, there has been some controversy about John Atanasoff, who built a small-scale electronic computer in the early 1940s [Atanasoff 1940]. His machine, designed at Iowa State University, was a special-purpose computer that was never completely operational. Mauchly briefly visited Atanasoff before he built ENIAC. The presence of the Atanasoff machine, together with delays in filing the ENIAC patents (the work was classified and patents could not be filed until after the war) and the distribution of von Neumann's EDVAC paper, were used to break the Eckert-Mauchly patent [Larson 1973]. Though controversy still rages over Atanasoff's role, Eckert and Mauchly are usually given credit for building the first working, general-purpose, electronic computer [Stern 1980]. Atanasoff, however, demonstrated several important innovations included in later computers. One of the most important was the use of a binary representation for numbers. Atanasoff deserves much credit for his work, and he might fairly be given credit for the world's first special-purpose electronic computer. Another early machine that deserves some credit was a special-purpose machine built by Konrad Zuse in Germany in the late 1930s and early 1940s. This machine was electromechanical and, because of the war, never extensively pursued.

In the same time period as ENIAC, Howard Aiken was designing an electromechanical computer called the Mark-I at Harvard. The Mark-I was built by a team of engineers from IBM. He followed the Mark-I by a relay machine, the Mark-II, and a pair of vacuum tube machines, the Mark-III and Mark-IV. The Mark-III and Mark-IV were being built after the first stored-program machines. Because they had separate memories for instructions and data, the machines were regarded as reactionary by the advocates of stored-program computers. The term *Harvard architecture* was coined to describe this type of machine. Though clearly different from the original sense, this term is used today to apply to machines with a single main memory but with separate instruction and data caches.

The Whirlwind project [Redmond and Smith 1980] began at MIT in 1947 and was aimed at applications in real-time radar signal processing. While it led to several inventions, its overwhelming innovation was the creation of magnetic core memory, the first reliable and inexpensive memory technology. Whirlwind had 2048 16-bit words of magnetic core. Magnetic cores served as the main memory technology for nearly 30 years.

Commercial Developments

In December 1947, Eckert and Mauchly formed Eckert-Mauchly Computer Corporation. Their first machine, the BINAC, was built for Northrop and was shown in August 1949. After some financial difficulties, the Eckert-Mauchly Computer Corporation was acquired by Remington-Rand, where they built the UNIVAC I, designed to be sold as a general-purpose computer. First delivered in June 1951, the UNIVAC I sold for $250,000 and was the first successful commercial computer—48 systems were built! Today, this early machine, along with many other fascinating pieces of computer lore, can be seen at the Computer Museum in Boston, Massachusetts.

IBM, which earlier had been in the punched card and office automation business, didn't start building computers until 1950. The first IBM computer, the IBM 701, shipped in 1952 and eventually sold 19 units. In the early 1950s, many people were pessimistic about the future of computers, believing that the market and opportunities for these "highly specialized" machines were quite limited.

Several books describing the early days of computing have been written by the pioneers [Wilkes 1985, 1995; Goldstine 1972]. There are numerous independent histories, often built around the people involved [Slater 1987], as well as a journal, *Annals of the History of Computing,* devoted to the history of computing.

The history of some of the computers invented after 1960 can be found in Chapter 2 (the IBM 360, the DEC VAX, the Intel 80x86, and the early RISC machines), Chapters 3 and 4 (the pipelined processors, including Stretch and the CDC 6600), and Appendix B (vector processors including the TI ASC, CDC Star, and Cray processors).

Development of Quantitative Performance Measures: Successes and Failures

In the earliest days of computing, designers set performance goals—ENIAC was to be 1000 times faster than the Harvard Mark-I, and the IBM Stretch (7030) was to be 100 times faster than the fastest machine in existence. What wasn't clear, though, was how this performance was to be measured. In looking back over the years, it is a consistent theme that each generation of computers obsoletes the performance evaluation techniques of the prior generation.

The original measure of performance was time to perform an individual operation, such as addition. Since most instructions took the same execution time, the timing of one gave insight into the others. As the execution times of instructions in a machine became more diverse, however, the time for one operation was no longer useful for comparisons. To take these differences into account, an *instruction mix* was calculated by measuring the relative frequency of instructions in a computer across many programs. The Gibson mix [Gibson 1970] was an early popular instruction mix. Multiplying the time for each instruction times its weight in the mix gave the user the *average instruction execution time*. (If measured in clock cycles, average instruction execution time is the same as average CPI.) Since instruction sets were similar, this was a more accurate comparison than add times. From average instruction execution time, then, it was only a small step to MIPS (as we have seen, the one is the inverse of the other). MIPS has the virtue of being easy for the layman to understand, hence its popularity.

As CPUs became more sophisticated and relied on memory hierarchies and pipelining, there was no longer a single execution time per instruction; MIPS could not be calculated from the mix and the manual. The next step was benchmarking using kernels and synthetic programs. Curnow and Wichmann [1976] created the Whetstone synthetic program by measuring scientific programs written in Algol 60. This program was converted to FORTRAN and was widely used to characterize scientific program performance. An effort with similar goals to Whetstone, the Livermore FORTRAN Kernels, was made by McMahon [1986] and researchers at Lawrence Livermore Laboratory in an attempt to establish a benchmark for supercomputers. These kernels, however, consisted of loops from real programs.

As it became clear that using MIPS to compare architectures with different instructions sets would not work, a notion of relative MIPS was created. When the VAX-11/780 was ready for announcement in 1977, DEC ran small benchmarks that were also run on an IBM 370/158. IBM marketing referred to the 370/158 as a 1-MIPS computer, and since the programs ran at the same speed, DEC marketing called the VAX-11/780 a 1-MIPS computer. Relative MIPS for a machine M was defined based on some reference machine as

$$\text{MIPS}_M = \frac{\text{Performance}_M}{\text{Performance}_{\text{reference}}} \times \text{MIPS}_{\text{reference}}$$

The popularity of the VAX-11/780 made it a popular reference machine for relative MIPS, especially since relative MIPS for a 1-MIPS computer is easy to calculate: If a machine was five times faster than the VAX-11/780, for that benchmark its rating would be 5 relative MIPS. The 1-MIPS rating was unquestioned for four years, until Joel Emer of DEC measured the VAX-11/780 under a time-sharing load. He found that the VAX-11/780 native MIPS rating was 0.5. Subsequent VAXes that run 3 native MIPS for some benchmarks were therefore called 6-MIPS machines because they run six times faster than the VAX-11/780. By the early 1980s, the term MIPS was almost universally used to mean relative MIPS.

The 1970s and 1980s marked the growth of the supercomputer industry, which was defined by high performance on floating-point-intensive programs. Average instruction time and MIPS were clearly inappropriate metrics for this industry, hence the invention of MFLOPS. Unfortunately customers quickly forget the program used for the rating, and marketing groups decided to start quoting peak MFLOPS in the supercomputer performance wars.

SPEC (System Performance and Evaluation Cooperative) was founded in the late 1980s to try to improve the state of benchmarking and make a more valid basis for comparison. The group initially focused on workstations and servers in the UNIX marketplace, and that remains the primary focus of these benchmarks today. The first release of SPEC benchmarks, now called SPEC89, was a substantial improvement in the use of more realistic benchmarks. SPEC89 was replaced by SPEC92. This release enlarged the set of programs, made the inputs to some benchmarks bigger, and specified new run rules. To reduce the large number of benchmark-specific compiler flags and the use of targeted optimizations, in 1994 SPEC introduced rules for compilers and compilation switches to be used in determining the SPEC92 baseline performance:

1. The optimization options are safe: it is expected that they could generally be used on any program.

2. The same compiler and flags are used for all the benchmarks.

3. No assertion flags, which would tell the compiler some fact it could not derive, are allowed.

4. Flags that allow inlining of library routines normally considered part of the language are allowed, though other such inlining hints are disallowed by rule 5.

5. No program names or subroutine names are allowed in flags.

6. Feedback-based optimization is not allowed.

7. Flags that change the default size of a data item (for example, single precision to double precision) are not allowed.

Specifically permitted are flags that direct the compiler to compile for a particular implementation and flags that allow the compiler to relax certain numerical accuracy requirements (such as left-to-right evaluation). The intention is that the baseline results are what a casual user could achieve without extensive effort.

SPEC also has produced system-oriented benchmarks that can be used to benchmark a system including I/O and OS functions, as well as a throughput-oriented measure (SPECrate), suitable for servers. What has become clear is that maintaining the relevance of these benchmarks in an area of rapid performance improvement will be a continuing investment.

Implementation-Independent Performance Analysis

As the distinction between architecture and implementation pervaded the computing community in the 1970s, the question arose whether the performance of an architecture itself could be evaluated, as opposed to an implementation of the architecture. Many of the leading people in the field pursued this notion. One of the ambitious studies of this question performed at Carnegie Mellon University is summarized in Fuller and Burr [1977]. Three quantitative measures were invented to scrutinize architectures:

- S—Number of bytes for program code

- M—Number of bytes transferred between memory and the CPU during program execution for code and data (S measures size of code at compile time, while M is memory traffic during program execution.)

- R—Number of bytes transferred between registers in a canonical model of a CPU

Once these measures were taken, a weighting factor was applied to them to determine which architecture was "best." The VAX architecture was designed in the height of popularity of the Carnegie Mellon study, and by those measures it does very well. Architectures created since 1985, however, have poorer measures than the VAX using these metrics, yet their implementations do well against the VAX implementations. For example, Figure 1.20 compares S, M, and CPU time for the VAXstation 3100, which uses the VAX instruction set, and the DECstation 3100, which doesn't. The DECstation 3100 is about three to five times faster, even though its S measure is 35% to 70% worse and its M measure is 5% to 15% worse. The attempt to evaluate architecture independently of implementation was a valiant, if not successful, effort.

Program	S (code size in bytes)		M (megabytes code + data transferred)		CPU time (in secs)	
	VAX 3100	DEC 3100	VAX 3100	DEC 3100	VAX 3100	DEC 3100
Gnu C Compiler	409,600	688,128	18	21	291	90
Common TeX	158,720	217,088	67	78	449	95
spice	223,232	372,736	99	106	352	94

FIGURE 1.20   Code size and CPU time of the VAXstation 3100 and DECstation 3100 for Gnu C Compiler, TeX, and spice. Both machines were announced the same day by the same company, and they run the same operating system and similar technology. The difference is in the instruction sets, compilers, clock cycle time, and organization.

References

AMDAHL, G. M. [1967]. "Validity of the single processor approach to achieving large scale comput-ing capabilities," *Proc. AFIPS 1967 Spring Joint Computer Conf. 30* (April), Atlantic City, N.J., 483–485.

ATANASOFF, J. V. [1940]. "Computing machine for the solution of large systems of linear equations," Internal Report, Iowa State University, Ames.

BELL, C. G. [1984]. "The mini and micro industries," *IEEE Computer* 17:10 (October), 14–30.

BELL, C. G., J. C. MUDGE, AND J. E. MCNAMARA [1978]. *A DEC View of Computer Engineering*, Digital Press, Bedford, Mass.

BURKS, A. W., H. H. GOLDSTINE, AND J. VON NEUMANN [1946]. "Preliminary discussion of the logi-cal design of an electronic computing instrument," Report to the U.S. Army Ordnance Department, p. 1; also appears in *Papers of John von Neumann*, W. Aspray and A. Burks, eds., MIT Press, Cam-bridge, Mass., and Tomash Publishers, Los Angeles, Calif., 1987, 97–146.

CURNOW, H. J. AND B. A. WICHMANN [1976]. "A synthetic benchmark," *The Computer J.*, 19:1.

FLEMMING, P. J. AND J. J. WALLACE [1986]. "How not to lie with statistics: The correct way to summarize benchmarks results," *Comm. ACM* 29:3 (March), 218–221.

FULLER, S. H. AND W. E. BURR [1977]. "Measurement and evaluation of alternative computer architectures," *Computer* 10:10 (October), 24–35.

GIBSON, J. C. [1970]. "The Gibson mix," Rep. TR. 00.2043, IBM Systems Development Division, Poughkeepsie, N.Y. (Research done in 1959.)

GOLDSTINE, H. H. [1972]. *The Computer: From Pascal to von Neumann*, Princeton University Press, Princeton, N.J.

JAIN, R. [1991]. *The Art of Computer Systems Performance Analysis: Techniques for Experimental Design, Measurement, Simulation, and Modeling*, Wiley, New York.

LARSON, E. R. [1973]. "Findings of fact, conclusions of law, and order for judgment," File No. 4–67, Civ. 138, *Honeywell v. Sperry Rand and Illinois Scientific Development*, U.S. District Court for the State of Minnesota, Fourth Division (October 19).

LUBECK, O., J. MOORE, AND R. MENDEZ [1985]. "A benchmark comparison of three super-computers: Fujitsu VP-200, Hitachi S810/20, and Cray X-MP/2," *Computer* 18:12 (December), 10–24.

MCMAHON, F. M. [1986]. "The Livermore FORTRAN kernels: A computer test of numerical perfor-mance range," Tech. Rep. UCRL-55745, Lawrence Livermore National Laboratory, Univ. of Cali-fornia, Livermore (December).

rcentage of the execution time
w depends on the fraction of the
S f enhanced mode. Thus, we can-
S up with Amdahl's Law.

SL
S from fast mode?
M
31 on time has been converted to fast

SPEC
SPEC the Examples on page 31 and page 3
STERN ge to an instruction set. The base
Comp nd all operations work on the reg
TOUMA, Chapter 2). Measurements of th
stations ck cycle counts per instruction
WEICKER,
27:10 (O ck cycle counts directly
WILKES, M.
WILKES, M. it (ALU) operations in mem
WILKES, M. one source operand in mem
Digital Com le count of 2. Suppose that
for branches by 1, but it
xplains why adding regis
is change improve CPU

E X E R C

Each exercise ha chine that with a perfect
depends on in an

1.1 [20/10/10/15] structions have a miss
chine by adding a alty is 40 cycles. Find
faster than the norm w much faster the m
using vector mode th
you don't need to kn

a. [20] <1.6> Draw are asked to becom
performed in vec usage of high-level
vectorization." pensive operation
associated with

b. [10] <1.6> What p s with and witho

c. [10] <1.6> What p izing compiler
mum speedup attain eveal the follov
nized version

d. [15] <1.6> Suppose y tions in the v
to be 70%. The hardw ecutes two-t
rate with a significant instruction
compiler crew could in r instruction
performance. How muc g load and
current usage) would yo decision
ment would you recomme

1.2 [15/10] <1.6> Assume—as
an enhancement to a computer

Design

ne benchmark contains 195,578 basic floating-
led as shown in Figure 1.21.

Count
82,014
8,229
73,220
21,399
6,006
4,710
195,578

cy of floating-point
e benchmark.

iler with optimization turned on. The
.67 MHz, and it includes a floating-
g point to be calculated with the compiler flags. A single iteration of
13.6 seconds using software. As-
be 10, while the CPI using soft-

?

ecuted for both runs?

ns does it take to perform a

with the floating-point co-
point operations in Figure

plete packaged cost of a
ing and testing costs. We
iscussion of packaging

of packaging

st time

Since bad dies are discarded, die yield is in the denominator in the equation—the good must shoulder the costs of testing those that fail. (In practice, a bad die may take less time to test, but this effect is small, since moving the probes on the die is a mechanical process that takes a large fraction of the time.) Testing costs about $50 to $500 per hour, depending on the tester needed. High-end designs with many high-speed pins require the more expensive testers. For higher-end microprocessors test time would run $300 to $500 per hour. Die tests take about 5 to 90 seconds on average, depending on the simplicity of the die and the provisions to reduce testing time included in the chip.

The cost of a package depends on the material used, the number of pins, and the die area. The cost of the material used in the package is in part determined by the ability to dissipate power generated by the die. For example, a *plastic quad flat pack* (PQFP) dissipating less than 1 watt, with 208 or fewer pins, and containing a die up to 1 cm on a side costs $2 in 1995. A ceramic *pin grid array* (PGA) can handle 300 to 600 pins and a larger die with more power, but it costs $20 to $60. In addition to the cost of the package itself is the cost of the labor to place a die in the package and then bond the pads to the pins, which adds from a few cents to a dollar or two to the cost. Some good dies are typically lost in the assembly process, thereby further reducing yield. For simplicity we assume the final test yield is 1.0; in practice it is at least 0.95. We also ignore the cost of the final packaged test.

This exercise requires the information provided in Figure 1.22.

Microprocessor	Die area (mm^2)	Pins	Technology	Estimated wafer cost ($)	Package
MIPS 4600	77	208	CMOS, 0.6μ, 3M	3200	PQFP
PowerPC 603	85	240	CMOS, 0.6μ, 4M	3400	PQFP
HP 71x0	196	504	CMOS, 0.8μ, 3M	2800	Ceramic PGA
Digital 21064A	166	431	CMOS, 0.5μ, 4.5M	4000	Ceramic PGA
SuperSPARC/60	256	293	BiCMOS, 0.6μ, 3.5M	4000	Ceramic PGA

FIGURE 1.22 Characteristics of microprocessors. The technology entry is the process type, line width, and number of interconnect levels.

a. [15] <1.4> For each of the microprocessors in Figure 1.22, compute the number of good chips you would get per 20-cm wafer using the model on page 12. Assume a defect density of one defect per cm^2, a wafer yield of 95%, and assume $\alpha = 3$.

b. [10] <1.4> For each microprocessor in Figure 1.22, compute the cost per projected good die before packaging and testing. Use the number of good dies per wafer from part (a) of this exercise and the wafer cost from Figure 1.22.

c. [15] <1.3> Both package cost and test cost are proportional to pin count. Using the additional assumption shown in Figure 1.23, compute the cost per good, tested, and packaged part using the costs per good die from part (b) of this exercise.

d. [15] <1.3> There are wide differences in defect densities between semiconductor manufacturers. Find the costs for the largest processor in Figure 1.22 (total cost including packaging), assuming defect densities are 0.6 per cm^2 and assuming that defect densities are 1.2 per cm^2.

Object addressed	Aligned at byte offsets	Misaligned at byte offsets
Byte	0,1,2,3,4,5,6,7	Never
Half word	0,2,4,6	1,3,5,7
Word	0,4	1,2,3,5,6,7
Double word	0	1,2,3,4,5,6,7

FIGURE 2.4   Aligned and misaligned accesses of objects. The byte offsets are specified for the low-order three bits of the address.

Why would someone design a machine with alignment restrictions? Misalignment causes hardware complications, since the memory is typically aligned on a word or double-word boundary. A misaligned memory access will, therefore, take multiple aligned memory references.Thus, even in machines that allow misaligned access, programs with aligned accesses run faster.

Even if data are aligned, supporting byte and half-word accesses requires an alignment network to align bytes and half words in registers. Depending on the instruction, the machine may also need to sign-extend the quantity. On some machines a byte or half word does not affect the upper portion of a register. For stores only the affected bytes in memory may be altered. (Although all the machines discussed in this book permit byte and half-word accesses to memory, only the Intel 80x86 supports ALU operations on register operands with a size shorter than a word.)

Addressing Modes

We now know what bytes to access in memory given an address. In this subsection we will look at addressing modes—how architectures specify the address of an object they will access. In GPR machines, an addressing mode can specify a constant, a register, or a location in memory. When a memory location is used, the actual memory address specified by the addressing mode is called the *effective address*.

Figure 2.5 shows all the data-addressing modes that have been used in recent machines. Immediates or literals are usually considered memory-addressing modes (even though the value they access is in the instruction stream), although registers are often separated. We have kept addressing modes that depend on the program counter, called *PC-relative addressing*, separate. PC-relative addressing is used primarily for specifying code addresses in control transfer instructions. The use of PC-relative addressing in control instructions is discussed in section 2.4.

Figure 2.5 shows the most common names for the addressing modes, though the names differ among architectures. In this figure and throughout the book, we will use an extension of the C programming language as a hardware description notation. In this figure, only one non-C feature is used: The left arrow (←) is used

Addressing mode	Example instruction	Meaning	When used
Register	Add R4,R3	Regs[R4]←Regs[R4]+Regs[R3]	When a value is in a register.
Immediate	Add R4,#3	Regs[R4]←Regs[R4]+3	For constants.
Displacement	Add R4,100(R1)	Regs[R4]←Regs[R4]+Mem[100+Regs[R1]]	Accessing local variables.
Register deferred or indirect	Add R4,(R1)	Regs[R4]←Regs[R4]+Mem[Regs[R1]]	Accessing using a pointer or a computed address.
Indexed	Add R3,(R1 + R2)	Regs[R3]←Regs[R3]+Mem[Regs[R1]+Regs[R2]]	Sometimes useful in array addressing: R1 = base of array; R2 = index amount.
Direct or absolute	Add R1,(1001)	Regs[R1]←Regs[R1]+Mem[1001]	Sometimes useful for accessing static data; address constant may need to be large.
Memory indirect or memory deferred	Add R1,@(R3)	Regs[R1]←Regs[R1]+Mem[Mem[Regs[R3]]]	If R3 is the address of a pointer p, then mode yields *p.
Autoincrement	Add R1,(R2)+	Regs[R1]←Regs[R1]+Mem[Regs[R2]] Regs[R2]←Regs[R2]+d	Useful for stepping through arrays within a loop. R2 points to start of array; each reference increments R2 by size of an element, d.
Autodecrement	Add R1,-(R2)	Regs[R2]←Regs[R2]-d Regs[R1]←Regs[R1]+Mem[Regs[R2]]	Same use as autoincrement. Autodecrement/increment can also act as push/pop to implement a stack.
Scaled	Add R1,100(R2)[R3]	Regs[R1]← Regs[R1]+Mem[100+Regs[R2]+Regs[R3]*d]	Used to index arrays. May be applied to any indexed addressing mode in some machines.

FIGURE 2.5 **Selection of addressing modes with examples, meaning, and usage.** The extensions to C used in the hardware descriptions are defined above. In autoincrement/decrement and scaled addressing modes, the variable d designates the size of the data item being accessed (i.e., whether the instruction is accessing 1, 2, 4, or 8 bytes); this means that these addressing modes are only useful when the elements being accessed are adjacent in memory. In our measurements, we use the first name shown for each mode.

for assignment. We also use the array Mem as the name for main memory and the array Regs for registers. Thus, Mem[Regs[R1]] refers to the contents of the memory location whose address is given by the contents of register 1 (R1). Later, we will introduce extensions for accessing and transferring data smaller than a word.

Addressing modes have the ability to significantly reduce instruction counts; they also add to the complexity of building a machine and may increase the average CPI (clock cycles per instruction) of machines that implement those modes.

Immediate or Literal Addressing Mode

Immediates can be used in arithmetic operations, in comparisons (primarily for branches), and in moves where a constant is wanted in a register. The last case occurs for constants written in the code, which tend to be small, and for address constants, which can be large. For the use of immediates it is important to know whether they need to be supported for all operations or for only a subset. The chart in Figure 2.8 shows the frequency of immediates for the general classes of integer operations in an instruction set.

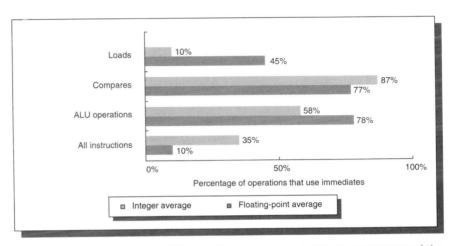

FIGURE 2.8   We see that for ALU operations about one-half to three-quarters of the operations have an immediate operand, while 75% to 85% of compare operations use an immediate operation. (For ALU operations, shifts by a constant amount are included as operations with immediate operands.) For loads, the load immediate instructions load 16 bits into either half of a 32-bit register. These load immediates are not loads in a strict sense because they do not reference memory. In some cases, a pair of load immediates may be used to load a 32-bit constant, but this is rare. The compares include comparisons against zero that are done in conditional branches based on this comparison. These measurements were taken on the DLX architecture with full compiler optimization (see section 2.7). The compiler attempts to use simple compares against zero for branches whenever possible, because these branches are efficiently supported in the architecture. Note that the bottom bars show that integer programs use immediates in about one-third of the instructions, while floating-point programs use immediates in about one-tenth of the instructions. Floating-point programs have many data transfers and operations on floating-point data that do not have immediate forms in the DLX instruction set. (These percentages are the averages of the same 10 programs as in Figure 2.7 on page 77.)

Another important instruction set measurement is the range of values for immediates. Like displacement values, the sizes of immediate values affect instruction lengths. As Figure 2.9 shows, immediate values that are small are most heavily used. Large immediates are sometimes used, however, most likely in addressing calculations. The data in Figure 2.9 were taken on a VAX because, unlike recent load-store architectures, it supports 32-bit long immediates. For these measurements the VAX has the drawback that many of its instructions have zero as an implicit operand. These include instructions to compare against zero and to store zero into a word. Because of the use of these instructions, the measurements show less frequent use of zero than on architectures without such instructions.

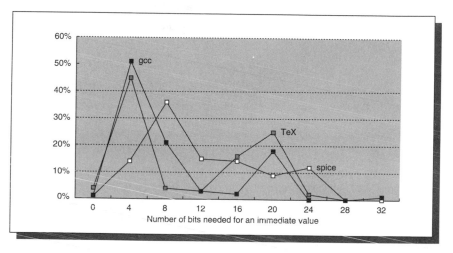

FIGURE 2.9   The distribution of immediate values is shown. The *x* axis shows the number of bits needed to represent the magnitude of an immediate value—0 means the immediate field value was 0. The vast majority of the immediate values are positive: Overall, less than 6% of the immediates are negative.These measurements were taken on a VAX, which supports a full range of immediates and sizes as operands to any instruction. The measured programs are gcc, spice, and TeX. Note that 50% to 70% of the immediates fit within 8 bits and 75% to 80% fit within 16 bits.

Summary: Memory Addressing

First, because of their popularity, we would expect a new architecture to support at least the following addressing modes: displacement, immediate, and register deferred. Figure 2.6 on page 76 shows they represent 75% to 99% of the addressing modes used in our measurements. Second, we would expect the size of the address for displacement mode to be at least 12 to 16 bits, since the caption in Figure 2.7 on page 77 suggests these sizes would capture 75% to 99% of the displacements. Third, we would expect the size of the immediate field to be at least 8 to 16 bits. As the caption in Figure 2.9 suggests, these sizes would capture 50% to 80% of the immediates.

Operator type	Examples
Arithmetic and logical	Integer arithmetic and logical operations: add, and, subtract, or
Data transfer	Loads-stores (move instructions on machines with memory addressing)
Control	Branch, jump, procedure call and return, traps
System	Operating system call, virtual memory management instructions
Floating point	Floating-point operations: add, multiply
Decimal	Decimal add, decimal multiply, decimal-to-character conversions
String	String move, string compare, string search
Graphics	Pixel operations, compression/decompression operations

FIGURE 2.10   Categories of instruction operators and examples of each. All machines generally provide a full set of operations for the first three categories. The support for system functions in the instruction set varies widely among architectures, but all machines must have some instruction support for basic system functions. The amount of support in the instruction set for the last four categories may vary from none to an extensive set of special instructions. Floating-point instructions will be provided in any machine that is intended for use in an application that makes much use of floating point. These instructions are sometimes part of an optional instruction set. Decimal and string instructions are sometimes primitives, as in the VAX or the IBM 360, or may be synthesized by the compiler from simpler instructions. Graphics instructions typically operate on many smaller data items in parallel; for example, performing eight 8-bit additions on two 64-bit operands.

2.4 | Operations in the Instruction Set

The operators supported by most instruction set architectures can be categorized, as in Figure 2.10. One rule of thumb across all architectures is that the most widely executed instructions are the simple operations of an instruction set. For example, Figure 2.11 shows 10 simple instructions that account for 96% of instructions executed for a collection of integer programs running on the popular Intel 80x86. Hence the implementor of these instructions should be sure to make these fast, as they are the common case.

Because the measurements of branch and jump behavior are fairly independent of other measurements, we examine the use of control-flow instructions next.

Instructions for Control Flow

There is no consistent terminology for instructions that change the flow of control. In the 1950s they were typically called *transfers*. Beginning in 1960 the name *branch* began to be used. Later, machines introduced additional names. Throughout this book we will use *jump* when the change in control is unconditional and *branch* when the change is conditional.

Rank	80x86 instruction	Integer average (% total executed)
1	load	22%
2	conditional branch	20%
3	compare	16%
4	store	12%
5	add	8%
6	and	6%
7	sub	5%
8	move register-register	4%
9	call	1%
10	return	1%
Total		96%

FIGURE 2.11   The top 10 instructions for the 80x86. These percentages are the average of the same five SPECint92 programs as in Figure 2.7 on page 77.

We can distinguish four different types of control-flow change:

1. Conditional branches

2. Jumps

3. Procedure calls

4. Procedure returns

We want to know the relative frequency of these events, as each event is different, may use different instructions, and may have different behavior. The frequencies of these control-flow instructions for a load-store machine running our benchmarks are shown in Figure 2.12.

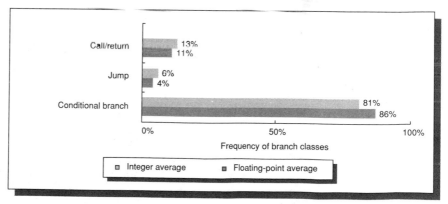

FIGURE 2.12   Breakdown of control flow instructions into three classes: calls or returns, jumps, and conditional branches. Each type is counted in one of three bars. Conditional branches clearly dominate. The programs and machine used to collect these statistics are the same as those in Figure 2.7.

The destination address of a control flow instruction must always be specified. This destination is specified explicitly in the instruction in the vast majority of cases—procedure return being the major exception—since for return the target is not known at compile time. The most common way to specify the destination is to supply a displacement that is added to the *program counter*, or PC. Control flow instructions of this sort are called *PC-relative*. PC-relative branches or jumps are advantageous because the target is often near the current instruction, and specifying the position relative to the current PC requires fewer bits. Using PC-relative addressing also permits the code to run independently of where it is loaded. This property, called *position independence*, can eliminate some work when the program is linked and is also useful in programs linked during execution.

To implement returns and indirect jumps in which the target is not known at compile time, a method other than PC-relative addressing is required. Here, there must be a way to specify the target dynamically, so that it can change at runtime. This dynamic address may be as simple as naming a register that contains the target address; alternatively, the jump may permit any addressing mode to be used to supply the target address. These register indirect jumps are also useful for three other important features: *case* or *switch* statements found in many programming languages (which select among one of several alternatives), *dynamically shared libraries* (which allow a library to be loaded only when it is actually invoked by the program), and *virtual functions* in object-oriented languages like C++ (which allow different routines to be called depending on the type of the data). In all three cases the target address is not known at compile time, and hence is usually loaded from memory into a register before the register indirect jump.

As branches generally use PC-relative addressing to specify their targets, a key question concerns how far branch targets are from branches. Knowing the distribution of these displacements will help in choosing what branch offsets to support and thus will affect the instruction length and encoding. Figure 2.13 shows the distribution of displacements for PC-relative branches in instructions. About 75% of the branches are in the forward direction.

Since most changes in control flow are branches, deciding how to specify the branch condition is important. The three primary techniques in use and their advantages and disadvantages are shown in Figure 2.14.

One of the most noticeable properties of branches is that a large number of the comparisons are simple equality or inequality tests, and a large number are comparisons with zero. Thus, some architectures choose to treat these comparisons as special cases, especially if a *compare and branch* instruction is being used. Figure 2.15 shows the frequency of different comparisons used for conditional branching. The data in Figure 2.8 said that a large percentage of the comparisons had an immediate operand, and while not shown, 0 was the most heavily used immediate. When we combine this with the data in Figure 2.15, we can see that a significant percentage (over 50%) of the integer compares in branches are simple tests for equality with 0.

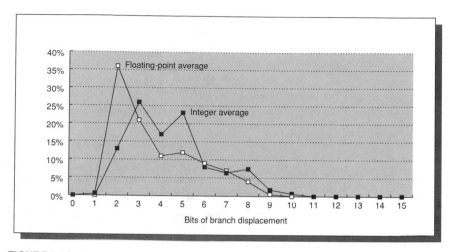

FIGURE 2.13   Branch distances in terms of number of instructions between the target and the branch instruction. The most frequent branches in the integer programs are to targets that are four to seven instructions away. This tells us that short displacement fields often suffice for branches and that the designer can gain some encoding density by having a shorter instruction with a smaller branch displacement. These measurements were taken on a load-store machine (DLX architecture). An architecture that requires fewer instructions for the same program, such as a VAX, would have shorter branch distances. Similarly, the number of bits needed for the displacement may change if the machine allows instructions to be arbitrarily aligned. A cumulative distribution of this branch displacement data is shown in Exercise 2.1 (see Figure 2.32 on page 119). The programs and machine used to collect these statistics are the same as those in Figure 2.7.

Name	How condition is tested	Advantages	Disadvantages
Condition code (CC)	Special bits are set by ALU operations, possibly under program control.	Sometimes condition is set for free.	CC is extra state. Condition codes constrain the ordering of instructions since they pass information from one instruction to a branch.
Condition register	Test arbitrary register with the result of a comparison.	Simple.	Uses up a register.
Compare and branch	Compare is part of the branch. Often compare is limited to subset.	One instruction rather than two for a branch.	May be too much work per instruction.

FIGURE 2.14   The major methods for evaluating branch conditions, their advantages, and their disadvantages. Although condition codes can be set by ALU operations that are needed for other purposes, measurements on programs show that this rarely happens. The major implementation problems with condition codes arise when the condition code is set by a large or haphazardly chosen subset of the instructions, rather than being controlled by a bit in the instruction. Machines with compare and branch often limit the set of compares and use a condition register for more complex compares. Often, different techniques are used for branches based on floating-point comparison versus those based on integer comparison. This is reasonable since the number of branches that depend on floating point comparisons is much smaller than the number depending on integer comparisons.

Procedure calls and returns include control transfer and possibly some state saving; at a minimum the return address must be saved somewhere. Some archi-

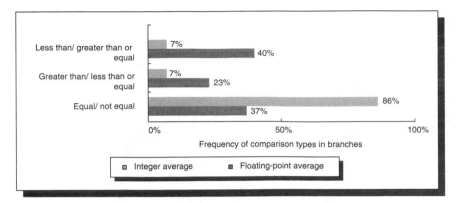

FIGURE 2.15   Frequency of different types of compares in conditional branches. This includes both the integer and floating-point compares in branches. Remember that earlier data in Figure 2.8 indicate that most integer comparisons are against an immediate operand. The programs and machine used to collect these statistics are the same as those in Figure 2.7.

tectures provide a mechanism to save the registers, while others require the compiler to generate instructions. There are two basic conventions in use to save registers. *Caller saving* means that the calling procedure must save the registers that it wants preserved for access after the call. *Callee saving* means that the called procedure must save the registers it wants to use. There are times when caller save must be used because of access patterns to globally visible variables in two different procedures. For example, suppose we have a procedure P1 that calls procedure P2, and both procedures manipulate the global variable x. If P1 had allocated x to a register it must be sure to save x to a location known by P2 before the call to P2. A compiler's ability to discover when a called procedure may access register-allocated quantities is complicated by the possibility of separate compilation and situations where P2 may not touch x but can call another procedure, P3, that may access x. Because of these complications, most compilers will conservatively caller save *any* variable that may be accessed during a call.

In the cases where either convention could be used, some programs will be more optimal with callee save and some will be more optimal with caller save. As a result, the most sophisticated compilers use a combination of the two mechanisms, and the register allocator may choose which register to use for a variable based on the convention. Later in this chapter we will examine the mismatch between sophisticated instructions for automatically saving registers and the needs of the compiler.

Summary: Operations in the Instruction Set

From this section we see the importance and popularity of simple instructions: load, store, add, subtract, move register-register, and, shift, compare equal, compare not equal, branch, jump, call, and return. Although there are many options for conditional branches, we would expect branch addressing in a new architecture to be able to jump to about 100 instructions either above or below the branch, implying a PC-relative branch displacement of at least 8 bits. We would also expect to see register-indirect and PC-relative addressing for jump instructions to support returns as well as many other features of current systems.

2.5 | Type and Size of Operands

How is the type of an operand designated? There are two primary alternatives: First, the type of an operand may be designated by encoding it in the opcode—this is the method used most often. Alternatively, the data can be annotated with tags that are interpreted by the hardware. These tags specify the type of the operand, and the operation is chosen accordingly. Machines with tagged data, however, can only be found in computer museums.

Usually the type of an operand—for example, integer, single-precision floating point, character—effectively gives its size. Common operand types include character (1 byte), half word (16 bits), word (32 bits), single-precision floating point (also 1 word), and double-precision floating point (2 words). Characters are almost always in ASCII and integers are almost universally represented as two's complement binary numbers. Until the early 1980s, most computer manufacturers chose their own floating-point representation. Almost all machines since that time follow the same standard for floating point, the IEEE standard 754. The IEEE floating-point standard is discussed in detail in Appendix A.

Some architectures provide operations on character strings, although such operations are usually quite limited and treat each byte in the string as a single character. Typical operations supported on character strings are comparisons and moves.

For business applications, some architectures support a decimal format, usually called *packed decimal* or *binary-coded decimal*—4 bits are used to encode the values 0–9, and 2 decimal digits are packed into each byte. Numeric character strings are sometimes called *unpacked decimal,* and operations—called *packing* and *unpacking*—are usually provided for converting back and forth between them.

Our benchmarks use byte or character, half word (short integer), word (integer), and floating-point data types. Figure 2.16 shows the dynamic distribution of the sizes of objects referenced from memory for these programs. The frequency of access to different data types helps in deciding what types are most important to support efficiently. Should the machine have a 64-bit access path, or would taking two cycles to access a double word be satisfactory? How important is it to support byte accesses as primitives, which, as we saw earlier, require an alignment network? In Figure 2.16, memory references are used to examine the types of data being accessed. In some architectures, objects in registers may be accessed as bytes or half words. However, such access is very infrequent—on the VAX, it accounts for no more than 12% of register references, or roughly 6% of all operand accesses in these programs. The successor to the VAX not only removed operations on data smaller than 32 bits, it also removed data transfers on these smaller sizes: The first implementations of the Alpha required multiple instructions to read or write bytes or half words.

Note that Figure 2.16 was measured on a machine with 32-bit addresses: On a 64-bit address machine the 32-bit addresses would be replaced by 64-bit addresses. Hence as 64-bit address architectures become more popular, we would expect that double-word accesses will be popular for integer programs as well as floating-point programs.

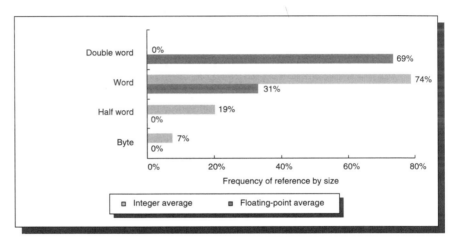

FIGURE 2.16   Distribution of data accesses by size for the benchmark programs. Access to the major data type (word or double word) clearly dominates each type of program. Half words are more popular than bytes because one of the five SPECint92 programs (eqntott) uses half words as the primary data type, and hence they are responsible for 87% of the data accesses (see Figure 2.31 on page 110). The double-word data type is used solely for double-precision floating-point in floating-point programs. These measurements were taken on the memory traffic generated on a 32-bit load-store architecture.

Summary: Type and Size of Operands

From this section we would expect a new 32-bit architecture to support 8-, 16-, and 32-bit integers and 64-bit IEEE 754 floating-point data; a new 64-bit address architecture would need to support 64-bit integers as well. The level of support for decimal data is less clear, and it is a function of the intended use of the machine as well as the effectiveness of the decimal support.

2.6 | Encoding an Instruction Set

Clearly the choices mentioned above will affect how the instructions are encoded into a binary representation for execution by the CPU. This representation affects not only the size of the compiled program, it affects the implementation of the CPU, which must decode this representation to quickly find the operation and its operands. The operation is typically specified in one field, called the *opcode*. As we shall see, the important decision is how to encode the addressing modes with the operations.

This decision depends on the range of addressing modes and the degree of independence between opcodes and modes. Some machines have one to five operands with 10 addressing modes for each operand (see Figure 2.5 on page 75). For such a large number of combinations, typically a separate *address specifier* is needed for each operand: the address specifier tells what addressing mode is used to access the operand. At the other extreme is a load-store machine with only one memory operand and only one or two addressing modes; obviously, in this case, the addressing mode can be encoded as part of the opcode.

When encoding the instructions, the number of registers and the number of addressing modes both have a significant impact on the size of instructions, since the addressing mode field and the register field may appear many times in a single instruction. In fact, for most instructions many more bits are consumed in encoding addressing modes and register fields than in specifying the opcode. The architect must balance several competing forces when encoding the instruction set:

1. The desire to have as many registers and addressing modes as possible.

2. The impact of the size of the register and addressing mode fields on the average instruction size and hence on the average program size.

3. A desire to have instructions encode into lengths that will be easy to handle in the implementation. As a minimum, the architect wants instructions to be in multiples of bytes, rather than an arbitrary length. Many architects have chosen to use a fixed-length instruction to gain implementation benefits while sacrificing average code size.

Since the addressing modes and register fields make up such a large percentage of the instruction bits, their encoding will significantly affect how easy it is for an implementation to decode the instructions. The importance of having easily decoded instructions is discussed in Chapter 3.

Figure 2.17 shows three popular choices for encoding the instruction set. The first we call *variable*, since it allows virtually all addressing modes to be with all operations. This style is best when there are many addressing modes and operations. The second choice we call *fixed*, since it combines the operation and the

compiler technology and its effect on hardware performance from the architecture and its performance, just as it was popular to try to separate an architecture from its implementation. This separation is essentially impossible with today's compilers and machines. Architectural choices affect the quality of the code that can be generated for a machine and the complexity of building a good compiler for it. Isolating the compiler from the hardware is likely to be misleading. In this section we will discuss the critical goals in the instruction set primarily from the compiler viewpoint. What features will lead to high-quality code? What makes it easy to write efficient compilers for an architecture?

The Structure of Recent Compilers

To begin, let's look at what optimizing compilers are like today. The structure of recent compilers is shown in Figure 2.18.

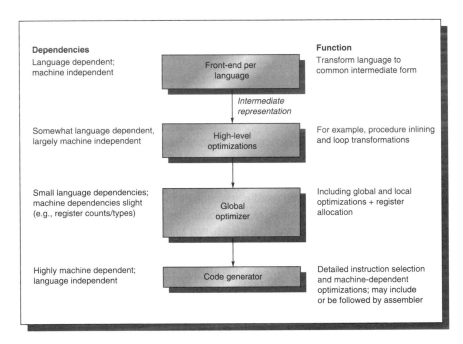

FIGURE 2.18 Current compilers typically consist of two to four passes, with more highly optimizing compilers having more passes. A *pass* is simply one phase in which the compiler reads and transforms the entire program. (The term *phase* is often used interchangeably with *pass*.) The optimizing passes are designed to be optional and may be skipped when faster compilation is the goal and lower quality code is acceptable. This structure maximizes the probability that a program compiled at various levels of optimization will produce the same output when given the same input. Because the optimizing passes are also separated, multiple languages can use the same optimizing and code-generation passes. Only a new front end is required for a new language. The high-level optimization mentioned here, *procedure inlining,* is also called *procedure integration.*

A compiler writer's first goal is correctness—all valid programs must be compiled correctly. The second goal is usually speed of the compiled code. Typically, a whole set of other goals follows these two, including fast compilation, debugging support, and interoperability among languages. Normally, the passes in the compiler transform higher-level, more abstract representations into progressively lower-level representations, eventually reaching the instruction set. This structure helps manage the complexity of the transformations and makes writing a bug-free compiler easier.

The complexity of writing a correct compiler is a major limitation on the amount of optimization that can be done. Although the multiple-pass structure helps reduce compiler complexity, it also means that the compiler must order and perform some transformations before others. In the diagram of the optimizing compiler in Figure 2.18, we can see that certain high-level optimizations are performed long before it is known what the resulting code will look like in detail. Once such a transformation is made, the compiler can't afford to go back and revisit all steps, possibly undoing transformations. This would be prohibitive, both in compilation time and in complexity. Thus, compilers make assumptions about the ability of later steps to deal with certain problems. For example, compilers usually have to choose which procedure calls to expand inline before they know the exact size of the procedure being called. Compiler writers call this problem the *phase-ordering problem*.

How does this ordering of transformations interact with the instruction set architecture? A good example occurs with the optimization called *global common subexpression elimination*. This optimization finds two instances of an expression that compute the same value and saves the value of the first computation in a temporary. It then uses the temporary value, eliminating the second computation of the expression. For this optimization to be significant, the temporary must be allocated to a register. Otherwise, the cost of storing the temporary in memory and later reloading it may negate the savings gained by not recomputing the expression. There are, in fact, cases where this optimization actually slows down code when the temporary is not register allocated. Phase ordering complicates this problem, because register allocation is typically done near the end of the global optimization pass, just before code generation. Thus, an optimizer that performs this optimization *must* assume that the register allocator will allocate the temporary to a register.

Optimizations performed by modern compilers can be classified by the style of the transformation, as follows:

1. *High-level optimizations* are often done on the source with output fed to later optimization passes.

2. *Local optimizations* optimize code only within a straight-line code fragment (called a *basic block* by compiler people).

3. *Global optimizations* extend the local optimizations across branches and introduce a set of transformations aimed at optimizing loops.

4. *Register allocation.*

5. *Machine-dependent optimizations* attempt to take advantage of specific architectural knowledge.

Because of the central role that register allocation plays, both in speeding up the code and in making other optimizations useful, it is one of the most important—if not the most important—optimizations. Recent register allocation algorithms are based on a technique called *graph coloring*. The basic idea behind graph coloring is to construct a graph representing the possible candidates for allocation to a register and then to use the graph to allocate registers. Although the problem of coloring a graph is NP-complete, there are heuristic algorithms that work well in practice.

Graph coloring works best when there are at least 16 (and preferably more) general-purpose registers available for global allocation for integer variables and additional registers for floating point. Unfortunately, graph coloring does not work very well when the number of registers is small because the heuristic algorithms for coloring the graph are likely to fail. The emphasis in the approach is to achieve 100% allocation of active variables.

It is sometimes difficult to separate some of the simpler optimizations—local and machine-dependent optimizations—from transformations done in the code generator. Examples of typical optimizations are given in Figure 2.19. The last column of Figure 2.19 indicates the frequency with which the listed optimizing transforms were applied to the source program. The effect of various optimizations on instructions executed for two programs is shown in Figure 2.20.

The Impact of Compiler Technology on the Architect's Decisions

The interaction of compilers and high-level languages significantly affects how programs use an instruction set architecture. There are two important questions: How are variables allocated and addressed? How many registers are needed to allocate variables appropriately? To address these questions, we must look at the three separate areas in which current high-level languages allocate their data:

■ The *stack* is used to allocate local variables. The stack is grown and shrunk on procedure call or return, respectively. Objects on the stack are addressed relative to the stack pointer and are primarily scalars (single variables) rather than arrays. The stack is used for activation records, *not* as a stack for evaluating expressions. Hence values are almost never pushed or popped on the stack.

Optimization name	Explanation	Percentage of the total number of optimizing transforms
High-level	**At or near the source level; machine-independent**	
Procedure integration	Replace procedure call by procedure body	N.M.
Local	**Within straight-line code**	
Common subexpression elimination	Replace two instances of the same computation by single copy	18%
Constant propagation	Replace all instances of a variable that is assigned a constant with the constant	22%
Stack height reduction	Rearrange expression tree to minimize resources needed for expression evaluation	N.M.
Global	**Across a branch**	
Global common subexpression elimination	Same as local, but this version crosses branches	13%
Copy propagation	Replace all instances of a variable A that has been assigned X (i.e., $A = X$) with X	11%
Code motion	Remove code from a loop that computes same value each iteration of the loop	16%
Induction variable elimination	Simplify/eliminate array-addressing calculations within loops	2%
Machine-dependent	**Depends on machine knowledge**	
Strength reduction	Many examples, such as replace multiply by a constant with adds and shifts	N.M.
Pipeline scheduling	Reorder instructions to improve pipeline performance	N.M.
Branch offset optimization	Choose the shortest branch displacement that reaches target	N.M.

FIGURE 2.19 Major types of optimizations and examples in each class. The third column lists the static frequency with which some of the common optimizations are applied in a set of 12 small FORTRAN and Pascal programs. The percentage is the portion of the static optimizations that are of the specified type. These data tell us about the relative frequency of occurrence of various optimizations. There are nine local and global optimizations done by the compiler included in the measurement. Six of these optimizations are covered in the figure, and the remaining three account for 18% of the total static occurrences. The abbreviation *N.M.* means that the number of occurrences of that optimization was not measured. Machine-dependent optimizations are usually done in a code generator, and none of those was measured in this experiment. Data from Chow [1983] (collected using the Stanford UCODE compiler).

- The *global data area* is used to allocate statically declared objects, such as global variables and constants. A large percentage of these objects are arrays or other aggregate data structures.

- The *heap* is used to allocate dynamic objects that do not adhere to a stack discipline. Objects in the heap are accessed with pointers and are typically not scalars.

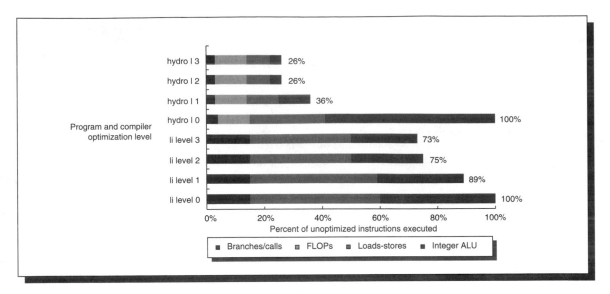

FIGURE 2.20   Change in instruction count for the programs hydro2d and li from the SPEC92 as compiler optimization levels vary. Level 0 is the same as unoptimized code. These experiments were perfomed on the MIPS compilers. Level 1 includes local optimizations, code scheduling, and local register allocation. Level 2 includes global optimizations, loop transformations (*software pipelining*), and global register allocation. Level 3 adds procedure integration.

Register allocation is much more effective for stack-allocated objects than for global variables, and register allocation is essentially impossible for heap-allocated objects because they are accessed with pointers. Global variables and some stack variables are impossible to allocate because they are *aliased*, which means that there are multiple ways to refer to the address of a variable, making it illegal to put it into a register. (Most heap variables are effectively aliased for today's compiler technology.) For example, consider the following code sequence, where & returns the address of a variable and * dereferences a pointer:

```
p = &a        -- gets address of a in p
a = ...       -- assigns to a directly
*p = ...      -- uses p to assign to a
...a...       -- accesses a
```

The variable a could not be register allocated across the assignment to *p without generating incorrect code. Aliasing causes a substantial problem because it is often difficult or impossible to decide what objects a pointer may refer to. A compiler must be conservative; many compilers will not allocate *any* local variables of a procedure in a register when there is a pointer that may refer to *one* of the local variables.

How the Architect Can Help the Compiler Writer

Today, the complexity of a compiler does not come from translating simple statements like A = B + C. Most programs are *locally simple,* and simple translations work fine. Rather, complexity arises because programs are large and globally complex in their interactions, and because the structure of compilers means that decisions must be made about what code sequence is best one step at a time.

Compiler writers often are working under their own corollary of a basic principle in architecture: *Make the frequent cases fast and the rare case correct.* That is, if we know which cases are frequent and which are rare, and if generating code for both is straightforward, then the quality of the code for the rare case may not be very important—but it must be correct!

Some instruction set properties help the compiler writer. These properties should not be thought of as hard and fast rules, but rather as guidelines that will make it easier to write a compiler that will generate efficient and correct code.

1. *Regularity*—Whenever it makes sense, the three primary components of an instruction set—the operations, the data types, and the addressing modes—should be *orthogonal.* Two aspects of an architecture are said to be orthogonal if they are independent. For example, the operations and addressing modes are orthogonal if for every operation to which a certain addressing mode can be applied, all addressing modes are applicable. This helps simplify code generation and is particularly important when the decision about what code to generate is split into two passes in the compiler. A good counterexample of this property is restricting what registers can be used for a certain class of instructions. This can result in the compiler finding itself with lots of available registers but none of the right kind!

2. *Provide primitives, not solutions*—Special features that "match" a language construct are often unusable. Attempts to support high-level languages may work only with one language, or do more or less than is required for a correct and efficient implementation of the language. Some examples of how these attempts have failed are given in section 2.9.

3. *Simplify trade-offs among alternatives*—One of the toughest jobs a compiler writer has is figuring out what instruction sequence will be best for every segment of code that arises. In earlier days, instruction counts or total code size might have been good metrics, but—as we saw in the last chapter—this is no longer true. With caches and pipelining, the trade-offs have become very complex. Anything the designer can do to help the compiler writer understand the costs of alternative code sequences would help improve the code. One of the most difficult instances of complex trade-offs occurs in a register-memory architecture in deciding how many times a variable should be referenced before it is cheaper to load it into a register. This threshold is hard to compute and, in fact, may vary among models of the same architecture.

Registers for DLX

DLX has 32 32-bit general-purpose registers (GPRs), named R0, R1, ..., R31. Additionally, there is a set of floating-point registers (FPRs), which can be used as 32 single-precision (32-bit) registers or as even-odd pairs holding double-precision values. Thus, the 64-bit floating-point registers are named F0, F2, ..., F28, F30. Both single- and double-precision floating-point operations (32-bit and 64-bit) are provided.

The value of R0 is always 0. We shall see later how we can use this register to synthesize a variety of useful operations from a simple instruction set.

A few special registers can be transferred to and from the integer registers. An example is the floating-point status register, used to hold information about the results of floating-point operations. There are also instructions for moving between a FPR and a GPR.

Data types for DLX

The data types are 8-bit bytes, 16-bit half words, and 32-bit words for integer data and 32-bit single precision and 64-bit double precision for floating point. Half words were added to the minimal set of recommended data types supported because they are found in languages like C and popular in some programs, such as the operating systems, concerned about size of data structures. They will also become more popular as Unicode becomes more widely used. Single-precision floating-point operands were added for similar reasons. (Remember the early warning that you should measure many more programs before designing an instruction set.)

The DLX operations work on 32-bit integers and 32- or 64-bit floating point. Bytes and half words are loaded into registers with either zeros or the sign bit replicated to fill the 32 bits of the registers. Once loaded, they are operated on with the 32-bit integer operations.

Addressing modes for DLX data transfers

The only data addressing modes are immediate and displacement, both with 16-bit fields. Register deferred is accomplished simply by placing 0 in the 16-bit displacement field, and absolute addressing with a 16-bit field is accomplished by using register 0 as the base register. This gives us four effective modes, although only two are supported in the architecture.

DLX memory is byte addressable in Big Endian mode with a 32-bit address. As it is a load-store architecture, all memory references are through loads or stores between memory and either the GPRs or the FPRs. Supporting the data types mentioned above, memory accesses involving the GPRs can be to a byte, to a half word, or to a word. The FPRs may be loaded and stored with single-precision or double-precision words (using a pair of registers for DP). All memory accesses must be aligned.

DLX Instruction Format

Since DLX has just two addressing modes, these can be encoded into the opcode. Following the advice on making the machine easy to pipeline and decode, all instructions are 32 bits with a 6-bit primary opcode. Figure 2.21 shows the instruction layout. These formats are simple while providing 16-bit fields for displacement addressing, immediate constants, or PC-relative branch addresses.

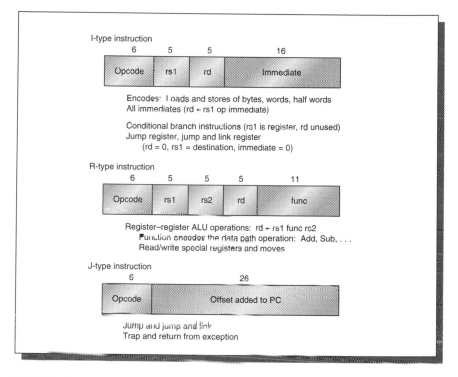

FIGURE 2.21   Instruction layout for DLX. All instructions are encoded in one of three types.

DLX Operations

DLX supports the list of simple operations recommended above plus a few others. There are four broad classes of instructions: loads and stores, ALU operations, branches and jumps, and floating-point operations.

Any of the general-purpose or floating-point registers may be loaded or stored, except that loading R0 has no effect. Single-precision floating-point numbers occupy a single floating-point register, while double-precision values occupy a pair. Conversions between single and double precision must be done explicitly. The floating-point format is IEEE 754 (see Appendix A). Figure 2.22 gives examples

Example instruction	Instruction name	Meaning
LW R1,30(R2)	Load word	$Regs[R1] \leftarrow_{32} Mem[30+Regs[R2]]$
LW R1,1000(R0)	Load word	$Regs[R1] \leftarrow_{32} Mem[1000+0]$
LB R1,40(R3)	Load byte	$Regs[R1] \leftarrow_{32} (Mem[40+Regs[R3]]_0)^{24} \#\# Mem[40+Regs[R3]]$
LBU R1,40(R3)	Load byte unsigned	$Regs[R1] \leftarrow_{32} 0^{24} \#\# Mem[40+Regs[R3]]$
LH R1,40(R3)	Load half word	$Regs[R1] \leftarrow_{32} (Mem[40+Regs[R3]]_0)^{16} \#\# Mem[40+Regs[R3]] \#\# Mem[41+Regs[R3]]$
LF F0,50(R3)	Load float	$Regs[F0] \leftarrow_{32} Mem[50+Regs[R3]]$
LD F0,50(R2)	Load double	$Regs[F0] \#\# Regs[F1] \leftarrow_{64} Mem[50+Regs[R2]]$
SW R3,500(R4)	Store word	$Mem[500+Regs[R4]] \leftarrow_{32} Regs[R3]$
SF F0,40(R3)	Store float	$Mem[40+Regs[R3]] \leftarrow_{32} Regs[F0]$
SD F0,40(R3)	Store double	$Mem[40+Regs[R3]] \leftarrow_{32} Regs[F0];$ $Mem[44+Regs[R3]] \leftarrow_{32} Regs[F1]$
SH R3,502(R2)	Store half	$Mem[502+Regs[R2]] \leftarrow_{16} Regs[R3]_{16..31}$
SB R2,41(R3)	Store byte	$Mem[41+Regs[R3]] \leftarrow_8 Regs[R2]_{24..31}$

FIGURE 2.22 The load and store instructions in DLX. All use a single addressing mode and require that the memory value be aligned. Of course, both loads and stores are available for all the data types shown.

of the load and store instructions. A complete list of the instructions appears in Figure 2.25 (page 104). To understand these figures we need to introduce a few additional extensions to our C description language:

- A subscript is appended to the symbol $\leftarrow$ whenever the length of the datum being transferred might not be clear. Thus, $\leftarrow_n$ means transfer an n-bit quantity. We use $x, y \leftarrow z$ to indicate that z should be transferred to x and y.

- A subscript is used to indicate selection of a bit from a field. Bits are labeled from the most-significant bit starting at 0. The subscript may be a single digit (e.g., $Regs[R4]_0$ yields the sign bit of R4) or a subrange (e.g., $Regs[R3]_{24..31}$ yields the least-significant byte of R3).

- The variable Mem, used as an array that stands for main memory, is indexed by a byte address and may transfer any number of bytes.

- A superscript is used to replicate a field (e.g., 0^{24} yields a field of zeros of length 24 bits).

- The symbol ## is used to concatenate two fields and may appear on either side of a data transfer.

A summary of the entire description language appears on the back inside cover. As an example, assuming that R8 and R10 are 32-bit registers:

$$Regs[R10]_{16..31} \leftarrow {}_{16}(Mem[Regs[R8]]_0)^8 \; \#\# \; Mem[Regs[R8]]$$

means that the byte at the memory location addressed by the contents of R8 is sign-extended to form a 16-bit quantity that is stored into the lower half of R10. (The upper half of R10 is unchanged.)

All ALU instructions are register-register instructions. The operations include simple arithmetic and logical operations: add, subtract, AND, OR, XOR, and shifts. Immediate forms of all these instructions, with a 16-bit sign-extended immediate, are provided. The operation LHI (load high immediate) loads the top half of a register, while setting the lower half to 0. This allows a full 32-bit constant to be built in two instructions, or a data transfer using any constant 32-bit address in one extra instruction.

As mentioned above, R0 is used to synthesize popular operations. Loading a constant is simply an add immediate where one of the source operands is R0, and a register-register move is simply an add where one of the sources is R0. (We sometimes use the mnemonic LI, standing for load immediate, to represent the former and the mnemonic MOV for the latter.)

There are also compare instructions, which compare two registers (=, ≠, <, >, ≤, ≥). If the condition is true, these instructions place a 1 in the destination register (to represent true); otherwise they place the value 0. Because these operations "set" a register, they are called set-equal, set-not-equal, set-less-than, and so on. There are also immediate forms of these compares. Figure 2.23 gives some examples of the arithmetic/logical instructions.

Example instruction	Instruction name	Meaning
ADD R1,R2,R3	Add	$Regs[R1] \leftarrow Regs[R2]+Regs[R3]$
ADDI R1,R2,#3	Add immediate	$Regs[R1] \leftarrow Regs[R2]+3$
LHI R1,#42	Load high immediate	$Regs[R1] \leftarrow 42\#\#0^{16}$
SLLI R1,R2,#5	Shift left logical immediate	$Regs[R1] \leftarrow Regs[R2]<<5$
SLT R1,R2,R3	Set less than	if $(Regs[R2]<Regs[R3])$ $Regs[R1] \leftarrow 1$ else $Regs[R1] \leftarrow 0$

FIGURE 2.23 Examples of arithmetic/logical instructions on DLX, both with and without immediates.

Control is handled through a set of jumps and a set of branches. The four jump instructions are differentiated by the two ways to specify the destination address and by whether or not a link is made. Two jumps use a 26-bit signed offset added to the program counter (of the instruction sequentially following the jump) to determine the destination address; the other two jump instructions specify a register that contains the destination address. There are two flavors of jumps: plain jump, and jump and link (used for procedure calls). The latter places the return address—the address of the next sequential instruction—in R31.

All branches are conditional. The branch condition is specified by the instruction, which may test the register source for zero or nonzero; the register may contain a data value or the result of a compare. The branch target address is specified with a 16-bit signed offset that is added to the program counter, which is pointing to the next sequential instruction. Figure 2.24 gives some typical branch and jump instructions. There is also a branch to test the floating-point status register for floating-point conditional branches, described below.

Example instruction	Instruction name	Meaning
J name	Jump	$PC \leftarrow name;\ ((PC+4) - 2^{25}) \leq name <$ $((PC+4) + 2^{25})$
JAL name	Jump and link	$Regs[R31] \leftarrow PC+4;\ PC \leftarrow name;$ $((PC+4) - 2^{25}) \leq name < ((PC+4) + 2^{25})$
JALR R2	Jump and link register	$Regs[R31] \leftarrow PC+4;\ PC \leftarrow Regs[R2]$
JR R3	Jump register	$PC \leftarrow Regs[R3]$
BEQZ R4,name	Branch equal zero	$if\ (Regs[R4]==0)\ PC \leftarrow name;$ $((PC+4) - 2^{15}) \leq name < ((PC+4) + 2^{15})$
BNEZ R4,name	Branch not equal zero	$if\ (Regs[R4]!=0)\ PC \leftarrow name;$ $((PC+4) - 2^{15}) \leq name < ((PC+4) + 2^{15})$

FIGURE 2.24 Typical control-flow instructions in DLX. All control instructions, except jumps to an address in a register, are PC-relative. If the register operand is R0, BEQZ will always branch, but the compiler will usually prefer to use a jump with a longer offset over this "unconditional branch."

Floating-point instructions manipulate the floating-point registers and indicate whether the operation to be performed is single or double precision. The operations MOVF and MOVD copy a single-precision (MOVF) or double-precision (MOVD) floating-point register to another register of the same type. The operations MOVFP2I and MOVI2FP move data between a single floating-point register and an integer register; moving a double-precision value to two integer registers requires two instructions. Integer multiply and divide that work on 32-bit floating-point registers are also provided, as are conversions from integer to floating point and vice versa.

The floating-point operations are add, subtract, multiply, and divide; a suffix D is used for double precision and a suffix F is used for single precision (e.g., ADDD, ADDF, SUBD, SUBF, MULTD, MULTF, DIVD, DIVF). Floating-point compares set a bit in the special floating-point status register that can be tested with a pair of branches: BFPT and BFPF, branch floating-point true and branch floating-point false.

One slightly unusual DLX characteristic is that it uses the floating-point unit for integer multiplies and divides. As we shall see in Chapters 3 and 4, the control for the slower floating-point operations is much more complicated than for integer addition and subtraction. Since the floating-point unit already handles floating point multiply and divide, it is not much harder for it to perform the relatively slow operations of integer multiply and divide. Hence DLX requires that operands to be multiplied or divided be placed in floating-point registers.

Figure 2.25 contains a list of all DLX operations and their meaning. To give an idea which instructions are popular, Figure 2.26 shows the frequency of instructions and instruction classes for five SPECint92 programs and Figure 2.27 shows the same data for five SPECfp92 programs. To give a more intuitive feeling, Figures 2.28 and 2.29 show the data graphically for all instructions that are responsible on average for more than 1% of the instructions executed.

Effectiveness of DLX

It would seem that an architecture with simple instruction formats, simple address modes, and simple operations would be slow, in part because it has to execute more instructions than more sophisticated designs. The performance equation from the last chapter reminds us that execution time is a function of more than just instruction count:

$$\text{CPU time} = \text{Instruction count} \times \text{CPI} \times \text{Clock cycle time}$$

To see whether reduction in instruction count is offset by increases in CPI or clock cycle time, we need to compare DLX to a sophisticated alternative.

One example of a sophisticated instruction set architecture is the VAX. In the mid 1970s, when the VAX was designed, the prevailing philosophy was to create instruction sets that were close to programming languages to simplify compilers. For example, because programming languages had loops, instruction sets should have loop instructions, not just simple conditional branches; they needed call instructions that saved registers, not just simple jump and links; they needed case instructions, not just jump indirect; and so on. Following similar arguments, the VAX provided a large set of addressing modes and made sure that all addressing modes worked with all operations. Another prevailing philosophy was to minimize code size. Recall that DRAMs have grown in capacity by a factor of four every three years; thus in the mid 1970s DRAM chips contained less than 1/1000 the capacity of today's DRAMs, so code space was also critical. Code space was

Instruction	doduc	ear	hydro2d	mdljdp2	su2cor	FP average
load	1.4%	0.2%	0.1%	1.1%	3.6%	1%
store	1.3%	0.1%		0.1%	1.3%	1%
add	13.6%	13.6%	10.9%	4.7%	9.7%	11%
sub	0.3%		0.2%		0.7%	0%
mul						0%
div						0%
compare	3.2%	3.1%	1.2%	0.3%	1.3%	2%
load imm	2.2%		0.2%	2.2%	0.9%	1%
cond branch	8.0%	10.1%	11.7%	9.3%	2.6%	8%
jump	0.9%	0.4%		0.4%	0.1%	0%
call	0.5%	1.9%			0.3%	1%
return, jmp ind	0.6%	1.9%			0.3%	1%
shift	2.0%	0.2%	2.4%	1.3%	2.3%	2%
and	0.4%	0.1%			0.3%	0%
or		0.2%	0.1%	0.1%	0.1%	0%
other (xor, not)						0%
load FP	23.3%	19.8%	24.1%	25.9%	21.6%	23%
store FP	5.7%	11.4%	9.9%	10.0%	9.8%	9%
add FP	8.8%	7.3%	3.6%	8.5%	12.4%	8%
sub FP	3.8%	3.2%	7.9%	10.4%	5.9%	6%
mul FP	12.0%	9.6%	9.4%	13.9%	21.6%	13%
div FP	2.3%		1.6%	0.9%	0.7%	1%
compare FP	4.2%	6.4%	10.4%	9.3%	0.8%	6%
mov reg-reg FP	2.1%	1.8%	5.2%	0.9%	1.9%	2%
other FP	2.4%	8.4%	0.2%	0.2%	1.2%	2%

FIGURE 2.27   DLX instruction mix for five programs from SPECfp92. Note that integer register-register move instructions are included in the add instruction. Blank entries have the value 0.0%.

goals for VAX and MIPS have led to very different architectures. The VAX goals, simple compilers and code density, led to powerful addressing modes, powerful instructions, efficient instruction encoding, and few registers. The MIPS goals were high performance via pipelining, ease of hardware implementation, and compatibility with highly optimizing compilers. These goals led to simple instructions, simple addressing modes, fixed-length instruction formats, and a large number of registers.

Figure 2.30 shows the ratio of the number of instructions executed, the ratio of CPIs, and the ratio of performance measured in clock cycles. Since the organizations

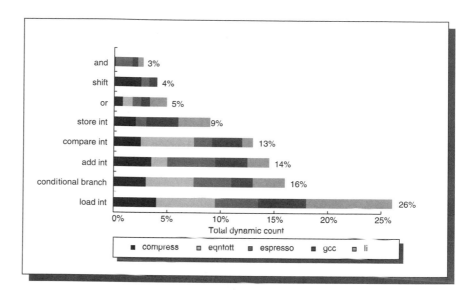

FIGURE 2.28 Graphical display of instructions executed of the five programs from SPECint92 in Figure 2.26. These instruction classes collectively are responsible on average for 92% of instructions executed.

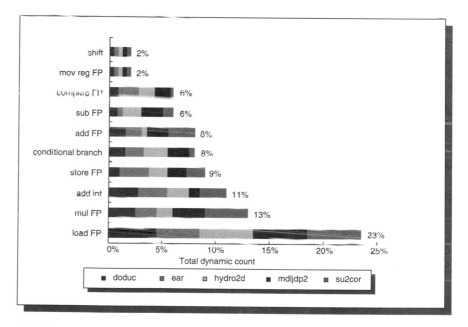

FIGURE 2.29 Graphical display of instructions executed of the five programs from SPECfp92 in Figure 2.27. These instruction classes collectively are responsible on average for just under 90% of instructions executed.

The VAX designers provided a simpler instruction, JSB, that is much faster since it only pushes the return PC on the stack and jumps to the procedure. However, most VAX compilers use the more costly CALLS instructions. The call instructions were included in the architecture to standardize the procedure linkage convention. Other machines have standardized their calling convention by agreement among compiler writers and without requiring the overhead of a complex, very general-procedure call instruction.

Fallacy: There is such a thing as a typical program.

Many people would like to believe that there is a single "typical" program that could be used to design an optimal instruction set. For example, see the synthetic benchmarks discussed in Chapter 1. The data in this chapter clearly show that programs can vary significantly in how they use an instruction set. For example, Figure 2.31 shows the mix of data transfer sizes for four of the SPEC92 programs: It would be hard to say what is typical from these four programs. The variations are even larger on an instruction set that supports a class of applications, such as decimal instructions, that are unused by other applications.

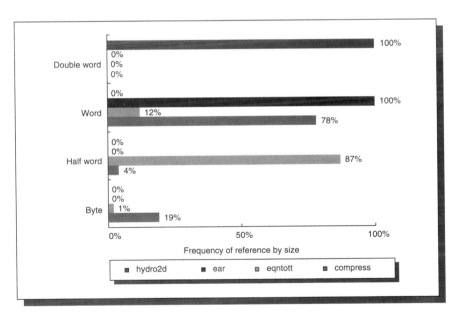

FIGURE 2.31   Data reference size of four programs from SPEC92. Although you can calculate an average size, it would be hard to claim the average is typical of programs.

Fallacy: An architecture with flaws cannot be successful.

The 80x86 provides a dramatic example: The architecture is one only its creators could love (see Appendix D). Succeeding generations of Intel engineers have tried to correct unpopular architectural decisions made in designing the 80x86. For example, the 80x86 supports segmentation, whereas all others picked paging; the 80x86 uses extended accumulators for integer data, but other machines use general-purpose registers; and it uses a stack for floating-point data when everyone else abandoned execution stacks long before. Despite these major difficulties, the 80x86 architecture—because of its selection as the microprocessor in the IBM PC—has been enormously successful.

Fallacy: You can design a flawless architecture.

All architecture design involves trade-offs made in the context of a set of hardware and software technologies. Over time those technologies are likely to change, and decisions that may have been correct at the time they were made look like mistakes. For example, in 1975 the VAX designers overemphasized the importance of code-size efficiency, underestimating how important ease of decoding and pipelining would be 10 years later. Almost all architectures eventually succumb to the lack of sufficient address space. However, avoiding this problem in the long run would probably mean compromising the efficiency of the architecture in the short run.

2.10 | Concluding Remarks

The earliest architectures were limited in their instruction sets by the hardware technology of that time. As soon as the hardware technology permitted, architects began looking for ways to support high-level languages. This search led to three distinct periods of thought about how to support programs efficiently. In the 1960s, stack architectures became popular. They were viewed as being a good match for high-level languages—and they probably were, given the compiler technology of the day. In the 1970s, the main concern of architects was how to reduce software costs. This concern was met primarily by replacing software with hardware, or by providing high-level architectures that could simplify the task of software designers. The result was both the high-level-language computer architecture movement and powerful architectures like the VAX, which has a large number of addressing modes, multiple data types, and a highly orthogonal architecture. In the 1980s, more sophisticated compiler technology and a renewed emphasis on machine performance saw a return to simpler architectures, based mainly on the load-store style of machine.

Today, there is widespread agreement on instruction set design. However, in the next decade we expect to see change in the following areas:

- The 32-bit address instruction sets are being extended to 64-bit addresses, expanding the width of the registers (among other things) to 64 bits. Appendix C gives three examples of architectures that have gone from 32 bits to 64 bits.

The term "machine language programmer" meant that compatibility would hold, even in assembly language, while "timing independent" allowed different implementations.

The IBM 360 was the first machine to sell in large quantities with both byte addressing using 8-bit bytes and general-purpose registers. The 360 also had register-memory and limited memory-memory instructions.

In 1964, Control Data delivered the first supercomputer, the CDC 6600. As Thornton [1964] discusses, he, Cray, and the other 6600 designers were the first to explore pipelining in depth. The 6600 was the first general-purpose, load-store machine. In the 1960s, the designers of the 6600 realized the need to simplify architecture for the sake of efficient pipelining. This interaction between architectural simplicity and implementation was largely neglected during the 1970s by microprocessor and minicomputer designers, but it was brought back in the 1980s.

In the late 1960s and early 1970s, people realized that software costs were growing faster than hardware costs. McKeeman [1967] argued that compilers and operating systems were getting too big and too complex and taking too long to develop. Because of inferior compilers and the memory limitations of machines, most systems programs at the time were still written in assembly language. Many researchers proposed alleviating the software crisis by creating more powerful, software-oriented architectures. Tanenbaum [1978] studied the properties of high-level languages. Like other researchers, he found that most programs are simple. He then argued that architectures should be designed with this in mind and should optimize program size and ease of compilation. Tanenbaum proposed a stack machine with frequency-encoded instruction formats to accomplish these goals. However, as we have observed, program size does not translate directly to cost/performance, and stack machines faded out shortly after this work.

Strecker's article [1978] discusses how he and the other architects at DEC responded to this by designing the VAX architecture. The VAX was designed to simplify compilation of high-level languages. Compiler writers had complained about the lack of complete orthogonality in the PDP-11. The VAX architecture was designed to be highly orthogonal and to allow the mapping of a high-level-language statement into a single VAX instruction. Additionally, the VAX designers tried to optimize code size because compiled programs were often too large for available memories.

The VAX-11/780 was the first machine announced in the VAX series. It is one of the most successful and heavily studied machines ever built. The cornerstone of DEC's strategy was a single architecture, VAX, running a single operating system, VMS. This strategy worked well for over 10 years. The large number of papers reporting instruction mixes, implementation measurements, and analysis of the VAX make it an ideal case study [Wiecek 1982; Clark and Levy 1982]. Bhandarkar and Clark [1991] give a quantitative analysis of the disadvantages of the VAX versus a RISC machine, essentially a technical explanation for the demise of the VAX.

While the VAX was being designed, a more radical approach, called *high-level-language computer architecture* (HLLCA), was being advocated in the research community. This movement aimed to eliminate the gap between high-level languages and computer hardware—what Gagliardi [1973] called the "semantic gap"—by bringing the hardware "up to" the level of the programming language. Meyers [1982] provides a good summary of the arguments and a history of high-level-language computer architecture projects.

HLLCA never had a significant commercial impact. The increase in memory size on machines and the use of virtual memory eliminated the code-size problems arising from high-level languages and operating systems written in high-level languages. The combination of simpler architectures together with software offered greater performance and more flexibility at lower cost and lower complexity.

In the early 1980s, the direction of computer architecture began to swing away from providing high-level hardware support for languages. Ditzel and Patterson [1980] analyzed the difficulties encountered by the high-level-language architectures and argued that the answer lay in simpler architectures. In another paper [Patterson and Ditzel 1980], these authors first discussed the idea of reduced instruction set computers (RISC) and presented the argument for simpler architectures. Their proposal was rebutted by Clark and Strecker [1980].

The simple load-store machines from which DLX is derived are commonly called RISC architectures. The roots of RISC architectures go back to machines like the 6600, where Thornton, Cray, and others recognized the importance of instruction set simplicity in building a fast machine. Cray continued his tradition of keeping machines simple in the CRAY-1. However, DLX and its close relatives are built primarily on the work of three research projects: the Berkeley RISC processor, the IBM 801, and the Stanford MIPS processor. These architectures have attracted enormous industrial interest because of claims of a performance advantage of anywhere from two to five times over other machines using the same technology.

Begun in 1975, the IBM project was the first to start but was the last to become public. The IBM machine was designed as an ECL minicomputer, while the university projects were both MOS-based microprocessors. John Cocke is considered to be the father of the 801 design. He received both the Eckert-Mauchly and Turing awards in recognition of his contribution. Radin [1982] describes the highlights of the 801 architecture. The 801 was an experimental project that was never designed to be a product. In fact, to keep down cost and complexity, the machine was built with only 24-bit registers.

In 1980, Patterson and his colleagues at Berkeley began the project that was to give this architectural approach its name (see Patterson and Ditzel [1980]). They built two machines called RISC-I and RISC-II. Because the IBM project was not widely known or discussed, the role played by the Berkeley group in promoting the RISC approach was critical to the acceptance of the technology. The Berkeley group went on to build RISC machines targeted toward Smalltalk, described by Ungar et al. [1984], and LISP, described by Taylor et al. [1986].

In 1981, Hennessy and his colleagues at Stanford published a description of the Stanford MIPS machine. Efficient pipelining and compiler-assisted scheduling of the pipeline were both key aspects of the original MIPS design.

These early RISC machines—the 801, RISC-II, and MIPS—had much in common. Both university projects were interested in designing a simple machine that could be built in VLSI within the university environment. All three machines used a simple load-store architecture, fixed-format 32-bit instructions, and emphasized efficient pipelining. Patterson [1985] describes the three machines and the basic design principles that have come to characterize what a RISC machine is. Hennessy [1984] provides another view of the same ideas, as well as other issues in VLSI processor design.

In 1985, Hennessy published an explanation of the RISC performance advantage and traced its roots to a substantially lower CPI—under 2 for a RISC machine and over 10 for a VAX-11/780 (though not with identical workloads). A paper by Emer and Clark [1984] characterizing VAX-11/780 performance was instrumental in helping the RISC researchers understand the source of the performance advantage seen by their machines.

Since the university projects finished up, in the 1983–84 time frame, the technology has been widely embraced by industry. Many manufacturers of the early computers (those made before 1986) claimed that their products were RISC machines. However, these claims were often born more of marketing ambition than of engineering reality.

In 1986, the computer industry began to announce processors based on the technology explored by the three RISC research projects. Moussouris et al. [1986] describe the MIPS R2000 integer processor, while Kane's book [1986] is a complete description of the architecture. Hewlett-Packard converted their existing minicomputer line to RISC architectures; the HP Precision Architecture is described by Lee [1989]. IBM never directly turned the 801 into a product. Instead, the ideas were adopted for a new, low-end architecture that was incorporated in the IBM RT-PC and described in a collection of papers [Waters 1986]. In 1990, IBM announced a new RISC architecture (the RS 6000), which is the first superscalar RISC machine (see Chapter 4). In 1987, Sun Microsystems began delivering machines based on the SPARC architecture, a derivative of the Berkeley RISC-II machine; SPARC is described in Garner et al. [1988]. The PowerPC joined the forces of Apple, IBM, and Motorola. Appendix C summarizes several RISC architectures.

Prior to the RISC architecture movement, the major trend had been highly microcoded architectures aimed at reducing the semantic gap. DEC, with the VAX, and Intel, with the iAPX 432, were among the leaders in this approach. Today it is hard to find a computer company without a RISC product. With the 1994 announcement that Hewlett Packard and Intel will eventually have a common architecture, the end of the 1970s architectures draws near.

References

AMDAHL, G. M., G. A. BLAAUW, AND F. P. BROOKS, JR. [1964]. "Architecture of the IBM System 360," *IBM J. Research and Development* 8:2 (April), 87–101.

BARTON, R. S. [1961]. "A new approach to the functional design of a computer," *Proc. Western Joint Computer Conf.,* 393–396.

BELL, G., R. CADY, H. MCFARLAND, B. DELAGI, J. O'LAUGHLIN, R. NOONAN, AND W. WULF [1970]. "A new architecture for mini-computers: The DEC PDP-11," *Proc. AFIPS SJCC*, 657–675.

BHANDARKAR, D., AND D. W. CLARK [1991]. "Performance from architecture: Comparing a RISC and a CISC with similar hardware organizations," *Proc. Fourth Conf. on Architectural Support for Programming Languages and Operating Systems*, IEEE/ACM (April), Palo Alto, Calif., 310–19.

CHOW, F. C. [1983]. *A Portable Machine-Independent Global Optimizer—Design and Measurements*, Ph.D. Thesis, Stanford Univ. (December).

CLARK, D. AND H. LEVY [1982]. "Measurement and analysis of instruction set use in the VAX-11/780," *Proc. Ninth Symposium on Computer Architecture* (April), Austin, Tex., 9–17.

CLARK, D. AND W. D. STRECKER [1980]. "Comments on 'the case for the reduced instruction set computer'," *Computer Architecture News* 8:6 (October), 34–38.

CRAWFORD, J. AND P. GELSINGER [1988]. *Programming the 80386,* Sybex Books, Alameda, Calif.

DITZEL, D. R. AND D. A. PATTERSON [1980]. "Retrospective on high-level language computer architecture," in *Proc. Seventh Annual Symposium on Computer Architecture,* La Baule, France (June), 97–104.

EMER, J. S. AND D. W. CLARK [1984]. "A characterization of processor performance in the VAX-11/780," *Proc. 11th Symposium on Computer Architecture* (June), Ann Arbor, Mich., 301–310.

GAGLIARDI, U. O. [1973]. "Report of workshop 4–Software-related advances in computer hardware," *Proc. Symposium on the High Cost of Software*, Menlo Park, Calif., 99–120.

GARNER, R., A. AGARWAL, F. BRIGGS, E. BROWN, D. HOUGH, B. JOY, S. KLEIMAN, S. MUNCHNIK, M. NAMJOO, D. PATTERSON, J. PENDLETON, AND R. TUCK [1988]. "Scalable processor architecture (SPARC)," *COMPCON, IEEE* (March), San Francisco, 278–283.

HAUCK, E. A., AND B. A. DENT [1968]. "Burroughs' B6500/B7500 stack mechanism," *Proc. AFIPS SJCC*, 245–251.

HENNESSY, J. [1984]. "VLSI processor architecture," *IEEE Trans. on Computers* C-33:11 (December), 1221–1246.

HENNESSY, J. [1985]. "VLSI RISC processors," *VLSI Systems Design* VI:10 (October), 22–32.

HENNESSY, J., N. JOUPPI, F. BASKETT, AND J. GILL [1981]. "MIPS: A VLSI processor architecture," *Proc. CMU Conf. on VLSI Systems and Computations* (October), Computer Science Press, Rockville, Md.

KANE, G. [1986]. *MIPS R2000 RISC Architecture*, Prentice Hall, Englewood Cliffs, N.J.

LEE, R. [1989]. "Precision architecture," *Computer* 22:1 (January), 78–91.

LEVY, H. AND R. ECKHOUSE [1989]. *Computer Programming and Architecture: The VAX,* Digital Press, Boston.

LUNDE, A. [1977]. "Empirical evaluation of some features of instruction set processor architecture," *Comm. ACM* 20:3 (March), 143–152.

MCKEEMAN, W. M. [1967]. "Language directed computer design," *Proc. 1967 Fall Joint Computer Conf.,* Washington, D.C., 413–417.

MEYERS, G. J. [1978]. "The evaluation of expressions in a storage-to-storage architecture," *Computer Architecture News* 7:3 (October), 20–23.

MEYERS, G. J. [1982]. *Advances in Computer Architecture*, 2nd ed., Wiley, New York.

MOUSSOURIS, J., L. CRUDELE, D. FREITAS, C. HANSEN, E. HUDSON, S. PRZYBYLSKI, T. RIORDAN, AND C. ROWEN [1986]. "A CMOS RISC processor with integrated system functions," *Proc. COMPCON, IEEE* (March), San Francisco, 191.

PATTERSON, D. [1985]. "Reduced instruction set computers," *Comm. ACM* 28:1 (January), 8–21.

PATTERSON, D. A. AND D. R. DITZEL [1980]. "The case for the reduced instruction set computer," *Computer Architecture News* 8:6 (October), 25–33.

RADIN, G. [1982]. "The 801 minicomputer," *Proc. Symposium Architectural Support for Programming Languages and Operating Systems* (March), Palo Alto, Calif., 39–47.

STRECKER, W. D. [1978]. "VAX-11/780: A virtual address extension of the PDP-11 family," *Proc. AFIPS National Computer Conf.* 47, 967–980.

TANENBAUM, A. S. [1978]. "Implications of structured programming for machine architecture," *Comm. ACM* 21:3 (March), 237–246.

TAYLOR, G., P. HILFINGER, J. LARUS, D. PATTERSON, AND B. ZORN [1986]. "Evaluation of the SPUR LISP architecture," *Proc. 13th Symposium on Computer Architecture* (June), Tokyo.

THORNTON, J. E. [1964]. "Parallel operation in Control Data 6600," *Proc. AFIPS Fall Joint Computer Conf.* 26, part 2, 33–40.

UNGAR, D., R. BLAU, P. FOLEY, D. SAMPLES, AND D. PATTERSON [1984]. "Architecture of SOAR: Smalltalk on a RISC," *Proc. 11th Symposium on Computer Architecture* (June), Ann Arbor, Mich., 188–197.

WAKERLY, J. [1989]. *Microcomputer Architecture and Programming,* J. Wiley, New York.

WATERS, F., ED. [1986]. *IBM RT Personal Computer Technology,* IBM, Austin, Tex., SA 23-1057.

WIECEK, C. [1982]. "A case study of the VAX 11 instruction set usage for compiler execution," *Proc. Symposium on Architectural Support for Programming Languages and Operating Systems* (March), IEEE/ACM, Palo Alto, Calif., 177–184.

WULF, W. [1981]. "Compilers and computer architecture," *Computer* 14:7 (July), 41–47.

E X E R C I S E S

2.1 [20/15/10] <2.3,2.8> We are designing instruction set formats for a load-store architecture and are trying to decide whether it is worthwhile to have multiple offset lengths for branches and memory references. We have decided that both branch and memory references can have only 0-, 8-, and 16-bit offsets. The length of an instruction would be equal to 16 bits + offset length in bits. ALU instructions will be 16 bits. Figure 2.32 contains the data in cumulative form. Assume an additional bit is needed for the sign on the offset.

For instruction set frequencies, use the data for DLX from the average of the five benchmarks for the load-store machine in Figure 2.26. Assume that the miscellaneous instructions are all ALU instructions that use only registers.

a. [20] <2.3,2.8> Suppose offsets were permitted to be 0, 8, or 16 bits in length, including the sign bit. What is the average length of an executed instruction?

b. [15] <2.3,2.8> Suppose we wanted a fixed-length instruction and we chose a 24-bit instruction length (for everything, including ALU instructions). For every offset of longer than 8 bits, an additional instruction is required. Determine the number of

Offset bits	Cumulative data references	Cumulative branches
0	17%	0%
1	17%	0%
2	23%	24%
3	32%	49%
4	40%	64%
5	48%	79%
6	54%	87%
7	57%	93%
8	60%	98%
9	61%	99%
10	69%	100%
11	71%	100%
12	75%	100%
13	78%	100%
14	80%	100%
15	100%	100%

FIGURE 2.32 **The second and third columns contain the cumulative percentage of the data references and branches, respectively, that can be accommodated with the corresponding number of bits of magnitude in the displacement.** These are the average distances of all 10 programs in Figure 2.7.

instruction bytes fetched in this machine with fixed instruction size versus those fetched with a byte-variable-sized instruction as defined in part (a).

c. [10] <2.3,2.8> Now suppose we use a fixed offset length of 16 bits so that no additional instruction is ever required. How many instruction bytes would be required? Compare this result to your answer to part (b), which used 8-bit fixed offsets that used additional instruction words when larger offsets were required.

2.2 [15/10] <2.2> Several researchers have suggested that adding a register-memory addressing mode to a load-store machine might be useful. The idea is to replace sequences of

```
LOAD    R1,0(Rb)
ADD     R2,R2,R1
```

by

```
ADD     R2,0(Rb)
```

Assume the new instruction will cause the clock cycle to increase by 10%. Use the instruction frequencies for the gcc benchmark on the load-store machine from Figure 2.26. The new instruction affects only the clock cycle and not the CPI.

a.   [15] <2.2> What percentage of the loads must be eliminated for the machine with the new instruction to have at least the same performance?

b.   [10] <2.2> Show a situation in a multiple instruction sequence where a load of R1 followed immediately by a use of R1 (with some type of opcode) could not be replaced by a single instruction of the form proposed, assuming that the same opcode exists.

2.3 [20] <2.2> Your task is to compare the memory efficiency of four different styles of instruction set architectures. The architecture styles are

1.   *Accumulator*—All operations occur between a single register and a memory location.

2.   *Memory-memory*—All three operands of each instruction are in memory.

3.   *Stack*—All operations occur on top of the stack. Only push and pop access memory; all other instructions remove their operands from stack and replace them with the result. The implementation uses a stack for the top two entries; accesses that use other stack positions are memory references.

4.   *Load-store*—All operations occur in registers, and register-to-register instructions have three operands per instruction. There are 16 general-purpose registers, and register specifiers are 4 bits long.

To measure memory efficiency, make the following assumptions about all four instruction sets:

■   The opcode is always 1 byte (8 bits).

■   All memory addresses are 2 bytes (16 bits).

■   All data operands are 4 bytes (32 bits).

■   All instructions are an integral number of bytes in length.

There are no other optimizations to reduce memory traffic, and the variables A, B, C, and D are initially in memory.

Invent your own assembly language mnemonics and write the best equivalent assembly language code for the high-level-language fragment given. Write the four code sequences for

```
A = B + C;
B = A + C;
D = A - B;
```

Calculate the instruction bytes fetched and the memory-data bytes transferred. Which architecture is most efficient as measured by code size? Which architecture is most efficient as measured by total memory bandwidth required (code + data)?

2.4 [Discussion] <2.2–2.9> What are the *economic* arguments (i.e., more machines sold) for and against changing instruction set architecture?

2.5 [25] <2.1–2.5> Find an instruction set manual for some older machine (libraries and private bookshelves are good places to look). Summarize the instruction set with the discriminating characteristics used in Figure 2.2. Write the code sequence for this machine for the statements in Exercise 2.3. The size of the data need not be 32 bits as in Exercise 2.3 if the word size is smaller in the older machine.

2.6 [20] <2.8> Consider the following fragment of C code:

```
for (i=0; i<=100; i++)
        {A[i] = B[i] + C;}
```

Assume that A and B are arrays of 32-bit integers, and C and i are 32-bit integers. Assume that all data values and their addresses are kept in memory (at addresses 0, 5000, 1500, and 2000 for A, B, C, and i, respectively) except when they are operated on. Assume that values in registers are lost between iterations of the loop.

Write the code for DLX; how many instructions are required dynamically? How many memory-data references will be executed? What is the code size in bytes?

2.7 [20] <App. D> Repeat Exercise 2.6, but this time write the code for the 80x86.

2.8 [20] <2.8> For this question use the code sequence of Exercise 2.6, but put the scalar data—the value of i, the value of C, and the addresses of the array variables (but not the actual array)—in registers and keep them there whenever possible.

Write the code for DLX; how many instructions are required dynamically? How many memory-data references will be executed? What is the code size in bytes?

2.9 [20] <App. D> Make the same assumptions and answer the same questions as the prior exercise, but this time write the code for the 80x86.

2.10 [15] <2.8> When designing memory systems it becomes useful to know the frequency of memory reads versus writes and also accesses for instructions versus data. Using the average instruction-mix information for DLX in Figure 2.26, find

- the percentage of all memory accesses for data

- the percentage of data accesses that are reads

- the percentage of all memory accesses that are reads

Ignore the size of a datum when counting accesses.

2.11 [18] <2.8> Compute the effective CPI for DLX using Figure 2.26. Suppose we have made the following measurements of average CPI for instructions:

Instruction	Clock cycles
All ALU instructions	1.0
Loads-stores	1.4
Conditional branches	
Taken	2.0
Not taken	1.5
Jumps	1.2

Assume that 60% of the conditional branches are taken and that all instructions in the miscellaneous category of Figure 2.26 are ALU instructions. Average the instruction frequencies of gcc and espresso to obtain the instruction mix.

2.12 [20/10] <2.3,2.8> Consider adding a new index addressing mode to DLX. The addressing mode adds two registers and an 11-bit signed offset to get the effective address.

Our compiler will be changed so that code sequences of the form

```
ADD R1, R1, R2
LW  Rd, 100(R1)(or store)
```

will be replaced with a load (or store) using the new addressing mode. Use the overall average instruction frequencies from Figure 2.26 in evaluating this addition.

a.   [20] <2.3,2.8> Assume that the addressing mode can be used for 10% of the displacement loads and stores (accounting for both the frequency of this type of address calculation and the shorter offset). What is the ratio of instruction count on the enhanced DLX compared to the original DLX?

b.   [10] <2.3,2.8> If the new addressing mode lengthens the clock cycle by 5%, which machine will be faster and by how much?

2.13 [25/15] <2.7> Find a C compiler and compile the code shown in Exercise 2.6 for one of the machines covered in this book. Compile the code both optimized and unoptimized.

a.   [25] <2.7> Find the instruction count, dynamic instruction bytes fetched, and data accesses done for both the optimized and unoptimized versions.

b.   [15] <2.7> Try to improve the code by hand and compute the same measures as in part (a) for your hand-optimized version.

2.14 [30] <2.8> Small synthetic benchmarks can be very misleading when used for measuring instruction mixes. This is particularly true when these benchmarks are optimized. In this exercise and Exercises 2.15–2.17, we want to explore these differences. These programming exercises can be done with any load-store machine.

Compile Whetstone with optimization. Compute the instruction mix for the top 20 most frequently executed instructions. How do the optimized and unoptimized mixes compare? How does the optimized mix compare to the mix for spice on the same or a similar machine?

2.15 [30] <2.8> Follow the same guidelines as the prior exercise, but this time use Dhrystone and compare it with TeX.

2.16 [30] <2.8> Many computer manufacturers now include tools or simulators that allow you to measure the instruction set usage of a user program. Among the methods in use are machine simulation, hardware-supported trapping, and a compiler technique that instruments the object-code module by inserting counters. Find a processor available to you that includes such a tool. Use it to measure the instruction set mix for one of TeX, gcc, or spice. Compare the results to those shown in this chapter.

2.17 [30] <2.3,2.8> DLX has only three operand formats for its register-register operations. Many operations might use the same destination register as one of the sources. We could introduce a new instruction format into DLX called R_2 that has only two operands and is a total of 24 bits in length. By using this instruction type whenever an operation had only two different register operands, we could reduce the instruction bandwidth required for a program. Modify the DLX simulator to count the frequency of register-register operations with only two different register operands. Using the benchmarks that come with the simulator, determine how much more instruction bandwidth DLX requires than DLX with the R_2 format.

2.18 [25] <App. C> How much do the instruction set variations among the RISC machines discussed in Appendix C affect performance? Choose at least three small programs (e.g., a sort), and code these programs in DLX and two other assembly languages. What is the resulting difference in instruction count?

3 Pipelining

It is quite a three-pipe problem.

Sir Arthur Conan Doyle
The Adventures of Sherlock Holmes

3.1	What Is Pipelining?	125
3.2	The Basic Pipeline for DLX	132
3.3	The Major Hurdle of Pipelining—Pipeline Hazards	139
3.4	Data Hazards	146
3.5	Control Hazards	161
3.6	What Makes Pipelining Hard to Implement?	178
3.7	Extending the DLX Pipeline to Handle Multicycle Operations	187
3.8	Crosscutting Issues: Instruction Set Design and Pipelining	199
3.9	Putting It All Together: The MIPS R4000 Pipeline	201
3.10	Fallacies and Pitfalls	209
3.11	Concluding Remarks	211
3.12	Historical Perspective and References	212
	Exercises	214

3.1 | What Is Pipelining?

Pipelining is an implementation technique whereby multiple instructions are overlapped in execution. Today, pipelining is the key implementation technique used to make fast CPUs.

A pipeline is like an assembly line. In an automobile assembly line, there are many steps, each contributing something to the construction of the car. Each step operates in parallel with the other steps, though on a different car. In a computer pipeline, each step in the pipeline completes a part of an instruction. Like the assembly line, different steps are completing different parts of different instructions in parallel. Each of these steps is called a *pipe stage* or a *pipe segment*. The stages are connected one to the next to form a pipe—instructions enter at one end, progress through the stages, and exit at the other end, just as cars would in an assembly line.

In an automobile assembly line, *throughput* is defined as the number of cars per hour and is determined by how often a completed car exits the assembly line. Likewise, the throughput of an instruction pipeline is determined by how often an instruction exits the pipeline. Because the pipe stages are hooked together, all the stages must be ready to proceed at the same time, just as we would require in an assembly line. The time required between moving an instruction one step down the pipeline is a *machine cycle*. Because all stages proceed at the same time, the length of a machine cycle is determined by the time required for the slowest pipe stage, just as in an auto assembly line, the longest step would determine the time between advancing the line. In a computer, this machine cycle is usually one clock cycle (sometimes it is two, rarely more), although the clock may have multiple phases.

The pipeline designer's goal is to balance the length of each pipeline stage, just as the designer of the assembly line tries to balance the time for each step in the process. If the stages are perfectly balanced, then the time per instruction on the pipelined machine—assuming ideal conditions—is equal to

$$\frac{\text{Time per instruction on unpipelined machine}}{\text{Number of pipe stages}}$$

Under these conditions, the speedup from pipelining equals the number of pipe stages, just as an assembly line with n stages can ideally produce cars n times as fast. Usually, however, the stages will not be perfectly balanced; furthermore, pipelining does involve some overhead. Thus, the time per instruction on the pipelined machine will not have its minimum possible value, yet it can be close.

Pipelining yields a reduction in the average execution time per instruction. Depending on what you consider as the base line, the reduction can be viewed as decreasing the number of clock cycles per instruction (CPI), as decreasing the clock cycle time, or as a combination. If the starting point is a machine that takes multiple clock cycles per instruction, then pipelining is usually viewed as reducing the CPI. This is the primary view we will take. If the starting point is a machine that takes one (long) clock cycle per instruction, then pipelining decreases the clock cycle time.

Pipelining is an implementation technique that exploits parallelism among the instructions in a sequential instruction stream. It has the substantial advantage that, unlike some speedup techniques (see Chapter 8 and Appendix B), it is not visible to the programmer. In this chapter we will first cover the concept of pipelining using DLX and a simple version of its pipeline. We use DLX because its simplicity makes it easy to demonstrate the principles of pipelining. In addition, to simplify the diagrams we do not include the jump instructions of DLX; adding them does not involve new concepts—only bigger diagrams. The principles of pipelining in this chapter apply to more complex instruction sets than DLX or its RISC relatives, although the resulting pipelines are more complex. Using the DLX example, we will look at the problems pipelining introduces and the performance attainable under typical situations. Section 3.9 examines the MIPS R4000 pipeline, which is similar to other recent machines with extensive pipelining. Chapter 4 looks at more advanced pipelining techniques being used in the highest-performance processors.

Before we proceed to basic pipelining, we need to review a simple implementation of an unpipelined version of DLX.

A Simple Implementation of DLX

To understand how DLX can be pipelined, we need to understand how it is implemented *without* pipelining. This section shows a simple implementation where every instruction takes at most five clock cycles. We will extend this basic implementation to a pipelined version, resulting in a much lower CPI. Our unpipelined implementation is not the most economical or the highest-performance implementation without pipelining. Instead, it is designed to lead naturally to a pipelined implementation. We will indicate where the implementation could be improved later in this section. Implementing the instruction set requires the introduction of several temporary registers that are not part of the architecture; these are introduced in this section to simplify pipelining.

In sections 3.1–3.5 we focus on a pipeline for an integer subset of DLX that consists of load-store word, branch, and integer ALU operations. Later in the chapter, we will incorporate the basic floating-point operations. Although we discuss only a subset of DLX, the basic principles can be extended to handle all the instructions.

Every DLX instruction can be implemented in at most five clock cycles. The five clock cycles are as follows.

1. *Instruction fetch cycle* (IF):

$$IR \leftarrow Mem[PC]$$
$$NPC \leftarrow PC + 4$$

Operation: Send out the PC and fetch the instruction from memory into the instruction register (IR); increment the PC by 4 to address the next sequential instruction. The IR is used to hold the instruction that will be needed on subsequent clock cycles; likewise the register NPC is used to hold the next sequential PC.

2. *Instruction decode/register fetch cycle* (ID):

$$A \leftarrow Regs[IR_{6..10}];$$
$$B \leftarrow Regs[IR_{11..15}];$$
$$Imm \leftarrow ((IR_{16})^{16}\#\#IR_{16..31})$$

Operation: Decode the instruction and access the register file to read the registers. The outputs of the general-purpose registers are read into two temporary registers (A and B) for use in later clock cycles. The lower 16 bits of the IR are also sign-extended and stored into the temporary register Imm, for use in the next cycle.

device, which may be memory, a general-purpose register, the PC, or a temporary register (i.e., LMD, Imm, A, B, IR, NPC, ALUOutput, or Cond). The temporary registers hold values between clock cycles for one instruction, while the other storage elements are visible parts of the state and hold values between successive instructions.

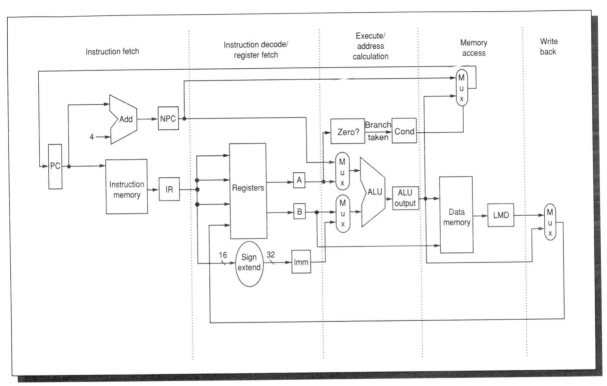

FIGURE 3.1   The implementation of the DLX datapath allows every instruction to be executed in four or five clock cycles. Although the PC is shown in the portion of the datapath that is used in instruction fetch and the registers are shown in the portion of the datapath that is used in instruction decode/register fetch, both of these functional units are read as well as written by an instruction. Although we show these functional units in the cycle corresponding to where they are read, the PC is written during the memory access clock cycle and the registers are written during the write back clock cycle. In both cases, the writes in later pipe stages are indicated by the multiplexer output (in memory access or write back) that carries a value back to the PC or registers. These backward-flowing signals introduce much of the complexity of pipelining, and we will look at them more carefully in the next few sections.

In this implementation, branch and store instructions require four cycles and all other instructions require five cycles. Assuming the branch frequency of 12% and a store frequency of 5% from the last chapter, this leads to an overall CPI of 4.83. This implementation, however, is not optimal either in achieving the best performance or in using the minimal amount of hardware given the performance level. The CPI could be improved without affecting the clock rate by completing ALU instructions during the MEM cycle, since those instructions are idle during that cycle. Assuming ALU instructions occupy 47% of the instruction mix, as we measured in Chapter 2, this improvement would lead to a CPI of 4.35, or an improvement of 4.82/4.35 = 1.1. Beyond this simple change, any other attempts to decrease the CPI may increase the clock cycle time, since such changes would need to put more activity into a clock cycle. Of course, it may still be beneficial to trade an increase in the clock cycle time for a decrease in the CPI, but this requires a detailed analysis and is unlikely to produce large improvements, especially if the initial distribution of work among the clock cycles is reasonably balanced.

Although all machines today are pipelined, this multicycle implementation is a reasonable approximation of how most machines would have been implemented in earlier times. A simple finite-state machine could be used to implement the control following the five-cycle structure shown above. For a much more complex machine, microcode control could be used. In either event, an instruction sequence like that above would determine the structure of the control.

In addition to these CPI improvements, there are some hardware redundancies that could be eliminated in this multicycle implementation. For example, there are two ALUs: one to increment the PC and one used for effective address and ALU computation. Since they are not needed on the same clock cycle, we could merge them by adding additional multiplexers and sharing the same ALU. Likewise, instructions and data could be stored in the same memory, since the data and instruction accesses happen on different clock cycles.

Rather than optimize this simple implementation, we will leave the design as it is in Figure 3.1, since this provides us with a better base for the pipelined implementation.

As an alternative to the multicycle design discussed in this section, we could also have implemented the machine so that every instruction takes one long clock cycle. In such cases, the temporary registers would be deleted, since there would not be any communication across clock cycles within an instruction. Every instruction would execute in one long clock cycle, writing the result into the data memory, registers, or PC at the end of the clock cycle. The CPI would be one for such a machine. However, the clock cycle would be roughly equal to five times the clock cycle of the multicycle machine, since every instruction would need to traverse all the functional units. Designers would never use this single-cycle implementation for two reasons. First, a single-cycle implementation would be very inefficient for most machines that have a reasonable variation among the amount of work, and hence in the clock cycle time, needed for different instructions. Second, a single-cycle implementation requires the duplication of functional units that could be shared in a multicycle implementation. Nonetheless, this single-cycle datapath allows us to illustrate how pipelining can improve the clock cycle time, as opposed to the CPI, of a machine.

3.2 | The Basic Pipeline for DLX

We can pipeline the datapath of Figure 3.1 with almost no changes by starting a new instruction on each clock cycle. (See why we chose that design!) Each of the clock cycles from the previous section becomes a *pipe stage:* a cycle in the pipeline. This results in the execution pattern shown in Figure 3.2, which is the typical way a pipeline structure is drawn. While each instruction takes five clock cycles to complete, during each clock cycle the hardware will initiate a new instruction and will be executing some part of the five different instructions.

	Clock number								
Instruction number	**1**	**2**	**3**	**4**	**5**	**6**	**7**	**8**	**9**
Instruction *i*	IF	ID	EX	MEM	WB				
Instruction *i* + 1		IF	ID	EX	MEM	WB			
Instruction *i* + 2			IF	ID	EX	MEM	WB		
Instruction *i* + 3				IF	ID	EX	MEM	WB	
Instruction *i* + 4					IF	ID	EX	MEM	WB

FIGURE 3.2   Simple DLX pipeline. On each clock cycle, another instruction is fetched and begins its five-cycle execution. If an instruction is started every clock cycle, the performance will be up to five times that of a machine that is not pipelined. The names for the stages in the pipeline are the same as those used for the cycles in the implementation on pages 127–129: IF = instruction fetch, ID = instruction decode, EX = execution, MEM = memory access, and WB = write back.

Your instinct is right if you find it hard to believe that pipelining is as simple as this, because it's not. In this and the following sections, we will make our DLX pipeline "real" by dealing with problems that pipelining introduces.

To begin with, we have to determine what happens on every clock cycle of the machine and make sure we don't try to perform two different operations with the same datapath resource on the same clock cycle. For example, a single ALU cannot be asked to compute an effective address and perform a subtract operation at the same time. Thus, we must ensure that the overlap of instructions in the pipeline cannot cause such a conflict. Fortunately, the simplicity of the DLX instruction set makes resource evaluation relatively easy. Figure 3.3 shows a simplified version of the DLX datapath drawn in pipeline fashion. As you can see, the major functional units are used in different cycles and hence overlapping the execution of multiple instructions introduces relatively few conflicts. There are three observations on which this fact rests.

First, the basic datapath of the last section already used separate instruction and data memories, which we would typically implement with separate instruction and data caches (discussed in Chapter 5). The use of separate caches eliminates a conflict for a single memory that would arise between instruction fetch

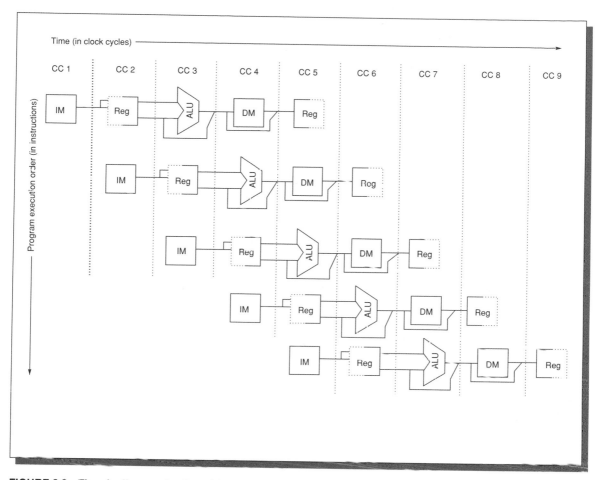

FIGURE 3.3 The pipeline can be thought of as a series of datapaths shifted in time. This shows the overlap among the parts of the datapath, with clock cycle 5 (CC 5) showing the steady state situation. Because the register file is used as a source in the ID stage and as a destination in the WB stage, It appears Iwice. We show that It is read in one stage and written in another by using a solid line, on the right or left, respectively, and a dashed line on the other side. The abbreviation IM is used for instruction memory, DM for data memory, and CC for clock cycle.

and data memory access. Notice that if our pipelined machine has a clock cycle that is equal to that of the unpipelined version, the memory system must deliver five times the bandwidth. This is one cost of higher performance.

Second, the register file is used in the two stages: for reading in ID and for writing in WB. These uses are distinct, so we simply show the register file in two places. This does mean that we need to perform two reads and one write every clock cycle. What if a read and write are to the same register? For now, we ignore this problem, but we will focus on it in the next section.

Third, Figure 3.3 does not deal with the PC. To start a new instruction every clock, we must increment and store the PC every clock, and this must be done during the IF stage in preparation for the next instruction. The problem arises when we consider the effect of branches, which changes the PC also, but not until the MEM stage. This is not a problem in our multicycle, unpipelined datapath, since the PC is written once in the MEM stage. For now, we will organize our pipelined datapath to write the PC in IF and write either the incremented PC or the value of the branch target of an earlier branch. This introduces a problem in how branches are handled that we will explain in the next section and explore in detail in section 3.5.

Because every pipe stage is active on every clock cycle, all operations in a pipe stage must complete in one clock cycle and any combination of operations must be able to occur at once. Furthermore, pipelining the datapath requires that values passed from one pipe stage to the next must be placed in registers. Figure 3.4 shows the DLX pipeline with the appropriate registers, called *pipeline registers* or *pipeline latches*, between each pipeline stage. The registers are labeled with the names of the stages they connect. Figure 3.4 is drawn so that connections through the pipeline registers from one stage to another are clear.

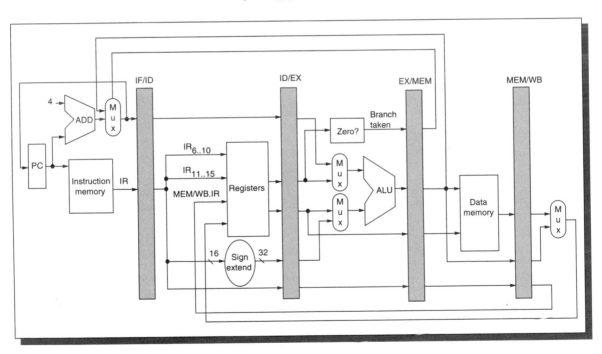

FIGURE 3.4   The datapath is pipelined by adding a set of registers, one between each pair of pipe stages. The registers serve to convey values and control information from one stage to the next. We can also think of the PC as a pipeline register, which sits before the IF stage of the pipeline, leading to one pipeline register for each pipe stage. Recall that the PC is an edge-triggered register written at the end of the clock cycle; hence there is no race condition in writing the PC. The selection multiplexer for the PC has been moved so that the PC is written in exactly one stage (IF). If we didn't move it, there would be a conflict when a branch occurred, since two instructions would try to write different values into the PC. Most of the datapaths flow from left to right, which is from earlier in time to later. The paths flowing from right to left (which carry the register write-back information and PC information on a branch) introduce complications into our pipeline, which we will spend much of this chapter overcoming.

All of the registers needed to hold values temporarily between clock cycles within one instruction are subsumed into these pipeline registers. The fields of the instruction register (IR), which is part of the IF/ID register, are labeled when they are used to supply register names. The pipeline registers carry both data and control from one pipeline stage to the next. Any value needed on a later pipeline stage must be placed in such a register and copied from one pipeline register to the next, until it is no longer needed. If we tried to just use the temporary registers we had in our earlier unpipelined datapath, values could be overwritten before all uses were completed. For example, the field of a register operand used for a write on a load or ALU operation is supplied from the MEM/WB pipeline register rather than from the IF/ID register. This is because we want a load or ALU operation to write the register designated by that operation, not the register field of the instruction currently transitioning from IF to ID! This destination register field is simply copied from one pipeline register to the next, until it is needed during the WB stage.

Any instruction is active in exactly one stage of the pipeline at a time; therefore, any actions taken on behalf of an instruction occur between a pair of pipeline registers. Thus, we can also look at the activities of the pipeline by examining what has to happen on any pipeline stage depending on the instruction type. Figure 3.5 shows this view. Fields of the pipeline registers are named so as to show the flow of data from one stage to the next. Notice that the actions in the first two stages are independent of the current instruction type; they must be independent because the instruction is not decoded until the end of the ID stage. The IF activity depends on whether the instruction in EX/MEM is a taken branch. If so, then the branch target address of the branch instruction in EX/MEM is written into the PC at the end of IF; otherwise the incremented PC will be written back. (As we said earlier, this effect of branches leads to complications in the pipeline that we deal with in the next few sections.) The fixed position encoding of the register source operands is critical to allowing the registers to be fetched during ID.

To control this simple pipeline we need only determine how to set the control for the four multiplexers in the datapath of Figure 3.4. The two multiplexers in the ALU stage are set depending on the instruction type, which is dictated by the IR field of the ID/EX register. The top ALU input multiplexer is set by whether the instruction is a branch or not, and the bottom multiplexer is set by whether the instruction is a register-register ALU operation or any other type of operation. The multiplexer in the IF stage chooses whether to use the value of the incremented PC or the value of the EX/MEM.ALUOutput (the branch target) to write into the PC. This multiplexer is controlled by the field EX/MEM.cond. The fourth multiplexer is controlled by whether the instruction in the WB stage is a load or a ALU operation. In addition to these four multiplexers, there is one additional multiplexer needed that is not drawn in Figure 3.4, but whose existence is clear from looking at the WB stage of an ALU operation. The destination register field is in one of two different places depending on the instruction type (register-register ALU versus either ALU immediate or load). Thus, we will need a multiplexer to choose the correct portion of the IR in the MEM/WB register to specify the register destination field, assuming the instruction writes a register.

Stage	Any instruction		
IF	IF/ID.IR ← Mem[PC]; IF/ID.NPC,PC ← (if ((EX/MEM.opcode == branch) & EX/MEM.cond){EX/MEM. ALUOutput} else {PC+4});		
ID	ID/EX.A ← Regs[IF/ID.IR$_{6..10}$]; ID/EX.B ← Regs[IF/ID.IR$_{11..15}$]; ID/EX.NPC ← IF/ID.NPC; ID/EX.IR ← IF/ID.IR; ID/EX.Imm ← (IF/ID.IR$_{16}$)^{16}##IF/ID.IR$_{16..31}$;		

	ALU instruction	**Load or store instruction**	**Branch instruction**
EX	EX/MEM.IR ← ID/EX.IR; EX/MEM.ALUOutput← ID/EX.A *func* ID/EX.B; or EX/MEM.ALUOutput ← ID/EX.A *op* ID/EX.Imm; EX/MEM.cond ← 0;	EX/MEM.IR← ID/EX.IR EX/MEM.ALUOutput ← ID/EX.A + ID/EX.Imm; EX/MEM.cond ← 0; EX/MEM.B← ID/EX.B;	EX/MEM.ALUOutput ← ID/EX.NPC+ID/EX.Imm; EX/MEM.cond ← (ID/EX.A *op* 0);
MEM	MEM/WB.IR ← EX/MEM.IR; MEM/WB.ALUOutput ← EX/MEM.ALUOutput;	MEM/WB.IR ← EX/MEM.IR; MEM/WB.LMD ← Mem[EX/MEM.ALUOutput]; or Mem[EX/MEM.ALUOutput] ← EX/MEM.B;	
WB	Regs[MEM/WB.IR$_{16..20}$] ← MEM/WB.ALUOutput; or Regs[MEM/WB.IR$_{11..15}$] ← MEM/WB.ALUOutput;	For load only: Regs[MEM/WB.IR$_{11..15}$] ← MEM/WB.LMD;	

FIGURE 3.5   Events on every pipe stage of the DLX pipeline. Let's review the actions in the stages that are specific to the pipeline organization. In IF, in addition to fetching the instruction and computing the new PC, we store the incremented PC both into the PC and into a pipeline register (NPC) for later use in computing the branch target address. This structure is the same as the organization in Figure 3.4, where the PC is updated in IF from one or two sources. In ID, we fetch the registers, extend the sign of the lower 16 bits of the IR, and pass along the IR and NPC. During EX, we perform an ALU operation or an address calculation; we pass along the IR and the B register (if the instruction is a store). We also set the value of cond to 1 if the instruction is a taken branch. During the MEM phase, we cycle the memory, write the PC if needed, and pass along values needed in the final pipe stage. Finally, during WB, we update the register field from either the ALU output or the loaded value. For simplicity we always pass the entire IR from one stage to the next, though as an instruction proceeds down the pipeline, less and less of the IR is needed.

Basic Performance Issues in Pipelining

Pipelining increases the CPU instruction throughput—the number of instructions completed per unit of time—but it does not reduce the execution time of an individual instruction. In fact, it usually slightly increases the execution time of each instruction due to overhead in the control of the pipeline. The increase in instruction throughput means that a program runs faster and has lower total execution time, even though no single instruction runs faster!

The fact that the execution time of each instruction does not decrease puts limits on the practical depth of a pipeline, as we will see in the next section. In addition to limitations arising from pipeline latency, limits arise from imbalance among the pipe stages and from pipelining overhead. Imbalance among the pipe stages reduces performance since the clock can run no faster than the time needed for the slowest pipeline stage. Pipeline overhead arises from the combination of pipeline register delay and clock skew. The pipeline registers add setup time, which is the time that a register input must be stable before the clock signal that triggers a write occurs, plus propagation delay to the clock cycle. Clock skew, which is maximum delay between when the clock arrives at any two registers, also contributes to the lower limit on the clock cycle. Once the clock cycle is as small as the sum of the clock skew and latch overhead, no further pipelining is useful, since there is no time left in the cycle for useful work.

EXAMPLE   Consider the unpipelined machine in the previous section. Assume that it has 10-ns clock cycles and that it uses four cycles for ALU operations and branches and five cycles for memory operations. Assume that the relative frequencies of these operations are 40%, 20%, and 40%, respectively. Suppose that due to clock skew and setup, pipelining the machine adds 1 ns of overhead to the clock. Ignoring any latency impact, how much speedup in the instruction execution rate will we gain from a pipeline?

ANSWER   The average instruction execution time on the unpipelined machine is

$$
\begin{aligned}
\text{Average instruction execution time} \ &= \ \text{Clock cycle} \ \times \text{Average CPI} \\
&= \ 10 \ \text{ns} \times ((40\% + 20\%) \times 4 + 40\% \times 5) \\
&= \ 10 \ \text{ns} \times 4.4 \\
&= \ 44 \ \text{ns}
\end{aligned}
$$

In the pipelined implementation, the clock must run at the speed of the slowest stage plus overhead, which will be 10 + 1 or 11 ns; this is the average instruction execution time. Thus, the speedup from pipelining is

$$
\begin{aligned}
\text{Speedup from pipelining} \ &= \ \frac{\text{Average instruction time unpipelined}}{\text{Average instruction time pipelined}} \\
&= \ \frac{44 \ \text{ns}}{11 \ \text{ns}} = 4 \ \text{times}
\end{aligned}
$$

The 1-ns overhead essentially establishes a limit on the effectiveness of pipelining. If the overhead is not affected by changes in the clock cycle, Amdahl's Law tells us that the overhead limits the speedup.   ■

Alternatively, if our base machine already has a CPI of 1 (with a longer clock cycle), then pipelining will enable us to have a shorter clock cycle. The datapath of the previous section can be made into a single-cycle datapath by simply removing the latches and letting the data flow from one cycle of execution to the next. How would the speedup of the pipelined version compare to the single-cycle machine?

EXAMPLE   Assume that the times required for the five functional units, which operate in each of the five cycles, are as follows: 10 ns, 8 ns, 10 ns, 10 ns, and 7 ns. Assume that pipelining adds 1 ns of overhead. Find the speedup versus the single-cycle datapath.

ANSWER   Since the unpipelined machine executes all instructions in a single clock cycle, its average time per instruction is simply the clock cycle time. The clock cycle time is equal to the sum of the times for each step in the execution:

$$\text{Average instruction execution time} = 10 + 8 + 10 + 10 + 7$$
$$= 45 \text{ ns}$$

The clock cycle time on the pipelined machine must be the largest time for any stage in the pipeline (10 ns) plus the overhead of 1 ns, for a total of 11 ns. Since the CPI is 1, this yields an average instruction execution time of 11 ns. Thus,

$$\text{Speedup from pipelining} = \frac{\text{Average instruction time unpipelined}}{\text{Average instruction time pipelined}}$$
$$= \frac{45 \text{ ns}}{11 \text{ ns}} = 4.1 \text{ times}$$

Pipelining can be thought of as improving the CPI, which is what we typically do, as increasing the clock rate—especially compared to another pipelined machine, or sometimes as doing both.   ■

Because the latches in a pipelined design can have a significant impact on the clock speed, designers have looked for latches that permit the highest possible clock rate. The Earle latch (invented by J. G. Earle [1965]) has three properties that make it especially useful in pipelined machines. First, it is relatively insensitive to clock skew. Second, the delay through the latch is always a constant two-gate delay, avoiding the introduction of skew in the data passing through the latch. Finally, two levels of logic can be performed in the latch without increasing the latch delay time. This means that two levels of logic in the pipeline can be overlapped with the latch, so the overhead from the latch can be hidden. We will not be analyzing the pipeline designs in this chapter at this level of detail. The interested reader should see Kunkel and Smith [1986].

The pipeline we now have for DLX would function just fine for integer instructions if every instruction were independent of every other instruction in the pipeline. In reality, instructions in the pipeline can depend on one another; this is the topic of the next section. The complications that arise in the floating-point pipeline will be treated in section 3.7, and section 3.9 will look at a complete real pipeline.

3.3 | The Major Hurdle of Pipelining— Pipeline Hazards

There are situations, called *hazards*, that prevent the next instruction in the instruction stream from executing during its designated clock cycle. Hazards reduce the performance from the ideal speedup gained by pipelining. There are three classes of hazards:

1. *Structural hazards* arise from resource conflicts when the hardware cannot support all possible combinations of instructions in simultaneous overlapped execution.

2. *Data hazards* arise when an instruction depends on the results of a previous instruction in a way that is exposed by the overlapping of instructions in the pipeline.

3. *Control hazards* arise from the pipelining of branches and other instructions that change the PC.

Hazards in pipelines can make it necessary to *stall* the pipeline. In Chapter 1, we mentioned that the processor could stall on an event such as a cache miss. Stalls arising from hazards in pipelined machines are more complex than the simple stall for a cache miss. Eliminating a hazard often requires that some instructions in the pipeline be allowed to proceed while others are delayed. For the pipelines we discuss in this chapter, when an instruction is stalled, all instructions issued *later* than the stalled instruction—and hence not as far along in the pipeline—are also stalled. Instructions issued *earlier* than the stalled instruction—and hence farther along in the pipeline—must continue, since otherwise the hazard will never clear. As a result, no new instructions are fetched during the stall. In contrast to this process of stalling only a portion of the pipeline, a cache miss stalls *all* the instructions in the pipeline both before and after the instruction causing the miss. (For the simple pipelines of this chapter there is no advantage in selecting stalling instructions on a cache miss, but in future chapters we will examine pipelines and caches that reduce cache miss costs by selectively stalling on a cache miss.) We will see several examples of how pipeline stalls operate in this section—don't worry, they aren't as complex as they might sound!

Performance of Pipelines with Stalls

A stall causes the pipeline performance to degrade from the ideal performance. Let's look at a simple equation for finding the actual speedup from pipelining, starting with the formula from the previous section.

$$\text{Speedup from pipelining} = \frac{\text{Average instruction time unpipelined}}{\text{Average instruction time pipelined}}$$

$$= \frac{\text{CPI unpipelined} \times \text{Clock cycle unpipelined}}{\text{CPI pipelined} \times \text{Clock cycle pipelined}}$$

$$= \frac{\text{CPI unpipelined}}{\text{CPI pipelined}} \times \frac{\text{Clock cycle unpipelined}}{\text{Clock cycle pipelined}}$$

Remember that pipelining can be thought of as decreasing the CPI or the clock cycle time. Since it is traditional to use the CPI to compare pipelines, let's start with that assumption. The ideal CPI on a pipelined machine is almost always 1. Hence, we can compute the pipelined CPI:

$$\text{CPI pipelined} = \text{Ideal CPI} + \text{Pipeline stall clock cycles per instruction}$$

$$= 1 + \text{Pipeline stall clock cycles per instruction}$$

If we ignore the cycle time overhead of pipelining and assume the stages are perfectly balanced, then the cycle time of the two machines can be equal, leading to

$$\text{Speedup} = \frac{\text{CPI unpipelined}}{1 + \text{Pipeline stall cycles per instruction}}$$

One important simple case is where all instructions take the same number of cycles, which must also equal the number of pipeline stages (also called the *depth of the pipeline*). In this case, the unpipelined CPI is equal to the depth of the pipeline, leading to

$$\text{Speedup} = \frac{\text{Pipeline depth}}{1 + \text{Pipeline stall cycles per instruction}}$$

If there are no pipeline stalls, this leads to the intuitive result that pipelining can improve performance by the depth of the pipeline.

Alternatively, if we think of pipelining as improving the clock cycle time, then we can assume that the CPI of the unpipelined machine, as well as that of the pipelined machine, is 1. This leads to

$$\text{Speedup from pipelining} = \frac{\text{CPI unpipelined}}{\text{CPI pipelined}} \times \frac{\text{Clock cycle unpipelined}}{\text{Clock cycle pipelined}}$$

$$= \frac{1}{1 + \text{Pipeline stall cycles per instruction}} \times \frac{\text{Clock cycle unpipelined}}{\text{Clock cycle pipelined}}$$

In cases where the pipe stages are perfectly balanced and there is no overhead, the clock cycle on the pipelined machine is smaller than the clock cycle of the unpipelined machine by a factor equal to the pipelined depth:

$$\text{Clock cycle pipelined} = \frac{\text{Clock cycle unpipelined}}{\text{Pipeline depth}}$$

$$\text{Pipeline depth} = \frac{\text{Clock cycle unpipelined}}{\text{Clock cycle pipelined}}$$

This leads to the following:

$$\text{Speedup from pipelining} = \frac{1}{1 + \text{Pipeline stall cycles per instruction}} \times \frac{\text{Clock cycle unpipelined}}{\text{Clock cycle pipelined}}$$

$$= \frac{1}{1 + \text{Pipeline stall cycles per instruction}} \times \text{Pipeline depth}$$

Thus, if there are no stalls, the speedup is equal to the number of pipeline stages, matching our intuition for the ideal case.

Structural Hazards

When a machine is pipelined, the overlapped execution of instructions requires pipelining of functional units and duplication of resources to allow all possible combinations of instructions in the pipeline. If some combination of instructions cannot be accommodated because of resource conflicts, the machine is said to have a *structural hazard*. The most common instances of structural hazards arise when some functional unit is not fully pipelined. Then a sequence of instructions using that unpipelined unit cannot proceed at the rate of one per clock cycle. Another common way that structural hazards appear is when some resource has not been duplicated enough to allow all combinations of instructions in the pipeline to execute. For example, a machine may have only one register-file write port, but under certain circumstances, the pipeline might want to perform two writes in a clock cycle. This will generate a structural hazard. When a sequence of instructions encounters this hazard, the pipeline will stall one of the instructions until the required unit is available. Such stalls will increase the CPI from its usual ideal value of 1.

Some pipelined machines have shared a single-memory pipeline for data and instructions. As a result, when an instruction contains a data-memory reference, it will conflict with the instruction reference for a later instruction, as shown in Figure 3.6. To resolve this, we stall the pipeline for one clock cycle when the data memory access occurs. Figure 3.7 shows our pipeline datapath figure with the stall cycle added. A stall is commonly called a *pipeline bubble* or just *bubble*, since it floats through the pipeline taking space but carrying no useful work. We will see another type of stall when we talk about data hazards.

Rather than draw the pipeline datapath every time, designers often just indicate stall behavior using a simpler diagram with only the pipe stage names, as in Figure 3.8. The form of Figure 3.8 shows the stall by indicating the cycle when no action occurs and simply shifting instruction 3 to the right (which delays its

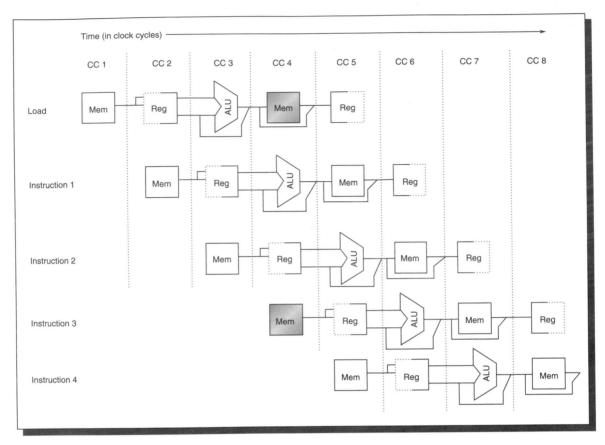

FIGURE 3.6   A machine with only one memory port will generate a conflict whenever a memory reference occurs. In this example the load instruction uses the memory for a data access at the same time instruction 3 wants to fetch an instruction from memory.

execution start and finish by one cycle). The effect of the pipeline bubble is actually to occupy the resources for that instruction slot as it travels through the pipeline, just as Figure 3.7 shows. Although Figure 3.7 shows how the stall is actually implemented, the performance impact indicated by the two figures is the same: Instruction 3 does not complete until clock cycle 9, and no instruction completes during clock cycle 8.

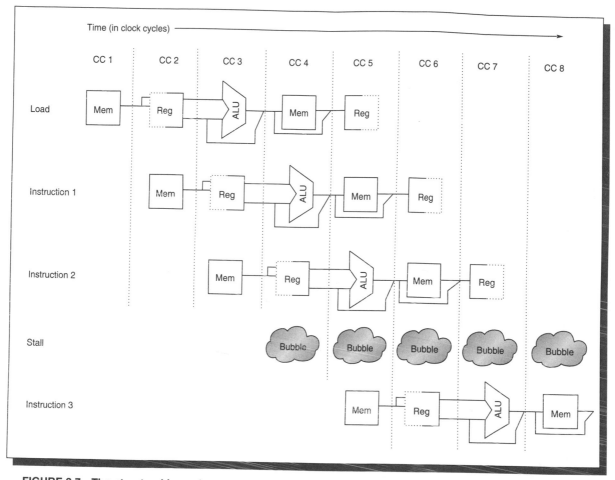

FIGURE 3.7 The structural hazard causes pipeline bubbles to be inserted. The effect is that no instruction will finish during clock cycle 8, when instruction 3 would normally have finished. Instruction 1 is assumed to not be a load or store; otherwise, instruction 3 cannot start execution.

Ch...

Instruction	1	2
Load instruction	IF	ID
Instruction $i + 1$		IF
Instruction $i + 2$		
Instruction $i + 3$		
Instruction $i + 4$		
Instruction $i + 5$		
Instruction $i + 6$		

FIGURE 3.8 A pipeline stalled for a str
tion effectively steals an instruction-fetch
(which normally would initiate instruction i
pipeline before the stalled instruction can p
no instruction completes on clock cycle 8. S
horizontal row and instruction 3 being move
not begin execution until cycle 5. We use th

EXAMPLE Let's se
data refe
pipelined
machine v
er than the
other perfo
hazard fast

ANSWER There are s
plest is to co

Clearly, the machi
the ratio of the ave
without the hazard

---

esigner could provide
by splitting the cache
ing a set of buffers,
s. Both the split cache
pter 5.

tructural hazards will always
ow structural hazards? There
ency of the unit. Pipelining all
too costly. For example, ma-
a cache access every cycle (to
le) require twice as much total
idth at the pins. Likewise, fully
ots of gates. If the structural haz-
cost to avoid it. It is also usual-
he that isn't fully pipelined, with a
pelined unit. The shorter latency
introduce overhead. For example,
ting-point unit choose shorter laten-
pelining. As we will see shortly, re-
s and may overcome the disadvantage

pipelined floating-point units. For
ontation of DLX with a floating-point
se the multiplier could accept a new
cles. (This rate is called the *repeat* or
hazard have a large or small perfor-
n DLX? For simplicity, assume that
ormly distributed.

Since it has ng-point multiply has a frequency of
is simply the celine can handle up to a 20% frequency
chine with the every five clock cycles. This means that
pipelining the floating-point multiply on
Average long as the floating-point multiplies are
uniformly. In the best case, multiplies a
ns, and there is no performance penalt
iplies are all clustered with no interve
nstructions take 5 cycles each. Assur
to an increase of 0.7 in the CPI.

---

performance of mdljdp2 on a machine with
peline shows that this structural hazard
than 3%. One reason this loss is so low
he next section) cause the pipeline to
s that might cause structural hazards
r benchmarks make heavier use of
ata hazards, and thus would show a
r we will examine the contributions
LX pipeline.

lative timing of instructions by
and control hazards. Data haz-
ad/write accesses to operands
tially executing instructions
execution of these instruc-

truction. As shown in
WB pipe stage, but
problem is called a
SUB instruction will
by the SUB instruc-
ical to assume that
instruction prior to
ween the ADD and
he value of R1 at
vior is obviously

can see from
cycle 5. Thus,
vill receive the

ad occurs in
be made to
chnique, im-
the register file reads
he first half. This technique,

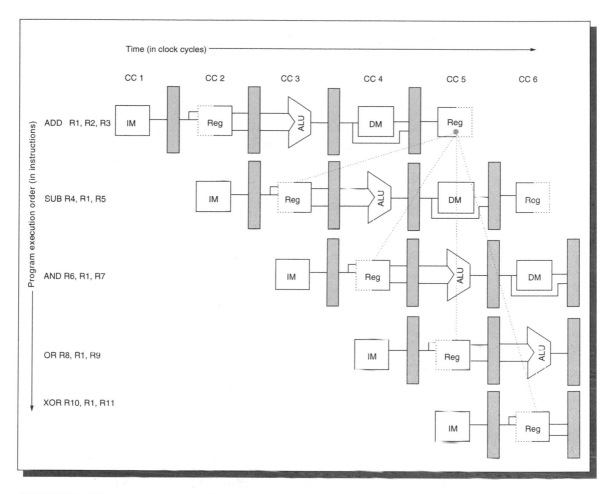

FIGURE 3.9 The use of the result of the ADD instruction in the next three instructions causes a hazard, since the register is not written until after those instructions read it.

which is hinted at in earlier figures by placing the dashed box around the register file, allows the OR instruction in the example in Figure 3.9 to execute correctly.

The next subsection discusses a technique to eliminate the stalls for the hazard involving the SUB and AND instructions.

Minimizing Data Hazard Stalls By Forwarding

The problem posed in Figure 3.9 can be solved with a simple hardware technique called *forwarding* (also called *bypassing* and sometimes *short-circuiting*). The key insight in forwarding is that the result is not really needed by the SUB until after the ADD actually produces it. If the result can be moved from where the ADD produces it, the EX/MEM register, to where the SUB needs it, the ALU input latches, then the need for a stall can be avoided. Using this observation, forwarding works as follows:

1. The ALU result from the EX/MEM register is always fed back to the ALU input latches.

2. If the forwarding hardware detects that the previous ALU operation has written the register corresponding to a source for the current ALU operation, control logic selects the forwarded result as the ALU input rather than the value read from the register file.

Notice that with forwarding, if the SUB is stalled, the ADD will be completed and the bypass will not be activated. This is also true for the case of an interrupt between the two instructions.

As the example in Figure 3.9 shows, we need to forward results not only from the immediately previous instruction, but possibly from an instruction that started two cycles earlier. Figure 3.10 shows our example with the bypass paths in place and highlighting the timing of the register read and writes. This code sequence can be executed without stalls.

Forwarding can be generalized to include passing a result directly to the functional unit that requires it: A result is forwarded from the output of one unit to the input of another, rather than just from the result of a unit to the input of the same unit. Take, for example, the following sequence:

```
ADD     R1,R2,R3
LW      R4,0(R1)
SW      12(R1),R4
```

To prevent a stall in this sequence, we would need to forward the values of R1 and R4 from the pipeline registers to the ALU and data memory inputs. Figure 3.11 shows all the forwarding paths for this example. In DLX, we may require a forwarding path from any pipeline register to the input of any functional unit. Because the ALU and data memory both accept operands, forwarding paths are needed to their inputs from both the ALU/MEM and MEM/WB registers. In addition, DLX uses a zero detection unit that operates during the EX cycle, and forwarding to that unit will be needed as well. Later in this section we will explore all the necessary forwarding paths and the control of those paths.

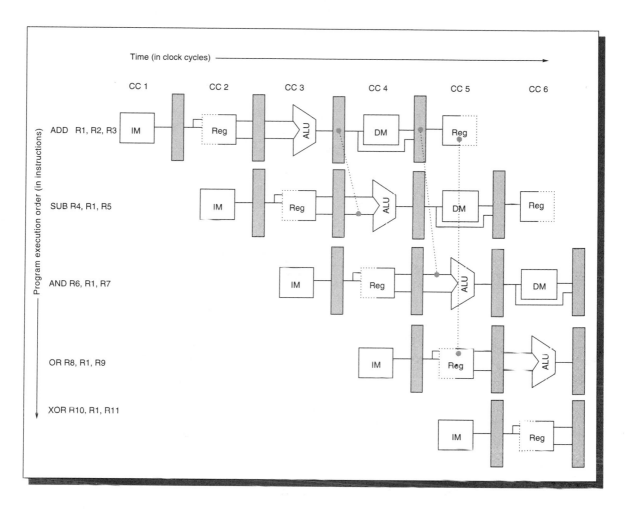

FIGURE 3.10 A set of instructions that depend on the ADD result use forwarding paths to avoid the data hazard. The inputs for the SUB and AND instructions forward from the EX/MEM and the MEM/WB pipeline registers, respectively, to the first ALU input. The OR receives its result by forwarding through the register file, which is easily accomplished by reading the registers in the second half of the cycle and writing in the first half, as the dashed lines on the registers indicate. Notice that the forwarded result can go to either ALU input; in fact, both ALU inputs could use forwarded inputs from either the same pipeline register or from different pipeline registers. This would occur, for example, if the AND instruction was AND R6, R1, R4.

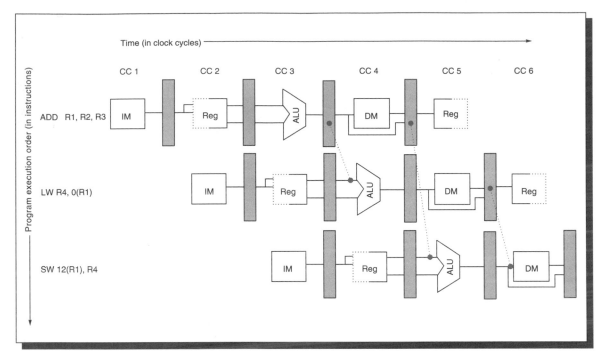

FIGURE 3.11   Stores require an operand during MEM, and forwarding of that operand is shown here. The result of the load is forwarded from the memory output in MEM/WB to the memory input to be stored. In addition, the ALU output is forwarded to the ALU input for the address calculation of both the load and the store (this is no different than forwarding to another ALU operation). If the store depended on an immediately preceding ALU operation (not shown above), the result would need to be forwarded to prevent a stall.

Data Hazard Classification

A hazard is created whenever there is a dependence between instructions, and they are close enough that the overlap caused by pipelining would change the order of access to an operand. Our example hazards have all been with register operands, but it is also possible for a pair of instructions to create a dependence by writing and reading the same memory location. In our DLX pipeline, however, memory references are always kept in order, preventing this type of hazard from arising. Cache misses could cause the memory references to get out of order if we allowed the processor to continue working on later instructions, while an earlier instruction that missed the cache was accessing memory. For the DLX pipeline we stall the entire pipeline on a cache miss, effectively making the instruction that contained the miss run for multiple clock cycles. In the next chapter, we will discuss machines that allow loads and stores to be executed in an order different from that in the program, which will introduce new problems. All the data hazards discussed in this chapter involve registers within the CPU.

Data hazards may be classified as one of three types, depending on the order of read and write accesses in the instructions. By convention, the hazards are named by the ordering in the program that must be preserved by the pipeline. Consider two instructions i and j, with i occurring before j. The possible data hazards are

- RAW *(read after write)* — j tries to read a source before i writes it, so j incorrectly gets the old value. This is the most common type of hazard and the kind that we used forwarding to overcome in Figures 3.10 and 3.11.

- WAW *(write after write)* — j tries to write an operand before it is written by i. The writes end up being performed in the wrong order, leaving the value written by i rather than the value written by j in the destination. This hazard is present only in pipelines that write in more than one pipe stage (or allow an instruction to proceed even when a previous instruction is stalled). The DLX integer pipeline writes a register only in WB and avoids this class of hazards. If we made two changes to the DLX pipeline, WAW hazards would be possible. First, we could move write back for an ALU operation into the MEM stage, since the data value is available by then. Second, suppose that the data memory access took two pipe stages. Here is a sequence of two instructions showing the execution in this revised pipeline, highlighting the pipe stage that writes the result:

LW R1,0(R2)	IF	ID	EX	MEM1	MEM2	**WB**
ADD R1,R2,R3		IF	ID	EX	**WB**	

Unless this hazard is avoided, execution of this sequence on this revised pipeline will leave the result of the first write (the LW) in R1, rather than the result of the ADD!

Allowing writes in different pipe stages introduces other problems, since two instructions can try to write during the same clock cycle. When we discuss the DLX FP pipeline (section 3.7), which has both writes in different stages and different pipeline lengths, we will deal with both write conflicts and WAW hazards in detail.

- WAR *(write after read)* — j tries to write a destination before it is read by i, so i incorrectly gets the new value. This cannot happen in our example pipeline because all reads are early (in ID) and all writes are late (in WB). This hazard occurs when there are some instructions that write results early in the instruction pipeline, and other instructions that read a source late in the pipeline.

Because of the natural structure of a pipeline, which typically reads values before it writes results, such hazards are rare. Pipelines for complex instruction sets that support autoincrement addressing and require operands to be read late in the pipeline could create a WAR hazard. If we modified the DLX pipeline as in the above example and also read some operands late, such as the source value for a store instruction, a WAR hazard could occur. Here is the pipeline timing for such a potential hazard, highlighting the stage where the conflict occurs:

SW 0(R1),R2	IF	ID	EX	MEM1	**MEM2**	WB
ADD R2,R3,R4		IF	ID	EX	**WB**	

If the SW reads R2 during the second half of its MEM2 stage and the ADD writes R2 during the first half of its WB stage, the SW will incorrectly read and store the value produced by the ADD. In the DLX pipeline, reading all operands from the register file during ID avoids this hazard; however, in the next chapter, we will see how these hazards occur more easily when instructions are executed out of order.

Note that the RAR *(read after read)* case is not a hazard.

Data Hazards Requiring Stalls

Unfortunately, not all potential data hazards can be handled by bypassing. Consider the following sequence of instructions:

```
LW    R1,0(R2)
SUB   R4,R1,R5
AND   R6,R1,R7
OR    R8,R1,R9
```

The pipelined datapath with the bypass paths for this example is shown in Figure 3.12. This case is different from the situation with back-to-back ALU operations. The LW instruction does not have the data until the end of clock cycle 4 (its MEM cycle), while the SUB instruction needs to have the data by the beginning of that clock cycle. Thus, the data hazard from using the result of a load instruction cannot be completely eliminated with simple hardware. As Figure 3.12 shows, such a forwarding path would have to operate backward in time—a capability not yet available to computer designers! We *can* forward the result immediately to the ALU from the MEM/WB registers for use in the AND operation, which begins two clock cycles after the load. Likewise, the OR instruction has no problem, since it receives the value through the register file. For the SUB instruction, the forwarded result arrives too late—at the end of a clock cycle, when it is needed at the beginning.

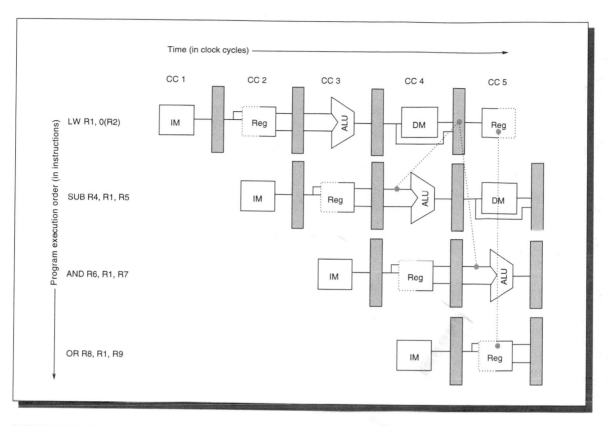

FIGURE 3.12   The load instruction can bypass its results to the AND and OR instructions, but not to the SUB, since that would mean forwarding the result in "negative time."

The load instruction has a delay or latency that cannot be eliminated by forwarding alone. Instead, we need to add hardware, called a *pipeline interlock*, to preserve the correct execution pattern. In general, a *pipeline interlock* detects a hazard and stalls the pipeline until the hazard is cleared. In this case, the interlock stalls the pipeline, beginning with the instruction that wants to use the data until the source instruction produces it. This pipeline interlock introduces a stall or bubble, just as it did for the structural hazard in section 3.3. The CPI for the stalled instruction increases by the length of the stall (one clock cycle in this case). The pipeline with the stall and the legal forwarding is shown in Figure 3.13. Because the stall causes the instructions starting with the SUB to move one cycle later in time, the forwarding to the AND instruction now goes through the register file, and no forwarding at all is needed for the OR instruction. The insertion of the bubble causes the number of cycles to complete this sequence to grow by one. No instruction is started during clock cycle 4 (and none

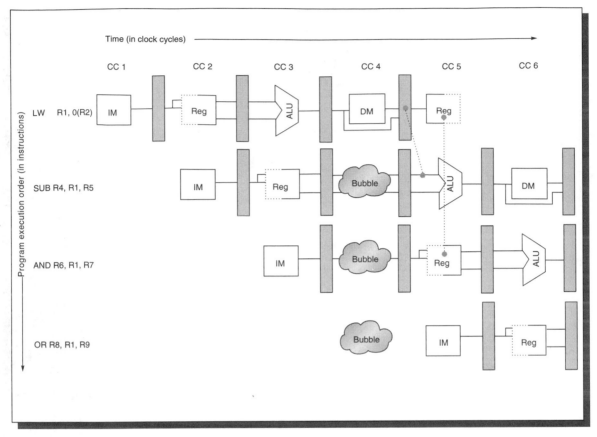

FIGURE 3.13   The load interlock causes a stall to be inserted at clock cycle 4, delaying the SUB instruction and those that follow by one cycle. This delay allows the value to be successfully forwarded on the next clock cycle.

finishes during cycle 6). Figure 3.14 shows the pipeline before and after the stall using a diagram containing only the pipeline stages. We will make extensive use of this more concise form for showing interlocks and stalls in this chapter and the next.

LW R1,0(R2)	IF	ID	EX	MEM	WB			
SUB R4,R1,R5		IF	ID	EX	MEM	WB		
AND R6,R1,R7			IF	ID	EX	MEM	WB	
OR R8,R1,R9				IF	ID	EX	MEM	WB

LW R1,0(R2)	IF	ID	EX	MEM	WB			
SUB R4,R1,R5		IF	ID	stall	EX	MEM	WB	
AND R6,R1,R7			IF	stall	ID	EX	MEM	WB
OR R8,R1,R9				stall	IF	ID	EX	MEM	WB

FIGURE 3.14   In the top half, we can see why a stall is needed: the MEM cycle of the load produces a value that is needed in the EX cycle of the SUB, which occurs at the same time. This problem is solved by inserting a stall, as shown in the bottom half.

EXAMPLE   Suppose that 30% of the instructions are loads, and half the time the instruction following a load instruction depends on the result of the load. If this hazard creates a single-cycle delay, how much faster is the ideal pipelined machine (with a CPI of 1) that does not delay the pipeline than the real pipeline? Ignore any stalls other than pipeline stalls.

ANSWER   The ideal machine will be faster by the ratio of the CPIs. The CPI for an instruction following a load is 1.5, since it stalls half the time. Because loads are 30% of the mix, the effective CPI is $(0.7 \times 1 + 0.3 \times 1.5) = 1.15$. This means that the ideal machine is 1.15 times faster. ∎

In the next subsection we consider compiler techniques to reduce these penalties. After that, we look at how to implement hazard detection, forwarding, and interlocks.

Compiler Scheduling for Data Hazards

Many types of stalls are quite frequent. The typical code-generation pattern for a statement such as A = B + C produces a stall for a load of the second data value (C). Figure 3.15 shows that the store of A need not cause another stall, since the result of the addition can be forwarded to the data memory for use by the store.

Rather than just allow the pipeline to stall, the compiler could try to schedule the pipeline to avoid these stalls by rearranging the code sequence to eliminate the hazard. For example, the compiler could try to avoid generating code with a load followed by the immediate use of the load destination register. This technique, called *pipeline scheduling* or *instruction scheduling,* was first used in the 1960s and became an area of major interest in the 1980s, as pipelined machines became more widespread.

LW R1,B	IF	ID	EX	MEM	WB				
LW R2,C		IF	ID	EX	MEM	WB			
ADD R3,R1,R2			IF	ID	stall	EX	MEM	WB	
SW A,R3				IF	stall	ID	EX	MEM	WB

FIGURE 3.15 The DLX code sequence for A = B + C. The ADD instruction must be stalled to allow the load of C to complete. The SW need not be delayed further because the forwarding hardware passes the result from the MEM/WB directly to the data memory input for storing.

EXAMPLE   Generate DLX code that avoids pipeline stalls for the following sequence:

```
a = b + c;
d = e - f;
```

Assume loads have a latency of one clock cycle.

ANSWER   Here is the scheduled code:

```
LW      Rb,b
LW      Rc,c
LW      Re,e    ; swap instructions to avoid stall
ADD     Ra,Rb,Rc
LW      Rf,f
SW      a,Ra    ; store/load exchanged to avoid stall
SUB     Rd,Re,Rf
SW      d,Rd
```

Both load interlocks (LW Rc, c to ADD Ra, Rb, Rc and LW Rf, f to
SUB Rd, Re, Rf) have been eliminated. There is a dependence between
the ALU instruction and the store, but the pipeline structure allows the result to be forwarded. Notice that the use of different registers for the first
and second statements was critical for this schedule to be legal. In particular, if the variable e was loaded into the same register as b or c, this
schedule would be illegal. In general, pipeline scheduling can increase
the register count required. In the next chapter, we will see that this increase can be substantial for machines that can issue multiple instructions in one clock.   ■

Many modern compilers try to use instruction scheduling to improve pipeline
performance. In the simplest algorithms, the compiler simply schedules using
other instructions in the same basic block. A *basic block* is a straight-line code sequence with no transfers in or out, except at the beginning or end. Scheduling
such code sequences is easy, since we know that every instruction in the block is
executed if the first one is. We can simply make a graph of the dependences
among the instructions and order the instructions so as to minimize the stalls. For
a simple pipeline like the DLX integer pipeline with only short latencies (the only
delay is one cycle on loads), a scheduling strategy focusing on basic blocks is adequate. Figure 3.16 shows the frequency that stalls are required for load results,
assuming a single-cycle delay for loads. As you can see, this process is more effective for floating-point programs that have significant amounts of parallelism
among instructions. As pipelining becomes more extensive and the effective
pipeline latencies grow, more ambitious scheduling schemes are needed; these
are discussed in detail in the next chapter.

Implementing the Control for the DLX Pipeline

The process of letting an instruction move from the instruction decode stage (ID)
into the execution stage (EX) of this pipeline is usually called *instruction issue*;
an instruction that has made this step is said to have *issued*. For the DLX integer
pipeline, all the data hazards can be checked during the ID phase of the pipeline.

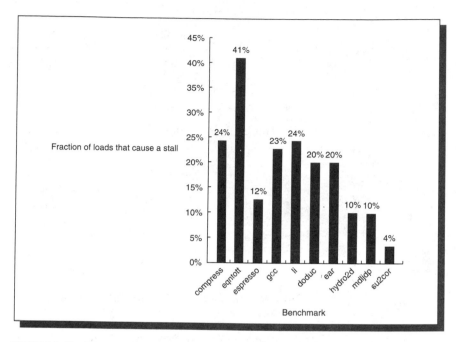

FIGURE 3.16 **Percentage of the loads that result in a stall with the DLX pipeline.** This chart shows the frequency of stalls remaining in scheduled code that was globally optimized before scheduling. Global optimization actually makes scheduling relatively harder because there are fewer candidates for scheduling into delay slots, as we discuss in *Fallacies and Pitfalls*. The pipeline slot after a load is often called the *load delay* or *delay slot*. In general, it is easier to schedule the delay slots in FP programs, since they are more regular and the analysis is easier. Hence fewer loads stall in the FP programs: an average of 13% of the loads versus 25% on the integer programs. The actual performance impact depends on the load frequency, which varies from 19% to 34% with an average of 24%. The contribution to CPI runs from 0.01 cycles per instruction to 0.15 cycles per instruction.

If a data hazard exists, the instruction is stalled before it is issued. Likewise, we can determine what forwarding will be needed during ID and set the appropriate controls then. Detecting interlocks early in the pipeline reduces the hardware complexity because the hardware never has to suspend an instruction that has updated the state of the machine, unless the entire machine is stalled. Alternatively, we can detect the hazard or forwarding at the beginning of a clock cycle that uses an operand (EX and MEM for this pipeline). To show the differences in these two approaches, we will show how the interlock for a RAW hazard with the source coming from a load instruction (called a *load interlock*) can be implemented by a check in ID, while the implementation of forwarding paths to the ALU inputs can be done during EX. Figure 3.17 lists the variety of circumstances that we must handle.

Situation	Example code sequence	Action

No dependence	LW **R1**,45(R2)
	ADD R5,R6,R7
	SUB R8,R6,R7
	OR R9,R6,R7
		No hazard possible because no dependence exists on R1 in the immediately following three instructions.

Dependence requiring stall	LW **R1**,45(R2)
	ADD R5,**R1**,R7
	SUB R8,R6,R7
	OR R9,R6,R7
		Comparators detect the use of R1 in the ADD and stall the ADD (and SUB and OR) before the ADD begins EX.

Dependence overcome by forwarding	LW **R1**,45(R2)
	ADD R5,R6,R7
	SUB R8,**R1**,R7
	OR R9,R6,R7
		Comparators detect use of R1 in SUB and forward result of load to ALU in time for SUB to begin EX.

Dependence with accesses in order	LW **R1**,45(R2)
	ADD R5,R6,R7
	SUB R8,R6,R7
	OR R9,**R1**,R7
		No action required because the read of R1 by OR occurs in the second half of the ID phase, while the write of the loaded data occurred in the first half.

FIGURE 3.17   Situations that the pipeline hazard detection hardware can see by comparing the destination and sources of adjacent instructions. This table indicates that the only comparison needed is between the destination and the sources on the two instructions following the instruction that wrote the destination. In the case of a stall, the pipeline dependences will look like the third case once execution continues. Of course hazards that involve R0 can be ignored since the register always contains 0, and the test above could be extended to do this.

Let's start with implementing the load interlock. If there is a RAW hazard with the source instruction being a load, the load instruction will be in the EX stage when an instruction that needs the load data will be in the ID stage. Thus, we can describe all the possible hazard situations with a small table, which can be directly translated to an implementation. Figure 3.18 shows a table that detects all load interlocks when the instruction using the load result is in the ID stage.

Opcode field of ID/EX ($ID/EX.IR_{0..5}$)	Opcode field of IF/ID ($IF/ID.IR_{0..5}$)	Matching operand fields
Load	Register-register ALU	$ID/EX.IR_{11..15} == IF/ID.IR_{6..10}$
Load	Register-register ALU	$ID/EX.IR_{11..15} == IF/ID.IR_{11..15}$
Load	Load, store, ALU immediate, or branch	$ID/EX.IR_{11..15} == IF/ID.IR_{6..10}$

FIGURE 3.18   The logic to detect the need for load interlocks during the ID stage of an instruction requires three comparisons. Lines 1 and 2 of the table test whether the load destination register is one of the source registers for a register-register operation in ID. Line 3 of the table determines if the load destination register is a source for a load or store effective address, an ALU immediate, or a branch test. Remember that the IF/ID register holds the state of the instruction in ID, which potentially uses the load result, while ID/EX holds the state of the instruction in EX, which is the potential load instruction.

Once a hazard has been detected, the control unit must insert the pipeline stall and prevent the instructions in the IF and ID stages from advancing. As we said in section 3.2, all the control information is carried in the pipeline registers. (Carrying the instruction along is enough, since all control is derived from it.) Thus, when we detect a hazard we need only change the control portion of the ID/EX pipeline register to all 0s, which happens to be a no-op (an instruction that does nothing, such as ADD R0,R0,R0). In addition, we simply recirculate the contents of the IF/ID registers to hold the stalled instruction. In a pipeline with more complex hazards, the same ideas would apply: We can detect the hazard by comparing some set of pipeline registers and shift in no-ops to prevent erroneous execution.

Implementing the forwarding logic is similar, though there are more cases to consider. The key observation needed to implement the forwarding logic is that the pipeline registers contain both the data to be forwarded as well as the source and destination register fields. All forwarding logically happens from the ALU or data memory output to the ALU input, the data memory input, or the zero detection unit. Thus, we can implement the forwarding by a comparison of the destination registers of the IR contained in the EX/MEM and MEM/WB stages against the source registers of the IR contained in the ID/EX and EX/MEM registers. Figure 3.19 shows the comparisons and possible forwarding operations where the destination of the forwarded result is an ALU input for the instruction currently in EX. The Exercises ask you to add the entries when the result is forwarded to the data memory. The last possible forwarding destination is the zero detect unit, whose forwarding paths look the same as those that are needed when the destination instruction is an ALU immediate.

In addition to the comparators and combinational logic that we need to determine when a forwarding path needs to be enabled, we also need to enlarge the multiplexers at the ALU inputs and add the connections from the pipeline registers that are used to forward the results. Figure 3.20 shows the relevant segments of the pipelined datapath with the additional multiplexers and connections in place.

For DLX, the hazard detection and forwarding hardware is reasonably simple; we will see that things become somewhat more complicated when we extend this pipeline to deal with floating point. Before we do that, we need to handle branches.

Pipeline register containing source instruction	Opcode of source instruction	Pipeline register containing destination instruction	Opcode of destination instruction	Destination of the forwarded result	Comparison (if equal then forward)
EX/MEM	Register-register ALU	ID/EX	Register-register ALU, ALU immediate, load, store, branch	Top ALU input	EX/MEM.IR$_{16..20}$ == ID/EX.IR$_{6..10}$
EX/MEM	Register-register ALU	ID/EX	Register-register ALU	Bottom ALU input	EX/MEM.IR$_{16..20}$ == ID/EX.IR$_{11..15}$
MEM/WB	Register-register ALU	ID/EX	Register-register ALU, ALU immediate, load, store, branch	Top ALU input	MEM/WB.IR$_{16..20}$ == ID/EX.IR$_{6..10}$
MEM/WB	Register-register ALU	ID/EX	Register-register ALU	Bottom ALU input	MEM/WB.IR$_{16..20}$ == ID/EX.IR$_{11..15}$
EX/MEM	ALU immediate	ID/EX	Register-register ALU, ALU immediate, load, store, branch	Top ALU input	EX/MEM.IR$_{11..15}$ == ID/EX.IR$_{6..10}$
EX/MEM	ALU immediate	ID/EX	Register-register ALU	Bottom ALU input	EX/MEM.IR$_{11..15}$ == ID/EX.IR$_{11..15}$
MEM/WB	ALU immediate	ID/EX	Register-register ALU, ALU immediate, load, store, branch	Top ALU input	MEM/WB.IR$_{11..15}$ == ID/EX.IR$_{6..10}$
MEM/WB	ALU immediate	ID/EX	Register-register ALU	Bottom ALU input	MEM/WB.IR$_{11..15}$ == ID/EX.IR$_{11..15}$
MEM/WB	Load	ID/EX	Register-register ALU, ALU immediate, load, store, branch	Top ALU input	MEM/WB.IR$_{11..15}$ == ID/EX.IR$_{6..10}$
MEM/WB	Load	ID/EX	Register-register ALU	Bottom ALU input	MEM/WB.IR$_{11..15}$ == ID/EX.IR$_{11..15}$

FIGURE 3.19   Forwarding of data to the two ALU inputs (for the instruction in EX) can occur from the ALU result (in EX/MEM or in MEM/WB) or from the load result in MEM/WB. There are 10 separate comparisons needed to tell whether a forwarding operation should occur. The top and bottom ALU inputs refer to the inputs corresponding to the first and second ALU source operands, respectively, and are shown explicitly in Figure 3.1 on page 130 and in Figure 3.20 on page 161. Remember that the pipeline latch for destination instruction in EX is ID/EX, while the source values come from the ALUOutput portion of EX/MEM or MEM/WB or the LMD portion of MEM/WB. There is one complication not addressed by this logic: dealing with multiple instructions that write the same register. For example, during the code sequence ADD R1, R2, R3; ADDI R1, R1, #2; SUB R4, R3, R1, the logic must ensure that the SUB instruction uses the result of the ADDI instruction rather than the result of the ADD instruction. The logic shown above can be extended to handle this case by simply testing that forwarding from MEM/WB is enabled only when forwarding from EX/MEM is not enabled for the same input. Because the ADDI result will be in EX/MEM, it will be forwarded, rather than the ADD result in MEM/WB.

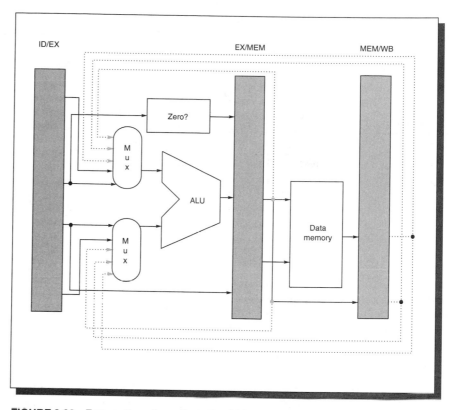

FIGURE 3.20   Forwarding of results to the ALU requires the addition of three extra in-puts on each ALU multiplexer and the addition of three paths to the new inputs. The paths correspond to a bypass of (1) the ALU output at the end of the EX, (2) the ALU output at the end of the MEM stage, and (3) the memory output at the end of the MEM stage.

3.5 | Control Hazards

Control hazards can cause a greater performance loss for our DLX pipeline than do data hazards. When a branch is executed, it may or may not change the PC to something other than its current value plus 4. Recall that if a branch changes the PC to its target address, it is a *taken* branch; if it falls through, it is *not taken*, or *untaken*. If instruction *i* is a taken branch, then the PC is normally not changed until the end of MEM, after the completion of the address calculation and comparison, as shown in Figure 3.4 (page 134) and Figure 3.5 (page 136).

The simplest method of dealing with branches is to stall the pipeline as soon as we detect the branch until we reach the MEM stage, which determines the new PC. Of course, we do not want to stall the pipeline until we know that the instruction is a branch; thus, the stall does not occur until after the ID stage, and the pipeline behavior looks like that shown in Figure 3.21. This control hazard stall must be implemented differently from a data hazard stall, since the IF cycle of the instruction following the branch must be repeated as soon as we know the branch outcome. Thus, the first IF cycle is essentially a stall, because it never performs useful work. This stall can be implemented by setting the IF/ID register to zero for the three cycles. You may have noticed that if the branch is untaken, then the repetition of the IF stage is unnecessary since the correct instruction was indeed fetched. We will develop several schemes to take advantage of this fact shortly, but first, let's examine how we could reduce the worst-case branch penalty.

Branch instruction	IF	ID	EX	MEM	WB					
Branch successor		IF	*stall*	*stall*	IF	ID	EX	MEM	WB	
Branch successor + 1						IF	ID	EX	MEM	WB
Branch successor + 2							IF	ID	EX	MEM
Branch successor + 3								IF	ID	EX
Branch successor + 4									IF	ID
Branch successor + 5										IF

FIGURE 3.21   A branch causes a three-cycle stall in the DLX pipeline: One cycle is a repeated IF cycle and two cycles are idle. The instruction after the branch is fetched, but the instruction is ignored, and the fetch is restarted once the branch target is known. It is probably obvious that if the branch is not taken, the second IF for branch successor is redundant. This will be addressed shortly.

Three clock cycles wasted for every branch is a significant loss. With a 30% branch frequency and an ideal CPI of 1, the machine with branch stalls achieves only about *half* the ideal speedup from pipelining! Thus, reducing the branch penalty becomes critical. The number of clock cycles in a branch stall can be reduced by two steps:

1. Find out whether the branch is taken or not taken earlier in the pipeline.

2. Compute the taken PC (i.e., the address of the branch target) earlier.

To optimize the branch behavior, *both* of these must be done—it doesn't help to know the target of the branch without knowing whether the next instruction to execute is the target or the instruction at PC + 4. Both steps should be taken as early in the pipeline as possible.

In DLX, the branches (BEQZ and BNEZ) require testing a register for equality to zero. Thus, it is possible to complete this decision by the end of the ID cycle by moving the zero test into that cycle. To take advantage of an early decision on whether the branch is taken, both PCs (taken and untaken) must be computed early. Computing the branch target address during ID requires an additional adder because the main ALU, which has been used for this function so far, is not usable until EX. Figure 3.22 shows the revised pipelined datapath. With the separate adder and a branch decision made during ID, there is only a one-clock-cycle stall on branches. Although this reduces the branch delay to one cycle, it means that an ALU instruction followed by a branch on the result of the instruction will in-

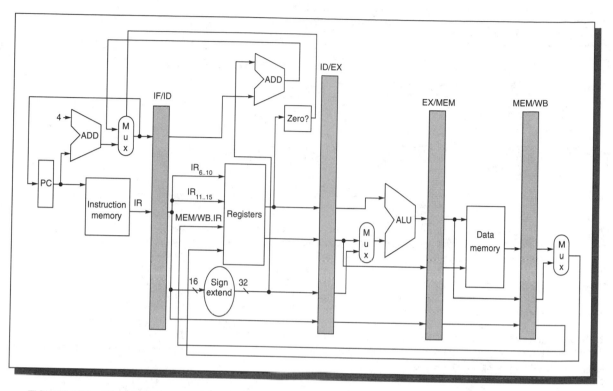

FIGURE 3.22 The stall from branch hazards can be reduced by moving the zero test and branch target calculation into the ID phase of the pipeline. Notice that we have made two important changes, each of which removes one cycle from the three cycle stall for branches. The first change is to move both the branch address target calculation and the branch condition decision to the ID cycle. The second change is to write the PC of the instruction in the IF phase, using either the branch target address computed during ID or the incremented PC computed during IF. In comparison, Figure 3.4 obtained the branch target address from the EX/MEM register and wrote the result during the MEM clock cycle. As mentioned in Figure 3.4, the PC can be thought of as a pipeline register (e.g., as part of ID/IF), which is written with the address of the next instruction at the end of each IF cycle.

cur a data hazard stall. Figure 3.23 shows the branch portion of the revised pipeline table from Figure 3.5 (page 136).

In some machines, branch hazards are even more expensive in clock cycles than in our example, since the time to evaluate the branch condition and compute the destination can be even longer. For example, a machine with separate decode and register fetch stages will probably have a *branch delay*—the length of the control hazard—that is at least one clock cycle longer. The branch delay, unless it is dealt with, turns into a branch penalty. Many older machines that implement more complex instruction sets have branch delays of four clock cycles or more, and large, deeply pipelined machines often have branch penalties of six or seven. In general, the deeper the pipeline, the worse the branch penalty in clock cycles. Of course, the relative performance effect of a longer branch penalty depends on the overall CPI of the machine. A high CPI machine can afford to have more expensive branches because the percentage of the machine's performance that will be lost from branches is less.

Pipe stage	Branch instruction
IF	`IF/ID.IR ← Mem[PC];` **`IF/ID.NPC,PC ← (if ((IF/ID.opcode == branch) & (Regs[IF/ID.IR`**$_{6..10}$**`]`** **`op 0)) {IF/ID.NPC +`** **`(IF/ID.IR`**$_{16}$**`)`**^{16}**`##IF/ID.IR`**$_{16..31}$**`} else {PC+4});`**

ID	`ID/EX.A ← Regs[IF/ID.IR`$_{6..10}$`];  ID/EX.B ← Regs[IF/ID.IR`$_{11..15}$`];`
	`ID/EX.IR ← IF/ID.IR;`
	`ID/EX.Imm ← (IF/ID.IR`$_{16}$`)`^{16}`##IF/ID.IR`$_{16..31}$

EX	
MEM	
WB	

FIGURE 3.23 This revised pipeline structure is based on the original in Figure 3.5, page 136. It uses a separate adder, as in Figure 3.22, to compute the branch target address during ID. The operations that are new or have changed are in bold. Because the branch target address addition happens during ID, it will happen for all instructions; the branch condition (`Regs[IF/ID.IR`$_{6..10}$`]` op 0) will also be done for all instructions. The selection of the sequential PC or the branch target PC still occurs during IF, but it now uses values from the ID/EX register, which correspond to the values set by the previous instruction. This change reduces the branch penalty by two cycles: one from evaluating the branch target and condition earlier and one from controlling the PC selection on the same clock rather than on the next clock. Since the value of cond is set to 0, unless the instruction in ID is a taken branch, the machine must decode the instruction before the end of ID. Because the branch is done by the end of ID, the EX, MEM, and WB stages are unused for branches. An additional complication arises for jumps that have a longer offset than branches. We can resolve this by using an additional adder that sums the PC and lower 26 bits of the IR.

Before talking about methods for reducing the pipeline penalties that can arise from branches, let's take a brief look at the dynamic behavior of branches.

Branch Behavior in Programs

Because branches can dramatically affect pipeline performance, we should look at their behavior to get some ideas about how the penalties of branches and jumps might be reduced. We already know something about branch frequencies from our programs in Chapter 2. Figure 3.24 reviews the overall frequency of control-flow operations for our SPEC subset on DLX and gives the breakdown between branches and jumps. Conditional branches are also broken into forward and backward branches.

The integer benchmarks show conditional branch frequencies of 14% to 16%, with much lower unconditional branch frequencies (though li has a large number because of its high procedure call frequency). For the FP benchmarks, the behavior is much more varied with a conditional branch frequency of 3% up to 12%, but an overall average for both conditional branches and unconditional branches that is lower than for the integer benchmarks. Forward branches dominate backward branches by about 3.7 to 1 on average.

Since the performance of pipelining schemes for branches may depend on whether or not branches are taken, this data becomes critical. Figure 3.25 shows the frequency of forward and backward branches that are taken as a fraction of all conditional branches. Totaling the two columns shows that 67% of the condition-

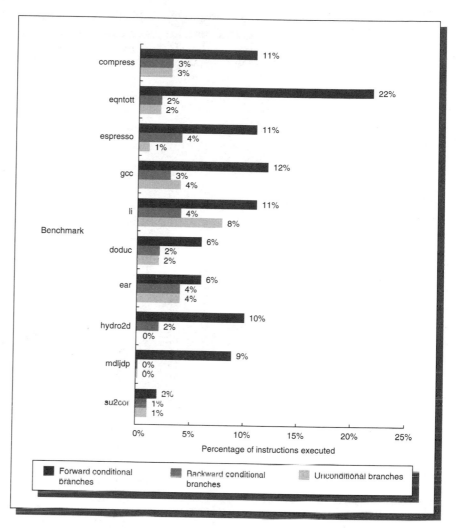

FIGURE 3.24   The frequency of instructions (branches, jumps, calls, and returns) that may change the PC. The unconditional column includes unconditional branches and jumps (these differ in how the target address is specified), procedure calls, and returns. In all the cases except li, the number of unconditional PC changes is roughly equally divided between those that are for calls or returns and those that are unconditional jumps. In li, calls and returns outnumber jumps and unconditional branches by a factor of 3 (6% versus 2%). Since the compiler uses loop unrolling (described in detail in Chapter 4) as an optimization, the backward conditional branch frequency will be lower, especially for the floating-point programs. Overall, the integer programs average 13% forward conditional branches, 3% backward conditional branches, and 4% unconditional branches. The FP programs average 7%, 2%, and 1%, respectively.

al branches are taken on average. By combining the data in Figures 3.24 and 3.25, we can compute the fraction of forward branches that are taken, which is the probability that a forward branch will be taken. Since backward branches often form loops, we would expect that the probability of a backward branch being taken is higher than the probability of a forward branch being taken. Indeed, the data, when combined, show that 60% of the forward branches are taken on average and 85% of the backward branches are taken.

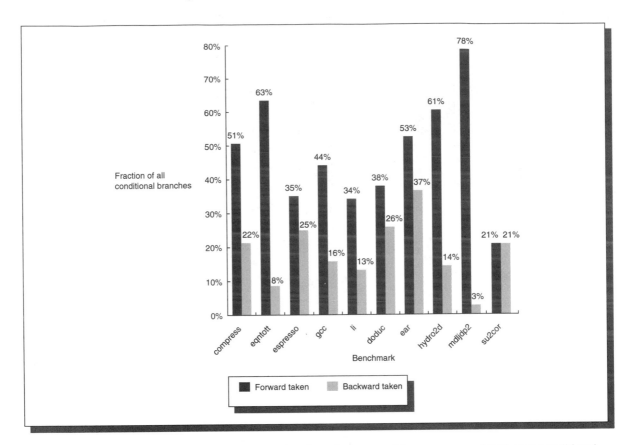

FIGURE 3.25   **Together the forward and backward taken branches account for an average of 67% of all conditional branches.** Although the backward branches are outnumbered, they are taken with a frequency that is almost 1.5 times higher, contributing substantially to the taken branch frequency. On average, 62% of the branches are taken in the integer programs and 70% in the FP programs. Note the wide disparity in behavior between a program like su2cor and mdljdp2; these variations make it challenging to predict the branch behavior very accurately. As in Figure 3.24, the use of loop unrolling affects this data since it removes backward branches that had a high probability of being taken.

Reducing Pipeline Branch Penalties

There are many methods for dealing with the pipeline stalls caused by branch delay; we discuss four simple compile-time schemes in this subsection. In these four schemes the actions for a branch are static—they are fixed for each branch during the entire execution. The software can try to minimize the branch penalty using knowledge of the hardware scheme and of branch behavior. After discussing these schemes, we examine compile-time branch prediction, since these branch optimizations all rely on such technology. In the next chapter, we look both at more powerful compile-time schemes (such as loop unrolling) that reduce the frequency of loop branches and at dynamic hardware-based prediction schemes.

The simplest scheme to handle branches is to *freeze* or *flush* the pipeline, holding or deleting any instructions after the branch until the branch destination is known. The attractiveness of this solution lies primarily in its simplicity both for hardware and software. It is the solution used earlier in the pipeline shown in Figure 3.21. In this case the branch penalty is fixed and cannot be reduced by software.

A higher performance, and only slightly more complex, scheme is to treat every branch as not taken, simply allowing the hardware to continue as if the branch were not executed. Here, care must be taken not to change the machine state until the branch outcome is definitely known. The complexity that arises from having to know when the state might be changed by an instruction and how to "back out" a change might cause us to choose the simpler solution of flushing the pipeline in machines with complex pipeline structures.

In the DLX pipeline, this *predict-not-taken* or *predict-untaken* scheme is implemented by continuing to fetch instructions as if the branch were a normal instruction. The pipeline looks as if nothing out of the ordinary is happening. If the branch is taken, however, we need to turn the fetched instruction into a no-op (simply by clearing the IF/ID register) and restart the fetch at the target address. Figure 3.26 shows both situations.

Untaken branch instruction	IF	ID	EX	MEM	WB				
Instruction $i + 1$		IF	ID	EX	MEM	WB			
Instruction $i + 2$			IF	ID	EX	MEM	WB		
Instruction $i + 3$				IF	ID	EX	MEM	WB	
Instruction $i + 4$					IF	ID	EX	MEM	WB

Taken branch instruction	IF	ID	EX	MEM	WB				
Instruction $i + 1$		IF	**idle**	**idle**	**idle**	**idle**			
Branch target			IF	ID	EX	MEM	WB		
Branch target + 1				IF	ID	EX	MEM	WB	
Branch target + 2					IF	ID	EX	MEM	WB

FIGURE 3.26 The predict-not-taken scheme and the pipeline sequence when the branch is untaken (top) and taken (bottom). When the branch is untaken, determined during ID, we have fetched the fall-through and just continue. If the branch is taken during ID, we restart the fetch at the branch target. This causes all instructions following the branch to stall one clock cycle.

An alternative scheme is to treat every branch as taken. As soon as the branch is decoded and the target address is computed, we assume the branch to be taken and begin fetching and executing at the target. Because in our DLX pipeline we don't know the target address any earlier than we know the branch outcome, there is no advantage in this approach for DLX. In some machines—especially those with implicitly set condition codes or more powerful (and hence slower) branch conditions—the branch target is known before the branch outcome, and a predict-taken scheme might make sense. In either a predict-taken or predict-not-taken scheme, the compiler can improve performance by organizing the code so that the most frequent path matches the hardware's choice. Our fourth scheme provides more opportunities for the compiler to improve performance.

A fourth scheme in use in some machines is called *delayed branch*. This technique is also used in many microprogrammed control units. In a delayed branch, the execution cycle with a branch delay of length n is

```
branch instruction
sequential successor₁
sequential successor₂
........
sequential successorₙ
branch target if taken
```

The sequential successors are in the *branch-delay slots*. These instructions are executed whether or not the branch is taken. The pipeline behavior of the DLX pipeline, which would have one branch-delay slot, is shown in Figure 3.27. In

Untaken branch instruction	IF	ID	EX	MEM	WB				
Branch-delay instruction ($i + 1$)		IF	ID	EX	MEM	WB			
Instruction $i + 2$			IF	ID	EX	MEM	WB		
Instruction $i + 3$				IF	ID	EX	MEM	WB	
Instruction $i + 4$					IF	ID	EX	MEM	WB

Taken branch instruction	IF	ID	EX	MEM	WB				
Branch-delay instruction ($i + 1$)		IF	ID	EX	MEM	WB			
Branch target			IF	ID	EX	MEM	WB		
Branch target + 1				IF	ID	EX	MEM	WB	
Branch target + 2					IF	ID	EX	MEM	WB

FIGURE 3.27   The behavior of a delayed branch is the same whether or not the branch is taken. The instructions in the delay slot (there is only one delay slot for DLX) are executed. If the branch is untaken, execution continues with the instruction after the branch-delay instruction; if the branch is taken, execution continues at the branch target. When the instruction in the branch-delay slot is also a branch, the meaning is unclear: if the branch is not taken, what should happen to the branch in the branch-delay slot? Because of this confusion, architectures with delay branches often disallow putting a branch in the delay slot.

practice, all machines with delayed branch have a single instruction delay, and we focus on that case.

The job of the compiler is to make the successor instructions valid and useful. A number of optimizations are used. Figure 3.28 shows the three ways in which the branch delay can be scheduled. Figure 3.29 shows the different constraints for each of these branch-scheduling schemes, as well as situations in which they win.

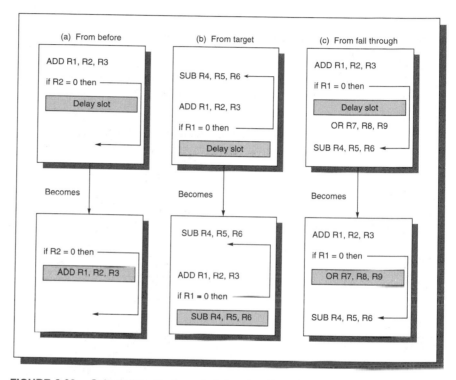

FIGURE 3.28   Scheduling the branch-delay slot. The top box in each pair shows the code before scheduling; the bottom box shows the scheduled code. In (a) the delay slot is scheduled with an independent instruction from before the branch. This is the best choice. Strategies (b) and (c) are used when (a) is not possible. In the code sequences for (b) and (c), the use of R1 in the branch condition prevents the ADD instruction (whose destination is R1) from being moved after the branch. In (b) the branch-delay slot is scheduled from the target of the branch; usually the target instruction will need to be copied because it can be reached by another path. Strategy (b) is preferred when the branch is taken with high probability, such as a loop branch. Finally, the branch may be scheduled from the not-taken fall through as in (c). To make this optimization legal for (b) or (c), it must be OK to execute the moved instruction when the branch goes in the unexpected direction. By OK we mean that the work is wasted, but the program will still execute correctly. This is the case, for example in case (b), if R4 were an unused temporary register when the branch goes in the unexpected direction.

Scheduling strategy	Requirements	Improves performance when?
(a) From before	Branch must not depend on the rescheduled instructions.	Always.
(b) From target	Must be OK to execute rescheduled instructions if branch is not taken. May need to duplicate instructions.	When branch is taken. May enlarge program if instructions are duplicated.
(c) From fall through	Must be OK to execute instructions if branch is taken.	When branch is not taken.

FIGURE 3.29   Delayed-branch scheduling schemes and their requirements. The origin of the instruction being scheduled into the delay slot determines the scheduling strategy. The compiler must enforce the requirements when looking for instructions to schedule the delay slot. When the slots cannot be scheduled, they are filled with no-op instructions. In strategy (b), if the branch target is also accessible from another point in the program—as it would be if it were the head of a loop—the target instructions must be copied and not just moved.

The limitations on delayed-branch scheduling arise from (1) the restrictions on the instructions that are scheduled into the delay slots and (2) our ability to predict at compile time whether a branch is likely to be taken or not. Shortly, we will see how we can better predict branches statically at compile time. To improve the ability of the compiler to fill branch delay slots, most machines with conditional branches have introduced a *cancelling* or *nullifying* branch. In a cancelling branch, the instruction includes the direction that the branch was predicted. When the branch behaves as predicted, the instruction in the branch-delay slot is simply executed as it would normally be with a delayed branch. When the branch is incorrectly predicted, the instruction in the branch-delay slot is simply turned into a no-op. Figure 3.30 shows the behavior of a predicted-taken cancelling branch, both when the branch is taken and untaken.

Untaken branch instruction	IF	ID	EX	MEM	WB			
Branch-delay instruction ($i+1$)		IF	idle	idle	idle	idle		
Instruction $i+2$			IF	ID	EX	MEM	WB	
Instruction $i+3$				IF	ID	EX	MEM	WB
Instruction $i+4$					IF	ID	EX	MEM	WB

Taken branch instruction	IF	ID	EX	MEM	WB			
Branch-delay instruction ($i+1$)		IF	ID	EX	MEM	WB		
Branch target			IF	ID	EX	MEM	WB	
Branch target + 1				IF	ID	EX	MEM	WB
Branch target + 2					IF	ID	EX	MEM	WB

FIGURE 3.30   The behavior of a predicted-taken cancelling branch depends on whether the branch is taken or not. The instruction in the delay slot is executed only if the branch is taken and is otherwise made into a no-op.

The advantage of cancelling branches is that they eliminate the requirements on the instruction placed in the delay slot, enabling the compiler to use scheduling schemes (b) and (c) of Figure 3.28 without meeting the requirements shown for these schemes in Figure 3.29. Most machines with cancelling branches provide both a noncancelling form (i.e., a regular delayed branch) and a cancelling form, usually cancel if not taken. This combination gains most of the advantages, but does not allow scheduling scheme (c) to be used unless the requirements of Figure 3.29 are met.

Figure 3.31 shows the effectiveness of the branch scheduling in DLX with a single branch-delay slot and both a noncancelling branch and a cancel-if-untaken form. The compiler uses a standard delayed branch whenever possible and then opts for a cancel-if-not-taken branch (also called *branch likely*). The second column shows that almost 20% of the branch delay slots are filled with no-ops. These occur when it is not possible to fill the delay slot, either because the potential candidates are unknown (e.g., for a jump register that will be used in a case statement) or because the successors are also branches. (Branches are not allowed in branch-delay slots because of the confusion in semantics.) The table shows that the

Benchmark	% conditional branches	% conditional branches with empty slots	% conditional branches that are cancelling	% cancelling branches that are cancelled	% branches with cancelled delay slots	Total % branches with empty or cancelled delay slot
compress	14%	18%	31%	43%	13%	31%
eqntott	24%	24%	50%	24%	12%	36%
espresso	15%	29%	19%	21%	4%	33%
gcc	15%	16%	33%	34%	11%	27%
li	15%	20%	55%	48%	26%	46%
Integer average	17%	21%	38%	34%	13%	35%
doduc	8%	33%	12%	62%	7%	40%
ear	10%	37%	36%	14%	5%	42%
hydro2d	12%	0%	69%	24%	17%	17%
mdljdp2	9%	0%	86%	10%	9%	9%
su2cor	3%	7%	17%	57%	10%	17%
FP average	8%	16%	44%	33%	10%	25%
Overall average	12%	18%	41%	34%	12%	30%

FIGURE 3.31   Delayed and cancelling delay branches for DLX allow branch hazards to be hidden 70% of the time on average for these 10 SPEC benchmarks. Empty delay slots cannot be filled at all (most often because the branch target is another branch) in 18% of the branches. Just under half the conditional branches use a cancelling branch, and most of these are not cancelled (65%). The behavior varies widely across benchmarks. When the fraction of conditional branches is added in, the contribution to CPI varies even more widely.

remaining 80% of the branch delay slots are filled nearly equally by standard delayed branches and by cancelling branches. Most of the cancelling branches are not cancelled and hence contribute to useful computation. Figure 3.32 summarizes the performance of the combination of delayed branch and cancelling branch. Overall, 70% of the branch delays are usefully filled, reducing the stall penalty to 0.3 cycles per conditional branch.

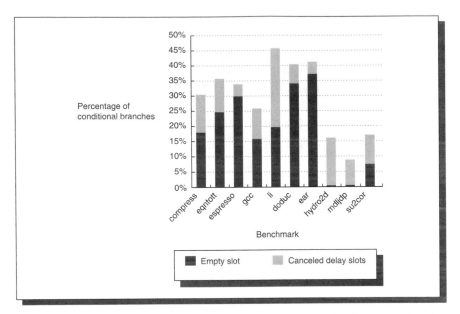

FIGURE 3.32   The performance of delayed and cancelling branches is summarized by showing the fraction of branches either with empty delay slots or with a cancelled delay slot. On average 30% of the branch delay slots are wasted. The integer programs are, on average, worse, wasting an average of 35% of the slots versus 25% for the FP programs. Notice, though, that two of the FP programs waste more branch delay slots than four of the five integer programs.

Delayed branches are an architecturally visible feature of the pipeline. This is the source both of their primary advantage—allowing the use of simple compiler scheduling to reduce branch penalties—and their primary disadvantage—exposing an aspect of the implementation that is likely to change. In the early RISC machines with single-cycle branch delays, the delayed branch approach was attractive, since it yielded good performance with minimal hardware costs. More recently, with deeper pipelines and longer branch delays, a delayed branch approach is less useful since it cannot easily hide the longer delays. With these longer branch delays, most architects have found it necessary to include more powerful hardware schemes for branch prediction (which we will explore in the next chapter), making the delayed branch superfluous.This has led to recent RISC architectures that include both delayed and nondelayed branches or that include only nondelayed branches, relying on hardware prediction.

There is a small additional hardware cost for delayed branches. For a single-cycle delayed branch, the only case that exists in practice, a single extra PC is needed. To understand why an extra PC is needed for the single-cycle delay case, consider when the interrupt occurs for the instruction in the branch-delay slot. If the branch was taken, then the instruction in the delay slot and the branch target have addresses that are not sequential. Thus, we need to save the PCs of both instructions and restore them after the interrupt to restart the pipeline. The two PCs can be kept with the control in the pipeline latches and passed along with the instruction. This makes saving and restoring them easy.

Performance of Branch Schemes

What is the effective performance of each of these schemes? The effective pipeline speedup with branch penalties, assuming an ideal CPI of 1, is

$$\text{Pipeline speedup} = \frac{\text{Pipeline depth}}{1 + \text{Pipeline stall cycles from branches}}$$

Because of the following:

$$\text{Pipeline stall cycles from branches} = \text{Branch frequency} \times \text{Branch penalty}$$

we obtain

$$\text{Pipeline speedup} = \frac{\text{Pipeline depth}}{1 + \text{Branch frequency} \times \text{Branch penalty}}$$

The branch frequency and branch penalty can have a component from both unconditional and conditional branches. However, the latter dominate since they are more frequent.

Using the DLX measurements in this section, Figure 3.33 shows several hardware options for dealing with branches, along with their performances given as branch penalty and as CPI (assuming a base CPI of 1).

Scheduling scheme	Branch penalty per conditional branch		Penalty per unconditional branch	Average branch penalty per branch		Effective CPI with branch stalls	
	Integer	FP		Integer	FP	Integer	FP
Stall pipeline	1.00	1.00	1.00	1.00	1.00	1.17	1.15
Predict taken	1.00	1.00	1.00	1.00	1.00	1.17	1.15
Predict not taken	0.62	0.70	1.0	0.69	0.74	1.12	1.11
Delayed branch	0.35	0.25	0.0	0.30	0.21	1.06	1.03

FIGURE 3.33 Overall costs of a variety of branch schemes with the DLX pipeline. These data are for our DLX pipeline using the average measured branch frequencies from Figure 3.24 on page 165, the measurements of taken/untaken frequencies from 3.25 on page 166, and the measurements of delay-slot filling from Figure 3.31 on page 171. Shown are both the penalties per branch and the resulting overall CPI including only the effect of branch stalls and assuming a base CPI of 1.

Remember that the numbers in this section are *dramatically* affected by the length of the pipeline delay and the base CPI. A longer pipeline delay will cause an increase in the penalty and a larger percentage of wasted time. A delay of only one clock cycle is small—the R4000 pipeline, which we examine in section 3.9, has a conditional branch delay of three cycles. This results in a much higher penalty.

EXAMPLE   For an R4000-style pipeline, it takes three pipeline stages before the branch target address is known and an additional cycle before the branch condition is evaluated, assuming no stalls on the registers in the conditional comparison. This leads to the branch penalties for the three simplest prediction schemes listed in Figure 3.34.

Branch scheme	Penalty unconditional	Penalty untaken	Penalty taken
Flush pipeline	2	3	3
Predict taken	2	3	2
Predict untaken	2	0	3

FIGURE 3.34   Branch penalties for the three simplest prediction schemes for a deeper pipeline.

Find the effective addition to the CPI arising from branches for this pipeline, using the data from the 10 SPEC benchmarks in Figures 3.24 and 3.25.

ANSWER   We find the CPIs by multiplying the relative frequency of unconditional, conditional untaken, and conditional taken branches by the respective penalties. These frequencies for the 10 SPEC programs are 4%, 6%, and 10%, respectively. The results are shown in Figure 3.35.

	Addition to the CPI			
Branch scheme	Unconditional branches	Untaken conditional branches	Taken conditional branches	All branches
Frequency of event	4%	6%	10%	20%
Stall pipeline	0.08	0.18	0.30	0.56
Predict taken	0.08	0.18	0.20	0.46
Predict untaken	0.08	0.00	0.30	0.38

FIGURE 3.35   CPI penalties for three branch-prediction schemes and a deeper pipeline.

The differences among the schemes are substantially increased with this longer delay. If the base CPI was 1 and branches were the only source of stalls, the ideal pipeline would be 1.56 times faster than a pipeline that used the stall-pipeline scheme. The predict-untaken scheme would be 1.13 times better than the stall-pipeline scheme under the same assumptions.

As we will see in section 3.9, the R4000 uses a mixed strategy with a one-cycle, cancelling delayed branch for the first cycle of the branch penalty. For an unconditional branch, a single-cycle stall is always added. For conditional branches, the remaining two cycles of the branch penalty use a predict-not-taken scheme. We will see measurements of the effective branch penalties for this strategy later.
■

Static Branch Prediction: Using Compiler Technology

Delayed branches are a technique that exposes a pipeline hazard so that the compiler can reduce the penalty associated with the hazard. As we saw, the effectiveness of this technique partly depends on whether we correctly guess which way a branch will go. Being able to accurately predict a branch at compile time is also helpful for scheduling data hazards. Consider the following code segment:

```
        LW      R1,0(R2)
        SUB     R1,R1,R3
        BEQZ    R1,L
        OR      R4,R5,R6
        ADD     R10,R4,R3
L:      ADD     R7,R8,R9
```

The dependence of the SUB and BEQZ on the LW instruction means that a stall will be needed after the LW. Suppose we knew that this branch was almost always taken and that the value of R7 was not needed on the fall-through path. Then we could increase the speed of the program by moving the instruction ADD R7,R8,R9 to the position after the LW. Correspondingly, if we knew the branch was rarely taken and that the value of R4 was not needed on the taken path, then we could contemplate moving the OR instruction after the LW. In addition, we can also use the information to better schedule any branch delay, since choosing how to schedule the delay depends on knowing the branch behavior.

To perform these optimizations, we need to predict the branch statically when we compile the program. In the next chapter, we will examine the use of dynamic prediction based on runtime program behavior. We will also look at a variety of compile-time methods for scheduling code; these techniques require static branch prediction and thus the ideas in this section are critical.

There are two basic methods we can use to statically predict branches: by examination of the program behavior and by the use of profile information collected from earlier runs of the program. We saw in Figure 3.25 (page 166) that most branches were taken for both forward and backward branches. Thus, the simplest scheme is to predict a branch as taken. This scheme has an average misprediction rate for the 10 programs in Figure 3.25 of the untaken branch frequency (34%). Unfortunately, the misprediction rate ranges from not very accurate (59%) to highly accurate (9%).

Another alternative is to predict on the basis of branch direction, choosing backward-going branches to be taken and forward-going branches to be not taken. For some programs and compilation systems, the frequency of forward taken branches may be significantly less than 50%, and this scheme will do better than just predicting all branches as taken. In our SPEC programs, however, more than half of the forward-going branches are taken. Hence, predicting all branches as taken is the better approach. Even for other benchmarks or compilers, direction-based prediction is unlikely to generate an overall misprediction rate of less than 30% to 40%.

A more accurate technique is to predict branches on the basis of profile information collected from earlier runs. The key observation that makes this worthwhile is that the behavior of branches is often bimodally distributed; that is, an individual branch is often highly biased toward taken or untaken. Figure 3.36 shows the success of branch prediction using this strategy. The same input data were used for runs and for collecting the profile; other studies have shown that changing the input so that the profile is for a different run leads to only a small change in the accuracy of profile-based prediction.

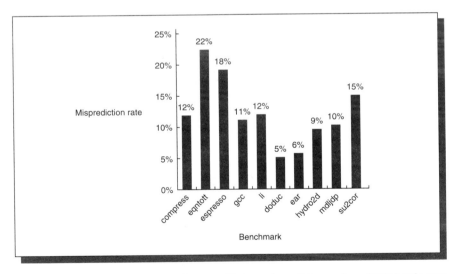

FIGURE 3.36   Misprediction rate for a profile-based predictor varies widely but is generally better for the FP programs, which have an average misprediction rate of 9% with a standard deviation of 4%, than for the integer programs, which have an average misprediction rate of 15% with a standard deviation of 5%. The actual performance depends on both the prediction accuracy and the branch frequency, which varies from 3% to 24% in Figure 3.31 (page 171); we will examine the combined effect in Figure 3.37.

While we can derive the prediction accuracy of a predict-taken strategy and measure the accuracy of the profile scheme, as in Figure 3.36, the wide range of frequency of conditional branches in these programs, from 3% to 24%, means that the overall frequency of a mispredicted branch varies widely. Figure 3.37 shows the number of instructions executed between mispredicted branches for both a profile-based and a predict-taken strategy. The number varies widely, both because of the variation in accuracy and the variation in branch frequency. On average, the predict-taken strategy has 20 instructions per mispredicted branch and the profile-based strategy has 110. However, these averages are very different for integer and FP programs, as the data in Figure 3.37 show.

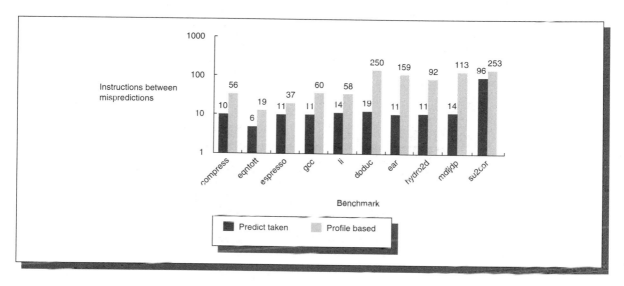

FIGURE 3.37 Accuracy of a predict-taken strategy and a profile-based predictor as measured by the number of instructions executed between mispredicted branches and shown on a log scale. The average number of instructions between mispredictions is 20 for the predict-taken strategy and 110 for the profile-based prediction; however, the standard deviations are large: 27 instructions for the predict-taken strategy and 85 instructions for the profile-based scheme. This wide variation arises because programs such as su2cor have both low conditional branch frequency (3%) and predictable branches (85% accuracy for profiling), while eqntott has eight times the branch frequency with branches that are nearly 1.5 times *less* predictable. The difference between the FP and integer benchmarks as groups is large. For the predict-taken strategy, the average distance between mispredictions for the integer benchmarks is 10 instructions, while it is 30 instructions for the FP programs. With the profile scheme, the distance between mispredictions for the integer benchmarks is 46 instructions, while it is 173 instructions for the FP benchmarks.

Summary: Performance of the DLX Integer Pipeline

We close this section on hazard detection and elimination by showing the total distribution of idle clock cycles for our integer benchmarks when run on the DLX pipeline with software for pipeline scheduling. (After we examine the DLX FP pipeline in section 3.7, we will examine the overall performance of the FP benchmarks.) Figure 3.38 shows the distribution of clock cycles lost to load and branch

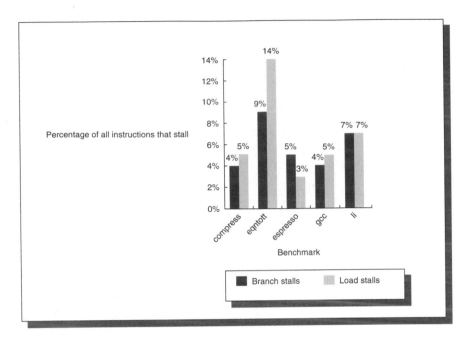

FIGURE 3.38   Percentage of the instructions that cause a stall cycle. This assumes a perfect memory system; the clock-cycle count and instruction count would be identical if there were no integer pipeline stalls. It also assumes the availability of both a basic delayed branch and a cancelling delayed branch, both with one cycle of delay. According to the graph, from 8% to 23% of the instructions cause a stall (or a cancelled instruction), leading to CPIs from pipeline stalls that range from 1.09 to 1.23. The pipeline scheduler fills load delays before branch delays, and this affects the distribution of delay cycles.

delays, which is obtained by combining the separate measurements shown in Figures 3.16 (page 157) and 3.31 (page 171).

Overall the integer programs exhibit an average of 0.06 branch stalls per instruction and 0.05 load stalls per instruction, leading to an average CPI from pipelining (i.e., assuming a perfect memory system) of 1.11. Thus, with a perfect memory system and no clock overhead, pipelining could improve the performance of these five integer SPECint92 benchmarks by 5/1.11 or 4.5 times.

3.6 | What Makes Pipelining Hard to Implement?

Now that we understand how to detect and resolve hazards, we can deal with some complications that we have avoided so far. The first part of this section considers the challenges of exceptional situations where the instruction execution order is changed in unexpected ways. In the second part of this section, we discuss some of the challenges raised by different instruction sets.

Dealing with Exceptions

Exceptional situations are harder to handle in a pipelined machine because the overlapping of instructions makes it more difficult to know whether an instruction can safely change the state of the machine. In a pipelined machine, an instruction is executed piece by piece and is not completed for several clock cycles. Unfortunately, other instructions in the pipeline can raise exceptions that may force the machine to abort the instructions in the pipeline before they complete. Before we discuss these problems and their solutions in detail, we need to understand what types of situations can arise and what architectural requirements exist for supporting them.

Types of Exceptions and Requirements

The terminology used to describe exceptional situations where the normal execution order of instruction is changed varies among machines. The terms *interrupt*, *fault*, and *exception* are used, though not in a consistent fashion. We use the term *exception* to cover all these mechanisms, including the following:

 I/O device request

 Invoking an operating system service from a user program

 Tracing instruction execution

 Breakpoint (programmer-requested interrupt)

 Integer arithmetic overflow

 FP arithmetic anomaly (see Appendix A)

 Page fault (not in main memory)

 Misaligned memory accesses (if alignment is required)

 Memory-protection violation

 Using an undefined or unimplemented instruction

 Hardware malfunctions

 Power failure

When we wish to refer to some particular class of such exceptions, we will use a longer name, such as I/O interrupt, floating-point exception, or page fault. Figure 3.39 shows the variety of different names for the common exception events above.

Although we use the name *exception* to cover all of these events, individual events have important characteristics that determine what action is needed in the hardware. The requirements on exceptions can be characterized on five semi-independent axes:

Exception type	Synchronous vs. asynchronous	User request vs. coerced	User maskable vs. nonmaskable	Within vs. between instructions	Resume vs. terminate
I/O device request	Asynchronous	Coerced	Nonmaskable	Between	Resume
Invoke operating system	Synchronous	User request	Nonmaskable	Between	Resume
Tracing instruction execution	Synchronous	User request	User maskable	Between	Resume
Breakpoint	Synchronous	User request	User maskable	Between	Resume
Integer arithmetic overflow	Synchronous	Coerced	User maskable	Within	Resume
Floating-point arithmetic overflow or underflow	Synchronous	Coerced	User maskable	Within	Resume
Page fault	Synchronous	Coerced	Nonmaskable	Within	Resume
Misaligned memory accesses	Synchronous	Coerced	User maskable	Within	Resume
Memory-protection violations	Synchronous	Coerced	Nonmaskable	Within	Resume
Using undefined instructions	Synchronous	Coerced	Nonmaskable	Within	Terminate
Hardware malfunctions	Asynchronous	Coerced	Nonmaskable	Within	Terminate
Power failure	Asynchronous	Coerced	Nonmaskable	Within	Terminate

FIGURE 3.40   Five categories are used to define what actions are needed for the different exception types shown in Figure 3.39. Exceptions that must allow resumption are marked as resume, although the software may often choose to terminate the program. Synchronous, coerced exceptions occurring within instructions that can be resumed are the most difficult to implement. We might expect that memory protection access violations would always result in termination; however, modern operating systems use memory protection to detect events such as the first attempt to use a page or the first write to a page. Thus, processors should be able to resume after such exceptions.

Stopping and Restarting Execution

As in unpipelined implementations, the most difficult exceptions have two properties: (1) they occur within instructions (that is, in the middle of the instruction execution corresponding to EX or MEM pipe stages), and (2) they must be restartable. In our DLX pipeline, for example, a virtual memory page fault resulting from a data fetch cannot occur until sometime in the MEM stage of the instruction. By the time that fault is seen, several other instructions will be in execution. A page fault must be restartable and requires the intervention of another process, such as the operating system. Thus, the pipeline must be safely shut down and the state saved so that the instruction can be restarted in the correct state. Restarting is usually implemented by saving the PC of the instruction at which to restart. If the restarted instruction is not a branch, then we will continue to fetch the sequential successors and begin their execution in the normal fashion. If the restarted instruction is a branch, then we will reevaluate the branch condition and begin fetching from either the target or the fall through. When an exception occurs, the pipeline control can take the following steps to save the pipeline state safely:

1. Force a trap instruction into the pipeline on the next IF.

2. Until the trap is taken, turn off all writes for the faulting instruction and for all instructions that follow in the pipeline; this can be done by placing zeros into the pipeline latches of all instructions in the pipeline, starting with the instruction that generates the exception, but not those that precede that instruction. This prevents any state changes for instructions that will not be completed before the exception is handled.

3. After the exception-handling routine in the operating system receives control, it immediately saves the PC of the faulting instruction. This value will be used to return from the exception later.

When we use delayed branches, as mentioned in the last section, it is no longer possible to re-create the state of the machine with a single PC because the instructions in the pipeline may not be sequentially related. So we need to save and restore as many PCs as the length of the branch delay plus one. This is done in the third step above.

After the exception has been handled, special instructions return the machine from the exception by reloading the PCs and restarting the instruction stream (using the instruction RFE in DLX). If the pipeline can be stopped so that the instructions just before the faulting instruction are completed and those after it can be restarted from scratch, the pipeline is said to have *precise exceptions*. Ideally, the faulting instruction would not have changed the state, and correctly handling some exceptions requires that the faulting instruction have no effects. For other exceptions, such as floating-point exceptions, the faulting instruction on some machines writes its result before the exception can be handled. In such cases, the hardware must be prepared to retrieve the source operands, even if the destination is identical to one of the source operands. Because floating-point operations may run for many cycles, it is highly likely that some other instruction may have written the source operands (as we will see in the next section, floating point operations often complete out of order). To overcome this, many recent high-performance machines have introduced two modes of operation. One mode has precise exceptions and the other (fast or performance mode) does not. Of course, the precise exception mode is slower, since it allows less overlap among floating-point instructions. In some high-performance machines, including Alpha 21064, Power-2, and MIPS R8000, the precise mode is often much slower (>10 times) and thus useful only for debugging of codes.

Supporting precise exceptions is a requirement in many systems, while in others it is "just" valuable because it simplifies the operating system interface. At a minimum, any machine with demand paging or IEEE arithmetic trap handlers must make its exceptions precise, either in the hardware or with some software support. For integer pipelines, the task of creating precise exceptions is easier, and accommodating virtual memory strongly motivates the support of precise since there may be dependences on the updated state: Consider a VAX instruction that autoincrements the same register multiple times. Thus, to maintain a precise exception model, most machines with such instructions have the ability to back out any state changes made before the instruction is committed. If an exception occurs, the machine uses this ability to reset the state of the machine to its value before the interrupted instruction started. In the next section, we will see that a more powerful DLX floating-point pipeline can introduce similar problems, and the next chapter introduces techniques that substantially complicate exception handling.

A related source of difficulties arises from instructions that update memory state during execution, such as the string copy operations on the VAX or 360. To make it possible to interrupt and restart these instructions, the instructions are defined to use the general-purpose registers as working registers. Thus the state of the partially completed instruction is always in the registers, which are saved on an exception and restored after the exception, allowing the instruction to continue. In the VAX an additional bit of state records when an instruction has started updating the memory state, so that when the pipeline is restarted, the machine knows whether to restart the instruction from the beginning or from the middle of the instruction. The 80x86 string instructions also use the registers as working storage, so that saving and restoring the registers saves and restores the state of such instructions.

A different set of difficulties arises from odd bits of state that may create additional pipeline hazards or may require extra hardware to save and restore. Condition codes are a good example of this. Many machines set the condition codes implicitly as part of the instruction. This approach has advantages, since condition codes decouple the evaluation of the condition from the actual branch. However, implicitly set condition codes can cause difficulties in scheduling any pipeline delays between setting the condition code and the branch, since most instructions set the condition code and cannot be used in the delay slots between the condition evaluation and the branch.

Additionally, in machines with condition codes, the processor must decide when the branch condition is fixed. This involves finding out when the condition code has been set for the last time before the branch. In most machines with implicitly set condition codes, this is done by delaying the branch condition evaluation until all previous instructions have had a chance to set the condition code.

Of course, architectures with explicitly set condition codes allow the delay between condition test and the branch to be scheduled; however, pipeline control must still track the last instruction that sets the condition code to know when the branch condition is decided. In effect, the condition code must be treated as an operand that requires hazard detection for RAW hazards with branches, just as DLX must do on the registers.

A final thorny area in pipelining is multicycle operations. Imagine trying to pipeline a sequence of VAX instructions such as this:

```
MOVL    R1,R2
ADDL3   42(R1),56(R1)+,@(R1)
SUBL2   R2,R3
MOVC3   @(R1)[R2],74(R2),R3
```

These instructions differ radically in the number of clock cycles they will require, from as low as one up to hundreds of clock cycles. They also require different numbers of data memory accesses, from zero to possibly hundreds. The data hazards are very complex and occur both between and within instructions. The simple solution of making all instructions execute for the same number of clock cycles is unacceptable, because it introduces an enormous number of hazards and bypass conditions and makes an immensely long pipeline. Pipelining the VAX at the instruction level is difficult, but a clever solution was found by the VAX 8800 designers. They pipeline the *microinstruction* execution: a microinstruction is a simple instruction used in sequences to implement a more complex instruction set. Because the microinstructions are simple (they look a lot like DLX), the pipeline control is much easier. While it is not clear that this approach can achieve quite as low a CPI as an instruction-level pipeline for the VAX, it is much simpler, possibly leading to a shorter clock cycle.

In comparison, load-store machines have simple operations with similar amounts of work and pipeline more easily. If architects realize the relationship between instruction set design and pipelining, they can design architectures for more efficient pipelining. In the next section we will see how the DLX pipeline deals with long-running instructions, specifically floating-point operations.

3.7 | Extending the DLX Pipeline to Handle Multicycle Operations

We now want to explore how our DLX pipeline can be extended to handle floating-point operations. This section concentrates on the basic approach and the design alternatives, closing with some performance measurements of a DLX floating-point pipeline.

It is impractical to require that all DLX floating-point operations complete in one clock cycle, or even in two. Doing so would mean accepting a slow clock, or using enormous amounts of logic in the floating point units, or both. Instead, the floating-point pipeline will allow for a longer latency for operations. This is easier to grasp if we imagine the floating-point instructions as having the same pipeline as the integer instructions, with two important changes. First, the EX cycle may be repeated as many times as needed to complete the operation—the number of repetitions can vary for different operations. Second, there may be multiple floating-point functional units. A stall will occur if the instruction to be issued will either cause a structural hazard for the functional unit it uses or cause a data hazard.

The pipeline structure can also be shown using the familiar diagrams from earlier in the chapter, as Figure 3.45 shows for a set of independent FP operations and FP loads and stores. Naturally, the longer latency of the FP operations increases the frequency of RAW hazards and resultant stalls, as we will see later in this section.

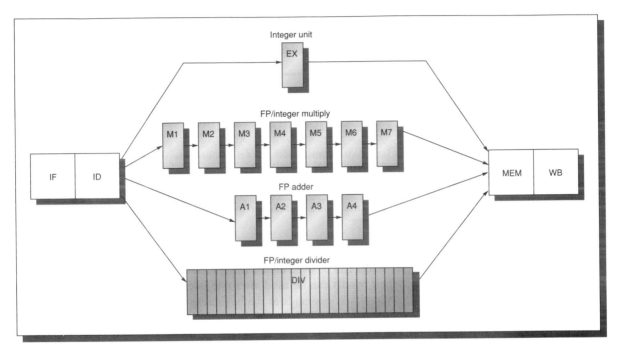

FIGURE 3.44 A pipeline that supports multiple outstanding FP operations. The FP multiplier and adder are fully pipelined and have a depth of seven and four stages, respectively. The FP divider is not pipelined, but requires 24 clock cycles to complete. The latency in instructions between the issue of an FP operation and the use of the result of that operation without incurring a RAW stall is determined by the number of cycles spent in the execution stages. For example, the fourth instruction after an FP add can use the result of the FP add. For integer ALU operations, the depth of the execution pipeline is always one and the next instruction can use the results. Both FP loads and integer loads complete during MEM, which means that the memory system must provide either 32 or 64 bits in a single clock.

MULTD	IF	ID	*M1*	M2	M3	M4	M5	M6	**M7**	MEM	WB
ADDD		IF	ID	*A1*	A2	A3	**A4**	MEM	WB		
LD			IF	ID	*EX*	**MEM**	WB				
SD				IF	ID	*EX*	*MEM*	WB			

FIGURE 3.45 The pipeline timing of a set of independent FP operations. The stages in italics show where data is needed, while the stages in bold show where a result is available. FP loads and stores use a 64-bit path to memory so that the pipelining timing is just like an integer load or store.

The structure of the pipeline in Figure 3.44 requires the introduction of the additional pipeline registers (e.g., A1/A2, A2/A3, A3/A4) and the modification of the connections to those registers. The ID/EX register must be expanded to connect ID to EX, DIV, M1, and A1; we can refer to the portion of the register associated with one of the next stages with the notation ID/EX, ID/DIV, ID/M1, or ID/A1. The pipeline register between ID and all the other stages may be thought of as logically separate registers and may, in fact, be implemented as separate registers. Because only one operation can be in a pipe stage at a time, the control information can be associated with the register at the head of the stage.

Hazards and Forwarding in Longer Latency Pipelines

There are a number of different aspects to the hazard detection and forwarding for a pipeline like that in Figure 3.44:

1. Because the divide unit is not fully pipelined, structural hazards can occur. These will need to be detected and issuing instructions will need to be stalled.

2. Because the instructions have varying running times, the number of register writes required in a cycle can be larger than 1.

3. WAW hazards are possible, since instructions no longer reach WB in order. Note that WAR hazards are not possible, since the register reads always occur in ID.

4. Instructions can complete in a different order than they were issued, causing problems with exceptions; we deal with this in the next subsection.

5. Because of longer latency of operations, stalls for RAW hazards will be more frequent.

The increase in stalls arising from longer operation latencies is fundamentally the same as that for the integer pipeline. Before describing the new problems that arise in this FP pipeline and looking at solutions, let's examine the potential impact of RAW hazards. Figure 3.46 shows a typical FP code sequence and the resultant stalls. At the end of this section, we'll examine the performance of this FP pipeline for our SPEC subset.

Now look at the problems arising from writes, described as (2) and (3) in the list above. If we assume the FP register file has one write port, sequences of FP operations, as well as an FP load together with FP operations, can cause conflicts for the register write port. Consider the pipeline sequence shown in Figure 3.47: In clock cycle 11, all three instructions will reach WB and want to write the register file. With only a single register file write port, the machine must serialize the instruction completion. This single register port represents a structural hazard. We could increase the number of write ports to solve this, but that solution may be unattractive since the additional write ports would be used only rarely. This is because the maximum steady state number of write ports needed is 1. Instead, we choose to detect and enforce access to the write port as a structural hazard.

Instruction	Clock cycle number																
	1	2	3	4	5	6	7	8	9	10	11	12	13	14	15	16	17
LD F4,0(R2)	IF	ID	EX	MEM	WB												
MULTD F0,F4,F6		IF	ID	stall	M1	M2	M3	M4	M5	M6	M7	MEM	WB				
ADDD F2,F0,F8			IF	stall	ID	stall	stall	stall	stall	stall	stall	A1	A2	A3	A4	MEM	
SD 0(R2),F2				IF	stall	stall	stall	stall	stall	stall	stall	ID	EX	stall	stall	stall	MEM

FIGURE 3.46   A typical FP code sequence showing the stalls arising from RAW hazards. The longer pipeline substantially raises the frequency of stalls versus the shallower integer pipeline. Each instruction in this sequence is dependent on the previous and proceeds as soon as data are available, which assumes the pipeline has full bypassing and forwarding. The SD must be stalled an extra cycle so that its MEM does not conflict with the ADDD. Extra hardware could easily handle this case.

Instruction	Clock cycle number										
	1	2	3	4	5	6	7	8	9	10	11
MULTD F0,F4,F6	IF	ID	M1	M2	M3	M4	M5	M6	M7	MEM	WB
...		IF	ID	EX	MEM	WB					
...			IF	ID	EX	MEM	WB				
ADDD F2,F4,F6				IF	ID	A1	A2	A3	A4	MEM	WB
...					IF	ID	EX	MEM	WB		
...						IF	ID	EX	MEM	WB	
LD F2,0(R2)							IF	ID	EX	MEM	WB

FIGURE 3.47   Three instructions want to perform a write back to the FP register file simultaneously, as shown in clock cycle 11. This is *not* the worst case, since an earlier divide in the FP unit could also finish on the same clock. Note that although the MULTD, ADDD, and LD all are in the MEM stage in clock cycle 10, only the LD actually uses the memory, so no structural hazard exists for MEM.

There are two different ways to implement this interlock. The first is to track the use of the write port in the ID stage and to stall an instruction before it issues, just as we would for any other structural hazard. Tracking the use of the write port can be done with a shift register that indicates when already-issued instructions will use the register file. If the instruction in ID needs to use the register file at the same time as an instruction already issued, the instruction in ID is stalled for a cycle. On each clock the reservation register is shifted one bit. This implementation has an advantage: It maintains the property that all interlock detection and stall insertion occurs in the ID stage. The cost is the addition of the shift register and write conflict logic. We will assume this scheme throughout this section.

An alternative scheme is to stall a conflicting instruction when it tries to enter either the MEM or WB stage. If we wait to stall the conflicting instructions until they want to enter the MEM or WB stage, we can choose to stall either instruction. A simple, though sometimes suboptimal, heuristic is to give priority to the unit with the longest latency, since that is the one most likely to have caused another instruction to be stalled for a RAW hazard. The advantage of this scheme is that it does not require us to detect the conflict until the entrance of the MEM or WB stage, where it is easy to see. The disadvantage is that it complicates pipeline control, as stalls can now arise from two places. Notice that stalling before entering MEM will cause the EX, A4, or M7 stage to be occupied, possibly forcing the stall to trickle back in the pipeline. Likewise, stalling before WB would cause MEM to back up.

Our other problem is the possibility of WAW hazards. To see that these exist, consider the example in Figure 3.47. If the LD instruction were issued one cycle earlier and had a destination of F2, then it would create a WAW hazard, because it would write F2 one cycle earlier than the ADDD. Note that this hazard only occurs when the result of the ADDD is overwritten *without* any instruction ever using it! If there were a use of F2 between the ADDD and the LD, the pipeline would need to be stalled for a RAW hazard, and the LD would not issue until the ADDD was completed. We could argue that, for our pipeline, WAW hazards only occur when a useless instruction is executed, but we must still detect them and make sure that the result of the LD appears in F2 when we are done. (As we will see in section 3.10, such sequences sometimes *do* occur in reasonable code.)

There are two possible ways to handle this WAW hazard. The first approach is to delay the issue of the load instruction until the ADDD enters MEM. The second approach is to stamp out the result of the ADDD by detecting the hazard and changing the control so that the ADDD does not write its result. Then, the LD can issue right away. Because this hazard is rare, either scheme will work fine—you can pick whatever is simpler to implement. In either case, the hazard can be detected during ID when the LD is issuing. Then stalling the LD or making the ADDD a no-op is easy. The difficult situation is to detect that the LD might finish before the ADDD, because that requires knowing the length of the pipeline and the current position of the ADDD. Luckily, this code sequence (two writes with no intervening read) will be very rare, so we can use a simple solution: If an instruction in ID wants to write the same register as an instruction already issued, do not issue the instruction to EX. In the next chapter, we will see how additional hardware can eliminate stalls for such hazards. First, let's put together the pieces for implementing the hazard and issue logic in our FP pipeline.

In detecting the possible hazards, we must consider hazards among FP instructions, as well as hazards between an FP instruction and an integer instruction. Except for FP loads-stores and FP-integer register moves, the FP and integer registers are distinct. All integer instructions operate on the integer registers, while the floating-point operations operate only on their own registers. Thus, we need only consider FP loads-stores and FP register moves in detecting hazards between FP and integer instructions. This simplification of pipeline control is an additional advantage of having separate register files for integer and floating-point data. (The main advantages are a doubling of the number of registers, without making either set larger, and an increase in bandwidth without adding more ports to either set. The main disadvantage, beyond the need for an extra register file, is the small cost of occasional moves needed between the two register sets.) Assuming that the pipeline does all hazard detection in ID, there are three checks that must be performed before an instruction can issue:

1. *Check for structural hazards*—Wait until the required functional unit is not busy (this is only needed for divides in this pipeline) and make sure the register write port is available when it will be needed.

2. *Check for a RAW data hazard*—Wait until the source registers are not listed as pending destinations in a pipeline register that will not be available when this instruction needs the result. A number of checks must be made here, depending on both the source instruction, which determines when the result will be available, and the destination instruction, which determines when the value is needed. For example, if the instruction in ID is an FP operation with source register F2, then F2 cannot be listed as a destination in ID/A1, A1/A2, or A2/A3, which correspond to FP add instructions that will not be finished when the instruction in ID needs a result. (ID/A1 is the portion of the output register of ID that is sent to A1.) Divide is somewhat more tricky, if we want to allow the last few cycles of a divide to be overlapped, since we need to handle the case when a divide is close to finishing as special. In practice, designers might ignore this optimization in favor of a simpler issue test.

3. *Check for a WAW data hazard*—Determine if any instruction in A1,..., A4, D, M1,..., M7 has the same register destination as this instruction. If so, stall the issue of the instruction in ID.

Although the hazard detection is more complex with the multicycle FP operations, the concepts are the same as for the DLX integer pipeline. The same is true for the forwarding logic. The forwarding can be implemented by checking if the destination register in any of EX/MEM, A4/MEM, M7/MEM, D/MEM, or MEM/WB registers is one of the source registers of a floating-point instruction. If so, the appropriate input multiplexer will have to be enabled so as to choose the forwarded data. In the Exercises, you will have the opportunity to specify the logic for the RAW and WAW hazard detection as well as for forwarding.

Multicycle FP operations also introduce problems for our exception mechanisms, which we deal with next.

Maintaining Precise Exceptions

Another problem caused by these long-running instructions can be illustrated with the following sequence of code:

```
DIVF    F0,F2,F4
ADDF    F10,F10,F8
SUBF    F12,F12,F14
```

This code sequence looks straightforward; there are no dependences. A problem arises, however, because an instruction issued early may complete after an instruction issued later. In this example, we can expect ADDF and SUBF to complete *before* the DIVF completes. This is called *out-of-order completion* and is common in pipelines with long-running operations. Because hazard detection will prevent any dependence among instructions from being violated, why is out-of-order completion a problem? Suppose that the SUBF causes a floating-point arithmetic exception at a point where the ADDF has completed but the DIVF has not. The result will be an imprecise exception, something we are trying to avoid. It may appear that this could be handled by letting the floating-point pipeline drain, as we do for the integer pipeline. But the exception may be in a position where this is not possible. For example, if the DIVF decided to take a floating-point arithmetic exception after the add completed, we could not have a precise exception at the hardware level. In fact, because the ADDF destroys one of its operands, we could not restore the state to what it was before the DIVF, even with software help.

This problem arises because instructions are completing in a different order than they were issued. There are four possible approaches to dealing with out-of-order completion. The first is to ignore the problem and settle for imprecise exceptions. This approach was used in the 1960s and early 1970s. It is still used in some supercomputers, where certain classes of exceptions are not allowed or are handled by the hardware without stopping the pipeline. It is difficult to use this approach in most machines built today because of features such as virtual memory and the IEEE floating-point standard, which essentially require precise exceptions through a combination of hardware and software. As mentioned earlier, some recent machines have solved this problem by introducing two modes of execution: a fast, but possibly imprecise mode and a slower, precise mode. The slower precise mode is implemented either with a mode switch or by insertion of explicit instructions that test for FP exceptions. In either case the amount of overlap and reordering permitted in the FP pipeline is significantly restricted so that effectively only one FP instruction is active at a time. This solution is used in the DEC Alpha 21064 and 21164, in the IBM Power-1 and Power-2, and in the MIPS R8000.

A second approach is to buffer the results of an operation until all the operations that were issued earlier are complete. Some machines actually use this solution, but it becomes expensive when the difference in running times among operations is large, since the number of results to buffer can become large. Furthermore, results from the queue must be bypassed to continue issuing instructions while waiting for the longer instruction. This requires a large number of comparators and a very large multiplexer.

There are two viable variations on this basic approach. The first is a *history file*, used in the CYBER 180/990. The history file keeps track of the original values of registers. When an exception occurs and the state must be rolled back earlier than some instruction that completed out of order, the original value of the register can be restored from the history file. A similar technique is used for autoincrement and autodecrement addressing on machines like VAXes. Another approach, the *future file*, proposed by J. Smith and A. Pleszkun [1988], keeps the newer value of a register; when all earlier instructions have completed, the main register file is updated from the future file. On an exception, the main register file has the precise values for the interrupted state. In the next chapter (section 4.6), we will see extensions of this idea, which are used in processors such as the PowerPC 620 and MIPS R10000 to allow overlap and reordering while preserving precise exceptions.

A third technique in use is to allow the exceptions to become somewhat imprecise, but to keep enough information so that the trap-handling routines can create a precise sequence for the exception. This means knowing what operations were in the pipeline and their PCs. Then, after handling the exception, the software finishes any instructions that precede the latest instruction completed, and the sequence can restart. Consider the following worst-case code sequence:

$Instruction_1$—A long-running instruction that eventually interrupts execution.

$Instruction_2, ..., Instruction_{n-1}$—A series of instructions that are not completed.

$Instruction_n$—An instruction that is finished.

Given the PCs of all the instructions in the pipeline and the exception return PC, the software can find the state of $instruction_1$ and $instruction_n$. Because $instruction_n$ has completed, we will want to restart execution at $instruction_{n+1}$. After handling the exception, the software must simulate the execution of $instruction_1, ..., instruction_{n-1}$. Then we can return from the exception and restart at $instruction_{n+1}$. The complexity of executing these instructions properly by the handler is the major difficulty of this scheme. There is an important simplification for simple DLX-like pipelines: If $instruction_2, ..., instruction_n$ are all integer instructions, then we know that if $instruction_n$ has completed, all of $instruction_2, ..., instruction_{n-1}$ have also completed. Thus, only floating-point operations need to be handled. To make this scheme tractable, the number of floating-point instructions that can be overlapped in execution can be limited. For example, if we only overlap two instructions, then only the interrupting instruction need be completed by software. This restriction may reduce the potential throughput if the FP pipelines are deep or if there is a significant number of FP functional units. This approach is used in the SPARC architecture to allow overlap of floating-point and integer operations.

The final technique is a hybrid scheme that allows the instruction issue to continue only if it is certain that all the instructions before the issuing instruction will complete without causing an exception. This guarantees that when an exception occurs, no instructions after the interrupting one will be completed and all of the instructions before the interrupting one can be completed. This sometimes means stalling the machine to maintain precise exceptions. To make this scheme work, the floating-point functional units must determine if an exception is possible early in the EX stage (in the first three clock cycles in the DLX pipeline), so as to prevent further instructions from completing. This scheme is used in the MIPS R2000/3000, the R4000, and the Intel Pentium. It is discussed further in Appendix A.

Performance of a DLX FP Pipeline

The DLX FP pipeline of Figure 3.44 on page 190 can generate both structural stalls for the divide unit and stalls for RAW hazards (it also can have WAW hazards, but this rarely occurs in practice). Figure 3.48 shows the number of stall cycles for each type of floating-point operation on a per instance basis (i.e., the first bar for each FP benchmark shows the number of FP result stalls for each FP add, subtract, or compare). As we might expect, the stall cycles per operation track the latency of the FP operations, varying from 46% to 59% of the latency of the functional unit.

Figure 3.49 gives the complete breakdown of integer and floating-point stalls for the five FP SPEC benchmarks we are using. There are four classes of stalls shown: FP result stalls, FP compare stalls, load and branch delays, and floating-point structural delays. The compiler tries to schedule both load and FP delays before it schedules branch delays. The total number of stalls per instruction varies from 0.65 to 1.21.

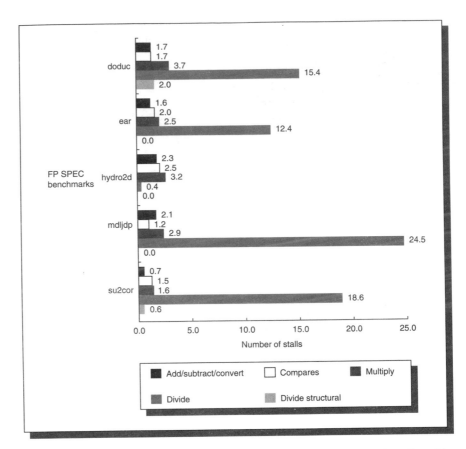

FIGURE 3.48   Stalls per FP operation for each major type of FP operation. Except for the divide structural hazards, these data do not depend on the frequency of an operation, only on its latency and the number of cycles before the result is used. The number of stalls from RAW hazards roughly tracks the latency of the FP unit. For example, the average number of stalls per FP add, subtract, or convert is 1.7 cycles, or 56% of the latency (3 cycles). Likewise, the average number of stalls for multiplies and divides are 2.8 and 14.2, respectively, or 46% and 59% of the corresponding latency. Structural hazards for divides are rare, since the divide frequency is low.

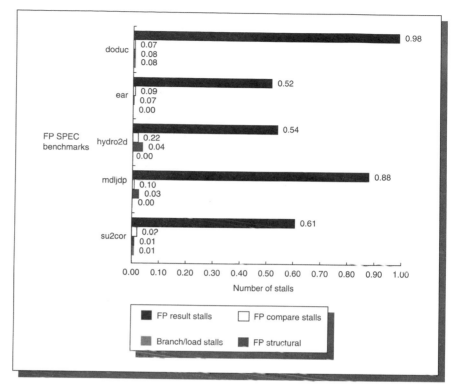

FIGURE 3.49 The stalls occurring for the DLX FP pipeline for the five FP SPEC benchmarks. The total number of stalls per instruction ranges from 0.65 for su2cor to 1.21 for doduc, with an average of 0.87. FP result stalls dominate in all cases, with an average of 0.71 stalls per instruction or 82% of the stalled cycles. Compares generate an average of 0.1 stalls per instruction and are the second largest source. The divide structural hazard is only significant for doduc.

3.8 Crosscutting Issues: Instruction Set Design and Pipelining

For many years the interaction between instruction sets and implementations was believed to be small, and implementation issues were not a major focus in designing instruction sets. In the 1980s it became clear that the difficulty and inefficiency of pipelining could both be increased by instruction set complications. Here are some examples, many of which are mentioned earlier in the chapter:

- Variable instruction lengths and running times can lead to imbalance among pipeline stages, causing other stages to back up. They also severely complicate hazard detection and the maintenance of precise exceptions. Of course, some-

- EX—Execution, which includes effective address calculation, ALU operation, and branch target computation and condition evaluation.

- DF—Data fetch, first half of data cache access.

- DS—Second half of data fetch, completion of data cache access.

- TC—Tag check, determine whether the data cache access hit.

- WB—Write back for loads and register-register operations.

In addition to substantially increasing the amount of forwarding required, this longer latency pipeline increases both the load and branch delays. Figure 3.51 shows that load delays are two cycles, since the data value is available at the end of DS. Figure 3.52 shows the shorthand pipeline schedule when a use immediately follows a load. It shows that forwarding is required for the result of a load instruction to a destination that is three or four cycles later.

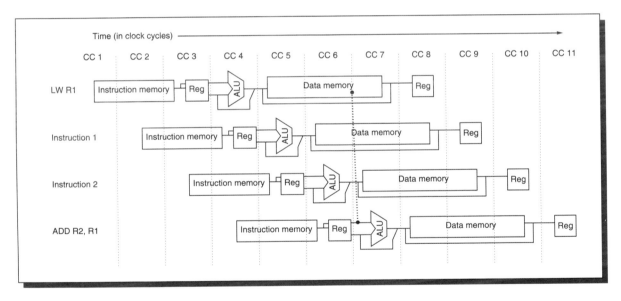

FIGURE 3.51   The structure of the R4000 integer pipeline leads to a two-cycle load delay. A two-cycle delay is possible because the data value is available at the end of DS and can be bypassed. If the tag check in TC indicates a miss, the pipeline is backed up a cycle, when the correct data are available.

Figure 3.53 shows that the basic branch delay is three cycles, since the branch condition is computed during EX. The MIPS architecture has a single-cycle delayed branch. The R4000 uses a predict-not-taken strategy for the remaining two cycles of the branch delay. As Figure 3.54 shows, untaken branches are simply one-cycle delayed branches, while taken branches have a one-cycle delay slot

Instruction number	Clock number								
	1	2	3	4	5	6	7	8	9
`LW R1, . . .`	IF	IS	RF	EX	DF	DS	TC	WB	
`ADD R2,R1, . . .`		IF	IS	RF	stall	stall	EX	DF	DS
`SUB R3,R1, . . .`			IF	IS	stall	stall	RF	EX	DF
`OR R4,R1, . . .`				IF	stall	stall	IS	RF	EX

FIGURE 3.52   A load instruction followed by an immediate use results in a two-cycle stall. Normal forwarding paths can be used after two cycles, so the ADD and SUB get the value by forwarding after the stall. The OR instruction gets the value from the register file. Since the two instructions after the load could be independent and hence not stall, the bypass can be to instructions that are three or four cycles after the load.

followed by two idle cycles. The instruction set provides a branch likely instruction, which we described earlier and which helps in filling the branch delay slot. Pipeline interlocks enforce both the two-cycle branch stall penalty on a taken branch and any data hazard stall that arises from use of a load result.

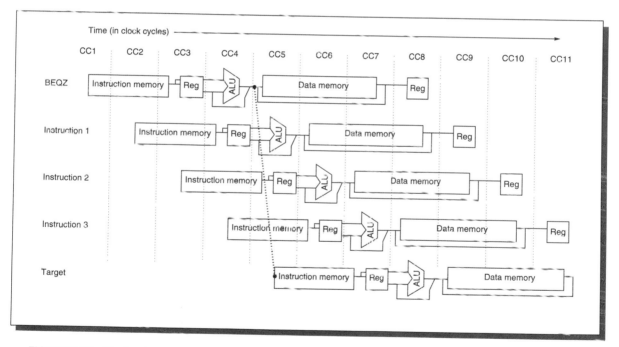

FIGURE 3.53   The basic branch delay is three cycles, since the condition evaluation is performed during EX.

Operation	Issue/stall	Clock cycle												
		0	1	2	3	4	5	6	7	8	9	10	11	12
Multiply	Issue	U	M	M	M	M	N	**N+A**	**R**					
Add	Issue		U	S+A	A+R	R+S									
	Issue			U	S+A	A+R	R+S								
	Issue				U	S+A	A+R	R+S							
	Stall					U	S+A	**A+R**	**R+S**						
	Stall						U	**S+A**	**A+R**	R+S					
	Issue							U	S+A	A+R	R+S				
	Issue								U	S+A	A+R	R+S			

FIGURE 3.57   An FP multiply issued at clock 0 is followed by a *single* FP add issued between clocks 1 and 7. The second column indicates whether an instruction of the specified type stalls when it is issued *n* cycles later, where *n* is the clock cycle number in which the U stage of the second instruction occurs. The stage or stages that cause a stall are highlighted. Note that this table deals with only the interaction between the multiply and *one* add issued between clocks 1 and 7. In this case, the add will stall if it is issued four or five cycles after the multiply; otherwise, it issues without stalling. Notice that the add will be stalled for two cycles if it issues in cycle 4 since on the next clock cycle it will still conflict with the multiply; if, however, the add issues in cycle 5, it will stall for only one clock cycle, since that will eliminate the conflicts.

Operation	Issue/stall	Clock cycle												
		0	1	2	3	4	5	6	7	8	9	10	11	12
Add	Issue	U	S+A	A+R	R+S									
Multiply	Issue		U	M	M	M	M	N	N+A	R				
	Issue			U	M	M	M	M	N	N+A	R				

FIGURE 3.58   A multiply issuing after an add can always proceed without stalling, since the shorter instruction clears the shared pipeline stages before the longer instruction reaches them.

whether that second instruction will issue or stall for each position. Of course, there could be three instructions active, in which case the possibilities for stalls are much higher and the figures more complex.

Operation	Issue/stall	Clock cycle											
		25	26	27	28	29	30	31	32	33	34	35	36
Divide	issued in cycle 0...	D	D	D	D	D	D+A	D+R	D+A	D+R	A	R	
Add	Issue		U	S+A	A+R	R+S							
	Issue			U	S+A	A+R	R+S						
	Stall				U	S+A	A+R	R+S					
	Stall					U	S+A	A+R	R+S				
	Stall						U	S+A	A+R	R+S			
	Stall							U	S+A	A+R	R+S		
	Stall								U	S+A	A+R	R+S	
	Stall									U	S+A	A+R	R+S
	Issue										U	S+A	A+R
	Issue											U	S+A
	Issue												U

FIGURE 3.59   An FP divide can cause a stall for an add that starts near the end of the divide. The divide starts at cycle 0 and completes at cycle 35; the last 10 cycles of the divide are shown. Since the divide makes heavy use of the rounding hardware needed by the add, it stalls an add that starts in any of cycles 28 to 33. Notice the add starting in cycle 28 will be stalled until cycle 34. If the add started right after the divide it would not conflict, since the add could complete before the divide needed the shared stages, just as we saw in Figure 3.58 for a multiply and add. As in the earlier figure, this example assumes *exactly* one add that reaches the U stage between clock cycles 26 and 35.

Operation	Issue/stall	Clock cycle												
		0	1	2	3	4	5	6	7	8	9	10	11	12
Add	Issue	U	S+A	A+R	R+S									
Divide	Stall		U	A	R	D	D	D	D	D	D	D	D	D
	Issue			U	A	R	D	D	D	D	D	D	D	D
	Issue				U	A	R	D	D	D	D	D	D	D

FIGURE 3.60   A double-precision add is followed by a double-precision divide. If the divide starts one cycle after the add, the divide stalls, but after that there is no conflict.

Performance of the R4000 Pipeline

In this section we examine the stalls that occur for the SPEC92 benchmarks when running on the R4000 pipeline structure. There are four major causes of pipeline stalls or losses:

1. Load stalls—Delays arising from the use of a load result one or two cycles after the load.

```
            BNEZ    R1,foo
            DIVD    F0,F2,F4 ; moved into delay slot
                    ; from fall through
            .....
            .....
foo:   LD       F0,qrs
```

If the branch is taken, then before the DIVD can complete, the LD will reach WB, causing a WAW hazard. The hardware must detect this and may stall the issue of the LD. Another way this can happen is if the second write is in a trap routine. This occurs when an instruction that traps and is writing results continues and completes after an instruction that writes the same register in the trap handler. The hardware must detect and prevent this as well.

Pitfall: Extensive pipelining can impact other aspects of a design, leading to overall worse cost/performance.

The best example of this phenomenon comes from two implementations of the VAX, the 8600 and the 8700. When the 8600 was initially delivered, it had a cycle time of 80 ns. Subsequently, a redesigned version, called the 8650, with a 55-ns clock was introduced. The 8700 has a much simpler pipeline that operates at the microinstruction level, yielding a smaller CPU with a faster clock cycle of 45 ns. The overall outcome is that the 8650 has a CPI advantage of about 20%, but the 8700 has a clock rate that is about 20% faster. Thus, the 8700 achieves the same performance with much less hardware.

Fallacy: Increasing the number of pipeline stages always increases performance.

Two factors combine to limit the performance improvement gained by pipelining. Limited parallelism in the instruction stream means that increasing the number of pipeline stages, called the pipeline depth, will eventually increase the CPI, due to dependences that require stalls. Second, clock skew and latch overhead combine to limit the decrease in clock period obtained by further pipelining. Figure 3.63 shows the trade-off between the number of pipeline stages and performance for the first 14 of the Livermore Loops. The performance flattens out when the number of pipeline stages reaches 4 and actually drops when the execution portion is pipelined 16 deep. Although this study is limited to a small set of FP programs, the trade-off of increasing CPI versus increasing clock rate by more pipelining arises constantly.

Pitfall: Evaluating a compile-time scheduler on the basis of unoptimized code.

Unoptimized code—containing redundant loads, stores, and other operations that might be eliminated by an optimizer—is much easier to schedule than "tight" optimized code. This holds for scheduling both control delays (with delayed

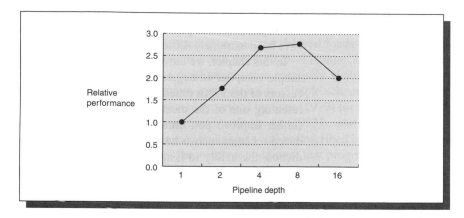

FIGURE 3.63 The depth of pipelining versus the speedup obtained. The x-axis shows the number of stages in the EX portion of the floating-point pipeline. A single-stage pipeline corresponds to 32 levels of logic, which might be appropriate for a single FP operation. Data based on Table 2 in Kunkel and Smith [1986].

branches) and delays arising from RAW hazards. In gcc running on an R3000, which has a pipeline almost identical to that of DLX, the frequency of idle clock cycles increases by 18% from the unoptimized and scheduled code to the optimized and scheduled code. Of course, the optimized program is much faster, since it has fewer instructions. To fairly evaluate a scheduler you must use optimized code, since in the real system you will derive good performance from other optimizations in addition to scheduling.

3.11 | Concluding Remarks

Pipelining has been and is likely to continue to be one of the most important techniques for enhancing the performance of processors. Improving performance via pipelining was the key focus of many early computer designers in the late 1950s through the mid 1960s. In the late 1960s through the late 1970s, the attention of computer architects was focused on other things, including the dramatic improvements in cost, size, and reliability that were achieved by the introduction of integrated circuit technology. In this period pipelining played a secondary role in many designs. Since pipelining was not a primary focus, many instruction sets designed in this period made pipelining overly difficult and reduced its payoff. The VAX architecture is perhaps the best example.

In the late 1970s and early 1980s several researchers realized that instruction set complexity and implementation ease, particularly ease of pipelining, were related. The RISC movement led to a dramatic simplification in instruction sets that allowed rapid progress in the development of pipelining techniques. As we will

EMER, J. S. AND D. W. CLARK [1984]. "A characterization of processor performance in the VAX-11/780," *Proc. 11th Symposium on Computer Architecture* (June), Ann Arbor, Mich., 301–310.

FISHER, J. AND FREUDENBERGER, S. [1992]. "Predicting conditional branch directions from previous runs of a program," *Proc. Fifth Conf. on Architectural Support for Programming Languages and Operating Systems,* IEEE/ACM (October), Boston, 85–95.

GIBBONS, P. B. AND S. S. MUCHNIK [1986]. "Efficient instruction scheduling for a pipelined processor," *SIGPLAN '86 Symposium on Compiler Construction,* ACM (June), Palo Alto, Calif., 11–16.

GROSS, T. R. [1983]. *Code Optimization of Pipeline Constraints,* Ph.D. Thesis (December), Computer Systems Lab., Stanford Univ.

HEINRICH, J. [1993]. *MIPS R4000 User's Manual,* Prentice Hall, Englewood Cliffs, N.J.

HENNESSY, J. L. AND T. R. GROSS [1983]. "Postpass code optimization of pipeline constraints," *ACM Trans. on Programming Languages and Systems* 5:3 (July), 422–448.

IBM [1990]. "The IBM RISC System/6000 processor" (collection of papers), *IBM J. of Research and Development* 34:1 (January).

KELLER R. M. [1975]. "Look-ahead processors," *ACM Computing Surveys* 7:4 (December), 177–195.

KILLIAN, E. [1991]. "MIPS R4000 technical overview–64 bits/100 MHz or bust," *Hot Chips III Symposium Record* (August), Stanford University, 1.6–1.19.

KOGGE, P. M. [1981]. *The Architecture of Pipelined Computers,* McGraw-Hill, New York.

KUNKEL, S. R. AND J. E. SMITH [1986]. "Optimal pipelining in supercomputers," *Proc. 13th Symposium on Computer Architecture* (June), Tokyo, 404–414.

MCFARLING, S. AND J. L. HENNESSY [1986]. "Reducing the cost of branches," *Proc. 13th Symposium on Computer Architecture* (June), Tokyo, 396-403.

RAMAMOORTHY, C. V. AND H. F. LI [1977]. "Pipeline architecture," *ACM Computing Surveys* 9:1 (March), 61–102.

RYMARCZYK, J. [1982]. "Coding guidelines for pipelined processors," *Proc. Symposium on Architectural Support for Programming Languages and Operating Systems,* IEEE/ACM (March), Palo Alto, Calif., 12–19.

SITES, R. [1979]. *Instruction Ordering for the CRAY-1 Computer,* Tech. Rep. 78-CS-023 (July), Dept. of Computer Science, Univ. of Calif., San Diego.

SMITH, J. E. AND A. R. PLESZKUN [1988]. "Implementing precise interrupts in pipelined processors," *IEEE Trans. on Computers* 37:5 (May), 562–573.

WEISS, S. AND J. E. SMITH [1984]. "Instruction issue logic for pipelined supercomputers," *Proc. 11th Symposium on Computer Architecture* (June), Ann Arbor, Mich., 110–118.

.

E X E R C I S E S

3.1 [15/15/15] <3.4,3.5> Use the following code fragment:

```
loop:   LW      R1,0(R2)
        ADDI    R1,R1,#1
        SW      0(R2),R1
        ADDI    R2,R2,#4
        SUB     R4,R3,R2
        BNEZ    R4,Loop
```

Assume that the initial value of R3 is R2 + 396.

Throughout this exercise use the DLX integer pipeline and assume all memory accesses are cache hits.

a. [15] <3.4,3.5> Show the timing of this instruction sequence for the DLX pipeline *without* any forwarding or bypassing hardware but assuming a register read and a write in the same clock cycle "forwards" through the register file, as in Figure 3.10. Use a pipeline timing chart like Figure 3.14 or 3.15. Assume that the branch is handled by flushing the pipeline. If all memory references hit in the cache, how many cycles does this loop take to execute?

b. [15] <3.4,3.5> Show the timing of this instruction sequence for the DLX pipeline with normal forwarding and bypassing hardware. Use a pipeline timing chart like Figure 3.14 or 3.15. Assume that the branch is handled by predicting it as not taken. If all memory references hit in the cache, how many cycles does this loop take to execute?

c. [15] <3.4,3.5> Assuming the DLX pipeline with a single-cycle delayed branch and normal forwarding and bypassing hardware, schedule the instructions in the loop including the branch-delay slot. You may reorder instructions and modify the individual instruction operands, but do not undertake other loop transformations that change the number or opcode of the instructions in the loop (that's for the next chapter!). Show a pipeline timing diagram and compute the number of cycles needed to execute the entire loop.

3.2 [15/15/15] <3.4,3.5,3.7> Use the following code fragment:

```
Loop:   LD      F0,0(R2)
        LD      F4,0(R3)
        MULTD   F0,F0,F4
        ADDD    F2,F0,F2
        ADDI    R2,R2,#8
        ADDI    R3,R3,#8
        SUB     R5,R4,R2
        BNEZ    R5,Loop
```

Assume that the initial value of R4 is R2 + 792.

For this exercise assume the standard DLX integer pipeline (as shown in Figure 3.10) and the standard DLX FP pipeline as described in Figures 3.43 and 3.44. If structural hazards are due to write-back contention, assume the earliest instruction gets priority and other instructions are stalled.

a. [15] <3.4,3.5,3.7> Show the timing of this instruction sequence for the DLX FP pipeline *without* any forwarding or bypassing hardware but assuming a register read and a write in the same clock cycle "forwards" through the register file, as in Figure 3.10. Use a pipeline timing chart like Figure 3.14 or 3.15. Assume that the branch is handled by flushing the pipeline. If all memory references hit in the cache, how many cycles does this loop take to execute?

b.   [15] <3.4,3.5,3.7> Show the timing of this instruction sequence for the DLX FP pipeline with normal forwarding and bypassing hardware. Use a pipeline timing chart like Figure 3.14 or 3.15. Assume that the branch is handled by predicting it as not taken. If all memory references hit in the cache, how many cycles does this loop take to execute?

c.   [15] <3.4,3.5,3.7> Assuming the DLX FP pipeline with a single-cycle delayed branch and full bypassing and forwarding hardware, schedule the instructions in the loop including the branch-delay slot. You may reorder instructions and modify the individual instruction operands, but do not undertake other loop transformations that change the number or opcode of the instructions in the loop (that's for the next chapter!). Show a pipeline timing diagram and compute the time needed in cycles to execute the entire loop.

3.3 [12/13/20/20/15/15] <3.2,3.4,3.5> For these problems, we will explore a pipeline for a register-memory architecture. The architecture has two instruction formats: a register-register format and a register-memory format. There is a single-memory addressing mode (offset + base register).

There is a set of ALU operations with format:

```
ALUop Rdest, Rsrc₁, Rsrc₂
```

or

```
ALUop Rdest, Rsrc₁, MEM
```

where the ALUop is one of the following: Add, Subtract, And, Or, Load ($Rsrc_1$ ignored), Store. Rsrc or Rdest are registers. MEM is a base register and offset pair.

Branches use a full compare of two registers and are PC-relative. Assume that this machine is pipelined so that a new instruction is started every clock cycle. The following pipeline structure—similar to that used in the VAX 8700 micropipeline (Clark [1987])—is

IF	RF	ALU1	MEM	ALU2	WB			
	IF	RF	ALU1	MEM	ALU2	WB		
		IF	RF	ALU1	MEM	ALU2	WB	
			IF	RF	ALU1	MEM	ALU2	WB
				IF	RF	ALU1	MEM	ALU2	WB
					IF	RF	ALU1	MEM	ALU2	WB

The first ALU stage is used for effective address calculation for memory references and branches. The second ALU cycle is used for operations and branch comparison. RF is both a decode and register-fetch cycle. Assume that when a register read and a register write of the same register occur in the same clock the write data is forwarded.

a.   [12] <3.2> Find the number of adders needed, counting any adder or incrementer; show a combination of instructions and pipe stages that justify this answer. You need only give one combination that maximizes the adder count.

b. [13] <3.2> Find the number of register read and write ports and memory read and write ports required. Show that your answer is correct by showing a combination of instructions and pipeline stage indicating the instruction and the number of read ports and write ports required for that instruction.

c. [20] <3.4> Determine any *data forwarding* for any ALUs that will be needed. Assume that there are separate ALUs for the ALU1 and ALU2 pipe stages. Put in all forwarding among ALUs needed to avoid or reduce stalls. Show the relationship between the two instructions involved in forwarding using the format of the table in Figure 3.19 but ignoring the last two columns. Be careful to consider forwarding across an intervening instruction, e.g.,

```
ADD     R1, ...
any instruction
ADD     ..., R1, ...
```

d. [20] <3.4> Show all data forwarding requirements needed to avoid or reduce stalls when either the source or destination unit is not an ALU. Use the same format as Figure 3.19, again ignoring the last two columns. Remember to forward to and from memory references.

e. [15] <3.4> Show all the remaining hazards that involve at least one unit other than an ALU as the source or destination unit. Use a table like that in Figure 3.18, but listing the length of hazard in place of the last column.

f. [15] <3.5> Show all control hazard types by example and state the length of the stall. Use a format like Figure 3.21, labeling each example.

3.4 [10] <3.2> Consider the example on page 137 that compares the unpipelined and pipelined machine. Assume that 1 ns overhead is fixed and that each pipe stage is balanced and takes 10 ns in the five-stage pipeline. Plot the speedup of the pipelined machine versus the unpipelined machine as the number of pipeline stages is increased from five stages to 20 stages, considering only the impact of the pipelining overhead and assuming that the work can be evenly divided as the stages are increased (which is not generally true). Also plot the "perfect" speedup that would be obtained if there was no overhead.

3.5 [12] <3.1–3.5> A machine is called "underpipelined" if additional levels of pipelining can be added without changing the pipeline-stall behavior appreciably. Suppose that the DLX integer pipeline was changed to four stages by merging EX and MEM and lengthening the clock cycle by 50%. How much faster would the conventional DLX pipeline be versus the underpipelined DLX on integer code only? Make sure you include the effect of any change in pipeline stalls using the data for gcc in Figure 3.38 (page 178).

3.6 [20] <3.4> Add the forwarding entries for stores and for the zero detect unit (for branches) to the table in Figure 3.19. *Hint:* Remember the tricky case:

```
ADD     R1, ...
any instruction
SW      ..., R1
```

How is the forwarding handled for this case?

3.7 [20] <3.4,3.9> Create a table showing the forwarding logic for the R4000 integer pipeline using the same format as that in Figure 3.19. Include only the DLX instructions we considered in Figure 3.19.

3.8 [15] <3.4,3.9> Create a table showing the R4000 integer hazard detection using the same format as that in Figure 3.18. Include only the instructions in the DLX subset that we considered in section 3.4.

3.9 [15] <3.5> Suppose the branch frequencies (as percentages of all instructions) are as follows:

Conditional branches	20%
Jumps and calls	5%
Conditional branches	60% are taken

We are examining a four-deep pipeline where the branch is resolved at the end of the second cycle for unconditional branches and at the end of the third cycle for conditional branches. Assuming that only the first pipe stage can always be done independent of whether the branch goes and ignoring other pipeline stalls, how much faster would the machine be without any branch hazards?

3.10 [20/20] <3.4> Suppose that we have the pipeline layout shown in Figure 3.64.

Stage	Function
1	Instruction fetch
2	Operand decode
3	Execution or memory access (branch resolution)

FIGURE 3.64   Pipeline stages.

All data dependences are between the register written in stage 3 of instruction i and a register read in stage 2 of instruction $i + 1$, before instruction i has completed. The probability of such an interlock occurring is $1/p$.

We are considering a change in the machine organization that would write back the result of an instruction during an effective fourth pipe stage. This would decrease the length of the clock cycle by d (i.e., if the length of the clock cycle was T, it is now T − d). The probability of a dependence between instruction i and instruction $i + 2$ is p^{-2}. (Assume that the value of p^{-1} excludes instructions that would interlock on $i + 2$.) The branch would also be resolved during the fourth stage.

a.   [20] <3.4> Assume that we add no additional forwarding hardware for the four-stage pipeline. Considering only the data hazard, find the lower bound on d that makes this a profitable change. Assume that each result has exactly one use and that the basic clock cycle has length T.

b.   [20] <3.4> Now assume that we have used forwarding to eliminate the extra hazard introduced by the change. That is, for all *data* hazards the pipeline length is *effectively* 3. This design may still not be worthwhile because of the impact of control hazards coming from a four-stage versus a three-stage pipeline. Assume that only stage 1 of the pipeline can be safely executed before we decide whether a branch goes or not. We want to know the impact of branch hazards before this longer pipeline does not yield high performance. Find an upper bound on the percentages of conditional branches in programs in terms of the ratio of d to the original clock-cycle time, so that the longer pipeline has better performance. If d is a 10% reduction, what is the maximum percentage of conditional branches before we lose with this longer pipeline? Assume the taken-branch frequency for conditional branches is 60%.

3.11 [20] <3.4,3.7> Construct a table like Figure 3.18 that shows the data hazard stalls for the DLX FP pipeline as shown in Figure 3.44. Consider both integer-FP and FP-FP interactions but ignore divides (FP and integer).

3.12 [20] <3.4,3.7> Construct the forwarding table for the DLX FP pipeline of Figure 3.44 as we did in Figure 3.19. Consider both FP to FP forwarding and forwarding of FP loads to the FP units but ignore FP and integer divides.

3.13 [25] <3.4,3.7> Suppose DLX had only one register set. Construct the forwarding table for the FP and integer instructions using the format of Figure 3.19. Assume the DLX pipeline in Figure 3.44. Ignore FP and integer divides.

3.14 [15] <3.4,3.7> Construct a table like Figure 3.18 to check for WAW stalls in the DLX FP pipeline of Figure 3.44. Do not consider integer or FP divides.

3.15 [20] <3.4,3.7> Construct a table like Figure 3.18 that shows the structural stalls for the R4000 FP pipeline.

3.16 [35] <3.2–3.7> Change the DLX instruction simulator to be pipelined. Measure the frequency of empty branch-delay slots, the frequency of load delays, and the frequency of FP stalls for a variety of integer and FP programs. Also, measure the frequency of forwarding operations. Determine the performance impact of eliminating forwarding and stalling.

3.17 [35] <3.7> Using a DLX simulator, create a DLX pipeline simulator. Explore the impact of lengthening the FP pipelines, assuming both fully pipelined and unpipelined FP units. How does clustering of FP operations affect the results? Which FP units are most susceptible to changes in the FP pipeline length?

3.18 [40] <3.3–3.5> Write an instruction scheduler for DLX that works on DLX assembly language. Evaluate your scheduler using either profiles of programs or a pipeline simulator. If the DLX C compiler does optimization, evaluate your scheduler's performance both with and without optimization.

4

Advanced Pipelining and Instruction-Level Parallelism

"Who's first?"

"America."

"Who's second?"

"Sir, there is no second."

> *Dialog between two observers of the sailing race later named "The America's Cup" and run every few years.*
>
> *This quote was the inspiration for John Cocke's naming of the IBM research processor as "America." This processor was the precursor to the RS/6000 series and the first superscalar microprocessor.*

4.1	Instruction-Level Parallelism: Concepts and Challenges	221
4.2	Overcoming Data Hazards with Dynamic Scheduling	240
4.3	Reducing Branch Penalties with Dynamic Hardware Prediction	262
4.4	Taking Advantage of More ILP with Multiple Issue	278
4.5	Compiler Support for Exploiting ILP	289
4.6	Hardware Support for Extracting More Parallelism	299
4.7	Studies of ILP	318
4.8	Putting It All Together: The PowerPC 620	335
4.9	Fallacies and Pitfalls	349
4.10	Concluding Remarks	352
4.11	Historical Perspective and References	354
	Exercises	362

4.1 | Instruction-Level Parallelism: Concepts and Challenges

In the last chapter we saw how pipelining can overlap the execution of instructions when they are independent of one another. This potential overlap among instructions is called *instruction-level parallelism* (ILP) since the instructions can be evaluated in parallel. In this chapter, we look at a wide range of techniques for extending the pipelining ideas by increasing the amount of parallelism exploited among instructions. We start by looking at techniques that reduce the impact of data and control hazards and then turn to the topic of increasing the ability of the processor to exploit parallelism. We discuss the compiler technology used to increase the ILP and examine the results of a study of available ILP. The *Putting It All Together* section covers the PowerPC 620, which supports most of the advanced pipelining techniques described in this chapter.

In this section, we discuss features of both programs and processors that limit the amount of parallelism that can be exploited among instructions. We conclude the section by looking at simple compiler techniques for enhancing the exploitation of pipeline parallelism by a compiler.

The CPI of a pipelined machine is the sum of the base CPI and all contributions from stalls:

$$\text{Pipeline CPI} = \text{Ideal pipeline CPI} + \text{Structural stalls} + \text{RAW stalls}$$
$$+ \text{WAR stalls} + \text{WAW stalls} + \text{Control stalls}$$

The *ideal pipeline CPI* is a measure of the maximum performance attainable by the implementation. By reducing each of the terms of the right-hand side, we minimize the overall pipeline CPI and thus increase the instruction throughput per clock cycle. While the focus of the last chapter was on reducing the RAW stalls and the control stalls, in this chapter we will see that the techniques we introduce to further reduce the RAW and control stalls, as well as reduce the ideal CPI, can increase the importance of dealing with structural, WAR, and WAW stalls. The equation above allows us to characterize the various techniques we examine in this chapter by what component of the overall CPI a technique reduces. Figure 4.1 shows some of the techniques we examine and how they affect the contributions to the CPI.

Technique	Reduces	Section
Loop unrolling	Control stalls	4.1
Basic pipeline scheduling	RAW stalls	4.1 (also Chapter 3)
Dynamic scheduling with scoreboarding	RAW stalls	4.2
Dynamic scheduling with register renaming	WAR and WAW stalls	4.2
Dynamic branch prediction	Control stalls	4.3
Issuing multiple instructions per cycle	Ideal CPI	4.4
Compiler dependence analysis	Ideal CPI and data stalls	4.5
Software pipelining and trace scheduling	Ideal CPI and data stalls	4.5
Speculation	All data and control stalls	4.6
Dynamic memory disambiguation	RAW stalls involving memory	4.2, 4.6

FIGURE 4.1   The major techniques examined in this chapter are shown together with the component of the CPI equation that the technique affects. Data stalls are stalls arising from any type of data hazard, namely RAW (read after write), WAR (write after read), or WAW (write after write).

Before we examine these techniques in detail, we need to define the concepts on which these techniques are built. These concepts, in the end, determine the limits on how much parallelism can be exploited.

Instruction-Level Parallelism

All the techniques in this chapter exploit parallelism among instruction sequences. As we stated above, this type of parallelism is called instruction-level parallelism or ILP. The amount of parallelism available within a basic block (a straight-line code sequence with no branches in except to the entry and no branches out except at the exit) is quite small. For example, in Chapter 3 we saw that the average dynamic branch frequency in integer programs was about 15%, meaning that between six and seven instructions execute between a pair of branches. Since these instructions are likely to depend upon one another, the amount of overlap we can exploit within a basic block is likely to be much less than six. To obtain substantial performance enhancements, we must exploit ILP across multiple basic blocks.

The simplest and most common way to increase the amount of parallelism available among instructions is to exploit parallelism among iterations of a loop. This type of parallelism is often called *loop-level parallelism*. Here is a simple example of a loop, which adds two 1000-element arrays, that is completely parallel:

```
for (i=1; i<=1000; i=i+1)
        x[i] = x[i] + y[i];
```

Every iteration of the loop can overlap with any other iteration, although within each loop iteration there is little opportunity for overlap.

There are a number of techniques we will examine for converting such loop-level parallelism into instruction-level parallelism. Basically, such techniques work by unrolling the loop either statically by the compiler or dynamically by the hardware. We will look at a detailed example of loop unrolling later in this section.

An important alternative method for exploiting loop-level parallelism is the use of vector instructions. Essentially, a vector instruction operates on a sequence of data items. For example, the above code sequence could execute in four instructions on a typical vector processor: two instructions to load the vectors x and y from memory, one instruction to add the two vectors, and an instruction to store back the result vector. Of course, these instructions would be pipelined and have relatively long latencies, but these latencies may be overlapped. Vector instructions and the operation of vector processors are described in detail in Appendix B. Although the development of the vector ideas preceded most of the techniques we examine in this chapter for exploiting parallelism, processors that exploit ILP are replacing the vector-based processors; the reasons for this technology shift are discussed in more detail later in this chapter and in the historical perspectives at the end of the chapter.

Basic Pipeline Scheduling and Loop Unrolling

To keep a pipeline full, parallelism among instructions must be exploited by finding sequences of unrelated instructions that can be overlapped in the pipeline. To avoid a pipeline stall, a dependent instruction must be separated from the source instruction by a distance in clock cycles equal to the pipeline latency of that source instruction. A compiler's ability to perform this scheduling depends both on the amount of ILP available in the program and on the latencies of the functional units in the pipeline. Throughout this chapter we will assume the FP unit latencies shown in Figure 4.2, unless different latencies are explicitly stated. We assume the standard DLX integer pipeline, so that branches have a delay of one clock cycle. We assume that the functional units are fully pipelined or replicated (as many times as the pipeline depth), so that an operation of any type can be issued on every clock cycle and there are no structural hazards.

Instruction producing result	Instruction using result	Latency in clock cycles
FP ALU op	Another FP ALU op	3
FP ALU op	Store double	2
Load double	FP ALU op	1
Load double	Store double	0

FIGURE 4.2   Latencies of FP operations used in this chapter. The first column shows the originating instruction type. The second column is the type of the consuming instruction. The last column is the number of intervening clock cycles needed to avoid a stall. These numbers are similar to the average latencies we would see on an FP unit, like the one we described for DLX in the last chapter. The major change versus the DLX FP pipeline was to reduce the latency of FP multiply; this helps keep our examples from becoming unwieldy. The latency of a floating-point load to a store is zero, since the result of the load can be bypassed without stalling the store. We will continue to assume an integer load latency of 1 and an integer ALU operation latency of 0.

In this subsection, we look at how the compiler can increase the amount of available ILP by unrolling loops. This example serves both to illustrate an important technique as well as to motivate the definitions and program transformations described in the rest of this section. Our example uses a simple loop that adds a scalar value to an array in memory. Here is a typical version of the source:

```
for (i=1000; i>0; i=i-1)
    x[i] = x[i] + s;
```

We can see that this loop is parallel by noticing that the body of each iteration is independent. We will formalize this notion later in this section and describe how we can test whether loop iterations are independent later in the chapter. First, let's work through this simple example, showing how we can use the parallelism to improve its performance for a DLX-like pipeline with the latencies shown above.

The first step is to translate the above segment to DLX assembly language. In the following code segment, R1 is initially the address of the element in the array with the highest address, and F2 contains the scalar value, s. For simplicity, we assume that the element (x[1]) with the lowest address is at 8; if it were located elsewhere, the loop would require one additional integer instruction to perform the comparison with R1.

The straightforward DLX code, not scheduled for the pipeline, looks like this:

```
Loop:   LD      F0,0(R1)        ;F0=array element
        ADDD    F4,F0,F2        ;add scalar in F2
        SD      0(R1),F4        ;store result
        SUBI    R1,R1,#8        ;decrement pointer
                                ;8 bytes (per DW)
        BNEZ    R1,Loop         ;branch R1!=zero
```

Let's start by seeing how well this loop will run when it is scheduled on a simple pipeline for DLX with the latencies from Figure 4.2.

EXAMPLE   Show how the loop would look on DLX, both scheduled and unscheduled, including any stalls or idle clock cycles. Schedule for both delays from floating-point operations and from the delayed branch.

ANSWER   Without any scheduling the loop will execute as follows:

			Clock cycle issued
Loop:	LD	F0,0(R1)	1
	stall		2
	ADDD	F4,F0,F2	3
	stall		4
	stall		5
	SD	0(R1),F4	6
	SUBI	R1,R1,#8	7
	stall		8
	BNEZ	R1,Loop	9
	stall		10

This requires 10 clock cycles per iteration: one stall for the LD, two for the ADDD, one for the SUBI (since a branch reads the operand in ID), and one for the delayed branch. We can schedule the loop to obtain only one stall:

```
Loop:   LD      F0,0(R1)
        SUBI    R1,R1,#8
        ADDD    F4,F0,F2
        stall
        BNEZ    R1,Loop         ;delayed branch
        SD      8(R1),F4        ;altered & interchanged
                                 with SUBI
```

Execution time has been reduced from 10 clock cycles to 6. The stall after ADDD is for the use by the SD.   ■

Notice that to schedule the delayed branch, the compiler had to determine that it could swap the SUBI and SD by changing the address to which the SD stored:

the address was 0(R1) and is now 8(R1). This is not a trivial observation, since most compilers would see that the SD instruction depends on the SUBI and would refuse to interchange them. A smarter compiler could figure out the relationship and perform the interchange. The chain of dependent instructions from the LD to the ADDD and then to the SD determines the clock cycle count for this loop. This chain must take at least 6 cycles because of dependencies and pipeline latencies.

In the above example, we complete one loop iteration and store back one array element every 6 clock cycles, but the actual work of operating on the array element takes just 3 (the load, add, and store) of those 6 clock cycles. The remaining 3 clock cycles consist of loop overhead—the SUBI and BNEZ—and a stall. To eliminate these 3 clock cycles we need to get more operations within the loop relative to the number of overhead instructions. A simple scheme for increasing the number of instructions relative to the branch and overhead instructions is *loop unrolling*. This is done by simply replicating the loop body multiple times, and adjusting the loop termination code.

Loop unrolling can also be used to improve scheduling. Because it eliminates the branch, it allows instructions from different iterations to be scheduled together. In this case, we can eliminate the load delay stall by creating additional independent instructions within the loop body. The compiler can then schedule these instructions into the load delay slot. If we simply replicated the instructions when we unrolled the loop, the resulting use of the same registers could prevent us from effectively scheduling the loop. Thus, we will want to use different registers for each iteration, increasing the required register count.

EXAMPLE   Show our loop unrolled so that there are four copies of the loop body, assuming R1 is initially a multiple of 32, which means that the number of loop iterations is a multiple of 4. Eliminate any obviously redundant computations and do not reuse any of the registers.

ANSWER   Here is the result after merging the SUBI instructions and dropping the unnecessary BNEZ operations that are duplicated during unrolling.

```
Loop:   LD      F0,0(R1)
        ADDD    F4,F0,F2
        SD      0(R1),F4        ;drop SUBI & BNEZ
        LD      F6,-8(R1)
        ADDD    F8,F6,F2
        SD      -8(R1),F8       ;drop SUBI & BNEZ
        LD      F10,-16(R1)
        ADDD    F12,F10,F2
        SD      -16(R1),F12     ;drop SUBI & BNEZ
        LD      F14,-24(R1)
        ADDD    F16,F14,F2
        SD      -24(R1),F16
        SUBI    R1,R1,#32
        BNEZ    R1,Loop
```

We have eliminated three branches and three decrements of R1. The addresses on the loads and stores have been compensated to allow the SUBI instructions on R1 to be merged. Without scheduling, every operation is followed by a dependent operation and thus will cause a stall. This loop will run in 28 clock cycles—each LD has 1 stall, each ADDD 2, the SUBI 1, the branch 1, plus 14 instruction issue cycles—or 7 clock cycles for each of the four elements. Although this unrolled version is currently slower than the scheduled version of the original loop, this will change when we schedule the unrolled loop. Loop unrolling is normally done early in the compilation process, so that redundant computations can be exposed and eliminated by the optimizer.   ■

In real programs we do not usually know the upper bound on the loop. Suppose it is n, and we would like to unroll the loop to make k copies of the body. Instead of a single unrolled loop, we generate a pair of consecutive loops. The first executes (n mod k) times and has a body that is the original loop. The second is the unrolled body surrounded by an outer loop that iterates (n/k) times.

In the above Example, unrolling improves the performance of this loop by eliminating overhead instructions, although it increases code size substantially. What will happen to the performance increase when the loop is scheduled on DLX?

EXAMPLE   Show the unrolled loop in the previous example after it has been scheduled on DLX.

ANSWER
```
Loop:  LD    F0,0(R1)
       LD    F6,-8(R1)
       LD    F10,-16(R1)
       LD    F14,-24(R1)
       ADDD  F4,F0,F2
       ADDD  F8,F6,F2
       ADDD  F12,F10,F2
       ADDD  F16,F14,F2
       SD    0(R1),F4
       SD    -8(R1),F8
       SUBI  R1,R1,#32
       SD    16(R1),F12
       BNEZ  R1,Loop
       SD    8(R1),F16    ;8-32 = -24
```

The execution time of the unrolled loop has dropped to a total of 14 clock cycles, or 3.5 clock cycles per element, compared with 7 cycles per element before scheduling and 6 cycles when scheduled but not unrolled.   ■

The gain from scheduling on the unrolled loop is even larger than on the original loop. This is because unrolling the loop exposes more computation that can be scheduled to minimize the stalls; the code above has no stalls. Scheduling the loop in this fashion necessitates realizing that the loads and stores are independent and can be interchanged.

Loop unrolling is a simple but useful method for increasing the size of straight-line code fragments that can be scheduled effectively. This transformation is useful in a variety of processors, from simple pipelines like those in DLX to the pipelines described in section 4.4 that issue more than one instruction per cycle.

Summary of the Loop Unrolling and Scheduling Example

Throughout this chapter we will look at both hardware and software techniques that allow us to take advantage of instruction-level parallelism to fully utilize the potential of the functional units in a processor. The key to most of these techniques is to know when and how the ordering among instructions may be changed. In our example we made many such changes, which to us, as human beings, were obviously allowable. In practice, this process must be performed in a methodical fashion either by a compiler or by hardware. To obtain the final unrolled code we had to make the following decisions and transformations:

1. Determine that it was legal to move the SD after the SUBI and BNEZ, and find the amount to adjust the SD offset.

2. Determine that unrolling the loop would be useful by finding that the loop iterations were independent, except for the loop maintenance code.

3. Use different registers to avoid unnecessary constraints that would be forced by using the same registers for different computations.

4. Eliminate the extra tests and branches and adjust the loop maintenance code.

5. Determine that the loads and stores in the unrolled loop can be interchanged by observing that the loads and stores from different iterations are independent. This requires analyzing the memory addresses and finding that they do not refer to the same address.

6. Schedule the code, preserving any dependences needed to yield the same result as the original code.

The key requirement underlying all of these transformations is an understanding of how an instruction depends on another and how the instructions can be changed or reordered given the dependences. The next subsection defines these ideas and describes the restrictions that any hardware or software system must maintain.

Dependences

Determining how one instruction depends on another is critical not only to the scheduling process we used in the earlier example but also to determining how much parallelism exists in a program and how that parallelism can be exploited. In particular, to exploit instruction-level parallelism we must determine which instructions can be executed in parallel. If two instructions are *parallel*, they can execute simultaneously in a pipeline without causing any stalls, assuming the pipeline has sufficient resources (and hence no structural hazards exist). Two instructions that are dependent are not parallel. Likewise, two instructions that are dependent cannot be reordered. Instructions that can be reordered are parallel and vice versa. The key in both cases is to determine whether an instruction is dependent on another instruction.

Data Dependences

There are three different types of dependences: data dependences, name dependences, and control dependences. An instruction j is *data dependent* on instruction i if either of the following holds:

- Instruction i produces a result that is used by instruction j, or

- Instruction j is data dependent on instruction k, and instruction k is data dependent on instruction i.

The second condition simply states that one instruction is dependent on another if there exists a chain of dependences of the first type between the two instructions. This dependence chain can be as long as the entire program. In our example, the sequences

```
Loop:   LD      F0,0(R1)  ;F0=array element
        ADDD    F4,F0,F2  ;add scalar in F2
        SD      0(R1),F4  ;store result
```

and

```
        SUBI    R1,R1,8   ;decrement pointer
                          ;8 bytes (per DW)
        BNEZ    R1,Loop   ; branch R1!=zero
```

are both dependent sequences, as shown by the arrows, with each instruction depending on the previous one. The arrows here and in following examples show the order that must be preserved for correct execution. The arrow points from an instruction that must precede the instruction that the arrowhead points to.

If two instructions are data dependent they cannot execute simultaneously or be completely overlapped. The dependence implies that there would be a chain of one or more RAW hazards between the two instructions. Executing the instructions simultaneously will cause a processor with pipeline interlocks to detect a hazard and stall, thereby reducing or eliminating the overlap. In a processor without interlocks that relies on compiler scheduling, the compiler cannot schedule dependent instructions in such a way that they completely overlap, since the program will not execute correctly. The presence of a data dependence in an instruction sequence reflects a data dependence in the source code from which the instruction sequence was generated. The effect of the original data dependence must be preserved.

Dependences are a property of *programs*. Whether a given dependence results in an actual hazard being detected and whether that hazard actually causes a stall are properties of the *pipeline organization*. This difference is critical to understanding how instruction-level parallelism can be exploited. In our example, there is a data dependence between the SUBI and the BNEZ; this dependence causes a stall because we moved the branch test for the DLX pipeline to the ID stage. Had the branch test stayed in EX, this dependence would not cause a stall. (Of course, the branch delay would then still be 2 cycles, rather than 1.) The presence of the dependence indicates the potential for a hazard, but the actual hazard and the *length of any stall* is a property of the pipeline. The importance of the data dependences is that a dependence (1) indicates the possibility of a hazard, (2) determines the order in which results must be calculated, and (3) sets an upper bound on how much parallelism can possibly be exploited. Such limits are explored in section 4.7.

Since a data dependence can limit the amount of instruction-level parallelism we can exploit, a major focus of this chapter is overcoming the limitations. This is done in two different ways: maintaining the dependence but avoiding a hazard, and eliminating a dependence by transforming the code. Scheduling the code is the primary method used to avoid a hazard without altering the dependence. We used this technique in several places in our example both before and after unrolling; the dependence LD, ADDD, SD was scheduled to avoid hazards, but the dependence remains in the code. We will see techniques for implementing scheduling of code both in hardware and in software. In our earlier example, we also eliminated dependences, though we did not show this step explicitly.

EXAMPLE   Show how the process of optimizing the loop overhead by unrolling the loop actually eliminates data dependences. In this example and those used in the remainder of this chapter, we use nondelayed branches for simplicity; it is easy to extend the examples to use delayed branches.

ANSWER   Here is the unrolled but unoptimized code with the extra SUBI instructions, but without the branches. (Eliminating the branches is another type of transformation, since it involves control rather than data.) The arrows

show the data dependences that are within the unrolled body and involve
the SUBI instructions:

```
Loop:   LD      F0,0(R1)
        ADDD    F4,F0,F2
        SD      0(R1),F4
        SUBI    R1,R1,#8      ;drop BNEZ
        LD      F6,0(R1)
        ADDD    F8,F6,F2
        SD      0(R1),F8
        SUBI    R1,R1,#8      ;drop BNEZ
        LD      F10,0(R1)
        ADDD    F12,F10,F2
        SD      0(R1),F12
        SUBI    R1,R1,#8      ;drop BNEZ
        LD      F14,0(R1)
        ADDD    F16,F14,F2
        SD      0(R1),F16
        SUBI    R1,R1,#8
        BNEZ    R1,LOOP
```

As the arrows show, the SUBI instructions form a dependent chain that involves the SUBI, LD, and SD instructions. This forces the body to execute
in order, as well as making the SUBI instructions necessary, which increases the instruction count. The compiler removes this dependence by
symbolically computing the intermediate values of R1 and folding the
computation into the offset of the LD and SD instructions and by changing
the final SUBI into a decrement by 32. This makes the three SUBI unnecessary, and the compiler can remove them. There are other types of dependences in this code, but we will deal with them shortly.   ■

Removing a real data dependence, as we did in the example above, requires
knowledge of the global structure of the program and typically a fair amount of
analysis. Thus, techniques for doing such optimizations are carried out by compilers, in contrast to the avoidance of hazards by scheduling, which can be performed both in hardware and software.

A data value may flow between instructions either through registers or through
memory locations. When the data flow occurs in a register, detecting the dependence is reasonably straightforward since the register names are fixed in the instructions, although it gets more complicated when branches intervene.
Dependences that flow through memory locations are more difficult to detect

since two addresses may refer to the same location, but look different: For example, `100(R4)` and `20(R6)` may be identical. In addition, the effective address of a load or store may change from one execution of the instruction to another (so that `20(R4)` and `20(R4)` will be different), further complicating the detection of a dependence. In this chapter, we examine both hardware and software techniques for detecting data dependences that involve memory locations. The compiler techniques for detecting such dependences are critical in uncovering loop-level parallelism, as we will see shortly.

Name Dependences

The second type of dependence is a *name dependence*. A name dependence occurs when two instructions use the same register or memory location, called a *name*, but there is no flow of data between the instructions associated with that name. There are two types of name dependences between an instruction *i* that precedes instruction *j* in program order:

1. An *antidependence* between instruction *i* and instruction *j* occurs when instruction *j* writes a register or memory location that instruction *i* reads and instruction *i* is executed first. An antidependence corresponds to a WAR hazard, and the hazard detection for WAR hazards forces the ordering of an antidependent instruction pair.

2. An *output dependence* occurs when instruction *i* and instruction *j* write the same register or memory location. The ordering between the instructions must be preserved. Output dependences are preserved by detecting WAW hazards.

Both antidependences and output dependences are name dependences, as opposed to true data dependences, since there is no value being transmitted between the instructions. This means that instructions involved in a name dependence can execute simultaneously or be reordered, if the name (register number or memory location) used in the instructions is changed so the instructions do not conflict. This renaming can be more easily done for register operands and is called *register renaming*. Register renaming can be done either statically by a compiler or dynamically by the hardware.

EXAMPLE   Unroll our example loop, eliminating the excess loop overhead, but using the same registers in each loop copy. Indicate both the data and name dependences within the body. Show how renaming eliminates name dependences that reduce parallelism.

ANSWER   Here's the loop unrolled but with the same registers in use for each copy. The data dependences are shown with gray arrows and the name dependences with black arrows. As in earlier examples, the direction of the arrow indicates the ordering that must be preserved for correct execution of the code:

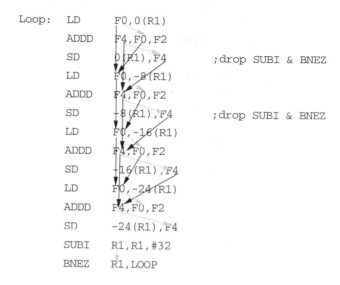

```
Loop:   LD      F0,0(R1)
        ADDD    F4,F0,F2
        SD      0(R1),F4            ;drop SUBI & BNEZ
        LD      F0,-8(R1)
        ADDD    F4,F0,F2
        SD      -8(R1),F4           ;drop SUBI & BNEZ
        LD      F0,-16(R1)
        ADDD    F4,F0,F2
        SD      +16(R1),F4
        LD      F0,-24(R1)
        ADDD    F4,F0,F2
        SD      -24(R1),F4
        SUBI    R1,R1,#32
        BNEZ    R1,LOOP
```

The name dependences force the instructions in the loop to be almost completely ordered, allowing only the order of the LD following each SD to be interchanged. When the registers used for each copy of the loop body are renamed only the true dependences within each body remain:

```
Loop:   LD      F0,0(R1)
        ADDD    F4,F0,F2
        SD      0(R1),F4            ;drop SUBI & BNEZ
        LD      F6,-8(R1)
        ADDD    F8,F6,F2
        SD      -8(R1),F8           ;drop SUBI & BNEZ
        LD      F10,-16(R1)
        ADDD    F12,F10,F2
        SD      16(R1),F12
        LD      F14,-24(R1)
        ADDD    F16,F14,F2
        SD      -24(R1),F16
        SUBI    R1,R1,#32
        BNEZ    R1,LOOP
```

With the renaming, the copies of each loop body become independent and can be overlapped or executed in parallel. This renaming process can be performed either by the compiler or in hardware. In fact, we will see how the entire unrolling and renaming process can be done in the hardware. ∎

Control Dependences

The last type of dependence is a *control dependence*. A control dependence determines the ordering of an instruction with respect to a branch instruction so that the non-branch instruction is executed only when it should be. Every instruction, except for those in the first basic block of the program, is control dependent on some set of branches, and, in general, these control dependences must be preserved. One of the simplest examples of a control dependence is the dependence of the statements in the "then" part of an if statement on the branch. For example, in the code segment:

```
if p1 {
        S1;
};
if p2 {
        S2;
}
```

S1 is control dependent on p1, and S2 is control dependent on p2 but not on p1. There are two constraints on control dependences:

1. An instruction that is control dependent on a branch cannot be moved before the branch so that its execution is no longer controlled by the branch. For example, we cannot take an instruction from the then portion of an if statement and move it before the if statement.

2. An instruction that is not control dependent on a branch cannot be moved after the branch so that its execution is controlled by the branch. For example, we cannot take a statement before the if statement and move it into the then portion.

It is sometimes possible to violate these constraints and still have a correct execution. Before we examine this further, let's see how control dependences limit parallelism in our example.

EXAMPLE   Show the unrolled code sequence before the loop overhead is optimized away. Indicate the control dependences. How are the control dependences removed?

ANSWER Here is the unrolled code sequence with the branches still in place. The branches for the first three loop iterations have the conditions complemented, because we want the fall-through case (when the branch is untaken) to execute another loop iteration. The control dependences within the unrolled body are shown with arrows.

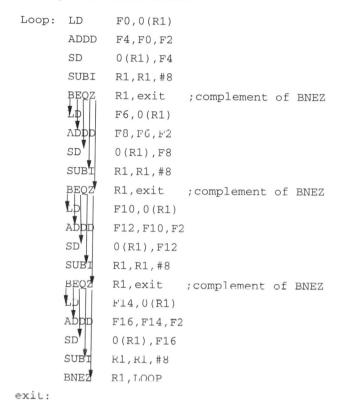

```
Loop:   LD      F0,0(R1)
        ADDD    F4,F0,F2
        SD      0(R1),F4
        SUBI    R1,R1,#8
        BEQZ    R1,exit     ;complement of BNEZ
        LD      F6,0(R1)
        ADDD    F8,F6,F2
        SD      0(R1),F8
        SUBI    R1,R1,#8
        BEQZ    R1,exit     ;complement of BNEZ
        LD      F10,0(R1)
        ADDD    F12,F10,F2
        SD      0(R1),F12
        SUBI    R1,R1,#8
        BEQZ    R1,exit     ;complement of BNEZ
        LD      F14,0(R1)
        ADDD    F16,F14,F2
        SD      0(R1),F16
        SUBI    R1,R1,#8
        BNEZ    R1,LOOP
exit:
```

The presence of the intermediate branches (BEQZ instructions) prevents the overlapping of iterations for scheduling since moving the instructions would require changing the control dependences. Furthermore, the presence of the intermediate branches prevents the removal of the SUBI instructions since the value computed by each SUBI is used in the branch. Hence the first goal is to remove the intermediate branches.

Removing the branches changes the control dependences. In this case, we know that the content of R1 is a multiple of 32 and that the number of loop iterations is a multiple of 4. This insight allows us to determine that the three intermediate BEQZ instructions will never be taken. Since they are never taken, the branches are no-ops and no instructions are control dependent on the branches. After removing the branches, we can then optimize the data dependences involving the SUBI instructions, as we did in the example on page 230. ■

Because parallelism exists naturally in loops, it is useful to extend our techniques for detecting dependences to loops. The next subsection describes how we can use the concept of a dependence to determine whether an entire loop can be executed in parallel.

Loop-Level Parallelism: Concepts and Techniques

Loop-level parallelism is normally analyzed at the source level or close to it, while most analysis of ILP is done once instructions have been generated by the compiler. Loop-level analysis involves determining what dependences exist among the operands in the loop across the iterations of the loop. For now, we will consider only data dependences, which arise when an operand is written at some point and read at a later point. Name dependences also exist and may be removed by renaming techniques like those we used earlier. The analysis of loop-level parallelism focuses on determining whether data accesses in later iterations are data dependent on data values produced in earlier iterations. Our earlier example is loop-level parallel. The computational work in each iteration is independent of previous iterations. To easily see this, we really want to look at the source representation:

```
for (i=1000; i>0; i=i-1)
        x[i] = x[i] + s;
```

There is a dependence in the loop body between the two uses of x[i], but this dependence is within a single iteration. There is no dependence between instructions in different iterations. Thus, the loop is parallel. Of course, once this loop is translated to assembly language, the loop implementation creates a loop-carried dependence, involving the register used for addressing and decrementing (R1 in our code). For this reason, loop-level parallelism is usually analyzed at or near the source level, with loops still represented in high-level form. Let's look at a more complex example.

EXAMPLE   Consider a loop like this one:

```
for (i=1; i<=100; i=i+1) {
        A[i+1] = A[i] + C[i]; /* S1 */
        B[i+1] = B[i] + A[i+1]; /* S2 */
}
```

Assume that A, B, and C are distinct, nonoverlapping arrays. (In practice, the arrays may sometimes be the same or may overlap. Because the arrays may be passed as parameters to a procedure, which includes this loop, determining whether arrays overlap or are identical requires sophisticated, interprocedural analysis of the program.) What are the data dependences among the statements S1 and S2 in the loop?

ANSWER   There are two different dependences:

1. S1 uses a value computed by S1 in an earlier iteration, since iteration i computes A[i+1], which is read in iteration i+1. The same is true of S2 for B[i] and B[i+1].

2. S2 uses the value, A[i+1], computed by S1 in the same iteration.

■

These two dependences are different and have different effects. To see how they differ, let's assume that only one of these dependences exists at a time. Consider the dependence of statement S1 on an earlier iteration of S1. This dependence is a *loop-carried dependence*, meaning that the dependence exists between different iterations of the loop. Furthermore, since the statement S1 is dependent on itself, successive iterations of statement S1 must execute in order.

The second dependence above (S2 depending on S1) is within an iteration and not loop-carried. Thus, if this were the only dependence, multiple iterations of the loop could execute in parallel, as long as each pair of statements in an iteration were kept in order. This is the same type of dependence that exists in our initial example, in which we can fully exploit the parallelism present in the loop through unrolling.

It is also possible to have a loop-carried dependence that does not prevent parallelism, as the next example shows.

EXAMPLE   Consider a loop like this one:

```
for (i=1; i<=100; i=i+1) {
        A[i] = A[i] + B[i];    /* S1 */
        B[i+1] = C[i] + D[i];  /* S2 */
}
```

What are the dependences between S1 and S2? Is this loop parallel? If not, show how to make it parallel.

ANSWER   Statement S1 uses the value assigned in the previous iteration by statement S2, so there is a loop-carried dependence between S2 and S1. Despite this loop-carried dependence, this loop can be made parallel. Unlike the earlier loop, this dependence is not circular: Neither statement depends on itself, and while S1 depends on S2, S2 does not depend on S1. A loop is parallel if it can be written without a cycle in the dependences, since the absence of a cycle means that the dependences give a partial ordering on the statements.

Although there are no circular dependences in the above loop, it must be transformed to conform to the partial ordering and expose the parallelism. Two observations are critical to this transformation:

1. There is no dependence from S1 to S2. If there were, then there would be a cycle in the dependences and the loop would not be parallel. Since this other dependence is absent, interchanging the two statements will not affect the execution of S2.

2. On the first iteration of the loop, statement S1 depends on the value of B[1] computed prior to initiating the loop.

These two observations allow us to replace the loop above with the following code sequence:

```
A[1] = A[1] + B[1];
for (i=1; i<=99; i=i+1) {
        B[i+1] = C[i] + D[i];
        A[i+1] = A[i+1] + B[i+1];
}
B[101] = C[100] + D[100];
```

The dependence between the two statements is no longer loop-carried, so that iterations of the loop may be overlapped, provided the statements in each iteration are kept in order. There are a variety of such transformations that restructure loops to expose parallelism, as we will see in section 4.5.   ■

The key focus of the rest of this chapter is on techniques that exploit instruction-level parallelism. The data dependences in a compiled program act as a limit on how much ILP can be exploited. The challenge is to approach that limit by trying to minimize the actual hazards and associated stalls that arise. The techniques we examine become ever more sophisticated in an attempt to exploit all the available parallelism while maintaining the necessary true data dependences in the code. Both the compiler and the hardware have a role to play: The compiler tries to eliminate or minimize dependences, while the hardware tries to prevent dependences from becoming stalls.

4.2 | Overcoming Data Hazards with Dynamic Scheduling

In Chapter 3 we assumed that our pipeline fetches an instruction and issues it, unless there is a data dependence between an instruction already in the pipeline and the fetched instruction that cannot be hidden with bypassing or forwarding. Forwarding logic reduces the effective pipeline latency so that the certain dependences do not result in hazards. If there is a data dependence that cannot be hidden, then the hazard detection hardware stalls the pipeline (starting with the instruction that uses the result). No new instructions are fetched or issued until the dependence is cleared. We also examined compiler techniques for scheduling the instructions so as to separate dependent instructions and minimize the number of actual hazards and resultant stalls. This approach, which has been called *static scheduling*, was first used in the 1960s and became popular in the 1980s as pipelining became widespread.

Several early processors used another approach, called *dynamic scheduling*, whereby the hardware rearranges the instruction execution to reduce the stalls. Dynamic scheduling offers several advantages: It enables handling some cases when dependences are unknown at compile time (e.g., because they may involve a memory reference), and it simplifies the compiler. Perhaps most importantly, it also allows code that was compiled with one pipeline in mind to run efficiently on a different pipeline. As we will see, these advantages are gained at a cost of a significant increase in hardware complexity.

While a dynamically scheduled processor cannot remove true data dependences, it tries to avoid stalling when dependences are present. In contrast, static pipeline scheduling, like that we have already seen, tries to minimize stalls by separating dependent instructions so that they will not lead to hazards. Of course, static scheduling can also be used on code destined to run on a processor with a dynamically scheduled pipeline. We will examine two different schemes, with the second one extending the ideas of the first to attack WAW and WAR hazards as well as RAW stalls.

Dynamic Scheduling: The Idea

A major limitation of the pipelining techniques we have used so far is that they all use in-order instruction issue: If an instruction is stalled in the pipeline, no later instructions can proceed. Thus, if there is a dependence between two closely spaced instructions in the pipeline, a stall will result. If there are multiple functional units, these units could lie idle. If instruction j depends on a long-running instruction i, currently in execution in the pipeline, then all instructions after j must be stalled until i is finished and j can execute. For example, consider this code:

```
DIVD    F0,F2,F4
ADDD    F10,F0,F8
SUBD    F12,F8,F14
```

The SUBD instruction cannot execute because the dependence of ADDD on DIVD causes the pipeline to stall; yet SUBD is not data dependent on anything in the pipeline. This is a performance limitation that can be eliminated by not requiring instructions to execute in order.

In the DLX pipeline developed in the last chapter, both structural and data hazards were checked during instruction decode (ID): When an instruction could execute properly, it was issued from ID. To allow us to begin executing the SUBD in the above example, we must separate the issue process into two parts: checking the structural hazards and waiting for the absence of a data hazard. We can still check for structural hazards when we issue the instruction; thus, we still use in-order instruction issue. However, we want the instructions to begin execution as soon as their data operands are available. Thus, the pipeline will do *out-of-order execution*, which implies *out-of-order completion*.

Out-of-order completion creates major complications in handling exceptions. In the dynamically scheduled processors addressed in this section, exceptions are imprecise, since instructions may complete before an instruction issued earlier raises an exception. Thus, it is difficult to restart after an interrupt. Rather than address these problems in this section, we will discuss a solution for precise exceptions in the context of a processor with speculation in section 4.6. The approach discussed in section 4.6 can be used to solve the simpler problem that arises in these dynamically scheduled processors. For floating-point exceptions other solutions may be possible, as discussed in Appendix A.

In introducing out-of-order execution, we have essentially split the ID pipe stage into two stages:

1. *Issue*—Decode instructions, check for structural hazards.

2. *Read operands*—Wait until no data hazards, then read operands.

An instruction fetch stage precedes the issue stage and may fetch either into a single-entry latch or into a queue; instructions are then issued from the latch or queue. The EX stage follows the read operands stage, just as in the DLX pipeline. As in the DLX floating-point pipeline, execution may take multiple cycles, depending on the operation. Thus, we may need to distinguish when an instruction *begins execution* and when it *completes execution*; between the two times, the instruction is *in execution*. This allows multiple instructions to be in execution at the same time. In addition to these changes to the pipeline structure, we will also change the functional unit design by varying the number of units, the latency of operations, and the functional unit pipelining, so as to better explore these more advanced pipelining techniques.

Dynamic Scheduling with a Scoreboard

In a dynamically scheduled pipeline, all instructions pass through the issue stage in order (in-order issue); however, they can be stalled or bypass each other in the second stage (read operands) and thus enter execution out of order. *Scoreboarding* is a technique for allowing instructions to execute out of order when there are sufficient resources and no data dependences; it is named after the CDC 6600 scoreboard, which developed this capability.

Before we see how scoreboarding could be used in the DLX pipeline, it is important to observe that WAR hazards, which did not exist in the DLX floating-point or integer pipelines, may arise when instructions execute out of order. Suppose in the earlier example, the SUBD destination is F8, so that the code sequence is

```
DIVD    F0,F2,F4
ADDD    F10,F0,F8
SUBD    F8,F8,F14
```

Now there is an antidependence between the ADDD and the SUBD: If the pipeline executes the SUBD before the ADDD, it will violate the antidependence, yielding incorrect execution. Likewise, to avoid violating output dependences, WAW hazards (e.g., as would occur if the destination of the SUBD were F10) must also be detected. As we will see, both these hazards are avoided in a scoreboard by stalling the later instruction involved in the antidependence.

The goal of a scoreboard is to maintain an execution rate of one instruction per clock cycle (when there are no structural hazards) by executing an instruction as early as possible. Thus, when the next instruction to execute is stalled, other instructions can be issued and executed if they do not depend on any active or stalled instruction. The scoreboard takes full responsibility for instruction issue and execution, including all hazard detection. Taking advantage of out-of-order execution requires multiple instructions to be in their EX stage simultaneously. This can be achieved with multiple functional units, with pipelined functional units, or with both. Since these two capabilities—pipelined functional units and multiple functional units—are essentially equivalent for the purposes of pipeline control, we will assume the processor has multiple functional units.

The CDC 6600 had 16 separate functional units, including 4 floating-point units, 5 units for memory references, and 7 units for integer operations. On DLX, scoreboards make sense primarily on the floating-point unit since the latency of the other functional units is very small. Let's assume that there are two multipliers, one adder, one divide unit, and a single integer unit for all memory references, branches, and integer operations. Although this example is simpler than the CDC 6600, it is sufficiently powerful to demonstrate the principles without having a mass of detail or needing very long examples. Because both DLX and the CDC 6600 are load-store architectures, the techniques are nearly identical for the two processors. Figure 4.3 shows what the processor looks like.

Every instruction goes through the scoreboard, where a record of the data dependences is constructed; this step corresponds to instruction issue and replaces part of the ID step in the DLX pipeline. The scoreboard then determines when the instruction can read its operands and begin execution. If the scoreboard decides the instruction cannot execute immediately, it monitors every change in the hardware and decides when the instruction *can* execute. The scoreboard also controls when an instruction can write its result into the destination register. Thus, all hazard detection and resolution is centralized in the scoreboard. We will see a picture of the scoreboard later (Figure 4.4 on page 247), but first we need to understand the steps in the issue and execution segment of the pipeline.

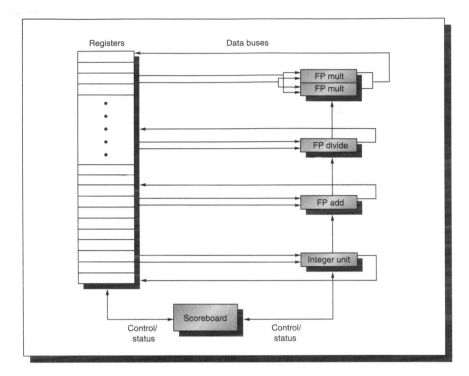

FIGURE 4.3   The basic structure of a DLX processor with a scoreboard. The scoreboard's function is to control instruction execution (vertical control lines). All data flows between the register file and the functional units over the buses (the horizontal lines, called trunks in the CDC 6600). There are two FP multipliers, an FP divider, an FP adder, and an integer unit. One set of buses (two inputs and one output) serves a group of functional units. The details of the scoreboard are shown in Figures 4.4–4.7.

Each instruction undergoes four steps in executing. (Since we are concentrating on the FP operations, we will not consider a step for memory access.) Let's first examine the steps informally and then look in detail at how the scoreboard keeps the necessary information that determines when to progress from one step to the next. The four steps, which replace the ID, EX, and WB steps in the standard DLX pipeline, are as follows:

1. *Issue*—If a functional unit for the instruction is free and no other active instruction has the same destination register, the scoreboard issues the instruction to the functional unit and updates its internal data structure. This step replaces a portion of the ID step in the DLX pipeline. By ensuring that no other active functional unit wants to write its result into the destination register, we guarantee that WAW hazards cannot be present. If a structural or WAW hazard exists, then the instruction issue stalls, and no further instructions will

issue until these hazards are cleared. When the issue stage stalls, it causes the buffer between instruction fetch and issue to fill; if the buffer is a single entry, instruction fetch stalls immediately. If the buffer is a queue with multiple instructions, it stalls when the queue fills; later we will see how a queue is used in the PowerPC 620 to connect fetch and issue.

2. *Read operands*—The scoreboard monitors the availability of the source operands. A source operand is available if no earlier issued active instruction is going to write it. When the source operands are available, the scoreboard tells the functional unit to proceed to read the operands from the registers and begin execution. The scoreboard resolves RAW hazards dynamically in this step, and instructions may be sent into execution out of order. This step, together with issue, completes the function of the ID step in the simple DLX pipeline.

3. *Execution*—The functional unit begins execution upon receiving operands. When the result is ready, it notifies the scoreboard that it has completed execution. This step replaces the EX step in the DLX pipeline and takes multiple cycles in the DLX FP pipeline.

4. *Write result*—Once the scoreboard is aware that the functional unit has completed execution, the scoreboard checks for WAR hazards and stalls the completing instruction, if necessary.

   A WAR hazard exists if there is a code sequence like our earlier example with ADDD and SUBD that both use F8. In that example we had the code

   ```
   DIVD   F0,F2,F4
   ADDD   F10,F0,F8
   SUBD   F8,F8,F14
   ```

   ADDD has a source operand F8, which is the same register as the destination of SUBD. But ADDD actually depends on an earlier instruction. The scoreboard will still stall the SUBD in its write result stage until ADDD reads its operands. In general, then, a completing instruction cannot be allowed to write its results when

   - there is an instruction that has not read its operands that precedes (i.e., in order of issue) the completing instruction, and

   - one of the operands is the same register as the result of the completing instruction.

   If this WAR hazard does not exist, or when it clears, the scoreboard tells the functional unit to store its result to the destination register. This step replaces the WB step in the simple DLX pipeline.

At first glance, it might appear that the scoreboard will have difficulty separating RAW and WAR hazards. Exercise 4.6 will help you understand how the scoreboard distinguishes these two cases and thus knows when to prevent a WAR hazard by stalling an instruction that is ready to write its results.

Because the operands for an instruction are read only when both operands are available in the register file, this scoreboard does not take advantage of forwarding. Instead registers are only read when they are both available. This is not as large a penalty as you might initially think. Unlike our simple pipeline of Chapter 3, instructions will write their result into the register file as soon as they complete execution (assuming no WAR hazards), rather than wait for a statically assigned write slot that may be several cycles away. The effect is reduced pipeline latency and benefits of forwarding. There is still one additional cycle of latency that arises since the write result and read operand stages cannot overlap. We would need additional buffering to eliminate this overhead.

Based on its own data structure, the scoreboard controls the instruction progression from one step to the next by communicating with the functional units. There is a small complication, however. There are only a limited number of source operand buses and result buses to the register file, which represents a structural hazard. The scoreboard must guarantee that the number of functional units allowed to proceed into steps 2 and 4 do not exceed the number of buses available. We will not go into further detail on this, other than to mention that the CDC 6600 solved this problem by grouping the 16 functional units together into four groups and supplying a set of buses, called *data trunks*, for each group. Only one unit in a group could read its operands or write its result during a clock.

Now let's look at the detailed data structure maintained by a DLX scoreboard with five functional units. Figure 4.4 shows what the scoreboard's information looks like part way through the execution of this simple sequence of instructions:

```
LD      F6,34(R2)
LD      F2,45(R3)
MULTD   F0,F2,F4
SUBD    F8,F6,F2
DIVD    F10,F0,F6
ADDD    F6,F8,F2
```

There are three parts to the scoreboard:

1. *Instruction status*—Indicates which of the four steps the instruction is in.

2. *Functional unit status*—Indicates the state of the functional unit (FU). There are nine fields for each functional unit:

   Busy—Indicates whether the unit is busy or not.

   Op—Operation to perform in the unit (e.g., add or subtract).

Fi—Destination register.

Fj, Fk—Source-register numbers.

Qj, Qk—Functional units producing source registers Fj, Fk.

Rj, Rk—Flags indicating when Fj, Fk are ready and not yet read. Set to No after operands are read.

3. *Register result status*—Indicates which functional unit will write each register, if an active instruction has the register as its destination. This field is set to blank whenever there are no pending instructions that will write that register.

Instruction		Instruction status			
		Issue	Read operands	Execution complete	Write result
LD	F6,34(R2)	√	√	√	√
LD	F2,45(R3)	√	√	√	
MULTD	F0,F2,F4	√			
SUBD	F8,F6,F2	√			
DIVD	F10,F0,F6	√			
ADDD	F6,F8,F2				

Functional unit status									
Name	Busy	Op	Fi	Fj	Fk	Qj	Qk	Rj	Rk
Integer	Yes	Load	F2	R3				No	
Mult1	Yes	Mult	F0	F2	F4	Integer		No	Yes
Mult2	No								
Add	Yes	Sub	F8	F6	F2		Integer	Yes	No
Divide	Yes	Div	F10	F0	F6	Mult1		No	Yes

Register result status									
	F0	F2	F4	F6	F8	F10	F12	...	F30
FU	Mult1	Integer			Add	Divide			

FIGURE 4.4 Components of the scoreboard. Each instruction that has issued or is pending issue has an entry in the instruction status table. There is one entry in the functional-unit status table for each functional unit. Once an instruction issues, the record of its operands is kept in the functional-unit status table. Finally, the register-result table indicates which unit will produce each pending result; the number of entries is equal to the number of registers. The instruction status table says that (1) the first LD has completed and written its result, and (2) the second LD has completed execution but has not yet written its result. The MULTD, SUBD, and DIVD have all issued but are stalled, waiting for their operands. The functional-unit status says that the first multiply unit is waiting for the integer unit, the add unit is waiting for the integer unit, and the divide unit is waiting for the first multiply unit. The ADDD instruction is stalled because of a structural hazard; it will clear when the SUBD completes. If an entry in one of these scoreboard tables is not being used, it is left blank. For example, the Rk field is not used on a load and the Mult2 unit is unused, hence their fields have no meaning. Also, once an operand has been read, the Rj and Rk fields are set to No. Figure 4.7 and Exercise 4.6 show why this last step is crucial.

Now let's look at how the code sequence begun in Figure 4.4 continues execution. After that, we will be able to examine in detail the conditions that the scoreboard uses to control execution.

EXAMPLE   Assume the following EX cycle latencies (chosen to illustrate the behavior and not representative) for the floating-point functional units: Add is 2 clock cycles, multiply is 10 clock cycles, and divide is 40 clock cycles. Using the code segment in Figure 4.4 and beginning with the point indicated by the instruction status in Figure 4.4, show what the status tables look like when MULTD and DIVD are each ready to go to the write-result state.

ANSWER   There are RAW data hazards from the second LD to MULTD and SUBD, from MULTD to DIVD, and from SUBD to ADDD. There is a WAR data hazard between DIVD and ADDD. Finally, there is a structural hazard on the add functional unit for ADDD. What the tables look like when MULTD and DIVD are ready to write their results is shown in Figures 4.5 and 4.6, respectively.

Instruction	Instruction status			
	Issue	**Read operands**	**Execution complete**	**Write result**
LD F6,34(R2)	√	√	√	√
LD F2,45(R3)	√	√	√	√
MULTD F0,F2,F4	√	√	√	
SUBD F8,F6,F2	√	√	√	√
DIVD F10,F0,F6	√			
ADDD F5,F8,F2	√	√	√	

Functional unit status									
Name	**Busy**	**Op**	**Fi**	**Fj**	**Fk**	**Qj**	**Qk**	**Rj**	**Rk**
Integer	No								
Mult1	Yes	Mult	F0	F2	F4			No	No
Mult2	No								
Add	Yes	Add	F6	F8	F2			No	No
Divide	Yes	Div	F10	F0	F6	Mult1		No	Yes

Register result status								
	F0	**F2**	**F4**	**F6**	**F8**	**F10**	**F12**	**...**	**F30**
FU	Mult1				Add		Divide		

FIGURE 4.5   Scoreboard tables just before the MULTD goes to write result. The DIVD has not yet read either of its operands, since it has a dependence on the result of the multiply. The ADDD has read its operands and is in execution, although it was forced to wait until the SUBD finished to get the functional unit. ADDD cannot proceed to write result because of the WAR hazard on F6, which is used by the DIVD. The Q fields are only relevant when a functional unit is waiting for another unit.

	Instruction status			
Instruction	**Issue**	**Read operands**	**Execution complete**	**Write result**
LD F6,34(R2)	√	√	√	√
LD F2,45(R3)	√	√	√	√
MULTD F0,F2,F4	√	√	√	√
SUBD F8,F6,F2	√	√	√	√
DIVD F10,F0,F6	√	√	√	
ADDD F6,F8,F2	√	√	√	√

	Functional unit status								
Name	**Busy**	**Op**	**Fi**	**Fj**	**Fk**	**Qj**	**Qk**	**Rj**	**Rk**
Integer	No								
Mult1	No								
Mult2	No								
Add	No								
Divide	Yes	Div	F10	F0	F6			No	No

	Register result status								
	F0	**F2**	**F4**	**F6**	**F8**	**F10**	**F12**	**...**	**F30**
FU						Divide			

FIGURE 4.6   Scoreboard tables just before the DIVD goes to write result. ADDD was able to complete as soon as DIVD passed through read operands and got a copy of F6. Only the DIVD remains to finish.

■

Now we can see how the scoreboard works in detail by looking at what has to happen for the scoreboard to allow each instruction to proceed. Figure 4.7 shows what the scoreboard requires for each instruction to advance and the bookkeeping action necessary when the instruction does advance. The scoreboard, like a number of other structures that we examine in this chapter, records operand specifier information, such as register numbers. For example, we must record the source registers when an instruction is issued. Because we refer to the contents of a register as Regs[D] where D is a register name, there is no ambiguity. For example, Fj[FU] ← S1 causes the register *name* S1 to be placed in Fj[FU], rather than the *contents* of the register of register S1.

Instruction status	Wait until	Bookkeeping
Issue	Not Busy [FU] and not Result [D]	`Busy[FU]←` yes; `Op[FU]←` op; `Fi[FU]←D;` `Fj[FU]←` S1; `Fk[FU]←` S2; `Qj←` Result[S1]; `Qk←` Result[S2]; `Rj←` not Qj; `Rk←` not Qk; Result[D]`←` FU;
Read operands	Rj and Rk	`Rj←` No; `Rk←` No; `Qj←0`; `Qk←0`
Execution complete	Functional unit done	
Write result	$\forall f((\text{Fj}[f] \neq \text{Fi}[FU]$ or Rj[f] = No) & (Fk[f] $\neq$ Fi[FU] or Rk[f] = No))	$\forall f$(if Qj[f]=FU then Rj[f]`←` Yes); $\forall f$(if Qk[f]=FU then Rk[f]`←` Yes); `Result[Fi[FU]]←` 0; `Busy[FU]←` No

FIGURE 4.7   Required checks and bookkeeping actions for each step in instruction execution. FU stands for the functional unit used by the instruction, D is the destination register name, S1 and S2 are the source register names, and op is the operation to be done. To access the scoreboard entry named Fj for functional unit FU we use the notation Fj[FU]. Result[D] is the value of the result register field for register D. The test on the write-result case prevents the write when there is a WAR hazard, which exists if another instruction has this instruction's destination (Fi[FU]) as a source (Fj[f] or Fk[f]) and if some other instruction has written the register (Rj = Yes or Rk = Yes). The variable f is used for any functional unit.

The costs and benefits of scoreboarding are interesting considerations. The CDC 6600 designers measured a performance improvement of 1.7 for FOR-TRAN programs and 2.5 for hand-coded assembly language. However, this was measured in the days before software pipeline scheduling, semiconductor main memory, and caches (which lower memory-access time). The scoreboard on the CDC 6600 had about as much logic as one of the functional units, which is surprisingly low. The main cost was in the large number of buses—about four times as many as would be required if the processor only executed instructions in order (or if it only initiated one instruction per execute cycle). The recently increasing interest in dynamic scheduling is motivated by attempts to issue more instructions per clock (so the cost of more buses must be paid anyway) and by ideas like speculation (explored in section 4.6) that naturally build on dynamic scheduling.

A scoreboard uses the available ILP to minimize the number of stalls arising from the program's true data dependences. In eliminating stalls, a scoreboard is limited by several factors:

1. *The amount of parallelism available among the instructions*—This determines whether independent instructions can be found to execute. If each instruction depends on its predecessor, no dynamic scheduling scheme can reduce stalls. If the instructions in the pipeline simultaneously must be chosen from the same basic block (as was true in the 6600), this limit is likely to be quite severe.

2. *The number of scoreboard entries*—This determines how far ahead the pipeline can look for independent instructions. The set of instructions examined as candidates for potential execution is called the *window*. The size of the scoreboard determines the size of the window. In this section, we assume a window

does not extend beyond a branch, so the window (and the scoreboard) always contains straight-line code from a single basic block. Section 4.6 shows how the window can be extended beyond a branch.

3. *The number and types of functional units*—This determines the importance of structural hazards, which can increase when dynamic scheduling is used.

4. *The presence of antidependences and output dependences*—These lead to WAR and WAW stalls.

This entire chapter focuses on techniques that attack the problem of exposing and better utilizing available ILP. The second and third factors can be attacked by increasing the size of the scoreboard and the number of functional units; however, these changes have cost implications and may also affect cycle time. WAW and WAR hazards become more important in dynamically scheduled processors, because the pipeline exposes more name dependences. WAW hazards also become more important if we use dynamic scheduling with a branch prediction scheme that allows multiple iterations of a loop to overlap.

The next subsection looks at a technique called *register renaming* that dynamically eliminates name dependences so as to avoid WAR and WAW hazards. Register renaming does this by replacing the register names (such as those kept in the scoreboard) with the names of a larger set of virtual registers. The register renaming scheme also is the basis for implementing forwarding.

Another Dynamic Scheduling Approach— The Tomasulo Approach

Another approach to allow execution to proceed in the presence of hazards was used by the IBM 360/91 floating-point unit. This scheme was invented by Robert Tomasulo and is named after him. Tomasulo's scheme combines key elements of the scoreboarding scheme with the introduction of register renaming. There are many variations on this scheme, though the key concept of renaming registers to avoid WAR and WAW hazards is the most common characteristic.

The IBM 360/91 was completed about three years after the CDC 6600, just before caches appeared in commercial processors. IBM's goal was to achieve high floating-point performance from an instruction set and from compilers designed for the entire 360 computer family, rather than from specialized compilers for the high-end processors. The 360 architecture had only four double-precision floating-point registers, which limits the effectiveness of compiler scheduling; this fact was another motivation for the Tomasulo approach. In addition, the IBM 360/91 had long memory accesses and long floating-point delays, which Tomasulo's algorithm was designed to overcome. At the end of the section, we will see that Tomasulo's algorithm can also support the overlapped execution of multiple iterations of a loop.

We explain the algorithm, which focuses on the floating-point unit, in the context of a pipelined, floating-point unit for DLX. The primary difference between DLX and the 360 is the presence of register-memory instructions in the latter processor. Because Tomasulo's algorithm uses a load functional unit, no significant changes are needed to add register-memory addressing modes. The primary addition is another bus. The IBM 360/91 also had pipelined functional units, rather than multiple functional units. The only difference between these is that a pipelined unit can start at most one operation per clock cycle. Since there are really no fundamental differences, we describe the algorithm as if there were multiple functional units. The IBM 360/91 could accommodate three operations for the floating-point adder and two for the floating-point multiplier. In addition, up to six floating-point loads, or memory references, and up to three floating-point stores could be outstanding. Load data buffers and store data buffers are used for this function. Although we will not discuss the load and store units, we do need to include the buffers for operands.

Tomasulo's scheme shares many ideas with the scoreboard scheme, so we assume that you understand the scoreboard thoroughly. In the last section, we saw how a compiler could rename registers to avoid WAW and WAR hazards. In Tomasulo's scheme this functionality is provided by the *reservation stations*, which buffer the operands of instructions waiting to issue, and by the issue logic. The basic idea is that a reservation station fetches and buffers an operand as soon as it is available, eliminating the need to get the operand from a register. In addition, pending instructions designate the reservation station that will provide their input. Finally, when successive writes to a register appear, only the last one is actually used to update the register. As instructions are issued, the register specifiers for pending operands are renamed to the names of the reservation station in a process called *register renaming*. This combination of issue logic and reservation stations provides renaming and eliminates WAW and WAR hazards. This additional capability is the major conceptual difference between scoreboarding and Tomasulo's algorithm. Since there can be more reservation stations than real registers, the technique can eliminate hazards that could not be eliminated by a compiler. As we explore the components of Tomasulo's scheme, we will return to the topic of register renaming and see exactly how the renaming occurs and how it eliminates hazards.

In addition to the use of register renaming, there are two other significant differences in the organization of Tomasulo's scheme and scoreboarding. First, hazard detection and execution control are distributed: The reservation stations at each functional unit control when an instruction can begin execution at that unit. This function is centralized in the scoreboard. Second, results are passed directly to functional units from the reservation stations where they are buffered, rather than going through the registers. This is done with a common result bus that allows all units waiting for an operand to be loaded simultaneously (on the 360/91 this is called the *common data bus* or CDB). In comparison, the scoreboard writes results into registers, where waiting functional units may have to contend for them. The number of result buses in either the scoreboard or Tomasulo's scheme can be varied. In the actual implementations, the CDC 6600 had multiple completion buses (two in the floating-point unit), while the IBM 360/91 had only one.

Figure 4.8 shows the basic structure of a Tomasulo-based floating-point unit for DLX; none of the execution control tables are shown. The reservation stations hold instructions that have been issued and are awaiting execution at a functional unit, the operands for that instruction if they have already been computed or the source of the operands otherwise, as well as the information needed to control the instruction once it has begun execution at the unit. The load buffers and store buffers hold data or addresses coming from and going to memory. The floating-point registers are connected by a pair of buses to the functional units and by a single bus to the store buffers. All results from the functional units and from memory are sent on the common data bus which goes everywhere except to the load buffer. All the buffers and reservation stations have tag fields, employed by hazard control.

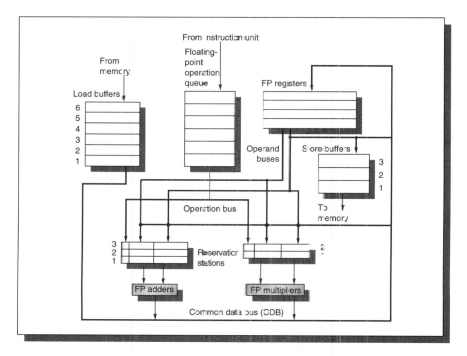

FIGURE 4.8 The basic structure of a DLX FP unit using Tomasulo's algorithm. Floating-point operations are sent from the instruction unit into a queue when they are issued. The reservation stations include the operation and the actual operands, as well as information used for detecting and resolving hazards. There are load buffers to hold the results of outstanding loads that are waiting for the CDB. Similarly, store buffers are used to hold the destination memory addresses of outstanding stores waiting for their operands. All results from either the FP units or the load unit are put on the CDB, which goes to the FP register file as well as to the reservation stations and store buffers. The FP adders implement addition and subtraction, while the FP multipliers do multiplication and division.

Before we describe the details of the reservation stations and the algorithm, let's look at the steps an instruction goes through—just as we did for the scoreboard. Since operands are transmitted differently than in a scoreboard, there are only three steps:

1. *Issue*—Get an instruction from the floating-point operation queue. If the operation is a floating-point operation, issue it if there is an empty reservation station, and send the operands to the reservation station if they are in the registers. If the operation is a load or store, it can issue if there is an available buffer. If there is not an empty reservation station or an empty buffer, then there is a structural hazard and the instruction stalls until a station or buffer is freed. This step also performs the process of renaming registers.

2. *Execute*—If one or more of the operands is not yet available, monitor the CDB while waiting for it to be computed. When an operand becomes available, it is placed into the corresponding reservation station. When both operands are available, execute the operation. This step checks for RAW hazards.

3. *Write result*—When the result is available, write it on the CDB and from there into the registers, into any reservation stations waiting for this result, and to any waiting store buffers.

Although these steps are fundamentally similar to those in the scoreboard, there are three important differences. First, there is no checking for WAW and WAR hazards—these are eliminated when the register operands are renamed during issue. Second, the CDB is used to broadcast results rather than waiting on the registers. Third, the loads and stores are treated as basic functional units.

The data structures used to detect and eliminate hazards are attached to the reservation stations, the register file, and the load and store buffers. Although different information is attached to different objects, everything except the load buffers contains a tag field per entry. These tags are essentially names for an extended set of virtual registers used in renaming. In this example, the tag field is a four-bit quantity that denotes one of the five reservation stations or one of the six load buffers; as we will see this produces the equivalent of eleven registers that can be designated as result registers (as opposed to the four double-precision registers that the 360 architecture contains). In a processor with more real registers, we would want renaming to provide an even larger set of virtual registers. The tag field describes which reservation station contains the instruction that will produce a result needed as a source operand. Once an instruction has issued and is waiting for a result, it refers to the operand by the reservation station number, rather than by the number of the destination register written by the instruction producing the value. Unused values, such as zero, indicate that the operand is already available in the registers. Because there are more reservation stations than actual register numbers, WAW and WAR hazards are eliminated by renaming results using reservation station numbers. Although in Tomasulo's scheme the reservation stations are used as the extended virtual registers, other approaches could use a register set with additional registers or a structure like the reorder buffer, which we will see in section 4.6.

In describing the operation of this scheme, scoreboard terminology is used wherever this will not lead to confusion. The terminology used by the IBM 360/91 is also shown, for historical reference. It is important to remember that the tags in the Tomasulo scheme refer to the buffer or unit that will produce a result; the register names are discarded when an instruction issues to a reservation station.

Each reservation station has six fields:

Op—The operation to perform on source operands S1 and S2.

Qj, Qk—The reservation stations that will produce the corresponding source operand; a value of zero indicates that the source operand is already available in Vj or Vk, or is unnecessary. (The IBM 360/91 calls these SINKunit and SOURCEunit.)

Vj, Vk—The value of the source operands. These are called SINK and SOURCE on the IBM 360/91. Note that only one of the V field or the Q field is valid for each operand.

Busy—Indicates that this reservation station and its accompanying functional unit are occupied.

The register file and store buffer each have a field, Qi:

Qi—The number of the reservation station that contains the operation whose result should be stored into this register or into memory. If the value of Qi is blank (or 0), no currently active instruction is computing a result destined for this register or buffer. For a register, this means the value is simply the register contents.

The load and store buffers each require a busy field, indicating when a buffer is available because of completion of a load or store assigned there; the register file will have a blank Qi field when it is not busy.

Before we examine the algorithm in detail, let's see what the information tables look like for the following code sequence:

```
1.    LD      F6,34(R2)
2.    LD      F2,45(R3)
3.    MULTD   F0,F2,F4
4.    SUBD    F8,F6,F2
5.    DIVD    F10,F0,F6
6.    ADDD    F6,F8,F2
```

We saw what the scoreboard looked like for this program when only the first load had written its result. Figure 4.9 depicts the reservation stations and the register tags. The numbers appended to the names add, mult, and load stand for the tag for that reservation station—Add1 is the tag for the result from the first add unit. In addition we have included an instruction status table. This table is included only to help you understand the algorithm; it is *not* actually a part of the hardware. Instead, the state of each operation that has issued is kept in a reservation station.

Instruction		Instruction status		
		Issue	Execute	Write result
LD	F6,34(R2)	√	√	√
LD	F2,45(R3)	√	√	
MULTD	F0,F2,F4	√		
SUBD	F8,F6,F2	√		
DIVD	F10,F0,F6	√		
ADDD	F6,F8,F2	√		

Reservation stations						
Name	Busy	Op	Vj	Vk	Qj	Qk
Add1	Yes	SUB	Mem[34+Regs[R2]]			Load2
Add2	Yes	ADD			Add1	Load2
Add3	No					
Mult1	Yes	MULT		Regs[F4]	Load2	
Mult2	Yes	DIV		Mem[34+Regs[R2]]	Mult1	

Register status									
Field	F0	F2	F4	F6	F8	F10	F12	...	F30
Qi	Mult1	Load2		Add2	Add1	Mult2			

FIGURE 4.9   Reservation stations and register tags. All of the instructions have issued, but only the first load instruction has completed and written its result to the CDB. The instruction status table is not actually present, but the equivalent information is distributed throughout the hardware. The Vj and Vk fields show the value of an operand in our hardware description language. The load and store buffers are not shown. Load buffer 2 is the only busy load buffer and it is performing on behalf of instruction 2 in the sequence—loading from memory address R3 + 45. Remember that an operand is specified by either a Q field or a V field at any time.

There are two important differences from scoreboards that are immediately observable in these tables. First, the value of an operand is stored in the reservation station in one of the V fields as soon as it is available; it is not read from the register file nor from a reservation station once the instruction has issued. Second, the ADDD instruction, which was blocked in the scoreboard by a WAR hazard at the WB stage, has issued and could complete before the DIVD initiates.

The major advantages of the Tomasulo scheme are (1) the distribution of the hazard detection logic, and (2) the elimination of stalls for WAW and WAR hazards. The first advantage arises from the distributed reservation stations and the use of the CDB. If multiple instructions are waiting on a single result, and each instruction already has its other operand, then the instructions can be released simultaneously by the broadcast on the CDB. In the scoreboard the waiting instructions must all read their results from the registers when register buses are available.

WAW and WAR hazards are eliminated by renaming registers using the reservation stations, and by the process of storing operands into the reservation station as soon as they are available. For example, in our code sequence in Figure 4.9 we have issued both the DIVD and the ADDD, even though there is a WAR hazard involving F6. The hazard is eliminated in one of two ways. First, if the instruction providing the value for the DIVD has completed, then Vk will store the result, allowing DIVD to execute independent of the ADDD (this is the case shown).

On the other hand, if the LD had not completed, then Qk would point to the Load1 reservation station, and the DIVD instruction would be independent of the ADDD. Thus, in either case, the ADDD can issue and begin executing. Any uses of the result of the DIVD would point to the reservation station, allowing the ADDD to complete and store its value into the registers without affecting the DIVD. We'll see an example of the elimination of a WAW hazard shortly. But let's first look at how our earlier example continues execution.

EXAMPLE   Assume the same latencies for the floating-point functional units as we did for Figure 4.6: Add is 2 clock cycles, multiply is 10 clock cycles, and divide is 40 clock cycles. With the same code segment, show what the status tables look like when the MULTD is ready to write its result.

ANSWER   The result is shown in the three tables in Figure 4.10. Unlike the example with the scoreboard, ADDD has completed since the operands of DIVD are copied, thereby overcoming the WAR hazard. Notice that even if the load of F6 was delayed, the add into F6 could be executed without triggering a WAW hazard.

Instruction		Instruction status		
Instruction		**Issue**	**Execute**	**Write result**
LD	F6,34(R2)	√	√	√
LD	F2,45(R3)	√	√	√
MULTD	F0,F2,F4	√	√	
SUBD	F8,F6,F2	√	√	√
DIVD	F10,F0,F6	√		
ADDD	F6,F8,F2	√	√	√

Reservation stations						
Name	**Busy**	**Op**	**Vj**	**Vk**	**Qj**	**Qk**
Add1	No					
Add2	No					
Add3	No					
Mult1	Yes	MULT	Mem[45+Regs[R3]]	Regs[F4]		
Mult2	Yes	DIV		Mem[34+Regs[R2]]	Mult1	

Register status									
Field	**F0**	**F2**	**F4**	**F6**	**F8**	**F10**	**F12**	**...**	**F30**
Qi	Mult1					Mult2			

FIGURE 4.10   Multiply and divide are the only instructions not finished. This is different from the scoreboard case, because the elimination of WAR hazards allowed the ADDD to finish right after the SUBD on which it depended.

■

Figure 4.11 gives the steps that each instruction must go through. Load and stores are only slightly special. A load can execute as soon as it is available. When execution is completed and the CDB is available, a load puts its result on the CDB like any functional unit. Stores receive their values from the CDB or from the register file and execute autonomously; when they are done they turn the busy field off to indicate availability, just like a load buffer or reservation station.

To understand the full power of eliminating WAW and WAR hazards through dynamic renaming of registers, we must look at a loop. Consider the following simple sequence for multiplying the elements of an array by a scalar in F2:

```
Loop:   LD      F0,0(R1)
        MULTD   F4,F0,F2
        SD      0(R1),F4
        SUBI    R1,R1,#8
        BNEZ    R1,Loop    ; branches if R1≠0
```

Instruction status	Wait until	Action or bookkeeping

Issue	Station or buffer empty	`if (Register[S1].Qi ≠0)`
		`    {RS[r].Qj← Register[S1].Qi}`
		`else {RS[r].Vj←S1; RS[r].Qj← 0};`
		`if (Register[S2].Qi≠0)`
		`    {RS[r].Qk← Register[S2].Qi}`
		`else {RS[r].Vk←S2; RS[r].Qk← 0};`
		`RS[r].Busy← yes;`
		`Register[D].Qi=r;`

Execute	(RS[r].Qj=0) and (RS[r].Qk=0)	None—operands are in Vj and Vk

Write result	Execution completed at r and CDB available	`∀x(if (Register[x].Qi=r)    {Fx← result;`
		`    Register[x].Qi← 0});`
		`∀x(if (RS[x].Qj=r) {RS[x].Vj← result;`
		`    RS[x].Qj ← 0});`
		`∀x(if (RS[x].Qk=r) {RS[x].Vk← result;`
		`    RS[x].Qk← 0});`
		`∀x(if (Store[x].Qi=r) {Store[x].V← result;`
		`    Store[x].Qi ← 0});`
		`RS[r].Busy← No`

FIGURE 4.11 Steps in the algorithm and what is required for each step. For the issuing instruction, D is the destination, S1 and S2 are the source register numbers, and r is the reservation station or buffer that D is assigned to. RS is the reservation-station data structure. The value returned by a reservation station or by the load unit is called result. Register is the register data structure (not the register file), while Store is the store-buffer data structure. When an instruction is issued, the destination register has its Qi field set to the number of the buffer or reservation station to which the instruction is issued. If the operands are available in the registers, they are stored in the V fields. Otherwise, the Q fields are set to indicate the reservation station that will produce the values needed as source operands. The instruction waits at the reservation station until both its operands are available, indicated by zero in the Q fields. The Q fields are set to zero either when this instruction is issued, or when an instruction on which this instruction depends completes and does its write back. When an instruction has finished execution and the CDB is available, it can do its write back. All the buffers, registers, and reservation stations whose value of Qj or Qk is the same as the completing reservation station update their values from the CDB and mark the Q fields to indicate that values have been received. Thus, the CDB can broadcast its result to many destinations in a single clock cycle, and if the waiting instructions have their operands, they can all begin execution on the next clock cycle. There is a subtle timing difficulty that arises in Tomasulo's algorithm; we discuss this in Exercise 4.24.

If we predict that branches are taken, using reservation stations will allow multiple executions of this loop to proceed at once. This advantage is gained without unrolling the loop—in effect, the loop is unrolled dynamically by the hardware. In the 360 architecture, the presence of only four FP registers would severely limit the use of unrolling, since we would generate many WAW and WAR hazards. As we saw earlier on page 227, when we unroll a loop and schedule it to avoid interlocks, many more registers are required. Tomasulo's algorithm supports the overlapped execution of multiple copies of the same loop with only a small number of registers used by the program. The reservation stations extend the real register set via the renaming process.

Let's assume we have issued all the instructions in two successive iterations of the loop, but none of the floating-point loads-stores or operations has completed. The reservation stations, register-status tables, and load and store buffers at this point are shown in Figure 4.12. (The integer ALU operation is ignored, and it is assumed the branch was predicted as taken.) Once the system reaches this state, two copies of the loop could be sustained with a CPI close to 1.0 provided the multiplies could complete in four clock cycles. If we ignore the loop overhead, which is not reduced in this scheme, the performance level achieved matches what we would obtain with compiler unrolling and scheduling, assuming we had enough registers.

An additional element that is critical to making Tomasulo's algorithm work is shown in this example. The load instruction from the second loop iteration could easily complete before the store from the first iteration, although the normal sequential order is different. The load and store can safely be done in a different order, provided the load and store access different addresses. This is checked by examining the addresses in the store buffer whenever a load is issued. If the load address matches the store-buffer address, we must stop and wait until the store buffer gets a value; we can then access it or get the value from memory. This dynamic disambiguation of addresses is an alternative to the techniques that a compiler would use when interchanging a load and store.

This dynamic scheme can yield very high performance, provided the cost of branches can be kept small, an issue we address in the next section. The major drawback of this approach is the complexity of the Tomasulo scheme, which requires a large amount of hardware. In particular, there are many associative stores that must run at high speed, as well as complex control logic. Lastly, the performance gain is limited by the single completion bus (CDB). While additional CDBs can be added, each CDB must interact with all the pipeline hardware, including the reservation stations. In particular, the associative tag-matching hardware would need to be duplicated at each station for each CDB.

In Tomasulo's scheme two different techniques are combined: the renaming of registers to a larger virtual set of registers and the buffering of source operands from the register file. Source operand buffering resolves WAR hazards that arise when the operand is available in the registers. As we will see later, it is also possible to eliminate WAR hazards by the renaming of a register together with the buffering of a result until no outstanding references to the earlier version of the register remain. This approach will be used when we discuss hardware speculation.

Tomasulo's scheme is appealing if the designer is forced to pipeline an architecture for which it is difficult to schedule code or that has a shortage of registers. On the other hand, the advantages of the Tomasulo approach versus compiler scheduling for a efficient single-issue pipeline are probably fewer than the costs of implementation. But, as processors become more aggressive in their issue capability and designers are concerned with the performance of difficult-to-schedule code (such as most nonnumeric code), techniques such as register renaming and dynamic scheduling will become more important. Later in this chapter, we will see that they are one important component of most schemes for incorporating hardware speculation.

The key components for enhancing ILP in Tomasulo's algorithm are dynamic scheduling, register renaming, and dynamic memory disambiguation. It is difficult to assess the value of these features independently. When we examine the studies of ILP in section 4.7, we will look at how these features affect the amount of parallelism discovered.

Corresponding to the dynamic hardware techniques for scheduling around data dependences are dynamic techniques for handling branches efficiently. These techniques are used for two purposes: to predict whether a branch will be taken and to find the target more quickly. *Hardware branch prediction*, the name for these techniques, is the next topic we discuss.

		Instruction status		
Instruction	**From iteration**	**Issue**	**Execute**	**Write result**
LD F0,0(R1)	1	√	√	
MULTD F4,F0,F2	1	√		
SD 0(R1),F4	1	√		
LD F0,0(R1)	2	√	√	
MULTD F4,F0,F2	2	√		
SD 0(R1),F4	2	√		

			Reservation stations			
Name	**Busy**	**Op**	**Vj**	**Vk**	**Qj**	**Qk**
Add1	No					
Add2	No					
Add3	No					
Mult1	Yes	MULT		Regs[F2]	Load1	
Mult2	Yes	MULT		Regs[F2]	Load2	

				Register status				
Field	**F0**	**F2**	**F4**	**F6**	**F8**	**F10**	**F12**	...	**F30**
Qi	Load2		Mult2						

	Load buffers		
Field	**Load 1**	**Load 2**	**Load 3**
Address	Regs[R1]	Regs[R1]-8	
Busy	Yes	Yes	No

	Store buffers		
Field	**Store 1**	**Store 2**	**Store 3**
Qi	Mult1	Mult2	
Busy	Yes	Yes	No
Address	Regs[R1]	Regs[R1]-8	

FIGURE 4.12 Two active iterations of the loop with no instruction yet completed. Load and store buffers are included, with addresses to be loaded from and stored to. The loads are in the load buffer; entries in the multiplier reservation stations indicate that the outstanding loads are the sources. The store buffers indicate that the multiply destination is their value to store.

4.3 | Reducing Branch Penalties with Dynamic Hardware Prediction

The previous section describes techniques for overcoming data hazards. The frequency of branches and jumps demands that we also attack the potential stalls arising from control dependences. Indeed, as the amount of ILP we attempt to exploit grows, control dependences rapidly become the limiting factor. Although schemes in this section are helpful in processors that try to maintain one instruction issue per clock, for two reasons they are *crucial* to any processor that tries to issue more than one instruction per clock. First, branches will arrive up to n times faster in an n-issue processor and providing an instruction stream will probably require that we predict the outcome of branches. Second, Amdahl's Law reminds us that relative impact of the control stalls will be larger with the lower potential CPI in such machines.

In the last chapter, we examined a variety of static schemes for dealing with branches; these schemes are static since the action taken does not depend on the dynamic behavior of the branch. We also examined the delayed branch scheme, which allows software to optimize the branch behavior by scheduling it at compile time. This section focuses on using hardware to dynamically predict the outcome of a branch—the prediction will change if the branch changes its behavior while the program is running.

We start with a simple branch prediction scheme and then examine approaches that increase the accuracy of our branch prediction mechanisms. After that, we look at more elaborate schemes that try to find the instruction following a branch even earlier. The goal of all these mechanisms is to allow the processor to resolve the outcome of a branch early, thus preventing control dependences from causing stalls. The effectiveness of a branch prediction scheme depends not only on the accuracy, but also on the cost of a branch when the prediction is correct and when the prediction is incorrect. These branch penalties depend on the structure of the pipeline, the type of predictor, and the strategies used for recovering from misprediction. Later in this chapter we will look at some typical examples.

Basic Branch Prediction and Branch-Prediction Buffers

The simplest dynamic branch-prediction scheme is a *branch-prediction buffer* or *branch history table*. A branch-prediction buffer is a small memory indexed by the lower portion of the address of the branch instruction. The memory contains a bit that says whether the branch was recently taken or not. This is the simplest sort of buffer; it has no tags and is useful only to reduce the branch delay when it is longer than the time to compute the possible target PCs. We don't know, in fact, if the prediction is correct—it may have been put there by another branch that has the same low-order address bits. But this doesn't matter. The prediction is a hint that is assumed to be correct, and fetching begins in the predicted direction. If the hint turns out to be wrong, the prediction bit is inverted and stored back. Of course, this buffer is effectively a cache where every access is a hit, and, as we will see, the performance of the buffer depends on both how often the prediction is for the branch of interest and how accurate the prediction is when it matches. We can use all the caching techniques to improve the accuracy of finding the prediction matching this branch, as we will see shortly. Before we do that, it is useful to make a small, but important, improvement in the accuracy of the branch prediction scheme.

This simple one-bit prediction scheme has a performance shortcoming: Even if a branch is almost always taken, we will likely predict incorrectly twice, rather than once, when it is not taken. The following example shows this.

EXAMPLE   Consider a loop branch whose behavior is taken nine times in a row, then not taken once. What is the prediction accuracy for this branch, assuming the prediction bit for this branch remains in the prediction buffer?

ANSWER   The steady-state prediction behavior will mispredict on the first and last loop iterations. Mispredicting the last iteration is inevitable since the prediction bit will say taken (the branch has been taken nine times in a row at that point). The misprediction on the first iteration happens because the bit is flipped on prior execution of the last iteration of the loop, since the branch was not taken on that iteration. Thus, the prediction accuracy for this branch that is taken 90% of the time is only 80% (two incorrect predictions and eight correct ones). In general, for branches used to form loops—a branch is taken many times in a row and then not taken once—a one-bit predictor will mispredict at twice the rate that the branch is not taken. Ideally, the accuracy of the predictor would match the taken branch frequency for these highly regular branches. ■

To remedy this, two-bit prediction schemes are often used. In a two-bit scheme, a prediction must miss twice before it is changed. Figure 4.13 shows the finite-state processor for a two-bit prediction scheme.

The two-bit scheme is actually a specialization of a more general scheme that has an n-bit saturating counter for each entry in the prediction buffer. With an n-bit counter, the counter can take on values between 0 and $2^n - 1$: when the counter is greater than or equal to one half of its maximum value (2^{n-1}), the branch is predicted as taken; otherwise, it is predicted untaken. As in the two-bit scheme, the counter is incremented on a taken branch and decremented on an untaken branch. Studies of n-bit predictors have shown that the two-bit predictors do almost as well, and thus most systems rely on two-bit branch predictors rather than the more general n-bit predictors.

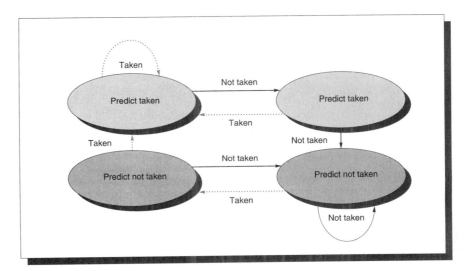

FIGURE 4.13   The states in a two-bit prediction scheme. By using two bits rather than one, a branch that strongly favors taken or not taken—as many branches do—will be mispredicted only once. The two bits are used to encode the four states in the system.

A branch-prediction buffer can be implemented as a small, special "cache" accessed with the instruction address during the IF pipe stage, or as a pair of bits attached to each block in the instruction cache and fetched with the instruction. If the instruction is decoded as a branch and if the branch is predicted as taken, fetching begins from the target as soon as the PC is known. Otherwise, sequential fetching and executing continue. If the prediction turns out to be wrong, the prediction bits are changed as shown in Figure 4.13.

While this scheme is useful for most pipelines, the DLX pipeline finds out both whether the branch is taken and what the target of the branch is at roughly the same time, assuming no hazard in accessing the register specified in the conditional branch. (Remember that this is true for the DLX pipeline because the branch does a compare of a register against zero during the ID stage, which is when the effective address is also computed.) Thus, this scheme does not help for the simple DLX pipeline; we will explore a scheme that can work for DLX a little later. First, let's see how well branch prediction works in general.

What kind of accuracy can be expected from a branch-prediction buffer using two bits per entry on real applications? For the SPEC89 benchmarks a branch-prediction buffer with 4096 entries results in a prediction accuracy ranging from over 99% to 82%, or a *misprediction rate* of 1% to 18%, as shown in Figure 4.14. To show the differences more clearly, we plot misprediction frequency rather than prediction frequency. A 4K-entry buffer, like that used for these results, is considered very large; smaller buffers would have worse results.

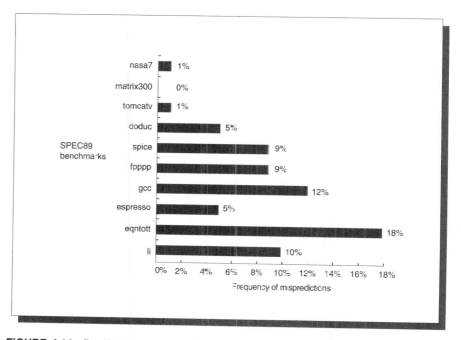

FIGURE 4.14   Prediction accuracy of a 4096-entry two-bit prediction buffer for the SPEC89 benchmarks. The misprediction rate for the integer benchmarks (gcc, espresso, eqntott, and li) is substantially higher (average of 11%) than that for the FP programs (average of 4%). Even omitting the FP kernels (nasa7, matrix300, and tomcatv) still yields a higher accuracy for the FP benchmarks than for the integer benchmarks. These data, as well as the rest of the data in this section, are taken from a branch prediction study done using the IBM Power architecture and optimized code for that system. See Pan et al. [1992].

Knowing just the prediction accuracy, as shown in Figure 4.14, is not enough to determine the performance impact of branches, even given the branch costs and penalties for misprediction. We also need to take into account the branch frequency, since the importance of accurate prediction is larger in programs with higher branch frequency. For example, the integer programs—li, eqntott, espresso, and gcc—have higher branch frequencies than those of the more easily predicted FP programs.

As we try to exploit more ILP, the accuracy of our branch prediction becomes critical. As we can see in Figure 4.14, the accuracy of the predictors for integer programs, which typically also have higher branch frequencies, is lower than for the loop-intensive scientific programs. We can attack this problem in two ways: by increasing the size of the buffer and by increasing the accuracy of the scheme we use for each prediction. A buffer with 4K entries is already quite large and, as Figure 4.15 shows, performs quite comparably to an infinite buffer. The data in Figure 4.15 make it clear that the hit rate of the buffer is not the limiting factor.

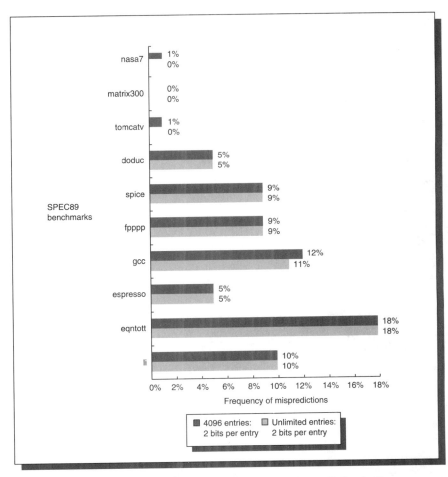

FIGURE 4.15   Prediction accuracy of a 4096-entry two-bit prediction buffer versus an infinite buffer for the SPEC89 benchmarks.

As we mentioned above, increasing the number of bits per predictor also has little impact.

These two-bit predictor schemes use only the recent behavior of a branch to predict the future behavior of that branch. It may be possible to improve the prediction accuracy if we also look at the recent behavior of *other* branches rather than just the branch we are trying to predict. Consider a small code fragment from the SPEC92 benchmark eqntott (the worst case for the two-bit predictor):

```
if (aa==2)
        aa=0;
if (bb==2)
        bb=0;
if (aa!=bb) {
```

Here is the DLX code that we would typically generate for this code fragment assuming that aa and bb are assigned to registers R1 and R2:

```
            SUBUI(3x)   R3,R1,#2
            BNEZ        R3,L1      ;branch b1   (aa!=2)
            ADD         R1,R0,R0   ;aa=0
    L1:     SUBUI(3x)   R3,R2,#2
            BNEZ        R3,L2      ;branch b2   (bb!=2)
            ADD         R2,R0,R0   ;bb=0
    L2:     SUBU(1x)    R3,R1,R2   ;R3=aa-bb
            BEQZ        R3,L3      ;branch b3   (aa==bb)
```

Let's label these branches b1, b2, and b3. The key observation is that the behavior of branch b3 is correlated with the behavior of branches b1 and b2. Clearly, if branches b1 and b2 are both not taken (i.e., the if conditions both evaluate to true and aa and bb are both assigned 0), then b3 will be taken, since aa and bb are clearly equal. A predictor that uses only the behavior of a single branch to predict the outcome of that branch can never capture this behavior.

Branch predictors that use the behavior of other branches to make a prediction are called *correlating predictors* or *two-level predictors*. To see how such predictors work, let's choose a simple hypothetical case. Consider the following simplified code fragment (chosen for illustrative purposes):

```
if  (d==0)
        d=1;
if  (d==1)
```

Here is the typical code sequence generated for this fragment, assuming that d is assigned to R1:

```
            BNEZ        R1,L1      ;branch b1 (d!=0)
            ADDI        R1,R0,#1   ;d==0, so d=1
    L1:     SUBUI(3x)   R3,R1,#1
            BNEZ        R3,L2      ;branch b2 (d!=1)
    ...
    L2:
```

The branches corresponding to the two if statements are labeled b1 and b2. The possible execution sequences for an execution of this fragment, assuming d has values 0, 1, and 2, are shown in Figure 4.16. To illustrate how a correlating predictor works, assume the sequence above is executed repeatedly and ignore other branches in the program (including any branch needed to cause the above sequence to repeat).

Initial value of d	d==0?	b1	Value of d before b2	d==1?	b2
0	Yes	Not taken	1	Yes	Not taken
1	No	Taken	1	Yes	Not taken
2	No	Taken	2	No	Taken

FIGURE 4.16   Possible execution sequences for a code fragment.

From Figure 4.16, we see that if b1 is not taken, then b2 will be not taken. A correlating predictor can take advantage of this, but our standard predictor cannot. Rather than consider all possible branch paths, consider a sequence where d alternates between 2 and 0. A one-bit predictor initialized to not taken has the behavior shown in Figure 4.17. As the figure shows, *all* the branches are mispredicted!

d=?	b1 prediction	b1 action	New b1 prediction	b2 prediction	b2 action	New b2 prediction
2	NT	T	T	NT	T	T
0	T	NT	NT	T	NT	NT
2	NT	T	T	NT	T	T
0	T	NT	NT	T	NT	NT

FIGURE 4.17   Behavior of a one-bit predictor initialized to not taken. T stands for taken, NT for not taken.

Alternatively, consider a predictor that uses one bit of correlation. The easiest way to think of this is that every branch has two separate prediction bits: one prediction assuming the last branch executed was not taken and another prediction that is used if the last branch executed was taken. Note that, in general, the last branch executed is *not* the same instruction as the branch being predicted, though this can occur in simple loops consisting of a single basic block (since there are no other branches in the loops).

We write the pair of prediction bits together, with the first bit being the prediction if the last branch in the program is not taken and the second bit being the prediction if the last branch in the program is taken. The four possible combinations and the meanings are listed in Figure 4.18.

Prediction bits	Prediction if last branch not taken	Prediction if last branch taken
NT/NT	Not taken	Not taken
NT/T	Not taken	Taken
T/NT	Taken	Not taken
T/T	Taken	Taken

FIGURE 4.18   Combinations and meaning of the taken/not taken prediction bits. T stands for taken, NT for not taken.

The action of the one-bit predictor with one bit of correlation, when initialized to NT/NT is shown in Figure 4.19.

d=?	b1 prediction	b1 action	New b1 prediction	b2 prediction	b2 action	New b2 prediction
2	NT/NT	T	T/NT	NT/NT	T	NT/T
0	T/NT	NT	T/NT	NT/T	NT	NT/T
2	T/NT	T	T/NT	NT/T	T	NT/T
0	T/NT	NT	T/NT	NT/T	NT	NT/T

FIGURE 4.19 The action of the one-bit predictor with one bit of correlation, initialized to not taken/not taken. T stands for taken, NT for not taken. The prediction used is shown in bold

In this case, the only misprediction is on the first iteration, when d = 2. The correct prediction of b1 is because of the choice of values for d, since b1 is not obviously correlated with the previous prediction of b2. The correct prediction of b2, however, shows the advantage of correlating predictors. Even if we had chosen different values for d, the predictor for b2 would correctly predict the case when b1 is not taken on every execution of b2 after one initial incorrect prediction.

The predictor in Figures 4.18 and 4.19 is called a (1,1) predictor since it uses the behavior of the last branch to choose from among a pair of one-bit branch predictors. In the general case an (m,n) predictor uses the behavior of the last m branches to choose from 2^m branch predictors, each of which is a n-bit predictor for a single branch. The attraction of this type of correlating branch predictor is that it can yield higher prediction rates than the two-bit scheme and requires only a trivial amount of additional hardware. The simplicity of the hardware comes from a simple observation: The global history of the most recent m branches can be recorded in an m-bit shift register, where each bit records whether the branch was taken or not taken. The branch-prediction buffer can then be indexed using a concatenation of the low-order bits from the branch address with the m-bit global history. For example, Figure 4.20 shows a (2,2) predictor and how the prediction is accessed.

There is one subtle effect in this implementation. Because the prediction buffer is not a cache, the counters indexed by a single value of the global predictor may in fact correspond to different branches at some point in time. This is no different from our earlier observation that the prediction may not correspond to the current branch. In Figure 4.20 we draw the buffer as a two-dimensional object to ease understanding. In reality, the buffer can simply be implemented as a linear memory array that is two bits wide; the indexing is done by concatenating the global history bits and the number of required bits from the branch address. For the example in Figure 4.20, a (2,2) buffer with 64 total entries, the four low-order address bits of the branch (word address) and the two global bits form a six-bit index that can be used to index the 64 counters.

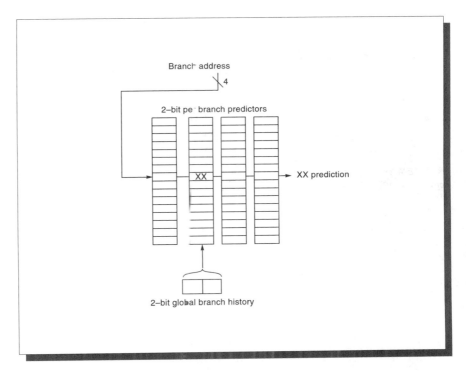

FIGURE 4.20   A (2,2) branch-prediction buffer uses a two-bit global history to choose from among four predictors for each branch address. Each predictor is in turn a two-bit predictor for that particular branch. The branch-prediction buffer shown here has a total of 64 entries; the branch address is used to choose four of these entries and the global history is used to choose one of the four. The two-bit global history can be implemented as a shifter register that simply shifts in the behavior of a branch as soon as it is known.

How much better do the correlating branch predictors work when compared with the standard two-bit scheme? To compare them fairly, we must compare predictors that use the same number of state bits. The number of bits in an (m,n) predictor is

$$2^m \times n \times \text{Number of prediction entries selected by the branch address}$$

A two-bit predictor with no global history is simply a (0,2) predictor.

EXAMPLE   How many bits are in the (0,2) branch predictor we examined earlier? How many bits are in the branch predictor shown in Figure 4.20?

ANSWER   The earlier predictor had 4K entries selected by the branch address. Thus the total number of bits is

$$2^0 \times 2 \times 4K = 8K.$$

The predictor in Figure 4.20 has

$$2^2 \times 2 \times 16 = 128 \text{ bits}$$

∎

To compare the performance of a correlating predictor with that of our simple two-bit predictor examined in Figure 4.14, we need to determine how many entries we should assume for the correlating predictor.

EXAMPLE   How many branch-selected entries are in a (2,2) predictor that has a total of 8K bits in the prediction buffer?

ANSWER   We know that

$$2^2 \times 2 \times \text{Number of prediction entries selected by the branch} = 8K.$$

Hence

$$\text{Number of prediction entries selected by the branch} = 1K.$$

∎

Figure 4.21 compares the performance of the earlier two-bit simple predictor with 4K entries and a (2,2) predictor with 1K entries. As you can see, this predictor not only outperforms a simple two-bit predictor with the same total number of state bits, it often outperforms a two-bit predictor with an unlimited number of entries.

There are a wide spectrum of correlating predictors, with the (0,2) and (2,2) predictors being among the most interesting. The Exercises ask you to explore the performance of a third extreme: a predictor that does not rely on the branch address. For example, a (12,2) predictor that has a total of 8K bits does not use the branch address in indexing the predictor, but instead relies solely on the global branch history. Surprisingly, this degenerate case can outperform a noncorrelating two-bit predictor if enough global history is used and the table is large enough!

Further Reducing Control Stalls: Branch-Target Buffers

To reduce the branch penalty on DLX, we need to know from what address to fetch by the end of IF. This means we must know whether the as-yet-undecoded instruction is a branch and, if so, what the next PC should be. If the instruction is a branch and we know what the next PC should be, we can have a branch penalty of zero. A branch-prediction cache that stores the predicted address for the next instruction after a branch is called a *branch-target buffer* or *branch-target cache*.

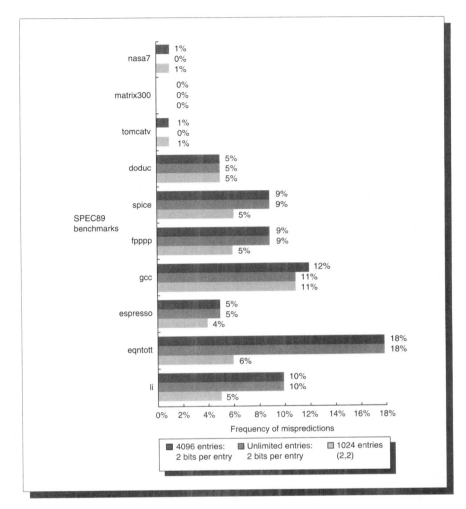

FIGURE 4.21   Comparison of two-bit predictors. A noncorrelating predictor for 4096 bits is first, followed by a noncorrelating two-bit predictor with unlimited entries and a two-bit predictor with two bits of global history and a total of 1024 entries.

For the standard DLX pipeline, a branch-*prediction* buffer is accessed during the ID cycle, so that at the end of ID we know the branch-target address (since it is computed during ID), the fall-through address (computed during IF), and the prediction. Thus, by the end of ID we know enough to fetch the next predicted instruction. For a branch-*target* buffer, we access the buffer during the IF stage using the instruction address of the fetched instruction, a possible branch, to index the buffer. If we get a hit, then we know the predicted instruction address at the end of the IF cycle, which is one cycle earlier than for a branch-prediction buffer.

Because we are predicting the next instruction address and will send it out *before* decoding the instruction, we *must* know whether the fetched instruction is predicted as a taken branch. Figure 4.22 shows what the branch-target buffer looks like. If the PC of the fetched instruction matches a PC in the buffer, then the corresponding predicted PC is used as the next PC. In Chapter 5 we will discuss caches in much more detail; we will see that the hardware for this branch-target buffer is essentially identical to the hardware for a cache.

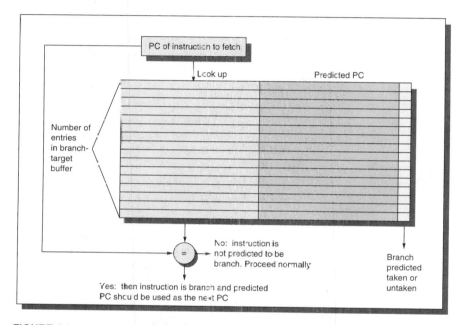

FIGURE 4.22 A branch-target buffer. The PC of the instruction being fetched is matched against a set of instruction addresses stored in the first column; these represent the addresses of known branches. If the PC matches one of these entries, then the instruction being fetched is a taken branch, and the second field, predicted PC, contains the prediction for the next PC after the branch. Fetching begins immediately at that address. The third field, which is optional, may be used for extra prediction state bits.

If a matching entry is found in the branch-target buffer, fetching begins immediately at the predicted PC. Note that (unlike a branch-prediction buffer) the entry must be for this instruction, because the predicted PC will be sent out before it is known whether this instruction is even a branch. If we did not check whether the entry matched this PC, then the wrong PC would be sent out for instructions that were not branches, resulting in a slower processor. We only need to store the predicted-taken branches in the branch-target buffer, since an untaken branch follows the same strategy (fetch the next sequential instruction) as a nonbranch. Complications arise when we are using a two-bit predictor, since this requires that we store information for both taken and untaken branches. One way to resolve this is to use both a target buffer and a prediction buffer, which is the solution used by the PowerPC 620—the topic of section 4.8. We assume that the buffer only holds PC-relative conditional branches, since this makes the target address a constant; it is not hard to extend the mechanism to work with indirect branches.

Figure 4.23 shows the steps followed when using a branch-target buffer and where these steps occur in the pipeline. From this we can see that there will be no branch delay if a branch-prediction entry is found in the buffer and is correct. Otherwise, there will be a penalty of at least two clock cycles. In practice, this penalty could be larger, since the branch-target buffer must be updated. We could assume that the instruction following a branch or at the branch target is not a branch, and do the update during that instruction time; however, this does complicate the control. Instead, we will take a two-clock-cycle penalty when the branch is not correctly predicted or when we get a miss in the buffer. Dealing with the mispredictions and misses is a significant challenge, since we typically will have to halt instruction fetch while we rewrite the buffer entry. Thus, we would like to make this process fast to minimize the penalty.

To evaluate how well a branch-target buffer works, we first must determine the penalties in all possible cases. Figure 4.24 contains this information.

EXAMPLE   Determine the total branch penalty for a branch-target buffer assuming the penalty cycles for individual mispredictions from Figure 4.24. Make the following assumptions about the prediction accuracy and hit rate:

- prediction accuracy is 90%

- hit rate in the buffer is 90%

ANSWER   Using a 60% taken branch frequency, this yields the following:

$$\text{Branch penalty} = \text{Percent buffer hit rate} \times \text{Percent incorrect predictions} \times 2$$
$$+ (1 - \text{Percent buffer hit rate}) \times \text{Taken branches} \times 2$$
$$\text{Branch penalty} = (90\% \times 10\% \times 2)$$
$$+ (10\% \times 60\% \times 2)$$
$$\text{Branch penalty} = 0.18 + 0.12 = 0.30 \text{ clock cycles}$$

This compares with a branch penalty for delayed branches, which we evaluated in section 3.5 of the last chapter, of about 0.5 clock cycles per branch. Remember, though, that the improvement from dynamic branch prediction will grow as the branch delay grows; in addition, better predictors will yield a larger performance advantage.   ■

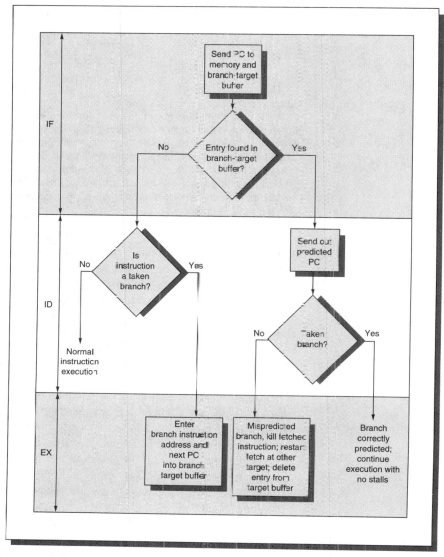

FIGURE 4.23 The steps involved in handling an instruction with a branch-target buffer. f the PC of an instruction is found in the buffer, then the instruction must be a branch that is predicted taken; thus, fetching immediately begins from the predicted PC in ID. If the entry is not found and it subsequently turns out to be a taken branch, it is entered in the buffer along with the target, which is known at the end of ID. f the entry is found, but the instruction turns out not to be a taken branch, it is removed from the buffer. If the instruction is a branch, is found, and is correctly predicted, then execution proceeds with no delays. If the prediction is incorrect, we suffer a one-clock-cycle delay fetching the wrong instruction and restart the fetch one clock cycle later, leading to a total mispredict penalty of two clock cycles. If the branch is not found in the buffer and the instruction turns out to be a branch, we will have proceeded as if the instruction were a branch and can turn this into an assume-not-taken strategy. The penalty will differ depending on whether the branch is actually taken or not.

Instruction in buffer	Prediction	Actual branch	Penalty cycles
Yes	Taken	Taken	0
Yes	Taken	Not taken	2
No		Taken	2
No		Not taken	0

FIGURE 4.24   Penalties for all possible combinations of whether the branch is in the buffer and what it actually does, assuming we store only taken branches in the buffer. There is no branch penalty if everything is correctly predicted and the branch is found in the target buffer. If the branch is not correctly predicted, the penalty is equal to one clock cycle to update the buffer with the correct information (during which an instruction cannot be fetched) and one clock cycle, if needed, to restart fetching the next correct instruction for the branch. If the branch is not found and taken, a two-cycle penalty is encountered, during which time the buffer is updated.

One variation on the branch-target buffer is to store one or more *target instructions* instead of, or in addition to, the predicted *target address*. This variation has two potential advantages. First, it allows the branch-target buffer access to take longer than the time between successive instruction fetches. This could allow a larger branch-target buffer. Second, buffering the actual target instructions allows us to perform an optimization called *branch folding*. Branch folding can be used to obtain zero-cycle unconditional branches, and sometimes zero-cycle conditional branches. Consider a branch-target buffer that buffers instructions from the predicted path and is being accessed with the address of an unconditional branch. The only function of the unconditional branch is to change the PC. Thus, when the branch-target buffer signals a hit and indicates that the branch is unconditional, the pipeline can simply substitute the instruction from the branch-target buffer in place of the instruction that is returned from the cache (which is the unconditional branch). If the processor is issuing multiple instructions per cycle, then the buffer will need to supply multiple instructions to obtain the maximum benefit. In some cases, it may be possible to eliminate the cost of a conditional branch when the condition codes are preset; we will see how this scheme can be used in the IBM PowerPC processor in the *Putting It All Together* section.

Another method that designers have studied and are including in the most recent processors is a technique for predicting indirect jumps, that is, jumps whose destination address varies at runtime. While high-level language programs will generate such jumps for indirect procedure calls, select or case statements, and FORTRAN-computed gotos, the vast majority of the indirect jumps come from procedure returns. For example, for the SPEC benchmarks procedure returns account for 85% of the indirect jumps on average. Thus, focusing on procedure returns seems appropriate.

Though procedure returns can be predicted with a branch-target buffer, the accuracy of such a prediction technique can be low if the procedure is called from multiple sites and the calls from one site are not clustered in time. To overcome this problem, the concept of a small buffer of return addresses operating as a stack has been proposed. This structure caches the most recent return addresses: pushing a return address on the stack at a call and popping one off at a return. If the cache is sufficiently large (i.e., as large as the maximum call depth), it will predict the returns perfectly. Figure 4.25 shows the performance of such a return buffer with 1–16 elements for a number of the SPEC benchmarks. We will use this type of return predictor when we examine the studies of ILP in section 4.7.

Branch prediction schemes are limited both by prediction accuracy and by the penalty for misprediction. As we have seen, typical prediction schemes achieve prediction accuracy in the range of 80–95% depending on the type of program and the size of the buffer. In addition to trying to increase the accuracy of the predictor, we can try to reduce the penalty for misprediction. This is done by fetching from both the predicted and unpredicted direction. This requires that the memory system be dual-ported, have an interleaved cache, or fetch from one path and then the other. While this adds cost to the system, it may be the only way to reduce branch penalties below a certain point. Caching addresses or instructions from multiple paths in the target buffer is another alternative that some processors have used.

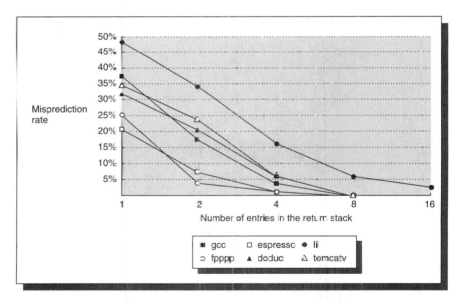

FIGURE 4.25 Prediction accuracy for a return address buffer operated as a stack. The accuracy is the fraction of return addresses predicted correctly. Since call depths are typically not large, with some exceptions, a modest buffer works well. On average returns account for 81% of the indirect jumps in these six benchmarks.

We have seen a variety of software-based static schemes and hardware-based dynamic schemes for trying to boost the performance of our pipelined processor. These schemes attack both the data dependences (discussed in the previous subsections) and the control dependences (discussed in this subsection). Our focus to date has been on sustaining the throughput of the pipeline at one instruction per clock. In the next section we will look at techniques that attempt to exploit more parallelism by issuing multiple instructions in a clock cycle.

4.4 | Taking Advantage of More ILP with Multiple Issue

Processors are being produced with the potential for very many parallel operations on the instruction level. ...Far greater extremes in instruction-level parallelism are on the horizon.

> J. Fisher [1981], in the paper that inaugurated
> the term "instruction-level parallelism"

The techniques of the previous two sections can be used to eliminate data and control stalls and achieve an ideal CPI of 1. To improve performance further we would like to decrease the CPI to less than one. But the CPI cannot be reduced below one if we issue only one instruction every clock cycle. The goal of the *multiple-issue processors* discussed in this section is to allow multiple instructions to issue in a clock cycle. Multiple-issue processors come in two flavors: *superscalar* processors and *VLIW* (very long instruction word) processors. Superscalar processors issue varying numbers of instructions per clock and may be either statically scheduled by the compiler or dynamically scheduled using techniques based on scoreboarding and Tomasulo's algorithm. In this section, we examine simple versions of both a statically scheduled superscalar and a dynamically scheduled superscalar. VLIWs, in contrast, issue a fixed number of instructions formatted either as one large instruction or as a fixed instruction packet. VLIW processors are inherently statically scheduled by the compiler. Section 4.5 explores compiler technology useful for scheduling both VLIWs and superscalars.

To explain and compare the techniques in this section we will assume the pipeline latencies we used earlier in section 4.1 (Figure 4.2) and the same example code segment, which adds a scalar to an array in memory:

```
Loop:   LD     F0,0(R1)    ;F0=array element
        ADDD   F4,F0,F2    ;add scalar in F2
        SD     0(R1),F4    ;store result
        SUBI   R1,R1,#8    ;decrement pointer
                           ;8 bytes (per DW)
        BNEZ   R1,LOOP     ; branch R1!=zero
```

We begin by looking at a simple superscalar processor.

A Superscalar Version of DLX

In a typical superscalar processor, the hardware might issue from one to eight instructions in a clock cycle. Usually, these instructions must be independent and will have to satisfy some constraints, such as no more than one memory reference issued per clock. If some instruction in the instruction stream is dependent or doesn't meet the issue criteria, only the instructions preceding that one in sequence will be issued, hence the variability in issue rate. In contrast, in VLIWs, the compiler has complete responsibility for creating a package of instructions that can be simultaneously issued, and the hardware does not dynamically make any decisions about multiple issue. Thus, we say that a superscalar processor has dynamic issue capability, while a VLIW processor has static issue capability. Superscalar processors may also be statically or dynamically scheduled; for now, we assume static scheduling, but we will explore the use of dynamic scheduling in conjunction with speculation in section 4.6.

What would the DLX processor look like as a superscalar? Let's assume two instructions can be issued per clock cycle. One of the instructions can be a load, store, branch, or integer ALU operation, and the other can be any floating-point operation. As we will see, issue of an integer operation in parallel with a floating-point operation is much simpler and less demanding than arbitrary dual issue. This configuration is, in fact, very close to the organization used in the HP 7100 processor.

Issuing two instructions per cycle will require fetching and decoding 64 bits of instructions. To keep the decoding simple, we could require that the instructions be paired and aligned on a 64-bit boundary, with the integer portion appearing first. The alternative is to examine the instructions and possibly swap them when they are sent to the integer or FP datapath; however, this introduces additional requirements for hazard detection. In either case, the second instruction can be issued only if the first instruction can be issued. Remember that the hardware makes this decision dynamically, issuing only the first instruction if the conditions are not met. Figure 4.26 shows how the instructions look as they go into the pipeline in pairs. This table does not address how the floating-point operations extend the EX cycle, but it is no different in the superscalar case than it was for the ordinary DLX pipeline; the concepts of section 3.7 apply directly.

With this pipeline, we have substantially boosted the rate at which we can issue floating-point instructions. To make this worthwhile, however, we need either pipelined floating-point units or multiple independent units. Otherwise, the floating-point datapath will quickly become the bottleneck, and the advantages gained by dual issue will be small.

By issuing an integer and a floating-point operation in parallel, the need for additional hardware, beyond the usual hazard detection logic, is minimized—integer and floating-point operations use different register sets and different functional units on load-store architectures. Furthermore, enforcing the issue restriction as a structural hazard (which it is, since only specific pairs of instructions can

Instruction type	Pipe stages							
Integer instruction	IF	ID	EX	MEM	WB			
FP instruction	IF	ID	EX	MEM	WB			
Integer instruction		IF	ID	EX	MEM	WB		
FP instruction		IF	ID	EX	MEM	WB		
Integer instruction			IF	ID	EX	MEM	WB	
FP instruction			IF	ID	EX	MEM	WB	
Integer instruction				IF	ID	EX	MEM	WB
FP instruction				IF	ID	EX	MEM	WB

FIGURE 4.26   Superscalar pipeline in operation. The integer and floating-point instructions are issued at the same time, and each executes at its own pace through the pipeline. This scheme will only improve the performance of programs with a fair fraction of floating-point operations.

issue), requires only looking at the opcodes. The only difficulties that arise are when the integer instruction is a floating-point load, store, or move. This creates contention for the floating-point register ports and may also create a new RAW hazard when the floating-point operation that could be issued in the same clock cycle is dependent on the first instruction of the pair.

The register port problem could be solved by requiring the FP loads and stores to issue by themselves. This solution treats the case of an FP load, store, or move that is paired with an FP operation as a structural hazard. This is easy to implement, but it has substantial performance drawbacks. This hazard could instead be eliminated by providing two additional ports, a read and a write, on the floating-point register file.

When the fetched instruction pair consists of an FP load and an FP operation that is dependent on it, we must detect the hazard and avoid issuing the FP operation. Except for this case, other possible hazards are essentially the same as for our single-issue pipeline. We will, however, need some additional bypass paths to prevent unnecessary stalls.

There is another difficulty that may limit the effectiveness of a superscalar pipeline. In our simple DLX pipeline, loads had a latency of one clock cycle, which prevented one instruction from using the result without stalling. In the superscalar pipeline, the result of a load instruction cannot be used on the *same* clock cycle or on the *next* clock cycle. This means that the next three instructions cannot use the load result without stalling. The branch delay also becomes three instructions, since a branch must be the first instruction of a pair. To effectively exploit the parallelism available in a superscalar processor, more ambitious compiler or hardware scheduling techniques, as well as more complex instruction decoding, will be needed.

Let's see how well loop unrolling and scheduling work on a superscalar version of DLX with the delays in clock cycles from Figure 4.2 on page 224.

EXAMPLE   Below is the loop we unrolled and scheduled earlier in section 4.1. How would it be scheduled on a superscalar pipeline for DLX?

```
Loop:   LD      F0,0(R1)      ;F0=array element
        ADDD    F4,F0,F2      ;add scalar in F2
        SD      0(R1),F4      ;store result
        SUBI    R1,R1,#8      ;decrement pointer
                              ;8 bytes (per DW)
        BNEZ    R1,Loop       ;branch R1!=zero
```

ANSWER   To schedule it without any delays, we will need to unroll the loop to make five copies of the body. After unrolling, the loop will contain five each of LD, ADDD, and SD; one SUBI; and one BNEZ. The unrolled and scheduled code is shown in Figure 4.27.

	Integer instruction		FP instruction	Clock cycle
Loop:	LD	F0,0(R1)		1
	LD	F6,-8(R1)		2
	LD	F10,-16(R1)	ADDD F4,F0,F2	3
	LD	F14,-24(R1)	ADDD F8,F6,F2	4
	LD	F18,-32(R1)	ADDD F12,F10,F2	5
	SD	0(R1),F4	ADDD F16,F14,F2	6
	SD	-8(R1),F8	ADDD F20,F18,F2	7
	SD	-16(R1),F12		8
	SUBI	R1,R1,#40		9
	SD	16(R1),F16		10
	BNEZ	R1,Loop		11
	SD	8(R1),F20		12

FIGURE 4.27   The unrolled and scheduled code as it would look on a superscalar DLX.

This unrolled superscalar loop now runs in 12 clock cycles per iteration, or 2.4 clock cycles per element, versus 3.5 for the scheduled and unrolled loop on the ordinary DLX pipeline. In this Example, the performance of the superscalar DLX is limited by the balance between integer and floating-point computation. Every floating-point instruction is issued together with an integer instruction, but there are not enough floating-point instructions to keep the floating-point pipeline full. When scheduled, the original loop ran in 6 clock cycles per iteration. We have improved on that by a factor of 2.5, more than half of which came from loop unrolling. Loop unrolling took us from 6 to 3.5 (a factor of 1.7), while superscalar execution gave us a factor of 1.5 improvement.   ■

Ideally, our superscalar processor will pick up two instructions and issue them both if the first is an integer and the second is a floating-point instruction. If they do not fit this pattern, which can be quickly detected, then they are issued sequentially. This points to two of the major advantages of a superscalar processor over a VLIW processor. First, there is little impact on code density, since the processor detects whether the next instruction can issue, and we do not need to lay out the instructions to match the issue capability. Second, even unscheduled programs, or those compiled for older implementations, can be run. Of course, such programs may not run well; one way to overcome this is to use dynamic scheduling.

Multiple Instruction Issue with Dynamic Scheduling

Multiple instruction issue can also be applied to dynamically scheduled processors. We could start with either the scoreboard scheme or Tomasulo's algorithm. Let's assume we want to extend Tomasulo's algorithm to support issuing two instructions per clock cycle, one integer and one floating point. We do not want to issue instructions to the reservation stations out of order, since this makes the bookkeeping extremely complex. Rather, by employing separate data structures for the integer and floating-point registers, we can simultaneously issue a floating-point instruction and an integer instruction to their respective reservation stations, as long as the two issued instructions do not access the same register set.

Unfortunately, this approach bars issuing two instructions with a dependence in the same clock cycle, such as a floating-point load (an integer instruction) and a floating-point add. Of course, we cannot execute these two instructions in the same clock, but we would like to issue them to the reservation stations where they will later be serialized. In the superscalar processor of the previous section, the compiler is responsible for finding independent instructions to issue. If a hardware-scheduling scheme cannot find a way to issue two dependent instructions in the same clock, there will be little advantage to a hardware-scheduled scheme versus a compiler-based scheme.

Luckily, there are two approaches that can be used to achieve dual issue. The first assumes that the register renaming portion of instruction-issue logic can be made to run in one-half of a clock. This permits two instructions to be processed in one clock cycle, so that they can begin executing on the same clock cycle.

The second approach is based on the observation that with the issue restrictions assumed, it will only be FP loads and moves from the GP to the FP registers that will create dependences among instructions that we can issue together. If we had a more complex set of issue capabilities, there would be additional possible dependences that we would need to handle.

The need for reservation tables for loads and moves can be eliminated by using queues for the result of a load or a move. Queues can also be used to allow stores to issue early and wait for their operands, just as they did in Tomasulo's algorithm. Since dynamic scheduling is most effective for data moves, while static scheduling is highly effective in register-register code sequences, we could use static scheduling to eliminate reservation stations completely and rely only on the queues for loads and stores. This style of processor organization, where the load-store units have queues to allow slippage with respect to other functional units, has been called a *decoupled architecture*. Several machines have used variations on this idea.

A processor that dynamically schedules loads and stores may cause loads and stores to be reordered. This may result in violating a data dependence through memory and thus requires some detection hardware for this potential hazard. We can detect such hazards with the same scheme we used for the single-issue version of Tomasulo's algorithm: We dynamically check whether the memory source address specified by a load is the same as the target address of an outstanding, uncompleted store. If there is such a match, we can stall the load instruction until the store completes. Since the address of the store has already been computed and resides in the store buffer, we can use an associative check (possibly with only a subset of the address bits) to determine whether a load conflicts with a store in the buffer. There is also the possibility of WAW and WAR hazards through memory, which must be prevented, although they are much less likely than a true data dependence. (In contrast to these dynamic techniques for detecting memory dependences, we will discuss compiler-based approaches in the next section.)

For simplicity, let us assume that we have pipelined the instruction issue logic so that we can issue two operations that are dependent but use different functional units. Let's see how this would work with the same code sequence we used earlier.

EXAMPLE   Consider the execution of our simple loop on a DLX pipeline extended with Tomasulo's algorithm and with multiple issue. Assume that both a floating-point and an integer operation can be issued on every clock cycle, even if they are related, provided the integer instruction is the first instruction. Assume one integer functional unit and a separate FP functional unit for each operation type. The number of cycles of latency per instruction is the same. Assume that issue and write results take one cycle each and that there is dynamic branch-prediction hardware. Create a table showing when each instruction issues, begins execution, and writes its result to the CDB for the first two iterations of the loop. Here is the original loop:

```
Loop:   LD     F0,0(R1)
        ADDD   F4,F0,F2
        SD     0(R1),F4
        SUBI   R1,R1,#8
        BNEZ   R1,Loop
```

ANSWER   The loop will be dynamically unwound and, whenever possible, instructions will be issued in pairs. The result is shown in Figure 4.28. The loop runs in 4 clock cycles per result, assuming no stalls are required on loop exit.

Iteration number	Instructions	Issues at clock-cycle number	Executes at clock-cycle number	Memory access at clock-cycle number	Writes result at clock-cycle number
1	LD F0,0(R1)	1	2	3	3
1	ADDD F4,F0,F2	1	4		6
1	SD 0(R1),F4	2	3	7	
1	SUBI R1,R1,#8	3	4		5
1	BNEZ R1,Loop	4	5		
2	LD F0,0(R1)	5	6	8	8
2	ADDD F4,F0,F2	5	9		11
2	SD 0(R1),F4	6	7	12	
2	SUBI R1,R1,#8	7	8		9
2	BNEZ R1,Loop	8	9		

FIGURE 4.28   The time of issue, execution, and writing result for a dual-issue version of our Tomasulo pipeline. The write-result stage does not apply to either stores or branches, since they do not write any registers. We assume a result is written to the CDB at the end of the clock cycle it is available in. This also assumes a wider CDB. For LD and SD, the execution is effective address calculation. We assume one memory pipeline.

∎

The number of dual issues is small because there is only one floating-point operation per iteration. The relative number of dual-issued instructions would be helped by the compiler partially unwinding the loop to reduce the instruction count by eliminating loop overhead. With that transformation, the loop would run as fast as scheduled code on a superscalar processor. We will return to this transformation in the Exercises. Alternatively, if the processor were "wider," that is, could issue more integer operations per cycle, larger improvements would be possible.

The VLIW Approach

With a VLIW we can reduce the amount of hardware needed to implement a multiple-issue processor, and the potential savings in hardware increases as we increase the issue width. For example, our two-issue superscalar processor requires that we examine the opcodes of two instructions and the six register specifiers and that we dynamically determine whether one or two instructions can issue and dispatch them to the appropriate functional units. Although the hardware required for a two-issue processor is modest and we could extend the mechanisms to handle three or four instructions (or more if the issue restrictions were chosen carefully), it becomes increasingly difficult to determine whether a significant number of instructions can all issue simultaneously without knowing both the order of the instructions before they are fetched and what dependencies might exist among them.

An alternative is an *LIW* (long instruction word) or *VLIW* (very long instruction word) architecture. VLIWs use multiple, independent functional units. Rather than attempting to issue multiple, independent instructions to the units, a VLIW packages the multiple operations into one very long instruction, hence the name. Since the burden for choosing the instructions to be issued simultaneously falls on the compiler, the hardware in a superscalar to make these issue decisions is unneeded. Since this advantage of a VLIW increases as the maximum issue rate grows, we focus on a wider-issue processor.

A VLIW instruction might include two integer operations, two floating-point operations, two memory references, and a branch. An instruction would have a set of fields for each functional unit—perhaps 16 to 24 bits per unit, yielding an instruction length of between 112 and 168 bits. To keep the functional units busy, there must be enough parallelism in a straight-line code sequence to fill the available operation slots. This parallelism is uncovered by unrolling loops and scheduling code across basic blocks using a global scheduling technique. In addition to eliminating branches by unrolling loops, global scheduling techniques allow the movement of instructions across branch points. In the next section, we will discuss *trace scheduling*, one of these techniques developed specifically for VLIWs; the references also provide pointers to other approaches. For now, let's assume we have a technique to generate long, straight-line code sequences for building up VLIW instructions and examine how well these processors operate.

EXAMPLE   Suppose we have a VLIW that could issue two memory references, two FP operations, and one integer operation or branch in every clock cycle. Show an unrolled version of the array sum loop for such a processor. Unroll as many times as necessary to eliminate any stalls. Ignore the branch-delay slot.

ANSWER   The code is shown in Figure 4.29. The loop has been unrolled to make seven copies of the body, which eliminates all stalls (i.e., completely empty issue cycles), and runs in 9 cycles. This yields a running rate of seven results in 9 cycles, or 1.29 cycles per result.   ■

Limitations in Multiple-Issue Processors

What are the limitations of a multiple-issue approach? If we can issue five operations per clock cycle, why not 50? The difficulty in expanding the issue rate comes from three areas:

1.   Inherent limitations of ILP in programs

2.   Difficulties in building the underlying hardware

3.   Limitations specific to either a superscalar or VLIW implementation.

Memory reference 1	Memory reference 2	FP operation 1	FP operation 2	Integer operation/branch
LD F0,0(R1)	LD F6,-8(R1)			
LD F10,-16(R1)	LD F14,-24(R1)			
LD F18,-32(R1)	LD F22,-40(R1)	ADDD F4,F0,F2	ADDD F8,F6,F2	
LD F26,-48(R1)		ADDD F12,F10,F2	ADDD F16,F14,F2	
		ADDD F20,F18,F2	ADDD F24,F22,F2	
SD 0(R1),F4	SD -8(R1),F8	ADDD F28,F26,F2		
SD -16(R1),F12	SD -24(R1),F16			
SD -32(R1),F20	SD -40(R1),F24			SUBI R1,R1,#56
SD 8(R1),F28				BNEZ R1,Loop

FIGURE 4.29   VLIW instructions that occupy the inner loop and replace the unrolled sequence. This code takes nine cycles assuming no branch delay; normally the branch delay would also need to be scheduled. The issue rate is 23 operations in nine clock cycles, or 2.5 operations per cycle. The efficiency, the percentage of available slots that contained an operation, is about 60%. To achieve this issue rate requires a larger number of registers than DLX would normally use in this loop. The VLIW code sequence above requires at least eight FP registers, while the same code sequence for the base DLX processor can use as few as two FP registers or as many as five when unrolled and scheduled. In the superscalar example in Figure 4.27, six registers were needed.

Limits on available ILP are the simplest and most fundamental. For example, in a statically scheduled processor, unless loops are unrolled very many times, there may not be enough operations to fill the available instruction issue slots. At first glance, it might appear that five instructions that could execute in parallel would be sufficient to keep our example VLIW completely busy. This, however, is not the case. Several of these functional units—the memory, the branch, and the floating-point units—will be pipelined and have a multicycle latency, requiring a larger number of operations that can execute in parallel to prevent stalls. For example, if the floating-point pipeline has a latency of five clocks, and if we want to schedule both FP pipelines without stalling, there must be 10 FP operations that are independent of the most recently issued FP operation. In general, we need to find a number of independent operations roughly equal to the average pipeline depth times the number of functional units. This means that roughly 15 to 20 operations could be needed to keep a multiple-issue processor with five functional units busy.

The second cost, the hardware resources for a multiple-issue processor, arises from the hardware needed both to issue and to execute multiple instructions per cycle. The hardware for executing multiple operations per cycle seems quite straightforward: duplicating the floating-point and integer functional units is easy and cost scales linearly. However, there is a large increase in the memory bandwidth and register-file bandwidth. For example, even with a split floating-point and integer register file, our VLIW processor will require six read ports (two for each load-store and two for the integer part) and three write ports (one for each non-FP unit) on the integer register file and six read ports (one for each load-store and two for each FP) and four write ports (one for each load-store or FP) on the floating-point register file. This bandwidth cannot be supported without an increase in the silicon area of the register file and possible degradation of clock speed. Our five-unit VLIW also has two data memory ports, which are substantially more expensive than register ports If we wanted to expand the number of issues further, we would need to continue adding memory ports. Adding only arithmetic units would not help, since the processor would be starved for memory bandwidth. As the number of data memory ports grows, so does the complexity of the memory system. To allow multiple memory accesses in parallel, we could break the memory into banks containing different addresses with the hope that the operations in a single instruction do not have conflicting accesses, or the memory may be truly dual-ported, which is substantially more expensive. Yet another approach is used in the IBM Power-2 design: The memory is accessed twice per clock cycle, but even with an aggressive memory system, this approach may be too slow for a high-speed processor. These memory system alternatives are discussed in more detail in the next chapter. The complexity and access time penalties of a multiported memory hierarchy are probably the most serious hardware limitations faced by any type of multiple-issue processor, whether VLIW or superscalar.

The hardware needed to support instruction issue varies significantly depending on the multiple-issue approach. At one end of the spectrum are the dynamically scheduled superscalar processors that have a substantial amount of hardware involved in implementing either scoreboarding or Tomasulo's algorithm. In addition to the silicon that such mechanisms consume, dynamic scheduling substantially complicates the design, making it more difficult to achieve high clock rates, as well as significantly increasing the task of verifying the design. At the other end of the spectrum are VLIWs, which require little or no additional hardware for instruction issue and scheduling, since that function is handled completely by the compiler. Between these two extremes lie most existing superscalar processors, which use a combination of static scheduling by the compiler with the hardware making the decision of how many of the next n instructions to issue. Depending on what restrictions are made on the order of instructions and what types of dependences must be detected among the issue candidates, statically scheduled superscalars will have issue logic either closer to that of a VLIW or more like that of a dynamically scheduled processor. Much of the challenge in designing multiple-issue processors lies in assessing the costs and performance advantages of a wide spectrum of possible hardware mechanisms versus the compiler-driven alternatives.

Finally, there are problems that are specific to either the superscalar or VLIW model. We have already discussed the major challenge for a superscalar processor, namely the instruction issue logic. For the VLIW model, there are both technical and logistical problems. The technical problems are the increase in code size and the limitations of lock-step operation. Two different elements combine to increase code size substantially for a VLIW. First, generating enough operations in a straight-line code fragment requires ambitiously unrolling loops, which increases code size. Second, whenever instructions are not full, the unused functional units translate to wasted bits in the instruction encoding. In Figure 4.29, we saw that only about 60% of the functional units were used, so almost half of each instruction was empty. To combat this problem, clever encodings are sometimes used. For example, there may be only one large immediate field for use by any functional unit. Another technique is to compress the instructions in main memory and expand them when they are read into the cache or are decoded. Because a VLIW is statically scheduled and operates lock-step, a stall in any functional unit pipeline must cause the entire processor to stall, since all the functional units must be kept synchronized. While we may be able to schedule the deterministic functional units to prevent stalls, predicting which data accesses will encounter a cache stall and scheduling them is very difficult. Hence, a cache miss must cause the entire processor to stall. As the issue rate and number of memory references becomes large, this lock-step structure makes it difficult to effectively use a data cache, thereby increasing memory complexity and latency.

Binary code compatibility is the major logistical problem for VLIWs. This problem exists within a generation of processors, even though the processors may implement the same basic instructions. The problem is that different numbers of issues and functional unit latencies require different versions of the code. Thus, migrating between successive implementations or even between implementations with different issue widths is more difficult than it may be for a superscalar design. Of course, obtaining improved performance from a new superscalar design may require recompilation. Nonetheless, the ability to run old binary files is a practical advantage for the superscalar approach. One possible solution to this problem, and the problem of binary code compatibility in general, is object-code translation or emulation. This technology is developing quickly and could play a significant role in future migration schemes.

The major challenge for all multiple-issue processors is to try to exploit large amounts of ILP. When the parallelism comes from unrolling simple loops in FP programs, the original loop probably could have been run efficiently on a vector processor (described in Appendix B). It is not clear that a multiple-issue processor is preferred over a vector processor for such applications; the costs are similar, and the vector processor is typically the same speed or faster. The potential advantages of a multiple-issue processor versus a vector processor are twofold. First, a multiple-issue processor has the potential to extract some amount of parallelism from less regularly structured code, and, second, it has the ability to use a less expensive memory system. For these reasons it appears clear that multiple-issue approaches will be the primary method for taking advantage of instruction-level parallelism, and vectors will primarily be an extension to these processors.

4.5 | Compiler Support for Exploiting ILP

In this section we discuss compiler technology for increasing the amount of parallelism that we can exploit in a program. We begin by examining techniques to detect dependences and eliminate name dependences.

Detecting and Eliminating Dependences

Finding the dependences in a program is an important part of three tasks: (1) good scheduling of code, (2) determining which loops might contain parallelism, and (3) eliminating name dependences. The complexity of dependence analysis arises because of the presence of arrays and pointers in languages like C. Since scalar variable references explicitly refer to a name, they can usually be analyzed quite easily, with aliasing because of pointers and reference parameters causing some complications and uncertainty in the analysis.

Our analysis needs to find all dependences and determine whether there is a cycle in the dependences, since that is what prevents us from running the loop in parallel. Consider the following example:

```
for (i=1;i<=100;i=i+1) {
        A[i] = B[i] + C[i]
        D[i] = A[i] * E[i]
}
```

Because the dependence involving A is not loop-carried, we can unroll the loop and find parallelism; we just cannot exchange the two references to A. If a loop has loop-carried dependences but no circular dependences (recall the Example in section 4.1), we can transform the loop to eliminate the dependence and then unrolling will uncover parallelism. In many parallel loops the amount of parallelism is limited only by the number of unrollings, which is limited only by the number of loop iterations. Of course, in practice, to take advantage of that much parallelism would require many functional units and possibly an enormous number of registers. The absence of a loop-carried dependence simply tells us that we have a large amount of parallelism *available*.

The code fragment above illustrates another opportunity for improvement. The second reference to A need not be translated to a load instruction, since we know that the value is computed and stored by the previous statement; hence, the second reference to A can simply be a reference to the register into which A was computed. Performing this optimization requires knowing that the two references are always to the same memory address and that there is no intervening access to the same location. Normally, data dependence analysis only tells that one reference *may* depend on another; a more complex analysis is required to determine that two references *must be* to the exact same address. In the example above, a simple version of this analysis suffices, since the two references are in the same basic block.

Often loop-carried dependences are in the form of a *recurrence*:

```
for (i=2;i<=100;i=i+1) {
      Y[i] = Y[i-1] + Y[i];
}
```

A recurrence is when a variable is defined based on the value of that variable in an earlier iteration, often the one immediately preceding, as in the above fragment. Detecting a recurrence can be important for two reasons: Some architectures (especially vector computers) have special support for executing recurrences, and some recurrences can be the source of a reasonable amount of parallelism. To see how the latter can be true, consider this loop:

```
for (i=6;i<=100;i=i+1) {
      Y[i] = Y[i-5] + Y[i];
}
```

On the iteration i, the loop references element $i - 5$. The loop is said to have a *dependence distance* of 5. Many loops with carried dependences have a dependence distance of 1. The larger the distance, the more potential parallelism can be obtained by unrolling the loop. For example, if we unroll the first loop, with a dependence distance of 1, successive statements are dependent on one another; there is still some parallelism among the individual instructions, but not much. If we unroll the loop that has a dependence distance of 5, there is a sequence of five instructions that have no dependences, and thus much more ILP. Although many loops with loop-carried dependences have a dependence distance of 1, cases with larger distances do arise, and the longer distance may well provide enough parallelism to keep a processor busy.

How does the compiler detect dependences in general? Nearly all dependence analysis algorithms work on the assumption that array indices are *affine*. In simplest terms, a one-dimensional array index is affine if it can be written in the form $a \times i + b$, where a and b are constants, and i is the loop index variable. The index of a multidimensional array is affine if the index in each dimension is affine.

Determining whether there is a dependence between two references to the same array in a loop is thus equivalent to determining whether two affine functions can have the same value for different indices between the bounds of the loop. For example, suppose we have stored to an array element with index value

$a \times i + b$ and loaded from the same array with index value $c \times i + d$, where i is the for-loop index variable that runs from m to n. A dependence exists if two conditions hold:

1. There are two iteration indices, j and k, both within the limits of the for loop. That is $m \leq j \leq n, m \leq k \leq n$.

2. The loop stores into an array element indexed by $a \times j + b$ and later fetches from that *same* array element when it is indexed by $c \times k + d$. That is, $a \times j + b = c \times k + d$.

In general, we cannot determine whether a dependence exists at compile time. For example, the values of a, b, c, and d may not be known (they could be values in other arrays), making it impossible to tell if a dependence exists. In other cases, the dependence testing may be very expensive but decidable at compile time. For example, the accesses may depend on the iteration indices of multiple nested loops. Many programs, however, contain primarily simple indices where $a, b, c,$ and d are all constants. For these cases, it is possible to devise reasonable compile-time tests for dependence.

As an example, a simple and sufficient test for the absence of a dependence is the *greatest common divisor*, or GCD, test. It is based on the observation that if a loop-carried dependence exists, then GCD (c,a) must *divide* $(d - b)$. (Remember that an integer, x, *divides* another integer, y, if there is no remainder when we do the division y/x and get an integer quotient.)

EXAMPLE   Use the GCD test to determine whether dependences exist in the following loop:

```
for (i=1; i<=100; i=i+1) {
      X[2*i+3] = X[2*i] * 5.0;
}
```

ANSWER   Given the values $a = 2, b = 3, c = 2,$ and $d = 0$, then GCD$(a,c) = 2$, and $d - b = -3$. Since 2 does not divide -3, no dependence is possible.   ∎

The GCD test is sufficient to guarantee that no dependence exists (you can show this in the Exercises); however, there are cases where the GCD test succeeds but no dependence exists. This can arise, for example, because the GCD test does not take the loop bounds into account.

In general, determining whether a dependence actually exists is NP-complete. In practice, however, many common cases can be analyzed precisely at low cost. Recently, approaches using a hierarchy of exact tests increasing in generality and cost have been shown to be both accurate and efficient. (A test is exact if it precisely determines whether a dependence exists. Although the general case is NP-complete, there exist exact tests for restricted situations that are much cheaper.)

In addition to detecting the presence of a dependence, a compiler wants to classify the types of dependence. This allows a compiler to recognize name dependences and eliminate them at compile time by renaming and copying.

EXAMPLE   The following loop has multiple types of dependences. Find all the true dependences, output dependences, and antidependences, and eliminate the output dependences and antidependences by renaming.

```
for (i=1; i<=100; i=i+1) {
    Y[i] = X[i] / c; /*S1*/
    X[i] = X[i] + c; /*S2*/
    Z[i] = Y[i] + c; /*S3*/
    Y[i] = c - Y[i]; /*S4*/
}
```

ANSWER   The following dependences exist among the four statements:

1. There are true dependences from S1 to S3 and from S1 to S4 because of Y[i]. These are not loop carried, so they do not prevent the loop from being considered parallel. These dependences will force S3 and S4 to wait for S1 to complete.

2. There is an antidependence from S1 to S2, based on X[i].

3. There is an antidependence from S3 to S4 for Y[i].

4. There is an output dependence from S1 to S4, based on Y[i].

The following version of the loop eliminates these false (or pseudo) dependences.

```
for (i=1; i<=100; i=i+1 {
    /* Y renamed to T to remove output dependence*/
    T[i] = X[i] / c;
    /* X renamed to X1 to remove antidependence*/
    X1[i] = X[i] + c;
    /* Y renamed to T to remove antidependence */
    Z[i] = T[i] + c;
    Y[i] = c - T[i];
}
```

After the loop the variable X has been renamed X1. In code that follows the loop, the compiler can simply replace the name X by X1. In this case, renaming does not require an actual copy operation but can be done by substituting names or by register allocation. In other cases, however, renaming will require copying.   ∎

Dependence analysis is a critical technology for exploiting parallelism. At the instruction level it provides information needed to interchange memory references when scheduling, as well as to determine the benefits of unrolling a loop. For detecting loop-level parallelism, dependence analysis is the basic tool. Effectively compiling programs to either vector computers or multiprocessors depends critically on this analysis. In addition, it is useful in scheduling instructions to determine whether memory references are potentially dependent. The major drawback of dependence analysis is that it applies only under a limited set of circumstances, namely among references within a single loop nest and using affine index functions. Thus, there are a wide variety of situations in which dependence analysis *cannot* tell us what we might want to know, including

- when objects are referenced via pointers rather than array indices;

- when array indexing is indirect through another array, which happens with many representations of sparse arrays;

- when a dependence may exist for some value of the inputs, but does not exist in actuality when the code is run since the inputs never take on certain values;

- when an optimization depends on knowing more than just the possibility of a dependence, but needs to know on *which* write of a variable does a read of that variable depend.

The rapid progress in dependence analysis algorithms has led us to a situation where we are often limited by the lack of applicability of the analysis rather than a shortcoming in dependence analysis per se.

Software Pipelining: Symbolic Loop Unrolling

We have already seen that one compiler technique, loop unrolling, is useful to uncover parallelism among instructions by creating longer sequences of straightline code. There are two other important techniques that have been developed for this purpose: *software pipelining* and *trace scheduling*.

Software pipelining is a technique for reorganizing loops such that each iteration in the software-pipelined code is made from instructions chosen from different iterations of the original loop. This is most easily understood by looking at the scheduled code for the superscalar version of DLX, which appeared in Figure 4.27 on page 281. The scheduler in this example essentially interleaves instructions from different loop iterations, so as to separate the dependent instructions that occur within a single loop iteration. A software-pipelined loop interleaves instructions from different iterations without unrolling the loop, as illustrated in Figure 4.30. This technique is the software counterpart to what Tomasulo's algorithm does in hardware. The software-pipelined loop for the earlier example would contain one load, one add, and one store, each from a different iteration. There is also some start-up code that is needed before the loop begins as well as code to finish up after the loop is completed. We will ignore these in this discussion, for simplicity; the topic is addressed in the Exercises.

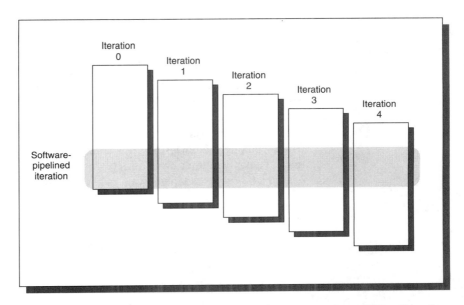

FIGURE 4.30   A software-pipelined loop chooses instructions from different loop iterations, thus separating the dependent instructions within one iteration of the original loop. The start-up and finish-up code will correspond to the portions above and below the software-pipelined iteration.

EXAMPLE   Show a software-pipelined version of this loop, which increments all the elements of an array whose starting address is in R1 by the contents of F2:

```
Loop:   LD      F0,0(R1)
        ADDD    F4,F0,F2
        SD      0(R1),F4
        SUBI    R1,R1,#8
        BNEZ    R1,Loop
```

You may omit the start-up and clean-up code.

ANSWER   Software pipelining symbolically unrolls the loop and then selects instructions from each iteration. Since the unrolling is symbolic, the loop overhead instructions (the SUBI and BNEZ) need not be replicated. Here's the body of the unrolled loop without overhead instructions, highlighting the instructions taken from each iteration:

```
Iteration i:      LD     F0,0(R1)
                  ADDD   F4,F0,F2
                  SD     0(R1),F4
Iteration i+1:    LD     F0,0(R1)
                  ADDD   F4,F0,F2
                  SD     0(R1),F4
Iteration i+2:    LD     F0,0(R1)
                  ADDD   F4,F0,F2
                  SD     0(R1),F4
```

The selected instructions are then put together in the loop with the loop control instructions:

```
Loop:  SD     16(R1),F4     ;stores into M[i]
       ADDD   F4,F0,F2      ;adds to M[i-1]
       LD     F0,0(R1)      ;loads M[i-2]
       SUBI   R1,R1,#8
       BNEZ   R1,Loop
```

This loop can be run at a rate of 5 cycles per result, ignoring the start-up and clean-up portions, and assuming that SUBI is scheduled after the ADDD and the LD instruction, with an adjusted offset, is placed in the branch delay slot. Because the load and store are separated by offsets of 16 (two iterations), the loop should run for two fewer iterations. (We address this and the start-up and clean-up portions in Exercise 4.18.) Notice that the reuse of registers (e.g., F4, F0, and R1) requires the hardware to avoid the WAR hazards that would occur in the loop. This should not be a problem in this case, since no data-dependent stalls should occur.

By looking at the unrolled version we can see what the start-up code and finish code will need to be. For start-up, we will need to execute any instructions that correspond to iteration 1 and 2 that will not be executed. These instructions are the LD for iterations 1 and 2 and the ADDD for iteration 1. For the finish code, we need to execute any instructions that will not be executed in the final two iterations. These include the ADDD for the last iteration and the SD for the last two iterations. ∎

Register management in software-pipelined loops can be tricky. The example above is not too hard since the registers that are written on one loop iteration are read on the next. In other cases, we may need to increase the number of iterations between when we issue an instruction and when the result is used. This occurs when there are a small number of instructions in the loop body and the latencies are large. In such cases, a combination of software pipelining and loop unrolling is needed. An example of this is shown in the Exercises.

Software pipelining can be thought of as *symbolic* loop unrolling. Indeed, some of the algorithms for software pipelining use loop-unrolling algorithms to figure out how to software pipeline the loop. The major advantage of software pipelining over straight loop unrolling is that software pipelining consumes less code space. Software pipelining and loop unrolling, in addition to yielding a better scheduled inner loop, each reduce a different type of overhead. Loop unrolling reduces the overhead of the loop—the branch and counter-update code. Software pipelining reduces the time when the loop is not running at peak speed to once per loop at the beginning and end. If we unroll a loop that does 100 iterations a constant number of times, say 4, we pay the overhead 100/4 = 25 times—every time the inner unrolled loop is initiated. Figure 4.31 shows this behavior graphically. Because these techniques attack two different types of overhead, the best performance can come from doing both.

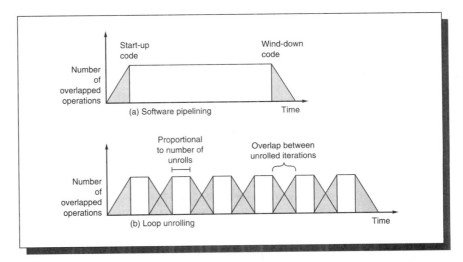

FIGURE 4.31   The execution pattern for (a) a software-pipelined loop and (b) an unrolled loop. The shaded areas are the times when the loop is not running with maximum overlap or parallelism among instructions. This occurs once at the beginning and once at the end for the software-pipelined loop. For the unrolled loop it occurs m/n times if the loop has a total of m iterations and is unrolled n times. Each block represents an unroll of n iterations. Increasing the number of unrollings will reduce the start-up and clean-up overhead. The overhead of one iteration overlaps with the overhead of the next, thereby reducing the impact. The total area under the polygonal region in each case will be the same, since the total number of operations is just the execution rate multiplied by the time.

Trace Scheduling: Using Critical Path Scheduling

The other technique used to generate additional parallelism is *trace scheduling*. Trace scheduling extends loop unrolling with a technique for finding parallelism across conditional branches other than loop branches. Trace scheduling is useful for processors with a very large number of issues per clock where loop unrolling may not be sufficient by itself to uncover enough ILP to keep the processor busy. Trace scheduling is a combination of two separate processes. The first process, called *trace selection,* tries to find a likely sequence of basic blocks whose operations will be put together into a smaller number of instructions; this sequence is called a *trace*. Loop unrolling is used to generate long traces, since loop branches are taken with high probability. Additionally, by using static branch prediction, other conditional branches are also chosen as taken or not taken, so that the resultant trace is a straight-line sequence resulting from concatenating many basic blocks. Once a trace is selected, the second process, called *trace compaction*, tries to squeeze the trace into a small number of wide instructions. Trace compaction attempts to move operations as early as it can in a sequence (trace), packing the operations into as few wide instructions (or issue packets) as possible.

Trace compaction is global code scheduling, where we want to compact the code into the shortest possible sequence that preserves the data and control dependences. The data dependences force a partial order on operations, while the control dependences dictate instructions across which code cannot be easily moved. Data dependences are overcome by unrolling and using dependence analysis to determine if two references refer to the same address. Control dependences are also reduced by unrolling. The major advantage of trace scheduling over simpler pipeline-scheduling techniques is that it provides a scheme for reducing the effect of control dependences by moving code across conditional non-loop branches using the predicted behavior of the branch. While such movements cannot guarantee speedup, if the prediction information is accurate, the compiler can determine whether such code movement is likely to lead to faster code. Figure 4.32 shows a code fragment, which may be thought of as an iteration of an unrolled loop, and the trace selected.

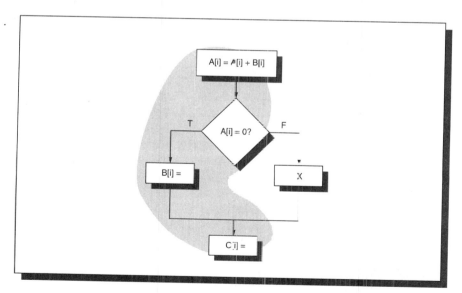

FIGURE 4.32 A code fragment and the trace selected shaded with gray. This trace would be selected first if the probability of the true branch being taken were much higher than the probability of the false branch being taken. The branch from the decision (A[i]=0) to X is a branch out of the trace, and the branch from X to the assignment to C is a branch into the trace. These branches are what make compacting the trace difficult.

Once the trace is selected as shown in Figure 4.32, it must be compacted so as to fill the processor's resources. Compacting the trace involves moving the assignments to variables B and C up to the block before the branch decision. The movement of the code associated with B is speculative: it will speed the computation up only when the path containing the code would be taken. Any global scheduling scheme, including trace scheduling, performs such movement under a set of constraints. In trace scheduling, branches are viewed as jumps into or out of the selected trace, which is assumed to the most probable path. When code is moved across such trace entry and exit points, additional bookkeeping code may be needed on the entry or exit point. The key assumption is that the selected trace is the most probable event, otherwise, the cost of the bookkeeping code may be excessive. This movement of code alters the control dependences, and the bookkeeping code is needed to maintain the correct dynamic data dependence. In the case of moving the code associated with C, the bookkeeping costs are the only cost, since C is executed independent of the branch. For a code movement that is speculative, like that associated with B, we must not introduce any new exceptions. Compilers avoid changing the exception behavior by not moving certain classes of instructions, such as memory references, that can cause exceptions. In the next section, we will see how hardware support can ease the process of speculative code motion as well as remove control dependences.

What is involved in moving the assignments to B and C? The computation of and assignment to B is control-dependent on the branch, while the computation of C is not. Moving these statements can only be done if they either do not change the control and data dependences or if the effect of the change is not visible and thus does not affect program execution. To see what's involved, let's look at a typical code generation sequence for the flowchart in Figure 4.32. Assuming that the addresses for A, B, C are in R1, R2, and R3, respectively, here is such a sequence:

```
           LW      R4,0(R1)        ; load A
           LW      R5,0(R2)        ; load B
           ADDI    R4,R4,R5        ; Add to A
           SW      0(R1),R4        ; Store A
           . . .
           BNEZ    R4,elsepart     ; Test A
           . . .                   ; then part
           SW      0(R2),...       ; Stores to B
           j       join            ; jump over else
elsepart:...                       ; else part
           X                       ; code for X
           . . .
join:  ...                         ; after if
           SW      0(R3),...       ; store C[i]
```

Let's first consider the problem of moving the assignment to B to before the BNEZ instruction. Since B is control-dependent on that branch before it is moved but not after, we must ensure the execution of the statement cannot cause any exception, since that exception would not have been raised in the original program if the else part of the statement were selected. The movement of B must also not affect the data flow, since that will result in changing the value computed.

Moving B will change the data flow of the program, if B is referenced before it is assigned either in X or after the if statement. In either case moving the assignment to B will cause some instruction, i (either in X or later in the program), to become data-dependent on the moved version of the assignment to B rather than on an earlier assignment to B that occurs before the loop and on which i originally depended. One could imagine more clever schemes to allow B to be moved even when the value is used: for example, in the first case, we could make a shadow copy of B before the if statement and use that shadow copy in X. Such schemes are generally not used, both because they are complex to implement and because they will slow down the program if the trace selected is not optimal and the operations end up requiring additional instructions to execute.

Moving the assignment to C up to before the first branch requires two steps. First, the assignment is moved over the join point of the else part into the trace (a trace entry) in the portion corresponding to the then part. This makes the instructions for C control-dependent on the branch and means that they will not execute if the else path, which is not on the trace, is chosen. Hence, instructions that were data-dependent on the assignment to C, and which execute after this code fragment, will be affected. To ensure the correct value is computed for such instructions, a copy is made of the instructions that compute and assign to C on the branch into the trace, that is, at the end of X on the else path. Second, we can move C from the then case of the branch across the branch condition, if it does not affect any data flow into the branch condition. If C is moved to before the if test, the copy of C in the else branch can be eliminated, since it will be redundant.

Loop unrolling, software pipelining, and trace scheduling all aim at trying to increase the amount of ILP that can be exploited by a processor issuing more than one instruction on every clock cycle. The effectiveness of each of these techniques and their suitability for various architectural approaches are among the hottest topics being actively pursued by researchers and designers of high-speed processors.

4.6 | Hardware Support for Extracting More Parallelism

Techniques such as loop unrolling, software pipelining, and trace scheduling can be used to increase the amount of parallelism available when the behavior of branches is fairly predictable at compile time. When the behavior of branches is not well known, compiler techniques alone may not be able to uncover much ILP. This section introduces several techniques that can help overcome such limitations. The first is an extension of the instruction set to include *conditional* or *predicated instructions*. Such instructions can be used to eliminate branches and to assist in allowing the compiler to move instructions past branches. As we will see, conditional or predicated instructions enhance the amount of ILP, but still have significant limitations. To exploit more parallelism, designers have explored an idea called *speculation*, which allows the execution of an instruction before the processor knows that the instruction should execute (i.e., it avoids control dependence stalls). We discuss two different approaches to speculation. The first is static speculation performed by the compiler with hardware support. In such schemes, the compiler chooses to make an instruction speculative and the hardware helps by making it easier to ignore the outcome of an incorrectly speculated instruction. Conditional instructions can also be used to perform limited speculation. Speculation can also be done dynamically by the hardware using branch prediction to guide the speculation process; such schemes are the subject of the third portion of this section.

Conditional or Predicated Instructions

The concept behind conditional instructions is quite simple: An instruction refers to a condition, which is evaluated as part of the instruction execution. If the condition is true, the instruction is executed normally; if the condition is false, the execution continues as if the instruction was a no-op. Many newer architectures include some form of conditional instructions. The most common example of such an instruction is conditional move, which moves a value from one register to another if the condition is true. Such an instruction can be used to completely eliminate the branch in simple code sequences.

EXAMPLE   Consider the following code:

```
if (A==0) {S=T;}
```

Assuming that registers R1, R2, and R3 hold the values of A, S, and T, respectively, show the code for this statement with the branch and with the conditional move.

ANSWER   The straightforward code using a branch for this statement is (remember that we are assuming normal rather than delayed branches)

```
        BNEZ    R1,L
        MOV     R2,R3
L:
```

Using a conditional move that performs the move only if the third operand is equal to zero, we can implement this statement in one instruction:

```
CMOVZ  R2,R3,R1
```

The conditional instruction allows us to convert the control dependence present in the branch-based code sequence to a data dependence. (This transformation is also used for vector computers, where it is called *if-conversion*.) For a pipelined processor, this moves the place where the dependence must be resolved from near the front of the pipeline, where it is resolved for branches, to the end of the pipeline where the register write occurs.   ■

One use for conditional move is to implement the absolute value function: A = abs (B), which is implemented as if (B<0) {A=-B;} else {A=B;}. This if statement can be implemented as a pair of conditional moves, or as one unconditional move (A = B) and one conditional move (A = −B).

In the example above or in the compilation of absolute value, conditional moves are used to change a control dependence into a data dependence. This enables us to eliminate the branch and possibly improve the pipeline behavior. Conditional instructions can also be used to improve scheduling in superscalar or VLIW processors by the use of speculation. A conditional instruction can be used to speculatively move an instruction that is time-critical.

EXAMPLE   Here is a code sequence for a two-issue superscalar that can issue a combination of one memory reference and one ALU operation, or a branch by itself, every cycle:

First instruction slot	Second instruction slot
LW R1,40(R2)	ADD R3,R4,R5
	ADD R6,R3,R7
BEQZ R10,L	
LW R8,20(R10)	
LW R9,0(R8)	

This sequence wastes a memory operation slot in the second cycle and will incur a data dependence stall if the branch is not taken, since the second LW after the branch depends on the prior load. Show how the code can be improved using a conditional form of LW.

ANSWER   Call the conditional version load word LWC and assume the load occurs unless the third operand is 0. The LW immediately following the branch can be converted to a LWC and moved up to the second issue slot:

First instruction slot	Second instruction slot
LW R1,40(R2)	ADD R3,R4,R5
LWC R8,20(R10),R10	ADD R6,R3,R7
BEQZ R10,L	
LW R9,0(R8)	

This improves the execution time by several cycles since it eliminates one instruction issue slot and reduces the pipeline stall for the last instruction in the sequence. Of course, if the compiler mispredicts the branch, the conditional instruction will have no effect and will not improve the running time. This is why the transformation is speculative.   ∎

To use a conditional instruction successfully in examples like this, we must ensure that the speculated instruction does not introduce an exception. Thus the semantics of the conditional instruction must define the instruction to have no effect if the condition is *not* satisfied. This means that the instruction cannot write the result destination nor cause any exceptions if the condition is not satisfied. The property of not causing exceptions is quite critical, as the Example above shows: If register R10 contains zero, the instruction LW R8,20(R10) executed unconditionally is likely to cause a protection exception, and this exception should not occur. It is this property that prevents a compiler from simply moving the load of R8 across the branch. Of course, if the condition is satisfied, the LW may still cause a legal and resumable exception (e.g., a page fault), and the hardware must take the exception when it knows that the controlling condition is true.

Conditional instructions are certainly helpful for implementing short alternative control flows. Nonetheless, the usefulness of conditional instructions is significantly limited by several factors:

- Conditional instructions that are annulled (i.e., whose conditions are false) still take execution time. Therefore, moving an instruction across a branch and making it conditional will slow the program down whenever the moved instruction would not have been normally executed. An important exception to this occurs when the cycles used by the moved instruction when it is not performed would have been idle anyway (as in the superscalar example above). Moving an instruction across a branch is essentially speculating on the outcome of the branch. Conditional instructions make this easier but do not eliminate the execution time taken by an incorrect guess. In simple cases, where we trade a conditional move for a branch and a move, using conditional moves is almost always better. When longer code sequences are made conditional, the benefits are more limited.

- Conditional instructions are most useful when the condition can be evaluated early. If the condition and branch cannot be separated (because of data dependences in determining the condition), then a conditional instruction will help less, though it may still be useful since it delays the point when the condition must be known till nearer the end of the pipeline.

- The use of conditional instructions is limited when the control flow involves more than a simple alternative sequence. For example, moving an instruction across multiple branches requires making it conditional on both branches, which requires two conditions to be specified, an unlikely capability, or requires additional instructions to compute the "and" of the conditions.

- Conditional instructions may have some speed penalty compared with unconditional instructions. This may show up as a higher cycle count for such instructions or a slower clock rate overall. If conditional instructions are more expensive, they will need to be used judiciously.

For these reasons, many architectures have included a few simple conditional instructions (with conditional move being the most frequent), but few architectures include conditional versions for the majority of the instructions. Figure 4.33 shows the conditional operations available in a variety of recent architectures.

Alpha	HP PA		MIPS	SPARC
Conditional move	Any register-register instruction can nullify the following instruction, making it conditional.		Conditional move	Conditional move

FIGURE 4.33   Conditional instructions available in four different RISC architectures. Conditional move was one of the few user instructions added to the Intel P6 processor.

Compiler Speculation with Hardware Support

As we saw in Chapter 3, many programs have branches that can be accurately predicted at compile time either from the program structure or by using a profile. In such cases, the compiler may want to speculate either to improve the scheduling or to increase the issue rate. Conditional instructions provide some limited ability to speculate, but they are really more useful when control dependences can be completely eliminated, such as in an if-then with a small then body. In trying to speculate, the compiler would like to not only make instructions control independent, it would also like to move them so that the speculated instructions execute before the branch!

In moving instructions across a branch the compiler must ensure that exception behavior is not changed and that the dynamic data dependence remains the same. We have already seen, in examining trace scheduling, how the compiler can move instructions across branches and how to compensate for such speculation so that

marked as speculative, the program could be terminated. In such a scheme, as in the next one, renaming will often be needed to prevent speculative instructions from destroying live values. Renaming is usually restricted to register values. Because of this restriction, the targets of stores cannot be destroyed and stores cannot be speculative. The small number of registers and the cost of spilling will act as one constraint on the amount of speculation. Of course, the major constraint remains the cost of executing speculative instructions when the compiler's branch prediction is incorrect.

Speculation with Poison Bits

The use of poison bits allows compiler speculation with less change to the exception behavior. In particular, incorrect programs that caused termination without speculation will still cause exceptions when instructions are speculated. The scheme is simple: A poison bit is added to every register and another bit is added to every instruction to indicate whether the instruction is speculative. The poison bit of the destination register is set whenever a speculative instruction results in a terminating exception; all other exceptions are handled immediately. If a speculative instruction uses a register with a poison bit turned on, the destination register of the instruction simply has its poison bit turned on. If a normal instruction attempts to use a register source with its poison bit turned on, the instruction causes a fault. In this way, any program that would have generated an exception still generates one, albeit at the first instance where a result is used by an instruction that is not speculative. Since poison bits exist only on register values and not memory values, stores are not speculative and thus trap if either operand is "poison."

EXAMPLE   Consider the code fragment from page 305 and show how it would be compiled with speculative instructions and poison bits. Show where an exception for the speculative memory reference would be recognized. Assume R14, R15 are unused and available.

ANSWER   Here is the code (an "*" on the opcode indicates a speculative instruction):

```
          LW     R1,0(R3)     ;load A
          LW*    R14,0(R2)    ;speculative load B
          BEQZ   R1,L3        ;
          ADDI   R14,R1,#4    ;
    L3:   SW     0(R3),R14    ;exception for speculative LW
```

If the speculative LW* generates a terminating exception, the poison bit of R14 will be turned on. When the nonspeculative SW instruction occurs, it will raise an exception if the poison bit for R14 is on.   ∎

One complication that must be overcome is how the OS can save the user registers if the poison bit is set. A special instruction is needed to save and reset the state of the poison bits to avoid this problem.

Speculative Instructions with Renaming

The main disadvantages of the two previous schemes are the need to introduce copies to deal with register renaming and the possibility of exhausting the registers. The former problem reduces efficiency, while the latter can make speculation not worthwhile. An alternative is to move instructions past branches, flagging them as speculative, and providing renaming and buffering in the hardware, much as Tomasulo's algorithm does. This concept has been called *boosting*, and it is closely related to the full hardware-based scheme we consider next. A boosted instruction is executed speculatively based on a future branch. The results of the instruction are forwarded to and used by other boosted instructions. When the branch following the boosted instruction is reached, if the boosted instruction contains a correct prediction of the branch, then results are committed to the registers; otherwise, the results are discarded. Boosted instructions allow the execution of an instruction that is dependent on a branch before the branch is resolved, but the final action to commit the instruction is taken only after the branch is resolved. It is possible to support boosting of instructions across multiple branches, but we consider only the case of boosting across one branch.

EXAMPLE   Consider the code fragment from page 305 and show how it would be compiled with boosted instructions. Show where the instruction would finally commit. Can the sequence be compiled without needing any additional registers?

ANSWER   We use a "+" after the opcode to indicate that the instruction is boosted across the next branch and predicts the branch as taken. Here is the new code:

```
        LW     R1,0(R3)     ;load A
        LW+    R1,0(R2)     ;boosted load B
        BEQZ   R1,L3        ;other branch of the if
        ADDI   R1,R1,#4     ;the else clause
L3:     SW     0(R3),R1     ;nonspeculative store
```

The extra register is no longer necessary, since if the branch is not taken, the result of the speculative load is never written to R1, so R1 can be used in the code sequence. Remember that the result of the boosted instruction is not written into R1 until after the branch. Hence, the branch uses the value of R1 produced by the first, nonboosted load. Other boosted instructions could use the results of the boosted load.   ■

Boosting can be implemented by one of several techniques that are closely related to the techniques needed to implement hardware-based speculation, the topic of the next section.

Hardware-Based Speculation

Hardware-based speculation combines three key ideas: dynamic branch prediction to choose which instructions to execute, speculation to allow the execution of instructions before the control dependences are resolved, and dynamic scheduling to deal with the scheduling of different combinations of basic blocks. Hardware-based speculation uses the dynamic data dependences to choose when to execute instructions. This method of executing programs is essentially a *dataflow execution*: operations execute as soon as their operands are available.

The advantages of hardware-based speculation versus software-based speculation include the following:

1. To speculate extensively, we must be able to disambiguate memory references. This is difficult to do at compile time for integer programs that contain pointers. In a hardware-based scheme, dynamic runtime disambiguation of memory addresses is done using the techniques we saw earlier for Tomasulo's algorithm. This allows us to move loads past stores at runtime.

2. Hardware-based speculation is better when hardware-based branch prediction is superior to software-based branch prediction done at compile time. This is true for many integer programs. For example, a profile-based static predictor has a misprediction rate of about 16% for four of the five integer SPEC programs we use, while a hardware predictor has a misprediction rate of about 11%. Because speculated instructions may slow down the computation when the prediction is incorrect, this difference is significant.

3. Hardware-based speculation maintains a completely precise exception model even for speculated instructions.

4. Hardware-based speculation does not require compensation or bookkeeping code.

5. Hardware-based speculation with dynamic scheduling does not require different code sequences to achieve good performance for different implementations of an architecture. Compiler-based speculation and scheduling often requires code sequences tuned to the machine, and older or different code sequences can result in much lower performance. In contrast, while hardware speculation and scheduling can benefit from scheduling and tuning processors, using the hardware-based approaches is expected to work well even with older or different code sequences. While this advantage is the hardest to quantify, it may be the most important in the long run. Interestingly, this was one of the motivations for the IBM 360/91.

Against these advantages stands a major disadvantage: supporting speculation in hardware is complex and requires substantial hardware resources.

The approach we examine here, and the one implemented in a number of processors (PowerPC 620, MIPS R10000, Intel P6, and AMD K5), is to combine speculative execution with dynamic scheduling based on Tomasulo's algorithm. The 360/91 did this to a certain extent since it could use branch prediction to fetch instructions and assign them to reservation stations. Speculation involves going further and actually executing the instructions as well as executing other instructions dependent on the speculated instructions. Just as with Tomasulo's algorithm, we explain hardware speculation in the context of the floating-point unit, but the ideas are easily applicable to the integer unit, as we will see in the *Putting It All Together* section.

The hardware that implements Tomasulo's algorithm can be extended to support speculation. To do so, we must separate the bypassing of results among instructions, which is needed to execute an instruction speculatively, from the actual completion of an instruction. By making this separation, we can allow an instruction to execute and to bypass its results to other instructions, without allowing the instruction to perform any updates that cannot be undone, until we know that the instruction is no longer speculative. Using the bypass is like performing a speculative register read, since we do not know whether the instruction providing the source register value is providing the correct result until the instruction is no longer speculative. When an instruction is no longer speculative, we allow it to update the register file or memory; we call this additional step in the instruction execution sequence *instruction commit*.

The key idea behind implementing speculation is to allow instructions to execute out of order but to force them to commit *in order* and to prevent any irrevocable action (such as updating state or taking an exception) until an instruction commits. In the simple single-issue DLX pipeline we could ensure that instructions committed in order, and only after any exceptions for that instruction had been detected, simply by moving writes to the end of the pipeline. When we add speculation, we need to separate the process of completing execution from instruction commit, since instructions may finish execution considerably before they are ready to commit. Adding this commit phase to the instruction execution sequence requires some changes to the sequence as well as an additional set of hardware buffers that hold the results of instructions that have finished execution but have not committed. This hardware buffer, which we call the *reorder buffer*, is also used to pass results among instructions that may be speculated.

The reorder buffer provides additional virtual registers in the same way as the reservation stations in Tomasulo's algorithm extend the register set. The reorder buffer holds the result of an instruction between the time the operation associated with the instruction completes and the time the instruction commits. Hence, the reorder buffer is a source of operands for instructions, just as the reservation stations provide operands in Tomasulo's algorithm. The key difference is that in Tomasulo's algorithm, once an instruction writes its result, any subsequently issued instructions will find the result in the register file. With speculation, the register file is not updated until the instruction commits (and we know definitively that the instruction should execute); thus, the reorder buffer supplies operands in the interval between completion of execution and instruction commit. The reorder buffer is not unlike the store buffer in Tomasulo's algorithm, and we integrate the function of the store buffer into the reorder buffer for simplicity. Since the reorder buffer is responsible for holding results until they are stored into the registers, it also replaces the function of the load buffers.

Each entry in the reorder buffer contains three fields: the instruction type, the destination field, and the value field. The instruction type field indicates whether the instruction is a branch (and has no destination result), a store (which has a memory address destination), or a register operation (ALU operation or load, which have register destinations). The destination field supplies the register number (for loads and ALU operations) or the memory address (for stores), where the instruction result should be written. The value field is used to hold the value of the instruction result until the instruction commits. We will see an example of reorder buffer entries shortly.

Figure 4.34 shows the hardware structure of the processor including the reorder buffer. The reorder buffer completely replaces the load and store buffers. Although the renaming function of the reservation stations is replaced by the reorder buffer, we still need a place to buffer operations (and operands) between the time they issue and the time they begin execution. This function is still provided by the reservation stations. Since every instruction has a position in the reorder buffer until it commits (and the results are posted to the register file), we tag a result using the reorder buffer entry number rather than using the reservation station number. This requires that the reorder buffer assigned for an instruction must be tracked in the reservation stations. In section 4.8, we will explore an alternative implementation that uses extra registers for renaming and the reorder buffer only to track when instructions can commit.

Here are the four steps involved in instruction execution:

1. *Issue*—Get an instruction from the floating-point operation queue. Issue the instruction if there is an empty reservation station and an empty slot in the reorder buffer, send the operands to the reservation station if they are in the registers or the reorder buffer, and update the control entries to indicate the buffers are in use. The number of the reorder buffer allocated for the result is also sent to the reservation station, so that the number can be used to tag the result when it is placed on the CDB. If either all reservations are full or the reorder buffer is full, then instruction issue is stalled until both have available entries. This stage is sometimes called *dispatch* in a dynamically scheduled machine.

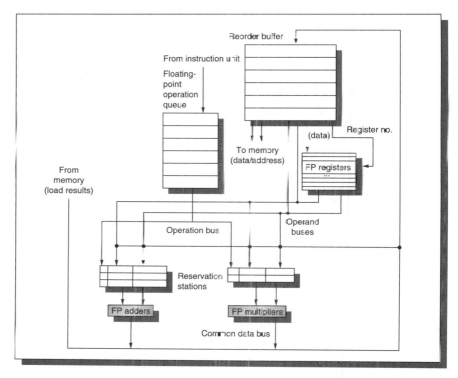

FIGURE 4.34   The basic structure of a DLX FP unit using Tomasulo's algorithm and extended to handle speculation. Comparing this to Figure 4.8 on page 253, which implemented Tomasulo's algorithm, the major changes are the addition of the reorder buffer and the elimination of the load and store buffers (their functions are subsumed by the reorder buffer). This mechanism can be extended to multiple issue by making the CDB (common data bus) wider to allow for multiple completions per clock.

2. *Execute*—If one or more of the operands is not yet available, monitor the CDB (common data bus) while waiting for the register to be computed. This step checks for RAW hazards. When both operands are available at a reservation station, execute the operation. Some dynamically scheduled processors call this step *issue*, but we use the terminology based on the CDC 6600.

3. *Write result*—When the result is available, write it on the CDB (with the reorder buffer tag sent when the instruction issued) and from the CDB into the reorder buffer, as well as to any reservation stations waiting for this result. (It is also possible to read results from the reorder buffer, rather than from the CDB, just as the scoreboard reads results from the registers rather than from a completion bus. The trade-offs are similar to those that exist in a central scoreboard scheme versus a broadcast scheme using a CDB.) Mark the reservation station as available.

4. *Commit*—When an instruction, other than a branch with incorrect prediction, reaches the head of the reorder buffer and its result is present in the buffer, update the register with the result (or perform a memory write if the operation is a store) and remove the instruction from the reorder buffer. When a branch with incorrect prediction reaches the head of the reorder buffer, it indicates that the speculation was wrong. The reorder buffer is flushed and execution is restarted at the correct successor of the branch. If the branch was correctly predicted, the branch is finished. Some machines call this *completion* or *graduation.*

Once an instruction commits, its entry in the reorder buffer is reclaimed and the register or memory destination is updated, eliminating the need for the reorder buffer entry. To avoid changing the reorder buffer numbers as instructions commit, we implement the reorder buffer as a circular queue, so that positions in the reorder buffer change only when an instruction is committed. If the reorder buffer fills, we simply stop issuing instructions until an entry is made free. Now, let's examine how this scheme would work with the same example we used for Tomasulo's algorithm.

EXAMPLE   Assume the same latencies for the floating-point functional units as in earlier examples: Add is 2 clock cycles, multiply is 10 clock cycles, and divide is 40 clock cycles. Using the code segment below, the same one we used earlier, show what the status tables look like when the MULTD is ready to go to commit.

```
LD      F6,34(R2)
LD      F2,45(R3)
MULTD   F0,F2,F4
SUBD    F8,F6,F2
DIVD    F10,F0,F6
ADDD    F6,F8,F2
```

ANSWER   The result is shown in the three tables in Figure 4.35. Note that although the SUBD instruction has completed execution, it does not commit until the MULTD commits. Note that all tags in the Qj and Qk fields as well as in the register status fields have been replaced with reorder buffer numbers, and the Dest field designates the reorder buffer number that is the destination for the result.   ∎

The above Example illustrates the key important difference between a processor with speculation and a processor with dynamic scheduling. Compare the content of Figure 4.35 with that of Figure 4.10 (page 258), which shows the same

Reservation stations							
Name	**Busy**	**Op**	**Vj**	**Vk**	**Qj**	**Qk**	**Dest**
Add1	No						
Add2	No						
Add3	No						
Mult1	No	MULTD	Mem[45+Regs[R3]]	Regs[F4]			#3
Mult2	Yes	DIVD		Mem[34+Regs[R2]]	#3		#5

Reorder buffer					
Entry	**Busy**	**Instruction**	**State**	**Destination**	**Value**
1	No	LD F6,34(R2)	Commit	F6	Mem[34+Regs[R2]]
2	No	LD F2,45(R3)	Commit	F2	Mem[45+Regs[R3]]
3	Yes	MULTD F0,F2,F4	Write result	F0	#2 x Regs[F4]
4	Yes	SUBD F8,F6,F2	Write result	F8	#1 – #2
5	Yes	DIVD F10,F0,F6	Execute	F10	
6	Yes	ADDD F6,F8,F2	Write result	F6	#4 + #2

FP register status									
Field	**F0**	**F2**	**F4**	**F6**	**F8**	**F10**	**F12**	**...**	**F30**
Reorder #	3			6	4	5			
Busy	Yes	No	No	Yes	Yes	Yes	No	...	No

FIGURE 4.35   Only the two LD instructions have committed, though several others have completed execution. The SUBD and ADDD instructions will not commit until the MULTD instruction commits, though the results of the instructions are available and can be used as sources for other instructions. The value column indicates the value being held, the format #X is used to refer to a value field of reorder buffer entry X.

code sequence in operation on a processor with Tomasulo's algorithm. The key difference is that in the example above, no instruction after the earliest uncompleted instruction (MULTD above) is allowed to complete. In contrast, in Figure 4.10 the SUBD and ADDD instructions have also completed.

One implication of this difference is that the processor with the reorder buffer can dynamically execute code while maintaining a precise interrupt model. For example, if the MULTD instruction caused an interrupt, we could simply wait until it reached the head of the reorder buffer and take the interrupt, flushing any other pending instructions. Because instruction commit happens in order, this yields a precise exception. By contrast, in the example using Tomasulo's algorithm, the SUBD and ADDD instructions could both complete before the MULTD raised the exception. The result is that the registers F8 and F6 (destinations of the SUBD and ADDD instructions) could be overwritten, and the interrupt would be imprecise. Some users and architects have decided that imprecise floating-point exceptions are acceptable in high-performance processors, since the program will likely terminate; see Appendix A for further discussion of this topic. Other types of exceptions, such as page faults, are much more difficult to accommodate if they are imprecise, since the program must transparently resume execution after handling such an exception. The use of a reorder buffer with in-order instruction commit provides precise exceptions, in addition to supporting speculative execution, as the next Example shows.

EXAMPLE   Consider the code example used earlier for Tomasulo's algorithm and shown in Figure 4.12 on page 261 in execution:

```
Loop:   LD      F0,0(R1)
        MULTD   F4,F0,F2
        SD      0(R1),F4
        SUBI    R1,R1,#8
        BNEZ    R1,Loop         ; branches if R1≠0
```

Assume that we have issued all the instructions in the loop twice. Let's also assume that the LD and MULTD from the first iteration have committed and all other instructions have completed execution. In an implementation that uses dynamic scheduling for both the integer and floating-point units, the store would wait in the reorder buffer for both the effective address operand (R1 in this example) and the value (F4 in this example); however, since we are only considering the floating-point resources, assume the effective address for the store is computed by the time the instruction is issued.

ANSWER   The result is shown in the three tables in Figure 4.36.

Reservation stations							
Name	**Busy**	**Op**	**Vj**	**Vk**	**Qj**	**Qk**	**Dest**
Mult1	No	MULTD	Mem[0+Regs[R1]]	Regs[F2]			#2
Mult2	No	MULTD	Mem[0+Regs[R1]]	Regs[F2]			#7

Reorder buffer					
Entry	**Busy**	**Instruction**	**State**	**Destination**	**Value**
1	No	LD F0,0(R1)	Commit	F0	Mem[0+Regs[R1]]
2	No	MULTD F4,F0,F2	Commit	F4	#1 x Regs[F2]
3	Yes	SD 0(R1),F4	Write result	0+Regs[R1]	#2
4	Yes	SUBI R1,R1,#8	Write result	R1	Regs[R1]–8
5	Yes	BNEZ R1,Loop	Write result		
6	Yes	LD F0,0(R1)	Write result	F0	Mem[#4]
7	Yes	MULTD F4,F0,F2	Write result	F4	#6 x Regs[F2]
8	Yes	SD 0(R1),F4	Write result	0+#4	#7
9	Yes	SUBI R1,R1,#8	Write result	R1	#4 – 8
10	Yes	BNEZ R1,Loop	Write result		

FP register status								
Field	**F0**	**F2**	**F4**	**F6**	**F8**	**F10**	**F12**	**...**	**F30**
Reorder #	6		7						
Busy	Yes	No	Yes	No	No	No	No	...	No

FIGURE 4.36   Only the LD **and** MULTD **instructions have committed, though all the others have completed execution.** The remaining instructions will be committed as fast as possible.

■

Because neither the register values nor any memory values are actually written until an instruction commits, the processor can easily undo its speculative actions when a branch is found to be mispredicted. Suppose that in the above example (Figure 4.36), the branch BNEZ is not taken the first time. The instructions prior to the branch will simply commit when each reaches the head of the reorder buffer; when the branch reaches the head of that buffer, the buffer is simply cleared and the processor begins fetching instructions from the other path. In practice, machines that speculate try to recover as early as possible after a branch is mispredicted. This can be done by clearing the reorder buffer for all entries that appear after the mispredicted branch, allowing those that are before the branch in the reorder buffer to continue, and restarting the fetch at the correct branch successor. In speculative processors, performance is more sensitive to the branch prediction mechanisms, since the impact of a misprediction will be higher. Thus, all the aspects of handling branches—prediction accuracy, misprediction detection, and misprediction recovery—increase in importance.

Exceptions are handled by not recognizing the exception until it is ready to commit. If a speculated instruction raises an exception, the exception is recorded in the reorder buffer. If a branch misprediction arises and the instruction should not have been executed, the exception is flushed along with the instruction when the reorder buffer is cleared. If the instruction reaches the head of the reorder buffer, then we know it is no longer speculative and the exception should really be taken. We can also try to handle exceptions as soon as they arise, but this is more challenging for exceptions than for branch mispredict.

Figure 4.37 shows the steps of execution for an instruction, as well as the conditions that must be satisfied to proceed to the step and the actions taken. We show the case where mispredicted branches are not resolved until commit.

Although this explanation of speculative execution has focused on floating point, the techniques easily extend to the integer registers and functional units. Indeed, speculation may be more useful in integer programs, since such programs tend to have code where the branch behavior is less predictable. Additionally, these techniques can be extended to work in a multiple-issue processor by allowing multiple instructions to issue and commit every clock. Indeed, speculation is probably most interesting in such processors, since less ambitious techniques can probably exploit sufficient ILP within basic blocks when assisted by a compiler using unrolling.

A speculative processor can be extended to multiple issue (see the Exercises) using the same techniques we employed when extending a Tomasulo-based processor in section 4.4. The same techniques for implementing the instruction issue unit can be used: We process multiple instructions per clock assigning reservation stations and reorder buffers to the instructions. The challenge here is in deciding what instructions can issue and in performing the renaming within the allowable clock period. We also need to widen the CDB to allow multiple instructions to complete within a clock cycle. The challenge lies in monitoring the multiple completion buses for operands without impacting the clock cycle. In section 4.7 we will examine the importance of speculation on the amount of ILP that can be extracted. Section 4.8 examines a speculative multiple-issue machine, the Power-PC 620, and its performance.

The alternative to hardware-based speculation is compiler-based speculation. Such approaches are useful when branches cannot be eliminated by techniques such as loop unrolling but are statically predictable, so that the compiler can choose how to speculate. Whether speculation will be supported primarily in hardware or primarily in software is a point of current debate.

Of course, all the techniques described in the last chapter and in this one cannot take advantage of more parallelism than is provided by the application. The question of how much parallelism is available has been hotly debated and is the topic of the next section.

Instruction status	Wait until	Action or bookkeeping
| Issue | Reservation station (r) and reorder buffer (b) both available | ```
if (Register[S1].Busy)
    /* an executing instruction writes S1 */
    {h← Register[S1].Reorder
    if (Reorder[h].Ready)
        /* Instruction has completed already */
        {RS[r].Vj← Reorder[h].Value; RS[r].Qj ← 0;}
    else /* Wait for instruction */
        {RS[r].Qj← h;}
} else /* Data must be in registers */
        {RS[r].Vj← Regs[S1]; RS[r].Qj← 0;};
if (Register[S2].Busy)
    /* an executing instruction writes S1 */
    {h← Register[S2].Reorder;
    if (Reorder[h].Ready)
        /* Instruction has completed already */
        {RS[r].Vk← Reorder[h].Value; RS[r].Qk ← 0;}
    else /* Wait for instruction */
        {RS[r].Qk← h;}
} else /* Data must be in registers */
        {RS[r].Vk← Regs[S2]; RS[r].Qk← 0;};
/* assign tracking fields of reservation station,
   register data structure, and reorder buffer */
RS[r].Busy← Yes; RS[r].Dest← b;
Register[D].Qi=b; Register[D].Busy← Yes;
Reorder[h].Instruction ← opcode;
Reorder[b].Dest← D; Reorder[b].Ready← No;
``` |
| Execute | (RS[r].Qj=0) and (RS[r].Qk=0) | None—operands are in Vj and Vk |
| Write result | Execution completed at *r* and CDB available, value is *result* (for a store, there are two results, *dest* is the stores destination address in memory, while *result* is the value to be stored) | ```
b←RS[r].Reorder;
/* if x waiting for this reorder buffer, update it */
∀x(if (RS[x].Qj=b) {RS[x].Vj← result; RS[x].Qj ← 0});
∀x(if (RS[x].Qk=b) {RS[x].Vk← result; RS[x].Qk ← 0});
/* free reservation station; update reorder buffer */
RS[r].Busy← No;
Reorder[b].Value← result; Reorder[b].Ready← Yes;
if (Reorder[h].Instruction=Store)
    {Reorder[b].Address← dest;}
``` |
| Commit | Instruction is at the head of the reorder buffer (entry h) and instruction has completed Write result. | ```
r = Reorder[h].Dest; /* register dest, if it exists
*/
if (Reorder[h].Instruction==Branch)
    {if (branch is mispredicted)
        {clear reorder buffer and Register status;
         fetch correct branch successor;};}
else if (Reorder[h].Instruction==Store)
    /* preform the store operation */
    {Mem[Reorder[h].Address]← Reorder[h].Value;}
else /* put the result in the register destination */
    {Regs[r]← Reorder[h].Value;};
Reorder[h].Busy← No;  /* free up reorder buffer entry */
/* free up dest register if no one else writing it */
if (Register[r].Qi==h) {Register[r].Busy← No;};
``` |

FIGURE 4.37   Steps in the algorithm and what is required for each step. For the issuing instruction, D is the destination, S1 and S2 are the sources, and r is the reservation station allocated and b is the assigned reorder buffer entry. RS is the reservation-station data structure. The value returned by a reservation station is called the result. Register is the register data structure, Regs represents the actual registers, while Reorder is the reorder buffer data structure. Just as in Tomasulo's algorithm there is a subtle timing problem; see Exercise 4.24 for further discussion. Similarly, some of the details in handling stores have been simplified; as an exercise, the reader should consider the implication of the fact that stores have two input operands, but that the operands are not needed at the same time.
```

4.7 | Studies of ILP

Exploiting ILP to increase performance began with the first pipelined processors in the 1960s. In the 1980s and 1990s, these techniques were key to achieving rapid performance improvements. The question of how much ILP exists is critical to our long-term ability to enhance performance at a rate that exceeds the increase in speed of the base integrated-circuit technology. On a shorter scale, the critical question of what is needed to exploit more ILP is crucial to both computer designers and compiler writers. The data in this section also provide us with a way to examine the value of ideas that we have introduced in this chapter, including memory disambiguation, register renaming, and speculation.

In this section we review one of the studies done of these questions. The historical section describes several studies, including the source for the data in this section. All these studies of available parallelism operate by making a set of assumptions and seeing how much parallelism is available under those assumptions. The data we examine here are from a study that makes the fewest assumptions; in fact, the ultimate hardware model is completely unrealizable. Nonetheless, all such studies assume a certain level of compiler technology and some of these assumptions could affect the results, despite the use of incredibly ambitious hardware. In the future, advances in compiler technology together with significantly new and different hardware techniques may be able to overcome some limitations assumed in these studies; however, it is unlikely that such advances *when coupled with realistic hardware* will overcome these limits in the near future. Instead, developing new hardware and software techniques to overcome the limits seen in these studies will continue to be one of the most important challenges in computer design.

The Hardware Model

To see what the limits of ILP might be, we first need to define an ideal processor. An ideal processor is one where all artificial constraints on ILP are removed. The only limits on ILP in such a processor are true data dependences either through registers or memory.

The assumptions made for an ideal or perfect processor are as follows:

1. *Register renaming*—There are an infinite number of virtual registers available and hence all WAW and WAR hazards are avoided.

2. *Branch prediction*—Branch prediction is perfect. All conditional branches are predicted exactly.

3. *Jump prediction*—All jumps (including jump register used for return and computed jumps) are perfectly predicted. When combined with perfect branch prediction, this is equivalent to having a processor with perfect speculation and an unbounded buffer of instructions available for execution.

4. *Memory-address alias analysis*—All memory addresses are known exactly and a load can be moved before a store provided that the addresses are not identical.

Initially, we examine a processor that can issue an unlimited number of instructions at once looking arbitrarily far ahead in the computation. For all the processor models we examine, there are no restrictions on what types of instructions can execute in a cycle. For the unlimited-issue case, this means there may be an unlimited number of loads or stores issuing in one clock cycle. In addition, all functional unit latencies are assumed to be one cycle, so that any sequence of dependent instructions can issue on successive cycles. Latencies longer than one cycle would decrease the number of issues per cycle, although not the number of instructions under execution at any point. (The instructions in execution at any point are often referred to as *in-flight*.)

Of course, this processor is completely unrealizable. For example, the HP 8000 is one of the widest superscalar processors announced to date. The 8000 issues up to six instructions per clock (with significant restrictions on the instruction types, including at most two memory references), supports limited renaming, has multicycle latencies, and uses branch prediction. After looking at the parallelism available for the perfect processor, we will examine the impact of restricting various features.

To measure the available parallelism, a set of programs were compiled and optimized with the standard MIPS optimizing compilers. The programs were instrumented and executed to produce a trace of the instruction and data references. Every instruction in the trace is then scheduled as early as possible, limited only by the data dependences. Since a trace is used, perfect branch prediction and perfect alias analysis are easy to do. With these mechanisms, instructions may be scheduled much earlier than they would otherwise, moving across large numbers of instructions on which they are not data dependent, including branches, since branches are perfectly predicted.

Figure 4.38 shows the average amount of parallelism available for six of the SPEC92 benchmarks. Throughout this section the parallelism is measured by the

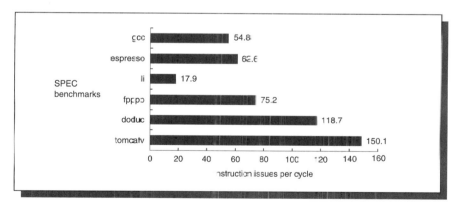

FIGURE 4.38   ILP available in a perfect processor for six of the SPEC benchmarks. The first three programs are integer programs, while the last three are floating-point programs. The floating-point programs are loop-intensive and have large amounts of loop-level parallelism.

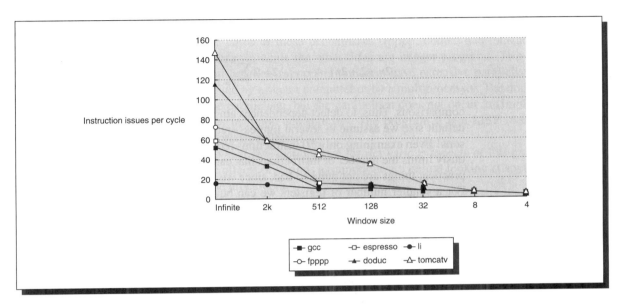

FIGURE 4.39   The effects of reducing the size of the window. The window is the group of instructions from which an instruction can issue. The start of the window is the earliest uncompleted instruction, while the last instruction in the window is determined by the window size. The instructions in the window are obtained by perfectly predicting branches and selecting instructions until the window is full.

window sizes is not that different among the floating-point and integer programs implies a structure where there are non-loop-carried dependences within loop bodies, but few loop-carried dependences in programs such as tomcatv. At small window sizes, the processors simply cannot see the instructions in the next loop iteration that could be issued in parallel with instructions from the current iteration. This is an example of where better compiler technology could uncover higher amounts of ILP, since it can find the loop-level parallelism and schedule the code to take advantage of it, even with small window sizes. Software pipelining, for example, could do this.

We know that large window sizes are impractical, and the data in Figures 4.39 and 4.40 tell us that issue rates will be considerably reduced with realistic windows, thus we will assume a base window size of 2K entries and a maximum issue capability of 64 instructions for the rest of this analysis. As we will see in the next few sections, when the rest of the processor is not perfect, a 2K window and a 64-issue limitation do not constrain the processor.

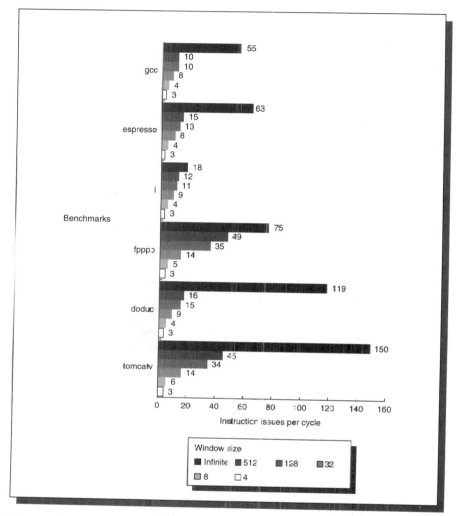

FIGURE 4.40   The effect of window size shown by each application by plotting the average number of instruction issues per clock cycle. The most interesting observation is that at modest window sizes, the amount of parallelism found in the integer and floating-point programs is similar.

The Effects of Realistic Branch and Jump Prediction

Our ideal processor assumes that branches can be perfectly predicted: The outcome of any branch in the program is known before the first instruction is executed! Of course, no real processor can ever achieve this. Figures 4.41 and 4.42 show the effects of more realistic prediction schemes in two different formats.

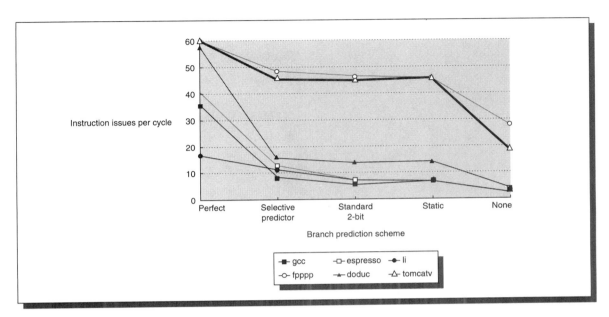

FIGURE 4.41   The effect of branch-prediction schemes. This graph shows the impact of going from a perfect model of branch prediction (all branches predicted correctly arbitrarily far ahead) to various dynamic predictors (selective and two-bit), to compile time, profile-based prediction, and finally to using no predictor. The predictors are described precisely in the text.

Our data is for several different branch-prediction schemes varying from perfect to no predictor. We assume a separate predictor is used for jumps. Jump predictors are important primarily with the most accurate branch predictors, since the branch frequency is higher and the accuracy of the branch predictors dominates.

The five levels of branch prediction shown in these figures are

1. *Perfect*—All branches and jumps are perfectly predicted at the start of execution.

2. *Selective history predictor*—The prediction scheme uses a correlating two-bit predictor and a noncorrelating two-bit predictor together with a selector, which chooses the best predictor for each branch. The prediction buffer contains 2^{13} (8K) entries, each consisting of three two-bit fields, two of which are predictors and the third is a selector. The correlating predictor is indexed using the exclusive-or of the branch address and the global branch history. The noncorrelating predictor is the standard two-bit predictor indexed by the branch address. The selector table is also indexed by the branch address and specifies whether the correlating or noncorrelating predictor should be used. The selector is incremented or decremented just as we would for a standard two-bit

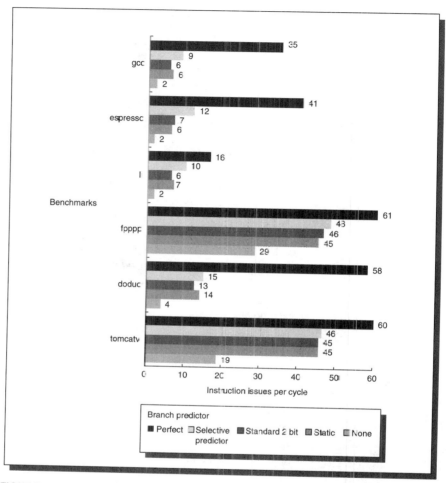

FIGURE 4.42 The effect of branch-prediction schemes sorted by application. This graph highlights the differences among the programs with extensive loop-level parallelism (tomcatv and fpppp) and those without (the integer programs and doduc).

predictor. This predictor, which uses a total of 48K bits, outperforms both the correlating and noncorrelating predictors, achieving an accuracy of at least 97% for these six SPEC benchmarks. Jump prediction is done with a pair of 2K-entry predictors, one organized as a circular buffer for predicting returns and one organized as a standard predictor and used for computed jumps (as in case statement or computed gotos). These jump predictors are nearly perfect.

3. *Standard two-bit predictor with 512 two-bit entries*—In addition, we assume a 16-entry buffer to predict returns.

4. *Static*—A static predictor uses the profile history of the program and predicts that the branch is always taken or always not taken based on the profile, as we discussed in the last chapter.

5. *None*—No branch prediction is used, though jumps are still predicted. Parallelism is largely limited to within a basic block.

Since we do *not* charge additional cycles for a mispredicted branch, the effect of varying the branch prediction is to vary the amount of parallelism that can be exploited across basic blocks by speculation.

Figure 4.42 shows that the branch behavior of two of the floating-point programs is much simpler than the other programs, primarily because these two programs have many fewer branches and the few branches that exist are highly predictable. This allows significant amounts of parallelism to be exploited with realistic prediction schemes. In contrast, for all the integer programs and for doduc, the FP benchmark with the least loop-level parallelism, even the difference between perfect branch prediction and the ambitious selective predictor is dramatic. Like the window size data, these figures tell us that to achieve significant amounts of parallelism in integer programs, the processor must select and execute instructions that are widely separated. When branch prediction is not highly accurate, the mispredicted branches become a barrier to finding the parallelism.

As we have seen, branch prediction is critical, even with a window size of 2K instructions and an issue limit of 64. For the rest of the studies, in addition to the window and issue limit, we assume as a base an ambitious predictor that uses two levels of prediction and a total of 8K entries. This predictor, which requires more than 150K bits of storage, slightly outperforms the selective predictor described above (by about 0.5–1%). We also assume a pair of 2K jump and return predictors, as described above.

The Effects of Finite Registers

Our ideal processor eliminates all name dependences among register references using an infinite set of virtual registers. While several processors have used register renaming for this purpose, most have only a few extra virtual registers. For example, the PowerPC 620 provides 12 extra FP registers and eight extra integer registers in addition to the 32 FP and 32 integer registers provided for in the architecture; these renaming registers are also used to hold speculative results in the 620, but not in these experiments where speculation is perfect. Figures 4.43 and 4.44 show the effect of reducing the number of registers available for renaming, again using the same data in two different forms. Both the FP and GP registers are increased by the number of registers shown on the axis or in the legend.

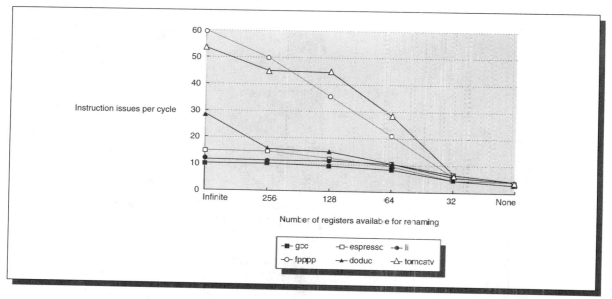

FIGURE 4.43   The effect of finite numbers of registers available for renaming. Both the number of FP registers and the number of GP registers are increased by the number shown on the x axis. The effect is most dramatic on the FP programs, although having only 32 extra GP and 32 extra FP registers has a significant impact on all the programs. As stated earlier, we assume a window size of 2K entries and a maximum issue width of 64 instructions. Recall that DLX supplies 31 integer registers and 16 FP registers (the base number provided under "None").

At first, the results in these figures might seem somewhat surprising: you might expect that name dependences should only slightly reduce the parallelism available. Remember though, exploiting large amounts of parallelism requires evaluating many independent threads of execution. Thus, many registers are needed to hold live variables from these threads. Figure 4.43 shows that the impact of having only a finite number of registers is significant if extensive parallelism exists. Although these graphs show a large impact on the floating-point programs, the impact on the integer programs is small primarily because the limitations in window size and branch prediction have limited the ILP substantially, making renaming less valuable. In addition, notice that the reduction in available parallelism is significant even if 32 additional registers are available for renaming, which is more than the number of registers available on any existing processor as of 1995.

While register renaming is obviously critical to performance, an infinite number of registers is obviously not practical. Thus, for the next section, we assume that there are 256 registers available for renaming—far more than any anticipated processor has.

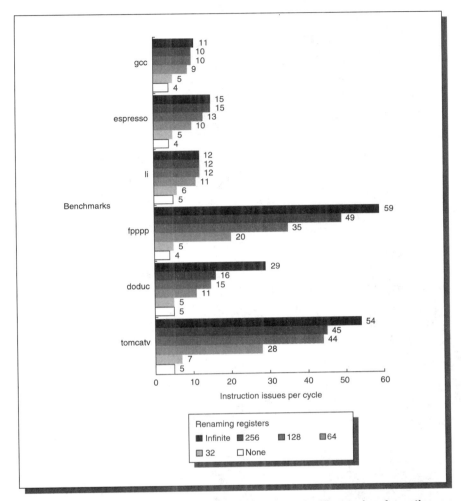

FIGURE 4.44 **The reduction in available parallelism is significant when fewer than an unbounded number of renaming registers are available.** For the integer programs, the impact of having more than 64 registers is not seen here. To use more than 64 registers requires uncovering lots of parallelism, which for the integer programs requires essentially perfect branch prediction.

The Effects of Imperfect Alias Analysis

Our optimal model assumes that it can perfectly analyze all memory dependences, as well as eliminate all register name dependences. Of course, perfect alias analysis is not possible in practice: The analysis cannot be perfect at compile time, and it requires a potentially unbounded number of comparisons at runtime. Figures 4.45 and 4.46 show the impact of three other models of memory alias analysis, in addition to perfect analysis. The three models are

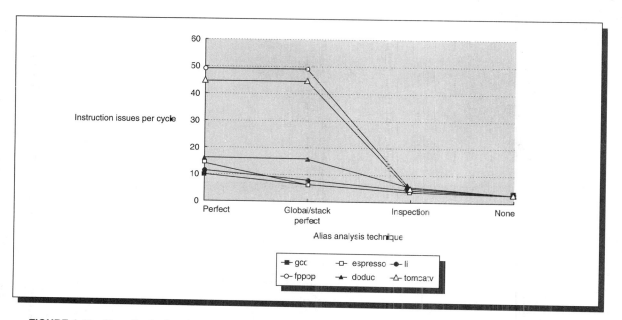

FIGURE 4.45   The effect of various alias analysis techniques on the amount of ILP. Anything less than perfect analysis has a dramatic impact on the amount of parallelism found in the integer programs, while global/stack analysis is perfect (and unrealizable) for the FORTRAN programs. As we said earlier, we assume a maximum issue width of 64 instructions and a window of 2K instructions.

1. *Global/stack perfect*—This model does perfect predictions for global and stack references and assumes all heap references conflict. This represents an idealized version of the best compiler-based analysis schemes currently in production. Recent and ongoing research on alias analysis for pointers should improve the handling of pointers to the heap.

2. *Inspection*—This model examines the accesses to see if they can be determined not to interfere at compile time. For example, if an access uses R10 as a base register with an offset of 20, then another access that uses R10 as a base register with an offset of 100 cannot interfere. In addition, addresses based on registers that point to different allocation areas (such as the global area and the stack area) are assumed never to alias. This analysis is similar to that performed by many existing commercial compilers, though newer compilers can do better through the use of dependence analysis, at least for loop-oriented programs.

3. *None*—All memory references are assumed to conflict.

As one might expect, for the FORTRAN programs (where no heap references exist), there is no difference between perfect and global/stack perfect analysis. The global/stack perfect analysis is optimistic, since no compiler could ever find

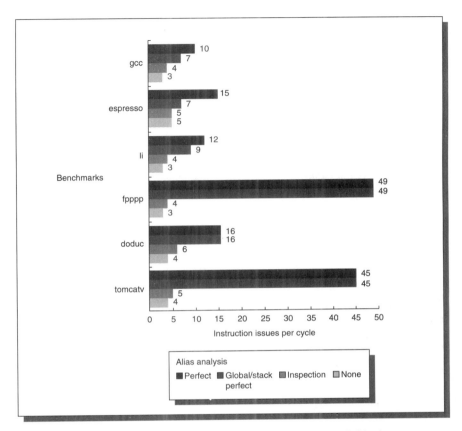

FIGURE 4.46   The effect of varying levels of alias analysis on individual programs.

all array dependences exactly. The fact that perfect analysis of global and stack references is still a factor of two better than inspection indicates that either so-phisticated compiler analysis or dynamic analysis on the fly will be required to obtain much parallelism.

ILP for Realizable Processors

In this section we look at the performance of processors with realistic levels of hardware support that might be attainable in the next five to 10 years. In particu-lar we assume the following fixed attributes:

1. Up to 64 instruction issues per clock with no issue restrictions.

2. A selective predictor with 1K entries and a 16-entry return predictor.

3. Perfect disambiguation of memory references done dynamically—this is ambitious but perhaps attainable for small window sizes.

4. Register renaming with 64 additional integer and 64 additional FP registers.

Figures 4.47 and 4.48 show the result for this configuration as we vary the window size. This configuration is still substantially more complex and expensive than existing implementations in 1995. Nonetheless, it gives a useful bound on what future implementations might yield. The data in these figures is likely to be very optimistic for another reason. There are no issue restrictions among the 64 instructions: they may all be memory references. No one would even contemplate this capability in a single processor at this time. Unfortunately, it is quite difficult to bound the performance of a processor with reasonable issue restrictions; not only is the space of possibilities quite large, but the existence of issue restrictions requires that the parallelism be evaluated with an accurate instruction scheduler, making the cost of studying processors with large numbers of issues very expensive.

In addition, remember that in interpreting these results, cache misses and non-unit latencies have not been taken into account, and both these effects will have significant impact (see the Exercises).

Figure 4.47 shows the parallelism versus window size. The most startling observation is that with the realistic processor constraints listed above, the effect of the window size for the integer programs is not so severe as for FP programs. This points to the key difference between these two types of programs: The

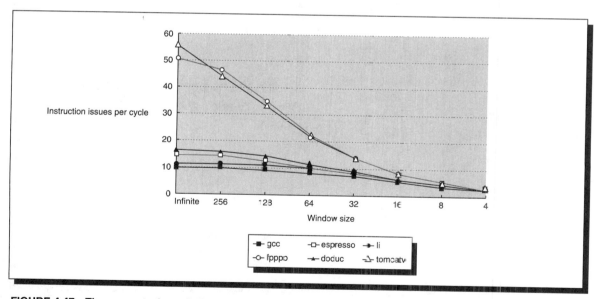

FIGURE 4.47   **The amount of parallelism available for a wide variety of window sizes and a fixed implementation with up to 64 issues per clock.**

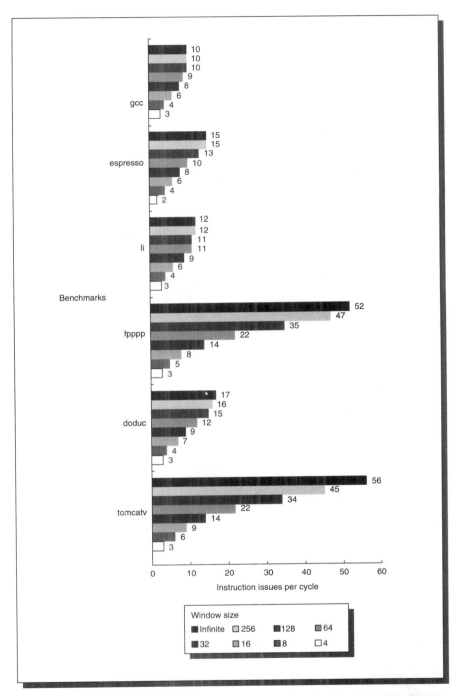

FIGURE 4.48 **The amount of parallelism available versus the window size for a variety of integer and floating-point programs with up to 64 arbitrary instruction issues per clock.**

availability of loop-level parallelism in two of the FP programs means that the amount of ILP that can be exploited is higher, but that for integer programs other factors—such as branch prediction, register renaming, and less parallelism to start with—are all important limitations. As we will see in the next section, for today's speculative machines the actual performance levels are much lower than those shown in Figure 4.47.

Given the difficulty of increasing the instruction rates with realistic hardware designs, designers face a challenge in deciding how best to use the limited resources available on a integrated circuit. One of the most interesting trade-offs is between simpler processors with larger caches and higher clock rates versus more emphasis on instruction-level parallelism with a slower clock and smaller caches. The following Example illustrates the challenges.

EXAMPLE   Consider the following three hypothetical, but not atypical, processors, which we run with the SPEC gcc benchmark:

1.   A simple DLX pipe running with a clock rate of 300 MHz and achieving a pipeline CPI of 1.1. This processor has a cache system that yields 0.03 misses per instruction.

2.   A deeply pipelined version of DLX with slightly smaller caches and a 400 MHz clock rate. The pipeline CPI of the processor is 1.5, and the smaller caches yield 0.035 misses per instruction on average.

3.   A speculative superscalar with a 32-entry window. It achieves 75% of the ideal issue rate measured for this window size. (Use the data in Figure 4.47 on page 331.) This processor has the smallest caches, which leads to 0.05 misses per instruction. This processor has a 200-MHz clock.

Assume that the main memory time (which sets the miss penalty) is 200 ns. Determine the relative performance of these three processors.

ANSWER   First, we use the miss penalty and miss rate information to compute the contribution to CPI from cache misses for each configuration. We do this with the following formula:

$$\text{Cache CPI} = \text{Misses per instruction} \times \text{Miss penalty}$$

We need to compute the miss penalties for each system:

$$\text{Miss penalty} = \frac{\text{Memory access time}}{\text{Clock cycle}}$$

The clock cycle times for the processors are 3.3 ns, 2.5 ns, and 5 ns, respectively. Hence, the miss penalties are

$$\text{Miss penalty}_1 = \frac{200 \text{ ns}}{3.33 \text{ ns}} = 60 \text{ cycles}$$

$$\text{Miss penalty}_2 = \frac{200 \text{ ns}}{2.5 \text{ ns}} = 80 \text{ cycles}$$

$$\text{Miss penalty}_3 = \frac{200 \text{ ns}}{5 \text{ ns}} = 40 \text{ cycles}$$

Applying this for each cache:

Cache $\text{CPI}_1 = 0.03 \times 60 = 1.8$
Cache $\text{CPI}_2 = 0.035 \times 80 = 2.8$
Cache $\text{CPI}_3 = 0.05 \times 40 = 2.0$

We know the pipeline CPI contribution for everything but processor 3; its pipeline CPI is given by

$$\text{Pipeline CPI}_3 = \frac{1}{\text{Issue rate}} = \frac{1}{8 \times 0.75} = \frac{1}{6} = 0.167$$

Now we can find the CPI for each processor by adding the pipeline and cache CPI contributions.

$\text{CPI}_1 = 1.1 + 1.8 = 2.9$
$\text{CPI}_2 = 1.5 + 2.8 = 4.3$
$\text{CPI}_3 = 0.167 + 2.0 = 2.167$

Since this is the same architecture we can compare instruction execution rates to determine relative performance:

$$\text{Instruction execution rate} = \frac{\text{CR}}{\text{CPI}}$$

$$\text{Instruction execution rate}_1 = \frac{300 \text{ MHz}}{2.9} = 103 \text{ MIPS}$$

$$\text{Instruction execution rate}_2 = \frac{400 \text{ MHz}}{4.3} = 93 \text{ MIPS}$$

$$\text{Instruction execution rate}_3 = \frac{200 \text{ MHz}}{2.167} = 92 \text{ MIPS}$$

So the simplest design is the fastest. Of course, the designer building either system 2 or system 3 will probably be alarmed by the large fraction of the system performance lost to cache misses. In the next chapter we'll see the most common solution to this problem: adding another level of caches.   ∎

Before we move to the next chapter, let's see how some of the advanced ideas in this chapter are put to use in a real processor.

4.8 | **Putting It All Together: The PowerPC 620**

The PowerPC 620 is an implementation of the 64-bit version of the PowerPC architecture; this implementation embodies many of the ideas discussed in section 4.6, including out-of-order execution and speculation. It is very similar to several other processors that provide this facility, including the MIPS R10000 and the HP PA 8000, and somewhat more ambitious in organization than other multiple-issue processors, such as the Alpha 21164 and UltraSPARC. The Power-PC 620 and 604 are very similar. The 604 implements only the 32-bit instruction set and provides fewer buffers; its overall organization, however, is essentially identical to that of the 620.

The structure of the PowerPC 620 is shown in Figure 4.49. The 620 can fetch, issue, and complete up to four instructions per clock. There are six separate execution units, each of which can initiate execution independently from its own reservation stations. The six units are as follows:

- Two simple integer units, XSU0 and XSU1, which handle simple integer operations, such as add, subtract, and simple logical operations. All operations here take a single cycle.

- One complex integer function unit, MCFXU, which handles integer multiply and divide. Operations in this unit have a latency of 3 to 20 clock cycles and provide early availability for multiplies with short input values. The operations in this unit vary from being fully pipelined (for multiplies with short integer values) to unpipelined (for integer divide).

- One load-store unit, LSU, which handles loads and stores and has a execution latency for integer loads of 1 cycle and for FP loads of 2 cycles. The LSU is fully pipelined and has its own effective address adder. The LSU contains both load and store buffers and allows loads to bypass pending stores by checking for address conflicts once the effective address of both instructions is known. The load and store buffers hold requests once the effective address calculation is completed. The load buffer simply holds the effective address until the cache access can be completed, whereupon the result is written to the GP or FP result buses. The store buffer is actually two separate queues: one that holds the effective address of the target until the data are available, and a second that holds both the effective address and the data until the store is ready to commit, which happens in order. When the store is ready to commit, the store buffer sends the data to the cache and frees the buffer entry. The cache has two banks so that a load and a store to separate banks can proceed in parallel. When a load causes a cache miss, the load is moved to a single-entry buffer that holds the pending load until the miss is handled. Other loads and stores can be processed at this point, and if the requests hit in the cache, the instructions can complete execu-

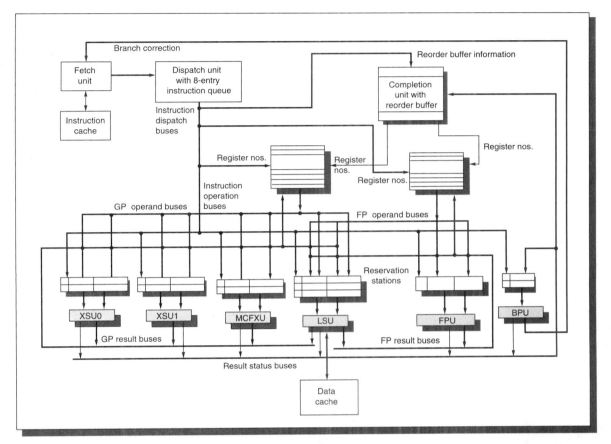

FIGURE 4.49   The PowerPC 620 has six different functional units, each with its own reservation stations and a 16-entry reorder buffer, contained in the instruction completion unit. Renaming is implemented for both the integer and floating-point registers, and the additional renaming registers are part of the respective register files. The condition register used for branches (see Appendix C for a description of conditional branches in the PowerPC architecture) is a 32-bit register grouped as a set of eight 4-bit fields. The BPU provides an additional 16 rename buffers that can each rename one 4-bit field. The condition register and rename buffers are inside the BPU and hence are not shown separately. All the major data flows in the processor are shown here, but not all the control signals. The load and store buffers are not shown, but are present inside the LSU.

tion. Because there is a single-entry buffer, when a second instruction misses, it is returned to the reservation station. This allows up to four cache misses to occur (one in the buffer and three in the reservation stations) before the load-store is completely stalled. This capability, called nonblocking, is described in more detail in Chapter 5.

- One floating-point unit, FPU, which has a latency for use of its result by another floating-point operation of 2 cycles for multiply, add, or multiply-add and 31 clock cycles for DP FP divide. The FPU is fully pipelined except for divide.

■ One branch unit, BPU, which completes branches and informs the fetch unit of mispredictions. The branch unit includes the condition register, used for conditional branches in the PowerPC architecture. The branch unit allows branches to be evaluated independently of the rest of the instructions. In particular, branches do not take issue slots or cycles in the other functional units. When condition registers are set early enough, conditional branches can be executed in parallel with no additional delay.

The 620 operates much like the speculative processor we saw in section 4.6, with one major extension: The register set is extended with a set of renaming registers. These are used to hold speculative results until the instruction commits, at which time the result is written from the renaming registers to the standard integer or floating-point registers. The reorder buffer, which is part of the completion unit, does not contain the speculative results, but only the information needed to complete the instruction when it commits. The primary advantage of this scheme, which is similar to the one used in the MIPS R10000, is that all the operands are available from a single location: the extended register file, consisting of the architectural plus renaming registers. In the 620, there are eight extra integer and 12 extra FP registers. When an instruction issues, it is allocated a rename register; when execution completes, the result is written into the rename register; and when it commits, the result is moved from the rename register to one of the architected registers. With the available rename registers, at most eight integer and 12 FP instructions can be in flight. Operands are still read into reservation stations as soon as they are available, either from the register file when the instruction is dispatched or from the result buses, the counterpart to the CDB (the Common Data Bus used in Tomasulo's scheme), when the operand is produced.

The instructions flow through a pipeline that varies from five to seven clock cycles in typical cases and much longer for operations like divide, which are not pipelined. All instructions pass through the following pipe stages:

1. *Fetch*—Loads the decode queue with instructions from the cache and determines the address of the next instruction. A 256-entry two-way set-associative branch-target buffer is used as the first source for predicting the next fetch address. There is also a 2048-entry branch-prediction buffer used when the branch-target buffer does not hit but a branch is present in the instruction stream. Both the target and prediction buffers are updated, if necessary, when the instruction completes using information from the BPU. In addition, there is a stack of return address registers used to predict subroutine returns.

2. *Instruction decode*—Instructions are decoded and prepared for issue. All time-critical portions of decode are done here. The next four instructions are passed to the next pipeline stage.

3. *Instruction issue*—Issues the instructions to the appropriate reservation station. Operands are read from the register file in this stage, either into the functional unit or into the reservation stations. A rename register is allocated to hold the result of the instruction and a reorder buffer entry is allocated to

ensure in-order completion. In some speculative and dynamically scheduled machines, this process is called *dispatch,* rather than issue. We use the term *issue,* since the process corresponds to the issue process of the CDC 6600, the first dynamically scheduled machine.

4. *Execution*—This stage proceeds when the operands are all available in a reservation station. One of six functional units executes the instruction. The simple integer units XSU0 and XSU1 have a one-stage execution pipeline. The MCFXU has a pipeline depth of between one and three, though integer divide is not fully pipelined and takes more clock cycles (a total of 20 cycles). The FPU has a three-stage pipeline, while the LSU has a two-cycle pipeline. At the end of execution, the result is written into the appropriate result bus and from there into any reservation stations that are waiting for the result, as well as into the rename buffer allocated for this instruction. The completion unit is notified that the instruction has completed. If the instruction is a branch, and the branch was mispredicted, the instruction fetch unit and completion unit are notified, causing instruction fetch to restart at the corrected address and causing the completion unit to discard the speculated instructions and free the rename buffers holding speculated results. When an instruction moves to the functional unit, we say that it has *initiated execution*; some machines use the term *issue* for this transition. An instruction frees up the reservation station when it initiates execution, allowing another instruction to issue to that station. If the instruction is ready to execute when it first issues to the reservation station, it can initiate on the next clock cycle freeing up the reservation station. In such cases, the instruction effectively spends no time in the reservation station: it acts simply as a latch between stages. When an instruction has finished execution and is ready to move to the next stage, we say it has *completed execution.*

5. *Commit*—This occurs when all previous instructions have been committed. Up to four instructions may complete per cycle. The results in the rename register are written into the register file and the rename buffer freed. Upon completion of a store instruction, the LSU is also notified, so that the corresponding store buffer may be sent to the cache. Some machines use the term *instruction completion* for this stage. In a small number of cases, an extra stage may be added for write backs that cannot complete during commit because of a shortage of write ports.

Figure 4.50 shows the basic structure of the PowerPC 620 pipeline and how the stages are connected by buffers, allowing one stage to slip with respect to another. When an instruction commits, all information about that instruction is removed and its results are written into architecturally visible state (registers, PC, or memory).

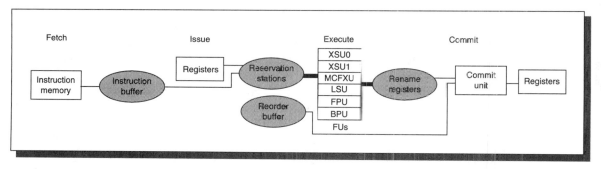

FIGURE 4.50   The pipeline stages of the 620 are linked with a set of buffers, which are shown in grey. These buffers allow slippage between stages of the pipeline. For example, the fetch stage places instructions in the instruction buffer where they are removed by the issue stage. The buffers limit the slippage: If the buffer fills, the stage filling the buffer must stall; if the buffer empties, the stage emptying the buffer must stall. The reservation stations, each of which is associated with a particular functinal unit, and the reorder buffer link issue with the rest of the pipeline. The rename registers are used for results by the execute stage, until the commit unit writes the renamed register to an architectural register. The data cache is essentially part of the load-store unit (LSU). Unless a stall occurs, instructions spend at most one cycle in each stage, except for execute.

Performance of the PowerPC 620 Pipeline

In this section we look at the performance characteristics of the PowerPC 620, examining the critical factors that determine performance. We use seven of the SPEC92 benchmarks in this evaluation: compress, eqntott, espresso, li, alvinn, hydro2d, and tomcatv.

Before we start, we need to understand what it means to stall a multiple-issue processor with dynamic scheduling and speculation. Let's start with the multiple-issue part. In a simple single-issue pipeline, the number of instructions completing in a clock cycle is 0 or 1, and the instruction portion of the CPI ratio for a given clock cycle either increases by 0, in which case a stall occurred, or increases by 1, in which case a stall did not occur. In a multiple-issue processor, the pipeline may be partially stalled—completing fewer instructions than its maximum capability. For example, in the 620 up to four instructions may be completed per clock cycle. Thus a stall is no longer binary: the contribution to the denominator of the CPI for a given clock cycle may vary from 0 to 4. Clearly, the processor is stalled when the contribution is 0, and not stalled when the contribution is 4; in between, the processor is partly stalled since the CPI corresponding to that cycle cannot reach its ideal value of 0.25. To keep this clear, we will focus on what fraction of the instruction slots are empty. If 50% of the instruction slots are empty at instruction commit in a given clock cycle, then two instructions commit that clock cycle, and the CPI for that clock cycle is 0.5. For multiple-issue machines, it is convenient to use IPC (instructions per clock) as the metric, rather than its reciprocal, CPI. We follow this practice in the measurements.

As a further complication, the dynamic scheduling in the pipeline means that we cannot simply track empty instruction slots down the pipeline in a rigid fashion. Once instructions reach the execution stage, dynamic scheduling can reorder the instructions. The instruction throughput, however, cannot *increase* as instructions proceed down the pipeline: If the issue unit processes only two instructions in a given cycle, at least two empty instruction slots will appear in a later clock cycle at the instruction commit stage. These commit slots may come up at different times, but they must appear. No stage can exceed the instruction processing rate achieved by earlier stages. In fact, because of the imposition of additional constraints as instructions flow down the pipeline, we can expect that each stage of execution will somewhat decrease the throughput. For the 620, this effect appears minor, primarily because the execute stage is wider than the issue stage and because instruction commit has few constraints.

Because of the buffering between stages, the performance is limited by the stage that falls behind on any given clock cycle. This means that empty instruction slots created by a given unit that would decrease performance can actually be hidden by the presence of stalls that create additional slots in another unit. For example, the instruction fetch unit may provide only three instructions on a given cycle, leaving one instruction slot empty. If, however, the issue unit processes only two instructions, then the lost slot generated by the fetch unit is essentially hidden by the issue unit. From a designer's viewpoint, we would like to place the burden for the partial stall on the issue unit. Notice that in doing so, we cannot conclude that eliminating the empty slots by redesigning the issue unit will improve the CPI by the corresponding amount. Instead, it will expose the empty slots in the fetch unit. Such interactions are a major source of complexity in the design and performance analysis of pipelines that provide buffering between stages. As a final complication, remember that the buffers are finite. As a result, if a given stage is stalled sufficiently, it also affects the earlier stages, since they will have to stall when the buffers are full. The buffers provide for limited slippage between stages. The goal is that the total number of empty instruction slots is less than the sum of the number of empty slots generated by each unit.

In looking at the 620 performance data, we will focus on the instruction throughput of the issue stage as the critical performance measurement. Focusing on issue makes sense for two reasons. First, it is a good measure of steady-state performance, since in equilibrium instructions cannot issue faster than they execute or commit. Second, the issue stage is the location of some key bottlenecks that are common in many dynamically scheduled machines. Although we will focus on the issue stage, both the fetch stage and the execute stage affect the performance of instruction issue since the fetch and execute stages are responsible for filling the input buffer and emptying the output buffer, respectively, of the issue stage. Thus, we examine the ability of the fetch and execute stages to prevent a stall in the issue stage. Figure 4.51 gives a preview of the pipeline performance, showing how the difference between the ideal IPC (4) and the actual IPC (1.2–1.3) is distributed to the various pipeline stages. We investigate this difference and its causes in more detail in this section.

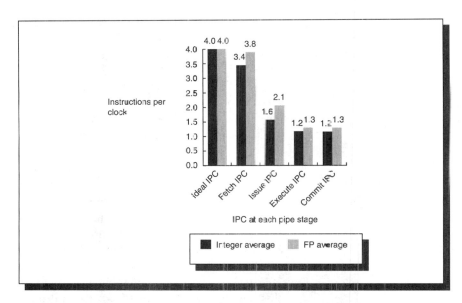

FIGURE 4.51   An overview of the performance of the 620 pipeline showing the IPC at each pipe stage. The ideal IPC is 4. Losses occurring in fetch, primarily due to branch mispredict, bring the IPC down to 3.6 on average. Issue stage incurs stalls for both limitations in the issue structure and mismatch in the functional unit capacity versus need. After issue the IPC is about 1.8. Losses occurring due to a lack of ILP and finite buffers cause the execute stage to back up. This eventually leads to a stall in the issue stage, but we count it in the execute stage. By the end of execute, the IPC is between 1.2 and 1.3. More detailed versions of these data appear throughout this section.

In a machine with speculation, the processor can be active doing work that is later discarded. In examining the performance we ignore such instructions, since they do not contribute to useful work. In particular, we charge the fetch stage for mispredicted branches and do not count stalls for such instructions in the later stages. Notice that incorrect speculation can reduce performance by competing for resources against instructions that must be completed, but we do not expect such effects to be large in well-designed machines. This downside to speculation puts increased importance on the accuracy of branch prediction. After looking at the performance of the various stages we summarize the overall processor performance. The data examined in this section all comes from measurements made on a PowerPC 620 simulator described by Diep, Nelson, and Shen [1995].

Performance of the Fetch Stage

The instruction fetch stage fetches up to four instructions per cycle and places them into the eight-entry instruction buffer. This stage can become a bottleneck whenever it cannot keep at least four instructions in the instruction buffer. Notice that if the instruction buffer has at least four instructions, then the failure of the fetch stage to return four instructions cannot be seen as a stall. In fact, if the buffer is completely full, then downstream pipe stages must be stalled and the fetch unit can do nothing but wait.

On average, the fetch stage is able to keep 5.2 instruction buffers full and is often not a limit on performance. Fetch does limit performance whenever it does not have four instructions available for issue. There are three circumstances under which the fetch unit can fail to keep the instruction buffer full:

1. *A branch misprediction*—No *useful* instructions are added to the buffer; the fetch unit is effectively stalled. In reality, instructions are added to the buffer, but since the instructions come from the wrong path, we count this as a stall, treating it as if no instructions were placed in the buffer. This is the dominant cause of a complete stall in the instruction fetch unit, since it can lead to an effectively empty instruction buffer. Branch mispredict is a much more serious problem for the selected integer programs, where the mispredict rate is 10%, than for the selected FP programs, where the rate is about 3%. This effect shows up clearly in Figure 4.51, where it is the dominant cause of the difference in throughput of the fetch stage for the integer and FP programs. In fact, 75% of the loss in fetch for the integer programs arises from having an empty buffer.

2. *An instruction cache miss*—No instructions are added to the buffer; the fetch unit is completely stalled. With the programs chosen and the assumption about a perfect off-chip cache, I-cache misses are not a serious problem.

3. *Partial cache line fill*—The next group of four instructions crosses a cache block, and only the instructions on the same cache block, which is 8 words long, are fetched. This effect can be significant when branch targets are in the middle of cache blocks. It is a major contributor to having 1–3 buffers full and is responsible for most of the throughput loss in the fetch stage of the FP programs.

Figure 4.52 shows the contribution of these factors to the total effective loss of instruction slots by the fetch unit. On average the integer benchmarks lose 15% (0.6 out of 4.0) of their peak performance, while the FP benchmarks lose 5% (0.2 out of 4.0).

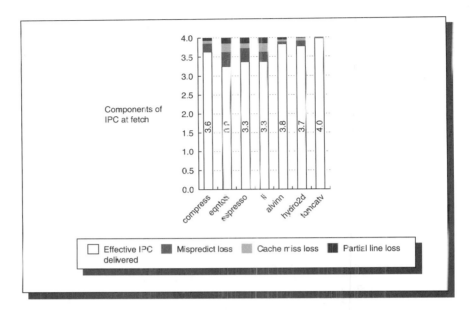

FIGURE 4.52   The average number of instructions that the fetch unit can provide to the issue unit varies between 3.2 and 4, with an average of 3.4 for the integer benchmarks and 3.8 for the FP benchmarks. This means that the fetch stage loses about 0.6 IFC for integer programs and 0.2 IPC for FP programs. These data are computed by determining how often the instruction buffer has 0 through 3 instructions and weighting the frequency by the issue potential that is lost, which is the difference between 4 and the number of entries in the buffer. The portion of the ideal IPC of 4 lost to each of the three causes is shown; these data make the assumption that the timing of one of these events is independent of the state of the instruction buffer. All of the measurements in this section include the effects of the on-chip cache misses, assuming the presence of another level of cache off-chip with a 100% hit rate. The miss penalty to the off-chip cache is 8 cycles, which is probably slightly optimistic. Multilevel cache structures are discussed in detail in the next chapter; the assumption of 100% hits in the next level has only a small effect on the SPEC benchmarks.

Instruction Issue

Instruction issue tries to send four instructions to the appropriate reservation units on every clock cycle. We measure and analyze the performance of the 620 by focusing on the instruction issue stage. Instruction issue can fail to process four instructions for two primary reasons. First, there are limitations in the instruction issue processing stage where certain combinations of instructions cannot simultaneously issue. Second, lack of progress in the execution and completion stages leads to the unavailability of buffers that are required to issue an instruction. Because instruction issue is in order, the first event that prevents issuing an instruction terminates the issue packet. Thus, if the conflicts that prevent issue were uniformly distributed across the four potentially issuing instructions, the average number of instruction issues would be given by $p + p^2 + p^3 + p^4$, where p is the probability that any one instruction can issue. If the probability of not issuing is significant, the average number of issues per clock drops quickly, as shown in Figure 4.53.

Probability (cannot issue a given instruction) = $(1 - p)$	Probability (issue a given instruction) = p	Average number of instruction issues
0.1	0.9	3.1
0.2	0.8	2.4
0.3	0.7	1.8
0.4	0.6	1.3
0.5	0.5	0.9

FIGURE 4.53   Number of instruction issues out of four possible issues. p is the probability that any one instruction can issue. The first instruction to stall ends the issue packet.

This clearly shows the importance of preventing unnecessary stalls in instruction issue.

Five possible conflicts can prevent an instruction from being issued:

1. No reservation station available: There is no reservation station of the appropriate type available.

2. No rename registers are available.

3. Reorder buffer is full.

4. Two operations to the same functional unit: The reservation stations in front of each functional unit share a single write port, so only one operation can issue to the reservation stations for a unit in a clock cycle.

5. Miscellaneous conflicts: Includes shortages of read ports for the registers, conflicts that occur when special registers are accessed, and serialization imposed by special instructions. The last is quite rare and essentially never occurs in the SPEC benchmarks (less than 0.01%). The use of special registers is significant only in li, while register port shortages occur for both tomcatv and hydro2d. These three classes of stalls are combined, but only one of the two primary types is significant in the benchmarks.

The first three of these conflicts arise because the execution or completion stages have not processed instructions that were previously issued; the last two conflicts are internal limitations in the implementation. Figure 4.54 shows the reduction in IPC because of these cases.

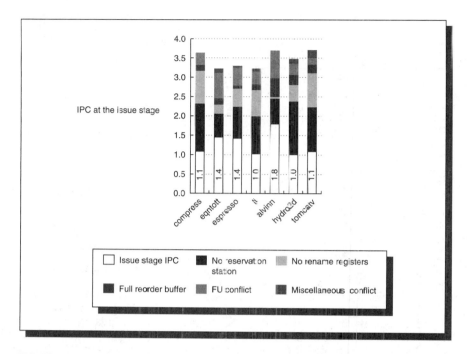

FIGURE 4.54   The IPC throughput rate for the issue stage is arrived at by subtracting stalls that arise in issue from the IPC rate sustained by the fetch stage. The top of each bar shows the IPC from the fetch stage, while the bottom section of each bar shows the effective IPC after the issue stage. The difference is divided between two classes of stalls, those that arise because the later stages have not freed up buffers and those that arise from an implementation limitation in the issue stage (the FU and miscellaneous conflicts). Multiple potential stalls can arise in the same clock cycle for the same instruction. We count the stall as arising from the first cause in the following order: miscellaneous stalls, no reservation station, no rename buffers, no reorder buffer entries, and FU conflict.

Because instruction issue is in order, the first of these conflicts that occurs when examining the instructions in order limits the instruction issue count for that clock cycle. Figure 4.55 shows the same data as Figure 4.54, but organized to show how often various events are responsible for issuing fewer than four instructions per cycle. More than one of these events can occur for a given instruction in a clock cycle. The data in Figure 4.54 assume that the cause is associated with the first event that triggers the stall in the order given above. The dominant cause of stalls is lack of available buffers to issue to (with an average of 54%, this occurs on slightly more than one-half of the cycles), with reservation stations accounting for the largest cause of shortage (33% of the cycles).

Benchmark	No stalls: 4 issues	Stall: no res. station	Stall: no rename buffer	Stall: no reorder buffer	Total stalls: no buffers	Stall: 2 instrs. to FU	Misc. stall	Total issue limit stalls
compress	24%	36%	24%	6%	66%	10%	0%	10%
eqntott	41%	22%	8%	4%	34%	21%	4%	25%
espresso	33%	32%	14%	2%	48%	18%	1%	19%
li	31%	34%	17%	4%	55%	11%	3%	14%
alvinn	31%	23%	1%	21%	45%	24%	0%	24%
hydro2d	17%	43%	17%	8%	68%	12%	3%	15%
tomcatv	6%	37%	34%	9%	80%	7%	7%	14%
Integer avg.	32%	31%	16%	4%	51%	15%	2%	17%
FP avg.	34%	28%	10%	8%	46%	19%	2%	21%
Total avg.	28%	33%	12%	9%	54%	16%	2%	18%

FIGURE 4.55 The sources of all stalls in the issue unit is shown in three broad groups. The first category shows the frequency that four instructions are issued, i.e., no stalls are incurred. The second group shows the frequency of stalls due to full buffers, with the last column totaling the frequency of full buffer stalls. This group arises because the execution and commit stages have failed to complete instructions, which would free up buffers. We will examine the reasons for lack of progress in the execute stage in the next section. The last group are stalls due to restrictions in the issue stage, and the last column sums the two types of these stalls. As in Figure 4.54, there may be multiple reasons for stalling an instruction, so the stall is counted according to the guidelines in Figure 4.54. Notice that the number of cycles where no stalls occur varies widely from 6% to 41%; likewise, in many cases (35% on average) zero instructions issue. This frequency also varies widely from 18% for alvinn to 45% for li and hydro2d.

Performance of the Execution Stage

Once instructions have issued, they wait at the assigned reservation station until the functional unit and the operands are available, whereupon the instruction initiates execution at a functional unit. There are six different functional units allowing up to six initiations per clock. Until an instruction in a reservation station issues, the buffers for the instruction are occupied, potentially causing a stall in the issue stage.

An instruction at a reservation station may be delayed for four reasons:

1. *Source operand unavailable*—One of the source operands is not yet ready.

2. *Functional unit unavailable*—Another instruction is using the functional unit. For fully pipelined units, this happens only when two instructions are ready to initiate on the same clock cycle, but for unpipelined units (integer multiply/ divide, FP divide), the functional unit blocks further initiation until the operation completes.

3. *Out-of-order disallowed*—Both the branch unit and the FP unit require that instructions initiate in order. Thus, an instruction may be stalled until its predecessor initiates.This is a limitation of the execution unit.

4. *Serialization*—A few instructions require totally in-order execution. For example, instructions that access the non-renamed special registers must execute totally in order. Such instructions wait at the reservation station for all prior instructions to commit.

Full buffer stalls in the issue stage are responsible for a loss of 1.6 IPC for the integer programs and 2.0 IPC in the FP programs. We can decompose this loss into the four components above, if we make the assumption that initiating execution for any instruction will free an equivalent number of buffers, allowing issue to continue. Figure 4.56 shows this distribution.

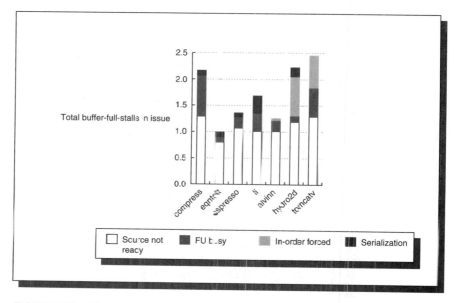

FIGURE 4.56   The stalls in the issue stage because of full buffers (reservation station, rename registers, or reorder buffer) can be attributed to lack of progress in the execution unit. An occupied reservation station fails to begin execution for one of the four reasons shown above. The frequency of these events is used to attribute the total number of full buffer stalls from the issue stage.

When the issue stage stalls and an instruction in a reservation station fails to initiate for one of the four reasons shown above, a designer could contemplate one of three possible reasons:

1. If the source operand is not available and issue stalls because the buffers are full, this indicates that the amount of instruction-level parallelism available, given the limited window size dictated by the buffering, is insufficient. If the code had more parallelism, then fewer reservation stations would have to wait

for results, leading to more initiations and a need for fewer buffers. Alternatively, the designer could increase the number of buffers, leading to a larger window and possibly increased instruction-level parallelism.

2. If the instruction in a reservation station does not initiate because the FU is in use and issue is also stalled, then the basic problem is that the FU capacity is not sufficient to handle the dynamic instruction distribution, at least at that point in the execution. Increasing the number of functional units of different classes would help, as would increasing the pipelining in the unpipelined units. For example, from Figure 4.56 and a knowledge of the instruction distribution, we can see the load-store FU is overcommitted in compress.

3. The final two reasons for a reservation station not initiating (out-of-order disallowed and serialization) are both execution-stage implementation choices, which could be eliminated by reorganizing the execution unit, though an alternative structure might have other drawbacks.

Performance of Instruction Commit

Instruction commit is totally stalled only when the instruction at the head of the reorder buffer has not completed execution. The failure to commit instructions during the cycle can eventually lead to a full reorder buffer, which in turn stalls the instruction issue stage. Instruction commit is basically limited by instruction issue and execute. In some infrequent situations, a lack of write-back ports—there are four integer write ports and two FP write ports—can also lead to a partial stall in instruction commit. Like execution stalls, a completion stall leads to not freeing up rename registers and reorder buffer entries, which can lead to a stall in the issue stage. Completion stalls, however, are very infrequent: on average, execution stalls are seven times more frequent for the FP programs and 100 times more frequent for the integer programs. As a result, instruction commit is not a bottleneck.

Summary: Overall Performance

From the data in earlier figures, we can determine that the IPC runs from just under 1 to just under 1.8 for these benchmarks. The gap between the effective IPC and the ideal IPC of 4.0 can be viewed as three parts:

1. *The limitation caused by the functional units*—This limitation arises because the 620 does not have four copies of each functional unit. For these benchmarks the bottleneck is the load-store unit. This loss counts only the average shortage of FU capacity for the entire program. Short-term higher demands for a functional unit are counted as ILP/finite buffer stalls.

2. *Losses in specific stages*—Fetch, issue, and execute all have losses associated specifically with that stage.

3. *Limited instruction-level parallelism and finite buffering*—Stalls that arise because of lack of parallelism or insufficient buffering. Cache misses that actually result in stall cycles are counted here; cache misses may occur without generating any stalls.

Figure 4.57 shows how the peak IPC of 4 is divided between the actual IPC (1.0 to 1.8) and the various possible stalls.

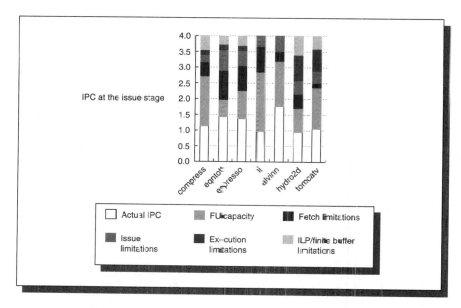

FIGURE 4.57   The breakdown of the ideal IPC of 4.0 into its components. The actual IPC averages 1.2 for the integer programs and 1.3 for the FP programs. The largest difference is the IPC loss due to the functional unit balance not matching the frequency of instructions. Losses in fetch, issue, and execution are the next largest components. ILP and limitations of finite buffering are last. The limits are calculated in this same order, so that the shortage of load-store execution slots is counted as a FU capacity loss, rather than as an ILP/finite buffer loss. Although the ILP/finite buffering limitations are small overall, this arises largely because the other limitations prevent the lack of ILP or finite buffering from becoming overly constraining.

4.9 | Fallacies and Pitfalls

Fallacy: Processors with lower CPIs will always be faster.

Although a lower CPI is certainly better, sophisticated pipelines typically have slower clock rates than processors with simple pipelines. In applications with limited ILP or where the parallelism cannot be exploited by the hardware resources, the faster clock rate often wins. The IBM Power-2 is a machine designed for high-performance FP and capable of sustaining four instructions per clock, including two FP and two load-store instructions; its clock rate was a modest 71.5 MHz. The DEC Alpha 21064 is a dual-issue machine with one load-store or FP operation per clock, but an aggressive 200-MHz clock rate. Comparing the low CPI Power-2 against the high CPI 21064 shows that on a few benchmarks, including some FP programs, the fast clock rate of Alpha leads to better performance (see Figure 4.58). Of course, this fallacy is nothing more than a restatement of a pitfall from Chapter 2 about comparing processors using only one part of the performance equation.

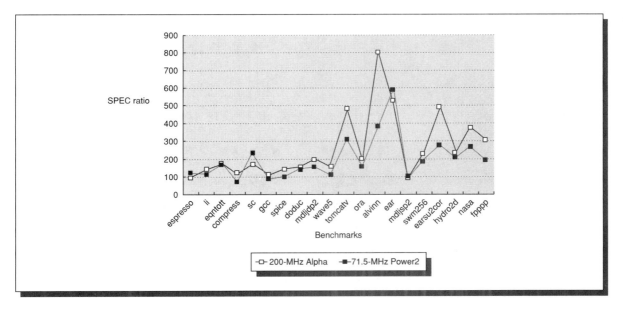

FIGURE 4.58 The performance of the low-CPI Power-2 design versus the high-CPI Alpha 21064. Overall, the 21064 is about 1.1 times faster on integer and 1.4 times faster on FP, indicating that the CPI for the 21064 is 2 to 2.5 times higher than for the Power-2, assuming instruction counts are identical.

> *Pitfall: Emphasizing a reduction in CPI by increasing issue rate while sacrificing clock rate can lead to lower performance.*

The TI SuperSPARC design is a flexible multiple-issue processor capable of issuing up to three instructions per cycle. It had a 1994 clock rate of 60 MHz. The HP PA 7100 processor is a simple dual-issue processor (integer and FP combination) with a 99-MHz clock rate in 1994. The HP processor is faster on all the SPEC benchmarks except two of the integer benchmarks and one FP benchmark, as shown in Figure 4.59. On average, the two processors are close on integer, but the

HP processor is about 1.5 times faster on the FP benchmarks. Of course, differences in compiler technology, as well as the processor, could contribute to the performance differences.

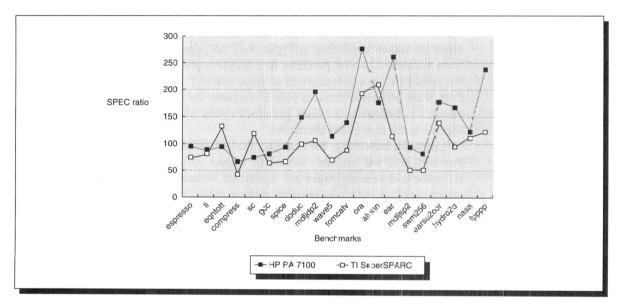

SPEC ratio

Benchmarks

HP PA 7100   TI SuperSPARC

FIGURE 4.59 **The performance of a 99-MHz HP PA 7100 processor versus a 60-MHz SuperSPARC.** The comparison is based on 1994 measurements.

The potential of multiple-issue techniques has caused many designers to focus on reducing CPI while possibly not focusing adequately on the trade-off in cycle time incurred when implementing these sophisticated techniques. This inclination arises at least partially because it is easier with good simulation tools to evaluate the impact of enhancements that affect CPI than it is to evaluate the cycle time impact. There are two factors that lead to this outcome. First, it is difficult to know the clock rate impact of an approach until the design is well underway, and then it may be too late to make large changes in the organization. Second, the design simulation tools available for determining and improving CPI are generally better than those available for determining and improving cycle time. In understanding the complex interaction between cycle time and various organizational approaches, the experience of the designers seems to be one of the most valuable factors.

Pitfall: Improving only one aspect of a multiple-issue processor and expecting overall performance improvement.

4.11 | Historical Perspective and References

This section describes some of the major advances in compiler technology and advanced pipelining and ends with some of the recent literature on multiple-issue processors. The basic concepts—data dependence and its limitation in exploiting parallelism—are old ideas that were studied in the 1960s. Ideas such as data flow computation derived from observations that programs were limited by data dependence. Loop unrolling is a similarly old idea, practiced by early computer programmers on processors with very expensive branches.

The Introduction of Dynamic Scheduling

In 1964 CDC delivered the first CDC 6600. The CDC 6600 was unique in many ways. In addition to introducing scoreboarding, the CDC 6600 was the first processor to make extensive use of multiple functional units. It also had peripheral processors that used a time-shared pipeline. The interaction between pipelining and instruction set design was understood, and the instruction set was kept simple to promote pipelining. The CDC 6600 also used an advanced packaging technology. Thornton [1964] describes the pipeline and I/O processor architecture, including the concept of out-of-order instruction execution. Thornton's book [1970] provides an excellent description of the entire processor, from technology to architecture, and includes a foreword by Cray. (Unfortunately, this book is currently out of print.) The CDC 6600 also has an instruction scheduler for the FORTRAN compilers, described by Thorlin [1967].

The IBM 360/91 introduced many new concepts, including tagging of data, register renaming, dynamic detection of memory hazards, and generalized forwarding. Tomasulo's algorithm is described in his 1967 paper. Anderson, Sparacio, and Tomasulo [1967] describe other aspects of the processor, including the use of branch prediction. Many of the ideas in the 360/91 faded from use for nearly 25 years before being broadly employed in the 1990s.

Branch Prediction Schemes

Basic dynamic hardware branch prediction schemes are described by J. E. Smith [1981] and by A. Smith and Lee [1984]. Ditzel and McLellan [1987] describe a novel branch-target buffer for CRISP, which implements branch folding. McFarling and Hennessy [1986] did a quantitative comparison of a variety of compile-time and runtime branch prediction schemes. Fisher and Freudenberger [1992] evaluated a range of compile-time branch prediction schemes using the metric of distance between mispredictions. The correlating predictor we examine was described by Pan, So, and Rameh in 1992. Yeh and Patt [1992,1993] have written several papers on multilevel predictors that use branch histories for each branch. McFarling's competitive prediction scheme is described in his 1993 technical report.

The Development of Multiple-Issue Processors

The concept of multiple-issue designs has been around for a while, though most early processors followed an LIW or VLIW design approach. Charlesworth [1981] reports on the Floating Point Systems AP-120B, one of the first wide-instruction processors containing multiple operations per instruction. Floating Point Systems applied the concept of software pipelining in both a compiler and by hand-writing assembly language libraries to use the processor efficiently. Since the processor was an attached processor, many of the difficulties of implementing multiple issue in general-purpose processors, for example, virtual memory and exception handling, could be ignored. The Stanford MIPS processor had the ability to place two operations in a single instruction, though this capability was dropped in commercial variants of the architecture, primarily for performance reasons. Along with his colleagues at Yale, Fisher [1983] proposed creating a processor with a very wide instruction (512 bits), and named this type of processor a VLIW. Code was generated for the processor using trace scheduling, which Fisher [1981] had developed originally for generating horizontal microcode. The implementation of trace scheduling for the Yale processor is described by Fisher et al. [1984] and by Ellis [1986]. The Multiflow processor (see Colwell et al. [1987]) was based on the concepts developed at Yale, although many important refinements were made to increase the practicality of the approach. Among these was a controllable store buffer that provided support for a form of speculation. Although more than 100 Multiflow processors were sold, a variety of problems, including the difficulties of introducing a new instruction set from a small company and the competition provided from RISC microprocessors that changed the economics in the minicomputer market, led to failure of Multiflow as a company. Around the same time, Cydrome was founded to build a VLIW-style processor (see Rau et al. [1989]), which was also unsuccessful commercially. Dehnert, Hsu, and Bratt [1989] explain the architecture and performance of the Cydrome Cydra 5, a processor with a wide-instruction word that provides dynamic register renaming and additional support for software pipelining. The Cydra 5 is a unique blend of hardware and software, including conditional instructions, aimed at extracting ILP. Cydrome relied on more hardware than the Multiflow processor and achieved competitive performance primarily on vector-style codes. In the end, Cydrome suffered from problems similar to those of Multiflow and was not a commercial success. Both Multiflow and Cydrome, though unsuccessful as commercial entities, produced a number of people with extensive experience in exploiting ILP as well as advanced compiler technology; many of those people have gone on to incorporate their experience and the pieces of the technology in newer processors. Recently, Fisher and Rau [1993] edited a comprehensive collection of papers covering the hardware and software of these two important processors.

Rau had also developed a scheduling technique called *polycyclic scheduling*, which is a basis for most software pipelining schemes (see Rau, Glaeser, and Picard [1982]). Rau's work built on earlier work by Davidson and his colleagues on the design of optimal hardware schedulers for pipelined processors. Other LIW processors have included the Apollo DN 10000 and the Intel i860, both of which could dual issue FP and integer operations.

One of the interesting approaches used in early VLIW processors, such as the AP-120B and i860, was the idea of a pipeline organization that requires operations to be "pushed through" a functional unit and the results to be caught at the end of the pipeline. In such processors, operations advance only when another operation pushes them from behind (in sequence). Furthermore, an instruction specifies the destination for an instruction issued earlier that will be pushed out of the pipeline when this new operation is pushed in. Such an approach has the advantage that it does not specify a result destination when an operation first issues but only when the result register is actually written. This eliminates the need to detect WAW and WAR hazards in the hardware. The disadvantage is that it increases code size since no-ops may be needed to push results out when there is a dependence on an operation that is still in the pipeline and no other operations of that type are immediately needed. Instead of the "push-and-catch" approach used in these two processors, almost all designers have chosen to use *self-draining pipelines* that specify the destination in the issuing instruction and in which an issued instruction will complete without further action. The advantages in code density and simplifications in code generation seem to outweigh the advantages of the more unusual structure.

IBM did pioneering work on multiple issue. In the 1960s, a project called ACS was underway. It included multiple-issue concepts, but never reached product stage. John Cocke made a subsequent proposal for a superscalar processor that dynamically makes issue decisions; he described the key ideas in several talks in the mid 1980s and coined the name *superscalar*. He called the design America; it is described by Agerwala and Cocke [1987]. The IBM Power-1 architecture (the RS/6000 line) is based on these ideas (see Bakoglu et al. [1989]).

J. E. Smith [1984] and his colleagues at Wisconsin proposed the decoupled approach that included multiple issue with limited dynamic pipeline scheduling. A key feature of this processor is the use of queues to maintain order among a class of instructions (such as memory references) while allowing it to slip behind or ahead of another class of instructions. The Astronautics ZS-1 described by Smith et al. [1987] embodies this approach with queues to connect the load-store unit and the operation units. The Power-2 design uses queues in a similar fashion. J. E. Smith [1989] also describes the advantages of dynamic scheduling and compares that approach to static scheduling.

The concept of speculation has its roots in the original 360/91, which performed a very limited form of speculation. The approach used in recent processors combines the dynamic scheduling techniques of the 360/91 with a buffer to allow in-order commit. J. E. Smith and Pleszkun [1988] explored the use of buffering to maintain precise interrupts and described the concept of a reorder buffer. Sohi [1990] describes adding renaming and dynamic scheduling, making it possible to use the mechanism for speculation. Patt and his colleagues have described another approach, called HPSm, that is also an extension of Tomasulo's algorithm [Hwu and Patt 1986] and supports speculative-like execution.

The use of speculation as a technique in multiple-issue processors was evaluated by Smith, Johnson, and Horowitz [1989] using the reorder buffer technique; their goal was to study available ILP in nonscientific code using speculation and multiple issue. In a subsequent book, M. Johnson [1990] describes the design of a speculative superscalar processor.

What is surprising about the development of multiple-issue processors is that many of the early processors were not successful. Recent superscalars with modest issue capabilities (e.g., the DEC 21064 or HP 7100), however, have shown that the techniques can be used together with aggressive clock rates to build very fast processors, and designs like the Power-2 and TFP [Hsu 1994] processor show that very high issue-rate processors can be successful in the FP domain.

Compiler Technology

Loop-level parallelism and dependence analysis was developed primarily by D. Kuck and his colleagues at the University of Illinois in the 1970s. They also coined the commonly used terminology of *antidependence* and *output dependence* and developed several standard dependence tests, including the GCD and Banerjee tests. The latter test was named after Uptal Banerjee and comes in a variety of flavors. Recent work on dependence analysis has focused on using a variety of exact tests ending with an algorithm called Fourier-Motzkin, which is a linear programming algorithm. D. Maydan and W. Pugh both showed that the sequences of exact tests were a practical solution.

In the area of uncovering and scheduling ILP, much of the early work was connected to the development of VLIW processors, described earlier. Lam [1988] developed algorithms for software pipelining and evaluated their use on Warp, a wide-instruction-word processor designed for special-purpose applications. Weiss and J. E. Smith [1987] compare software pipelining versus loop unrolling as techniques for scheduling code on a pipelined processor. Recently several groups have been looking at techniques for scheduling code for processors with conditional and speculative execution, but without full support for dynamic hardware scheduling. For example, Smith, Horowitz, and Lam [1992] created a concept called boosting that contains a hardware facility for supporting speculation but relies on compiler scheduling of speculated instructions. The sentinel concept, developed by Hwu and his colleagues [Mahlke et al. 1992] is a more general form of this idea.

Studies of ILP

A series of early papers, including Tjaden and Flynn [1970] and Riseman and Foster [1972], concluded that only small amounts of parallelism could be available at the instruction level without investing an enormous amount of hardware. These papers dampened the appeal of multiple instruction issue for more than ten years. Nicolau and Fisher [1984] published a paper based on their work with trace scheduling and asserted the presence of large amounts of potential ILP in scientific programs.

Since then there have been many studies of the available ILP. Such studies have been criticized since they presume some level of both hardware support and compiler technology. Nonetheless, the studies are useful to set expectations as well as to understand the sources of the limitations. Wall has participated in several such strategies, including Jouppi and Wall [1989], Wall [1991], and Wall [1993]. While the early studies were criticized as being conservative (e.g., they didn't include speculation), the latest study is by far the most ambitious study of ILP to date and the basis for the data in section 4.8. Sohi and Vajapeyam [1989] give measurements of available parallelism for wide-instruction-word processors. Smith, Johnson, and Horowitz [1989] also used a speculative superscalar processor to study ILP limits. At the time of their study, they anticipated that the processor they specified was an upper bound on reasonable designs. Recent and upcoming processors, however, are likely to be at least as ambitious as their processor. Most recently, Lam and Wilson [1992] have looked at the limitations imposed by speculation and shown that additional gains are possible by allowing processors to speculate in multiple directions, which requires more than one PC. Such ideas represent one possible alternative for future processor architectures, since they represent a hybrid organization between a conventional uniprocessor and a conventional multiprocessor.

Recent Advanced Microprocessors

The years 1994–95 saw the announcement of a wide superscalar processor (3 or more issues per clock) by every major processor vendor: Intel P6, AMD K5, Sun UltraSPARC, Alpha 21164, MIPS R10000, PowerPC 604/620, and HP 8000. In 1995, the trade-offs between processors with more dynamic issue and speculation and those with more static issue and higher clock rates remains unclear. In practice, many factors, including the implementation technology, the memory hierarchy, the skill of the designers, and the type of applications benchmarked, all play a role in determining which approach is best. Figure 4.60 shows some of the most interesting recent processors, their characteristics, and suggested references. What is clear is that some level of multiple issue is here to stay and will be included in all processors in the foreseeable future.

| Processor | Year shipped in systems | Initial clock rate (MHz) | Issue structure | Schedul-ing | Issue capabilities | | | | | SPEC (measure or estimate) |
					Maxi-mum	Load-store	Integer ALU	FP	Branch	
IBM Power-1	1991	66	Dynamic	Static	4	1	1	1	1	60 int 80 FP
HP 7100	1992	100	Static	Static	2	1	1	1	1	80 int 150 FP
DEC Al-pha 21064	1992	150	Dynamic	Static	2	1	1	1	1	100 int 150 FP
Super-SPARC	1993	50	Dynamic	Static	3	1	1	1	1	75 int 85 FP
IBM Power-2	1994	67	Dynamic	Static	6	2	2	2	2	95 int 270 FP
MIPS TFP	1994	75	Dynamic	Static	4	2	2	2	1	100 int 310 FP
Intel Pentium	1994	66	Dynamic	Static	2	2	2	1	1	65 int 65 FP
DEC Alpha 21164	1995	300	Static	Static	4	2	2	2	1	330 int 500 FP
Sun Ultra–SPARC	1995	167	Dynamic	Static	4	1	1	1	1	275 int 305 FP
Intel P6	1995	150	Dynamic	Dynamic	3	1	2	1	1	> 200 int
AMD K5	1995	100	Dynamic	Dynamic	4	2	2	1	1	130
HaL R1	1995	154	Dynamic	Dynamic	4	1	2	1	1	255 int 330 FP
PowerPC 620	1995	133	Dynamic	Dynamic	4	1	2	1	1	225 int 300 FP
MIPS R10000	1996	200	Dynamic	Dynamic	4	1	2	2	1	300 int 600 FP
HP 8000	1996	200	Dynamic	Static	4	2	2	2	1	> 360 int > 550 FP

FIGURE 4.60 Recent high-performance processors and their characteristics and suggested references. For the last seven systems (starting with the UltraSPARC), the SPEC numbers are estimates, since no system has yet shipped. Issue structure refers to whether the hardware (dynamic) or compiler (static) is responsible for arranging instructions into issue packets; scheduling similarly describes whether the hardware dynamically schedules instructions or not. To read more about these processors the following references are useful: *IBM Journal of Research and Development* (contains issues on Power and PowerPC designs), the *Digital Technical Journal* (contains issues on various Alpha processors), and *Proceedings of the Hot Chips Symposium* (annual meeting at Stanford, which reviews the newest microprocessors).

References

AGERWALA, T. AND J. COCKE [1987]. "High performance reduced instruction set processors," IBM Tech. Rep. (March).

ANDERSON, D. W., F. J. SPARACIO, AND R. M. TOMASULO [1967]. "The IBM 360 Model 91: Processor philosophy and instruction handling," *IBM J. Research and Development* 11:1 (January), 8–24.

BAKOGLU, H. B., G. F. GROHOSKI, L. E. THATCHER, J. A. KAHLE, C. R. MOORE, D. P. TUTTLE, W. E. MAULE, W. R. HARDELL, D. A. HICKS, M. NGUYEN PHU, R. K. MONTOYE, W. T. GLOVER, AND S. DHAWAN [1989]. "IBM second-generation RISC processor organization," *Proc. Int'l Conf. on Computer Design*, IEEE (October), Rye, N.Y., 138–142.

CHARLESWORTH, A. E. [1981]. "An approach to scientific array processing: The architecture design of the AP-120B/FPS-164 family," *Computer* 14:9 (September), 18–27.

COLWELL, R. P., R. P. NIX, J. J. O'DONNELL, D. B. PAPWORTH, AND P. K. RODMAN [1987]. "A VLIW architecture for a trace scheduling compiler," *Proc. Second Conf. on Architectural Support for Programming Languages and Operating Systems,* IEEE/ACM (March), Palo Alto, Calif., 180–192.

DEHNERT, J. C., P. Y.-T. HSU, AND J. P. BRATT [1989]. "Overlapped loop support on the Cydra 5," *Proc. Third Conf. on Architectural Support for Programming Languages and Operating Systems* (April), IEEE/ACM, Boston, 26–39.

DIEP, T. A., C. NELSON, AND J. P. SHEN [1995]. "Performance evaluation of the PowerPC 620 micro-architecture," *Proc. 22th Symposium on Computer Architecture* (June), Santa Margherita, Italy.

DITZEL, D. R. AND H. R. MCLELLAN [1987]. "Branch folding in the CRISP microprocessor: Reducing the branch delay to zero," *Proc. 14th Symposium on Computer Architecture* (June), Pittsburgh, 2–7.

ELLIS, J. R. [1986]. *Bulldog: A Compiler for VLIW Architectures*, MIT Press, Cambridge, Mass.

FISHER, J. A. [1981]. "Trace scheduling: A technique for global microcode compaction," *IEEE Trans. on Computers* 30:7 (July), 478–490.

FISHER, J. A. [1983]. "Very long instruction word architectures and ELI-512," *Proc. Tenth Symposium on Computer Architecture* (June), Stockholm, 140–150.

FISHER, J. A., J. R. ELLIS, J. C. RUTTENBERG, AND A. NICOLAU [1984]. "Parallel processing: A smart compiler and a dumb processor," *Proc. SIGPLAN Conf. on Compiler Construction* (June), Palo Alto, Calif., 11–16.

FISHER, J. A. AND S. M. FREUDENBERGER [1992]. "Predicting conditional branches from previous runs of a program," *Proc. Fifth Conf. on Architectural Support for Programming Languages and Operating Systems,* IEEE/ACM (October), Boston, 85-95.

FISHER, J. A. AND B. R. RAU [1993]. *Journal of Supercomputing* (January), Kluwer.

FOSTER, C. C. AND E. M. RISEMAN [1972]. "Percolation of code to enhance parallel dispatching and execution," *IEEE Trans. on Computers* C-21:12 (December), 1411–1415.

HSU, P. Y.-T. [1994]. "Designing the TFP microprocessor," *IEEE Micro.* 14:2, 23–33.

HWU, W.-M. AND Y. PATT [1986]. "HPSm, a high performance restricted data flow architecture having minimum functionality," *Proc. 13th Symposium on Computer Architecture* (June), Tokyo, 297–307.

IBM [1990]. "The IBM RISC System/6000 processor," collection of papers, *IBM J. Research and Development* 34:1 (January), 119 pages.

JOHNSON, M. [1990]. *Superscalar Microprocessor Design*, Prentice Hall, Englewood Cliffs, N.J.

JOUPPI, N. P. AND D. W. WALL [1989]. "Available instruction-level parallelism for superscalar and superpipelined processors," *Proc. Third Conf. on Architectural Support for Programming Languages and Operating Systems,* IEEE/ACM (April), Boston, 272–282.

LAM, M. [1988]. "Software pipelining: An effective scheduling technique for VLIW processors," *SIGPLAN Conf. on Programming Language Design and Implementation,* ACM (June), Atlanta, Ga., 318–328.

LAM, M. S. AND R. P. WILSON [1992]. "Limits of control flow on parallelism," *Proc. 19th Symposium on Computer Architecture* (May), Gold Coast, Australia, 46–57.

MAHLKE, S. A., W. Y. CHEN, W.-M. HWU, B. R. RAU, AND M. S. SCHLANSKER [1992]. "Sentinel scheduling for VLIW and superscalar processors," *Proc. Fifth Conf. on Architectural Support for Programming Languages and Operating Systems* (October), Boston, IEEE/ACM, 238–247.

MCFARLING, S. [1993] "Combining branch predictors," WRL Technical Note TN-36 (June), Digital Western Research Laboratory, Palo Alto, Calif.

MCFARLING, S. AND J. HENNESSY [1986]. "Reducing the cost of branches," *Proc. 13th Symposium on Computer Architecture* (June), Tokyo, 396–403.

NICOLAU, A. AND J. A. FISHER [1984]. "Measuring the parallelism available for very long instruction word architectures," *IEEE Trans. on Computers* C-33:11 (November), 968–976.

PAN, S.-T., K. SO, AND J. T. RAMEH [1992]. "Improving the accuracy of dynamic branch prediction using branch correlation," *Proc. Fifth Conf. on Architectural Support for Programming Languages and Operating Systems,* IEEE/ACM (October), Boston, 76-84.

RAU, B. R., C. D. GLAESER, AND R. L. PICARD [1982]. "Efficient code generation for horizontal architectures: Compiler techniques and architectural support," *Proc. Ninth Symposium on Computer Architecture* (April), 131–139.

RAU, B. R., D. W. L. YEN, W. YEN, AND R. A. TOWLE [1989]. "The Cydra 5 departmental supercomputer: Design philosophies, decisions, and trade-offs." *IEEE Computers* 22:1 (January), 12–34.

RISEMAN, E. M. AND C. C. FOSTER [1972]. "Percolation of code to enhance parallel dispatching and execution," *IEEE Trans. on Computers* C-21:12 (December), 1411–1415.

SMITH, A. AND J. LEE [1984]. "Branch prediction strategies and branch-target buffer design," *Computer* 17:1 (January), 6–22

SMITH, J. E. [1981]. "A study of branch prediction strategies," *Proc. Eighth Symposium on Computer Architecture* (May), Minneapolis, 135–148.

SMITH, J. E. [1984]. "Decoupled access/execute computer architectures," *ACM Trans. on Computer Systems* 2:4 (November), 289–308.

SMITH, J. E. [1989]. "Dynamic instruction scheduling and the Astronautics ZS-1," *Computer* 22:7 (July), 21–35.

SMITH, J. E. AND A. R. PLESZKUN [1988]. "Implementing precise interrupts in pipelined processors," *IEEE Trans. on Computers* 37:5 (May), 562–573. This paper is based on an earlier paper that appeared in *Proc. 12th Symposium on Computer Architecture,* June 1988.

SMITH, J. E., G. E. DERMER, B. D. VANDERWARN, S. D. KLINGER, C. M. ROZEWSKI, D. L. FOWLER, K. R. SCIDMORE, AND J. P. LAUDON [1987]. "The ZS-1 central processor," *Proc. Second Conf. on Architectural Support for Programming Languages and Operating Systems,* IEEE/ACM (March). Palo Alto, Calif., 199–204.

SMITH, M. D., M. HOROWITZ, AND M. S. LAM [1992]. "Efficient superscalar performance through boosting," *Proc. Fifth Conf. on Architectural Support for Programming Languages and Operating Systems* (October), Boston, IEEE/ACM, 248–259.

SMITH, M. D., M. JOHNSON, AND M. A. HOROWITZ [1989]. "Limits on multiple instruction issue," *Proc. Third Conf. on Architectural Support for Programming Languages and Operating Systems,* IEEE/ACM (April), Boston, 290–302.

SOHI, G. S. [1990]. "Instruction issue logic for high-performance, interruptible, multiple functional unit, pipelined computers," *IEEE Trans. on Computers* 39:3 (March), 349-359.

SOHI, G. S. AND S. VAJAPEYAM [1989]. "Tradeoffs in instruction format design for horizontal architectures," *Proc. Third Conf. on Architectural Support for Programming Languages and Operating Systems,* IEEE/ACM (April), Boston, 15–25.

THORLIN, J. F. [1967]. "Code generation for PIE (parallel instruction execution) computers," *Proc. Spring Joint Computer Conf.* 27.

THORNTON, J. E. [1964]. "Parallel operation in the Control Data 6600," *Proc. AFIPS Fall Joint Computer Conf., Part II,* 26, 33–40.

THORNTON, J. E. [1970]. *Design of a Computer, the Control Data 6600,* Scott, Foresman, Glenview, Ill.

TJADEN, G. S. AND M. J. FLYNN [1970]. "Detection and parallel execution of independent instructions," *IEEE Trans. on Computers* C-19:10 (October), 889–895.

TOMASULO, R. M. [1967]. "An efficient algorithm for exploiting multiple arithmetic units," *IBM J. Research and Development* 11:1 (January), 25–33.

WALL, D. W. [1991]. "Limits of instruction-level parallelism," *Proc. Fourth Conf. on Architectural Support for Programming Languages and Operating Systems* (April), Santa Clara, Calif., IEEE/ACM, 248–259.

WALL, D. W. [1993]. *Limits of Instruction-Level Parallelism,* Research Rep. 93/6, Western Research Laboratory, Digital Equipment Corp. (November).

WEISS, S. AND J. E. SMITH [1984]. "Instruction issue logic for pipelined supercomputers," *Proc. 11th Symposium on Computer Architecture* (June), Ann Arbor, Mich., 110–118.

WEISS, S. AND J. E. SMITH [1987]. "A study of scalar compilation techniques for pipelined supercomputers," *Proc. Second Conf. on Architectural Support for Programming Languages and Operating Systems* (March), IEEE/ACM, Palo Alto, Calif., 105–109.

WEISS, S. AND J. E. SMITH [1994]. *Power and PowerPC,* Morgan Kaufmann, San Francisco.

YEH, T. AND Y. N. PATT [1992]. "Alternative implementations of two-level adaptive branch prediction," *Proc. 19th Symposium on Computer Architecture* (May), Gold Coast, Australia, 124–134.

YEH, T. AND Y. N. PATT [1993]. "A comparison of dynamic branch predictors that use two levels of branch history," *Proc. 20th Symposium on Computer Architecture* (May), San Diego, 257–266.

E X E R C I S E S

4.1 [15] <4.1> List all the dependences (output, anti, and true) in the following code fragment. Indicate whether the true dependences are loop-carried or not. Show why the loop is not parallel.

```
for (i=2;i<100;i=i+1) {
    a[i] = b[i] + a[i];    /* S1 */
    c[i-1] = a[i] + d[i];  /* S2 */
    a[i-1] = 2 * b[i];     /* S3 */
    b[i+1] = 2 * b[i];     /* S4 */
}
```

4.2 [15] <4.1> Here is an unusual loop. First, list the dependences and then rewrite the loop so that it is parallel.

```
for (i=1;i<100;i=i+1) {
    a[i] = b[i] + c[i];    /* S1 */
    b[i] = a[i] + d[i];    /* S2 */
    a[i+1] = a[i] + e[i];  /* S3 */
}
```

4.3 [10] <4.1> For the following code fragment, list the control dependences. For each control dependence, tell whether the statement can be scheduled before the if statement based on the data references. Assume that all data references are shown, that all values are defined before use, and that only b and c are used again after this segment. You may ignore any possible exceptions.

```
if (a>c) {
        d = c + 5;
        a = b + d + e;}
else {
        e = e + 2;
        f = f + 2;
        c = c + f;
}
b = a + f;
```

4.4 [15] <4.1> Assuming the pipeline latencies from Figure 4.2, unroll the following loop as many times as necessary to schedule it without any delays, collapsing the loop overhead instructions. Assume a one-cycle delayed branch. Show the schedule. The loop computes Y[i] = a × X[i] + Y[i], the key step in a Gaussian elimination.

```
loop:    LD      F0,0(R1)
         MULTD   F0,F0,F2
         LD      F4,0(R2)
         ADDD    F0,F0,F4
         SD      0(R2),F0
         SUBI    R1,R1,8
         SUBI    R2,R2,8
         BNEZ    R1,loop
```

4.5 [15] <4.1> Assume the pipeline latencies from Figure 4.2 and a one-cycle delayed branch. Unroll the following loop a sufficient number of times to schedule it without any delays. Show the schedule after eliminating any redundant overhead instructions. The loop is a dot product (assuming F2 is initially 0) and contains a recurrence. Despite the fact that the loop is not parallel, it can be scheduled with no delays.

```
loop:    LD      F0,0(R1)
         LD      F4,0(R2)
         MULTD   F0,F0,F4
         ADDD    F2,F0,F2
         SUBI    R1,R1,#8
         SUBI    R2,R2,#8
         BNEZ    R1,loop
```

4.6 [20] <4.2> It is critical that the scoreboard be able to distinguish RAW and WAR hazards, since a WAR hazard requires stalling the instruction doing the writing until the instruction reading an operand initiates execution, while a RAW hazard requires delaying the reading instruction until the writing instruction finishes—just the opposite. For example, consider the sequence:

```
MULTD   F0,F6,F4
SUBD    F8,F0,F2
ADDD    F2,F10,F2
```

The SUBD depends on the MULTD (a RAW hazard) and thus the MULTD must be allowed to complete before the SUBD; if the MULTD were stalled for the SUBD due to the inability to distinguish between RAW and WAR hazards, the processor will deadlock. This sequence contains a WAR hazard between the ADDD and the SUBD, and the ADDD cannot be allowed to complete until the SUBD begins execution. The difficulty lies in distinguishing the RAW hazard between MULTD and SUBD, and the WAR hazard between the SUBD and ADDD.

Describe how the scoreboard for a machine with two multiply units and two add units avoids this problem and show the scoreboard values for the above sequence assuming the ADDD is the only instruction that has completed execution (though it has not written its result). (*Hint*: Think about how WAW hazards are prevented and what this implies about active instruction sequences.)

4.7 [12] <4.2> A shortcoming of the scoreboard approach occurs when multiple functional units that share input buses are waiting for a single result. The units cannot start simultaneously, but must serialize. This is not true in Tomasulo's algorithm. Give a code sequence that uses no more than 10 instructions and shows this problem. Assume the hardware configuration from Figure 4.3, for the scoreboard, and Figure 4.8, for Tomasulo's scheme. Use the FP latencies from Figure 4.2 (page 224). Indicate where the Tomasulo approach can continue, but the scoreboard approach must stall.

4.8 [15] <4.2> Tomasulo's algorithm also has a disadvantage versus the scoreboard: only one result can complete per clock, due to the CDB. Use the hardware configuration from Figures 4.3 and 4.8 and the FP latencies from Figure 4.2 (page 224). Find a code sequence of no more than 10 instructions where the scoreboard does not stall, but Tomasulo's algorithm must due to CDB contention. Indicate where this occurs in your sequence.

4.9 [45] <4.2> One benefit of a dynamically scheduled processor is its ability to tolerate changes in latency or issue capability without requiring recompilation. This was a primary motivation behind the 360/91 implementation. The purpose of this programming assignment is to evaluate this effect. Implement a version of Tomasulo's algorithm for DLX to issue one instruction per clock; your implementation should also be capable of in-order issue. Assume fully pipelined functional units and the latencies shown in Figure 4.61.

Unit	Latency
Integer	7
Branch	9
Load-store	11
FP add	13
FP mult	15
FP divide	17

FIGURE 4.61 Latencies for functional units.

A one-cycle latency means that the unit and the result are available for the next instruction. Assume the processor takes a one-cycle stall for branches, in addition to any data-dependent stalls shown in the above table. Choose 5–10 small FP benchmarks (with loops) to run; compare the performance with and without dynamic scheduling. Try scheduling the loops by hand and see how close you can get with the statically scheduled processor to the dynamically scheduled results.

Change the processor to the configuration shown in Figure 4.62.

Unit	Latency
Integer	19
Branch	21
Load-store	23
FP add	25
FP mult	27
FP divide	29

FIGURE 4.62 Latencies for functional units, configuration 2.

Rerun the loops and compare the performance of the dynamically scheduled processor and the statically scheduled processor.

4.10 [15] <4.3> Suppose we have a deeply pipelined processor, for which we implement a branch-target buffer for the conditional branches only. Assume that the misprediction penalty is always 4 cycles and the buffer miss penalty is always 3 cycles. Assume 90% hit rate and 90% accuracy, and 15% branch frequency. How much faster is the processor with the branch-target buffer versus a processor that has a fixed 2-cycle branch penalty? Assume a base CPI without branch stalls of 1.

4.11 [10] <4.3> Determine the improvement from branch folding for unconditional branches. Assume a 90% hit rate, a base CPI without unconditional branch stalls of 1, and an unconditional branch frequency of 5%. How much improvement is gained by this enhancement versus a processor whose effective CPI is 1.1?

4.12 [30] <4.4> Implement a simulator to evaluate the performance of a branch-prediction buffer that does not store branches that are predicted as untaken. Consider the following prediction schemes: a one-bit predictor storing only predicted taken branches, a two-bit predictor storing all the branches, a scheme with a target buffer that stores only predicted taken branches and a two-bit prediction buffer. Explore different sizes for the buffers keeping the total number of bits (assuming 32-bit addresses) the same for all schemes. Determine what the branch penalties are, using Figure 4.24 as a guideline. How do the different schemes compare both in prediction accuracy and in branch cost?

4.13 [30] <4.4> Implement a simulator to evaluate various branch prediction schemes. You can use the instruction portion of a set of cache traces to simulate the branch-prediction buffer. Pick a set of table sizes (e.g., 1K bits, 2K bits, 8K bits, and 16K bits). Determine the performance of both (0,2) and (2,2) predictors for the various table sizes. Also compare the performance of the degenerate predictor that uses no branch address information for these table sizes. Determine how large the table must be for the degenerate predictor to perform as well as a (0,2) predictor with 256 entries.

4.14 [20/22/22/22/22/25/25/25/20/22/22] <4.1,4.2,4.4> In this Exercise, we will look at how a common vector loop runs on a variety of pipelined versions of DLX. The loop is the so-called SAXPY loop (discussed extensively in Appendix B) and the central operation in

Gaussian elimination. The loop implements the vector operation $Y = a \times X + Y$ for a vector of length 100. Here is the DLX code for the loop:

```
foo:    LD      F2,0(R1)        ;load X(i)
        MULTD   F4,F2,F0        ;multiply a*X(i)
        LD      F6,0(R2)        ;load Y(i)
        ADDD    F6,F4,F6        ;add a*X(i) + Y(i)
        SD      0(R2),F6        ;store Y(i)
        ADDI    R1,R1,#8        ;increment X index
        ADDI    R2,R2,#8        ;increment Y index
        SGTI    R3,R1,done      ;test if done
        BEQZ    R3,foo          ; loop if not done
```

For (a)–(e), assume that the integer operations issue and complete in one clock cycle (including loads) and that their results are fully bypassed. Ignore the branch delay. You will use the FP latencies shown in Figure 4.2 (page 224). Assume that the FP unit is fully pipelined.

a. [20] <4.1> For this problem use the standard single-issue DLX pipeline with the pipeline latencies from Figure 4.2. Show the number of stall cycles for each instruction and what clock cycle each instruction begins execution (i.e., enters its first EX cycle) on the first iteration of the loop. How many clock cycles does each loop iteration take?

b. [22] <4.1> Unroll the DLX code for SAXPY to make four copies of the body and schedule it for the standard DLX integer pipeline and a fully pipelined FPU with the FP latencies of Figure 4.2. When unwinding, you should optimize the code as we did in section 4.1. Significant reordering of the code will be needed to maximize performance. How many clock cycles does each loop iteration take?

c. [22] <4.2> Using the DLX code for SAXPY above, show the state of the scoreboard tables (as in Figure 4.4) when the SGTI instruction reaches write result. Assume that issue and read operands each take a cycle. Assume that there is one integer functional unit that takes only a single execution cycle (the latency to use is 0 cycles, including loads and stores). Assume the FP unit configuration of Figure 4.3 with the FP latencies of Figure 4.2. The branch should not be included in the scoreboard.

d. [22] <4.2> Use the DLX code for SAXPY above and a fully pipelined FPU with the latencies of Figure 4.2. Assume Tomasulo's algorithm for the hardware with one integer unit taking one execution cycle (a latency of 0 cycles to use) for all integer operations. Show the state of the reservation stations and register-status tables (as in Figure 4.9) when the SGTI writes its result on the CDB. Do not include the branch.

e. [22] <4.2> Using the DLX code for SAXPY above, assume a scoreboard with the FP functional units described in Figure 4.3, plus one integer functional unit (also used for load-store). Assume the latencies shown in Figure 4.63. Show the state of the scoreboard (as in Figure 4.4) when the branch issues for the second time. Assume the branch was correctly predicted taken and took one cycle. How many clock cycles does each loop iteration take? You may ignore any register port/bus conflicts.

f. [25] <4.2> Use the DLX code for SAXPY above. Assume Tomasulo's algorithm for the hardware using one fully pipelined FP unit and one integer unit. Assume the latencies shown in Figure 4.63.

Instruction producing result	Instruction using result	Latency in clock cycles
FP multiply	FP ALU op	6
FP add	FP ALU op	4
FP multiply	FP store	5
FP add	FP store	3
Integer operation (including load)	Any	0

FIGURE 4.63 Pipeline latencies where latency is number of cycles between producing and consuming instruction.

Show the state of the reservation stations and register status tables (as in Figure 4.9) when the branch is executed for the second time. Assume the branch was correctly predicted as taken. How many clock cycles does each loop iteration take?

g. [25] <4.1,4.4> Assume a superscalar architecture that can issue any two independent operations in a clock cycle (including two integer operations). Unwind the DLX code for SAXPY to make four copies of the body and schedule it assuming the FP latencies of Figure 4.2. Assume one fully pipelined copy of each functional unit (e.g., FP adder, FP multiplier) and two integer functional units with latency to use of 0. How many clock cycles will each iteration on the original code take? When unwinding, you should optimize the code as in section 4.1. What is the speedup versus the original code?

h. [25] <4.4> In a superpipelined processor, rather than have multiple functional units, we would fully pipeline all the units. Suppose we designed a superpipelined DLX that had twice the clock rate of our standard DLX pipeline and could issue any two unrelated instructions in the same time that the normal DLX pipeline issued one operation. If the second instruction is dependent on the first, only the first will issue. Unroll the DLX SAXPY code to make four copies of the loop body and schedule it for this superpipelined processor, assuming the FP latencies of Figure 4.63. Also assume the load to use latency is 1 cycle, but other integer unit latencies are 0 cycles. How many clock cycles does each loop iteration take? Remember that these clock cycles are half as long as those on a standard DLX pipeline or a superscalar DLX.

i. [20] <4.4> Start with the SAXPY code and the processor used in Figure 4.29. Unroll the SAXPY loop to make four copies of the body, performing simple optimizations (as in section 4.1). Assume all integer unit latencies are 0 cycles and the FP latencies are given in Figure 4.2. Fill in a table like Figure 4.28 for the unrolled loop. How many clock cycles does each loop iteration take?

j. [22] <4.2,4.6> Using the DLX code for SAXPY above, assume a speculative processor with the functional unit organization used in section 4.6 and a single integer functional unit. Assume the latencies shown in Figure 4.63. Show the state of the processor (as in Figure 4.35) when the branch issues for the second time. Assume the branch was correctly predicted taken and took one cycle. How many clock cycles does each loop iteration take?

k. [22] <4.2,4.6> Using the DLX code for SAXPY above, assume a speculative processor like Figure 4.34 that can issue one load-store, one integer operation, and one FP operation each cycle. Assume the latencies in clock cycles of Figure 4.63. Show the state of the processor (as in Figure 4.35) when the branch issues for the second time. Assume the branch was correctly predicted taken and took one cycle. How many clock cycles does each loop iteration take?

4.15 [15] <4.5> Here is a simple code fragment:

```
for (i=2;i<=100;i+=2)
    a[i] = a[50*i+1];
```

To use the GCD test, this loop must first be "normalized"—written so that the index starts at 1 and increments by 1 on every iteration. Write a normalized version of the loop (change the indices as needed), then use the GCD test to see if there is a dependence.

4.16 [15] <4.1,4.5> Here is another loop:

```
for (i=2,i<=100;i+=2)
    a[i] = a[i-1];
```

Normalize the loop and use the GCD test to detect a dependence. Is there a loop-carried, true dependence in this loop?

4.17 [25] <4.5> Show that if for two array elements $A(a \times i + b)$ and $A(c \times i + d)$ there is a true dependence, then $GCD(c,a)$ divides $(d - b)$.

4.18 [15] <4.5> Rewrite the software pipelining loop shown in the Example on page 294 in section 4.5, so that it can be run by simply decrementing R1 by 16 before the loop starts. After rewriting the loop, show the start-up and finish-up code. *Hint*: To get the loop to run properly when R1 is decremented, the SD should store the result of the *original* first iteration. You can achieve this by adjusting load-store offsets.

4.19 [20] <4.5> Consider the loop that we software pipelined on page 294 in section 4.5. Suppose the latency of the ADDD was five cycles. The software pipelined loop now has a stall. Show how this loop can be written using both software pipelining and loop unrolling to eliminate any stalls. The loop should be unrolled as few times as possible (once is enough). You need not show loop start-up or clean-up.

4.20 [15/15] <4.6> Consider our speculative processor from section 4.6. Since the reorder buffer contains a value field, you might think that the value field of the reservation stations could be eliminated.

a. [15] <4.6> Show an example where this is the case and an example where the value field of the reservation stations is still needed. Use the speculative machine shown in Figure 4.34. Show DLX code for both examples. How many value fields are needed in each reservation station?

b. [15] <4.6> Find a modification to the rules for instruction commit that allows elimination of the value fields in the reservation station. What are the negative side effects of such a change?

4.21 [20] <4.6> Our implementation of speculation uses a reorder buffer and introduces the concept of instruction commit, delaying commit and the irrevocable updating of the registers until we know an instruction will complete. There are two other possible implementation techniques, both originally developed as a method for preserving precise interrupts when issuing out of order. One idea introduces a future file that keeps future values of a register; this idea is similar to the reorder buffer. An alternative is to keep a history buffer that records values of registers that have been speculatively overwritten.

Design a speculative processor like the one in section 4.6 but using a history buffer. Show the state of the processor, including the contents of the history buffer, for the example in Figure 4.36. Show the changes needed to Figure 4.37 for a history buffer implementation. Describe exactly how and when entries in the history buffer are read and written, including what happens on an incorrect speculation.

4.22 [30/30] <4.8> This exercise involves a programming assignment to evaluate what types of parallelism might be expected in more modest, and more realistic, processors than those studied in section 4.7. These studies can be done using traces available with this text or obtained from other tracing programs. For simplicity, assume perfect caches. For a more ambitious project, assume a real cache. To simplify the task, make the following assumptions:

■ Assume perfect branch and jump prediction: hence you can use the trace as the input to the window, without having to consider branch effects—the trace is perfect.

■ Assume there are 64 spare integer and 64 spare floating-point registers; this is easily implemented by stalling the issue of the processor whenever there are more live registers required.

■ Assume a window size of 64 instructions (the same for alias detection). Use greedy scheduling of instructions in the window. That is, at any clock cycle, pick for execution the first *n* instructions in the window that meet the issue constraints.

a. [30] <4.8> Determine the effect of limited instruction issue by performing the following experiments:

■ Vary the issue count from 4–16 instructions per clock.

■ Assuming eight issues per clock: determine what the effect of restricting the processor to two memory references per clock is.

b. [30] <4.8> Determine the impact of latency in instructions. Assume the following latency models for a processor that issues up to 16 instructions per clock:

■ Model 1: All latencies are one clock.

■ Model 2: Load latency and branch latency are one clock; all FP latencies are two clocks.

■ Model 3: Load and branch latency is two clocks; all FP latencies are five clocks.

Remember that with limited issue and a greedy scheduler, the impact of latency effects will be greater.

4.23 [Discussion] <4.3,4.6> Dynamic instruction scheduling requires a considerable investment in hardware. In return, this capability allows the hardware to run programs that could not be run at full speed with only compile-time, static scheduling. What trade-offs should be taken into account in trying to decide between a dynamically and a statically scheduled implementation? What situations in either hardware technology or program characteristics are likely to favor one approach or the other? Most speculative schemes rely on dynamic scheduling; how does speculation affect the arguments in favor of dynamic scheduling?

4.24 [Discussion] <4.3> There is a subtle problem that must be considered when implementing Tomasulo's algorithm. It might be called the "two ships passing in the night problem." What happens if an instruction is being passed to a reservation station during the same clock period as one of its operands is going onto the common data bus? Before an instruction is in a reservation station, the operands are fetched from the register file; but once it is in the station, the operands are always obtained from the CDB. Since the instruction and its operand tag are in transit to the reservation station, the tag cannot be matched against the tag on the CDB. So there is a possibility that the instruction will then sit in the reservation station forever waiting for its operand, which it just missed. How might this problem be solved? You might consider subdividing one of the steps in the algorithm into multiple parts. (This intriguing problem is courtesy of J. E. Smith.)

4.25 [Discussion] <4.4-4.6> Discuss the advantages and disadvantages of a superscalar implementation, a superpipelined implementation, and a VLIW approach in the context of DLX. What levels of ILP favor each approach? What other concerns would you consider in choosing which type of processor to build? How does speculation affect the results?

5 | Memory-Hierarchy Design

Ideally one would desire an indefinitely large memory capacity such that any particular . . . word would be immediately available. . . . We are . . . forced to recognize the possibility of constructing a hierarchy of memories, each of which has greater capacity than the preceding but which is less quickly accessible.

A. W. Burks, H. H. Goldstine, and J. von Neumann
*Preliminary Discussion of the Logical Design
of an Electronic Computing Instrument* (1946)

5.1	Introduction	373
5.2	The ABCs of Caches	375
5.3	Reducing Cache Misses	390
5.4	Reducing Cache Miss Penalty	411
5.5	Reducing Hit Time	422
5.6	Main Memory	427
5.7	Virtual Memory	439
5.8	Protection and Examples of Virtual Memory	447
5.9	Crosscutting Issues in the Design of Memory Hierarchies	457
5.10	Putting It All Together: The Alpha AXP 21064 Memory Hierarchy	461
5.11	Fallacies and Pitfalls	466
5.12	Concluding Remarks	471
5.13	Historical Perspective and References	472
	Exercises	476

5.1 Introduction

Computer pioneers correctly predicted that programmers would want unlimited amounts of fast memory. An economical solution to that desire is a *memory hierarchy*, which takes advantage of locality and cost/performance of memory technologies. The *principle of locality*, presented in the first chapter, says that most programs do not access all code or data uniformly (see section 1.6, page 38). This principle, plus the guideline that smaller hardware is faster, led to the hierarchy based on memories of different speeds and sizes. Since fast memory is expensive, a memory hierarchy is organized into several levels—each smaller, faster, and more expensive per byte than the next level. The goal is to provide a memory system with cost almost as low as the cheapest level of memory and speed almost as fast as the fastest level. The levels of the hierarchy usually subset one another; all data in one level is also found in the level below, and all data in that lower level is found in the one below it, and so on until we reach the bottom of the hierarchy. Note that each level maps addresses from a larger memory to a smaller but faster memory higher in the hierarchy. As part of address mapping, the memory hierarchy is given the responsibility of address checking; hence protection schemes for scrutinizing addresses are also part of the memory hierarchy.

The importance of the memory hierarchy has increased with advances in performance of processors. For example, in 1980 microprocessors were often designed without caches, while in 1995 they often come with two levels of caches. As noted in Chapter 1, microprocessor performance improved 55% per year since 1987, and 35% per year until 1986. Figure 5.1 plots CPU performance projections against the historical performance improvement in main memory access time. Clearly there is a processor-memory performance gap that computer architects must try to close.

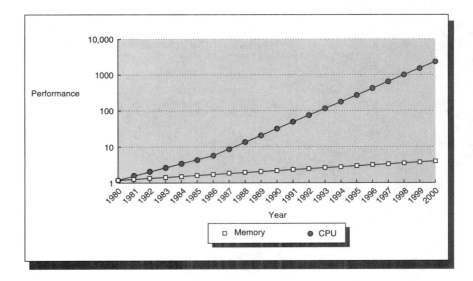

FIGURE 5.1   Starting with 1980 performance as a baseline, the performance of memory and CPUs are plotted over time. The memory baseline is 64-KB DRAM in 1980, with three years to the next generation and a 7% per year performance improvement in latency (see Figure 5.30 on page 429). The CPU line assumes a 1.35 improvement per year until 1986, and a 1.55 improvement thereafter. Note that the vertical axis must be on a logarithmic scale to record the size of the CPU-DRAM performance gap.

In addition to giving us the trends that highlight the importance of the memory hierarchy, Chapter 1 gives us a formula to evaluate the effectiveness of the memory hierarchy:

$$\text{Memory stall cycles} = \text{Instruction count} \times \text{Memory references per instruction} \times \text{Miss rate} \times \text{Miss penalty}$$

where *Miss rate* is the fraction of accesses that are not in the cache and *Miss penalty* is the additional clock cycles to service the miss. Recall that a *block* is the minimum unit of information that can be present in the cache (*hit* in the cache) or not (*miss* in the cache).

This chapter uses a related formula to evaluate many examples of using the principle of locality to improve performance while keeping the memory system affordable. This common principle allows us to pose four questions about *any* level of the hierarchy:

Q1: Where can a block be placed in the upper level? (*Block placement*)

Q2: How is a block found if it is in the upper level? (*Block identification*)

Q3: Which block should be replaced on a miss? (*Block replacement*)

Q4: What happens on a write? (*Write strategy*)

The answers to these questions help us understand the different trade-offs of memories at different levels of a hierarchy; hence we ask these four questions on every example.

To put these abstract ideas into practice, throughout the chapter we show examples from the four levels of the memory hierarchy in a computer using the Alpha AXP 21064 microprocessor. Toward the end of the chapter we evaluate the impact of these levels on performance using the SPEC92 benchmark programs.

5.2 | The ABCs of Caches

Cache: a safe place for hiding or storing things.

Webster's New World Dictionary of the American Language,
Second College Edition (1976)

Cache is the name generally given to the first level of the memory hierarchy encountered once the address leaves the CPU. Since the principle of locality applies at many levels, and taking advantage of locality to improve performance is so popular, the term *cache* is now applied whenever buffering is employed to reuse commonly occurring items; examples include *file caches*, *name caches*, and so on. We start our description of caches by answering the four common questions for the first level of the memory hierarchy; you'll see similar questions and answers later.

Q1: Where can a block be placed in a cache?

Figure 5.2 shows that the restrictions on where a block is placed create three categories of cache organization:

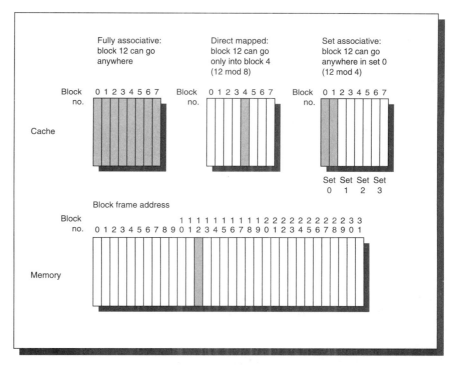

FIGURE 5.2 **This example cache has eight block frames and memory has 32 blocks.** Real caches contain hundreds of block frames and real memories contain millions of blocks. The set-associative organization has four sets with two blocks per set, called *two-way set associative*. Assume that there is nothing in the cache and that the block address in question identifies lower-level block 12. The three options for caches are shown left to right. In fully associative, block 12 from the lower level can go into any of the eight block frames of the cache. With direct mapped, block 12 can only be placed into block frame 4 (12 modulo 8). Set associative, which has some of both features, allows the block to be placed anywhere in set 0 (12 modulo 4). With two blocks per set, this means block 12 can be placed either in block 0 or block 1 of the cache.

- If each block has only one place it can appear in the cache, the cache is said to be *direct mapped*. The mapping is usually

(Block address) MOD *(Number of blocks in cache)*

- If a block can be placed anywhere in the cache, the cache is said to be *fully associative*.

- If a block can be placed in a restricted set of places in the cache, the cache is said to be *set associative*. A *set* is a group of blocks in the cache. A block is first mapped onto a set, and then the block can be placed anywhere within that set. The set is usually chosen by *bit selection*; that is,

(Block address) MOD *(Number of sets in cache)*

If there are *n* blocks in a set, the cache placement is called *n-way set associative*.

The range of caches from direct mapped to fully associative is really a continuum of levels of set associativity: Direct mapped is simply one-way set associative and a fully associative cache with *m* blocks could be called *m*-way set associative; equivalently, direct mapped can be thought of as having *m* sets and fully associative as having one set. The vast majority of processor caches today are direct mapped, two-way set associative, or four-way set associative, for reasons we shall see shortly.

Q2: How is a block found if it is in the cache?

Caches have an address tag on each block frame that gives the block address. The tag of every cache block that might contain the desired information is checked to see if it matches the block address from the CPU. As a rule, all possible tags are searched in parallel because speed is critical.

There must be a way to know that a cache block does not have valid information. The most common procedure is to add a *valid bit* to the tag to say whether or not this entry contains a valid address. If the bit is not set, there cannot be a match on this address.

Before proceeding to the next question, let's explore the relationship of a CPU address to the cache. Figure 5.3 shows how an address is divided. The first division is between the *block address* and the *block offset*. The block frame address can be further divided into the *tag* field and the *index* field. The block offset field selects the desired data from the block, the index field selects the set, and the tag field is compared against it for a hit. While the comparison could be made on more of the address than the tag, there is no need because of the following:

- Checking the index would be redundant, since it was used to select the set to be checked; an address stored in set 0, for example, must have 0 in the index field or it couldn't be stored in set 0.

- The offset is unnecessary in the comparison since the entire block is present or not, and hence all block offsets must match.

FIGURE 5.3   The three portions of an address in a set-associative or direct-mapped cache. The tag is used to check all the blocks in the set and the index is used to select the set. The block offset is the address of the desired data within the block.

If the total cache size is kept the same, increasing associativity increases the number of blocks per set, thereby decreasing the size of the index and increasing the size of the tag. That is, the tag-index boundary in Figure 5.3 moves to the right with increasing associativity, with the end case of fully associative caches having no index field.

Q3: Which block should be replaced on a cache miss?

When a miss occurs, the cache controller must select a block to be replaced with the desired data. A benefit of direct-mapped placement is that hardware decisions are simplified—in fact, so simple that there is no choice: Only one block frame is checked for a hit, and only that block can be replaced. With fully associative or set-associative placement, there are many blocks to choose from on a miss. There are two primary strategies employed for selecting which block to replace:

- *Random*—To spread allocation uniformly, candidate blocks are randomly selected. Some systems generate pseudorandom block numbers to get reproducible behavior, which is particularly useful when debugging hardware.

- *Least-recently used* (LRU)—To reduce the chance of throwing out information that will be needed soon, accesses to blocks are recorded. The block replaced is the one that has been unused for the longest time. LRU makes use of a corollary of locality: If recently used blocks are likely to be used again, then the best candidate for disposal is the least-recently used block.

A virtue of random replacement is that it is simple to build in hardware. As the number of blocks to keep track of increases, LRU becomes increasingly expensive and is frequently only approximated. Figure 5.4 shows the difference in miss rates between LRU and random replacement.

Q4: What happens on a write?

Reads dominate processor cache accesses. All instruction accesses are reads, and most instructions don't write to memory. Figure 2.26 on page 105 in Chapter 2 suggests a mix of 9% stores and 26% loads for DLX programs, making writes 9%/(100% + 26% + 9%) or about 7% of the overall memory traffic and

	Associativity					
	Two-way		Four-way		Eight-way	
Size	**LRU**	**Random**	**LRU**	**Random**	**LRU**	**Random**
16 KB	5.18%	5.69%	4.67%	5.29%	4.39%	4.96%
64 KB	1.88%	2.01%	1.54%	1.66%	1.39%	1.53%
256 KB	1.15%	1.17%	1.13%	1.13%	1.12%	1.12%

FIGURE 5.4   Miss rates comparing least-recently used versus random replacement for several sizes and associativities. These data were collected for a block size of 16 bytes using one of the VAX traces containing user and operating system code. There is little difference between LRU and random for larger-size caches in this trace. Although not included in the table, a first-in, first-out order replacement policy is worse than random or LRU.

9%/(26% + 9%) or about 25% of the data cache traffic. Making the common case fast means optimizing caches for reads, especially since processors traditionally wait for reads to complete but need not wait for writes. Amdahl's Law (section 1.6, page 29) reminds us, however, that high-performance designs cannot neglect the speed of writes.

Fortunately, the common case is also the easy case to make fast. The block can be read from cache at the same time that the tag is read and compared, so the block read begins as soon as the block address is available. If the read is a hit, the requested part of the block is passed on to the CPU immediately. If it is a miss, there is no benefit—but also no harm; just ignore the value read.

Such is not the case for writes. Modifying a block cannot begin until the tag is checked to see if the address is a hit. Because tag checking cannot occur in parallel, writes normally take longer than reads. Another complexity is that the processor also specifies the size of the write, usually between 1 and 8 bytes; only that portion of a block can be changed. In contrast, reads can access more bytes than necessary without fear.

The write policies often distinguish cache designs. There are two basic options when writing to the cache:

- *Write through* (or *store through*)—The information is written to both the block in the cache *and* to the block in the lower-level memory.

- *Write back* (also called *copy back* or *store in*)—The information is written only to the block in the cache. The modified cache block is written to main memory only when it is replaced.

To reduce the frequency of writing back blocks on replacement, a feature called the *dirty bit* is commonly used. This status bit indicates whether the block is *dirty* (modified while in the cache) or *clean* (not modified). If it is clean, the block is not written on a miss, since the lower level has identical information to the cache.

Both write back and write through have their advantages. With write back, writes occur at the speed of the cache memory, and multiple writes within a block require only one write to the lower-level memory. Since some writes don't go to memory, write back uses less memory bandwidth, making write back attractive in multiprocessors. With write through, read misses never result in writes to the lower level, and write through is easier to implement than write back. Write through also has the advantage that the next lower level has the most current copy of the data. This is important for I/O and for multiprocessors, which we examine in Chapters 6 and 8. As we shall see, I/O and multiprocessors are fickle: they want write back for processor caches to reduce the memory traffic and write through to keep the cache consistent with lower levels of the memory hierarchy.

When the CPU must wait for writes to complete during write through, the CPU is said to *write stall*. A common optimization to reduce write stalls is a *write buffer*, which allows the processor to continue as soon as the data is written to the buffer, thereby overlapping processor execution with memory updating. As we shall see shortly, write stalls can occur even with write buffers.

Since the data are not needed on a write, there are two common options on a write miss:

■ *Write allocate* (also called *fetch on write*)—The block is loaded on a write miss, followed by the write-hit actions above. This is similar to a read miss.

■ *No-write allocate* (also called *write around*)—The block is modified in the lower level and not loaded into the cache.

Although either write-miss policy could be used with write through or write back, write-back caches generally use write allocate (hoping that subsequent writes to that block will be captured by the cache) and write-through caches often use no-write allocate (since subsequent writes to that block will still have to go to memory).

An Example: The Alpha AXP 21064 Data Cache and Instruction Cache

To give substance to these ideas, Figure 5.5 shows the organization of the data cache in the Alpha AXP 21064 microprocessor that is found in the DEC 3000 Model 800 workstation. The cache contains 8192 bytes of data in 32-byte blocks with direct-mapped placement, write through with a four-block write buffer, and no-write allocate on a write miss.

Let's trace a cache hit through the steps of a hit as labeled in Figure 5.5. (The four steps are shown as circled numbers.) As we shall see later (Figure 5.41), the 21064 microprocessor presents a 34-bit physical address to the cache for tag comparison. The address coming into the cache is divided into two fields: the 29-bit block address and 5-bit block offset. The block address is further divided into an address tag and cache index. Step 1 shows this division.

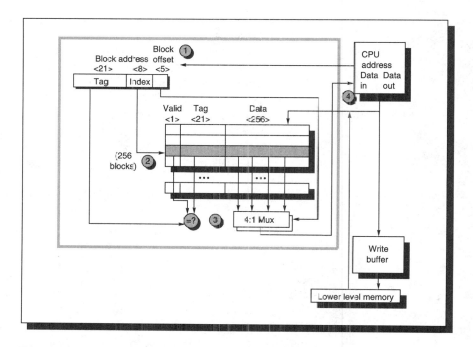

FIGURE 5.5   The organization of the data cache in the Alpha AXP 21064 microprocessor. The 8-KB cache is direct mapped with 32-byte blocks. It has 256 blocks selected by the 8-bit index. The four steps of a read hit, shown as circled numbers in order of occurrence, label this organization. Although we show a 4:1 multiplexer to select the desired 8 bytes, in reality the data RAM is organized 8 bytes wide and the multiplexer is unnecessary: 2 bits of the block offset join the index to supply the RAM address to select the proper 8 bytes (see Figure 5.8). Although not exercised in this example, the line from memory to the cache is used on a miss to load the cache.

The cache index selects the tag to be tested to see if the desired block is in the cache. The size of the index depends on cache size, block size, and set associativity. The 21064 cache is direct mapped, so set associativity is set to one, and we calculate the index as follows:

$$2^{\text{index}} = \frac{\text{Cache size}}{\text{Block size} \times \text{Set associativity}} = \frac{8192}{32 \times 1} = 256 = 2^8$$

Hence the index is 8 bits wide, and the tag is 29 – 8 or 21 bits wide.

Index selection is step 2 in Figure 5.5. Remember that direct mapping allows the data to be read and sent to the CPU in parallel with the tag being read and checked.

After reading the tag from the cache, it is compared to the tag portion of the block address from the CPU. This is step 3 in the figure. To be sure the tag contains valid information, the valid bit must be set or else the results of the comparison are ignored.

Assuming the tag does match, the final step is to signal the CPU to load the data from the cache. The 21064 allows two clock cycles for these four steps, so the instructions in the following two clock cycles would stall if they tried to use the result of the load.

Handling writes is more complicated than handling reads in the 21064, as it is in any cache. If the word to be written is in the cache, the first three steps are the same. After the tag comparison indicates a hit, the data are written. (Section 5.5 shows how the 21064 avoids the extra time on write hits that this description implies.)

Since this is a write-through cache, the write process isn't yet over. The data are also sent to a write buffer that can contain up to four blocks that each can hold four 64-bit words. If the write buffer is empty, the data and the full address are written in the buffer, and the write is finished from the CPU's perspective; the CPU continues working while the write buffer prepares to write the word to memory. If the buffer contains other modified blocks, the addresses are checked to see if the address of this new data matches the address of the valid write buffer entry; if so, the new data are combined with that entry, called *write merging*. Without this optimization, four stores to sequential addresses would fill the buffer, even though these four words easily fit within a single block of the write buffer when merged. Figure 5.6 shows a write buffer with and without write merging. If the buffer is full and there is no address match, the cache (and CPU) must wait until the buffer has an empty entry.

So far we have assumed the common case of a cache hit. What happens on a miss? On a read miss, the cache sends a stall signal to the CPU telling it to wait, and 32 bytes are read from the next level of the hierarchy. The path to the next lower level is 16 bytes wide in the DEC 3000 model 800 workstation, one of several models that use the 21064. That takes 5 clock cycles per transfer, or 10 clock cycles for all 32 bytes. Since the data cache is direct mapped, there is no choice on which block to replace. Replacing a block means updating the data, the address tag, and the valid bit. On a write miss, the CPU writes "around" the cache to lower-level memory and does not affect the cache; that is, the 21064 follows the no-write-allocate rule.

We have seen how it works, but the *data* cache cannot supply all the memory needs of the processor: the processor also needs instructions. Although a single cache could try to supply both, it can be a bottleneck. For example, when a load or store instruction is executed, the pipelined processor will simultaneously request both a data word *and* an instruction word. Hence a single cache would present a structural hazard for loads and stores, leading to stalls. One simple way to conquer this problem is to divide it: one cache is dedicated to instructions and another to data. Separate caches are found in most recent processors, including the Alpha AXP 21064. It has an 8-KB instruction cache that is nearly identical to its 8-KB data cache in Figure 5.5.

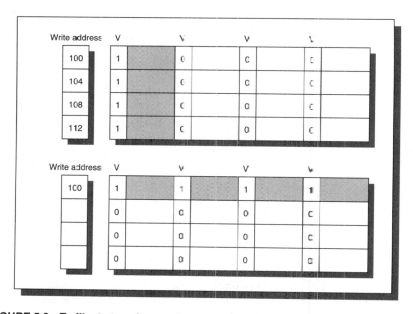

FIGURE 5.6 **To illustrate write merging, the write buffer on top does not use it while the write buffer on the bottom does.** Each buffer has four entries, and each entry holds four 64-bit words. The address for each entry is on the left, with valid bits (V) indicating whether or not the next sequential four bytes are occupied in this entry. The four writes are merged into a single buffer entry with write merging; without it, all four entries are used. Without write merging, the blocks to the right in the upper drawing would only be used for instructions that wrote multiple words at the same time. (The Alpha is a 64-bit architecture so its buffer is really 8 bytes per word.)

The CPU knows whether it is issuing an instruction address or a data address, so there can be separate ports for both, thereby doubling the bandwidth between the memory hierarchy and the CPU. Separate caches also offer the opportunity of optimizing each cache separately: different capacities, block sizes, and associativities may lead to better performance. (In contrast to the instruction caches and data caches of the 21064, the terms *unified* or *mixed* are applied to caches that can contain either instructions or data.)

Figure 5.7 shows that instruction caches have lower miss rates than data caches. Separating instructions and data removes misses due to conflicts between instruction blocks and data blocks, but the split also fixes the cache space devoted to each type. Which is more important to miss rates? A fair comparison of separate instruction and data caches to unified caches requires the total cache size to be the same. For example, a separate 1-KB instruction cache and 1-KB data cache should be compared to a 2-KB unified cache. Calculating the average miss rate with separate instruction and data caches necessitates knowing the percentage of memory references to each cache. Figure 2.26 on page 105 suggests the

Size	Instruction cache	Data cache	Unified cache
1 KB	3.06%	24.61%	13.34%
2 KB	2.26%	20.57%	9.78%
4 KB	1.78%	15.94%	7.24%
8 KB	1.10%	10.19%	4.57%
16 KB	0.64%	6.47%	2.87%
32 KB	0.39%	4.82%	1.99%
64 KB	0.15%	3.77%	1.35%
128 KB	0.02%	2.88%	0.95%

FIGURE 5.7   Miss rates for instruction, data, and unified caches of different sizes. The data are for a direct-mapped cache with 32-byte blocks for an average of SPEC92 benchmarks on the DECstation 5000 [Gee et al. 1993]. The percentage of instruction references is about 75%.

split is 100%/(100% + 26% + 9%) or about 75% instruction references to (26% + 9%)/(100% + 26% + 9%) or about 25% data references. Splitting affects performance beyond what is indicated by the change in miss rates, as we shall see in a little bit.

Cache Performance

Because instruction count is independent of the hardware, it is tempting to evaluate CPU performance using that number. As we saw in Chapter 1, however, such indirect performance measures have waylaid many a computer designer. The corresponding temptation for evaluating memory-hierarchy performance is to concentrate on miss rate, because it, too, is independent of the speed of the hardware. As we shall see, miss rate can be just as misleading as instruction count. A better measure of memory-hierarchy performance is the average time to access memory:

$$\text{Average memory access time} = \text{Hit time} + \text{Miss rate} \times \text{Miss penalty}$$

where *Hit time* is the time to hit in the cache; we have seen the other two terms before. The components of average access time can be measured either in absolute time—say, 2 nanoseconds on a hit—or in the number of clock cycles that the CPU waits for the memory—such as a miss penalty of 50 clock cycles. Remember that average memory access time is still an indirect measure of performance; although it is a better measure than miss rate, it is not a substitute for execution time.

This formula can help us decide between split caches and a unified cache.

EXAMPLE   Which has the lower miss rate: a 16-KB instruction cache with a 16-KB data cache or a 32-KB unified cache? Use the miss rates in Figure 5.7 to help calculate the correct answer. Assume a hit takes 1 clock cycle and the miss penalty is 50 clock cycles, and a load or store hit takes 1 extra clock cycle on a unified cache since there is only one cache port to satisfy two simultaneous requests. Using the pipelining terminology of the previous chapter, the unified cache leads to a structural hazard. What is the average memory access time in each case? Assume write-through caches with a write buffer and ignore stalls due to the write buffer.

ANSWER As stated above, about 75% of the memory accesses are instruction references. Thus, the overall miss rate for the split caches is

$$(75\% \times 0.64\%) + (25\% \times 6.47\%) = 2.10\%$$

According to Figure 5.7, a 32-KB unified cache has a slightly lower miss rate of 1.99%.

The average memory access time formula can be divided into instruction and data accesses:

Average memory access time

$= \%$ instructions $\times$ (Hit time + Instruction miss rate $\times$ Miss penalty) +
$\%$ data $\times$ (Hit time + Data miss rate $\times$ Miss penalty)

So the time for each organization is

Average memory access time$_{\text{split}}$

$= 75\% \times (1 + 0.64\% \times 50) + 25\% \times (1 + 6.47\% \times 50)$
$= (75\% \times 1.32) + (25\% \times 4.235) = 0.990 + 1.059 = 2.05$

Average memory access time$_{\text{unified}}$

$= 75\% \times (1 + 1.99\% \times 50) + 25\% \times (1 + 1 + 1.99\% \times 50)$
$= (75\% \times 1.995) + (25\% \times 2.995) = 1.496 + 0.749 = 2.24$

Hence the split caches in this example—which offer two memory ports per clock cycle, thereby avoiding the structural hazard—have a better average memory access time than the single-ported unified cache even though their effective miss rate is *higher*. ∎

In Chapter 1 we saw another formula for the memory hierarchy:

CPU time = (CPU execution clock cycles + Memory stall clock cycles) × Clock cycle time

To simplify evaluation of cache alternatives, sometimes designers assume that all memory stalls are due to cache misses since the memory hierarchy typically dominates other reasons for stalls, such as contention due to I/O devices using memory. We use this simplifying assumption here, but it is important to account for *all* memory stalls when calculating final performance!

The CPU time formula above raises the question whether the clock cycles for a cache hit should be considered part of CPU execution clock cycles or part of memory stall clock cycles. Although either convention is defensible, the most widely accepted is to include hit clock cycles in CPU execution clock cycles.

Memory stall clock cycles can then be defined in terms of the number of memory accesses per program, miss penalty (in clock cycles), and miss rate for reads and writes:

$$\text{Memory stall clock cycles} = \text{Reads} \times \text{Read miss rate} \times \text{Read miss penalty}$$
$$+ \text{Writes} \times \text{Write miss rate} \times \text{Write miss penalty}$$

We often simplify the complete formula by combining the reads and writes and finding the average miss rates and miss penalty for reads *and* writes:

$$\text{Memory stall clock cycles} = \text{Memory accesses} \times \text{Miss rate} \times \text{Miss penalty}$$

This formula is an approximation since the miss rates and miss penalties are often different for reads and writes.

Factoring instruction count (IC) from execution time and memory stall cycles, we now get a CPU time formula that includes memory accesses per instruction, miss rate, and miss penalty:

$$\text{CPU time} = \text{IC} \times \left(\text{CPI}_{\text{execution}} + \frac{\text{Memory accesses}}{\text{Instruction}} \times \text{Miss rate} \times \text{Miss penalty} \right) \times \text{Clock cycle time}$$

Some designers prefer measuring miss rate as *misses per instruction* rather than misses per memory reference:

$$\frac{\text{Misses}}{\text{Instruction}} = \frac{\text{Memory accesses} \times \text{Miss rate}}{\text{Instruction}}$$

The advantage of this measure is that it is independent of the hardware implementation. For example, the 21064 instruction prefetch unit can make repeated references to a single word (see section 5.10), which can artificially reduce the miss rate if measured as misses per memory reference rather than per instruction executed. The drawback is that misses per instruction is architecture dependent; for example, the average number of memory accesses per instruction may be very different for an 80x86 versus DLX. Thus misses per instruction is most popular with architects working with a single computer family. They then use this version of the CPU time formula:

$$\text{CPU time} = \text{IC} \times \left(\text{CPI}_{\text{execution}} + \frac{\text{Memory stall clock cycles}}{\text{Instruction}} \right) \times \text{Clock cycle time}$$

We can now explore the impact of caches on performance.

EXAMPLE   Let's use a machine similar to the Alpha AXP as a first example. Assume the cache miss penalty is 50 clock cycles, and all instructions normally take 2.0 clock cycles (ignoring memory stalls). Assume the miss rate is 2%, and there is an average of 1.33 memory references per instruction. What is the impact on performance when behavior of the cache is included?

ANSWER $$\text{CPU time} = \text{IC} \times \left(\text{CPI}_{\text{execution}} + \frac{\text{Memory stall clock cycles}}{\text{Instruction}} \right) \times \text{Clock cycle time}$$

The performance, including cache misses, is

$$\text{CPU time}_{\text{with cache}} = \text{IC} \times (2.0 + (1.33 \times 2\% \times 50)) \times \text{Clock cycle time}$$
$$= \text{IC} \times 3.33 \times \text{Clock cycle time}$$

The clock cycle time and instruction count are the same, with or without a cache, so CPU time increases with CPI from 2.0 for a "perfect cache" to 3.33 with a cache that can miss. Hence, including the memory hierarchy in the CPI calculations stretches the CPU time by a factor of 1.67. Without any memory hierarchy at all the CPI would increase to $2.0 + 50 \times 1.33$ or 68.5—a factor of over 30 times longer! ∎

As this example illustrates, cache behavior can have enormous impact on performance. Furthermore, cache misses have a double-barreled impact on a CPU with a low CPI and a fast clock:

1. The lower the $\text{CPI}_{\text{execution}}$, the higher the *relative* impact of a fixed number of cache miss clock cycles.

2. When calculating CPI, the cache miss penalty is measured in CPU clock cycles for a miss. Therefore, even if memory hierarchies for two computers are identical, the CPU with the higher clock rate has a larger number of clock cycles per miss and hence the memory portion of CPI is higher.

The importance of the cache for CPUs with low CPI and high clock rates is thus greater, and, consequently, greater is the danger of neglecting cache behavior in assessing performance of such machines. Amdahl's Law strikes again!

Although minimizing average memory access time is a reasonable goal and we will use it in much of this chapter, keep in mind that the final goal is to reduce CPU execution time. The next example shows how these two can differ.

EXAMPLE What is the impact of two different cache organizations on the performance of a CPU? Assume that the CPI with a perfect cache is 2.0 and the clock cycle time is 2 ns, that there are 1.3 memory references per instruction, and that the size of both caches is 64 KB and both have a block size of 32 bytes. One cache is direct mapped and the other is two-way set associative. Figure 5.8 shows that for set-associative caches we must add a multiplexer to select between the blocks in the set depending on the tag match. Since the speed of the CPU is tied directly to the speed of a cache hit, assume the CPU clock cycle time must be stretched 1.10 times to accommodate the selection multiplexer of the set-associative cache. To the first approximation, the cache miss penalty is 70 ns for either cache organization. (In practice it must be rounded up or down to an integer number of clock cycles.) First, calculate the average memory access time, and then CPU performance. Assume the hit time is one clock cycle. Assume that the miss rate of a direct-mapped 64-KB cache is 1.4%, and the miss rate for a two-way set-associative cache of the same size is 1.0%.

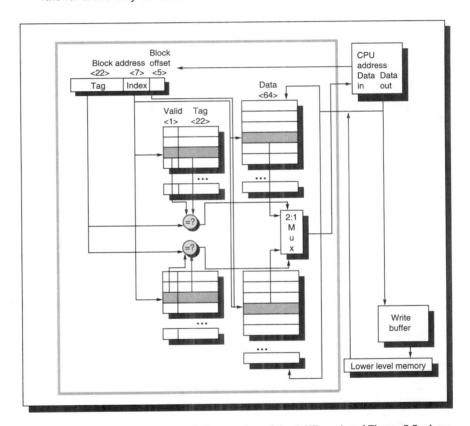

FIGURE 5.8   A two-way set-associative version of the 8-KB cache of Figure 5.5, showing the extra multiplexer in the path. Unlike the prior figure, the data portion of the cache is drawn more realistically, with the two leftmost bits of the block offset combined with the index to address the desired 64-bit word in memory, which is then sent to the CPU.

ANSWER   Average memory access time is

$$\text{Average memory access time} = \text{Hit time} + \text{Miss rate} \times \text{Miss penalty}$$

Thus, the time for each organization is

Average memory access time$_{1\text{-way}}$ = 2.0 + (.014 × 70) = 2.98 ns
Average memory access time$_{2\text{-way}}$ = 2.0 × 1.10 + (.010 × 70) = 2.90 ns

The average memory access time is better for the two-way set-associative cache.

CPU performance is

$$\text{CPU time} = IC \times \left(CPI_{\text{Execution}} + \frac{\text{Misses}}{\text{Instruction}} \times \text{Miss penalty} \right) \times \text{Clock cycle time}$$

$$= IC \times \left[(CPI_{\text{Execution}} \times \text{Clock cycle time}) \right.$$

$$\left. + \left(\frac{\text{Memory accesses}}{\text{Instruction}} \times \text{Miss rate} \times \text{Miss penalty} \times \text{Clock cycle time} \right) \right]$$

Substituting 70 ns for (Miss penalty × Clock cycle time), the performance of each cache organization is

$$\text{CPU time}_{1\text{-way}} = IC \times (2 \times 2.0 + (1.3 \times 0.014 \times 70)) = 5.27 \times IC$$

$$\text{CPU time}_{2\text{-way}} = IC \times (2 \times 2.0 \times 1.10 + (1.3 \times 0.010 \times 70)) = 5.31 \times IC$$

and relative performance is

$$\frac{\text{CPU time}_{2\text{-way}}}{\text{CPU time}_{1\text{-way}}} = \frac{5.31 \times \text{Instruction count}}{5.27 \times \text{Instruction count}} = \frac{5.31}{5.27} = 1.01$$

In contrast to the results of average memory access time comparison, the direct-mapped cache leads to slightly better average performance because the clock cycle is stretched for *all* instructions for the two-way case, even if there are fewer misses. Since CPU time is our bottom-line evaluation, and since direct mapped is simpler to build, the preferred cache is direct mapped in this example.   ∎

Improving Cache Performance

The increasing gap between CPU and main memory speeds shown in Figure 5.1 has attracted the attention of many architects. A bibliographic search for the years 1989–95 revealed more than 1600 research papers on the subject of caches. Your authors' job was to survey all 1600 papers, decide what is and is not worthwhile, translate the results into a common terminology, reduce the results to their essence, write in an intriguing fashion, and provide just the right amount of detail! Fortunately, the average memory access time formula gave us a framework to present cache optimizations as well as the techniques for improving caches:

Average memory access time = Hit time + Miss rate × Miss penalty

Hence we organize 15 cache optimizations into three categories:

- Reducing the miss rate (Section 5.3)

- Reducing the miss penalty (Section 5.4)

- Reducing the time to hit in the cache (Section 5.5)

Figure 5.29 on page 427 concludes with a summary of the implementation complexity and the performance benefits of the 15 techniques presented.

5.3 | Reducing Cache Misses

Most cache research has concentrated on reducing the miss rate, so that is where we start our exploration. To gain better insights into the causes of misses, we start with a model that sorts all misses into three simple categories:

- *Compulsory*—The very first access to a block *cannot be* in the cache, so the block must be brought into the cache. These are also called *cold start misses* or *first reference misses.*

- *Capacity*—If the cache cannot contain all the blocks needed during execution of a program, capacity misses will occur because of blocks being discarded and later retrieved.

- *Conflict*—If the block placement strategy is set associative or direct mapped, conflict misses (in addition to compulsory and capacity misses) will occur because a block can be discarded and later retrieved if too many blocks map to its set. These are also called *collision misses* or *interference misses.*

Figure 5.9 shows the relative frequency of cache misses, broken down by the "three C's." Figure 5.10 presents the same data graphically. The top graph shows absolute miss rates; the bottom graph plots percentage of all the misses by type of miss as a function of cache size. To show the benefit of associativity, conflict misses are divided into misses caused by each decrease in associativity. Here are the four divisions:

- *Eight-way*—conflict misses due to going from fully associative (no conflicts) to eight-way associative

- *Four-way*—conflict misses due to going from eight-way associative to four-way associative

- *Two-way*—conflict misses due to going from four-way associative to two-way associative

- *One-way*—conflict misses due to going from two-way associative to one-way associative (direct mapped)

Cache size	Degree associative	Total miss rate	Miss rate components (relative percent) (*Sum = 100% of total miss rate*)					
			Compulsory		Capacity		Conflict	
1 KB	1-way	0.133	0.002	1%	0.080	60%	0.052	39%
1 KB	2-way	0.105	0.002	2%	0.080	76%	0.023	22%
1 KB	4-way	0.095	0.002	2%	0.080	84%	0.013	14%
1 KB	8-way	0.087	0.002	2%	0.080	92%	0.005	6%
2 KB	1-way	0.098	0.002	2%	0.044	45%	0.052	53%
2 KB	2-way	0.076	0.002	2%	0.044	58%	0.030	39%
2 KB	4-way	0.064	0.002	3%	0.044	69%	0.018	28%
2 KB	8-way	0.054	0.002	4%	0.044	82%	0.008	14%
4 KB	1-way	0.072	0.002	3%	0.031	43%	0.039	54%
4 KB	2-way	0.057	0.002	3%	0.031	55%	0.024	42%
4 KB	4-way	0.049	0.002	4%	0.031	64%	0.016	32%
4 KB	8-way	0.039	0.002	5%	0.031	80%	0.006	15%
8 KB	1-way	0.046	0.002	4%	0.023	51%	0.021	45%
8 KB	2-way	0.038	0.002	5%	0.023	61%	0.013	34%
8 KB	4-way	0.035	0.002	5%	0.023	66%	0.010	28%
8 KB	8-way	0.029	0.002	6%	0.023	79%	0.004	15%
16 KB	1-way	0.029	0.002	7%	0.015	52%	0.012	42%
16 KB	2-way	0.022	0.002	9%	0.015	68%	0.005	23%
16 KB	4-way	0.020	0.002	10%	0.015	74%	0.003	17%
16 KB	8-way	0.018	0.002	10%	0.015	80%	0.002	9%
32 KB	1-way	0.020	0.002	10%	0.010	52%	0.008	38%
32 KB	2-way	0.014	0.002	14%	0.010	74%	0.002	12%
32 KB	4-way	0.013	0.002	15%	0.010	79%	0.001	6%
32 KB	8-way	0.013	0.002	15%	0.010	81%	0.001	4%
64 KB	1-way	0.014	0.002	14%	0.007	50%	0.005	36%
64 KB	2-way	0.010	0.002	20%	0.007	70%	0.001	10%
64 KB	4-way	0.009	0.002	21%	0.007	75%	0.000	3%
64 KB	8-way	0.009	0.002	22%	0.007	78%	0.000	0%
128 KB	1-way	0.010	0.002	20%	0.004	40%	0.004	40%
128 KB	2-way	0.007	0.002	29%	0.004	58%	0.001	14%
128 KB	4-way	0.006	0.002	31%	0.004	61%	0.001	8%
128 KB	8-way	0.006	0.002	31%	0.004	62%	0.000	7%

FIGURE 5.9   Total miss rate for each size cache and percentage of each according to the "three C's." Compulsory misses are independent of cache size, while capacity misses decrease as capacity increases, and conflict misses decrease as associativity increases. Gee et al. [1993] calculated the average D-cache miss rate for the SPEC92 benchmark suite with 32-byte blocks and LRU replacement on a DECstation 5000. Figure 5.10 shows the same information graphically. The compulsory rate was calculated as the miss rate of a fully associative 1-MB cache. Note that the 2:1 cache rule of thumb (inside front cover) is supported by the statistics in this table: a direct-mapped cache of size *N* has about the same miss rate as a 2-way set-associative cache of size *N*/2.

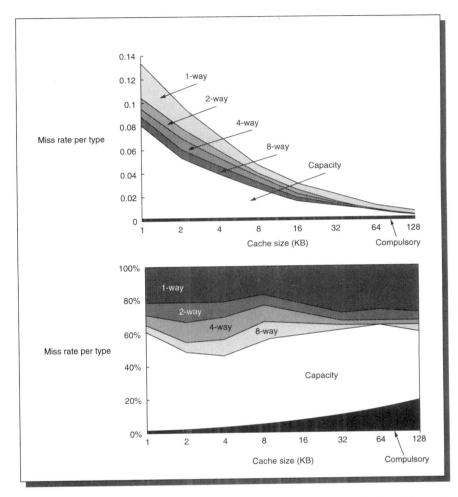

FIGURE 5.10   Total miss rate (top) and distribution of miss rate (bottom) for each size cache according to three C's for the data in Figure 5.9. The top diagram is the actual D-cache miss rates, while the bottom diagram is scaled to the direct-mapped miss ratios.

As we can see from the figures, the compulsory miss rate of the SPEC92 programs is very small, as it is for many long-running programs.

Having identified the three C's, what can a computer designer do about them? Conceptually, conflicts are the easiest: Fully associative placement avoids all conflict misses. Full associativity is expensive in hardware, however, and may slow the processor clock rate (see the example above), leading to lower overall performance.

There is little to be done about capacity except to enlarge the cache. If the upper-level memory is much smaller than what is needed for a program, and a significant percentage of the time is spent moving data between two levels in the hierarchy, the memory hierarchy is said to *thrash*. Because so many replacements are required, thrashing means the machine runs close to the speed of the lower-level memory, or maybe even slower because of the miss overhead.

Another approach to improving the three C's is to make blocks larger to reduce the number of compulsory misses, but, as we shall see, large blocks can increase other kinds of misses.

The three C's give insight into the cause of misses, but this simple model has its limits; it gives you insight into average behavior but may not explain an individual miss. For example, changing cache size changes conflict misses as well as capacity misses, since a larger cache spreads out references to more blocks. Thus, a miss might move from a capacity miss to a conflict miss as cache size changes. Note that the three C's also ignore replacement policy, since it is difficult to model and since, in general, it is less significant. In specific circumstances the replacement policy can actually lead to anomalous behavior, such as poorer miss rates for larger associativity, which is contradictory to the three C's model.

Alas, many of the techniques that reduce miss rates also increase hit time or miss penalty. The desirability of reducing miss rates using the seven techniques presented in the rest of this section must be balanced against the goal of making the whole system fast. This first example shows the importance of a balanced perspective.

First Miss Rate Reduction Technique: Larger Block Size

This simplest way to reduce miss rate is to increase the block size. Figure 5.11 shows the trade-off of block size versus miss rate for a set of programs and cache sizes. Larger block sizes will reduce compulsory misses. This reduction occurs because the principle of locality has two components: temporal locality and spatial locality. Larger blocks take advantage of spatial locality.

At the same time, larger blocks increase the miss penalty. Since they reduce the number of blocks in the cache, larger blocks may increase conflict misses and even capacity misses if the cache is small. Clearly there is little reason to increase the block size to such a size that it *increases* the miss rate, but there is also no benefit to reducing miss rate if it increases the average memory access time; the increase in miss penalty may outweigh the decrease in miss rate.

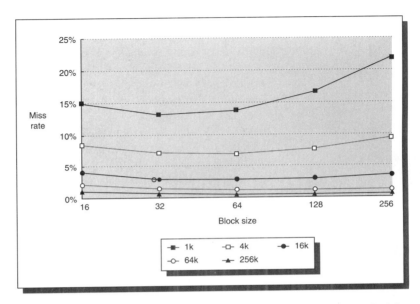

FIGURE 5.11   Miss rate versus block size for five different-sized caches. Each line represents a cache of different size. Figure 5.12 shows the data used to plot these lines. This graph is based on the same measurements found in Figure 5.10.

	Cache size				
Block size	**1K**	**4K**	**16K**	**64K**	**256K**
16	15.05%	8.57%	3.94%	2.04%	1.09%
32	13.34%	7.24%	2.87%	1.35%	0.70%
64	13.76%	7.00%	2.64%	1.06%	0.51%
128	16.64%	7.78%	2.77%	1.02%	0.49%
256	22.01%	9.51%	3.29%	1.15%	0.49%

FIGURE 5.12   Actual miss rate versus block size for five different-sized caches in Figure 5.11. Note that for a 1-KB cache, 64-byte, 128-byte, and 256-byte blocks have a higher miss rate than 32-byte blocks. In this example, the cache would have to be 256 KB in order for a 256-byte block to decrease misses.

EXAMPLE   Figure 5.12 shows the actual miss rates plotted in Figure 5.11. Assume the memory system takes 40 clock cycles of overhead and then delivers 16 bytes every 2 clock cycles. Thus, it can supply 16 bytes in 42 clock cycles, 32 bytes in 44 clock cycles, and so on. Which block size has the minimum average memory access time for each cache size in Figure 5.12?

ANSWER   Average memory access time is

$$\text{Average memory access time} = \text{Hit time} + \text{Miss rate} \times \text{Miss penalty}$$

If we assume the hit time is one clock cycle independent of block size, then the access time for a 16-byte block in a 1-KB cache is

$$\text{Average memory access time} = 1 + (15.05\% \times 42) = 7.321 \text{ clock cycles}$$

and for a 256-byte block in a 256-KB cache the average memory access time is

$$\text{Average memory access time} = 1 + (0.49\% \times 72) = 1.353 \text{ clock cycles}$$

Figure 5.13 shows the average memory access time for all block and cache sizes between those two extremes. The boldfaced entries show the fastest block size for a given cache size: 32 bytes for 1-KB, 4-KB, and 16-KB caches and 64 bytes for the larger caches. These sizes are, in fact, popular block sizes for processor caches today.

Block size	Miss penalty	Cache size				
		1K	**4K**	**16K**	**64K**	**256K**
16	42	7.321	4.599	2.655	1.857	1.458
32	44	**6.870**	**4.186**	**2.263**	1.594	1.308
64	48	7.605	4.360	2.267	**1.509**	**1.245**
128	56	10.318	5.357	2.551	1.571	1.274
256	72	16.847	7.847	3.369	1.828	1.353

FIGURE 5.13   Average memory access time versus block size for five different-sized caches in Figure 5.11. The smallest average time per cache size is boldfaced.

As in all of these techniques, the cache designer is trying to minimize both the miss rate and the miss penalty. The selection of block size depends on both the latency and bandwidth of the lower-level memory: high latency and high bandwidth encourage large block size since the cache gets many more bytes per miss for a small increase in miss penalty. Conversely, low latency and low bandwidth encourage smaller block sizes since there is little time saved from a larger block—twice the miss penalty of a small block may be close to the penalty of a block twice the size—and the larger number of small blocks may reduce conflict misses.

After seeing the positive and negative impact of larger block size on compulsory and capacity misses, we next look at the potential of higher associativity to reduce conflict misses.

One solution that reduces conflict misses without impairing clock rate is to add a small, fully associative cache between a cache and its refill path. Figure 5.15 shows the organization. This *victim cache* contains only blocks that

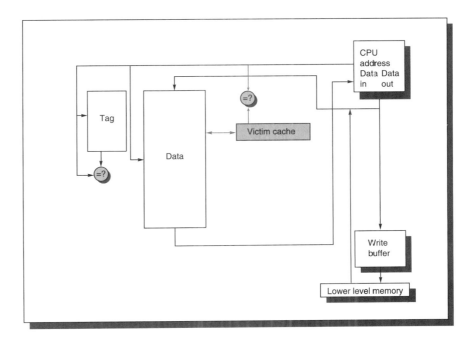

FIGURE 5.15   **Placement of victim cache in the memory hierarchy.**

are discarded from a cache because of a miss—"victims"—and are checked on a miss to see if they have the desired data before going to the next lower-level memory. If it is found there, the victim block and cache block are swapped. Jouppi [1990] found that victim caches of one to five entries are effective at reducing conflict misses, especially for small, direct-mapped data caches. Depending on the program, a four-entry victim cache removed 20% to 95% of the conflict misses in a 4-KB direct-mapped data cache.

Fourth Miss Rate Reduction Technique: Pseudo-Associative Caches

Another approach to getting the miss rate of set-associative caches and the hit speed of direct mapped is called *pseudo-associative* or *column associative*. A cache access proceeds just as in the direct-mapped cache for a hit. On a miss, however, before going to the next lower level of the memory hierarchy, another cache entry is checked to see if it matches there. A simple way is to invert the most significant bit of the index field to find the other block in the "pseudo set."

Pseudo-associative caches then have one fast and one slow hit time—corresponding to a regular hit and a pseudo hit—in addition to the miss penalty. Figure 5.16 shows the relative times. The danger is if many of the fast hit times of the direct-mapped cache became slow hit times in the pseudo-associative cache, then the performance would be degraded by this optimization. Hence it is important to be able to indicate for each set which block should be the fast hit and which should be the slow one; one way is simply to swap the contents of the blocks.

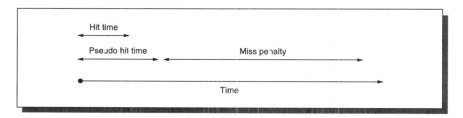

FIGURE 5.16 Relationship between a regular hit time, pseudo hit time, and miss penalty.

Let's do an example to see how well pseudo-associativity works.

EXAMPLE   Assume that it takes two extra cycles to find the entry in the alternative location if it is not found in the direct-mapped location: one cycle to check and one cycle to swap. Using the parameters from the previous example, which of direct-mapped, two-way set-associative, and pseudo-associative organizations is fastest for 2-KB and 128-KB sizes?

ANSWER   The average memory access time for pseudo-associative caches starts with the standard formula:

$$\text{Average memory access time}_{\text{pseudo}} = \text{Hit time}_{\text{pseudo}} + \text{Miss rate}_{\text{pseudo}} \times \text{Miss penalty}_{\text{pseudo}}$$

Let's start with the last part of the equation. The pseudo miss penalty is one cycle more than a normal miss penalty, to account for the time to check the alternative location. To determine the miss rate we need to see when misses occur. As long as we invert the most significant bit of the index to find the other block, the two blocks in the "pseudo set" are selected using the same index that would be used in a two-way set-associative cache and hence have the same miss rates. Thus the last part of the equation is

$$\text{Miss rate}_{\text{pseudo}} \times \text{Miss penalty}_{\text{pseudo}} = \text{Miss rate}_{\text{2-way}} \times \text{Miss penalty}_{\text{1-way}}$$

Returning to the beginning of the equation, the hit time for a pseudo-associative cache is the time to hit in a direct-mapped cache plus the fraction of accesses that are found in the pseudo-associative search times the extra time it takes to find the hit:

$$\text{Hit time}_{\text{pseudo}} = \text{Hit time}_{\text{1-way}} + \text{Alternate hit rate}_{\text{pseudo}} \times 2$$

The hit rate for the pseudo-associative search is the difference between the hits that would occur in a two-way set-associative cache and the number of hits in a direct-mapped cache:

$$\begin{aligned}
\text{Alternate hit rate}_{\text{pseudo}} &= \text{Hit rate}_{\text{2-way}} - \text{Hit rate}_{\text{1-way}} \\
&= (1 - \text{Miss rate}_{\text{2-way}}) - (1 - \text{Miss rate}_{\text{1-way}}) \\
&= \text{Miss rate}_{\text{1-way}} - \text{Miss rate}_{\text{2-way}}
\end{aligned}$$

But it is slightly more complex. The miss rate is of a direct-mapped cache half the size—since half of the cache is reserved for alternate locations—while the whole cache has the contents of a two-way set-associative cache. Putting the pieces back together:

$$\text{Average memory access time}_{\text{pseudo}} = \text{Hit time}_{\text{1-way}} + (\text{Miss rate}_{\text{1-way}} - \text{Miss rate}_{\text{2-way}}) \times 2 + \text{Miss rate}_{\text{2-way}} \times \text{Miss penalty}_{\text{1-way}}$$

Figure 5.9 supplies the values we need to plug into our formulas:

$$\text{Average memory access time}_{\text{pseudo 2 KB}} = 1 + (0.113 - 0.076) \times 2 + (0.076 \times (50 + 1)) = 1 + 0.074 + 3.876 = 4.950$$

$$\text{Average memory access time}_{\text{pseudo 128 KB}} = 1 + (0.014 - 0.007) \times 2 + (0.007 \times (50 + 1)) = 1 + 0.014 + 0.357 = 1.371$$

From Figure 5.14 in the last example we know these results for 2-KB caches:

$$\text{Average memory access time}_{\text{1-way}} = 5.90 \text{ clock cycles}$$
$$\text{Average memory access time}_{\text{2-way}} = 4.90 \text{ clock cycles}$$

For 128-KB caches the times are

$$\text{Average memory access time}_{\text{1-way}} = 1.50 \text{ clock cycles}$$
$$\text{Average memory access time}_{\text{2-way}} = 1.45 \text{ clock cycles}$$

The pseudo-associative cache is fastest for the 128-KB cache while the two-way set associative is fastest for the 2-KB cache.   ■

Although an attractive idea on paper, variable hit times can complicate a pipelined CPU design. Hence the authors expect the most likely use of pseudo-associativity is with caches further from the processor (see the description of second-level caches in the next section).

Fifth Miss Rate Reduction Technique: Hardware Prefetching of Instructions and Data

Victim caches and pseudo-associativity both promise to improve miss rates without affecting the processor clock rate. A third way is to prefetch items before they are requested by the processor. Both instructions and data can be prefetched, either directly into the caches or into an external buffer that can be more quickly accessed than main memory.

Instruction prefetch is frequently done in hardware outside of the cache. For example, the Alpha AXP 21064 microprocessor fetches two blocks on a miss: the requested block and the next consecutive block. The requested block is placed in the instruction cache when it returns, and the prefetched block is placed into the instruction stream buffer. If the requested block is present in the instruction stream buffer, the original cache request is canceled, the block is read from the stream buffer, and the next prefetch request is issued. There is never more than one 32-byte block in the 21064 instruction stream buffer. Jouppi [1990] found that a single instruction stream buffer would catch 15% to 25% of the misses from a 4-KB direct-mapped instruction cache with 16-byte blocks. With 4 blocks in the instruction stream buffer the hit rate improves to about 50%, and with 16 blocks to 72%.

A similar approach can be applied to data accesses. Jouppi found that a single data stream buffer caught about 25% of the misses from the 4-KB direct-mapped cache. Instead of having a single stream, there could be multiple stream buffers beyond the data cache, each prefetching at different addresses. Jouppi found that four data stream buffers increased the data hit rate to 43%. Palacharla and Kessler [1994] looked at a set of scientific programs and considered stream buffers that could handle either instructions or data. They found that eight stream buffers could capture 50% to 70% of all misses from a processor with two 64-KB four-way set-associative caches, one for instructions and the other for data.

EXAMPLE   What is the effective miss rate of the Alpha AXP 21064 using instruction prefetching? How much bigger an instruction cache would be needed in the Alpha AXP 21064 to match the average access time if prefetching were removed?

ANSWER   We assume it takes 1 extra clock cycle if the instruction misses the cache but is found in the prefetch buffer. Here is our revised formula:

$$\text{Average memory access time}_{\text{prefetch}} = \text{Hit time} + \text{Miss rate} \times \text{Prefetch hit rate} \times 1 + \text{Miss rate} \times (1 - \text{Prefetch hit rate}) \times \text{Miss penalty}$$

Let's assume the prefetch hit rate is 25%. Figure 5.7 on page 384 gives the miss rate for an 8-KB instruction cache as 1.10%. Using the parameters from the Example on page 386, the hit time is 2 clock cycles, and the miss penalty is 50 clock cycles:

$$\text{Average memory access time}_{\text{prefetch}} = 2 + (1.10\% \times 25\% \times 1) + (1.10\% \times (1 - 25\%) \times 50) = 2 + 0.00275 + 0.413 = 2.415$$

To find the effective miss rate with the equivalent performance, we start with the original formula and solve for the miss rate:

$$\text{Average memory access time} = \text{Hit time} + \text{Miss rate} \times \text{Miss penalty}$$

$$\text{Miss rate} = \frac{\text{Average memory access time} - \text{Hit time}}{\text{Miss penalty}}$$

$$\text{Miss rate} = \frac{2.415 - 2}{50} = \frac{0.415}{50} = 0.83\%$$

Our calculation suggests that the effective miss rate of prefetching with an 8-KB cache is 0.83%. Figure 5.7 on page 384 gives the miss rate of a 16-KB instruction cache as 0.64%, so 8 KB with prefetching is midway between the 1.10% and 0.64% miss rates of the 8-KB and 16-KB caches. ∎

Prefetching relies on utilizing memory bandwidth that otherwise would be unused, and can actually lower performance if it interferes with demand misses. Help from compilers can reduce useless prefetching.

Sixth Miss Rate Reduction Technique: Compiler-Controlled Prefetching

An alternative to hardware prefetching is for the compiler to insert prefetch instructions to request the data before they are needed. There are several flavors of prefetch:

■ *Register prefetch* will load the value into a register.

■ *Cache prefetch* loads data only into the cache and not the register.

Either of these can be *faulting* or *nonfaulting*; that is, the address does or does not cause an exception for virtual address faults and protection violations. Using this terminology, a normal load instruction could be considered a "faulting register prefetch instruction." Nonfaulting prefetches simply turn into no-ops if they would normally result in an exception. The most effective prefetch is "semantically invisible" to a program: it doesn't change the contents of registers or memory and it cannot cause virtual memory faults. This section assumes nonfaulting cache prefetch, also called *nonbinding* prefetch.

Prefetching makes sense only if the processor can proceed while the prefetched data are being fetched; that is, the caches continue to supply instructions and data while waiting for the prefetched data to return. Such a nimble cache is called a *nonblocking* cache or *lockup-free* cache; we'll discuss it in more detail later.

Like hardware-controlled prefetching, the goal is to overlap execution with the prefetching of data. Loops are the key targets, as they lend themselves to prefetch optimizations. If the miss penalty is small, the compiler just unrolls the loop once or twice and it schedules the prefetches with the execution. If the miss penalty is large, it uses software pipelining (page 290 in Chapter 4) or unrolls many times to prefetch data for a future iteration.

Issuing prefetch instructions incurs an instruction overhead, however, so care must be taken to ensure that such overheads do not exceed the benefits. By concentrating on references that are likely to be cache misses, programs can avoid unnecessary prefetches while improving average memory access time significantly.

EXAMPLE   For the code below, determine which accesses are likely to cause data cache misses. Next, insert prefetch instructions to reduce misses. Finally, calculate the number of prefetch instructions executed and the misses avoided due to prefetching. Let's assume we have an 8-KB direct-mapped data cache with 16-byte blocks. It is a write-back cache that does write allocate, and that the elements of a and b are 8 bytes long as they are double-precision floating-point arrays with 3 rows and 100 columns for a and 101 rows and 3 columns for b. Let's also assume they are not in the cache at the start of the program.

```
for (i = 0; i < 3; i = i+1)
    for (j = 0; j < 100; j = j+1)
        a[i][j] = b[j][0] * b[j+1][0];
```

ANSWER   The compiler will first determine which accesses are likely to cause cache misses; otherwise, we will waste time on issuing prefetch instructions for data that would be hits. Elements of a are written in the order that they are stored in memory, so a will benefit from spatial locality: the even values of j will miss and the odd values will hit. Since a has 3 rows and 100 columns, its accesses will lead to $\frac{3 \times 100}{2}$ or 150 misses. The array b does not benefit from spatial locality since the accesses are not in the order it is stored. The array b does benefit twice from temporal locality: the same elements are accessed for each iteration of i, and each iteration of j uses the same value of b as the last iteration. Ignoring potential conflict misses, the misses due to b will be for b[j+1][0] accesses when i = 0, and also the first access to b[j][0] when j = 0. Since j goes from 0 to 99 when i = 0, accesses to b lead to 100 + 1 or 101 misses. Thus this loop will miss the data cache approximately 150 + 101 or 251 times.

To simplify our optimization, we will not worry about prefetching the first accesses of the loop nor suppressing the prefetches at the end of the loop; if these were *faulting* prefetches, we could not take this luxury. Given our analysis of misses, we split the loop so the first loop will prefetch b as well as a, and the second loop will just prefetch a, since b will have already been prefetched. Let's assume that the miss penalty is so large we need to prefetch at least seven iterations in advance.

```
for (j = 0; j < 100; j = j+1) {
    prefetch(b[j+7][0]);
    /* b(j,0) for 7 iterations later */
    prefetch(a[0][j+7]);
    /* a(0,j) for 7 iterations later */
    a[0][j] = b[j][0] * b[j+1][0];};
for (i = 1; i < 3; i = i+1)
    for (j = 0; j < 100; j = j+1) {
        prefetch(a[i][j+7]);
        /* a(i,j) for +7 iterations */
        a[i-1][j] = b[j][0] *b[j+1][0];}
```

This revised code prefetches a[i][7] through a[i][99] and b[7][0] through b[99][0], reducing the number of nonprefetched misses to

$$\frac{3 \times 7}{2} + 8 = 11 + 8 = 19$$

The cost of avoiding 232 cache misses is executing 400 prefetch instructions, very likely a good trade-off.   ■

EXAMPLE   Calculate the time saved in the example above. Ignore instruction cache misses and assume there are no conflict or capacity misses in the data cache. Assume that prefetches can overlap with each other and with cache misses, thereby transferring at the maximum memory bandwidth. Here are the key loop times ignoring cache misses: the original loop takes 7 clock cycles per iteration, the first prefetch loop takes 9 clock cycles per iteration, and the second prefetch loop takes 8 clock cycles per iteration (including the overhead of the outer for loop). A miss takes 50 clock cycles.

ANSWER   The original doubly nested loop executes the multiply 3×100 or 300 times. Since the loop takes 7 clock cycles per iteration, the total is 300×7 or 2100 clock cycles plus cache misses. Cache misses add 251×50 or 12,550 clock cycles, giving a total of 14,650 clock cycles. The first prefetch loop iterates 100 times; at 9 clock cycles per iteration the total is 900 clock cycles plus cache misses. They add 11×50 or 550 clock cycles for cache misses, giving a total of 1450. The second loop executes 2×100 or 200 times, and at 8 clock cycles per iteration it takes 1600 clock cycles plus 8×50 or 400 clock cycles for cache misses. This gives a total of 2000 clock cycles. From the prior example we know that this code executes 400 prefetch instructions during the $1450 + 2000$ or 3450 clock cycles to execute these two loops. If we assume that the prefetches are completely overlapped with the rest of the execution, then the prefetch code is 14,650/3450 or 4.2 times faster.   ■

Seventh Miss Rate Reduction Technique: Compiler Optimizations

Thus far our techniques to reduce misses have required changes to or additions to the hardware: larger blocks, higher associativity, pseudo-associativity, hardware prefetching, or prefetch instructions. This final technique reduces miss rates without any hardware changes!

This magical reduction comes from optimized software—the hardware designer's favorite solution. The increasing performance gap between processors and main memory has inspired compiler writers to scrutinize the memory hierarchy to see if compile time optimizations can improve performance. Once again research is split between improvements in instruction misses and improvements in data misses.

Code can easily be rearranged without affecting correctness; for example, reordering the procedures of a program might reduce instruction miss rates by reducing conflict misses. McFarling [1989] looked at using profiling information to determine likely conflicts between groups of instructions, and reordered the instructions to reduce misses by 50% for a 2-KB direct-mapped instruction cache with 4-byte blocks, and by 75% in an 8-KB cache. McFarling got the best performance when it was possible to prevent some instructions from ever entering the cache, but even without that feature, optimized programs on a direct-mapped cache had lower miss rates than unoptimized programs on an eight-way set-associative cache of the same size.

Data have even fewer restrictions on location than code. The goal of such transformations is to try to improve the spatial and temporal locality of the data. For example, array calculations can be changed to operate on all the data in a cache block rather than blindly striding through arrays in the order the programmer happened to place the loop.

To give a feeling of this type of optimization, we will show four examples, transforming the C code by hand to reduce cache misses. Figure 5.17 shows the performance improvement in using these optimizations on a subset of the SPEC92 floating-point benchmarks.

Merging Arrays

This first technique reduces misses by improving spatial locality. Some programs reference multiple arrays in the same dimension with the same indices at the same time. The danger is that these accesses will interfere with each other, leading to conflict misses. This danger is removed by combining these independent matrices into a single compound array so that a single cache block can contain the desired elements.

```
/* Before */
int val[SIZE];
int key[SIZE];
```

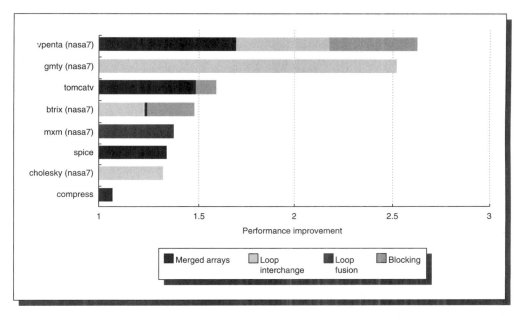

FIGURE 5.17   **Lebeck and Wood [1994] performed the four optimizations in this section by hand on three SPEC92 programs and five separate portions of the nasa7 benchmark.**

```
/* After */
struct merge {
        int val;
        int key;
};
struct merge merged_array[SIZE];
```

An interesting characteristic of this example is that the proper coding practice of using an array of records would achieve the same benefits as this optimization.

Loop Interchange

Some programs have nested loops that access data in memory in nonsequential order. Simply exchanging the nesting of the loops can make the code access the data in the order it is stored. Like the prior example, this technique reduces misses by improving spatial locality; reordering maximizes use of data in a cache block before it is discarded.

```
/* Before */
for (j = 0; j < 100; j = j+1)
      for (i = 0; i < 5000; i = i+1)
            x[i][j] = 2 * x[i][j];

/* After */
for (i = 0; i < 5000; i = i+1)
      for (j = 0; j < 100; j = j+1)
            x[i][j] = 2 * x[i][j];
```

The original code would skip through memory in strides of 100 words, while the revised version accesses all the words in the cache block before going to the next one. This optimization improves cache performance without affecting the number of instructions executed, unlike the prior example.

Loop Fusion

Some programs have separate sections of code that access the same arrays with the same loops, performing different computations on the common data. By "fusing" the code into a single loop, the data that are fetched into the cache can be used repeatedly before being swapped out. Hence, in contrast to our first two techniques, the target of this optimization is reducing misses via improved temporal locality.

```
/* Before */
for (i = 0; i < N; i = i+1)
      for (j = 0; j < N; j = j+1)
            a[i][j] = 1/b[i][j] * c[i][j];

for (i = 0; i < N; i = i+1)
      for (j = 0; j < N; j = j+1)
            d[i][j] = a[i][j] + c[i][j];

/* After */
for (i = 0; i < N; i = i+1)
      for (j = 0; j < N; j = j+1)
      {
            a[i][j] = 1/b[i][j] * c[i][j];
            d[i][j] = a[i][j] + c[i][j];
      }
```

The original code would take all the misses to access arrays a and c twice, once in the first loop and then again in the second. In the fused loop, the second statement freeloads on the cache accesses of the first statement.

Blocking

This optimization, perhaps the most famous of the cache optimizations, again tries to reduce misses via improved temporal locality. We are again dealing with multiple arrays, with some arrays accessed by rows and some by columns. Storing the arrays row by row (*row major order*) or column by column (*column major order*) does not solve the problem because both rows and columns are used in every iteration of the loop. Such orthogonal accesses mean the earlier transformations, such as loop interchange, are not helpful.

Instead of operating on entire rows or columns of an array, blocked algorithms operate on submatrices or *blocks*. The goal is to maximize accesses to the data loaded into the cache before the data are replaced. The code example below, which performs matrix multiplication, helps motivate the optimization:

```
/* Before */
for (i = 0; i < N; i = i+1)
        for (j = 0; j < N; j = j+1)
                {r = 0;
                for (k = 0; k < N; k = k+1) {
                        r = r + y[i][k]*z[k][j];};
                x[i][j] = r;
                };
```

The two inner loops read all N by N elements of z, access the same N elements in a row of y repeatedly, and write one row of N elements of x. Figure 5.18 gives a

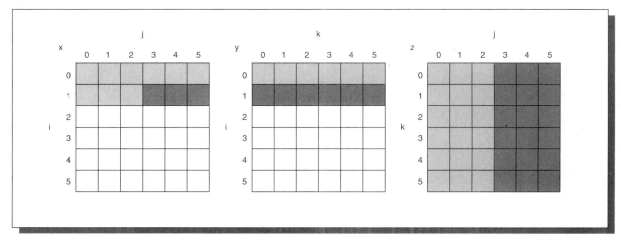

FIGURE 5.18   A snapshot of the three arrays x, y, and z when i = 1. The age of accesses to the array elements is indicated by shade: white means not yet touched, light means older accesses and dark means newer accesses. The variables i, j, and k are shown along the rows or columns used to access the arrays.

snapshot of the accesses to the three arrays, with a dark shade indicating a recent access, a light shade indicating an older access, and white meaning not yet accessed.

The number of capacity misses clearly depends on N and the size of the cache. If it can hold all three N by N matrices, then all is well, provided there are no cache conflicts. If the cache can hold one N by N matrix and one row of N, then at least the ith row of y and the array z may stay in the cache. Less than that and misses may occur for both x and z. In the worst case, there would be $2N^3 + N^2$ words read from memory for N^3 operations.

To ensure that the elements being accessed can fit in the cache, the original code is changed to compute on a submatrix of size B by B by having the two inner loops compute in steps of size B rather than going from beginning to end of x and z. B is called the *blocking factor*. (Assume x is initialized to zero.)

```
/* After */
for (jj = 0; jj < N; jj = jj+B)
for (kk = 0; kk < N; kk = kk+B)
for (i = 0; i < N; i = i-1)
        for (j = jj; j < min(jj+B,N); j = j+1)
            {r = 0;
             for (k = kk; k < min(kk+B,N); k = k+1) {
                    r = r + y[i][k]*z[k][j];};
             x[i][j] = x[i][j] + r;
            };
```

Figure 5.19 illustrates the accesses to the three arrays using blocking. Looking only at capacity misses, the total number of memory words accessed is $2N^3/B + N^2$, which is an improvement by about a factor of B. Thus blocking exploits a combination of spatial and temporal locality, since y benefits from spatial locality and z benefits from temporal locality.

Although we have aimed at reducing cache misses, blocking can also be used to help register allocation. By taking a small blocking size such that the block can be held in registers, we can minimize the number of loads and stores in the program.

Traditionally blocking has been aimed at reducing capacity misses, under the simplifying assumption that conflict misses are either not significant or can be removed by more associative caches. Since blocking reduces the number of words that are active in a cache at a given time, choosing a blocking size smaller than capacity can also reduce conflict misses. Figure 5.20 gives a qualitative view of this trade-off.

These last two subsections have concentrated on the potential benefit of cache-aware compilers and programs. Given that increasing gap in processor speed and memory access times, this benefit will only increase in importance over time.

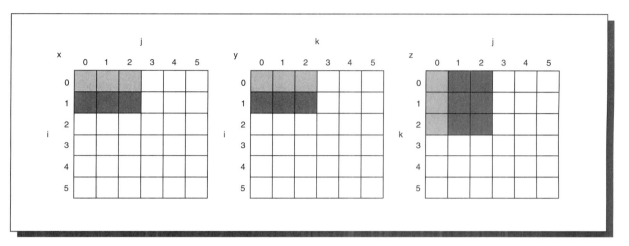

FIGURE 5.19 The age of accesses to the arrays x, y, and z. Note in contrast to Figure 5.18 the smaller number of elements accessed.

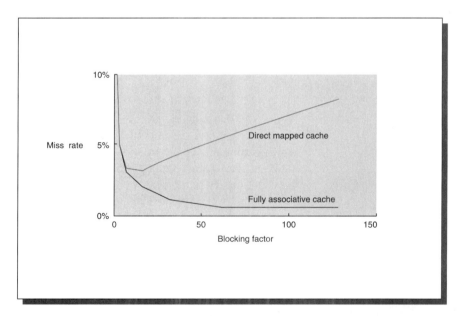

FIGURE 5.20   The impact of conflict misses in caches that aren't fully associative on block size. For example, Lam, Rothberg, and Wolf [1991] found one case where a blocking factor of 24 had a fifth the number of misses of a blocking factor of 48, despite both fitting into the cache.

Now that we have spent more than 20 pages on techniques that reduce cache misses, it is time to look at reducing the next component of average memory access time.

5.4 | Reducing Cache Miss Penalty

Reducing cache misses has been the traditional focus of cache research, but the cache performance formula assures us that improvements in miss penalty can be just as beneficial as improvements in miss rate. Moreover, Figure 5.1 shows that technology trends have improved the speed of processors faster than DRAMs, making the relative cost of miss penalties increase over time. We give five optimizations here to address this problem. Perhaps the most interesting optimization is the final one, which adds another level of cache to reduce miss penalty.

First Miss Penalty Reduction Technique: Giving Priority to Read Misses over Writes

With a write-through cache the most important improvement is a write buffer (page 380) of the proper size (see the pitfall on page 470 in section 5.11). Write buffers, however, do complicate memory accesses in that they might hold the updated value of a location needed on a read miss.

EXAMPLE   Look at this code sequence:

```
SW  512(R0),R3      ; M[512] ← R3     (cache index 0)
LW  R1,1024(R0)     ; R1 ← M[1024]    (cache index 0)
LW  R2,512(R0)      ; R2 ← M[512]     (cache index 0)
```

Assume a direct-mapped, write-through cache that maps 512 and 1024 to the same block, and a four-word write buffer. Will the value in R2 always be equal to the value in R3?

ANSWER   Using the terminology from Chapter 3, this is a read-after-write data hazard in memory. Let's follow a cache access to see the danger. The data in R3 are placed into the write buffer after the store. The following load uses the same cache index and is therefore a miss. The second load instruction tries to put the value in location 512 into register R2; this also results in a miss. If the write buffer hasn't completed writing to location 512 in memory, the read of location 512 will put the old, wrong value into the cache block, and then into R2. Without proper precautions, R3 would not be equal to R2!   ∎

ANSWER   The average miss penalty is five clock cycles for critical word first. For back-to-back reads of both halves of the cache block, only one cycle is saved since the pipeline will only move one instruction further until it must stall on the missing data.   ∎

As this example illustrates, the benefits of critical word first and early restart depend on the size of the block and the likelihood of another access to the portion of the block that has not yet been fetched.

The next technique takes overlap between the CPU and cache miss penalty even further to reduce the average miss penalty.

Fourth Miss Penalty Reduction Technique: Nonblocking Caches to Reduce Stalls on Cache Misses

Early restart still waits for the requested word to arrive before the CPU can continue execution. For pipelined machines that allow out-of-order completion using a scoreboard or Tomasulo-style control (section 4.2 in Chapter 4), the CPU need not stall on a cache miss. For example, the CPU could continue fetching instructions from the instruction cache while waiting for the data cache to return the missing data. A *nonblocking cache* or *lockup-free cache* escalates the potential benefits of such a scheme by allowing the data cache to continue to supply cache hits during a miss. This "hit under miss" optimization reduces the effective miss penalty by being helpful during a miss instead of ignoring the requests of the CPU. A subtle and complex option is that the cache may further lower the effective miss penalty if it can overlap multiple misses: a "hit under multiple miss" or "miss under miss" optimization. The second option is beneficial only if the memory system can service multiple misses (see page 434). Be aware that hit under miss significantly increases the complexity of the cache controller as there can be multiple outstanding memory accesses.

Figure 5.22 shows the average time in clock cycles for cache misses for an 8-KB data cache as the number of outstanding misses is varied. Floating-point programs benefit from increasing complexity, while integer programs get almost all of the benefit from a simple hit-under-one-miss scheme.

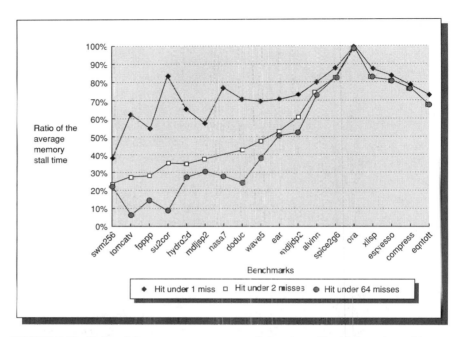

FIGURE 5.22   Ratio of the average memory stall time for a blocking cache to hit-under-miss schemes as the number of outstanding misses is varied for 18 SPEC92 programs. The hit-under-64-misses line allows one miss for every register in the machine. The first 14 programs are floating-point programs: the average for hit under 1 miss is 76%, for 2 misses is 51%, and for 64 misses is 39%. The final four are integer programs, and the three averages are 81%, 73%, and 78%, respectively. These data were collected for an 8-KB direct-mapped data cache with 32-byte blocks and a 16-clock-cycle miss penalty. These data were generated using the VLIW Multiflow Compiler, which scheduled loads away from use [Farkas and Jouppi 1994].

EXAMPLE   For the cache described in Figure 5.22, which is more important for floating-point programs: two-way set associativity or hit under one miss? What about for integer programs? Assume the following average miss rates for 8-KB data caches: 11.4% for floating-point programs with a direct-mapped cache, 10.7% for these programs with a two-way set-associative cache, 7.4% for integer programs with a direct-mapped cache, and 6.0% for integer programs with a two-way set-associative cache. Assume the average memory stall time is just the product of the miss rate and the miss penalty.

ANSWER   The numbers for Figure 5.22 were based on a miss penalty of 16 clock cycles. Although this is low for a miss penalty, let's stick with it for consistency. For floating-point programs the average memory stall times are

$$\text{Miss rate}_{DM} \times \text{Miss penalty} = 11.4\% \times 16 = 1.84$$

$$\text{Miss rate}_{2\text{-way}} \times \text{Miss penalty} = 10.7\% \times 16 = 1.71$$

The memory stalls of two-way are thus 1.71/1.84 or 93% of direct-mapped cache. The caption of Figure 5.22 says hit under one miss reduces the average memory stall time to 76% of a blocking cache, so for floating-point programs the direct-mapped data cache supporting hit under one miss gives better performance than a two-way set-associative cache that blocks on a miss.

For integer programs the calculation is

$$\text{Miss rate}_{DM} \times \text{Miss penalty} = 7.4\% \times 16 = 1.18$$

$$\text{Miss rate}_{2\text{-way}} \times \text{Miss penalty} = 6.0\% \times 16 = 0.96$$

The memory stalls of two-way are thus 0.96/1.18 or 81% of direct-mapped cache. The caption of Figure 5.22 says hit under one miss reduces the average memory stall time to 81% of a blocking cache, so the two options give about the same performance for integer programs. One potential advantage of hit under miss is that it cannot affect the hit time, as associativity can.   ■

Fifth Miss Penalty Reduction Technique: Second-Level Caches

The first four techniques to reduce miss penalty have impact on the CPU. This final technique ignores the CPU, concentrating on the interface between the cache and main memory.

The performance gap between processors and memory leads the architect to this question: Should I make the cache faster to keep pace with the speed of CPUs, or make the cache larger to overcome the widening gap between the CPU and main memory? One answer is, both. By adding another level of cache between the original cache and memory, the first-level cache can be small enough to match the clock cycle time of the fast CPU, while the second-level cache can be large enough to capture many accesses that would go to main memory, thereby lessening the effective miss penalty.

While the concept of adding another level in the hierarchy is straightforward, it complicates performance analysis. Definitions for a second level of cache are not always straightforward. Let's start with the definition of *average memory access time* for a two-level cache. Using the subscripts L1 and L2 to refer, respectively, to a first-level and a second-level cache, the original formula is

$$\text{Average memory access time} = \text{Hit time}_{L1} + \text{Miss rate}_{L1} \times \text{Miss penalty}_{L1}$$

and

$$\text{Miss penalty}_{L1} = \text{Hit time}_{L2} + \text{Miss rate}_{L2} \times \text{Miss penalty}_{L2}$$

so

$$\text{Average memory access time} = \text{Hit time}_{L1} + \text{Miss rate}_{L1} \times (\text{Hit time}_{L2} + \text{Miss rate}_{L2} \times \text{Miss penalty}_{L2})$$

In this formula, the second-level miss rate is measured on the leftovers from the first-level cache. To avoid ambiguity, these terms are adopted here for a two-level cache system:

- *Local miss rate*—The number of misses in the cache divided by the total number of memory accesses to this cache; this is Miss rate$_{L2}$ above for the second-level cache.

- *Global miss rate*—The number of misses in the cache divided by the total number of memory accesses generated by the CPU; using the terms above, the global miss rate of the second-level cache is Miss rate$_{L1}$ × Miss rate$_{L2}$.

This local miss rate is large because the first-level cache skims the cream of the memory accesses, and this is why the global miss rate is the more useful measure: it indicates what fraction of the memory accesses that leave the CPU go all the way to memory.

EXAMPLE   Suppose that in 1000 memory references there are 40 misses in the first-level cache and 20 misses in the second-level cache. What are the various miss rates?

ANSWER   The miss rate (either local or global) for the first-level cache is 40/1000 or 4%. The local miss rate for the second-level cache is 20/40 or 50%. The global miss rate of the second-level cache is 20/1000 or 2%.   ∎

Note that these formulas are for combined reads and writes, assuming a write-back first-level cache. Obviously, a write-through first-level cache will send *all* writes to the second level, not just the misses, and a write buffer would be used.

Figures 5.23 and 5.24 show how miss rates and relative execution time change with the size of a second-level cache for one design. From these figures we can gain two insights. The first is that the global cache miss rate is very similar to the

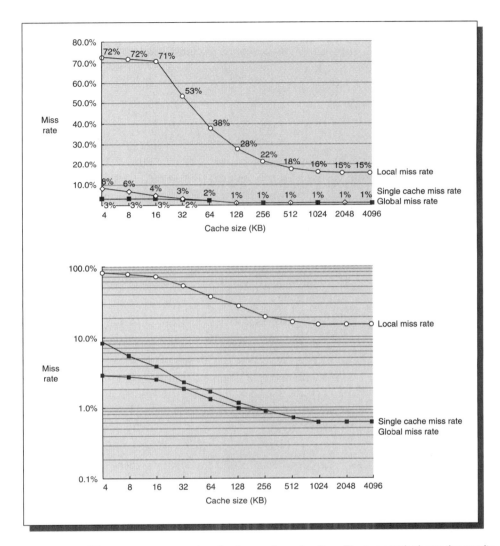

FIGURE 5.23   Miss rates versus cache size for reads and writes. The top graph shows the results plotted on a linear scale as we have done with earlier figures, while the bottom graph shows the results plotted on a log scale. As miss rates shrink, the log scale makes the differences easier to follow. The miss rate of a single-level cache versus size is plotted against the local miss rate and global miss rate of a second-level cache using a 32-KB first-level cache. Second-level caches *smaller* than the 32-KB first level make little sense, as reflected in the high miss rates. After 256 KB the single cache and global miss rates are virtually identical. Przybylski [1990] used four traces from the VAX system and four user programs from the MIPS R2000 that were randomly interleaved to duplicate the effect of process switches.

single cache miss rate of the second-level cache, provided that the second-level cache is much larger than the first-level cache. Hence our intuition and knowledge about the first-level caches apply. The second insight is that the local cache rate is *not* a good measure of secondary caches; it is a function of the miss rate of the first-level cache, and hence can vary by changing the first-level cache. Thus, the global cache miss rate should be used when evaluating second-level caches.

With these definitions in place, we can consider the parameters of second-level caches. The foremost difference between the two levels is that the speed of the first-level cache affects the clock rate of the CPU, while the speed of the second-level cache only affects the miss penalty of the first-level cache. Thus, we can consider many alternatives in the second-level cache that would be ill chosen for the first-level cache. There are but two questions for the design of the second-level cache: Will it lower the average memory access time portion of the CPI, and how much does it cost?

The initial decision is the size of a second-level cache. Since everything in the first-level cache is likely to be in the second-level cache, the second-level cache should be much bigger than the first. If second-level caches are just a little bigger, the local miss rate will be high. This observation inspires design of huge second-level caches—the size of main memory in older computers! Large size means that the second-level cache may have practically no capacity misses, leaving a few compulsory and conflict misses for our attention. One question is whether set associativity makes more sense for second-level caches.

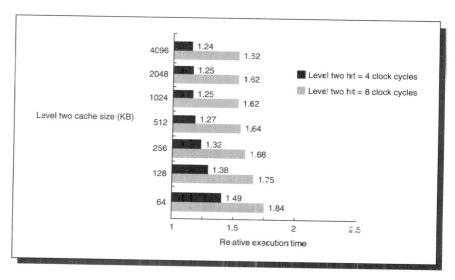

FIGURE 5.24   Relative execution time by second-level cache size. Przybylski [1990] collected these data using a 32-KB first-level write-back cache, varying the size of the second-level cache. The two bars are for different clock cycles for a level two cache hit. The reference execution time of 1.00 is for a 4096-KB second-level cache with a one-clock-cycle latency on a second-level hit. These data were collected the same way as in Figure 5.23.

Summarizing the second-level cache considerations, the essence of cache design is balancing fast hits and few misses. Most optimizations that help one hurt the other. For second-level caches, there are many fewer hits than in the first-level cache, so the emphasis shifts to fewer misses. This insight leads to larger caches with higher associativity and larger blocks.

5.5   Reducing Hit Time

Now that we have examined ways to improve cache performance by reducing misses (in section 5.3) and by reducing miss penalty (in section 5.4), we are ready to reduce the third component of the average memory access time.

Hit time is critical because it affects the clock rate of the processor; on many machines today the cache access time limits the clock cycle rate, even for machines that take multiple clock cycles to access the cache. Hence a fast hit time is multiplied in importance beyond the average memory access time formula because it helps everything. This section gives two general techniques and then one optimization for write hits.

First Hit Time Reduction Technique: Small and Simple Caches

A time-consuming portion of a cache hit is using the index portion of the address to read the tag memory and then compare it to the address. Our guideline from Chapter 1 suggests that smaller hardware is faster, and a small cache certainly helps the hit time. It is also critical to keep the cache small enough to fit on the same chip as the processor to avoid the time penalty of going off-chip. Some designs strike a compromise by keeping the tags on-chip and the data off-chip, promising a fast tag check, yet providing the greater capacity of separate memory chips. The second suggestion is to keep the cache simple, such as using direct mapping (see page 396). A main benefit of direct-mapped caches is that the designer can overlap the tag check with the transmission of the data. This effectively reduces hit time. Hence the pressure of a fast clock cycle encourages small and simple cache designs for first-level caches.

Second Hit Time Reduction Technique: Avoiding Address Translation During Indexing of the Cache

Even a small and simple cache must cope with the translation of a virtual address from the CPU to a physical address to access memory. As described below in section 5.7, processors treat main memory as just another level of the memory hierarchy, and thus the address of the virtual memory that exists on disk must be mapped onto the main memory.

The guideline of making the common case fast suggests that we use virtual addresses for the cache, since hits are much more common than misses. Such caches are termed *virtual caches*, with *physical cache* used to identify the traditional cache that uses physical addresses. Virtual addressing eliminates address translation time from a cache hit. Then why doesn't everyone build virtually addressed caches? One reason is that every time a process is switched, the virtual addresses refer to different physical addresses, requiring the cache to be flushed. Figure 5.26 shows the impact on miss rates of this flushing. One solution is to

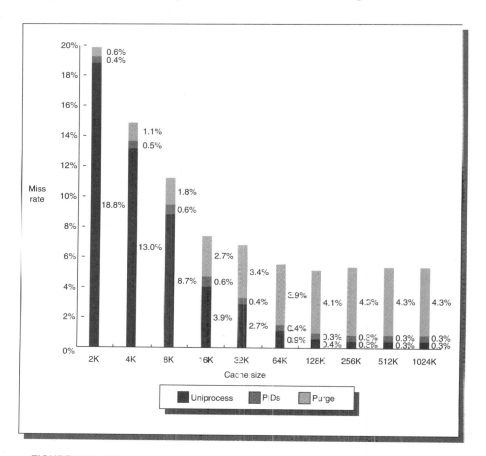

FIGURE 5.26 Miss rate versus virtually addressed cache size of a program measured three ways: without process switches (uniprocess), with process switches using a process-identifier tag (PIDs), and with process switches but without PIDs (purge). PIDs increase the uniprocess absolute miss rate by 0.3% to 0.6% and save 0.6% to 4.3% over purging. Agarwal [1987] collected these statistics for the Ultrix operating system running on a VAX, assuming direct-mapped caches with a block size of 16 bytes. Note that the miss rate goes up from 128K to 256K. Such nonintuitive behavior can occur in caches because changing size changes the mapping of memory blocks onto cache blocks, which can change the conflict miss rate.

increase the width of the cache address tag with a *process-identifier tag* (PID). If the operating system assigns these tags to processes, it only need flush the cache when a PID is recycled; that is, the PID distinguishes whether or not the data in the cache are for this program. Figure 5.26 shows the improvement in miss rates by using PIDs to avoid cache flushes.

Another reason why virtual caches are not more popular is that operating systems and user programs may use two different virtual addresses for the same physical address. These duplicate addresses, called *synonyms* or *aliases*, could result in two copies of the same data in a virtual cache; if one is modified, the other will have the wrong value. With a physical cache this wouldn't happen, since the accesses would first be translated to the same physical cache block. Hardware solutions, called *anti-aliasing*, guarantee every cache block a unique physical address.

Software can make this problem much easier by forcing aliases to share some address bits. The version of UNIX from Sun Microsystems, for example, requires all aliases to be identical in the last 18 bits of their addresses; this restriction is called *page coloring*. Note that page coloring is simply set-associative mapping applied to virtual memory: the 4-KB (2^{12}) pages are mapped using 64 (2^6) sets to ensure that the physical and virtual addresses match in the last 18 bits. This restriction means a direct-mapped cache that is 2^{18} (256K) bytes or smaller can never have duplicate physical addresses for blocks.

The final area of concern with virtual addresses is I/O. I/O typically uses physical addresses and thus would require mapping to virtual addresses to interact with a virtual cache. (The impact of I/O on caches is further discussed below in section 5.9.)

Another technique to get fast hits is to break address translation and cache access into separate pipeline stages, giving fast cycle time and slow hits. This increases the number of pipeline stages for a memory access, leading to greater penalty on mispredicted branches and more clock cycles between the issue of the load and the use of the data (see section 3.9).

One alternative to get the best of both virtual and physical caches is to use the page offset—the part unaffected by address translation—to index the cache while sending the virtual part to be translated. This alternative allows the comparison to be with physical addresses and yet overlap the time to read the tags with address translation. The limitation of this virtually indexed, physically tagged alternative is that a direct-mapped cache can be no bigger than the page size. This is an advantage of the 8-KB caches of the Alpha AXP 21064; the minimum page size is 8 KB, so the 8-bit index can be taken from the physical part of the address.

One way to keep the index small enough to be taken from the physical part of the address and still have a large cache is to use high associativity. Recall that the size of the index is controlled by this formula:

$$2^{\text{index}} = \frac{\text{Cache size}}{\text{Block size} \times \text{Set associativity}}$$

The IBM 3033 cache, as an extreme example, is 16-way set associative, even though studies show there is little benefit to miss rates above eight-way set associativity. This high associativity allows a 64-KB cache to be addressed with a physical index despite the limitation of 4-KB pages in the IBM architecture. Figure 5.27 shows the relationship of index to page offset.

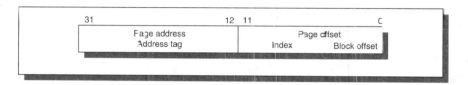

FIGURE 5.27   Relationship of index field and page offset in the IBM 3033 cache. The 4-KB page means the last 12 bits of the address are not translated, and hence some of it can be used to index the cache.

One alternative to higher associativity is for the operating system to implement page coloring by guaranteeing that the last few bits of the virtual and physical page address are identical. Such cooperating allows a larger index than first with the page offset and still compares physical addresses.

Another alternative to higher associativity is to have a small piece of hardware that guesses the mapping of the last few bits of virtual address bits to physical address. This might be a small table that uses a hashing function on the virtual address. This guess is used with the physical portion of the address to index the cache, with the translated address used to match the tag selected by this hybrid index. If the tag matches, we have a hit. If the tag doesn't match, either the data were not in the cache or we had a bad guess of the mapping of the last few bits of virtual address. The cache would presumably retry with the correct index to decide whether the access was a hit or a real miss.

Keeping caches small and simple and techniques to avoid delays of address translation will make both read hits and write hits faster. The next subsection concentrates only on writes.

Third Hit Time Reduction Technique: Pipelining Writes for Fast Write Hits

Write hits usually take longer than read hits because the tag must be checked before writing the data; otherwise the wrong address would be written. One technique, used by the Alpha AXP 21064 and other machines, pipelines the writes. Figure 5.28 shows the hardware organization of pipelined writes. First, tags and data are split so that they can be addressed independently. On a write, the cache compares the tag with the current write address, as usual. The difference comes

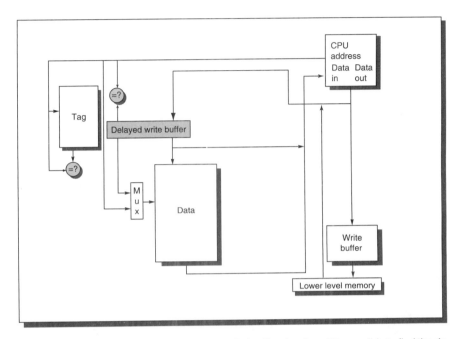

FIGURE 5.28   The hardware organization of pipelined writes. It is possible to find the desired data in the delayed write buffer. In that case, either the write buffer supplies the newer data or the write buffer could complete and then the new data are read from the cache.

with the write to the data portion of the cache that occurs during the tag comparison; it must be using some other address since the current write address is still being checked. The trick is that the cache uses the address and data from the *previous* write, which has already been determined to be a hit. Thus the logical pipeline is between writes—the second stage of the write occurs during the first stage of the next write (or during a cache miss). Therefore, writes can be performed back to back at one per clock cycle because the CPU does not have to wait for the tag check before writing. Reads play no part in this pipeline since they already operate in parallel with the tag check, and so no help is needed.

Cache Optimization Summary

The techniques in sections 5.3 to 5.5 to improve miss rate, miss penalty, and hit time generally impact the other components of the average memory access equation as well as the complexity of the memory hierarchy. Figure 5.29 summarizes these techniques and estimates the impact on complexity, with + meaning that the technique improves the factor, – meaning it hurts that factor, and blank meaning it has no impact. Note that few techniques help more than one category, and none help all three.

Technique	Miss rate	Miss penalty	Hit time	Hardware complexity	Comment
Larger block size	+	–		0	Trivial; RS/6000 550 uses 128
Higher associativity	+		–	1	e.g., MIPS R10000 is 4-way
Victim caches	+			2	Similar technique in HP 7200
Pseudo-associative caches	+			2	Used in L2 of MIPS R10000
Hardware prefetching of instructions and data	+			2	Data are harder to prefetch; tried in a few machines; Alpha 21064
Compiler-controlled prefetching	+			3	Needs nonblocking cache too; several machines support it
Compiler techniques to reduce cache misses	+			0	Software is challenge; some machines give compiler option
Giving priority to read misses over writes		+		1	Trivial for uniprocessor, and widely used
Subblock placement		+		1	Used primarily to reduce tags
Early restart and critical word first		+		2	Used in MIPS R10000, IBM 620
Nonblocking caches		+		3	Used in Alpha 21064, R10000
Second-level caches		+		2	Costly hardware; harder if block size L1 $\neq$ L2; widely used
Small and simple caches	–		+	0	Trivial; widely used
Avoiding address translation during indexing of the cache			+	2	Trivial if small cache; used in Alpha 21064
Pipelining writes for fast write hits			+	1	Used in Alpha 21064

FIGURE 5.29   Summary of cache optimizations and impact on the three aspects of cache performance and on cache complexity. + means that the technique improves the factor, – means it hurts that factor, and blank means it has no impact. The complexity measure is subjective, with 0 being the easiest and 3 being a challenge.

5.6 | Main Memory

... the one single development that put computers on their feet was the invention of a reliable form of memory, namely, the core memory. ... Its cost was reasonable, it was reliable and, because it was reliable, it could in due course be made large. [p. 209]

Maurice Wilkes, *Memoirs of a Computer Pioneer* (1985)

Main memory is the next level down in the hierarchy. Main memory satisfies the demands of caches and serves as the I/O interface, as it is the destination of input as well as the source for output. Performance measures of main memory emphasize both latency and bandwidth. (Memory bandwidth is the number of bytes read or written per unit time.) Traditionally, main memory latency (which affects the cache miss penalty) is the primary concern of the cache, while main memory bandwidth is the primary concern of I/O. With the popularity of second-level caches and their larger block sizes, main memory bandwidth becomes important to caches as well. In fact, cache designers may take advantage of the high memory bandwidth by increasing block size. The relationship of main memory and I/O is discussed in Chapter 6.

Memory Technology

Memory latency is traditionally quoted using two measures—access time and cycle time. *Access time* is the time between when a read is requested and when the desired word arrives, while *cycle time* is the minimum time between requests to memory. One reason that cycle time is greater than access time is that the memory needs the address lines to be stable between accesses.

As early DRAMs grew in capacity, the cost of a package with all the necessary address lines was an issue. The solution was to multiplex the address lines, thereby cutting the number of address pins in half. One half of the address is sent first, called the *row access strobe* or *RAS*. It is followed by the other half of the address, sent during the *column access strobe* or *CAS*. These names come from the internal chip organization, since the memory is organized as a rectangular matrix addressed by rows and columns.

An additional requirement of DRAM derives from the property signified by its first letter, *D*, for *dynamic*. DRAMs use only a single transistor to store a bit, but reading that bit can disturb the information. To prevent loss of information, each bit must be "refreshed" periodically. Fortunately, all the bits in a row can be refreshed simultaneously just by reading that row. Hence every DRAM in the memory system must access every row within a certain time window, such as 8 milliseconds. Memory controllers include hardware to periodically refresh the DRAMs.

This requirement means that the memory system is occasionally unavailable because it is sending a signal telling every chip to *refresh*. The time for a refresh is typically a full memory access (RAS and CAS) for each row of the DRAM. Since the memory matrix in a DRAM is conceptually square, the number of steps in a refresh is usually the square root of the DRAM capacity. DRAM designers try to keep time spent refreshing to be less than 5% of the total time.

In contrast to DRAMs are SRAMs—the first letter standing for *static*. The dynamic nature of the circuits in DRAM require data to be written back after being read, hence the difference between the access time and the cycle time as well as the need to refresh. SRAMs use four to six transistors per bit to prevent the information from being disturbed when read. Thus, unlike DRAMs, there is no difference between access time and cycle time, and there is no need to refresh SRAM. In DRAM designs the emphasis is on capacity, while SRAM designs are concerned with both speed *and* capacity. Because of this concern, SRAM address lines are not multiplexed.) For memories designed in comparable technologies, the capacity of DRAMs is roughly 4 o 8 times that of SRAMs. The cycle time of SRAMs is 8 to 16 times faster than DRAMs, but they are also 8 to 16 times as expensive.

The main memory of virtually every computer sold since 1975 is composed of semiconductor DRAMs (and virtually all caches use SRAM); the exception that proves the rule is Cray supercomputers such as the C-90, which use SRAM for main memory.

Amdahl suggested a rule of thumb that memory capacity should grow linearly with CPU speed to keep a balanced system (see section 1.4), and CPU designers rely on DRAMs to supply that demand: they expect a four-fold improvement in capacity every three years in the base technology, or 60% per year. Unfortunately, the performance of DRAMs is growing at a much slower rate. Figure 5.30 shows a performance improvement in row access time of about 22% per generation, or 7% per year.

Year of introduction	Chip size	Row access strobe (RAS)		Column access strobe (CAS)	Cycle time
		Slowest DRAM	Fastest DRAM		
1980	64 Kbit	180 ns	50 ns	75 ns	250 ns
1983	256 Kbit	150 ns	20 ns	50 ns	220 ns
1986	1 Mbit	120 ns	00 ns	25 ns	190 ns
1989	4 Mbit	100 ns	80 ns	20 ns	165 ns
1992	16 Mbit	80 ns	60 ns	15 ns	120 ns
1995	64 Mbit	65 ns	50 ns	10 ns	90 ns

FIGURE 5.30 Times of fast and slow DRAMs with each generation. The improvement by a factor of two in column access accompanied the switch from NMOS DRAMs to CMOS DRAMs. With three years per generation, the performance improvement of row access time is about 7% per year. Data in the last row represent predicted performance for 64-Mbit DRAMs.

As we saw in Figure 5.1 on page 374, the CPU-DRAM performance gap is clearly a problem today—Amdahl's Law warns us what will happen if we ignore one portion of the computation while trying to speed up the rest. The previous sections describe what can be done with cache organization to reduce this performance gap, but simply making caches larger or adding more levels of caches may not be a cost-effective way to eliminate the gap. Innovative organizations of main memory are needed as well. In the next section we examine techniques for organizing memory to improve bandwidth, concluding with techniques especially for DRAMs.

Organizations for Improving Main Memory Performance

Although caches are interested in low latency memory, it is generally easier to improve memory bandwidth with new organizations than it is to reduce latency. Caches benefit from bandwidth improvement by allowing each cache block size to increase without a large increase in the miss penalty.

Let's illustrate these organizations with the case of satisfying a cache miss. Assume the performance of the basic memory organization is

- 4 clock cycles to send the address

- 24 clock cycles for the access time per word

- 4 clock cycles to send a word of data

Given a cache block of four words, the miss penalty is $4 \times (4 + 24 + 4)$ or 128 clock cycles, with a memory bandwidth of one-eighth byte (16/128) per clock cycle.

Figure 5.31 shows some of the options to faster memory systems. The next four solutions assume generic memory, either DRAM or SRAM. DRAM-specific solutions form the last subsection.

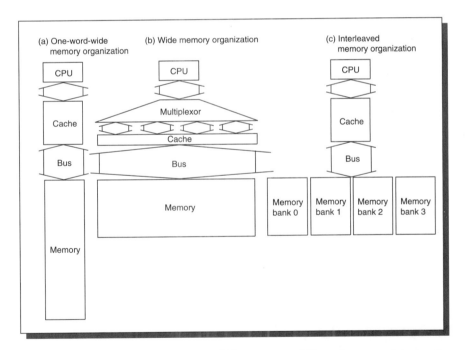

FIGURE 5.31 Three examples of bus width, memory width, and memory interleaving to achieve higher memory bandwidth. (a) is the simplest design, with everything the width of one word; (b) shows a wider memory, bus, and cache; while (c) shows a narrow bus and cache with an interleaved memory.

The simplest approach to increasing memory bandwidth, then, is to make the memory wider; we examine this first.

First Technique for Higher Bandwidth: Wider Main Memory

First-level caches are often organized with a physical width of one word because most CPU accesses are that size. Systems without second-level caches often design main memory to match the width of the cache. Doubling or quadrupling the width of the cache and the memory will therefore double or quadruple the memory bandwidth. With a main memory width of two words, the miss penalty in our example would drop from 4×32 or 128 clock cycles to 2×32 or 64 clock cycles. At four words wide the miss penalty is just 1×32 clock cycles. The bandwidth is then one-quarter byte per clock cycle at two words wide and one-half byte per clock cycle when the memory is four words wide.

There is cost in the wider connection between the CPU and memory, typically called a memory *bus*. CPUs will still access the cache a word at a time, so there now needs to be a multiplexer between the cache and the CPU—and that multiplexer may be on the critical timing path. Second-level caches can help since the multiplexing can be between first- and second-level caches, not on the critical path. Another drawback is that since main memory is traditionally expandable by the customer, the minimum increment is doubled or quadrupled when the width is doubled or quadrupled. Finally, memories with error correction have difficulties with writes to a portion of the protected block (e.g., a write of a byte); the rest of the data must be read so that the new error correction code can be calculated and stored when the data are written. If the error correction is done over the full width, the wider memory will increase the frequency of such "read-modify-write" sequences because more writes become partial block writes. Many designs of wider memory have separate error correction every 32 bits since most writes are that size.

One example of wide main memory is the Alpha AXP 21064 whose second-level cache, memory bus, and memory are all 256 bits wide. To allow customers to purchase small amounts of memory without sacrificing width, DEC sells older generations of DRAM for small memories as well as current DRAMs for the larger memory systems (see section 5.10).

Second Technique for Higher Bandwidth: Simple Interleaved Memory

Increasing width is one way to improve bandwidth, but another is to take advantage of the potential parallelism of having many DRAMs in a memory system. Memory chips can be organized in banks to read or write multiple words at a time rather than a single word. In general, the purpose of interleaved memory is to try to take advantage of the potential memory bandwidth of *all* the DRAMs in the

The memory system goal is to deliver information from a new bank each clock cycle for sequential accesses. To see why this formula holds, imagine there were fewer banks than clock cycles to access a word in a bank; say, 8 banks with an access time of 10 clock cycles. After 10 clock cycles the CPU could get a word from bank 0, and then bank 0 would begin fetching the next desired word as the CPU received the following 7 words from the other 7 banks. At clock cycle 18 the CPU would be at the door of bank 0, waiting for it to supply the next word. The CPU would have to wait until clock cycle 20 for the word to appear. Hence we want more banks than clock cycles to access a bank to avoid waiting.

We will discuss conflicts on nonsequential accesses to banks in the following subsections. For now, we note that having many banks reduces the chance of these bank conflicts.

Ironically, as capacity per memory chip increases, there are fewer chips in the same-sized memory system, making multiple banks much more expensive. For example, a 64-MB main memory takes 512 memory chips of $1 M \times 1$ bit, easily organized into 16 banks of 32 memory chips. But it takes only eight $64\text{-}M \times 1$-bit memory chips for 64 MB, making one bank the limit. Even though the Amdahl/ Case rule of thumb for balanced computer systems recommends increasing memory capacity with increasing CPU performance, many manufacturers will want to have a small memory option in the baseline model. This shrinking number of DRAMs is the main disadvantage of interleaved memory banks. DRAMs organized with wider paths, such as $16 M \times 4$ bits or $8 M \times 8$ bits, will postpone this weakness.

A second disadvantage of memory banks is again the difficulty of main memory expansion. Either the memory system must support multiple generations of DRAM, as in the DEC 3000 model 800, or the minimum increment will be to, say, double main memory.

Third Technique for Higher Bandwidth: Independent Memory Banks

The original motivation for memory banks was higher memory bandwidth by interleaving sequential accesses. This hardware is not much more difficult since the banks can share address lines with a memory controller, enabling each bank to use the data portion of the memory bus. A generalization of interleaving is to allow multiple independent accesses, where multiple memory controllers allow banks (or sets of word-interleaved banks) to operate independently. Each bank needs separate address lines and possibly a separate data bus. For example, an input device may use one controller and one bank, the cache read may use another, and a cache write may use a third. Nonblocking caches (page 414) allow the CPU to proceed beyond a cache miss, potentially allowing multiple cache misses to be serviced simultaneously. Such a design only makes sense with memory banks; otherwise the multiple reads will be serviced by a single memory port and get only a small benefit of overlapping access with transmission. Multiprocessors that share a common memory provide further motivation for memory banks (see Chapter 8).

Thus the term *memory bank* has potentially two conflicting definitions. We use the term *superbank* to mean all memory active on one block transfer and the term *bank* for the portion within a superbank that is word interleaved. Figure 5.33 shows this relationship. If there is no confusion, we'll just use the shorter term *bank* to mean a collection of memory.

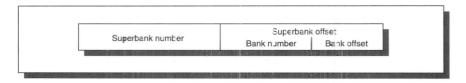

FIGURE 5.33   The relationship of superbanks and banks.

Fourth Technique for Higher Bandwidth: Avoiding Memory Bank Conflicts

If the memory system is being designed to support multiple independent requests—as in the case of miss-under-miss caches, direct memory access I/O that can read data from noncontiguous addresses ("gather") or write data to noncontiguous addresses ("scatter"), multiprocessors (see Chapter 8), or vector computers (see Appendix B)—the effectiveness of the system will depend on the frequency that independent requests will go to different banks. Sequential accesses work well with traditional interleaving, as do any accesses that differ by an odd number. The problem is when this difference between addresses is an even number. One solution, used by larger computers, is to statistically reduce the chances by having many banks; the NEC SX/3, for instance, has up to 128 banks.

The problem with such a solution is that data memory references are not random, and may go to the same bank no matter how many banks are provided. Suppose we have 128 memory banks, interleaved on a word basis, and execute this code:

```
int x[255][512];
    for (j = 0; j < 512; j = j+1)
        for (i = 0; i < 256; i = i+1)
            x[i][j] = 2 * x[i][j];
```

Since the 512 is an even multiple of 128, all the elements of a column will be in the same memory bank and code will stall on data cache misses no matter how sophisticated a CPU or memory system.

There are both software and hardware solutions to the bank conflict problem. The compiler could do the loop interchange optimization (see page 407) to avoid accessing the same bank. A simpler solution would be for the programmer or the compiler to expand the size of the array so that it is not a power of two, thereby forcing the addresses above to go to different banks.

Before describing a hardware solution, let's review how addressing of banks works. The mapping of an address to a location in a memory bank can be expressed as two problems:

$$\text{Bank number} = \text{Address MOD Number of banks}$$

$$\text{Address within bank} = \lfloor \text{Address / Number of banks} \rfloor$$

Traditional memory systems keep both the number of banks and the amount of memory per bank a power of two to make this calculation trivial.

One hardware solution to reduce the number of bank conflicts is to have a prime number of banks! Such a number would seem to demand more hardware to perform a complex calculation: the modulo and the division mentioned above. Furthermore, this complex calculation would lengthen each memory access.

Fortunately, there are several hardware schemes to calculate modulo quickly, especially if the prime number of memory banks is one less than a power of two (see Exercise 5.10). In this case division can be replaced by the following simple calculation:

$$\text{Address within bank} = \text{Address MOD Number of words in bank}$$

Since the number of words in a bank is very likely a power of two, we have replaced division by a prime number by bit selection.

The proof of this simplification is based on the *Chinese Remainder Theorem*. This 2000-year-old observation states that as long as two sets of integers a_i and b_i follow these rules:

$$b_i = x \text{ MOD } a_i, \ 0 \le b_i < a_i, \ 0 \le x < a_0 \times a_1 \times a_2 \times \ldots$$

and that a_i and a_j are co-prime if $i \ne j$, then the integer x has only one solution of each pair of integers a_i and b_i (two integers are *co-prime* if they have no common prime number as a factor). The Chinese Remainder Theorem guarantees that there is no ambiguity with this mapping of addresses to banks because the following conditions hold:

- Bank number = Address MOD Number of banks ($b_0 = x \text{ MOD } a_0$).

- Address within bank = Address MOD Number of words in bank ($b_1 = x \text{ MOD } a_1$).

- Bank number < Number of banks ($0 \le b_0 < a_0$).

- Address within a bank < Number of words in bank ($0 \le b_1 < a_1$).

- Address < Number of banks $\times$ Number of words in a bank ($0 \le x < a_0 \times a_1$).

■ The number of banks and the number of words in a bank are co-prime (a_0 and a_1 are co-prime).

The first two conditions above are simply the definition of the mapping. The next three conditions are trivially true because an N-word address goes from 0 to $N-1$. The last condition is true since the number of banks is a prime number greater than two and the number of words in a bank is a power of two.

Figure 5.34 shows three memory modules, each with eight words, showing the traditional sequentially interleaved mapping of addresses on the left and the new mapping on the right.

Address within bank	Memory bank					
	Sequentially interleaved			Modulo interleaved		
	0	1	2	0	1	2
0	0	1	2	0	16	8
1	3	4	5	9	1	17
2	6	7	8	18	10	2
3	9	10	11	3	19	11
4	12	13	14	12	4	20
5	15	16	17	21	13	5
6	18	19	20	6	22	14
7	21	22	23	15	7	23

FIGURE 5.34 Three memory banks with sequentially interleaved addressing on the left, requiring a division as part of addressing of the word within a module, and the new mapping, which requires only modulo to a power of two. For example, address 5 is mapped to the second word of memory bank 2 on the left and to the sixth word of memory bank 2 on the right.

Fifth Technique for Higher Bandwidth: DRAM-Specific Interleaving

Thus far we have seen four techniques that improve memory bandwidth: wider memory, interleaved memory, banked memory, and bank conflict avoidance. These techniques work with any memory technology, and have been used or discussed since before DRAMs were invented. This section presents techniques that take advantage of the nature of DRAMs.

As mentioned earlier, DRAM access is divided into row access and column access. DRAMs must buffer a row of bits inside the DRAM for the column access, and this row is usually the square root of the DRAM size—8 Kbits for 64 Mbits, 16 Kbits for 256 Mbits, and so on. To improve performance, all DRAMs come with timing signals that allow repeated accesses to the buffer without another row access time. There are three versions for this optimization:

- *Nibble mode*—The DRAM can supply three extra bits from sequential locations for every row access strobe.

- *Page mode*—The buffer acts like a SRAM; by changing column address, random bits can be accessed in the buffer until the next row access or refresh time.

- *Static column*—Very similar to page mode, except that it's not necessary to toggle the column access strobe line every time the column address changes.

Starting with the 1-Mbit generation, most DRAMs can perform any of the three options, with the optimization selected at the time the die is packaged by choosing which pads to wire up. These operations change the definition of cycle time for DRAMs. Figure 5.35 shows the traditional cycle time plus the fastest speed between accesses in the optimized mode.

	Row access				Optimized time
Chip size	**Slowest DRAM**	**Fastest DRAM**	**Column access**	**Cycle time**	**nibble, page, static column**
64 Kbits	180 ns	150 ns	75 ns	250 ns	150 ns
256 Kbits	150 ns	120 ns	50 ns	220 ns	100 ns
1 Mbits	120 ns	100 ns	25 ns	190 ns	50 ns
4 Mbits	100 ns	80 ns	20 ns	165 ns	40 ns
16 Mbits	80 ns	60 ns	15 ns	120 ns	30 ns
64 Mbits	65 ns	50 ns	10 ns	90 ns	25 ns

FIGURE 5.35 DRAM cycle time for the optimized accesses. This figure is the same as Figure 5.30 (page 429), with a column added to show the optimized cycle time for the three modes. Starting with the 1-Mbit DRAM, optimized cycle time is about four times faster than unoptimized cycle time. It is so much faster that page mode was renamed *fast page mode*. The optimized cycle time is the same no matter which of the three optimized modes is selected.

The advantage of such optimizations is that they use the circuitry already on the DRAMs, adding little cost to the system while achieving almost a fourfold improvement in bandwidth. For example, nibble mode was designed to take advantage of the same program behavior as interleaved memory. The chip reads 4 bits at a time internally, supplying 4 bits externally in the time of four optimized cycles. Unless the bus transfer time is faster than the optimized cycle time, the cost of four-way interleaved memory is only more complicated timing control. Page mode and static column could also be used to get even higher interleaving with slightly more complex control. DRAMs also tend to have weak tristate buffers, implying traditional interleaving with more memory chips must include buffer chips for each memory bank.

Recently new breeds of DRAMs have been produced that further optimize the interface between the DRAM and CPU. One example is from RAMBUS. This company takes the standard DRAM core and provides a new interface, making a single chip act more like a memory system than a memory component. RAMBUS has dropped RAS/CAS, replacing it with a bus that allows other accesses over the bus between the sending of the address and return of the data. (Such a bus is called a *packet-switched bus* or *split-transaction* bus, described in Chapters 6 and 7.) This bus allows a single chip to act as a memory bank. A chip can return a variable amount of data from a single request, and even perform its own refresh. RAMBUS offers a byte-wide interface, and a clock signal so that the chip can be tightly synchronized to the CPU clock. Once the address pipeline is full, a single chip can deliver one byte every 2 ns.

Most main memory systems use techniques such as page mode to reduce the CPU-DRAM performance gap. Unlike traditional interleaved memories, there are no disadvantages using such a mode as DRAMs scale upward in capacity. On the other hand, the new breed of DRAMs such as RAMBUS might cost a premium of, say, 20% per megabyte over traditional DRAMs to provide the greater bandwidth. The marketplace will determine whether the more radical DRAMs such as RAMBUS will become popular for main memory, or whether the price premium restricts them to niche markets.

One example niche market is computer graphics, where a DRAM with a fast serial output line is used to drive displays. This special DRAM is called a *video RAM* or *VRAM*; RAMBUS is challenging VRAMs in this market.

5.7 | Virtual Memory

… a system has been devised to make the core drum combination appear to the programmer as a single level store, the requisite transfers taking place automatically.

Kilburn et al. [1962]

At any instant in time computers are running multiple processes, each with its own address space. (Processes are described in the next section.) It would be too expensive to dedicate a full-address-space worth of memory for each process, especially since many processes use only a small part of their address space. Hence, there must be a means of sharing a smaller amount of physical memory among many processes. One way to do this, *virtual memory*, divides physical memory into blocks and allocates them to different processes. Inherent in such an approach must be a *protection* scheme that restricts a process to the blocks belonging only to that process. Most forms of virtual memory also reduce the time to start a program, since not all code and data need be in physical memory before a program can begin.

on any machine ranges from 2^{16} bytes up to 2^{32} bytes; the smallest segment is 1 byte. Figure 5.38 shows how the two approaches might divide code and data.

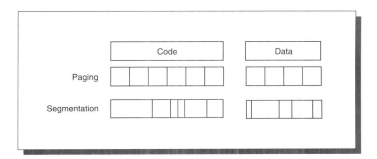

FIGURE 5.38   Example of how paging and segmentation divide a program.

The decision to use paged virtual memory versus segmented virtual memory affects the CPU. Paged addressing has a single fixed-size address divided into page number and offset within a page, analogous to cache addressing. A single address does not work for segmented addresses; the variable size of segments requires one word for a segment number and one word for an offset within a segment, for a total of two words. An unsegmented address space is simpler for the compiler.

The pros and cons of these two approaches have been well documented in operating systems textbooks; Figure 5.39 summarizes the arguments. Because of

	Page	**Segment**
Words per address	One	Two (segment and offset)
Programmer visible?	Invisible to application programmer	May be visible to application programmer
Replacing a block	Trivial (all blocks are the same size)	Hard (must find contiguous, variable-size, unused portion of main memory)
Memory use inefficiency	Internal fragmentation (unused portion of page)	External fragmentation (unused pieces of main memory)
Efficient disk traffic	Yes (adjust page size to balance access time and transfer time)	Not always (small segments may transfer just a few bytes)

FIGURE 5.39   Paging versus segmentation. Both can waste memory, depending on the block size and how well the segments fit together in main memory. Programming languages with unrestricted pointers require both the segment and the address to be passed. A hybrid approach, called *paged segments*, shoots for the best of both worlds: segments are composed of pages, so replacing a block is easy, yet a segment may be treated as a logical unit.

the replacement problem (the third line of the figure), few machines today use pure segmentation. Some machines use a hybrid approach, called *paged segments*, in which a segment is an integral number of pages. This simplifies replacement because memory need not be contiguous, and the full segments need not be in main memory. A more recent hybrid is for a machine to offer multiple page sizes, with the larger sizes being powers of two times the smallest page size. The Alpha AXP 21064, for example, allows 8 KB, 64 KB ($2^3 \times 8$ KB), 512 KB ($2^6 \times 8$ KB), and 4096 KB ($2^9 \times 8$ KB) to act as a single page.

We are now ready to answer the four memory-hierarchy questions for virtual memory.

Q1: Where can a block be placed in main memory?

The miss penalty for virtual memory involves access to a rotating magnetic storage device and is therefore quite high. Given the choice of lower miss rates or a simpler placement algorithm, operating systems designers normally pick lower miss rates because of the exorbitant miss penalty. Thus, operating systems allow blocks to be placed anywhere in main memory. According to the terminology in Figure 5.2 (page 376), this strategy would be labeled fully associative.

Q2: How is a block found if it is in main memory?

Both paging and segmentation rely on a data structure that is indexed by the page or segment number. This data structure contains the physical address of the block. For segmentation, the offset is added to the segment's physical address to obtain the final physical address. For paging, the offset is simply concatenated to this physical page address (see Figure 5.40).

This data structure, containing the physical page addresses, usually takes the form of a *page table*. Indexed by the virtual page number, the size of the table is the number of pages in the virtual address space. Given a 28-bit virtual address, 4-KB pages, and 4 bytes per page table entry, the size of the page table would be 256 KB. To reduce the size of this data structure, some machines apply a hashing function to the virtual address so that the data structure need only be the length of the number of *physical* pages in main memory; this number could be much smaller than the number of virtual pages. Such a structure is called an *inverted page table*. Using the example above, a 64-MB physical memory would only need 128 KB (8×64 MB/4 KB) for an inverted page table; the extra 4 bytes per page table entry is for the virtual address.

To reduce address translation time, computers use a cache dedicated to these address translations, called a *translation look-aside buffer*, or simply *translation buffer*. They are described in more detail shortly.

Q3: Which block should be replaced on a virtual memory miss?

As mentioned above, the overriding operating system guideline is minimizing page faults. Consistent with this guideline, almost all operating systems try to

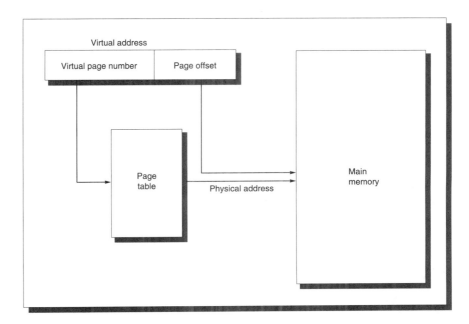

FIGURE 5.40   The mapping of a virtual address to a physical address via a page table.

replace the least-recently used (LRU) block, because that is the one least likely to be needed. To help the operating system estimate LRU, many machines provide a *use bit* or *reference bit*, which is set whenever a page is accessed. The operating system periodically clears the use bits and later records them so it can determine which pages were touched during a particular time period. By keeping track in this way, the operating system can select a page that is among the least-recently referenced.

Q4: What happens on a write?

The level below main memory contains rotating magnetic disks that take millions of clock cycles to access. Because of the great discrepancy in access time, no one has yet built a virtual memory operating system that can write through main memory straight to disk on every store by the CPU. (This remark should not be interpreted as an opportunity to become famous by being the first to build one!) Thus, the write strategy is always write back. Since the cost of an unnecessary access to the next-lower level is so high, virtual memory systems usually include a dirty bit so that the only blocks written to disk are those that have been altered since they were loaded from the disk.

Techniques for Fast Address Translation

Page tables are usually so large that they are stored in main memory, and sometimes paged themselves. This means that every memory access logically takes at least twice as long, with one memory access to obtain the physical address and a second access to get the data. This cost is far too dear.

One remedy is to remember the last translation, so that the mapping process is skipped if the current address refers to the same page as the last one. A more general solution is to again rely on the principle of locality; if the accesses have locality, then the *address translations* for the accesses must also have locality. By keeping these address translations in a special cache, a memory access rarely requires a second access to translate the data. This special address translation cache is referred to as a *translation look-aside buffer* or TLB, also called a *translation buffer* or TB.

A TLB entry is like a cache entry where the tag holds portions of the virtual address and the data portion holds a physical page frame number, protection field, valid bit, and usually a use bit and dirty bit. To change the physical page frame number or protection of an entry in the page table, the operating system must make sure the old entry is not in the TLB; otherwise, the system won't behave properly. Note that this dirty bit means the corresponding *page* is dirty, not that the address translation in the TLB is dirty nor that a particular block in the data cache is dirty.

Figure 5.41 shows the Alpha AXP 21064 data TLB organization, with each step of a translation labeled. The TLB uses fully associative placement; thus, the translation begins (steps 1 and 2) by sending the virtual address to all tags. Of course, the tag must be marked valid to allow a match. At the same time, the type of memory access is checked for a violation (also in step 2) against protection information in the TLB.

For reasons similar to those in the cache case, there is no need to include the 13 bits of the Alpha AXP 21064 page offset in the TLB. The matching tag sends the corresponding physical address through the 32:1 multiplexer (step 3). The page offset is then combined with the physical page frame to form a full 34-bit physical address (step 4).

As mentioned on page 422, one architectural challenge stems from the difficulty of combining caches with virtual memory. Small caches can restrict the index to the page offset so that the index can proceed immediately. While the cache address tags are being read, the virtual portion of the address (the page frame address) is sent to the TLB to be translated. The address comparison is then between the physical address from the TLB and the cache tag; hence the cache index is virtual but the tags are physical.

Address translation can easily be on the critical path determining the clock cycle of the processor, since even in the simplest cache the TLB values must be read and compared. Thus the TLB is usually smaller and faster than the cache-address-tag memory, so that simultaneous TLB reading does not stretch the cache

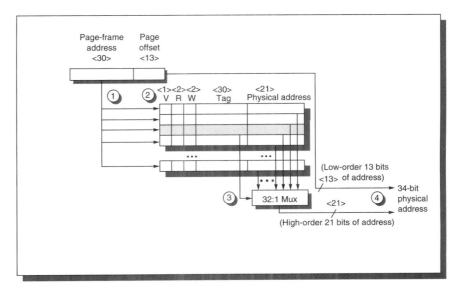

FIGURE 5.41   Operation of the Alpha AXP 21064 data TLB during address translation. The four steps of a TLB hit are shown as circled numbers. The three left fields of an entry are valid (V), read permissions (R), and write permissions (W). Note that there is no specific reference, use bit, or dirty bit. Hence, a page replacement algorithm such as LRU must rely on disabling reads and writes occasionally to record reads and writes to pages to measure usage and whether or not pages are dirty. The advantage of these omissions is that the TLB need not be written during normal memory accesses.

hit time. For example, in the Alpha AXP 21064, the data TLB has 32 blocks and the data cache has 256 blocks. Because of its critical nature, TLB access is sometimes pipelined.

Selecting a Page Size

The most obvious architectural parameter is the page size. Choosing the page is a question of balancing forces that favor a larger page size versus those favoring a smaller size. The following favor a larger size:

- The size of the page table is inversely proportional to the page size; memory (or other resources used for the memory map) can therefore be saved by making the pages bigger.

- As mentioned on page 424 in section 5.5, a larger page size simplifies fast cache hit times.

- Transferring larger pages to or from secondary storage, possibly over a network, is more efficient than transferring smaller pages.

- The number of TLB entries are restricted, so a larger page size means that more memory can be mapped efficiently, thereby reducing the number of TLB misses.

It is for this final reason that recent microprocessors have decided to support multiple page sizes; for some programs, TLB misses can be as significant on CPI as the cache misses.

The main motivation for a smaller page size is conserving storage. A small page size will result in less wasted storage when a contiguous region of virtual memory is not equal in size to a multiple of the page size. The term for this unused memory in a page is *internal fragmentation*. Assuming that each process has three primary segments (text, heap, and stack), the average wasted storage per process will be 1.5 times the page size. This is negligible for machines with megabytes of memory and page sizes in the range of 4 KB to 8 KB. Of course, when the page sizes become very large (more than 32 KB), lots of storage (both main and secondary) may be wasted, as well as I/O bandwidth. A final concern is process start-up time; many processes are small, so larger page sizes would lengthen the time to invoke a process.

5.8 | Protection and Examples of Virtual Memory

The invention of multiprogramming, where a computer would be shared by several programs running concurrently, led to new demands for protection and sharing among programs. These are closely tied to virtual memory in computers today, and so we cover the topic here along with two examples of virtual memory.

Multiprogramming leads to the concept of a *process*. Metaphorically, a process is a program's breathing air and living space—that is, a running program plus any state needed to continue running it. Time-sharing is a variation of multiprogramming that shares the CPU and memory with several interactive users at the same time, giving the illusion that all users have their own machines. Thus, at any instant it must be possible to switch from one process to another. This is called a *process switch* or *context switch*.

A process must operate correctly whether it executes continuously from start to finish, or is interrupted repeatedly and switched with other processes. The responsibility for maintaining correct process behavior is shared by the computer designer, who must ensure that the CPU portion of the process state can be saved and restored, and the operating system designer, who must guarantee that processes do not interfere with each others' computations. The safest way to protect the state of one process from another would be to copy the current information to disk. But a process switch would then take seconds—far too long for a time-sharing environment. This problem is solved by operating systems partitioning main memory so that several different processes have their state in memory at the same time. This means that the operating system designer needs help from the computer designer to provide protection so that one process cannot modify another. Besides protection, the computers also provide for sharing of code and data between processes, to allow communication between processes or to save memory by reducing the number of copies of identical information.

Protecting Processes

The simplest protection mechanism is a pair of registers that checks every address to be sure that it falls between the two limits, traditionally called *base* and *bound*. An address is valid if

$$\text{Base} \leq \text{Address} \leq \text{Bound}$$

In some systems the address is considered an unsigned number that is always added to the base, so the limit test is just

$$(\text{Base} + \text{Address}) \leq \text{Bound}$$

If user processes are allowed to change the base and bounds registers, then users can't be protected from each other. The operating system, however, must be able to change the registers so that it can switch processes. Hence, the computer designer has three more responsibilities in helping the operating system designer protect processes from each other:

1. Provide at least two modes, indicating whether the running process is a user process or an operating system process. This latter process is sometimes called a *kernel* process, a *supervisor* process, or an *executive* process.

2. Provide a portion of the CPU state that a user process can use but not write. This includes the base/bound registers, a user/supervisor mode bit(s), and the exception enable/disable bit. Users are prevented from writing this state because the operating system cannot control user processes if users can change the address range checks, give themselves supervisor privileges, or disable exceptions.

3. Provide mechanisms whereby the CPU can go from user mode to supervisor mode and vice versa. The first direction is typically accomplished by a *system call*, implemented as a special instruction that transfers control to a dedicated location in supervisor code space. The PC is saved from the point of the system call, and the CPU is placed in supervisor mode. The return to user mode is like a subroutine return that restores the previous user/supervisor mode.

Base and bound constitute the minimum protection system, while virtual memory offers a more fine-grained alternative to this simple model. As we have seen, the CPU address must go through a mapping from virtual to physical address. This mapping provides the opportunity for the hardware to check further for errors in the program or to protect processes from each other. The simplest way of doing this is to add permission flags to each page or segment. For example, since few programs today intentionally modify their own code, an operating system can detect accidental writes to code by offering read-only protection to pages. This page-level protection can be extended by adding user/kernel protection to prevent a user program from trying to access pages that belong to the kernel. As long as the CPU provides a read/write signal and a user/kernel signal, it is easy for the address translation hardware to detect stray memory accesses before they can do damage. Such reckless behavior simply interrupts the CPU and invokes the operating system.

Processes are thus protected from one another by having their own page tables, each pointing to distinct pages of memory. Obviously, user programs must be prevented from modifying their page tables or protection would be circumvented.

Protection can be escalated, depending on the apprehension of the computer designer or the purchaser. Rings added to the CPU protection structure expand memory access protection from two levels (user and kernel) to many more. Like a military classification system of top secret, secret, confidential, and unclassified, concentric *rings* of security levels allow the most trusted to access anything, the second most trusted to access everything except the innermost level, and so on until the "civilian" programs, which are the least trusted and, hence, have the most limited range of accesses. There may also be restrictions on what pieces of memory can contain code—execute protection—and even on the entrance point between the levels. The Intel Pentium protection structure, which uses rings, is described later in this section. It is not clear today whether rings are an improvement in practice over the simple system of user and kernel modes.

As the designer's apprehension escalates to trepidation, these simple rings may not suffice. Restricting the freedom given a program in the inner sanctum requires a new classification system. Instead of a military model, the analogy of this system is to keys and locks: A program can't unlock access to the data unless it has the key. For these keys, or *capabilities*, to be useful, the hardware and operating system must be able to explicitly pass them from one program to another without allowing a program itself to forge them. Such checking requires a great deal of hardware support if time for checking keys is to be kept low.

A Paged Virtual Memory Example: The Alpha AXP Memory Management and the 21064 TLB

The Alpha AXP architecture uses a combination of segmentation and paging, providing protection while minimizing page table size. The 64-bit address space is first divided into three segments: *seg0* (bits 63 – 41 = 0...00), *kseg* (bits 63 – 41 = 0...01), and *seg1* (bits 63 to 41 = 1...11) kseg is reserved for the operating system kernel, has uniform protection for the whole space, and does not use memory management. User processes use seg0, which is mapped into pages with individual protection. Figure 5.42 shows the layout of seg0 and seg1. seg0 grows from address 0 upward, while seg1 grows downward to 0. Many systems today use some such combination of predivided segments and paging. This approach provides many advantages: segmentation divides the address space and conserves page table space, while paging provides virtual memory, relocation, and protection.

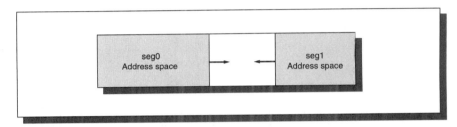

FIGURE 5.42   The organization of seg0 and seg1 in the Alpha. User processes live in seg0, while seg1 is used for portions of the page tables. seg0 includes a downward growing stack, text and data, and an upward growing heap.

Even with this division, the size of page tables for the 64-bit address space is alarming. Hence the Alpha uses a three-level hierarchical page table to map the address space to keep the size reasonable. The addresses for each of these page tables come from three "level" fields, labeled level1, level2, and level3. Figure 5.43 shows address translation in the Alpha AXP. Address translation starts with adding the level1 address field to the page table base register and then reading memory from this location to get the base of the second-level page table. The level2 address field is in turn added to this newly fetched address, and memory is accessed again to determine the base of the third page table. The level3 address field is added to this base address, and memory is read using this sum to (finally) get the physical address of the page being referenced. This address is concatenated with the page offset to get the full physical address. Each page table in the Alpha AXP architecture is constrained to fit within a single page, so all page table addresses are physical addresses that need no further translation.

The Alpha uses a 64-bit *page table entry* (*PTE*) in each of these page tables. The first 32 bits contain the physical page frame number, and the other half includes the following five protection fields:

- *Valid*—Says that the page frame number is valid for hardware translation

- *User read enable*—Allows user programs to read data within this page

- *Kernel read enable*—Allows the kernel to read data within this page

- *User write enable*—Allows user programs to write data within this page

- *Kernel write enable*—Allows the kernel to write data within this page

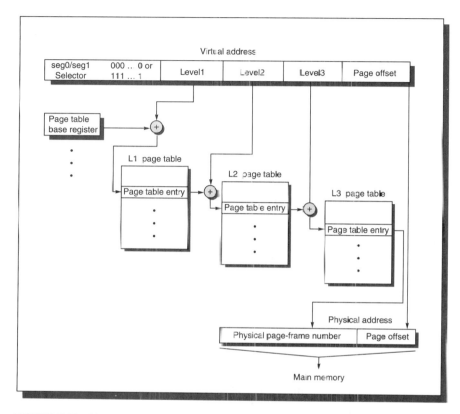

FIGURE 5.43   The mapping of an Alpha virtual address. Each page table is exactly one page long, so each level field is n bits wide where 2^n = page size/8. The Alpha AXP architecture document allows the page size to grow from 8 KB in the current implementations to 16 KB, 32 KB, or 64 KB in the future. The virtual address for each page size grows from the current 43 bits to 47, 51, or 55 bits and the maximum physical address size grows from the current 41 bits to 45, 47, or 48 bits. The 21064 uses 8-KB pages, but it implements just 34 bits of the maximum 41-bit physical address possible in this scheme.

In addition, the PTE has fields reserved for systems software to use as it pleases. Since the Alpha goes through three levels of tables on a TLB miss, there are three potential places to check protection restrictions. The Alpha obeys only the third-level PTE, checking the first two only to be sure the valid bit is set.

Since the PTEs are 8 bytes long, the page tables are exactly one page long, and the Alpha AXP 21064 has 8-KB pages, each page table has 1024 PTEs. Each of the three level fields are 10 bits long and the page offset is 13 bits, which leaves $64 - (3 \times 10 + 13)$ or 21 bits to be defined. If this is a seg0 address, the most-significant bit is a 0, and for seg1 the two most-significant bits are 11_{two}. Alpha requires all bits to the left of the level1 field to be identical. For seg0 these 21 bits

of the use of such protected sharing, suppose a payroll program writes checks and also updates the year-to-date information on total salary and benefits payments. Thus, we want to give the program the ability to read the salary and year-to-date information, and modify the year-to-date information but not the salary. We shall see the mechanism to support such features shortly. In the rest of this subsection, we will look at the big picture of the Pentium protection and examine its motivation.

Adding Bounds Checking and Memory Mapping

The first step in enhancing the Intel processor was getting the segmented addressing to check bounds as well as supply a base. Rather than a base address, as in the 8086, segment registers in the Pentium contain an index to a virtual memory data structure called a *descriptor table*. Descriptor tables play the role of page tables in the Alpha. On the Pentium the equivalent of a page table entry is a *segment descriptor*. It contains fields found in PTEs:

- A *present bit*—equivalent to the PTE valid bit, used to indicate this is a valid translation

- A *base field*—equivalent to a page frame address, containing the physical address of the first byte of the segment

- An *access bit*—like the reference bit or use bit in some architectures that is helpful for replacement algorithms

- An *attributes field*—specifies the valid operations and protection levels for operations that use this segment

There is also a *limit field*, not found in paged systems, which establishes the upper bound of valid offsets for this segment. Figure 5.45 shows examples of Pentium segment descriptors.

Pentium provides an optional paging system in addition to this segmented addressing, where the upper portion of the 32-bit address selects the segment descriptor and the middle portion is used as an index into the page table selected by the descriptor. We describe below the protection system that does not rely on paging.

Adding Sharing and Protection

To provide for protected sharing, half of the address space is shared by all processes and half is unique to each process, called *global address space* and *local address space*, respectively. Each half is given a descriptor table with the appropriate name. A descriptor pointing to a shared segment is placed in the global descriptor table, while a descriptor for a private segment is placed in the local descriptor table.

A program loads a Pentium segment register with an index to the table *and* a bit saying which table it desires. The operation is checked according to the

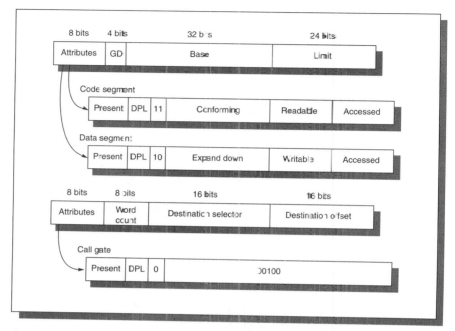

FIGURE 5.45 The Pentium segment descriptors are distinguished by bits in the attributes field. *Base, limit, present, readable,* and *writable* are all self-explanatory. D gives the default addressing size of the instructions: 16 bits or 32 bits. G gives the granularity of the segment limit: 0 means in bytes and 1 means in 4-KB pages. G is set to 1 when paging is turned on to set the size of the page tables. DPL means *descriptor privilege level*—this is checked against the code privilege level to see if the access will be allowed. *Conforming* says the code takes on the privilege level of the code being called rather than the privilege level of the caller; it is used for library routines. The *expand-down field* flips the check to let the base field be the high-water mark and the limit field be the low-water mark. As one might expect, this is used for stack segments that grow down. *Word count* controls the number of words copied from the current stack to the new stack on a call gate. The other two fields of the call gate descriptor, *destination selector* and *destination offset,* select the descriptor of the destination of the call and the offset into it, respectively. There are many more than these three segment descriptors in the Pentium.

attributes in the descriptor, the physical address being formed by adding the offset in the CPU to the base in the descriptor, provided the offset is less than the limit field. Every segment descriptor has a separate 2-bit field to give the legal access level of this segment. A violation occurs only if the program tries to use a segment with a lower protection level in the segment descriptor.

We can now show how to invoke the payroll program mentioned above to update the year-to-date information without allowing it to update salaries. The program could be given a descriptor to the information that has the writable field clear, meaning it can read but not write the data. A trusted program can then be supplied that will only write the year-to-date information and is given a descriptor with the writable field set (Figure 5.45). The payroll program invokes the trusted code using a code segment descriptor with the conforming field set. This means the called program takes on the privilege level of the code being called rather than the privilege level of the caller. Hence, the payroll program can read the salaries and call a trusted program to update the year-to-date totals, yet the payroll program cannot modify the salaries. If a Trojan horse exists in this system, to be effective it must be located in the trusted code whose only job is to update the year-to-date information. The argument for this style of protection is that limiting the scope of the vulnerability enhances security.

Adding Safe Calls from User to OS Gates and Inheriting Protection Level for Parameters

Allowing the user to jump into the operating system is a bold step. How, then, can a hardware designer increase the chances of a safe system without trusting the operating system or any other piece of code? The Pentium approach is to restrict where the user can enter a piece of code, to safely place parameters on the proper stack, and to make sure the user parameters don't get the protection level of the called code.

To restrict entry into others' code, the Pentium provides a special segment descriptor, or *call gate*, identified by a bit in the attributes field. Unlike other descriptors, call gates are full physical addresses of an object in memory; the offset supplied by the CPU is ignored. As stated above, their purpose is to prevent the user from randomly jumping anywhere into a protected or more-privileged code segment. In our programming example, this means the only place the payroll program can invoke the trusted code is at the proper boundary. This restriction is needed to make conforming segments work as intended.

What happens if caller and callee are "mutually suspicious," so that neither trusts the other? The solution is found in the word count field in the bottom descriptor in Figure 5.45. When a call instruction invokes a call gate descriptor, the descriptor copies the number of words specified in the descriptor from the local stack onto the stack corresponding to the level of this segment. This allows the user to pass parameters by first pushing them onto the local stack. The hardware then safely transfers them onto the correct stack. A return from a call gate will pop the parameters off both stacks and copy any return values to the proper stack. Note that this model is incompatible with the current practice of passing parameters in registers.

This scheme still leaves open the potential loophole of having the operating system use the user's address, passed as parameters, with the operating system's security level, instead of with the user's level. The Pentium solves this problem by dedicating 2 bits in every CPU segment register to the *requested protection level*. When an operating system routine is invoked, it can execute an instruction that sets this 2-bit field in all address parameters with the protection level of the user that called the routine. Thus, when these address parameters are loaded into the segment registers, they will set the requested protection level to the proper value. The Pentium hardware then uses the requested protection level to prevent any foolishness: No segment can be accessed from the system routine using those parameters if it has a more-privileged protection level than requested.

Summary: Protection on the Alpha versus the Pentium

If the Pentium protection model looks harder to build than the Alpha model, that's because it is. This effort must be especially frustrating for the Pentium engineers, since few customers use the elaborate protection mechanism. Also, the fact that the protection model is a mismatch for the simple paging protection of UNIX means it will be used only by someone writing an operating system especially for this computer. NT from Microsoft is the best candidate, but only time will tell whether the performance cost of such protection is justified for a personal computer operating system.

One wild card is the increasing popularity of the Internet, where virtually any machine can become an information provider, and hence almost anyone could access the desktop computer. This openness leads to extraordinary sharing of information, but it also gives a powerful opportunity for malicious behavior.

We conclude this section with questions rather than answers: Will the considerable protection engineering effort, which must be borne by each generation of the 80x86 family, be put to good use? Will it prove any safer in practice than its paging system? Will the popularity of the Internet lead to demands of increased support for protection in all computers?

5.9 | Crosscutting Issues in the Design of Memory Hierarchies

This section describes four topics discussed in other chapters that are fundamental to memory-hierarchy design.

Superscalar CPU and Number of Ports to the Cache

One complexity of the advanced designs of Chapter 4 is that multiple instructions can be issued within a single clock cycle. Clearly, if there is not sufficient peak bandwidth from the cache to match the peak demands of the instructions, there is little benefit to designing such parallelism in the processor. As mentioned above, similar reasoning applies to CPUs that want to continue executing instructions on a cache miss: clearly the memory hierarchy must also be nonblocking or the CPU benefits little.

For example, the IBM RS/6000 Power 2 model 900 can issue up to six instructions per clock cycle, and its data cache can supply two 128-bit accesses per clock cycle. The RS/6000 does this by making the instruction cache and data cache wide and by making two reads to the data cache each clock cycle, certainly likely to be the critical path in the 71.5-MHz machine.

Speculative Execution and the Memory System

Inherent in CPUs that support speculative execution or conditional instructions is the possibility of generating invalid addresses that would not occur without speculative execution. Not only would this be incorrect behavior if exceptions were taken, the benefits of speculative execution would be swamped by false exception overhead. Hence the memory system must identify speculatively executed instructions and conditionally executed instructions and suppress the corresponding exception.

By similar reasoning, we cannot allow such instructions to cause the cache to stall on a miss, for again unnecessary stalls could overwhelm the benefits of speculation. Hence these CPUs must be matched with nonblocking caches (see page 414).

Compiler Optimization: Instruction-Level Parallelism versus Reducing Cache Misses

Sometimes the compiler must choose between improving instruction-level parallelism and improving cache performance. For example, the code below,

```
for (i = 0; i < 512; i = i+1)
    for (j = 1; j < 512; j = j+1)
        x[i][j] = 2 * x[i][j-1];
```

accesses the data in the order they are stored, thereby minimizing cache misses. Unfortunately, the dependency limits parallel execution. Unrolling the loop shows this dependency:

```
for (i = 0; i < 512; i = i+1)
    for (j = 1; j < 512; j = j+4){
        x[i][j]   = 2 * x[i][j-1];
        x[i][j+1] = 2 * x[i][j];
        x[i][j+2] = 2 * x[i][j+1];
        x[i][j+3] = 2 * x[i][j+2];
    };
```

Each of the last three statements has a RAW dependency on the prior statement. We can improve parallelism by interchanging the two loops:

```
for (j = 1; j < 512; j = j+1)
     for (i = 0; i < 512; i = i+1)
               x[i][j] = 2 * x[i][j-1];
```

Unrolling the loop shows this parallelism:

```
for (j = 1; j < 512; j = j+1)
     for (i = 0; i < 512; i = i+4) {
          x[i][j]   = 2 * x[i][j-1];
          x[i+1][j] = 2 * x[i+1][j-1];
          x[i+2][j] = 2 * x[i+2][j-1];
          x[i+3][j] = 2 * x[i+3][j-1];
          };
```

Now all four statements in the loop are independent! Alas, increasing parallelism leads to accesses that hop through memory, reducing spatial locality and cache hit rates.

I/O and Consistency of Cached Data

Because of caches, data can be found in memory and in the cache. As long as the CPU is the sole device changing or reading the data and the cache stands between the CPU and memory, there is little danger in the CPU seeing the old or *stale* copy. I/O devices give the opportunity for other devices to cause copies to be inconsistent or for other devices to read the stale copies. Figure 5.46 illustrates the problem, generally referred to as the *cache-coherency* problem.

The question is this: Where does the I/O occur in the computer—between the I/O device and the cache or between the I/O device and main memory? If input puts data into the cache and output reads data from the cache, both I/O and the CPU see the same data, and the problem is solved. The difficulty in this approach is that it interferes with the CPU. I/O competing with the CPU for cache access will cause the CPU to stall for I/O. Input will also interfere with the cache by displacing some information with the new data that is unlikely to be accessed by the CPU soon. For example, on a page fault the CPU may need to access a few words in a page, but a program is not likely to access every word of the page if it were loaded into the cache. Given the integration of caches onto the same integrated circuit, it is also difficult for that interface to be visible.

The goal for the I/O system in a computer with a cache is to prevent the stale-data problem while interfering with the CPU as little as possible. Many systems, therefore, prefer that I/O occur directly to main memory, with main memory

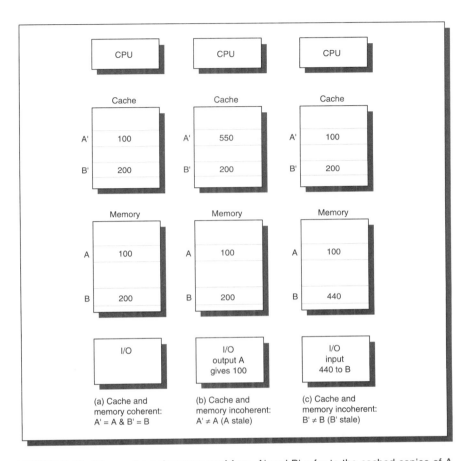

FIGURE 5.46   The cache-coherency problem. A' and B' refer to the cached copies of A and B in memory. (a) shows cache and main memory in a coherent state. In (b) we assume a write-back cache when the CPU writes 550 into A. Now A' has the value but the value in memory has the old, stale value of 100. If an output used the value of A from memory, it would get the stale data. In (c) the I/O system inputs 440 into the memory copy of B, so now B' in the cache has the old, stale data.

acting as an I/O buffer. If a write-through cache is used, then memory has an up-to-date copy of the information, and there is no stale-data issue for output. (This is a reason many machines use write through.) Input requires some extra work. The software solution is to guarantee that no blocks of the I/O buffer designated for input are in the cache. In one approach, a buffer page is marked as noncach-able; the operating system always inputs to such a page. In another approach, the operating system flushes the buffer addresses from the cache after the input oc-curs. A hardware solution is to check the I/O addresses on input to see if they are in the cache; to avoid slowing down the cache to check addresses, sometimes a duplicate set of tags are used to allow checking of I/O addresses in parallel with processor cache accesses. If there is a match of I/O addresses in the cache, the cache entries are invalidated to avoid stale data. All these approaches can also be used for output with write-back caches. More about this is found in Chapter 6.

The cache-coherency problem applies to multiprocessors as well as I/O. Unlike I/O, where multiple data copies are a rare event—one to be avoided whenever possible—a program running on multiple processors will want to have copies of the same data in several caches. Performance of a multiprocessor program depends on the performance of the system when sharing data. The protocols to maintain coherency for multiple processors are called *cache-coherency protocols,* and are described in Chapter 8.

5.10 | Putting It All Together: The Alpha AXP 21064 Memory Hierarchy

Thus far we have given glimpses of the Alpha AXP 21064 memory hierarchy; this section unveils the full design and shows the performance of its components for the SPEC92 programs. Figure 5.47 gives the overall picture of this design.

Let's really start at the beginning, when the Alpha is turned on. Hardware on the chip loads the instruction cache from an external PROM. This initialization allows the 8-KB instruction cache to omit a valid bit, for there are always valid instructions in the cache; they just might not be the ones your program is interested in. The hardware does clear the valid bits in the data cache. The PC is set to the kseg segment so that the instruction addresses are not translated, thereby avoiding the TLB.

One of the first steps is to update the instruction TLB with valid page table entries (PTEs) for this process. Kernel code updates the TLB with the contents of the appropriate page table entry for each page to be mapped. The instruction TLB has eight entries for 8-KB pages and four for 4-MB pages. (The 4-MB pages are used by large programs such as the operating system or data bases that will likely touch most of their code.) A miss in the TLB invokes the Privileged Architecture Library (PAL code) software that updates the TLB. PAL code is simply machine language routines with some implementation-specific extensions to allow access to low-level hardware, such as the TLB. PAL code runs with exceptions disabled, and instruction accesses are not checked for memory management violations, allowing PAL code to fill the TLB.

Once the operating system is ready to begin executing a user process, it sets the PC to the appropriate address in segment seg0.

We are now ready to follow memory hierarchy in action: Figure 5.47 is labeled with the steps of this narrative. The page frame portion of this address is sent to the TLB (step 1), while the 8-bit index from the page offset is sent to the direct-mapped 8-KB (256 32-byte blocks) instruction cache (step 2). The fully associative TLB simultaneously searches all 12 entries to find a match between the address and a valid PTE (step 3). In addition to translating the address, the TLB checks to see if the PTE demands that this access result in an exception. An exception might occur if either this access violates the protection on the page or if

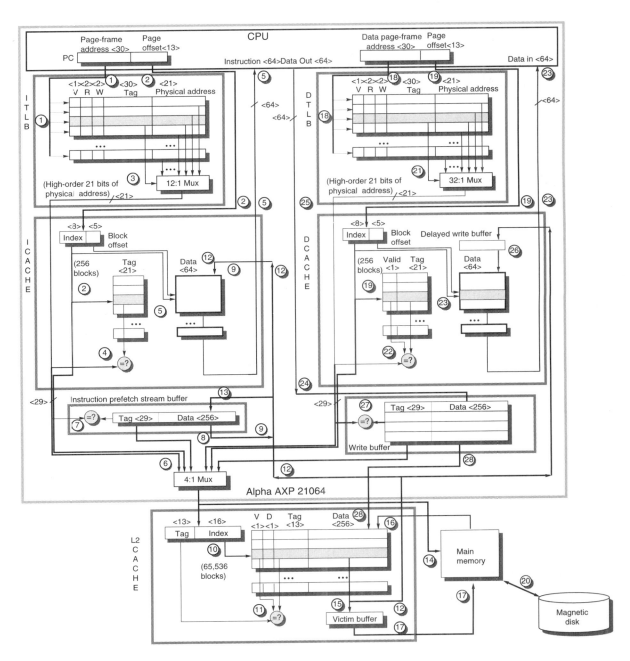

FIGURE 5.47 The overall picture of the Alpha AXP 21064 memory hierarchy. Individual components can be seen in greater detail in Figures 5.5 (page 381), 5.28 (page 426), and 5.41 (page 446). While the data TLB has 32 entries, the instruction TLB has just 12.

the page is not in main memory. If there is no exception, and if the translated physical address matches the tag in the instruction cache (step 4), then the proper 8 bytes of the 32-byte block are furnished to the CPU using the lower bits of the page offset (step 5), and the instruction stream access is done.

A miss, on the other hand, simultaneously starts an access to the second-level cache (step 6) and checks the prefetch instruction stream buffer (step 7). If the desired instruction is found in the stream buffer (step 8), the critical 8 bytes are sent to the CPU, the full 32-byte block of the stream buffer is written into the instruction cache (step 9), and the request to the second-level cache is canceled. Steps 6 to 9 take just a single clock cycle.

If the instruction is not in the prefetch stream buffer, the second-level cache continues trying to fetch the block. The 21064 microprocessor is designed to work with direct-mapped second-level caches from 128 KB to 8 MB with a miss penalty between 3 and 16 clock cycles. For this section we use the memory system of the DEC 3000 model 800 Alpha AXP. It has a 2-MB (65,536 32-byte blocks) second-level cache, so the 29-bit block address is divided into a 13-bit tag and a 16-bit index (step 10). The cache reads the tag from that index and if it matches (step 11), the cache returns the critical 16 bytes in the first 5 clock cycles and the other 16 bytes in the next 5 clock cycles (step 12). The path between the first- and second-level cache is 128 bits wide (16 bytes). At the same time, a request is made for the next sequential 32-byte block, which is loaded into the instruction stream buffer in the next 10 clock cycles (step 13).

The instruction stream does not rely on the TLB for address translation. It simply increments the physical address of the miss by 32 bytes, checking to make sure that the new address is within the same page. If the incremented address crosses a page boundary, then the prefetch is suppressed.

If the instruction is not found in the secondary cache, the translated physical address is sent to memory (step 14). The DEC 3000 model 800 divides memory into four memory mother boards (MMB), each of which contains two to eight SIMMs (single inline memory modules). The SIMMs come with eight DRAMs for information plus one DRAM for error protection per side, and the options are single- or double-sided SIMMs using 1-Mbit, 4-Mbit, or 16-Mbit DRAMs. Hence the memory capacity of the model 800 is 8 MB ($4 \times 2 \times 8 \times 1 \times 1/8$) to 1024 MB ($4 \times 8 \times 8 \times 16 \times 2/8$), always organized 256 bits wide. The average time to transfer 32 bytes from memory to the secondary cache is 36 clock cycles after the processor makes the request. The second-level cache loads this data 16 bytes at a time.

Since the second-level cache is a write-back cache, any miss can lead to some old block being written back to memory. The 21064 places this "victim" block into a victim buffer to get out of the way of new data (step 15). The new data are loaded into the cache as soon as they arrive (step 16), and then the old data are written from the victim buffer (step 17). There is a single block in the victim buffer, so a second miss would need to stall until the victim buffer empties.

due to the memory hierarchy for the SPEC92 programs and three commercial programs. The three commercial programs tax the memory much more heavily, with secondary cache misses alone responsible for 20% to 28% of the execution time.

Figure 5.48 also shows the miss rates for each component. The SPECint92 programs have about a 2% instruction miss rate, a 13% data cache miss rate, and a 0.6% second-level cache miss rate. For SPECfp92 the averages are 1%, 21%, and 0.3%, respectively. The commercial workloads really exercise the memory hierarchy; the averages of the three miss rates are 6%, 32%, and 10%. Figure 5.49 shows the same data graphically. This figure makes clear that the primary performance limits of the superscalar 21064 are instruction stalls, which result from branch mispredictions, and the other category, which includes data dependencies.

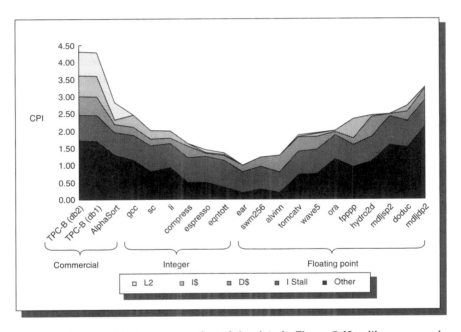

FIGURE 5.49   Graphical representation of the data in Figure 5.48, with programs in each of the three classes sorted by total CPI.

5.11 | Fallacies and Pitfalls

As the most naturally quantitative of the computer architecture disciplines, memory hierarchy would seem to be less vulnerable to fallacies and pitfalls. Yet the authors were limited here not by lack of warnings, but by lack of space!

Pitfall: Too small an address space.

Just five years after DEC and Carnegie Mellon University collaborated to design the new PDP-11 computer family, it was apparent that their creation had a fatal flaw. An architecture announced by IBM six years *before* the PDP-11 was still thriving, with minor modifications, 25 years later. And the DEC VAX, criticized for including unnecessary functions, has sold 100,000 units since the PDP-11 went out of production. Why?

The fatal flaw of the PDP-11 was the size of its addresses as compared to the address sizes of the IBM 360 and the VAX. Address size limits the program length, since the size of a program and the amount of data needed by the program must be less than $2^{\text{address size}}$. The reason the address size is so hard to change is that it determines the minimum width of anything that can contain an address: PC, register, memory word, and effective-address arithmetic. If there is no plan to expand the address from the start, then the chances of successfully changing address size are so slim that it normally means the end of that computer family. Bell and Strecker [1976] put it like this:

There is only one mistake that can be made in computer design that is difficult to recover from—not having enough address bits for memory addressing and memory management. The PDP-11 followed the unbroken tradition of nearly every known computer. [p. 2]

A partial list of successful machines that eventually starved to death for lack of address bits includes the PDP-8, PDP-10, PDP-11, Intel 8080, Intel 8086, Intel 80186, Intel 80286, Motorola AMI 6502, Zilog Z80, CRAY-1, and CRAY X-MP. A few companies already offer computers with 64-bit flat addresses, and the authors expect that the rest of the industry will offer 64-bit address machines before the third edition of this book!

Fallacy: Predicting cache performance of one program from another.

Figure 5.50 shows the instruction miss rates and data miss rates for three programs from the SPEC92 benchmark suite as cache size varies. Depending on the program, the data miss rate for a direct-mapped 4-KB cache is either 28%, 12%, or 8%, and the instruction miss rate for a direct-mapped 1-KB cache is either 10%, 3%, or 0%. Figure 5.48 on page 465 shows that commercial programs such as databases will have significant miss rates even in a 2-MB second-level cache, which is not the case for the SPEC92 programs. Clearly it is not safe to generalize cache performance from one of these programs to another.

Nor is it safe to generalize cache measurements from one architecture to another. Figure 5.48 for the DEC Alpha with 8-KB caches running gcc shows miss rates of 17% for data and 4.67% for instructions, yet the DEC MIPS machine running the same program and cache size measured in Figure 5.48 suggests 10% for data and 4% for instructions.

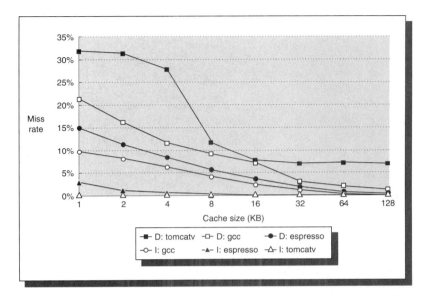

FIGURE 5.50 Instruction and data miss rates for direct-mapped caches with 32-byte blocks for running three programs for DEC 5000 as cache size varies from 1 KB to 128 KB. The programs espresso, gcc, and tomcatv are from the SPEC92 benchmark suite.

Pitfall: Simulating enough instructions to get accurate performance measures of the memory hierarchy.

There are really two pitfalls here. One is trying to predict performance of a large cache using a small trace, and the other is that a program's locality behavior is not constant over the run of the entire program. Figure 5.51 shows the cumulative average memory access time for four programs over the execution of billions of instructions. For these programs, the average memory access times for the first billion instructions executed is very different from their average memory access times for the second billion. While two of the programs need to execute half of the total number of instructions to get a good estimate of the average memory access time, SOR needs to get to the three-quarters mark, and TV needs to finish completely before the accurate measure appears.

The first edition of this book included another example of this pitfall. The compulsory miss ratios were erroneously high (e.g., 1%) because of tracing too few memory accesses. A program with an infinite cache miss ratio of 1% running on a machine accessing memory 10 million times per second would touch hundreds of megabytes of new memory every minute:

$$\frac{10{,}000{,}000 \text{ accesses}}{\text{Second}} \times \frac{0.01 \text{ misses}}{\text{Access}} \times \frac{32 \text{ bytes}}{\text{Miss}} \times \frac{60 \text{ seconds}}{\text{Minute}} = \frac{192{,}000{,}000 \text{ bytes}}{\text{Minute}}$$

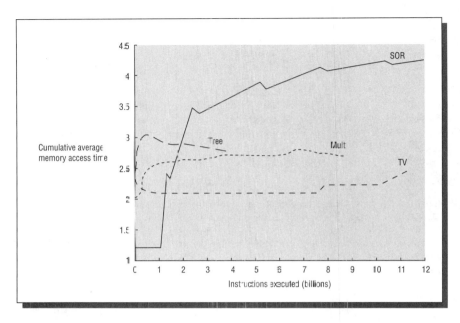

FIGURE 5.51 Average memory access times for four programs over execution time of billions of instructions. The assumed memory hierarchy was a 4-KB instruction cache and 4-KB data cache with 16-byte blocks, and a 512-KB second-level cache with 128-byte blocks using the Titan RISC instruction set. The first-level data cache is write through with a four-entry write buffer, and the second-level cache is write back. The miss penalty for the first-level cache to second-level cache is 12 clock cycles, and the miss penalty from the second-level cache to main memory is 200 clock cycles. SOR is a FORTRAN program for successive over-relaxation, Tree is a Scheme program that builds and searches a tree, Mult is a multi-programmed workload consisting of six smaller programs, and TV is a Pascal program for timing verification of VLSI circuits. (This figure taken from Figure 3-5 on page 276 of the paper by Borg, Kessler, and Wall [1990].)

Data on typical page fault rates and process sizes do not support the conclusion that memory is touched at this rate.

Pitfall: Ignoring the impact of the operating system on the performance of the memory hierarchy.

Figure 5.52 shows the memory stall time due to the operating system spent on three large workloads. About 25% of the stall time is either spent in misses in the operating system or results from misses in the application programs because of interference with the operating system.

			Time						
	Misses		**% time due to appl. misses**		**% time due directly to OS misses**				**% time OS misses & appl. conflicts**
Workload	**% in appl**	**% in OS**	**Inherent appl. misses**	**OS conflicts w. appl.**	**OS instr misses**	**Data misses for migration**	**Data misses in block operations**	**Rest of OS misses**	
Pmake	47%	53%	14.1%	4.8%	10.9%	1.0%	6.2%	2.9%	25.8%
Multipgm	53%	47%	21.6%	3.4%	9.2%	4.2%	4.7%	3.4%	24.9%
Oracle	73%	27%	25.7%	10.2%	10.6%	2.6%	0.6%	2.8%	26.8%

FIGURE 5.52 Misses and time spent in misses for applications and operating system. Collected on Silicon Graphics POWER stat on 4D/340, a multiprocessor with four 33-MHz R3000 CPUs running three application workloads under a UNIX System V—Pmake: a parallel compile of 56 files; Multipgm: the parallel numeric program MP3D running concurrently with Pmake and f ve-screen edit session; and Oracle: running a restricted version of the TP-1 benchmark using the Oracle database. Each CPU has a 64-KB instruction cache and a two-level data cache with 64 KB in the first level and 256 KB in the second level; all caches are direct mapped with 16-byte blocks. Data from Torrellas, Gupta, and Hennessy [1992].

Pitfall: Basing the size of the write buffer on the speed of memory and the average mix of writes.

This seems like a reasonable approach:

$$\text{Write buffer size} \ = \ \frac{\text{Memory references}}{\text{Clock cycle}} \times \text{Write percentage}$$
$$\times \text{Clock cycles to write memory}$$

If there is one memory reference per clock cycle, 10% of the memory references are writes, and writing a word of memory takes 10 cycles, then a one-word buffer is added ($1 \times 10\% \times 10 = 1$). Calculating for the Alpha AXP 21064,

$$\text{Write buffer size} \ = \ \frac{1.36 \text{ memory references}}{2.0 \text{ clock cycles}} \times 0.1 \text{ writes} \times \frac{15 \text{ clock cycles}}{\text{Write}} \ = \ 1.0$$

Thus, a one-word buffer seems sufficient.

The pitfall is that when writes come close together, the CPU must stall until the prior write is completed. Hence the calculation above says that a one-word buffer would be utilized 100% of the time. Queuing theory tells us if utilization is close to 100%, then writes will normally stall the CPU.

The proper question to ask is how large a buffer is needed to keep utilization low so that the buffer rarely fills, thereby keeping CPU write stall time low. The impact of write buffer size can be established by simulation or estimated with a queuing model.

5.12 | Concluding Remarks

The difficulty of building a memory system to keep pace with faster CPUs is underscored by the fact that the raw material for main memory is the same as that found in the cheapest computer. It is the principle of locality that saves us here— its soundness is demonstrated at all levels of the memory hierarchy in current computers, from disks to TLBs. Figure 5.53 summarizes the attributes of the memory-hierarchy examples described in this chapter.

	TLB	First-level cache	Second-level cache	Virtual memory
Block size	4–8 bytes (1 PTE)	4–32 bytes	32–255 bytes	4096–16,384 bytes
Hit time	1 clock cycle	1–2 clock cycles	6–15 clock cycles	10–100 clock cycles
Miss penalty	10–30 clock cycles	8–66 clock cycles	30–200 clock cycles	700,000–6,000,000 clock cycles
Miss rate (local)	0.1–2%	0.5–20%	15–30%	0.00001–0.001%
Size	32–8192 bytes (8–1024 PTEs)	1–128 KB	256 KB–16 MB	16–8192 MB
Backing store	First-level cache	Second-level cache	Page-mode DRAM	Disks
Q1: block placement	Fully associative or set associative	Direct mapped	Direct mapped or set associative	Fully associative
Q2: block identification	Tag/block	Tag/block	Tag/block	Table
Q3: block replacement	Random	N.A. (direct mapped)	Random	≈ LRU
Q4: write strategy	Flush on a write to page table	Write through or write back	Write back	Write back

FIGURE 5.53 Summary of the memory-hierarchy examples in this chapter.

Yet the design decisions at these levels interact, and the architect must take the whole system view to make wise decisions. The primary challenge for the memory-hierarchy designer is in choosing parameters that work well together, not in inventing new techniques. The increasingly fast CPUs are spending a larger fraction of time waiting for memory, which has led to new inventions that have increased the number of choices: variable page size, pseudo-associative caches, and cache-aware compilers weren't found in the first edition of this book. Fortunately, there tends to be a technological "sweet spot" in balancing cost, performance, and complexity: missing the target wastes performance, hardware, design time, debug time, or possibly all four. Architects hit the target by careful, quantitative analysis.

5.13 | Historical Perspective and References

While the pioneers of computing knew of the need for a memory hierarchy and coined the term, the automatic management of two levels was first proposed by Kilburn et al. [1962] and demonstrated with the Atlas computer at the University of Manchester. This was the year *before* the IBM 360 was announced. While IBM planned for its introduction with the next generation (System/370), the operating system TSS wasn't up to the challenge in 1970. Virtual memory was announced for the 370 family in 1972, and it was for this machine that the term "translation look-aside buffer" was coined [Case and Padegs 1978]. The only computers today without virtual memory are a few supercomputers, embedded processors, and older personal computers.

Both the Atlas and the IBM 360 provided protection on pages, and the GE 645 was the first system to provide paged segmentation. The Intel 80286, the first 80x86 to have the protection mechanisms described on pages 453 to 457, was inspired by the Multics protection software that ran on the GE 645. Over time, machines evolved more elaborate mechanisms. The most elaborate mechanism was *capabilities*, which reached its highest interest in the late 1970s and early 1980s [Fabry 1974; Wulf, Levin, and Harbison 1981]. Wilkes [1982], one of the early workers on capabilities, had this to say:

Anyone who has been concerned with an implementation of the type just described [capability system], or has tried to explain one to others, is likely to feel that complexity has got out of hand. It is particularly disappointing that the attractive idea of capabilities being tickets that can be freely handed around has become lost ....

Compared with a conventional computer system, there will inevitably be a cost to be met in providing a system in which the domains of protection are small and frequently changed. This cost will manifest itself in terms of additional hardware, decreased runtime speed, and increased memory occupancy. It is at present an open question whether, by adoption of the capability approach, the cost can be reduced to reasonable proportions.

Today there is little interest in capabilities either from the operating systems or the computer architecture communities, although there is growing interest in protection and security.

Bell and Strecker [1976] reflected on the PDP-11 and identified a small address space as the only architectural mistake that is difficult to recover from. At the time of the creation of PDP-11, core memories were increasing at a very slow rate, and the competition from 100 other minicomputer companies meant that DEC might not have a cost-competitive product if every address had to go through the 16-bit datapath twice, hence the architect's decision to add just 4 more address bits than the predecessor of the PDP-11. The architects of the IBM 360 were aware of the importance of address size and planned for the architecture to extend to 32 bits of address. Only 24 bits were used in the IBM 360, however, because the low-end 360 models would have been even slower with the larger addresses in 1964. Unfortunately, the architects didn't reveal their plans to the software people, and the expansion effort was foiled by programmers who stored extra information in the upper 8 "unused" address bits. Virtually every machine since then, including the Alpha AXP, will check to make sure the unused bits stay unused, and trap if the bits have the wrong value.

A few years after the Atlas paper Wilkes published the first paper describing the concept of a cache [1965]:

The use is discussed of a fast core memory of, say, 32,000 words as slave to a slower core memory of, say, one million words in such a way that in practical cases the effective access time is nearer that of the fast memory than that of the slow memory. [p. 270]

This two-page paper describes a direct-mapped cache. While this is the first publication on caches, the first implementation was probably a direct-mapped instruction cache built at the University of Cambridge. It was based on tunnel diode memory, the fastest form of memory available at the time. Wilkes states that G. Scarott suggested the idea of a cache memory.

Subsequent to that publication, IBM started a project that led to the first commercial machine with a cache, the IBM 360/85 [Liptay 1968]. Gibson [1967] describes how to measure program behavior as memory traffic as well as miss rate and shows how the miss rate varies between programs. Using a sample of 20 programs (each with 3 million references!), Gibson also relied on average memory access time to compare systems with and without caches. This was over 25 years ago, and yet many used miss rates until recently.

Conti, Gibson, and Pitkowsky [1968] describe the resulting performance of the 360/85. The 360/91 outperforms the 360/85 on only 3 of the 11 programs in the paper, even though the 360/85 has a slower clock cycle time (80 ns versus 60 ns), smaller memory interleaving (4 versus 16), and a slower main memory (1.04 μsec versus 0.75 μsec). This paper was also the first to use the term "cache." Strecker [1976] published the first comparative cache design paper examining caches for the PDP-11. Smith [1982] later published a thorough survey paper, using the terms "spatial locality" and "temporal locality"; this paper has served as a reference for many computer designers. While most studies have relied on simulations, Clark [1983] used a hardware monitor to record cache misses of the VAX-11/780 over several days. Hill [1987] proposed the three C's used in section 5.3 to explain cache misses. One of the first papers on nonblocking caches is by Kroft [1981].

This chapter relies on the measurements of SPEC92 benchmarks collected by Gee et al. [1993] for DEC 5000s. There are several other papers used in this chapter that are cited in the captions of the figures that use the data: Borg, Kessler, and Wall [1990]; Farkas and Jouppi [1994]; Jouppi [1990]; Lam, Rothberg, and Wolf [1991]; Mowry, Lam, and Gupta [1992]; Lebeck and Wood [1994]; and Torrellas, Gupta, and Hennessy [1992]. For more details on prime numbers of memory modules, read Gao [1993]; for more on pseudo-associative caches, see Agarwal and Pudar [1993]. Caches remain an active area of research.

The Alpha AXP architecture is described in detail by Bhandarkar [1995] and by Sites [1992], and a good source of data on implementations is the *Digital Technical Journal,* issue no. 4 of 1992, which is dedicated to articles on Alpha.

References

AGARWAL, A. [1987]. *Analysis of Cache Performance for Operating Systems and Multiprogramming,* Ph.D. Thesis, Stanford Univ., Tech. Rep. No. CSL-TR-87-332 (May).

AGARWAL, A. AND S. D. PUDAR [1993]. "Column-associative caches: A technique for reducing the miss rate of direct-mapped caches," 20th Annual Int'l Symposium on Computer Architecture ISCA '20, San Diego, Calif., May 16–19. *Computer Architecture News* 21:2 (May), 179–90.

BAER, J.-L. AND W.-H. WANG [1988]. "On the inclusion property for multi-level cache hierarchies," *Proc. 15th Annual Symposium on Computer Architecture* (May–June), Honolulu, 73–80.

BELL, C. G. AND W. D. STRECKER [1976]. "Computer structures: What have we learned from the PDP-11?," *Proc. Third Annual Symposium on Computer Architecture* (January), Pittsburgh, 1–14.

BHANDARKAR, D. P. [1995]. *Alpha Architecture Implementations,* Digital Press, Newton, Mass.

BORG, A., R. E. KESSLER, AND D. W. WALL [1990]. "Generation and analysis of very long address traces," *Proc. 17th Annual Int'l Symposium on Computer Architecture* (Cat. No. 90CH2887–8), Seattle, May 28–31, IEEE Computer Society Press, Los Alamitos, Calif., 270–9.

CASE, R. P. AND A. PADEGS [1978]. "The architecture of the IBM System/370," *Communications of the ACM* 21:1, 73–96. Also appears in D. P. Siewiorek, C. G. Bell, and A. Newell, *Computer Structures: Principles and Examples* (1982), McGraw-Hill, New York, 830–855.

CLARK, D. W. [1983]. "Cache performance of the VAX-11/780," *ACM Trans. on Computer Systems* 1:1, 24–37.

CONTI, C., D. H. GIBSON, AND S. H. PITKOWSKY [1968]. "Structural aspects of the System/360 Model 85, Part I: General organization," *IBM Systems J.* 7:1, 2–14.

CRAWFORD, J. H. AND P. P. GELSINGER [1987]. *Programming the 80386,* Sybex, Alameda, Calif.

FABRY, R. S. [1974]. "Capability based addressing," *Comm. ACM* 17:7 (July), 403–412.

FARKAS, K. I. AND N. P. JOUPPI [1994]. "Complexity/performance tradeoffs with non-blocking loads," *Proc. 21st Annual Int'l Symposium on Computer Architecture*, Chicago (April).

GAO, Q. S. [1993]. "The Chinese remainder theorem and the prime memory system," 20th Annual Int'l Symposium on Computer Architecture ISCA '20, San Diego, May 16–19, 1993. *Computer Architecture News* 21:2 (May), 337–40.

GEE, J. D., M. D. HILL, D. N. PNEVMATIKATOS, AND A. J. SMITH [1993]. "Cache performance of the SPEC92 benchmark suite," *IEEE Micro* 13:4 (August), 17–27.

GIBSON, D. H. [1967]. "Considerations in block-oriented systems design," *AFIPS Conf. Proc.* 30, SJCC, 75–80.

HANDY, J. [1993]. *The Cache Memory Book*, Academic Press, Boston.

HILL, M. D. [1987]. *Aspects of Cache Memory and Instruction Buffer Performance*, Ph.D. Thesis, University of Calif. at Berkeley, Computer Science Division, Tech. Rep. UCB/CSD 87/381 (November).

HILL, M. D. [1988]. "A case for direct mapped caches," *Computer* 21:12 (December), 25–40.

JOUPPI, N. P. [1990]. "Improving direct-mapped cache performance by the addition of a small fully-associative cache and prefetch buffers," *Proc. 17th Annual Int'l Symposium on Computer Architecture* (Cat. No. 90CH2887–8), Seattle, May 28–31, 1990. IEEE Computer Society Press, Los Alamitos, Calif., 364–73.

KILBURN, T., D. B. G. EDWARDS, M. J. LANIGAN, AND F. H. SUMNER [1962]. "One-level storage system," *IRE Trans. on Electronic Computers* EC-11 (April) 223–235. Also appears in D. P. Siewiorek, C. G. Bell, and A. Newell, *Computer Structures: Principles and Examples* (1982), McGraw-Hill, New York, 135–148.

KROFT, D. [1981]. "Lockup-free instruction fetch/prefetch cache organization," *Proc. Eighth Annual Symposium on Computer Architecture* (May 12–14), Minneapolis, 81–87.

LAM, M. S., E. E. ROTHBERG, AND M. E. WOLF [1991]. "The cache performance and optimizations of blocked algorithms," Fourth Int'l Conf. on Architectural Support for Programming Languages and Operating Systems, Santa Clara, Calif., April 8–11. *SIGPLAN Notices* 26:4 (April), 63–74.

LEBECK, A. R. AND D. A. WOOD [1994]. "Cache profiling and the SPEC benchmarks: A case study," *Computer* 27:10 (October), 15–26.

LIPTAY, J. S. [1968]. "Structural aspects of the System/360 Model 85, Part II: The cache," *IBM Systems J.* 7:1, 15–21.

MCFARLING, S. [1989]. "Program optimization for instruction caches," *Proc. Third Int'l Conf. on Architectural Support for Programming Languages and Operating Systems* (April 3–6), Boston, 183–191.

MOWRY, T. C., S. LAM, AND A. GUPTA [1992]. "Design and evaluation of a compiler algorithm for prefetching," Fifth Int'l Conf. on Architectural Support for Programming Languages and Operating Systems (ASPLOS-V), Boston, October 12–15, *SIGPLAN Notices* 27:9 (September), 62–73.

PALACHARLA, S. AND R. E. KESSLER [1994]. "Evaluating stream buffers as a secondary cache replacement," *Proc. 21st Annual Int'l Symposium on Computer Architecture*, Chicago, April 18–21, IEEE Computer Society Press, Los Alamitos, Calif., 24–33.

PRZYBYLSKI, S. A. [1990]. *Cache Design: A Performance-Directed Approach*, Morgan Kaufmann Publishers, San Mateo, Calif.

PRZYBYLSKI, S. A., M. HOROWITZ, AND J. L. HENNESSY [1988]. "Performance tradeoffs in cache design," *Proc. 15th Annual Symposium on Computer Architecture* (May–June), Honolulu, 290–298.

SAAVEDRA-BARRERA, R. H. [1992]. *CPU Performance Evaluation and Execution Time Prediction Using Narrow Spectrum Benchmarking*, Ph.D. Dissertation, University of Calif., Berkeley (May).

SAMPLES, A. D. AND P. N. HILFINGER [1988]. "Code reorganization for instruction caches," Tech. Rep. UCB/CSD 88/447 (October), University of Calif., Berkeley.

SITES, R. L. (ED.) [1992]. *Alpha Architecture Reference Manual*, Digital Press, Burlington, Mass.

SMITH, A. J. [1982]. "Cache memories," *Computing Surveys* 14:3 (September), 473–530.

SMITH, J. E. AND J. R. GOODMAN [1983]. "A study of instruction cache organizations and replacement policies," *Proc. 10th Annual Symposium on Computer Architecture* (June 5–7), Stockholm, 132–137.

STRECKER, W. D. [1976]. "Cache memories for the PDP-11?," *Proc. Third Annual Symposium on Computer Architecture* (January), Pittsburgh, 155–158.

TORRELLAS, J., A. GUPTA, AND J. HENNESSY [1992]. "Characterizing the caching and synchronization performance of a multiprocessor operating system," *Fifth Int'l Conf. on Architectural Support for Programming Languages and Operating Systems* (ASPLOS-V), Boston, October 12–15, *SIGPLAN Notices* 27:9 (September), 162–174.

WANG, W.-H., J.-L. BAER, AND H. M. LEVY [1989]. "Organization and performance of a two-level virtual-real cache hierarchy," *Proc. 16th Annual Symposium on Computer Architecture* (May 28– June 1), Jerusalem, 140–148.

WILKES, M. [1965]. "Slave memories and dynamic storage allocation," *IEEE Trans. Electronic Computers* EC-14:2 (April), 270–271.

WILKES, M. V. [1982]. "Hardware support for memory protection: Capability implementations," *Proc. Symposium on Architectural Support for Programming Languages and Operating Systems* (March 1–3), Palo Alto, Calif., 107–116.

WULF, W. A., R. LEVIN, AND S. P. HARBISON [1981]. *Hydra/C.mmp: An Experimental Computer System,* McGraw-Hill, New York.

E X E R C I S E S

5.1 [15/15/12/12] <5.1,5.2> Let's try to show how you can make *unfair* benchmarks. Here are two machines with the same processor and main memory but different cache organizations. Assume the miss time is 10 times a cache hit time for both machines. Assume writing a 32-bit word takes 5 times as long as a cache hit (for the write-through cache) and that writing a whole 32-byte block takes 10 times as long as a cache-read hit (for the write-back cache). The caches are unified; that is, they contain both instructions and data.

Cache A: 128 sets, two elements per set, each block is 32 bytes, and it uses write through and no-write allocate.

Cache B: 256 sets, one element per set, each block is 32 bytes, and it uses write back and does allocate on write misses.

    a.   [15] <1.5,5.2> Describe a program that makes machine A run as much faster as possible than machine B. (Be sure to state any further assumptions you need, if any.)

    b.   [15] <1.5,5.2> Describe a program that makes machine B run as much faster as possible than machine A. (Be sure to state any further assumptions you need, if any.)

    c.   [12] <1.5,5.2> Approximately how much faster is the program in part (a) on machine A than machine B?

    d.   [12] <1.5,5.2> Approximately how much faster is the program in part (b) on machine B than on machine A?

5.2 [15/10/12/12/12/12/12/12/12/12] <5.3,5.4> In this exercise, we will run a program to evaluate the behavior of a memory system. The key is having accurate timing and then having the program stride through memory to invoke different levels of the hierarchy. Below is the code in C for UNIX systems. The first part is a procedure that uses a standard UNIX utility to get an accurate measure of the user CPU time; this procedure may need to change to work on some systems. The second part is a nested loop to read and write memory at different strides and cache sizes. To get accurate cache timing, this code is repeated many times. The third part times the nested loop overhead only so that it can be subtracted from overall measured times to see how long the accesses were. The last part prints the time per access as the size and stride varies. You may need to change CACHE_MAX depending on the question you are answering and the size of memory on the system you are measuring. The code below was taken from a program written by Andrea Dusseau of U.C. Berkeley, and was based on a detailed description found in Saavedra-Barrera [1992].

```
#include <stdio.h>
#include <sys/times.h>
#include <sys/types.h>
#include <time.h>
#define CACHE_MIN (1024) /* smallest cache */
#define CACHE_MAX (1024*1024) /* largest cache */
#define SAMPLE 10 /* to get a larger time sample */
#ifndef CLK_TCK
#define CLK_TCK 60 /* number clock ticks per second */
#endif
int x[CACHE_MAX]; /* array going to stride through */

double get_seconds() { /* routine to read time */
    struct tms rusage;
    times(&rusage); /* UNIX utility: time in clock ticks */
    return (double) (rusage.tms_utime)/CLK_TCK;
}
void main() {
int register i, index, stride, limit, temp;
int steps, tsteps, csize;
double sec0, sec; /* timing variables */

for (csize=CACHE_MIN; csize <= CACHE_MAX; csize=csize*2)
    for (stride=1; stride <= csize/2; stride=stride*2) {
        sec = 0; /* initialize timer */
        limit = csize-stride+1; /* cache size this loop */

        steps = 0;
            do { /* repeat until collect 1 second */
        sec0 = get_seconds(); /* start timer */
        for (i=SAMPLE*stride;i!=0;i=i-1) /* larger sample */
          for (index=0; index < limit; index=index+stride)
                x[index] = x[index] + 1; /* cache access */
        steps = steps + 1; /* count while loop iterations */
        sec = sec + (get_seconds() - sec0);/* end timer */
        } while (sec < 1.0); /* until collect 1 second */

        /* Repeat empty loop to subtract loop overhead */
        tsteps = 0; /* used to match no. while iterations */
            do { /* repeat until same no. iterations as above */
        sec0 = get_seconds(); /* start timer */
        for (i=SAMPLE*stride;i!=0;i=i-1) /* larger sample */
          for (index=0; index < limit; index=index-stride)
                temp = temp + index; /* dummy code */
        tsteps = tsteps + 1; /* count while iterations */
        sec = sec - (get_seconds() - sec0);/* - overhead */
        } while (tsteps<steps); /* until = no. iterations */

        printf("Size:%7d Stride:%7d read-write:%14.0f ns\n",
            csize*sizeof(int), stride*sizeof(int), (double)
        sec*1e9/(steps*SAMPLE*stride*((limit-1)/stride-1)));
    }; /* end of both outer for loops */
}
```

The program above assumes that program addresses track physical addresses, which is true on the few machines that use virtually addressed caches. In general, virtual addresses tend to follow physical addresses shortly after rebooting, so you may need to reboot the machine in order to get smooth lines in your results.

To answer the questions below, assume that the sizes of all components of the memory hierarchy are powers of 2.

a.   [15] <5.3,5.4> Plot the experimental results with elapsed time on the y-axis and the memory stride on the x-axis. Use logarithmic scales for both axes, and draw a line for each cache size.

b.   [10] <5.3,5.4> How many levels of cache are there?

c.   [12] <5.3,5.4> What is the size of the first-level cache? Block size? *Hint*: Assume the size of the page is much larger than the size of a block in a secondary cache (if any), and the size of a second-level cache block is greater than or equal to the size of a block in a first-level cache.

d.   [12] <5.3,5.4> What is the size of the second-level cache (if any)? Block size?

e.   [12] <5.3,5.4> What is the associativity of the first-level cache? Second-level cache?

f.   [12] <5.3,5.4> What is the page size?

g.   [12] <5.3,5.4> How many entries are in the TLB?

h.   [12] <5.3,5.4> What is the miss penalty for the first-level cache? Second-level?

i.   [12] <5.3,5.4> What is the time for a page fault to secondary memory? *Hint*: A page fault to magnetic disk should be measured in milliseconds.

j.   [12] <5.3,5.4> What is the miss penalty for the TLB?

k.   [12] <5.3,5.4> Is there anything else you have discovered about the memory hierarchy from these measurements?

5.3 [10/10/10] <5.2> Figure 5.54 shows the output from running the program in Exercise 5.2 on a SPARCstation 1+, which has a single unified cache.

a.   [10] <5.2> What is the size of the cache?

b.   [10] <5.2> What is the block size of the cache?

c.   [10] <5.2> What is the miss penalty for the first-level cache?

5.4 [15/15] <5.2> You purchased an Acme computer with the following features:

■   95% of all memory accesses are found in the cache.

■   Each cache block is two words, and the whole block is read on any miss.

■   The processor sends references to its cache at the rate of 10^9 words per second.

■   25% of those references are writes.

■   Assume that the memory system can support 10^9 words per second, reads or writes.

■   The bus reads or writes a single word at a time (the memory system cannot read or write two words at once).

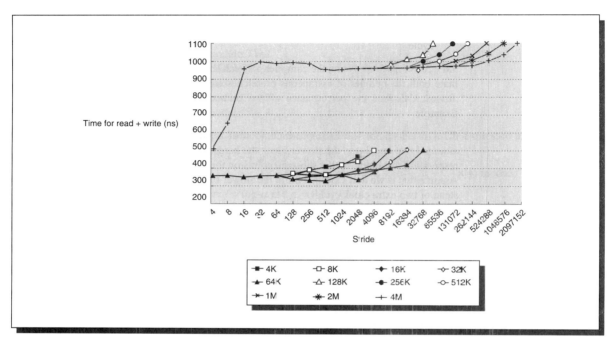

FIGURE 5.54   Results of running program in Exercise 5.2 on a SPARCstation 1+.

■   Assume at any one time, 30% of the blocks in the cache have been modified.

■   The cache uses write allocate on a write miss.

You are considering adding a peripheral to the system, and you want to know how much of the memory system bandwidth is already used. Calculate the percentage of memory system bandwidth used on the average in the two cases below. Be sure to state your assumptions.

a.   [15] <5.2> The cache is write through.

b.   [15] <5.2> The cache is write back.

5.5 [15/15] <5.5> One difference between a write-through cache and a write-back cache can be in the time it takes to write. During the first cycle, we detect whether a hit will occur, and during the second (assuming a hit) we actually write the data. Let's assume that 50% of the blocks are dirty for a write-back cache. For this question, assume that the write buffer for write through will never stall the CPU (no penalty). Assume a cache read hit takes 1 clock cycle, the cache miss penalty is 50 clock cycles, and a block write from the cache to main memory takes 50 clock cycles. Finally, assume the instruction cache miss rate is 0.5% and the data cache miss rate is 1%.

a.   [15] <5.5> Using statistics for the average percentage of loads and stores from DLX in Figure 2.26 on page 105. estimate the performance of a write-through cache with a two-cycle write versus a write-back cache with a two-cycle write for each of the programs.

6 | Storage Systems

I/O certainly has been lagging in the last decade.

Seymour Cray
Public Lecture (1976)

Also, I/O needs a lot of work.

David Kuck
*Keynote Address, 15th Annual Symposium
on Computer Architecture* (1988)

6.1	Introduction	485
6.2	Types of Storage Devices	486
6.3	Buses—Connecting I/O Devices to CPU/Memory	496
6.4	I/O Performance Measures	504
6.5	Reliability, Availability, and RAID	521
6.6	Crosscutting Issues: Interfacing to an Operating System	525
6.7	Designing an I/O System	528
6.8	Putting It All Together: UNIX File System Performance	539
6.9	Fallacies and Pitfalls	548
6.10	Concluding Remarks	553
6.11	Historical Perspective and References	553
	Exercises	557

6.1 Introduction

Input/output has been the orphan of computer architecture. Historically neglected by CPU enthusiasts, the prejudice against I/O is institutionalized in the most widely used performance measure, CPU time (page 32). The quality of a computer's I/O system—whether it has the best or worst in the world—cannot be measured by CPU time, which by definition ignores I/O. The second-class citizenship of I/O is even apparent in the label *peripheral* applied to I/O devices.

This attitude is contradicted by common sense. A computer without I/O devices is like a car without wheels—you can't get very far without them. And while CPU time is interesting, response time—the time between when the user types a command and when results appear—is surely a better measure of performance. The customer who pays for a computer cares about response time, even if the CPU designer doesn't.

I/O's revenge is at hand. Suppose we have a difference between CPU time and response time of 10%, and we speed up the CPU by a factor of 10, while neglecting I/O. Amdahl's Law tells us that we will get a speedup of only 5 times, with half the potential of the CPU wasted. Similarly, making the CPU 100 times faster without improving the I/O would obtain a speedup of only 10 times, squandering 90% of the potential. If, as predicted in Chapter 1, performance of CPUs improves at 55% per year and I/O does not improve, every task will become I/O-bound. There would be no reason to buy faster CPUs—and no jobs for CPU designers.

To reflect the increasing importance of I/O, we have expanded its coverage in this second edition. We now have two I/O chapters: this chapter covers storage I/O, and the next covers network I/O. Although two chapters cannot fully vindicate I/O, they may at least atone for some of the sins of the past and restore some balance.

Are CPUs Ever Idle?

Some suggest that the prejudice against I/O is well founded. I/O speed doesn't matter, they argue, since there is always another process to run while one process waits for a peripheral.

There are several points to make in reply. First, this is an argument that performance is measured as *throughput*—more tasks per hour—rather than as response time. Plainly, if users didn't care about response time, interactive software never would have been invented, and there would be no workstations or personal computers today; section 6.4 gives experimental evidence on the importance of response time. It may also be expensive to rely on performing other processes while waiting for I/O, since the main memory must be large or else the paging traffic from process switching would actually increase I/O. Furthermore, with desktop computing there is only one person per CPU, and thus fewer processes than in timesharing; many times the only waiting process is the human being! And some applications, such as transaction processing (section 6.4), place strict limits on response time as part of the performance analysis.

Thus, I/O performance can limit system performance and effectiveness.

6.2 | Types of Storage Devices

Rather than discuss the characteristics of all storage devices, we will concentrate on the devices with the highest capacity: magnetic disks, magnetic tapes, CD-ROMS, and automated tape libraries.

Magnetic Disks

I think Silicon Valley was misnamed. If you look back at the dollars shipped in products in the last decade there has been more revenue from magnetic disks than from silicon. They ought to rename the place Iron Oxide Valley.

Al Hoagland, One of the Pioneers of Magnetic Disks (1982)

In spite of repeated attacks by new technologies, magnetic disks have dominated secondary storage since 1965. Magnetic disks play two roles in computer systems:

- Long-term, nonvolatile storage for files, even when no programs are running

- A level of the memory hierarchy below main memory used for virtual memory during program execution (see section 5.7)

In this chapter we are not talking about floppy disks, but the original "hard" disks.

As descriptions of magnetic disks can be found in countless books, we will only list the key characteristics, with the terms illustrated in Figure 6.1. A magnetic disk consists of a collection of *platters* (1 to 20), rotating on a spindle at, say, 3600 revolutions per minute (RPM). These platters are metal disks covered with magnetic recording material on both sides. Disk diameters vary by a factor of six, from 1.3 to 8 inches. Traditionally, the widest disks have the highest performance and the smallest disks have the lowest cost per disk drive.

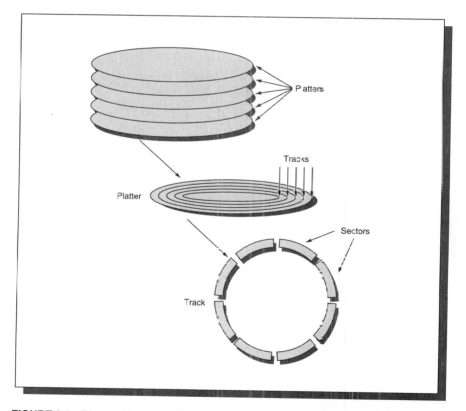

FIGURE 6.1 Disks are organized into platters, tracks, and sectors. Both sides of a platter are coated so that information can be stored on both surfaces. A cylinder refers to a track at the same position on every platter.

The disk surface is divided into concentric circles, designated *tracks*. There are typically 500 to 2500 tracks on each surface. Each track in turn is divided into *sectors* that contain the information; each track might have 64 sectors. A sector is the smallest unit that can be read or written. The sequence recorded on the magnetic media is a sector number, a gap, the information for that sector including error correction code, a gap, the sector number of the next sector, and so on.

Traditionally, all tracks have the same number of sectors; the outer tracks, which are longer, record information at a lower density than the inner tracks. Recording more sectors on the outer tracks than on the inner tracks, called *constant bit density*, is becoming more widespread with the advent of intelligent interface standards such as SCSI (see section 6.3). IBM mainframes allow users to select the size of the sectors, although almost all other systems fix their size.

To read and write information into a sector, a movable *arm* containing a *read/write head* is located over each surface. Bits are recorded using a run-length limited code, which improves the recording density of the magnetic media. The arms for each surface are connected together and move in conjunction, so that every arm is over the same track of every surface. The term *cylinder* is used to refer to all the tracks under the arms at a given point on all surfaces.

To read or write a sector, the disk controller sends a command to move the arm over the proper track. This operation is called a *seek*, and the time to move the arm to the desired track is called *seek time*. Average seek time is the subject of considerable misunderstanding.

Disk manufacturers report minimum seek time, maximum seek time, and average seek time in their manuals. The first two are easy to measure, but the average was open to wide interpretation. The industry decided to calculate average seek time as the sum of the time for all possible seeks divided by the number of possible seeks. Average seek times are advertised to be 8 ms to 12 ms, but, depending on the application and operating system, the actual average seek time may be only 25% to 33% of the advertised number, due to locality of disk references. Section 6.9 has a detailed example.

The time for the requested sector to rotate under the head is the *rotation latency* or *rotational delay*. Many disks rotate at 3600 RPM, and an average latency to the desired information is halfway around the disk; the average rotation time for many disks is therefore

$$\text{Average rotation time } = \frac{0.5}{3600 \text{ RPM}} = 0.0083 \text{ sec} = 8.3 \text{ ms}$$

Note that there are two mechanical components to a disk access: several milliseconds on average for the arm to move over the desired track and then several milliseconds on average for the desired sector to rotate under the read/write head.

The next component of disk access, *transfer time,* is the time it takes to transfer a block of bits, typically a sector, under the read-write head. This time is a function of the block size, rotation speed, recording density of a track, and speed of the electronics connecting disk to computer. Transfer rates in 1995 are typically 2 to 8 MB per second.

Between the disk controller and main memory is a hierarchy of controllers and data paths, whose complexity varies (and the cost of the computer with it). For example, whenever the transfer time is a small portion of a full access, the designer will want to disconnect the memory device during the access so that others can transfer their data. This is true for disk controllers in high-performance systems, and, as we shall see later, for buses and networks. There is also a desire to amortize this long access by reading more than simply what is requested; this is called *read ahead*. The hope is that a nearby request will be for the next sector, which will already be available.

To handle the complexities of disconnect/connect and read ahead, there is usually, in addition to the disk drive, a device called a *disk controller*. Thus, the final component of disk-access time is *controller time*, which is the overhead the controller imposes in performing an I/O access. When referring to the performance of a disk in a computer system, the time spent waiting for a disk to become free (*queuing delay*) is added to this time.

EXAMPLE   What is the average time to read or write a 512-byte sector for a typical disk? The advertised average seek time is 9 ms, the transfer rate is 4 MB/sec, it rotates at 7200 RPM, and the controller overhead is 1 ms. Assume the disk is idle so that there is no queuing delay.

ANSWER   Average disk access is equal to average seek time + average rotational delay + transfer time + controller overhead. Using the calculated, average seek time, the answer is

$$9 \text{ ms} + \frac{0.5}{7200 \text{ RPM}} + \frac{0.5 \text{ KB}}{4.0 \text{ MB/sec}} + 1 \text{ ms} = 9 - 4.15 + 0.125 + 1 = 14.3 \text{ ms}$$

Assuming the measured seek time is 33% of the calculated average, the answer is

$$3 \text{ ms} + 4.2 \text{ ms} + 0.1 \text{ ms} - 1 \text{ ms} = 8.3 \text{ ms}$$

■

Figure 6.2 shows the characteristics of a 1993 magnetic disk. Large-diameter drives have many more megabytes to amortize the cost of electronics, so the traditional wisdom used to be that they had the lowest cost per megabyte. But this advantage is offset for the small drives by the much higher sales volume, which lowers manufacturing costs. Hence the best price per megabyte is typically a medium-width disk, which has enough capacity to offset the cost of the mechanical components and enough volume to take advantage of high manufacturing volume.

Characteristics	Seagate ST31401N Elite-2 SCSI Drive
Disk diameter (inches)	5.25
Formatted data capacity (GB)	2.8
Cylinders	2627
Tracks per cylinder	21
Sectors per track	≈ 99
Bytes per sector	512
Rotation speed (RPM)	5400
Average seek in ms (random cylinder to cylinder)	11.0
Minimum seek in ms	1.7
Maximum seek in ms	22.5
Data transfer rate in MB/sec	≈ 4.6

FIGURE 6.2   Characteristics of a 1993 magnetic disk.

The Future of Magnetic Disks

The disk industry has concentrated on improving the capacity of disks. Improvement in capacity is customarily expressed as *areal density*, measured in bits per square inch:

$$\text{Areal density} = \frac{\text{Tracks}}{\text{Inch}} \text{ on a disk surface} \times \frac{\text{Bits}}{\text{Inch}} \text{ on a track}$$

Through about 1988 the rate of improvement of areal density was 29% per year, thus doubling density every three years. Since that time the rate has improved to 60% per year, quadrupling density every three years and matching the traditional rate of DRAMs. In 1995 the highest density in commercial products is 644 million bits per square inch, with 3000 million bits per square inch demonstrated in the labs.

Cost per megabyte has dropped at least at the same rate of improvement of areal density, with smaller drives playing the larger role in this improvement. Figure 6.3 plots price per personal computer disk between 1983 and 1995, showing both the rapid drop in price and the increase in capacity. Figure 6.4 translates these costs into price per megabyte, showing that it has improved more than a hundredfold over those 12 years. In fact, between 1992 and 1995 the rate of improvement in cost per megabyte of personal computer disks was about 2.0 times per year, a considerable increase over the previous rate of about 1.3 to 1.4 times per year between 1986 and 1992.

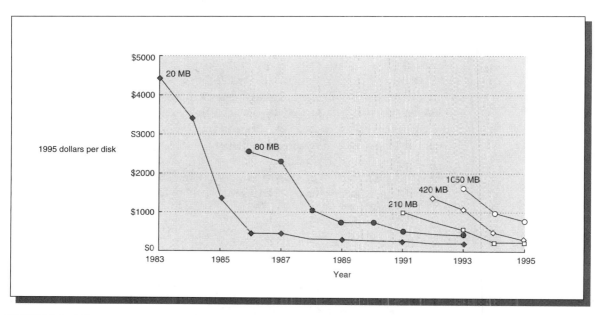

FIGURE 6.3   Price per personal computer disk over time. The prices are in 1995 dollars, adjusted for inflation using the Producer Price Index. The costs were collected from advertisements from the January edition of *Byte* magazine, using the lowest price of a disk of a particular size in that issue. In a few cases, the price was adjusted slightly to get a consistent disk capacity (e.g., shrinking the price of an 86-MB disk by 80/86 to get a point for the 80-MB line).

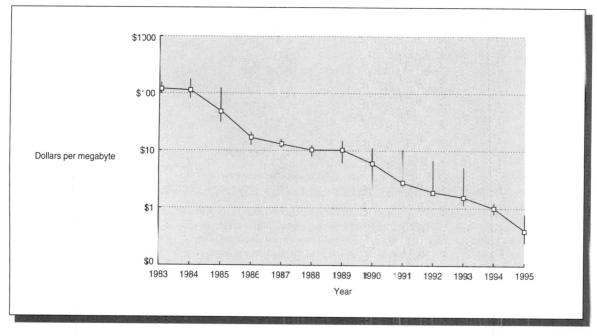

FIGURE 6.4   Price per megabyte of personal computer disk over time. The center point is the median price per MB, with the low point on the line being the minimum and the high point being the maximum. These data were collected in the same way as for Figure 6.3, except that more disks are included on this graph.

Because it is easier to spin the smaller mass, smaller-diameter disks save power as well as volume. Smaller drives also have fewer cylinders, so the seek distances are shorter. In 1995, 3.5-inch or 2.5-inch drives are probably the leading technology, and the future will see even smaller drives. Increasing density (bits per inch on a track) has improved transfer times, and there has been some small improvement in seek speed. Rotation speeds have improved from the standard 3600 RPM in the 1980s to 5400–7200 RPM in the 1990s.

Magnetic disks have been challenged many times for supremacy of secondary storage. One reason has been the fabled *access time gap* as shown in Figure 6.5. The price of a megabyte of disk storage in 1995 is about 100 times cheaper than the price of a megabyte of DRAM in a system, but DRAM is about 100,000 times faster. Many a scientist has tried to invent a technology to fill that gap, but thus far all have failed.

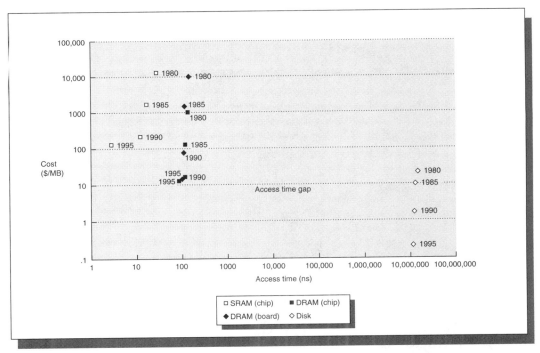

FIGURE 6.5   Cost versus access time for SRAM, DRAM, and magnetic disk in 1980, 1985, 1990, and 1995. (Note the difference in cost between a DRAM chip and DRAM chips packaged on a board and ready to plug into a computer.) The two-order-of-magnitude gap in cost and access times between semiconductor memory and rotating magnetic disks has inspired a host of competing technologies to try to fill it. So far, such attempts have been made obsolete before production by improvements in magnetic disks, DRAMs, or both. Note that between 1990 and 1995 the cost per megabyte of SRAM and DRAM chips made less improvement, while disk cost made dramatic improvement. Also, since 1990 SIMM modules have shrunk the gap between the cost of DRAM (board) and DRAM (chip).

Using DRAMs as Disks

One challenger to disks for dominance of secondary storage is *solid state disks* (SSDs), built from DRAMs with a battery to make the system nonvolatile; another is *expanded storage* (ES), a large memory that allows only block transfers to or from main memory. ES acts like a software-controlled cache (the CPU stalls during the block transfer), while SSDs involve the operating system just like a transfer from magnetic disks. The advantages of SSDs and ES are nonvolatility, trivial seek times, higher potential transfer rate, and possibly higher reliability. Unlike just a larger main memory, SSDs and ES are autonomous: They require special commands to access their storage, and thus are "safe" from some software errors that write over main memory. The block-access nature of SSDs and ES allows error correction to be spread over more words, which means lower cost for greater error recovery. For example, IBM's ES uses the greater error recovery to allow it to be constructed from less reliable (and less expensive) DRAMs without sacrificing product availability. SSDs, unlike main memory and ES, may be shared by multiple CPUs because they function as separate units. Placing DRAMs in an I/O device rather than memory is also one way to get around the address-space limits of the current 32-bit computers. The disadvantage of SSDs and ES is cost, which is at least 50 times per megabyte the cost of magnetic disks.

When the first edition of this book was written, disks were growing at 29% per year and DRAMs at 60% per year. One exercise asked when DRAMs would match the cost per bit of magnetic disks. Now that disks have at least matched the DRAM growth rate and will apparently do so for many years, the question has changed from What year? to What must change for it to happen?

Optical Disks

Another challenger to magnetic disks is *optical compact disks,* or *CDs.* The *CD-ROM* is removable and inexpensive to manufacture, but it is a read-only medium. Its low manufacturing cost has made it a favorite medium for distributing information, but not as a rewritable storage device. The high capacity and low cost mean that CD-ROMs may well replace floppy disks as the favorite medium for distributing personal computer software.

So far, magnetic disk challengers have never had a product to market at the right time. By the time a new product ships, disks have made advances as predicted earlier, and costs have dropped accordingly.

Unfortunately, the data distribution responsibilities of CDs mean that their rate of improvement is governed by standards committees, and it appears that magnetic storage grows more quickly than human beings can agree on CD standards. Writable optical disks, however, may have the potential to compete with new tape technologies for archival storage.

Magnetic Tapes

Magnetic tapes have been part of computer systems as long as disks because they use the same technology as disks, and hence follow the same density improvements. The inherent cost/performance difference between disks and tapes is based on their geometries:

- Fixed rotating platters offer random access in milliseconds, but disks have a limited storage area and the storage medium is sealed within each reader.

- Long strips wound on removable spools of "unlimited" length mean many tapes can be used per reader, but tapes require sequential access that can take seconds.

This relationship has made tapes the technology of choice for backups to disk.

One of the limits of tapes has been the speed at which the tapes can spin without breaking or jamming. A relatively recent technology, called *helical scan tapes*, solves this problem by keeping the tape speed the same but recording the information on a diagonal to the tape with a tape reader that spins much faster than the tape is moving. This technology increases recording density by about a factor of 20 to 50. Helical scan tapes were developed for the low-cost VCRs and camcorders, which brings down the cost of the tapes and readers.

One drawback to tapes is that they wear out: Helical tapes last for hundreds of passes, while the traditional longitudinal tapes wear out in thousands to millions of passes. The helical scan read/write heads also wear out quickly, typically rated for 2000 hours of continuous use. Finally, there are typically long rewind, eject, load, and spin-up times for helical scan tapes. In the archival backup market, such performance characteristics have not mattered, and hence there has been more engineering focus on increasing density than on overcoming these limitations.

Automated Tape Libraries

Tape capacities are enhanced by inexpensive robots to automatically load and store tapes, offering a new level of storage hierarchy. These robo-line tapes mean access to terabytes of information in tens of seconds, without the intervention of a human operator. Figure 6.6 shows the Storage Technologies Corporation (STC) PowderHorn, which loads 6000 tapes, giving a total capacity of 60 terabytes. Putting this capacity into perspective, in 1995 the Library of Congress is estimated to have 30 terabytes of text, if books could be magically transformed into ASCII characters.

One interesting characteristic of automated tape libraries is that economy of scale can apply, unlike almost all other parts of the computer industry. Figure 6.7 shows that the price per gigabyte drops by a factor of four when going from the small systems (less than 100 GB in 1995) to the large systems (greater than 1000 GB). The drawback of such large systems is the limited bandwidth of this massive storage.

Now that we have described several storage devices, we must discover how to connect them to a computer.

FIGURE 6.6   The STC PowderHorn. This storage silo holds 6000 tape cartridges; using the 3590 cartridge announced in 1995, the total capacity is 60 terabytes. It has a performance level of up to 350 cartridge exchanges per hour. (Courtesy STC.)

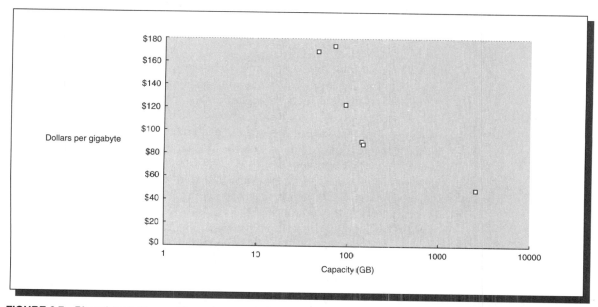

FIGURE 6.7   Plot of capacity per library versus dollars per gigabyte for several 1995 tape libraries. Note that the x axis is a log scale. In 1995 large libraries are one-quarter the cost per gigabyte of small libraries. The danger of comparing disk to tape at small capacities is the subject of the fallacy discussed on page 548.

6.3 | Buses—Connecting I/O Devices to CPU/Memory

In a computer system, the various subsystems must have interfaces to one another; for instance, the memory and CPU need to communicate, and so do the CPU and I/O devices. This is commonly done with a *bus*. The bus serves as a shared communication link between the subsystems. The two major advantages of the bus organization are low cost and versatility. By defining a single interconnection scheme, new devices can be added easily and peripherals may even be moved between computer systems that use a common bus. The cost is low, since a single set of wires is shared in multiple ways.

The major disadvantage of a bus is that it creates a communication bottleneck, possibly limiting the maximum I/O throughput. When I/O must pass through a central bus, this bandwidth limitation is as real as—and sometimes more severe than—memory bandwidth. In commercial systems, where I/O is frequent, and in supercomputers, where the necessary I/O rates are high because the CPU performance is high, designing a bus system capable of meeting the demands of the processor is a major challenge.

One reason bus design is so difficult is that the maximum bus speed is largely limited by physical factors: the length of the bus and the number of devices (and, hence, bus loading). These physical limits prevent arbitrary bus speedup. The desire for high I/O rates (low latency) and high I/O throughput can also lead to conflicting design requirements.

Buses are traditionally classified as *CPU-memory buses* or *I/O buses*. I/O buses may be lengthy, may have many types of devices connected to them, have a wide range in the data bandwidth of the devices connected to them, and normally follow a bus standard. CPU-memory buses, on the other hand, are short, generally high speed, and matched to the memory system to maximize memory-CPU bandwidth. During the design phase, the designer of a CPU-memory bus knows all the types of devices that must connect together, while the I/O bus designer must accept devices varying in latency and bandwidth capabilities. To lower costs, some computers have a single bus for both memory and I/O devices.

Let's review a typical *bus transaction*, as seen in Figure 6.8. A bus transaction includes two parts: sending the address and receiving or sending the data. Bus transactions are usually defined by what they do to memory: A *read* transaction transfers data *from* memory (to either the CPU or an I/O device), and a *write* transaction writes data to the memory. In a read transaction, the address is first sent down the bus to the memory, together with the appropriate control signals indicating a read. In Figure 6.8, this means deasserting the read signal. The memory responds by returning the data on the bus with the appropriate control signals, in this case deasserting the wait signal. A write transaction requires that the CPU or I/O device send both address and data and requires no return of data. Usually the CPU must wait between sending the address and receiving the data on a read, but the CPU often does not wait on writes.

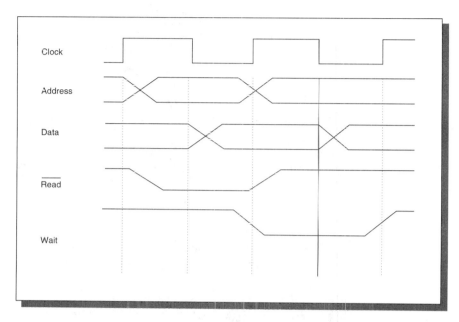

FIGURE 6.8 Typical bus read transaction. This bus is synchronous. The read begins when the read signal is asserted, and data are not ready until the wait signal is deasserted.

Bus Design Decisions

The design of a bus presents several options, as Figure 6.9 shows. Like the rest of the computer system, decisions will depend on cost and performance goals. The first three options in the figure are clear choices—separate address and data lines, wider data lines, and multiple-word transfers all give higher performance at more cost.

Option	High performance	Low cost
Bus width	Separate address and data lines	Multiplex address and data lines
Data width	Wider is faster (e.g., 64 bits)	Narrower is cheaper (e.g., 8 bits)
Transfer size	Multiple words have less bus overhead	Single-word transfer is simpler
Bus masters	Multiple (requires arbitration)	Single master (no arbitration)
Split transaction?	Yes—separate request and reply packets get higher bandwidth (need multiple masters)	No—continuous connection is cheaper and has lower latency
Clocking	Synchronous	Asynchronous

FIGURE 6.9 The main options for a bus. The advantage of separate address and data buses is primarily on writes.

The next item in the table concerns the number of *bus masters*. These are devices that can initiate a read or write transaction; the CPU, for instance, is always a bus master. A bus has multiple masters when there are multiple CPUs or when I/O devices can initiate a bus transaction. If there are multiple masters, an arbitration scheme is required among the masters to decide who gets the bus next. Arbitration is often a fixed priority, as is the case with daisy-chained devices or an approximately fair scheme that randomly chooses which master gets the bus.

With multiple masters, a bus can offer higher bandwidth by going to packets, as opposed to holding the bus for the full transaction. This technique is called *split transactions*. (Some systems call this ability *connect/disconnect*, a *pipelined bus,* or a *packet-switched bus*.) Figure 6.10 shows the split-transaction bus. The read transaction is broken into a read-request transaction that contains the address and a memory-reply transaction that contains the data. Each transaction must now be tagged so that the CPU and memory can tell what is what. Split transactions make the bus available for other masters while the memory reads the words from the requested address. It also normally means that the CPU must arbitrate for the bus to send the data and the memory must arbitrate for the bus to return the data. Thus, a split-transaction bus has higher bandwidth, but it usually has higher latency than a bus that is held during the complete transaction.

The final item in Figure 6.9, *clocking*, concerns whether a bus is synchronous or asynchronous. If a bus is *synchronous,* it includes a clock in the control lines and a fixed protocol for address and data relative to the clock. Since little or no logic is needed to decide what to do next, these buses can be both fast and

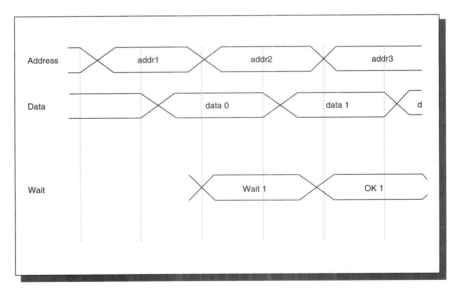

FIGURE 6.10   A split-transaction bus. Here the address on the bus corresponds to a later memory access.

inexpensive. They have two major disadvantages, however. Everything on the bus must run at the same clock rate, and because of clock-skew problems, synchronous buses cannot be long. CPU-memory buses are typically synchronous.

An *asynchronous* bus, on the other hand, is not clocked. Instead, self-timed, handshaking protocols are used between bus sender and receiver. Figure 6.11 shows the steps of a master performing a write on an asynchronous bus.

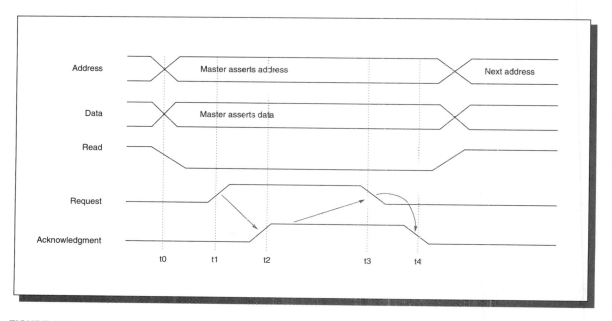

FIGURE 6.11 A master performing a write. The state of the transaction at each time step is as follows. Master has obtained control and asserts address, direction, and data, then waits a specified amount of time for slaves to decode target; t1: Master asserts request line; t2: Slave asserts ack, indicating data received; t3: Master releases req; t4: Slave releases ack.

Asynchrony makes it much easier to accommodate a wide variety of devices and to lengthen the bus without worrying about clock skew or synchronization problems. If a synchronous bus can be used, it is usually faster than an asynchronous bus because it avoids the overhead of synchronizing the bus for each transaction. The choice of synchronous versus asynchronous bus has implications not only for data bandwidth but also for an I/O system's capacity in terms of physical distance and number of devices that can be connected to the bus; asynchronous buses scale better with technological changes. I/O buses are typically asynchronous. Figure 6.12 suggests when to use one over the other.

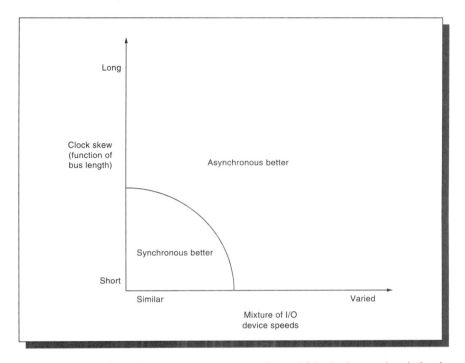

FIGURE 6.12   Preferred bus type as a function of length/clock skew and variation in I/O device speed. Synchronous is best when the distance is short and the I/O devices on the bus all transfer at similar speeds.

Bus Standards

The number and variety of I/O devices are not fixed on most computer systems, permitting customers to tailor computers to their needs. As the interface to which devices are connected, the I/O bus can also be considered an expansion bus for adding I/O devices over time. Standards that let the computer designer and I/O-device designer work independently, therefore, play a large role in determining the choice of buses. As long as both the computer-system designer and the I/O-device designer meet the requirements, any I/O device can connect to any computer. In fact, an I/O bus standard is the document that defines how to connect them.

Machines sometimes grow to be so popular that their I/O buses become de facto standards; examples are the PDP-11 Unibus and the IBM PC-AT Bus. Once many I/O devices have been built for a popular machine, other computer designers will build their I/O interface so that those devices can plug into their machines as well. Sometimes standards also come from an explicit standards effort on the part of I/O device makers. The *intelligent peripheral interface* (IPI) and Ethernet are examples of standards that resulted from the cooperation of manufacturers. If standards are successful, they are eventually blessed by a sanctioning body like ANSI or IEEE. Occasionally, a bus standard comes top-down directly from a standards committee—PCI is one example.

Examples of Buses

Figure 6.13 summarizes characteristics of five I/O buses, and Figure 6.14 summarizes three CPU-memory buses found in servers.

	S bus	**MicroChannel**	**PCI**	**IPI**	**SCSI 2**
Data width (primary)	32 bits	32 bits	32 to 64 bits	16 bits	8 to 16 bits
Clock rate	16 to 25 MHz	Asynchronous	33 MHz	Asynchronous	10 MHz or asynchronous
Number of bus masters	Multiple	Multiple	Multiple	Single	Multiple
Bandwidth, 32-bit reads	33 MB/sec	20 MB/sec	33 MB/sec	25 MB/sec	20 MB/sec or 6 MB/sec
Bandwidth, peak	89 MB/sec	75 MB/sec	132 MB/sec	25 MB/sec	20 MB/sec or 6 MB/sec
Standard	None	—	—	ANSI X3.129	ANSI X3.131

FIGURE 6.13 Summary of I/O buses. The first two started as CPU-memory buses and evolved into I/O buses.

	HP Summit	**SGI Challenge**	**Sun XDBus**
Data width (primary)	128 bits	256 bits	144 bits
Clock rate	60 MHz	48 MHz	66 MHz
Number of bus masters	Multiple	Multiple	Multiple
Bandwidth, peak	960 MB/sec	1200 MB/sec	1056 MB/sec
Standard	None	None	None

FIGURE 6.14 Summary of CPU-memory buses found in 1994 servers. All use split transactions to enhance bandwidth. The number of slots on the bus for masters or slaves is 16, 9, and 10, respectively.

Interfacing Storage Devices to the CPU

Having described I/O devices and looked at some of the issues of the connecting bus, we are ready to discuss the CPU end of the interface. The first question is how the physical connection of the I/O bus should be made. The two choices are connecting it to memory or to the cache. In the following section we will discuss the pros and cons of connecting an I/O bus directly to the cache; in this section we examine the more usual case in which the I/O bus is connected to the main memory bus. Figure 6.15 shows a typical organization. In low-cost systems, the I/O bus *is* the memory bus; this means an I/O command on the bus could interfere with a CPU instruction fetch, for example.

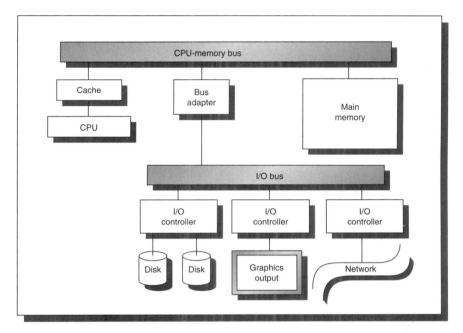

FIGURE 6.15   A typical interface of I/O devices and an I/O bus to the CPU-memory bus.

Once the physical interface is chosen, the question becomes, How does the CPU address an I/O device that it needs to send or receive data? The most common practice is called *memory-mapped* I/O. In this scheme, portions of the address space are assigned to I/O devices. Reads and writes to those addresses may cause data to be transferred; some portion of the I/O space may also be set aside for device control, so commands to the device are just accesses to those memory-mapped addresses.

The alternative practice is to use dedicated I/O opcodes in the CPU. In this case, the CPU sends a signal that this address is for I/O devices. Examples of computers with I/O instructions are the Intel 80x86 and the IBM 370 computers. I/O opcodes have been waning in popularity.

No matter which addressing scheme is selected, each I/O device has registers to provide status and control information. Either through loads and stores in memory-mapped I/O or through special instructions, the CPU sets flags to determine the operation the I/O device will perform.

Any I/O event is rarely a single operation. For example, the DEC LP11 line printer has two I/O device registers: one for status information and one for data to be printed. The status register contains a *done bit*, set by the printer when it has printed a character, and an *error bit*, indicating that the printer is jammed or out of paper. Each byte of data to be printed is put into the data register; the CPU must then wait until the printer sets the done bit before it can place another character in the buffer.

This simple interface, in which the CPU periodically checks status bits to see if it is time for the next I/O operation, is called *polling*. As you might expect, the fact that CPUs are so much faster than I/O devices means that polling may waste a lot of CPU time. This was recognized long ago, leading to the invention of interrupts to notify the CPU when it is time to do something for the I/O device.

Interrupt-driven I/O, used by most systems for at least some devices, allows the CPU to work on some other process while waiting for the I/O device. For example, the LP11 has a mode that allows it to interrupt the CPU whenever the done bit or error bit is set. In general-purpose applications, interrupt-driven I/O is the key to multitasking operating systems and good response times.

The drawback to interrupts is the operating system overhead on each event. In real-time applications with hundreds of I/O events per second, this overhead can be intolerable. One hybrid solution for real-time systems is to use a clock to periodically interrupt the CPU, at which time the CPU polls all I/O devices.

Delegating I/O Responsibility from the CPU

Interrupt-driven I/O relieves the CPU from waiting for every I/O event, but there are still many CPU cycles spent in transferring data. Transferring a disk block of 2048 words, for instance, would require at least 2048 loads and 2048 stores, as well as the overhead for the interrupt. Since I/O events so often involve block transfers, *direct memory access* (DMA) hardware is added to many computer systems to allow transfers of numbers of words without intervention by the CPU.

DMA is a specialized processor that transfers data between memory and an I/O device while the CPU goes on with other tasks. Thus, it is external to the CPU and must act as a master on the bus. The CPU first sets up the DMA registers, which contain a memory address and number of bytes to be transferred. Once the DMA transfer is complete, the controller interrupts the CPU. There may be multiple DMA devices in a computer system; for example, DMA is frequently part of the controller for an I/O device.

Increasing the intelligence of the DMA device can further unburden the CPU. Devices called *I/O processors* (or *I/O controllers*, or *channel controllers*) operate either from fixed programs or from programs downloaded by the operating system. The operating system typically sets up a queue of *I/O control blocks* that contain information such as data location (source and destination) and data size. The I/O processor then takes items from the queue, doing everything requested and sending a single interrupt when the task specified in the I/O control blocks is complete. Whereas the LP11 line printer would cause 4800 interrupts to print a 60-line by 80-character page, an I/O processor could save 4799 of those interrupts.

I/O processors are similar to multiprocessors in that they facilitate several processes being executed simultaneously in the computer system. I/O processors are less general than CPUs, however, since they have dedicated tasks, and thus parallelism is also much more limited. Also, an I/O processor doesn't normally

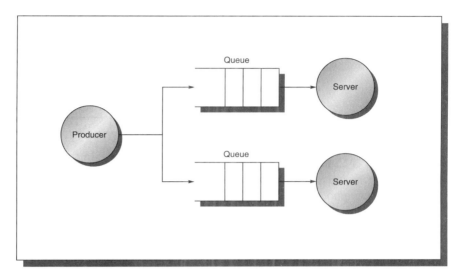

FIGURE 6.18   The single-producer, single-server model of Figure 6.16 is extended with another server and buffer. This increases I/O system throughput and takes less time to service producer tasks. Increasing the number of servers is a common technique in I/O systems. There is a potential imbalance problem with two buffers: Unless data is placed perfectly in the buffers, sometimes one server will be idle with an empty buffer while the other server is busy with many tasks in its buffer.

1. *Entry time*—The time for the user to enter the command. The graphics system in Figure 6.19 took 0.25 seconds on average to enter a command versus 4.0 seconds for the keyboard system.

2. *System response time*—The time between when the user enters the command and the complete response is displayed.

3. *Think time*—The time from the reception of the response until the user begins to enter the next command.

The sum of these three parts is called the *transaction time*. Several studies report that user productivity is inversely proportional to transaction time; *transactions per hour* is a measure of the work completed per hour by the user.

   The results in Figure 6.19 show that reduction in response time actually decreases transaction time by more than just the response time reduction: Cutting system response time by 0.7 seconds saves 4.9 seconds (34%) from the conventional transaction and 2.0 seconds (70%) from the graphics transaction. This implausible result is explained by human nature: People need less time to think when given a faster response.

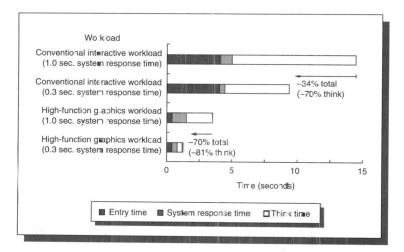

FIGURE 6.19   A user transaction with an interactive computer divided into entry time, system response time, and user think time for a conventional system and graphics system. The entry times are the same, independent of system response time. The entry time was 4 seconds for the conventional system and 0.25 seconds for the graphics system. (From Brady [1986].)

Whether these results are explained as a better match to the human attention span or getting people "on a roll," several studies report this behavior. In fact, as computer responses drop below one second, productivity seems to make a more than linear jump. Figure 6.20 compares transactions per hour (the inverse of transaction time) of a novice, an average engineer, and an expert performing physical design tasks on graphics displays. System response time magnified talent: a novice with subsecond response time was as productive as an experienced professional with slower response, and the experienced engineer in turn could outperform the expert with a similar advantage in response time. In all cases the number of transactions per hour jumps more than linearly with subsecond response time.

Since humans may be able to get much more work done per day with better response time, it is possible to attach an economic benefit to the customer of lowering response time into the subsecond range [IBM 1982], thereby helping the architect decide how to tip the balance between response time and throughput.

A Little Queuing Theory

With an appreciation of the importance of response time we can give a set of simple theorems that will help calculate response time and throughput of an entire I/O system. Let's start with a black box approach to I/O systems, as in Figure 6.21. In our example the CPU is making I/O requests that arrive at the I/O device, and the requests "depart" when the I/O device fulfills them.

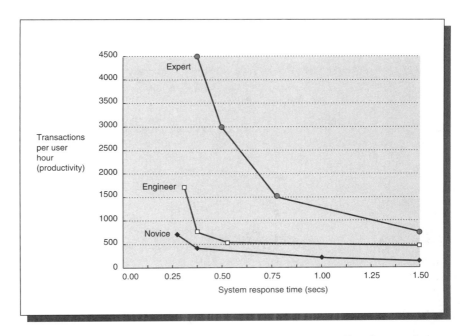

FIGURE 6.20   Transactions per hour versus computer response time for a novice, experienced engineer, and expert doing physical design on a graphics system. *Transactions per hour* is a measure of productivity. (From IBM [1982].)

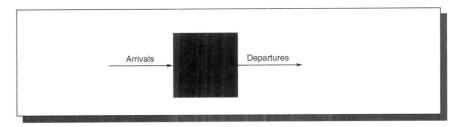

FIGURE 6.21   Treating the I/O system as a black box. This leads to a simple but important observation: If the system is in steady state, then the number of tasks entering the systems must equal the number of tasks leaving the system.

We are usually interested in the long term, or steady state, of a system rather than in the initial start-up conditions. Hence we make the simplifying assumption that we are evaluating systems in equilibrium: the input rate must be equal to the output rate. This leads us to *Little's Law*, which relates the average number of tasks in the system, the average arrival rate of new tasks, and the average time to perform a task:

$$\text{Mean number of tasks in system} \; = \; \text{Arrival rate} \times \text{Mean response time}$$

Little's Law applies to any system in equilibrium, as long as nothing inside the black box is creating new tasks or destroying them. This simple equation is surprisingly powerful, as we shall see.

If we open the black box, we see Figure 6.22. The areas where the tasks accumulate, waiting to be serviced, is called the *queue*, or *waiting line*, and the device performing the requested service is called the *server*.

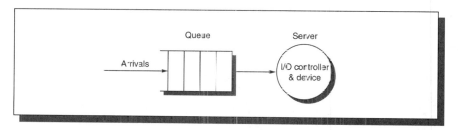

FIGURE 6.22 The single server model for this section. In this situation an I/O request "departs" by being completed by the server.

Little's Law and a series of definitions lead to several useful equations:

$Time_{server}$—Average time to service a task; service rate is $1/Time_{server}$, traditionally represented by the symbol μ in many texts.

$Time_{queue}$—Average time per task in the queue.

$Time_{system}$—Average time/task in the system, or the response time, the sum of $Time_{queue}$ and $Time_{server}$.

Arrival rate—Average number of arriving tasks/second, traditionally represented by the symbol λ in many texts.

$Length_{server}$—Average number of tasks in service.

$Length_{queue}$—Average length of queue.

$Length_{system}$—Average number of tasks in system, the sum of $Length_{queue}$ and $Length_{server}$.

One common misunderstanding can be made clearer by these definitions: whether the question is how long a task must wait in the queue before service starts ($Time_{queue}$) or how long a task takes until it is completed ($Time_{system}$). The latter term is what we mean by response time, and the relationship between the terms is $Time_{system} = Time_{queue} + Time_{server}$.

Using the terms above we can restate Little's Law as

$$Length_{system} = Arrival\ rate \times Time_{system}$$

We can also talk about how busy a system is from these definitions. Server utilization is simply

$$\text{Server utilization} = \frac{\text{Arrival rate}}{\text{Service rate}}$$

The value must be between 0 and 1, for otherwise there would be more tasks arriving than could be serviced, violating our assumption that the system is in equilibrium. Utilization is also called *traffic intensity* and is represented by the symbol ρ in many texts.

EXAMPLE   Suppose an I/O system with a single disk gets about 10 I/O requests per second and the average time for a disk to service an I/O request is 50 ms. What is the utilization of the I/O system?

ANSWER   The service rate is then

$$\frac{1}{50 \text{ ms}} = \frac{1}{0.05 \text{ sec}} = 20 \text{ I/O per second (IOPS)}$$

Using the equation above,

$$\text{Server utilization} = \frac{\text{Arrival rate}}{\text{Service rate}} = \frac{10 \text{ IOPS}}{20 \text{ IOPS}} = 0.50$$

So the I/O system utilization is 0.5.   ■

Little's Law can be applied to the components of the black box as well, since they must also be in equilibrium:

$$\text{Length}_{\text{queue}} = \text{Arrival rate} \times \text{Time}_{\text{queue}}$$
$$\text{Length}_{\text{server}} = \text{Arrival rate} \times \text{Time}_{\text{server}}$$

EXAMPLE   Suppose the average time to satisfy a disk request is 50 ms and the I/O system with many disks gets about 200 I/O requests per second. What is the mean number of I/O requests at the disk server?

ANSWER   Using the equation above,

$$\text{Length}_{\text{server}} = \text{Arrival rate} \times \text{Time}_{\text{server}} = \frac{200}{\text{sec}} \times 0.05 \text{ sec} = 10$$

So there are 10 requests on average at the disk server.   ■

How the queue delivers tasks to the server is called the *queue discipline*. The simplest and most common discipline is *first-in-first-out* (FIFO). If we assume FIFO we can relate time waiting in the queue to the mean number of tasks in the queue:

$$\text{Time}_{system} = \text{Length}_{queue} \times \text{Time}_{server} + \text{Mean time to complete service of tasks when new task arrives}$$

That is, the system response time is the number of tasks in the queue times the mean service time plus the time it takes the server to complete whatever tasks are being serviced when a new task arrives.

The last component of the equation is not as simple as it first appears. A new task can arrive at any instant, so we have no basis to know how long the existing task has been in the server. Although such requests are random events, if we know something about the distribution of events we can predict performance.

To estimate this answer we need to know a little about distributions of *random variables*. A variable is random if it takes one of a specified set of values with a specified probability; that is, you cannot know exactly what its next value will be, but you do know the probability of all possible values.

One way to characterize the distribution of values of a random variable is a *histogram*, which divides the range between the minimum and maximum values into subranges called *buckets*. Histograms then plot the number in each bucket as columns. Histograms work well for distributions that are discrete values—for example, the number of I/O requests. For distributions that are not discrete values, such as time waiting for an I/O request, we need a curve to plot the values over the full range so that we can accurately estimate the value. Stated alternatively, we need a histogram with an infinite number of buckets.

Hence, to be able to solve the last part of the equation above we need to characterize the distribution of this random variable. The mean time and some measure of the variance is sufficient for that characterization. For the first term we use the *weighted arithmetic mean time* (see page 25 in Chapter 1 for a slightly different version of the formula):

$$\text{Weighted mean time} = \frac{f_1 \times T_1 - f_2 \times T_2 + \dots + f_n \times T_n}{f_1 - f_2 + \dots + f_n}$$

where T_i is the time for task i and f_i is the frequency of occurrence of task i.

To characterize variability about the mean, many people use the standard deviation. Let's use the *variance* instead, which is simply the square of the standard deviation. Given the weighted mean, the variance can be calculated as

$$\text{Variance} = \frac{f_1 \times T_1^2 + f_2 \times T_2^2 + \dots + f_n \times T_n^2}{f_1 + f_2 + \dots + f_n} - \text{Weighted mean time}^2$$

The problem with variance is that you must remember the units. Let's assume the distribution is of time. If time is on the order of 100 milliseconds, then squaring it yields 10,000 square milliseconds. This unit is certainly unusual. It would be more convenient if we had a unitless measure.

To avoid this unit problem, we use the *squared coefficient of variance*, traditionally called *C*:

$$C = \frac{\text{Variance}}{\text{Weighted mean time}^2}$$

For reasons stated earlier, we are trying to characterize random events, but to be able to predict performance we need random events with certain nice properties. Figure 6.23 gives a few examples. An *exponential distribution*, with most of the times short relative to average but with a few long ones, has a C value of 1. In a *hypoexponential distribution*, most values are close to average and C is less than 1. In a *hyperexponential distribution*, most values are further from the average and C is greater than 1. The disk service is best measured with a C of about 1.5. As we shall see, the value of C affects the simplicity of the queuing formulas.

Distribution type	C	% less than average	90% of distribution is less than
Hypoexponential	0.5	57%	2.0 times average
Exponential	1.0	63%	2.3 times average
Hyperexponential	2.0	69%	2.8 times average

FIGURE 6.23 Examples of value of squared coefficient of variance C and variability of distributions given an unlimited number of tasks (*infinite population*).

Note that we are using a constant to characterize variability about the mean. Since C does not vary over time, the past history of events has no impact on the probability of an event occurring now. This forgetful property is called *memoryless* and is a key assumption used to predict behavior.

Finally, we can answer the question about the length of time a new task must wait for the server to complete a task, called the *average residual service time*:

$$\text{Average residual service time} = 1/2 \times \text{Weighted mean time} \times (1 + C)$$

Although we won't derive this formula, we can appeal to intuition. When the distribution is not random and all possible values are equal to the average, the variance is 0 and so C is 0. The average residual service time is then just half the average service time, as we would expect.

EXAMPLE   Using the definitions and formulas above, derive the average time waiting in the queue ($Time_{queue}$) in terms of the average service time ($Time_{server}$), server utilization, and the squared coefficient of variance (C).

ANSWER   All tasks in the queue ($Length_{queue}$) ahead of the new task must be completed before the task can be serviced; each takes on average $Time_{server}$. If a task is at the server, it takes average residual service time to complete. The chance the server is busy is *server utilization*, hence the expected time for service is Server utilization × Average residual service time. This leads to our initial formula:

$$Time_{queue} = Length_{queue} \times Time_{server} + \text{Server utilization} \times \text{Average residual service time}$$

Replacing average residual service time by its definition and $Length_{queue}$ by Arrival rate × $Time_{queue}$ yields

$$Time_{queue} = \text{Server utilization} \times (1/2 \times Time_{server} \times (1+C)) + (\text{Arrival rate} \times Time_{queue}) \times Time_{server}$$

Rearranging the last term, let us replace Arrival rate × $Time_{server}$ by Server utilization since

$$\text{Server utilization} = \frac{\text{Arrival rate}}{1/Time_{server}} = \text{Arrival rate} \times Time_{server}$$

It works as follows:

$$Time_{queue} = \text{Server utilization} \times (1/2 \times Time_{server} \times (1+C)) + (\text{Arrival rate} \times Time_{server}) \times Time_{queue}$$
$$= \text{Server utilization} \times (1/2 \times Time_{server} \times (1+C)) + \text{Server utilization} \times Time_{queue}$$

Rearranging terms and simplifying gives us the desired equation:

$$Time_{queue} = \text{Server utilization} \times (1/2 \times Time_{server} \times (1+C)) + \text{Server utilization} \times Time_{queue}$$
$$Time_{queue} - \text{Server utilization} \times Time_{queue} = \text{Server utilization} \times (1/2 \times Time_{server} \times (1+C))$$
$$Time_{queue} \times (1 - \text{Server utilization}) = \frac{\text{Server utilization} \times (Time_{server} \times (1+C))}{2}$$
$$Time_{queue} = \frac{Time_{server} \times (1+C) \times \text{Server utilization}}{2 \times (1 - \text{Server utilization})}$$

Note that when we have an exponential distribution, then C = 1.0, so this formula simplifies to

$$\text{Time}_{queue} = \text{Time}_{server} \times \frac{\text{Server utilization}}{(1 - \text{Server utilization})}$$

■

These equations and this subsection are based on an area of applied mathematics called *queuing theory*, which offers equations to predict behavior of such random variables. Real systems are too complex for queuing theory to provide exact analysis, and hence queuing theory works best when only approximate answers are needed. This subsection is a simple introduction, and interested readers can find many books on the topic.

Requests for service from an I/O system can be modeled by a random variable, because the operating system is normally switching between several processes that generate independent I/O requests. We also model I/O service times by a random variable given the probabilistic nature of disks in terms of seek and rotational delays.

Queuing theory makes a sharp distinction between past events, which can be characterized by measurements using simple arithmetic, and future events, which are predictions requiring mathematics. In computer systems we commonly predict the future from the past; one example is least recently used block placement (see Chapter 5). Hence the distinction between measurements and predicted distributions is often blurred here, and we use measurements to verify the type of distribution and then rely on the distribution thereafter.

Let's review the assumptions about the queuing model:

■ The system is in equilibrium.

■ The times between two successive requests arriving, called the *interarrival times*, are exponentially distributed.

■ The number of requests is unlimited (this is called an *infinite population model* in queuing theory).

■ The server can start on the next customer immediately after finishing with the prior one.

■ There is no limit to the length of the queue, and it follows the first-in-first-out order discipline.

■ All tasks in line must be completed.

Such a queue is called *M/G/1*:

M = exponentially random request arrival (C = 1), with M standing for the memoryless property mentioned above

G = general service distribution (i.e., not necessarily exponential)

I = single server

When service times are exponentially distributed, this model becomes an *M/M/1* queue and we can use the simple equation for waiting time at the end of the last example. The M/M/1 model is a simple and widely used model.

The assumption of exponential distribution is commonly used in queuing examples for two reasons, one good and one bad. The good reason is that a collection of many arbitrary distributions acts as an exponential distribution. Many times in computer systems a particular behavior is the result of many components interacting, so an exponential distribution of interarrival times is the right model. The bad reason is that the math is simpler if you assume exponential distributions.

Let's put queuing theory to work in a few Examples.

EXAMPLE   Suppose a processor sends 10 disk I/Os per second, these requests are exponentially distributed, and the average disk service time is 20 ms. Answer the following questions:

1.   On average, how utilized is the disk?

2.   What is the average time spent in the queue?

3.   What is the 90th percentile of the queuing time?

4.   What is the average response time for a disk request, including the queuing time and disk service time?

ANSWER   Let's restate these facts:

Average number of arriving tasks/second is 10.

Average disk time to service a task is 20 ms (0.02 sec).

The server utilization is then

$$\text{Server utilization} = \frac{\text{Arrival rate}}{\text{Service rate}} = \frac{10}{1/0.02} = 0.2$$

Since the interarrival times are exponentially distributed, we can use the simplified formula for the average time spent waiting in line:

$$\text{Time}_{queue} = \text{Time}_{server} \times \frac{\text{Server utilization}}{(1 - \text{Server utilization})} = 20 \text{ ms} \times \frac{0.2}{1-0.2} = 20 \times \frac{0.2}{0.8} = 20 \times 0.25 = 5 \text{ ms}$$

From Figure 6.23 (page 512), the 90th percentile is 2.3 times the mean waiting time, so it is 11.5 ms. The average response time is

$$\text{Time}_{queue} + \text{Time}_{server} = 5 + 20 \text{ ms} = 25 \text{ ms}$$

■

EXAMPLE   Suppose we get a new, faster disk. Recalculate the answers to the questions above, assuming the disk service time is 10 ms.

ANSWER   The disk utilization is then

$$\text{Server utilization} = \frac{\text{Arrival rate}}{\text{Service rate}} = \frac{10}{1/0.01} = 0.1$$

Since the service distribution is exponential, we can use the simplified formula for the average time spent waiting in line:

$$\text{Time}_{queue} = \text{Time}_{server} \times \frac{\text{Server utilization}}{(1 - \text{Server utilization})} = 10 \text{ ms} \times \frac{0.1}{1 - 0.1} = 10 \times \frac{0.1}{0.9} = 10 \times 0.11 = 1.11 \text{ ms}$$

The 90th percentile of the mean waiting time is 2.56 ms.

The average response time is 10 + 1.11 ms or 11.11 ms, 2.25 times faster than the old response time even though the new service time is only 2.0 times faster.   ∎

Section 6.7 has more examples using queuing theory to predict performance.

Examples of Benchmarks of Disk Performance

The prior subsection tries to predict the performance of storage subsystems. We also need to measure the performance of real systems to collect the values of parameters needed for prediction, to determine if the queuing theory assumptions hold, and to suggest what to do if the assumptions don't hold.

This subsection describes three benchmarks, each illustrating novel concerns regarding storage systems versus processors.

Transaction Processing Benchmarks

Transaction processing (TP, or OLTP for on-line transaction processing) is chiefly concerned with *I/O rate*: the number of disk accesses per second, as opposed to *data rate*, measured as bytes of data per second. TP generally involves changes to a large body of shared information from many terminals, with the TP system guaranteeing proper behavior on a failure. If, for example, a bank's computer fails when a customer withdraws money, the TP system would guarantee that the account is debited if the customer received the money and that the account is unchanged if the money was not received. Airline reservations systems as well as banks are traditional customers for TP.

Two dozen members of the TP community conspired to form a benchmark for the industry and, to avoid the wrath of their legal departments, published the report anonymously [1985]. This benchmark, called *DebitCredit*, simulates bank tellers and has as its bottom line the number of debit/credit transactions per second (TPS). The DebitCredit performs the operation of a customer depositing or withdrawing money. *TPC-A* and *TPC-B* are more tightly specified versions of this original benchmark. The organization responsible for standardizing TPC-A and TPC-B have also developed benchmarks on complex query processing (*TPC-C*) and decision support (*TPC-D*).

Disk I/O for DebitCredit is random reads and writes of 100-byte records along with occasional sequential writes. Depending on how cleverly the transaction-processing system is designed, each transaction results in between 2 and 10 disk I/Os and takes between 5000 and 20,000 CPU instructions per disk I/O. The variation depends largely on the efficiency of the transaction-processing software, although in part it depends on the extent to which disk accesses can be avoided by keeping information in main memory. Hence, TPC measures the database software as well as the underlying machine.

The main performance measurement is the peak TPS, under the restriction that 90% of the transactions have less than a two-second response time. The benchmark requires that for TPS to increase, the number of tellers and the size of the account file must also increase. Figure 6.24 shows this unusual relationship in which more TPS requires more users. This scaling is to ensure that the benchmark really measures disk I/O; otherwise a large main memory dedicated to a database cache with a small number of accounts would unfairly yield a very high TPS. (Another perspective is that the number of accounts must grow, since a person is not likely to use the bank more frequently just because the bank has a faster computer!)

TPS	Number of ATMs	Account file size
10	1000	0.1 GB
100	10,000	1.0 GB
1000	100,000	10.0 GB
10,000	1,000,000	100.0 GB

FIGURE 6.24 Relationship among TPS, tellers, and account file size. The DebitCredit benchmark requires that the computer system handle more tellers and larger account files before it can claim a higher transaction-per-second milestone. The benchmark is supposed to include "terminal handling" overhead, but this metric is sometimes ignored.

Another novel feature of TPC-A and TPC-B is that they address how to compare the performance of systems with different configurations. In addition to reporting TPS, benchmarkers must also report the cost per TPS, based on the five-year cost of the computer system hardware and software.

SPEC System-Level File Server (SFS) Benchmark

The SPEC benchmarking effort is best known for its characterization of processor performance, but it branches out into other fields as well. In 1990 seven companies agreed on a synthetic benchmark, called SFS, to evaluate systems running the Sun Microsystems network file service NFS. This synthetic mix was based on measurements on NFS systems to propose a reasonable mix of reads, writes, and file operations such as examining a file. SFS supplies default parameters for comparative performance: For example, half of all writes are done in 8-KB blocks and half are done in partial blocks of 1, 2, or 4 KB. For reads the mix is 85% full blocks and 15% partial blocks.

Like TPC-B, SFS scales the size of the file system according to the reported throughput: For every 100 NFS operations per second, the capacity must increase by 1 GB. It also limits the average response time, in this case to 50 ms. Figure 6.25 shows average response time versus throughput for three systems. Unfortunately, unlike TPC-B, SFS does not normalize for different configurations. The fastest system in Figure 6.25 has 12 times the number of CPUs and disks as the slowest system, but SPEC leaves it to you to calculate price versus performance.

Self-Scaling I/O Benchmark

A different approach to I/O performance analysis was proposed by Chen and Patterson [1994b]. The first step is a *self-scaling benchmark,* which automatically and dynamically adjusts *several* aspects of its workload according to the performance characteristics of the system being measured. By doing so, the benchmark automatically scales across current and future systems. This scaling is more general than the scaling found in TPC-B and SFS, for scaling here varies five parameters, according to the characteristics of the system being measured, rather than just one.

This first step aids in understanding system performance by reporting how performance varies according to each of five workload parameters. These five parameters determine the first-order performance effects in I/O systems:

1. *Number of unique bytes touched*—This is the number of unique data bytes read or written in a workload; essentially, it is the total size of the data set.

2. *Percentage of reads.*

3. *Average I/O request size*—It chooses sizes from a distribution with a coefficient of variance (C) of one.

4. *Percentage of sequential requests*—This is the percentage of requests that sequentially follow the prior request. When set at 50%, on average half of the accesses are to the next sequential address.

5. *Number of processes*—This is the concurrency in the workload, that is, the number of processes simultaneously issuing I/O.

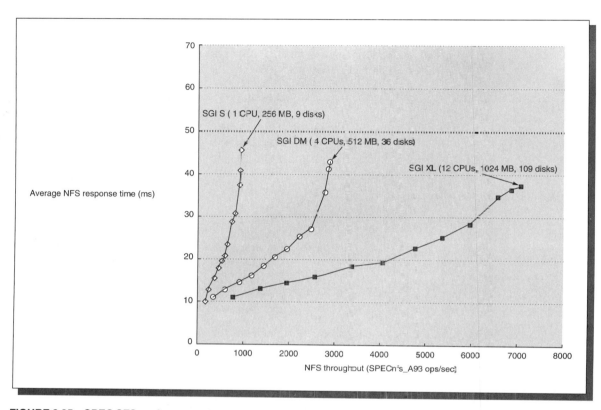

FIGURE 6.25   SPEC SFS performance for three SGI Challenge servers. The dashed line represents the 50-ms average response time limit imposed by SPEC. Reported in March 1995, these systems all ran IRIX version 5.3 with the EFS file system and all used the R4400 microprocessor. The XL model processors ran at 200 MHz and the other two used 150 MHz. Each system had one 1-GB disk with the rest being 2-GB disks, most spinning at 7200 RPM. SPEC SFS also divides the peak rate by 10 and calls this quotient SPECnsf_A93 users/second. The numbers of such users per second for these three machines are 84, 283, and 702, respectively.

The benchmark first chooses a nominal value for each of the five parameters based on the system's performance. It then varies each parameter in turn while the other four parameters remain at their fixed, nominal values. The one exception is the first parameter, since it determines whether all accesses go to the file cache or to disk. Because of the very different performance for file cache and disk accesses, the benchmark automatically picks two values for the number of bytes accessed.

The resulting I/O performance is then plotted for each of the parameters. Figure 6.26 shows the performance for workstations and mainframes, using the nominal parameter values collected by the self-scaling benchmark as a function of unique bytes touched. These plots give insight into appropriate workloads and resulting performance. The width of the high-performance parts of the curves is determined by the size of the file cache. For example, the HP 730 offers the highest performance, provided the workload fits in its small file cache, and workloads that would need to go to disk on other systems can be satisfied by the very large file cache of the Convex.

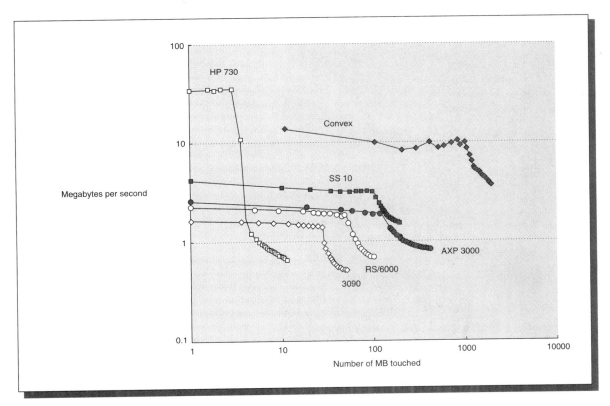

FIGURE 6.26   Performance versus megabytes touched for several workstations and mainframes (see section 6.8). Note the log-log scale. These results use the nominal values selected by the self-scaling benchmark. For example, 50% of accesses are reads and 50% are writes. The primary difference between the systems is the average access size of 120 KB for the Convex; adjusting for a common access size would halve Convex performance but make little change to the other lines in this plot.

The self-scaling benchmark increases our understanding of a system and scales the workload to remain relevant as technology advances. It complicates the task of comparing results from two systems, however. The problem is that the benchmark may choose different workloads on which to measure each system.

Hence, the second part of this new approach is to estimate the performance of other workloads. It estimates performance for unmeasured workloads by assuming that the *shape* of a performance curve for one parameter is independent of the values of the other parameters. This assumption leads to an overall performance equation of

$$\text{Perf}(X, Y, Z, \ldots) = \text{Perf}(X_{nominal}, Y_{nominal}, Z_{nominal}, \ldots) \times f_X(X) \times f_Y(Y) \times f_Z(Z) \times \ldots$$

where X, Y, Z, ... are the parameters. Suppose the nominal values were 50% reads and 50% of accesses as sequential, but the desired workload had 60% reads and 60% sequential, and all other parameters matched the nominal values. The predicted performance is the nominal performance multiplied by the measured ratio of 60% reads to 50% reads and by the measured ratio at 60% sequential to 50% sequential. Chen and Patterson [1994b] have shown that this technique yields accurate performance estimates, within 10% for most workloads.

We use this benchmark to evaluate systems in section 6.8.

6.5 Reliability, Availability, and RAID

Although throughput and response time have their analogues in processor design, reliability is given considerably more attention in storage than in processors. This brings us to two terms that are often confused—*reliability* and *availability*. The term reliability is commonly used interchangeably with availability: if something breaks, but the user can still use the system, it seems as if the system still works and hence it seems more reliable. Here is a clearer distinction:

Reliability—Is anything broken?

Availability—Is the system still available to the user?

Adding hardware can therefore improve availability (for example, ECC on memory), but it cannot improve reliability (the DRAM is still broken). Reliability can only be improved by bettering environmental conditions, by building from more reliable components, or by building with fewer components. Another term, *data integrity*, refers to consistent reporting when information is lost because of failure; this is very important to some applications.

One innovation that improves both availability and performance of storage systems is *disk arrays*. The argument for arrays is that since price per megabyte is independent of disk size, potential throughput can be increased by having many disk drives and, hence, many disk arms. For example, Figure 6.25 (page 519) shows how NFS throughput increases as the systems expand from 9 disks to 109 disks. Simply spreading data over multiple disks, called *striping*, automatically forces accesses to several disks. (Although arrays improve throughput, latency is not necessarily improved.) The drawback to arrays is that with more devices, reliability drops: N devices generally have $1/N$ the reliability of a single device.

So, while a disk array can never be more reliable than a smaller number of larger disks when each disk has the same failure rate, availability can be improved by adding redundant disks. That is, if a single disk fails, the lost information can be reconstructed from redundant information. The only danger is in having another disk failure between the time a disk fails and the time it is replaced (termed *mean time to repair,* or MTTR). Since the *mean time to failure* (MTTF) of disks is five or more years, and the MTTR is measured in hours, redundancy can make the availability of 100 disks much higher than that of a single disk. These systems have become known by the acronym *RAID,* standing for *redundant array of inexpensive disks.*

There are several approaches to redundancy that have different overhead and performance. Figure 6.27 shows the RAID levels and gives an example of how eight disks would have to be supplemented by redundant or check disks at each level plus the number of failures that the system would survive.

RAID level		Failures survived	Data disks	Check disks
0	Nonredundant	0	8	0
1	Mirrored	1	8	8
2	Memory-style ECC	1	8	4
3	Bit-interleaved parity	1	8	1
4	Block-interleaved parity	1	8	1
5	Block-interleaved distributed parity	1	8	1
6	P+Q redundancy	2	8	2

FIGURE 6.27   RAID levels, their availability, and their overhead in redundant disks. The paper that introduced the term RAID [Patterson, Gibson, and Katz 1987] used a numerical classification for these schemes that has become popular; in fact, the nonredundant disk array is sometimes called RAID 0.

One problem is discovering when a disk fails. Fortunately, magnetic disks provide information about their correct operation. There is extra information recorded in each sector to discover errors within that sector. As long as we transfer at least one sector and check the error detection information when reading sectors, electronics associated with disks will with very high probability discover when a disk fails or loses information.

We cover here the most popular of these RAID levels; readers interested in more detail should see the paper by Chen et al. [1994].

Mirroring (RAID 1)

The traditional solution to disk failure, called *mirroring* or *shadowing*, uses twice as many disks. Whenever data is written to one disk, that data is also written to a redundant disk, so that there are always two copies of the information. If a disk fails, the system just goes to the "mirror" to get the desired information. Mirroring is the most expensive solution.

Bit-Interleaved Parity (RAID 3)

The cost of higher availability can be reduced to $1/N$, where N is the number of disks in a protection group. Rather than have a complete copy of the original data for each disk, we need only add enough redundant information to restore the lost information on a failure. Reads or writes go to all disks in the group, with one extra disk to hold the check information in case there is a failure.

Parity is one such scheme. Readers unfamiliar with parity can think of the redundant disk as having the sum of all the data in the other disks. When a disk fails, then you subtract all the data in the good disks from the parity disk; the remaining information must be the missing information. Parity is simply the sum modulo 2. The assumption is that failures are so rare that taking longer to recover from failure but reducing redundant storage is a good trade-off.

Just as direct-mapped associative placement in caches can be considered a special case of set-associative placement (see section 5.2), the mirroring can be considered the special case of one data disk and one parity disk ($N = 1$). Parity can be accomplished by duplicating the data, so mirrored disks have the advantage of simplifying parity calculation. Duplicating data also means that the controller can improve read performance by reading from the disk of the pair that has the shortest seek distance, although this optimization means writes must wait for the arm with the longer seek since arms are no longer synchronized. Of course, the redundancy of $N = 1$ has the highest overhead for increasing disk availability.

Block-Interleaved Distributed Parity (RAID 5)

This level uses the same organization of disks, but data is accessed differently. In the prior organization every access went to all disks. Some applications would prefer to do smaller accesses, allowing independent accesses to occur in parallel. That is the purpose of this next RAID level. Since error-detection information in each sector is checked on reads to see if data is correct, such "small reads" to each disk can occur independently as long as the minimum access is one sector.

Writes are another matter. It would seem that each small write would demand that all other disks be accessed to read the rest of the information needed to recalculate the new parity. In our example, a "small write" would require reading the other three data disks, adding the new information, and then writing the new parity to the parity disk and the new data to the data disk. The key insight to reduce this overhead is that parity is simply a sum of information; by watching which bits change when we write the new information, we need only change the corresponding bits on the parity disk. We must read the old data, compare old data to the new data to see which bits change, read the old parity, change the corresponding bits, then write the new data and new parity. Thus the small write involves four disk accesses for two disks instead of accessing all disks.

This scheme supports mixtures of large reads, large writes, small reads, and small writes. One drawback to the system is that the parity disk must be updated on every write, so it is the bottleneck for sequential writes. To fix the parity-write bottleneck, the parity information is spread throughout all the disks so that there is no single bottleneck for writes. Figure 6.28 shows how data are distributed in this disk array organization.

As the organization on the right shows, the parity associated with each row of data blocks is no longer restricted to a single disk. This organization allows for multiple writes to occur simultaneously as long as the stripe units are not located in the same disks. For example, a write to block 8 on the right must also access its parity block P2, thereby occupying the first and third disks. A second write to block 5 on the right, implying an update to its parity block P1, accesses the second and fourth disks and thus could occur at the same time as the prior write.

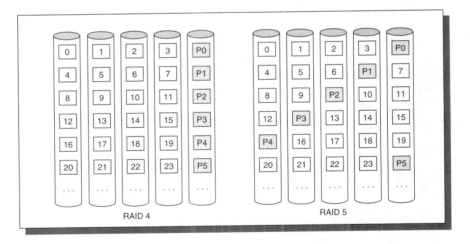

FIGURE 6.28   Block-interleaved parity (RAID 4) versus distributed block-interleaved parity (RAID 5). By distributing parity blocks to all disks, some small writes can be performed in parallel.

The higher throughput, measured either as megabytes per second or as I/Os per second, and the ability to recover from failures make RAID attractive. When combined with the advantages of smaller volume and lower power of small-diameter drives, RAIDs are playing an increasing role in storage systems.

6.6 | Crosscutting Issues: Interfacing to an Operating System

In a manner analogous to the way compilers use an instruction set, operating systems control what I/O techniques implemented by the hardware will actually be used. For example, many I/O controllers used in early UNIX systems were 16-bit microprocessors. To avoid problems with 16-bit addresses in controllers, UNIX was changed to limit the maximum I/O transfer to 63 KB or less. Thus, a new I/O controller designed to efficiently transfer 1-MB files would never see more than 63 KB at a time under UNIX, no matter how large the files.

Caches Cause Problems for Operating Systems—Stale Data

The prevalence of caches in computer systems has added to the responsibilities of the operating system. Caches imply the possibility of two copies of the data—one each for cache and main memory—while virtual memory can result in three copies—for cache, memory, and disk. This brings up the possibility of *stale data*: the CPU or I/O system could modify one copy without updating the other copies (see section 5.9). Either the operating system or the hardware must make sure that the CPU reads the most recently input data and that I/O outputs the correct data, in the presence of caches and virtual memory. Whether the stale-data problem arises depends in part on where the I/O is connected to the computer. If it is connected to the CPU cache, as shown in Figure 6.29, there is no stale-data problem; all I/O devices and the CPU see the most accurate version in the cache, and existing mechanisms in the memory hierarchy ensure that other copies of the data will be updated. The side effect is lost CPU performance, since I/O will replace blocks in the cache with data that are unlikely to be needed by the process running in the CPU at the time of the transfer. In other words, all I/O data goes through the cache, but little of it is referenced. This arrangement also requires arbitration between the CPU and I/O to decide who accesses the cache. If I/O is connected to memory, as in Figure 6.15 (page 502), then it doesn't interfere with CPU, provided the CPU has a cache. In this situation, however, the stale-data problem occurs. Alternatively, I/O can just invalidate data—either all data that might match (no tag check) or only data that matches.

There are two parts to the stale-data problem:

1. The I/O system sees stale data on output because memory is not up-to-date.

2. The CPU sees stale data in the cache on input after the I/O system has updated memory.

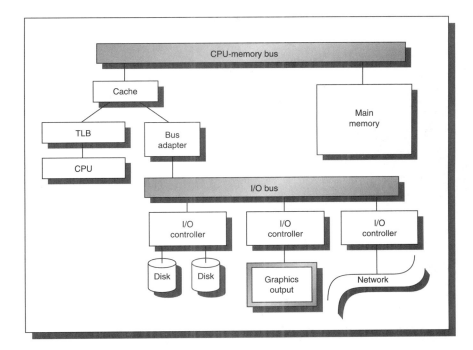

FIGURE 6.29   Example of I/O connected directly to the cache.

The first dilemma is how to output correct data if there is a cache and I/O is connected to memory. A write-through cache solves this by ensuring that memory will have the same data as the cache. A write-back cache requires the operating system to flush output addresses to make sure they are not in the cache. This flush takes time, even if the data is not in the cache, since address checks are sequential. Alternatively, the hardware can check cache tags during output to see if they are in a write-back cache, and only interact with the cache if the output tries to read data that is in the cache.

The second problem is ensuring that the cache won't have stale data after input. The operating system can guarantee that the input data area can't possibly be in the cache. If it can't guarantee this, the operating system flushes input addresses to make sure they are not in the cache. Again, this takes time, whether or not the input addresses are in the cache. As before, extra hardware can be added to check tags during an input and invalidate the data if there is a conflict. These problems are basically the same as cache coherency in a multiprocessor, discussed in Chapter 8; I/O can be thought of as a second dedicated processor in a multiprocessor.

DMA and Virtual Memory

Given the use of virtual memory, there is the matter of whether DMA should transfer using virtual addresses or physical addresses. Here are a couple of problems with DMA using physically mapped I/O:

- Transferring a buffer that is larger than one page will cause problems, since the pages in the buffer will not usually be mapped to sequential pages in physical memory.

- Suppose DMA is ongoing between memory and a frame buffer, and the operating system removes some of the pages from memory (or relocates them). The DMA would then be transferring data to or from the wrong page of memory.

One answer is *virtual DMA*. It allows the DMA to use virtual addresses that are mapped to physical addresses during the DMA. Thus, a buffer must be sequential in virtual memory, but the pages can be scattered in physical memory. The operating system could update the address tables of a DMA if a process is moved using virtual DMA, or the operating system could "lock" the pages in memory until the DMA is complete. Figure 6.30 shows address-translation registers added to the DMA device.

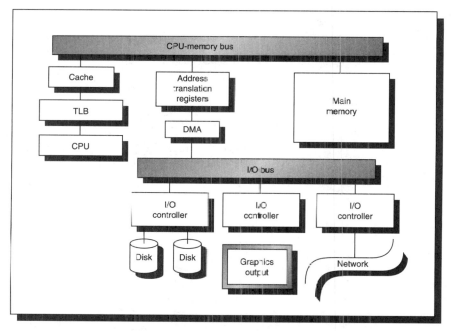

FIGURE 6.30 **Virtual DMA requires a register for each page to be transferred in the DMA controller, showing the protection bits and the physical page corresponding to each virtual page.**

6.7 | Designing an I/O System

The art of I/O is finding a design that meets goals for cost and variety of devices while avoiding bottlenecks to I/O performance. This means that components must be balanced between main memory and the I/O device, because performance—and hence effective cost/performance—can only be as good as the weakest link in the I/O chain. The architect must also plan for expansion so that customers can tailor the I/O to their applications. This expansibility, both in numbers and types of I/O devices, has its costs in longer I/O buses, larger power supplies to support I/O devices, and larger cabinets.

In designing an I/O system, analyze performance, cost, and capacity using varying I/O connection schemes and different numbers of I/O devices of each type. Here is a series of six steps to follow in designing an I/O system. The answers for each may be dictated by market requirements or simply by cost/performance goals.

1. List the different types of I/O devices to be connected to the machine, or list the standard buses that the machine will support.

2. List the physical requirements for each I/O device. This includes volume, power, connectors, bus slots, expansion cabinets, and so on.

3. List the cost of each I/O device, including the portion of cost of any controller needed for this device.

4. Record the CPU resource demands of each I/O device. This should include

    ■   Clock cycles for instructions used to initiate an I/O, to support operation of an I/O device (such as handling interrupts), and complete I/O

    ■   CPU clock stalls due to waiting for I/O to finish using the memory, bus, or cache

    ■   CPU clock cycles to recover from an I/O activity, such as a cache flush

5. List the memory and I/O bus resource demands of each I/O device. Even when the CPU is not using memory, the bandwidth of main memory and the I/O bus is limited.

6. The final step is assessing the performance of the different ways to organize these I/O devices. Performance can only be properly evaluated with simulation, though it may be estimated using queuing theory.

You then select the best organization, given your performance and cost goals.

Cost/performance goals affect the selection of the I/O scheme and physical design. Performance can be measured either as megabytes per second or I/Os per second, depending on the needs of the application. For high performance, the only limits should be speed of I/O devices, number of I/O devices, and speed of memory and CPU. For low cost, the only expenses should be those for the I/O devices themselves and for cabling to the CPU. Cost/performance design, of course, tries for the best of both worlds.

To make these ideas clearer, let's go through several examples.

EXAMPLE   First, let's look at the impact on the CPU of reading a disk page directly into the cache. Make the following assumptions:

- Each page is 16 KB, and the cache-block size is 64 bytes.

- The addresses corresponding to the new page are *not* in the cache.

- The CPU will not access any of the data in the new page.

- 95% of the blocks that were displaced from the cache will be read in again, and each will cause a miss.

- The cache uses write back, and 50% of the blocks are dirty on average.

- The I/O system buffers a full cache block before writing to the cache (this is called a *speed-matching buffer*, matching transfer bandwidth of the I/O system and memory).

- The accesses and misses are spread uniformly to all cache blocks.

- There is no other interference between the CPU and I/O for the cache slots.

- There are 15,000 misses every 1 million clock cycles when there is *no* I/O.

- The miss penalty is 30 clock cycles, plus 30 more cycles to write the block if it was dirty.

Assuming one page is brought in every 1 million clock cycles, what is the impact on performance?

ANSWER   Each page fills 16,384/64 or 256 blocks. I/O transfers do not cause cache misses on their own because entire cache blocks are transferred. However, they do displace blocks already in the cache. If half of the displaced blocks are dirty, it takes 128×30 clock cycles to write them back to memory. There are also misses from 95% of the blocks displaced in the cache because they are referenced later, adding another $95\% \times 256$, or 244 misses. Since this data was placed into the cache from the I/O system, all these blocks are dirty and will need to be written back when replaced. Thus, the total is on average $128 \times 30 + 244 \times 60$ more clock cycles than the original $1,000,000 + 7500 \times 30 + 7500 \times 60$. This turns into a 1% decrease in performance:

$$\frac{128 \times 30 + 244 \times 60}{1,000,000 + 7500 \times 30 + 7500 \times 60} = \frac{18,480}{1,675,000} = 0.011$$

■

Now let's take a long look at the cost/performance of different I/O organizations. A simple way to perform this analysis is to look at maximum throughput, assuming that resources can be used at 100% of their maximum rate without side effects from interference. (A later example takes a more realistic view.)

EXAMPLE   Assume the following performance and cost information:

- A 500-MIPS CPU costing $30,000.

- A 16-byte-wide memory with a 100-ns cycle time.

- 200 MB/sec I/O bus with room for 20 SCSI-2 buses and controllers.

- SCSI-2 buses that can transfer 20 MB/sec and support up to 15 disks per bus (these are also called SCSI *strings*).

- A $1500 SCSI-2 controller that adds 1 ms of overhead to perform a disk I/O.

- An operating system that uses 10,000 CPU instructions for a disk I/O.

- A choice of a large disk containing 8 GB or a small disk containing 2 GB, each costing $0.25 per MB.

- Both disks rotate at 7200 RPM, have an 8-ms average seek time, and can transfer 6 MB/sec.

- The storage capacity must be 200 GB.

- The average I/O size is 16 KB.

Evaluate the cost per I/O per second (IOPS) of using small or large drives. Assume that every disk I/O requires an average seek and average rotational delay. Use the optimistic assumption that all devices can be used at 100% of capacity and that the workload is evenly divided among all disks.

ANSWER   I/O performance is limited by the weakest link in the chain, so we evaluate the maximum performance of each link in the I/O chain for each organization to determine the maximum performance of that organization.

Let's start by calculating the maximum number of IOPS for the CPU, main memory, and I/O bus. The CPU I/O performance is determined by the speed of the CPU and the number of instructions to perform a disk I/O:

$$\text{Maximum IOPS for CPU} = \frac{500 \text{ MIPS}}{10,000 \text{ instructions per I/O}} = 50,000$$

The maximum performance of the memory system is determined by the memory cycle time, the width of the memory, and the size of the I/O transfers:

$$\text{Maximum IOPS for main memory} = \frac{(1/100 \text{ ns}) \times 16}{16 \text{ KB per I/O}} \approx 10,000$$

The I/O bus maximum performance is limited by the bus bandwidth and the size of the I/O:

$$\text{Maximum IOPS for the I/O bus} = \frac{200 \text{ MB/sec}}{16 \text{ KB per I/O}} \approx 12,500$$

Thus, no matter which disk is selected, the CPU and main memory limit the maximum performance to no more than 10,000 IOPS.

Now it's time to look at the performance of the next link in the I/O chain, the SCSI-2 controllers. The time to transfer 16 KB over the SCSI-2 bus is

$$\text{SCSI-2 bus transfer time} = \frac{16 \text{ KB}}{20 \text{ MB/sec}} = 0.8 \text{ ms}$$

Adding the 1-ms SCSI-2 controller overhead means 1.8 ms per I/O, making the maximum rate per controller

$$\text{Maximum IOPS per SCSI-2 controller} = \frac{1}{1.8 \text{ ms}} = 556 \text{ IOPS}$$

All the organizations will use several controllers, so 556 IOPS is not the limit for the whole system.

The final link in the chain is the disks themselves. The time for an average disk I/O is

$$\text{I/O time} = 8 \text{ ms} + \frac{0.5}{7200 \text{ RPM}} + \frac{16 \text{ KB}}{6 \text{ MB/sec}} = 8 + 4.2 + 2.7 = 14.9 \text{ ms}$$

so the disk performance is

$$\text{Maximum IOPS (using average seeks) per disk} = \frac{1}{14.9 \text{ ms}} \approx 67 \text{ IOPS}$$

The number of disks in each organization depends on the size of each disk: 200 GB can be either 25 8-GB disks or 100 2-GB disks. The maximum number of I/Os for all the disks is

$$\text{Maximum IOPS for 25 8-GB disks} = 25 \times 67 = 1675$$
$$\text{Maximum IOPS for 100 2-GB disks} = 100 \times 67 = 6700$$

Thus, provided there are enough SCSI-2 strings, the disks become the new limit to maximum performance: 1675 IOPS for the 8-GB disks and 6700 for the 2-GB disks.

Although we have determined the performance of each link of the I/O chain, we still have to determine how many SCSI-2 buses and controllers to use and how many disks to connect to each controller, as this may further limit maximum performance. The I/O bus is limited to 20 SCSI-2 controllers, and the limit is 15 disks per SCSI-2 string. The minimum number of controllers for the 8-GB disks is

$$\text{Minimum number of SCSI-2 strings for 25 8-GB disks} = \left\lceil \frac{25}{15} \right\rceil \text{ or } 2$$

and for 2-GB disks

$$\text{Minimum number of SCSI-2 strings for 100 2-GB disks} = \left\lceil \frac{100}{15} \right\rceil \text{ or } 7$$

We can calculate the maximum IOPS for each configuration:

$$\text{Maximum IOPS for 2 SCSI-2 strings} = 2 \times 556 = 1112$$
$$\text{Maximum IOPS for 7 SCSI-2 strings} = 7 \times 556 = 3892$$

The maximum performance of this number of controllers is slightly lower than the disk I/O throughput, so let's also calculate the number of controllers so they don't become a bottleneck. One way is to find the number of disks they can support per string:

$$\text{Number of disks per SCSI string at full bandwidth} = \left\lfloor \frac{556}{67} \right\rfloor = \lfloor 8.3 \rfloor \text{ or } 8$$

and then calculate the number of strings:

$$\text{Number of SCSI strings for full bandwidth 8-GB disks} = \left\lceil \frac{25}{8} \right\rceil = \lceil 3.1 \rceil \text{ or } 4$$

$$\text{Number of SCSI strings for full bandwidth 2-GB disks} = \left\lceil \frac{100}{8} \right\rceil = \lceil 12.5 \rceil \text{ or } 13$$

This establishes the performance of four organizations: 25 8-GB disks with 2 or 4 SCSI-2 strings and 100 2-GB disks with 7 or 13 SCSI-2 strings. Using the format

$$\text{Min(CPU limit, memory limit, I/O bus limit, disk limit, string limit)}$$

the maximum performance of each option is limited by the bottleneck (in boldface):

8-GB disks, 2 strings = Min(50,000, 10,000, 12,500, 1675,**1112**) = 1112 IOPS
8-GB disks, 4 strings = Min(50,000, 10,000, 12,500, **1675**, 2224) = 1675 IOPS
2-GB disks, 7 strings = Min(50,000, 10,000, 12,500, 6700, **3892**) = 3892 IOPS
2-GB disks, 13 strings = Min(50,000, 10,000, 12,500, **6700**, 7228) = 6700 IOPS

We can now calculate the cost for each organization:

8-GB disks, 2 strings = \$30,000 + 2 × \$1500 + 25 × (8192 × \$0.25) = \$84,200
8-GB disks, 4 strings = \$30,000 + 4 × \$1500 + 25 × (8192 × \$0.25) = \$87,200
2-GB disks, 7 strings = \$30,000 + 7 × \$1500 + 100 × (2048 × \$0.25) = \$91,700
2-GB disks, 13 strings = \$30,000 + 13 × \$1500 + 100 × (2048 × \$0.25) = \$100,700

Finally, the cost per IOPS for each of the four configurations is \$76, \$52, \$24, and \$15, respectively. Calculating the maximum number of average I/Os per second, assuming 100% utilization of the critical resources, the best cost/performance is the organization with the small disks and the largest number of controllers. The small disks have about 3.5 times better cost/performance than the large disks in this example. The only drawback is that the larger number of disks will affect system availability unless some form of redundancy is added (see section 6.5). ∎

This example assumed that resources can be used 100%. It is instructive to see what the bottleneck is in each organization.

EXAMPLE   For the organizations in the last example, calculate the percentage of utilization of each resource in the computer system.

ANSWER   Figure 6.31 gives the answer. Either the disks or the SCSI buses are the bottleneck.

Resource	8-GB disks, 2 strings	8-GB disks, 4 strings	2-GB disks, 7 strings	2-GB disks, 13 strings
CPU	2%	3%	8%	13%
Memory	11%	17%	39%	67%
I/O bus	9%	13%	31%	54%
SCSI-2 buses	100%	75%	100%	93%
Disks	66%	100%	58%	100%
IOPS	1112	1675	3892	6700

FIGURE 6.31   The percentage of utilization of each resource and peak IOPS given the four organizations in the previous example. Either the SCSI-2 buses or the disks are the bottleneck.

∎

While it is useful to learn where the bottleneck is, it's more important to see the impact on response time as we approach 100% utilization of a resource. Let's do this for one configuration from Figure 6.31.

EXAMPLE   Recalculate performance for, say, the second column in Figure 6.31, but this time in terms of response time. Assume that all requests are in a single wait line. To simplify the calculation, ignore the SCSI-2 strings and just calculate for the 25 disks. According to Figure 6.31, the peak I/O rate is 1675 IOPS. Plot the mean response time for the following number of I/Os per second: 1000, 1100, 1200, 1300, 1400, 1500, 1550, 1600, 1625, 1650, 1670. Assume the time between requests is exponentially distributed.

ANSWER   To be able to calculate the average response time, we need the equation for an M/M/m queue; that is, for m servers rather than one. From Jain [1991] we get the formulas for that queue:

$$\text{Server utilization} = \frac{\text{Arrival rate}}{\dfrac{1}{\text{Time}_{\text{server}}/m}} = \text{Arrival rate} \times \frac{\text{Time}_{\text{server}}}{m}$$

$$\text{Time}_{\text{system}} = \text{Time}_{\text{server}} \times \left(1 + \frac{\text{Prob} \ (>=m)}{m \times 1 - \text{Util}_{\text{server}}}\right)$$

That is, the average service time for m servers is simply the average service time of one server divided by the number of servers.

From the example above we know that we have 25 disks and that the mean service time is 14.9 ms. Figure 6.32 shows the utilization and mean response time for each of the request rates, and Figure 6.33 plots the response times as the request rate varies.

Request rate	Utilization	Mean response time (ms)
1000	60%	15.8
1100	66%	16.0
1200	72%	16.4
1300	77%	16.9
1400	83%	17.9
1500	89%	19.9
1550	92%	22.1
1600	95%	27.1
1625	97%	33.1
1650	98%	49.8
1670	100%	137.0

FIGURE 6.32   Utilization and mean response time for 25 large disks in the prior example, ignoring the impact of SCSI-2 buses and controllers.

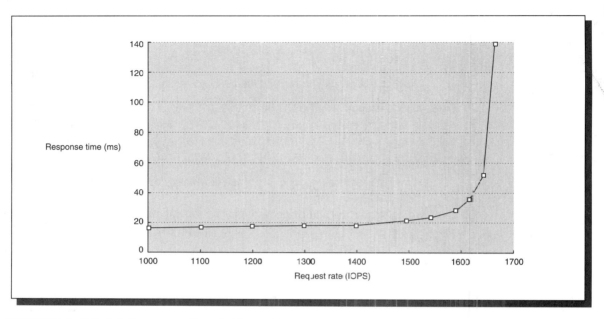

FIGURE 6.33   X-Y plot of response times in Figure 6.32.

Figure 6.33 shows the severe increase in response time when trying to use 100% of a server. A variety of rules of thumb have been evolved to guide I/O designers to keep response time and contertion low:

- No I/O bus should be utilized more than 75%.

- No disk string should be utilized more than 40%.

- No disk arm should be seeking more than 60% of the time.

- No disk should be used more than 80% of the time.

EXAMPLE   Recalculate performance in the example above using these rules of thumb, and show the utilization of each component.

ANSWER   Figure 6.31 shows that the I/O bus is far below the suggested guidelines, so we concentrate on the disks, utilization of disk seeking, and SCSI-2 bus. The new limit on IOPS for disks used 80% of the time is 67 × 0.8 = 54 IOPS. The utilization of seek time per disk is

$$\frac{\text{Time of average seek}}{\text{Time between I/Os}} = \frac{8}{\frac{1}{54\text{ IOPS}}} = \frac{8}{18.5} = 43\%$$

which is below the rule of thumb. The biggest impact is on the SCSI-2 bus:

$$\text{Suggested IOPS per SCSI-2 string} = \frac{1}{1.8 \text{ ms}} \times 40\% = 222 \text{ IOPS}$$

With this data we can recalculate IOPS for each organization:

8-GB disks, 2 strings   = Min(50,000,10,000, 9375, 1350, **444**)   = 444 IOPS
8-GB disks, 4 strings   = Min(50,000,10,000, 9375, 1350, **888**)   = 888 IOPS
2-GB disks, 7 strings   = Min(50,000,10,000, 9375, 5400, **1554**) = 1554 IOPS
2-GB disks, 13 strings = Min(50,000,10,000, 9375, 5400, **2886**) = 2886 IOPS

Under these assumptions, the small disks have about 3.5 times the performance of the large disks.

Clearly, the string bandwidth is the bottleneck now. The number of disks per string that would not exceed the guideline is

$$\text{Number of disks per SCSI-2 string at full bandwidth} = \left\lfloor \frac{222}{54} \right\rfloor = \lfloor 4.1 \rfloor = 4$$

and the ideal number of strings is

$$\text{Number of SCSI-2 strings with 8-GB disks} = \left\lceil \frac{25}{4} \right\rceil = \lceil 6.3 \rceil = 7$$

$$\text{Number of SCSI-2 strings for full bandwidth with 2-GB disks} = \left\lceil \frac{100}{4} \right\rceil = 25$$

This suggestion is fine for 8-GB disks, but the I/O bus is limited to 20 SCSI-2 controllers and strings so that becomes the limit for 2-GB disks:

8-GB disks, 7 strings   = Min(50,000, 10,000, 9375, **1350**, 1554) = 1350 IOPS
2-GB disks, 20 strings = Min(50,000, 10,000, 9375, 5400, **4440**) = 4440 IOPS

Notice that the IOPS for the large disks is in the flat part of the response time graph in Figure 6.33, as we would hope. We can now calculate the cost for each organization:

8-GB disks, 7 strings   = $30,000 + 7 \times $1500 + 25 \times (8192 \times $0.25)   = $91,700
2-GB disks, 20 strings = $30,000 + 20 \times $1500 + 100 \times (2048 \times $0.25) = $111,200

The respective cost per IOPS is $68 versus $25, or an advantage of about 2.7 for the small disks. Compared with the earlier naive assumption that we could use 100% of resources, the cost per IOPS increased $10 to $15. Figure 6.34 shows the new utilization of each resource by following these guidelines. Following the rule of thumb of 40% string utilization sets the performance limit in every case. Exercise 6.18 explores what happens when this SCSI limit is relaxed.

Resource	8-GB disks, 2 strings	8-GB disks, 4 strings	2-GB disks, 7 strings	2-GB disks, 13 strings	8-GB disks, 7 strings	2-GB disks, 20 strings
CPU	1%	2%	3%	6%	3%	9%
Memory	4%	9%	16%	29%	16%	44%
I/O bus	4%	7%	12%	23%	12%	36%
SCSI-2 buses	40%	40%	40%	40%	40%	40%
Disks	27%	53%	23%	43%	23%	66%
Seek utilization	14%	28%	12%	23%	12%	36%
IOPS	444	888	1554	2886	1350	4400

FIGURE 6.34 The percentage of utilization of each resource, given the six organizations in this Example, which tries to limit utilization of key resources to the rules of thumb given above.

■

Queuing theory can also help us to answer questions about I/O controllers and buses.

EXAMPLE The SCSI controller will send requests down the bus to the device and then get data back on a read. One issue is the impact of returning the data in a single 16-KB transfer versus four 4-KB transfers. How long does it take for the drive to see the request for each workload? Assume that there are many disks on the SCSI bus, that the time between arriving SCSI requests is exponential, that the bus is occupied during the entire transfer, that the overhead for each SCSI activity is 1 ms plus the time to transfer the data, and that the CPU issues 100 disk reads per second on this SCSI bus.

ANSWER The times between arrivals are exponential, but we need the distribution of the service times on the SCSI bus. For the 16-KB transfer size there are just two sizes: very small and 16 KB, and so the times are 1 ms or

$$1 \text{ ms} + \frac{16 \text{ KB}}{20 \text{ MB/sec}} = 1 + 0.8 = 1.8 \text{ ms}$$

In fact, for each CPU request taking 1 ms there is exactly one transfer taking 1.8 ms, so the distribution is half 1-ms service times and half 1.8-ms service times. A 4-KB transfer takes

$$1 \text{ ms} + \frac{4 \text{ KB}}{20 \text{ MB/sec}} = 1 + 0.2 = 1.2 \text{ ms}$$

For every request of 1.0 ms there are four 1.2-ms transfers. Neither distribution is exponential, so we must use the general model for service interarrival times. Since the SCSI bus acts as a single queue following the FIFO discipline, we must use the M/G/1 model to answer this question.

The proper formula to predict the time before a single transfer comes from page 513:

$$\text{Time}_{queue} = \frac{\text{Time}_{server} \times (1 + C) \times \text{Server utilization}}{2 \times (1 - \text{Server utilization})}$$

Thus we must first calculate Time_{server}, Server utilization, and C.

For a single transfer, the average time before the disk can transfer is

$$\text{Time}_{server} = \text{Weighted mean time} = \frac{f_1 \times T_1 + f_2 \times T_2 + \dots + f_n \times T_n}{f_1 + f_2 + \dots + f_n} = \frac{0.5 \times 1 + 0.5 \times 1.8}{0.5 + 0.5} = 1.4 \text{ ms}$$

$$\text{Server utilization} = \frac{\text{Arrival rate}}{1/\text{Time}_{server}} = \text{Arrival rate} \times \text{Time}_{server} = (100 \times (1 + 1))/\text{sec} \times 1.4 \text{ ms} = 200/\text{sec} \times 0.0014 \text{ sec} = 0.28$$

$$\text{Variance} = \frac{f_1 \times T_1^2 + f_2 \times T_2^2 + \dots + f_n \times T_n^2}{f_1 + f_2 + \dots + f_n} - \text{Time}_{server}^2$$

$$\text{Variance} = \frac{0.5 \times 1^2 + 0.5 \times 1.8^2}{0.5 + 0.5} - 1.4^2 = 0.5 + 1.62 - 1.96 = 2.12 - 1.96 = 0.16$$

$$C = \frac{\text{Variance}}{\text{Time}_{server}^2} = \frac{0.16}{1.4^2} = \frac{0.16}{1.96} = 0.082$$

$$\text{Time}_{queue} = \frac{\text{Time}_{server} \times (1 + C) \times \text{Server utilization}}{2 \times (1 - \text{Server utilization})} = \frac{1.4 \text{ ms} \times (1 + 0.082) \times 0.28}{2 \times (1 - 0.16)} = \frac{0.424}{1.440} \text{ ms} = 0.294 \text{ ms}$$

For the case where the transfer is broken into four 4-KB pieces, the time is

$$\text{Time}_{\text{server}} = \text{Weighted mean time} = \frac{f_1 \times T_1 + f_2 \times T_2 - \ldots + f_n \times T_n}{f_1 + f_2 + \ldots + f_n} = \frac{0.2 \times 1 + 0.8 \times 1.2}{0.2 + 0.8} = 1.16 \text{ ms}$$

$$\text{Server utilization} = \text{Arrival rate} \times \text{Time}_{\text{server}} = (100 \times (1 + 4))/\text{sec} \times 1.16 \text{ ms} = 500/\text{sec} \times 0.0016 \text{ sec} = 0.58$$

$$\text{Variance} = \frac{f_1 \times T_1^2 + f_2 \times T_2^2 + \ldots + f_n \times T_n^2}{f_1 + f_2 + \ldots + f_n} - \text{Time}_{\text{server}}^2$$

$$\text{Variance} = \frac{0.2 \times 1^2 + 0.8 \times 1.2^2}{0.2 + 0.8} - 1.16^2 = 0.2 + 1.152 - 1.346 = 1.352 - 1.346 = 0.006$$

$$C = \frac{\text{Variance}}{\text{Time}_{\text{server}}^2} = \frac{0.006}{1.16^2} = \frac{0.006}{1.346} = 0.005$$

$$\text{Time}_{\text{queue}} = \frac{\text{Time}_{\text{server}} \times (1 + C) \times \text{Server utilization}}{2 \times (1 - \text{Server utilization})} = \frac{1.16 \text{ ms} \times (1 + 0.005) \times 0.58}{2 \times (1 - 0.58)} = \frac{0.676}{0.840} \text{ ms} = 0.805 \text{ ms}$$

For these parameters, the single large transfer wins: 0.3 ms versus 0.8 ms. Although it might seem better to break the transfer into smaller pieces so that a request doesn't have to wait for the long transfer, the collective SCSI overhead on each transfer increases bus utilization so as to overcome the benefits of the shorter transfers.   ■

6.8 | Putting It All Together: UNIX File System Performance

This section compares the file-system performance of several operating systems and hardware systems in use in 1995 (see Figure 6.35). It is based on a paper by Chen and Patterson [1994a].

As a preview, this evaluation once again shows that I/O performance is limited by the weakest link in the chain between the disk and the operating system. The hardware determines potential I/O performance, but the operating system determines how much of that potential is delivered. In particular, for UNIX systems the file cache is critical to I/O performance. The main observations are that file cache performance of UNIX on mainframes and mini-supercomputers is no better than workstations, and that file caching policy is of overriding importance. Optimized memory systems can increase read performance, but the operating-system policy on writes can result in orders of magnitude differences in file cache performance.

Given the warnings above, we *cannot* say that IBM mainframes have lower disk performance than workstations, nor that Convex has the fastest disk subsystem. We *can* say that the IBM 3090-600J running AIX/ESA under VM performs 32-KB reads to a single IBM 3390 disk drive much more slowly than a Convex C240 running Convex OS10 reads 32-KB blocks from a four-disk RAID.

The conclusions we draw from Figure 6.36 are that many workstation I/O subsystems can sustain the performance of a high-speed single disk, that a RAID disk array can deliver much higher performance, and that the performance of a single mainframe disk on a 3090 model 600J running AIX/ESA under VM is no faster than many workstations.

Basic File Cache Performance

For UNIX systems the most important factor in I/O performance is not how fast the disk is, or how efficiently it is used, but *whether* it is used. Operating systems designers' concern for performance led them to cache-like optimizations, using main memory as a "cache" for disk traffic to improve I/O performance. Since main memory is much faster than disks, file caches yield a substantial performance improvement and are found in every UNIX operating system. Figure 6.37 shows the change in disk I/Os versus a cacheless system measured as miss rate.

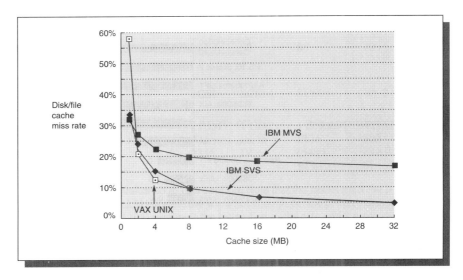

FIGURE 6.37   The effectiveness of a file cache or disk cache on reducing disk I/Os versus cache size. Ousterhout et al. [1985] collected the VAX UNIX data on VAX-11/785s with 8 MB to 16 MB of main memory, running 4.2 BSD UNIX using a 16-KB block size. Smith [1985] collected the IBM SVS and IBM MVS traces on IBM 370/168 using a one-track block size (which varied from 7294 bytes to 19,254 bytes, depending on the disk). The difference between a file cache and a disk cache is that the file cache uses logical block numbers while a disk cache uses addresses that have been mapped to the physical sector and track on a disk. This difference is similar to the difference between a virtually addressed and a physically addressed cache (see section 5.5).

Figure 6.38 shows this file cache performance for the machines of Figure 6.35. The first thing to notice is the change in scale of the chart: machines read from their file caches 3 to 25 times faster than from their disks. The performance of the file cache is determined by the processor, cache, CPU-memory bus, main memory, and operating system. Except for the size of memory and perhaps the operating system, there is little choice in these components when selecting a computer. Hence observations about commercial systems can be drawn about file cache performance with much more confidence than with the disks, since this portion of the system will be common at most sites.

The biggest surprise is that the mainframe and mini-supercomputers did not lead this chart, given their much greater cost and reputation for high-bandwidth memory systems and CPU-memory buses. At the top of the list is the Alpha AXP/3000 and HP 730 workstation running HP/UX version 8, both delivering over 30 MB per second. Unlike most workstations, the Alpha 3000 and HP 730 have interleaved main memories; that may explain their fast file cache performance. The IBM RS/6000 model 550 comes in third, and it also has high memory bandwidth. This chart also shows rapid file cache improvement in workstations. For example, both the SparcStation 10 and DEC Alpha AXP/3000 are more than four times faster than their predecessors, the SparcStation 1 and the DecStation 5000.

In addition, Figure 6.38 shows the impact of operating systems on I/O performance; the Sprite operating system offers 1.7 times the file cache performance of Ultrix running on the same DecStation 5000 hardware. Sprite does fewer copies when reading data from the file cache than does Ultrix, hence its higher performance. Fewer copies are important for networks as well as storage, as we shall see in the next chapter.

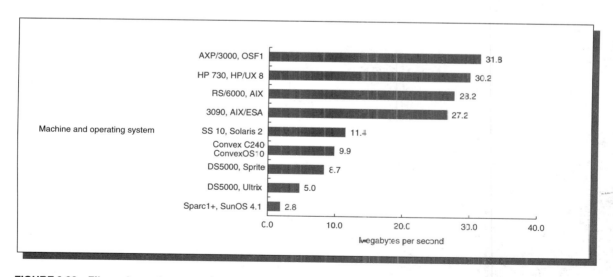

FIGURE 6.38 File cache performance for machines in Figure 6.35. This plot is for 32-KB reads with the number of bytes touched limited to fit within the file cache of each system. Figure 6.39 (page 545) shows the size of the file caches that achieve this performance. (See the caption of Figure 6.39 for details on measurements.)

The Impact of Operating System Policies on File Cache Performance

Given that UNIX systems have common ancestors, we expected that the operating system policies toward I/O would be the same on all machines. Instead, we find that different systems have very different I/O policies, and some policies alter I/O performance by factors of 10 to 75. Even though the machines measured vary significantly in cost, these policies can be more important than the underlying hardware. These file systems are aimed largely at the same customers running the same applications, which calls into question the low performance of some of these policies.

File Cache Size

Since main memory must be used for running programs as well as for the file cache, the first policy decision is how much main memory should be allocated to the file cache. The second is whether or not the size of the file cache can change dynamically. Early UNIX systems give the file cache a fixed percentage of main memory; this percentage is determined at the time of system generation, and is typically set to 10%. Recent systems allow the barrier between file cache and program memory to vary, allowing file caches to grow to be virtually the full size of the main memory if warranted by the workload. File servers, for example, will surely use much more of their main memory for file cache than will most client workstations.

Figure 6.39 shows these maximum file cache sizes, both in percentage of main memory and in absolute size. The reason for the large variation in percentage of main memory is the file cache size policy. HP/UX version 8, Ultrix, and AIX/ESA all reserve small, fixed portions of main memory for the file cache.

Figure 6.37 (page 542) shows that UNIX workloads benefit from larger file caches, so this fixed-size policy surely hurts I/O performance. Note that Sprite, running on the same hardware as Ultrix, has more than six times the file cache size, and that the SparcStation 1 has a file cache almost as large as the IBM 3090, even though the mainframe has four times the physical memory of the workstation. When the flexible file cache boundary policy is combined with large main memories, we can get astounding file caches: the Convex C240 file cache is almost 900 MB! Thus workloads that would require disk accesses on other machines will instead access main memory on the Convex.

Write Policy

Thus far we have unrealistically left the O out of I/O. There is often some confusion about the definition and implications of alternative write strategies for caches. To lessen that confusion, we first review write policies of processor caches.

Write through with write buffers and write back applies to file caches as well as processor caches. The operating systems community uses the term *asynchronous writes* for writes that allow the processor to continue after updating a write

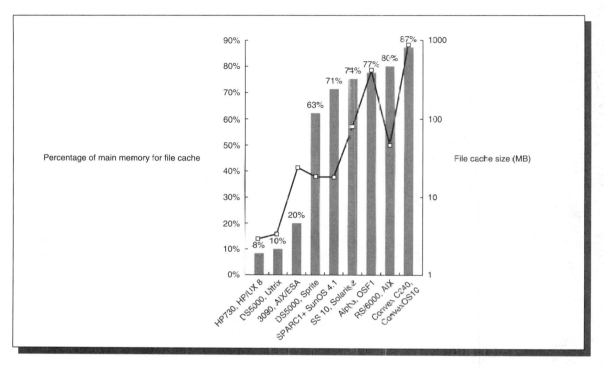

FIGURE 6.39 File cache size. The bar graph shows the maximum percentage of main memory for the file cache, while the line graph shows the maximum size in megabytes, using the log scale on the right. Thus the HP 730 HP/UX version 8 uses only 8% of its 32-MB main memory for its file cache, or just 2.7 MB, and the Convex C240 uses 87% of its 1024-MB main memory, or 890 MB, for its file cache.

buffer. If writes occur infrequently, then this buffer works well; if writes are frequent, then the processor may eventually have to stall until the write buffer empties, limiting the speed to that of the next level of the memory hierarchy. Note that a write buffer does not reduce the number of writes to the next level. It just allows the processor to continue while I/O is in progress, provided that the write buffer is not full.

Figure 6.40 shows the file cache performance as we vary the mix of reads and writes. Clearly HP/UX and Sprite use a write-back cache; while it is hard to see with this figure, the Sun OS 4.1 write performance is nearly as fast as reads and much faster than disks, so it also uses write back. We can tell that the other operating systems use write through because their write performance matches disk speed. Note that three of the highest performers in Figure 6.38—RS/6000, IBM 3090, and Alpha AXP/3000—fall to the back of the pack unless the percentage of reads is more than 90%.

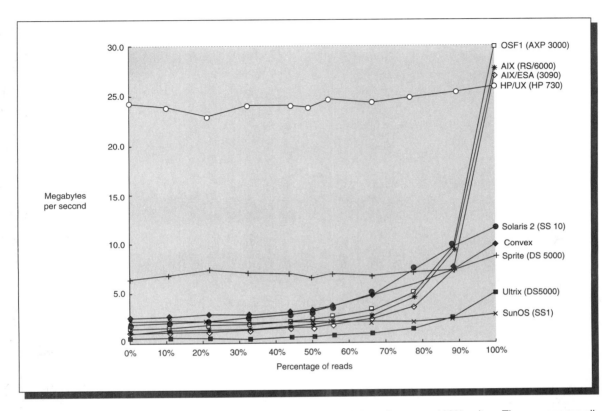

FIGURE 6.40   File cache performance versus read percentage. 0% reads means 100% writes. These accesses all fit within the file caches of the respective machines. Note that the high performance of the file caches of the AXP/3000, RS/6000, and 3090 are only evident for workloads with ≥ 90% reads. Access sizes are 32 KB. (See the caption of Figure 6.36 for details on measurements.)

The effectiveness of caches for writes also depends on the policy of flushing dirty data to the disk; to protect against losing information in case of failures, applications will occasionally issue a command that forces modified data out of the cache and onto the disk. Most UNIX operating systems have a policy of periodically writing dirty data to disk to give a safety window for all applications; typically, the window is 30 seconds.

The short lives of files means that files will be deleted or overwritten and so their data need not be written to disk. Baker et al. [1991] found that this 30-second window captures 65% to 80% of the lifetimes for all files. Hartman and Ousterhout [1993] reported that 36% to 63% of the bytes written do not survive a 30-second window; this number jumps to 60% to 95% in a 1000-second window. Given that such short lifetimes mean that file cache blocks will be rewritten, it seems wise for more operating system policy makers to consider write-back caches provided a 30-second window meets the failure requirements.

Write Policy for Client/Server Computing

Thus far we have been ignoring the network and the possibility that the files exist on a file server. Figure 6.41 shows performance for three combinations of clients and servers:

- An HP 712/60 client running HP-UX 9.05 with an Auspex file server (a 10 SPARC multiprocessor designed for file service)

- An IBM RS6000/520 client running AIX 3.0 with a RS6000/320H server

- A Sun SPARC 10/50 client running Solaris 2.3 with a Sun SPARC 10/50 server

All client/server pairs were connected by an Ethernet local area network. Figure 6.41 shows file cache performance as a percentage of reads when the files are reached over the networks.

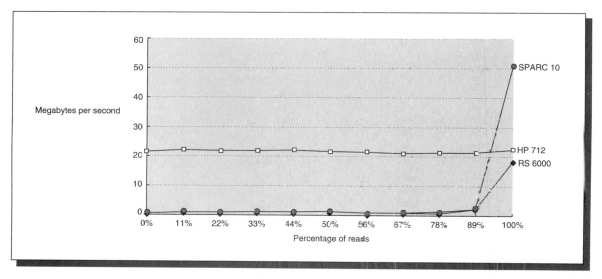

FIGURE 6.41   File cache performance versus percentage of reads for client/server computing. An IBM RS 6000 is 75 times slower than an HP 712 running the DUX network file system.

This experiment brings us to the issue of consistency of files in multiple file caches. The concern is that multiple copies of files in the client caches and on the server create the possibility that someone will access the wrong version of the data. This raises a policy question: How do you ensure that no one accesses stale data? The NFS solution, used by SunOS, is to make all client writes go to the server's disk when the file is closed. It would seem that if the 30-second delay was satisfactory for writes to local disk, then a 30-second delay would also be acceptable before client writes must be sent to the server, thereby allowing the same benefits to accrue. Hence HP/UX 9 offers an alternative network protocol, called

DUX, which allows client-level caching of writes. The server keeps track of potential conflicts and takes the appropriate action only when the file is shared and someone is writing it. Using a shared-bus multiprocessor as a rough analogy to our workstations on the local area network, DUX offers write back with cache coherency, while NFS does write through without write buffers.

The 100%-read case—the rightmost portion of the graph—shows the differences in performance of the hardware, where SPARC 10 is twice as fast as the HP 712. The rest of the graph shows the differences in performance due to the write policies of their operating systems. The HP system is the clear winner: It is 75 times faster than the RS/6000 and 25 times faster than the SPARC 10 for workloads with mostly writes, and still 14 to 20 times faster even when only 20% of the accesses are writes. Put another way, for all but the most heavily read-oriented workloads, the RS/6000 and SPARC 10 clients operate at disk speed while the HP client runs at main memory speed.

Conclusion

Hardware determines the potential I/O performance, but the operating system determines how much of that potential is delivered. As a result of the studies in this section, we conclude the following:

- File caching policy determines performance of most I/O events, and hence is the place to start when trying to improve I/O performance.

- File cache performance in workstations is improving rapidly, with more than fourfold improvements in three years for DEC (AXP/3000 vs. DecStation 5000) and Sun (SparcStation 10 vs. SparcStation 1+).

- File cache performance of UNIX on mainframes and mini-supercomputers is no better than on workstations.

- Workstations can take advantage of high-performance disks.

- RAID systems can deliver much higher disk performance, but cannot overcome weaknesses in file cache policy.

Given the varying decisions in this matter by companies serving the same market, we hope this section motivates file cache designers to give greater emphasis to quantitative evaluations of policy decisions.

6.9 | Fallacies and Pitfalls

Pitfall: Comparing the price of media with the price of the packaged system.

This happens most frequently when new memory technologies are compared with magnetic disks. For example, comparing the DRAM-chip price with magnetic-disk packaged price in Figure 6.5 (page 492) suggests the difference is less than a factor of 10, but it's much greater when the price of packaging DRAM is included. A common mistake with removable media is to compare the media cost not including the drive to read the media. For example, a CD-ROM costs only $2 per gigabyte in 1995, but including the cost of the optical drive may bring the price closer to $200 per gigabyte.

Figure 6.7 (page 495) suggests another example. When comparing a single disk to a tape library, it would seem that tape libraries have little benefit. There are two mistakes in this comparison. The first is that economy of scale applies to tape libraries, and so the economical end is for large tape libraries. The second is that it is more than twice as expensive per gigabyte to purchase a disk storage subsystem that can store terabytes than it is to buy one that can store gigabytes. Reasons for increased cost include packing, interfaces, redundancy to make a system with many disks sufficiently reliable, and so on. These same factors don't apply to tape libraries since they are designed to be sufficiently reliable to store terabytes without extra redundancy. These two mistakes change the ratio by a factor of 10 when comparing large tape libraries with large disk subsystems.

Fallacy: The time of an average seek of a disk in a computer system is the time for a seek of one-third the number of cylinders.

This fallacy comes from confusing the way manufacturers market disks with the expected performance and with the false assumption that seek times are linear in distance. The one-third-distance rule of thumb comes from calculating the distance of a seek from one random location to another random location, not including the current cylinder and assuming there are a large number of cylinders. In the past, manufacturers listed the seek of this distance to offer a consistent basis for comparison. (As mentioned on page 488, today they calculate the "average" by timing all seeks and dividing by the number.) Assuming (incorrectly) that seek time is linear in distance, and using the manufacturer's reported minimum and "average" seek times, a common technique to predict seek time is

$$\text{Time}_{seek} = \text{Time}_{minimum} + \frac{\text{Distance}}{\text{Distance}_{average}} \times (\text{Time}_{average} - \text{Time}_{minimum})$$

The fallacy concerning seek time is twofold. First, seek time is *not* linear with distance; the arm must accelerate to overcome inertia, reach its maximum traveling speed, decelerate as it reaches the requested position, and then wait to allow the arm to stop vibrating (*settle time*). Moreover, sometimes the arm must pause to control vibrations. Figure 6.42 plots time versus seek distance for a sample disk. It also shows the error in the simple seek-time formula above. For short seeks, the acceleration phase plays a larger role than the maximum traveling speed, and this phase is typically modeled as the square root of the distance. For disks with more than 200 cylinders, Chen and Lee [1995] modeled the seek distance as

$$\text{Seek time (Distance)} = a \times \sqrt{\text{Distance} - 1} - b \times (\text{Distance} - 1) + c$$

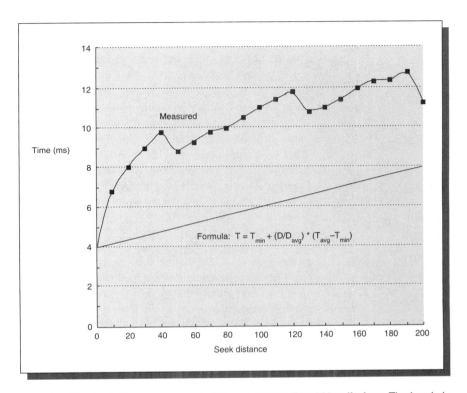

FIGURE 6.42   Seek time versus seek distance for the first 200 cylinders. The Imprimis Sabre 97209 contains 1.2 GB using 1635 cylinders and has the IPI-2 interface [Imprimis 1989]. This is an 8-inch disk. Note that longer seeks can take less time than shorter seeks. For example, a 40-cylinder seek takes almost 10 ms, while a 50-cylinder seek takes less than 9 ms.

where a, b, and c are selected for a particular disk so that this formula will match the quoted times for Distance = 1, Distance = max, and Distance = 1/3 max. Figure 6.43 plots this equation versus the fallacy equation for the disk in Figure 6.2.

The second problem is that the average in the product specification would only be true if there was no locality to disk activity. Fortunately, there is both temporal and spatial locality (see page 393 in Chapter 5): disk blocks get used more than once, and disk blocks near the current cylinder are more likely to be used than those farther away. For example, Figure 6.44 shows sample measurements of seek distances for two workloads: a UNIX timesharing workload and a business-processing workload. Notice the high percentage of disk accesses to the same cylinder, labeled distance 0 in the graphs, in both workloads.

Thus, this fallacy couldn't be more misleading. (The Exercises debunk this fallacy in more detail.)

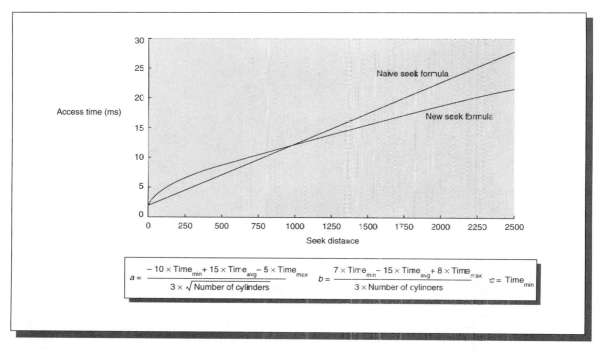

FIGURE 6.43 **Seek time versus seek distance for sophisticated model versus naive model for the disk in Figure 6.2 (page 490).** Chen and Lee [1995] found the equations shown above for parameters a, b, and c worked well for several disks.

Pitfall: Moving functions from the CPU to the I/O processor to improve performance.

There are many examples of this pitfall, although I/O processors can enhance performance. A problem inherent with a family of computers is that the migration of an I/O feature usually changes the instruction set architecture or system architecture in a programmer-visible way, causing all future machines to have to live with a decision that made sense in the past. If CPUs are improved in cost/performance more rapidly than the I/O processor (and this will likely be the case), then moving the function may result in a slower machine in the next CPU.

The most telling example comes from the IBM 360. It was decided that the performance of the ISAM system, an early database system, would improve if some of the record searching occurred in the disk controller itself. A key field was associated with each record, and the device searched each key as the disk rotated until it found a match. It would then transfer the desired record. For the disk to find the key, there had to be an extra gap in the track. This scheme is applicable to searches through indices as well as data.

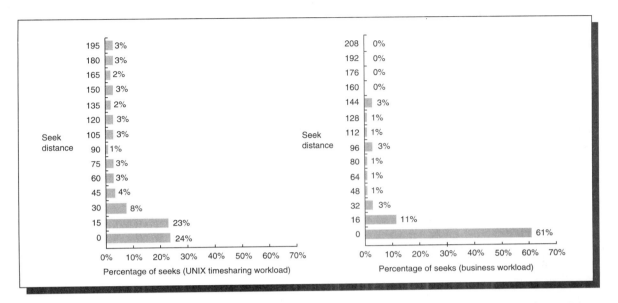

FIGURE 6.44 Sample measurements of seek distances for two systems. The measurements on the left were taken on a UNIX timesharing system. The measurements on the right were taken from a business-processing application in which the disk seek activity was scheduled. Seek distance of 0 means the access was made to the same cylinder. The rest of the numbers show the collective percentage for distances between numbers on the y axis. For example, 11% for the bar labeled 16 in the business graph means that the percentage of seeks between 1 and 16 cylinders was 11%. The UNIX measurements stopped at 200 cylinders, but this captured 85% of the accesses. The total was 1000 cylinders. The business measurements tracked all 816 cylinders of the disks. The only seek distances with 1% or greater of the seeks that are not in the graph are 224 with 4% and 304, 336, 512, and 624 each having 1%. This total is 94%, with the difference being small but nonzero distances in other categories. Measurements courtesy of Dave Anderson of Imprimis.

The speed at which a track can be searched is limited by the speed of the disk and of the number of keys that can be packed on a track. On an IBM 3330 disk, the key is typically 10 characters, but the total gap between records is equivalent to 191 characters if there were a key. (The gap is only 135 characters if there is no key, since there is no need for an extra gap for the key.) If we assume that the data is also 10 characters and that the track has nothing else on it, then a 13,165-byte track can contain

$$\frac{13,165}{191 + 10 + 10} = 62 \text{ key-data records}$$

This performance is

$$\frac{16.7 \text{ ms (1 revolution)}}{62} \approx .25 \text{ ms/key search}$$

In place of this scheme, we could put several key-data pairs in a single block and have smaller interrecord gaps. Assuming there are 15 key-data pairs per block and the track has nothing else on it, then

$$\frac{13,165}{135 + 15 \times (10 + 10)} = \frac{13,165}{135 + 300} = 30 \text{ blocks of key-data pairs}$$

The revised performance is then

$$\frac{16.7 \text{ ms (1 revolution)}}{30 \times 15} \approx 0.04 \text{ ms/key search}$$

Yet as CPUs got faster, the CPU time for a search was trivial. Although the strategy made early machines faster, programs that use the search-key operation in the I/O processor run almost six times slower on today's machines!

6.10 Concluding Remarks

According to Amdahl's Law, ignorance of I/O will lead to wasted performance as CPUs get faster. Disk performance is growing at 4% to 6% per year, while CPU performance is growing at a much faster rate. This performance gap has led to novel organizations to try to bridge it: file caches to improve latency and RAIDs to improve throughput. The future demands for I/O include better algorithms, better organizations, and more caching in a struggle to keep pace.

Nevertheless, the impressive improvement in capacity and cost per megabyte of disks and tape have made digital libraries plausible, whereby all of humankind's knowledge could be at the beck and call of your fingertips. Getting those requests to the libraries and the information back is the challenge of interconnection networks, the topic of the next chapter.

6.11 Historical Perspective and References

Mass storage is a term used there to imply a unit capacity in excess of one million alphanumeric characters...

Hoagland [1963]

Magnetic recording was invented to record sound, and by 1941 magnetic tape was able to compete with other storage devices. It was the success of the ENIAC in 1947 that led to the push to use tapes to record digital information. Reels of magnetic tapes dominated removable storage through the 1970s. In the 1980s the IBM 3480 cartridge became the de facto standard, at least for mainframes. It can transfer at 3 MB/sec since it reads 18 tracks in parallel. The capacity is just 200

MB for this 1/2-inch tape. In 1995 3M and IBM announced the IBM 3590, which transfers at 9 MB/sec and stores 10,000 MB. This device records the tracks in a zig-zag fashion rather than just longitudinally, so that the head reverses direction to follow the track. Its official name is *serpentine recording*. The other competitor is helical scan, which rotates the head to get the increased recording density. In 1995 the 8-mm tapes contain 6000 MB and transfer at about 1 MB/sec. Whatever their density and cost, the serial nature of tapes creates an appetite for storage devices with random access.

The magnetic disk first appeared in 1956 in the IBM Random Access Method of Accounting and Control (RAMAC) machine. This disk used 50 platters that were 24 inches in diameter, with a total capacity of 5 MB and an access time of 1 second. IBM maintained its leadership in the disk industry, and many of the future leaders of competing disk industries started their careers at IBM. The disk industry is responsible for 90% of the mass storage market.

Although RAMAC contained the first disk, the breakthrough in magnetic recording was found in later disks with air-bearing read-write heads. These allowed the head to ride on a cushion of air created by the fast-moving disk surface. This cushion meant the head could both follow imperfections in the surface and yet be very close to the surface. In 1995 heads fly 4 microinches above the surface, whereas the RAMAC drive was 1000 microinches away. Subsequent advances have been largely from improved quality of components and higher precision.

The second breakthough was the so-called Winchester disk design in about 1965. Before this time the cost of the electronics to control the disk meant that the media had to be removable. The integrated circuit lowered the costs of not only CPUs, but also of disk controllers and the electronics to control the arms. This price reduction meant that the media could be sealed with the reader. The sealed system meant the heads could fly closer to the surface, which led to increases in areal density. The IBM 1311 disk in 1962 had an areal density of 50,000 bits per square inch and a cost of about $800 per megabyte, and in 1995 IBM sells a disk using 640 million bits per square inch with a street price of about $0.25 per megabyte. (See Hospodor and Hoagland [1993] for more on magnetic storage trends.)

The personal computer created a market for small form-factor disk drives, since the 14-inch disk drives used in mainframes were bigger than the PC. In 1995 the 3.5-inch drive is the market leader, although the smaller 2.5-inch drive needed for portable computers is catching up quickly in sales volume. It remains to be seen whether hand-held devices, requiring even smaller disks, will become as popular as PCs or portables. These smaller disks inspired RAID; Chen et al. [1994] survey the RAID ideas and future directions.

One attraction of a personal computer is that you don't have to share it with anyone. This means that response time is predictable, unlike timesharing systems. Early experiments in the importance of fast response time were performed by Doherty and Kelisky [1979]. They showed that if computer-system response time increased one second, then user think time did also. Thadhani [1981] showed a jump in productivity as computer response times dropped to one second and another jump as they dropped to one-half second. His results inspired a flock of studies, and they supported his observations [IBM 1982]. In fact, some studies were started to disprove his results! Brady [1986] proposed differentiating entry time from think time (since entry time was becoming significant when the two were lumped together) and provided a cognitive model to explain the more-than-linear relationship between computer response time and user think time.

The ubiquitous microprocessor has inspired not only personal computers in the 1970s, but also the current trend to moving controller functions into I/O devices in the late 1980s and 1990s. I/O devices continued this trend by moving controllers into the devices themselves. These are called *intelligent devices*, and some bus standards (e.g., IPI and SCSI) have been created specifically for them. Intelligent devices can relax the timing constraints by handling many of the low-level tasks and queuing the results. For example, many SCSI-compatible disk drives include a track buffer on the disk itself, supporting read ahead and connect/disconnect. Thus, on a SCSI string some disks can be seeking and others loading their track buffer while one is transferring data from its buffer over the SCSI bus. The controller in the original RAMAC, built from vacuum tubes, only needed to move the head over the desired track, wait for the data to pass under the head, and transfer data with calculated parity.

SCSI, which stands for *small computer systems interface*, is an example of one company inventing a bus and generously encouraging other companies to build devices that would plug into it. This bus, originally called SASI, was invented by Shugart and was later standardized by the IEEE. Perhaps the first multivendor bus was the PDP-11 Unibus in 1970 from DEC. Alas, this open-door policy on buses is in contrast to companies with proprietary buses using patented interfaces, thereby preventing competition from plug-compatible vendors. This practice also raises costs and lowers availability of I/O devices that plug into proprietary buses, since such devices must have an interface designed just for that bus. The PCI bus being pushed by Intel gives us hope in 1995 of a return to open, standard I/O buses inside computers. There are also several candidates to be the successor to SCSI, most using simpler connectors and serial cables.

The machines of the RAMAC era gave us I/O interrupts as well as storage devices. The first machine to extend interrupts from detecting arithmetic abnormalities to detecting asynchronous I/O events is credited as the NBS DYSEAC in 1954 [Leiner and Alexander 1954]. The following year, the first machine with DMA was operational, the IBM SAGE. Just as today's DMA has, the SAGE had address counters that performed block transfers in parallel with CPU operations. (Smotherman [1989] explores the history of I/O in more depth.)

References

ANON, ET AL. [1985]. "A measure of transaction processing power," Tandem Tech. Rep. TR 85.2. Also appeared in *Datamation*, April 1, 1985.

BAKER, M. G., J. H. HARTMAN, M. D. KUPFER, K. W. SHIREIFF, AND J. K. OUSTERHOUT [1991]. "Measurements of a distributed file system," *Proc. 13th ACM Symposium on Operating Systems Principles* (October), 198–212.

6.3 [20] <6.9> Using the formulas in the fallacy starting on page 549, including the caption of Figure 6.43 (page 551) and the statistics in Figure 6.44 (page 552), calculate the average seek distance on the disk in Figure 6.2 (page 490). Use the midpoint of a range as the seek distance. For example, use 98 as the seek distance for the entry representing 91–105 in Figure 6.44. For the business workload, just ignore the missing 5% of the seeks. For the UNIX workload, assume the missing 15% of the seeks have an average distance of 300 cylinders. If you were misled by the fallacy, you might calculate the average distance as 884/3. What is the measured distance for each workload?

6.4 [20] <6.9> Figure 6.2 (page 490) gives the manufacturer's average seek time. Using the formulas in the fallacy starting on page 549, including the equations in Figure 6.43 (page 551), and the statistics in Figure 6.44 (page 552), what is the average seek time for each workload on the disk in Figure 6.2 using the measurements? Make the same assumptions as in Exercise 6.3.

6.5 [20/15/15/15/15/15] <6.4> The I/O bus and memory system of a computer are capable of sustaining 1000 MB/sec without interfering with the performance of an 800-MIPS CPU (costing $50,000). Here are the assumptions about the software:

- Each transaction requires 2 disk reads plus 2 disk writes.

- The operating system uses 15,000 instructions for each disk read or write.

- The database software executes 40,000 instructions to process a transaction.

- The transfer size is 100 bytes.

You have a choice of two different types of disks:

- A small disk that stores 500 MB and costs $100.

- A big disk that stores 1250 MB and costs $250.

Either disk in the system can support on average 30 disk reads or writes per second.

Answer parts (a)–(f) using the TPS benchmark in section 6.4. Assume that the requests are spread evenly to all the disks, that there is no waiting time due to busy disks, and that the account file must be large enough to handle 1000 TPS according to the benchmark ground rules.

a.   [20] <6.4> How many TPS transactions per second are possible with each disk organization, assuming that each uses the minimum number of disks to hold the account file?

b.   [15] <6.4> What is the system cost per transaction per second of each alternative for TPS?

c.   [15] <6.4> How fast does a CPU need to be to make the 1000 MB/sec I/O bus a bottleneck for TPS? (Assume that you can continue to add disks.)

d.   [15] <6.4> As manager of MTP (Mega TP), you are deciding whether to spend your development money building a faster CPU or improving the performance of the software. The database group says they can reduce a transaction to 1 disk read and 1 disk write and cut the database instructions per transaction to 30,000. The hardware group can build a faster CPU that sells for the same amount as the slower CPU with the same development budget. (Assume you can add as many disks as needed to get higher performance.) How much faster does the CPU have to be to match the performance gain of the software improvement?

e. [15] <6.4> The MTP I/O group was listening at the door during the software presentation. They argue that advancing technology will allow CPUs to get faster without significant investment, but that the cost of the system will be dominated by disks if they don't develop new small, faster disks. Assume the next CPU is 100% faster at the same cost and that the new disks have the same capacity as the old ones. Given the new CPU and the old software, what will be the cost of a system with enough old small disks so that they do not limit the TPS of the system?

f. [15] <6.4> Start with the same assumptions as in part (e). Now assume that you have as many new disks as you had old small disks in the original design. How fast must the new disks be (I/Os per second) to achieve the same TPS rate with the new CPU as the system in part (e)? What will the system cost?

6.6 [20] <6.4> Assume that we have the following two magnetic-disk configurations: a single disk and an array of four disks. Each disk has 20 surfaces, 885 tracks per surface, and 16 sectors/track. Each sector holds 1K bytes, and it revolves at 7200 RPM. Use the seek-time formula in the fallacy starting on page 549, including the equations in Figure 6.43 (page 551). The time to switch between surfaces is the same as to move the arm one track. In the disk array all the spindles are synchronized—sector 0 in every disk rotates under the head at the exact same time—and the arms on all four disks are always over the same track. The data is "striped" across all four disks, so four consecutive sectors on a single-disk system will be spread one sector per disk in the array. The delay of the disk controller is 2 ms per transaction, either for a single disk or for the array. Assume the performance of the I/O system is limited only by the disks and that there is a path to each disk in the array. Calculate the performance in both I/Os per second and megabytes per second of these two disk organizations, assuming the request pattern is random reads of 4 KB of sequential sectors. Assume the 4 KB are aligned under the same arm on each disk in the array.

6.7 [20]<6.4> Start with the same assumptions as in Exercise 6.5 (e). Now calculate the performance in both I/Os per second and megabytes per second of these two disk organizations assuming the request pattern is reads of 4 KB of sequential sectors where the average seek distance is 10 tracks. Assume the 4 KB are aligned under the same arm on each disk in the array.

6.8 [20] <6.4> Start with the same assumptions as in Exercise 6.5 (e). Now calculate the performance in both I/Os per second and megabytes per second of these two disk organizations assuming the request pattern is random reads of 1 MB of sequential sectors. (If it matters, assume the disk controller allows the sectors to arrive in any order.)

6.9 [20] <6.2> Assume that we have one disk defined as in Exercise 6.5 (e). Assume that we read the next sector after any read and that *all* read requests are one sector in length. We store the extra sectors that were read ahead in a disk cache. Assume that the probability of receiving a request for the sector we read ahead at some time in the future (before it must be discarded because the disk-cache buffer fills) is 0.1. Assume that we must still pay the controller overhead on a disk-cache read hit, and the transfer time for the disk cache is 250 ns per word. Is the read-ahead strategy faster? (*Hint*: Solve the problem in the steady state by assuming that the disk cache contains the appropriate information and a request has just missed.)

6.10 [20/10/20/20] <6.4–6.6> Assume the following information about our DLX machine:

- Loads 2 cycles.

- Stores 2 cycles.

- All other instructions are 1 cycle.

Use the summary instruction mix information on DLX for gcc from Chapter 2.

Here are the cache statistics for a write-through cache:

- Each cache block is four words, and the whole block is read on any miss.

- Cache miss takes 23 cycles.

- Write through takes 16 cycles to complete, and there is no write buffer.

Here are the cache statistics for a write-back cache:

- Each cache block is four words, and the whole block is read on any miss.

- Cache miss takes 23 cycles for a clean block and 31 cycles for a dirty block.

- Assume that on a miss, 30% of the time the block is dirty.

Assume that the bus

- Is only busy during transfers

- Transfers on average 1 word / clock cycle

- Must read or write a single word at a time (it is not faster to access two at once)

a. [20] <6.4–6.6> Assume that DMA I/O can take place simultaneously with CPU cache hits. Also assume that the operating system can guarantee that there will be no stale-data problem in the cache due to I/O. The sector size is 1 KB. Assume the cache miss rate is 5%. On the average, what percentage of the bus is used for each cache write policy? (This measured is called the *traffic ratio* in cache studies.)

b. [10] <6.4–6.6> Start with the same assumptions as in part (a). If the bus can be loaded up to 80% of capacity without suffering severe performance penalties, how much memory bandwidth is available for I/O for each cache write policy? The cache miss rate is still 5%.

c. [20] <6.4–6.6> Start with the same assumptions as in part (a). Assume that a disk sector read takes 1000 clock cycles to initiate a read, 100,000 clock cycles to find the data on the disk, and 1000 clock cycles for the DMA to transfer the data to memory. How many disk reads can occur per million instructions executed for each write policy? How does this change if the cache miss rate is cut in half?

d. [20] <6.4–6.6> Start with the same assumptions as in part (c). Now you can have any number of disks. Assuming ideal scheduling of disk accesses, what is the maximum number of sector reads that can occur per million instructions executed?

6.11 [50] < 6.4> Take your favorite computer and write a program that achieves maximum bandwidth to and from disks. What is the percentage of the bandwidth that you achieve compared with what the I/O device manufacturer claims?

6.12 [20] <6.2,6.5> Search the World Wide Web to find descriptions of recent magnetic disks of different diameters. Be sure to include at least the information in Figure 6.2 on page 490.

6.13 [20] <6.9> Using data collected in Exercise 6.12, plot the two projections of seek time as used in Figure 6.43 (page 551). What seek distance has the largest percentage of difference between these two predictions? If you have the real seek distance data from Exercise 6.12, add that data to the plot and see on average how close each projection is to the real seek times.

6.14 [15] <6.2,6.5> Using the answer to Exercise 6.13, which disk would be a good building block to build a 100-GB storage subsystem using mirroring (RAID 1)? Why?

6.15 [15] <6.2,6.5> Using the answer to Exercise 6.13, which disk would be a good building block to build a 1000-GB storage subsystem using distributed parity (RAID 5)? Why?

6.16 [15] <6.4> Starting with the Example on page 515, calculate the average length of the queue and the average length of the system.

6.17 [15] <6.4> Redo the Example that starts on page 515, but this time assume the distribution of disk service times has a squared coefficient of variance of 2.0 (C = 2.0), versus 1.0 in the Example. How does this change affect the answers?

6.18 [20] <6.7> The I/O utilization rules of thumb on page 535 are just guidelines and are subject to debate. Redo the Example starting on page 535, but increase the limit of SCSI utilization to 50%, 60%, ..., until it is never the bottleneck. How does this change affect the answers? What is the new bottleneck? (*Hint*: Use a spreadsheet program to find answers)

6.19 [15]<6.2> Tape libraries were invented as archival storage, and hence have relatively few readers per tape. Calculate how long it would take to read all the data for a system with 6000 tapes, 10 readers that read at 9 MB/sec, and 30 seconds per tape to put the old tape away and load a new tape.

6.20 [25]<6.2>Extend the figures, showing price per system and price per megabyte of disks by collecting data from advertisements in the January issues of *Byte* magazine after 1995. How fast are prices changing now?

7 Interconnection Networks

"The Medium is the Message" because it is the medium that
shapes and controls the search and form of human associations
and actions.

Marshall McLuhan
Understanding Media (1964)

The marvels—of film, radio, and television—are marvels of
one-way communication, which is not communication at all.

Milton Mayer
*On the Remote Possibility of
Communication* (1967)

7.1	Introduction	563
7.2	A Simple Network	565
7.3	Connecting the Interconnection Network to the Computer	573
7.4	Interconnection Network Media	576
7.5	Connecting More Than Two Computers	579
7.6	Practical Issues for Commercial Interconnection Networks	597
7.7	Examples of Interconnection Networks	601
7.8	Crosscutting Issues for Interconnection Networks	605
7.9	Internetworking	608
7.10	Putting It All Together: An ATM Network of Workstations	613
7.11	Fallacies and Pitfalls	622
7.12	Concluding Remarks	625
7.13	Historical Perspective and References	626
	Exercises	629

7.1 | Introduction

Thus far we have covered the components of a single computer, which has been the traditional focus of computer architecture. In this chapter we see how to connect computers together, forming a community of computers. Figure 7.1 shows the generic components of this community: computer nodes, hardware and software interfaces, links to the interconnection network, and the interconnection network. Interconnection networks are also called *networks* or *communication subnets*, and nodes are sometimes called *end systems* or *hosts*. This topic is vast, with whole books written about portions of this figure. The goal of this chapter is to help you understand the architectural implications of interconnection network technology, providing introductory explanations of the key ideas and references to more detailed descriptions.

Let's start with the generic types of interconnections. Depending on the number of nodes and their proximity, these interconnections are given different names:

- *Massively parallel processor (MPP) network*—This interconnection network can connect thousands of nodes, and the maximum distance is typically less than 25 meters. The nodes are typically found in a row of adjacent cabinets.

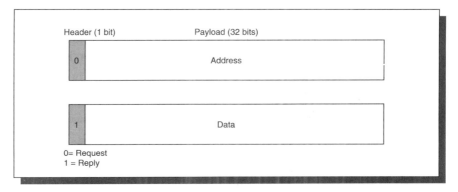

FIGURE 7.3   Message format for our simple network. Messages must have extra information beyond the data.

All interconnection networks involve software. Even this simple example invokes software to translate requests and replies into messages with the appropriate headers. An application program must usually cooperate with the operating system to send a message to another machine, since the network will be shared with all the processes running on the two machines, and the operating system cannot allow messages for one process to be received by another. Thus the messaging software must have some way to distinguish between processes; this distinction may be included in an expanded header. Although hardware support can reduce the amount of work, most is done by software.

In addition to protection, network software is often responsible for ensuring that messages are reliably delivered. The twin responsibilities are ensuring that the message is not garbled in transit, or lost in transit.

The first responsibility is met by adding a *checksum* field to the message format; this redundant information is calculated when the message is first sent and checked upon receipt. The receiver then sends an acknowledgment if the message passes the test.

One way to meet the second responsibility is to have a timer record the time each message is sent and to presume the message is lost if the timer expires before an acknowledgment arrives. The message is then re-sent.

The software steps to send a message are as follows:

1. The application copies data to be sent into an operating system buffer.

2. The operating system calculates the checksum, includes it in the header or trailer of the message, and then starts the timer.

3. The operating system sends the data to the network interface hardware and tells the hardware to send the message.

Message reception is in just the reverse order:

3. The system copies the data from the network interface hardware into the operating system buffer.

2. The system calculates the checksum over the data. If the checksum matches the sender's checksum, the receiver sends an acknowledgment back to the sender; if not, it deletes the message, assuming that the sender will resend the message when the associated timer expires.

1. If the data pass the test, the system copies the data to the user's address space and signals the application to continue.

The sender must still react to the acknowledgment:

■   When the sender gets the acknowledgment, it releases the copy of the message from the system buffer.

■   If the sender gets the time-out instead, it resends the data and restarts the timer.

Here we assume that the operating system keeps the message in its buffer to support retransmission in case of failure. Figure 7.4 shows how the message format looks now.

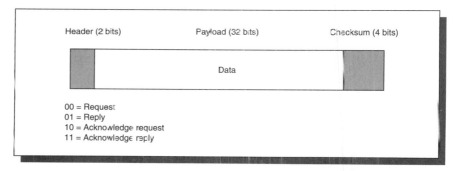

FIGURE 7.4   Message format for our simple network. Note that the checksum is in the trailer.

The sequence of steps that software follows to communicate is called a *protocol* and generally has the symmetric but reversed steps between sending and receiving. Our example is similar to the *UDP/IP* protocol used by some UNIX systems. Note that this protocol is for sending a *single* message. When an application does not require a response before sending the next message, the sender can overlap the time to send with the transmission delays and the time to receive.

A protocol must handle many more issues than reliability. For example, if two machines are from different manufacturers, they might order bytes differently within a word (see section 2.3 of Chapter 2). The software must reverse the order of bytes in each word as part of the delivery system. It must also guard against the possibility of duplicate messages if a delayed message were to become unstuck. Finally, it must work when the receiver's FIFO becomes full, suggesting feedback to control the flow of messages from the sender (see section 7.5).

Now that we have covered the steps in sending and receiving a message, we can discuss performance. Figure 7.5 shows the many performance parameters of interconnection networks. These terms are often used loosely, leading to confusion, so we define them here precisely:

- *Bandwidth*—This most widely used term refers to the maximum rate at which the interconnection network can propagate information once the message enters the network. Traditionally, the headers and trailers as well as the payload are counted in the bandwidth calculation, and the units are megabits/second rather than megabytes/second. The term *throughput* is sometimes used to mean network bandwidth delivered to an application.

- *Time of flight*—The time for the first bit of the message to arrive at the receiver, including the delays due to repeaters or other hardware in the network. Time of flight can be milliseconds for a WAN or nanoseconds for an MPP.

- *Transmission time*—The time for the message to pass through the network (not including time of flight) and equal to the size of the message divided by the bandwidth. This measure assumes there are no other messages to contend for the network.

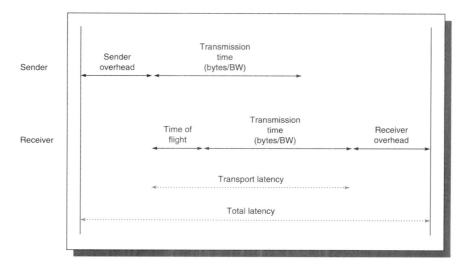

FIGURE 7.5 Performance parameters of interconnection networks. Depending on whether it is an MPP, LAN, or WAN, the relative lengths of the time of flight and transmission may be quite different from those shown here. (Based on a presentation by Greg Papadopolous, Sun Microsystems.)

- *Transport latency*—The sum of time of flight and transmission time, it is the time that the message spends in the interconnection network, not including the overhead of injecting the message into the network nor pulling it out when it arrives.

- *Sender overhead*—The time for the processor to inject the message into the interconnection network, including both hardware and software components. Note that the processor is busy for the entire time, hence the use of the term *overhead*. Once the processor is free, any subsequent delays are considered part of the transport latency.

- *Receiver overhead*—The time for the processor to pull the message from the interconnection network, including both hardware and software components. In general, the receiver overhead is larger than the sender overhead: for example, the receiver may pay the cost of an interrupt.

The total latency of a message can be expressed algebraically:

$$\text{Total latency} = \text{Sender overhead} + \text{Time of flight} + \frac{\text{Message size}}{\text{Bandwidth}} + \text{Receiver overhead}$$

As we shall see, for many applications and networks, the overheads dominate the total message latency.

EXAMPLE   Assume a network with a bandwidth of 10 Mbits/second has a sending overhead of 230 microseconds and a receiving overhead of 270 microseconds. Assume two machines are 100 meters apart and one wants to send a 1000-byte message to another (including the header), and the message format allows 1000 bytes in a single message. Calculate the total latency to send the message from one machine to another. Next, perform the same calculation but assume the machines are now 1000 km apart.

ANSWER   The speed of light is 299,792.5 kilometers per second, and signals propagate at about 50% of the speed of light in a conductor, so time of flight can be estimated. Let's plug the parameters for the shorter distance into the formula above:

$$\text{Total latency} = \text{Sender overhead} + \text{Time of flight} + \frac{\text{Message size}}{\text{Bandwidth}} + \text{Receiver overhead}$$

$$= 230 \ \mu\text{secs} + \frac{0.1 \text{km}}{0.5 \times 299{,}792.5 \text{ km/sec}} + \frac{1000 \text{ bytes}}{10 \text{ Mbits/sec}} + 270 \ \mu\text{secs}$$

$$= 230 \ \mu\text{secs} + \frac{0.1 \times 10^6}{0.5 \times 299{,}792.5} \ \mu\text{secs} + \frac{1000 \times 8}{10} \ \mu\text{secs} + 270 \ \mu\text{secs}$$

$$= 230 \ \mu\text{secs} + 0.67 \ \mu\text{secs} + 800 \ \mu\text{secs} + 270 \ \mu\text{secs}$$

$$= 1301 \ \mu\text{secs}$$

Substituting the longer distance into the third equation yields

$$\text{Total latency} = 230 \ \mu\text{secs} + \frac{1000 \times 10^6}{0.5 \times 299{,}792.5} \ \mu\text{secs} + \frac{1000 \times 8}{10} \ \mu\text{secs} + 270 \ \mu\text{secs}$$

$$= 230 \ \mu\text{secs} + 6671 \ \mu\text{secs} + 800 \ \mu\text{secs} + 270 \ \mu\text{secs}$$

$$= 7971 \ \mu\text{secs}$$

The increased fraction of the latency required by time of flight for long distances, as well as the greater likelihood of errors over long distances, are why wide area networks use more sophisticated and time-consuming protocols. Increased latency affects the structure of programs that try to hide this latency, requiring quite different solutions if the latency is 1, 100, or 10,000 microseconds.

As mentioned above, when an application does not require a response before sending the next message, the sender can overlap the sending overhead with the transport latency and receiver overhead. ∎

We can simplify the performance equation by combining sender overhead, receiver overhead, and time of flight into a single term called *Overhead*:

$$\text{Total latency} \approx \text{Overhead} + \frac{\text{Message size}}{\text{Bandwidth}}$$

We can use this formula to calculate the effective bandwidth delivered by the network as message size varies:

$$\text{Effective bandwidth} = \frac{\text{Message size}}{\text{Total latency}}$$

Let's use this simpler equation to explore the impact of overhead and message size on effective bandwidth.

EXAMPLE   Plot the effective bandwidth versus message size for overheads of 1, 25, and 500 microseconds and for network bandwidths of 10, 100, and 1000 Mbits/second. Vary message size from 16 bytes to 4 megabytes. For what message sizes is the effective bandwidth virtually the same as the raw network bandwidth? Assuming a 500-microsecond overhead, for what message sizes is the effective bandwidth always less than 10 Mbits/second?

ANSWER   Figure 7.6 plots effective bandwidth versus message size using the simplified equation above. The notation "oX,bwY" means an overhead of X microseconds and a network bandwidth of Y Mbits/second. Message sizes must be four megabytes for effective bandwidth to be about the same as network bandwidth, thereby amortizing the cost of high overhead. Assuming the high overhead, message sizes less than 4096 bytes will not break the 10 Mbits/second barrier no matter what the actual network bandwidth.

Thus we must lower overhead as well as increase network bandwidth unless messages are very large.   ■

Many applications send far more small messages than large messages. Figure 7.7 shows the size of Network File System (NFS) messages for 239 machines at Berkeley collected over a period of one week. One plot is cumulative in messages sent, and the other is cumulative in data bytes sent. The maximum NFS message size is just over 8 KB, yet 95% of the messages are less than 192 bytes long.

Even this simple network has brought up the issues of protection, reliability, heterogeneity, software protocols, and a more sophisticated performance model. The next four sections address other key questions:

- Where do you connect the network to the computer?

- Which media are available to connect computers together?

- What issues arise if you want to connect more than two computers?

- What practical issues arise for commercial networks?

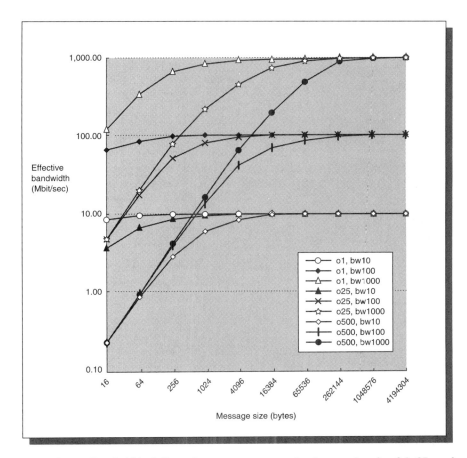

FIGURE 7.6   Bandwidth delivered versus message size for overheads of 1, 25, and 500 microseconds and for network bandwidths of 10, 100, and 1000 Mbits/second. The notation "oX,bwY" means an overhead of X microseconds and a network bandwidth of Y Mbits/second. Note that with 500 microseconds of overhead and a network bandwidth of 1000 Mbits/second, only the 4-MB message size gets an effective bandwidth of 1000 Mbits/second. In fact, message sizes must be greater than 4 KB for the effective bandwidth to exceed 10 Mbits/second.

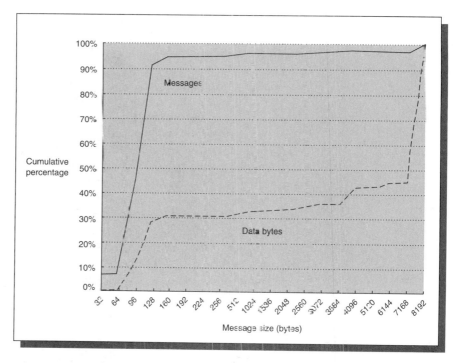

FIGURE 7.7 Cumulative percentage of messages and data transferred as message size varies for NFS traffic in the Computer Science Department at University of California at Berkeley. Each x-axis entry includes all bytes up to the next one; e.g., 32 represents 32 bytes to 63 bytes. More than half the bytes are sent in 8-KB messages, but 95% of the messages are less than 192 bytes. Figure 7.39 (page 622) shows the details of this measurement.

7.3 | Connecting the Interconnection Network to the Computer

Where the network attaches to the computer affects both the network interface hardware and software. Questions include whether to use the memory bus or the I/O bus, whether to use polling or interrupts, and how to avoid invoking the operating system.

Computers have a hierarchy of buses with different cost/performance. For example, a personal computer in 1995 has a memory bus, a PCI bus for fast I/O devices, and an ISA bus for slow I/O devices. I/O buses follow open standards and have less stringent electrical requirements. Memory buses, on the other hand, provide higher bandwidth and lower latency than I/O buses. Typically, MPPs plug into the memory bus, and LANs and WANs plug into the I/O bus.

Where to connect the network to the machine depends on the performance goals and whether you hope to buy a standard network interface card or are willing to design or buy one that only works with the memory bus on your model of computer.

The location of the network connection significantly affects the software interface to the network as well as the hardware. As mentioned in section 6.6, one key is whether the interface is consistent with the processor's caches: the sender may have to flush the cache before each send, and the receiver may have to flush its cache before each receive to prevent the stale data problem. Such flushes increase send and receive overhead. A memory bus is more likely to be cache-coherent than an I/O bus and therefore more likely to avoid these extra cache flushes.

A related question of where to connect to the computer is how to connect to the software: Do you use programmed I/O or direct memory access (DMA) to send a message? (See section 6.6.) In general, large messages are best sent by DMA. Whether to use DMA to send small messages depends on the efficiency of the interface to the DMA. The DMA interface is usually memory-mapped, and so each interaction is typically at the speed of main memory rather than of a cache access. If DMA setup takes many accesses, each running at uncached memory speeds, then the sender overhead may be so high that it is faster to simply send the data directly to the interface.

Interconnection networks follow biblical advice: It's easier to send than to receive. One question is how the receiver should be notified when a message arrives. Should it poll the network interface waiting for a message to arrive, or should it perform other tasks and then pay the overhead to service an interrupt when it arrives? The issue is the time wasted polling before the message arrives versus the time wasted in interrupting the processor and restoring its state.

EXAMPLE   The CM-5 is an MPP that allows users to send messages without invoking the operating system and allows the receiver to either poll or use interrupts. First plot the average overhead for polling and interrupts as a function of message arrival. Then propose a message reception scheme for the CM-5 that will work well as the rate varies. The time per poll is 1.6 microseconds: 0.6 to poll the interface card and 1.0 to check the type of message and get it from the interface card. The time per interrupt is 19 microseconds. The times are 4.9 microseconds and 3.75 microseconds to enable or disable interrupts, respectively, because the CM-5 operating system kernel must be invoked.

ANSWER   For polling, the wasted time is simply the time between messages less the time to execute the simplest code to handle the message, which takes 0.5 microseconds. Interrupts cannot process messages any faster than the interrupt overhead time plus the time to handle a message, so the fastest time between interrupts is 19.5 microseconds. Figure 7.8 plots these curves.

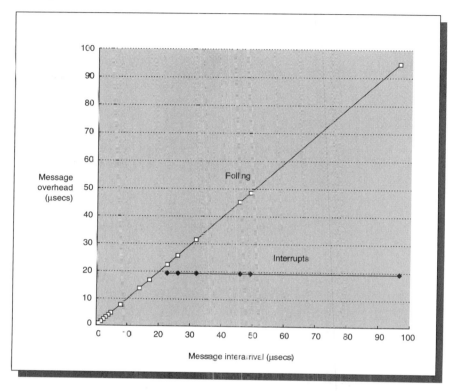

FIGURE 7.8   Message overhead versus message interarrival times for the CM-5. Liu and Culler [1994] took these measurements.

Given the parameters above, we want to avoid enabling and disabling interrupts, since the cost of invoking the kernel is large relative to the cost of receiving messages. The CM-5 uses the following scheme: Have interrupts enabled at all times, but on an interrupt the routine will poll for incoming messages before returning to the interrupted program. The virtue of this scheme is that it works well no matter what the load. When messages are arriving slowly, the overhead cost should be that of the interrupt code; when they arrive quickly, the cost should be that of polling, since the interrupt code will not return until all the messages have been received. ■

When selecting the network interface hardware, where to plug it into the machine, and how to interface to the software, try to follow these guidelines:

- Avoid invoking the operating system in the common case.

- Minimize the number of times operating at uncached memory speeds to interact with the network interface (such as to check status).

7.4 Interconnection Network Media

There is an old network saying: Bandwidth problems can be cured with money. Latency problems are harder because the speed of light is fixed—you can't bribe God.

David Clark, MIT

Just as there is a memory hierarchy, there is a hierarchy of media to interconnect computers that varies in cost, performance, and reliability. Network media have another figure of merit, the maximum distance between nodes. This section covers three popular examples, and Figure 7.9 illustrates them.

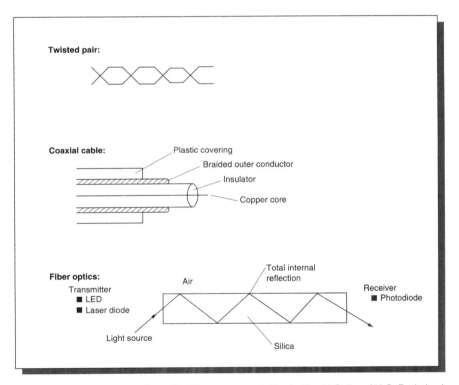

FIGURE 7.9   Three network media. (From a presentation by David Culler of U.C. Berkeley.)

The first medium is *twisted pairs* of copper wires. These are two insulated wires, each about 1 mm thick. They are twisted together to reduce electrical interference, since two parallel lines form an antenna but a twisted pair does not. As they can transfer a few megabits per second over several kilometers without amplification, twisted pair were the mainstay of the telephone system. Telephone companies bundled together (and sheathed) many pairs coming into a building. Twisted pairs can also offer tens of megabits per second of bandwidth over shorter distances, making them plausible for LANs.

Coaxial cable was developed for the cable television companies to deliver a higher rate over a few kilometers. To offer high bandwidth and good noise immunity, a single stiff copper wire is surrounded by insulating material, and then the insulator is surrounded by cylindrical conductor, often woven as a braided mesh. A 50-ohm baseband coaxial cable delivers 10 megabits per second over a kilometer.

Connecting to this heavily insulated media is more challenging. The original technique was a *T junction*: the cable is cut in two and a connector is inserted that reconnects the cable and adds a third wire to a computer. A less invasive solution is a *vampire tap*: a hole of precise depth and width is first drilled into the cable, terminating in the copper core. A connector is then screwed in without having to cut the cable.

As the supply of copper has dwindled and to keep up with the demands of bandwidth and distance, it became clear that the telephone company would need to find new media. The solution could be more expensive provided that it offered much higher bandwidth and that supplies were plentiful. The answer was to replace copper with plastic and electrons with photons. *Fiber optics* transmits digital data as pulses of light: for example, light might mean 1 and no light might mean 0.

A fiber optic network has three components:

1. the transmission medium, a fiber optic cable;

2. the light source, an LED or laser diode;

3. the light detector, a photodiode.

Note that unlike twisted pairs or coax, fibers are one-way, or *simplex,* media. A two-way, or *full duplex,* connection between two nodes requires two fibers.

Since light is bent or refracted at interfaces, it can slowly be spread out as it travels down the cable unless the diameter of the cable is limited to one wavelength of light; then it transfers in a straight line. Thus fiber optic cables are of two forms:

1. *Multimode fiber*—Allows the light to be dispersed and uses inexpensive LEDs as a light source. It is useful for transmissions up to 2 kilometers and in 1995 transmits up to 600 megabits per second.

2. *Single-mode fiber*—This single-wavelength fiber requires more expensive laser diodes for light sources and currently transmits gigabits per second for hundreds of kilometers, making it the medium of choice for telephone companies.

Although single-mode fiber is a better transmitter, it is much more difficult to attach connectors to single-mode; it is less reliable and more expensive, and the cable itself has restrictions on the degree it can be bent. Hence when ease of connection is more important than very long distance, such as in a LAN, multimode fiber is likely to be popular.

Connecting fiber optics to a computer is more challenging than connecting cable. The vampire tap solution of cable fails because it loses light. There are two forms of T-boxes:

1. Taps are fused onto the optical fiber. Each tap is passive, so a failure cuts off just a single computer.

2. In an active repeater, light is converted to electrical signals, sent to the computer, converted back to light, and then sent down the cable. If an active repeater fails, it blocks the network.

In both cases, fiber optics has the additional cost of optical-to-electrical and electrical-to-optical conversion as part of the computer interface.

The product of the bandwidth and maximum distance forms a single figure of merit: gigabit-kilometers per second. According to Desurvire [1992], since 1975 optical fibers have increased transmission capacity by tenfold every four years by this measure.

Figure 7.10 shows the typical distance, bandwidth, and cost of the three media. Compared to the electrical media, fiber optics are more difficult to tap, have more expensive interfaces, go for longer distances, and are less likely to experience degradation due to noise.

Media	Bandwidth	Maximum distance	Bandwidth × distance	Cost per meter	Cost for termi- nation	Labor cost to install	Cost per computer interface
Twisted pair copper wire	1 Mb/sec (20 Mb/sec)	2 km (0.1 km)	0.02 Gb-km/sec	$0.23	$4.60	$2.00	≈$2
Coaxial cable	10 Mb/sec	1 km	0.01 Gb-km/sec	$1.64	$220.00	$15.00	≈$5
Multimode optical fiber	600 Mb/sec	2 km	1.20 Gb-km/sec	$1.03	$11.80	$10.00	≈$1000
Single-mode optical fiber	2000 Mb/sec	100 km	200.00 Gb-km/sec	$1.64	$23.90	$10.00	≈$1000

FIGURE 7.10   Figures of merit for several network media in 1995. The coaxial cable is the Thick Net Ethernet standard (see Figure 7.9) using a vampire tap for termination. Twisted-pair Ethernet lowers cost by using the media in the first row. Since an optical fiber is a one-way, or simplex, media, the costs per meter and for termination in this figure are for two strands to supply two-way, or full duplex, communication. The major costs for fiber are the electrical-optical interfaces.

Let's compare these media in an example.

EXAMPLE   Suppose you have 100 magnetic tapes, each containing 10 GB. Assume
that you have enough tape readers to keep any network busy. How long
will it take to transmit the data over a distance of one kilometer using each
of the media in Figure 7.10? How do they compare to delivering the tapes
by car?

ANSWER   The amount of data is 1000 GB. The time for each medium is given below:

$$\text{Twisted pair} = \frac{1000 \times 1024 \times 8 \text{ Mb}}{1 \text{ Mb/sec}} = 8,192,000 \text{ secs} = 95 \text{ days}$$

$$\text{Coaxial cable} = \frac{1000 \times 1024 \times 8 \text{ Mb}}{10 \text{ Mb/sec}} = 819,200 \text{ secs} = 9.5 \text{ days}$$

$$\text{Multimode fiber} = \frac{1000 \times 1024 \times 8 \text{ Mb}}{600 \text{ Mb/sec}} = 13,653 \text{ secs} = 3.8 \text{ hours}$$

$$\text{Single-mode fiber} = \frac{1000 \times 1024 \times 8 \text{ Mb}}{2000 \text{ Mb/sec}} = 4096 \text{ secs} = 1.1 \text{ hours}$$

$$\text{Car} = \text{Time to load car} + \text{Transport time} + \text{Time to unload car}$$

$$= 300 \text{ secs} + \frac{1 \text{ km}}{50 \text{ kph}} + 300 \text{ secs} = 300 \text{ secs} + 72 \text{ secs} + 300 \text{ secs}$$

$$= 672 \text{ secs} = 11.2 \text{ min}$$

A car filled with tapes is a high-bandwidth medium!   ■

7.5 | Connecting More Than Two Computers

Thus far we have discussed two computers communicating over private lines, but
what makes interconnection networks interesting is the ability to connect hundreds of computers together. And what makes them more interesting also makes
them more challenging to build.

Shared versus Switched Media

Certainly the simplest way to connect multiple computers is to have them share a
single interconnection medium, just as I/O devices share a single I/O bus. The
most popular LAN, Ethernet, is simply a bus that can be shared by hundreds of
computers.

Given that the medium is shared, there must be a mechanism to coordinate the
use of the shared medium so that only one message is sent at a time. If the network is small, it may be possible to have an additional central arbiter to give

permission to send a message. (Of course, this leaves open the question of how the nodes talk to the arbiter.)

Centralized arbitration is impractical for networks with a large number of nodes spread out over a kilometer, so we must distribute arbitration. A node first listens to make sure it doesn't send a message while another message is on the network. If the interconnection is idle, the node tries to send. Of course, some other node may decide to send at the same instant. When two nodes send at the same time, it is called a *collision*. Let's assume that the network interface can detect any resulting collisions by listening to what is sent to hear if the data were garbled by other data appearing on the line. Listening to avoid and detect collisions is called *carrier sensing and collision detection.*

To avoid repeated head-on collisions, each node whose message was garbled waits (or "backs off") a random time before resending. Subsequent collisions result in exponentially increasing time between attempts to retransmit. Although this approach is not guaranteed to be fair—some subsequent node may transmit while those that collided are waiting—it does control congestion. If the network does not have high demand from many nodes, this simple approach works well. Under high utilization, performance degrades since the medium is shared.

Shared media have some of the same advantages and disadvantages as buses: they are inexpensive, but they have limited bandwidth. The alternative to sharing the media is to have a dedicated line to a switch that in turn provides a dedicated line to all destinations. Figure 7.11 shows the potential bandwidth improvement of switches: *Aggregate bandwidth* is many times that of the single shared medium.

Switches allow communication directly from source to destination, without intermediate nodes to interfere with these signals. Such *point-to-point* communication is faster than a line shared between many nodes because there is no arbitration and the interface is simpler electrically. Of course, it does pay the added latency of going through the switch.

Every node of a shared line will see every message, even if it is just to check to see whether or not the message is for that node, so this style of communication is sometimes called *broadcast* to contrast it with point-to-point. The shared medium makes it easy to broadcast a message to every node, and even to broadcast to subsets of nodes, called *multicasting.*

Switches allow multiple pairs of nodes to communicate simultaneously, giving these interconnections much higher *aggregate* bandwidth than the speed of a shared link to a node. Switches also allow the interconnection network to scale to a very large number of nodes. Switches are called *data switching exchanges, multistage interconnection networks,* or even *interface message processors* (*IMPs*). Depending on the distance of the node to the switch, the network medium is either copper wire or optical fiber.

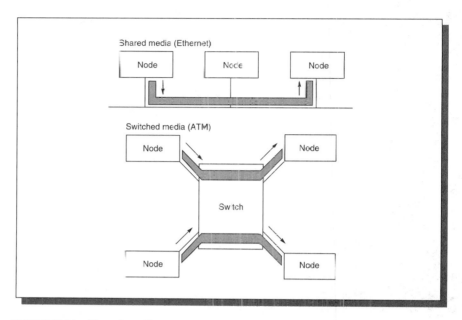

FIGURE 7.11   Shared medium versus switch. Ethernet is a shared medium and ATM is a switch-based medium. All nodes on the Ethernet must share the 10 Mb/sec interconnection, but switches like ATM can support multiple 155 Mb/sec transfers simultaneously.

EXAMPLE   Compare 16 nodes connected three ways: a single 10 Mb/sec coaxial cable; a switch connected via twisted pairs, each running at 10 Mb/sec; and a switch connected via optical fibers, each running at 100 Mb/sec. The single coax is 500 meters long, and the average length of each segment to a switch is 50 meters. Both switches can support the full bandwidth, with the slower version costing $10,000 and the faster version costing $15,000. Assume each switch adds 50 microseconds to the latency. Calculate the aggregate bandwidth, transport latency, and cost of each alternative. Assume the average message size is 125 bytes.

ANSWER   The aggregate bandwidth of each example is the simplest calculation: 10 Mb/sec for the single coax; 16×10, or 160 Mb/sec for the switched twisted pairs; and 16×100, or 1600 Mb/sec for the switched optical fibers.
        The transport time is

$$\text{Transport time} = \text{Time of flight} + \frac{\text{Message size}}{\text{Bandwidth}}$$

For coax we just plug in the distance, bandwidth, and message size:

$$\text{Transport time}_{coax} = \frac{500/1000 \times 10^6}{0.5 \times 299,792.5} \text{ }\mu\text{secs} + \frac{125 \times 8}{10} \text{ }\mu\text{secs}$$

$$= 3.3 \text{ }\mu\text{secs} + 100 \text{ }\mu\text{secs}$$

$$= 103.3 \text{ }\mu\text{secs}$$

For the switches, the distance is twice the average segment, since there is one segment from the sender to the switch and one from the switch to the receiver. We must also add the latency for the switch.

$$\text{Transport time}_{tp} = 2 \times \left(\frac{50/1000 \times 10^6}{0.5 \times 299,792.5} \right) \text{ }\mu\text{secs} + 50 \text{ }\mu\text{secs} + \frac{125 \times 8}{10} \text{ }\mu\text{secs}$$

$$= 0.7 \text{ }\mu\text{secs} + 50 \text{ }\mu\text{secs} + 100 \text{ }\mu\text{secs}$$

$$= 150.7 \text{ }\mu\text{secs}$$

$$\text{Transport time}_{fiber} = 2 \times \left(\frac{50/1000 \times 10^6}{0.5 \times 299,792.5} \right) \text{ }\mu\text{secs} + 50 \text{ }\mu\text{secs} + \frac{125 \times 8}{100} \text{ }\mu\text{secs}$$

$$= 0.7 \text{ }\mu\text{secs} + 50 \text{ }\mu\text{secs} + 10 \text{ }\mu\text{secs}$$

$$= 60.7 \text{ }\mu\text{secs}$$

Figure 7.12 shows the costs of each option, based on Figure 7.10. We assumed that the switches included the termination and interfaces. Since the media is connected to both the nodes and to the switch, we doubled the labor costs.

	Coax	Twisted pair	Fiber optic
Termination	$3520	$74	$189
Labor	$240	$64	$320
Node interfaces	$80	$32	$16,000
Media	$820	$184	$824
Switch		$10,000	$15,000
Total	$4660	$10,354	$32,333

FIGURE 7.12   Costs of single coax, twisted pair using switch, and fiber optics using switch, using costs in Figure 7.10 (page 578).

The high costs of the thick coaxial cable and vampire taps, illustrated in this example, have led to the use of twisted pairs for shorter distance LANs. Although the continuing silicon revolution will lower the price of the switch, the challenge for the optical fiber is to bring down the cost of the electrical-optical interfaces.   ∎

Switches allow communication to harvest the same rapid advance from silicon as have processors and main memory. Whereas the switches from telecommunications companies were once the size of mainframe computers, today we see single-chip switches in MPPs. Just as single-chip processors led to processors replacing logic in a surprising number of places, single-chip switches will increasingly replace buses and shared media interconnection networks.

Switch Topology

The number of different topologies that have been discussed in publications would be difficult to count, but the number that have been used commercially is just a handful, with MPP designers being the most visible and imaginative. MPPs have used regular topologies to simplify packaging and scalability. The topologies of LANs and WANs are more haphazard, having more to do with the challenges of long distance or simply the connection of equipment purchased over several years.

Figure 7.13 illustrates two of the popular switch organizations, with the path from node P_0 to node P_6 shown in gray in each topology. A fully connected, or *crossbar*, interconnection allows any node to communicate with any other node in one pass through the interconnection. An *Omega* interconnection uses less hardware than the crossbar interconnection ($n/2 \log_2 n$ vs. n^2 switches), but contention is more likely to occur between messages, depending on the pattern of communication. The term *blocking* is used to describe this form of contention. For example, in the Omega interconnection in Figure 7.13 a message from P_1 to P_7 is blocked while waiting for a message from P_0 to P_6. Of course, if two nodes try to send to the same destination—both P_0 and P_1 send to P_6—there will be contention for that link, even in the crossbar.

Another switch is based on a tree with bandwidth added higher in the tree to match the requirements of common communications patterns. This topology, commonly called a *fat tree*, is shown in Figure 7.14. Interconnections are normally drawn as graphs, with each arc of the graph representing a link of the communication interconnection, with nodes shown as black squares and switches shown as shaded circles. This figure shows that there are multiple paths between any two nodes; for example, between node 0 and node 8 there are four paths. If messages are randomly assigned to different paths, communication can take advantage of the full bandwidth of the fat-tree topology.

Thus far the switch has been separate from the processor and memory and assumed to be located in a central location. Looking inside this switch we see many smaller switches. The term *multistage switch* is sometimes used to refer to centralized units to reflect the multiple steps that a message may travel before it reaches a computer. Instead of centralizing these small switching elements, an alternative is to place one small switch at every computer, yielding a distributed switching unit.

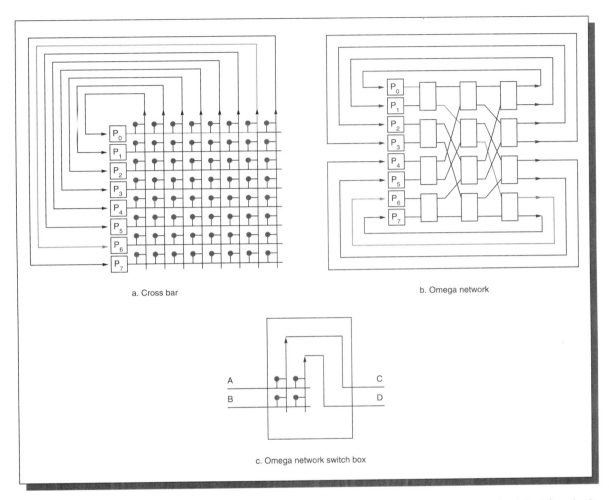

a. Cross bar

b. Omega network

c. Omega network switch box

FIGURE 7.13   Popular switch topologies for eight nodes. The links are unidirectional; data come in at the left and exit out the right link. The switch box in (c) can pass A to C and B to D or B to C and A to D. The crossbar uses n^2 switches, where n is the number of processors, while the Omega network uses $n/2 \log_2 n$ of the large switch boxes, each of which is logically composed of four of the smaller switches. In this case the crossbar uses 64 switches versus 12 switch boxes or 48 switches in the Omega network. The crossbar, however, can simultaneously route any permutation of traffic pattern between processors. The Omega network cannot.

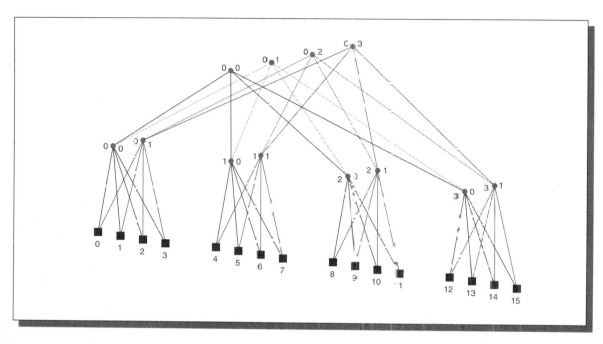

FIGURE 7.14   A fat-tree topology for 16 nodes. The shaded circles are switches, and the squares at the bottom are processor-memory nodes. A simple 4-ary tree would only have the links at the front of the figure; that is, the tree with the root labeled 0,0. This three-dimensional view suggests the increase in bandwidth via extra links at each level over a simple tree, so bandwidth between each level of a fat tree is normally constant rather than being reduced by a factor of four as in a 4-ary tree. Multiple paths and random routing give it the ability to route common patterns well, which ensures no single pattern from a broad class of communication patterns will do badly. In the CM-5 fat-tree implementation, the switches have four downward connections and two or four upward connections; in this figure the switches have two upward connections.

Given a distributed switch, the question is how to connect the switches together. Figure 7.15 shows that a low-cost alternative to full interconnection is a network that connects a sequence of nodes together. This topology is called a *ring*. Since some nodes are not directly connected, some messages will have to hop along intermediate nodes until they arrive at the final destination. Unlike shared lines, a ring is capable of many simultaneous transfers the first node can send to the second at the same time as the third node can send to the fourth, for example. Rings are not quite as good as this sounds because the average message must travel through $n/2$ switches, where n is the number of nodes. To first order, a ring is like a pipelined bus: on the plus side are point-to-point links, and on the minus side are "bus repeater" delays.

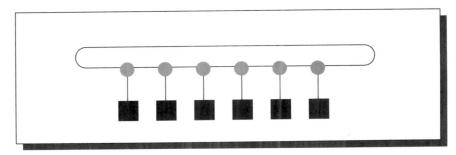

FIGURE 7.15   A ring network topology.

One variation of rings used in local area networks is the *token ring*. To simplify arbitration, a single slot, or *token,* is passed around the ring to determine which node is allowed to send a message; a node can send only when it gets the token. (A token is simply a special bit pattern.) In this section we will evaluate the ring as a topology with more bandwidth rather than one that may be simpler to arbitrate than a long shared medium.

A straightforward but expensive alternative to a ring is to have a dedicated communication link between every switch. The tremendous improvement in performance of fully connected switches is offset by the enormous increase in cost, typically going up with the square of the number of nodes. This cost inspires designers to invent new topologies that are between the cost of rings and the performance of fully connected networks. The evaluation of success depends in large part on the nature of the communication in the interconnection network. Real machines frequently add extra links to these simple topologies to improve performance and reliability. Figure 7.16 illustrates three popular topologies for MPPs.

One popular measure for MPP interconnections, in addition to the ones covered in section 7.2, is the *bisection bandwidth*. This measure is calculated by dividing the interconnect into two roughly equal parts, each with half the nodes. You then sum the bandwidth of the lines that cross that imaginary dividing line. For fully connected interconnections the bisection bandwidth is $(n/2)^2$, where n is the number of nodes.

Since some interconnections are not symmetric, the question arises as to where to draw the imaginary line when bisecting the interconnect. Bisection bandwidth is a worst-case metric, so the answer is to choose the division that makes interconnection performance worst; stated alternatively, calculate all possible bisection bandwidths and pick the smallest. Figure 7.17 summarizes these different topologies using bisection bandwidth and the number of links for 64 nodes.

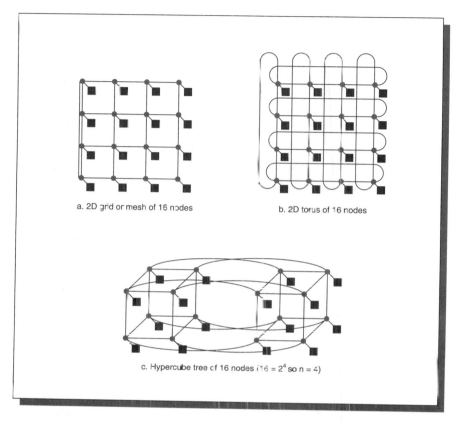

a. 2D grid or mesh of 16 nodes

b. 2D torus of 16 nodes

c. Hypercube tree of 16 nodes ($16 = 2^4$ so n = 4)

FIGURE 7.16 Network topologies that have appeared in commercial MPPs. The shaded circles represent switches, and the black squares represent nodes. Even though a switch has many links, generally only one goes to the node. Frequently these basic topologies have been supplemented with extra arcs to improve performance and reliability. For example, the switches in the left and right columns of the 2D grid are connected together using the unused ports on each switch to form the 2D torus. The Boolean hypercube topology is an n-dimensional interconnect for 2^n nodes, requiring n ports per switch (plus one for the processor), and thus n nearest neighbor nodes.

Evaluation category	Bus	Ring	2D torus	6-cube	Fully connected
Performance					
Bisection bandwidth	1	2	16	32	1024
Cost					
Ports per switch	NA	3	5	7	64
Total number of lines	1	128	192	256	2080

FIGURE 7.17 Relative cost and performance of several interconnects for 64 nodes. The bus is the standard reference at unit cost, and of course there can be more than one data line along each link between nodes. Note that any network topology that scales the bisection bandwidth linearly must scale the number of interconnection lines faster than linearly. Figure 7.13a on page 584 is an example of a fully connected network.

EXAMPLE   Let's examine the difference between the bisection bandwidths of each topology in Figure 7.17 for 64 nodes. Assume all-to-all communication: each node does a single transfer to every other node. We simplify the communication cost model for this example: it takes one time unit to go from switch to switch, and there is no cost in or out of the processor. Assuming every link of every interconnect is the same speed and that a node can send as many messages as it wants at a time, how long does it take for complete communication? (See Exercise 7.8 for a more realistic version of this example.)

ANSWER   For each node to send a message to every other node, we need to send 64 × 63 or 4032 messages. Here are the cases in increasing order of difficulty of explanation:

- *Bus*—Transfers are done sequentially, so it takes 4032 time units.

- *Fully connected*—All transfers are done in parallel, taking one time unit.

- *Ring*—This is easiest to see step by step. In the first step each node sends a message to the node with the next higher address, with node 63 sending to node 0. This takes one step for all 64 transfers to the nearest neighbor. The second step sends to the node address + 2 modulo 64. Since this goes through two links, it takes two time units. It would seem that this would continue until we send to the node address + 63 modulo 64 taking 63 time units, but remember that these are bidirectional links. Hence, sending from node 1 to node 1 + 63 modulo 64 = 0 takes just one time unit because there is a link connecting them together. Then the calculation for the ring is

$$\text{Time}_{\text{Ring}} = 1 + 2 + \ldots + 31 + 32 + 31 + \ldots + 2 + 1$$

$$= \frac{31 \times 32}{2} + 32 + \frac{31 \times 32}{2} = 496 + 32 + 496$$

$$= 1024$$

- *2D torus*—There are eight rows and eight columns in our torus of 64 nodes. Remember that the top and bottom rows of a torus are just one link away, as are the leftmost and rightmost columns. This allows us to treat the communication as we did the ring, in that there are no special cases at the edges. Let's first calculate the time to send a message to all the nodes in the same row. This time is the same as a ring with just eight nodes:

$$\text{Time}_{\text{Row}} = 1 + 2 + 3 + 4 + 3 + 2 + 1$$

$$= \frac{3 \times 4}{2} + 4 + \frac{3 \times 4}{2} = 6 + 4 + 6$$

$$= 16$$

To send a message to all the elements in the row below, all eight messages must first take one time unit to get to that row. The time for the eight messages to get to the proper node within that row is the same as the time to send a message to all elements of a row:

$$\text{Time}_{\text{Row below}} = 8 \times 1 + \text{Time}_{\text{Row}}$$

This can be generalized as the time it takes to send eight messages to each row plus the time to distribute the messages within a row:

$$
\begin{aligned}
\text{Time}_{2D} &= \text{Time}_{\text{Row}} + (8 \times 1 + \text{Time}_{\text{Row}}) + (8 \times 2 + \text{Time}_{\text{Row}}) + \ldots \\
&\quad + (8 \times 4 + \text{Time}_{\text{Row}}) + \ldots + (8 \times 1 + \text{Time}_{\text{Row}}) \\
&= \text{Time}_{\text{Row}} + (8 \times 1 + 8 \times 2 + 8 \times 3 + 8 \times 4 + 8 \times 3 + 8 \times 2 + 8 \times 1) + 7 \times \text{Time}_{\text{Row}} \\
&= 8 \times \text{Time}_{\text{Row}} + 8 \times (1 + 2 + 3 + 4 + 3 + 2 + 1) \\
&= 256
\end{aligned}
$$

This is only sending one message at a time per node, even though each node has multiple links. The communication pattern suggested above first uses vertical and then horizontal links, using only half the potential interconnection bandwidth. By carefully selecting pairs of communications that have the same number of vertical hops as the other has horizontal hops and vice versa, the time for complete communication can be cut approximately in half.

- *6-cube*—The number of nodes at each distance in a 6-cube can be found from Pascal's Triangle: 6 at distance 1, 15 at 2, 20 at 3, 15 at 4, 6 at 5, and 1 at distance 6. The number of hops for a node to send to all other nodes is

  $(1 \times 6) + (2 \times 15) + (3 \times 20) + (4 \times 15) + (5 \times 6) + (6 * 1) = 6 + 30 + 60 + 60 + 30 + 6 = 192$

Since every node must send this message, the total number required is $64 \times 192 = 12,228$. Since the interconnection network has $64 \times (6/2) = 192$ links, it will take $12,228/192 = 64$ cycles to complete all hops.

Figure 7.18 summarizes the calculations from this example.

Evaluation category	Bus	Ring	2D torus	6-cube	Fully connected
Time all-to-all	4032	1024	256	64	1
Time north & east	112	8	1	1	1

FIGURE 7.18   Summary of the communication times for all-to-all and for nearest northern and eastern neighbors calculated in the surrounding examples.

■

EXAMPLE   A common communication pattern in scientific programs is to consider the nodes as elements of a two-dimensional array and then have communication to the nearest neighbor in a given direction. (This is sometimes called NEWS communication, standing for north, east, west, and south, the directions on the compass.) Map an eight-by-eight array onto the 64 nodes in each topology, and assume every link of every interconnect is the same speed. How long does it take for each node to send one message to its northern neighbor and one to its eastern neighbor? Ignore nodes that have no northern or eastern neighbors.

ANSWER   In this case we want to send $2 \times (64 - 8)$, or 112, messages. Here are the cases, again in increasing order of difficulty of explanation:

■ *Bus*—The placement of the eight-by-eight array makes no difference for the bus, since all nodes are equally distant. The 112 transfers are done sequentially, taking 112 time units.

■ *Fully connected*—Again the nodes are equally distant; all transfers are done in parallel, taking one time unit.

■ *Ring*—Here the nodes are differing distances. Assume the first row of the array is placed on nodes 0 to 7, the second row on nodes 8 to 15, and so on. It takes just one time unit to send to the eastern neighbor, for this is a send from node n to node $n + 1$. The northern neighbor is exactly eight nodes away in this scheme, so it takes eight time units for each node to send to its northern neighbor. The ring total is nine time units.

■ *2D torus*—There are eight rows and eight columns in our grid of 64 nodes, which is a perfect match to the NEWS communication. It takes just two time units to send to the northern and eastern neighbors.

■ *6-cube*—It is possible to place the array so that it will take just two time units for this communication pattern, as in the case of the 2D grid.

Figure 7.18 also summarizes the calculations from this example.   ■

The simple analysis of interconnection networks in this section ignores several important practical considerations in the construction of an interconnection network. First, these three-dimensional drawings must be mapped onto chips, boards, and cabinets that are essentially two-dimensional media, often tree-like. For example, due to the fixed height of cabinets, an n-node Intel Paragon uses an $n/16 \times 16$ rectangular grid rather than the ideal of $\sqrt{n} \times \sqrt{n}$. Another consideration is the internal speed of the switch: if it is fixed, then more links per switch means lower bandwidth per link, potentially affecting the desirability of different topologies. Yet another consideration is that the latency through a switch depends on the complexity of the routing pattern, which in turn depends on the topology.

Topologies that appear elegant when sketched on the blackboard may look awkward when constructed from chips, cables, boards, and boxes. The bottom line is that quality of implementation matters more than topology. To put these topologies in perspective, Figure 7.19 lists those used in commercial MPPs.

Institution	Name	Number of nodes	Basic topology	Data bits/link	Network clock rate	Peak BW/link (MB/sec)	Bisection (MB/sec)	Year
Thinking Machines	CM-2	1024 to 4096	12-cube	1	7 MHz	1	1024	1987
nCube	nCube/ten	1 to 1024	10-cube	1	10 MHz	1.2	640	1987
Intel	iPSC/2	16 to 128	7-cube	1	16 MHz	2	345	1988
Maspar	MP-1216	32 to 512	2D grid + multistage Omega	1	25 MHz	3	1300	1989
Intel	Delta	540	2D grid	16	40 MHz	40	640	1991
Thinking Machines	CM-5	32 to 2048	Multistage fat tree	4	40 MHz	20	10,240	1991
Meiko	CS-2	32 to 1024	Multistage fat tree	8	70 MHz	50	50,000	1992
Intel	Paragon	4 to 2048	2D grid	16	100 MHz	175	6400	1992
IBM	SP-2	2 to 512	Multistage fat tree	8	40 MHz	40	20,480	1993
Cray Research	T3D	16 to 2048	3D torus	16	150 MHz	300	76,800	1993

FIGURE 7.19 Characteristics of interconnections of some commercial MPPs. The bisection bandwidth is given for the largest machine. The 2D grid of the Intel Delta is 16 rows by 35 columns. The fat-tree topology of the CM-5 is restricted in the lower two levels, hence the lower bandwidth in the bisection. Note that the Cray T3D has two processors per node and the Intel Paragon has from two to as many as four processors per node.

Connection-Oriented versus Connectionless Communication

Before computers arrived on the scene, the telecommunications industry allowed communication around the world. An operator sets up a *connection* between a caller and a callee, and once the connection is established, a conversation can continue for hours. To share transmission lines over long distances, the telecommunications industry uses switches to multiplex several conversations on the same lines. Since audio transmissions have relatively low bandwidth, the solution was to divide the bandwidth of the transmission line into a fixed number of slots, with each slot assigned to a conversation. This technique is called *frequency-division multiplexing*.

Although a good match for voice, frequency-division multiplexing is inefficient for sending data. The problem is that the time slot is dedicated to the conversation whether or not there is anything being said. Hence the long distance lines are "busy" based on the *number* of conversations, and not on the *amount* of information being sent at a particular time. An alternative style of communication is called *connectionless*, where each package is routed to the destination by looking at its address. The postal system is a good example of connectionless communication.

Closely related to the idea of connection versus connectionless communication are the terms *circuit switching* and *packet switching*. Circuit switching is the traditional way to offer a connection-based service. A circuit is established from source to destination to carry the conversation, reserving bandwidth until the circuit is broken. The alternative to circuit-switched transmission is to divide the information into *packets,* or *frames*, with each packet including the destination of the packet plus a portion of the information. Queuing theory in section 6.4 tells us that packets cannot use all of the bandwidth, but in general this *packet-switched* approach allows more use of the bandwidth of the medium and is the traditional way to support connectionless communication.

EXAMPLE　Let's compare a single 100 Mbits/sec packet switched network with ten 10 Mbits/sec packet-switched networks. Assume that the mean size of a packet is 250 bytes, the arrival rate is 25,000 packets per second, and the interarrival times are exponentially distributed. What is the mean response time for each alternative? What is the intuitive reason behind the difference?

ANSWER　From section 6.4 in the prior chapter, we can use an M/M/1 queue to calculate the mean response time for the single fast network:

$$\text{Service rate} = \frac{100 \times 10^6}{250 \times 8} = \frac{100 \times 10^6}{2000} = 50,000 \text{ packets per second}$$

$$\text{Time}_{server} = \frac{1}{50,000} = 0.00002 \text{ secs} = 20 \text{ } \mu\text{secs}$$

$$\text{Utilization} = \frac{\text{Arrival rate}}{\text{Service rate}} = \frac{25,000}{50,000} = 0.5$$

$$\text{Time}_{queue} = \text{Time}_{server} \times \frac{\text{Server utilization}}{(1 - \text{Server utilization})} = 20 \text{ } \mu\text{secs} \times \frac{0.5}{1 - 0.5} = 20 \times \frac{0.5}{0.5} = 20 \text{ } \mu\text{secs}$$

$$\text{Mean response time} = \text{Time}_{queue} - \text{Time}_{server} = 20 + 20 = 40 \text{ } \mu\text{secs}$$

The 10 slow networks can be modeled by an M/M/m queue, and the appropriate formulas are found in section 6.7:

$$\text{Service rate} = \frac{10 \times 10^6}{250 \times 8} = \frac{10 \times 10^6}{2000} = 5000 \text{ packets per second}$$

$$\text{Time}_{server} = \frac{1}{5000} = 0.0002 \text{ secs} = 200 \text{ } \mu\text{secs}$$

$$\text{Utilization} = \frac{\text{Arrival rate}}{m \times \text{Service rate}} = \frac{25,000}{10 \times 5000} = \frac{25,000}{50,000} = 0.5$$

$$\text{Time}_{queue} = \text{Time}_{server} \times \frac{\text{Server utilization}}{m \times (1 - \text{Server utilization})} = 200 \text{ } \mu\text{secs} \times \frac{0.5}{10 \times (1 - 0.5)} = 20 \times \frac{0.5}{0.5} = 20 \text{ } \mu\text{secs}$$

$$\text{Mean response time} = \text{Time}_{queue} + \text{Time}_{server} = 20 + 200 = 220 \text{ } \mu\text{secs}$$

The intuition is clear from the results: the service time is much less for the faster networks even though the queuing times are the same. This intuition is the argument for "statistical multiplexing" using packets; queuing times are not worse for a single faster network, and the latency for a single packet is much less. Stated alternatively, you get better latency when you use an unloaded fast network, and data traffic is bursty so it works. ∎

Although connections are traditionally aligned with circuit switching, it is certainly possible to provide the user the appearance of a logical connection on top of a packet-switched network. TCP/IP, as we shall see in section 7.9, is a connection-oriented service that operates over packet-switched networks.

Routing: Delivering Messages

Given that the path between nodes may be difficult to navigate depending upon the topology, the system must be able to route the message to the desired node. Shared media has a simple solution: The message is broadcast to *all* nodes that share the media, and each node looks at an address within the message to see whether the message is for that node. This routing also made it easy to broadcast one message to all nodes by reserving one address for everyone; broadcast is much harder to support in switch-based networks.

Switched media use three solutions for routing. In *source-based routing,* the message specifies the path to the destination. Since the network merely follows directions, it can be simpler. One alternative is the *virtual circuit,* whereby a circuit is established between source and destination, and the message simply names the circuit to follow. Another approach is a *destination-based routing*, where the message merely contains a destination address, and the switch must pick a path to deliver the message. Destination-based routing may be *deterministic* and always follow the same path, or it may be *adaptive*, allowing the network to pick different routes to avoid failures or congestion. Closely related to adaptive routing is *randomized routing,* whereby the network will randomly pick between several equally good paths to spread the traffic throughout the network, thereby avoiding hot spots.

Switches in wide area networks route messages using a *store-and-forward* policy; each switch waits for the full message to arrive in the switch before it is sent on to the next switch. The alternative is for the switch to examine the header, decide where to send the message, and then start forwarding it immediately without waiting for the rest of the message. This alternative is called either *cut-through* routing or *wormhole* routing and is popular in MPP networks. In wormhole routing, when the head of the message is blocked, the message stays strung out over the network, potentially blocking other messages. Cut-through routing lets the tail continue when the head is blocked, compressing the strung-out message into a single switch. Clearly, cut-through routing requires a buffer large enough to hold the largest packet, while wormhole routing needs only to buffer the piece of the packet that is sent between switches.

The advantage of both cut-through and wormhole routing over store-and-forward is that latency reduces from a function of the number of intermediate switches *multiplied* by the size of the packet to the time for the first part of the packet to negotiate the switches *plus* the transmission time.

EXAMPLE   The CM-5 uses wormhole routing, with each switch buffer being just 4 bits per port. Compare efficiency of store-and-forward versus wormhole routing for a 128-node machine using a CM-5 interconnection sending a 16-byte payload. Assume each switch takes 0.25 microseconds and that the transfer rate is 20 MB/sec.

ANSWER   Each switch in the CM-5 is one node of the 4-ary fat tree. The CM-5 interconnection for 128 nodes is four levels high, so a message goes through seven intermediate switches. Each CM-5 packet has four bytes of header information, so the length of this packet is 20 bytes. The time to transfer 20 bytes over one CM-5 link is

$$\frac{20}{20 \text{ MB/sec}} = 1 \text{ μsec}$$

Then the time for store and forward is

$$(\text{Switches} \times \text{Switch delay}) - ((\text{Switches} + 1) \times \text{Transfer time}) = (7 \times 0.25) + (8 \times 1) = 9.75 \text{ }\mu\text{secs}$$

while wormhole routing is

$$(\text{Switches} \times \text{Switch delay}) + \text{Transfer time} = (7 \times 0.25) + 1 = 2.75 \text{ }\mu\text{secs}$$

For this example, wormhole routing improves latency by more than a factor of three.

■

A final routing issue is the order in which packets arrive. Some networks require that packets arrive in the order in which they are sent. The alternative removes this restriction, requiring software to reassemble the packets in proper order.

Congestion Control

One advantage of a circuit-switched network is that once a circuit is established, it ensures there is sufficient bandwidth to deliver all the information that can be sent along that circuit. Thus interconnection bandwidth is reserved as circuits are established rather than consumed as data are sent, and if the network is full, no more circuits can be established. You may have encountered this blockage when trying to place a long distance phone call on a popular holiday, as the telephone system tells you that "all circuits are busy" and asks you to please call back at a later time.

Packet-switched networks do not reserve interconnect bandwidth in advance, so the interconnection network can become clogged with too many packets. Just as with rush hour traffic, a traffic jam of packets increases packet latency. Packets take longer to arrive, and in extreme cases fewer packets per second are delivered by the interconnect, just as is the case for the poor rush-hour commuters. There is even the computer equivalent of gridlock: *deadlock* is achieved when packets in the interconnect can make no forward progress no matter what sequence of events happens. Chapter 8 addresses how to avoid this ultimate congestion.

These problems are exacerbated with higher bandwidth and longer distance networks, as this Example illustrates.

EXAMPLE   Assume a 155 Mbits/sec network stretching from San Francisco to New York City. How many bytes will be in flight? What is the number if the network is upgraded to 1000 Mbits/sec?

ANSWER   The speed of light is still 299,792.5 kilometers per second, signals go at about 50% of the speed of light in a conductor, and the distance between San Francisco and New York City is 4120 km. Calculating time of flight:

$$\text{Time of flight} = \frac{4120 \text{ km}}{0.5 \times 299{,}792.5 \text{ km/sec}} = 0.0275 \text{ secs}$$

Let's assume the network delivers 50% of the peak bandwidth. The number of bytes in transit on a 155 Mbits/sec network is

$$\text{Bytes in transit} = \text{Delivered bandwidth} \times \text{Time of Flight}$$
$$= \frac{0.5 \times 155 \text{ Mbits/sec}}{8} \times 0.0275 \text{ secs} = 9.7 \text{ MB/sec} \times 0.0275 \text{ secs}$$
$$= 260 \text{ KB}$$

At 1000 Mbits/sec the number is

$$\text{Bytes in transit} = \frac{0.5 \times 1000 \text{ Mbits/sec}}{8} \times 0.0275 \text{ secs} = 62.5 \text{ MB/sec} \times 0.0275 \text{ secs}$$
$$= 1678 \text{ KB}$$

Clearly a megabyte of messages will be a challenge to control and to store.

■

The solution to congestion is to prevent new packets from entering the network until traffic is reduced. Using our automobile analogy, this is the role of the metering lights on freeway on-ramps that control the rate of cars entering the freeway. There are three basic schemes used for congestion control in computer interconnection networks, each with its own weaknesses: packet discarding, flow control, and choke packets.

The simplest, and most callous, is *packet discarding*. If a packet arrives at a switch and there is no room in the buffer, the packet is discarded. This scheme relies on higher-level software that handles errors in transmission to resend lost packets. Internetworking protocols such as UDP discard packets.

The second scheme is to rely on *flow control* between pairs of receivers and senders. The idea is to use feedback to tell the sender when it is allowed to send the next packet. One version of feedback is via separate wires between adjacent senders and receivers that tell the sender to stop immediately when the receiver cannot accept another message. This *back-pressure* feedback is rapidly sent back to the original sender over dedicated lines, causing all links between the two end points to be frozen until the receiver can make room for the next message. Back-pressure flow control is common in MPPs. A more sophisticated variation of feedback is for the ultimate destination to give the original sender the right to send n packets before getting permission to send more. The collection of n packets is typically called a *window*, with the window's size determining the minimum frequency of communication from receiver to sender. The goal of the window is to send enough packets to overlap the latency of the interconnection with the overhead to send and receive a packet. The TCP protocol uses a window.

This brings us to a point of confusion on terminology in many papers and textbooks. Note that flow control describes just two nodes of the interconnection and not the total interconnection network between all end systems. *Congestion control* refers to schemes that reduce traffic when the collective traffic of all nodes is too large for the network to handle. Hence flow control helps congestion control, but it is not a universal solution.

The third scheme is based on *choke packets*. The observation is that you only want to limit traffic when the network is congested. The idea is for each switch to see how busy it is, entering a warning state when it passes a threshold. Each packet received by the switch in a warning state will be sent back to the source via a choke packet that includes the intended destination. The source is expected to reduce traffic to that destination by a fixed percentage. Since it likely will have already sent many packets along that path, it waits for all the packets in transit to be returned before taking choke packets seriously.

7.6 | Practical Issues for Commercial Interconnection Networks

There are two practical issues in addition to the technical issues described so far that are important considerations for some interconnection networks: standardization and fault tolerance.

Standardization

Standards are useful in many places in computer design, but with interconnection networks they are often critical. Advantages of successful standards include low cost and stability: the customer has many vendors to choose from, which both keeps price close to cost due to competition and makes the viability of the interconnection independent of the stability of a single company. Components designed to be used in a standard interconnection may also have a larger market, and this higher volume can lower the vendor's costs, further benefitting the customer. Finally, a standard allows many companies to build products with interfaces to the standard, so the customer does not have to wait for a single company to develop interfaces to all the products the customer might be interested in.

One drawback of standards is that it takes a long time for committees to agree on the definition of standards, which is a problem when technology is changing quickly. Another problem is *when* to standardize: on one hand, designers would like to have a standard before anything is built; on the other, it would be better if something is built before standardization to avoid legislating useless features or omitting important ones. When done too early, it is often done entirely by committee, which is somewhat like asking all of France to prepare a single dish of food. Standards can also suppress innovation, since the interfaces are fixed by the standard.

MPP interconnection networks are traditionally proprietary, while LANs and WANs use standards. WANs involve many types of companies and must connect to many brands of computers, so it is difficult to imagine a proprietary WAN ever being successful. The ubiquitous nature of the Ethernet shows the popularity of standards for LANs as well as WANs, and it seems unlikely that many customers would tie the viability of their LAN to the stability of a single company.

Since an MPP is really a single brand of computer from a single company, the customer is already betting on a single company, removing one of the main arguments for interconnect standards. Thus the few MPPs that used standard interconnections did so to take advantage of the lower cost of components developed for these standards.

Node Failure Tolerance

The second practical issue refers to whether or not the interconnection relies on all the nodes being operational in order for the interconnection to work properly. Since software failures are generally much more frequent than hardware failures, the question is whether a software crash on a single node can prevent the rest of the nodes from communicating.

Clearly WANs would be useless if they demanded that thousands of computers spread across a continent be continuously available, and so they all tolerate the failures of individual nodes. LANs connect dozens to hundreds of computers together, and again it would be impractical to require that no computer ever fail. All successful LANs normally survive node failures.

Although some MPPs have the ability to work around failed nodes and switches, it is not clear that MPP operating systems support this feature. The close cooperation of the software on an MPP during communication also makes it unlikely that the interconnection would be useful if a single node crashed.

EXAMPLE   Figure 7.20 shows the number of failures of 58 workstations on a local area network for a period of just over one year. Suppose that one local area network is based on a network that requires all machines to be operational for the interconnection network to send data; if a node crashes, it cannot accept messages, so the interconnection becomes choked with data waiting to be delivered. An alternative is the traditional local area network, which can operate in the presence of node failures; the interconnection simply discards messages for a node that decides not to accept them. Assuming that you need to have both your workstation and the connecting LAN to get your work done, how much greater are your chances of being prevented from getting your work done using the failure-intolerant LAN versus traditional LANs? Assume the down time for a crash is less than 30 minutes. Calculate using the one-hour intervals from this figure.

ANSWER   Assuming the numbers for Figure 7.20, the percentage of hours that you can't get your work done using the failure-intolerant network is

$$\frac{\text{Intervals with failures}}{\text{Total intervals}} = \frac{\text{Total intervals} - \text{Intervals no failures}}{\text{Total intervals}}$$

$$= \frac{8974 - 3605}{8974} = \frac{369}{8974} = 4.1\%$$

The percentage of hours that you can't get your work done using the traditional network is just the time your workstation has crashed. Assuming that these failures are equally distributed among workstations, the percentage is

$$\frac{\text{Failures/Machines}}{\text{Total intervals}} = \frac{654/58}{8974} = \frac{11.28}{8974} = 0.13\%$$

Hence you are more than 30 times more likely to be prevented from getting your work done with the failure-intolerant LAN than with the traditional LAN, according to the failure statistics in Figure 7.20. Stated alternatively, the person responsible for maintaining the LAN would receive a thirtyfold increase in phone calls from irate users!   ■

One practical issue is tied to node failure tolerance: If the interconnection can survive a failure, can it also continue operation while a new node is added to the interconnection? If not, the interconnection must be disabled each time a new node is added. Disabling is impractical for both WANs and LANs.

Finally, we have been discussing the ability of the network to operate in the presence of failed nodes. Clearly as important to the happiness of the network administrator is the reliability of the network media and switches themselves, for their failure is certain to frustrate much of the user community.

Failed machines per time interval	One-hour intervals with number of failed machines in first column	Total failures per one-hour interval	One-day intervals with number of failed machines in first column	Total failures per one-day interval
0	8605	0	184	0
1	264	264	105	105
2	50	100	35	70
3	25	75	11	33
4	10	40	6	24
5	7	35	9	45
6	3	18	6	36
7	1	7	4	28
8	1	8	4	32
9	2	18	2	18
10	2	20		
11	1	11	2	22
12			1	12
17	1	17		
20	1	20		
21	1	21	1	21
31			1	31
38			1	38
58			1	58
Total	**8974**	**654**	**373**	**573**

FIGURE 7.20   Measurement of reboots of 58 DECstation 5000s running Ultrix over a 373-day period. These reboots are distributed into time intervals of one hour and one day. The first column is used to sort the intervals according to the number of machines that failed in that interval. The next two columns concern one-hour intervals, and the last two columns concern one-day intervals. The second and fourth columns show the number of intervals for each number of failed machines. The third and fifth columns are just the product of the number of failed machines and the number of intervals. For example, there were 50 occurrences of one-hour intervals with two failed machines, for a total of 100 failed machines, and there were 35 days with two failed machines, for a total of 70 failures. As we would expect, the number of failures per interval changes with the size of the interval. For example, the day with 31 failures might include one hour with 11 failures and one hour with 20 failures. The last row shows the total number of each column: the number of failures don't agree because multiple reboots of the same machine in the same interval do not result in separate entries. (These data were collected by Randy Wang of U.C. Berkeley.)

7.7 | **Examples of Interconnection Networks**

To further understand these issues, this section explores examples and the solutions used in each context. Figure 7.21 lists several examples and Figure 7.22 shows the packet formats for three examples. Figure 7.23 shows where networks are connected on several systems and the level of processing available on the network interface card. We discuss a few networks in more detail.

The first example is the Ethernet: It has been extraordinarily successful with the 10 Mbits/sec standard proposed in 1978 used practically everywhere today. Many classes of computers include Ethernet as a standard interface. This packet-switched network uses carrier sensing with exponential backoff to arbitrate for the network, and has been codified as IEEE 802.3.

Given that computers are hundreds of times faster than they were in 1978 and the shared interconnection is no faster, engineers have invented temporary solutions until a faster interconnect can take Ethernet's place. One solution is to use multiple Ethernets to connect machines and to connect these smaller Ethernets with devices that can take traffic from one Ethernet and pass it on to another as needed. These devices allow individual Ethernets to operate in parallel, thereby increasing the aggregate interconnection bandwidth of a collection of computers. In effect these devices provide similar functionality to the switches described above for point-to-point networks.

Figure 7.24 shows the potential parallelism. Depending on how they pass traffic and what kinds of interconnections they can put together, these devices are named differently:

- *Bridges*—These devices connect LANs together, passing traffic from one side to another depending on the addresses in the packet. Bridges operate at the Ethernet protocol level and are usually simpler and cheaper than routers, discussed next.

- *Routers* or *gateways*—These devices connect LANs to WANs or WANs to WANs and resolve incompatible addressing. Generally slower than bridges, they operate at the internetworking protocol level (see section 7.9). Routers divide the interconnect into separate smaller subnets, which simplifies manageability and improves security.

Since these devices were not planned as part of the Ethernet standard, their ad hoc nature has added to the difficulty and cost of maintaining LANs.

	MPP				LAN				WAN
	CM-5	IBM SP-2	Intel Paragon	Cray T3D	Ethernet	100-Mb Ethernet	Switched Ethernet	FDDI	ATM
Length (meters)	25	10?	10?	10.3	500/ 2500	200	500/2500	4000	100/1000
Number data lines	4	8	16	16	1	1	1	1	1
Clock rate (MHz)	40	40	100	150	10	100	10	100	155/622...
Switch?	Yes	Yes	Yes	Yes	No	No	Yes	No	Yes
Nodes	≤2048	≤512	≤1024	≤2048	≤254	≤254	≤254	≤254	≈10000
Material	Copper	Copper	Copper	Copper	Copper	Copper	Copper	Fiber	Copper/fiber
Bisection BW (Mbits/sec)	40x Nodes	320x Nodes	1600x Nodes$^{1/2}$	2400x Nodes$^{2/3}$	10	100	10x Nodes	100	155x Nodes
Peak link BW (Mbits/sec)	160	320	1600	2400	10	100	10	100	155/622
Measured link BW	160	284	1400	1120	9			97	10
Latency (μsecs)	5	1	1	0.2	15	1.5	≈50	10	≈50
Send + receive overheads (μsecs)	15	39	24	0.7	440	440	440	≈500	630
Topology	Fat tree	Fat tree	2D mesh	3D torus	Line	Line	Star	Ring	Star
Connectionless?	Yes	Yes	Yes	Yes	Yes	Yes	Yes	Yes	No
Store & forward?	No	No	No	No	No	No	No	No	Yes
Congestion control	Back-pressure	Back-pressure	Back-pressure	Back-pressure	Carrier sense	Carrier sense	Carrier sense	Token	
Standard	No	No	No	No	IEEE 802.3				ATM Forum
Fault tolerance	No	Yes	No	No	Yes	Yes	Yes	Yes	Yes

FIGURE 7.21   Several examples of MPP, LAN, and WAN interconnection networks. The overhead figure is hardware and software overhead, measured on SPARCStation-10s for the LANs and WAN (see section 7.10).

One potential successor to Ethernet is FDDI, which stands for *fiber-distributed data interface*. This optical-based interconnection was specified at 100 Mbits/sec

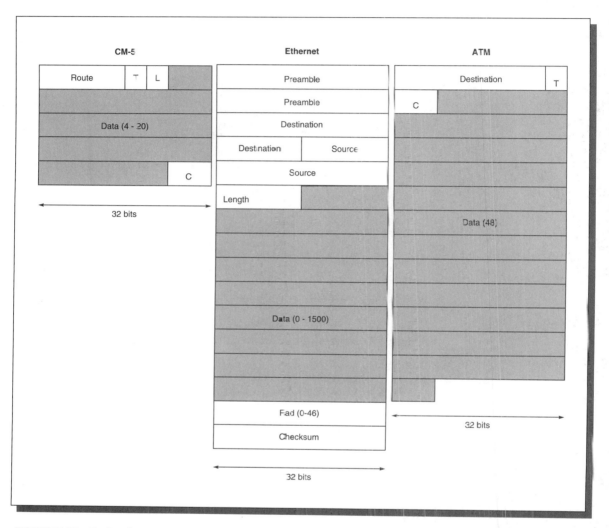

FIGURE 7.22 Packet format for CM-5, Ethernet, and ATM. ATM calls their messages "cells" instead of packets, so this is more properly called the ATM cell format (see section 7 10). The width of each drawing is 32 bits. All three formats have destination addressing fields, encoded differently for each situation. All three also have a checksum field (C) to catch transmission errors, although the ATM checksum field is calculated only over the header; ATM relies on higher-level protocols to catch errors in the data. Both CM-5 and the Ethernet have a length field (L), since the packets hold a variable amount of data, with the former counted in 32-bit words and the latter in bytes. The CM-5 and ATM headers have a type field (T) that gives the type of packet. The remaining Ethernet fields are a preamble to a low the receiver to recover the clock from the self-clocking code used on the Ethernet, the source address, and a pad field to make sure the smallest packet is 64 bytes (including the header).

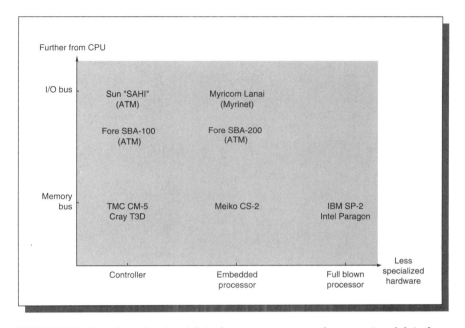

FIGURE 7.23   Location of network interface versus processing on network interface for several interconnection networks. The fallacy on page 623 refers to the increasing processing performance. (From a presentation by Lok Liu of U.C. Berkeley.)

and could use much longer cables than Ethernet. Unfortunately, FDDI inherited Ethernet's weakness in that all machines shared the interconnection medium, with only one packet on the medium at a time, so FDDI still needed bridges and routers. FDDI is currently most widely used as a "backbone" network, which simply means connecting LANs together via their routers rather than connecting desktop computers.

Today, there are three more promising LAN candidates. The first candidate is one of two competing standards that offer a 100 Mbits/sec version of the Ethernet. The second builds on the trend toward many smaller networks by making switches a part of the standard. *Switched Ethernet* simply includes fast, multiport switches so that the bandwidth to a single machine is no higher, but the aggregate bandwidth of the LAN is much higher. Twisted pairs can connect the machine to the switch, lowering the costs of wiring. The third candidate, *asynchronous transfer mode* (ATM), is described in section 7.10.

At the opposite performance end of the LAN networks is the MPP network found in the Cray Research T3D. Using 16-bit links clocked at 150 MHz yields 2400 megabits (300 MB) per second per link. The distributed switch using a

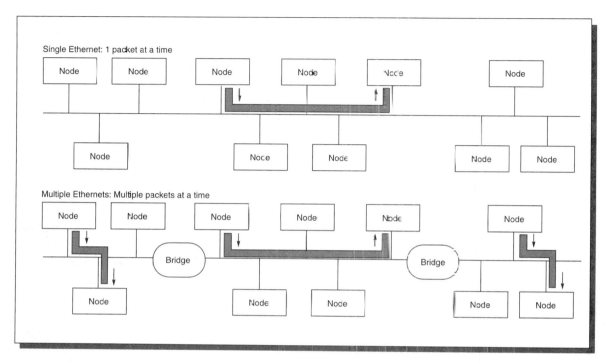

FIGURE 7.24   The potential increased bandwidth cf using many Ethernets and bridges.

three-dimensional torus topology has a bisection bandwidth of between about 10% and 25% of a fully connected system—38,400 to 244,000 Mbits/second—depending on the number of nodes. This proprietary network, which can scale up to 2048 nodes, has a one-way trip latency of less than one microsecond, including hardware and software overhead. Although the T3D network does not face the LAN challenges of distance and security, it still shows that LANs have a long way to go before pushing the envelope of networking bandwidth and latency.

7.8 Crosscutting Issues for Interconnection Networks

This section describes four topics discussed in other chapters that are fundamental to interconnections.

Efficient Interface to Memory Hierarchy versus Interconnection Network

Traditional evaluations of processor performance, such as SPECint and SPECfp, encourage the memory hierarchy to be closely integrated with the processor, as the efficiency of the memory hierarchy translates directly into processor performance. Hence microprocessors have first-level caches on chips along with buffers for writes, and usually have second-level caches immediately next to the chip. Benchmarks such as SPECint and SPECfp do not reward good interfaces to interconnection networks, and hence many machines make the access time to the network delayed by the full memory hierarchy: Writes must lumber their way through full write buffers, and reads must go through the cycles of first- and second-level cache misses before reaching the interconnection. This results in newer systems having higher latencies to interconnections than older machines.

Let's compare three machines. A 40-MHz SPARCstation-2, a 50-MHz SPARCstation-20 without an external cache, and a 50-MHz SPARCstation-20 with an external cache. According to SPECint95, this list is in order of increasing performance. The time to access the I/O bus (S-bus), however, increases in this sequence: 200 ns, 500 ns, and 1000 ns. The SPARCstation-2 is fastest because it has a single bus for memory and I/O, and there is only one level to the cache. The SPARCstation-20 memory access must first go over the memory bus (M-bus) and then to the I/O bus, adding 300 ns. Machines with a second-level cache pay an extra penalty of 500 ns before accessing the I/O bus.

Compute-Optimized Processors versus Receiver Overhead

The overhead to receive a message likely involves an interrupt, which bears the cost of flushing and then restarting the processor pipeline. As mentioned earlier, to read the network status and to receive the data from the network interface likely operates at cache miss speeds. As microprocessors become more superscalar and go to faster clock rates, the number of missed instruction issue opportunities per message reception seems likely to rise quickly over time.

Where to Draw the Hardware/Software Dividing Line for Interconnection Network Functions

The choice of hardware versus software support for interconnection networks has many of the same trade-offs as in other parts of a computer. Examples of features implemented in hardware with some systems and in software with others are message routing, message error detection, and retransmission.

Early MPPs required each processor along a path to route a message from switch to switch. This software overhead dominated switch latency, and thus all recent MPPs have hardware routing. Hardware routing in turn affects the complexity of the topologies of the interconnection, since hardware simplicity demands a simple routing algorithm.

Another example of the hardware/software implementation decision is reliable delivery of messages. TCP checks to make sure that messages are delivered reliably by including checksums, yet LANs like Ethernet will also include checksums in hardware to determine whether packets have been reliably delivered. Some interconnection interfaces hold onto a packet until it has been acknowledged by the receiving hardware, retransmitting in case of failure. These same functions are provided in software by TCP. Reliable delivery is one area of considerable duplication in effort between the hardware and software rather than a clear division of responsibilities (see the pitfall on page 623).

Protection and User Access to the Network

The challenge is to ensure safe communication across a network without invoking the operating system in the common case. The Cray Research T3D offers an interesting case study. It supports a global address space, so loads and stores can access memory across the network. Protection is ensured because each access is checked by the TLB.

To support transfer of larger objects, a block transfer engine (BLT) was added to the hardware. Protection of access requires invoking the operating system, before using the BLT, to check the range of accesses to be sure there will be no protection violations.

Figure 7.25 compares the bandwidth delivered as the size of the object varies for reads and writes. For very large reads, 512 KB, the BLT does achieve the highest performance: 140 MB/sec. But simple loads get higher performance for 8 KB or less. For the write case, both achieve a peak of 90 MB/sec, presumably because of the limitations of the memory bus. But for writes, BLT can only match the performance of simple stores for transfers of 2 MB; anything smaller and it's faster to send stores. Clearly a BLT that avoided invoking the operating system in the common case would be more useful.

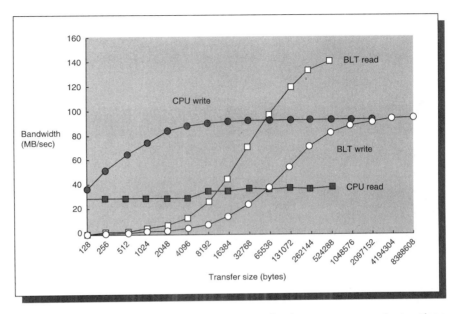

FIGURE 7.25   Bandwidth versus transfer size for simple memory access instructions versus a block transfer device on the Cray Research T3D. (Arpaci et al. [1995].)

7.9 | Internetworking

Undoubtedly one of the most important innovations in the communications community has been internetworking. It allows computers on independent and incompatible networks to communicate reliably and efficiently. The need to cross networks is illustrated by Figure 7.26, which shows the networks and machines involved in transferring a file from Stanford University to the University of California at Berkeley, a distance of about 75 km.

The low cost of internetworking is remarkable. For example, it is vastly less expensive to send electronic mail than to make a coast-to-coast telephone call and leave a message on an answering machine. This dramatic cost improvement is achieved using the same long-haul communication lines as the telephone call, which makes the improvement even more impressive.

The enabling technologies for internetworking are software standards that allow reliable communication without demanding reliable networks. The underlying principle of these successful standards is that they were composed as a hierarchy of layers, each layer taking responsibility for a portion of the overall communication task. Each computer, network, and switch implements its layer of the standards, relying on the other components to faithfully fulfill their responsibilities. These layered software standards are called *protocol families* or *protocol*

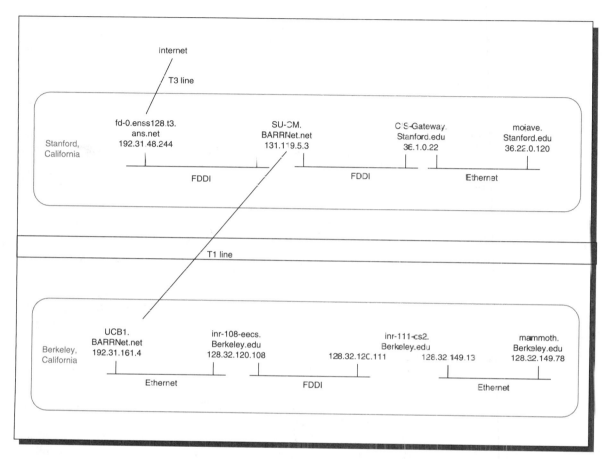

FIGURE 7.26 The connection established between mojave.stanford.edu and mammoth.berkeley.edu. FDDI is a 100 Mbits/sec LAN, while a T1 line is a 1.5 Mbits/sec telecommunications line and a T3 is a 45 Mbits/sec telecommunications line. BARRNet stands for Bay Area Research Network. Note that inr-111-cs2.Berkeley.edu is a router with two Internet addresses, one for each port.

suites. They enable applications to work with any interconnection without extra work by the application programmer. Figure 7.27 suggests the hierarchical model of communication.

The most popular internetworking standard is *TCP/IP,* which stands for *transmission control protocol/internet protocol.* This protocol family is the basis of the humbly named *Internet,* which connects tens of millions of computers around the world. This popularity means TCP/IP is used even when communicating locally across compatible networks; for example, the network file system NFS uses IP even though it is very likely to be communicating across a homogenous LAN such as Ethernet.

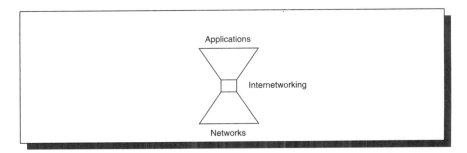

FIGURE 7.27   The role of internetworking. The width is intended to indicate the relative number of items at each level.

We use TCP/IP as our protocol family example; other protocol families follow similar lines. Section 7.13 gives the history of TCP/IP.

The goal of a family of protocols is to simplify the standard by dividing responsibilities hierarchically among layers, with each layer offering services needed by the layer above. The application program is at the top, and at the bottom is the physical communication medium, which sends the bits. Just as abstract data types simplify the programmer's task by shielding the programmer from details of the implementation of the data type, this layered strategy makes the standard easier to understand.

The key to protocol families is that communication occurs *logically at the same level* of the protocol in both sender and receiver, but it is *implemented via services of the lower level.* This style of communication is called *peer-to-peer.* As an analogy, imagine that General A needs to send a message to General B on the battlefield. General A writes the message, puts it in an envelope addressed to General B, and gives it to a colonel with orders to deliver it. This colonel puts it in an envelope and writes the name of the corresponding colonel who reports to General B, and gives it to a major with instructions for delivery. The major does the same thing and gives it to a captain, who gives it to a lieutenant, who gives it to a sergeant. The sergeant takes the envelope from the lieutenant, puts it into an envelope with the name of a sergeant who is in General B's division, and finds a private with orders to take the large envelope. The private borrows a motorcycle and delivers the envelope to the sergeant. Once it arrives, it is passed up the chain of command, with each person removing an outer envelope with his name on it and passing on the inner envelope to his superior. As far as General B can tell, the note is from another general. Neither general knows who was involved in transmitting the envelope, nor how it was transported from one division to the other.

Protocol families follow this analogy more closely than you might think, as Figure 7.28 shows. The original message is given a header and possibly a trailer to be sent by the lower-level protocol. The next-lower protocol in turn adds its own header to the message, possibly breaking it up into smaller messages if it is

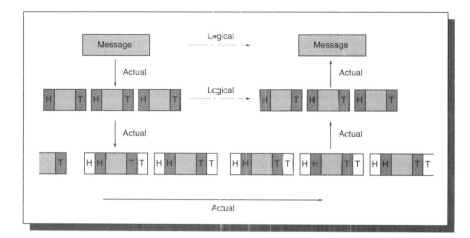

FIGURE 7.28 A generic protocol stack with two layers. Note that communication is peer-to-peer, with headers and trailers for the peer added at each sending layer and removed by each receiving layer. Each layer is intended to offer services to the one above to shield it from unnecessary details.

too large for this layer. Recalling our analogy, a long message from the general would be divided and placed in several envelopes if it could not fit in one. This division of the message and appending of headers and trailers continues until the message descends to the physical transmission medium. The message is then sent to the destination. Each level of the protocol family on the receiving end will check the message at its level and peel off its headers and trailers, passing it on to the next higher level and putting the pieces back together. This nesting of protocol layers for a specific message is often referred to as a *protocol stack*, reflecting the last-in-first-out nature of the addition and removal of headers.

As in our analogy, the danger in this layered approach is the considerable latency added to message delivery. Clearly one way to reduce latency is to reduce the number of layers. But keep in mind that protocol families are used to define a standard, not to force how the standard is implemented. Just as there are many ways to implement an instruction set architecture, there are many ways to implement a protocol family.

Our protocol stack example is TCP/IP. Let's assume that the bottom protocol layer is Ethernet. The next level up is the Internet Protocol or IP layer; the official term for an IP packet is *datagram*. The IP layer routes the datagram to the destination machine, which may involve many intermediate machines or switches. IP makes a best effort to deliver the packets, but does not guarantee delivery, content, or order of datagrams. The TCP layer above IP makes the guarantee of reliable, in-order delivery and prevents corruption of datagrams.

Following the example in Figure 7.28, assume an application program wants to send a message to a machine via an Ethernet. It starts with TCP. The largest

Our example is 16 SPARCstation-10 workstations connected via two brands of ATM switches. Figure 7.30 shows details of the organization. The SPARCstation-10 uses a 50-MHz SuperSPARC microprocessor, which consists of a

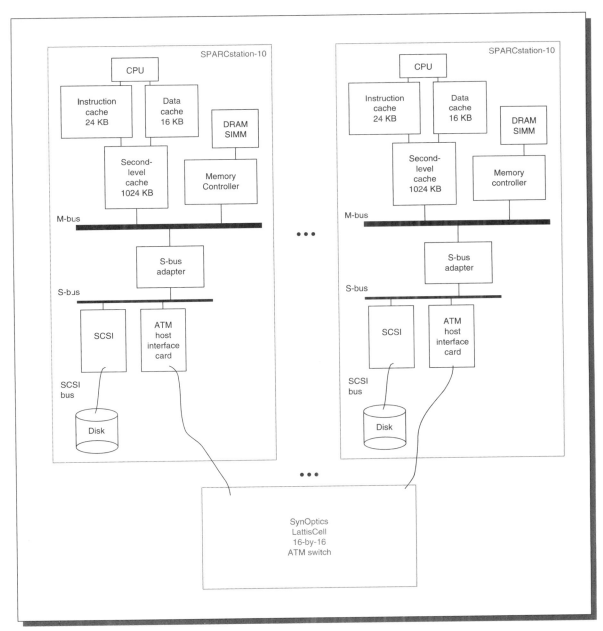

FIGURE 7.30   The organization of the SPARCstation-10 and the ATM switch. The switch is described in Figure 7.35.

superscalar CPU and instruction and data caches on a single chip. This chip interfaces to a 1-MB second-level cache that stands between the microprocessor and the 40-MHz M-bus. The M-bus connects to memory and to a bus interface to the 20-MHz S-bus, Sun's I/O bus. It is on the S-bus that we find the ATM *host interface card*, which interfaces to the 16-by-16 ATM switch.

Let's follow a transfer through the levels before we talk in detail about the components. The transfer proceeds down the TCP and IP layers until it reaches ATM. At the top of the ATM software is the ATM adaptation layer. Figure 7.31 shows this relationship between layers and Figure 7.32 shows AAL-5, the fifth proposal for an ATM standard protocol.

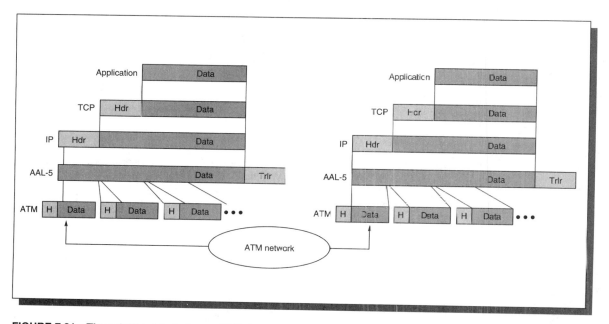

FIGURE 7.31   The relationship between TPC, IP, and AAL-5 layers. The ATM Forum hopes that over time adaptation layers such as AAL-5 will replace protocol suites such as TCP/IP.

The next layer of ATM software breaks up the data payload into the 48-byte units transferred in each ATM cell. Figure 7.33 shows the details of the ATM header. Unlike Ethernet, ATM is based on connections set up in advance before data are transmitted between two machines. For this example, we assume that the connections have already been established between machines, so that we do not need to establish a connection. These connections are called *virtual channels*, with the *virtual channel identifier* (VCI) used to pick the proper connection for each ATM cell. The ATM switch uses the VCI to send the cell to the proper output port. The header also provides a *virtual path identifier* (VPI); *virtual paths*

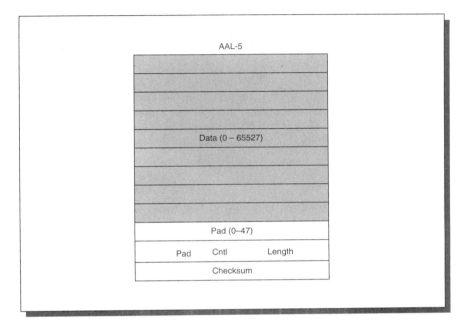

FIGURE 7.32 The AAL-5 format of ATM. The evolving ATM standard has at least five proposals for AALs, but in our view AAL-5 is the most likely winner for LANs when shipping datagrams. Lower-level protocols set bits in packets to show the end of the transfer. The pad field ensures that the data payload plus the AAL-5 trailer is a multiple of 48 bytes, the data size of an ATM cell. The control field (Cntl) is reserved for future use. Length and checksum fields are self-explanatory. The total size including trailer and pad is 64 KB.

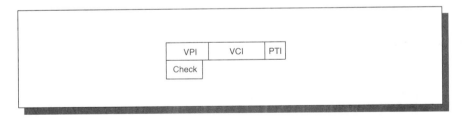

FIGURE 7.33 The ATM header format. The VPI field is 12 bits, VCI is 16 bits, the PTI field is 4 bits, and the checksum field is 8 bits. The main use of the payload type indicator field is to mark the end of the AAL-5 packet. This format is used for the ATM network-to-network interface.

simply represent bundles of virtual channels and may be used by ATM switches to route many channels at once rather than individually. The payload type indicator field is used by AAL-5 to mark the end of a packet.

Note that ATM uses a fixed-sized unit of transmission to simplify the design of switches and interfaces. These units are called *cells*, since use of the term *packet* in a connection-based system might lead to confusion. The cell selects the *connection* rather than including the *destination address* in every cell.

Once all cells composing the AAL-5 message are delivered to the appropriate machine, the cells arrive in order and are passed to the AAL-5 layer software. The layer checks the data and passes them up to the IP software, proceeding up the protocol stack.

The Host Interface Card

The ATM *host interface card* lives on the S-bus and interfaces a node to the ATM switch. The Fore Systems SBA-200 ATM adapter is a rather sophisticated network interface. It is the successor to Fore's simple SBA-100 adapter, which contained only send and receive FIFOs. The three key features of the SBA-200 are a 25-MHz Intel i960CA used as communications coprocessor, a DMA interface to the host bus, and an AAL5-compatible hardware CRC generator/checker. In addition, the SBA-200 has 256 KB of static RAM, which serves as program and data memory for the i960 and can be accessed directly from the host workstation processor. Figure 7.34 shows a block diagram of the SBA-200.

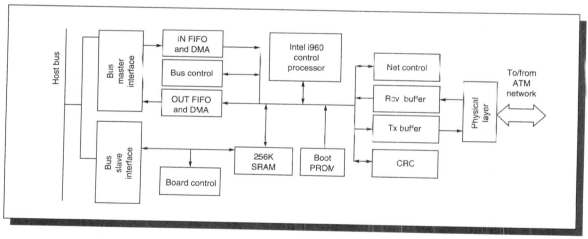

FIGURE 7.34 The Fore Systems SBA-200 host interface card. The processor and SRAM are in the center, the DMA unit in the upper-left corner, the direct access to the SRAM and to a few board control registers in the lower-left corner, and a simple send/receive FIFO interface to the fiber augmented with the CRC generator/checker on the right-hand side.

The inclusion of a processor on the network interface card is the most visible feature of the SBA-200. The main role of the i960 is to free the host workstation CPU from performing the ATM adaptation layer (AAL) segmentation and reassembly of data payload into cells. The host CPU hands a data descriptor to the i960, which breaks the data blocks into cells and generates the cell headers and trailers, including appropriate checksums, or CRCs. On the receiving side, the i960 reassembles arriving cells into data blocks and hands a descriptor to the host once the data are complete.

The role of the DMA interface is twofold: It allows the ATM adaptor to transfer packets to and from main memory without host processor intervention, and it allows data to be transferred using burst bus transactions. The SBA-200's DMA interface can transfer data at over 30 Mbytes/sec in eight-word bursts.

The software support for the SBA-200 consists of two major components: the firmware that is downloaded into the SBA-200's SRAM at boot time and controls the operation of the i960, and the device driver that communicates with the i960 from the host. The apparent rationale underlying the design of Fore's hardware and software is to off-load the specifics of the ATM adaptation layer processing from the host processor as much as possible and to provide a data block interface to the device driver.

The Switches

Each host interface card is connected to a 16-by-16 ATM switch. Depending on the distance to the switch, the media can be either twisted pair copper wire or optical fiber. The latter option requires expensive electrical-to-optical interfaces, but stretches the distance between the host interface card and switch from meters to kilometers.

The Bay Networks LattisCell 10114 switch itself is a multistage switch similar to the Omega switch in Figure 7.13 (page 584), with an internal bandwidth that is twice the demand of the sixteen 155 Mbits/sec ports: 5 Gbits/sec. Figure 7.35 gives details of the switch.

Another ATM switch is the Fore Systems ASX-200. Inside this 2.5 Gbits/sec switch is simply a 40-MHz, 64-bit-wide bus! Capable of handling up to 24 155 Mbits/sec ports, the latency through the switch is less than 10 microseconds. It includes a SPARC microprocessor for routing and up to 700 KB of output buffer per port.

Performance of SPARCstations and ATM

To put ATM in context, this section compares the performance of two of the initial ATM switches to an Ethernet LAN. For each experiment, two Sparc 10s running Solaris 2.3 were connected to an ATM switch via OC-3C SONET links, which have a line rate of 155 Mbits/sec. The network interface was the Fore Systems SBA-200 ATM interface and two ATM switches were tested, the Fore Systems ASX-200 and the Bay Networks LattisCell 10114. The approximate 1995 prices of the components are shown in Figure 7.36.

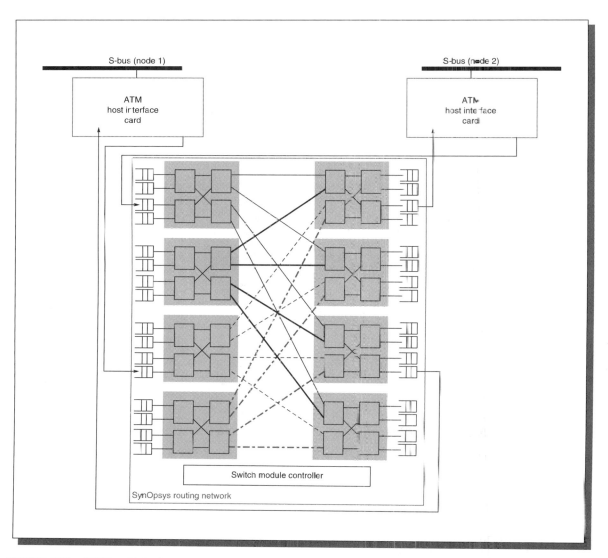

FIGURE 7.35 ATM host interface cards and 16-by-16 LattisCell ATM switch from Synoptics. The switch connection is called a Delta connection, which is a relative of the Omega switch. The switch also has a copy network that is identical to the routing network to support multicast; it is placed before the router. The switch module finds the outgoing destination port of the switch by indexing into a table using the incoming VCI port number.

Figure 7.37 shows the TCP throughput as the size of the TCP packets are increased for Ethernet and ATM. Sending larger packets amortizes the overhead of TCP, IP, and the ATM driver. Figure 7.38 shows the one-way trip latencies for the same systems.

Network	Host Interfaces	Switch
Ethernet	≈$50	NA
ATM	≈$1000	≈$50,000 (ASX-200)
		≈$30,000 (LattisCell 10114)

FIGURE 7.36   Approximate 1995 prices of measured networks.

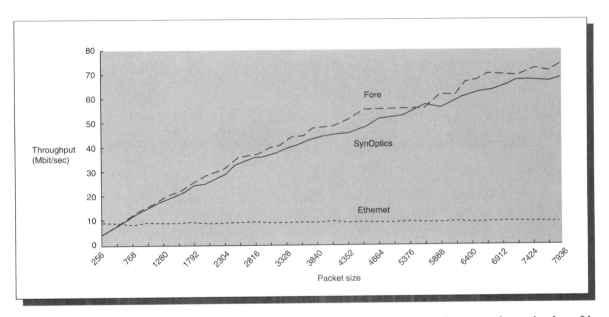

FIGURE 7.37   TCP throughput of ATM versus Ethernet between two machines as datagram size varies from 64 bytes to 8 KB. The Fore Systems switch offers roughly 5% to 10% higher bandwidth. Measurements were gathered by running user-level programs that exchanged data over TCP sockets. All measurements were done for point-to-point connections with little or no additional network traffic flowing through the switch. We measured the time to receive 5000 TCP packets and calculated the effective bandwidth (number of bytes received/elapsed time). Since these experiments measure user data, it does not give credit to the headers and trailers that are part of TCP, IP, AAL5, or ATM. If they were counted, the delivered throughput would be closer to 90 Mbits/second. (Measurements were taken by Kim Keeton of U.C. Berkeley.)

The most surprising result here is that the bandwidth for messages under 512 bytes is worse over the ATM network than it is over the Ethernet! The reason is that the vast majority of the time is spent in the operating system networking layers and the latency of the network itself is insignificant in comparison in both cases. The Ethernet turns out to be faster because its device drivers have been improved over many years and are thus better optimized.

To see the impact, let's estimate the times to replay the trace of NFS traffic from Figure 7.7 on page 573 on Ethernet and ATM. Measurements show the one-

Data size	Ethernet	ASX-200	LattisCell 10114
8	504	690	865
256	726	811	989
1024	1422	908	1083
4096	4174	1379	1589
8192	8631	1993	2274

FIGURE 7.38   One-way trip times in microseconds for different data payloads and networks. Measurements were gathered by running user-level programs that exchanged data over UDP sockets. All measurements were done for point-to-point connections with little or no additional network traffic flowing through the switch. The round-trip test was performed by sending messages over UDP in a request-response communication pattern. Reported above is one-half of the round-trip times. Single round-trip times were collected until a 95% confidence interval was obtained, or a minimum of 35 iterations were measured—whichever came first. (Measurements were taken by Kim Keeton of U.C. Berkeley.)

way time for the smallest packet on an unloaded Ethernet to be 504 microseconds, versus the 690 microseconds for ATM. We model the time as the fixed overhead per message plus a per-data-byte overhead. Our ATM measurements suggest a peak rate of 78 Mbits/sec using TCP/IP for the Fore ATM Switch and 9 Mbits/sec for Ethernet. Figure 7.39 shows the overhead time, transmission time, and total time to send all the NFS messages over Ethernet and ATM. The peak link speed of ATM is 15 times faster and the measured link speed for 8-KB datagrams is almost 9 times faster, but the higher overheads offset the benefits so that ATM would transmit these messages only 1.2 times faster.

Overall the performance is depressing: using a reliable transport protocol (TCP), we can utilize little more than half the network bandwidth. In addition, the small messages prevalent in request-response-style communication fare worse over ATM than over Ethernet. Why is this so? The answer is twofold: First, the UNIX networking layers are not designed for networks of this speed, and second, the driver-firmware interface used by Fore is inefficient.

The problem with the UNIX network layers is that they were designed a decade ago for much slower networks and workstations with much less memory. The same layers with the same algorithms are used for SLIP connections across 9.6 Kbits/second modems as well as for 155 Mbits/second ATM connections.

Another problem is caused by the fact that the driver-firmware interface is at the level of data blocks. This level requires the i960 to traverse descriptors and follow pointers in main memory using DMA accesses that are good for high bandwidth but not low latency. The result is that even if all the UNIX networking inefficiencies were alleviated, the round-trip times would still be several hundred microseconds. See page 623 for the fallacy concerning off-loading the main processor.

Size	No. messages	Overhead (secs)		No. data bytes	Transmission (secs)		Total time (secs)	
		ATM	Ethernet		ATM	Ethernet	ATM	Ethernet
32	771,060	532	389	33,817,052	4	48	536	436
64	56,923	39	29	4,101,088	0	5	40	34
96	4,082,014	2817	2057	428,346,316	46	475	2863	2532
128	5,574,092	3846	2809	779,600,736	83	822	3929	3631
160	328,439	227	166	54,860,484	6	56	232	222
192	16,313	11	8	3,316,416	0	3	12	12
224	4820	3	2	1,135,380	0	1	3	4
256	24,766	17	12	9,150,720	1	9	18	21
512	32,159	22	16	25,494,920	3	23	25	40
1024	69,834	48	35	70,578,564	8	72	56	108
1536	8842	6	4	15,762,180	2	14	8	19
2048	9170	6	5	20,621,760	2	19	8	23
2560	20,206	14	10	56,319,740	6	51	20	61
3072	13,549	9	7	43,184,992	4	39	14	46
3584	4200	3	2	16,152,228	2	14	5	17
4096	67,808	47	34	285,606,596	29	255	76	290
5120	6143	4	3	35,434,680	4	32	8	35
6144	5858	4	3	37,934,684	4	34	8	37
7168	4140	3	2	31,769,300	3	28	6	30
8192	287,577	198	145	2,390,688,480	245	2132	444	2277
Total	11,387,913	7858	5740	4,352,876,316	452	4132	8310	9872

FIGURE 7.39   Total time on Ethernet and ATM, calculating the total overhead and transmission time separately. Note that the size of the headers needs to be added to the data bytes to calculate transmission time. (NFS measurements taken by Mike Dahlin of U.C. Berkeley.)

7.11 | Fallacies and Pitfalls

Interconnection networks are filled with myths and hazards; this section has just a few warnings, so proceed carefully.

Pitfall: Using bandwidth as the only measure of network performance.

Many network companies apparently believe that given sophisticated protocols like TCP/IP that maximize delivered bandwidth, there is only one figure of merit for networks. This may be true for some applications, such as video, where there is little interaction between the sender and the receiver, but many applications, such as NFS, are of a request-response nature, and so for every large message there must be one or more small messages. Figure 7.39 shows that latency is as important as bandwidth.

Pitfall: Ignoring software overhead when determining message overhead.

Low software overhead requires cooperation with the operating system as well as with the communication libraries. As an example, the CM-5 has a software overhead of 20 µsecs to send a message and a hardware overhead of 0.5 microseconds. The Intel Paragon reduced the hardware overhead to just 0.2 microseconds, but the initial release of software has a software overhead of 250 microseconds. Later releases reduced this overhead to 25 microseconds, which still dominates the hardware overhead. Figure 7.39 shows a similar pitfall for ATM.

This pitfall is simply Amdahl's Law applied to networks: Faster network hardware is superfluous if there is not a corresponding decrease in software overhead.

Pitfall: Adding functions to interconnection systems that violate the end-to-end argument.

This argument is against providing features at a lower level that only partially satisfy the communication demand that can only be accomplished at the highest level. Saltzer, Reed, and Clark [1984] give the end-to-end argument as

> *The function in question can completely and correctly be specified only with the knowledge and help of the application standing at the endpoints of the communication system. Therefore, providing that questioned function as a feature of the communication system itself is not possible. [page 278]*

Their example of the pitfall was a network at MIT that used several gateways, each of which added a checksum from one gateway to the next. The programmers of the application assumed the checksum guaranteed accuracy, incorrectly believing that the message was protected while stored in the memory of each gateway. One gateway developed a transient failure that swapped one pair of bytes per million bytes transferred. Over time the source code of one operating system was repeatedly passed through the gateway, thereby corrupting the code. The only solution was to correct the infected source files by comparing to paper listings and repairing the code by hand! Had the checksums been calculated and checked by the application running on the end systems, safety would have been assured.

Fallacy: Adding a processor to the network interface card improves performance.

Microprocessors make it very tempting to add intelligence to a network interface card. Like the pitfall in the last chapter (page 551), the danger is that the processor is much slower and that the additional processor will add to the latency of an operation. Here are two examples.

The Meiko CS-2 MPP uses a 66-MHz HyperSPARC microprocessor in the computation node and added a SPARC-compatible microprocessor built from gate arrays to the network interface card. Their custom design has a much slower clock rate and no caches, and hence the main processor is about 40 times faster. The Meiko's communication has higher overhead than the CM-5, which has simpler hardware despite the use of similar nodes on both MPPs.

To avoid the problem above, the Intel Paragon MPP uses the identical microprocessor twice: once for computation and once for communication. The two 50-MHz i860 XP microprocessors use a common bus that is cache-coherent, further simplifying the software model.

Liu and Culler [1995] measure the Paragon performance for sending eight words using two processors versus one processor. The latency for a single processor is 3.1 microseconds but grows to 9.1 microseconds for the dual processor! The basic reason for the slowdown is that extra work must be performed transferring the data between the cache of the communication microprocessor and the cache of the computation microprocessor. Sending a message requires the following steps on the Paragon:

1. The computation processor stores the messages into the message queue in shared memory for the communication processor to access.

2. The cache block for the queue is likely already in the communication processor, since there is little else for it to do. Since the i860 XP uses an invalidation-based protocol, the store by the first processor invalidates the block in the second. The communication processor is polling, so each time the computation processor writes one word, it is read into the cache of the communication processor and then invalidated by a subsequent write. There is also the extra cost of executing the instructions that write to memory and then read the message back. Each cache-to-cache transfer takes two bus transactions.

3. When the full message is in the cache of the communication processor, the processor sends it to the network interface card, which sends it over the network to the receiver's network interface card.

4. The receiver's communication processor loads the message into its registers.

5. Similar to step 2 above, there begins a sequence of stores by the communication processor and loads by the computation processor to move the data from one cache to the other, which may involve a repeated sequence of invalidates and partial copies.

The extra processor adds steps 2 and 5, which are the most time-consuming steps in the process.

The reasons designers add an extra processor are to avoid the overhead of invoking the operating system and to communicate in parallel with the computation. This works best for DMA-like transfers of large messages, but can interfere with latency of small messages.

Pitfall: Using TCP/IP as LAN protocol.

The network designers on the first workstations decided it would be elegant to use a single protocol stack no matter where the destination of the message: across a room or across an ocean, the TCP/IP overhead must be paid. This might have been a wise decision especially given the unreliability of early Ethernet hardware, but it sets a high software overhead barrier for commercial systems. Such an obstacle lowers the enthusiasm for low-latency network interface hardware and low-latency interconnection networks if the software is just going to waste hundreds of microseconds when the message must travel only dozens of meters.

TCP/IP advocates point out that the protocol itself is theoretically not as burdensome as the current implementations, but progress has been modest in systems shipped commercially.

7.12 | Concluding Remarks

Networking is one of the most exciting fields in computer science and engineering today. The Internet and World Wide Web pervade our society and will likely revolutionize how we access information. Although we couldn't have the Internet without the telecommunication media, it is protocol suites such as TCP/IP that make electronic communication practical. More than almost any other area of computer science and engineering, these protocols embrace the concept that failures are the norm, and so the system must operate reliably in the presence of failures. Interconnection network hardware and software blend telecommunications with data communications, calling into question whether they should remain as separate academic disciplines or be combined into a single field.

The silicon revolution has made its way to the switch: just as the "killer micro" changed computing, whatever turns out to be the "killer network" will transform communication. We are seeing the same dramatic change in cost/performance in switches as the mainframe-minicomputer-microprocessor change did to processors. Inexpensive switches mean that network bandwidth can scale with the number of nodes, even in the local area network.

The combination of fast rate of improvement in processors and in switch-based LANs offers an interesting challenge to conventional computer design. Although the desktop computer is clearly the most cost-effective solution for problems that run fast enough on the desktop, there are many alternatives for problems that are bigger than the desktop. For example, both MPPs and shared-memory processors leverage the same microprocessor as on the desktop to provide larger-scale computing. The problem has been higher prices and delays of introduction for nodes in the multiprocessor versus the high volume and fast-moving desktop computer. The ability to upgrade nodes and switches independently may offer the same flexibility and competition in price and quality as are enjoyed by buyers of stereo components. In 1995, clusters or networks of workstations have the potential to pose a serious challenge to the other candidates for large-scale computing. Challenges to be overcome include the high overhead of communication, the Achilles' heel of such collections of low-cost machines, and providing operating systems that can coordinate hundreds of machines [Anderson, Culler, and Patterson 1995].

The dramatic improvement in cost/performance of communications has enabled millions of people around the world to find others with common interests. We are not near any performance plateaus, so we expect rapid advance in both local and wide area networks. As the quotes at the beginning of this chapter suggest, the authors believe this revolution in two-way communication will change the form of human associations and actions.

7.13 | Historical Perspective and References

This chapter has taken the unusual perspective that computers inside a cabinet of an MPP and computers on an intercontinental WAN share many of the same concerns. Although this observation may be true, their histories are very different.

Wide Area Networks

The earliest of the data interconnection networks are WANs. The forerunner of the Internet is the ARPANET, which in 1969 connected computer science departments across the U.S. that had research grants funded by the Advanced Research Project Agency (ARPA), a U.S. government agency. It was originally envisioned as using reliable communications at lower levels; it was the practical experience with failures of underlying technology that led to the failure-tolerant TCP/IP, which is the basis for the Internet today. Vint Cerf and Robert Kahn are credited with developing the TCP/IP protocols in the mid 1970s, winning the ACM Software Award in recognition of that achievement. Kahn [1972] is an early reference on the ideas of ARPANET.

In 1975 there were roughly 100 networks in the ARPANET and only 200 in 1983; in 1995 the Internet encompasses 50,000 networks worldwide, about half of which are in the United States. Interestingly, the key networks that made the Internet possible, such as ARPANET and NSFNET, have been replaced by fully commercial systems, and yet the Internet still thrives. The exciting application of the Internet is the World Wide Web, developed by a programmer at the European Center for Particle Research (CERN) in 1989 for information access. In 1992 a young programmer at the University of Illinois developed a graphical interface for Web called Mosaic, which became immensely popular. In May 1995 there are over 30,000 Web sites, and the number is doubling every two months.

One interesting sociological phenomenon is the ongoing battle between the advocates of ATM and the Internet protocols. The dream of ATM is a seamless software interface from the local area network to the wide area network, replacing the cumbersome TCP/IP protocol stack with a uniform protocol such as

AAL-5. The Internet advocates think ATM is a fine piece of underlying technology, but you still need TCP/IP because networks will continue to be heterogeneous: ISDN to the home, wireless to the portable, ATM to the office. Thus we are more likely to see contention than synergy between ATM and TCP/IP.

ATM is just the latest of the ongoing standards set by the telecommunications industry, and it is undoubtedly the future for this community. Communication forces standardization by competitive companies, sometimes leading to anomalies. For example, the telecommunication companies in North America wanted to use 64-byte packets to match their existing equipment, while the Europeans wanted 32-byte packets to match their existing equipment. The 48-byte compromise of the new standard was reached to ensure that neither group had an advantage in the marketplace!

Local Area Networks

ARPA's success with wide area networks led directly to the most popular local area networks. Many researchers at Xerox Palo Alto Research Center had been funded by ARPA while working at universities, and so they all knew the value of networking. This group invented the forerunner of today's workstations [Thacker et al. 1982] and Ethernets in 1974 [Metcalfe and Boggs 1976]. It was Boggs' experience as a ham radio operator that led to a design that did not need a central arbiter, but instead listened before use and then varied back-off times in case of conflicts.

This first Ethernet provided a 3 Mbits/sec interconnection, which seemed like an unlimited amount of communication bandwidth with computers of that era, relying on the interconnect technology developed for the cable television industry. The announcement by Digital Equipment Corporation, Intel, and Xerox of a standard for 10 Mbits/sec Ethernet was critical to the commercial success of Ethernet. This announcement short-circuited a lengthy IEEE standards effort, which eventually did publish IEEE 802.3 as an standard for Ethernets.

It is long past time to replace the Ethernet, and there have been several unsuccessful candidates. Unfortunately, the FDDI committee took a very long time to agree on the standard and the resulting interfaces were expensive. It is also a shared medium when switches are becoming affordable.

As mentioned earlier, the failure of FDDI on the desktop has led the LAN community to look elsewhere, and at the time of this writing there are three promising candidates: switched Ethernet, 100-Mbit Ethernet, and ATM.

Massively Parallel Processors

The final component of interconnect networks is found in massively parallel processors (MPPs). One forerunner of today's MPPs is the Cosmic Cube [Seitz 1985], which used Ethernet interface chips to connect 8086 computers in a hypercube. MPP interconnections have improved considerably since then, with messages routed automatically through intermediate switches to their final destinations at high bandwidths and with low latency. Considerable research has gone into the benefits over different topologies in both construction and program behavior. Whether due to faddishness or changes in technology is hard to say, but topologies certainly become very popular and then disappear. The hypercube, widely popular in the 1980s, has almost disappeared from MPPs of the 1990s. Cut-through routing, however, has been preserved and is covered by Dally and Seitz [1986].

By the second edition of this book, MPPs have fallen on hard times: Thinking Machines, Kendall Square Research, and Cray Computer Corporation declared bankruptcy, and Intel Supercomputer announced a reorganization. Although the Cray T3D and N-cube MPP continue unchanged, the MPP standard bearer in 1995 is clearly the IBM SP-2. It uses processor boards from the RS/6000 model 590 workstation, the AIX operating systems from the workstations, and a switch from an MPP research project. The conventionally configured maximum size of the SP-2 is 128 nodes, with two special orders at 512 nodes. The M of MPP stands for massive, and massive is certainly smaller in 1995 than it was in the 1980s.

The Future

At the time of writing this second edition, a new class of networks is emerging: *system area networks*. These recent networks are designed for a single room or single floor and thus the length is ten to hundreds of meters, falling between an MPP interconnection network and a LAN. Close distance means the wires can be wider and faster at lower cost, network hardware can ensure error-free delivery, and less handshaking time is consumed when cascading switches together. There is also less reason to go to the cost of optical fiber, since the distance advantage of fiber is less important for SANs. The limited size of the networks also makes source-based routing plausible, further simplifying the network. Both Tandem Computers and Myricom sell SANs.

Will ATM, Ethernet successors, or SANs be the killer network of the next decade? In 1995 it is very hard to tell. A wonderful characteristic of computer architecture is that such issues will not remain academic debates, unresolved as people rehash the same arguments time and again. Instead, the battle will be fought in the marketplace, with well-funded and talented groups giving their best shots at shaping the future. The best combination of technology and follow-through has often determined commercial success.

Thus time will tell us who wins and who loses; we shall know the score by the next edition of this text.

References

ALLES, A. [1993]. *ATM in Private Networking*, Interop 93 Tutorial.

ANDERSON, T. E., D. E. CULLER, D. PATTERSON [1995]. "A case for NOW (networks of workstations)," *IEEE Micro* 15:1 (February), 54–64.

ARPACI, R. H., D. E. CULLER, A. KRISHNAMURTHY, S. G. STEINBERG, AND K. YELICK [1995]. "Empirical evaluation of the CRAY-T3D A compiler perspective," *Proc. 23rd Int'l Symposium on Computer Architecture* (June), Italy.

ATM FORUM [1994]. *ATM User-Network Interface Specification: Version 3.1.*, PTR Prentice Hall, Englewood Cliffs, N.J

BREWER, E. A. AND B. C. KUSZMAUL [1994]. "How to get good performance from the CM-5 data network." *Proc. Eighth Int'l Parallel Processing Symposium* (April), Cancun, Mexico.

COMER, D. [1993]. *Internetworking with TCP/IP*, 2nd ed., Prentice Hall, Englewood Cliffs, N.J.

DALLY, W. J. AND C. I. SEITZ [1986]. "The torus routing chip," *Distributed Computing* 1:4, 187–96.

DESURVIRE, E. [1992]. "Lightwave communications: The fifth generation," *Scientific American* (International Edition) 266:1 (January), 96–103.

KAHN, R. E. [1972]. "Resource-sharing computer communication networks," *Proc. IEEE* 60:11 (November), 1397–1407.

LIU, L. T. AND D. E. CULLER [1994]. "Measurement of active message performance on the CM-5," Tech. Rep. UCB/CSD94-807, University of California, Berkeley.

LIU, L. T. AND D. E. CULLER [1995]. "An evaluation of the Intel Paragon communication architecture," submitted to *Supercomputing 95*, San Diego, Calif.

METCALFE, R. M. [1993] "Computer/network interface design: Lessons from Arpanet and Ethernet. *IEEE J. on Selected Areas in Communications* 11:2 (February), 173–80.

METCALFE, R. M. AND D. R. BOGGS [1976]. "Ethernet: Distributed packet switching for local computer networks," *Comm. ACM* 19:7 (July), 395–404.

PARTRIDGE, C. [1994]. *Gigabit Networking*. Addison-Wesley, Reading, Mass.

SALTZER, J. H., D. P. REED, D. D. CLARK [1984]. "End-to-end arguments in system design," *ACM Trans. on Computer Systems* 2:4 (November), 277–88.

SEITZ, C. L. [1985]. "The Cosmic Cube (concurrent computing)." *Communications of the ACM* 28:1 (January), 22–33.

TANENBAUM, A. S. [1988]. *Computer Networks*, 2nd ed., Prentice Hall, Englewood Cliffs, N.J.

THACKER, C. P., E. M. MCCREIGHT, B. W. LAMPSON, R. F. SPROULL, AND D. R. BOGGS [1982]. "Alto: A personal computer," in *Computer Structures: Principles and Examples*, D. P. Siewiorek, C. G. Bell, and A. Newell, eds., McGraw-Hill, New York, 549–572.

WALRAND, J. [1991]. *Communication Networks: A First Course*, Aksen Associates: Irwin, Homewood, Ill.

E X E R C I S E S

7.1 [15] <7.2> Assume the overhead to send a zero-length data packet on an Ethernet is 500 microseconds and that an unloaded network can transmit at 90% of the peak 10 Mbits/sec rating. Plot the delivered bandwidth as the data transfer size varies from 32 bytes to 1500.

7.2 [15] <7.2> One reason that ATM has a fixed transfer size is that when a short message is behind a long message, a node may need to wait for an entire transfer to complete. For applications that are time-sensitive, such as when transmitting voice or video, the large transfer size may result in transmission delays that are too long for the application. On an unloaded interconnection, what is the worst-case delay if a node must wait for one full-size Ethernet packet versus an ATM transfer? See Figure 7.22 (page 603) to find the packet sizes. For this question assume you can transmit at 100% of the 155 Mbits/sec of the ATM network and 100% of the 10 Mbits/sec Ethernet.

7.3 [20/10] <7.4>Is electronic communication always fastest for longer distances than the Example on page 579? Calculate the time to send 100 GB using 10 8-mm tapes and an overnight delivery service versus sending 100 GB by FTP over the Internet. Make the following four assumptions:

- The tapes are picked up at 4 P.M. Pacific time and delivered 4200 km away at 10 A.M. Eastern time (7 A.M. Pacific time).

- On one route the slowest link is a T1 line, which transfers at 1.5 Mbits/sec.

- On another route the slowest link is a 10 Mbits/sec Ethernet.

- You can use 50% of the slowest link between the two sites.

a.   [20] <7.4> Will all the bytes sent by either Internet route arrive before the overnight delivery person arrives?

b.   [10] <7.4> What is the bandwidth of overnight delivery? Calculate the average bandwidth of overnight delivery service for a 100-GB package.

7.4 [20/20/20/20] <7.9> If you have access to a UNIX system, use `ping` to explore the Internet. First read the manual page. Then use `ping` without option flags to be sure you can reach the following sites. It should say that X is alive. Depending on your system, you may be able to see the path by setting the flags to verbose mode (`-v`) and trace route mode (`-R`) to see the path between your machine and the example machine. Alternatively, you may need to use the program `traceroute` to see the path. If so, try its manual page. You may want to use the UNIX command `script` to make a record of your session.

a.   [20] <7.9> Trace the route to another machine on the same local area network.

b.   [20] <7.9> Trace the route to another machine on your campus that is *not* on the same local area network.

c.   [20] <7.9> Trace the route to another machine *off campus*. For example, if you have a friend you send email to, try tracing that route. See if you can discover what types of networks are used along that route.

d.   [20] <7.9> One of the more interesting sites is the McMurdo NASA government station in Antarctica. Trace the route to mcmvax.mcmurdo.gov.

7.5 [12/15/15] <7.5> Assume 64 nodes and 16 × 16 ATM switches in the following. (This exercise was suggested by Mark Hill.)

a.   [12] <7.5> Design a switch topology that has the minimum number of switches.

b. [15] <7.5> Design a switch topology that has the minium latency through the switches. Assume unit delay in the switches and zero delay for wires.

c. [15] <7.5> Design a switch topology that balances the bandwidth required for all links. Assume a uniform traffic pattern.

7.6 [20] <7.5> Redo the cut-through routing calculation for CM-5 on page 594 of different sizes: 64, 256, and 1024 nodes.

7.7 [15] <7.5> Calculate the time to perform a broadcast (from-one-to-all) on each of the topologies in Figure 7.17 on page 587, making the same assumptions as the two Examples on pages 588–590.

7.8 [20] <7.5> The two Examples on pages 588–590 assumed unlimited bandwidth between the node and the network interface. Redo the calculations in Figure 7.17 on page 587, this time assuming a node can only issue one message in a time unit.

7.9 [15] <7.5> Compare the interconnection latency of a crossbar, Omega network, and fat tree with eight nodes. Use Figure 7.13 on page 584 and add a fat tree similar to Figure 7.14 on page 585 as a third option. Assume that each switch costs a unit time delay. Assume the fat tree randomly picks a path, so give the best case and worst case for each example. How long will it take to send a message from node P0 to P6? How long will it take P1 and P7 to also communicate?

7.10 [15] <7.5> One interesting measure of the latency and bandwidth of an interconnection is to calculate the size of a message needed to achieve one-half of the peak bandwidth. This halfway point is sometimes referred to as $n_{1/2}$, taken from the vector processing. Using Figure 7.37 on page 620, estimate $n_{1/2}$ for TCP/IP message using ATM and the Ethernet.

7.11 [15] <7.9> Use FTP to transfer a file from a remote site and then between local sites on the same LAN. What is the difference in bandwidth for each transfer? Try the transfer at different times of day or days of the week. Is the WAN or LAN the bottleneck?

7.12 [15] <7.5> Draw the topology of a 6-cube similar to the drawing of the 4-cube in Figure 7.16 on page 587.

7.13 [12/12/12/15/15/18] <7.7> Use M/M/1 queuing model to answer this exercise. Measurements of a network bridge show that packets arrive at 200 packets per second and that the gateway forwards them in about 2 ms.

a. [12] <7.7> What is the utilization of the gateway?

b. [12] <7.7> What is the mean number of packets in the gateway?

c. [12] <7.7> What is the mean time spent in the gateway?

d. [15] <7.7> Plot the response time versus utilization as you vary the arrival rate.

e. [15] <7.7> For an M/M/1 queue, the probability of finding n or more tasks in the system is Utilization^r. What is the chance of an overflow of the FIFO if it can hold 10 messages?

f. [18] <7.7> How big must the gateway be to have packet loss due to FIFO overflow to be less than one packet per million?

7.14 [20] <7.7> The imbalance between the time of sending and receiving can cause problems in network performance. Sending too fast can cause the network to back up and increase the latency of messages, since the receivers will not be able to pull out the message fast enough. A technique called *bandwidth matching* proposes a simple solution: Slow down the sender so that it matches the performance of the receiver [Brewer 1994]. If two machines exchange an equal number of messages using a protocol like UDP, one will get ahead of the other, causing it to send all its messages first. After the receiver puts all these messages away, it will then send its messages. Estimate the performance for this case versus a bandwidth-matched case. Assume the send overhead is 200 microseconds, the receive overhead is 300 microseconds, time of flight is 5 microseconds, and latency is 10 microseconds, and that the two machines want to exchange 100 messages.

7.15 [40] <7.7> Compare the performance of UDP with and without bandwidth matching by slowing down the UDP send code to match the receive code as advised by bandwidth matching [Brewer 1994]. Devise an experiment to see how much performance changes as a result. How should you change the send rate when two nodes send to the same destination? What if one sender sends to two destinations?

8 Multiprocessors

The turning away from the conventional organization came in the middle 1960s, when the law of diminishing returns began to take effect in the effort to increase the operational speed of a computer. ... Electronic circuits are ultimately limited in their speed of operation by the speed of light... and many of the circuits were already operating in the nanosecond range.

Bouknight et al., *The Illiac IV System* [1972]

... sequential computers are approaching a fundamental physical limit on their potential computational power. Such a limit is the speed of light ...

A. L. DeCegama, *The Technology of Parallel Processing, Volume I* (1989)

... today's machines... are nearing an impasse as technologies approach the speed of light. Even if the components of a sequential processor could be made to work this fast, the best that could be expected is no more than a few million instructions per second.

Mitchell, *The Transputer: The Time Is Now* [1989]

8.1	Introduction	635
8.2	Characteristics of Application Domains	647
8.3	Centralized Shared-Memory Architectures	654
8.4	Distributed Shared-Memory Architectures	677
8.5	Synchronization	694
8.6	Models of Memory Consistency	708
8.7	Crosscutting Issues	721
8.8	Putting It All Together: The SGI Challenge Multiprocessor	728
8.9	Fallacies and Pitfalls	734
8.10	Concluding Remarks	740
8.11	Historical Perspective and References	745
	Exercises	755

8.1 Introduction

As the quotations that open this chapter show, the view that advances in uniprocessor architecture were nearing an end has been widely held at varying times To counter this view, we observe that during the period 1985–95, uniprocessor performance growth, driven by the microprocessor, was at its highest rate since the first transistorized computers in the late 1950s and early 1960s. On balance, your authors believe that parallel machines will definitely have a bigger role in the future. This view is driven by three observations. First, since microprocessors are likely to remain the dominant uniprocessor technology, the logical way to improve performance beyond a single processor is by connecting multiple microprocessors together. This is likely to be more cost-effective than designing a custom processor. Second, it is unclear whether the pace of architectural innovation that has contributed to the rapid rate of performance growth starting in 1985 can be sustained indefinitely. As we saw in Chapter 4, modern multiple-issue processors have become incredibly complex, and the increases achieved in performance for increasing complexity and increasing silicon seem to be diminishing. Third, there appears to be slow but steady progress on the major obstacle to widespread use of parallel machines, namely software.

Your authors, however, are extremely reluctant to predict the death of advances in uniprocessor architecture. Indeed, we believe that the rapid rate of performance growth will continue at least into the next millennium. Whether this pace of innovation can be sustained longer is difficult to predict and hard to bet against. Nonetheless, if the pace of progress in uniprocessors does slow down, multiprocessor architectures will become increasingly attractive.

That said, we are left with two problems. First, multiprocessor architecture is a large and diverse field, and much of the field is in its infancy, with ideas coming and going and more architectures failing than succeeding. Given that we are already on page 636, full coverage of the multiprocessor design space and its trade-offs would require another volume. Second, such coverage would necessarily entail discussing approaches that may not stand the test of time, something we have largely avoided to this point. For these reasons, we have chosen to focus on the mainstream of multiprocessor design: machines with small to medium numbers of processors (<100). Such designs vastly dominate in terms of both units and dollars. We will pay only slight attention to the larger-scale multiprocessor design space (>100 processors). The future architecture of such machines is so unsettled in the mid 1990s that even the viability of that marketplace is in doubt. In the past, the high-end scientific marketplace has been dominated by vector computers (see Appendix B), which in recent times have become small-scale parallel vector computers (typically 4 to 16 processors). There are several contending approaches and which, if any, will survive in the future remains unclear. We will return to this topic briefly at the end of the chapter, in section 8.10.

A Taxonomy of Parallel Architectures

We begin this chapter with a taxonomy so that you can appreciate both the breadth of design alternatives for multiprocessors and the context that has led to the development of the dominant form of multiprocessors. We briefly describe the alternatives and the rationale behind them; a longer description of how these different models were born (and often died) can be found in the historical perspectives at the end of the chapter.

The idea of using multiple processors both to increase performance and to improve availability dates back to the earliest electronic computers. About 30 years ago, Flynn proposed a simple model of categorizing all computers that is still useful today. He looked at the parallelism in the instruction and data streams called for by the instructions at the most constrained component of the machine, and placed all computers in one of four categories:

1. *Single instruction stream, single data stream* (SISD)—This is a uniprocessor.

2. *Single instruction stream, multiple data streams* (SIMD)—The same instruction is executed by multiple processors using different data streams. Each processor has its own data memory (hence multiple data), but there is a single instruction memory and control processor, which fetches and dispatches instructions. The processors are typically special purpose, since full generality is not required.

3. *Multiple instruction streams, single data stream* (MISD)—No commercial machine of this type has been built to date, but may be in the future.

4. *Multiple instruction streams, multiple data streams* (MIMD)—Each processor fetches its own instructions and operates on its own data. The processors are often off-the-shelf microprocessors.

This is a coarse model, as some machines are hybrids of these categories. Nonetheless, it is useful to put a framework on the design space.

As discussed in the historical perspectives, many of the early multiprocessors were SIMD, and the SIMD model received renewed attention in the 1980s. In the last few years, however, MIMD has clearly emerged as the architecture of choice for general-purpose multiprocessors. Two factors are primarily responsible for the rise of the MIMD machines:

1. MIMDs offer flexibility. With the correct hardware and software support, MIMDs can function as single-user machines focusing on high performance for one application, as multiprogrammed machines running many tasks simultaneously, or as some combination of these functions.

2. MIMDs can build on the cost-performance advantages of off-the-shelf microprocessors. In fact, nearly all multiprocessors built today use the same microprocessors found in workstations and small, single-processor servers.

Existing MIMD machines fall into two classes, depending on the number of processors involved, which in turn dictate a memory organization and interconnect strategy. We refer to the machines by their memory organization, because what constitutes a small or large number of processors is likely to change over time.

The first group, which we call *centralized shared-memory architectures*, have at most a few dozen processors in the mid 1990s. For multiprocessors with small processor counts, it is possible for the processors to share a single centralized memory and to interconnect the processors and memory by a bus. With large caches, the bus and the single memory can satisfy the memory demands of a small number of processors. Because there is a single main memory that has a uniform access time from each processor, these machines are sometimes called

UMAs for *uniform memory access*. This type of centralized shared-memory architecture is currently by far the most popular organization. Figure 8.1 shows what these machines look like. The architecture of such multiprocessors is the topic of section 8.3.

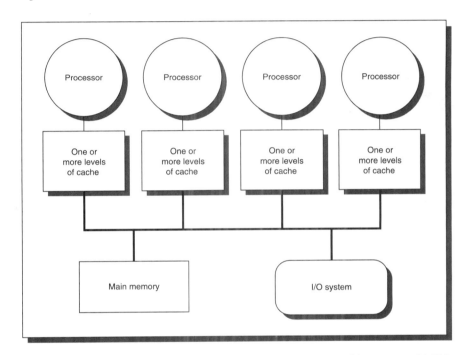

FIGURE 8.1   Basic structure of a centralized shared-memory multiprocessor. Multiple processor-cache subsystems share the same physical memory, typically connected by a bus.

The second group consists of machines with physically distributed memory. To support larger processor counts, memory must be distributed among the processors rather than centralized; otherwise the memory system would not be able to support the bandwidth demands of a larger number of processors. With the rapid increase in processor performance and the associated increase in a processor's memory bandwidth requirements, the scale of machine for which distributed memory is preferred over a single, centralized memory continues to decrease in number (which is another reason not to use small and large scale). Of course, moving to a distributed-memory organization raises the need for a high bandwidth interconnect, of which we saw examples in Chapter 7. Figure 8.2 shows what these machines look like.

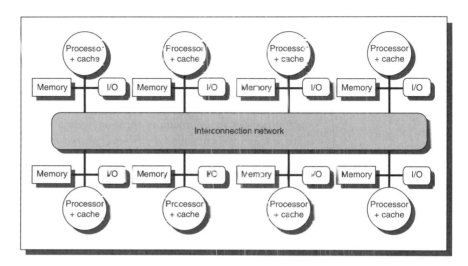

FIGURE 8.2   The basic architecture of a distributed-memory machine consists of individual nodes containing a processor, some memory, typically some I/O, and an interface to an interconnection network that connects all the nodes. Individual nodes may contain a small number of processors, which may be interconnected by a small bus or a different interconnection technology, which is often less scalable than the global interconnection network.

Distributing the memory among the nodes has two major benefits. First, it is a cost-effective way to scale the memory bandwidth, if most of the accesses are to the local memory in the node. Second, it reduces the latency for accesses to the local memory. These two advantages make distributed memory attractive at smaller processor counts as processors get ever faster and require more memory bandwidth and lower memory latency. The key disadvantage for a distributed memory architecture is that communicating data between processors becomes somewhat more complex and has higher latency because the processors no longer share a single centralized memory. As we will see shortly, the use of distributed memory leads to two different paradigms for interprocessor communication.

Typically, I/O as well as memory is distributed among the nodes of the multiprocessor, and the nodes may actually each contain a small number (2–8) of processors interconnected with a different technology. While this *clustering* of multiple processors in a node together with a memory and a network interface may be quite useful from a cost-efficiency viewpoint, it is not fundamental to how these machines work, and so we will focus on the one-processor-per-node style of machine throughout this chapter. The major architectural differences that distinguish among the distributed-memory machines are how communication is done and the logical architecture of the distributed memory.

messages are largely determined by the communication mechanism and its implementation. Why is latency crucial? Latency affects both performance and how easy it is to program a multiprocessor. Unless latency is hidden, it directly affects performance either by tying up processor resources or by causing the processor to wait. Overhead and occupancy are closely related, since many forms of overhead also tie up some part of the node, incurring an occupancy cost, which in turn limits bandwidth. Key features of a communication mechanism may directly affect overhead and occupancy. For example, how is the destination address for a remote communication named, and how is protection implemented? When naming and protection mechanisms are provided by the processor, as in a shared address space, the additional overhead is small. Alternatively, if these mechanisms must be provided by the operating system for each communication, this increases the overhead and occupancy costs of communication, which in turn reduce bandwidth and increase latency.

3. *Communication latency hiding*—How well can the mechanism hide latency by overlapping communication with computation or with other communication? Although measuring this is not as simple as measuring the first two, it is an important characteristic that can be quantified by measuring the running time on machines with the same communication latency but different support for latency hiding. We will see examples of latency hiding techniques for shared memory in sections 8.6 and 8.7. While hiding latency is certainly a good idea, it poses an additional burden on the software system and ultimately on the programmer. Furthermore, the amount of latency that can be hidden is application dependent. Thus it is usually best to reduce latency wherever possible.

Each of these performance measures is affected by the characteristics of the communications needed in the application. The size of the data items being communicated is the most obvious, since it affects both latency and bandwidth in a direct way, as well as affecting the efficacy of different latency hiding approaches. Similarly, the regularity in the communication patterns affects the cost of naming and protection, and hence the communication overhead. In general, mechanisms that perform well with smaller as well as larger data communication requests, and irregular as well as regular communication patterns, are more flexible and efficient for a wider class of applications. Of course, in considering any communication mechanism, designers must consider cost as well as performance.

Advantages of Different Communication Mechanisms

Each of these communication mechanisms has its advantages. For shared-memory communication, advantages include

- Compatibility with the well-understood mechanisms in use in centralized multiprocessors, which all use shared-memory communication.

- Ease of programming when the communication patterns among processors are complex or vary dynamically during execution. Similar advantages simplify compiler design.

- Lower overhead for communication and better use of bandwidth when communicating small items. This arises from the implicit nature of communication and the use of memory mapping to implement protection in hardware, rather than through the operating system.

- The ability to use hardware-controlled caching to reduce the frequency of remote communication by supporting automatic caching of all data, both shared and private. As we will see, caching reduces both latency and contention for accessing shared data.

The major advantages for message-passing communication include

- The hardware can be simpler, especially by comparison with a scalable shared-memory implementation that supports coherent caching of remote data.

- Communication is explicit, forcing programmers and compilers to pay attention to communication. This process may be painful for programmers and compiler writers, but it simplifies the abstraction of what is costly and what is not and focuses attention on costly communication. (If you think this advantage is a mixed bag, that's OK; so do many others.)

Of course, the desired communication model can be created on top of a hardware model that supports either of these mechanisms. Supporting message passing on top of shared memory is considerably easier. Because messages essentially send data from one memory to another, sending a message can be implemented by doing a copy from one portion of the address space to another. The major difficulties arise from dealing with messages that may be misaligned and of arbitrary length in a memory system that is normally oriented toward transferring aligned blocks of data organized as cache blocks. These difficulties can be overcome either with small performance penalties in software or with essentially no penalties, using a small amount of hardware support.

Supporting shared memory efficiently on top of hardware for message passing is much more difficult. Without explicit hardware support for shared memory, all shared-memory references need to involve the operating system to provide address translation and memory protection, as well as to translate memory references into message sends and receives. Loads and stores usually move small amounts of data, so the high overhead of handling these communications in software severely limits the range of applications for which the performance of software-based shared memory is acceptable. An ongoing area of research is the exploration of when a software-based model is acceptable and whether a software-based mechanism is usable for the highest level of communication in a hierarchically structured system. One promising direction is the use of virtual memory mechanisms to share objects at the page level, a technique called *shared virtual memory;* we discuss this approach in section 8.7.

In distributed-memory machines, the memory model and communication mechanisms distinguish the machines. Originally, distributed-memory machines were built with message passing, since it was clearly simpler and many designers and researchers did not believe that a shared address space could be built with distributed memory. More recently, shared-memory communication has been supported in virtually every machine designed for the latter half of the 1990s. What hardware communication mechanisms will be supported in the very largest machines (called *massively parallel processors,* or *MPPs*), which typically have more than 100 processors, is unclear; shared memory, message passing, and hybrid approaches are all contenders. Despite the symbolic importance of the MPPs, such machines are a small portion of the market and have little or no influence on the mainstream machines with tens of processors. We will return to a discussion of the possibilities and trends for MPPs in the concluding remarks and historical perspectives at the end of this chapter.

Although centralized memory machines using a bus interconnect still dominate in terms of market size, long-term technical trends favor distributing memory even in moderate-scale machines; we'll discuss these issues in more detail at the end of this chapter. These distributed shared-memory machines are a natural extension of the centralized multiprocessors that dominate the market, so we discuss these architectures in section 8.4. One important question that we address there is the question of caching and coherence.

Challenges of Parallel Processing

Two important hurdles, both explainable with Amdahl's Law, make parallel processing challenging. The first has to do with the limited parallelism available in programs and the second arises from the relatively high cost of communications. Limitations in available parallelism make it difficult to achieve good speedups in parallel machines, as our first Example shows.

EXAMPLE   Suppose you want to achieve a speedup of 80 with 100 processors. What fraction of the original computation can be sequential?

ANSWER   Amdahl's Law is

$$\text{Speedup} = \frac{1}{\dfrac{\text{Fraction}_{\text{enhanced}}}{\text{Speedup}_{\text{enhanced}}} + (1 - \text{Fraction}_{\text{enhanced}})}$$

For simplicity in this example, assume that the program operates in only two modes: parallel with all processors fully used, which is the enhanced mode, or serial with only one processor in use. With this simplification, the speedup in enhanced mode is simply the number of processors, while the fraction of enhanced mode is the time spent in parallel mode. Substituting into the equation above:

$$80 = \frac{1}{\dfrac{\text{Fraction}_{\text{parallel}}}{100} + (1 - \text{Fraction}_{\text{parallel}})}$$

Simplifying this equation yields

$$0.8 \times \text{Fraction}_{\text{parallel}} + 80 \times (1 - \text{Fraction}_{\text{parallel}}) = 1$$
$$80 - 79.2 \times \text{Fraction}_{\text{parallel}} = 1$$
$$\text{Fraction}_{\text{parallel}} = 0.9975$$

Thus to achieve a speedup of 80 with 100 processors, only 0.25% of original computation can be sequential. Of course, to achieve linear speedup (speedup of n with n processors), the entire program must usually be parallel with no serial portions. (One exception to this is *superlinear speedup* that occurs due to the increased memory and cache available when the processor counts increased. This effect is usually not very large.) In practice, programs do not just operate in fully parallel or sequential mode, but often use less than the full complement of the processors. Exercise 8.2 asks you to extend Amdahl's Law to deal with such a case.   ∎

The second major challenge involves the large latency of remote access in a parallel machine. In existing machines, communication of data between processors may cost anywhere from 50 clock cycles to over 10,000 clock cycles, depending on the communication mechanism, the type of interconnection network, and the scale of the machine. Figure 8 3 shows the typical round-trip delays to retrieve a word from a remote memory for several different parallel machines.

The effect of long communication delays is clearly substantial. Let's consider a simple Example.

Machine	Communication mechanism	Interconnection network	Processor count	Typical remote memory access time
SPARCCenter	Shared memory	Bus	≤ 20	1 μs
SGI Challenge	Shared memory	Bus	≤ 36	1 μs
Cray T3D	Shared memory	3D torus	32–2048	1 μs
Convex Exemplar	Shared memory	Crossbar + ring	8–64	2 μs
KSR-1	Shared memory	Hierarchical ring	32–256	2–6 μs
CM-5	Message passing	Fat tree	32–1024	10 μs
Intel Paragon	Message passing	2D mesh	32–2048	10–30 μs
IBM SP-2	Message passing	Multistage switch	2–512	30–100 μs

FIGURE 8.3   Typical remote access times to retrieve a word from a remote memory. In the case of shared-memory machines, this is the remote load time. For a message-passing machine, the value shown is the time to send a message and reply to the message.

EXAMPLE   Suppose we have an application running on a 32-processor machine, which has a 2000-ns time to handle reference to a remote memory. For this application, assume that all the references except those involving communication hit in the local memory hierarchy, which may be only slightly pessimistic. Processors are stalled on a remote request, and the cycle time of the processors is 10 ns. If the base CPI (assuming that all references hit in the cache) is 1.0, how much faster is the machine if there is no communication versus if 0.5% of the instructions involve a remote communication reference?

ANSWER   The effective CPI for the machine with 0.5% remote references is

$$\text{CPI} = \text{Base CPI} + \text{Remote request rate} \times \text{Remote request cost}$$
$$= 1.0 + 0.5\% \times \text{Remote request cost}$$

The Remote request cost is

$$\frac{\text{Remote access cost}}{\text{Cycle time}} = \frac{2000 \text{ ns}}{10 \text{ ns}} = 200 \text{ cycles}$$

Hence we can compute the CPI:

$$\text{CPI} = 1.0 + 0.5\% \times 200 = 2.0$$

The machine with all local references is 2.0/1.0 = 2 times faster. In practice, the performance analysis is much more complex, since some fraction of the noncommunication references will miss in the local hierarchy and the remote access time does not have a single constant value. For example, the cost of a remote reference could be quite a bit worse, since contention caused by many references trying to use the global interconnect can lead to increased delays.   ■

These problems—insufficient parallelism and long latency remote communication—are the two biggest challenges in using multiprocessors. The problem of inadequate application parallelism must be attacked primarily in software with new algorithms that can have better parallel performance. Reducing the impact of long remote latency can be attacked both by the architecture and by the programmer. For example, we can reduce the frequency of remote accesses with either hardware mechanisms, such as caching shared data, or with software mechanisms, such as restructuring the data to make more accesses local. We can try to tolerate the latency by using prefetch, which we examined in Chapter 5.

Much of this chapter focuses on techniques for reducing the impact of long remote communication latency. For example, sections 8.3 and 8.4 discuss how caching can be used to reduce remote access frequency, while maintaining a coherent view of memory. Section 8.5 discusses synchronization, which, because it inherently involves interprocessor communication, is an additional potential bottleneck. Section 8.6 talks about latency hiding techniques and memory consistency models for shared memory. Before we wade into these topics, it is helpful to have some understanding of the characteristics of parallel applications, both for better comprehension of the results we show using some of these applications and to gain a better understanding of the challenges in writing efficient parallel programs.

8.2 | Characteristics of Application Domains

In earlier chapters, we examined the performance and characteristics of applications with only a small amount of insight into the structure of the applications. For understanding the key elements of uniprocessor performance, such as caches and pipelining, general knowledge of an application is often adequate. In parallel processing, however, the additional performance-critical characteristics—such as load balance, synchronization, and sensitivity to memory latency—often depend on high-level characteristics of the application. These characteristics include factors like how data is distributed, the structure of a parallel algorithm, and the spatial and temporal access patterns to data. Therefore at this point we take the time to examine the two different classes of workloads that we will use for performance analysis in this chapter.

This section briefly describes the characteristics of two different domains of multiprocessor workloads: individual parallel programs and multiprogrammed workloads with operating systems included. Other major classes of workloads are databases, fileservers, and transaction processing systems. Constructing realistic versions of such workloads and accurately measuring them on multiprocessors, including any OS activity, is an extremely complex and demanding process, at the edge of what we can do with performance modeling tools. Future editions of this book may contain characterizations of such workloads. Happily, there is some evidence that the parallel processing and memory system behaviors of database and transaction processing workloads are similar to those of large multiprogrammed workloads, which include the OS activity. For the present, we have to be content with examining such a multiprogramming workload.

Parallel Applications

Our parallel applications workload consists of two applications and two computational kernels. The kernels are an FFT (fast Fourier transformation) and an LU decomposition, which were chosen because they represent commonly used techniques in a wide variety of applications and have performance characteristics typical of many parallel scientific applications. In addition, the kernels have small code segments whose behavior we can understand and directly track to specific architectural characteristics.

The two applications that we use in this chapter are Barnes and Ocean, which represent two important but very different types of parallel computation. We briefly describe each of these applications and kernels and characterize their basic behavior in terms of parallelism and communication. We describe how the problem is decomposed for a distributed shared-memory machine; certain data decompositions that we describe are not necessary on machines that have a single centralized memory.

The FFT Kernel

The *fast Fourier transform* (FFT) is the key kernel in applications that use spectral methods, which arise in fields ranging from signal processing to fluid flow to climate modeling. The FFT application we study here is a one-dimensional version of a parallel algorithm for a complex-number FFT. It has a sequential execution time for n data points of $n \log n$. The algorithm uses a high radix (equal to $\sqrt{n}$) that minimizes communication. The measurements shown in this chapter are collected for a million-point input data set.

There are three primary data structures: the input and output arrays of the data being transformed and the roots of unity matrix, which is precomputed and only read during the execution. All arrays are organized as square matrices. The six steps in the algorithm are as follows:

1. Transpose data matrix.

2. Perform 1D FFT on each row of data matrix.

3. Multiply the roots of unity matrix by the data matrix and write the result in the data matrix.

4. Transpose data matrix.

5. Perform 1D FFT on each row of data matrix.

6. Transpose data matrix.

The data matrices and the roots of unity matrix are partitioned among processors in contiguous chunks of rows, so that each processor's partition falls in its own local memory. The first row of the roots of unity matrix is accessed heavily by all processors and is often replicated, as we do, during the first step of the algorithm just shown.

The only communication is in the transpose phases, which require all-to-all communication of large amounts of data. Contiguous subcolumns in the rows assigned to a processor are grouped into blocks, which are transposed and placed into the proper location of the destination matrix. Every processor transposes one block locally and sends one block to each of the other processors in the system. Although there is no reuse of individual words in the transpose, with long cache blocks it makes sense to block the transpose to take advantage of the spatial locality afforded by long blocks in the source matrix.

The LU Kernel

LU is an LU factorization of a dense matrix and is representative of many dense linear algebra computations, such as QR factorization, Cholesky factorization, and eigenvalue methods. For a matrix of size $n \times n$ the running time is n^3 and the parallelism is proportional to n^2. Dense LU factorization can be performed efficiently by blocking the algorithm, using the techniques in Chapter 5, which leads to highly efficient cache behavior and low communication. After blocking the algorithm, the dominant computation is a dense matrix multiply that occurs in the innermost loop. The block size is chosen to be small enough to keep the cache miss rate low, and large enough to reduce the time spent in the less parallel parts of the computation. Relatively small block sizes (8×8 or 16×16) tend to satisfy both criteria. Two details are important for reducing interprocessor communication. First, the blocks of the matrix are assigned to processors using a 2D tiling: the $\frac{n}{B} \times \frac{n}{B}$ (where each block is $B \times B$) matrix of blocks is allocated by laying a grid of size $p \times p$ over the matrix of blocks in a cookie-cutter fashion until all the blocks are allocated to a processor. Second, the dense matrix multiplication is performed by the processor that owns the *destination* block. With this blocking and allocation scheme, communication during the reduction is both regular and predictable. For the measurements in this chapter, the input is a 512×512 matrix and a block of 16×16 is used.

A natural way to code the blocked LU factorization of a 2D matrix in a shared address space is to use a 2D array to represent the matrix. Because blocks are allocated in a tiled decomposition, and a block is not contiguous in the address space in a 2D array, it is very difficult to allocate blocks in the local memories of the processors that own them. The solution is to ensure that blocks assigned to a processor are allocated locally and contiguously by using a 4D array (with the first two dimensions specifying the block number in the 2D grid of blocks, and the next two specifying the element in the block).

The Barnes Application

Barnes is an implementation of the Barnes-Hut n-body algorithm solving a problem in galaxy evolution. *N-body algorithms* simulate the interaction among a large number of bodies that have forces interacting among them. In this instance the bodies represent collections of stars and the force is gravity. To reduce the computational time required to model completely all the individual interactions among the bodies, which grow as n^2, n-body algorithms take advantage of the fact that the forces drop off with distance. (Gravity, for example, drops off as $1/d^2$, where d is the distance between the two bodies.) The Barnes-Hut algorithm takes advantage of this property by treating a collection of bodies that are "far away" from another body as a single point at the center of mass of the collection and with mass equal to the collection. If the body is far enough from any body in the collection, then the error introduced will be negligible. The collections are structured in a hierarchical fashion, which can be represented in a tree. This algorithm yields an $n \log n$ running time with parallelism proportional to n.

The Barnes-Hut algorithm uses an octree (each node has up to eight children) to represent the eight cubes in a portion of space. Each node then represents the collection of bodies in the subtree rooted at that node, which we call a *cell*. Because the density of space varies and the leaves represent individual bodies, the depth of the tree varies. The tree is traversed once per body to compute the net force acting on that body. The force-calculation algorithm for a body starts at the root of the tree. For every node in the tree it visits, the algorithm determines if the center of mass of the cell represented by the subtree rooted at the node is "far enough away" from the body. If so, the entire subtree under that node is approximated by a single point at the center of mass of the cell, and the force this center of mass exerts on the body is computed. On the other hand, if the center of mass is not far enough away, the cell must be "opened" and each of its subtrees visited. The distance between the body and the cell, together with the error tolerances, determines which cells must be opened. This force calculation phase dominates the execution time. This chapter takes measurements using 16K bodies; the criterion for determining whether a cell needs to be opened is set to the middle of the range typically used in practice.

Obtaining effective parallel performance on Barnes-Hut is challenging because the distribution of bodies is nonuniform and changes over time, making partitioning the work among the processors and maintenance of good locality of reference difficult. We are helped by two properties: the system evolves slowly; and because gravitational forces fall off quickly, with high probability, each cell requires touching a small number of other cells, most of which were used on the last time step. The tree can be partitioned by allocating each processor a subtree. Many of the accesses needed to compute the force on a body in the subtree will be to other bodies in the subtree. Since the amount of work associated with a subtree varies (cells in dense portions of space will need to access more cells), the size of the subtree allocated to a processor is based on some measure of the work it has to do (e.g., how many other cells does it need to visit), rather than just on the number of nodes in the subtree. By partitioning the octree representation, we can obtain good load balance and good locality of reference, while keeping the partitioning cost low. Although this partitioning scheme results in good locality of reference, the resulting data references tend to be for small amounts of data and are unstructured. Thus this scheme requires an efficient implementation of shared-memory communication.

The Ocean Application

Ocean simulates the influence of eddy and boundary currents on large-scale flow in the ocean. It uses a restricted red-black Gauss-Seidel multigrid technique to solve a set of elliptical partial differential equations. *Red-black Gauss-Seidel* is an iteration technique that colors the points in the grid so as to consistently update each point based on previous values of the adjacent neighbors. *Multigrid methods* solve finite difference equations by iteration using hierarchical grids. Each grid in the hierarchy has fewer points than the grid below, and is an approximation to the lower grid. A finer grid increases accuracy and thus the rate of convergence, while requiring more execution time, since it has more data points. Whether to move up or down in the hierarchy of grids used for the next iteration is determined by the rate of change of the data values. The estimate of the error at every time-step is used to decide whether to stay at the same grid, move to a coarser grid, or move to a finer grid. When the iteration converges at the finest level, a solution has been reached. Each iteration has n^2 work for an $n \times n$ grid and the same amount of parallelism.

The arrays representing each grid are dynamically allocated and sized to the particular problem. The entire ocean basin is partitioned into square subgrids (as close as possible) that are allocated in the portion of the address space corresponding to the local memory of the individual processors, which are assigned responsibility for the subgrid. For the measurements in this chapter we use an input that has 130×130 grid points. There are five steps in a time iteration. Since data are exchanged between the steps, all the processors present synchronize at the end of each step before proceeding to the next. Communication occurs when the boundary points of a subgrid are accessed by the adjacent subgrid in nearest-neighbor fashion.

Figure 8.5 shows how the execution time breaks down for the eight processors using the parameters just listed. Execution time is broken into four components: idle—execution in the kernel mode idle loop; user—execution in user code; synchronization—execution or waiting for synchronization variables; and kernel—execution in the OS that is neither idle nor in synchronization access.

Mode	% instructions executed	% execution time
Idle	69%	64%
User	27%	27%
Sync	1%	2%
Kernel	3%	7%

FIGURE 8.5   The distribution of execution time in the multiprogrammed parallel make workload. The high fraction of idle time is due to disk latency when only one of the eight processes is active. These data and the subsequent measurements for this workload were collected with the SimOS system [Rosenblum 1995]. The actual runs and data collection were done by M. Rosenblum, S. Herrod, and E. Bugnion of Stanford University, using the SimOS simulation system.

Unlike the parallel scientific workload, this multiprogramming workload has a significant instruction cache performance loss, at least for the OS. The instruction cache miss rate in the OS for a 32-byte block size, two set-associative cache varies from 1.7% for a 32-KB cache to 0.2% for a 256-KB cache. User-level, instruction cache misses are roughly one-sixth of the OS rate, across the variety of cache sizes.

8.3 | Centralized Shared-Memory Architectures

Multis are a new class of computers based on multiple microprocessors. The small size, low cost, and high performance of microprocessors allow design and construction of computer structures that offer significant advantages in manufacture, price-performance ratio, and reliability over traditional computer families. ... Multis are likely to be the basis for the next, the fifth, generation of computers. [p. 463]

Bell [1985]

As we saw in Chapter 5, the use of large, multilevel caches can substantially reduce the memory bandwidth demands of a processor. If the main memory bandwidth demands of a single processor are reduced, multiple processors may be able to share the same memory. Starting in the 1980s, this observation, combined with the emerging dominance of the microprocessor, motivated many designers to create small-scale multiprocessors where several processors shared a single physical memory connected by a shared bus. Because of the small size of the processors and the significant reduction in the requirements for bus bandwidth achieved by large caches, such machines are extremely cost-effective, provided that a sufficient amount of memory bandwidth exists. Early designs of such machines were able to place an entire CPU and cache subsystem on a board, which plugged into the bus backplane. More recent designs have placed up to four processors per board; and by some time early in the next century, there may be multiple processors on a single die configured as a multiprocessor. Figure 8.1 on page 638 shows a simple diagram of such a machine.

The architecture supports the caching of both shared and private data. *Private data* is used by a single processor, while *shared data* is used by multiple processors, essentially providing communication among the processors through reads and writes of the shared data. When a private item is cached, its location is migrated to the cache, reducing the average access time as well as the memory bandwidth required. Since no other processor uses the data, the program behavior is identical to that in a uniprocessor. When shared data are cached, the shared value may be replicated in multiple caches. In addition to the reduction in access latency and required memory bandwidth, this replication also provides a reduction in contention that may exist for shared data items that are being read by multiple processors simultaneously. Caching of shared data, however, introduces a new problem: cache coherence.

What Is Multiprocessor Cache Coherence?

As we saw in Chapter 6, the introduction of caches caused a coherence problem for I/O operations, since the view of memory through the cache could be different from the view of memory obtained through the I/O subsystem. The same problem exists in the case of multiprocessors, because the view of memory held by two different processors is through their individual caches. Figure 8.6 illustrates the problem and shows how two different processors can have two different values for the same location. This is generally referred to as the *cache-coherence* problem.

Time	Event	Cache contents for CPU A	Cache contents for CPU B	Memory contents for location X
0				1
1	CPU A reads X	1		1
2	CPU B reads X	1	1	1
3	CPU A stores 0 into X	0	1	0

FIGURE 8.6   The cache-coherence problem for a single memory location (X), read and written by two processors (A and B). We initially assume that neither cache contains the variable and that X has the value 1. We also assume a write-through cache; a write-back cache adds some additional but similar complications. After the value of X has been written by A, A's cache and the memory both contain the new value, but B's cache does not, and if B reads the value of X, it will receive 1!

Informally, we could say that a memory system is coherent if any read of a data item returns the most recently written value of that data item. This definition, while intuitively appealing, is vague and simplistic; the reality is much more complex. This simple definition contains two different aspects of memory system behavior, both of which are critical to writing correct shared-memory programs. The first aspect, called *coherence,* defines what values can be returned by a read. The second aspect, called *consistency,* determines when a written value will be returned by a read. Let's look at coherence first.

A memory system is coherent if

1. A read by a processor, P, to a location X that follows a write by P to X, with no writes of X by another processor occurring between the write and the read by P, always returns the value written by P.

2. A read by a processor to location X that follows a write by another processor to X returns the written value if the read and write are sufficiently separated and no other writes to X occur between the two accesses.

3. Writes to the same location are serialized: that is, two writes to the same location by any two processors are seen in the same order by all processors. For example, if the values 1 and then 2 are written to a location, processors can never read the value of the location as 2 and then later read it as 1.

The first property simply preserves program order—we expect this property to be true even in uniprocessors. The second property defines the notion of what it means to have a coherent view of memory: If a processor could continuously read an old data value, we would clearly say that memory was incoherent.

The need for write serialization is more subtle, but equally important. Suppose we did not serialize writes, and processor P1 writes location X followed by P2 writing location X. Serializing the writes ensures that every processor will see the write done by P2 at some point. If we did not serialize the writes, it might be the case that some processor could see the write of P2 first and then see the write of P1, maintaining the value written by P1 indefinitely. The simplest way to avoid such difficulties is to serialize writes, so that all writes to the same location are seen in the same order; this property is called *write serialization.* Although the three properties just described are sufficient to ensure coherence, the question of when a written value will be seen is also important.

To understand why consistency is complex, observe that we cannot require that a read of X instantaneously see the value written for X by some other processor. If, for example, a write of X on one processor precedes a read of X on another processor by a very small time, it may be impossible to ensure that the read returns the value of the data written, since the written data may not even have left the processor at that point. The issue of exactly when a written value must be seen by a reader is defined by a *memory consistency model*—a topic discussed in section 8.6. Coherence and consistency are complementary: Coherence defines the behavior of reads and writes to the same memory location, while consistency defines the behavior of reads and writes with respect to accesses to other memory locations. For simplicity, and because we cannot explain the problem in full detail at this point, assume that we require that a write does not complete until all processors have seen the effect of the write and that the processor does not change the order of any write with any other memory access. This allows the processor to reorder reads, but forces the processor to finish a write in program order. We will rely on this assumption until we reach section 8.6, where we will see exactly the meaning of this definition, as well as the alternatives.

Basic Schemes for Enforcing Coherence

The coherence problem for multiprocessors and I/O, while similar in origin, has different characteristics that affect the appropriate solution. Unlike I/O, where multiple data copies are a rare event—one to be avoided whenever possible—a program running on multiple processors will want to have copies of the same data in several caches. In a coherent multiprocessor, the caches provide both *migration* and *replication* of shared data items. Coherent caches provide migration, since a data item can be moved to a local cache and used there in a transparent fashion; this reduces the latency to access a shared data item that is allocated remotely. Coherent caches also provide replication for shared data that is being simultaneously read, since the caches make a copy of the data item in the local cache. Replication reduces both latency of access and contention for a read shared data item. Supporting this migration and replication is critical to performance in accessing shared data. Thus, rather than trying to solve the problem by avoiding it in software, small-scale multiprocessors adopt a hardware solution by introducing a protocol to maintain coherent caches.

The protocols to maintain coherence for multiple processors are called *cache-coherence protocols*. Key to implementing a cache-coherence protocol is tracking the state of any sharing of a data block. There are two classes of protocols, which use different techniques to track the sharing status, in use:

- *Directory based*—The sharing status of a block of physical memory is kept in just one location, called the *directory;* we focus on this approach in section 8.4, when we discuss scalable shared-memory architecture.

- *Snooping*—Every cache that has a copy of the data from a block of physical memory also has a copy of the sharing status of the block, and no centralized state is kept. The caches are usually on a shared-memory bus, and all cache controllers monitor or *snoop* on the bus to determine whether or not they have a copy of a block that is requested on the bus. We focus on this approach in this section.

Snooping protocols became popular with multiprocessors using microprocessors and caches attached to a single shared memory because these protocols can use a preexisting physical connection—the bus to memory—to interrogate the status of the caches.

Alternative Protocols

There are two ways to maintain the coherence requirement described in the previous subsection. One method is to ensure that a processor has exclusive access to a data item before it writes that item. This style of protocol is called a *write invalidate protocol* because it invalidates other copies on a write. It is by far the most common protocol, both for snooping and for directory schemes. Exclusive access ensures that no other readable or writable copies of an item exist when the write occurs: all other cached copies of the item are invalidated. To see how this ensures coherence, consider a write followed by a read by another processor: Since the write requires exclusive access, any copy held by the reading processor must be invalidated (hence the protocol name). Thus, when the read occurs, it misses in the cache and is forced to fetch a new copy of the data. For a write, we require that the writing processor have exclusive access, preventing any other processor from being able to write simultaneously. If two processors do attempt to write the same data simultaneously, one of them wins the race (we'll see how we decide who wins shortly), causing the other processor's copy to be invalidated. For the other processor to complete its write, it must obtain a new copy of the data, which must now contain the updated value. Therefore, this protocol enforces write serialization. Figure 8.7 shows an example of an invalidation protocol for a snooping bus with write-back caches in action.

Processor activity	Bus activity	Contents of CPU A's cache	Contents of CPU B's cache	Contents of memory location X
				0
CPU A reads X	Cache miss for X	0		0
CPU B reads X	Cache miss for X	0	0	0
CPU A writes a 1 to X	Invalidation for X	1		0
CPU B reads X	Cache miss for X	1	1	1

FIGURE 8.7   An example of an invalidation protocol working on a snooping bus for a single cache block (X) with write-back caches. We assume that neither cache initially holds X and that the value of X in memory is 0. The CPU and memory contents show the value after the processor and bus activity have both completed. A blank indicates no activity or no copy cached. When the second miss by B occurs, CPU A responds with the value canceling the response from memory. In addition, both the contents of B's cache and the memory contents of X are updated. This is typical in most protocols and simplifies the protocol, as we will see shortly.

The alternative to an invalidate protocol is to update all the cached copies of a data item when that item is written. This type of protocol is called a *write update* or *write broadcast* protocol. To keep the bandwidth requirements of this protocol under control it is useful to track whether or not a word in the cache is shared—that is, is contained in other caches. If it is not, then there is no need to broadcast or update any other caches. Figure 8.8 shows an example of a write update protocol in operation. In the decade since these protocols were developed, invalidate has emerged as the winner for the vast majority of designs. To understand why, let's look at the qualitative performance differences.

Processor activity	Bus activity	Contents of CPU A's cache	Contents of CPU B's cache	Contents of memory location X
				0
CPU A reads X	Cache miss for X	0		0
CPU B reads X	Cache miss for X	0	0	0
CPU A writes a 1 to X	Write broadcast of X	1	1	1
CPU B reads X		1	1	1

FIGURE 8.8   An example of a write update or broadcast protocol working on a snooping bus for a single cache block (X) with write-back caches. We assume that neither cache initially holds X and that the value of X in memory is 0. The CPU and memory contents show the value after the processor and bus activity have both completed. A blank indicates no activity or no copy cached. When CPU A broadcasts the write, both the cache in CPU B and the memory location of X are updated.

The performance differences between write update and write invalidate protocols arise from three characteristics:

1. Multiple writes to the same word with no intervening reads require multiple write broadcasts in an update protocol, but only one initial invalidation in a write invalidate protocol.

2. With multiword cache blocks, each word written in a cache block requires a write broadcast in an update protocol, while only the first write to any word in the block needs to generate an invalidate in an invalidation protocol. An invalidation protocol works on cache blocks, while an update protocol must work on individual words (or bytes, when bytes are written). It is possible to try to merge writes in a write broadcast scheme, just as we did for write buffers in Chapter 5, but the basic difference remains.

3. The delay between writing a word in one processor and reading the written value in another processor is usually less in a write update scheme, since the written data are immediately updated in the reader's cache (assuming that the reading processor has a copy of the data). By comparison, in an invalidation

protocol, the reader is invalidated first, then later reads the data and is stalled until a copy can be read and returned to the processor.

Because bus and memory bandwidth is usually the commodity most in demand in a bus-based multiprocessor, invalidation has become the protocol of choice for almost all implementations. Update protocols also cause problems for memory consistency models, reducing the potential performance gains of update, mentioned in point 3, even further. In designs with very small processor counts (2–4) where the processors are tightly coupled, the larger bandwidth demands of update may be acceptable. Nonetheless, given the trends in increasing processor performance and the related increase in bandwidth demands, we can expect update schemes to be used very infrequently. For this reason, we will focus only on invalidate protocols for the rest of the chapter.

Basic Implementation Techniques

The key to implementing an invalidate protocol in a small-scale machine is the use of the bus to perform invalidates. To perform an invalidate the processor simply acquires bus access and broadcasts the address to be invalidated on the bus. All processors continuously snoop on the bus watching the addresses. The processors check whether the address on the bus is in their cache. If so, the corresponding data in the cache is invalidated. The serialization of access enforced by the bus also forces serialization of writes, since when two processors compete to write to the same location, one must obtain bus access before the other. The first processor to obtain bus access will cause the other processor's copy to be invalidated, causing writes to be strictly serialized. One implication of this scheme is that a write to a shared data item cannot complete until it obtains bus access.

In addition to invalidating outstanding copies of a cache block that is being written into, we also need to locate a data item when a cache miss occurs. In a write-through cache, it is easy to find the recent value of a data item, since all written data are always sent to the memory, from which the most recent value of a data item can always be fetched. (Write buffers can lead to some additional complexities, which are discussed in section 8.6.)

For a write-back cache, however, the problem of finding the most recent data value is harder, since the most recent value of a data item can be in a cache rather than in memory. Happily, write-back caches can use the same snooping scheme both for caches misses and for writes: Each processor snoops every address placed on the bus. If a processor finds that it has a dirty copy of the requested cache block, it provides that cache block in response to the read request and causes the memory access to be aborted. Since write-back caches generate lower requirements for memory bandwidth, they are greatly preferable in a multiprocessor, despite the slight increase in complexity. Therefore, we focus on implementation with write-back caches.

The normal cache tags can be used to implement the process of snooping. Furthermore, the valid bit for each block makes invalidation easy to implement. Read misses, whether generated by an invalidation or by some other event, are also straightforward since they simply rely on the snooping capability. For writes we'd like to know whether any other copies of the block are cached, because, if there are no other cached copies, then the write need not be placed on the bus in a write-back cache. Not sending the write reduces both the time taken by the write and the required bandwidth.

To track whether or not a cache block is shared we can add an extra state bit associated with each cache block, just as we have a valid bit and a dirty bit. By adding a bit indicating whether the block is shared, we can decide whether a write must generate an invalidate. When a write to a block in the shared state occurs, the cache generates an invalidation on the bus and marks the block as private. No further invalidations will be sent by that processor for that block. The processor with the sole copy of a cache block is normally called the *owner* of the cache block.

When an invalidation is sent, the state of the owner's cache block is changed from shared to unshared (or exclusive). If another processor later requests this cache block, the state must be made shared again. Since our snooping cache also sees any misses, it knows when the exclusive cache block has been requested by another processor and the state should be made shared.

Since every bus transaction checks cache-address tags, this could potentially interfere with CPU cache accesses. This potential interference is reduced by one of two techniques: duplicating the tags or employing a multilevel cache with *inclusion,* whereby the levels closer to the CPU are a subset of those further away. If the tags are duplicated, then the CPU and the snooping activity may proceed in parallel. Of course, on a cache miss the processor needs to arbitrate for and update both sets of tags. Likewise, if the snoop finds a matching tag entry, it needs to arbitrate for and access both sets of cache tags (to perform an invalidate or to update the shared bit), as well as possibly the cache data array to retrieve a copy of a block. Thus with duplicate tags the processor only needs to be stalled when it does a cache access at the same time that a snoop has detected a copy in the cache. Furthermore, snooping activity is delayed only when the cache is dealing with a miss.

If the CPU uses a multilevel cache with the inclusion property, then every entry in the primary cache is also in the secondary cache. Thus the snoop activity can be directed to the second-level cache, while most of the processor's activity is directed to the primary cache. If the snoop gets a hit in the secondary cache, then it must arbitrate for the primary cache to update the state and possibly retrieve the data, which usually requires a stall of the processor. Since many multiprocessors use a multilevel cache to decrease the bandwidth demands of the individual processors, this solution has been adopted in many designs. Sometimes it may even be useful to duplicate the tags of the secondary cache to further decrease contention between the CPU and the snooping activity. We discuss the inclusion property in more detail in section 8.8.

As you might imagine, there are many variations on cache coherence, depending on whether the scheme is invalidate based or update based, whether the cache is write back or write through, when updates occur, and if and how ownership is recorded. Figure 8.9 summarizes several snooping cache-coherence protocols and shows some machines that have used or are using that protocol.

Name	Protocol type	Memory-write policy	Unique feature	Machines using
Write Once	Write invalidate	Write back after first write	First snooping protocol described in literature	
Synapse N+1	Write invalidate	Write back	Explicit state where memory is the owner	Synapse machines; first cache-coherent machines available
Berkeley	Write invalidate	Write back	Owned shared state	Berkeley SPUR machine
Illinois	Write invalidate	Write back	Clean private state; can supply data from any cache with a clean copy	SGI Power and Challenge series
"Firefly"	Write broadcast	Write back when private, write through when shared	Memory updated on broadcast	No current machines; SPARCCenter 2000 closest.

FIGURE 8.9   Five snooping protocols summarized. Archibald and Baer [1986] use these names to describe the five protocols, and Eggers [1989] summarizes the similarities and differences as shown in this figure. The Firefly protocol was named for the experimental DEC Firefly multiprocessor, in which it appeared.

An Example Protocol

A bus-based coherence protocol is usually implemented by incorporating a finite state controller in each node. This controller responds to requests from the processor and from the bus, changing the state of the selected cache block, as well as using the bus to access data or to invalidate it. Figure 8.10 shows the requests

Request	Source	Function
Read hit	Processor	Read data in cache
Write hit	Processor	Write data in cache
Read miss	Bus	Request data from cache or memory
Write miss	Bus	Request data from cache or memory; perform any needed invalidates

FIGURE 8.10   The cache-coherence mechanism receives requests from both the processor and the bus and responds to these based on the type of request and the state of the cache block specified in the request.

generated by the processor-cache module in a node as well as those coming from the bus. For simplicity, the protocol we explain does not distinguish between a write hit and a write miss to a shared cache block: in both cases, we treat such an access as a write miss. When the write miss is placed on the bus, any processors with copies of the cache block invalidate it. In a write-back cache, if the block is exclusive in just one cache, that cache also writes back the block. Treating write hits to shared blocks as cache misses reduces the number of different bus transactions and simplifies the controller.

Figure 8.11 shows a finite-state transition diagram for a single cache block using a write-invalidation protocol and a write-back cache. For simplicity, the three states of the protocol are duplicated to represent transitions based on CPU requests (on the left), as opposed to transitions based on bus requests (on the right). Boldface type is used to distinguish the bus actions, as opposed to the conditions on which a state transition depends. The state in each node represents the state of the selected cache block specified by the processor or bus request.

All of the states in this cache protocol would be needed in a uniprocessor cache, where they would correspond to the invalid, valid (and clean), and dirty states. All of the state changes indicated by arcs in the left half of Figure 8.11 would be needed in a write-back uniprocessor cache; the only difference in a multiprocessor with coherence is that the controller must generate a write miss when the controller has a write hit for a cache block in the shared state. The state changes represented by the arcs in the right half of Figure 8.11 are needed only for coherence and would not appear at all in a uniprocessor cache controller.

In reality, there is only one finite-state machine per cache, with stimuli coming either from the attached CPU or from the bus. Figure 8.12 shows how the state transitions in the right half of Figure 8.11 are combined with those in the left half of the figure to form a single state diagram for each cache block.

To understand why this protocol works, observe that any valid cache block is either in the shared state in multiple caches or in the exclusive state in exactly one cache. Any transition to the exclusive state (which is required for a processor to write to the block) requires a write miss to be placed on the bus, causing all caches to make the block invalid. In addition, if some other cache had the block in exclusive state, that cache generates a write back, which supplies the block containing the desired address. Finally, if a read miss occurs on the bus to a block in the exclusive state, the owning cache also makes its state shared, forcing a subsequent write to require exclusive ownership. The actions in gray in Figure 8.12, which handle read and write misses on the bus, are essentially the snooping component of the protocol. One other property that is preserved in this protocol, and in most other protocols, is that any memory block in the shared state is always up to date in the memory. This simplifies the implementation, as we will see in detail in section 8.5.

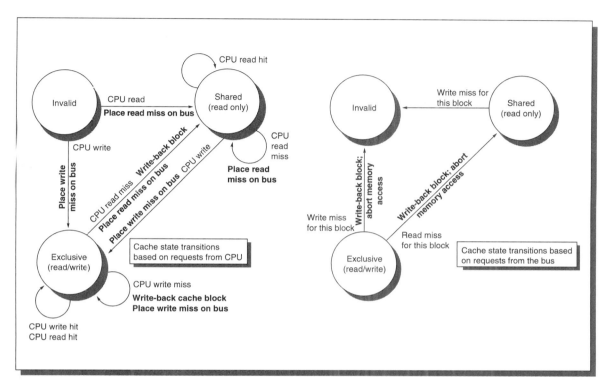

FIGURE 8.11 A write-invalidate, cache-coherence protocol for a write-back cache showing the states and state transitions for each block in the cache. The cache states are shown in circles with any access permitted by the CPU without a state transition shown in parenthesis under the name of the state. The stimulus causing a state change is shown on the transition arcs in regular type, and any bus actions generated as part of the state transition are shown on the transition arc in bold. The stimulus actions apply to a block in the cache, not to a specific address in the cache. Hence, a read miss to a line in the shared state is a miss for that cache block but for a different address. The left side of the diagram shows state transitions based on actions of the CPU associated with this cache; the right side shows transitions based on operations on the bus. A read miss in the exclusive or shared state and a write miss in the exclusive state occur when the address requested by the CPU does not match the address in the cache block. Such a miss is a standard cache replacement miss. An attempt to write a block in the shared state always generates a miss, even if the block is present in the cache, since the block must be made exclusive. Whenever a bus transaction occurs, all caches that contain the cache block specified in the bus transaction take the action dictated by the right half of the diagram. The protocol assumes that memory provides data on a read miss for a block that is clean in all caches. In actual implementations, these two sets of state diagrams are combined. This protocol is somewhat simpler than those in use in existing multiprocessors.

Although our simple cache protocol is correct, it omits a number of complications that make the implementation much trickier. The most important of these is that the protocol assumes that operations are *atomic*—that is, an operation can be done in such a way that no intervening operation can occur. For example, the protocol described assumes that write misses can be detected, acquire the bus, and receive a response as a single atomic action. In reality this is not true. Similarly, if we used a split transaction bus (see Chapter 6, section 6.3), then read misses would also not be atomic.

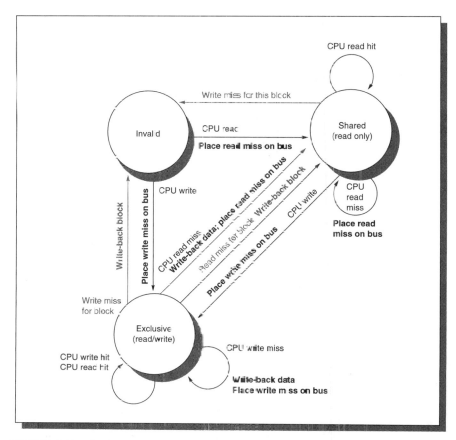

FIGURE 8.12 Cache-coherence state diagram with the state transitions induced by the local processor shown in black and by the bus activities shown in gray. As in Figure 8.11, the activities on a transition are shown in bold.

Nonatomic actions introduce the possibility that the protocol can *deadlock,* meaning that it reaches a state where it cannot continue. Appendix E deals with these complex issues, showing how the protocol can be modified to deal with nonatomic writes without introducing deadlock.

As stated earlier, this coherence protocol is actually simpler than those used in practice. There are two major simplifications. First, in this protocol all transitions to the exclusive state generate a write miss on the bus, and we assume that the requesting cache always fills the block with the contents returned. This simplifies the detailed implementation. Most real protocols distinguish between a write miss and a write hit, which can occur when the cache block is initially in the shared state. Such misses are called *ownership* or *upgrade* misses, since they involve changing the state of the block, but do not actually require a data fetch. To support such state changes, the protocol uses an *invalidate operation,* in addition to a write miss. With such operations, however, the actual implementation of the protocol becomes slightly more complex.

The second major simplification is that many machines distinguish between a cache block that is really shared and one that exists in the clean state in exactly one cache. This addition of a "clean and private" state eliminates the need to generate a bus transaction on a write to such a block. Another enhancement in wide use allows other caches to supply data on a miss to a shared block. The next part of this section examines the performance of these protocols for our parallel and multiprogrammed workloads.

Performance of Snooping Coherence Protocols

In a bus-based multiprocessor using an invalidation protocol, several different phenomena combine to determine performance. In particular, the overall cache performance is a combination of the behavior of uniprocessor cache miss traffic and the traffic caused by communication, which results in invalidations and subsequent cache misses. Changing the processor count, cache size, and block size can affect these two components of the miss rate in different ways, leading to overall system behavior that is a combination of the two effects.

Performance for the Parallel Program Workload

In this section, we use a simulator to study the performance of our four parallel programs. For these measurements, the problem sizes are as follows:

- *Barnes-Hut*—16K bodies run for six time steps (the accuracy control is set to 1.0, a typical, realistic value);

- *FFT*—1 million complex data points

- *LU*—A 512×512 matrix is used with 16×16 blocks

- *Ocean*—A 130×130 grid with a typical error tolerance

In looking at the miss rates as we vary processor count, cache size, and block size, we decompose the total miss rate into *coherence misses* and normal uniprocessor misses. The normal uniprocessor misses consist of capacity, conflict, and compulsory misses. We label these misses as capacity misses, because that is the dominant cause for these benchmarks. For these measurements, we include as a coherence miss any write misses needed to upgrade a block from shared to exclusive, even though no one is sharing the cache block. This reflects a protocol that does not distinguish between a private and shared cache block.

Figure 8.13 shows the data miss rates for our four applications, as we increase the number of processors from one to 16, while keeping the problem size constant. As we increase the number of processors, the total amount of cache increases, usually causing the capacity misses to drop. In contrast, increasing the processor count usually causes the amount of communication to increase, in turn causing the coherence misses to rise. The magnitude of these two effects differs by application.

In FFT, the capacity miss rate drops (from nearly 7% to just over 5%) but the coherence miss rate increases (from about 1% to about 2.7%), leading to a constant overall miss rate. Ocean shows a combination of effects, including some that relate to the partitioning of the grid and how grid boundaries map to cache blocks. For a typical 2D grid code the communication-generated misses are proportional to the boundary of each partition of the grid, while the capacity misses are proportional to the area of the grid. Therefore, increasing the total amount of cache while keeping the total problem size fixed will have a more significant effect on the capacity miss rate, at least until each subgrid fits within an individual processor's cache. The significant jump in miss rate between one and two processors occurs because of conflicts that arise from the way in which the multiple grids are mapped to the caches. This conflict is present for direct-mapped and two-way set associative caches, but fades at higher associativities. Such conflicts are not unusual in array-based applications, especially when there are multiple grids in use at once. In Barnes and LU the increase in processor count has little effect on the miss rate, sometimes causing a slight increase and sometimes causing a slight decrease.

Increasing the cache size has a beneficial effect on performance, since it reduces the frequency of costly cache misses. Figure 8.14 illustrates the change in miss rate as cache size is increased, showing the portion of the miss rate due to coherence misses and to uniprocessor capacity misses. Two effects can lead to a miss rate that does not decrease—at least not as quickly as we might expect—as cache size increases: inherent communication and plateaus in the miss rate. Inherent communication leads to a certain frequency of coherence misses that are not significantly affected by increasing cache size. Thus if the cache size is increased while maintaining a fixed problem size, the coherence miss rate eventually limits the decrease in cache miss rate. This effect is most obvious in Barnes, where the coherence miss rate essentially becomes the entire miss rate.

A less important effect is a temporary plateau in the capacity miss rate that arises when the application has some fraction of its data present in cache but some significant portion of the data set does not fit in the cache or in caches that are slightly bigger. In LU, a very small cache (about 4 KB) can capture the pair of 16×16 blocks used in the inner loop; beyond that the next big improvement in capacity miss rate occurs when both matrices fit in the caches, which occurs when the total cache size is between 4 MB and 8 MB, a data point we will see later. This *working set effect* is partly at work between 32 KB and 128 KB for FFT, where the capacity miss rate drops only 0.3%. Beyond that cache size, a faster decrease in the capacity miss rate is seen, as some other major data structure begins

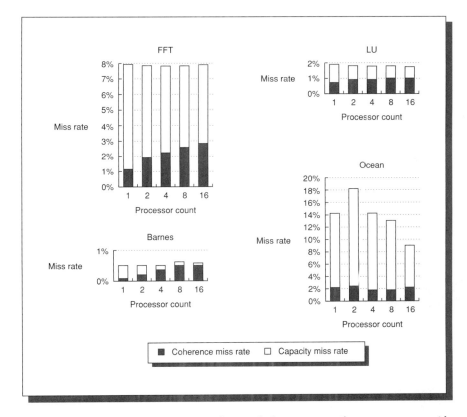

FIGURE 8.13   Data miss rates can vary in nonobvious ways as the processor count is increased from one to 16. The miss rates include both coherence and capacity miss rates. The compulsory misses in these benchmarks are all very small and are included in the capacity misses. Most of the misses in these applications are generated by accesses to data that is potentially shared, although in the applications with larger miss rates (FFT and Ocean), it is the capacity misses rather than the coherence misses that comprise the majority of the miss rate. Data is potentially shared if it is allocated in a portion of the address space used for shared data. In all except Ocean, the potentially shared data is heavily shared, while in Ocean only the boundaries of the subgrids are actually shared, although the entire grid is treated as a potentially shared data object. Of course, since the boundaries change as we increase the processor count (for a fixed-size problem), different amounts of the grid become shared. The anomalous increase in capacity miss rate for Ocean in moving from one to two processors arises because of conflict misses in accessing the subgrids. In all cases except Ocean, the fraction of the cache misses caused by coherence transactions rises when a fixed-size problem is run on an increasing number of processors. In Ocean, the coherence misses initially fall as we add processors due to a large number of misses that are write ownership misses to data that is potentially, but not actually, shared. As the subgrids begin to fit in the aggregate cache (around 16 processors), this effect lessens. The single processor numbers include write upgrade misses, which occur in this protocol even if the data is not actually shared, since it is in the shared state. For all these runs, the cache size is 64 KB, two-way set associative, with 32 blocks. Notice that the scale for each benchmark is different, so that the behavior of the individual benchmarks can be seen clearly.

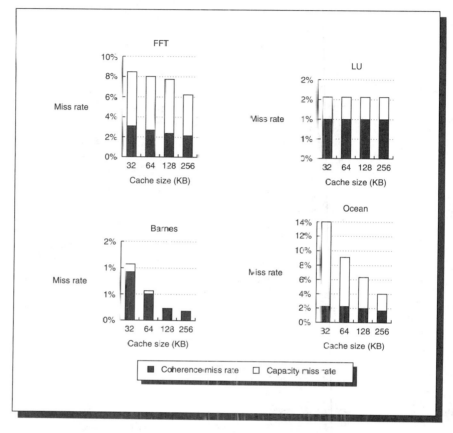

**FIGURE 8.14   The miss rate usually drops as the cache size is increased, although co-
herence misses dampen the effect.** The block size is 32 bytes and the cache is two-way
set-associative. The processor count is fixed at 16 processors. Observe that the scale for
each graph is different.

to reside in the cache. These plateaus are common in programs that deal with
large arrays in a structured fashion.

Increasing the block size is another way to change the miss rate in a cache. In
uniprocessors, larger block sizes are often optimal with larger caches. In multiprocessors, two new effects come into play: a reduction in spatial locality for
shared data and an effect called *false sharing*. Several studies have shown that
shared data have lower spatial locality than unshared data. This means that for
shared data, fetching larger blocks is less effective than in a uniprocessor, because the probability is higher that the block will be replaced before all its contents are referenced.

The second effect, false sharing, arises from the use of an invalidation-based coherence algorithm with a single valid bit per block. False sharing occurs when a block is invalidated (and a subsequent reference causes a miss) because some word in the block, other than the one being read, is written into. If the word written into is actually used by the processor that received the invalidate, then the reference was a true sharing reference and would have caused a miss independent of the block size or position of words. If, however, the word being written and the word read are different and the invalidation does not cause a new value to be communicated, but only causes an extra cache miss, then it is a false sharing miss. In a false sharing miss, the block is shared, but no word in the cache is actually shared, and the miss would not occur if the block size were a single word. The following Example makes the sharing patterns clear.

EXAMPLE   Assume that words x1 and x2 are in the same cache block in a clean state in the caches of P1 and P2, which have previously read both x1 and x2. Assuming the following sequence of events, identify each miss as a true sharing miss, a false sharing miss, or a hit. Any miss that would occur if the block size were one word is designated a true sharing miss.

Time	P1	P2
1	Write x1	
2		Read x2
3	Write x1	
4		Write x2
5	Read x2	

ANSWER   Here are classifications by time step:

1. This event is a true sharing miss, since x1 was read by P2 and needs to be invalidated from P2.

2. This event is a false sharing miss, since x2 was invalidated by the write of x1 in P1, but that value of x1 is not used in P2.

3. This event is a false sharing miss, since the block containing x1 is marked shared due to the read in P2, but P2 did not read x1.

4. This event is a false sharing miss for the same reason as step 3.

5. This event is a true sharing miss, since the value being read was written by P2.   ∎

Figure 8.15 shows the miss rates as the cache block size is increased for a 16-processor run with a 64-KB cache. The most interesting behavior is in Barnes, where the miss rate initially declines and then rises due to an increase in the number of coherence misses, which probably occurs because of false sharing. In the other benchmarks, increasing the block size decreases the overall miss rate. In Ocean and LU, the block size increase affects both the coherence and capacity miss rates about equally. In FFT, the coherence miss rate is actually decreased at a faster rate than the capacity miss rate. This is because the communication in FFT is structured to be very efficient. In less optimized programs, we would expect more false sharing and less spatial locality for shared data, resulting in more behavior like that of Barnes.

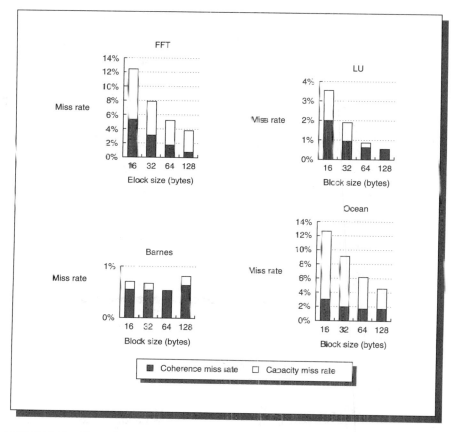

FIGURE 8.15 The data miss rate drops as the cache block size is increased. All these results are for a 16-processor run with a 64-KB cache and two-way set associativity. Once again we use different scales for each benchmark.

Although the drop in miss rates with longer blocks may lead you to believe that choosing a longer block size is the best decision, the bottleneck in bus-based multiprocessors is often the limited memory and bus bandwidth. Larger blocks mean more bytes on the bus per miss. Figure 8.16 shows the growth in bus traffic as the block size is increased. This growth is most serious in the programs that have a high miss rate, especially Ocean. The growth in traffic can actually lead to performance slowdowns due both to longer miss penalties and to increased bus contention.

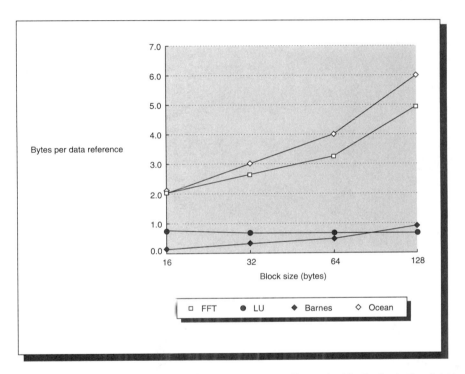

FIGURE 8.16   Bus traffic for data misses climbs steadily as the block size in the data cache is increased. The factor of 3 increase in traffic for Ocean is the best argument against larger block sizes. Remember that our protocol treats ownership misses the same as other misses, slightly increasing the penalty for large cache blocks; in both Ocean and FFT this effect accounts for less than 10% of the traffic.

Performance of the Multiprogramming and OS Workload

In this subsection we examine the cache performance of the multiprogrammed workload as the cache size and block size are changed. The workload remains the same as described in the previous section: two independent parallel makes, each using up to eight processors. Because of differences between the behavior of the kernel and that of the user processes, we keep these two components separate.

Remember, though, that the user processes execute more than eight times as many instructions, so that the overall miss rate is determined primarily by the miss rate in user code, which, as we will see, is often one-fifth of the kernel miss rate.

Figure 8.17 shows the data miss rate versus data cache size for the kernel and user components. The misses can be broken into three significant classes:

- Compulsory misses represent the first access to this block by this processor and are significant in this workload.

- Coherence misses represent misses due to invalidations.

- Normal capacity misses include misses caused by interference between the OS and the user process and between multiple user processes. Conflict misses are included in this category.

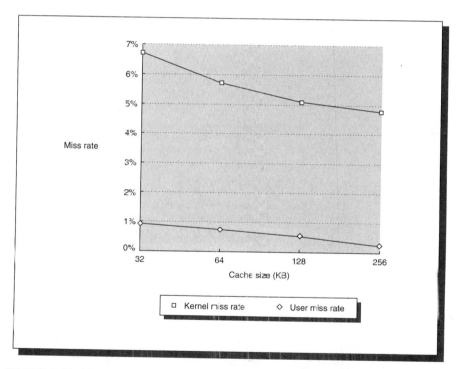

FIGURE 8.17 The data miss rate drops faster for the user code than for the kernel code as the data cache is increased from 32 KB to 256 KB with a 32-byte block. Although the user level miss rate drops by a factor of 3, the kernel level miss rate drops only by a factor of 1.3. As Figure 8.18 shows, this is due to a higher rate of compulsory misses and coherence misses.

For this workload the behavior of the operating system is more complex than the user processes. This is for two reasons. First, the kernel initializes all pages before allocating them to a user, which significantly increases the compulsory component of the kernel's miss rate. Second, the kernel actually shares data and thus has a nontrivial coherence miss rate. In contrast, user processes cause coherence misses only when the process is scheduled on a different processor; this component of the miss rate is small. Figure 8.18 shows the breakdown of the kernel miss rate as the cache size is increased.

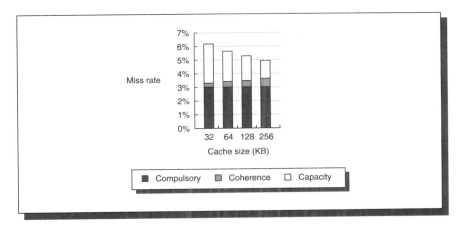

FIGURE 8.18   The components of the kernel data miss rate change as the data cache size is increased from 32KB to 256 KB. The compulsory miss rate component stays constant, since it is unaffected by cache size. The capacity component drops by more than a factor of two, while the coherence component nearly doubles. The increase in coherence misses occurs because the probability of a miss being caused by an invalidation increases with cache size, since fewer entries are bumped due to capacity.

Increasing the block size is likely to have more beneficial effects for this workload than for our parallel program workload, since a larger fraction of the misses arise from compulsory and capacity, both of which can be potentially improved with larger block sizes. Since coherence misses are relatively more rare, the negative effects of increasing block size should be small. Figure 8.19 shows how the miss rate for the kernel and user references changes as the block size is increased, assuming a 32 KB two-way set-associative data cache. Figure 8.20 confirms that, for the kernel references, the largest improvement is the reduction of the compulsory miss rate. As in the parallel programming workloads, the absence of large increases in the coherence miss rate as block size is increased means that false sharing effects are insignificant.

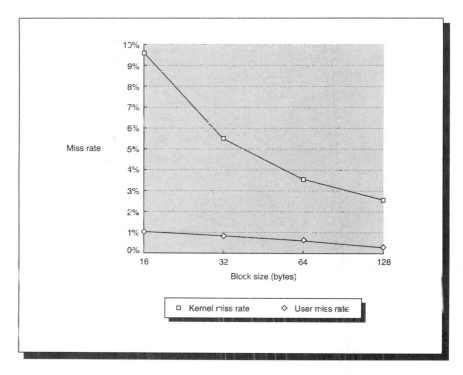

FIGURE 8.19   Miss rate drops steadily as the block size is increased for a 32-KB two-way set-associative data cache. As we might expect based on the higher compulsory component in the kernel, the improvement in miss rate for the kernel references is larger (almost a factor of 4 for the kernel references when going from 16-byte to 128-byte blocks versus just under a factor of 3 for the user references).

If we examine the number of bytes needed per data reference, as in Figure 8.21, we see that the behavior of the multiprogramming workload is like that of some programs in the parallel program workload. The kernel has a higher traffic ratio that grows quickly with block size. This is despite the significant reduction in compulsory misses; the smaller reduction in capacity and coherence misses drives an increase in total traffic. The user program has a much smaller traffic ratio that grows very slowly.

For the multiprogrammed workload, the OS is a much more demanding user of the memory system. If more OS or OS-like activity is included in the workload, it will become very difficult to build a sufficiently capable memory system.

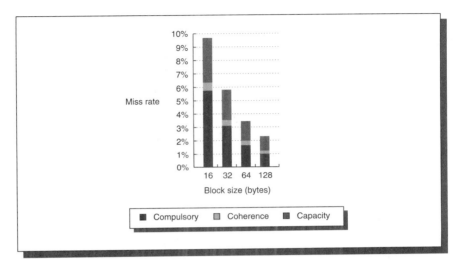

FIGURE 8.20   As we would expect, the increasing block size substantially reduces the compulsory miss rate in the kernel references. It also has a significant impact on the capacity miss rate, decreasing it by a factor of 2.4 over the range of block sizes. The increased block size has a small reduction in coherence traffic, which appears to stabilize at 64 bytes, with no change in the coherence miss rate in going to 128-byte lines. Because there are not significant reductions in the coherence miss rate as the block size increases, the fraction of the miss rate due to coherence grows from about 7% to about 15%.

Summary: Performance of Snooping Cache Schemes

In this section we examined the cache performance of both parallel program and multiprogrammed workloads. We saw that the coherence traffic can introduce new behaviors in the memory system that do not respond as easily to changes in cache size or block size that are normally used to improve uniprocessor cache performance. Coherence requests are a significant but not overwhelming component in the parallel processing workload. We can expect, however, that coherence requests will be more important in parallel programs that are less optimized.

In the multiprogrammed workload, the user and OS portions perform very differently, although neither has significant coherence traffic. In the OS portion, the compulsory and capacity contributions to the miss rate are much larger, leading to overall miss rates that are comparable to the worst programs in the parallel program workload. User cache performance, on the other hand, is very good and compares to the best programs in the parallel program workload.

The question of how these cache miss rates affect CPU performance depends on the rest of the memory system, including the latency and bandwidth of the bus and memory. We will return to overall performance in section 8.8, when we explore the design of the Challenge multiprocessor.

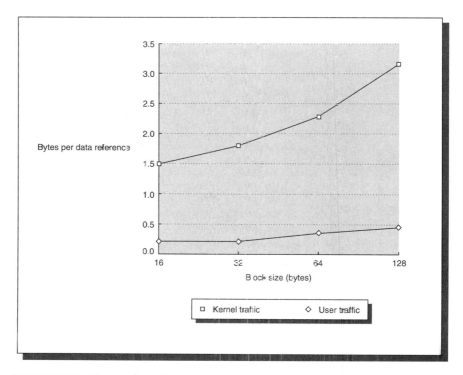

FIGURE 8.21   The number of bytes needed per data reference grows as block size is increased for both the kernel and user components. It is interesting to compare this chart against the same chart for the parallel program workload shown in Figure 8.16.

8.4 | Distributed Shared-Memory Architectures

A scalable machine supporting shared memory could choose to exclude or include cache coherence. The simplest scheme for the hardware is to exclude cache coherence, focusing instead on a scalable memory system. Several companies have built this style of machine: the Cray T3D is one well-known example. In such machines, memory is distributed among the nodes and all nodes are interconnected by a network. Access can be either local or remote—a controller inside each node decides, on the basis of the address, whether the data resides in the local memory or in a remote memory. In the latter case a message is sent to the controller in the remote memory to access the data.

These systems have caches, but to prevent coherence problems, shared data is marked as uncacheable and only private data is kept in the caches. Of course, software can still explicitly cache the value of shared data by copying the data from the shared portion of the address space to the local private portion of the address space that is cached. Coherence is then controlled by software. The advantage of such a mechanism is that little hardware support is required, although support for features such as block copy may be useful, since remote accesses fetch only single words (or double words) rather than cache blocks.

There are several major disadvantages to this approach. First, compiler mechanisms for transparent software cache coherence are very limited. The techniques that currently exist apply primarily to programs with well-structured loop-level parallelism, and these techniques have significant overhead arising from explicitly copying data. For irregular problems or problems involving dynamic data structures and pointers (including operating systems, for example), compiler-based software cache coherence is currently impractical. The basic difficulty is that software-based coherence algorithms must be conservative: every block that *might* be shared must be treated as if it *is* shared. This results in excess coherence overhead, because the compiler cannot predict the actual sharing accurately enough. Due to the complexity of the possible interactions, asking programmers to deal with coherence is unworkable.

Second, without cache coherence, the machine loses the advantage of being able to fetch and use multiple words in a single cache block for close to the cost of fetching one word. The benefits of spatial locality in shared data cannot be leveraged when single words are fetched from a remote memory for each reference. Support for a DMA mechanism among memories can help, but such mechanisms are often either costly to use (since they often require OS intervention) or expensive to implement since special-purpose hardware support and a buffer are needed. Furthermore, they are useful primarily when large block copies are needed (see Figure 7.25 on page 608 on the Cray T3D block copy).

Third, mechanisms for tolerating latency such as prefetch are more useful when they can fetch multiple words, such as a cache block, and where the fetched data remain coherent; we will examine this advantage in more detail later.

These disadvantages are magnified by the large latency of access to remote memory versus a local cache. For example, on the Cray T3D a local cache access has a latency of two cycles and is pipelined, while a remote access takes about 150 cycles.

For these reasons, cache coherence is an accepted requirement in small-scale multiprocessors. For larger-scale architectures, there are new challenges to extending the cache-coherent shared-memory model. Although the bus can certainly be replaced with a more scalable interconnection network, and we could certainly distribute the memory so that the memory bandwidth could also be scaled, the lack of scalability of the snooping coherence scheme needs to be addressed. A snooping protocol requires communication with all caches on every cache miss, including writes of potentially shared data. The absence of any centralized data structure that tracks the state of the caches is both the fundamental advantage of a snooping-based scheme, since it allows it to be inexpensive, as well as its Achilles' heel when it comes to scalability. For example, with only 16 processors and a block size of 64 bytes and a 64-KB data cache, the total bus bandwidth demand (ignoring stall cycles) for the four parallel programs in the workload ranges from almost 500 MB/sec (for Barnes) to over 9400 MB/sec (for Ocean), assuming a processor that issues a data reference every 5 ns, which is what a 1995 superscalar processor might generate. In comparison, the Silicon Graphics Challenge bus, the highest bandwidth bus-based multiprocessor in 1995, provides 1200 MB of bandwidth. Although the cache size used in these simulations is small, so is the problem size. Furthermore, although larger caches reduce the uniprocessor component of the traffic, they do not significantly reduce the parallel component of the miss rate.

Alternatively, we could build scalable shared-memory architectures that include cache coherency. The key is to find an alternative coherence protocol to the snooping protocol. One alternative protocol is a directory protocol. A directory keeps the state of every block that may be cached. Information in the directory includes which caches have copies of the block, whether it is dirty, and so on.

Existing directory implementations associate an entry in the directory with each memory block. In typical protocols, the amount of information is proportional to the product of the number of memory blocks and the number of processors. This is not a problem for machines with less than about a hundred processors, because the directory overhead will be tolerable. For larger machines, we need methods to allow the directory structure to be efficiently scaled. The methods that have been proposed either try to keep information for fewer blocks (e.g., only those in caches rather than all memory blocks) or try to keep fewer bits per entry.

To prevent the directory from becoming the bottleneck, directory entries can be distributed along with the memory, so that different directory accesses can go to different locations, just as different memory requests go to different memories. A distributed directory retains the characteristic that the sharing status of a block is always in a single known location. This property is what allows the coherence protocol to avoid broadcast. Figure 8.22 shows how our distributed-memory machine looks with the directories added to each node.

Directory-Based Cache-Coherence Protocols: The Basics

Just as with a snooping protocol, there are two primary operations that a directory protocol must implement: handling a read miss and handling a write to a shared, clean cache block. (Handling a write miss to a shared block is a simple combination of these two.) To implement these operations, a directory must track the state of each cache block. In a simple protocol, these states could be the following:

- *Shared*—One or more processors have the block cached, and the value in memory is up to date (as well as in all the caches).

- *Uncached*—No processor has a copy of the cache block.

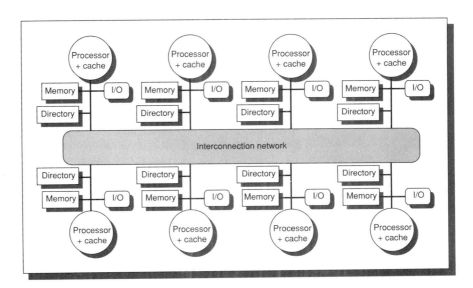

FIGURE 8.22   A directory is added to each node to implement cache coherence in a distributed-memory machine. Each directory is responsible for tracking the caches that share the memory addresses of the portion of memory in the node. The directory may communicate with the processor and memory over a common bus, as shown, or it may have a separate port to memory, or it may be part of a central node controller through which all intranode and internode communications pass.

- *Exclusive*—Exactly one processor has a copy of the cache block and it has written the block, so the memory copy is out of date. The processor is called the *owner* of the block.

In addition to tracking the state of each cache block, we must track the processors that have copies of the block when it is shared, since they will need to be invalidated on a write. The simplest way to do this is to keep a bit vector for each memory block. When the block is shared, each bit of the vector indicates whether the corresponding processor has a copy of that block. We can also use the bit vector to keep track of the owner of the block when the block is in the exclusive state. For efficiency reasons, we also track the state of each cache block at the individual caches.

The states and transitions for the state machine at each cache are identical to what we used for the snooping cache, although the actions on a transition are slightly different. We make the same simplifying assumptions that we made in the case of the snooping cache: attempts to write data that is not exclusive in the writer's cache always generate write misses, and the processors block until an access completes. Since the interconnect is no longer a bus and we want to avoid broadcast, there are two additional complications. First, we cannot use the interconnect as a single point of arbitration, a function the bus performed in the snooping case. Second, because the interconnect is message oriented (unlike the bus, which is transaction oriented), many messages must have explicit responses.

Before we see the protocol state diagrams, it is useful to examine a catalog of the message types that may be sent between the processors and the directories. Figure 8.23 shows the type of messages sent among nodes. The *local* node is the node where a request originates. The *home* node is the node where the memory location and the directory entry of an address reside. The physical address space is statically distributed, so the node that contains the memory and directory for a given physical address is known. For example, the high-order bits may provide the node number, while the low-order bits provide the offset within the memory on that node.

The *remote* node is the node that has a copy of a cache block, whether exclusive or shared. The local node may also be the home node, and vice versa. In either case the protocol is the same, although internode messages can be replaced by intranode transactions, which should be faster.

Message type	Source	Destination	Message contents	Function of this message
Read miss	Local cache	Home directory	P, A	Processor P has a read miss at address A; request data and make P a read sharer.
Write miss	Local cache	Home directory	P, A	Processor P has a write miss at address A; — request data and make P the exclusive owner.
Invalidate	Home directory	Remote cache	A	Invalidate a shared copy of data at address A.
Fetch	Home directory	Remote cache	A	Fetch the block at address A and send it to its home directory; change the state of A in the remote cache to shared.
Fetch/invalidate	Home directory	Remote cache	A	Fetch the block at address A and send it to its home directory; invalidate the block in the cache.
Data value reply	Home directory	Local cache	Data	Return a data value from the home memory.
Data write back	Remote cache	Home directory	A, data	Write back a data value for address A.

FIGURE 8.23 The possible messages sent among nodes to maintain coherence. The first two messages are miss requests sent by the local cache to the home. The third through fifth messages are messages sent to a remote cache by the home when the home needs the data to satisfy a read or write miss request. Data value replies are used to send a value from the home node back to the requesting node. Data value write backs occur for two reasons: when a block is replaced in a cache and must be written back to its home memory, and also in reply to fetch or fetch/invalidate messages from the home. Writing back the data value whenever the block becomes shared simplifies the number of states in the protocol, since any dirty block must be exclusive and any shared block is always available in the home memory.

In this section, we assume a simple model of memory consistency. To minimize the type of messages and the complexity of the protocol, we make an assumption that messages will be received and acted upon in the same order they are sent. This assumption may not be true in practice, and can result in additional complications, some of which we address in section 8.6 when we discuss memory consistency models. In this section, we use this assumption to ensure that invalidates sent by a processor are honored immediately.

An Example Directory Protocol

The basic states of a cache block in a directory-based protocol are exactly like those in a snooping protocol, and the states in the directory are also analogous to those we showed earlier. Thus we can start with simple state diagrams that show the state transitions for an individual cache block and then examine the state diagram for the directory entry corresponding to each block in memory. As in the snooping case, these state transition diagrams do not represent all the details of a coherence protocol; however, the actual controller is highly dependent on a number of details of the machine (message delivery properties, buffering structures, and so on). In this section we present the basic protocol state diagrams. The knotty issues involved in implementing these state transition diagrams are examined in Appendix E, along with similar problems that arise for snooping caches.

Figure 8.24 shows the protocol actions to which an individual cache responds. We use the same notation as in the last section, with requests coming from outside the node in gray and actions in bold. The state transitions for an individual cache are caused by read misses, write misses, invalidates, and data fetch requests; these operations are all shown in Figure 8.24. An individual cache also generates read and write miss messages that are sent to the home directory. Read and write misses require data value replies, and these events wait for replies before changing state.

The operation of the state transition diagram for a cache block in Figure 8.24 is essentially the same as it is for the snooping case: the states are identical, and the stimulus is almost identical. The write miss operation, which was broadcast on the bus in the snooping scheme, is replaced by the data fetch and invalidate operations that are selectively sent by the directory controller. Like the snooping protocol, any cache block must be in the exclusive state when it is written and any shared block must be up to date in memory.

In a directory-based protocol, the directory implements the other half of the coherence protocol. A message sent to a directory causes two different types of actions: updates of the directory state, and sending additional messages to satisfy the request. The states in the directory represent the three standard states for a block, but for all the cached copies of a memory block rather than for a single cache block. The memory block may be uncached by any node, cached in multiple nodes and readable (shared), or cached exclusively and writable in exactly

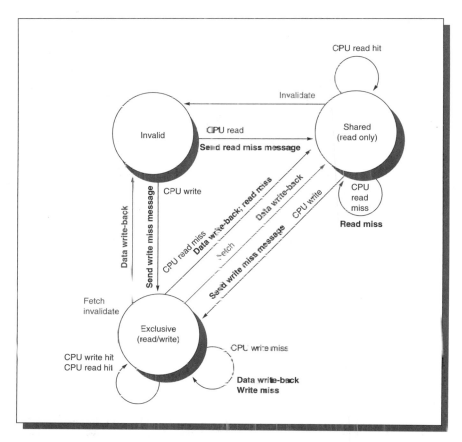

FIGURE 8.24 State transition diagram for an individual cache block in a directory-based system. Requests by the local processor are shown in black and those from the home directory are shown in gray. The states are identical to those in the snooping case, and the transactions are very similar, with explicit invalidate and write-back requests replacing the write misses that were formerly broadcast on the bus. As we did for the snooping controller, we assume that an attempt to write a shared cache block is treated as a miss; in practice, such a transaction can be treated as an ownership request or upgrade request and can deliver ownership without requiring that the cache block be fetched.

one node. In addition to the state of each block, the directory must track the set of processors that have a copy of a block; we use a set called *Sharers* to perform this function. In small-scale machines ($\leq$ 128 nodes), this set is typically kept as a bit vector. In larger machines, other techniques, which we discuss in the Exercises, are needed. Directory requests need to update the set Sharers and also read the set to perform invalidations.

Figure 8.25 shows the actions taken at the directory in response to messages received. The directory receives three different requests: read miss, write miss,

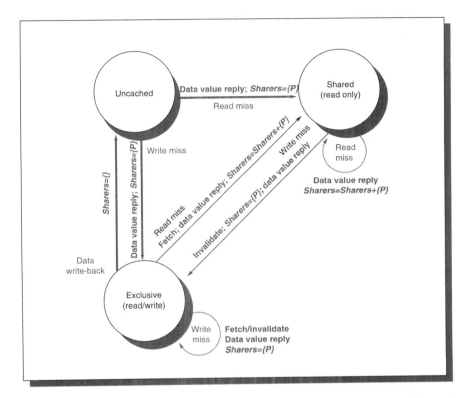

FIGURE 8.25   The state transition diagram for the directory has the same states and structure as the transition diagram for an individual cache. All actions are in gray because they are all externally caused. Bold indicates the action taken by the directory in response to the request. Bold italics indicate an action that updates the sharing set, Sharers, as opposed to sending a message.

and data write back. The messages sent in response by the directory are shown in bold, while the updating of the set Sharers is shown in bold italics. Because all the stimulus messages are external, all actions are shown in gray. Our simplified protocol assumes that some actions are atomic, such as requesting a value and sending it to another node; a realistic implementation cannot use this assumption.

To understand these directory operations, let's examine the requests received and actions taken state by state. When a block is in the uncached state the copy in memory is the current value, so the only possible requests for that block are

- *Read miss*—The requesting processor is sent the requested data from memory and the requestor is made the only sharing node. The state of the block is made shared.

- *Write miss*—The requesting processor is sent the value and becomes the Sharing node. The block is made exclusive to indicate that the only valid copy is cached. Sharers indicates the identity of the owner.

When the block is in the shared state the memory value is up to date, so the same two requests can occur:

- *Read miss*—The requesting processor is sent the requested data from memory and the requesting processor is added to the sharing set.

- *Write miss*—The requesting processor is sent the value. All processors in the set Sharers are sent invalidate messages, and the Sharers set is to contain the identity of the requesting processor. The state of the block is made exclusive.

When the block is in the exclusive state the current value of the block is held in the cache of the processor identified by the set sharers (the owner), so there are three possible directory requests:

- *Read miss*—The owner processor is sent a data fetch message, which causes the state of the block in the owner's cache to transition to shared and causes the owner to send the data to the directory, where it is written to memory and sent back to the requesting processor. The identity of the requesting processor is added to the set sharers, which still contains the identity of the processor that was the owner (since it still has a readable copy).

- *Data write-back*—The owner processor is replacing the block and therefore must write it back. This makes the memory copy up to date (the home directory essentially becomes the owner), the block is now uncached, and the sharer set is empty.

- *Write miss*—The block has a new owner. A message is sent to the old owner causing the cache to send the value of the block to the directory, from which it is sent to the requesting processor, which becomes the new owner. Sharers is set to the identity of the new owner, and the state of the block remains exclusive.

This state transition diagram in Figure 8.25 is a simplification, just as it was in the snooping cache case. In the directory case it is a larger simplification, since our assumption that bus transactions are atomic no longer applies. Appendix E explores these issues in depth.

In addition, the directory protocols used in real machines contain additional optimizations. In particular, in our protocol here when a read or write miss occurs for a block that is exclusive, the block is first sent to the directory at the home node. From there it is stored into the home memory and also sent to the original requesting node. Many protocols in real machines forward the data from the owner node to the requesting node directly (as well as performing the write back to the home). Such optimizations may not add complexity to the protocol, but they often move the complexity from one part of the design to another.

Performance of Directory-Based Coherence Protocols

The performance of a directory-based machine depends on many of the same factors that influence the performance of bus-based machines (e.g., cache size, processor count, and block size), as well as the distribution of misses to various locations in the memory hierarchy. The location of a requested data item depends on both the initial allocation and the sharing patterns. We start by examining the basic cache performance of our parallel program workload and then look at the effect of different types of misses.

Because the machine is larger and has longer latencies than our snooping-based multiprocessor, we begin with a slightly larger cache (128 KB) and a block size of 64 bytes. In distributed memory architectures, the distribution of memory requests between local and remote is key to performance, because it affects both the consumption of global bandwidth and the latency seen by requests. Therefore, for the figures in this section we separate the cache misses into local and remote requests. In looking at the figures, keep in mind that, for these applications, most of the remote misses that arise are coherence misses, although some capacity misses can also be remote, and in some applications with poor data distribution, such misses can be significant (see the Pitfall on page 738).

As Figure 8.26 shows, the miss rates with these cache sizes are not affected much by changes in processor count, with the exception of Ocean, where the miss rate rises at 64 processors. This rise occurs because of mapping conflicts in the cache that occur when the grid becomes small, leading to a rise in local misses, and because of a rise in the coherence misses, which are all remote.

Figure 8.27 shows how the miss rates change as the cache size is increased, assuming a 64-processor execution and 64-byte blocks. These miss rates decrease at rates that we might expect, although the dampening effect caused by little or no reduction in coherence misses leads to a slower decrease in the remote misses than in the local misses. By the time we reach the largest cache size shown, 512 KB, the remote miss rate is equal to or greater than the local miss rate. Larger caches would just continue to amplify this trend.

Finally, we examine the effect of changing the block size in Figure 8.28. Because these applications have good spatial locality, increases in block size reduce the miss rate, even for large blocks, although the performance benefits for going to the largest blocks are small. Furthermore, most of the improvement in miss rate comes in the local misses.

Rather than plot the memory traffic, Figure 8.29 plots the number of bytes required per data reference versus block size, breaking the requirement into local and global bandwidth. In the case of a bus, we can simply aggregate the demands of each processor to find the total demand for bus and memory bandwidth. For a scalable interconnect, we can use the data in Figure 8.29 to compute the required per-node global bandwidth and the estimated bisection bandwidth, as the next Example shows.

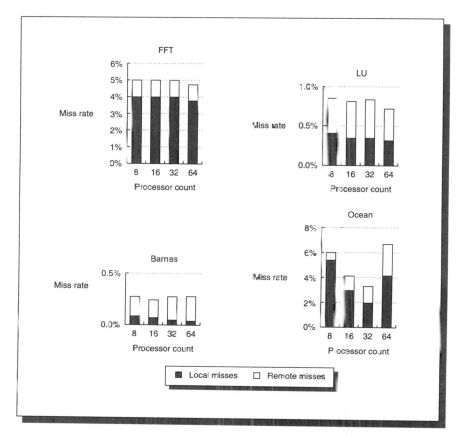

FIGURE 8.26   The data miss rate is often steady as processors are added for these benchmarks. Because of its grid structure, Ocean has an initially decreasing miss rate, which rises when there are 64 processors. For Ocean, the local miss rate drops from 5% at 8 processors to 2% at 32, before rising to 4% at 64. The remote miss rate in Ocean, driven primarily by communication, rises monotonically from 1% to 2.5%. Note that to show the detailed behavior of each benchmark, different scales are used on the y-axis. The cache for all these runs is 128 KB, two-way set associative, with 64-byte blocks. Remote misses include any misses that require communication with another node, whether to fetch the data or to deliver an invalidate. In particular, in this figure and other data in this sector, the measurement of remote misses includes write upgrade misses where the data is up to date in the local memory but cached elsewhere and, therefore, requires invalidations to be sent. Such invalidations do indeed generate remote traffic, but may or may not delay the write, depending on the consistency model (see section 8.6).

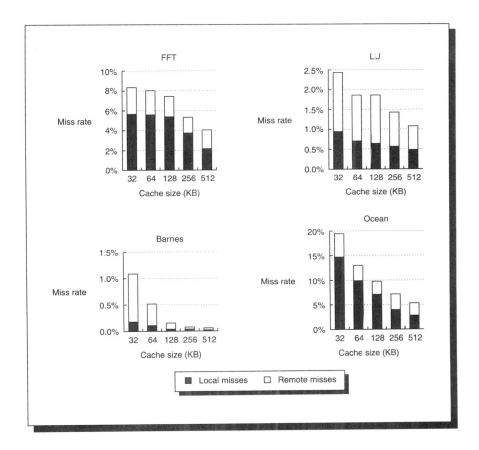

FIGURE 8.27   Miss rates decrease as cache sizes grow. Steady decreases are seen in the local miss rate, while the remote miss rate declines to varying degrees, depending on whether the remote miss rate had a large capacity component or was driven primarily by communication misses. In all cases, the decrease in the local miss rate is larger than the decrease in the remote miss rate. The plateau in the miss rate of FFT, which we mentioned in the last section, ends once the cache exceeds 128 KB. These runs were done with 64 processors and 64-byte cache blocks.

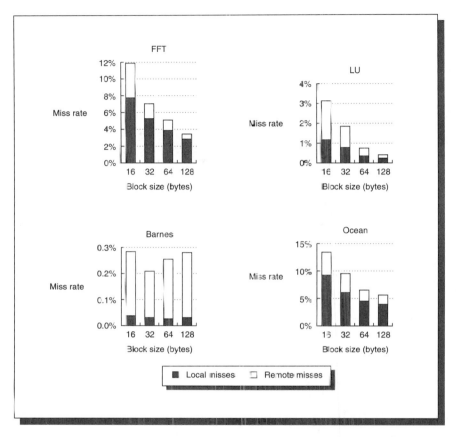

FIGURE 8.28   Data miss rate versus block size assuming a 128-KB cache and 64 processors in total. Although difficult to see, the coherence miss rate in Barnes actually rises for the largest block size, just as in the last section.

EXAMPLE   Assume a multiprocessor with 64 200-MHz processors that sustains one memory reference per clock. For a 64-byte block size, the remote miss rate is 0.7%. Find the per-node and estimated bisection bandwidth for FFT. Assume that the processor does not stall for remote memory requests; this might be true if, for example, all remote data were prefetched. How do these bandwidth requirements compare to various interconnection technologies?

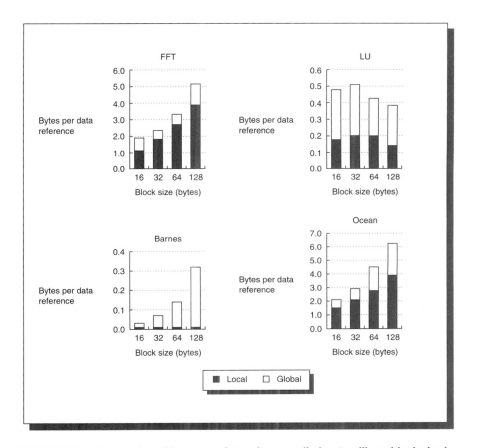

FIGURE 8.29 **The number of bytes per data reference climbs steadily as block size is increased.** These data can be used to determine the bandwidth required per node both internally and globally. The data assumes a 128-KB cache for each of 64 processors.

ANSWER The per-node bandwidth is simply the number of data bytes per reference times the reference rate: $0.7\% \times 200 \times 64 = 90$ MB/sec. This rate is about half the bandwidth of the fastest scalable MPP interconnects available in 1995. The FFT per-node bandwidth demand exceeds the fastest ATM interconnects available in 1995 by about a factor of 5, and slightly exceeds next-generation ATM.

FFT performs all-to-all communication, so the bisection bandwidth is equal to 32 times the per-node bandwidth, or 2880 MB/sec. For a 64-processor machine arranged in a 2D mesh, the bisection bandwidth grows as the square root of the number of processors. Thus for 64 processors the bisection bandwidth is 8 times the node bandwidth. In 1995, MPP-style interconnects offer about 200 MB/sec to a node for a total of 1600 MB/sec, or somewhat less than the required bandwidth. At 64 processors, a 3D mesh has double this bisection bandwidth (3200 MB/sec), which exceeds the required bandwidth. A next-generation 2D mesh is also expected to meet the bisection bandwidth requirement. A 1995 ATM-based 64 × 64 crossbar has about 1200 MB/sec of bisection bandwidth; a next-generation ATM offers four times this bandwidth, which exceeds the bisection bandwidth required, although it does not satisfy the per-node bandwidth. ∎

The previous Example looked at the bandwidth demands. The other key issue for a parallel program is remote memory access time, or latency. To get insight into this, we use a simple example of a directory-based machine. Figure 8.30 shows the parameters we assume for our simple machine. It assumes that the time to first word for a local memory access is 25 cycles and that the path to local memory is 8 bytes wide, while the network interconnect is 2 bytes wide. This model ignores the effects of contention, which are probably not too serious in the parallel benchmarks we examine, with the possible exception of FFT, which uses all-to-all communication. Contention could have a serious performance impact in other work loads.

Characteristic	Number of processor clock cycles
Cache hit	1
Cache miss to local memory	$25 + \dfrac{\text{block size in bytes}}{8}$
Cache miss to remote home directory	$75 + \dfrac{\text{block size in bytes}}{2}$
Cache miss to remotely cached data (3-hop miss)	$100 + \dfrac{\text{block size in bytes}}{2}$

FIGURE 8.30 Characteristics of the example directory-based machine. Misses can be serviced locally (including from the local directory), at a remote home node, or using the services of both the home node and another remote node that is caching an exclusive copy. This last case is called a 3-hop miss and has a higher cost because it requires interrogating both the home directory and a remote cache. Note that this simple model does not account for invalidation time. These network latencies are typical of what can be achieved in 1995–96 in an MPP-style network interfaced in hardware to each node and assuming moderately fast processors (150–200 MHz).

Figure 8.31 shows the cost in cycles for the average memory reference, assuming the parameters in Figure 8.30. Only the latencies for each reference type are counted. Each bar indicates the contribution from cache hits, local misses, remote misses, and 3-hop remote misses. The cost is influenced by the total frequency of cache misses and upgrades, as well as by the distribution of the location where the miss is satisfied. The cost for a remote memory reference is fairly steady as the processor count is increased, except for Ocean. The increasing miss rate in Ocean for 64 processors is clear in Figure 8.26. As the miss rate increases, we should expect the time spent on memory references to increase also.

Although Figure 8.31 shows the memory access cost, which is the dominant multiprocessor cost in these benchmarks, a complete performance model would need to consider the effect of contention in the memory system, as well as the losses arising from synchronization delays. In section 8.8 we will look at the actual performance of the SGI Challenge system on these benchmarks.

The coherence protocols that we have discussed so far have made several simplifying assumptions. In practice, real protocols must deal with two realities: nonatomicity of operations and finite buffering. We have seen why certain operations (such as a write miss) cannot be atomic. In DSM machines the presence of only a finite number of buffers to hold message requests and replies introduces additional possibilities for deadlock. The challenge for the designer is to create a protocol that works correctly and without deadlock, using nonatomic actions and finite buffers as the building blocks. These factors are fundamental challenges in all parallel machines, and the solutions are applicable to a wide variety of protocol design environments, both in hardware and in software.

Because this material is extremely complex and not necessary to comprehend the rest of the chapter, we have placed it in Appendix E. For the interested reader, Appendix E shows how the specific problems in our coherence protocols are solved and illustrates the general principles that are more globally applicable. It describes the problems arising in snooping cache implementations, as well as the more complex problems that arise in more distributed systems using directories. If you want to understand how these machines really work and why designing them is such a challenge, go read Appendix E!

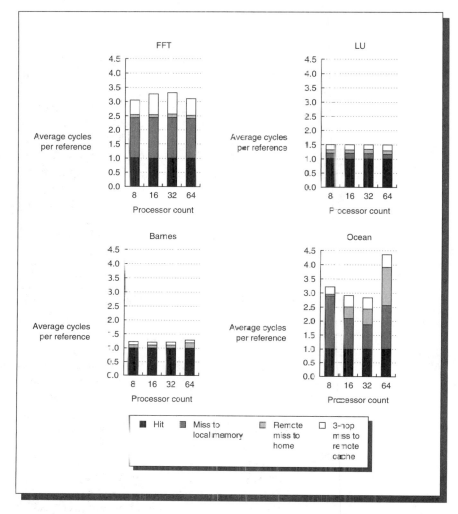

FIGURE 8.31 The effective latency of memory references in a DSM machine depends both on the relative frequency of cache misses and on the location of the memory where the accesses are served. These plots show the memory access cost (a metric called average memory access time in Chapter 5) for each of the benchmarks for 8, 16, 32, and 64 processors, assuming a 128-KB data cache that is two-way set associative with 64-byte blocks. The average memory access cost is composed of four different types of accesses, with the cost of each type given in Figure 8.30. For the Barnes and LU benchmarks, the low miss rates lead to low overall access times. In FFT, the higher access cost is determined by a higher local miss rate (4%) and a significant 3-hop miss rate (1%). Ocean shows the highest cost for memory accesses, as well as the only behavior that varies significantly with processor count. The high cost is driven primarily by a high local miss rate (average 1.4%). The memory access cost drops from 8 to 32 processors as the grids more easily fit in the individual caches. At 64 processors, the data set size is too small to map properly and both local misses and coherence misses rise, as we saw in Figure 8.26.

8.5 Synchronization

Synchronization mechanisms are typically built with user-level software routines that rely on hardware-supplied synchronization instructions. For smaller machines or low-contention situations, the key hardware capability is an uninterruptible instruction or instruction sequence capable of atomically retrieving and changing a value. Software synchronization mechanisms are then constructed using this capability. For example, we will see how very efficient spin locks can be built using a simple hardware synchronization instruction and the coherence mechanism. In larger-scale machines or high-contention situations, synchronization can become a performance bottleneck, because contention introduces additional delays and because latency is potentially greater in such a machine. We will see how contention can arise in implementing some common user-level synchronization operations and examine more powerful hardware-supported synchronization primitives that can reduce contention as well as latency.

We begin by examining the basic hardware primitives, then construct several well-known synchronization routines with the primitives, and then turn to performance problems in larger machines and solutions for those problems.

Basic Hardware Primitives

The key ability we require to implement synchronization in a multiprocessor is a set of hardware primitives with the ability to atomically read and modify a memory location. Without such a capability, the cost of building basic synchronization primitives will be too high and will increase as the processor count increases. There are a number of alternative formulations of the basic hardware primitives, all of which provide the ability to atomically read and modify a location, together with some way to tell if the read and write were performed atomically. These hardware primitives are the basic building blocks that are used to build a wide variety of user-level synchronization operations, including things such as locks and barriers. In general, architects do not expect users to employ the basic hardware primitives, but instead expect that the primitives will be used by system programmers to build a synchronization library, a process that is often complex and tricky. Let's start with one such hardware primitive and show how it can be used to build some basic synchronization operations.

One typical operation for building synchronization operations is the *atomic exchange*, which interchanges a value in a register for a value in memory. To see how to use this to build a basic synchronization operation, assume that we want to build a simple lock where the value 0 is used to indicate that the lock is free and a 1 is used to indicate that the lock is unavailable. A processor tries to set the lock by doing an exchange of 1, which is in a register, with the memory address corresponding to the lock. The value returned from the exchange instruction is 1 if some other processor had already claimed access and 0 otherwise. In the latter case, the value is also changed to be 1, preventing any competing exchange from also retrieving a 0.

For example, consider two processors that each try to do the exchange simultaneously: This race is broken since exactly one of the processors will perform the exchange first, returning 0, and the second processor will return 1 when it does the exchange. The key to using the exchange (or swap) primitive to implement synchronization is that the operation is atomic: the exchange is indivisible and two simultaneous exchanges will be ordered by the write serialization mechanisms. It is impossible for two processors trying to set the synchronization variable in this manner to both think they have simultaneously set the variable.

There are a number of other atomic primitives that can be used to implement synchronization. They all have the key property that they read and update a memory value in such a manner that we can tell whether or not the two operations executed atomically. One operation present in many older machines is *test-and-set,* which tests a value and sets it if the value passes the test. For example, we could define an operation that tested for 0 and set the value to 1, which can be used in a fashion similar to how we used atomic exchange. Another atomic synchronization primitive is *fetch-and-increment:* it returns the value of a memory location and atomically increments it. By using the value 0 to indicate that the synchronization variable is unclaimed, we can use fetch-and-increment, just as we used exchange. There are other uses of operations like fetch-and-increment, which we will see shortly.

A slightly different approach to providing this atomic read-and-update operation has been used in some recent machines. Implementing a single atomic memory operation introduces some challenges, since it requires both a memory read and a write in a single, uninterruptible instruction. This complicates the implementation of coherence, since the hardware cannot allow any other operations between the read and the write, and yet must not deadlock.

An alternative is to have a pair of instructions where the second instruction returns a value from which it can be deduced whether the pair of instructions was executed as if the instructions were atomic. The pair of instructions appears atomic if it appears as if all other operations executed by any processor appear before or after the pair. Thus when an instruction pair appears atomic, no other processor can change the value between the instruction pair.

The pair of instructions includes a special load called a *load linked* or *load locked* and a special store called a *store conditional.* These instructions are used in sequence: If the contents of the memory location specified by the load linked are changed before the store conditional to the same address occurs, then the store conditional fails. If the processor does a context switch between the two instructions, then the store conditional also fails. The store conditional is defined to return a value indicating whether or not the store was successful. Since the load linked returns the initial value and the store conditional returns 1 if it succeeds

and 0 otherwise, the following sequence implements an atomic exchange on the
memory location specified by the contents of R1:

```
try:    MOV    R3,R4        ;mov exchange value
        LL     R2,0(R1)     ;load linked
        SC     R3,0(R1)     ;store conditional
        BEQZ   R3,try       ;branch store fails
        MOV    R4,R2        ;put load value in R4
```

At the end of this sequence the contents of R4 and the memory location specified by R1 have been atomically exchanged (ignoring any effect from delayed
branches). Any time a processor intervenes and modifies the value in memory between the LL and SC instructions, the SC returns 0 in R3, causing the code sequence to try again.

An advantage of the load linked/store conditional mechanism is that it can be
used to build other synchronization primitives. For example, here is an atomic
fetch-and-increment:

```
try:    LL     R2,0(R1)     ;load linked
        ADDI   R3,R2,#1     ;increment
        SC     R3,0(R1)     ;store conditional
        BEQZ   R3,try       ;branch store fails
```

These instructions are typically implemented by keeping track of the address
specified in the LL instruction in a register, often called the *link register.* If an interrupt occurs, or if the cache block matching the address in the link register is invalidated (for example, by another SC), the link register is cleared. The SC
instruction simply checks that its address matches that in the link register; if so,
the SC succeeds; otherwise, it fails. Since the store conditional will fail after either another attempted store to the load linked address or any exception, care
must be taken in choosing what instructions are inserted between the two instructions. In particular, only register-register instructions can safely be permitted;
otherwise, it is possible to create deadlock situations where the processor can
never complete the SC. In addition, the number of instructions between the load
linked and the store conditional should be small to minimize the probability that
either an unrelated event or a competing processor causes the store conditional to
fail frequently.

Implementing Locks Using Coherence

Once we have an atomic operation, we can use the coherence mechanisms of a
multiprocessor to implement *spin locks:* locks that a processor continuously tries
to acquire, spinning around a loop. Spin locks are used when we expect the lock
to be held for a very short amount of time and when we want the process of lock-
ing to be low latency when the lock is available. Because spin locks tie up the

processor, waiting in a loop for the lock to become free, they are inappropriate in some circumstances.

The simplest implementation, which we would use if there were no cache coherence, would keep the lock variables in memory. A processor could continually try to acquire the lock using an atomic operation, say exchange, and test whether the exchange returned the lock as free. To release the lock, the processor simply stores the value 0 to the lock. Here is the code sequence to lock a spin lock whose address is in R1 using an atomic exchange:

```
            LI     R2,#1
lockit:     EXCH   R2,0(R1)    ;atomic exchange
            BNEZ   R2,lockit   ;already locked?
```

If our machine supports cache coherence, we can cache the locks using the coherence mechanism to maintain the lock value coherently. This has two advantages. First, it allows an implementation where the process of "spinning" (trying to test and acquire the lock in a tight loop) could be done on a local cached copy rather than requiring a global memory access on each attempt to acquire the lock. The second advantage comes from the observation that there is often locality in lock accesses: that is, the processor that used the lock last will use it again in the near future. In such cases, the lock value may reside in the cache of that processor, greatly reducing the time to acquire the lock.

To obtain the first advantage—being able to spin on a local cached copy rather than generating a memory request for each attempt to acquire the lock—requires a change in our simple spin procedure. Each attempt to exchange in the loop directly above requires a write operation. If multiple processors are attempting to get the lock, each will generate the write. Most of these writes will lead to write misses, since each processor is trying to obtain the lock variable in an exclusive state.

Thus we should modify our spin-lock procedure so that it spins by doing reads on a local copy of the lock until it successfully sees that the lock is available. Then it attempts to acquire the lock by doing a swap operation. A processor first reads the lock variable to test its state. A processor keeps reading and testing until the value of the read indicates that the lock is unlocked. The processor then races against all other processes that were similarly "spin waiting" to see who can lock the variable first. All processes use a swap instruction that reads the old value and stores a 1 into the lock variable. The single winner will see the 0, and the losers will see a 1 that was placed there by the winner. (The losers will continue to set the variable to the locked value, but that doesn't matter.) The winning processor executes the code after the lock and, when finished, stores a 0 into the lock variable to release the lock, which starts the race all over again. Here is the code to perform this spin lock (remember that 0 is unlocked and 1 is locked):

```
lockit: LW     R2,0(R1)    ;load of lock
        BNEZ   R2,lockit   ;not available-spin
        LI     R2,#1       ;load locked value
        EXCH   R2,0(R1)    ;swap
        BNEZ   R2,lockit   ;branch if lock wasn't 0
```

Let's examine how this "spin-lock" scheme uses the cache-coherence mechanisms. Figure 8.32 shows the processor and bus or directory operations for multiple processes trying to lock a variable using an atomic swap. Once the processor with the lock stores a 0 into the lock, all other caches are invalidated and must fetch the new value to update their copy of the lock. One such cache gets the copy of the unlocked value (0) first and performs the swap. When the cache miss of other processors is satisfied, they find that the variable is already locked, so they must return to testing and spinning.

Step	Processor P0	Processor P1	Processor P2	Coherence state of lock	Bus/directory activity
1	Has lock	Spins, testing if lock = 0	Spins, testing if lock = 0	Shared	None
2	Set lock to 0	(Invalidate received)	(Invalidate received)	Exclusive	Write invalidate of lock variable from P0
3		Cache miss	Cache miss	Shared	Bus/directory services P2 cache miss; write back from P0
4		(Waits while bus/ directory busy)	Lock = 0	Shared	Cache miss for P2 satisfied
5		Lock = 0	Executes swap, gets cache miss	Shared	Cache miss for P1 satisfied
6		Executes swap, gets cache miss	Completes swap: returns 0 and sets Lock =1	Exclusive	Bus/directory services P2 cache miss; generates invalidate
7		Swap completes and returns 1	Enter critical section	Shared	Bus/directory services P1 cache miss; generates write back
8		Spins, testing if lock = 0			None

FIGURE 8.32   Cache-coherence steps and bus traffic for three processors, P0, P1, and P2. This figure assumes write-invalidate coherence. P0 starts with the lock (step 1). P0 exits and unlocks the lock (step 2). P1 and P2 race to see which reads the unlocked value during the swap (steps 3–5). P2 wins and enters the critical section (steps 6 and 7), while P1's attempt fails so it starts spin waiting (steps 7 and 8). In a real system, these events will take many more than eight clock ticks, since acquiring the bus and replying to misses takes much longer.

This example shows another advantage of the load-linked/store-conditional primitives: the read and write operation are explicitly separated. The load linked need not cause any bus traffic. This allows the following simple code sequence, which has the same characteristics as the optimized version using exchange (R1 has the address of the lock):

```
lockit:  LL    R2,0(R1)    ;load linked
         BNEZ  R2,lockit   ;not available-spin
         LI    R2,#1       ;locked value
         SC    R2,0(R1)    ;store
         BEQZ  R2,lockit   ;branch if store fails
```

The first branch forms the spinning loop; the second branch resolves races when two processors see the lock available simultaneously.

Although our spin lock scheme is simple and compelling, it has difficulty scaling up to handle many processors because of the communication traffic generated when the lock is released. The next section discusses these problems in more detail, as well as techniques to overcome these problems in larger machines.

Synchronization Performance Challenges

To understand why the simple spin-lock scheme of the previous section does not scale well, imagine a large machine with all processors contending for the same lock. The directory or bus acts as a point of serialization for all the processors, leading to lots of contention, as well as traffic. The following Example shows how bad things can be.

EXAMPLE   Suppose there are 20 processors on a bus that each try to lock a variable simultaneously. Assume that each bus transaction (read miss or write miss) is 50 clock cycles long. You can ignore the time of the actual read or write of a lock held in the cache, as well as the time the lock is held (they won't matter much!). Determine the number of bus transactions required for all 20 processors to acquire the lock, assuming they are all spinning when the lock is released at time 0. About how long will it take to process the 20 requests? Assume that the bus is totally fair so that every pending request is serviced before a new request and that the processors are equally fast.

ANSWER   Figure 8.33 shows the sequence of events from the time of the release to the time to the next release. Of course, the number of processors contending for the lock drops by one each time the lock is acquired, which reduces the average cost to 1525 cycles. Thus for 20 lock-unlock pairs it will

```
local_sense = ! local_sense; /*toggle local_sense*/
lock (counterlock);/* ensure update atomic */
count=count+1;/* count arrivals */
unlock (counterlock);/* unlock */
if (count==total) { /* all arrived */
        count=0;/* reset counter */
        release=local_sense;/* release processes */
}
else { /* more to come */
        spin (release==local_sense);/*wait for signal*/
}
```

FIGURE 8.35   Code for a sense-reversing barrier. The key to making the barrier reusable is the use of an alternating pattern of values for the flag release, which controls the exit from the barrier. If a process races ahead to the next instance of this barrier while some other processes are still in the barrier, the fast process cannot trap the other processes, since it does not reset the value of release as it did in Figure 8.34.

EXAMPLE   Suppose there are 20 processors on a bus that each try to execute a barrier simultaneously. Assume that each bus transaction is 50 clock cycles, as before. You can ignore the time of the actual read or write of a lock held in the cache as the time to execute other nonsynchronization operations in the barrier implementation. Determine the number of bus transactions required for all 20 processors to reach the barrier, be released from the barrier, and exit the barrier. Assume that the bus is totally fair, so that every pending request is serviced before a new request and that the processors are equally fast. Don't worry about counting the processors out of the barrier. How long will the entire process take?

ANSWER   The following table shows the sequence of events for one processor to traverse the barrier, assuming that the first process to grab the bus does not have the lock.

Event	Duration in clocks for one processor	Duration in clocks for 20 processors
Time for each processor to grab lock, increment, release lock	1525	30,500
Time to execute release	50	50
Time for each processor to get the release flag	50	1000
Total	1625	31,550

> Our barrier operation takes a little longer than the 20-processor lock-unlock sequence we considered earlier. The total number of bus transactions is about 440.   ■

As we can see from these examples, synchronization performance can be a real bottleneck when there is substantial contention among multiple processes. When there is little contention and synchronization operations are infrequent, we are primarily concerned about the latency of a synchronization primitive—that is, how long it takes an individual process to complete a synchronization operation. Our basic spin-lock operation can do this in two bus cycles: one to initially read the lock and one to write it. We could improve this to a single bus cycle by a variety of methods. For example, we could simply spin on the swap operation. If the lock were almost always free, this could be better, but if the lock were not free it would lead to lots of bus traffic, since each attempt to lock the variable would lead to a bus cycle. In practice, the latency of our spin lock is not quite as bad as we have seen in this example, since the write miss for a data item present in the cache is treated as an upgrade and will be cheaper than a true read miss.

The more serious problem in these examples is the serialization of each process's attempt to complete the synchronization. This serialization is a problem when there is contention, because it greatly increases the time to complete the synchronization operation. For example, if the time to complete all 20 lock and unlock operations depended only on the latency in the uncontended case, then it would take 2000 rather than 40,000 cycles to complete the synchronization operations. The use of a bus interconnect exacerbates this problem, but serialization could be just as serious in a directory-based machine, where the latency would be large. The next section presents some solutions that are useful when either the contention is high or the processor count is large.

Synchronization Mechanisms for Larger-Scale Machines

What we would like are synchronization mechanisms that have low latency in uncontended cases and that minimize serialization in the case where contention is significant. We begin by showing how software implementations can improve the performance of locks and barriers when contention is high; we then explore two basic hardware primitives that reduce serialization while keeping latency low.

Software Implementations

The major difficulty with our spin-lock implementation is the delay due to contention when many processes are spinning on the lock. One solution is to artificially delay processes when they fail to acquire the lock. This is done by delaying attempts to reacquire the lock whenever the store-conditional operation fails. The best performance is obtained by increasing the delay exponentially whenever the attempt to acquire the lock fails. Figure 8.36 shows how a spin lock with *exponential back-off* is implemented. Exponential back-off is a common technique for reducing contention in shared resources, including access to shared networks and buses (see section 7.7). This implementation still attempts to preserve low latency when contention is small by not delaying the initial spin loop. The result is that if many processes are waiting, the back-off does not affect the processes on their first attempt to acquire the lock. We could also delay that process, but the result would be poorer performance when the lock was in use by only two processes and the first one happened to find it locked.

```
        LI      R3,#1           ;R3 = initial delay
lockit: LL      R2,0(R1)        ;load linked
        BNEZ    R2,lockit       ;not available-spin
        ADDI    R2,R2,#1        ;get locked value
        SC      R2,0(R1)        ;store conditional
        BNEZ    R2,gotit        ;branch if store succeeds
        SLL     R3,R3,#1        ;increase delay by factor of 2
        PAUSE   R3              ;delays by value in R3
        J       lockit
gotit:  use data protected by lock
```

FIGURE 8.36   A spin lock with exponential back-off. When the store conditional fails, the process delays itself by the value in R3. The delay can be implemented by decrementing R3 until it reaches 0. The exact timing of the delay is machine dependent, although it should start with a value that is approximately the time to perform the critical section and release the lock. The statement pause R3 should cause a delay of R3 of these time units. The value in R3 is increased by a factor of 2 every time the store conditional fails, which causes the process to wait twice as long before trying to acquire the lock again.

Another technique for implementing locks is to use queuing locks. We show how this works in the next section using a hardware implementation, but software implementations using arrays can achieve most of the same benefits (see Exercise 8.24). Before we look at hardware primitives, let's look at a better mechanism for barriers.

Our barrier implementation suffers from contention both during the *gather* stage, when we must atomically update the count, and at the *release* stage, when all the processes must read the release flag. The former is more serious because it requires exclusive access to the synchronization variable and thus creates much more serialization; in comparison, the latter generates only read contention. We can reduce the contention by using a *combining tree,* a structure where multiple requests are locally combined in tree fashion. The same combining tree can be used to implement the release process, reducing the contention there; we leave the last step for the Exercises.

Our combining tree barrier uses a predetermined *n*-ary tree structure. We use the variable *k* to stand for the fan-in; in practice $k = 4$ seems to work well. When the *k*th process arrives at a node in the tree, we signal the next level in the tree. When a process arrives at the root, we release all waiting processes. As in our earlier example, we use a sense-reversing technique. The following tree-based barrier uses a tree to combine the processes and a single signal to release the barrier.

```
struct node{ /* a node in the combining tree */
    int counterlock; /* lock for this node */
    int count; /* counter for this node */
    int parent; /* parent in the tree = 0..P-1 except for root
                   = -1*/
};
struct node tree [0..P-1]; /* the tree of nodes */
int local_sense; /* private per processor */
int release; /* global release flag */

/* function to implement barrier */
barrier (int mynode) {
    lock (tree[mynode].counterlock); /* protect count */
    tree[mynode].count=tree[mynode].count+1;
        /* increment count */
    unlock (tree[mynode].counterlock); /* unlock */
    if (tree[mynode].count==k) { /* all arrived at mynode */
        if (tree[mynode].parent >=0) {
            barrier(tree[mynode].parent);
        } else{
            release = local_sense;
        }
        tree[mynode].count = 0; /* reset for the next time */
    } else{
        spin (release==local_sense); /* wait */
    };
};
/* code executed by a processor to join barrier */
local_sense = ! local_sense;
barrier (mynode);
```

The tree is assumed to be prebuilt statically using the nodes in the array `tree`. Each node in the tree combines *k* processes and provides a separate counter and lock, so that at most *k* processes contend at each node. When the *k*th process reaches a node in the tree it goes up to the parent, incrementing the count at the parent. When the count in the parent node reaches *k*, the release flag is set. The count in each node is reset by the last process to arrive. Sense-reversing is used to avoid races as in the simple barrier. Exercises 8.22 and 8.23 ask you to analyze the time for the combining barrier versus the noncombining version. Some MPPs (e.g., the T3D and CM-5) have also included hardware support for barriers, but whether such facilities will be included in future machines is unclear.

Hardware Primitives

In this section we look at two hardware synchronization primitives. The first primitive deals with locks, while the second is useful for barriers and a number of other user-level operations that require counting or supplying distinct indices. In both cases we can create a hardware primitive where latency is essentially identical to our earlier version, but with much less serialization, leading to better scaling when there is contention.

The major problem with our original lock implementation is that it introduces a large amount of unneeded contention. For example, when the lock is released all processors generate both a read and a write miss, although at most one processor can successfully get the lock in the unlocked state. This happens on each of the 20 lock/unlock sequences. We can improve this situation by explicitly handing the lock from one waiting processor to the next. Rather than simply allowing all processors to compete every time the lock is released, we keep a list of the waiting processors and hand the lock to one explicitly, when its turn comes. This sort of mechanism has been called a *queuing lock*. Queuing locks can be implemented either in hardware, which we describe here, or in software using an array to keep track of the waiting processes. The basic concepts are the same in either case. Our hardware implementation assumes a directory-based machine where the individual processor caches are addressable. In a bus-based machine, a software implementation would be more appropriate and would have each processor using a different address for the lock, permitting the explicit transfer of the lock from one process to another.

How does a queuing lock work? On the first miss to the lock variable, the miss is sent to a synchronization controller, which may be integrated with the memory controller (in a bus-based system) or with the directory controller. If the lock is free, it is simply returned to the processor. If the lock is unavailable, the controller creates a record of the node's request (such as a bit in a vector) and sends the processor back a locked value for the variable, which the processor then spins on. When the lock is freed, the controller selects a processor to go ahead from the list of waiting processors. It can then either update the lock variable in the selected processor's cache or invalidate the copy, causing the processor to miss and fetch an available copy of the lock.

EXAMPLE   How many bus transaction and how long does it take to have 20 processors lock and unlock the variable using a queuing lock that updates the lock on a miss? Make the other assumptions about the system the same as before.

ANSWER   Each processor misses once on the lock initially and once to free the lock, so it takes only 40 bus cycles. The first 20 initial misses take 1000 cycles, followed by a 50-cycle delay for each of the 20 releases. This is a total of 2050 cycles—significantly better than the case with conventional coherence-based spin locks. ∎

There are a couple of key insights in implementing such a queuing lock capability. First, we need to be able to distinguish the initial access to the lock, so we can perform the queuing operation, and also the lock release, so we can provide the lock to another processor. The queue of waiting processes can be implemented by a variety of mechanisms. In a directory-based machine, this queue is akin to the sharing set, and similar hardware can be used to implement the directory and queuing lock operations. One complication is that the hardware must be prepared to reclaim such locks, since the process that requested the lock may have been context-switched and may not even be scheduled again on the same processor.

Queuing locks can be used to improve the performance of our barrier operation (see Exercise 8.15). Alternatively, we can introduce a primitive that reduces the amount of time needed to increment the barrier count, thus reducing the serialization at this bottleneck, which should yield comparable performance to using queuing locks. One primitive that has been introduced for this and for building other synchronization operations is *fetch-and-increment,* which atomically fetches a variable and increments its value. The returned value can be either the incremented value or the fetched value. Using fetch-and-increment we can dramatically improve our barrier implementation, compared to the simple code-sensing barrier.

EXAMPLE   Write the code for the barrier using fetch-and-increment. Making the same assumptions as in our earlier example and also assuming that a fetch-and-increment operation takes 50 clock cycles, determine the time for 20 processors to traverse the barrier. How many bus cycles are required?

ANSWER   Figure 8.37 shows the code for the barrier. This implementation requires 20 fetch-and-increment operations and 20 cache misses for the release operation. This is a total time of 2000 cycles and 40 bus/interconnect operations versus an earlier implementation that took over 15 times longer and 10 times more bus operations to complete the barrier. Of course, fetch-and-increment can also be used in implementing the combining tree barrier, reducing the serialization at each node in the tree.

```
local_sense = ! local_sense; /*toggle local_sense*/
fetch_and_increment(count);/* atomic update*/
if (count==total) { /* all arrived */
      count=0;/* reset counter */
      release=local_sense;/* release processes */
}
else { /* more to come */
      spin (release==local_sense);/*wait for signal*/
}
```

FIGURE 8.37 Code for a sense-reversing barrier using fetch-and-increment to do the counting.

∎

As we have seen, synchronization problems can become quite acute in larger-scale machines. When the challenges posed by synchronization are combined with the challenges posed by long memory latency and potential load imbalance in computations, we can see why getting efficient usage of large-scale parallel machines is very challenging. In section 8.8 we will examine the costs of synchronization on an existing bus-based multiprocessor for some real applications.

8.6 | Models of Memory Consistency

Cache coherence ensures that multiple processors see a consistent view of memory. It does not answer the question of *how* consistent the view of memory must be. By this we mean, When must a processor see a value that has been updated by another processor?

Since processors communicate through shared variables (both those for data values and those used for synchronization), the question boils down to this: In what order must a processor observe the data writes of another processor?

Since the only way to "observe the writes of another processor" is through reads, the question becomes, What properties must be enforced among reads and writes to different locations by different processors?

Although the question, how consistent?, seems simple, it is remarkably complicated, as we can see in the following example. Here are two code segments from processes P1 and P2, shown side by side:

```
P1:     A = 0;              P2:     B = 0;
        .....                       .....
        A = 1;                      B = 1;
L1:     if (B == 0) ...      L2:    if (A == 0) ...
```

Assume that the processes are running on different processors, and that locations A and B are originally cached by both processors with the initial value of 0. If writes always take immediate effect and are immediately seen by other processors, it will be impossible for *both* if statements (labeled L1 and L2) to evaluate their conditions as true, since reaching the if statement means that either A or B must have been assigned the value 1. But suppose the write invalidate is delayed, and the processor is allowed to continue during this delay; then it is possible that both P1 and P2 have not seen the invalidations for B and A (respectively) *before* they attempt to read the values. The question is, Should this behavior be allowed, and if so, under what conditions?

The most straightforward model for memory consistency is called *sequential consistency*. Sequential consistency requires that the result of any execution be the same as if the accesses executed by each processor were kept in order and the accesses among different processors were interleaved. This eliminates the possibility of some nonobvious execution in the previous example, because the assignments must be completed before the if statements are initiated. Figure 8.38 illustrates why sequential consistency prohibits an execution where both if statements evaluate to true.

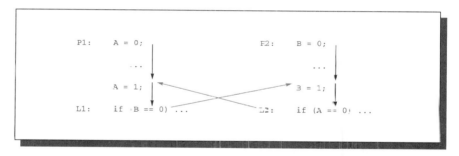

FIGURE 8.38   In sequential consistency, both if statements cannot evaluate to true, since the memory accesses within one process must be kept in program order and the reads of A and B must be interleaved so that one of them completes before the other. To see that this is true, consider the program order shown with black arrows. For both if statements to evaluate to true, the order shown by the two gray arrows must hold, since the reads must appear as if they happen before the writes. For both of these orders to hold and program order to hold, there must be a cycle in the order. The presence of the cycle means that it is impossible to write the accesses down in interleaved order. This means that the execution is not sequentially consistent. You can easily write down all possible orders to help convince yourself.

The simplest way to implement sequential consistency is to require a processor to delay the completion of any memory access until all the invalidations caused by that access are completed. Of course, it is equally simple to delay the next memory access until the previous one is completed. Remember that memory consistency involves operations among different variables: the two accesses that must be ordered are actually to different memory locations. In our example, we must delay the read of A or B (A==0 or B==0) until the previous write has completed (B=1 or A=1). Under sequential consistency, we cannot, for example, simply place the write in a write buffer and continue with the read. Although sequential consistency presents a simple programming paradigm, it reduces potential performance, especially in a machine with a large number of processors, or long interconnect delays, as we can see in the following Example.

EXAMPLE   Suppose we have a processor where a write miss takes 40 cycles to establish ownership, 10 cycles to issue each invalidate after ownership is established, and 50 cycles for an invalidate to complete and be acknowledged once it is issued. Assuming that four other processors share a cache block, how long does a write miss stall the writing processor if the processor is sequentially consistent? Assume that the invalidates must be explicitly acknowledged before the directory controller knows they are completed. Suppose we could continue executing after obtaining ownership for the write miss without waiting for the invalidates; how long would the write take?

ANSWER   When we wait for invalidates, each write takes the sum of the ownership time plus the time to complete the invalidates. Since the invalidates can overlap, we need only worry about the last one, which starts 10 + 10 + 10 + 10 = 40 cycles after ownership is established. Hence the total time is 40 + 40 + 50 = 130 cycles. In comparison, the ownership time is only 40 cycles. With appropriate write-buffer implementations it is even possible to continue before ownership is established.   ■

To provide better performance, designers have developed less restrictive memory consistency models that allow for faster hardware. Such models do affect how the programmer sees the machine, so before we discuss these less restrictive models, let's look at what the programmer expects.

The Programmer's View

Although the sequential consistency model has a performance disadvantage, from the viewpoint of the programmer it has the advantage of simplicity. The challenge is to develop a programming model that is simple to explain and yet allows a high performance implementation. One such programming model that allows us to have a more efficient implementation is to assume that programs are *synchronized*. A program is synchronized if all access to shared data is ordered by synchronization operations. A data reference is ordered by a synchronization operation if, in every possible execution, a write of a variable by one processor and an access (either a read or a write) of that variable by another processor are separated by a pair of synchronization operations, one executed after the write by the writing processor and one executed before the access by the second processor. Cases where variables may be updated without ordering by synchronization are called *data races,* because the execution outcome depends on the relative speed of the processors, and like races in hardware design, the outcome is unpredictable. This leads to another name for synchronized programs: *data-race-free.*

As a simple example, consider a variable being read and updated by two different processors. Each processor surrounds the read and update with a lock and an unlock, both to ensure mutual exclusion for the update and to ensure that the read is consistent. Clearly, every write is now separated from a read by the other processor by a pair of synchronization operations: one unlock (after the write) and one lock (before the read). Of course, if two processors are writing a variable with no intervening reads, then the writes must also be separated by synchronization operations.

We call the synchronization operation corresponding to the unlock a *release,* because it releases a potentially blocked processor, and the synchronization operation corresponding to a lock an *acquire,* because it acquires the right to read the variable. We use the terms acquire and release because they apply to a wide set of synchronization structures, not just locks and unlocks. The next Example shows where the acquires and releases are in several synchronization primitives taken from the previous section.

EXAMPLE   Show which operations are acquires and releases in the lock implementation on page 699 and the barrier implementation in Figure 8.34 on page 701.

ANSWER   Here is the lock code with the acquire operation shown in bold:

```
lockit:  LL    R2,0(R1)    ;load linked
         BNEZ  R2,lockit   ;not available-spin
         ADDI  R2,R2,#1    ;get locked value
         SC    0(R1),R2    ;store
         BEQZ  R2,lockit   ;branch if store fails
```

The release operation for this lock is simply a store operation (which is not shown, but looks like: sw(R1), R0).

Here is the code for the barrier operation with the acquires shown in bold and the releases in italics (there are two acquires and two releases in the barrier):

```
lock (counterlock);/* ensure update atomic */
if (count==0) release=0;/*first=>reset release */
count=count+1;/* count arrivals */
unlock(counterlock);/* release lock */
if (count==total) { /* all arrived */
      count=0;/* reset counter */
      release=1;/* release processes */
}
else{ /* more to come */

      spin (release==1);/* wait for arrivals */
}
```

■

We can now define when a program is synchronized using acquires and releases. A program is *synchronized* if every execution sequence containing a write by a processor and a subsequent access of the same data by another processor contains the following sequence of events:

```
write (x)
...
release (s)
...
acquire (s)
...
access(x)
```

It is easy to see that if all such execution sequences look like this, the program is synchronized in the sense that accesses to shared data are always ordered by synchronization and that data races are impossible.

It is a broadly accepted observation that most programs are synchronized. This observation is true primarily because if the accesses were unsynchronized, the behavior of the program would be quite difficult to determine because the speed of execution would determine which processor won a data race and thus affect the results of the program. Even with sequential consistency, reasoning about such programs is very difficult. Programmers could attempt to guarantee ordering by constructing their own synchronization mechanisms, but this is extremely tricky, can lead to buggy programs, and may not be supported architecturally, meaning that they may not work in future generations of the machine. Instead, almost all programmers will choose to use synchronization libraries that are correct and optimized for the machine and the type of synchronization. A standard synchronization library can classify the operations used for synchronization in the library as releases or acquires, or sometimes as both, as, for example, in the case of a barrier.

The major use of unsynchronized accesses is in programs that want to avoid synchronization cost and are willing to accept an inconsistent view of memory. For example, in a stochastic program we may be willing to have a read return an old value of a data item, because the program will still converge on the correct answer. In such cases we still require the system to behave in a coherent fashion, but we do not need to rely on a well-defined consistency model.

Beyond the synchronization operations, we also need to define the ordering of memory operations. There are two types of restrictions on memory orders: *write fences* and *read fences*. Fences are fixed points in a computation that ensure that no read or write is moved across the fence. For example, a write fence executed by processor P ensures that

- all writes by P that occur before P executed the write fence operation have completed, and

- no writes that occur after the fence in P are initiated before the fence.

In sequential consistency, all reads are read fences and all writes are write fences. This limits the ability of the hardware to optimize accesses, since order must be strictly maintained.

From a performance viewpoint, the processor would like to execute reads as early as possible and complete writes as late as possible. Fences act as boundaries, forcing the processor to order reads and writes with respect to the fence. Although a write fence is a two-way blockade, it is most often used to ensure that writes have completed, since the processor wants to delay write completion. Thus the typical effect of a write fence is to cause the program execution to stall until all outstanding writes have completed, including the delivery of any associated invalidations.

A read fence is also a two-way blockade, marking the earliest or latest point that a read may be executed. Most often a read fence is used to mark the earliest point that a read may be executed.

A *memory fence* is an operation that acts as both a read and a write fence. Memory fences enforce ordering among the accesses of different processes. Within a single process we require that program order always be preserved, so reads and writes of the same location cannot be interchanged.

The weaker consistency models discussed in the next section provide the potential for hiding read and write latency by defining fewer read and write fences. In particular, synchronization accesses act as the fences rather than ordinary accesses.

Relaxed Models for Memory Consistency

Since most programs are synchronized and since a sequential consistency model imposes major inefficiencies, we would like to define a more relaxed model that allows higher performance implementations and still preserves a simple programming model for synchronized programs. In fact, there are a number of relaxed models that all maintain the property that the execution semantics of a synchronized program is the same under the model as it would be under a sequential consistency model. The relaxed models vary in how tightly they constrain the set of possible execution sequences, and thus in how many constraints they impose on the implementation.

To understand the variations among the relaxed models and the possible implications for an implementation, it is simplest if we define the models in terms of what orderings among reads and writes *performed by a single processor* are preserved by each model. There are four such orderings:

1. R → R: a read followed by a read.

2. R → W: a read followed by a write, which is always preserved if the operations are to the same address, since this is an antidependence.

3. W → W: a write followed by a write, which is always preserved if they are to the same address, since this is an output dependence.

4. W → R: a write followed by a read, which is always preserved if they are to the same address, since this is a true dependence.

If there is a dependence between the read and the write, then uniprocessor program semantics demand that the operations be ordered. If there is no dependence, the memory consistency model determines what orders must be preserved. A sequential consistency model requires that all four orderings be preserved and is thus equivalent to assuming a single centralized memory module that serializes all processor operations, or to assuming that all reads and writes are memory barriers.

When an order is relaxed, it simply means that we allow an operation executed later by the processor to complete first. For example, relaxing the ordering W→R means that we allow a read that is later than a write to complete before the write has completed. Remember that a write does not complete until all its invalidations complete, so letting the read occur after the write miss has been handled but before the invalidations are done does not preserve the ordering.

A consistency model does not, in reality, restrict the ordering of events. Instead, it says what possible orderings can be *observed*. For example, in sequential consistency, the system must appear to preserve the four orderings just described, although in practice it can allow reordering. This subtlety allows implementations to use tricks that reorder events without allowing the reordering to be observed. Under sequential consistency an implementation can, for example, allow a processor, P, to initiate another write before an earlier write is completed, as long as P does not allow the value of the later write to be seen before the earlier write has completed. For simplicity, we discuss what orderings must be preserved, with the understanding that the implementation has the flexibility to preserve fewer orderings if only the preserved orderings are visible.

The consistency model must also define the orderings imposed between synchronization variable accesses, which act as fences, and all other accesses. When a machine implements sequential consistency, all reads and writes, including synchronization accesses, are fences and are thus kept in order. For weaker models, we need to specify the ordering restrictions imposed by synchronization accesses, as well as the ordering restrictions involving ordinary variables. The simplest ordering restriction is that every synchronization access is a memory fence. If we let S stand for a synchronization variable access, we could also write this with the ordering notation just shown as S→W, S→R, W→S, and R→S. Remember that a synchronization access is also an R or a W and its ordering is affected by other synchronization accesses, which means there is an implied ordering S→S.

The first model we examine relaxes the ordering between a write and a read (to a different address), eliminating the order W→R; this model was first used in the IBM 370 architecture. Such models allow the buffering of writes with bypassing by reads, which occurs whenever the processor allows a read to proceed before it guarantees that an earlier write by that processor has been seen by all the other processors. This model allows a machine to hide some of the latency of a write operation. Furthermore, by relaxing only this one ordering, many applications, even those that are unsynchronized, operate correctly, although a synchronization operation is necessary to ensure that a write completes before a read is done. If a synchronization operation is executed before the read (i.e. a pattern W...S...R), then the orderings W→S and S→R ensure that the write completes before the read. *Processor consistency* and *total store ordering* (TSO) have been used as names for this model, and many machines have implicitly selected this model. This model is equivalent to making the writes be write fences. We summarize all the models, showing the orderings imposed, in Figure 8.39 and show an example in Figure 8.40.

If we also allow nonconflicting writes to potentially complete out of order, by relaxing the W →W ordering, we arrive at a model that has been called *partial store ordering* (PSO). From an implementation viewpoint, it allows pipelining or overlapping of write operations, rather than forcing one operation to complete before another. A write operation need only cause a stall when a synchronization operation, which causes a write fence, is encountered.

The third major class of relaxed models eliminates the R → R and R → W orderings, in addition to the other two orders. This model, which is called *weak ordering*, does not preserve ordering among references, except for the following:

- A read or write is completed before any synchronization operation executed in program order by the processor after the read or write.

- A synchronization operation is always completed before any reads or writes that occur in program order after the operation.

As Figure 8.39 shows, the only orderings imposed in weak order are those created by synchronization operations. Although we have eliminated the R → R and R → W orderings, the processor can only take advantage of this if it has nonblocking reads. Otherwise the processor implicitly implements these two orders, since no further instructions can be executed until the R is completed. Even with nonblocking reads, the processor may be limited in the advantage it obtains from relaxing the read orderings, since the primary advantage occurs when the R causes a cache miss and the processor is unlikely to be able to keep busy for the tens to hundreds of cycles that handling the cache miss may take. In general, the major advantage of all weaker consistency models comes in hiding write latencies rather than read latencies.

A more relaxed model can be obtained by extending weak ordering. This model, called *release consistency,* distinguishes between synchronization operations that are used to *acquire* access to a shared variable (denoted S_A) and those that *release* an object to allow another processor to acquire access (denoted S_R). Release consistency is based on the observation that in synchronized programs an acquire operation must precede a use of shared data, and a release operation must follow any updates to shared data and also precede the time of the next acquire. This allows us to slightly relax the ordering by observing that a read or write that precedes an acquire need not complete before the acquire, and also that a read or write that follows a release need not wait for the release. Thus the orderings that are preserved involve only S_A and S_R, as shown in Figure 8.39; as the example in Figure 8.40 shows, this model imposes the fewest orders of the five models.

To compare release consistency to weak ordering, consider what orderings would be needed for weak ordering, if we decompose each S in the orderings to S_A and S_R. This would lead to eight orderings involving synchronization accesses and ordinary accesses plus four orderings involving only synchronization accesses. With such a description, we can see that four of the orderings required under weak ordering are *not* imposed under release consistency: W → S_A, R→ S_A, S_R → R, and S_R → W.

Release consistency provides one of the least restrictive models that is easily checkable, and ensures that synchronized programs will see a sequentially consistent execution. While most synchronization operations are either an acquire or a release (an acquire normally reads a synchronization variable and atomically updates it, while a release usually just writes it), some operations, such as a barrier, act as both an acquire and a release and cause the ordering to be equivalent to weak ordering.

Model	Used in	Ordinary orderings	Synchronization orderings
Sequential consistency	Most machines as an optional mode	$R \rightarrow R, R \rightarrow W, W \rightarrow R,$ $W \rightarrow W$	$S \rightarrow W, S \rightarrow R, R \rightarrow S, W \rightarrow S, S \rightarrow S$
Total store order or processor consistency	IBMS/370, DEC VAX, SPARC	$R \rightarrow R, R \rightarrow W, W \rightarrow W$	$S \rightarrow W, S \rightarrow R, R \rightarrow S, W \rightarrow S, S \rightarrow S$
Partial store order	SPARC	$R \rightarrow R, R \rightarrow W$	$S \rightarrow W, S \rightarrow R, R \rightarrow S, W \rightarrow S, S \rightarrow S$
Weak ordering	PowerPC		$S \rightarrow W, S \rightarrow R, R \rightarrow S, W \rightarrow S, S \rightarrow S$
Release consistency	Alpha, MIPS		$S_A \rightarrow W, S_A \rightarrow R, R \rightarrow S_R, W \rightarrow S_R,$ $S_A \rightarrow S_A, S_A \rightarrow S_R, S_R \rightarrow S_A, S_R \rightarrow S_R$

FIGURE 8.39   The orderings imposed by various consistency models are shown for both ordinary accesses and synchronization accesses. The models grow from most restrictive (sequential consistency) to least restrictive (release consistency), allowing increased flexibility in the implementation. The weaker models rely on fences created by synchronization operations, as opposed to an implicit fence at every memory operation. S_A and S_F stand for acquire and release operations, respectively, and are needed to define release consistency. If we used the notation S_A and S_R for each S consistently, each ordering with one S would become two orderings (e.g., $S \rightarrow W$ becomes $S_A \rightarrow W$, $S_R \rightarrow W$), and each $S \rightarrow S$ would become the four orderings shown in the last line of the bottom-right table entry.

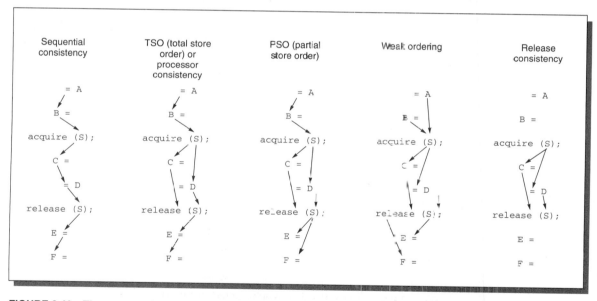

FIGURE 8.40   These examples of the five consistency models discussed in this section show the reduction in the number of orders imposed as the models become more relaxed. Only the minimum orders are shown with arrows. Orders implied by transitivity, such as the write of C before the release of S in the sequential consistency model or the acquire before the release in weak ordering or release consistency, are not shown.

It is also possible to consider even weaker orderings. For example, in release consistency we do not associate memory locations with particular synchronization variables. If we required that the same synchronization variable, V, always be acquired before accessing a particular memory location, M, for example, we could relax the ordering of access to M and acquires and releases of all other synchronization variables other than V. The orderings discussed so far are relatively straightforward to implement. Weaker orderings, such as the previous example, are harder to implement, and it is unclear whether the advantages of weaker orderings would justify their implementation.

Implementation of Relaxed Models

Relaxed models of consistency can usually be implemented with little additional hardware. Most of the complexity lies in implementing memory or interconnect systems that can take advantage of a relaxed model. For example, if the memory or interconnect does not allow multiple outstanding accesses from a processor, then the benefits of the more ambitious relaxed models will be small. Fortunately, most of the benefit can be obtained by having a small number of outstanding writes and one outstanding read.

In this section we describe straightforward implementations of processor consistency and release consistency. Our directory protocols already satisfy the constraints of sequential consistency, since the processor stalls until an operation is complete and the directory first invalidates all sharers before responding to a write miss.

Processor consistency (or TSO) is typically implemented by allowing read misses to bypass pending writes. A write buffer that can support a check to determine whether any pending write in the buffer is to the same address as a read miss, together with a memory and interconnection system that can support two outstanding references per node, is sufficient to implement this scheme. Qualitatively, the advantage of processor consistency over sequential consistency is that it allows the latency of write misses to be hidden.

Release consistency allows additional write latency to be hidden, and if the processor supports nonblocking reads, allows the read latency to be hidden also. To allow write latency to be hidden as much as possible, the processor must allow multiple outstanding writes and allow read misses to bypass outstanding writes. To maximize performance, writes should complete and clear the write buffer as early as possible, which allows any dependent reads to go forward. Supporting early completion of writes requires allowing a write to complete as soon as data are available and before all pending invalidations are completed (since our consistency model allows this). To implement this scheme, either the directory or the original requester can keep track of the invalidation count for each outstanding write. After each invalidation is acknowledged, the pending invalidation count for that write is decreased. We must ensure that all pending invalidates to all out-standing writes complete before we allow a release to complete, so we simply check the pending invalidation counts on any outstanding write when a release is executed. The release is held up until all such invalidations for all outstanding writes complete. In practice, we limit the number of outstanding writes, so that it is easy to track the writes and pending invalidates.

To hide read latency we must have a machine that has nonblocking reads; otherwise, when the processor blocks, little progress will be made. If reads are nonblocking we can simply allow them to execute, knowing that the data dependences will preserve correct execution. It is unlikely, however, that the addition of nonblocking reads to a relaxed consistency model will substantially enhance performance. The limited gain occurs because the read miss times in a multiprocessor are likely to be large and the processor can provide only limited ability to hide this latency. For example, if the reads are nonblocking but the processor executes in order, then the processor will almost certainly block for the read after a few cycles. If the processor supports nonblocking reads and out-of-order execution, it will block as soon as any of its buffers, such as the reorder buffer or reservation stations, are full. (See Chapter 4 for a discussion of full buffer stalls in dynamically scheduled machines.) This is likely to happen in at most tens of cycles, while a miss may cost a hundred cycles. Thus, although the gain may be limited, there is a positive synergy between nonblocking loads and relaxed consistency models.

Performance of Relaxed Models

The performance potential of a more relaxed consistency model depends on both the capabilities of the machine and the particular application. To examine the performance of a memory consistency model, we must first define a hardware environment. The hardware configurations we consider have the following properties:

- The pipeline issues one instruction per clock cycle and is either statically or dynamically scheduled. All functional unit latencies are one cycle.

- Cache misses take 50 clock cycles.

- The CPU includes a write buffer of depth 16.

- The caches are 64 KB and have 16-byte blocks.

To give a flavor of the tradeoffs and performance potential with different hardware capabilities, we consider four hardware models:

1. *SSBR (statically scheduled with blocking reads)*—The processor is statically scheduled and reads that miss in the cache immediately block.

2. *SS (statically scheduled)*—The processor is statically scheduled but reads do not cause the processor to block until the result is used.

3. *DS16 (dynamically scheduled with a 16-entry reorder buffer)*—The processor is dynamically scheduled and has a reorder buffer that allows up to 16 outstanding instructions of any type, including 16 memory access instructions.

4. *DS64 (dynamically scheduled with a 64-entry reorder buffer)*—The processor is dynamically scheduled and has a reorder buffer that allows up to 64 outstanding instructions of any type. This reorder buffer is potentially large enough to hide the total cache miss latency of 50 cycles.

Figure 8.41 shows the relative performance for two of the parallel program benchmarks, LU and Ocean, for these four hardware models and for two different consistency models: total store order (TSO) and release consistency. The performance is shown relative to the performance under a straightforward implementation of sequential consistency. Relaxed models offer a much larger performance gain on Ocean than on LU. This is simply because Ocean has a much higher miss rate and has a significant fraction of write misses. In interpreting the data in Figure 8.41, remember that the caches are fairly small. Most designers would increase the cache size before including nonblocking reads or even beginning to think about dynamic scheduling. This would dramatically reduce the miss rate and the possible advantage from the relaxed model at least for these applications.

Final Remarks on Consistency Models

At the present time, most machines being built support some sort of weak consistency model, varying from processor consistency to release consistency, and almost all also support sequential consistency as an option. Since synchronization is highly machine specific and error prone, the expectation is that most programmers will use standard synchronization libraries and will write synchronized programs, making the choice of a weak consistency model invisible to the programmer and yielding higher performance. Yet to be developed are ideas of how to deal with nondeterministic programs that do not rely on getting the latest values. One possibility is that programmers will not need to rely at all on the timing of updates to variables in such programs; the other possibility is that machine-specific models of update behavior will be needed and used. As remote access latencies continue to increase relative to processor performance, and as features that increase the potential advantage of relaxed models, such as nonblocking caches, are included in more processors, the importance of choosing a consistency model that delivers both a convenient programming model and high performance will increase.

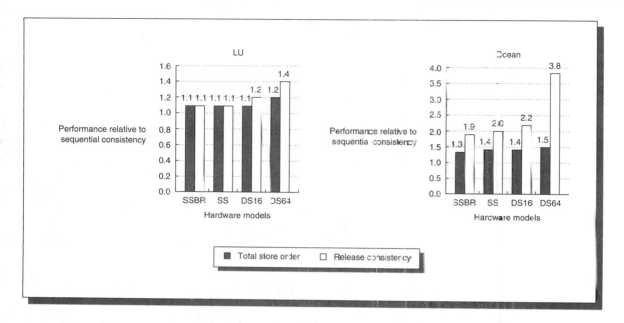

FIGURE 8.41   The performance of relaxed consistency models on a variety of hardware mechanisms, varying from quite reasonable to highly ambitious. The caches are 64 KB, direct mapped, with 16-byte blocks. Misses take 50 cycles. With SSBR most of the write latency is hidden in these benchmarks. It takes dynamic scheduling to hide read latency, and to completely hide read latency a buffer larger than the latency is needed (DS64). For larger cache sizes, the miss rate of Ocean continues to fall and so does the advantage of a relaxed model. For example at a 256-KB cache with 64-byte blocks and 16 processors, the miss rate is 2%. This leads to an upper bound of 2.0 on the benefits from a relaxed model.

8.7 | Crosscutting Issues

Because multiprocessors redefine many system characteristics, they introduce interesting design problems across the spectrum. In this section we give several examples: accurate performance measurement, two examples involving memory systems, an example of the interaction between compilers and the memory consistency model, and a method for using virtual memory support to implement shared memory.

Performance Measurement of Parallel Machines

One of the most controversial issues in parallel processing has been how to measure the performance of parallel machines. Of course, the straightforward answer is to measure a benchmark as supplied and to examine wall-clock time. Measuring wall-clock time obviously makes sense; in a parallel processor, measuring

CPU time can be misleading because the processors may be idle but unavailable for other uses.

Users and designers are often interested in knowing not just how well a machine performs with a certain fixed number of processors, but also how the performance scales as more processors are added. In many cases, it makes sense to scale the application or benchmark, since if the benchmark is unscaled, effects arising from limited parallelism and increases in communication can lead to results that are pessimistic when the expectation is that more processors will be used to solve larger problems. Thus it is often useful to measure the speedup as processors are added both for a fixed-size problem and for a scaled version of the problem, providing an unscaled and a scaled version of the speedup curves. The choice of how to measure the uniprocessor algorithm is also important to avoid anomalous results, since using the parallel version of the benchmark may understate the uniprocessor performance and thus overstate the speedup. This is discussed with an example in section 8.9.

Once we have decided to measure scaled speedup, the question is *how* to scale the application. Let's assume that we have determined that running a benchmark of size n on p processors makes sense. The question is how to scale the benchmark to run on $m \times p$ processors. There are two obvious ways to scale the problem: keeping the amount of memory used per processor constant; and keeping the total execution time, assuming perfect speedup, constant. The first method, called *memory-constrained scaling,* specifies running a problem of size $m \times n$ on $m \times p$ processors. The second method, called *time-constrained scaling,* requires that we know the relationship between the running time and the problem size, since the former is kept constant. For example, suppose the running time of the application with data size n on p processors is proportional to n^2/p. Then with time-constrained scaling, the problem to run is the problem whose ideal running time on $m \times p$ processors is still n^2/p. The problem with this ideal running time has size $\sqrt{m} \times n$.

EXAMPLE   Suppose we have a problem whose execution time for a problem of size n is proportional to n^3. Suppose the actual running time on a 10-processor machine is 1 hour. Under the time-constrained and memory-constrained scaling models, find the size of the problem to run and the effective running time for a 100-processor machine.

ANSWER   For the time-constrained problem, the ideal running time is the same, 1 hour, so the problem size is $\sqrt[3]{10} \times n$. For memory-constrained scaling, the size of the problem is $10n$ and the ideal execution time is $10^3/10$, or 100 hours! Since most users will be reluctant to run a problem on an order of magnitude more processors for 100 times longer, this size problem is probably unrealistic.   ■

In addition to the scaling methodology, there are questions as to how the program should be scaled when increasing the problem size affects the quality of the result. Since many parallel programs are simulations of physical phenomena, changing the problem size changes the quality of the result, and we must change the application to deal with this effect. As a simple example, consider the effect of time to convergence for solving a differential equation. This time typically increases as the problem size increases, since, for example, we often require more iterations for the larger problem. Thus when we increase the problem size, the total running time may scale faster than the basic algorithmic scaling would indicate. For example, suppose that the number of iterations grows as the log of the problem size. Then for a problem whose algorithmic running time is linear in the size of the problem, the effective running time actually grows proportional to $n \log n$. If we scaled from a problem of size m on 10 processors, purely algorithmic scaling would allow us to run a problem of size $10\,m$ on 100 processors. Accounting for the increase in iterations means that a problem of size $k \times m$, where $k \log k = 10$, will have the same running time on 100 processors. This yields a scaling of $5.72\,m$, rather than $10\,m$. In practice, scaling to deal with error requires a good understanding of the application and may involve other factors, such as error tolerances (for example, it affects the cell-opening criteria in Barnes-Hut). In turn, such effects often significantly affect the communication or parallelism properties of the application as well as the choice of problem size.

Scaled speedup is not the same as unscaled (or true) speedup; confusing the two has led to erroneous claims. Scaled speedup has an important role, but only when the scaling methodology is sound and the results are clearly reported as using a scaled version of the application.

Memory System Issues

As we have seen in this chapter, memory system issues are at the core of the design of shared-memory multiprocessors. Indeed, multiprocessing introduces many new memory system complications that do not exist in uniprocessors. In this section we look at two implementation issues that have a significant impact on the design and implementation of a memory system in a multiprocessor context.

Inclusion and Its Implementation

Many multiprocessors use multilevel cache hierarchies to reduce both the demand on the global interconnect and the latency of cache misses. If the cache also provides *multilevel inclusion*—every level of cache hierarchy is a subset of the level further away from the processor—then we can use the multilevel structure to reduce the contention between coherence traffic and processor traffic, as explained earlier. Thus most multiprocessors with multilevel caches enforce the inclusion property. This restriction is also called the *subset property,* because each cache is a subset of the cache below it in the hierarchy.

At first glance, preserving the multilevel inclusion property seems trivial. Consider a two-level example: any miss in L1 either hits in L2 or generates a miss in L2, causing it to be brought into both L1 and L2. Likewise, any invalidate that hits in L2 must be sent to L1, where it will cause the block to be invalidated, if it exists.

The catch is what happens when the block size of L1 and L2 are different. Choosing different block sizes is quite reasonable, since L2 will be much larger and have a much longer latency component in its miss penalty, and thus will want to use a larger block size. What happens to our "automatic" enforcement of inclusion when the block sizes differ? A block in L2 represents multiple blocks in L1, and a miss in L2 causes the replacement of data that is equivalent to multiple L1 blocks. For example, if the block size of L2 is four times that of L1, then a miss in L2 will replace the equivalent of four L1 blocks. Let's consider a detailed example.

EXAMPLE   Assume that L2 has a block size four times that of L1. Show how a miss for an address that causes a replacement in L1 and L2 can lead to violation of the inclusion property.

ANSWER   Assume that L1 and L2 are direct mapped and that the block size of L1 is *b* bytes and the block size of L2 is 4*b* bytes. Suppose L1 contains blocks with starting addresses *x* and *x* + *b* and that *x* mod 4*b* = 0, meaning that *x* also is the starting address of a block in L2. That single block in L2 contains the L1 blocks *x*, *x* + *b*, *x* + 2*b*, and *x* + 3*b*. Suppose the processor generates a reference to block *y* that maps to the block containing *x* in both caches and hence misses. Since L2 missed, it fetches 4*b* bytes and replaces the block containing *x*, *x* + *b*, *x* + 2*b*, and *x* + 3*b*, while L1 takes *b* bytes and replaces the block containing *x*. Since L1 still contains *x* + *b*, but L2 does not, the inclusion property no longer holds.   ■

To maintain inclusion with multiple block sizes, we must probe the higher levels of the hierarchy when a replacement is done at the lower level to ensure that any words replaced in the lower level are invalidated in the higher-level caches. Most systems chose this solution rather than the alternative of not relying on inclusion and snooping the higher-level caches. In the Exercises we explore inclusion further and show that similar problems exist if the associativity of the levels is different.

Nonblocking Caches and Latency Hiding

We saw the idea of nonblocking or lockup-free caches in Chapter 5, where the concept was used to reduce cache misses by overlapping them with execution and by pipelining misses. There are additional benefits in the multiprocessor case. The first is that the miss penalties are likely to be larger, meaning there is more latency to hide, and the opportunity for pipelining misses is also probably larger, since the memory and interconnect system can often handle multiple outstanding memory references.

A machine needs nonblocking caches to take advantage of weak consistency models. For example, to implement a model like processor consistency requires that writes be nonblocking with respect to reads so that a processor can continue either immediately, by buffering the write, or as soon as it establishes ownership of the block and updates the cache. Relaxed consistency models allow further reordering of misses, but nonblocking caches are needed to take full advantage of this flexibility. With the more extensive use of nonblocking caches and dynamic scheduling, we can expect the potential benefits of relaxed consistency models to increase.

Finally, nonblocking support is critical to implementing prefetching. Prefetching, which we also discussed in Chapter 5, is even more important in multiprocessors than in uniprocessors, due to longer memory latencies. In Chapter 5 we described why it is important that prefetches not affect the semantics of the program, since this allows them to be inserted anywhere in the program without changing the results of the computation.

In a multiprocessor, maintaining the absence of any semantic impact from the use of prefetches requires that prefetched data be kept coherent. A prefetched value is kept coherent if, when the value is actually accessed by a load instruction, the most recently written value is returned, even if that value was written after the prefetch. This is exactly the property that cache coherence gives us for other variables in memory. A prefetch that brings a data value closer, and guarantees that on the actual memory access to the data (a load of the prefetched value) the most recent value of the data item is obtained, is called *nonbinding,* since the data value is not bound to a local copy, which would be incoherent. By contrast, a prefetch that moves a data value into a general-purpose register is binding, since the register value is a new variable, as opposed to a cache block, which is a coherent copy of a variable. A nonbinding prefetch maintains the coherence properties of any other value in memory, while a binding prefetch appears more like a register load, since it removes the data from the coherent address space.

Why is nonbinding prefetch critical? Consider a simple but typical example: a data value written by one processor and used by another. In this case, the consumer would like to prefetch the value as early as possible; but suppose the producing process is delayed for some reason. Then the prefetch may fetch the old value of the data item. If the prefetch is nonbinding, the copy of the old data is invalidated when the value is written, maintaining coherence. If the prefetch is binding, however, then the old, incoherent value of the data is used by the prefetching process. Because of the long memory latencies, a prefetch may need to be placed a hundred or more instructions earlier than the data use, if we aim to hide the entire latency. This makes the nonbinding property vital to ensure coherent usage of the prefetch in multiprocessors.

Implementing prefetch requires the same sort of support that a lockup-free cache needs, since there are multiple outstanding memory accesses. This causes several complications:

1. A local node will need to keep track of the multiple outstanding accesses, since the replies may return in a different order than they were sent. This can be handled by adding tags to the requests, or by incorporating the address of the memory block in the reply.

2. Before issuing a request, the node must ensure that it has not already issued a request for the same block, since two requests for the same block could lead to incorrect operation of the protocol. In particular, if the node issues a write miss to a block, while it has such a write miss outstanding both our snooping protocol and directory protocol fail to operate properly.

3. Our implementation of the directory and snooping controllers assumes that the processor stalls on a miss. Stalling allows the cache controller to simply wait for a reply when it has generated a request. With a nonblocking cache, stalling is not possible and the actual implementation must deal with additional processor requests.

Compiler Optimization and the Consistency Model

Another reason for defining a model for memory consistency is to specify the range of legal compiler optimizations that can be performed on shared data. In explicitly parallel programs, unless the synchronization points are clearly defined and the programs are synchronized, the compiler could not interchange a read and a write of two different shared data items, because such transformations might affect the semantics of the program. This prevents even relatively simple optimizations, such as register allocation of shared data, because such a process usually interchanges reads and writes. In implicitly parallelized programs—for example, those written in High Performance FORTRAN (HPF)—programs must be synchronized and the synchronization points are known, so this issue does not arise.

Using Virtual Memory Support to Build Shared Memory

Suppose we wanted to support a shared address space among a group of workstations connected to a network. One approach is to use the virtual memory mechanism and operating system (OS) support to provide shared memory. This approach, which was first explored more than 10 years ago, has been called *distributed virtual memory (DVM)* or *shared virtual memory (SVM)*. The key observation that this idea builds on is that the virtual memory hardware has the ability to control access to portions of the address space for both reading and writing. By using the hardware to check and intercept accesses and the operating system to ensure coherence, we can create a coherent, shared address space across the distributed memory of multiple processors.

In SVM, pages become the units of coherence, rather than cache blocks. The OS can allow pages to be replicated in read-only fashion, using the virtual memory support to protect the pages from writing. When a process attempts to write such a page, it traps to the operating system. The operating system on that processor can then send messages to the OS on each node that shares the page, requesting that the page be invalidated. Just as in a directory system, each page has a home node, and the operating system running in that node is responsible for tracking who has copies of the page.

The mechanisms are quite similar to those at work in coherent shared memory. The key differences are that the unit of coherence is a page and that software is used to implement the coherence algorithms. It is exactly these two differences that lead to the major performance differences. A page is considerably bigger than a cache block, and the possibilities for poor usage of a page and for false sharing are very high. This leads to much less stable performance and sometimes even lower performance than a uniprocessor. Because the coherence algorithms are implemented in software, they have much higher overhead.

The result of this combination is that shared virtual memory has become an acceptable substitute for loosely coupled message passing, since in both cases the frequency of communication must be low, and communication that is structured in larger blocks is favored. Distributed virtual memory is not currently competitive with schemes that have hardware-supported, coherent memory, such as the distributed shared-memory schemes we examined in section 8.4: Most programs written for coherent shared memory cannot be run efficiently on shared virtual memory.

Several factors could change the attractiveness of shared virtual memory. Better implementation and small amounts of hardware support could reduce the overhead in the operating system. Compiler technology, as well as the use of smaller or multiple page sizes, could allow the system to reduce the disadvantages of coherence at a page-level granularity. The concept of software-supported shared memory remains an important and active area of research, and such techniques may play an important role in improving the hardware mechanisms; in using more loosely coupled machines, such as networks of workstations; or in allowing coherent shared memory to be extended to larger or more distributed machines possibly built with DSM clusters.

8.8 Putting It All Together: The SGI Challenge Multiprocessor

In this section we examine the design and performance of the Silicon Graphics Challenge multiprocessor. The Challenge is a bus-based, cache-coherent design with a wide, high-speed bus, capable of holding up to 36 MIPS R4400 processors with 4 processors on a board, and up to 16 GB of eight-way interleaved memory. The Power Challenge design uses the much higher performance R8000 (TFP) microprocessors but with the same bus, memory, and I/O system; with two processors per board a Power Challenge can hold up to 18 processors. Our discussion will focus on the bus, coherence hardware, and synchronization support, and our measurements use a 150-MHz R4400-based Challenge system.

The Challenge System Bus (POWERpath-2)

The core of the Challenge design is a wide (256 data bits; 40 address bits), 50-MHz bus (using reduced voltage swing) called POWERpath-2. This bus interconnects all the major system components and provides support for coherence. Figure 8.42 is a diagram of the system configuration.

The POWERpath-2 implements a write-invalidate coherence scheme using four states: the three states we saw in section 8.3 and an additional state representing a block that is clean but exclusive in one cache. The basic coherence protocol is a slight extension over the three-state protocol we examined in detail. When a block that is not shared by any cache is read, the block is placed in the clean exclusive state. Additional read misses of the same block by other processors change the block to the shared state. A write miss causes the block to be transferred to the exclusive (dirty exclusive) state. The major advantage of this protocol is that there is no need to generate a write miss, or an invalidate, when a block is upgraded from clean exclusive to dirty exclusive. Although this is unlikely to be a large effect for accesses to truly shared data (since such data will often be in some processor's cache), it does improve the performance of accesses to private data and to data that are potentially but not actually shared. In particular, data that are not actually shared behave as if the machine were a uniprocessor, where a cache miss would not be needed to write a block already resident in the cache. Implementing the clean exclusive state is straightforward, because the processor sees any attempt to read or write the block and can change the state accordingly.

The POWERpath-2 bus supports split transactions and can have up to eight pending memory reads outstanding, including reads needed to satisfy a write miss. All pending reads are tracked at each processor board, and *resource identifiers,* unique numbers between 0 and 7 (since there are eight outstanding operations), are assigned to reads as they arrive. The resource identifiers are used to tag

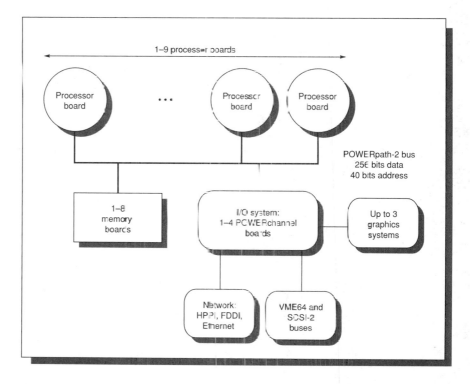

FIGURE 8.42 The Challenge system structure relies on a fast wide bus to interconnect the system and to allow expansion. Each processor board holds four R4400 processors or two R8000 processors. Each memory board holds up to 2 GB. In the largest configuration there are 15 POWERpath-2 bus slots, which can be configured with up to a maximum of nine CPU boards (36 R4400s or 18 R8000s), eight memory boards (16 GB), five VME64 buses (with up to 20 more in an extension box), 32 SCSI-2 channels, eight Ethernets, four HPPI channels, four FDDI connections, and up to three graphics subsystems. This configuration allows four disks in the main cabinet and almost 500 disks with expansion cabinets, for a total of multiple terabytes. For further information about the Challenge design, see http://www.sgi.com/.

results, so that processors know when a response to their request is on the bus. If all eight resource identifiers are in use, a read must wait for one to become free, which happens when an outstanding read completes.

In Appendix E we discuss the difficulties raised by a split transaction bus. In particular, the cache-coherence algorithm of section 8.3 will not work correctly if two writes or a write and a read for the same cache block can be interleaved on the bus. (The interested reader should see Appendix E for an example and further details.) To prevent this problem, a processor board will not issue an invalidate (or write miss) for the same address as any pending read. Thus each processor module keeps track of the requested address for the eight possible outstanding reads. If a write miss occurs for a read that is pending, the processor is stalled and the write is delayed. If a processor board receives a read miss for an address for which a read is pending, the later read can "piggyback" on the earlier read. When the response to the earlier read appears (tagged with the correct resource ID), the bus interface simply grabs the data and uses it to satisfy the later cache miss.

For each of the eight read resources there is an inhibit line, which is used to indicate that a read request should not be responded to by the memory. Snoops can take variable amounts of time, depending on the state of the processor and the block, so this signal is critical to implementing coherence. When a processor receives a snoop request, it asserts the inhibit line until it completes its snoop. If the snoop either finds that the cache does not have the block or finds the block in a clean state, the processor drops the inhibit line. If all the processors drop the inhibit line, the memory will respond, since it knows that all the processor copies are clean. If a processor finds a dirty copy of the block, it requests the bus and places the data on the bus, after which it drops the inhibit line. Both the requesting processor and the memory receive the data and write it. In this latter case, since there are separate tags for snooping, and retrieving a value from the first- or second-level cache takes much longer than detecting the presence of the data, this solution of letting memory respond when its copy is valid is considerably faster than always intervening.

The data and address buses are separately arbitrated and used. Write-back requests use both buses, read responses use only the data bus, and invalidate and read requests use only the address bus. Since the buses are separately arbitrated and assigned, the combined pair of buses can simultaneously carry a new read request and a response to an earlier request.

On POWERpath-2, each bus transaction consists of five bus clock cycles, each 20 ns in length, that are executed in parallel by the bus controllers on each board. These five cycles are arbitration, resolution, address, decode, and acknowledge. On the address bus, one address is sent in the five-cycle bus transaction. On the data bus, four 256-bit data transfers are performed during the five-cycle bus transaction. Thus the sustained bus transfer rate is

$$(256/8) \text{ bytes/transfer} \times (1000/20) \text{ bus cycles/microsecond}$$

$$\times (4/5) \text{ transfers/bus cycle} = 1.28 \text{ GB/sec}$$

To obtain high bandwidth from memory, each memory board provides a 576-bit path to the DRAMs (512 bits of data and 64 bits of ECC), allowing a single memory cycle to provide the data for two bus transfers. Thus with two-way interleaving a single memory board can support the full bus bandwidth. The total time to satisfy a read miss for a 128-byte cache block with no contention is 22 bus clock cycles:

1. The initial read request is one bus transaction of five bus clock cycles.

2. The latency until memory is ready to transfer is 12 bus clock cycles.

3. The reply transfers all 128 bytes in one reply transaction (four 256-bit transfers), taking five bus clock cycles.

Thus, latency of the access from the processor viewpoint is 22 bus clock cycles, assuming that the memory access can start when the address is received and the reply transaction can start immediately after the data is available. The bus is split transaction, so other requests and replies can occur during the memory access time.

Thus to calculate the secondary cache miss time, we need to compute the latency of each step from the point a memory address is issued until the processor is restarted after the miss:

1. The first step is the initial detection of the miss and generation of the memory request by the processor. This process consists of three steps: detecting a miss in the primary on-chip cache; initiating a secondary (off-chip) cache access and detecting a miss in the secondary cache; and driving the complete address off-chip through the system bus. This process takes about 40 processor clock cycles.

2. The next step is the bus and memory system component, which we know takes 22 bus clock cycles.

3. The next step is reloading the cache line. The R4400 is stalled until the entire cache block is reloaded, so the reload time is added into the miss time. The memory interface on the processor is 64 bits and operates at the external bus timing of 50 MHz, which is the same as the bus timing. Thus reloading the 128-byte cache block takes 16 bus clock cycles.

4. Finally, 10 additional processor clock cycles are used to reload the primary cache and restart the pipeline.

The total miss penalty for a secondary cache miss consists of 50 processor clocks plus 38 bus clocks. For a 150-MHz R4400, each bus clock (20 ns) is three processor clocks (6.67 ns), so the miss time is 164 processor clocks, or 1093 ns. This number is considerably larger than it would be for a uniprocessor memory access, as we discuss in section 8.9. The next section discusses performance.

Performance of the Parallel Program Workload on Challenge

Figure 8.43 shows the speedup for our applications running on up to 16 processors. The speedups for 16 processors vary from 10.5 to 15.0. Because these benchmarks have been tuned to improve memory behavior, the uniprocessor version of the parallel benchmark is better than the original uniprocessor version. Thus we report speedup relative to the uniprocessor parallel version. To understand what's behind the speedups, we can examine the components of the execution time.

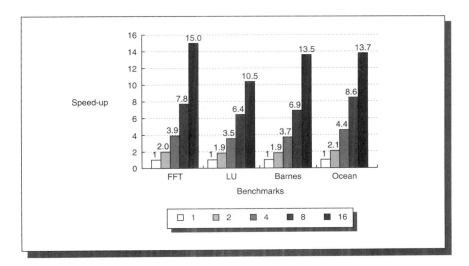

FIGURE 8.43   The speedups for the parallel benchmarks are shown versus processor count for a 150-MHz R4400 Challenge system. The superlinear speedup for Ocean running on two processors occurs because of the doubling of the available cache.

Figure 8.44 shows how the total execution time is composed of three components: CPU time, memory overhead or stall time, and synchronization wait time. With the data in Figure 8.44, we can explain the speedup behavior of these programs. For example, FFT shows the most linear speedup, as can be seen by the nearly constant processor utilization. Both Barnes and Ocean have some drop-off in speedup due to slight increases in synchronization overhead. LU has the most significant loss of speedup, which arises from a significant increase in synchronization overhead. Interestingly, this synchronization overhead actually represents load imbalance, which becomes a serious problem as the ratio between a fixed problem size and the number of processors decreases. Figure 8.44 also reminds us that speedup is a dangerous measure to use by itself. For example, Barnes and Ocean have nearly identical speedup at 16 processors, but the 16 processors are busy 70% of the time in Barnes and only 43% of the time in Ocean. Clearly, Barnes makes much more effective use of the Challenge multiprocessor.

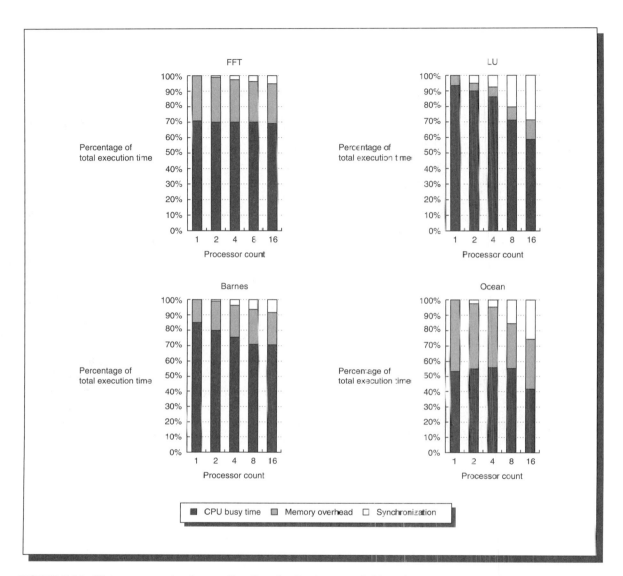

FIGURE 8.44   The components of execution time for the four parallel benchmarks running on a Challenge multi-processor with 1 to 16 150-MHz R4400. Although memory stalls are a problem with all processor counts, synchronization stalls become more severe as the processor count is increased. Synchronization stalls often result from load balancing, as in LU, or from contention arising when synchronization becomes very frequent, as in Ocean. These applications have been tuned to have good locality and low miss rates, which keep memory stalls from becoming an increasing problem with larger processor counts.

8.9 | Fallacies and Pitfalls

Given the lack of maturity in our understanding of parallel computing, there are many hidden pitfalls that will be uncovered either by careful designers or by unfortunate ones. Given the large amount of hype that often surrounds multiprocessors, especially at the high end, common fallacies abound. We have included a selection of these.

Pitfall: Measuring performance of multiprocessors by linear speedup versus execution time.

"Mortar shot" graphs—plotting performance versus number of processors showing linear speedup, a plateau, and then a falling off—have long been used to judge the success of parallel processors. Although speedup is one facet of a parallel program, it is not a direct measure of performance. The first question is the power of the processors being scaled: A program that linearly improves performance to equal 100 Intel 8080s may be slower than the sequential version on a workstation. Be especially careful of floating-point-intensive programs; processing elements without hardware assist may scale wonderfully but have poor collective performance.

Comparing execution times is fair only if you are comparing the best algorithms on each machine. Comparing the identical code on two machines may seem fair, but it is not; the parallel program may be slower on a uniprocessor than a sequential version. Developing a parallel program will sometimes lead to algorithmic improvements, so that comparing the previously best-known sequential program with the parallel code—which seems fair—will not compare equivalent algorithms. To reflect this issue, the terms *relative speedup* (same program) and *true speedup* (best program) are sometimes used. Results that suggest *superlinear* performance, when a program on n processors is more than n times faster than the equivalent uniprocessor, may indicate that the comparison is unfair, although there are instances where "real" superlinear speedups have been encountered. For example, when Ocean is run on two processors, the combined cache produces a small superlinear speedup (2.1 vs. 2.0), as shown in Figure 8.43.

In summary, comparing performance by comparing speedups is at best tricky and at worst misleading. Comparing the speedups for two different machines does not necessarily tell us anything about the relative performance of the machines. Even comparing two different algorithms on the same machine is tricky, since we must use true speedup, rather than relative speedup, to obtain a valid comparison.

Fallacy: Amdahl's Law doesn't apply to parallel computers.

In 1987, the head of a research organization claimed that Amdahl's Law (see section 1.6) had been broken by an MIMD machine. This hardly meant, however, that the law has been overturned for parallel computers; the neglected portion of the program will still limit performance. To understand the basis of the media reports, let's see what Amdahl [1967] originally said:

A fairly obvious conclusion which can be drawn at this point is that the effort expended on achieving high parallel processing rates is wasted unless it is accompanied by achievements in sequential processing rates of very nearly the same magnitude. [p. 483]

One interpretation of the law was that since portions of every program must be sequential, there is a limit to the useful economic number of processors—say 100. By showing linear speedup with 1000 processors, this interpretation of Amdahl's Law was disproved.

The basis for the statement that Amdahl's Law had been "overcome" was the use of scaled speedup. The researchers scaled the benchmark to have a data set size that is 1000 times larger and compared the uniprocessor and parallel execution times of the scaled benchmark. For this particular algorithm the sequential portion of the program was constant independent of the size of the input, and the rest was fully parallel—hence, linear speedup with 1000 processors.

We have already described the dangers of relating scaled speedup as true speedup. Additional problems with this sort of scaling methodology, which can result in unrealistic running times, were examined in section 8.7.

Fallacy: Multiprocessors are "free"

This fallacy has two different interpretations, and both are erroneous. The first is, given that modern microprocessors contain support for snooping caches, we can build small-scale, bus-based multiprocessors for no additional cost in dollars (other than the microprocessor cost) or sacrifice of performance. Many designers believed this to be true and have even tried to build machines to prove it.

To understand why this doesn't work, you need to compare a design with no multiprocessing extensibility against a design that allows for a moderate level of multiprocessing (say 2–4 processors). The 2–4 processor design requires some sort of bus and a coherence controller that is more complicated than the simple memory controller required for the uniprocessor design. Furthermore, the memory access time is almost always faster in the uniprocessor case, since the processor can be directly connected to memory with only a simple single-master bus. Thus the strictly uniprocessor solution typically has better performance and lower cost than the 1-processor configuration of even a very small multiprocessor. For example, a typical Silicon Graphics workstation using 150-MHz R4400 has a miss penalty that is under 80 processor clocks versus the 164 processor clocks seen on a Challenge.

It also became popular in the 1980s to believe that the multiprocessor design was free in the sense that an MP could be quickly constructed from state-of-the-art microprocessors and then quickly updated using newer processors as they

components, the OS algorithms and data structures must be rethought in a multiprocessor context. Placing locks on smaller portions of the page table effectively eliminates the problem.

Pitfall: Neglecting data distribution in a distributed shared-memory machine.

Consider the Ocean benchmark running on a 32-processor DSM architecture. As Figure 8.26 (page 687) shows, the miss rate is 3.1%. Because the grid used for the calculation is allocated in a tiled fashion (as described on page 654), 2.5% of the accesses are local capacity misses and 0.6% are remote communication misses needed to access data at the boundary of each grid. Assuming a 30-cycle local memory access cost and a 100-cycle remote memory access cost, the average miss has a cost of 43.5 cycles.

If the grid was allocated in a straightforward fashion by round-robin allocation of the pages, we could expect 1/32 of the misses to be local and the rest to be remote. This would lead to local miss rate of $3.1\% \times 1/32 = 0.1\%$ and a remote miss rate of 3.0%, for an average miss cost of 96.8 cycles. If the average CPI without cache misses is 1.5, and 45% of the instructions are data references, the version with tiled allocation is

$$\frac{1.5 + 45\% \times 3.1\% \times 96.8}{1.5 + 45\% \times 3.1\% \times 43.5} = \frac{1.5 + 1.35}{1.5 + 0.61} = \frac{2.85}{2.11} = 1.35 \text{ times faster}$$

This analysis only considers latency, and assumes that contention effects do not lead to increased latency, which is very optimistic. Round-robin is also not the worst possible data allocation: if the grid fit in a subset of the memory and was allocated to only a subset of the nodes, contention for memory at those nodes could easily lead to a difference in performance of more than a factor of 2.

Fallacy: Linear speedups are needed to make multiprocessors cost-effective.

It is widely recognized that one of the major benefits of parallel computing is to offer a "shorter time to solution" than the fastest uniprocessor. Many people, however, also hold the view that parallel processors cannot be as cost-effective as uniprocessors unless they can achieve perfect linear speedup. This argument says that because the cost of the machine is a linear function of the number of processors, anything less than linear speedup means that the ratio of performance/cost decreases, making a parallel processor less cost-effective than using a uniprocessor.

The problem with this argument is that cost is not only a function of processor count, but also depends on memory (as well as I/O). The effect of including memory in the system cost was pointed out by Wood and Hill [1995], and we use an example from their article to demonstrate the effect of looking at a complete system. They compare a uniprocessor server, the Challenge DM (a deskside unit with one processor and up to 6 GB of memory), against a multiprocessor Challenge XL, the rack-mounted multiprocessor we examined in section 8.8.

(The XL also has faster processors than those of the Challenge DM—150 MHz versus 100 MHz—but we will ignore this difference.)

First, Wood and Hill introduce a cost function: $cost$ (p, m), which equals the list price of a machine with p processors and m megabytes of memory. For the Challenge DM:

$$cost(1, m) = \$38,400 + \$100 \times m$$

For the Challenge XL:

$$cost(p, m) = \$81,600 + \$20,000 \times p + \$100 \times m$$

Suppose our computation requires 1 GB of memory on either machine. Then the cost of the DM is $138,400, while the cost of the Challenge XL is $181,600 + $20,000 × p. For different numbers of processors, we can compute what speedups are necessary to make the use of parallel processing on the XL *more* cost effective than that of the uniprocessor. For example, the cost of an 8-processor XL is $341,600, which is about 2.5 times higher than the DM, so if we have a speedup on 8 processors of more than 2.5, the multiprocessor is actually *more* cost effective than the uniprocessor. If we are able to achieve linear speedup, the 8-processor XL system is actually more than *three times* more cost effective! Things get better with more processors: On 16 processors, we need to achieve a speedup of only 3.6, or less than 25% parallel efficiency, to make the multiprocessor as cost effective as the uniprocessor.

The use of a multiprocessor may involve some additional memory overhead, although this number is likely to be small for a shared-memory architecture. If we assume an extremely conservative number of 100% overhead (i.e., double the memory is required on the multiprocessor), the 8-processor machine needs to achieve a speedup of 3.2 to break even, and the 16-processor machine needs to achieve a speedup of 4.3 to break even. Surprisingly, the XL can even be cost effective when compared against a headless workstation used as a server. For example, the cost function for a Challenge S, which can have at most 256 MB of memory, is

$$cost(1, m) = \$16,600 + \$100 \times m$$

For problems small enough to fit in 256 MB of memory on both machines, the XL breaks even with a speedup of 6.3 on 8 processors and 10.1 on 16 processors.

In comparing the cost/performance of two computers, we must be sure to include accurate assessments of both total system cost and what performance is achievable. For many applications with larger memory demands, such a comparison can dramatically increase the attractiveness of using a multiprocessor.

8.10 | Concluding Remarks

For over a decade prophets have voiced the contention that the organization of a single computer has reached its limits and that truly significant advances can be made only by interconnection of a multiplicity of computers in such a manner as to permit cooperative solution. ...Demonstration is made of the continued validity of the single processor approach. ... [p. 483]

Amdahl [1967]

The dream of building computers by simply aggregating processors has been around since the earliest days of computing. However, progress in building and using effective and efficient parallel processors has been slow. This rate of progress has been limited by difficult software problems as well as by a long process of evolving architecture of multiprocessors to enhance usability and improve efficiency. We have discussed many of the software challenges in this chapter, including the difficulty of writing programs that obtain good speedup due to Amdahl's law, dealing with long remote access or communication latencies, and minimizing the impact of synchronization. The wide variety of different architectural approaches and the limited success and short life of many of the architectures to date has compounded the software difficulties. We discuss the history of the development of these machines in section 8.11.

Despite this long and checkered past, progress in the last 10 years leads to some reasons to be optimistic about the future of parallel processing and multiprocessors. This optimism is based on a number of observations about this progress and the long-term technology directions:

1. The use of parallel processing in some domains is beginning to be understood. Probably first among these is the domain of scientific and engineering computation. This application domain has an almost limitless thirst for more computation. It also has many applications that have lots of natural parallelism. Nonetheless, it has not been easy: programming parallel processors even for these applications remains very challenging. Another important, and much larger (in terms of market size), application area is large-scale data base and transaction processing systems. This application domain also has extensive natural parallelism available through parallel processing of independent requests, but its needs for large-scale computation, as opposed to purely access to large-scale storage systems, are less well understood. There are also several contending architectural approaches that may be viable—a point we discuss shortly.

2. It is now widely held that one of the most effective ways to build computers that offer more performance than that achieved with a single-chip micro-

processor is by building a multiprocessor that leverages the significant price/performance advantages of mass-produced microprocessors. This is likely to become more true in the future.

3. Multiprocessors are highly effective for multiprogrammed workloads that are often the dominant use of mainframes and large servers, including file servers, which handle a restricted type of multiprogrammed workload. In the future, such workloads may well constitute a large portion of the market need for higher-performance machines. When the workload wants to share resources, such as file storage, or can efficiently timeshare a resource, such as a large memory, a multiprocessor can be a very efficient host. Furthermore, the OS software needed to efficiently execute multiprogrammed workloads is becoming commonplace.

While there is reason to be optimistic about the growing importance of multiprocessors, many areas of parallel architecture remain unclear. Two particularly important questions are, How will the largest-scale multiprocessors (the massively parallel processors, or MPPs) be built? and What is the role of multiprocessing as a long-term alternative to higher-performance uniprocessors?

The Future of MPP Architecture

Hennessy and Patterson should move MPPs to Chapter 11.

> Jim Gray, when asked about coverage of MPPs
> in the second edition of this book, alludes to
> Chapter 11 bankruptcy protection in U.S. law (1995)

Small-scale multiprocessors built using snooping-bus schemes are extremely cost-effective. Recent microprocessors have even included much of the logic for cache coherence in the processor chip and several allow the buses of two or more processors to be directly connected—implementing a coherent bus with no additional logic. With modern integration levels, multiple processors can be placed on a board, or even on a single multi-chip module (MCM), resulting in a highly cost-effective multiprocessor. Using DSM technology it is possible to configure such 2–4 processor nodes into a coherent structure with relatively small amounts of additional hardware. It is premature to predict that such architectures will dominate the middle range of processor counts (16–64), but it appears at the present that this approach is the most attractive.

What is totally unclear at the present is how the very largest machines will be constructed. The difficulties that designers face include the relatively small market for very large machines (> 64 nodes and often > $5 million) and the need for machines that scale to larger processor counts to be extremely cost-effective at the lower processor counts where most of the machines will be sold. At the present there appear to be four slightly different alternatives for large-scale machines:

1. Large-scale machines that simply scale up naturally, using proprietary interconnect and communications controller technology. This is the approach that has been followed so far in machines like the Intel Paragon, using a message passing approach, and Cray T3D, using a shared memory without cache coherence. There are two primary difficulties with such designs. First, the machines are not cost-effective at small scales, where the cost of scalability is not valued. Second, these machines have programming models that are incompatible, in varying degrees, with the mainstream of smaller and midrange machines.

2. Large-scale machines constructed from clusters of mid range machines with combinations of proprietary and standard technologies to interconnect such machines. This cluster approach gets its cost-effectiveness through the use of cost-optimized building blocks. In some approaches, the basic architectural model (e.g., coherent shared memory) is extended. The Convex Exemplar fits in this class. The disadvantage of trying to build this extended machine is that more custom design and interconnect are needed. Alternatively, the programming model can be changed from shared memory to message passing or to a different variation on shared memory, such as shared virtual memory, which may be totally transparent. The disadvantage of such designs is the potential change in the programming model; the advantage is that the large-scale machine can make use of more off-the-shelf technology, including standard networks. Another example of such a machine is the SGI Challenge array, which is built from SGI Challenge machines and uses standard HPPI for its interconnect. Overall, this class of machine, while attractive, remains experimental.

3. Designing machines that use off-the-shelf uniprocessor nodes and a custom interconnect. The advantage of such a machine is the cost-effectiveness of the standard uniprocessor node, which is often a repackaged workstation; the disadvantage is that the programming model will probably need to be message passing even at very small node counts. In some application environments where little or no sharing occurs, this may be acceptable. In addition, the cost of the interconnect, because it is custom, can be significant, making the machine costly, especially at small node counts. The IBM SP-2 is the best example of this approach today.

4. Designing a machine using *all* off-the-shelf components, which promises the lowest cost. The leverage in this approach lies in the use of commodity technology everywhere: in the processors (PC or workstation nodes), in the interconnect (high-speed local area network technology, such as ATM), and in the software (standard operating systems and programming languages). Of

course, such machines will use message passing, and communication is likely to have higher latency and lower bandwidth than in the alternative designs. Like the previous class of designs, for applications that do not need high bandwidth or low-latency communication, this approach can be extremely cost-effective. Databases and file servers, for example, may be a good match to these machines. Also, for multiprogrammed workloads, where each user process is independent of the others, this approach is very attractive. Today these machines are built as workstation clusters or as NOWs (networks of workstations) or COWs (clusters of workstations). The VAXCluster approach successfully used this organization for multiprogrammed and transaction-oriented workloads, albeit with minicomputers rather than desktop machines.

Each of these approaches has advantages and disadvantages, and the importance of the shortcomings of any one approach are dependent on the application class. In 1995 it is unclear which if any of these models will win out for larger-scale machines. For some classes of applications, one of these approaches may even become dominant for small to midrange machines. Finally, some hybridization of these ideas may emerge, given the similarity in several of the approaches.

The Future of Microprocessor Architecture

As we saw in Chapter 4, architects are using ever more complex techniques to try to exploit more instruction-level parallelism. As we also saw in that chapter, the prospects for finding ever-increasing amounts of instruction-level parallelism in a manner that is efficient to exploit are somewhat limited. Likewise, there are increasingly difficult problems to be overcome in building memory hierarchies for high-performance processors. Of course, continued technology improvements will allow us to continue to advance clock rate. But the use of technology improvements that allow a faster gate speed alone is not sufficient to maintain the incredible growth of performance that the industry has experienced in the past 10 years. Maintaining a rapid rate of performance growth will depend to an increasing extent on exploiting the dramatic growth in effective silicon area, which will continue to grow much faster than the basic speed of the process technology.

Unfortunately, for the past five or more years, increases in performance have come at the cost of ever-increasing inefficiencies in the use of silicon area, external connections, and power. This diminishing-returns phenomenon has not yet slowed the growth of performance in the mid 1990s, but we cannot sustain the rapid rate of performance improvements without addressing these concerns through new innovations in computer architecture.

Unlike the prophets quoted at the beginning of the chapter, your authors do not believe that we are about to "hit a brick wall" in our attempts to improve single-processor performance. Instead, we may see a gradual slowdown in performance growth, with the eventual growth being limited primarily by improvements in the speed of the technology. When these limitation will become serious is hard to say, but possibly as early as the beginning of the next century. Even if such a slow-down were to occur, performance might well be expected to grow at the annual rate of 1.35 that we saw prior to 1985.

Furthermore, we do not want to rule out the possibility of a breakthrough in uniprocessor design. In the early 1980s, many people predicted the end of growth in uniprocessor performance, only to see the arrival of RISC technology and an unprecedented 10-year growth in performance averaging 1.6 times per year!

With this in mind, we cautiously ask whether the long-term direction will be to use increased silicon to build multiple processors on a single chip. Such a direction is appealing from the architecture viewpoint—it offers a way to scale performance without increasing complexity. It also offers an approach to easing some of the challenges in memory-system design, since a distributed memory can be used to scale bandwidth while maintaining low latency for local accesses. The challenge lies in software and in what architecture innovations may be used to make the software easier.

Evolution Versus Revolution and the Challenges to Paradigm Shifts in the Computer Industry

Figure 8.45 shows what we mean by the *evolution-revolution spectrum* of computer architecture innovation. To the left are ideas that are invisible to the user (presumably excepting better cost, better performance, or both). This is the evolutionary end of the spectrum. At the other end are revolutionary architecture ideas. These are the ideas that require new applications from programmers who must learn new programming languages and models of computation, and must invent new data structures and algorithms.

Revolutionary ideas are easier to get excited about than evolutionary ideas, but to be adopted they must have a much higher payoff. Caches are an example of an evolutionary improvement. Within 5 years after the first publication about caches, almost every computer company was designing a machine with a cache. The RISC ideas were nearer to the middle of the spectrum, for it took closer to 10 years for most companies to have a RISC product. Most multiprocessors have tended to the revolutionary end of the spectrum, with the largest-scale machines (MPPs) being more revolutionary than others. Most programs written to use multiprocessors as parallel engines have been written especially for that class of machines, if not for the specific architecture.

The challenge for both hardware and software designers that would propose that multiprocessors and parallel processing become the norm, rather than the exception, is the disruption to the established base of programs. There are two possible ways this paradigm shift could be facilitated: if parallel processing offers the only alternative to enhance performance, and if advances in hardware and software technology can construct a gentle ramp that allows the movement to parallel processing, at least with small numbers of processors, to be more evolutionary.

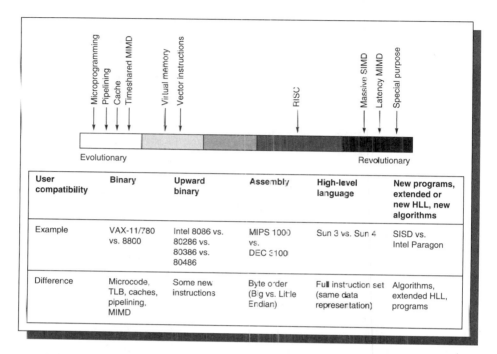

FIGURE 8.45 The evolution-revolution spectrum of computer architecture. The second through fifth columns are distinguished from the final column in that applications and operating systems can be ported from other computers rather than written from scratch. For example, RISC is listed in the middle of the spectrum because user compatibility is only at the level of high-level languages, while microprogramming allows binary compatibility, and latency-oriented MIMDs require changes to algorithms and extending HLLs. Timeshared MIMD means MIMDs justified by running many independent programs at once, while latency MIMD means MIMDs intended to run a single program faster.

8.11 Historical Perspective and References

There is a tremendous amount of history in parallel processing; in this section we divide our discussion by both time period and architecture. We start with the SIMD approach and the Illiac IV. We then turn to a short discussion of some other early experimental machines and progress to a discussion of some of the great debates in parallel processing. Next we discuss the historical roots of the present machines and conclude by discussing recent advances.

The Rise and Fall of SIMD Computers

The cost of a general multiprocessor is, however, very high and further design options were considered which would decrease the cost without seriously degrading the power or efficiency of the system. The options consist of recentralizing one of the three major components.... Centralizing the [control unit] gives rise to the basic organization of [an]... array processor such as the Illiac IV.

Bouknight et al. [1972]

The SIMD model was one of the earliest models of parallel computing, dating back to the first large-scale multiprocessor, the Illiac IV. The key idea in that machine, as in more recent SIMD machines, is to have a single instruction that operates on many data items at once, using many functional units.

The earliest ideas on SIMD-style computers are from Unger [1958] and Slotnick, Borck, and McReynolds [1962]. Slotnick's Solomon design formed the basis of the Illiac IV, perhaps the most infamous of the supercomputer projects. While successful in pushing several technologies that proved useful in later projects, it failed as a computer. Costs escalated from the $8 million estimate in 1966 to $31 million by 1972, despite construction of only a quarter of the planned machine. Actual performance was at best 15 MFLOPS, versus initial predictions of 1000 MFLOPS for the full system [Hord 1982]. Delivered to NASA Ames Research in 1972, the computer took three more years of engineering before it was usable. These events slowed investigation of SIMD, with Danny Hillis [1985] resuscitating this style in the Connection Machine, which had 65,636 1-bit processors.

Real SIMD computers need to have a mixture of SISD and SIMD instructions. There is an SISD host computer to perform operations such as branches and address calculations that do not need parallel operation. The SIMD instructions are broadcast to all the execution units, each of which has its own set of registers. For flexibility, individual execution units can be disabled during a SIMD instruction. In addition, massively parallel SIMD machines rely on interconnection or communication networks to exchange data between processing elements.

SIMD works best in dealing with arrays in for-loops. Hence, to have the opportunity for massive parallelism in SIMD there must be massive amounts of data, or *data parallelism*. SIMD is at its weakest in case statements, where each execution unit must perform a different operation on its data, depending on what data it has. The execution units with the wrong data are disabled so that the proper units can continue. Such situations essentially run at $1/n$th performance, where n is the number of cases.

The basic trade-off in SIMD machines is performance of a processor versus number of processors. Recent machines emphasize a large degree of parallelism over performance of the individual processors. The Connection Machine 2, for example, offered 65,536 single bit-wide processors, while the Illiac IV had 64 64-bit processors.

After being resurrected in the 1980s, first by Thinking Machines and then by MasPar, the SIMD model has once again been put to bed as a general-purpose multiprocessor architecture, for two main reasons. First, it is too inflexible. A number of important problems cannot use such a style of machine, and the architecture does not scale down in a competitive fashion; that is, small-scale SIMD machines often have worse cost/performance compared with that of the alternatives. Second, SIMD cannot take advantage of the tremendous performance and cost advantages of microprocessor technology. Instead of leveraging this low-cost technology, designers of SIMD machines must build custom processors for their machines.

Although SIMD computers have departed from the scene as general-purpose alternatives, this style of architecture will continue to have a role in special-purpose designs. Many special-purpose tasks are highly data parallel and require a limited set of functional units. Thus designers can build in support for certain operations, as well as hardwire interconnection paths among functional units. Such organizations are often called *array processors,* and they are useful for tasks like image and signal processing.

Other Early Experiments

It is difficult to distinguish the first multiprocessor. Surprisingly, the first computer from the Eckert-Mauchly Corporation, for example, had duplicate units to improve availability. Holland [1959] gave early arguments for multiple processors.

Two of the best-documented multiprocessor projects were undertaken in the 1970s at Carnegie Mellon University. The first of these was C.mmp [Wulf and Bell 1972; Wulf and Harbison 1978], which consisted of 16 PDP-11s connected by a crossbar switch to 16 memory units. It was among the first multiprocessors with more than a few processors, and it had a shared-memory programming model. Much of the focus of the research in the C.mmp project was on software, especially in the OS area. A later machine, Cm* [Swan et al. 1977], was a cluster-based multiprocessor with a distributed memory and a nonuniform access time. The absence of caches and a long remote access latency made data placement critical. This machine and a number of application experiments are well described by Gehringer, Siewiorek, and Segall [1987]. Many of the ideas in these machines would be reused in the 1980s when the microprocessor made it much cheaper to build multiprocessors.

Great Debates in Parallel Processing

The quotes at the beginning of this chapter give the classic arguments for abandoning the current form of computing, and Amdahl [1967] gave the classic reply in support of continued focus on the IBM 370 architecture. Arguments for the advantages of parallel execution can be traced back to the 19th century [Menabrea 1842]! Yet the effectiveness of the multiprocessor for reducing latency of individual important programs is still being explored. Aside from these debates about the advantages and limitations of parallelism, several hot debates have focused on how to build multiprocessors.

How to Build High-Performance Parallel Processors

One of the longest-raging debates in parallel processing has been over how to build the fastest multiprocessors—using many small processors or a smaller number of faster processors. This debate goes back to the 1960s and 1970s. Figure 8.46 shows the state of the industry in 1990, plotting number of processors

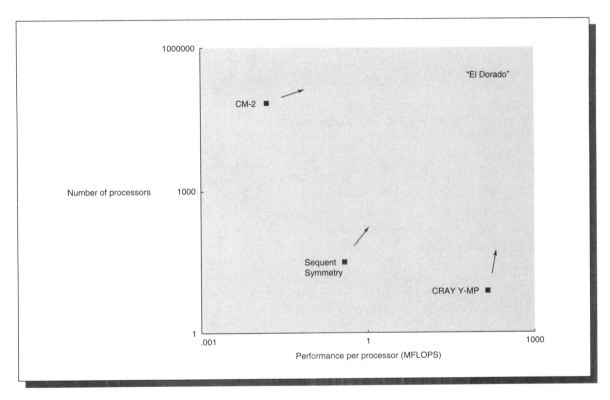

FIGURE 8.46   Danny Hillis, architect of the Connection Machines, has used a figure similar to this to illustrate the multiprocessor industry. (Hillis's x-axis was processor width rather than processor performance.) Processor performance on this graph is approximated by the MFLOPS rating of a single processor for the DAXPY procedure of the Linpack benchmark for a 1000 x 1000 matrix. Generally it is easier for programmers when moving to the right, while moving up is easier for the hardware designer because there is more hardware replication. The massive parallelism question is, Which is the quickest path to the upper right corner? The computer design question is, Which has the best cost/performance or is more scalable for equivalent cost/performance?

versus performance of an individual processor. The massive parallelism question is whether taking the high road or the low road in Figure 8.46 will get us to El Dorado—the highest-performance multiprocessor. In the last few years, much of this debate has subsided. Microprocessor-based machines are assumed to be the basis for the highest-performance multiprocessors. Perhaps the biggest change is the perception that machines built from microprocessors will probably have hundreds and perhaps a few thousand processors, but not the tens of thousands that had been predicted earlier.

In the last five years, the middle road has emerged as the most viable direction. It combines moderate numbers of high-performance microprocessors. This road relies on advances in our ability to program parallel machines as well as on continued progress in microprocessor performance and advances in parallel architecture.

Predictions of the Future

It's hard to predict the future, yet in 1989 Gordon Bell made two predictions for 1995. We included these predictions in the first edition of the book, when the outcome was completely unclear. We discuss them in this section, together with an assessment of the accuracy of the prediction.

The first is that a computer capable of sustaining a teraFLOPS—one million MFLOPS—will be constructed by 1995, either using a multicomputer with 4K to 32K nodes or a Connection Machine with several million processing elements [Bell 1989]. To put this prediction in perspective, each year the Gordon Bell Prize acknowledges advances in parallelism, including the fastest real program (highest MFLOPS). In 1989 the winner used an eight-processor Cray Y-MP to run at 1680 MFLOPS. On the basis of these numbers, machines and programs would have to have improved by a factor of 3.6 each year for the fastest program to achieve 1 TFLOPS in 1995. In 1994, the winner achieved 140,000 MFLOPS (0.14 TFLOPS) using a 1904-node Paragon, which contains 3808 processors. This represents a year-to-year improvement of 2.4, which is still quite impressive.

What has become recognized since 1989 is that although we may have the technology to build a teraFLOPS machine, it is not clear either that anyone could afford it or that it would be cost-effective. For example, based on the 1994 winner, a sustained teraFLOPS would require a machine that is about seven times larger and would likely cost close to $100 million. If factors of 2 in year-to-year performance improvement can be sustained, the price of a teraFLOPS might reach a reasonable level in 1997 or 1998. Gordon Bell argued this point in a series of articles and lectures in 1992–93, using the motto "No teraFLOPS before its time."

The second Bell prediction concerns the number of data streams in supercomputers shipped in 1995. Danny Hillis believed that although supercomputers with a small number of data streams may be the best sellers, the biggest machines will be machines with many data streams, and these will perform the bulk of the computations. Bell bet Hillis that in the last quarter of calendar year 1995 more sustained MFLOPS will be shipped in machines using few data streams (≤ 100)

rather than many data streams (≥1000). This bet concerns only supercomputers, defined as machines costing more than $1 million and used for scientific applications. Sustained MFLOPS is defined for this bet as the number of floating-point operations per *month,* so availability of machines affects their rating. The loser must write and publish an article explaining why his prediction failed; your authors will act as judge and jury.

In 1989, when this bet was made, it was totally unclear who would win. Although it is a little too early to convene the court, a survey of the current publicly known supercomputers shows only six machines in existence in the world with more than 1000 data streams. It is quite possible that during the last quarter of 1995, *no* machines with ≥1000 data streams will ship. In fact, it appears that much smaller microprocessor-based machines (≤ 20 programs) are becoming dominant. A recent survey of the 500 highest-performance machines in use (based on Linpack ratings), called the Top 500, showed that the largest number of machines were bus-based shared-memory multiprocessors!

More Recent Advances and Developments

With the exception of the parallel vector machines (see Appendix B), all other recent MIMD computers have been built from off-the-shelf microprocessors using a bus and logically central memory or an interconnection network and a distributed memory. A number of experimental machines built in the 1980s further refined and enhanced the concepts that form the basis for many of today's multiprocessors.

The Development of Bus-Based Coherent Machines

Although very large mainframes were built with multiple processors in the 1970s, multiprocessors did not become highly successful until the 1980s. Bell [1985] suggests the key was that the smaller size of the microprocessor allowed the memory bus to replace the interconnection network hardware, and that portable operating systems meant that multiprocessor projects no longer required the invention of a new operating system. In this paper, Bell defines the terms *multiprocessor* and *multicomputer* and sets the stage for two different approaches to building larger-scale machines.

The first bus-based multiprocessor with snooping caches was the Synapse N+1 described by Frank [1984]. Goodman [1983] wrote one of the first papers to describe snooping caches. The late 1980s saw the introduction of many commercial bus-based, snooping-cache architectures, including the Silicon Graphics 4D/240 [Baskett et al. 1988], the Encore Multimax [Wilson 1987], and the Sequent Symmetry [Lovett and Thakkar 1988]. The mid 1980s saw an explosion in the development of alternative coherence protocols, and Archibald and Baer [1986] provide a good survey and analysis, as well as references to the original papers.

Toward Large-Scale Multiprocessors

In the effort to build large-scale multiprocessors, two different directions were explored: message passing multicomputers and scalable shared-memory multiprocessors. Although there had been many attempts to build mesh and hypercube-connected multiprocessors, one of the first machines to successfully bring together all the pieces was the Cosmic Cube built at Caltech [Seitz 1985]. It introduced important advances in routing and interconnect technology and substantially reduced the cost of the interconnect, which helped make the multicomputer viable. The Intel iPSC 860, a hypercube-connected collection of i860s, was based on these ideas. More recent machines, such as the Intel Paragon, have used networks with lower dimensionality and higher individual links. The Paragon also employed a separate i860 as a communications controller in each node, although a number of users have found it better to use both i860 processors for computation as well as communication. The Thinking Machines CM-5 made use of off-the-shelf microprocessors and a fat tree interconnect (see Chapter 7). It provided user-level access to the communication channel, thus significantly improving communication latency. In 1995, these two machines represent the state of the art in message-passing multicomputers.

Early attempts at building a scalable shared-memory multiprocessor include the IBM RP3 [Pfister et al. 1985], the NYU Ultracomputer [Schwartz 1980; Elder et al. 1985], the University of Illinois Cedar project [Gajksi et al. 1983], and the BBN Butterfly and Monarch [BBN Laboratories 1986; Rettberg et al. 1990]. These machines all provided variations on a nonuniform distributed-memory model, but did not support cache coherence, which substantially complicated programming. The RP3 and Ultracomputer projects both explored new ideas in synchronization (fetch-and-operate) as well as the idea of combining references in the network. In all four machines, the interconnect networks turned out to be more costly than the processing nodes, raising problems for smaller versions of the machine. The Cray T3D builds on these ideas, using a noncoherent shared address space but building on the advances in interconnect technology developed in the multicomputer domain.

Extending the shared-memory model with scalable cache coherence was done by combining a number of ideas. Directory-based techniques for cache coherence were actually known before snooping cache techniques. In fact, the first cache-coherence protocols actually used directories, as described by Tang [1976] and implemented in the IBM 3081. Censier and Feautrier [1978] described a directory coherence scheme with tags in memory. The idea of distributing directories with the memories to obtain a scalable implementation of cache coherence (now called distributed shared memory, or DSM) was first described by Agarwal et al. [1988] and served as the basis for the Stanford DASH multiprocessor (see Lenoski et al. [1990, 1992]). The Kendall Square Research KSR-1 [Burkhardt et al.1992] was the first commercial implementation of scalable coherent shared memory. It extended the basic DSM approach to implement a concept called *COMA* (*cache-only memory architecture*), which makes the main memory a cache, as described in Exercise 8.13. The Convex Exemplar implements scalable coherent shared memory using a two-level architecture: at the lowest level eight-processor modules are built using a crossbar. A ring can then connect up to 32 of these modules, for a total of 256 processors.

Developments in Synchronization and Consistency Models

A wide variety of synchronization primitives have been proposed for shared-memory multiprocessors. Mellor-Crummey and Scott [1991] provide an overview of the issues as well as efficient implementations of important primitives, such as locks and barriers. An extensive bibliography supplies references to other important contributions, including developments in spin locks, queuing locks, and barriers.

Lamport [1979] introduced the concept of sequential consistency and what correct execution of parallel programs means. Dubois, Scheurich, and Briggs [1988] introduced the idea of weak ordering (originally in 1986). In 1990, Adve and Hill provided a better definition of weak ordering and also defined the concept of data-race-free; at the same conference, Gharachorloo [1990] and his colleagues introduced release consistency and provided the first data on the performance of relaxed consistency models.

Other References

There is an almost unbounded amount of information on multiprocessors and multicomputers: Conferences, journal papers, and even books seem to appear faster than any single person can absorb the ideas. No doubt many of these papers will go unnoticed—not unlike the past. Most of the major architecture conferences contain papers on multiprocessors. An annual conference, *Supercomputing XY* (where X and Y are the last two digits of the year), brings together users, architects, software developers, and vendors and publishes the proceedings in book and CD-ROM form. Two major journals, *Journal of Parallel and Distributed Computing* and the *IEEE Transactions on Parallel and Distributed Systems,* contain papers on all aspects of parallel processing. Several books focusing on parallel processing are included in the following references. Eugene Miya of NASA Ames has collected an online bibliography of parallel-processing papers that contains more than 10,000 entries. To get information about receiving the bibliography, see http://unix.hensa.ac.uk/parallel/bibliographies/parallelism-biblos-FAQ. Also see [Miya 1985]. In addition to documenting the discovery of concepts now used in practice, these references also provide descriptions of many ideas that have been explored and found wanting, as well as ideas whose time has just not yet come.

References

ADVE, S. V. AND M. D. HILL [1990]. "Weak ordering—A new definition," *Proc. 17th Int'l Symposium on Computer Architecture* (June), Seattle, 2–14.

AGARWAL, A., J. L. HENNESSY, R. SIMONI, AND M.A HOROWITZ [1988]. "An evaluation of directory schemes for cache coherence," *Proc. 15th Int'l Symposium on Computer Architecture* (June), 280–289.

ALMASI, G. S. AND A. GOTTLIEB [1989]. *Highly Parallel Computing,* Benjamin/Cummings, Redwood City, Calif.

AMDAHL, G. M. [1967]. "Validity of the single processor approach to achieving large scale computing capabilities," *Proc. AFIPS Spring Joint Computer Conf.* 30, Atlantic City, N.J. (April), 483–485.

ARCHIBALD, J. AND J.-L BAER [1986]. "Cache coherence protocols: Evaluation using a multiprocessor simulation model," *ACM Trans. on Computer Systems* 4:4 (November), 273–298.

BASKETT, F., T. JERMOLUK, AND D. SOLOMON [1988]. "The 4D-MP graphics superworkstation: Computing + graphics = 40 MIPS + 40 MFLOPS and 10,000 lighted polygons per second," *Proc. COMPCON Spring,* San Francisco, 468–471.

BBN LABORATORIES [1986]. "Butterfly parallel processor overview," Tech. Rep. 6148, BBN Laboratories, Cambridge, Mass.

BELL, C. G. [1985]. "Multis: A new class of multiprocessor computers," *Science* 228 (April 26), 462–467.

BELL, C. G. [1989]. "The future of high performance computers in science and engineering," *Comm. ACM* 32:9 (September), 1091–1101.

BOUKNIGHT, W. J, S. A. DENEBERG, D. E. MCINTYRE, J. M. RANDALL, A. H. SAMEH, AND D. L. SLOTNICK [1972]. "The Illiac IV system," *Proc. IEEE* 60:4, 369–379. Also appears in D. P. Siewiorek, C. G. Bell, and A. Newell, *Computer Structures: Principles and Examples,* McGraw-Hill, New York (1982), 306–316.

BURKHARDT, H. III, S. FRANK, B. KNOBE, AND J. ROTHNIE [1992]. "Overview of the KSR1 computer system," Tech. Rep. KSR-TR-9202001, Kendall Square Research, Boston (February).

CENSIER, L. AND P. FEAUTRIER [1978]. "A new solution to coherence problems in multicache systems," *IEEE Trans. on Computers* C-27:12 (December), 1112–1118.

DUBOIS, M., C. SCHEURICH, AND F. BRIGGS [1988]. "Synchronization, coherence, and event ordering," *IEEE Computer* 9-21 (February).

EGGERS, S. [1989]. *Simulation Analysis of Data Sharing in Shared Memory Multiprocessors,* Ph.D. Thesis, Univ. of California, Berkeley. Computer Science Division Tech. Rep. UCB/CSD 89/501 (April).

ELDER, J., A. GOTTLIEB, C. K. KRUSKAL, K. P. MCAULIFFE, L. RANDOLPH, M. SNIR, P. TELLER, AND J. WILSON [1985]. "Issues related to MIMD shared-memory computers: The NYU Ultracomputer approach," *Proc. 12th Int'l Symposium on Computer Architecture* (June), Boston, 126–135.

FLYNN, M. J. [1966]. "Very high-speed computing systems," *Proc. IEEE* 54:12 (December), 1901–1909.

FRANK, S. J. [1984] "Tightly coupled multiprocessor systems speed memory access time," *Electronics* 57:1 (January), 164–169.

GAJSKI, D., D. KUCK, D. LAWRIE, AND A. SAMEH [1983]. "CEDAR—A large scale multiprocessor," *Proc. Int'l Conf. on Parallel Processing* (August), 524–529.

GEHRINGER, E. F., D. P. SIEWIOREK, AND Z. SEGALL [1987]. *Parallel Processing: The Cm* Experience,* Digital Press, Bedford, Mass.

GHARACHORLOO, K., D. LENOSKI, J. LAUDON, P. GIBBONS, A. GUPTA, AND J. L. HENNESSY [1990]. "Memory consistency and event ordering in scalable shared-memory multiprocessors," *Proc. 17th Int'l Symposium on Computer Architecture* (June), Seattle, 15–26.

GOODMAN, J. R. [1983]. "Using cache memory to reduce processor memory traffic," *Proc. 10th Int'l Symposium on Computer Architecture* (June), Stockholm, Sweden, 124–131.

HILLIS, W. D. [1985]. *The Connection Machine,* MIT Press, Cambridge, Mass.

HOCKNEY, R. W. AND C. R. JESSHOPE [1988]. *Parallel Computers-2, Architectures, Programming and Algorithms,* Adam Hilger Ltd., Bristol, England.

HOLLAND, J. H. [1959]. "A universal computer capable of executing an arbitrary number of subprograms simultaneously," *Proc. East Joint Computer Conf.* 16, 108–113.

HORD, R. M. [1982]. *The Illiac-IV, The First Supercomputer,* Computer Science Press, Rockville, Md.

HWANG, K. [1993]. *Advanced Computer Architecture and Parallel Programming,* McGraw-Hill, New York.

LAMPORT, L. [1979]. "How to make a multiprocessor computer that correctly executes multiprocess programs," *IEEE Trans. on Computers* C-28:9 (September), 241–248.

LENOSKI, D., J. LAUDON, K. GHARACHORLOO, A. GUPTA, AND J. L. HENNESSY [1990]. "The Stanford DASH multiprocessor," *Proc. 17th Int'l Symposium on Computer Architecture* (June), Seattle, 148–159.

LENOSKI, D., J. LAUDON, K. GHARACHORLOO, W.-D. WEBER, A. GUPTA, J. L. HENNESSY, M. A. HOROWITZ, AND M. LAM [1992]. "The Stanford DASH multiprocessor," *IEEE Computer* 25:3 (March).

LOVETT, T. AND S. THAKKAR [1988]. "The Symmetry multiprocessor system," *Proc. 1988 Int'l Conf. of Parallel Processing*, University Park, Penn., 303–310.

MELLOR-CRUMMEY, J. M. AND M. L. SCOTT [1991]. "Algorithms for scalable synchronization on shared-memory multiprocessors," *ACM Trans. on Computer Systems* 9:1 (February), 21–65.

MENABREA, L. F. [1842]. "Sketch of the analytical engine invented by Charles Babbage," Bibiothèque Universelle de Genève (October).

MITCHELL, D. [1989]. "The Transputer: The time is now," *Computer Design* (RISC supplement), 40–41.

MIYA, E. N. [1985]. "Multiprocessor/distributed processing bibliography," *Computer Architecture News* (ACM SIGARCH) 13:1, 27–29.

PFISTER, G. F., W. C. BRANTLEY, D. A. GEORGE, S. L. HARVEY, W. J. KLEINFEKDER, K. P. MCAULIFFE, E. A. MELTON, V. A. NORTON, AND J. WEISS [1985]. "The IBM research parallel processor prototype (RP3): Introduction and architecture," *Proc. 12th Int'l Symposium on Computer Architecture* (June), Boston, 764–771.

RETTBERG, R. D., W. R. CROWTHER, P. P. CARVEY, AND R. S. TOWLINSON [1990]. "The Monarch parallel processor hardware design," *IEEE Computer* 23:4 (April).

ROSENBLUM, M., S. A. HERROD, E. WITCHEL, AND A. GUTPA [1995]. "Complete computer simulation: The SimOS approach," to appear in *IEEE Parallel and Distributed Technology* 3:4 (fall).

SCHWARTZ, J. T. [1980]. "Ultracomputers," *ACM Trans. on Programming Languages and Systems* 4:2, 484–521.

SEITZ, C. [1985]. "The Cosmic Cube," *Comm. ACM* 28:1 (January), 22–31.

SLOTNICK, D. L., W. C. BORCK, AND R. C. MCREYNOLDS [1962]. "The Solomon computer," *Proc. Fall Joint Computer Conf.* (December), Philadelphia, 97–107.

STONE, H. [1991]. *High Performance Computers,* Addison-Wesley, New York.

SWAN, R. J., A. BECHTOLSHEIM, K. W. LAI, AND J. K. OUSTERHOUT [1977]. "The implementation of the Cm* multi-microprocessor," *Proc. AFIPS National Computing Conf.*, 645–654.

SWAN, R. J., S. H. FULLER, AND D. P. SIEWIOREK [1977]. "Cm*—A modular, multi-microprocessor," *Proc. AFIPS National Computer Conf.* 46, 637–644.

TANG, C. K. [1976]. "Cache design in the tightly coupled multiprocessor system," *Proc. AFIPS National Computer Conf.*, New York (June), 749–753.

UNGER, S. H. [1958]. "A computer oriented towards spatial problems," *Proc. Institute of Radio Enginers* 46:10 (October), 1744–1750.

WILSON, A. W., JR. [1987]. "Hierarchical cache/bus architecture for shared-memory multiprocessors," *Proc. 14th Int'l Symposium on Computer Architecture* (June), Pittsburgh, 244–252.

WOOD, D. A. AND M. D. HILL [1995]. "Cost-effective parallel computing," *IEEE Computer* 28:2 (February).

WULF, W. AND C. G. BELL [1972]. "C.mmp—A multi-mini-processor," *Proc. AFIPS Fall Joint Computing Conf.* 41, part 2, 765–777.

WULF, W. AND S. P. HARBISON [1978]. "Reflections in a pool of processors—An experience report on C.mmp/Hydra," *Proc. AFIPS 1978 National Computing Conf.* 48 (June), Anaheim, Calif., 939–951.

EXERCISES

8.1 [10] <8.1> Suppose we have an application that runs in three modes: all processors used, half the processors in use, and serial mode. Assume that 0.02% of the time is serial mode, and there are 100 processors in total. Find the maximum time that can be spent in the mode when half the processors are used, if our goal is a speedup of 80.

8.2 [15] <8.1> Assume that we have a function for an application of the form F(i,p), which gives the fraction of time that exactly i processors are usable given that a total of p processors are available. This means that

$$\sum_{i=1}^{\bar{p}} F(i,\bar{p}) = 1$$

Assume that when i processors are in use, the application runs i times faster. Rewrite Amdahl's Law so that it gives the speedup as a function of p for some application.

8.3 [15] <8.3> In small bus-based multiprocessors, write-through caches are sometimes used. One reason is that a write-through cache has a slightly simpler coherence protocol. Show how the basic snooping cache coherence protocol of Figure 8.12 on page 665 can be changed for a write-through cache. From the viewpoint of an implementor, what is the major hardware functionality that is not needed with a write-through cache compared with a write-back cache?

8.4 [20] <8.3> Add a clean private state to the basic snooping cache-coherence protocol (Figure 8.12 on page 665). Show the protocol in the format of Figure 8.12.

8.5 [15] <8.3> One proposed solution for the problem of false sharing is to add a valid bit per word (or even for each byte). This would allow the protocol to invalidate a word without removing the entire block, allowing a cache to keep a portion of a block in its cache while another processor wrote a different portion of the block. What extra complications are introduced into the basic snooping cache coherency protocol (Figure 8.12) if this capability is included? Remember to consider all possible protocol actions.

8.6 [12/10/15] <8.3> The performance differences for write invalidate and write update schemes can arise from both bandwidth consumption and latency. Assume a memory system with 64-byte cache blocks. Ignore the effects of contention.

a.   [12] <8.3> Write two parallel code sequences to illustrate the bandwidth differences between invalidate and update schemes. One sequence should make update look much better and the other should make invalidate look much better.

b.   [10] <8.3> Write a parallel code sequence to illustrate the latency advantage of an update scheme versus an invalidate scheme.

c.   [15] <8.3> Show, by example, that when contention is included, the latency of update may actually be worse. Assume a bus-based machine with 50-cycle memory and snoop transactions.

8.7 [15/15] <8.3–8.4> One possible approach to achieving the scalability of distributed shared memory and the cost-effectiveness of a bus design is to combine the two approaches, using a set of nodes with memories at each node, a hybrid cache-coherence scheme, and interconnected with a bus. The argument in favor of such a design is that the use of local memories and a coherence scheme with limited broadcast results in a reduction in bus traffic, allowing the bus to be used for a larger number of processors. For these Exercises, assume the same parameters as for the Challenge bus. Assume that remote snoops and memory accesses take the same number of cycles as a memory access on the Challenge bus. Ignore the directory processing time for these Exercises. Assume that the coherency scheme works as follows on a miss: If the data are up-to-date in the local memory, it is used there. Otherwise, the bus is used to snoop for the data. Assume that local misses take 25 bus clocks.

a.   [15] <8.3–8.4> Find the time for a read or write miss to data that are remote.

b.   [15] <8.3–8.4> Ignoring contention and using the data from the Ocean benchmark run on 16 processors for the frequency of local and remote misses (Figure 8.26 on page 687), estimate the average memory access time versus that for a Challenge using the same total miss rate.

8.8 [20/15] <8.4> If an architecture allows a relaxed consistency model, the hardware can improve the performance of write misses by allowing the write miss to proceed immediately, buffering the write data until ownership is obtained.

a.   [20] <8.4> Modify the directory protocol in Figure 8.24 on page 683 and in Figure 8.25 on page 684 to do this. Show the protocol in the same format as these two figures.

b.   [15] <8.4> Assume that the write buffer is large enough to hold the write until ownership is granted, and that write ownership and any required invalidates always complete before a release is reached. If the extra time to complete a write is 100 processor clock cycles and writes generate 40% of the misses, find the performance advantage for the relaxed consistency machines versus the original protocol using the FFT data on 32 processors (Figure 8.26 on page 687).

8.9 [12/15] <8.3,8.4,8.8> Although it is widely believed that buses are the ideal interconnect for small-scale multiprocessors, this may not always be the case. For example, increases in processor performance are lowering the processor count at which a more distributed implementation becomes attractive. Because a standard bus-based implementation uses the bus both for access to memory and for interprocessor coherency traffic, it has a uniform memory access time for both. In comparison, a distributed memory implementation may sacrifice on remote memory access, but it can have a much better local memory access time.

Consider the design of a DSM multiprocessor with 16 processors. Assume the R4400 cache miss overheads shown for the Challenge design (see pages 730–731). Assume that a memory access takes 150 ns from the time the address is available from either the local processor or a remote processor until the first word is delivered.

a. [12] <8.3,8.4,8.8> How much faster is a local access than on the Challenge?

b. [15] <8.3,8.4,8.8> Assume that the interconnect is a 2D grid with links that are 16 bits wide and clocked at 100 MHz, with a start-up time of five cycles for a message. Assume one clock cycle between nodes in the network, and ignore overhead in the messages and contention (i.e., assume that the network bandwidth is not the limit). Find the average remote memory access time, assuming a uniform distribution of remote requests. How does this compare to the Challenge case? What is the largest fraction of remote misses for which the DSM machine will have a lower average memory access time than that of the Challenge machine?

8.10 [20/15/30] <8.4> One downside of a straightforward implementation of directories using fully populated bit vectors is that the total size of the directory information scales as the product: Processor count × Memory blocks. If memory is grown linearly with processor count, then the total size of the directory grows quadratically in the processor count. In practice, because the directory needs only 1 bit per memory block (which is typically 32 to 128 bytes), this problem is not serious for small to moderate processor counts. For example, assuming a 128-byte block, the amount of directory storage compared to main memory is Processor count/1024, or about 10% additional storage with 100 processors. This problem can be avoided by observing that we only need to keep an amount of information that is proportional to the cache size of each processor. We explore some solutions in these Exercises.

a. [20] <8.4> One method to obtain a scalable directory protocol is to organize the machine as a logical hierarchy with the processors at the leaves of the hierarchy and directories positioned at the root of each subtree. The directory at each subtree root records which descendents cache which memory blocks, as well as which memory blocks with a home in that subtree are cached outside of the subtree. Compute the amount of storage needed to record the processor information for the directories, assuming that each directory is fully associative. Your answer should incorporate both the number of nodes at each level of the hierarchy as well as the total number of nodes.

b. [15] <8.4> Assume that each level of the hierarchy in part (a) has a lookup cost of 50 cycles plus a cost to access the data or cache of 50 cycles, when the point is reached. We want to compute the AMAT (average memory access time—see Chapter 5) for a 64-processor machine with four-node subtrees. Use the data from the Ocean benchmark run on 64 processors (Figure 8.26) and assume that all noncoherence misses occur within a subtree node and that coherence misses are uniformly distributed across the machine. Find the AMAT for this machine. What does this say about hierarchies?

c.   [30] <8.4> An alternative approach to implementing directory schemes is to implement bit vectors that are not dense. There are two such strategies: one reduces the number of bit vectors needed and the other reduces the number of bits per vector. Using traces, you can compare these schemes. First, implement the directory as a four-way set-associative cache storing full bit vectors, but only for the blocks that are cached outside of the home node. If a directory cache miss occurs, choose a directory entry and invalidate the entry. Second, implement the directory so that every entry has 8 bits. If a block is cached in only one node outside of its home, this field contains the node number. If the block is cached in more than one node outside its home, this field is a bit vector with each bit indicating a group of eight processors, at least one of which caches the block. Using traces of 64-processor execution, simulate the behavior of these two schemes. Assume a perfect cache for nonshared references, so as to focus on coherency behavior. Determine the number of extraneous invalidations as the directory cache size is increased.

8.11 [25/40] <8.7> Prefetching and relaxed consistency models are two methods of tolerating the latency of longer access in multiprocessors. Another scheme, originally used in the HEP multiprocessor and incorporated in the MIT Alewife multiprocessor, is to switch to another activity when a long-latency event occurs. This idea, called *multiple context* or *multithreading,* works as follows:

■   The processor has several register files and maintains several PCs (and related program states). Each register file and PC holds the program state for a separate parallel thread.

■   When a long-latency event occurs, such as a cache miss, the processor switches to another thread, executing instructions from that thread while the miss is being handled.

a.   [25] <8.7> Using the data for the Ocean benchmark running on 64 processors (Figure 8.26), determine how many contexts are needed to hide all the latency of remote accesses. Assume that local cache misses take 40 cycles and that remote misses take 120 cycles. Assume that the increased demands due to a higher request rate do not affect either the latency or the bandwidth of communications.

b.   [40] <8.7> Implement a simulator for a multiple-context directory-based machine. Use the simulator to evaluate the performance gains from multiple context. How significant are contention and the added bandwidth demands in limiting the gains?

8.12 [25] <8.7> Prove that in a two-level cache hierarchy, where L1 is closer to the processor, inclusion is maintained with no extra action if L2 has at least as much associativity as L1, both caches use LRU replacement, and both caches have the same block size.

8.13 [20] <8.4,8.9> As we saw in *Fallacies and Pitfalls,* data distribution can be important when an application has a nontrivial private data miss rate caused by capacity misses. This problem can be attacked with compiler technology (distributing the data in blocks) or through architectural support. One architectural technique is called cache-only memory architecture (COMA), a version of which was implemented in the KSR-1. The basic idea in COMA is to make the distributed memories into caches, so that blocks *can* be replicated and migrated at the memory level of the hierarchy, as well as in higher levels. Thus, a COMA architecture can change what would be remote capacity misses on a DSM architecture into local capacity misses, by creating copies of data in the local memory. This hardware capability allows the software to ignore the initial distribution of data to different memories. The hardware required to implement a cache in the local memory will usually lead to a slight increase in the memory access time of the memory on a COMA architecture.

Assume that we have a DSM and a COMA machine where remote coherence misses are uniformly distributed and take 100 clocks. Assume that all capacity misses on the COMA machine hit in the local memory and require 50 clock cycles. Assume that capacity misses take 40 cycles when they are local on the DSM machine and 75 cycles otherwise. Using the Ocean data for 32 processors (Figure 8.13), find what fraction of the capacity misses on the DSM machine must be local if the performance of the two machines is identical.

8.14 [15] <8.5> Some machines have implemented a special broadcast coherence protocol just for locks, sometimes even using a different bus. Evaluate the performance of the spin lock in the Example on page 699 assuming a write broadcast protocol.

8.15 [15] <8.5> Implement the barrier in Figure 8.34 on page 701, using queuing locks. Compare the performance to the spin-lock barrier

8.16 [15] <8.5> Implement the barrier in Figure 8.34 on page 701, using fetch-and-increment. Compare the performance to the spin-lock barrier.

8.17 [15] <8.5> Implement the barrier on page 705, so that barrier release is also done with a combining tree.

8.18 [28] <8.6> Write a set of programs so that you can distinguish the following consistency models: sequential consistency, processor consistency or total store order, partial store order, weak ordering, and release consistency. Using multiprocessors that you have access to, determine what consistency model different machines support. Note that, because of timing, you may need to try accesses multiple times to uncover all orderings allowed by a machine.

8.19 [30] <8.3–8.5> Using an available shared-memory multiprocessor, see if you can determine the organization and latencies of its memory hierarchy. For each level of the hierarchy, you can look at the total size, block size, and associativity, as well as the latency of each level of the hierarchy. If the machine uses a nonbus interconnection network, see if you can discover the topology, latency, and bandwidth characteristics of the network.

8.20 [20] <8.4> As we discussed earlier, the directory controller can send invalidates for lines that have been replaced by the local cache controller. To avoid such messages, and to keep the directory consistent, replacement hints are used. Such messages tell the controller that a block has been replaced. Modify the directory coherence protocol of section 8.4 to use such replacement hints.

8.21 [25] <8.6> Prove that for synchronized programs, a release consistency model allows only the same results as sequential consistency.

8.22 [15] <8.5> Find the time for n processes to synchronize using a standard barrier. Assume that the time for a single process to update the count and release the lock is c.

8.23 [15] <8.5> Find the time for n processes to synchronize using a combining tree barrier. Assume that the time for a single process to update the count and release the lock is c.

8.24 [25] <8.5> Implement a software version of the queuing lock for a bus-based system. Using the model in the Example on page 699, how long does it take for 20 processors to acquire and release the lock? You need only count bus cycles.

8.25 [20/30] <8.2–8.5> Both researchers and industry designers have explored the idea of having the capability to explicitly transfer data between memories. The argument in favor of such facilities is that the programmer can achieve better overlap of computation and communication by explicitly moving data when it is available. The first part of this exercise explores the potential on paper; the second explores the use of such facilities on real machines.

a. [20] <8.2–8.5> Assume that cache misses stall the processor, and that block transfer occurs into the local memory of a DSM node. Assume that remote misses cost 100 cycles and that local misses cost 40 cycles. Assume that each DMA transfer has an overhead of 10 cycles. Assuming that all the coherence traffic can be replaced with DMA into main memory followed by a cache miss, find the potential improvement for Ocean running on 64 processors (Figure 8.26).

b. [30] <8.2–8.5> Find a machine that implements both shared memory (coherent or incoherent) and a simple DMA facility. Implement a blocked matrix multiply using only shared memory and using the DMA facilities with shared memory. Is the latter faster? How much? What factors make the use of a block data transfer facility attractive?

8.26 [Discussion] <8.8> Construct a scenario whereby a truly revolutionary architecture— pick your favorite candidate—will play a significant role. *Significant* is defined as 10% of the computers sold, 10% of the users, 10% of the money spent on computers, or 10% of some other figure of merit.

8.27 [40] <8.2,8.7,8.9> A multiprocessor or multicomputer is typically marketed using programs that can scale performance linearly with the number of processors. The project here is to port programs written for one machine to the others and to measure their absolute performance and how it changes as you change the number of processors. What changes need to be made to improve performance of the ported programs on each machine? What is the ratio of processor performance according to each program?

8.28 [35] <8.2,8.7,8.9> Instead of trying to create fair benchmarks, invent programs that make one multiprocessor or multicomputer look terrible compared with the others, and also programs that always make one look better than the others. It would be an interesting result if you couldn't find a program that made one multiprocessor or multicomputer look worse than the others. What are the key performance characteristics of each organization?

8.29 [40] <8.2,8.7,8.9> Multiprocessors and multicomputers usually show performance increases as you increase the number of processors, with the ideal being n times speedup for n processors. The goal of this biased benchmark is to make a program that gets worse performance as you add processors. For example, this means that one processor on the multiprocessor or multicomputer runs the program fastest, two are slower, four are slower than two, and so on. What are the key performance characteristics for each organization that give inverse linear speedup?

8.30 [50] <8.2,8.7,8.9> Networked workstations can be considered multicomputers, albeit with somewhat slower, though perhaps cheaper, communication relative to computation. Port multicomputer benchmarks to a network using remote procedure calls for communication. How well do the benchmarks scale on the network versus the multicomputer? What are the practical differences between networked workstations and a commercial multicomputer?

A

Computer Arithmetic

by David Goldberg
(Xerox Palo Alto Research Center)

The Fast drives out the Slow even if the Fast is wrong.

W. Kahan

A.1	Introduction	A-1
A.2	Basic Techniques of Integer Arithmetic	A-2
A.3	Floating Point	A-13
A.4	Floating-Point Multiplication	A-17
A.5	Floating-Point Addition	A-22
A.6	Division and Remainder	A-28
A.7	More on Floating-Point Arithmetic	A-34
A.8	Speeding Up Integer Addition	A-38
A.9	Speeding Up Integer Multiplication and Division	A-46
A.10	Putting It All Together	A-61
A.11	Fallacies and Pitfalls	A-65
A.12	Historical Perspective and References	A-66
	Exercises	A-72

A.1 Introduction

Although computer arithmetic is sometimes viewed as a specialized part of CPU design, it is a very important part. This was brought home for Intel when their Pentium chip was discovered to have a bug in the divide algorithm. This floating-point flaw resulted in a flurry of bad publicity for Intel and also cost them a lot of money. Intel took a $300 million write-off to cover the cost of replacing the buggy chips.

In this appendix we will study some basic floating-point algorithms, including the division algorithm used on the Pentium. Although a tremendous variety of algorithms have been proposed for use in floating-point accelerators, actual implementations are usually based on refinements and variations of the few basic algorithms presented here. In addition to choosing algorithms for addition, subtraction, multiplication, and division, the computer architect must make other choices. What precisions should be implemented? How should exceptions be handled? This appendix will give you the background for making these and other decisions.

Our discussion of floating point will focus almost exclusively on the IEEE floating-point standard (IEEE 754) because of its rapidly increasing acceptance.

Although floating-point arithmetic involves manipulating exponents and shifting fractions, the bulk of the time in floating-point operations is spent operating on fractions using integer algorithms (but not necessarily sharing the hardware that implements integer instructions). Thus, after our discussion of floating point, we will take a more detailed look at integer algorithms.

Some good references on computer arithmetic, in order from least to most detailed, are Chapter 4 of Patterson and Hennessy [1994]; Chapter 7 of Hamacher, Vranesic, and Zaky [1984]; Gosling [1980]; and Scott [1985].

A.2 | Basic Techniques of Integer Arithmetic

Readers who have studied computer arithmetic before will find most of this section to be review.

Ripple-Carry Addition

Adders are usually implemented by combining multiple copies of simple components. The natural components for addition are *half adders* and *full adders*. The half adder takes two bits a and b as input and produces a sum bit s and a carry bit c_{out} as output. Mathematically, $s = (a + b) \bmod 2$, and $c_{out} = \lfloor (a + b)/2 \rfloor$, where $\lfloor \ \rfloor$ is the floor function. As logic equations, $s = a\bar{b} + \bar{a}b$ and $c_{out} = ab$, where ab means $a \wedge b$ and $a + b$ means $a \vee b$. The half adder is also called a (2,2) adder, since it takes two inputs and produces two outputs. The full adder is a (3,2) adder and is defined by $s = (a + b + c) \bmod 2$, $c_{out} = \lfloor (a + b + c)/2 \rfloor$, or the logic equations

A.2.1
$$s = a\bar{b}\bar{c} + \bar{a}b\bar{c} + \bar{a}\bar{b}c + abc$$

A.2.2
$$c_{out} = ab + ac + bc$$

The principal problem in constructing an adder for n-bit numbers out of smaller pieces is propagating the carries from one piece to the next. The most obvious way to solve this is with a *ripple-carry adder*, consisting of n full adders, as illustrated in Figure A.1. (In the figures in this appendix, the least-significant bit is always on the right.) The inputs to the adder are $a_{n-1}a_{n-2}\cdots a_0$ and $b_{n-1}b_{n-2}\cdots b_0$, where $a_{n-1}a_{n-2}\cdots a_0$ represents the number $a_{n-1}2^{n-1} + a_{n-2}2^{n-2} + \cdots + a_0$. The c_{i+1} output of the ith adder is fed into the c_{i+1} input of the next adder (the $(i + 1)$-th adder) with the lower-order carry-in c_0 set to 0. Since the low-order carry-in is wired to 0, the low-order adder could be a half adder. Later, however, we will see that setting the low-order carry-in bit to 1 is useful for performing subtraction.

In general, the time a circuit takes to produce an output is proportional to the maximum number of logic levels through which a signal travels. However, determining the exact relationship between logic levels and timings is highly technology dependent. Therefore, when comparing adders we will simply compare the

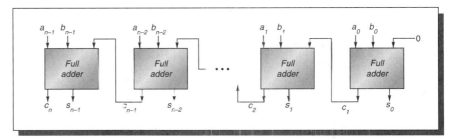

FIGURE A.1 Ripple-carry adder, consisting of n full adders. The carry-out of one full adder is connected to the carry-in of the adder for the next most-significant bit. The carries ripple from the least-significant bit (on the right) to the most-significant bit (on the left).

number of logic levels in each one. How many levels are there for a ripple-carry adder? It takes two levels to compute c_1 from a_0 and b_0. Then it takes two more levels to compute c_2 from c_1, a_1, b_1, and so on, up to c_n. So there are a total of $2n$ levels. Typical values of n are 32 for integer arithmetic and 53 for double-precision floating point. The ripple-carry adder is the slowest adder, but also the cheapest. It can be built with only n simple cells, connected in a simple, regular way.

Because the ripple-carry adder is relatively slow compared with the designs discussed in section A.8, you might wonder why it is used at all. In technologies like CMOS, even though ripple adders take time $O(n)$, the constant factor is very small. In such cases short ripple adders are often used as building blocks in larger adders.

Radix-2 Multiplication and Division

The simplest multiplier computes the product of two unsigned numbers, one bit at a time, as illustrated in Figure A.2(a). The numbers to be multiplied are $a_{n-1}a_{n-2}\cdots a_0$ and $b_{n-1}b_{n-2}\cdots b_0$, and they are placed in registers A and B, respectively. Register P is initially 0. Each multiply step has two parts.

Multiply Step

(*i*) If the least-significant bit of A is 1, then register B, containing $b_{n-1}b_{n-2}\cdots b_0$, is added to P; otherwise $00\cdots00$ is added to P. The sum is placed back into P.

(*ii*) Registers P and A are shifted right, with the carry-out of the sum being moved into the high-order bit of P, the low-order bit of P being moved into register A, and the rightmost bit of A, which is not used in the rest of the algorithm, being shifted out.

After n steps, the product appears in registers P and A, with A holding the lower-order bits.

The simplest divider also operates on unsigned numbers and produces the quotient bits one at a time. A hardware divider is shown in Figure A.2(b). To

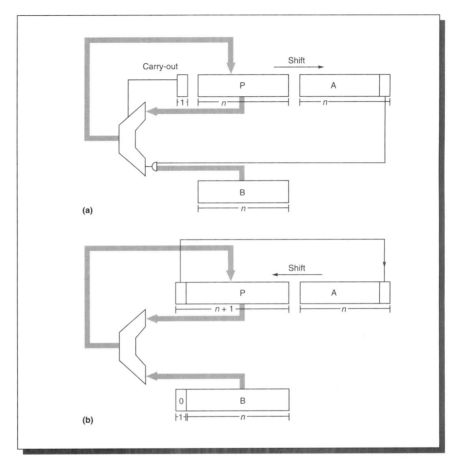

FIGURE A.2   Block diagram of (a) multiplier and (b) divider for *n*-bit unsigned integers. Each multiplication step consists of adding the contents of P to either B or 0 (depending on the low-order bit of A), replacing P with the sum, and then shifting both P and A one bit right. Each division step involves first shifting P and A one bit left, subtracting B from P, and, if the difference is nonnegative, putting it into P. If the difference is nonnegative, the low-order bit of A is set to 1.

compute *a/b,* put *a* in the A register, *b* in the B register, 0 in the P register, and then perform *n* divide steps. Each divide step consists of four parts:

Divide Step   (*i*)   Shift the register pair (P,A) one bit left.

(*ii*) Subtract the content of register B (which is $b_{n-1}b_{n-2}\cdots b_0$) from register P, putting the result back into P.

(*iii*) If the result of step 2 is negative, set the low-order bit of A to 0, otherwise to 1.

(*iv*) If the result of step 2 is negative, restore the old value of P by adding the contents of register B back into P.

After repeating this process n times, the A register will contain the quotient. and the P register will contain the remainder. This algorithm is the binary version of the paper-and-pencil method; a numerical example is illustrated in Figure A.3(a).

P	A	
00000	1110	Divide 14 = 1110_2 by 3 = 11_2. B always contains 0011_2
00001	110	step 1(i): shift.
−00011		step 1(ii): subtract.
−00010	1100	step 1(iii): result is negative, set quotient bit to 0.
00001	1100	step 1(iv): restore.
00011	100	step 2(i): shift.
−00011		step 2(ii): subtract.
00000	1001	step 2(iii): result is nonnegative, set quotient bit to 1.
00001	001	step 3(i): shift.
−00011		step 3(ii): subtract.
−00010	0010	step 3(iii): result is negative, set quotient bit to 0.
00001	0010	step 3(iv): restore.
00010	010	step 4(i): shift.
−00011		step 4(ii): subtract.
−00001	0100	step 4(iii): result is negative, set quotient bit to 0.
00010	0100	step 4(iv): restore. The quotient is 0100_2 and the remainder is 00010_2.

(a)

00000	1110	Divide 14 = 1110_2 by 3 = 11_2. B always contains 0011_2.
00001	110	step 1(i-b): shift.
+11101		step 1(ii-b): subtract b (add two's complement).
11110	1100	step 1(iii): P is negative, so set quotient bit 0.
11101	100	step 2(i-a): shift.
+00011		step 2(ii-a): add b.
00000	1001	step 2(iii): P is nonnegative, so set quotient bit to 1.
00001	001	step 3(i-b): shift.
+11101		step 3(ii-b): subtract b.
11110	0010	step 3(iii): P is negative, so set quotient bit to 0.
11100	010	step 4(i-a): shift.
+00011		step 4(i-a): add b.
11111	0100	step 4(iii): P is negative, so set quotient bit to 0.
+00011		Remainder is negative, so do final restore step.
00010		The quotient is 0100_2 and the remainder is 00010_2.

(b)

FIGURE A.3   Numerical example of (a) restoring division and (b) nonrestoring division.

binary equivalent (10001_2) doesn't fit into 4 bits. For unsigned numbers, detecting overflow is easy; it occurs exactly when there is a carry-out of the most-significant bit. For two's complement, things are trickier: Overflow occurs exactly when the carry into the high-order bit is different from the (to be discarded) carry-out of the high-order bit. In the example of $5 + -2$ above, a 1 is carried both into and out of the leftmost bit, avoiding overflow.

Negating a two's complement number involves complementing each bit and then adding 1. For instance, to negate 0011_2, complement it to get 1100_2 and then add 1 to get 1101_2. Thus, to implement $a - b$ using an adder, simply feed a and $\overline{b}$ (where $\overline{b}$ is the number obtained by complementing each bit of b) into the adder and set the low-order, carry-in bit to 1. This explains why the rightmost adder in Figure A.1 is a full adder.

Multiplying two's complement numbers is not quite as simple as adding them. The obvious approach is to convert both operands to be nonnegative, do an unsigned multiplication, and then (if the original operands were of opposite signs) negate the result. Although this is conceptually simple, it requires extra time and hardware. Here is a better approach: Suppose that we are multiplying a times b using the hardware shown in Figure A.2(a). Register A is loaded with the number a; B is loaded with b. Since the content of register B is always b, we will use B and b interchangeably. If B is potentially negative but A is nonnegative, the only change needed to convert the unsigned multiplication algorithm into a two's complement one is to ensure that when P is shifted, it is shifted arithmetically; that is, the bit shifted into the high-order bit of P should be the sign bit of P (rather than the carry-out from the addition). Note that our n-bit-wide adder will now be adding n-bit two's complement numbers between -2^{n-1} and $2^{n-1} - 1$.

Next, suppose a is negative. The method for handling this case is called *Booth recoding*. Booth recoding is a very basic technique in computer arithmetic and will play a key role in section A.9. The algorithm on page A-3 computes $a \times b$ by examining the bits of a from least significant to most significant. For example, if $a = 7 = 0111_2$, then part (i) will successively add B, add B, add B, and add 0. Booth recoding "recodes" the number 7 as $8 - 1 = 1000_2 - 0001_2 = 100\overline{1}$, where $\overline{1}$ represents -1. This gives an alternate way to compute $a \times b$; namely, successively subtract B, add 0, add 0, and add B. This is more complicated than the unsigned algorithm on page A-3, since it uses both addition and subtraction. The advantage shows up for negative values of a. With the proper recoding, we can treat a as though it were unsigned. For example, take $a = -4 = 1100_2$. Think of 1100_2 as the unsigned number 12, and recode it as $12 = 16 - 4 = 10000_2 - 0100_2 = 10\overline{1}00$. If the multiplication algorithm is only iterated n times ($n = 4$ in this case), the high-order digit is ignored, and we end up subtracting $0100_2 = 4$ times the multiplier—exactly the right answer. This suggests that multiplying using a recoded form of a will work equally well for both positive and negative numbers. And indeed, to deal with negative values of a, all that is required is to sometimes subtract b from P, instead of adding either b or 0 to P. Here are the precise rules: If the initial content of A is $a_{n-1}\cdots a_0$, then at the ith multiply step, the low-order bit of register A is a_i, and step (i) in the multiplication algorithm becomes

I.   If $a_i = 0$ and $a_{i-1} = 0$, then add 0 to P.

II. If $a_i = 0$ and $a_{i-1} = 1$, then add B to P.

III. If $a_i = 1$ and $a_{i-1} = 0$, then subtract B from P.

IV. If $a_i = 1$ and $a_{i-1} = 1$, then add 0 to P.

For the first step, when $i = 0$, take a_{i-1} to be 0.

EXAMPLE   When multiplying –6 times –5, what is the sequence of values in the (P,A) register pair?

ANSWER   See Figure A.4.

P	A	
0000	1010	Put –6 = 1010$_2$ into A, –5 = 1011$_2$ into B.
0000	1010	step 1(i): a_0 = a_{-1} = 0, so from rule I add 0.
0000	0101	step 1(ii): shift.
+ 0101		step 2(i): a_1 = 1, a_0 = 0. Rule III says subtract b (or add –b = –1011$_2$ = 0101$_2$).
0101	0101	
0010	1010	step 2(ii): shift.
+ 1011		step 3(i): a_2 = 0, a_1 = 1. Rule II says add b (1011).
1101	1010	
1110	1101	step 3(ii): shift. (Arithmetic shift—load 1 into leftmost bit.)
+ 0101		step 4(i): a_3 = 1, a_2 = 0. Rule III says subtract b.
0011	1101	
0001	1110	step 4(ii): shift. Final result is 00011110$_2$ = 30.

FIGURE A.4   Numerical example of Booth recoding. Multiplication of $a = -6$ by $b = -5$ to get 30.

The four cases above can be restated as saying that in the ith step you should add $(a_{i-1} - a_i)$B to P. With this observation, it is easy to verify that these rules work, because the result of all the additions is

$$\sum_{i=0}^{n-1} b(a_{i-1} - a_i)2^i = b\left(-a_{n-1}2^{n-1} + a_{n-2}2^{n-2} + \ldots + a_1 2 + a_0\right) + ba_{-1}$$

Using Equation A.2.3 (page A-7) together with $a_{-1} = 0$, the right-hand side is seen to be the value of $b \times a$ as a two's complement number.

The simplest way to implement the rules for Booth recoding is to extend the A register one bit to the right so that this new bit will contain a_{i-1}. Unlike the naive method of inverting any negative operands, this technique doesn't require extra steps or any special casing for negative operands. It has only slightly more control logic. If the multiplier is being shared with a divider, there will already be the capability for subtracting b, rather than adding it. To summarize, a simple method for handling two's complement multiplication is to pay attention to the sign of P when shifting it right, and to save the most recently shifted-out bit of A to use in deciding whether to add or subtract b from P.

Booth recoding is usually the best method for designing multiplication hardware that operates on signed numbers. For hardware that doesn't directly implement it, however, performing Booth recoding in software or microcode is usually too slow because of the conditional tests and branches. If the hardware supports arithmetic shifts (so that negative b is handled correctly), then the following method can be used. Treat the multiplier a as if it were an unsigned number, and perform the first $n - 1$ multiply steps using the algorithm on page A-3. If $a < 0$ (in which case there will be a 1 in the low-order bit of the A register at this point), then subtract b from P; otherwise ($a \geq 0$) neither add nor subtract. In either case, do a final shift (for a total of n shifts). This works because it amounts to multiplying b by $-a_{n-1}2^{n-1} + \cdots + a_1 2 + a_0$, which is the value of $a_{n-1}\cdots a_0$ as a two's complement number by Equation A.2.3. If the hardware doesn't support arithmetic shift, then converting the operands to be nonnegative is probably the best approach.

Two final remarks: A good way to test a signed-multiply routine is to try $-2^{n-1} \times -2^{n-1}$, since this is the only case that produces a $2n - 1$ bit result. Unlike multiplication, division is usually performed in hardware by converting the operands to be nonnegative and then doing an unsigned divide. Because division is substantially slower (and less frequent) than multiplication, the extra time used to manipulate the signs has less impact than it does on multiplication.

Systems Issues

When designing an instruction set, a number of issues related to integer arithmetic need to be resolved. Several of them are discussed here.

First, what should be done about integer overflow? This situation is complicated by the fact that detecting overflow differs depending on whether the operands are signed or unsigned integers. Consider signed arithmetic first. There are three approaches: Set a bit on overflow, trap on overflow, or do nothing on overflow. In the last case, software has to check whether or not an overflow occurred. The most convenient solution for the programmer is to have an enable bit. If this bit is turned on, then overflow causes a trap. If it is turned off, then overflow sets a bit (or alternatively, have two different add instructions). The advantage of this approach is that both trapping and nontrapping operations require only one instruction. Furthermore, as we will see in section A.7, this is analogous to how the IEEE floating-point standard handles floating-point overflow. Figure A.5 shows how some common machines treat overflow.

Machine	Trap on signed overflow?	Trap on unsigned overflow?	Set bit on signed overflow?	Set bit on unsigned overflow?
VAX	If enable is on	No	Yes. Add sets V bit.	Yes. Add sets C bit.
IBM 370	If enable is on	No	Yes. Add sets cond code.	Yes. Logical add sets cond code.
Intel 8086	No	No	Yes. Add sets V bit.	Yes. Add sets C bit.
MIPS R3000	Two add instructions: one always traps, the other never does.	No	No. Software must deduce it from sign of operands and result.	
SPARC	No	No	Addcc sets V bit. Add does not.	Addcc sets C bit. Add does not.

FIGURE A.5   Summary of how various machines handle integer overflow. Both the 8086 and SPARC have an instruction that traps if the V bit is set, so the cost of trapping on overflow is one extra instruction.

What about unsigned addition? Notice that none of the architectures in Figure A.5 traps on unsigned overflow. The reason for this is that the primary use of unsigned arithmetic is in manipulating addresses. It is convenient to be able to subtract from an unsigned address by adding. For example, when $n = 4$, we can subtract 2 from the unsigned address $10 = 1010_2$ by adding $14 = 1110_2$. This generates an overflow, but we would not want a trap to be generated.

A second issue concerns multiplication. Should the result of multiplying two n-bit numbers be a $2n$-bit result, or should multiplication just return the low-order n bits, signaling overflow if the result doesn't fit in n bits? An argument in favor of an n-bit result is that in virtually all high-level languages, multiplication is an operation in which arguments are integer variables and the result is an integer variable of the same type. Therefore, compilers won't generate code that utilizes a double-precision result. An argument in favor of a $2n$-bit result is that it can be used by an assembly language routine to substantially speed up multiplication of multiple-precision integers (by about a factor of 3).

A third issue concerns machines that want to execute one instruction every cycle. It is rarely practical to perform a multiplication or division in the same amount of time that an addition or register-register move takes. There are three possible approaches to this problem. The first is to have a single-cycle *multiply-step* instruction. This might do one step of the Booth algorithm. The second approach is to do integer multiplication in the floating-point unit and have it be part of the floating-point instruction set. (This is what DLX does.) The third approach is to have an autonomous unit in the CPU do the multiplication. In this case, the result either can be guaranteed to be delivered in a fixed number of cycles—and the compiler charged with waiting the proper amount of time—or there can be an interlock. The same comments apply to division as well. As examples, the original SPARC had a multiply-step instruction but no divide-step instruction, while the MIPS R3000 has an autonomous unit that does multiplication and division (newer versions of the SPARC architecture added an integer multiply instruction). The designers of the HP Precision Architecture did an especially thorough job of analyzing the frequency of the operands for multiplication and division, and they based their multiply and divide steps accordingly. (See Magenheimer et al. [1988] for details.)

The final issue involves the computation of integer division and remainder for negative numbers. For example, what is -5 DIV 3 and -5 MOD 3? When computing x DIV y and x MOD y, negative values of x occur frequently enough to be worth some careful consideration. (On the other hand, negative values of y are quite rare.) If there are built-in hardware instructions for these operations, they should correspond to what high-level languages specify. Unfortunately, there is no agreement among existing programming languages. See Figure A.6.

Language	Division	Remainder
FORTRAN	$-5/3 = -1$	MOD$(-5, 3) = -2$
Pascal	-5 DIV $3 = -1$	-5 MOD $3 = 1$
Ada	$-5/3 = -1$	-5 MOD $3 = 1$ -5 REM $3 = -2$
C	$-5/3$ undefined	-5 % 3 undefined
Modula-3	-5 DIV $3 = -2$	-5 MOD $3 = 1$

FIGURE A.6   Examples of integer division and integer remainder in various programming languages.

One definition for these expressions stands out as clearly superior. Namely x DIV $y = \lfloor x/y \rfloor$, so that 5 DIV 3 = 1, -5 DIV 3 = -2. And MOD should satisfy $x = (x$ DIV $y) \times y + x$ MOD y, so that x MOD $y \geq 0$. Thus 5 MOD 3 = 2, and -5 MOD 3 = 1. Some of the many advantages of this definition are

1. A calculation to compute an index into a hash table of size N can use MOD N and be guaranteed to produce a valid index in the range from 0 to $N - 1$.

2. In graphics, when converting from one coordinate system to another, there is no "glitch" near 0. For example, to convert from a value x expressed in a system that uses 100 dots per inch to a value y on a bitmapped display with 70 dots per inch, the formula $y = (70 \times x)$ DIV 100 maps one or two x coordinates into each y coordinate. But if DIV were defined as in Pascal to be x/y rounded to 0, then 0 would have three different points $(-1, 0, 1)$ mapped into it.

3. x MOD 2^k is the same as performing a bitwise AND with a mask of k bits, and x DIV 2^k is the same as doing a k-bit arithmetic right shift.

Finally, a potential pitfall worth mentioning concerns multiple-precision addition. Many instruction sets offer a variant of the add instruction that adds three operands: two n-bit numbers together with a third single-bit number. This third number is the carry from the previous addition. Since the multiple-precision number will typically be stored in an array, it is important to be able to increment the array pointer without destroying the carry bit.

A.3 | Floating Point

Many applications require numbers that aren't integers. There are a number of ways that non-integers can be represented. One is to use *fixed point*; that is, use integer arithmetic and simply imagine the binary point somewhere other than just to the right of the least-significant digit. Adding two such numbers can be done with an integer add, whereas multiplication requires some extra shifting. Other representations that have been proposed involve storing the logarithm of a number and doing multiplication by adding the logarithms, or using a pair of integers (a,b) to represent the fraction a/b. However, only one non-integer representation has gained widespread use, and that is *floating point*. In this system, a computer word is divided into two parts, an exponent and a significand. As an example, an exponent of -3 and significand of 1.5 might represent the number $1.5 \times 2^{-3} = 0.1875$. The advantages of standardizing a particular representation are obvious. Numerical analysts can build up high-quality software libraries, computer designers can develop techniques for implementing high-performance hardware, and hardware vendors can build standard accelerators. Given the predominance of the floating-point representation, it appears unlikely that any other representation will come into widespread use.

The semantics of floating-point instructions are not as clear-cut as the semantics of the rest of the instruction set, and in the past the behavior of floating-point operations varied considerably from one computer family to the next. The variations involved such things as the number of bits allocated to the exponent and significand, the range of exponents, how rounding was carried out, and the actions taken on exceptional conditions like underflow and overflow. Computer architecture books used to dispense advice on how to deal with all these details, but fortunately this is no longer necessary. That's because the computer industry is rapidly converging on the format specified by IEEE standard 754-1985 (also an international standard, IEC 559). The advantages of using a standard variant of floating point are similar to those for using floating point over other non-integer representations.

IEEE arithmetic differs from many previous arithmetics in the following major ways:

1. When rounding a "halfway" result to the nearest floating-point number, it picks the one that is even.

2. It includes the *special values* NaN, ∞, and $-\infty$.

3. It uses *denormal* numbers to represent the result of computations whose value is less than $1.0 \times 2^{E_{min}}$.

4. It rounds to nearest by default, but it also has three other rounding modes.

5. It has sophisticated facilities for handling exceptions.

To elaborate on (1), note that when operating on two floating-point numbers, the result is usually a number that cannot be exactly represented as another floating-point number. For example, in a floating-point system using base 10 and two significant digits, $6.1 \times 0.5 = 3.05$. This needs to be rounded to two digits. Should it be rounded to 3.0 or 3.1? In the IEEE standard, such halfway cases are rounded to the number whose low-order digit is even. That is, 3.05 rounds to 3.0, not 3.1. The standard actually has four *rounding modes*. The default is *round to nearest*, which rounds ties to an even number as just explained. The other modes are round toward 0, round toward $+\infty$, and round toward $-\infty$.

We will elaborate on the other differences in following sections. For further reading, see IEEE [1985], Cody et al. [1984], and Goldberg [1991].

Special Values and Denormals

Probably the most notable feature of the standard is that by default a computation continues in the face of exceptional conditions, such as dividing by 0 or taking the square root of a negative number. For example, the result of taking the square root of a negative number is a *NaN* (*N*ot *a N*umber), a bit pattern that does not represent an ordinary number. As an example of how NaNs might be useful, consider the code for a zero finder that takes a function F as an argument and evaluates F at various points to determine a zero for it. If the zero finder accidentally probes outside the valid values for F, F may well cause an exception. Writing a zero finder that deals with this case is highly language and operating-system dependent, because it relies on how the operating system reacts to exceptions and how this reaction is mapped back into the programming language. In IEEE arithmetic it is easy to write a zero finder that handles this situation and runs on many different systems. After each evaluation of F, it simply checks to see whether F has returned a NaN; if so, it knows it has probed outside the domain of F.

In IEEE arithmetic, if the input to an operation is a NaN, the output is NaN (e.g., 3 + NaN = NaN). Because of this rule, writing floating-point subroutines that can accept NaN as an argument rarely requires any special case checks. For example, suppose that arccos is computed in terms of arctan, using the formula arccos $x = 2$ arctan($\sqrt{(1-x)/(1+x)}$). If arctan handles an argument of NaN properly, arccos will automatically do so too. That's because if x is a NaN, $1 + x$, $1 - x$, $(1 + x)/(1 - x)$, and $\sqrt{(1 - x)/(1 + x)}$ will also be NaNs. No checking for NaNs is required.

While the result of $\sqrt{-1}$ is a NaN, the result of $1/0$ is not a NaN, but $+\infty$, which is another special value. The standard defines arithmetic on infinities (there is both $+\infty$ and $-\infty$) using rules such as $1/\infty = 0$. The formula arccos $x = 2 \arctan(\sqrt{(1 - x)/(1 + x)})$ illustrates how infinity arithmetic can be used. Since $\arctan x$ asymptotically approaches $\pi/2$ as x approaches ∞, it is natural to define $\arctan(\infty) = \pi/2$, in which case arccos(-1) will automatically be computed correctly as $2 \arctan(\infty) = \pi$.

The final kind of special values in the standard are *denormal* numbers. In many floating-point systems, if E_{min} is the smallest exponent, a number less than $1.0 \times 2^{E_{min}}$ cannot be represented, and a floating-point operation that results in a number less than this is simply flushed to 0. In the IEEE standard, on the other hand, numbers less than $1.0 \times 2^{E_{min}}$ are represented using significands less than 1. This is called *gradual underflow*. Thus, as numbers decrease in magnitude below $2^{E_{min}}$, they gradually lose their significance and are only represented by 0 when all their significance has been shifted out. For example, in base 10 with four significant figures, let $x = 1.234 \times 10^{E_{min}}$. Then $x/10$ will be rounded to $0.123 \times 10^{E_{min}}$, having lost a digit of precision. Similarly $x/100$ rounds to $0.012 \times 10^{E_{min}}$, and $x/1000$ to $0.001 \times 10^{E_{min}}$, while $x/10000$ is finally small enough to be rounded to 0. Denormals make dealing with small numbers more predictable by maintaining familiar properties such as $x = y \Leftrightarrow x - y = 0$. For example, in a flush-to-zero system (again in base 10 with four significant digits), if $x = 1.256 \times 10^{E_{min}}$ and $y = 1.234 \times 10^{E_{min}}$, then $x - y = 0.022 \times 10^{E_{min}}$, which flushes to zero. So even though $x \neq y$, the computed value of $x - y = 0$. This never happens with gradual underflow. In this example, $x - y = 0.022 \times 10^{E_{min}}$ is a denormal number, and so the computation of $x - y$ is exact.

Representation of Floating-Point Numbers

Let us consider how to represent single-precision numbers in IEEE arithmetic. Single-precision numbers are stored in 32 bits: 1 for the sign, 8 for the exponent, and 23 for the fraction. The exponent is a signed number represented using the bias method (see the subsection *Signed Numbers*, page A-7) with a bias of 127. The term *biased exponent* refers to the unsigned number contained in bits 1 through 8 and *unbiased exponent* (or just exponent) means the actual power to which 2 is to be raised. The fraction represents a number less than 1, but the *significand* of the floating-point number is 1 plus the fraction part. In other words, if e is the biased exponent (value of the exponent field) and f is the value of the fraction field, the number being represented is $1.f \times 2^{e-127}$.

EXAMPLE   What single-precision number does the following 32-bit word represent?

1 10000001 01000000000000000000000

ANSWER   Considered as an unsigned number, the exponent field is 129, making the value of the exponent $129 - 127 = 2$. The fraction part is $.01_2 = .25$, making the significand 1.25. Thus, this bit pattern represents the number $-1.25 \times 2^2 = -5$.   ∎

The fractional part of a floating-point number (.25 in the example above) must not be confused with the significand, which is 1 plus the fractional part. The leading 1 in the significand $1.f$ does not appear in the representation; that is, the leading bit is implicit. When performing arithmetic on IEEE format numbers, the fraction part is usually *unpacked*, which is to say the implicit one is made explicit.

Figure A.7 summarizes the parameters for single (and other) precisions. It shows the exponents for single precision to range from -126 to 127; accordingly, the biased exponent ranges from 1 to 254. The biased exponents of 0 and 255 are used to represent special values. This is summarized in Figure A.8. When the biased exponent is 255, a zero fraction field represents infinity, and a nonzero fraction field represents a NaN. Thus, there is an entire family of NaNs. When the biased exponent and the fraction field are 0, then the number represented is 0. Because of the implicit leading 1, ordinary numbers always have a significand greater than or equal to 1. Thus, a special convention such as this is required to represent 0. Denormalized numbers are implemented by having a word with a zero exponent field represent the number $0.f \times 2^{E_{min}}$.

	Single	**Single extended**	**Double**	**Double extended**
p (bits of precision)	24	≥ 32	53	≥ 64
E_{max}	127	≥ 1023	1023	≥ 16383
E_{min}	-126	≤ -1022	-1022	≤ -16382
Exponent bias	127		1023	

FIGURE A.7   Format parameters for the IEEE 754 floating-point standard. The first row gives the number of bits in the significand. The blanks are unspecified parameters.

The primary reason why the IEEE standard, like most other floating-point formats, uses biased exponents is that it means nonnegative numbers are ordered in the same way as integers. That is, the magnitude of floating-point numbers can be compared using an integer comparator. Another (related) advantage is that 0 is represented by a word of all 0's. The downside of biased exponents is that adding

Exponent	Fraction	Represents
$e = E_{min} - 1$	$f = 0$	± 0
$e = E_{min} - 1$	$f \neq 0$	$0.f \times 2^{E_{min}}$
$E_{min} \leq e \leq E_{max}$	—	$1.f \times 2^e$
$e = E_{max} + 1$	$f = 0$	$\pm \infty$
$e = E_{max} + 1$	$f \neq 0$	NaN

FIGURE A.8   Representation of special values. When the exponent of a number falls outside the range $E_{min} \leq e \leq E_{max}$, then that number has a special interpretation as indicated in the table.

them is slightly awkward, because it requires that the bias be subtracted from their sum.

A.4 | Floating-Point Multiplication

The simplest floating-point operation is multiplication, so we discuss it first. A binary floating-point number x is represented as a significand and an exponent, $x = s \times 2^e$. The formula

$$(s_1 \times 2^{e1}) \bullet (s_2 \times 2^{e2}) = (s_1 \bullet s_2) \times 2^{e1+e2}$$

shows that a floating-point multiply algorithm has several parts. The first part multiplies the significands using ordinary integer multiplication. Because floating-point numbers are stored in sign-magnitude form, the multiplier need only deal with unsigned numbers (although we have seen that Booth recoding handles signed two's complement numbers painlessly). The second part rounds the result. If the significands are unsigned p-bit numbers (e.g., $p = 24$ for single precision), then the product can have as many as $2p$ bits and must be rounded to a p-bit number. The third part computes the new exponent. Because exponents are stored with a bias, this involves subtracting the bias from the sum of the biased exponents.

EXAMPLE   How does the multiplication of the single precision numbers

$$1\ 10000010\ 000... = -1 \times 2^3$$

$$0\ 10000011\ 000... = 1 \times 2^4$$

proceed in binary?

If $r = 1$ and $s = 0$, we are in a halfway case, and round up according to the least significant bit of P. As an example, apply the decimal version of these rules to Figure A.9(b). After the multiplication, P = 126 and A = 501, with $g = 5$, $r = 0$, $s = 1$. Since the high-order digit of P is nonzero, case (2) applies and $r := g$, so that $r = 5$, as the arrow indicates in Figure A.9. Since $r = 5$, we could be in a halfway case, but $s = 1$ indicates that the result is in fact slightly over 1/2, so add 1 to P to obtain the correctly rounded product.

The precise rules for rounding depend on the rounding mode and are given in Figure A.11. Note that P is nonnegative, that is, it contains the magnitude of the result. A good discussion of more efficient ways to implement rounding is in Santoro, Bewick, and Horowitz [1989].

Rounding mode	Sign of result ≥ 0	Sign of result < 0
$-\infty$		$+1$ if $r \vee s$
$+\infty$	$+1$ if $r \vee s$	
0		
Nearest	$+1$ if $r \wedge p_0$ or $r \wedge s$	$+1$ if $r \wedge p_0$ or $r \wedge s$

FIGURE A.11 Rules for implementing the IEEE rounding modes. Let S be the magnitude of the preliminary result. Blanks mean that the p most-significant bits of S are the actual result bits. If the condition listed is true, add 1 to the pth most-significant bit of S. The symbols r and s represent the round and sticky bits, while p_0 is the pth most-significant bit of S.

EXAMPLE   In binary with $p = 4$, show how the multiplication algorithm computes the product -5×10 in each of the four rounding modes.

ANSWER   In binary, -5 is $-1.010_2 \times 2^2$ and $10 = 1.010_2 \times 2^3$. Applying the integer multiplication algorithm to the significands gives 01100100_2, so P = 0110_2, A = 0100_2, $g = 0$, $r = 1$, and $s = 0$. The high-order bit of P is 0, so case (1) applies. Thus P becomes 1100_2, and since the result is negative, Figure A.11 gives

round to $-\infty$ 1101_2 add 1 since $r \vee s = 1 \vee 0 =$ TRUE

round to $+\infty$ 1100_2

round to 0 1100_2

round to nearest 1100_2 no add since $r \wedge p_0 = 1 \wedge 0 =$ FALSE and

    $r \wedge s = 1 \wedge 0 =$ FALSE

The exponent is $2 + 3 = 5$, so the result is $-1.100_2 \times 2^5 = -48$, except when rounding to $-\infty$, in which case it is $-1.101_2 \times 2^5 = -52$.   ∎

Overflow occurs when the rounded result is too large to be represented. In single precision, this occurs when the result has an exponent of 128 or higher. If e_1 and e_2 are the two biased exponents, then $1 \le e_i \le 254$, and the exponent calculation $e_1 + e_2 - 127$ gives numbers between $1 + 1 - 127$ and $254 + 254 - 127$, or between -125 and 381. This range of numbers can be represented using 9 bits. So one way to detect overflow is to perform the exponent calculations in a 9-bit adder (see Exercise A.12). Remember that you must check for overflow *after* rounding—the example in Figure A.9(c) shows that this can make a difference.

Denormals

Checking for underflow is somewhat more complex because of denormals. In single precision, if the result has an exponent less than -126, that does not necessarily indicate underflow, because the result might be a denormal number. For example, the product of (1×2^{-64}) with (1×2^{-65}) is 1×2^{-129}, and -129 is below the legal exponent limit. But this result is a valid denormal number, namely 0.125×2^{-126}. In general, when the unbiased exponent of a product dips below -126, the resulting product must be shifted right and the exponent incremented until the exponent reaches -126. If this process causes the entire significand to be shifted out, then underflow has occurred. The precise definition of underflow is somewhat subtle—see section A.7 for details.

When one of the operands of a multiplication is denormal, its significand will have leading zeros, and so the product of the significands will also have leading zeros. If the exponent of the product is less than -126, then the result is denormal, so right shift and increment the exponent as before. If the exponent is greater than -126, the result may be a normalized number. In this case, *left* shift the product (while decrementing the exponent) until either it becomes normalized or the exponent drops to -126.

Denormal numbers present a major stumbling block to implementing floating-point multiplication, because they require performing a variable shift in the multiplier, which wouldn't otherwise be needed. Thus, high-performance, floating-point multipliers often do not handle denormalized numbers, but instead trap, letting software handle them. A few practical codes frequently underflow, even when working properly, and these programs will run quite a bit slower on systems that require denormals to be processed by a trap handler.

So far we haven't mentioned how to deal with operands of zero. This can be handled by either testing both operands before beginning the multiplication or testing the product afterward. If you test afterward, be sure to handle the case $0 \times \infty$ properly: this results in NaN, not 0. Once you detect that the result is 0, set the biased exponent to 0. Don't forget about the sign. The sign of a product is the XOR of the signs of the operands, even when the result is 0.

Precision of Multiplication

In the discussion of integer multiplication, we mentioned that designers must decide whether to deliver the low-order word of the product or the entire product. A similar issue arises in floating-point multiplication, where the exact product can be rounded to the precision of the operands or to the next higher precision. In the case of integer multiplication, none of the standard high-level languages contains a construct that would generate a "single times single gets double" instruction. The situation is different for floating point. Many languages allow assigning the product of two single-precision variables to a double-precision one, and the construction can also be exploited by numerical algorithms. The best-known case is using iterative refinement to solve linear systems of equations.

A.5 | Floating-Point Addition

Typically, a floating-point operation takes two inputs with p bits of precision and returns a p-bit result. The ideal algorithm would compute this by first performing the operation exactly, and then rounding the result to p bits (using the current rounding mode). The multiplication algorithm presented in the previous section follows this strategy. Even though hardware implementing IEEE arithmetic must return the same result as the ideal algorithm, it doesn't need to actually perform the ideal algorithm. For addition, in fact, there are better ways to proceed. To see this, consider some examples.

First, the sum of the binary 6-bit numbers 1.10011_2 and $1.10001_2 \times 2^{-5}$: When the summands are shifted so they have the same exponent, this is

$$
\begin{array}{r}
1.10011 \\
+ \quad .0000110001 \\
\end{array}
$$

Using a 6-bit adder (and discarding the low-order bits of the second addend) gives

$$
\begin{array}{r}
1.10011 \\
+ \quad .00001 \\
\hline
1.10100 \\
\end{array}
$$

The first discarded bit is 1. This isn't enough to decide whether to round up. The rest of the discarded bits, 0001, need to be examined. Or actually, we just need to record whether any of these bits are nonzero, storing this fact in a sticky bit just as in the multiplication algorithm. So for adding two p-bit numbers, a p-bit adder is sufficient, as long as the first discarded bit (round) and the OR of the rest of the bits (sticky) are kept. Then Figure A.11 can be used to determine if a round-up is necessary, just as with multiplication. In the example above, sticky is 1, so a round-up is necessary. The final sum is 1.10101_2.

Here's another example:

$$1.11011$$
$$+ \quad .0101001$$

A 6-bit adder gives

$$1.11011$$
$$+ \quad .01010$$
$$10.00101$$

Because of the carry-out on the left, the round bit isn't the first discarded bit; rather, it is the low-order bit of the sum (1). The discarded bits, 01, are OR'ed together to make sticky. Because round and sticky are both 1, the high-order 6 bits of the sum, 10.0010_2, must be rounded up for the final answer of 10.0011_2.

Next, consider subtraction and the following example:

$$1.00000$$
$$- \quad .00000101111$$

The simplest way of computing this is to convert $-.00000101111_2$ to its two's complement form, so the difference becomes a sum

$$1.00000$$
$$+ \quad 1.11111010001$$

Computing this sum in a 6-bit adder gives

$$1.00000$$
$$+1.11111$$
$$0.11111$$

Because the top bits canceled, the first discarded bit (the guard bit) is needed to fill in the least-significant bit of the sum, which becomes 0.111110_2, and the second discarded bit becomes the round bit. This is analogous to case (1) in the multiplication algorithm (see page A-19). The round bit of 1 isn't enough to decide whether to round up. Instead, we need to OR all the remaining bits (0001) into a sticky bit. In this case, sticky is 1, so the final result must be rounded up to 0.111111. This example shows that if subtraction causes the most significant bit to cancel, then one guard bit is needed. It is natural to ask whether two guard bits are needed for the case when the *two* most-significant bits cancel. The answer is no, because if x and y are so close that the top two bits of $x - y$ cancel, then $x - y$ will be exact, so guard bits aren't needed at all.

To summarize, addition is more complex than multiplication because, depending on the signs of the operands, it may actually be a subtraction. If it is an addition, there can be carry-out on the left, as in the second example. If it is subtraction, there can be cancellation, as in the third example. In each case, the position of the round bit is different. However, we don't need to compute the exact sum and then round. We can infer it from the sum of the high-order p bits together with the round and sticky bits.

The rest of this section is devoted to a detailed discussion of the floating-point addition algorithm. Let a_1 and a_2 be the two numbers to be added. The notations e_i and s_i are used for the exponent and significand of the addends a_i. This means that the floating-point inputs have been unpacked and that s_i has an explicit leading bit. To add a_1 and a_2, perform these eight steps.

1. If $e_1 < e_2$, swap the operands. This ensures that the difference of the exponents satisfies $d = e_1 - e_2 \geq 0$. Tentatively set the exponent of the result to e_1.

2. If the signs of a_1 and a_2 differ, replace s_2 by its two's complement.

3. Place s_2 in a p-bit register and shift it $d = e_1 - e_2$ places to the right (shifting in 1's if s_2 was complemented in previous step). From the bits shifted out, set g to the most-significant bit, r to the next most-significant bit, and set sticky to the OR of the rest.

4. Compute a preliminary significand $S = s_1 + s_2$ by adding s_1 to the p-bit register containing s_2. If the signs of a_1 and a_2 are different, the most-significant bit of S is 1, and there was no carry-out, then S is negative. Replace S with its two's complement. This can only happen when $d = 0$.

5. Shift S as follows. If the signs of a_1 and a_2 are the same and there was a carry-out in step 4, shift S right by one, filling in the high-order position with 1 (the carry-out). Otherwise shift it left until it is normalized. When left shifting, on the first shift fill in the low-order position with the g bit. After that, shift in zeros. Adjust the exponent of the result accordingly.

6. Adjust r and s. If S was shifted right in step 5, set $r :=$ low-order bit of S before shifting and $s := g$ OR r OR s. If there was no shift, set $r := g$, $s := r$ OR s. If there was a single left shift, don't change r and s. If there were two or more left shifts, $r := 0$, $s := 0$. (In the last case, two or more shifts can only happen when a_1 and a_2 have opposite signs and the same exponent, in which case the computation $s_1 + s_2$ in step 4 will be exact.)

7. Round S using Figure A.11; namely, if a table entry is non-empty, add 1 to the low-order bit of S. If rounding causes carry-out, shift S right and adjust the exponent. This is the significand of the result.

8. Compute the sign of the result. If a_1 and a_2 have the same sign, this is the sign of the result. If a_1 and a_2 have different signs, then the sign of the result depends on which of a_1, a_2 is negative, whether there was a swap in step 1, and whether S was replaced by its two's complement in step 4. See Figure A.12.

swap	compl	sign(c_1)	sign(a_2)	sign(result)
Yes		−	−	−
Yes		−	+	+
No	No	+	−	+
No	No	−	+	−
No	Yes	+	−	−
No	Yes	−	+	+

FIGURE A.12 Rules for computing the sign of a sum when the addends have different signs. The *swap* column refers to swapping the operands in step 1, while the *compl* column refers to performing a two's complement in step 2. Blanks are "don't care."

EXAMPLE Use the algorithm to compute the sum $(-1.001_2 \times 2^{-2}) + (-1.111_2 \times 2^0)$

ANSWER $s_1 = 1.001$, $e_1 = -2$, $s_2 = 1.111$, $e_2 = 0$

1. $e_1 < e_2$, so swap. $d = 2$. Tentative exp = 0.

2. Signs of both operands negative, don't negate s_2.

3. Shift s_2 (1.001 after swap) right by 2, giving $s_2 = .010$, $g = 0$, $r = 1$, $s = 0$.

4.   1.111
    +   .010
       (1)0.001 $S = 0.001$, with a carry-out.

5. Carry-out, so shift S right, $S = 1.000$, exp = exp + 1, so exp = 1.

6. r = low-order bit of sum = 1, $s = g \vee r \vee s = 0 \vee 1 \vee 0 = 1$.

7. r AND s = TRUE, so Figure A.11 says round up, $S = S + 1$ or $S = 1.001$.

8. Both signs negative, so sign of result is negative. Final answer:
    $-S \times 2^{exp} = -1.001_2 \times 2^1$.   ∎

EXAMPLE Use the algorithm to compute the sum $(-1.010_2) + 1.100_2$

ANSWER $s_1 = 1.010$, $e_1 = 0$, $s_2 = 1.100$, $e_2 = 0$

1. No swap, $d = 0$, tentative exp = 0.

2. Signs differ, replace s_2 with 0.100.

3. $d = 0$, so no shift. $r = g = s = 0$.

4.   1.010
   +   0.100
            —————
            1.110   Signs are different, most-significant bit is 1, no carry-
                     out, so must two's complement sum, giving $S = 0.010$.

5.   Shift left twice, so $S = 1.000$, exp = exp − 2, or exp = −2.

6.   Two left shifts, so $r = g = s = 0$.

7.   No addition required for rounding.

8.   Answer is sign $\times S \times 2^{exp}$ or sign $\times 1.000 \times 2^{-2}$. Get sign from Figure
     A.12. Since complement but no swap and sign(a_1) is −, the sign of
     sum is +. Thus answer = $1.000_2 \times 2^{-2}$.   ∎

Speeding Up Addition

Let's estimate how long it takes to perform the algorithm above. Step 2 may require an addition, step 4 requires one or two additions, and step 7 may require an
addition. If it takes T time units to perform a p-bit add (where $p = 24$ for single
precision, 53 for double), then it appears the algorithm will take at least $4T$ time
units. But that is too pessimistic. If step 4 requires two adds, then a_1 and a_2 have
the same exponent and different signs. But in that case the difference is exact, and
so no round-up is required in step 7. Thus only three additions will ever occur.
Similarly, it appears that a variable shift may be required both in step 3 and step
5. But if $|e_1 - e_2| \leq 1$, then step 3 requires a right shift of at most one place, so
only step 5 needs a variable shift. And if $|e_1 - e_2| > 1$, then step 3 needs a variable
shift, but step 5 will require a left shift of at most one place. So only a single variable shift will be performed. Still, the algorithm requires three sequential adds,
which, in the case of a 53-bit double-precision significand, can be rather time
consuming.

A number of techniques can speed up addition. One is to use pipelining. The
Putting It All Together section gives examples of how some commercial chips
pipeline addition. Another method (used on the Intel 860 [Kohn and Fu 1989]) is
to perform two additions in parallel. We now explain how this reduces the latency
from $3T$ to T.

There are three cases to consider. First, suppose that both operands have the
same sign. We want to combine the addition operations from steps 4 and 7. The
position of the high-order bit of the sum is not known ahead of time, because the
addition in step 4 may or may not cause a carry-out. Both possibilities are ac-
counted for by having two adders. The first adder assumes the add in step 4 will
not result in a carry-out. Thus the values of r and s can be computed before the
add is actually done. If r and s indicate a round-up is necessary, the first adder
will compute $S = s_1 + s_2 + 1$, where the notation +1 means adding 1 at the position
of the least-significant bit of s_1. This can be done with a regular adder by setting
the low-order carry-in bit to 1. If r and s indicate no round-up, the adder computes $S = s_1 + s_2$ as usual. One extra detail: when $r = 1$, $s = 0$, you will also need to

know the low-order bit of the sum, which can also be computed in advance very quickly. The second adder covers the possibility that there will be carry-out. The values of r and s and the position where the round-up 1 is added are different from above, but again they can be quickly computed in advance. It is not known whether there will be a carry-out until after the add is actually done, but that doesn't matter. By doing both adds in parallel, one adder is guaranteed to reduce the correct answer.

The next case is when a_1 and a_2 have opposite signs, but the same exponent. The sum $a_1 + a_2$ is exact in this case (no round-up is necessary), but the sign isn't known until the add is completed. So don't compute the two's complement (which requires an add) in step 2, but instead compute $\bar{s}_1 + s_2 + 1$ and $s_1 + \bar{s}_2 + 1$ in parallel. The first sum has the result of simultaneously complementing s_1 and computing the sum, resulting in $s_2 - s_1$. The second sum computes $s_1 - s_2$. One of these will be nonnegative and hence the correct final answer. Once again, all the additions are done in one step using two adders operating in parallel.

The last case, when a_1 and a_2 have opposite signs and different exponents, is more complex. If $|e_1 - e_2| > 1$, the location of the leading bit of the difference is in one of two locations, so there are two cases just as in addition. When $|e_1 - e_2| = 1$, cancellation is possible and the leading bit could be almost anywhere. However, only if the leading bit of the difference is in the same position as the leading bit of s_1 could a round-up be necessary. So one adder assumes a round-up, the other assumes no round-up. Thus the addition of step 4 and the rounding of step 7 can be combined. However, there is still the problem of the addition in step 2!

To eliminate this addition, consider the following diagram of step 4:

$$\begin{array}{ll} & \hspace{1em} \vert \!\!-\!\!-\!\!- p \!-\!\!-\!\!- \vert \\ s_1 & \hspace{1em} 1.xxxxxxx \\ s_2 & \hspace{0.3em} - \hspace{2em} 1.yyzzzzz \\ \hline \end{array}$$

If the bits marked z are all 0, then the high-order p bits of $S = s_1 - s_2$ can be computed as $s_1 + \bar{s}_2 + 1$. If at least one of the z bits is 1, use $s_1 + \bar{s}_2$. So $s_1 - s_2$ can be computed with one addition. However, we still don't know g and r for the two's complement of s_2, which are needed for rounding in step 7.

To compute $s_1 - s_2$ and get the proper g and r bits, combine steps 2 and 4 as follows. Don't complement s_2 in step 2. Extend the adder used for computing S two bits to the right (call the extended sum S'). If the preliminary sticky bit (computed in step 3) is 1, compute $S' = s_1' + \bar{s}_2'$, where s_1' has two 0 bits tacked onto the right, and s_2' has preliminary g and r appended. If the sticky bit is 0, compute $s_1' + \bar{s}_2' + 1$. Now the two low-order bits of S' have the correct values of g and r (the sticky bit was already computed properly in step 3). Finally, this modification can be combined with the modification that combines the addition from steps 4 and 7 to provide the final result in time T, the time for one addition.

A few more details need to be considered, as discussed in Santoro, Bewick, and Horowitz [1989] and Exercise A.17. Although the Santoro paper is aimed at multiplication, much of the discussion applies to addition as well. Also relevant is Exercise A.19, which contains an alternate method for adding signed magnitude numbers.

Denormalized Numbers

Unlike multiplication, for addition very little changes in the above description if one of the inputs is a denormal number. There must be a test to see if the exponent field is 0. If it is, then when unpacking the significand there will not be a leading 1. By setting the biased exponent to 1 when unpacking a denormal, the algorithm works unchanged.

To deal with denormalized outputs, step 5 must be modified slightly. Shift S until it is normalized, or until the exponent becomes E_{min} (that is, the biased exponent becomes 1). If the exponent is E_{min} and, after rounding, the high-order bit of S is 1, then the result is a normalized number and should be packed in the usual way, by omitting the 1. If, on the other hand, the high-order bit is 0, the result is denormal. When the result is unpacked, the exponent field must be set to 0. Section A.7 discusses the exact rules for detecting underflow.

Incidentally, detecting overflow is very easy. It can only happen if step 5 involves a shift right and the biased exponent at that point is bumped up to 255 in single precision (or 2047 for double precision), or if this occurs after rounding.

A.6 | Division and Remainder

In this section, we'll discuss floating-point division and remainder.

Iterative Division

We earlier discussed an algorithm for integer division. Converting it into a floating-point division algorithm is similar to converting the integer multiplication algorithm into floating point. The formula

$$(s_1 \times 2^{e_1}) / (s_2 \times 2^{e_2}) = (s_1 / s_2) \times 2^{e_1 - e_2}$$

shows that if the divider computes s_1/s_2, then the final answer will be this quotient multiplied by $2^{e_1-e_2}$. Referring to Figure A.2(b) (page A-4), the alignment of operands is slightly different from integer division. Load s_2 into B and s_1 into P. The A register is not needed to hold the operands. Then the integer algorithm for division (with the one small change of skipping the very first left shift) can be used, and the result will be of the form $q_0.q_1\cdots$. To round, simply compute two additional quotient bits (guard and round) and use the remainder as the sticky bit. The guard digit is necessary because the first quotient bit might be 0. However, since the numerator and denominator are both normalized, it is not possible for the two most-significant quotient bits to be 0. This algorithm produces one quotient bit in each step.

A different approach to division converges to the quotient at a quadratic rather than a linear rate. An actual machine that uses this algorithm will be discussed in section A.10. First, we will describe the two main iterative algorithms, and then we will discuss the pros and cons of iteration when compared with the direct algorithms. There is a general technique for constructing iterative algorithms, called *Newton's iteration*, shown in Figure A.13. First, cast the problem in the

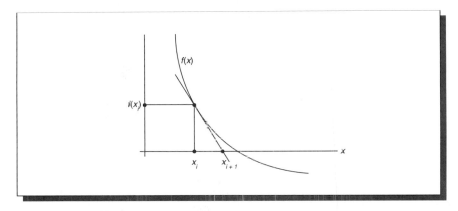

FIGURE A.13   Newton's iteration for zero finding. If x_i is an estimate for a zero of f, then x_{i+1} is a better estimate. To compute x_{i+1}, find the intersection of the x axis with the tangent line to f at $f(x_i)$.

form of finding the zero of a function. Then, starting from a guess for the zero, approximate the function by its tangent at that guess and form a new guess based on where the tangent has a zero. If x_i is a guess at a zero, then the tangent line has the equation

$$y - f(x_i) \; = \; f'(x_i)(x - x_i)$$

This equation has a zero at

A.6.1
$$x \; = \; x_{i+1} = x_i - \frac{f(x_i)}{f'(x_i)}$$

To recast division as finding the zero of a function, consider $f(x) = x^{-1} - b$. Since the zero of this function is at $1/b$, applying Newton's iteration to it will give an iterative method of computing $1/b$ from b. Using $f'(x) = -1/x^2$, Equation A.6.1 becomes

A.6.2
$$x_{i+1} \; = \; x_i - \frac{1/x_i - b}{-1/x_i^2} \; = x_i + x_i - x_i^2 b = x_i(2 - x_i b)$$

Thus, we could implement computation of a/b using the following method:

1. Scale b to lie in the range $1 \leq b < 2$ and get an approximate value of $1/b$ (call it x_0) using a table lookup.

2. Iterate $x_{i+1} = x_i(2 - x_ib)$ until reaching an x_n that is accurate enough.

3. Compute ax_n and reverse the scaling done in step 1.

Here are some more details. How many times will step 2 have to be iterated? To say that x_i is accurate to p bits means that $|(x_i - 1/b)/(1/b)| = 2^{-p}$, and a simple algebraic manipulation shows that when this is so, then $(x_{i+1} - 1/b)/(1/b) = 2^{-2p}$. Thus the number of correct bits doubles at each step. Newton's iteration is *self-correcting* in the sense that making an error in x_i doesn't really matter. That is, it treats x_i as a guess at $1/b$ and returns x_{i+1} as an improvement on it (roughly doubling the digits). One thing that would cause x_i to be in error is rounding error. More importantly, however, in the early iterations we can take advantage of the fact that we don't expect many correct bits by performing the multiplication in reduced precision, thus gaining speed without sacrificing accuracy. Another application of Newton's iteration is discussed in Exercise A.20.

The second iterative division method is sometimes called *Goldschmidt's algorithm*. It is based on the idea that to compute a/b, you should multiply the numerator and denominator by a number r with $rb \approx 1$. In more detail, let $x_0 = a$ and $y_0 = b$. At each step compute $x_{i+1} = r_ix_i$ and $y_{i+1} = r_iy_i$. Then the quotient $x_{i+1}/y_{i+1} = x_i/y_i = a/b$ is constant. If we pick r_i so that $y_i \to 1$, then $x_i \to a/b$, so the x_i converge to the answer we want. This same idea can be used to compute other functions. For example, to compute the square root of a, let $x_0 = a$ and $y_0 = a$, and at each step compute $x_{i+1} = r_i^2x_i$, $y_{i+1} = r_iy_i$. Then $x_{i+1}/y_{i+1}^2 = x_i/y_i^2 = 1/a$, so if the r_i are chosen to drive $x_i \to 1$, then $y_i \to \sqrt{a}$. This technique is used to compute square roots on the TI 8847.

Returning to Goldschmidt's division algorithm, set $x_0 = a$ and $y_0 = b$, and write $b = 1 - \delta$, where $|\delta| < 1$. If we pick $r_0 = 1 + \delta$, then $y_1 = r_0y_0 = 1 - \delta^2$. We next pick $r_1 = 1 + \delta^2$, so that $y_2 = r_1y_1 = 1 - \delta^4$, and so on. Since $|\delta| < 1$, $y_i \to 1$. With this choice of r_i, the x_i will be computed as $x_{i+1} = r_ix_i = (1 + \delta^{2^i})x_i = (1 + (1 - b)^{2^i})x_i$, or

A.6.3
$$x_{i+1} = a\,[1 + (1 - b)]\,[1 + (1 - b)^2\,]\,[1 + (1 - b)^4]\cdots[1 + (1 - b)^{2^i}]$$

There appears to be two problems with this algorithm. First, convergence is slow when b is not near 1 (that is, δ is not near 0); and second, the formula isn't self-correcting—since the quotient is being computed as a product of independent terms, an error in one of them won't get corrected. To deal with slow convergence, if you want to compute a/b, look up an approximate inverse to b (call it b'), and run the algorithm on ab'/bb'. This will converge rapidly since $bb' \approx 1$.

To deal with the self-correction problem, the computation should be run with a few bits of extra precision to compensate for rounding errors. However, Goldschmidt's algorithm does have a weak form of self-correction, in that the precise value of the r_i does not matter. Thus, in the first few iterations, when the full precision of $1 - \delta^2$ is not needed you can choose r_i to be a truncation of $1 + \delta^{2^i}$, which may make these iterations run faster without affecting the speed of convergence. If r_i is truncated, then y_i is no longer exactly $1 - \delta^{2^i}$. Thus, Equation A.6.3 can no longer be used, but it is easy to organize the computation so that it does not depend on the precise value of r_i. With these changes, Goldschmidt's algorithm is as follows (the notes in brackets show the connection with our earlier formulas).

1. Scale a and b so that $1 \le b < 2$.

2. Look up an approximation to $1/b$ (call it b') in a table.

3. Set $x_0 = ab'$ and $y_0 = bb'$.

4. Iterate until x_i is close enough to a/b:

   Loop

   $$r \approx 2 - y \qquad [\text{if } y_i = 1 + \delta_i \text{ then } r \approx 1 - \delta_i]$$

   $$y = y \times r \qquad [y_{i+1} = y_i \times r \approx 1 - \delta^2]$$

   $$x_{i+1} = x_i \times r \qquad [x_{i+1} = x_i \times r]$$

   End loop

The two iteration methods are related. Suppose in Newton's method that we unroll the iteration and compute each term x_{i+1} directly in terms of b, instead of recursively in terms of x_i. By carrying out this calculation (see Exercise A.22), we discover that

$$x_{i+1} = x_0(2 - x_0 b) [(1 + (x_0 b - 1)^2] [1 + (x_0 b - 1)^4] \ldots [1 + (x_0 b - 1)^{2^i}]$$

This formula is very similar to Equation A.6.3. In fact they are identical if a, b in A.6.3 are replaced with ax_0, bx_0 and $c = 1$. Thus if the iterations were done to infinite precision, the two methods would yield exactly the same sequence x_i.

The advantage of iteration is that it doesn't require special divide hardware. Instead, it can use the multiplier (which, however, requires extra control). Further, on each step, it delivers twice as many digits as in the previous step—unlike ordinary division, which produces a fixed number of digits at every step.

There are two disadvantages with inverting by iteration. The first is that the IEEE standard requires division to be correctly rounded, but iteration only delivers a result that is close to the correctly rounded answer. In the case of Newton's iteration, which computes $1/b$ instead of a/b directly, there is an additional problem. Even if $1/b$ was correctly rounded, there is no guarantee that a/b will be.

An example in decimal with $p = 2$ is $a = 13$, $b = 51$. Then $a/b = .2549...$, which rounds to .25. But $1/b = .0196...$, which rounds to .020, and then $a \times .020 = .26$, which is off by 1. The second disadvantage is that iteration does not give a remainder. This is especially troublesome if the floating-point divide hardware is being used to perform integer division, since a remainder operation is present in almost every high-level language.

Traditional folklore has held that the way to get a correctly rounded result from iteration is to compute $1/b$ to slightly more than $2p$ bits, compute a/b to slightly more than $2p$ bits, and then round to p bits. However, there is a faster way, which apparently was first implemented on the TI 8847. In this method, a/b is computed to about 6 extra bits of precision, giving a preliminary quotient q. By comparing qb with a (again with only 6 extra bits), it is possible to quickly decide whether q is correctly rounded or whether it needs to be bumped up or down by 1 in the least significant place. This algorithm is explored further in Exercise A.21.

One factor to take into account when deciding on division algorithms is the relative speed of division and multiplication. Since division is more complex than multiplication, it will run more slowly. A common rule of thumb is that division algorithms should try to achieve a speed that is about one-third that of multiplication. One argument in favor of this rule is that there are real programs (such as some versions of spice) where the ratio of division to multiplication is 1:3. Another place where a factor of 3 arises is in the standard iterative method for computing square root. This method involves one division per iteration, but it can be replaced by one using three multiplications. This is discussed in Exercise A.20.

Floating-Point Remainder

For nonnegative integers, integer division and remainder satisfy

$$a = (a \text{ DIV } b)b + a \text{ REM } b, \ \ 0 \leq a \text{ REM } b < b$$

A floating-point remainder x REM y can be similarly defined as $x = \text{INT}(x/y)y + x$ REM y. How should x/y be converted to an integer? The IEEE remainder function uses the round-to-even rule. That is, pick $n = \text{INT}(x/y)$ so that $|x/y - n| \leq 1/2$. If two different n satisfy this relation, pick the even one. Then REM is defined to be $x - yn$. Unlike integers where $0 \leq a$ REM $b < b$, for floating-point numbers $|x \text{ REM } y| \leq y/2$. Although this defines REM precisely, it is not a practical operational definition, because n can be huge. In single precision, n could be as large as $2^{127}/2^{-126} = 2^{253} \approx 10^{76}$.

There is a natural way to compute REM if a direct division algorithm is used. Proceed as if you were computing x/y. If $x = s_1 2^{e_1}$ and $y = s_2 2^{e_2}$ and the divider is as in Figure A.2(b) (page A-4), then load s_1 into P and s_2 into B. After $e_1 - e_2$ division steps, the P register will hold a number r of the form $x - yn$ satisfying $0 \leq r < y$. Since the IEEE remainder satisfies $|\text{REM}| \leq y/2$, REM is equal to either r or $r - y$. It is only necessary to keep track of the last quotient bit produced, which is needed to resolve halfway cases. Unfortunately, $e_1 - e_2$ can be a lot of steps, and floating-point units typically have a maximum amount of time they are allowed to spend on one instruction. Thus, it is usually not possible to implement REM directly. None of the chips discussed in section A.10 implements REM, but they could by providing a remainder-step instruction—this is what is done on the Intel 8087 family. A remainder step takes as arguments two numbers x and y and performs divide steps until either the remainder is in P or n steps have been performed, where n is a small number, such as the number of steps required for division in the highest-supported precision. Then REM can be implemented as a software routine that calls the REM step instruction $\lfloor (e_1 - e_2)/n \rfloor$ times, initially using x as the numerator, but then replacing it with the remainder from the previous REM step.

REM can be used for computing trigonometric functions. To simplify things, imagine that we are working in base 10 with five significant figures, and consider computing $\sin x$. Suppose that $x = 7$. Then we can reduce by $\pi = 3.1416$ and compute $\sin(7) = \sin(7 - 2 \times 3.1416) = \sin(0.7168)$ instead. But suppose we want to compute $\sin(2.0 \times 10^5)$. Then $2 \times 10^5/3.1416 = 63661.8$, which in our five-place system comes out to be 63662. Since multiplying 3.1416 times 63662 gives 200000.5392, which rounds to 2.0000×10^5, argument reduction reduces 2×10^5 to 0, which is not even close to being correct. The problem is that our five-place system does not have the precision to do correct argument reduction. Suppose we had the REM operator. Then we could compute 2×10^5 REM 3.1416 and get $-.53920$. However, this is still not correct because we used 3.1416, which is an approximation for π. The value of 2×10^5 REM π is $-.071513$.

Traditionally, there have been two approaches to computing periodic functions with large arguments. The first is to return an error for their value when x is large. The second is to store π to a very large number of places and do exact argument reduction. The REM operator is not much help in either of these situations. There is a third approach that has been used in some math libraries, such as the Berkeley UNIX 4.3bsd release. In these libraries, π is computed to the nearest floating-point number. Let's call this machine π, and denote it by π'. Then when computing $\sin x$, reduce x using x REM π'. As we saw in the above example, x REM π' is quite different from x REM π when x is large, so that computing $\sin x$ as $\sin(x\,\mathrm{REM}\,\pi')$ will not give the exact value of $\sin x$. However, computing trigonometric functions in this fashion has the property that all familiar identities (such as $\sin^2 x + \cos^2 x = 1$) are true to within a few rounding errors. Thus, using REM together with machine π provides a simple method of computing trigonometric functions that is accurate for small arguments and still may be useful for large arguments.

When REM is used for argument reduction, it is very handy if it also returns the low-order bits of n (where x REM $y = x - ny$). This is because a practical implementation of trigonometric functions will reduce by something smaller than 2π. For example, it might use $\pi/2$, exploiting identities such as $\sin(x - \pi/2) = -\cos x$, $\sin(x - \pi) = -\sin x$. Then the low bits of n are needed to choose the correct identity.

In our example above, $q = 3$ and $p = 2$, so $q \geq 2p + 2$ is not true. On the other hand, for IEEE arithmetic, double precision has $q = 53$, $p = 24$, so $q = 53 \geq 2p + 2 = 50$. Thus, single precision can be implemented by computing in double precision—that is, computing the answer exactly and then rounding to double—and then rounding to single precision.

Exceptions

The IEEE standard defines five exceptions: underflow, overflow, divide by zero, inexact, and invalid. By default, when these exceptions occur, they merely set a flag and the computation continues. The flags are *sticky*, meaning that once set they remain set until explicitly cleared. The standard strongly encourages implementations to provide a trap-enable bit for each exception. When an exception with an enabled trap handler occurs, a user trap handler is called, and the value of the associated exception flag is undefined. In section A.3 we mentioned that $\sqrt{-3}$ has the value NaN and $1/0$ is ∞. These are examples of operations that raise an exception. By default, computing $\sqrt{-3}$ sets the invalid flag and returns the value NaN. Similarly $1/0$ sets the divide-by-zero flag and returns ∞.

The underflow, overflow, and divide-by-zero exceptions are found in most other systems. The *invalid exception* is for the result of operations such as $\sqrt{-1}$, $0/0$, or $\infty - \infty$, which don't have any natural value as a floating-point number or as $\pm\infty$. The *inexact exception* is peculiar to IEEE arithmetic and occurs when either the result of an operation must be rounded or when it overflows. In fact, since $1/0$ and an operation that overflows both deliver ∞, the exception flags must be consulted to distinguish between them. The inexact exception is an unusual "exception," in that it is not really an exceptional condition because it occurs so frequently. Thus, enabling a trap handler for the inexact exception will most likely have a severe impact on performance. Enabling a trap handler doesn't affect whether an operation is exceptional except in the case of underflow. This is discussed below.

The IEEE standard assumes that when a trap occurs, it is possible to identify the operation that trapped and its operands. On machines with pipelining or multiple arithmetic units, when an exception occurs, it may not be enough to simply have the trap handler examine the program counter. Hardware support may be necessary to identify exactly which operation trapped.

Another problem is illustrated by the following program fragment.

```
r1 = r2 / r3
r2 = r4 + r5
```

These two instructions might well be executed in parallel. If the divide traps, its argument r2 could already have been overwritten by the addition, especially since addition is almost always faster than division. Computer systems that support trapping in the IEEE standard must provide some way to save the value of r2, either in hardware or by having the compiler avoid such a situation in the first place. This kind of problem is not peculiar to floating point. In the sequence

```
r1 = 0(r2)
r2 = r3
```

it would be efficient to execute r2 = r3 while waiting for memory. But if accessing 0(r2) causes a page fault, r2 might no longer be available for restarting the instruction r1 = 0(r2).

One approach to this problem, used in the MIPS R3010, is to identify instructions that may cause an exception early in the instruction cycle. For example, an addition can overflow only if one of the operands has an exponent of E_{max}, and so on. This early check is conservative: It might flag an operation that doesn't actually cause an exception. However, if such false positives are rare, then this technique will have excellent performance. When an instruction is tagged as being possibly exceptional, special code in a trap handler can compute it without destroying any state. Remember that all these problems occur only when trap handlers are enabled. Otherwise, setting the exception flags during normal processing is straightforward.

Underflow

We have alluded several times to the fact that detection of underflow is more complex than for the other exceptions. The IEEE standard specifies that if an underflow trap handler is enabled, the system must trap if the result is denormal. On the other hand, if trap handlers are disabled, then the underflow flag is set only if there is a loss of accuracy—that is, if the result must be rounded. The rationale is, if no accuracy is lost on an underflow, there is no point in setting a warning flag. But if a trap handler is enabled, the user might be trying to simulate flush-to-zero and should therefore be notified whenever a result dips below $1.0 \times 2^{E_{min}}$.

So if there is no trap handler, the underflow exception is signaled only when the result is denormal and inexact. But the definitions of *denormal* and *inexact* are both subject to multiple interpretations. Normally, inexact means there was a result that couldn't be represented exactly and had to be rounded. Consider the example (in a base 2 floating-point system with 3-bit significands) of $(1.11_2 \times 2^{-2}) \times (1.11_2 \times 2^{E_{min}}) = 0.110001_2 \times 2^{E_{min}}$, with round to nearest in effect. The delivered result is $0.11_2 \times 2^{E_{min}}$, which had to be rounded, causing inexact to be signaled. But is it correct to also signal underflow? Gradual underflow loses significance because the exponent range is bounded. If the exponent range were unbounded, the delivered result would be $1.10_2 \times 2^{E_{min}-1}$, exactly the same answer obtained with gradual underflow. The fact that denormalized numbers have fewer bits in their significand than normalized numbers therefore doesn't make any difference in this case. The commentary to the standard [Cody et al. 1984] encourages this as the criterion for setting the underflow flag. That is, it should be set whenever the delivered result is different from what would be delivered in a system with the same fraction size, but with a very large exponent range. However, owing to the difficulty of implementing this scheme, the standard allows setting the underflow flag whenever the result is denormal and different from the infinitely precise result.

There are two possible definitions of what it means for a result to be denormal. Consider the example of $1.10_2 \times 2^{-1}$ multiplied by $1.01_2 \times 2^{E_{min}}$. The exact product is $0.1111 \times 2^{E_{min}}$. The rounded result is the normal number $1.00_2 \times 2^{E_{min}}$. Should underflow be signaled? Signaling underflow means that you are using the *before rounding* rule, because the result was denormal before rounding. Not signaling underflow means that you are using the *after rounding* rule, because the result is normalized after rounding. The IEEE standard provides for choosing either rule; however, the one chosen must be used consistently for all operations.

To illustrate these rules, consider floating-point addition. When the result of an addition (or subtraction) is denormal, it is always exact. Thus the underflow flag never needs to be set for addition. That's because if traps are not enabled, then no exception is raised. And if traps are enabled, the value of the underflow flag is undefined, so again it doesn't need to be set.

One final subtlety should be mentioned concerning underflow. When there is no underflow trap handler, the result of an operation on p-bit numbers that causes an underflow is a denormal number with $p - 1$ or fewer bits of precision. When traps are enabled, the trap handler is provided with the result of the operation rounded to p bits and with the exponent wrapped around. Now there is a potential double-rounding problem. If the trap handler wants to return the denormal result, it can't just round its argument, because that might lead to a double-rounding error. Thus, the trap handler must be passed at least one extra bit of information if it is to be able to deliver the correctly rounded result.

A.8 | **Speeding Up Integer Addition**

The previous section showed that many steps go into implementing floating-point operations. However, each floating-point operation eventually reduces to an integer operation. Thus, increasing the speed of integer operations will also lead to faster floating point.

Integer addition is the simplest operation and the most important. Even for programs that don't do explicit arithmetic, addition must be performed to increment the program counter and to calculate addresses. Despite the simplicity of addition, there isn't a single best way to perform high-speed addition. We will discuss three techniques that are in current use: carry lookahead, carry skip, and carry select.

Carry Lookahead

An n-bit adder is just a combinational circuit. It can therefore be written by a logic formula whose form is a sum of products and can be computed by a circuit with two levels of logic. How do you figure out what this circuit looks like? From Equation A.2.1 (page A-2) the formula for the ith sum can be written as

A.8.1
$$s_i = a_i \overline{b}_i \overline{c}_i + \overline{a}_i b_i \overline{c}_i + \overline{a}_i \overline{b}_i c_i + a_i b_i c_i$$

where c_i is both the carry-in to the ith adder and the carry-out from the $(i-1)$-st adder.

The problem with this formula is that although we know the values of a_i and b_i—they are inputs to the circuit—we don't know c_i. So our goal is to write c_i in terms of a_i and b_i. To accomplish this, we first rewrite Equation A.2.2 (page A-2) as

A.8.2
$$c_i = g_{i-1} + p_{i-1} c_{i-1}, \quad g_{i-1} = a_{i-1} b_{i-1}, \quad p_{i-1} = a_{i-1} + b_{i-1}$$

Here is the reason for the symbols p and g: If g_{i-1} is true, then c_i is certainly true, so a carry is *generated*. Thus, g is for generate. If p_{i-1} is true, then if c_{i-1} is true, it is *propagated* to c_i. Start with Equation A.8.1 and use Equation A.8.2 to replace c_i with $g_{i-1} + p_{i-1} c_{i-1}$. Then, use Equation A.8.2 with $i-1$ in place of i to replace c_{i-1} with c_{i-2}, and so on. This gives the result

A.8.3
$$c_i = g_{i-1} + p_{i-1} g_{i-2} + p_{i-1} p_{i-2} g_{i-3} + \cdots + p_{i-1} p_{i-2} \cdots p_1 g_0 + p_{i-1} p_{i-2} \cdots p_1 p_0 c_0$$

An adder that computes carries using Equation A.8.3 is called a *carry-lookahead adder*, or CLA. A CLA requires one logic level to form p and g, two levels to form the carries, and two for the sum, for a grand total of five logic levels. This is a vast improvement over the $2n$ levels required for the ripple-carry adder.

Unfortunately, as is evident from Equation A.8.3 or from Figure A.14, a carry-lookahead adder on n bits requires a fan-in of $n+1$ at the OR gate as well as at the rightmost AND gate. Also, the p_{n-1} signal must drive n AND gates. In addition, the rather irregular structure and many long wires of Figure A.14 make it impractical to build a full carry-lookahead adder when n is large.

However, we can use the carry-lookahead idea to build an adder that has about $\log_2 n$ logic levels (substantially fewer than the $2n$ required by a ripple-carry adder) and yet has a simple, regular structure. The idea is to build up the p's and g's in steps. We have already seen that

$$c_1 = g_0 + c_0 p_0$$

This says there is a carry-out of the 0th position (c_1) either if there is a carry generated in the 0th position, or if there is a carry into the 0th position and the carry propagates. Similarly,

$$c_2 = G_{01} + P_{01} c_0$$

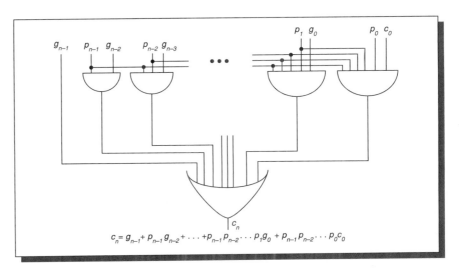

FIGURE A.14   Pure carry-lookahead circuit for computing the carry-out c_n of an n-bit adder.

G_{01} means there is a carry generated out of the block consisting of the first two bits. P_{01} means that a carry propagates through this block. P and G have the following logic equations:

$$G_{01} = g_1 + p_1 g_0$$

$$P_{01} = p_1 p_0$$

More generally, for any j with $i < j, j + 1 < k$, we have the recursive relations

A.8.4 $$c_{k+1} = G_{ik} + P_{ik} c_i$$

A.8.5 $$G_{ik} = G_{j+1,k} + P_{j+1,k} G_{ij}$$

A.8.6 $$P_{ik} = P_{ij} P_{j+1,k}$$

Equation A.8.5 says that a carry is generated out of the block consisting of bits i through k inclusive if it is generated in the high-order part of the block $(j + 1, k)$ or if it is generated in the low-order part of the block (i,j) and then propagated through the high part. These equations will also hold for $i \leq j < k$ if we set $G_{ii} = g_i$ and $P_{ii} = p_i$.

EXAMPLE   Express P_{03} and G_{03} in terms of p's and g's.

ANSWER   Using Equation A.8.6, $P_{03} = P_{01} P_{23} = P_{00} P_{11} P_{22} P_{33}$. Since $P_{ii} = p_i$, $P_{03} = p_0 p_1 p_2 p_3$. For G_{03}, Equation A.8.5 says $G_{03} = G_{23} + P_{23} G_{01} = (G_{33} + P_{33} G_{22}) + (P_{22} P_{33})(G_{11} + P_{11} G_{00}) = g_3 + p_3 g_2 + p_3 p_2 g_1 + p_3 p_2 p_1 g_0$.   ∎

With these preliminaries out of the way, we can now show the design of a practical CLA. The adder consists of two parts. The first part computes various values of P and G from p_i and g_i, using Equations A.8.5 and A.8.6; the second part uses these P and G values to compute all the carries via Equation A.8.4. The first part of the design is shown in Figure A.15. At the top of the diagram, input numbers $a_7 \cdots a_0$ and $b_7 \cdots b_0$ are converted to p's and g's using cells of type 1. Then various P's and G's are generated by combining cells of type 2 in a binary-tree structure. The second part of the design is shown in Figure A.16. By feeding c_0 in at the bottom of this tree, all the carry bits come out at the top. Each cell must know a pair of (P,G) values in order to do the conversion, and the value it needs is written inside the cells. Now compare Figures A.15 and A.16. There is a one-to-one correspondence between cells, and the value of (P,G) needed by the carry-generating cells is exactly the value known by the corresponding (P,G) generating cells. The combined cell is shown in Figure A.17. The numbers to be added flow into the top and downward through the tree, combining with c_0 at the bottom and flowing back up the tree to form the carries. Note that one thing is missing from Figure A.17: a small piece of extra logic to compute c_8 for the carry-out of the adder.

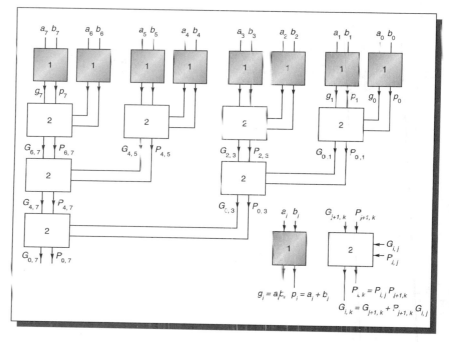

FIGURE A.15 First part of carry-lookahead tree. As signals flow from the top to the bottom, various values of P and G are computed.

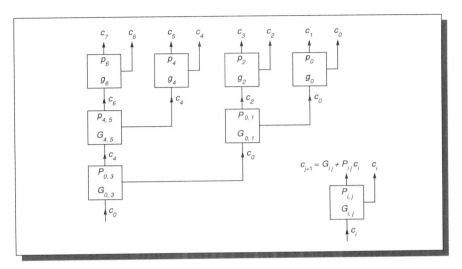

FIGURE A.16   Second part of carry-lookahead tree. Signals flow from the bottom to the top, combining with P and G to form the carries.

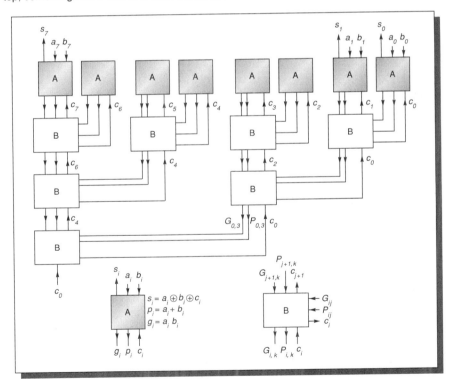

FIGURE A.17   Complete carry-lookahead tree adder. This is the combination of Figures A.15 and A.16. The numbers to be added enter at the top, flow to the bottom to combine with c_0, and then flow back up to compute the sum bits.

The bits in a CLA must pass through about $\log_2 n$ logic levels, compared with $2n$ for a ripple-carry adder. This is a substantial speed improvement, especially for a large n. Whereas the ripple-carry adder had n cells, however, the CLA has $2n$ cells, although in our layout they will take $n \log n$ space. The point is that a small investment in size pays off in a dramatic improvement in speed.

A number of technology-dependent modifications can improve CLAs. For example, if each node of the tree has three inputs instead of two, then the height of the tree will decrease from $\log_2 n$ to $\log_3 n$. Of course, the cells will be more complex and thus might operate more slowly, negating the advantage of the decreased height. For technologies where rippling works well, a hybrid design might be better. This is illustrated in Figure A.18. Carries ripple between adders at the top level, while the "B" boxes are the same as those in Figure A.17. This design will be faster if the time to ripple between four adders is faster than the time it takes to traverse a level of "B" boxes. (To make the pattern more clear, Figure A.18 shows a 16-bit adder, so the 8-bit adder of Figure A.17 corresponds to the right half of Figure A.18.)

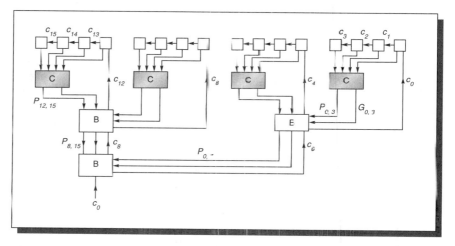

FIGURE A.18   Combination of CLA and ripple-carry adder. In the top row, carries ripple within each group of four boxes.

Carry-Skip Adders

A *carry-skip adder* sits midway between a ripple-carry adder and a carry-lookahead adder, both in terms of speed and cost. (A carry-skip adder is not called a CSA, as that name is reserved for carry-save adders.) The motivation for this adder comes from examining the equations for P and G. For example,

$$P_{03} = p_0 p_1 p_2 p_3$$

$$G_{03} = g_3 + p_3 g_2 + p_3 p_2 g_1 + p_3 p_2 p_1 g_0$$

Computing P is much simpler than computing G, and a carry-skip adder only computes the P's. Such an adder is illustrated in Figure A.19. Carries begin rippling simultaneously through each block. If any block generates a carry, then the carry-out of a block will be true, even though the carry-in to the block may not be correct yet. If at the start of each add operation the carry-in to each block is 0, then no spurious carry-outs will be generated. Thus, the carry-out of each block can thus be thought of as if it were the G signal. Once the carry-out from the least significant block is generated, it not only feeds into the next block, but is also fed through the AND gate with the P signal from that next block. If the carry-out and P signals are both true, then the carry *skips* the second block and is ready to feed into the third block, and so on. The carry-skip adder is only practical if the carry-in signals can be easily cleared at the start of each operation—for example, by precharging in CMOS.

To analyze the speed of a carry-skip adder, let's assume that it takes 1 time unit for a signal to pass through two logic levels. Then it will take k time units for a carry to ripple across a block of size k, and it will take 1 time unit for a carry to skip a block. The longest signal path in the carry-skip adder starts with a carry being generated at the 0th position. If the adder is n-bits wide, then it takes k time units to ripple through the first block, $n/k - 2$ time units to skip blocks, and k more to ripple through the last block. To be specific: If we have a 20-bit adder broken into groups of 4 bits, it will take $4 + (20/4 - 2) + 4 = 11$ time units to perform an add. Some experimentation reveals that there are more efficient ways to divide 20 bits into blocks. For example, consider five blocks with the least-significant 2 bits in the first block, the next 5 bits in the second block, followed by blocks of size 6, 5, and 2. Then the add time is reduced to 9 time units. This illustrates an important general principle. For a carry-skip adder, making the interior blocks larger will speed up the adder. In fact, the same idea of varying the block sizes can sometimes speed up other adder designs as well. Because of the large amount of rippling, a carry-skip adder is most appropriate for technologies where rippling is fast.

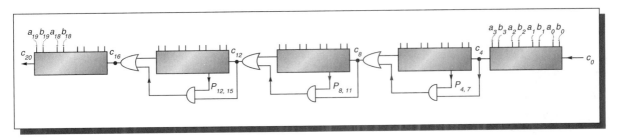

FIGURE A.19   Carry-skip adder. This is a 20-bit carry-skip adder ($n = 20$) with each block 4-bits wide ($k = 4$).

Carry-Select Adder

A *carry-select adder* works on the following principle: Two additions are performed in parallel, one assuming the carry-in is 0 and the other assuming the carry-in is 1. When the carry-in is finally known, the correct sum (which has been precomputed) is simply selected. An example of such a design is shown in Figure A.20. An 8-bit adder is divided into two halves, and the carry-out from the

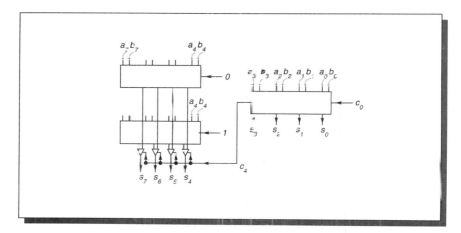

FIGURE A.20   Simple carry-select adder. At the same time that the sum of the low-order 4 bits are being computed, the high-order bits are being computed twice in parallel: once assuming that $c_4 = 0$ and once assuming $c_4 = 1$.

lower half is used to select the sum bits from the upper half. If each block is computing its sum using rippling (a linear-time algorithm), then the design in Figure A.20 is twice as fast at 50% more cost. However, note that the c_4 signal must drive many muxes, which may be very slow in some technologies. Instead of dividing the adder into halves, it could be divided into quarters for a still further speedup. This is illustrated in Figure A.21. If it takes k time units for a block to add k-bit numbers, and if it takes one time unit to compute the mux input from the two carry-out signals, then for optimal operation each block should be 1 bit wider than the next, as shown in Figure A.21. Therefore, as in the carry-skip adder, the best design involves variable-sized blocks.

As a summary of this section, the asymptotic time and space requirements for the different adders are given in Figure A.22. (The times for carry-skip and carry-select come from a careful choice of block size. See Exercise A.27 for the carry-skip adder.) These different adders shouldn't be thought of as disjoint choices, but rather as building blocks to be used in constructing an adder. The utility of these different building blocks is highly dependent on the technology used. For example, the carry-select adder works well when a signal can drive many muxes, and the carry-skip adder is attractive in technologies where signals can be cleared

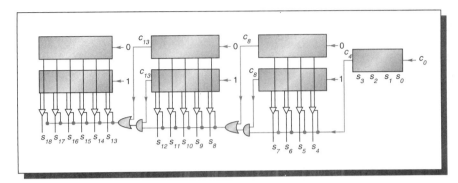

FIGURE A.21   Carry-select adder. As soon as the carry-out of the rightmost block is known, it is used to select the other sum bits.

Adder	Time	Space
Ripple	$O(n)$	$O(n)$
CLA	$O(\log n)$	$O(n \log n)$
Carry skip	$O(\sqrt{n})$	$O(n)$
Carry select	$O(\sqrt{n})$	$O(n)$

FIGURE A.22   Asymptotic time and space requirements for four different types of adders.

at the start of each operation. Knowing the asymptotic behavior of adders is useful in understanding them, but relying too much on that behavior is a pitfall. The reason is that asymptotic behavior is only important as n grows very large. But n for an adder is the bits of precision, and double precision today is the same as it was 20 years ago—about 53 bits. Although it is true that as computers get faster, computations get longer—and thus have more rounding error, which in turn requires more precision—this effect grows very slowly with time.

A.9 | Speeding Up Integer Multiplication and Division

The multiplication and division algorithms presented in section A.2 are fairly slow, producing 1 bit per cycle (although that cycle might be a fraction of the CPU instruction cycle time). In this section we discuss various techniques for higher-performance multiplication and division, including the division algorithm used in the Pentium chip.

Shifting Over Zeros

Although the technique of shifting over zeros is not currently used much, it is instructive to consider. It is distinguished by the fact that its execution time is operand dependent. Its lack of use is primarily attributable to its failure to offer enough speedup over bit-at-a-time algorithms. In addition, pipelining, synchronization with the CPU, and good compiler optimization are difficult with algorithms that run in variable time. In multiplication, the idea behind shifting over zeros is to add logic that detects when the low-order bit of the A register is 0 (see Figure A.2(a) on page A-4) and, if so, skips the addition step and proceeds directly to the shift step—hence the term *shifting over zeros*.

What about shifting for division? In nonrestoring division, an ALU operation (either an addition or subtraction) is performed at every step. There appears to be no opportunity for skipping an operation. But think about division this way: To compute a/b, subtract multiples of b from a, and then report how many subtractions were done. At each stage of the subtraction process the remainder must fit into the P register of Figure A.2(b) (page A-4). In the case when the remainder is a small positive number, you normally subtract b; but suppose instead you only shifted the remainder and subtracted b the next time. As long as the remainder was sufficiently small (its high-order bit 0), after shifting it still would fit into the P register, and no information would be lost. However, this method does require changing the way we keep track of the number of times b has been subtracted from a. This idea usually goes under the name of *SRT division*, for Sweeney, Robertson, and Tocher, who independently proposed algorithms of this nature. The main extra complication of SRT division is that the quotient bits cannot be determined immediately from the sign of P at each step, as they can be in ordinary nonrestoring division.

More precisely, to divide a by b where a and b are n-bit numbers, load a and b into the A and B registers, respectively, of Figure A.2 (page A-4).

SRT Division

1. If B has k leading zeros when expressed using n bits, shift all the registers left k bits.

2. For $i = 0, n - 1$,

    (a) If the top three bits of P are equal, set $q_i = 0$ and shift (P,A) one bit left.

    (b) If the top three bits of P are not all equal and P is negative, set $q_i = -1$ (also written as $\overline{1}$), shift (P,A) one bit left, and add B.

    (c) Otherwise set $q_i = 1$, shift (P,A) one bit left, and subtract B.

    End loop

3. If the final remainder is negative, correct the remainder by adding B, and correct the quotient by subtracting 1 from q_0. Finally, the remainder must be shifted k bits right, where k is the initial shift.

A numerical example is given in Figure A.23. Although we are discussing integer division, it helps in explaining the algorithm to imagine the binary point just left of the most-significant bit. This changes Figure A.23 from $01000_2/0011_2$ to $0.1000_2/.0011_2$. Since the binary point is changed in both the numerator and denominator, the quotient is not affected. The (P,A) register pair holds the remainder and is a two's complement number. For example, if P contains 11110_2 and A = 0, then the remainder is $1.1110_2 = -1/8$. If r is the value of the remainder, then $-1 \leq r < 1$.

P	A	
00000	1000	Divide 8 = 1000 by 3 = 0011. B contains 0011.
00010	0000	step 1: B had two leading 0s, so shift left by 2. B now contains 1100.
		step 2.1: Top three bits are equal. This is case (a), so
00100	0000	set $q_0 = 0$ and shift.
		step 2.2: Top three bits not equal and P ≥ 0 is case (c), so
01000	0001	set $q_1 = 1$ and shift.
+ 10100		Subtract B.
11100	0001	step 2.3: Top bits equal is case (a), so
11000	0010	set $q_2 = 0$ and shift.
		step 2.4: Top three bits unequal is case (b), so
10000	010$\overline{1}$	set $q_3 = -1$ and shift.
+ 01100		Add B.
11100		step 3. Remainder is negative so restore it and subtract 1 from q.
+ 01100		
01000		Must undo the shift in step 1, so right shift by 2 to get true remainder. Remainder = 10, quotient = 010$\overline{1}$ − 1 = 0010.

FIGURE A.23   SRT division of $1000_2/0011_2$. The quotient bits are shown in bold, using the notation $\overline{1}$ for −1.

Given these preliminaries, we can now analyze the SRT division algorithm. The first step of the algorithm shifts b so that $b \geq 1/2$. The rule for which ALU operation to perform is this: If $-1/4 \leq r < 1/4$ (true whenever the top three bits of P are equal), then compute $2r$ by shifting (P,A) left one bit; else if $r < 0$ (and hence $r < -1/4$, since otherwise it would have been eliminated by the first condition), then compute $2r + b$ by shifting and then adding, else $r \geq 1/4$ and subtract b from $2r$. Using $b \geq 1/2$, it is easy to check that these rules keep $-1/2 \leq r < 1/2$. For non-restoring division, we only have $|r| \leq b$, and we need P to be $n + 1$ bits wide. But for SRT division, the bound on r is tighter, namely $-1/2 \leq r < 1/2$. Thus, we can save a bit by eliminating the high-order bit of P (and b and the adder). In particular, the test for equality of the top three bits of P becomes a test on just two bits.

The algorithm might change slightly in an implementation of SRT division. After each ALU operation, the P register can be shifted as many places as necessary to make either $r \geq 1/4$ or $r < -1/4$. By shifting k places, k quotient bits are set equal to zero all at once. For this reason SRT division is sometimes described as one that keeps the remainder normalized to $|r| \geq 1/4$.

Notice that the value of the quotient bit computed in a given step is based on which operation is performed in that step (which in turn depends on the result of the operation from the previous step). This is in contrast to nonrestoring division, where the quotient bit computed in the ith step depends on the result of the operation in the same step. This difference is reflected in the fact that when the final remainder is negative, the last quotient bit must be adjusted in SRT division, but not in nonrestoring division. However, the key fact about the quotient bits in SRT division is that they can include $\overline{1}$. Although Figure A.23 shows the quotient bits being stored in the low-order bits of A, an actual implementation can't do this because you can't fit the three values $-1, 0, 1$ into one bit. Furthermore, the quotient must be converted to ordinary two's complement in a full adder. A common way to do this is to accumulate the positive quotient bits in one register and the negative quotient bits in another, and then subtract the two registers after all the bits are known. Because there is more than one way to write a number in terms of the digits $-1, 0, 1$, SRT division is said to use a *redundant* quotient representation.

The differences between SRT division and ordinary nonrestoring division can be summarized as follows:

1. ALU decision rule: In nonrestoring division, it is determined by the sign of P; in SRT, it is determined by the two most-significant bits of P.

2. Final quotient: In nonrestoring division, it is immediate from the successive signs of P; in SRT, there are three quotient digits $(1, 0, \overline{1})$, and the final quotient must be computed in a full n-bit adder.

3. Speed: SRT division will be faster on operands that produce zero quotient bits.

The simple version of the SRT division algorithm given above does not offer enough of a speedup to be practical in most cases. However, later on in this section we will study variants of SRT division that are quite practical.

Speeding Up Multiplication with a Single Adder

As mentioned before, shifting-over zero techniques are not used much in current hardware. We now discuss some methods that are in widespread use. Methods that increase the speed of multiplication can be divided into two classes: those that use a single adder and those that use multiple adders. Let's first discuss techniques that use a single adder.

In the discussion of addition we noted that, because of carry propagation, it is not practical to perform addition with two levels of logic. Using the cells of Figure A.17, adding two 64-bit numbers will require a trip through seven cells to compute the P's and G's, and seven more to compute the carry bits, which will

```
      P      A    L
    00000   1001         Multiply –7 = 1001 times –5 = 1011. B contains 1011.
  + 11011                Low order bits of A are 0, 1; L=0, so add B.
    11011   1001
    11110   1110   0     Shift right by two bits, shifting in 1s on the left.
  + 01010                Low order bits of A are 1, 0; L=0, so add –2b.
    01000   1110   0
    00010   0011   1     Shift right by two bits.
                         Product is 35 = 0100011.
```

FIGURE A.26   Multiplication of –7 times –5 using radix-4 Booth recoding. The column labeled L contains the last bit shifted out the right end of A.

Faster Multiplication with Many Adders

If the space for many adders is available, then multiplication speed can be improved. Figure A.27 shows a simple array multiplier for multiplying two 5-bit numbers, using three CSAs and one propagate adder. Part (a) is a block diagram of the kind we will use throughout this section. Parts (b) and (c) show the adder in more detail. All the inputs to the adder are shown in (b); the actual adders with their interconnections are shown in (c). Each row of adders in (c) corresponds to a box in (a). The picture is "twisted" so that bits of the same significance are in the same column. In an actual implementation, the array would most likely be laid out as a square instead.

The array multiplier in Figure A.27 performs the same number of additions as the design in Figure A.24, so its latency is not dramatically different from that of a single carry-save adder. However, with the hardware in Figure A.27, multiplication can be pipelined, increasing the total throughput. On the other hand, although this level of pipelining is sometimes used in array processors, it is not used in any of the single-chip, floating-point accelerators discussed in section A.10. Pipelining is discussed in general in Chapters 3 and 4 and by Kogge [1981] in the context of multipliers.

Sometimes the space budgeted on a chip for arithmetic may not hold an array large enough to multiply two double-precision numbers. In this case, a popular design is to use a two-pass arrangement such as the one shown in Figure A.28. The first pass through the array "retires" 5 bits of B. Then the result of this first pass is fed back into the top to be combined with the next three summands. The result of this second pass is then fed into a CPA. This design, however, loses the ability to be pipelined.

If arrays require as many addition steps as the much cheaper arrangements in Figures A.2 and A.24, why are they so popular? First of all, using an array has a smaller latency than using a single adder—because the array is a combinational circuit, the signals flow through it directly without being clocked. Although the

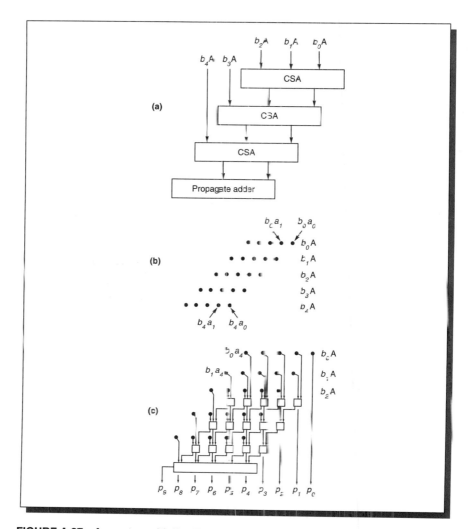

FIGURE A.27 An array multiplier. The 5-bit number in A is multiplied by $b_4b_3b_2b_1b_0$. Part (a) shows the block diagram, (b) shows the inputs to the array, and (c) expands the array to show all the adders.

two-pass adder of Figure A.28 would normally still use a clock the cycle time for passing through k arrays can be less than k times the clock that would be needed for designs like the ones in Figures A.2 or A.24. Second, the array is amenable to various schemes for further speedup. One of them is shown in Figure A.29. The idea of this design is that two adds proceed in parallel or, to put it another way, each stream passes through only half the adders. Thus, it runs at almost twice the speed of the multiplier in Figure A.27. This *even/odd* multiplier is popular in

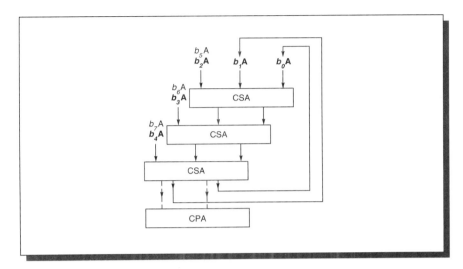

FIGURE A.28   Multipass array multiplier. Multiplies two 8-bit numbers with about half the hardware that would be used in a one-pass design like that of Figure A.27. At the end of the second pass, the bits flow into the CPA. The inputs used in the first pass are marked in bold.

VLSI because of its regular structure. Arrays can also be speeded up using asynchronous logic. One of the reasons why the multiplier of Figure A.2 (page A-4) needs a clock is to keep the output of the adder from feeding back into the input of the adder before the output has fully stabilized. Thus, if the array in Figure A.28 is long enough so that no signal can propagate from the top through the bottom in the time it takes for the first adder to stabilize, it may be possible to avoid clocks altogether. Williams et al. [1987] discuss a design using this idea, although it is for dividers instead of multipliers.

The techniques of the previous paragraph still have a multiply time of $O(n)$, but the time can be reduced to $\log n$ using a tree. The simplest tree would combine pairs of summands $b_0 A \cdots b_{n-1} A$, cutting the number of summands from n to $n/2$. Then these $n/2$ numbers would be added in pairs again, reducing to $n/4$, and so on, and resulting in a single sum after $\log n$ steps. However, this simple binary tree idea doesn't map into full (3,2) adders, which reduce three inputs to two rather than reducing two inputs to one. A tree that does use full adders, known as a *Wallace tree*, is shown in Figure A.30. When computer arithmetic units were built out of MSI parts, a Wallace tree was the design of choice for high-speed multipliers. There is, however, a problem with implementing it in VLSI. If you try to fill in all the adders and paths for the Wallace tree of Figure A.30, you will discover that it does not have the nice, regular structure of Figure A.27. This is why VLSI designers have often chosen to use other $\log n$ designs such as the *binary tree multiplier*, which is discussed next.

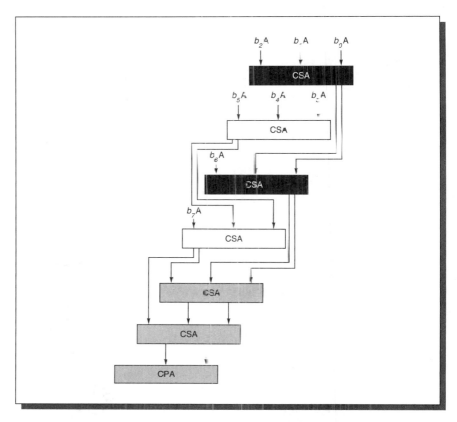

FIGURE A.29   Even/odd array. The first two adders work in parallel. Their results are fed into the third and fourth adders, which also work in parallel, and so on.

The problem with adding summands in a binary tree is coming up with a (2.1) adder that combines two digits and produces a single-sum digit. Because of carries, this isn't possible using binary notation, but it can be done with some other representation. We will use the *signed-digit representation* 1, $\overline{1}$, and 0, which we used previously to understand Booth's algorithm. This representation has two costs. First, it takes 2 bits to represent each signed digit. Second, the algorithm for adding two signed-digit numbers a_i and b_i is complex and requires examining $a_i a_{i-1} a_{i-2}$ and $b_i b_{i-1} b_{i-2}$. Although this means you must look 2 bits back, in binary addition you might have to look an arbitrary number of bits back because of carries.

We can describe the algorithm for adding two signed-digit numbers as follows. First, compute sum and carry bits s_i and c_{i+1} using Figure A.31. Then compute the final sum as $s_i + c_i$. The tables are set up so that this final sum does not generate a carry.

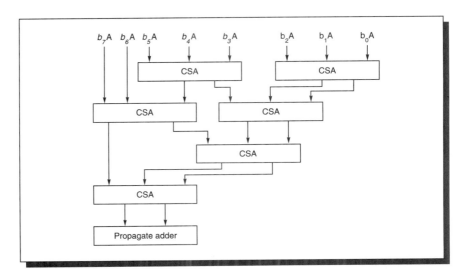

FIGURE A.30   Wallace tree multiplier. An example of a multiply tree that computes a product in $O(\log n)$ steps.

$$
\begin{array}{cccccc}
1 & 1 & \bar{1} & 0 & 1 \; x & \bar{1} \; x \\
+1 & +\bar{1} & +\bar{1} & +0 & +0 \; y & +0 \; y \\
\hline
1\,0 & 0\,0 & \bar{1}\,0 & 0\,0 & 1\,\bar{1} \quad \text{if } x \geq 0 \text{ and } y \geq 0 & 0\,\bar{1} \quad \text{if } x \geq 0 \text{ and } y \geq 0 \\
 & & & & 0\,1 \quad \text{otherwise} & \bar{1}\,1 \quad \text{otherwise}
\end{array}
$$

FIGURE A.31   Signed-digit addition table. The leftmost sum shows that when computing $1 + 1$, the sum bit is 0 and the carry bit is 1.

EXAMPLE   What is the sum of the signed-digit numbers $1\bar{1}0_2$ and 001_2 ?

ANSWER   The two low-order bits sum to $0 + 1 = 1\bar{1}$, the next pair sums to $\bar{1} + 0 = 0\bar{1}$, and the high-order pair sums to $1 + 0 = 01$, so the sum is $1\bar{1} + 0\bar{1}0 + 0100 = 10\bar{1}_2$.

This, then, defines a (2,1) adder. With this in hand, we can use a straightforward binary tree to perform multiplication. In the first step it adds $b_0A + b_1A$ in parallel with $b_2A + b_3A$, $\cdots$, $b_{n-2}A + b_{n-1}A$. The next step adds the results of these sums in pairs, and so on. Although the final sum must be run through a carry-propagate adder to convert it from signed-digit form to two's complement, this final add step is necessary in any multiplier using CSAs.

To summarize, both Wallace trees and signed-digit trees are $\log n$ multipliers. The Wallace tree uses fewer gates but is harder to lay out. The signed-digit tree has a more regular structure, but requires 2 bits to represent each digit and has more complicated add logic. As with adders, it is possible to combine different multiply techniques. For example, Booth recoding and arrays can be combined. In Figure A.27 instead of having each input be b_iA, we could have it be $b_ib_{i-1}A$. To avoid having to compute the multiple $3b$, we can use Booth recoding.

Faster Division with One Adder

The two techniques we discussed for speeding up multiplication with a single adder were carry-save adders and higher-radix multiplication. However, there is a difficulty when trying to utilize these approaches to speed up nonrestoring division. If the adder in Figure A.2(b) on page A-4 is replaced with a carry-save adder, then P will be replaced with two registers, one for the sum bits and one for the carry bits (compare with the multiplier in Figure A.24). At the end of each cycle, the sign of P is uncertain (since P is the unevaluated sum of the two registers), yet it is the sign of P that is used to compute the quotient digit and decide the next ALU operation. When a higher radix is used, the problem is deciding what value to subtract from P. In the paper-and-pencil method, you have to guess the quotient digit. In binary division there are only two possibilities. We were able to finesse the problem by initially guessing one and then adjusting the guess based on the sign of P. This doesn't work in higher radices because there are more than two possible quotient digits, rendering quotient selection potentially quite complicated: You would have to compute all the multiples of b and compare them to P.

Both the carry-save technique and higher-radix division can be made to work if we use a redundant quotient representation. Recall from our discussion of SRT division (page A-47) that by allowing the quotient digits to be -1, 0, or 1, there is often a choice of which one to pick. The idea in the previous algorithm was to choose 0 whenever possible, because that meant an ALU operation could be skipped. In carry-save division, the idea is that, because the remainder (which is the value of the (P,A) register pair) is not known exactly (being stored in carry-save form), the exact quotient digit is also not known. But thanks to the redundant representation, the remainder doesn't have to be known precisely in order to pick a quotient digit. This is illustrated in Figure A.32, where the x axis represents r_i, the remainder after i steps. The line labeled $q_i = 1$ shows the value that r_{i+1} would be if we choose $q_i = 1$, and similarly for the lines $q_i = 0$ and $q_i = -1$. We can choose any value for q_i, as long as $r_{i-1} = 2r_i - q_ib$ satisfies $|r_{i+1}| \leq b$. The allowable ranges are shown in the right half of Figure A.32. This shows that you don't need to know the precise value of r_i in order to choose a quotient digit q_i. You only need to know that r lies in an interval small enough to fit entirely within one of the overlapping bars shown in the right half of Figure A.32.

b	Range of P		q	b	Range of P		q
8	−12	−7	−2	12	−18	−10	−2
8	−6	−3	−1	12	−10	−4	−1
8	−2	1	0	12	−4	3	0
8	2	5	1	12	3	9	1
8	6	11	2	12	9	17	2
9	−14	−8	−2	13	−19	−11	−2
9	−7	−3	−1	13	−10	−4	−1
9	−3	2	0	13	−4	3	0
9	2	6	1	13	3	9	1
9	7	13	2	13	10	18	2
10	−15	−9	−2	14	−20	−11	−2
10	−8	−3	−1	14	−11	−4	−1
10	−3	2	0	14	−4	3	0
10	2	7	1	14	3	10	1
10	8	14	2	14	10	19	2
11	−16	−9	−2	15	−22	−12	−2
11	−9	−3	−1	15	−12	−4	−1
11	−3	2	0	15	−5	4	0
11	2	8	1	15	3	11	1
11	8	15	2	15	11	21	2

FIGURE A.34   Quotient digits for radix-4 SRT division with a propagate adder. The top row says that if the high-order 4 bits of b are $1000_2 = 8$, and if the top 6 bits of P are between $110100_2 = -12$ and $111001_2 = -7$, then -2 is a valid quotient digit.

```
     P          A
000000000  10010101    Divide 149 by 5. B contains 00000101.
000010010  10100000    step 1:     B had 5 leading 0s, so shift left by 5. B now
                                    contains 010C000, so use b = 10 section of table.
                        step 2.1:   Top 6 bits of P are 2, so
                                    shift left by 2. From table, can pick q to be
001001010  1000000                  0 or 1. Choose q_0 = 0.
                        step 2.2:   Top 6 bits of P are 9, so
100101010  000002                   shift left 2. q_1 = 2.
+ 011000000                         Subtract 2b.
111101010  000002      step 2.3:    Top bits = -3, so
110101000  00020                    shift left 2. Can pick 0 or -1 for q, pick q_2 = 0.
                        step 2.4:   Top bits = -11, so
010100000  0202                     shift left 2. q_3 = -2.
+ 101000000         —               Add 2b.
111100000              step 3:      Remainder is negative, so restore
+ 010100000                         by adding b and subtract 1 from q.
010000000              Answer:      q = 0202 - 1 = 29.
                                    To get remainder, undo shift in step 1 so
                                    remainder = 010000000 >> 5 = 4.
```

FIGURE A.35 Example of radix-4 SRT division. Division of 149 by 5.

A.10 Putting It All Together

In this section, we will compare the Weitek 3364, the MIPS R3010, and the Texas Instruments 8847 (see Figures A.36 and A.37). In many ways, these are ideal chips to compare. They each implement the IEEE standard for addition, subtraction, multiplication, and division on a single chip. All were introduced in 1988

Features	MIPS R3010	Weitek 3364	TI 8847
Clock cycle time (ns)	40	50	30
Size (mil^2)	114,857	147,600	156,180
Transistors	75,000	165,000	180,000
Pins	84	168	207
Power (watts)	3.5	1.5	1.5
Cycles/add	2	2	2
Cycles/mult	5	2	3
Cycles/divide	19	17	11
Cycles/sq root	–	30	14

FIGURE A.36 Summary of the three floating-point chips discussed in this section. The cycle times are for production parts available in June 1989. The cycle counts are for double-precision operations.

and run with a cycle time of about 40 nanoseconds. However, as we will see, they use quite different algorithms. The Weitek chip is well described in Birman et al. [1990], the MIPS chip is described in less detail in Rowen, Johnson, and Ries [1988], and details of the TI chip can be found in Darley et al. [1989].

These three chips have a number of things in common. They perform addition and multiplication in parallel, and they implement neither extended precision nor a remainder step operation. (Recall from section A.6 that it is easy to implement the IEEE remainder function in software if a remainder step instruction is available.) The designers of these chips probably decided not to provide extended precision because the most influential users are those who run portable codes, which can't rely on extended precision. However, as we have seen, extended precision can make for faster and simpler math libraries.

In the summary of the three chips given in Figure A.36, note that a higher transistor count generally leads to smaller cycle counts. Comparing the cycles/op numbers needs to be done carefully, because the figures for the MIPS chip are those for a complete system (R3000/3010 pair), while the Weitek and TI numbers are for stand-alone chips and are usually larger when used in a complete system.

The MIPS chip has the fewest transistors of the three. This is reflected in the fact that it is the only chip of the three that does not have any pipelining or hardware square root. Further, the multiplication and addition operations are not completely independent because they share the carry-propagate adder that performs the final rounding (as well as the rounding logic).

Addition on the R3010 uses a mixture of ripple, CLA, and carry select. A carry-select adder is used in the fashion of Figure A.20 (page A-45). Within each half, carries are propagated using a hybrid ripple-CLA scheme of the type indicated in Figure A.18 (page A-43). However, this is further tuned by varying the size of each block, rather than having each fixed at 4 bits (as they are in Figure A.18). The multiplier is midway between the designs of Figures A.2 (page A-4) and A.27 (page A-53). It has an array just large enough so that output can be fed back into the input without having to be clocked. Also, it uses radix-4 Booth recoding and the even-odd technique of Figure A.29 (page A-55). The R3010 can do a divide and multiply in parallel (like the Weitek chip but unlike the TI chip). The divider is a radix-4 SRT method with quotient digits -2, -1, 0, 1, and 2, and is similar to that described in Taylor [1985]. Double-precision division is about four times slower than multiplication. The R3010 shows that for chips using an $O(n)$ multiplier, an SRT divider can operate fast enough to keep a reasonable ratio between multiply and divide.

The Weitek 3364 has independent add, multiply, and divide units. It also uses radix-4 SRT division. However, the add and multiply operations on the Weitek chip are pipelined. The three addition stages are (1) exponent compare, (2) add followed by shift (or vice versa), and (3) final rounding. Stages (1) and (3) take only a half-cycle, allowing the whole operation to be done in two cycles, even though there are three pipeline stages. The multiplier uses an array of the style of Figure A.28 but uses radix-8 Booth recoding, which means it must compute 3 times the multiplier. The three multiplier pipeline stages are (1) compute $3b$, (2) pass through array, and (3) final carry-propagation add and round. Single precision passes through the array once, double precision twice. Like addition, the latency is two cycles.

The Weitek chip uses an interesting addition algorithm. It is a variant on the carry-skip adder pictured in Figure A.19 (page A-44). However, P_{ij}, which is the logical AND of many terms, is computed by rippling, performing one AND per ripple. Thus, while the carries propagate left within a block, the value of P_{ij} is propagating right within the next block, and the block sizes are chosen so that both waves complete at the same time. Unlike the MIPS chip, the 3364 has hardware square root, which shares the divide hardware. The ratio of double-precision multiply to divide is 2:17. The large disparity between multiply and divide is due to the fact that multiplication uses radix-8 Booth recoding, while division uses a radix-4 method. In the MIPS R3010, multiplication and division use the same radix.

The notable feature of the TI 8847 is that it does division by iteration (using the Goldschmidt algorithm discussed in section A.6). This improves the speed of division (the ratio of multiply to divide is 3:11), but means that multiplication and division cannot be done in parallel as on the other two chips. Addition has a two-stage pipeline. Exponent compare, fraction shift, and fraction addition are done in the first stage, normalization and rounding in the second stage. Multiplication uses a binary tree of signed-digit adders and has a three-stage pipeline. The first stage passes through the array, retiring half the bits; the second stage passes through the array a second time; and the third stage converts from signed-digit form to two's complement. Since there is only one array, a new multiply operation can only be initiated in every other cycle. However, by slowing down the clock, two passes through the array can be made in a single cycle. In this case, a new multiplication can be initiated in each cycle. The 8847 adder uses a carry-select algorithm rather than carry lookahead. As mentioned in section A.6, the TI carries 60 bits of precision in order to do correctly rounded division.

These three chips illustrate the different trade-offs made by designers with similar constraints. One of the most interesting things about these chips is the diversity of their algorithms. Each uses a different add algorithm, as well as a different multiply algorithm. In fact, Booth recoding is the only technique that is universally used by all the chips.

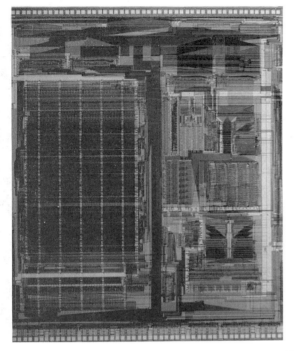

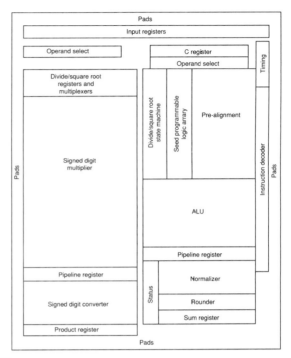

TI 8847

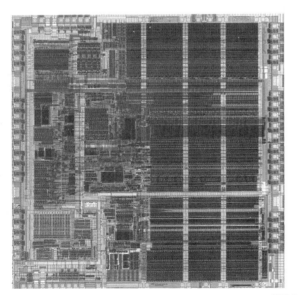

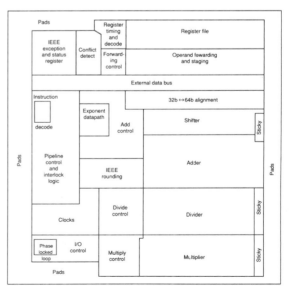

MIPS R3010

Figure continued on next page

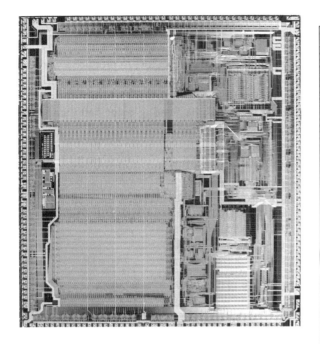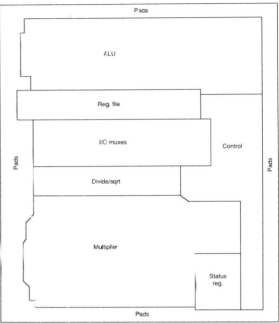

Weitek 3364

FIGURE A.37 Chip layout for the TI 8847, MIPS R3010, and Weitek 3364. In the left-hand columns are the photomicrographs; the right-hand columns show the corresponding floor plans.

A.11 Fallacies and Pitfalls

Fallacy: Underflows rarely occur in actual floating-point application code.

Although most codes rarely underflow, there are actual codes that underflow frequently. SDRWAVE [Kahaner 1988], which solves a one-dimensional wave equation, is one such example. This program underflows quite frequently, even when functioning properly. Measurements on one machine show that adding hardware support for gradual underflow would cause SDRWAVE to run about 50% faster.

Fallacy: Conversions between integer and floating point are rare.

In fact, in spice they are as frequent as divides. The assumption that conversions are rare leads to a mistake in the SPARC version 8 instruction set, which does not provide an instruction to move from integer registers to floating-point registers.

field and a 48-bit fraction field. Addition on Cray computers does not have a guard digit, and multiplication is even less accurate than addition. Thinking of multiplication as a sum of p numbers, each $2p$ bits long, Cray computers drop the low-order bits of each summand. Thus, analyzing the exact error characteristics of the multiply operation is not easy. Reciprocals are computed using iteration, and division of a by b is done by multiplying a times $1/b$. The errors in multiplication and reciprocation combine to make the last three bits of a divide operation unreliable. At least Cray computers serve to keep numerical analysts on their toes!

The IEEE standardization process began in 1977, inspired mainly by W. Kahan and based partly on Kahan's work with the IBM 7094 at the University of Toronto [Kahan 1968]. The standardization process was a lengthy affair, with gradual underflow causing the most controversy. (According to Cleve Moler, visitors to the U.S. were advised that the sights not to be missed were Las Vegas, the Grand Canyon, and the IEEE standards committee meeting.) The standard was finally approved in 1985. The Intel 8087 was the first major commercial IEEE implementation and appeared in 1981, before the standard was finalized. It contains features that were eliminated in the final standard, such as projective bits. According to Kahan, the length of double-extended precision was based on what could be implemented in the 8087. Although the IEEE standard was not based on any existing floating-point system, most of its features were present in some other system. For example, the CDC 6600 reserved special bit patterns for INDEFINITE and INFINITY, while the idea of denormal numbers appears in Goldberg [1967] as well as in Kahan [1968]. Kahan was awarded the 1989 Turing prize in recognition of his work on floating point.

Although floating point rarely attracts the interest of the general press, newspapers were filled with stories about floating-point division in November 1994. A bug in the division algorithm used on all of Intel's Pentium chips had just come to light. It was discovered by Thomas Nicely, a math professor at Lynchburg College in Virginia. Nicely found the bug when doing calculations involving reciprocals of prime numbers. News of Nicely's discovery first appeared in the press on the front page of the November 7 issue of *Electronic Engineering Times*. Intel's immediate response was to stonewall, asserting that the bug would only affect theoretical mathematicians. Intel told the press, "This doesn't even qualify as an errata . . . even if you're an engineer, you're not going to see this."

Under more pressure, Intel issued a white paper, dated November 30, explaining why they didn't think the bug was significant. One of their arguments was based on the fact that if you pick two floating-point numbers at random and divide one into the other, the chance that the resulting quotient will be in error is about 1 in 9 billion. However, Intel neglected to explain why they thought that the typical customer accessed floating-point numbers randomly.

Pressure continued to mount on Intel. One sore point was that Intel had known about the bug before Nicely discovered it, but had decided not to make it public. Finally, on December 20, Intel announced that they would unconditionally replace any Pentium chip that used the faulty algorithm and that they would take an unspecified charge against earnings, which turned out to be $300 million.

The Pentium uses a simple version of SRT division as discussed in section
A.9. The bug was introduced when they converted the quotient lookup table to a
PLA. Evidently there were a few elements of the table containing the quotient
digit 2 that Intel thought would never be accessed, and they optimized the PLA
design using this assumption. The resulting PLA returned 0 rather than 2 in these
situations. However, those entries were really accessed, and this caused the division bug. Even though the effect of the faulty PLA was to cause 5 out of 2048 table entries to be wrong, the Pentium only computes an incorrect quotient 1 out of
9 billion times on random inputs. This is explored in Exercise A.34.

References

ANDERSON, S. F., J. G. EARLE, R. E. GOLDSCHMIDT, AND D. M. POWERS [1967]. "The IBM System/
360 Model 91: Floating-point execution unit," *IBM J. Research and Development* 11, 34–53. Reprinted in Swartzlander [1990].

> *Good description of an early high-performance floating-point unit that used a pipelined
> Wallace-tree multiplier and iterative division.*

BELL, C. G. AND A. NEWELL [1971]. *Computer Structures: Readings and Examples,* McGraw-Hill,
New York.

BIRMAN, M., A. SAMUELS, G. CHU, T. CHUK, L. HU, J. MCLEOD, AND J. BARNES [1990]. "Developing the WRL3170/3171 SPARC floating-point coprocessors," *IEEE Micro* 10:1, 55–64.

> *These chips have the same floating-point core as the Weitek 3364, and this paper has a fairly
> detailed description of that floating-point design.*

BRENT, R. P. AND H. T. KUNG [1982]. "A regular layout for parallel adders," *IEEE Trans. on Computers* C-31, 260–264.

> *This is the paper that popularized CLAs in VLSI.*

BURGESS, N. AND T. WILLIAMS [1995]. "Choices of operand truncation in the SRT division algorithm," *IEEE Trans. on Computers* 44:7.

> *Analyzes how many bits of divisor and remainder need to be examined in SRT division.*

BURKS, A. W., H. H. GOLDSTINE, AND J. VON NEUMANN [1946]. "Preliminary discussion of the logical design of an electronic computing instrument," Report to the U.S. Army Ordnance Department,
p. 1; also appears in *Papers of John von Neumann,* W. Aspray and A. Burks, eds., MIT Press, Cambridge, Mass., and Tomash Publishers, Los Angeles, Calif., 1987, 97–146.

CODY, W. J., J. T. COONEN, D. M. GAY, K. HANSON, D. HOUGH, W. KAHAN, R. KARPINSKI,
J. PALMER, F. N. RIS, AND D. STEVENSON [1984]. "A proposed radix- and word-length-independent standard for floating-point arithmetic," *IEEE Micro* 4:4 86–100.

> *Contains a draft of the 854 standard, which is more general than 754. The significance of this
> article is that it contains commentary on the standard, most of which is equally relevant to
> 754. However, be aware that there are some differences between this draft and the final stan-
> dard.*

COONEN, J. [1984]. *Contributions to a Proposed Standard for Binary Floating-Point Arithmetic,*
Ph.D. Thesis, Univ. of Calif., Berkeley.

> *The only detailed discussion of how rounding modes can be used to implement efficient binary
> decimal conversion.*

DARLEY, H. M., ET AL. [1989]. "Floating point/integer processor with divide and square root functions," U.S. Patent 4,878,190, October 31, 1989.

> *Pretty readable as patents go. Gives a high-level view of the TI 8847 chip, but doesn't have all the details of the division algorithm.*

DEMMEL, J. W. AND X. LI [1994]. "Faster numerical algorithms via exception handling," *IEEE Trans. on Computers* 43:8, 983–992.

> *A good discussion of how the features unique to IEEE floating point can improve the performance of an important software library.*

FREIMAN, C. V. [1961]. "Statistical analysis of certain binary division algorithms," *Proc. IRE* 49:1, 91–103.

> *Contains an analysis of the performance of shifting-over-zeros SRT division algorithm.*

GOLDBERG, D. [1991]. "What every computer scientist should know about floating-point arithmetic," *Computing Surveys* 23:1, 5–48.

> *Contains an in-depth tutorial on the IEEE standard from the software point of view.*

GOLDBERG, I. B. [1967]. "27 bits are not enough for 8-digit accuracy," *Comm. ACM* 10:2, 105–106.

> *This paper proposes using hidden bits and gradual underflow.*

GOSLING, J. B. [1980]. *Design of Arithmetic Units for Digital Computers,* Springer-Verlag, New York.

> *A concise, well-written book, although it focuses on MSI designs.*

HAMACHER, V. C., Z. G. VRANESIC, AND S. G. ZAKY [1984]. *Computer Organization,* 2nd ed., McGraw-Hill, New York.

> *Introductory computer architecture book with a good chapter on computer arithmetic.*

HWANG, K. [1979]. *Computer Arithmetic: Principles, Architecture, and Design,* Wiley, New York.

> *This book contains the widest range of topics of the computer arithmetic books.*

IEEE [1985]. "IEEE standard for binary floating-point arithmetic," *SIGPLAN Notices* 22:2, 9–25.

> *IEEE 754 is reprinted here.*

KAHAN, W. [1968]. "7094-II system support for numerical analysis," *SHARE Secretarial Distribution* SSD-159.

> *This system had many features that were incorporated into the IEEE floating-point standard.*

KAHANER, D. K. [1988]. "Benchmarks for 'real' programs," *SIAM News* (November).

> *The benchmark presented in this article turns out to cause many underflows.*

KNUTH, D. [1981]. *The Art of Computer Programming,* vol. II, 2nd ed., Addison-Wesley, Reading, Mass.

> *Has a section on the distribution of floating-point numbers.*

KOGGE, P. [1981]. *The Architecture of Pipelined Computers,* McGraw-Hill, New York.

> *Has brief discussion of pipelined multipliers.*

KOHN, L. AND S.-W. FU [1989]. "A 1,000,000 transistor microprocessor," *IEEE Int'l Solid-State Circuits Conf.*, 54–55.

> *There are several articles about the i860, but this one contains the most details about its floating-point algorithms.*

KOREN, I. [1989]. *Computer Arithmetic Algorithms,* Prentice Hall, Englewood Cliffs, N.J.

LEIGHTON, F. T. [1992]. *Introduction to Parallel Algorithms and Architectures: Arrays, Trees, Hypercubes,* Morgan Kaufmann, San Mateo, Calif.

> *This is an excellent book, with emphasis on the complexity analysis of algorithms. Section 1.2.1 has a nice discussion of carry-lookahead addition on a tree.*

MAGENHEIMER, D. J., L. PETERS, K. W. PETTIS, AND D. ZURAS [1983]. "Integer multiplication and division on the HP Precision architecture," *IEEE Trans. on Computers* 37:8, 980–990.

Gives rationale for the integer- and divide-step instructions in the Precision architecture.

MARKSTEIN, P. W. [1990]. "Computation of elementary functions on the IBM RISC System/6000 processor," *IBM J. of Research and Development* 34:1, 111–119.

Explains how to use fused muliply-add to compute correctly rounded division and square root.

MEAD, C. AND L. CONWAY [1980]. *Introduction to VLSI Systems,* Addison-Wesley, Reading, Mass.

MONTOYE, R. K., E. HOKENEK, AND S. L. RUNYON [1990]. "Design of the IBM RISC System/6000 floating-point execution," *IBM J. of Research and Development* 34:1, 59–70.

Describes one implementation of fused multiply-add.

NGAI, T.-F. AND M. J. IRWIN [1985]. "Regular, area-time efficient carry-lookahead adders," *Proc. Seventh IEEE Symposium on Computer Arithmetic,* 9–15.

Describes a CLA like that of Figure A.17, where the bits flow up and then come back down.

PATTERSON, D.A. AND J.L. HENNESSY [1994]. *Computer Organization and Design: The Hardware/ Software Interface,* Morgan Kaufmann, San Francisco.

Chapter 4 is a gentler introduction to the first third of this appendix.

PENG, V., S. SAMUDRALA, AND M. GAVRIELOV [1987]. "On the implementation of shifters, multipliers, and dividers in VLSI floating point units," *Proc. Eighth IEEE Symposium on Computer Arithmetic,* 95–102.

Highly recommended survey of different techniques actually used in VLSI designs.

ROWEN, C., M. JOHNSON, AND P. RIES [1988]. "The MIPS R3010 floating-point coprocessor," *IEEE Micro* 53–62 (June).

SANTORO, M. R., G. BEWICK, AND M. A. HOROWITZ [1989]. "Rounding algorithms for IEEE multipliers," *Proc. Ninth IEEE Symposium on Computer Arithmetic,* 176–183.

A very readable discussion of how to efficiently implement rounding for floating-point multiplication.

SCOTT, N. R. [1985]. *Computer Number Systems and Arithmetic,* Prentice Hall, Englewood Cliffs, N.J.

SWARTZLANDER, E., ED. [1990]. *Computer Arithmetic,* IEEE Computer Society Press, Los Alamitos, Calif.

A collection of historical papers in two volumes.

TAKAGI, N., H. YASUURA, AND S. YAJIMA [1985]."High-speed VLSI multiplication algorithm with a redundant binary addition tree," *IEEE Trans. on Computers* C-34:9, 789–796.

A discussion of the binary-tree signed multiplier that was the basis for the design used in the TI 8847.

TAYLOR, G. S. [1981]. "Compatible hardware for division and square root," *Proc. Fifth IEEE Symposium on Computer Arithmetic,* 127–134.

Good discussion of a radix-4 SRT division algorithm.

TAYLOR, G. S. [1985]. "Radix 16 SRT dividers with overlapped quotient selection stages," *Proc. Seventh IEEE Symposium on Computer Arithmetic,* 64–71.

Describes a very sophisticated high-radix division algorithm.

WESTE, N. AND K. ESHRAGHIAN [1993]. *Principles of CMOS VLSI Design: A Systems Perspective,* 2nd ed., Addison-Wesley, Reading, Mass.

This textbook has a section on the layout of various kinds of adders.

WILLIAMS, T. E., M. HOROWITZ, R. L. ALVERSON, AND T. S. YANG [1987]. "A self-timed chip for division," *Advanced Research in VLSI, Proc. 1987 Stanford Conf.,* MIT Press, Cambridge, Mass.

> *Describes a divider that tries to get the speed of a combinational design without using the area that would be required by one.*

E X E R C I S E S

A.1 [12] <A.2> Using *n* bits, what is the largest and smallest integer that can be represented in the two's complement system?

A.2 [20/25] <A.2> In the subsection *Signed Numbers* (page A-7), it was stated that two's complement overflows when the carry into the high-order bit position is different from the carry-out from that position.

a.   [20] <A.2> Give examples of pairs of integers for all four combinations of carry-in and carry-out. Verify the rule stated above.

b.   [25] <A.2> Explain why the rule is always true.

A.3 [12] <A.2> Using 4-bit binary numbers, multiply -8×-8 using Booth recoding.

A.4 [15] <A.2> Equations A.2.1 and A.2.2 are for adding two *n*-bit numbers. Derive similar equations for subtraction, where there will be a borrow instead of a carry.

A.5 [25] <A.2> On a machine that doesn't detect integer overflow in hardware, show how you would detect overflow on a signed addition operation in software.

A.6 [15/15/20] <A.3> Represent the following numbers as single-precision and double-precision IEEE floating-point numbers.

a.   [15] <A.3> 10.

b.   [15] <A.3> 10.5.

c.   [20] <A.3> 0.1.

A.7 [12/12/12/12/12] <A.3> Below is a list of floating-point numbers. In single precision, write down each number in binary, in decimal, and give its representation in IEEE arithmetic.

a.   [12] <A.3> The largest number less than 1.

b.   [12] <A.3> The largest number.

c.   [12] <A.3> The smallest positive normalized number.

d.   [12] <A.3> The largest denormal number.

e.   [12] <A.3> The smallest positive number.

A.8 [15] <A.3> Is the ordering of nonnegative floating-point numbers the same as integers when denormalized numbers are also considered?

A.9 [20] <A.3> Write a program that prints out the bit patterns used to represent floating-point numbers on your favorite computer. What bit pattern is used for NaN?

A.10 [15] <A.4> Using $p = 4$, show how the binary floating-point multiply algorithm computes the product of 1.875×1.875.

A.11 [12/10] <A.4> Concerning the addition of exponents in floating-point multiply:

a. [12] <A.4> What would the hardware that implements the addition of exponents look like?

b. [10] <A.4> If the bias in single precision were 129 instead of 127, would addition be harder or easier to implement?

A.12 [15/12] <A.4> In the discussion of overflow detection for floating-point multiplication, it was stated that (for single precision) you can detect an overflowed exponent by performing exponent addition in a 9-bit adder.

a. [15] <A.4> Give the exact rule for detecting overflow.

b. [12] <A.4> Would overflow detection be any easier if you used a 10-bit adder instead?

A.13 [15/10] <A.4> Floating-point multiplication:

a. [15] <A.4> Construct two single-precision floating-point numbers whose product doesn't overflow until the final rounding step.

b. [10] <A.4> Is there any rounding mode where this phenomenon cannot occur?

A.14 [15] <A.4> Give an example of a product with a denormal operand but a normalized output. How large was the final shifting step? What is the maximum possible shift that can occur when the inputs are double-precision numbers?

A.15 [15] <A.5> Use the floating-point addition algorithm on page A-24 to compute $1.010_2 - .1001_2$ (in 4-bit precision).

A.16 [10/15/20/20/20] <A.5> In certain situations, you can be sure that $a + b$ is exactly representable as a floating-point number, that is, no rounding is necessary.

a. [10] <A.5> If a, b have the same exponent and different signs, explain why $a + b$ is exact. This was used in the subsection *Speeding Up Addition* on page A-27.

b. [15] <A.5> Give an example where the exponents differ by 1, a and b have different signs, and $a + b$ is not exact.

c. [20] <A.5> If $a \geq b \geq 0$, and the top two bits of a cancel when computing $a - b$, explain why the result is exact (this fact is mentioned on page A-23).

d. [20] <A.5> If $a \geq b \geq 0$, and the exponents differ by 1, show that $a - b$ is exact unless the high order bit of $a - b$ is in the same position as that of a (mentioned in *Speeding Up Addition*, page A-27).

e. [20] <A.5> If the result of $a - b$ or $a + b$ is denormal, show that the result is exact (mentioned in the subsection *Underflow*, page A-38).

A.17 [15/20] <A.5> Fast floating-point addition (using parallel adders) for $p = 5$.

a. [15] <A.5> Step through the fast addition algorithm for $a + b$, where $a = 1.0111_2$ and $b = .11011_2$.

b.   [20] <A.5> Suppose the rounding mode is toward $+\infty$. What complication arises in the above example for the adder that assumes a carry-out? Suggest a solution.

A.18 [12] <A.4,A.5> How would you use two parallel adders to avoid the final round-up addition in floating-point multiplication?

A.19 [30/10] <A.5> This problem presents a way to reduce the number of addition steps in floating-point addition from three to two using only a single adder.

a.   [30] <A.5> Let A and B be integers of opposite signs, with a and b be their magnitudes. Show that the following rules for manipulating the unsigned numbers a and b gives $A + B$.

   1.   Complement one of the operands.

   2.   Using end around carry to add the complemented operand and the other (uncomplemented) one.

   3.   If there was a carry-out, the sign of the result is the sign associated with the uncomplemented operand.

   4.   Otherwise, if there was no carry-out, complement the result, and give it the sign of the complemented operand.

b.   [10] <A.5> Use the above to show how steps 2 and 4 in the floating-point addition algorithm can be performed using only a single addition.

A.20 [20/15/20/15/20/15] <A.6> Iterative square root.

a.   [20] <A.6> Use Newton's method to derive an iterative algorithm for square root. The formula will involve a division.

b.   [15] <A.6> What is the fastest way you can think of to divide a floating-point number by 2?

c.   [20] <A.6> If division is slow, then the iterative square root routine will also be slow. Use Newton's method on $f(x) = 1/x^2 - a$ to derive a method that doesn't use any divisions.

d.   [15] <A.6> Assume that the ratio division by 2 : floating-point add : floating-point multiply is 1:2:4. What ratios of multiplication time to divide time makes each iteration step in the method of part(c) faster than each iteration in the method of part(a)?

e.   [20] <A.6> When using the method of part(a), how many bits need to be in the initial guess in order to get double-precision accuracy after three iterations? (You may ignore rounding error.)

f.   [15] <A.6> Suppose that when Spice runs on the TI 8847, it spends 16.7% of its time in the square root routine (this percentage has been measured on other machines). Using the values in Figure A.36 and assuming three iterations, how much slower would Spice run if square root was implemented in software using the method of part(a)?

A.21 [10/20/15/15/15] <A.6> Correctly rounded iterative division. Let a and b be floating-point numbers with p-bit significands ($p = 53$ in double precision). Let q be the exact quotient $q = a/b$, $1 \leq q < 2$. Suppose that $\overline{q}$ is the result of an iteration process, that $\overline{q}$ has a few extra bits of precision, and that $0 < q - \bar{q} < 2^{-p}$. For the following, it is important that $\bar{q} < q$, even when q can be exactly represented as a floating-point number.

a. [10] <A.6> If x is a floating-point number, and $1 \le x < 2$, what is the next representable number after x?

b. [20] <A.6> Show how to compute q' from $\bar{q}$, where q' has $p + 1$ bits of precision and $|q - q'| < 2^{-p}$.

c. [15] <A.6> Assuming round to nearest, show that the correctly rounded quotient is either q', $q' - 2^{-p}$, or $q' + 2^{-p}$.

d. [15] <A.6> Give rules for computing the correctly rounded quotient from q' based on the low-order bit of q' and the sign of $a - bq'$.

e. [15] <A.6> Solve part(c) for the other three rounding modes.

A.22 [15] <A.6> Verify the formula on page A-31. [*Hint:* If $x_n = x_0(2 - x_0 b) \times \prod_{i=1,n} [1 + (1 - x_0 b)^{2^i}]$, then $2 - x_n b = 2 - x_0 b(2 - x_0 b) \prod [1 + (1 - x_0 b)^{2^i}] = 2 - [1 - (1 - x_0 b)^2] \prod [1 + (1 - x_0 b)^{2^i}]$.]

A.23 [15] <A.7> Our example that showed that double rounding can give a different answer from rounding once used the round-to-even rule. If halfway cases are always rounded up, is double rounding still dangerous?

A.24 [10/10/20/20] <A.7> Some of the cases of the italicized statement in the *Precisions* subsection (page A-34) aren't hard to demonstrate.

a. [10] <A.7> What form must a binary number have if rounding to q bits followed by rounding to p bits gives a different answer than rounding directly to p bits?

b. [10] <A.7> Show that for multiplication of p-bit numbers, rounding to q bits followed by rounding to p bits is the same as rounding immediately to p bits if $q \ge 2p$.

c. [20] <A.7> If a and b are p-bit numbers with the same sign, show that rounding $a + b$ to q bits followed by a rounding to p bits is the same as rounding immediately to p bits if $q \ge 2p + 1$.

d. [20] <A.7> Do part (c) when a and b have opposite signs.

A.25 [Discussion] <A.7> In the MIPS approach to exception handling, you need a test for determining whether two floating-point operands could cause an exception. This should be fast and also not have too many false positives. Can you come up with a practical test? The performance cost of your design will depend on the distribution of floating-point numbers. This is discussed in Knuth [1981] and the Hamming paper in Swartzlander [1990].

A.26 [12/12/10] <A.8> Carry-skip adders.

a. [12] <A.8> Assuming that time is proportional to logic levels, how long does it take an n-bit adder divided into (fixed) blocks of length k bits to perform an addition?

b. [12] <A.8> What value of k gives the fastest adder?

c. [10] <A.8> Explain why the carry-skip adder takes time $0(\sqrt{n})$.

A.27 [10/15/20] <A.8> Complete the details of the block diagrams for the following adders.

a.　[10] <A.8> In Figure A.15, show how to implement the "1" and "2" boxes in terms of AND and OR gates.

b.　[15] <A.8> In Figure A.18, what signals need to flow from the adder cells in the top row into the "C" cells? Write the logic equations for the "C" box.

c.　[20] <A.8> Show how to extend the block diagram in A.17 so it will produce the carry-out bit c_8.

A.28 [15] <A.9> For ordinary Booth recoding, the multiple of b used in the ith step is simply $a_{i-1} - a_i$. Can you find a similar formula for radix-4 Booth recoding (overlapped triplets)?

A.29 [20] <A.9> Expand Figure A.29 in the fashion of A.27, showing the individual adders.

A.30 [25] <A.9> Write out the analogue of Figure A.25 for radix-8 Booth recoding.

A.31 [18] <A.9> Suppose that $a_{n-1}\ldots a_1 a_0$ and $b_{n-1}\ldots b_1 b_0$ are being added in a signed-digit adder as illustrated in the Example on page A-56. Write a formula for the ith bit of the sum, s_i, in terms of a_i, a_{i-1}, a_{i-2}, b_i, b_{i-1}, and b_{i-2}.

A.32 [15] <A.9> The text discussed radix-4 SRT division with quotient digits of $-2, -1, 0, 1, 2$. Suppose that 3 and -3 are also allowed as quotient digits. What relation replaces $|r_i| \leq 2b/3$?

A.33 [25/20/30] <A.9> Concerning the SRT division table, Figure A.34:

a.　[25] <A.9> Write a program to generate the results of Figure A.34.

b.　[20] <A.9> Note that Figure A.34 has a certain symmetry with respect to positive and negative values of P. Can you find a way to exploit the symmetry and only store the values for positive P?

c.　[30] <A.9> Suppose a carry-save adder is used instead of a propagate adder. The input to the quotient lookup table will be k bits of divisor, and l bits of remainder, where the remainder bits are computed by summing the top l bits of the sum and carry registers. What are k and l? Write a program to generate the analogue of Figure A.34.

A.34 [12/12/12]<A.9,A.12>The first several million Pentium chips produced had a flaw that caused division to sometimes return the wrong result. The Pentium uses a radix-4 SRT algorithm similar to the one illustrated in the Example on page A-59 (but with the remainder stored in carry-save format: see Exercise A.33(c)). According to Intel, the bug was due to five incorrect entries in the quotient lookup table.

a.　[12] <A.9,A.12> The bad entries should have had a quotient of plus or minus 2, but instead had a quotient of 0. Because of redundancy, it's conceivable that the algorithm could "recover" from a bad quotient digit on later iterations. Show that this is not possible for the Pentium flaw.

b.   [12] <A.9,A.12> Since the operation is a floating-point divide rather than an integer divide, the SRT division algorithm on page A-47 must be modified in two ways. First, step 1 is no longer needed, since the divisor is already normalized. Second, the very first remainder may not satisfy the proper bound ($|r| \leq 2b/3$ for Pentium, see page A-58). Show that skipping the very first left shift in step 2(a) of the SRT algorithm will solve this problem.

c.   [12] <A.9,A.12> If the faulty table entries were indexed by a remainder that could occur at the very first divide step (when the remainder is the divisor), random testing would quickly reveal the bug. This didn't happen. What does that tell you about the remainder values that index the faulty entries?

A.35 [12/12/12] <A.6,A.9> The discussion of the remainder-step instruction assumed that division was done using a bit-at-a-time algorithm. What would have to change if division were implemented using a higher-radix method?

A.36 [25] <A.9> In the array of Figure A.28, the fact that an array can be pipelined is not exploited. Can you come up with a design that feeds the output of the bottom CSA into the bottom CSAs instead of the top one, and that will run faster than the arrangement of Figure A.28?

instructions per clock. This obstacle is one reason that it has been difficult to build processors with high clock rates and very high issue rates.

The dual limitations imposed by deeper pipelines and issuing multiple instructions can be viewed from the standpoint of either clock rate or CPI: It is just as difficult to schedule a pipeline that is n times deeper as it is to schedule a processor that issues n instructions per clock cycle.

High-speed, pipelined processors are particularly useful for large scientific and engineering applications. A high-speed pipelined processor will usually use a cache to avoid forcing memory reference instructions to have very long latency. Unfortunately, big, long-running, scientific programs often have very large active data sets that are sometimes accessed with low locality, yielding poor performance from the memory hierarchy. This problem could be overcome by not caching these structures if it were possible to determine the memory-access patterns and pipeline the memory accesses efficiently. Novel cache architectures and compiler assistance through blocking and prefetching are decreasing these memory hierarchy problems, but they continue to be serious in some applications.

Vector processors provide high-level operations that work on *vectors*—linear arrays of numbers. A typical vector operation might add two 64-element, floating-point vectors to obtain a single 64-element vector result. The vector instruction is equivalent to an entire loop, with each iteration computing one of the 64 elements of the result, updating the indices, and branching back to the beginning.

Vector instructions have several important properties that solve most of the problems mentioned above:

- The computation of each result is independent of the computation of previous results, allowing a very deep pipeline *without* generating any data hazards. Essentially, the absence of data hazards was determined by the compiler or by the programmer when she decided that a vector instruction could be used.

- A single vector instruction specifies a great deal of work—it is equivalent to executing an entire loop. Thus, the instruction bandwidth requirement is reduced, and the Flynn bottleneck is considerably mitigated.

- Vector instructions that access memory have a known access pattern. If the vector's elements are all adjacent, then fetching the vector from a set of heavily interleaved memory banks works very well (as we saw in section 5.6). The high latency of initiating a main memory access versus accessing a cache is amortized, because a single access is initiated for the entire vector rather than to a single word. Thus, the cost of the latency to main memory is seen only once for the entire vector, rather than once for each word of the vector.

- Because an entire loop is replaced by a vector instruction whose behavior is predetermined, control hazards that would normally arise from the loop branch are nonexistent.

For these reasons, vector operations can be made faster than a sequence of scalar operations on the same number of data items, and designers are motivated to include vector units if the applications domain can use them frequently.

As mentioned above, vector processors pipeline the operations on the individual elements of a vector. The pipeline includes not only the arithmetic operations (multiplication, addition, and so on), but also memory accesses and effective address calculations. In addition, most high-end vector processors allow multiple vector operations to be done at the same time, creating parallelism among the operations on different elements. In this appendix, we focus on vector processors that gain performance by pipelining and instruction overlap.

B.2 | Basic Vector Architecture

A vector processor typically consists of an ordinary pipelined scalar unit plus a vector unit. All functional units within the vector unit have a latency of several clock cycles. This allows a shorter clock cycle time and is compatible with long-running vector operations that can be deeply pipelined without generating hazards. Most vector processors allow the vectors to be dealt with as floating-point numbers, as integers, or as logical data. Here we will focus on floating point. The scalar unit is basically no different from the type of advanced pipelined CPU discussed in Chapter 3.

There are two primary types of architectures for vector processors: *vector-register processors* and *memory-memory vector processors*. In a vector-register processor, all vector operations—except load and store—are among the vector registers. These architectures are the vector counterpart of a load-store architecture. All major vector computers shipped since the late 1980s use a vector-register architecture; these include the Cray Research processors (CRAY-1, CRAY-2, X-MP, Y-MP, and C-90), the Japanese supercomputers (NEC SX/2 and SX/3, Fujitsu VP200 and VP400, and the Hitachi S820), as well as the mini-supercomputers (Convex C-1 and C-2). In a memory-memory vector processor, all vector operations are memory to memory. The first vector computers were of this type, as were CDC's vector computers. From this point on we will focus on vector-register architectures only; we will briefly return to memory-memory vector architectures at the end of the appendix (section B.7) to discuss why they have not been as successful as vector-register architectures.

We begin with a vector-register processor consisting of the primary components shown in Figure B.1. This processor, which is loosely based on the CRAY-1, is the foundation for discussion throughout most of this appendix. We will call it DLXV; its integer portion is DLX, and its vector portion is the logical vector extension of DLX. The rest of this section examines how the basic architecture of DLXV relates to other processors.

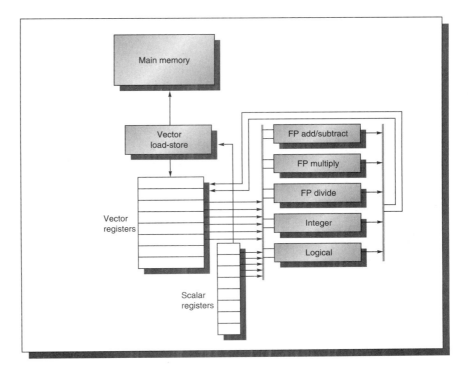

FIGURE B.1   The basic structure of a vector-register architecture, DLXV. This processor has a scalar architecture just like DLX. There are also eight 64-element vector registers, and all the functional units are vector functional units. Special vector instructions are defined both for arithmetic and for memory accesses. We show vector units for logical and integer operations. These are included so that DLXV looks like a standard vector processor, which usually includes these units. However, we will not be discussing these units except in the Exercises. The vector and scalar registers have a significant number of read and write ports to allow multiple simultaneous vector operations. These ports are connected to the inputs and outputs of the vector functional units by a set of crossbars (shown in thick gray lines). In section B.5 we add chaining, which will require additional interconnect capability.

The primary components of the instruction set architecture of DLXV are

■ *Vector registers*—Each vector register is a fixed-length bank holding a single vector. DLXV has eight vector registers, and each vector register holds 64 elements. Each vector register must have at least two read ports and one write port in DLXV. This will allow a high degree of overlap among vector operations to different vector registers. (We do not consider the problem of a shortage of vector register ports. In real machines this would result in a structural hazard.) The read and write ports, which total at least 16 read ports and eight write ports, are connected to the functional unit inputs or outputs by a pair of crossbars. (The CRAY-1 manages to implement the register file with only a single port per register using some clever implementation techniques.)

- *Vector functional units*—Each unit is fully pipelined and can start a new operation on every clock cycle. A control unit is needed to detect hazards, both from conflicts for the functional units (structural hazards) and from conflicts for register accesses (data hazards). DLXV has five functional units, as shown in Figure B.1. For simplicity, we will focus exclusively on the floating-point functional units. Depending on the vector processor, scalar operations either use the vector functional units or use a dedicated set. We assume the functional units are shared, but again, for simplicity, we ignore potential conflicts.

- *Vector load-store unit*—This is a vector memory unit that loads or stores a vector to or from memory. The DLXV vector loads and stores are fully pipelined, so that words can be moved between the vector registers and memory with a bandwidth of one word per clock cycle, after an initial latency. This unit would also normally handle scalar loads and stores.

- *A set of scalar registers*—Scalar registers can also provide data as input to the vector functional units, as well as compute addresses to pass to the vector load-store unit. These are the normal 32 general-purpose registers and 32 floating-point registers of DLX, though more read and write ports are needed. The scalar registers are also connected to the functional units by the pair of crossbars.

Figure B.2 shows the characteristics of some typical vector processors, including the size and count of the registers, the number and types of functional units, and the number of load-store units.

In DLXV, vector operations use the same names as DLX operations, but with the letter "V" appended. These are double-precision, floating-point vector operations. (We have omitted single-precision FP operations and integer and logical operations for simplicity.) Thus, ADDV is an add of two double-precision vectors. The vector instructions take as their input either a pair of vector registers (ADDV) or a vector register and a scalar register, designated by appending "SV" (ADDSV). In the latter case, the value in the scalar register is used as the input for all operations—the operation ADDSV will add the contents of a scalar register to each element in a vector register. Most vector operations have a vector destination register, though a few (population count) produce a scalar value, which is stored to a scalar register. The names LV and SV denote vector load and vector store, and they load or store an entire vector of double-precision data. One operand is the vector register to be loaded or stored; the other operand, which is a DLX general-purpose register, is the starting address of the vector in memory. Figure B.3 lists the DLXV vector instructions. In addition to the vector registers, we need two additional special-purpose registers: the vector-length and vector-mask registers. We will discuss these registers and their purpose in sections B.3 and B.5, respectively.

Processor	Year announced	Clock rate (MHz)	Registers	Elements per register (64-bit elements)	Functional units	Load-store units
CRAY-1	1976	80	8	64	6: add, multiply, reciprocal, integer add, logical, shift	1
CRAY X-MP CRAY Y-MP	1983 1988	120 166	8	64	8: FP add, FP multiply, FP reciprocal, integer add, 2 logical, shift, population count/parity	2 loads 1 store
CRAY-2	1985	166	8	64	5: FP add, FP multiply, FP reciprocal/sqrt, integer (add shift, population count), logical	1
Fujitsu VP100/200	1982	133	8–256	32–1024	3: FP or integer add/logical, multiply, divide	2
Hitachi S810/820	1983	71	32	256	4: 2 integer add/logical, 1 multiply-add, and 1 multiply/divide–add unit	4
Convex C-1	1985	10	8	128	4: multiply, add, divide, integer/logical	1
NEC SX/2	1984	160	8 + 8192	256 variable	16: 4 integer add/logical, 4 FP multiply/divide, 4 FP add, 4 shift	8
DLXV	1990	200	8	64	5: multiply, divide, add, integer add, logical	1
Cray C-90	1991	240	8	128	8: FP add, FP multiply, FP reciprocal, integer add, 2 logical, shift, population count/parity	4
Convex C-4	1994	135	16	128	3: each is full integer, logical, and FP (including multiply-add)	
NEC SX/4	1995	400	8 + 8192	256 variable	16: 4 integer add/logical, 4 FP multiply/divide, 4 FP add, 4 shift	8
Cray J-90	1995	100	8	64	4: FP add, FP multiply, FP reciprocal, integer/logical	
Cray T-90	1996	~500	8	128	8: FP add, FP multiply, FP reciprocal, integer add, 2 logical, shift, population count/parity	4

FIGURE B.2   Characteristics of several vector-register architectures. The vector functional units include all operation units used by the vector instructions. The functional units are floating point unless stated otherwise. If the processor is a multiprocessor, the entries correspond to the characteristics of one processor. Each vector load-store unit represents the ability to do an independent, overlapped transfer to or from the vector registers. The Fujitsu VP200's vector registers are configurable: The size and count of the 8 K 64-bit entries may be varied inversely to one another (e.g., eight registers each 1 K elements long, or 128 registers each 64 elements long). The NEC SX/2 has eight fixed registers of length 256, plus 8 K of configurable 64-bit registers. The reciprocal unit on the CRAY processors is used to do division (and square root on the CRAY-2). Add pipelines perform floating-point add and subtract. The multiply/divide–add unit on the Hitachi S810/820 performs an FP multiply or divide followed by an add or subtract (while the multiply-add unit performs a multiply followed by an add or subtract). Note that most processors use the vector FP multiply and divide units for vector integer multiply and divide, just like DLX, and several of the processors use the same units for FP scalar and FP vector operations. Several of the machines have different clock rates in the vector and scalar units; the clock rates shown are for the vector units.

Instruction	Operands	Function
ADDV ADDSV	V1,V2,V3 V1,F0,V2	Add elements of V2 and V3, then put each result in V1. Add F0 to each element of V2, then put each result in V1.
SUBV SUBVS SUBSV	V1,V2,V3 V1,V2,F0 V1,F0,V2	Subtract elements of V3 from V2, then put each result in V1. Subtract F0 from elements of V2, then put each result in V1. Subtract elements of V2 from F0, then put each result in V1.
MULTV MULTSV	V1,V2,V3 V1,F0,V2	Multiply elements of V2 and V3, then put each result in V1. Multiply F0 by each element of V2, then put each result in V1.
DIVV DIVVS DIVSV	V1,V2,V3 V1,V2,F0 V1,F0,V2	Divide elements of V2 by V3, then put each result in V1. Divide elements of V2 by F0, then put each result in V1. Divide F0 by elements of V2, then put each result in V1.
LV	V1,R1	Load vector register V1 from memory starting at address R1.
SV	R1,V1	Store vector register V1 into memory starting at address R1.
LVWS	V1,(R1,R2)	Load V1 from address at R1 with stride in R2, i.e., R1+i × R2.
SVWS	(R1,R2),V1	Store V1 from address at R1 with stride in R2, i.e., R1+i × R2.
LVI	V1,(R1+V2)	Load V1 with vector whose elements are at R1+V2 (i), i.e., V2 is an index.
SVI	(R1+V2),V1	Store V1 to vector whose elements are at R1+V2 (i), i.e., V2 is an index.
CVI	V1,R1	Create an index vector by storing the values 0, 1 × R1, 2 × R1, ..., 63 × R1 into V1.
S--V S--SV	V1,V2 F0,V1	Compare the elements (EQ, NE, GT, LT, GE, LE) in V1 and V2. If condition is true, put a 1 in the corresponding bit vector; otherwise put 0. Put resulting bit vector in vector-mask register (VM). The instruction S--SV performs the same compare but using a scalar value as one operand.
POP	R1,VM	Count the 1s in the vector-mask register and store count in R1.
CVM		Set the vector-mask register to all 1s.
MOVI2S MOVS2I	VLR,R1 R1,VLR	Move contents of R1 to the vector-length register. Move the contents of the vector-length register to R1.
MOVF2S MOVS2F	VM,F0 F0,VM	Move contents of F0 to the vector-mask register. Move contents of vector-mask register to F0.

FIGURE B.3   The DLXV vector instructions. Only the double-precision FP operations are shown. In addition to the vector registers, there are two special registers, VLR (discussed in section B.3) and VM (discussed in section B.5). The operations with stride are explained in section B.3, and the use of the index creation and indexed load-store operations are explained in section B.5.

A vector processor is best understood by looking at a vector loop on DLXV. Let's take a typical vector problem, which will be used throughout this appendix:

$$Y = a \times X + Y$$

X and Y are vectors, initially resident in memory, and a is a scalar. This is the so-called *SAXPY* or *DAXPY* loop that forms the inner loop of the Linpack benchmark. (SAXPY stands for single-precision a × X plus Y; DAXPY for double-precision a × X plus Y.) Linpack is a collection of linear algebra routines, and the routines for performing Gaussian elimination constitute what is known as the Linpack benchmark. The DAXPY routine, which implements the above loop, represents a small fraction of the source code of the Linpack benchmark, but it accounts for most of the execution time for the benchmark.

For now, let us assume that the number of elements, or length, of a vector register (64) matches the length of the vector operation we are interested in. (This restriction will be lifted shortly.)

EXAMPLE   Show the code for DLX and DLXV for the DAXPY loop. Assume that the starting addresses of X and Y are in Rx and Ry, respectively.

ANSWER   Here is the DLX code.

```
        LD      F0,a
        ADDI    R4,Rx,#512   ;last address to load
Loop:   LD      F2,0(Rx)     ;load X(i)
        MULTD   F2,F0,F2     ;a x X(i)
        LD      F4,0(Ry)     ;load Y(i)
        ADDD    F4,F2,F4     ;a x X(i) + Y(i)
        SD      0(Ry),F4     ;store into Y(i)
        ADDI    Rx,Rx,#8     ;increment index to X
        ADDI    Ry,Ry,#8     ;increment index to Y
        SUB     R20,R4,Rx    ;compute bound
        BNEZ    R20,Loop     ;check if done
```

Here is the code for DLXV for DAXPY.

```
        LD      F0,a         ;load scalar a
        LV      V1,Rx        ;load vector X
        MULTSV  V2,F0,V1     ;vector-scalar multiply
        LV      V3,Ry        ;load vector Y
        ADDV    V4,V2,V3     ;add
        SV      Ry,V4        ;store the result
```

There are some interesting comparisons between the two code segments in this Example. The most dramatic is that the vector processor greatly reduces the dynamic instruction bandwidth, executing only six instructions versus almost 600 for DLX. This reduction occurs both because the vector operations work on 64 elements and because the overhead instructions that constitute nearly half the loop on DLX are not present in the DLXV code.   ∎

Another important difference is the frequency of pipeline interlocks. In the straightforward DLX code every ADDD must wait for a MULTD, and every SD must wait for the ADDD. On the vector processor, each vector instruction operates on all the vector elements independently. Thus, pipeline stalls are required only once per vector operation, rather than once per vector element. In this example, the pipeline-stall frequency on DLX will be about 64 times higher than it is on DLXV. The pipeline stalls can be eliminated on DLX by using software pipelining or loop unrolling (as we saw in Chapter 4). However, the large difference in instruction bandwidth cannot be reduced.

Vector Execution Time

The execution time of a sequence of vector operations primarily depends on three factors: the length of the vectors being operated on, structural hazards among the operations, and the data dependences. Given the vector length and the *initiation rate*, which is the rate at which a vector unit consumes new operands and produces new results, we can compute the time for a single vector instruction. The initiation rate is usually one per clock cycle for individual operations. However, some supercomputers have vector instructions that can produce two or more results per clock, and others have units that may not be fully pipelined. For simplicity, we assume that initiation rates are one throughout this appendix. Thus, the execution time for a single vector instruction is approximately the vector length.

To simplify the discussion of vector execution and its timing, we will use the notion of a *convoy*, which is the set of vector instructions that could potentially begin execution together in one clock period. (Although the concept of a convoy is used in vector compilers, no standard terminology exists. Hence, we created the term *convoy*.) The instructions in a convoy *must not* contain any structural or data hazards (though we will relax this later); if such hazards were present, the instructions in the potential convoy would need to be serialized and initiated in different convoys. To keep the analysis simple, we assume that a convoy of instructions must complete execution before any other instructions (scalar or vector) can begin execution. We will relax this in section B.6 by using a less restrictive, but more complex, method for issuing instructions.

Accompanying the notion of a convoy is a timing metric, called a *chime*, that can be used for estimating the performance of a vector sequence consisting of convoys. A chime is an approximate measure of execution time for a vector sequence; a chime measurement is independent of vector length. Thus, a vector sequence that consists of m convoys executes in m chimes, and for a vector length of n, this is approximately $m \times n$ clock cycles. A chime approximation ignores some processor-specific overheads, many of which are dependent on vector length. Hence, measuring time in chimes is a better approximation for long vectors. We will use the chime measurement, rather than clock cycles per result, to explicitly indicate that certain overheads are being ignored.

If we know the number of convoys in a vector sequence, we know the execution time in chimes. One source of overhead ignored in measuring chimes is any limitation on initiating multiple vector instructions in a clock cycle. If only one vector instruction can be initiated in a clock cycle (the reality in most vector processors), the chime count will underestimate the actual execution time of a convoy. Because the vector length is typically much greater than the number of instructions in the convoy, we will simply assume that the convoy executes in one chime.

EXAMPLE   Show how the following code sequence lays out in convoys, assuming a single copy of each vector functional unit:

```
LV          V1,Rx        ;load vector X
MULTSV      V2,F0,V1     ;vector-scalar multiply
LV          V3,Ry        ;load vector Y
ADDV        V4,V2,V3     ;add
SV          Ry,V4        ;store the result
```

How many chimes will this vector sequence take? How many chimes per FLOP (floating-point operation) are needed?

ANSWER   The first convoy is occupied by the first LV instruction. The MULTSV is dependent on the first LV, so it cannot be in the same convoy. The second LV instruction can be in the same convoy as the MULTSV. The ADDV is dependent on the second LV, so it must come in yet a third convoy, and finally the SV depends on the ADDV, so it must go in a following convoy. This leads to the following layout of vector instructions into convoys:

1. LV

2. MULTSV   LV

3. ADDV

4. SV

The sequence requires four convoys and hence takes four chimes. Note that although we allow the MULTSV and the LV both to execute in convoy 2, most vector machines will take two clock cycles to initiate the instructions. Since the sequence takes a total of four chimes and there are two floating-point operations per result, the number of chimes per FLOP is two.   ■

The chime approximation is reasonably accurate for long vectors. For example, for 64-element vectors, the time in chimes is four, so the sequence would take about 256 clock cycles. The overhead of issuing convoy 2 in two separate clocks would be small.

Another source of overhead is far more significant than the issue limitation. The most important source of overhead ignored by the chime model is vector *start-up time*. The start-up time comes from the pipelining latency of the vector operation and is principally determined by how deep the pipeline is for the functional unit used. The start-up time increases the effective time to execute a convoy to more than one chime. Because of our assumption that convoys do not overlap in time, the start-up time delays the execution of subsequent convoys. Of course the instructions in successive convoys have either structural conflicts for some functional unit or are data dependent, so the assumption of no overlap is reasonable. The actual time to complete a convoy is determined by the sum of the vector length and the start-up time. If vector lengths were infinite, this start-up overhead would be amortized, but finite vector lengths expose it, as the following Example shows.

EXAMPLE Assume the start-up overhead for functional units is shown in Figure B.4.

Unit	Start-up overhead
Load and store unit	12 cycles
Multiply unit	7 cycles
Add unit	6 cycles

FIGURE B.4 Start-up overhead.

Show the time that each convoy can begin and the total number of cycles needed. How does the time compare to the chime approximation for a vector of length 64?

ANSWER Figure B.5 provides the answer in convoys, assuming that the vector length is n:

Convoy	Starting time	First-result time	Last-result time
1. LV	0	12	$11 + n$
2. MULTSV LV	$12 + n$	$12 + n + 12$	$23 + 2n$
3. ADDV	$24 + 2n$	$24 + 2n + 6$	$29 + 3n$
4. SV	$30 + 3n$	$30 + 3n - 12$	$41 + 4n$

FIGURE B.5 Starting times and first- and last-result times for convoys 1 through 4. The vector length is n.

One tricky question is when we assume the vector sequence is done; this determines whether the start-up time of the SV is visible or not. We assume that the instructions following cannot fit in the same convoy, and we have already assumed that convoys do not overlap. Thus the total time is given by the time until the last vector instruction in the last convoy completes. This is an approximation, and the start-up time of the last vector instruction may be seen in some sequences and not in others. For simplicity, we always include it.

The time per result for a vector of length 64 is $4 + (42/64) = 4.65$ clock cycles, while the chime approximation would be 4. The execution time with start-up overhead is 1.16 times higher. ∎

For simplicity, we will use the chime approximation for running time, incorporating start-up time effects only when we want more detailed performance or to illustrate the benefits of some enhancement. For long vectors, a typical situation, the overhead effect is not that large. Later in the appendix we will explore ways to reduce start-up overhead.

Start-up time for an instruction comes from the pipeline depth for the functional unit implementing that instruction. If the initiation rate is to be kept at one clock cycle per result, then

$$\text{Pipeline depth} = \left\lceil \frac{\text{Total functional unit time}}{\text{Clock cycle time}} \right\rceil$$

For example, if an operation takes 10 clock cycles, it must be pipelined 10 deep to achieve an initiation rate of one per clock cycle. Pipeline depth, then, is determined by the complexity of the operation and the clock cycle time of the processor. The pipeline depths of functional units vary widely—from two to 20 stages is not uncommon—though the most heavily used units have pipeline depths of four to eight clock cycles.

For DLXV, we will use the same pipeline depths as the CRAY-1, though more modern processors might have units with lower latency. All functional units are fully pipelined. As shown in Figure B.6, pipeline depths are six clock cycles for floating-point add and seven clock cycles for floating-point multiply. On DLXV, as on most vector processors, independent vector operations using different functional units can issue in the same convoy.

Operation	Start-up penalty
Vector add	6
Vector multiply	7
Vector divide	20
Vector load	12

FIGURE B.6   **Start-up penalties on DLXV.** These are the start-up penalties in clock cycles for DLXV vector operations.

Vector Load-Store Units and Vector Memory Systems

The behavior of the load-store vector unit is significantly more complicated than that of the arithmetic functional units. The start-up time for a load is the time to get the first word from memory into a register. If the rest of the vector can be supplied without stalling, then the vector initiation rate is equal to the rate at which new words are fetched or stored. Unlike simpler functional units, the initiation rate may not necessarily be one clock cycle.

Typically, penalties for start-ups on load-store units are higher than those for arithmetic functional units—up to 50 clock cycles on some processors. For DLXV we will assume a start-up time of 12 clock cycles; by comparison, the CRAY-1 and CRAY X-MP have load-store start-up times of between nine and 17 clock cycles. Figure B.6 summarizes the start-up penalties for DLXV vector operations.

To maintain an initiation rate of one word fetched or stored per clock, the memory system must be capable of producing or accepting this much data. This is usually done by creating multiple memory banks, as discussed in section 5.6. As we will see in the next section, having significant numbers of banks is useful for dealing with vector loads or stores that access rows or columns of data.

Most vector processors use memory banks rather than simple interleaving for two primary reasons:

1. Many vector computers support multiple loads or stores per clock. To support multiple simultaneous accesses, the memory system needs to have multiple banks and be able to control the addresses to the banks independently.

2. As we will see in the next section, many vector processors support the ability to load or store data words that are not sequential. In such cases, independent bank addressing, rather than interleaving, is required.

In Chapter 5 we saw that the desired access rate and the bank access time determined how many banks were needed to access a memory without a stall. The next Example shows how these timings work out in a vector processor.

EXAMPLE Suppose we want to fetch a vector of 64 elements starting at byte address 136, and a memory access takes six clocks. How many memory banks must we have? With what addresses are the banks accessed? When will the various elements arrive at the CPU?

ANSWER Six clocks per access require at least six banks, but because we want the number of banks to be a power of two, we choose to have eight banks. Figure B.7 shows what byte addresses each bank accesses within each time period. Remember that a bank begins a new access as soon as it has completed the old access.

Beginning at clock no.	Bank							
	0	1	2	3	4	5	6	7
0	192	136	144	152	160	168	176	184
6	256	200	208	216	224	232	240	248
14	320	264	272	280	288	296	304	312
22	384	328	336	344	352	360	368	376

FIGURE B.7 Memory addresses (in bytes) by bank number and time slot at which access begins. The exact time when a bank transmits its data is given by the address it accesses minus the starting address, divided by eight, plus the memory latency (six clocks). It is important to observe that bank 0 accesses a word in the next block (i.e., it accesses 192 rather than 128 and then 256 rather than 192, and so on). If bank 0 were to start at the lower address, we would require an extra cycle to transmit the data, and we would transmit one value unnecessarily. While this problem is not severe for this example, if we had 64 banks, up to 63 unnecessary clock cycles and transfers could occur. The fact that bank 0 does not access a word in the same block of eight distinguishes this type of memory system from interleaved memory. Normally, interleaved memory systems combine the bank address and the base starting address by concatenation rather than addition. Also, interleaved memories are almost always implemented with synchronized access. Memory banks require address latches for each bank, which are not normally needed in a system with only interleaving. This timing diagram is drawn as if all banks access in clock 0, clock 16, etc. In practice, since the bus allocations needed to return the words are staggered, the actual accesses are often staggered.

Figure B.8 shows the timing for the first few sets of accesses for an eight-bank system with a six-clock-cycle access latency. There are two important observations about Figures B.7 and B.8: First, notice that the exact address fetched by a bank is largely determined by the lower-order bits in the bank number; however, the initial access to a bank is always within eight double words of the starting address. Second, notice that once the initial latency is overcome (six clocks in this case), the pattern is to access a bank every n clock cycles, where n is the total number of banks ($n = 8$ in this case).

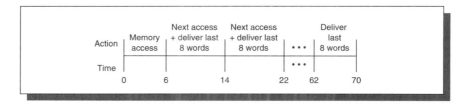

FIGURE B.8 Access timing for the first 64 double-precision words of the load. After the six-clock-cycle initial latency, eight double-precision words are returned every eight clock cycles.

The number of banks in the memory system and the pipeline depth in the functional units are essentially counterparts, since they determine the initiation rates for operations using these units. The processor cannot access a memory bank faster than the memory cycle time. Thus, if memory is built from DRAM, where the memory cycle time is about twice the access time, the processor needs twice as many banks as the above Example shows. For memory systems that support multiple simultaneous vector accesses or allow nonsequential accesses in vector loads or stores, the number of memory banks should be larger than the minimum, otherwise, memory bank conflicts will exist. We explore this in more detail in the next section.

B.3 | Two Real-World Issues: Vector Length and Stride

This section deals with two issues that arise in real programs: What do you do when the vector length in a program is not exactly 64? How do you deal with nonadjacent elements in vectors that reside in memory? First, let's consider the issue of vector length.

Vector-Length Control

A vector-register processor has a natural vector length determined by the number of elements in each vector register. This length, which is 64 for DLXV, is unlikely to match the real vector length in a program. Moreover, in a real program the length of a particular vector operation is often unknown at compile time. In fact, a single piece of code may require different vector lengths. For example, consider this code:

```
        do 10 i = 1,n
10      Y(i) = a * X(i) + Y(i)
```

The size of all the vector operations depends on n, which may not even be known until runtime! The value of n might also be a parameter to a procedure containing the above loop and therefore be subject to change during execution.

The solution to these problems is to create a *vector-length register* (VLR). The VLR controls the length of any vector operation, including a vector load or store The value in the VLR, however, cannot be greater than the length of the vector registers. This solves our problem as long as the real length is less than the *maximum vector length* (MVL) defined by the processor.

What if the value of n is not known at compile time, and thus may be greater than MVL? To tackle the second problem where the vector is longer than the maximum length, a technique called *strip mining* is used. Strip mining is the generation of code such that each vector operation is done for a size less than or equal to the MVL. We could strip-mine the loop in the same manner that we un-rolled loops in Chapter 4: Create one loop that handles any number of iterations that is a multiple of MVL and another loop that handles any remaining iterations, which must be less than MVL. In practice, compilers usually create a single strip-mined loop that is parameterized to handle both portions by changing the length. The strip-mined version of the DAXPY loop written in FORTRAN, the major language used for scientific applications, is shown with C-style comments:

```
      low = 1
      VL = (n mod MVL) /*find the odd size piece*/
      do 1 j = 0,(n / MVL) /*outer loop*/
          do 10 i = low, low+VL-1 /*runs for length VL*/
              Y(i) = a*X(i) + Y(i) /*main operation*/
10        continue
          low = low+VL /*start of next vector*/
          VL = MVL /*reset the length to max*/
1     continue
```

The term `n/MVL` represents truncating integer division (which is what FOR-TRAN does) and is used throughout this section. The effect of this loop is to block the vector into segments which are then processed by the inner loop. The length of the first segment is (n mod MVL) and all subsequent segments are of length MVL. This is depicted in Figure B.9.

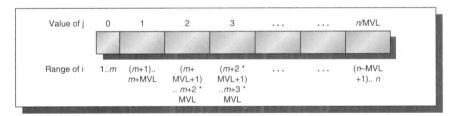

FIGURE B.9   A vector of arbitrary length processed with strip mining. All blocks but the first are of length MVL, utilizing the full power of the vector processor. In this figure, the variable *m* is used for the expression (n mod MVL).

The inner loop of the code above is vectorizable with length VL, which is equal to either (n mod MVL) or MVL. The VLR register must be set twice—once at each place where the variable VL in the code is assigned. With multiple vector operations executing in parallel, the hardware must copy the value of VLR when a vector operation issues, in case VLR is changed for a subsequent vector operation.

In addition to the start-up overhead, we need to account for the overhead of executing the strip-mined loop. This strip-mining overhead, which arises from the need to reinitiate the vector sequence and set the VLR, effectively adds to the vector start-up time, assuming that a convoy does not overlap with other instructions. If that overhead for a convoy is 10 cycles, then the effective overhead per 64 elements increases by 10 cycles, or 0.15 cycles per element.

There are two key factors that contribute to the running time of a strip-mined loop consisting of a sequence of convoys:

1. The number of convoys in the loop, which determines the number of chimes. We use the notation T_{chime} for the execution time in chimes.

2. The overhead for each strip-mined sequence of convoys. This overhead consists of the cost of executing the scalar code for strip mining each block, T_{loop}, plus the vector start-up cost for each convoy, T_{start}.

There may also be a fixed overhead associated with setting up the vector sequence the first time. In recent vector processors this overhead has become quite small, so we ignore it.

The components can be used to state the total running time for a vector sequence operating on a vector of length n, which we will call T_n:

$$T_n = \left\lceil \frac{n}{MVL} \right\rceil \times (T_{loop} + T_{start}) + n \times T_{chime}$$

The values of T_{start}, T_{loop}, and T_{chime} are compiler and processor dependent. The register allocation and scheduling of the instructions affect both what goes in a convoy and the start-up overhead of each convoy.

For simplicity, we will use a constant value for T_{loop} on DLXV. Based on a variety of measurements of CRAY-1 vector execution, the value chosen is 15 for T_{loop}. At first glance, you might think that this value is too small. The overhead in each loop requires setting up the vector starting addresses and the strides, incrementing counters, and executing a loop branch. In practice, these scalar instructions can be totally or partially overlapped with the vector instructions, minimizing the time spent on these overhead functions. The value of T_{loop} of course depends on the loop structure, but the dependence is slight compared with the connection between the vector code and the values of T_{chime} and T_{start}.

EXAMPLE   What is the execution time on DLXV for the vector operation A = B × s, where s is a scalar and the length of the vectors A and B is 200?

ANSWER   Assume the addresses of A and B are initially in Ra and Rb, s is in Fs, and recall that for DLX (and DLXV) R0 always holds 0. Since (200 mod 64) = 8, the first iteration of the strip-mined loop will execute for a vector length of eight elements, and the following iterations will execute for a vector length of 64 elements. The starting byte addresses of the next segment of each vector is eight times the vector length. Since the vector length is either eight or 64, we increment the address registers by $8 \times 8 = 64$ after the first segment and $8 \times 64 = 512$ for latter segments. The total number of bytes in the vector is $8 \times 200 = 1600$, and we test for completion by comparing the address of the next vector segment to the initial address plus 1600. Here is the actual code:

```
       ADDI    R2,R0,#1600    ;total # bytes in vector
       ADD     R2,R2,Ra       ;address of the end of A vector
       ADDI    R1,R0,#8       ;loads length of 1st segment
       MOVI2S  VLR,R1         ;load vector length in VLR
       ADDI    R1,R0,#64      ;length in bytes of 1st segment
       ADDI    R3,R0,#64      ;vector length other segments
Loop:  LV      V1,Rb          ;load B
       MULTSV  V2,Fs,V1       ;vector * scalar
       SV      Ra,V2          ;store A
       ADD     Ra,Ra,R1       ;address of next segment of A
       ADD     Rb,Rb,R1       ;address of next segment of B
       ADDI    R1,R0,#512     ;load byte offset next segment
       MOVI2S  VLR,R3         ;set length to 64 element
       SUB     R4,R2,Ra       ;at the end of A?
       BNEZ    R4,Loop        ;if not, go back
```

The three vector instructions in the loop are dependent and must go into three convoys, hence $T_{chime} = 3$. Let's use our basic formula:

$$T_n = \left\lceil \frac{n}{MVL} \right\rceil \times (T_{loop} + T_{start}) + n \times T_{chime}$$

$$T_{200} = 4 \times (15 + T_{start}) + 200 \times 3$$

$$T_{200} = 60 + (4 \times T_{start}) + 600 = 660 + (4 \times T_{start})$$

The value of T_{start} is the sum of

■   The vector load start-up of 12 clock cycles

■   A seven-clock-cycle start-up for the multiply

■   A 12-clock-cycle start-up for the store.

Thus, the value of T_{start} is given by

$$T_{start} = 12 + 7 + 12 = 31$$

So, the overall value becomes

$$T_{200} = 660 + 4 \times 31 = 784$$

The execution time per element with all start-up costs is then 784/200 = 3.9, compared with a chime approximation of three. In section B.6, we will be more ambitious—allowing overlapping of separate convoys. ∎

Figure B.10 shows the overhead and effective rates per element for the above example (A = B × s) with various vector lengths. A chime counting model would lead to three clock cycles per element, while the two sources of overhead add 0.9 clock cycles per element in the limit.

The next few sections introduce enhancements that reduce this time. We will see how to reduce the number of convoys and hence the number of chimes using a technique called *chaining*. The loop overhead can be reduced by further overlapping the execution of vector and scalar instructions, allowing the scalar loop overhead in one iteration to be executed while the vector instructions in the previous instruction are completing. Finally, the vector start-up overhead can also be eliminated, using a technique that allows overlap of vector instructions in separate convoys.

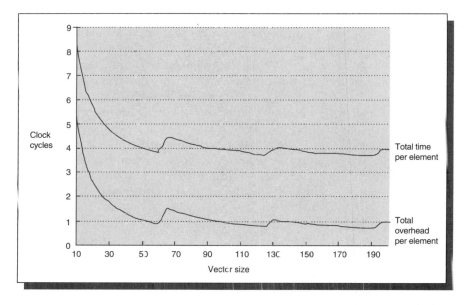

FIGURE B.10   This shows the total execution time per element and the total overhead time per element, versus the vector length for the Example on page B-17. For short vectors the total start-up time is more than one-half of the total time, while for long vectors it reduces to about one-third of the total time. The sudden jumps occur when the vector length crosses a multiple of 64, forcing another iteration of the strip-mining code and execution of a set of vector instructions. These operations increase T_n by $T_{loop} + T_{start}$.

Vector Stride

The second problem this section addresses is that the position in memory of adjacent elements in a vector may not be sequential. Consider the straightforward code for matrix multiply:

```
do 10 i = 1,100
    do 10 j = 1,100
        A(i,j) = 0.0
        do 10 k = 1,100
10          A(i,j) = A(i,j)+B(i,k)*C(k,j)
```

At the statement labeled 10 we could vectorize the multiplication of each row of B with each column of C and strip-mine the inner loop with k as the index variable.

To do so, we must consider how adjacent elements in B and adjacent elements in C are addressed. As we discussed in section 5.3, when an array is allocated memory it is linearized and must be laid out in either row-major or column-major order. This linearization means that either the elements in the row or the elements in the column are not adjacent in memory. For example, if the above loop were written in FORTRAN, which allocates column-major order, the elements of B that are accessed by iterations in the inner loop are separated by the row size times 8 (the number of bytes per entry) for a total of 800 bytes. In Chapter 5, we saw that blocking could be used to improve the locality in cache-based systems. In vector processors we do not have caches, so we need another technique to fetch elements of a vector that are not adjacent in memory.

This distance separating elements that are to be gathered into a single register is called the *stride*. In the current example, using column-major layout for the matrices means that matrix C has a stride of 1, or 1 double word (8 bytes), separating successive elements, and matrix B has a stride of 100, or 100 double words (800 bytes).

Once a vector is loaded into a vector register it acts as if it had logically adjacent elements. Thus a vector-register processor can handle strides greater than one, called *nonunit strides*, using only vector-load and vector-store operations with stride capability. This ability to access nonsequential memory locations and to reshape them into a dense structure is one of the major advantages of a vector processor over a cache-based processor. Caches inherently deal with unit stride data, so that while increasing block size can help reduce miss rates for large scientific data sets, increasing block size can have a negative effect for data that is accessed with nonunit stride. While blocking techniques can solve some of these problems (see section 5.3), the ability to efficiently access data that is not contiguous remains an advantage for vector processors on certain problems.

On DLXV, where the addressable unit is a byte, the stride for our example would be 800. The value must be computed dynamically, since the size of the matrix may not be known at compile time, or—just like vector length—may change for different executions of the same statement. The vector stride, like the vector starting address, can be put in a general-purpose register. Then the DLXV instruction LVWS (load vector with stride) can be used to fetch the vector into a vector register. Likewise, when a nonunit stride vector is being stored, SVWS (store vector with stride) can be used. In some vector processors the loads and stores always have a stride value stored in a register, so that only a single load and a single store instruction are required.

Complications in the memory system can occur from supporting strides greater than one. In Chapter 5 we saw that memory accesses could proceed at full speed if the number of memory banks was at least as large as the memory-access time in clock cycles. Once nonunit strides are introduced, however, it becomes possible to request accesses from the same bank at a higher rate than the memory-access time. When multiple accesses contend for a bank, a memory bank conflict occurs and one access must be stalled. A bank conflict, and hence a stall, will occur if

$$\frac{\text{Least common multiple (Stride, Number of banks)}}{\text{Stride}} < \text{Memory-access latency}$$

EXAMPLE   Suppose we have 16 memory banks with a read latency of 12 clocks. How long will it take to complete a 64-element vector load with a stride of 1? With a stride of 32?

ANSWER   Since the number of banks is larger than the read latency, for a stride of 1, the load will take $12 + 64 = 76$ clock cycles, or 1.2 clocks per element. The worst possible stride is a value that is a multiple of the number of memory banks, as in this case with a stride of 32 and 16 memory banks. Every access to memory will collide with the previous one. This leads to a read latency of 12 clock cycles per element and a total time for the vector load of 768 clock cycles. ∎

Memory bank conflicts will not occur if the stride and number of banks are relatively prime with respect to each other and there are enough banks to avoid conflicts in the unit-stride case. When there are no bank conflicts, multiword and unit strides run at the same rates. Increasing the number of memory banks to a number greater than the minimum to prevent stalls with a stride of length 1 will decrease the stall frequency for some other strides. For example, with 64 banks, a stride of 32 will stall on every other access, rather than every access. If we originally had a stride of 8 and 16 banks, every other access would stall; while with 64 banks, a stride of 8 will stall on every eighth access. If we have multiple memory pipelines, we will also need more banks to prevent conflicts. In 1995, most vector supercomputers have at least 64 banks, and some have as many as 1024 in the maximum memory configuration. Because bank conflicts can still occur in nonunit stride cases, many programmers favor unit stride accesses whenever possible.

B.4 | Effectiveness of Compiler Vectorization

Two factors affect the success with which a program can be run in vector mode. The first factor is the structure of the program itself: Do the loops have true data dependences, or can they be restructured so as not to have such dependences? This factor is influenced by the algorithms chosen and, to some extent, by how they are coded. The second factor is the capability of the compiler. While no compiler can vectorize a loop where no parallelism among the loop iterations exists, there is tremendous variation in the ability of compilers to determine whether a loop can be vectorized. The techniques used to vectorize programs are the same as those discussed in Chapter 4 for uncovering ILP; here we simply review how well these techniques work.

As an indication of the level of vectorization that can be achieved in scientific programs, let's look at the vectorization levels observed for the Perfect Club benchmarks, mentioned in Chapter 1. These benchmarks are large, real scientific applications. Figure B.11 shows the percentage of floating-point operations in

Benchmark name	FP operations	FP operations executed in vector mode
ADM	23%	68%
DYFESM	26%	95%
FLO52	41%	100%
MDG	28%	27%
MG3D	31%	86%
OCEAN	28%	58%
QCD	14%	1%
SPICE	16%	7%
TRACK	9%	23%
TRFD	22%	10%

FIGURE B.11   Level of vectorization among the Perfect Club benchmarks when executed on the CRAY X-MP. The first column contains the percentage of operations that are floating point, while the second contains the percentage of FP operations executed in vector instructions.

each benchmark and the percentage executed in vector mode on the CRAY X-MP. The wide variation in level of vectorization has been observed by several studies of the performance of applications on vector processors. While better compilers might improve the level of vectorization in some of these programs, most will require rewriting to achieve significant increases in vectorization. For example, a new program or a significant rewrite will be needed to obtain the benefits of a vector processor on SPICE.

There is also tremendous variation in how well compilers do in vectorizing programs. As a summary of the state of vectorizing compilers, consider the data in Figure B.12, which shows the extent of vectorization for different processors using a test suite of 100 hand-written FORTRAN kernels. The kernels were designed to test vectorization capability and can all be vectorized by hand; we will see several examples of these loops in the Exercises.

Processor	Compiler	Completely vectorized	Partially vectorized	Not vectorized
CDC CYBER-205	VAST-2 V2.21	62	5	33
Convex C-series	FC5.0	69	5	26
CRAY X-MP	CFT77 V3.0	69	3	28
CRAY X-MP	CFT V1.15	50	1	49
CRAY-2	CFT2 V3.1a	27	1	72
ETA-10	FTN 77 V1.0	62	7	31
Hitachi S810/820	FORT77/HAP V20-2B	67	4	29
IBM 3090/VF	VS FORTRAN V2.4	52	4	44
NEC SX/2	FORTRAN77 / SX V.040	66	5	29

FIGURE B.12   Result of applying vectorizing compilers to the 100 FORTRAN test kernels. For each processor we indicate how many loops were completely vectorized, partially vectorized, and unvectorized. These loops were collected by Callahan, Dongarra, and Levine [1988]. Two different compilers for the CRAY X-MP show the large dependence on compiler technology.

B.5 | Enhancing Vector Performance

Three techniques for improving the performance of vector processors are discussed in this section. The first deals with making a sequence of dependent vector operations run faster. The other two deal with expanding the class of loops that can be run in vector mode. The first technique, *chaining*, originated in the CRAY-1, but is now supported on most vector processors. The techniques discussed in the second and third parts of this section combat the effects of conditional execution and sparse matrices. The extensions are taken from a variety of processors including the most recent supercomputers.

Chaining—The Concept of Forwarding Extended to Vector Registers

Consider the simple vector sequence

```
MULTV   V1,V2,V3
ADDV    V4,V1,V5
```

In DLXV, as it currently stands, these two instructions must be put into two separate convoys, since the instructions are dependent. On the other hand, if the vector register, V1 in this case, is treated not as a single entity but as a group of individual registers, then the ideas of forwarding can be conceptually extended to work on individual elements of a vector. This insight, which will allow the ADDV to start earlier in this example, is called *chaining*. Chaining allows a vector operation to start as soon as the individual elements of its vector source operand become available: The results from the first functional unit in the chain are "forwarded" to the second functional unit. In practice, chaining is often implemented by allowing the processor to read and write a particular register at the same time, albeit to different elements. Early implementations of chaining worked like forwarding, but this restricted the timing of the source and destination instructions in the chain. Recent implementations use *flexible chaining*, which allows a vector instruction to chain to essentially any other active vector instruction, assuming that no structural hazard is generated. Flexible chaining requires more read and write ports for the vector register file, but it is the form of chaining used in most recent machines. We assume this type of chaining throughout the rest of this appendix.

Even though a pair of operations depend on one another, chaining allows the operations to proceed in parallel on separate elements of the vector. This permits the operations to be scheduled in the same convoy and reduces the number of chimes required. For the sequence above, a sustained rate (ignoring start-up) of two floating-point operations per clock cycle, or one chime, can be achieved, even though the operations are dependent! The total running time for the above sequence becomes

$$\text{Vector length} + \text{Start-up time}_{\text{ADDV}} + \text{Start-up time}_{\text{MULTV}}$$

Figure B.13 shows the timing of a chained and an unchained version of the above pair of vector instructions with a vector length of 64. This convoy requires one chime; however, because it uses chaining, the start-up overhead will be seen in the actual timing of the convoy. In Figure B.13, the total time for chained operation is 77 clock cycles, or 1.2 cycles per result. With 128 floating-point operations done in that time, 1.7 FLOPs per clock cycle are obtained. For the unchained version, there are 141 clock cycles or 0.9 FLOPs per clock cycle.

Although chaining allows us to reduce the chime component of the execution time by putting two dependent instructions in the same convoy, it does not

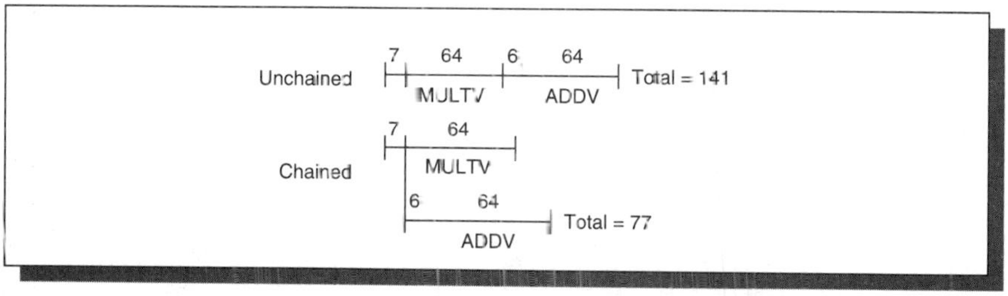

FIGURE B.13 Timings for a sequence of dependent vector operations ADDV and MULTV, both unchained and chained. The 6- and 7-clock-cycle delays are the latency of the adder and multiplier.

eliminate the start-up overhead. If we want an accurate running time estimate, we must count the start-up time both within and across convoys. With chaining the number of chimes for a sequence is determined by the number of different vector functional units available in the processor and the number required by the application. In particular, no convoy can contain a structural hazard. This means, for example, that a sequence containing two vector memory instructions must take at least two convoys, and hence two chimes, on a processor like DLXV with only one vector load-store unit.

We will see in section B.6 that chaining plays a major role in boosting vector performance. In fact, chaining is so important that virtually every vector processor now supports flexible chaining.

Conditionally Executed Statements

In the last section, we saw that many programs only achieved low to moderate levels of vectorization. Because of Amdahl's Law, the speedup on such programs will be very limited. Two reasons why higher levels of vectorization are not achieved are the presence of conditionals (if statements) inside loops and the use of sparse matrices. Programs that contain if statements in loops cannot be run in vector mode using the techniques we have discussed so far because the if statements introduce control dependences into a loop. Likewise, sparse matrices cannot be efficiently implemented using any of the capabilities we have seen so far; this is one factor in the lack of vectorization for SPICE. We discuss strategies for dealing with conditional execution here, leaving the discussion of sparse matrices to the following subsection.

Consider the following loop:

```
        do 100 i = 1, 64
            if (A(i).ne  0) then
                A(i) = A(i) - B(i)
            endif
100     continue
```

This loop cannot normally be vectorized because of the conditional execution of the body; however, if the inner loop could be run for the iterations for which $A(i) \neq 0$, then the subtraction could be vectorized. In Chapter 4, we saw that the conditionally executed instructions could turn such control dependences into data dependences, enhancing the ability to parallelize the loop. Vector processors can benefit from an equivalent capability for vectors.

The extension that is commonly used for this capability is *vector-mask control*. The vector-mask control uses a Boolean vector of length MVL to control the execution of a vector instruction just as conditionally executed instructions use a Boolean condition to determine whether an instruction is executed. When the *vector-mask register* is enabled, any vector instructions executed operate only on the vector elements whose corresponding entries in the vector-mask register are 1. The entries in the destination vector register that correspond to a 0 in the mask register are unaffected by the vector operation. If the vector-mask register is set by the result of a condition, only elements satisfying the condition will be affected. Clearing the vector-mask register sets it to all 1s, making subsequent vector instructions operate on all vector elements. The following code can now be used for the above loop, assuming that the starting addresses of A and B are in Ra and Rb, respectively:

```
LV     V1,Ra          ;load vector A into V1
LV     V2,Rb          ;load vector B
LD     F0,#0          ;load FP zero into F0
SNESV  F0,V1          ;sets VM(i) to 1 if V1(i)≠F0
SUBV   V1,V1,V2       ;subtract under vector mask
CVM                   ;set the vector mask to all 1s
SV     Ra,V1          ;store the result in A
```

Most recent vector processors provide vector-mask control. The vector-mask capability described here is available on some processors, but others allow the use of the vector mask with only a subset of the vector instructions.

Using a vector-mask register does, however, have disadvantages. When we examined conditionally executed instructions, we saw that such instructions still require execution time when the condition is not satisfied. Nonetheless, the elimination of a branch and the associated control dependences can make a conditional instruction faster even if it sometimes does useless work. Similarly, vector instructions executed with a vector mask still take execution time, even for the elements where the mask is 0. Likewise, even with a significant number of zeros in the mask, using vector-mask control may still be significantly faster than using scalar mode. In fact, the large difference in potential performance between vector and scalar mode makes the inclusion of vector-mask instructions critical.

Second, in some vector processors the vector mask serves only to disable the storing of the result into the destination register, and the actual operation still occurs. Thus, if the operation in the above example were a divide rather than a subtract and the test was on B rather than A, false floating-point exceptions might result since a division by 0 would occur. Processors that mask the operation as well as the storing of the result avoid this problem.

Sparse Matrices

There are techniques for allowing programs with sparse matrices to execute in vector mode. In a sparse matrix, the elements of a vector are usually stored in some compacted form and then accessed indirectly. Assuming a simplified sparse structure, we might see code that looks like this:

```
              do 100 i = 1,n
100              A(K(i)) = A(K(i)) - C(M(i))
```

This code implements a sparse vector sum on the arrays A and C, using index vectors K and M to designate the nonzero elements of A and C. (A and C must have the same number of nonzero elements—n of them.) Another common representation for sparse matrices uses a bit vector to say which elements exist and a dense vector for the nonzero elements. Often both representations exist in the same program. Sparse matrices are found in many codes, and there are many ways to implement them, depending on the data structure used in the program.

A primary mechanism for supporting sparse matrices is *scatter-gather operations* using index vectors. The goal of such operations is to support moving between a dense representation (i.e., zeros are not included) and normal representation (i.e., the zeros are included) of a sparse matrix. A *gather* operation takes an *index vector* and fetches the vector whose elements are at the addresses given by adding a base address to the offsets given in the index vector. The result is a nonsparse vector in a vector register. After these elements are operated on in dense form, the sparse vector can be stored in expanded form by a *scatter* store, using the same index vector. Hardware support for such operations is called *scatter-gather* and appears on several processors. The instructions LVI (load vector indexed) and SVI (store vector indexed) provide these operations in DLXV. For example, assuming that Ra, Rc, Rk, and Rm contain the starting addresses of the vectors in the above sequence, the inner loop of the sequence can be coded with vector instructions such as

```
LV     Vk,Rk          ;load K
LVI    Va,(Ra+Vk)     ;load A(K(I))
LV     Vm,Rm          ;load M
LVI    Vc,(Rc+Vm)     ;load C(M(I))
ADDV   Va,Va,Vc       ;add them
SVI    (Ra+Vk),Va     ;store A(K(I))
```

This technique allows code with sparse matrices to be run in vector mode. The source code above would *never* be automatically vectorized by a compiler because the compiler cannot know that the elements of K are distinct values, and thus that no dependences exist. Instead, a programmer directive would tell the compiler that it could run the loop in vector mode; without such directives, programs such as SPICE will not be vectorized even if the hardware support exists.

A scatter-gather capability is included on many of the recent supercomputers. Such operations rarely run at one element per clock, but they are still much faster than the alternative, which may be a scalar loop. If the sparsity properties of a matrix change, a new index vector must be computed. Many processors provide support for computing the index vector quickly. The CVI (create vector index) instruction in DLXV creates an index vector given a stride (m), where the values in the index vector are $0, m, 2 \times m, ..., 63 \times m$. Some processors provide an instruction to create a compressed index vector whose entries correspond to the positions with a 1 in the mask register. Other vector architectures provide a method to compress a vector. In DLXV, we define the CVI instruction to always create a compressed index vector using the vector mask. When the vector mask is all ones, a standard index vector will be created.

The indexed loads-stores and the CVI instruction provide an alternative method to support conditional vector execution. Here is a vector sequence that implements the loop we saw on page B-25:

```
LV        V1,Ra          ;load vector A into V1
LD        F0,#0          ;load FP zero into F0
SNESV     F0,V1          ;sets the VM to 1 if V1(i)≠F0
CVI       V2,#8          ;generates indices in V2
POP       R1,VM          ;find the number of 1's in VM
MOVI2S    VLR,R1         ;load vector length register
CVM                      ;clears the mask
LVI       V3,(Ra+V2)     ;load the nonzero A elements
LVI       V4,(Rb+V2)     ;load corresponding B elements
SUBV      V3,V3,V4       ;do the subtract
SVI       (Ra+V2),V3     ;store A back
```

Whether the implementation using scatter-gather is better than the conditionally executed version depends on the frequency with which the condition holds and the cost of the operations. Ignoring chaining, the running time of the first version (on page B-25) is $5n + c_1$. The running time of the second version, using indexed loads and stores with a running time of one element per clock, is $4n + 4 \times f \times n + c_2$, where f is the fraction of elements for which the condition is true (i.e., A $\neq 0$). If we assume that the values of c_1 and c_2 are comparable, or that they are much smaller than n, we can find when this second technique is better.

$$\text{Time}_1 = 5\,(n)$$
$$\text{Time}_2 = 4n + 4 \times f \times n$$

We want $\text{Time}_1 \geq \text{Time}_2$, so

$$5n \geq 4n + 4 \times f \times n$$
$$\frac{1}{4} \geq f$$

That is, the second method is faster if less than one-quarter of the elements are nonzero. In many cases the frequency of execution is much lower. If the index vector can be reused, or if the number of vector statements within the if statement grows, the advantage of the scatter-gather approach will increase sharply.

B.6   Putting It All Together: Performance of Vector Processors

In this section we look at different measures of performance for vector processors and what they tell us about the processor. To determine the performance of a processor on a vector problem we must look at the start-up cost and the sustained rate. The simplest and best way to report the performance of a vector processor on a loop is to give the execution time of the vector loop. For vector loops people often give the MFLOPS (millions of floating-point operations per second) rating rather than execution time. We use the notation R_n for the MFLOPS rating on a vector of length n. Using the measurements T_n (time) or R_n (rate) is equivalent if the number of FLOPs is agreed upon (see Chapter 1 for a longer discussion on MFLOPS). In any event, either measurement should include the overhead.

In this section we examine the performance of DLXV on our DAXPY loop by looking at performance from different viewpoints. We will continue to compute the execution time of a vector loop using the equation developed in section B.3. At the same time, we will look at different ways to measure performance using the computed time. The constant values for T_{loop} used in this section introduce some small amount of error, which will be ignored.

Measures of Vector Performance

Because vector length is so important in establishing the performance of a processor, length-related measures are often applied in addition to time and MFLOPS. These length-related measures tend to vary dramatically across different processors and are interesting to compare. (Remember, though, that *time* is always the measure of interest when comparing the relative speed of two processors.) Three of the most important length-related measures are

- R_∞—The MFLOPS rate on an infinite-length vector. Although this measure may be of interest when estimating peak performance, real problems do not have unlimited vector lengths, and the overhead penalties encountered in real problems will be larger.

- $N_{1/2}$—The vector length needed to reach one-half of R_∞. This is a good measure of the impact of overhead.

- N_v—The vector length needed to make vector mode faster than scalar mode. This measures both overhead and the speed of scalars relative to vectors.

Let's look at these measures for our DAXPY problem running on DLXV. When chained, the inner loop of the DAXPY code in convoys looks like Figure B.14 (assuming that Rx and Ry hold starting addresses).

LV V1,Rx	MULTSV V2,F0,V1	Convoy 1: chained load and multiply
LV V3,Ry	ADDV V4,V2,V3	Convoy 2: second load and ADD, chained
SV Ry,V4		Convoy 3: store the result

FIGURE B.14   The chained inner loop of the DAXPY code in convoys.

Recall our performance equation for the execution time of a vector loop with n elements, T_n:

$$T_n = T_{base} + \left\lceil \frac{n}{MVL} \right\rceil \times (T_{loop} + T_{start}) + n \times T_{chime}$$

Chaining allows the loop to run in three chimes (and no less, since there is one memory pipeline); thus $T_{chime} = 3$. If T_{chime} were a complete indication of performance, the loop would run at a MFLOPS rate of $2/3 \times$ clock rate (since there are 2 FLOPs per iteration). Thus, based only on the chime count, a 200-MHz DLXV would run this loop at 133 MFLOPS assuming no strip-mining or start-up overhead. There are several ways to improve the performance: add additional vector load-store units, allow convoys to overlap to reduce the impact of start-up overheads, and decrease the number of loads required by vector register allocation. We will examine the first two extensions in this section. The last optimization is actually used for the Cray-1, DLXV's cousin, to boost the performance by 50%. Reducing the number of loads requires an interprocedural optimization; we examine this transformation in Exercise B.6. Before we examine the first two extensions, let's see what the real performance, including overhead, is.

The Peak Performance of DLXV on DAXPY

First, we should determine what the peak performance, R_∞, really is, since we know it must differ from the ideal 133-MFLOPS rate. For now, we continue to use the simplifying assumption that a convoy cannot start until all the instructions in an earlier convoy have completed; later we will remove this restriction. Using this simplification, the start-up overhead for the vector sequence is simply the sum of the start-up times of the instructions:

$$T_{start} = 12 - 7 + 12 + 6 + 12 = 49$$

Using MVL = 64, $T_{loop} = 15$, $T_{start} = 49$, and $T_{chime} = 3$ in the performance equation, and assuming that n is not an exact multiple of 64, the time for an n-element operation is

$$T_n = \left\lceil \frac{n}{64} \right\rceil \times (15 + 49) + 3n$$

$$= (n + 64) + 3n$$

$$= 4n + 64$$

The sustained rate is actually over 4 clock cycles per iteration, rather than the theoretical rate of 3 chimes, which ignores overhead. The major part of the difference is the cost of the start-up overhead for each block of 64 elements (49 cycles versus 15 for the loop overhead).

We can now compute R_∞ for a 200-MHz clock as

$$R_\infty = \lim_{n \to \infty} \left(\frac{\text{Operations per iteration} \times \text{Clock rate}}{\text{Clock cycles per iteration}} \right)$$

The numerator is independent of n, hence

$$R_\infty = \frac{\text{Operations per iteration} \times \text{Clock rate}}{\lim_{n \to \infty} (\text{Clock cycles per iteration})}$$

$$\lim_{n \to \infty} (\text{Clock cycles per iteration}) = \lim_{n \to \infty} \left(\frac{T_n}{n} \right) = \lim_{n \to \infty} \left(\frac{4n + 64}{n} \right) = 4$$

$$R_\infty = \frac{2 \times 200 \text{ MHz}}{4} = 100 \text{ MFLOPS}$$

The performance without the start-up overhead, which is the peak performance given the vector functional unit structure, is now 1.33 times higher. In actuality the gap between peak and sustained performance for this benchmark is even larger!

Sustained Performance of DLXV on the Linpack Benchmark

The Linpack benchmark is a Gaussian elimination on a 100×100 matrix. Thus, the vector element lengths range from 99 down to 1. A vector of length k is used k times. Thus, the average vector length is given by

$$\frac{\sum\limits_{i=1}^{99} i^2}{\sum\limits_{i=1}^{99} i} = 66.3$$

Now we can obtain an accurate estimate of the performance of DAXPY using a vector length of 66.

$$T_{66} = 2 \times (15 + 49) + 66 \times 3 = 128 + 198 = 326$$

$$R_{66} = \frac{2 \times 66 \times 200}{326} \text{ MFLOPS} = 81 \text{ MFLOPS}$$

The peak number, ignoring start-up overhead, is 1.64 times higher than this estimate of sustained performance on the real vector lengths. In actual practice, the Linpack benchmark contains a nontrivial fraction of code that cannot be vectorized. Although this code accounts for less than 20% of the time before vectorization, it runs at less than one-tenth of the performance when counted as FLOPs. Thus, Amdahl's Law tells us that the overall performance will be significantly lower than the performance estimated from analyzing the inner loop.

Since vector length has a significant impact on performance, the $N_{1/2}$ and N_v measures are often used in comparing vector machines.

EXAMPLE   What is $N_{1/2}$ for just the inner loop of DAXPY for DLXV with a 200-MHz clock?

ANSWER   Using R_∞ as the peak rate, we want to know the vector length that will achieve about 50 MFLOPS. We start with the formula for MFLOPS assuming that the measurement is made for $N_{1/2}$ elements:

$$\text{MFLOPS} = \frac{\text{FLOPs executed in } N_{1/2} \text{ iterations}}{\text{Clock cycles to execute } N_{1/2} \text{ iterations}} \times \frac{\text{Clock cycles}}{\text{Second}} \times 10^{-6}$$

$$50 = \frac{2 \times N_{1/2}}{T_{N_{1/2}}} \times 200$$

Simplifying this and then assuming $N_{1/2} \le 64$, so that $T_{n \le 64} = 1 \times 64 + 3 \times n$, yields

$$T_{N_{1/2}} = 8 \times N_{1/2}$$

$$1 \times 64 + 3 \times N_{1/2} = 8 \times N_{1/2}$$

$$5 \times N_{1/2} = 64$$

$$N_{1/2} = 12.8$$

So $N_{1/2} = 13$; that is, a vector of length 13 gives approximately one-half the peak performance for the DAXPY loop on DLXV. ∎

EXAMPLE   What is the vector length, N_v, such that the vector operation runs faster than the scalar?

ANSWER   Again, we know that $N_v < 64$. The time to do one iteration in scalar mode can be estimated as $10 + 12 + 12 + 7 + 6 + 12 = 59$ clocks where 10 is the estimate of the loop overhead, known to be somewhat less than the strip-mining loop overhead. In the last problem, we showed that this vector loop runs in vector mode in time $T_{n \le 64} = 64 + 3 \times n$ clock cycles. Therefore,

$$64 + 3N_v = 59N_v$$
$$N_v = \left\lceil \frac{64}{56} \right\rceil$$
$$N_v = 2$$

For the DAXPY loop, vector mode is faster than scalar as long as the vector has at least two elements. This number is surprisingly small, as we will see in the next section (*Fallacies and Pitfalls*). ∎

DAXPY Performance on an Enhanced DLXV

DAXPY, like many vector problems, is memory limited. Consequently, performance could be improved by adding more memory-access pipelines. This is the major architectural difference between the CRAY X-MP (and later processors) and the CRAY-1. The CRAY X-MP has three memory pipelines, compared with the CRAY-1's single memory pipeline, and the X-MP has more flexible chaining. How does this affect performance?

EXAMPLE   What would be the value of T_{66} for DAXPY on DLXV if we added two more memory pipelines?

ANSWER   With three memory pipelines all the instructions fit in one convoy and take one chime. The start-up overheads are the same, so

$$T_{66} = \left\lceil \frac{66}{64} \right\rceil \times (T_{loop} + T_{start}) + 66 \times T_{chime}$$
$$T_{66} = 2 \times (15 + 49) + 66 \times 1 = 194$$

With three memory pipelines, we have reduced the clock-cycle count for sustained performance from 326 to 194, a factor of 1.7. Note the effect of Amdahl's Law: We improved the theoretical peak rate, as measured by the number of chimes by a factor of 3, but only achieved an overall improvement of a factor of 1.7 in sustained performance. ∎

Another improvement could come from allowing different convoys to overlap and also allowing the scalar loop overhead to overlap with the vector instructions. This requires that one vector operation be allowed to begin using a functional unit before another operation has completed and complicates the instruction issue logic. Allowing this overlap eliminates the separate start-up overhead for every convoy except the first and hides the loop overhead as well.

To achieve the maximum hiding of strip-mining overhead, we need to be able to overlap strip-mined instances of the loop, allowing two instances of a convoy as well as possibly two instances of the scalar code to be in execution simultaneously. This requires the same techniques we looked at in Chapter 4 to avoid WAR hazards, although because no overlapped read and write of a single vector element is possible, copying can be avoided. This technique, called *tailgating*, was used in the Cray-2. Alternatively, we could unroll the outer loop to create several instances of the vector sequence using different register sets (assuming sufficient registers), just as we did in Chapter 4. By allowing maximum overlap of the convoys and the scalar loop overhead, the start-up and loop overheads will only be seen *once* per vector sequence, independent of the number of convoys and the instructions in each convoy. In this way a processor with vector registers can have both low start-up overhead for short vectors and high peak performance for very long vectors.

EXAMPLE What would be the values of R_∞ and T_{66} for DAXPY on DLXV if we added two more memory pipelines and allowed the strip-mining and start-up overhead to be fully overlapped?

ANSWER

$$R_\infty = \lim_{n \to \infty} \left(\frac{\text{Operations per iteration} \times \text{Clock rate}}{\text{Clock cycles per iteration}} \right)$$

$$\lim_{n \to \infty} (\text{Clock cycles per iteration}) = \lim_{n \to \infty} \left(\frac{T_n}{n} \right)$$

Since the overhead is only seen once, $T_n = n + 49 + 15 = n + 64$. Thus,

$$\lim_{n \to \infty} \left(\frac{T_n}{n} \right) = \lim_{n \to \infty} \left(\frac{n + 64}{n} \right) = 1$$

$$R_\infty = \frac{2 \times 200 \text{ MHz}}{1} = 400 \text{ MFLOPS}$$

Adding the extra memory pipelines and more flexible issue logic yields an improvement in peak performance of a factor of 4. However, $T_{66} = 130$, so for shorter vectors, the sustained performance improvement is about $326/130 = 2.5$ times. ∎

In summary, we have examined several measures of vector performance. Theoretical peak performance can be calculated based purely on the value of T_{chime} as

$$\frac{\text{Number of FLOPs per iteration} \times \text{Clock rate}}{T_{chime}}$$

By including the loop overhead, we can calculate values for peak performance for an infinite-length vector (R_∞) and also for sustained performance, R_n for a vector of length n, which is computed as

$$R_n = \frac{\text{Number of FLOPs per iteration} \times n \times \text{Clock rate}}{T_n}$$

Using these measures we also can find $N_{1/2}$ and N_v, which give us another way of looking at the start-up overhead for vectors and the ratio of vector to scalar speed. A wide variety of measures of performance of vector processors are useful in understanding the range of performance that applications may see on a vector processor.

B.7 | Fallacies and Pitfalls

Pitfall: Concentrating on peak performance and ignoring start-up overhead.

Early vector processors such as the TI ASC and the CDC STAR-100 had long start-up times. For some vector problems, N_v could be greater than 100! Today, the supercomputers from Japan often have higher sustained rates than the Cray Research processors. But with start-up overheads that are 50–100% higher, the faster sustained rates often provide no real advantage. On the CYBER-205 the start-up overhead for DAXPY is 158 clock cycles, substantially increasing the break-even point. With a single vector unit, which contains 2 memory pipelines, the CYBER-205 can sustain a rate of 2 clocks per iteration. The time for DAXPY for a vector of length n is therefore roughly $158 + 2n$. If the clock rates of the CRAY-1 and the CYBER-205 were identical, the CRAY-1 would be faster until $n > 64$. Because the CRAY-1 clock is also faster (even though the 205 is newer), the crossover point is over 100. Comparing a four-vector-pipeline CYBER-205 (the maximum-size processor) with the CRAY X-MP that was delivered shortly after the 205, the 205 completes two results per clock cycle—twice as fast as the X-MP. However, vectors must be longer than about 200 for the CYBER-205 to be faster. The problem of start-up overhead has been the major difficulty for the memory-memory vector architectures, hence their lack of popularity.

Pitfall: Increasing vector performance, without comparable increases in scalar performance.

This was a problem on many early vector processors, and a place where Seymour Cray rewrote the rules. Many of the early vector processors had comparatively slow scalar units (as well as large start-up overheads). Even today, processors with higher peak vector performance can be outperformed by a processor with lower vector performance but better scalar performance. Good scalar performance keeps down overhead costs (strip mining, for example) and reduces the impact of Amdahl's Law. A good example of this comes from comparing a fast scalar processor and a vector processor with lower scalar performance. The Livermore FORTRAN kernels are a collection of 24 scientific kernels with varying degrees of vectorization. Figure B.15 shows the performance of two different processors on this benchmark. Despite the vector processor's higher peak performance, its low scalar performance makes it slower than a fast scalar processor. The next fallacy is closely related.

Processor	Minimum rate for any loop	Maximum rate for any loop	Harmonic mean of all 24 loops
MIPS M/120-5	0.80 MFLOPS	3.89 MFLOPS	1.85 MFLOPS
Stardent-1500	0.41 MFLOPS	10.08 MFLOPS	1.72 MFLOPS

FIGURE B.15   Performance measurements for the Livermore FORTRAN kernels on two different processors. Both the MIPS M/120-5 and the Stardent-1500 (formerly the Ardent Titan-1) use a 16.7-MHz MIPS R2000 chip for the main CPU. The Stardent-1500 uses its vector unit for scalar FP and has about half the scalar performance (as measured by the minimum rate) of the MIPS M/120, which uses the MIPS R2010 FP chip. The vector processor is more than a factor of 2.5 times faster for a highly vectorizable loop (maximum rate). However, the lower scalar performance of the Stardent-1500 negates the higher vector performance when total performance is measured by the harmonic mean on all 24 loops.

Fallacy: You can get vector performance without providing memory bandwidth.

As we saw with the DAXPY loop, memory bandwidth is quite important. DAXPY requires 1.5 memory references per floating-point operation, and this ratio is typical of many scientific codes. Even if the floating-point operations took no time, a CRAY-1 could not increase the performance of the vector sequence used, since it is memory limited. The CRAY-1 performance on Linpack jumped when the compiler used clever transformations to change the computation so that values could be kept in the vector registers. This lowered the number of memory references per FLOP and improved the performance by nearly a factor of 2! Thus, the memory bandwidth on the CRAY-1 became sufficient for a loop that formerly required more bandwidth.

B.8 | Concluding Remarks

In the late 1980s rapid performance increases in efficiently pipelined scalar processors led to a dramatic closing of the gap between vector supercomputers, costing millions of dollars, and fast, pipelined, VLSI microprocessors costing less than tens of thousands of dollars. In Chapter 1, we saw that a desk-side processor offered nearly the performance of a vector supercomputer introduced five years earlier for less than a tenth of the price. Comparing that processor against its contemporary, a Cray C-90, would show a reduced price-performance advantage, but still exceeding a factor of three times While the price advantage comes from the use of microprocessor technology, the high performance comes from the exploitation of instruction-level parallelism in the microprocessor, which allows CPIs to be under 1.

For scientific programs, an interesting counterpart to CPI is clock cycles per FLOP, or CPF. We saw in this chapter that for vector processors this number was typically in the range of 2 (for a CRAY X-MP style processor) to 4 (for a CRAY-1 style processor); a C-90 might reduce this number further but probably not below 1 to 1.5. In Chapter 4, we saw that the pipelined processor varied from about 6 (for DLX) down to about 2.5 (for a superscalar DLX with no memory system losses running a DAXPY-type loop). For processors like an IBM Power-2 or MIPS R8000 with multiple memory pipelines and a multiply-add instruction, this number could be as low as 1.

In addition to the use of vectors rather than multiple issue, the other major distinction between vector machines and advanced scalar machines is the use of vector memory systems versus caches. As we saw earlier in this appendix, vector memory systems can have significant advantages when accesses do not have unit stride. This performance advantage, however, comes at a significant price disadvantage. To keep the start-up penalties of vector loads small and to keep the number of required memory banks reasonable, many high-end vector machines use SRAM for the main memory. While SRAM has an access time several times lower than that of DRAM, it costs roughly 10 times as much per bit!

Recent trends in vector processor design have focused on high peak-vector performance and multiprocessing. Meanwhile, high-speed scalar processors concentrate on keeping the ratio of peak to sustained performance near 1. Thus, if the peak rates advance comparably, the sustained rates of the scalar processors will advance more quickly, and the scalar processors will continue to close the CPF gap. These multiple-issue scalar processors can rival or exceed the performance of vector processors with comparable clock speeds, especially for levels of vectorization below 70%.

In 1994, we saw two dramatic demonstrations that the gap between vector processors and superscalars may disappear in the future. First, microprocessors with clock rates exceeding those of the high-end Cray C-90 appeared. Second, microprocessors such as the MIPS R8000 (TFP) and the IBM Power-2 delivered CPF numbers competitive with vector processors by issuing multiple memory references and FP operations per cycle. In the near future, it is likely that designers will be able to use the advances in silicon technology to achieve low CPF performance while also achieving a high clock rate. At that point it may be primarily the memory systems that distinguish vector processors from microprocessor-based superscalars. Advances in compiler technology for cache-based systems, such as blocking and prefetching, are closing the performance gap in the memory system, while cache-based systems continue to have large cost advantages. New cache organizations, such as that used in the R8000 (a large pipelined cache for all FP data), are also helping to close the performance gap. New advances are likely to further narrow the advantages of vector-oriented memory systems both by reducing the performance gap and by narrowing the range of applications where a vector memory system is better than a cache-based system. Overall, a Cray C-90 processor has a SPECfp rating that is about 1.8 times higher than an R8000 processor and a price almost 20 times higher. On some benchmarks, however, the C-90 is over five times faster; while on others it is about half the speed of the R8000. Whether the range of applications for which the C-90 has a substantial performance advantage will remain large enough to justify the premium price for vector computers remains to be seen.

B.9 | Historical Perspective and References

The first vector processors were the CDC STAR-100 (see Hintz and Tate [1972]) and the TI ASC (see Watson [1972]), both announced in 1972. Both were memory-memory vector processors. They had relatively slow scalar units—the STAR used the same units for scalars and vectors—making the scalar pipeline extremely deep. Both processors had high start-up overhead and worked on vectors of several hundred to several thousand elements. The crossover between scalar and vector could be over 50 elements. It appears that not enough attention was paid to the role of Amdahl's Law on these two processors.

Cray, who worked on the 6600 and the 7600 at CDC, founded Cray Research and introduced the CRAY-1 in 1976 (see Russell [1978]). The CRAY-1 used a vector-register architecture to significantly lower start-up overhead. He also had efficient support for nonunit stride and invented chaining. Most importantly, the

CRAY-1 was the fastest scalar processor in the world at that time. This matching of good scalar and vector performance was probably the most significant factor in making the CRAY-1 a success. Some customers bought the processor primarily for its outstanding scalar performance. Many subsequent vector processors are based on the architecture of this first commercially successful vector processor. Baskett and Keller [1977] provide a good evaluation of the CRAY-1.

In 1981, CDC started shipping the CYBER-205 (see Lincoln [1982]). The 205 had the same basic architecture as the STAR, but offered improved performance all around as well as expandability of the vector unit with up to four vector pipelines, each with multiple functional units and a wide load-store pipe that provided multiple words per clock. The peak performance of the CYBER-205 greatly exceeded the performance of the CRAY-1. However, on real programs, the performance difference was much smaller.

The CDC STAR processor and its descendant, the CYBER-205, were memory-memory vector processors. To keep the hardware simple and support the high bandwidth requirements (up to three memory references per FLOP), these processors did not efficiently handle nonunit stride. While most loops have unit stride, a nonunit stride loop had poor performance on these processors because memory-to-memory data movements were required to gather together (and scatter back) the nonadjacent vector elements; these operations used special scatter-gather instructions. In addition, there was special support for sparse vectors that used a bit vector to represent the zeros and nonzeros and a dense vector of non-zero values. These more complex vector operations were slow because of the long memory latency, and it was often faster to use scalar mode for sparse or non-unit stride operations. Schneck [1987] described several of the early pipelined processors (e.g., Stretch) through the first vector processors including the 205 and CRAY-1. Dongarra [1986] did another good survey, focusing on more recent processors.

In 1983, Cray Research shipped the first CRAY X-MP (see Chen [1983]). With an improved clock rate (9.5 ns versus 12.5 on the CRAY-1), better chaining support, and multiple memory pipelines, this processor maintained the Cray Research lead in supercomputers. The CRAY-2, a completely new design configurable with up to four processors, was introduced later. A major feature of the CRAY-2 was the use of DRAM, which made it possible to have very large memories. The first CRAY-2 with its 256 M word (60-bit words) memory contained more memory than the total of all the Cray machines shipped to that point! The CRAY-2 had a much faster clock than the X-MP, but also much deeper pipelines; however, it lacked chaining, had an enormous memory latency, and had only one memory pipe per processor. In general, the CRAY-2 is only faster than the CRAY X-MP on problems that require its very large main memory.

The 1980s also saw the arrival of smaller-scale vector processors, called mini-supercomputers. Priced at roughly one-tenth the cost of a supercomputer ($0.5 to $1 million versus $5 to $10 million), these processors caught on quickly. Although many companies joined the market, the two companies that were most successful were Convex and Alliant. Convex started with a uniprocessor vector processor (C-1) and now offers a small multiprocessor (C-2); they emphasize Cray software capability. One of the keys to the success of Convex has been the effectiveness of their compiler (see Figure B.12 on page B-23) and the quality of their Unix OS implementation. The Convex example illustrates the increasing importance of software—even in the supercomputer business. Alliant [1987] concentrated more on the multiprocessor aspects; they built an eight-processor computer, with each processor offering vector capability. Alliant ceased operation in the early 1990s.

In 1983, processor vendors from Japan entered the supercomputer marketplace, starting with the Fujitsu VP100 and VP200 (Miura and Uchida [1983]), and later expanding to include the Hitachi S810 and the NEC SX/2 (see Watanabe [1987]). These processors have proved to be close to the CRAY X-MP in performance. In general, these three processors have much higher peak performance than the CRAY X-MP. However, because of large start-up overhead, their typical performance is often lower than the CRAY X-MP (see Figure 1.18 in Chapter 1). The CRAY X-MP favored a multiple-processor approach, first offering a two-processor version and later a four-processor. In contrast, the three Japanese processors had expandable vector capabilities.

In 1988, Cray Research introduced the CRAY Y-MP—a bigger and faster version of the X-MP. The Y-MP allows up to eight processors and lowers the cycle time to 6 ns. With a full complement of eight processors, the Y-MP was generally the fastest supercomputer, though the single-processor Japanese supercomputers may be faster than a one-processor Y-MP. In late 1989 Cray Research was split into two companies, both aimed at building high-end processors available in the early 1990s. Seymour Cray headed the spin-off, Cray Computer Corporation, until its demise in 1995. Their initial processor, the CRAY-3, was to be implemented in gallium arsenide, but they were unable to develop a reliable and cost-effective implementation technology. The CRAY-3 was cancelled and efforts were aimed at the CRAY-4, scheduled for delivery in 1995–96.

Cray Research focused on the C90, a new high-end processor with up to 16 processors and a clock rate of 240 MHz. This processor was delivered in 1991. Typical configurations are about $15 million. In 1993, Cray Research introduced their first highly parallel processor, the T3D. In 1995, they announced the availability of both a new low-end vector machine, the J90, and a high-end machine, the T90. The T90 is much like the C90, but offers a clock that is twice as fast (500 MHz), using three-dimensional packaging and optical clock distribution. Like the C90, the T90 costs in the tens of millions, though a single CPU is available for $2,500,000. The J90 is a CMOS-based vector machine using DRAM memory starting at $250,000, but with typical configurations running about $1 million. In mid 1995, Silicon Graphics acquired Cray Research, Inc.

In the early 1980s, CDC spun out a group, called ETA, to build a new supercomputer, the ETA-10, capable of 10 gigaFLOPS. The ETA processor delivered in the late 1980s (see Fazio [1987]) and used low-temperature CMOS in a configuration with up to 10 processors. Each processor retained the memory-memory architecture based on the CYBER-205. Although the ETA-10 achieved enormous peak performance, its scalar speed was not comparable. In 1989 CDC, the first supercomputer vendor, closed ETA and left the supercomputer design business.

In 1986, IBM introduced the System/370 vector architecture (see Moore et al. [1987]) and its first implementation in the 3090 Vector Facility. The architecture extends the System/370 architecture with 171 vector instructions. The 3090/VF is integrated into the 3090 CPU. Unlike most other vector processors, the 3090/VF routes its vectors through the cache.

The basis for modern vectorizing compiler technology and the notion of data dependence was developed by Kuck and his colleagues [1974] at the University of Illinois. Banerjee [1979] developed the test named after him. Padua and Wolfe [1986] gave a good overview of vectorizing compiler technology.

Benchmark studies of various supercomputers, including attempts to understand the performance differences, have been undertaken by Lubeck, Moore, and Mendez [1985], Bucher [1983], and Jordan [1987]. In Chapter 1, we discussed several benchmark suites aimed at scientific usage and often employed for supercomputer benchmarking, including Linpack and the Lawrence Livermore Laboratories FORTRAN kernels. The University of Illinois coordinated the collection of a set of benchmarks for supercomputers, called the Perfect Club. In 1993, the Perfect Club was integrated into SPEC, which will release a set of benchmarks aimed at high-end scientific processing sometime in 1995.

In less than 20 years vector processors have gone from unproven, new architectures to playing a significant role in the goal to provide engineers and scientists with ever-larger amounts of computing power. The enormous price-performance advantages of microprocessor technology may bring this era to an end. Recently, Cray, NEC, Fujitsu, and Convex announced and delivered large-scale multiprocessors based on microprocessors. By using advanced superscalar microprocessors, designers can build processors that exceed the peak performance of the fastest vector processors. The challenge, as we saw in Chapter 8, lies in programming these processors. As progress is made on this front, the role of vector processors in science and engineering may continue to decrease.

References

ALLIANT COMPUTER SYSTEMS CORP. [1987]. *Alliant FX/Series: Product Summary* (June), Acton, Mass.

BANERJEE, U. [1979]. *Speedup of Ordinary Programs*, Ph.D. Thesis, Dept. of Computer Science, Univ. of Illinois at Urbana-Champaign (October).

BASKETT, F. AND T. W. KELLER [1977]. "An Evaluation of the CRAY-1 Processor," in *High Speed Computer and Algorithm Organization*, D. J. Kuck, D. H. Lawrie, and A. H. Sameh, eds., Academic Press, San Diego, 71–84.

BUCHER, I. Y. [1983]. "The computational speed of supercomputers," *Proc. SIGMETRICS Conf. on Measuring and Modeling of Computer Systems,* ACM (August), 151–165.

CALLAHAN, D., J. DONGARRA, AND D. LEVINE [1988]. "Vectorizing compilers: A test suite and results," *Supercomputing '88,* ACM/IEEE (November), Orlando, Fla., 98–105.

CHEN, S. [1983]. "Large-scale and high-speed multiprocessor system for scientific applications," *Proc. NATO Advanced Research Work on High Speed Computing* (June); also in K. Hwang, ed., "Superprocessors: Design and applications," *IEEE* (August), 1984.

DONGARRA, J. J. [1986]. "A survey of high performance processors," *COMPCON, IEEE* (March), 8–11.

FAZIO, D. [1987]. "It's really much more fun building a supercomputer than it is simply inventing one," *COMPCON, IEEE* (February), 102–105.

FLYNN, M. J. [1966]. "Very high-speed computing systems," *Proc. IEEE* 54:12 (December), 1901–1909.

HINTZ, R. G. AND D. P. TATE [1972]. "Control data STAR-100 processor design," *COMPCON, IEEE* (September), 1–4.

JORDAN, K. E. [1987]. "Performance comparison of large-scale scientific processors: Scalar mainframes, mainframes with vector facilities, and supercomputers," *Computer* 20:3 (March), 10–23.

KUCK, D., P. P. BUDNIK, S.-C. CHEN, D. H. LAWRIE, R. A. TOWLE, R. E. STREBENDT, E. W. DAVIS, JR., J. HAN, P. W. KRASKA, AND Y. MURAOKA [1974]. "Measurements of parallelism in ordinary FORTRAN programs," *Computer* 7:1 (January), 37–46.

LINCOLN, N. R. [1982]. "Technology and design trade offs in the creation of a modern supercomputer," *IEEE Trans. on Computers* C-31:5 (May), 363–376.

LUBECK, O., J. MOORE, AND R. MENDEZ [1985]. "A benchmark comparison of three supercomputers: Fujitsu VP-200, Hitachi S810/20, and CRAY X-MP/2," *Computer* 18:1 (January), 10–29.

MIRANKER, G. S., J. RUBENSTEIN, AND J. SANGUINETTI [1988]. "Squeezing a Cray-class supercomputer into a single-user package," *COMPCON, IEEE* (March), 452–456.

MIURA, K. AND K. UCHIDA [1983]. "FACOM vector processing system: VP100/200," *Proc. NATO Advanced Research Work on High Speed Computing* (June); also in K. Hwang, ed., "Superprocessors: Design and applications," *IEEE* (August 1984), 59–73.

MOORE, B., A. PADEGS, R. SMITH, AND W. BUCHOLZ [1987]. "Concepts of the System/370 vector architecture," *Proc. 14th Symposium on Computer Architecture* (June), ACM/IEEE, Pittsburgh, 282–292.

PADUA, D. AND M. WOLFE [1986]. "Advanced compiler optimizations for supercomputers," *Comm. ACM* 29:12 (December), 1184–1201.

RUSSELL, R. M. [1978]. "The CRAY-1 processor system," *Comm. of the ACM* 21:1 (January), 63–72.

SCHNECK, P. B. [1987]. *Superprocessor Architecture,* Kluwer Academic Publishers, Norwell, Mass.

SMITH, B. J. [1981]. "Architecture and applications of the HEP multiprocessor system," *Real-Time Signal Processing IV* 298 (August), 241–248.

SPORER, M., F. H. MOSS, AND C. J. MATHAIS [1988]. "An introduction to the architecture of the Stellar Graphics supercomputer," *COMPCON, IEEE* (March), 464.

WATANABE, T. [1987]. "Architecture and performance of the NEC supercomputer SX system," *Parallel Computing* 5, 247–255.

WATSON, W. J. [1972]. "The TI ASC—A highly modular and flexible super processor architecture," *Proc. AFIPS Fall Joint Computer Conf.,* 221–228.

E X E R C I S E S

In these Exercises assume DLXV has a clock rate of 200 MHz and that $T_{loop} = 15$. Use the start-up times from the appendix, and assume that the store latency is always included in the running time.

B.1 [10] <B.1,B.2> Write a DLXV vector sequence that achieves the peak MFLOPS performance of the processor (use the functional unit and instruction description in section B.2). Assuming a 200-MHz clock rate, what is the peak MFLOPS?

B.2 [20/15/15] <B.1–B.6> Consider the following vector code run on a 200-MHz version of DLXV for a fixed vector length of 64:

```
LV      V1,Ra
MULTV   V2,V1,V3
ADDV    V4,V1,V3
SV      Rb,V2
SV      Rc,V4
```

Ignore all strip-mining overhead, but assume that the store latency must be included in the time to perform the loop. The entire sequence produces 64 results.

a. [20] <B.1–B.5> Assuming no chaining and a single memory pipeline, how many chimes are required? How many clock cycles per result (including both stores as one result) does this vector sequence require, including start-up overhead?

b. [15] <B.1–B.5> If the vector sequence is chained, how many clock cycles per result does this sequence require, including overhead?

c. [15] <B.1–B.6> Suppose DLXV had three memory pipelines and chaining. If there were no bank conflicts in the accesses for the above loop, how many clock cycles are required per result for this sequence?

B.3 [20/20/15/15/20/20/20] <B.2–B.6> Consider the following FORTRAN code:

```
        do 10 i=1,n
            A(i) = A(i) + E(i)
            B(i) = x * B(i)
10      continue
```

Use the techniques of section B.6 to estimate performance throughout this Exercise, assuming a 200-MHz version of DLXV.

a. [20] <B.2–B.6> Write the best DLXV vector code for the inner portion of the loop. Assume x is in F0 and the addresses of A and B are in Ra and Rb, respectively.

b. [20] <B.2–B.6> Find the total time for this loop on DLXV (T_{100}). What is the MFLOP rating for the loop (R_{100})?

c. [15] <B.2–B.6> Find R_∞ for this loop.

d. [15] <B.2–B.6> Find $N_{1/2}$ for this loop.

e. [20] <B.2–B.6> Find N_v for this loop. Assume the scalar code has been pipeline scheduled so that each memory reference takes six cycles and each FP operation takes three cycles. Assume the scalar overhead is also T_{loop}.

f.   [20] <B.2–B.6> Assume DLXV has two memory pipelines. Write vector code that takes advantage of the second memory pipeline. Show the layout in convoys.

g.   [20] <B.2–B.6> Compute T_{100} and R_{100} for DLXV with two memory pipelines.

B.4 [20/10] <B.3> Suppose we have a version of DLXV with eight memory banks (each a double word wide) and a memory-access time of eight cycles.

a.   [20] <B.3> If a load vector of length 64 is executed with a stride of 20 double words, how many cycles will the load take to complete?

b.   [10] <B.3> What percentage of the memory bandwidth do you achieve on a 64-element load at stride 20 versus stride 1?

B.5 [12/12] <B.4–B.6> Consider the following loop:

```
C = 0.0
do 10 i=1,64
        A(i) = A(i) + B(i)
        C = C + A(i)
10      continue
```

a.   [12] <B.4–B.6> Split the loop into two loops: one with no dependence and one with a dependence. Write these loops in FORTRAN—as a source-to-source transformation. This optimization is called *loop fission*.

b.   [12] <B.4–B.6> Write the DLXV vector code for the loop without a dependence.

B.6 [20/15/20/20] <B.4–B.6> The compiled Linpack performance of the CRAY-1 (designed in 1976) was almost doubled by a better compiler in 1989. Let's look at a simple example of how this might occur. Consider the DAXPY-like loop (where *k* is a parameter to the procedure containing the loop):

```
do 10 i=1,64
        do 10 j=1,64
                Y(k,j) = a*X(i,j) + Y(k,j)
10      continue
```

a.   [20] <B.4–B.6> Write the *straightforward* code sequence for just the inner loop in DLXV vector instructions.

b.   [15] <B.4–B.6> Using the techniques of section B.6, estimate the performance of this code on DLXV by finding T_{64} in clock cycles. You may assume that T_{loop} of overhead is incurred for each iteration of the outer loop. What limits the performance?

c.   [20] <B.4–B.6> Rewrite the DLXV code to reduce the performance limitation; show the resulting inner loop in DLXV vector instructions. (*Hint*: Think about what establishes T_{chime}; can you affect it?) Find the total time for the resulting sequence.

d.   [20] <B.4–B.6> Estimate the performance of your new version, using the techniques of section B.6 and finding T_{64}.

B.7 [15/15/25] <B.5> Consider the following code.

```
do 10 i=1,64
        if (B(i) .ne. 0) then
                A(i) = A(i) / B(i)
10      continue
```

Assume that the addresses of A and B are in Ra and Rb, respectively, and that F0 contains 0.

a.   [15] <B.5> Write the DLXV code for this loop using the vector-mask capability

b.   [15] <B.5> Write the DLXV code for this loop using scatter-gather.

c.   [25] <B.5> Estimate the performance (T_{100} in clock cycles) of these two vector loops, assuming a divide latency of 20 cycles. Assume that all vector instructions run at one result per clock, independent of the setting of the vector-mask register. Assume that 50% of the entries of B are 0. Considering hardware costs, which would you build if the above loop were typical?

B.8 [15/20/15/15] <B.1–B.6> In *Fallacies and Pitfalls* of Chapter 1, we saw that the difference between peak and sustained performance could be large: For one problem, a Hitachi S810 had a peak speed twice as high as that of the CRAY X-MP, while for another more realistic problem, the CRAY X-MP was twice as fast as the Hitachi processor. Let's examine why this might occur using two versions of DLXV and the following code sequences:

```
C                   Code sequence 1
          do 10 i=1,10000
                  A(i) = x * A(i) + y * A(i)
10        continue
```

```
C                   Code sequence 2
          do 10 i=1,100
                  A(i) = x * A(i)
10        continue
```

Assume there is a version of DLXV (call it DLXVII) that has two copies of every floating-point functional unit with full chaining among them. Assume that both DLXV and DLXVII have two load-store units. Because of the extra functional units and the increased complexity of assigning operations to units, all the overheads (T_{loop} and T_{start}) are doubled.

a.   [15] <B.1–B.6> Find the number of clock cycles for code sequence 1 on DLXV.

b.   [20] <B.1–B.6> Find the number of clock cycles on code sequence 1 for DLXVII. How does this compare to DLXV?

c.   [15] <B.1–B.6> Find the number of clock cycles on code sequence 2 for DLXV.

d.   [15] <B.1–B.6> Find the number of clock cycles on code sequence 2 for DLXVII. How does this compare to DLXV?

B.9 [20] <B.4> Here is a tricky piece of code with two-dimensional arrays. Does this loop have dependences? Can these loops be written so they are parallel? If so, how? Rewrite the *source* code so that it is clear that the loop can be vectorized, if possible.

```
          do 290 j = 2,n
            do 290 i = 2,j
                aa(i,j)= aa(i-1,j)*aa(i-1,j)+bb(i,j)
290       continue
```

C | Survey of RISC Architectures

RISC: any computer announced after 1985.

Steven Przybylski
A Designer of the Stanford MIPS

C.1   Introduction   C-1

C.2   Addressing Modes and Instruction Formats   C-3

C.3   Instructions: The DLX Subset   C-5

C.4   Instructions: Common Extensions to DLX   C-9

C.5   Instructions Unique to MIPS   C-13

C.6   Instructions Unique to SPARC   C-15

C.7   Instructions Unique to PowerPC   C-18

C.8   Instructions Unique to PA-RISC   C-19

C.9   Concluding Remarks   C-22

C.10 References   C-25

C.1 | Introduction

We cover four examples of reduced instruction set computer (RISC) architectures in this appendix:

- Hewlett Packard PA-RISC

- IBM and Motorola PowerPC

- SGI MIPS

- SPARC, developed originally by Sun Microsystems

We also include a discussion of DLX, the instruction set architecture invented for this book. (A review of DLX can be found on the back inside cover or in Figure 2.25 of Chapter 2.) There has never been another class of computers so similar. This similarity allows the presentation of four architectures in 25 pages, with DLX thrown in for good measure! Characteristics of these architectures are found in Figure C.1.

Readers of the first edition will note that the Intel i860 and Motorola M88000 now sleep with the fishes; HP PA-RISC and IBM PowerPC took their place in this appendix. Had we space for another architecture in our figures, the Digital Alpha AXP would join this group. Its similarities to MIPS made it the obvious candidate for omission.

	DLX	MIPS I	PA-RISC	PowerPC	SPARC V8
Date announced	1990	1986	1986	1993	1987
Instruction size (bits)	32	32	32	32	32
Address space (size, model)	32 bits, flat	32 bits, flat	48 bits, segmented	32 bits, flat	32 bits, flat
Data alignment	Aligned	Aligned	Aligned	Unaligned	Aligned
Data addressing modes	2	2	5	4	2
Protection	Page	Page	Page	Page	Page
Minimum page size	4 KB	4 KB	4 KB	4 KB	8 KB
I/O	Memory mapped	Memory mapped	Memory mapped	Memory mapped	Memory mapped
Integer registers (number, model, size)	31 GPR × 32 bits	31 GPR × 32 bits	31 GPR × 32 bits	32 GPR × 32 bits	31 GPR × 32 bits
Separate floating-point registers	32 × 32 or 16 × 64 bits	16 × 32 or 16 × 64 bits	56 × 32 or 28 × 64 bits	32 × 32 or 32 × 64 bits	32 × 32 or 16 × 64 bits
Floating-point format	IEEE 754 single, double	IEEE 754 single, double	IEEE 754 single, double	IEEE 754 single, double	IEEE 754 single, double

FIGURE C.1   Summary of the first version of five recent architectures. Except for number of data address modes and some instruction set details, the integer instruction sets of these architectures are very similar. Contrast this to Figure C.12 on page C-23. Later versions of these architectures all support a flat, 64-bit address space.

After discussing the addressing modes and instruction formats of our four RISC architectures, we present the survey of the instructions in three steps:

- Instructions found in DLX

- Instructions not found in DLX but found in two or more architectures

- The unique instructions and characteristics of each architecture

We conclude with a speculation about the future directions for RISCs.

The one complication in this second edition appendix is that some of the older RISCs have been extended over the years. As this book will be in print for several years, we decided to describe the latest version of the architectures, as computers with these instruction sets will be common soon even if they are not at the time of this writing: MIPS IV, PA-RISC 1.1; and SPARC version 9. We will also allude to version 2.0 of the PA-RISC instruction set occasionally, which will be published and shipped in systems shortly after the second edition of this book is complete. We give the evolution of the instruction sets in the final section.

C.2 | Addressing Modes and Instruction Formats

Figure C.2 shows the data addressing modes supported by each architecture. Since all have one register that always has the value 0 when used in address modes—in fact, it is r0 in every architecture—the absolute address mode with limited range can be synthesized using r0 as the base in displacement addressing. (Register 0 can be changed by ALU operations in PowerPC; register 0 is always zero in the other machines.) Similarly, register-indirect addressing is synthesized by using displacement addressing with an offset of 0. Simplified addressing modes is one distinguishing feature of RISC architectures.

Addressing mode	DLX	MIPS IV	PA-RISC 1.1	PowerPC	SPARC V9
Register + offset (displacement or based)	√	√	√	√	√
Register + register (indexed)	—	√ (FP)	√	√	√
Register + scaled register (scaled)	—	—	√	—	—
Register + offset & update register	—	—	√	√	—
Register + register & update register	—	—	√	√	—

FIGURE C.2 **Summary of data addressing modes.** PA-RISC also has short address versions of the offset addressing modes. MIPS IV has indexed addressing for floating-point loads and stores. (These addressing modes are described in Figure 2.5, page 75.)

References to code are normally PC-relative, although register indirect is supported for returning from procedures, for case statements, and for pointer function calls. One variation is that PC-relative branch addresses in everything but DLX are shifted left 2 bits before being added to the PC, thereby increasing the branch distance. This works because the length of all instructions is 32 bits and instructions must be aligned on 32-bit words in memory.

Figure C.3 shows the format of instructions, which includes the size of the address in the instructions. Each instruction set architecture uses these four primary instruction formats. The primary differences are subtle, concerning how to extend constant fields to 32 bits. Figure C.4 shows the variations.

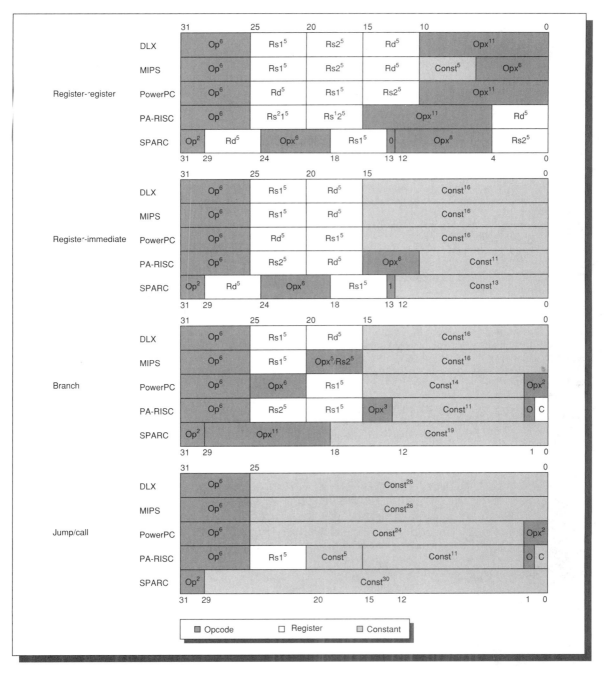

FIGURE C.3 Instruction formats for five architectures. These four formats are found in all five architectures. (The superscript notation in this figure means something different from our standard notation; it shows the width of a field in bits.) Although the register fields are located in similar pieces of the instruction, be aware that the destination and two source fields are scrambled. Here are the meanings of the abbreviations: Op = the main opcode, Opx = an opcode extension, Rd = the destination register, Rs1 = source register 1, Rs2 = source register 2, and Const = a constant (used as an immediate or as an address). Version 2.0 of PA-RISC will include a 16-bit add immediate format and a 17-bit address for calls. Note that our discussion of DLX in Chapters 2 and 3 numbers bits from left to right, while this figure uses right-to-left numbering.

Format: instruction category	DLX	MIPS IV	PA-RISC 1.1	PowerPC	SPARC V9
Branch: all	Sign	Sign	Sign	Sign	Sign
Jump/call: all	Sign	—	Sign	Sign	Sign
Register-immediate: data transfer	Sign	Sign	Sign	Sign	Sign
Register-immediate: arithmetic	Sign	Sign	Sign	Sign	Sign
Register-immediate: logical	Sign	Zero	—	Zero	Sign

FIGURE C.4 Summary of constant extension. The constants in the jump and call instructions of MIPS are not sign extended since they only replace the lower 28 bits of the PC, leaving the upper 4 bits unchanged (PA-RISC has no logical immediate instructions).

C.3 | Instructions: The DLX Subset

The similarities of each architecture allow simultaneous descriptions, starting with the operations equivalent to DLX.

DLX Instructions

Almost every instruction found in DLX is found in the other architectures, as Figure C.5 shows. (For reference, definitions of the DLX instructions are found in Figure 2.25 of Chapter 2 and on the back inside cover.) Instructions are listed under four categories: data transfer; arithmetic, logical; control; and floating point. A fifth category in the figure shows conventions for register usage and pseudo-instructions on each architecture. If a DLX instruction requires a short sequence of instructions in other architectures, these instructions are separated by semicolons in Figure C.5. (To avoid confusion, the destination register will *always* be the leftmost operand in this appendix, independent of the notation normally used with each architecture.)

Every architecture must have a scheme for compare and conditional branch, but despite all the similarities, each of these architectures has found a different way to perform the operation.

Instruction name	DLX	MIPS IV	PA-RISC 1.1	PowerPC	SPARC V9
Data transfer (instruction formats)	**R–I**	**R–I**	**R–I, R–R**	**R–I, R–R**	**R–I, R–R**
Load byte signed	LB	LB	LDB; EXTRS,8,31	LBZ; EXTSB	LDSB
Load byte unsigned	LBU	LBU	LDB,LDBX,LDBS	LBZ	LDUB
Load half word signed	LH	LH	LDH; EXTRS16,31	LHA	LDSH
Load half word unsigned	LHU	LHU	LDH,LDHX,LDHS	LHZ	LDUH
Load word	LW	LW	LDW,LDWX, LDWS	LW	LD
Load SP float	LF	LWC1	FLDWX,FLDWS	LFS	LDF
Load DP float	LD	LDC1	FLDDX,FLDDS	LFD	LDDF
Store byte	SB	SB	STB,STBX,STBS	STB	STB
Store half word	SH	SH	STH,STHX,STHS	STH	STH
Store word	SW	SW	STW,STWX,STWS	STW	ST
Store SP float	SF	SWC1	FSTWX,FSTWS	STFS	STF
Store DP float	SD	SWD1	FSTDX,FSTDS	STFD	STDF
Read, write special registers	MOVS2I, MOVI2S	MF, MT_	MFCTL, MTCTL	MFSPR, MF_, MTSPR, MT_	RD,WR, RDPR,WRPR, LDXFSR, STXFSR
Move int. to FP reg.	MOVI2FP	MFC1	STW; FLDWX	STW; LDFS	ST; LDF
Move FP to int. reg.	MOVFP2I	MTC1	FSTWX; LDW	STFS; LW	STF; LD
Arithmetic, logical (instruction formats)	**R–R, R–I**	**R–R, R–I**	**R–R, R–I**	**R–R, R–I**	**R–R, R–I**
Add	ADDU,ADDUI	ADDU, ADDIU	ADDL, LD0, ADDI, UADDCM	ADD,ADDI	ADD
Add (trap if overflow)	ADD,ADDI	ADD, ADDI	ADDO, ADDIO	ADDO; MCRXR; BC	ADDcc; TVS
Sub	SUBU,SUBUI	SUBU	SUB,SUBI	SUBF	SUB
Sub (trap if overflow)	SUB,SUBI	SUB	SUBTO,SUBIO	SUBF/oe	SUBcc; TVS
Multiply	MULTU, MULTUI	MULT, MULTU	SHiADD; ...; (i=1,2,3)	MULLW, MULLI	MULX
Multiply (trap if ovf)	MULT,MULTI	—	SHiADDO; ...;	—	—
Divide	DIVU,DIVUI	DIV,DIVU	DS; ...; DS	DIVW	DIVX
Divide (trap if ovf)	DIV,DIVI	—	—	—	—
And	AND,ANDI	AND,ANDI	AND	AND,ANDI	AND
Or	OR,ORI	OR,ORI	OR	OR,ORI	OR
Xor	XOR,XORI	XOR,XORI	XOR	XOR,XORI	XOR

Figure continued on next page

Instruction Name	DLX	MIPS IV	PA-RISC 1.1	PowerPC	SPARC V9
Arithmetic *(continued)* **(instruction formats)**	**R–I**	**R–I**	**R–I, R–R**	**R–I, R–R**	**R–I, R–R**
Load high part register	LHI	LUI	LDIL	ADDIS	SETHI (B fmt.)
Shift left logical	SLL,SLLI	SLLV,SLL	ZDEP 31-i, 32-i	RLWINM	SLL
Shift right logical	SRL,SRLI	SRLV,SRL	EXTRU 31, 32-i	RLWINM 32-i	SRL
Shift right arithmetic	SRA,SRAI	SRAV,SRA	EXTRS 31, 32-i	SRAW	SRA
Compare	S_(<,>,≤,≥, =,≠)	SLT/I, SL/ITU	COMB	CMP(I)CLR	SUBcc r0,...
Control **(instruction formats)**	**B, J/C**	**B, J/C**	**B, J/C**	**B, J/C**	**B, J/C**
Branch on integer compare	BEQ,BNE	BEQ,BNE, B_Z (<,>,≤,≥)	COMB, COMIB	BC	ER_Z, BPcc (<,>,≤,≥,=,≠)
Branch on floating-point compare	BFPT,BFPF	BC1T,BC1F	FSTWX f0; LDW t; BB t	BC	FBPfcc (<,>,≤,≥,=,...)
Jump, jump register	J,JR	J,JR	BL r0, BLR r0	B, BCLR, BCCTR	BA, JMPL r0,...
Call, call register	JAL,JALR	JAL,JALR	BL, BLE	BL,BLA, BCLRL, BCCTRL	CALL, JMPL
Trap	TRAP	BREAK	BREAK	TW, TWI	Ticc, SIR
Return from interrupt	RFE	JR; RFE	RFI,RFIR	RFI	DONE, RETRY, RETURN
Floating point **(instruction formats)**	**R–R**	**R–R**	**R–R**	**R–R**	**R–R**
Add single, double	ADDF, ADDD	ADD.S, ADD.D	FADD FADD/dbl	FADDS, FADD	FADDS, FADDD
Sub single, double	SUBF, SUBD	SUB.S, SUB.D	FSUB FSUB/dbl	FSUBS, FSUB	FSUBS, FSUBD
Mult single, double	MULF, MULD	MUL.S, MUL.D	FMPY FMPY/dbl	FMULS, FMUL	FMULS, FMULD
Div single, double	DIVF, DIVD	DIV.S, DIV.D	FDIV, FDIV/dbl	FDIVS, FDIV	FDIVS, FDIVD
Compare	_F, _D (<,>,≤,≥,=, ...)	C_.S, C_.D (<,>,≤,≥,=, ...)	FCMP, FCMP/ dbl (<,=,>)	FCMP	FCMPS, FCMPD
Move R–R	MOVF	MOV.S	FCPY	FMV	FMOVS/D/Q
Convert (single,double,integer) to (single,double,integer)	CVTF2D, CVTD2F, CVTF2I, CVTD2I, CVTI2F, CVTI2D	CVT.S.D, CVT.D.S, CVT.S.W, CVT.D.W, CVT.W.S, CVT.W.D	FCNVFF,s,d FCNVFF,d,s FCNVXF,s,s FCNVXF,d,d FCNVFX,s,s FCNVFX,d,s	—, FFSP, —, FCTIW, —, —	FSTOD, FDTOS, FSTOI, FDTOI, FITOS, FITOD

Figure continued on next page

Instruction Name	DLX	MIPS IV	PA-RISC 1.1	PowerPC	SPARC V9
Conventions					
Register with value 0	r0	r0	r0	r0 (addressing)	r0
Return address reg.	r31	r31	r2, r31	link (special)	r31
No-op	ADD r0,r0,r0	SLL r0,r0,r0	OR r0,r0,r0	ORI r0,r0,#0	SETHI r0,0
Move R–R integer	ADD ...,r0,...	ADD ...,r0,...	OR ...,r0,...	OR rx, ry, ry	OR ...,r0,...
Operand order	OP Rd,Rs1,Rs2	OP Rd,Rs1,Rs2	OP Rs1,Rs2,Rd	OP Rd,Rs1,Rs2	OP Rs1,Rs2,Rd

FIGURE C.5   Instructions equivalent to DLX. Dashes mean the operation is not available in that architecture, or not synthesized in a few instructions. Such a sequence of instructions is shown separated by semicolons. If there are several choices of instructions equivalent to DLX, they are separated by commas. Note that in the "Arithmetic, logical" category all machines but SPARC use separate instruction mnemonics to indicate an immediate operand; SPARC offers immediate versions of these instructions but uses a single mnemonic. (Of course these are separate opcodes!)

Compare and Conditional Branch

SPARC uses the traditional four condition code bits stored in the program status word: *negative, zero, carry,* and *overflow.* They can be set on any arithmetic or logical instruction; unlike earlier architectures, this setting is optional on each instruction. An explicit option leads to fewer problems in pipelined implementation. Although condition codes can be set as a side effect of an operation, explicit compares are synthesized with a subtract using r0 as the destination. SPARC conditional branches test condition codes to determine all possible unsigned and signed relations. Floating point uses separate condition codes to encode the IEEE 754 conditions, requiring a floating-point compare instruction. Version 9 expanded SPARC branches in four ways: a separate set of condition codes for 64-bit operations; a branch that tests the contents of a register and branches if the value is $=, \neq, <, \leq, \geq,$ or ≥ 0 (see MIPS below); three more sets of floating-point condition codes; and branch instructions that encode static branch prediction.

PowerPC also uses four condition codes: *less than, greater than, equal,* and *summary overflow,* but it has eight copies of them. This redundancy allows the PowerPC instructions to use different condition codes without conflict, essentially giving PowerPC eight extra 4-bit registers. Any of these eight condition codes can be the target of a compare instruction, and any can be the source of a conditional branch. The integer instructions have an option bit that behaves as if the integer op was followed by a compare to zero that sets the first condition "register." PowerPC also lets the second "register" be optionally set by floating-point instructions. PowerPC provides logical operations among these eight 4-bit condition code registers (CRAND, CROR, CRXOR, CRNAND, CRNOR, CREQV), allowing more complex conditions to be tested by a single branch.

MIPS uses the contents of registers to evaluate conditional branches. Any two registers can be compared for equality (BEQ) or inequality (BNE) and then the branch is taken if the condition holds. The set-on-less-than instructions (SLT, SLTI, SLTU, SLTIU) compare two operands and then set the destination register to 1 if less and to 0 otherwise. These instructions are enough to synthesize the full set of relations. Because of the popularity of comparisons to 0, MIPS includes special compare-and-branch instructions for all such comparisons: greater than or equal to zero (BGEZ), greater than zero (BGTZ), less than or equal to zero (BLEZ), and less than zero (BLTZ). Of course, equal and not equal to zero can be synthesized using r0 with BEQ and BNE. Like SPARC, MIPS I uses a condition code for floating point with separate floating-point compare and branch instructions; MIPS IV expands this to eight floating-point condition codes, with the floating-point comparisons and branch instructions specifying the condition to set or test.

PA-RISC has many branch options, which we'll see in section C.8. The most straightforward is a compare and branch instruction (COMB), which compares two registers, then branches depending on the standard relations, and tests the least-significant bit of the result of the comparison.

Figure C.6 summarizes the four schemes used for conditional branches.

	DLX	MIPS IV	PA-RISC 1.1	PowerPC	SPARC V9
Number of condition code bits (integer and FP)	1 FP	8 FP	1 FP	8 × 4 both	2 × 4 integer, 4 × 2 FP
Basic compare instructions (integer and FP)	1 integer, 1 FP	1 integer, 1 FP	4 integer, 1 FP	4 integer, 2 FP	1 FP
Basic branch instructions (integer and FP)	1 integer, 1 FP	2 integer, 1 FP	7 integer	1 both	3 integer, 1 FP
Compare register with register/const and branch	=,≠	=,≠	=,≠,<,≤,>,≥, even, odd	—	—
Compare register to zero and branch	=,≠	=,≠,<,≤,>,≥	=,≠,<,≤,>,≥, even, odd	—	=,≠,<,≤,>,≥

FIGURE C.6   Summary of five approaches to conditional branches. Floating-point branch on PA-RISC is accomplished by copying the FP status register into an integer register and then using the branch on bit instruction to test the FP comparison bit. Integer compare on SPARC is synthesized with an arithmetic instruction that sets the condition codes using r0 as the destination. PA-RISC 2.0 will have eight floating-point condition code bits.

C.4 | Instructions: Common Extensions to DLX

Figure C.7 lists instructions not found in Figure C.5 in the same four categories. Instructions are put in this list if they appear in more than one of the four architectures. The instructions are defined using the hardware description language, which is described on the page facing the inside back cover.

Name	Definition	MIPS IV	PA-RISC 1.1	PowerPC	SPARC V9
Data transfer					
Atomic swap R/M (for semaphores)	Temp←Rd; Rd← Mem[x]; Mem[x]←Temp	LL;SC	— (see C.8)	LWARX; STWCX	CASA, CASX
Load 64-bit integer	Rd←$_{64}$ Mem[x]	LD	(in 2.0)	LD	LDX
Store 64-bit int.	Mem[x]←$_{64}$ Rd	SD	(in 2.0)	STD	STX
Load 32-bit int. unsigned	Rd$_{32..63}$←$_{32}$ Mem[x]; Rd$_{0..31}$ ←$_{32}$ 0	LWU	(in 2.0)	LWZ	LDUW
Load 32-bit int. signed	Rd$_{32..63}$←$_{32}$ Mem[x]; Rd$_{0..31}$ ←$_{32}$ Mem[x]$_0^{32}$	LW	(in 2.0)	LWA	LDSW
Prefetch	Cache[x]←*hint*	PREF, PREFX	LDWX, LDWS, STWX, STWS	DCBT, DCBTST	PREFETCH
Load coprocessor	Coprocessor←Mem[x]	LWCi	CLDWX, CLDWS	—	—
Store coprocessor	Mem[x]←Coprocessor	SWCi	CSTWX, CSTWS	—	—
Endian	(Big/Little Endian?)	Either	Either	Either	Either
Cache flush	(Flush cache block at this address)	CP0op	FDC, FIC	DCBF	FLUSH
Shared memory synchronization	(All prior data transfers complete before next data transfers may start)	SYNC	SYNC	SYNC	MEMBAR
Arithmetic, logical					
64-bit integer arithmetic ops	Rd←$_{64}$Rs1 op$_{64}$ Rs2	DADD,DSUB DMULT, DDIV	(in 2.0)	ADD,SUBF, MULLD, DIVD	ADD, SUB, MULX, S/UDIVX
64-bit integer logical ops	Rd←$_{64}$Rs1 op$_{64}$ Rs2	AND,OR,XOR	(in 2.0)	AND,OR,XOR	AND,OR,XOR
64-bit shifts	Rd←$_{64}$Rs1 op$_{64}$ Rs2	DSLL,DSRA, DSRL	(in 2.0)	SLD,SRAD, SRLD	SLLX, SRAX, SRLX
Conditional move	if (cond) Rd← Rs	MOVN/Z	SUBc,n; ADD	—	MOVcc, MOVr
Support for multi-word integer add	CarryOut,Rd ← Rs1 + Rs2 + OldCarryOut	ADU;SLTU; ADDU	ADDC	ADDC, ADDE.	ADDcc
Support for multi-word integer sub	CarryOut,Rd ← Rs1 Rs2 + OldCarryOut	SUBU SLTU; SUBU	SUBB	SUBFC, SUBFE.	SUBcc
And not	Rd ← Rs1 & ~(Rs2)	—	ANDCM	ANDC	ANDN
Or not	Rd ← Rs1	~(Rs2)	—	—	ORC	ORN
Add high immediate	Rd$_{0..15}$←Rs1$_{0..15}$ + (Const<<16);	—	ADDIL (R-I)	ADDIS (R-I)	—
Coprocessor operations	(Defined by coprocessor)	COPi	COPR,i	—	IMPDEPi

Figure continued on next page

Name	Definition	MIPS IV	PA-RISC 1.1	PowerPC	SPARC V9
Control					
Optimized delayed branches	(Branch not always delayed)	BEQL,BNEL, B_ZL ($<,>,\leq,\geq$)	COMBT,n, COMBF,n	–	BPcc,A FPBcc,A
Conditional trap	if (COND) {R31←PC; PC ←0..0#i}	T_,T_I ($=,\neq,<,>,\leq,\geq$)	SUBc,n; BREAK	TW, TD, TWI, TDI	Tcc
No. control regs.	Misc. regs (virtual memory, interrupts,...)	≈12	32	33	29
Floating point					
Multiply & Add	Fd ← (Fs1 × Fs2) + Fs3	MADD.S/D	— (see C.8)	FMADD/S	
Multiply & Sub	Fd ← (Fs1 × Fs2) – Fs3	MSUB.S/D	— (see C.8)	FMSUB/S	
Neg Mult & Add	Fd ←–((Fs1 × Fs2)+Fs3)	NMADD.S/D		FNMADD/S	
Neg Mult & Sub	Fd ←–((Fs1 × Fs2)–Fs3)	NMSUB.S/D		FNMSUB/S	
Square Root	Fd ← SQRT(Fs)	SQRT.S/D	FSQRTsgl/ dbl	FSQRT/S	FSQRTS/D
Conditional Move	if (cond) Fd←Fs	MOVF/T, MOVF/T.S/D,	FTEST;FCPY	–	FMOVcc
Negate	Fd ← Fs ^ x80000000	NEG.S/D	(in 2.0)	FNEG	FNEGS/D/Q
Absolute value	Fd ← Fs & x7FFFFFFF	ABS.S/D	FABS/dbl	FABS	FABSS/D/Q

FIGURE C.7 Instructions not found in DLX but found in two or more of the four architectures.

Although most of the categories are self-explanatory, a few bear comment:

- The "atomic swap" row means a primitive that can exchange a register with memory without interruption. This is useful for operating system semaphores in uniprocessor as well as for multiprocessor synchronization (see section 8.5 of Chapter 8).

- The 64-bit data transfer and operation rows show how MIPS, PowerPC, and SPARC define 64-bit addressing and integer operations. SPARC simply defines all register and addressing operations to be 64 bits, adding only special instructions for 64-bit shifts, data transfers and branches. MIPS includes the same extensions, plus it adds separate 64-bit signed arithmetic instructions. PowerPC added 64-bit right shift, load, store, divide, and compare and has a separate mode determining whether instructions are interpreted as 32- or 64-bit operations; 64-bit operations will not work in a machine that only supports 32-bit mode. PA-RISC is expanded to 64-bit addressing and operations in version 2.0.

- The "prefetch" instruction supplies an address and hint to the implementation about the data. Hints include that the data is likely to be read or written soon.

likely to be read or written only once, or likely to be read or written many times. Prefetch does not cause exceptions. MIPS has a version that adds two registers to get the address for floating-point programs, unlike non-floating-point MIPS programs. (See pages 412–414 in Chapter 5 to learn more about prefetching.)

■ In the "Endian" row, "Big or Little" means there is a bit in the program status register that allows the processor to act either as Big Endian or Little Endian (see page 73 in Chapter 2). This can be accomplished by simply complementing some of the least-significant bits of the address in data transfer instructions.

■ The "shared memory synchronization" helps with cache-coherent multiprocessors: All loads and stores executed before the instruction must complete before loads and stores after it can start. (See section 8.5 of Chapter 8.)

■ The "coprocessor operations" row lists several categories that allow for the processor to be extended with special-purpose hardware.

One difference that needs a longer explanation is the optimized branches. Figure C.8 shows the options. The PowerPC offers branches that take effect immediately, like branches on earlier architectures. This avoids executing NOPs when there is no instruction to fill the delay slot; all the rest offer delayed branches. The other three provide a version of delayed branch that makes it easier to fill the delay slot. The SPARC "annulling" branch executes the instruction in the delay slot only if the branch is taken; otherwise the instruction is annulled. This means the instruction at the target of the branch can safely be copied into the delay slot since it will only be executed if the branch is taken. The restrictions are that the target is not another branch and that the target is known at compile time. (SPARC also offers a non-delayed jump because an unconditional branch with the annul bit set does *not* execute the following instruction.) Recent versions of the MIPS architecture have added a branch likely instruction that also annuls the following instruction if the branch is not taken. PA-RISC allows almost any instruction to annul the next instruction, including branches. Its "nullifying" branch option will execute the next instruction depending on the direction of the branch and whether it is taken (i.e., if a forward branch is *not* taken or a backward branch is taken). Presumably this choice was made to optimize loops, allowing the instructions following the exit branch and the looping branch to execute in the common case.

Now that we have covered the similarities, we will focus on the unique features of each architecture, ordering them by length of description of the unique features from shortest to longest.

	(Plain) Branch	Delayed branch	Annulling delayed branch	
Found in architectures	PowerPC	DLX, MIPS, PA-RISC, SPARC	MIPS, SPARC	PA-RISC
Execute following instruction	Only if branch *not* taken	Always	Only if branch taken	If forward branch *not* taken or backward branch taken

FIGURE C.8   **When the instruction following the branch is executed for three types of branches.**

C.5 | Instructions Unique to MIPS

MIPS has gone through four generations of instruction set evolution, and this evolution has generally added features found in other architectures. Here are the salient unique features of MIPS, the first several of which were found in the original instruction set.

Nonaligned Data Transfers

MIPS has special instructions to handle misaligned words in memory. A rare event in most programs, it is included for COBOL programs where the programmer can force misalignment by declarations. Although most RISCs trap if you try to load a word or store a word to a misaligned address, on all architectures misaligned words can be accessed without traps by using four load byte instructions and then assembling the result using shifts and logical ORs. The MIPS load and store word left and right instructions (LWL, LWR, SWL, SWR) allow this to be done in just two instructions: LWL loads the left portion of the register and LWR loads the right portion of the register. SWL and SWR do the corresponding stores. Figure C.9 shows how they work. There are also 64-bit versions of these instructions.

TLB Instructions

TLB misses are handled in software in MIPS, so the instruction set also has instructions for manipulating the registers of the TLB (see pages 455–456 in Chapter 5 for more on TLBs). These registers are considered part of the "system coprocessor" and thus can be accessed by the instructions that move between coprocessor registers and integer registers. The contents of a TLB entry are read by loading via read indexed TLB entry (TLBR) and written using either write indexed TLB entry (TLBWI) or write random TLB entry (TLBWR). The TLB contents are searched using probe TLB for matching entry (TLBP).

Remaining Instructions

Below is a list of the remaining unique details of the MIPS architecture:

- *NOR*—This logical instruction calculates ~(Rs1 | Rs2).

- *Constant shift amount*—Non-variable shifts use the 5-bit constant field shown in the register-register format in Figure C.3.

- *SYSCALL*—This special trap instruction is used to invoke the operating system.

- *Move to/from control registers*—CTCi and CFCi move between the integer registers and control registers.

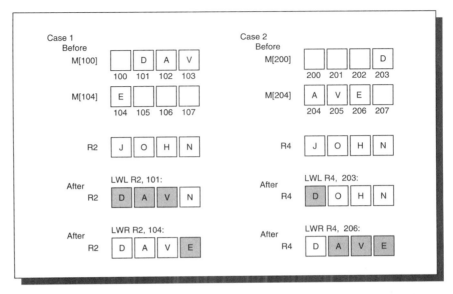

FIGURE C.9 MIPS instructions for unaligned word reads. This figure assumes operation in Big Endian mode. Case 1 first loads the 3 bytes 101,102, and 103 into the left of R2, leaving the least-significant byte undisturbed. The following LWR simply loads byte 104 into the least-significant byte of R2, leaving the other bytes of the register unchanged using LWL. Case 2 first loads byte 203 into the most-significant byte of R4, and the following LWR loads the other 3 bytes of R4 from memory bytes 204, 205, and 206. LWL reads the word with the first byte from memory, shifts to the left to discard the unneeded byte(s), and changes only those bytes in Rd. The byte(s) transferred are from the first byte until the lowest-order byte of the word. The following LWR addresses the last byte, right shifts to discard the unneeded byte(s), and finally changes only those bytes of Rd. The byte(s) transferred are from the last byte up to the highest-order byte of the word. Store word left (SWL) is simply the inverse of LWL, and store word right (SWR) is the inverse of LWR. Changing to Little Endian mode flips which bytes are selected and discarded. (If big-little, left-right, load-store seem confusing, don't worry, it works!)

- *Jump/call not PC-relative*—The 26-bit address of jumps and calls is not added to the PC. It is shifted left 2 bits and replaces the lower 28 bits of the PC. This would only make a difference if the program were located near a 256-MB boundary.

- *Load linked/store conditional*—This pair of instructions gives MIPS atomic operations for semaphores, allowing data to be read from memory, modified, and stored without fear of interrupts or other machines accessing the data in a multiprocessor (see section 8.5 of Chapter 8). There are both 32- and 64-bit versions of these instructions.

- *Reciprocal and reciprocal square root*—These instructions, which do *not* follow IEEE 754 guidelines of proper rounding, are included apparently for applications that value speed of divide and square root more than they value accuracy.

■ *Conditional procedure call instructions*—BGEZAL saves the return address and branches if the content of Rs1 is greater than or equal to zero, and BLTZAL does the same for less than zero. The purpose of these instructions is to get a PC-relative call. (There are "likely" versions of these instructions as well.)

There is no specific provision in the MIPS architecture for floating-point execution to proceed in parallel with integer execution, but the MIPS implementations of floating point allow this to happen by checking to see if arithmetic interrupts are possible early in the cycle (see Appendix A). Normally interrupts are not possible when integer and floating point operate in parallel.

C.6 Instructions Unique to SPARC

Several features are unique to SPARC.

Register Windows

The primary unique feature of SPARC is register windows, an optimization for reducing register traffic on procedure calls. Several banks of registers are used, with a new one allocated on each procedure call. Although this could limit the depth of procedure calls, the limitation is avoided by operating the banks as a circular buffer, providing unlimited depth. The knee of the cost-performance curve seems to be six to eight banks.

SPARC can have between two and 32 windows, typically using eight registers each for the globals, locals, incoming parameters, and outgoing parameters. (Given each window has 16 unique registers, an implementation of SPARC can have as few as 40 physical registers and as many as 520, although most have 128 to 136, so far.) Rather than tie window changes with call and return instructions, SPARC has the separate instructions SAVE and RESTORE. SAVE is used to "save" the caller's window by pointing to the next window of registers in addition to performing an add instruction. The trick is that the source registers are from the caller's window of the addition operation, while the destination register is in the callee's window. SPARC compilers typically use this instruction for changing the stack pointer to allocate local variables in a new stack frame. RESTORE is the inverse of SAVE, bringing back the caller's window while acting as an add instruction, with the source registers from the callee's window and the destination register in the caller's window. This automatically deallocates the stack frame. Compilers can also make use of it for generating the callee's final return value.

The danger of register windows is that the larger number of registers could slow down the clock rate. This was not the case for early implementations. The SPARC architecture (with register windows) and the MIPS R2000 architecture (without) have been built in several technologies since 1987. For several generations the SPARC clock rate has not been slower than the MIPS clock rate for implementations in similar technologies, probably because cache-access times dominate register-access times in these implementations. The current generation machines took different implementation strategies—superscalar vs. superpipelining—and it's unlikely that the number of registers by themselves determined the clock rate in either machine.

Another data transfer feature is alternate space option for loads and stores. This simply allows the memory system to identify memory accesses to input/output devices, or to control registers for devices such as the cache and memory-management unit.

Fast Traps

Version 9 SPARC includes support to make traps fast. It expands the single level of traps to at least four levels, allowing the window overflow and underflow trap handlers to be interrupted. The extra levels mean the handler does not need to check for page faults or misaligned stack pointers explicitly in the code, thereby making the handler faster. Two new instructions were added to return from this multilevel handler: RETRY (which retries the interrupted instruction) and DONE (which does not). To support user-level traps, the instruction RETURN will return from the trap in nonprivileged mode.

Support for LISP and Smalltalk

The primary remaining arithmetic feature is tagged addition and subtraction. The designers of SPARC spent some time thinking about languages like LISP and Smalltalk, and this influenced some of the features of SPARC already discussed: register windows, conditional trap instructions, calls with 32-bit instruction addresses, and multiword arithmetic (see Taylor et al. [1986] and Ungar et al. [1984]). A small amount of support is offered for tagged data types with operations for addition, subtraction, and hence comparison. The two least-significant bits indicate whether the operand is an integer (coded as 00), so TADDcc and TSUBcc set the overflow bit if either operand is not tagged as an integer or if the result is too large. A subsequent conditional branch or trap instruction can decide what to do. (If the operands are not integers, software recovers the operands, checks the types of the operands, and invokes the correct operation based on those types.) It turns out that the misaligned memory access trap can also be put to use for tagged data, since loading from a pointer with the wrong tag can be an invalid access. Figure C.10 shows both types of tag support.

Overlapped Integer and Floating-Point Operations

SPARC allows floating-point instructions to overlap execution with integer instructions. To recover from an interrupt during such a situation, SPARC has a queue of pending floating-point instructions and their addresses. RDPR allows the

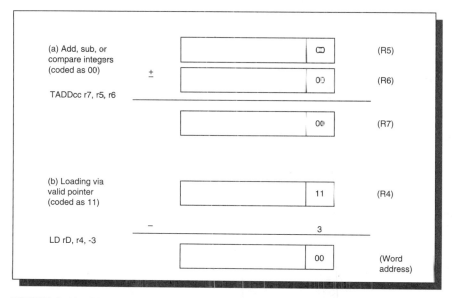

FIGURE C.10 SPARC uses the two least-significant bits to encode different data types for the tagged arithmetic instructions. (a) Integer arithmetic, which takes a single cycle as long as the operands and the result are integers. (b) The misaligned trap can be used to catch invalid memory accesses, such as trying to use an integer as a pointer. For languages with paired data like LISP, an offset of –3 can be used to access the even word of a pair (CAR) and +1 can be used for the odd word of a pair (CDR).

processor to empty the queue. The second floating-point feature is the inclusion of floating-point square root instructions FSQRTS, FSQRTD, and FSQRTQ.

Remaining Instructions

The remaining unique features of SPARC are

- *JMPL* uses Rd to specify the return address register, so specifying r31 makes it similar to JALR in DLX and specifying r0 makes it like JR.

- *LDSTUB* loads the value of the byte into Rd and then stores FF_{16} into the addressed byte. This version 8 instruction can be used to implement a semaphore.

- *CASA* (*CASXA*) atomically compares a value in a processor register to 32-bit (64-bit) value in memory; if and only if they are equal, it swaps the value in memory with the value in a second processor register. This version 9 instruction can be used to construct wait-free synchronization algorithms that do not require the use of locks.

- *XNOR* calculates the exclusive or with the complement of the second operand.

- *BPcc*, *BPr*, and *FBPcc* include a branch prediction bit so that the compiler can give hints to the machine about whether a branch is likely to be taken or not.

- *ILLTRAP* causes an illegal instruction trap. Muchnick [1988] explains how this is used for proper execution of aggregate returning procedures in C.

- *POPC* counts the number of bits set to one in an operand.

- *Non-faulting loads* allow compilers to move load instructions ahead of conditional control structures that control their use. Hence, non-faulting loads will be executed speculatively.

- *Quadruple precision floating-point arithmetic and data transfer* allow the floating-point registers to act as eight 128-bit registers for floating-point operations and data transfers.

- *Multiple-precision floating-point results for multiply* mean that two single-precision operands can result in a double-precision product and two double-precision operands can result in a quadruple-precision product. These instructions can be useful in complex arithmetic and some models of floating-point calculations.

C.7 | Instructions Unique to PowerPC

PowerPC is the result of several generations of IBM commercial RISC machines: IBM RT/PC, IBM Power-1, and IBM Power-2.

Branch Registers: Link and Counter

Rather than dedicate one of the 32 general-purpose registers to save the return address on procedure call, PowerPC puts the address into a special register called the *link register*. Since many procedures will return without calling another procedure, link doesn't always have to be saved away. Making the return address a special register makes the return jump faster since the hardware need not go through the register read pipeline stage for return jumps.

In a similar vein, PowerPC has a *count register* to be used in for loops where the program iterates for a fixed number of times. By using a special register the branch hardware can determine quickly whether a branch based on the count register is likely to branch, since the value of the register is known early in the execution cycle. Tests of the value of the count register in a branch instruction will automatically decrement the count register.

Given that the count register and link register are already located with the hardware that controls branches, and that one of the problems in branch prediction is getting the target address early in the pipeline (see Chapter 3, section 3.5), the PowerPC architects decided to make a second use of these registers. Either

register can hold a target address of a conditional branch. Thus PowerPC supple-
ments its basic conditional branch with two instructions that get the target address
from these registers (BCLR, BCCTR).

Remaining Instructions

Unlike other RISC machines, register 0 is not hardwired to the value 0. It cannot
be used as a base register, but in base+index addressing it can be used as the index. The other unique features of the PowerPC are

- *Load multiple* and *store multiple* save or restore up to 32 registers in a single
  instruction.

- LSW and STSW permit fetching and storing of fixed and variable-length strings
  that have arbitrary alignment.

- *Rotate with mask* instructions support bit field extraction and insertion. One
  version rotates the data and then performs logical AND with a mask of ones,
  thereby extracting a field. The other version rotates the data but only places the
  bits into the destination register where there is a corresponding 1 bit in the
  mask, thereby inserting a field.

- *Algebraic right shift* sets the carry bit (CA) if the operand is negative and any
  one bits are shifted out. Thus a signed divide by any constant power of two that
  rounds toward zero can be accomplished with a SRAWI followed by ADDZE,
  which adds CA to the register.

- *CBTLZ* will count leading zeros.

- *SUBFIC* computes (immediate – RA), which can be used to develop a one's or
  two's complement.

- *Logical shifted immediate* instructions shift the 16-bit immediate to the left 16
  bits before performing AND, OR, or XOR.

C.8 | Instructions Unique to PA-RISC

PA-RISC was expanded slightly in 1990 with version 1.1 and changed significantly in 2.0 with 64-bit extensions that will be in systems shipped in 1996. PA-
RISC perhaps has the most unusual features of any commercial RISC machine.
For example, it has the most addressing modes, instruction formats, and, as we
shall see, several instructions that are really the combination of two simpler instructions.

- *Load* and *clear* instructions provide a semaphore that reads a value from memory and then writes zero.

- *Store bytes short* optimizes unaligned data moves, moving either the leftmost or the rightmost bytes in a word to the effective address depending on the instruction options and condition code bits.

- Loads and stores work well with caches by having options that give hints about whether to load data into the cache if it's not already in the cache. For example, load with a destination of register 0 is defined to be a cache hint.

- *Multiply/add* and *multiply/subtract* are floating-point operations that can launch two independent floating-point operations in a single instruction. Version 2.0 of PA-RISC will have fused multiply-add like the PowerPC.

In addition to instructions, here are a few features that distinguish PA-RISC:

- The segmented address space above the 2^{32} boundary means that there must be instructions to manipulate the segment registers and branch instructions that can leave the current segment.

- The data addressing modes use either a 14-bit offset or a 5-bit offset, and the sum of the base register and the immediate can be used to update the base register. The decision of whether to use only the base register or the sum as the effective address is optional. For 5-bit offsets there is a bit in the instruction that makes the decision, but in the 14-bit offsets it depends on the sign bit offset: Negative means use the sum, positive means use the register. These options turn the standard 6-integer data transfers into 20 instructions. PA-RISC 2.0 makes the set of addressing options more orthogonal.

C.9 | Concluding Remarks

This appendix covers the addressing modes, instruction formats, and all instructions found in four recent RISC architectures. Although the later sections concentrate on the differences, it would not be possible to cover four architectures in these few pages if there were not so many similarities. In fact, we would guess that more than 90% of the instructions executed for any of these architectures would be found in Figure C.5 on pages C-6–C-8. To contrast this homogeneity, Figure C.12 gives a summary for four architectures from the 1970s in a format similar to that shown in Figure C.1 on page C-2. (Imagine trying to write a single appendix in this style for those architectures.) In the history of computing, there has never been such widespread agreement on computer architecture.

	IBM 360/370	**Intel 8086**	**Motorola 68000**	**DEC VAX**
Date announced	1964/1970	1978	1980	1977
Instruction size(s) (bits)	16,32,48	8,16,24,32, 40,48	16,32,48,64,80	8,16,24,32,..., 432
Addressing (size, model)	24 bits, flat/ 31 bits, flat	4+16 bits, segmented	24 bits, flat	32 bits, flat
Data aligned?	Yes 360/ No 370	No	16-bit aligned	No
Data addressing modes	2/3	5	9	≥ 14
Protection	Page	None	Optional	Page
Page size	2 KB & 4 KB	—	0.25 to 32 KB	0.5 KB
I/O	Opcode	Opcode	Memory mapped	Memory mapped
Integer registers (size, model, number)	16 GPR × 32 bits	8 dedicated data × 16 bits	8 data & 8 address × 32 bits	15 GPR × 32 bits
Separate floating-point registers	4 × 64 bits	Optional: 8 × 80 bits	Optional: 8 × 80 bits	0
Floating-point format	IBM (floating hexadecimal)	IEEE 754 single, double, extended	IEEE 754 single, double, extended	DEC

FIGURE C.12 Summary of four 1970s architectures. Unlike the architectures in Figure C.1 on page C-2, there is little agreement between these architectures in any category. (See Appendix D for more details on the 8086; in fact, the description of just this one machine is as long as this whole appendix!)

This style of architectures cannot remain static, however. Like people, instruction sets tend to get bigger as they get older. Figure C.13 shows the genealogy of these instruction sets, and Figure C.14 shows which features were added to or deleted from generations of machines over time.

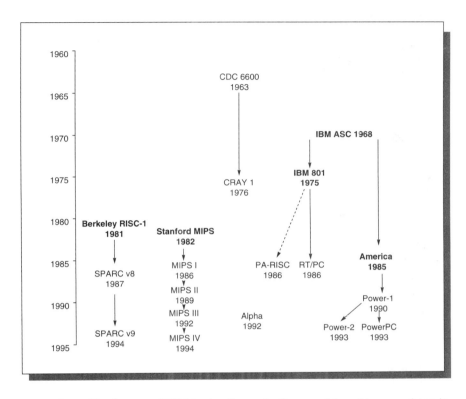

FIGURE C.13   The lineage of RISC instruction sets. Commercial machines are shown in plain text and research machines in **bold**. The CDC-6600 and Cray-1 were load-store machines with register 0 fixed at 0, and separate integer and floating-point registers. Instructions could not cross word boundaries. An early IBM research machine led to the 801 and America research projects, with the 801 leading to the unsuccessful RT/PC and America leading to the successful Power architecture. Some people who worked on the 801 later joined Hewlett Packard to work on the PA-RISC. The two university projects were the basis of MIPS and SPARC machines. DEC shipped workstations using MIPS microprocessors for three years before they brought out their own RISC instruction set, Alpha, which is very similar to MIPS III.

Feature	PA-RISC			SPARC		MIPS				Power		
	1.0	1.1	2.0	v. 8	v. 9	I	II	III	IV	1	2	PC
Interlocked loads	√	"	"	√	'		+	"	"	√	"	"
Load/store FP double	√	"	'	√	"		+	"	"	√	"	"
Semaphore	√	"	'	√	"		+	"	"	√	"	"
Square root	√	"	■	√	"		+	"	"		+	"
Single-precision FP ops	√	"	"	√	"	√	"	"	"			+
Memory synchronization	√	"	'	√	"		+	"	"	√	"	"
Coprocessor	√	"	"	√	−	√	"	"	"			
Base + index addressing	√	"	"	√	"				+	√	"	'
≈ 32 64-bit FP registers		"	"		+			+	"	√	"	'
Annulling delayed branch	√	"	"	√	"		+	"	"			
Branch register contents	√	"	"		+	√	"	"	"			
Big or Little Endian		+	"		+	√	"	"	"			+
Branch prediction bit					+		+	"	"	√	"	"
Conditional move					+				+	√	"	−
Prefetch data into cache			+		+				+	√	"	"
64-bit addressing/ int. ops			+		+			+	"			+
32-bit multiply, divide		+	"	+		√	"	"	'	√	"	
Load/store FP quad					+						+	−
Fused FP mul/add			+						−	√	"	"
String instructions	√	"	"							√	"	−

FIGURE C.14 **Features added to RISC machines.** √ means in the original machine, + means added later, " means continued from prior machine, and − means removed from architecture.

C.10 | References

BHANDARKAR, D. P. [1995]. *Alpha Architecture and Implementations*, Digital Press, Newton, Mass.

HEWLETT PACKARD [1994]. *PA-RISC 1.1 Architecture Reference Manual*, 3rd ed.

IBM [1994]. *The PowerPC Architecture*, Morgan Kaufmann, San Francisco.

KANE, G. [1988]. *MIPS RISC Architecture*, Prentice Hall, Englewood Cliffs, N. J.

MAGENHEIMER, D. J., L. PETERS, K. W. PETTIS, AND D. ZURAS [1988]. "Integer multiplication and division on the HP Precision Architecture," *IEEE Trans. on Computers*, 37:8, 980–990.

MUCHNICK, S. S. [1988] "Optimizing compilers for SPARC," *Sun Technology* (Summer) 1:3, 64–77.

SILICON GRAPHICS [1994]. *MIPS IV Instruction Set*, Revision 2.2.

SITES, R. L. (ED.) [1992]. *Alpha Architecture Reference Manual*, Digital Press, Newton, Mass.

Sun Microsystems [1989]. *The SPARC Architectural Manual*, Version 8, Part No. 800-1399-09, August 25, 1989.

Taylor, G., P. Hilfinger, J. Larus, D. Patterson, and B. Zorn [1986]. "Evaluation of the SPUR LISP architecture," *Proc. 13th Symposium on Computer Architecture (*June), Tokyo.

Ungar, D., R. Blau, P. Foley, D. Samples, and D. Patterson [1984]. "Architecture of SOAR: Smalltalk on a RISC," *Proc. 11th Symposium on Computer Architecture* (June), Ann Arbor, Mich., 188–197.

Weaver, D. L. and T. Germond [1994]. *The SPARC Architectural Manual*, Version 9, Prentice Hall, Englewood Cliffs, N. J.

Weiss, S. and J. E. Smith [1994]. *Power and PowerPC*, Morgan Kaufmann, San Francisco.

An Alternative to RISC: The Intel 80x86

The x86 isn't all that complex—it just doesn't make a lot of sense.

Mike Johnson
Leader of 80x86 Design at AMD,
Microprocessor Report (1994)

D.1	Introduction	D-1
D.2	80x86 Registers and Data Addressing Modes	D-2
D.3	80x86 Integer Operations	D-6
D.4	80x86 Floating-Point Operations	D-9
D.5	80x86 Instruction Encoding	D-11
D.6	Putting It All Together: Measurements of Instruction Set Usage	D-15
D.7	Concluding Remarks	D-22
D.8	Historical Perspective and References	D-23

D.1 Introduction

DLX was the vision of a single architect. The pieces of this architecture fit nicely together and the whole architecture can be described succinctly. Such is not the case of the 80x86: It is the product of several independent groups who evolved the architecture over more than 10 years, adding new features to the original instruction set as you might add clothing to a packed bag. Here are important 80x86 milestones:

- 1978—The Intel 8086 architecture was announced as an assembly-language-compatible extension of the then-successful Intel 8080, an 8-bit microprocessor. The 8086 is a 16-bit architecture, with all internal registers 16 bits wide. Whereas the 8080 was a straightforward accumulator machine, the 8086 extended the architecture with additional registers. Because nearly every register has a dedicated use, the 8086 falls somewhere between an accumulator machine and a general-purpose register machine, and can fairly be called an *extended accumulator* machine.

- 1980—The Intel 8087 floating-point coprocessor is announced. This architecture extends the 8086 with about 60 floating-point instructions. Its architects rejected extended accumulators to go with a hybrid of stacks and registers, essentially an *extended stack* architecture: A complete stack instruction set is supplemented by a limited set of register-memory instructions.

- 1982—The 80286 extended the 8086 architecture by increasing the address space to 24 bits, by creating an elaborate memory-mapping and protection model, and by adding a few instructions to round out the instruction set and to manipulate the protection model. Because it was important to run 8086 programs without change, the 80286 offered a *real addressing mode* to make the machine look just like an 8086.

- 1985—The 80386 extended the 80286 architecture to 32 bits. In addition to a 32-bit architecture with 32-bit registers and a 32-bit address space, the 80386 added new addressing modes and additional operations. The added instructions make the 80386 nearly a general-purpose register machine. The 80386 also added paging support in addition to segmented addressing (see Chapter 5). Like the 80286, the 80386 has a mode to execute 8086 programs without change.

This history illustrates the impact of the "golden handcuffs" of compatibility on the 80x86, as the existing software base at each step was too important to jeopardize with significant architectural changes. Fortunately, the subsequent 80486 in 1989, Pentium in 1992, and P6 in 1995 were aimed at higher performance, with only four instructions added to the user-visible instruction set: three to help with multiprocessing plus a conditional move instruction.

Whatever the artistic failures of the 80x86, keep in mind that there are more instances of this architectural family than of any other in the world, perhaps 200 million in 1995. Nevertheless, its checkered ancestry has led to an architecture that is difficult to explain and impossible to love.

We start our explanation with the registers and addressing modes, move on to the integer operations, then cover the floating-point operations, and conclude with an examination of instruction encoding.

D.2 | 80x86 Registers and Data Addressing Modes

The evolution of the instruction set can be seen in the registers of the 80x86 (Figure D.1). Original registers are shown in black, with the extensions of the 80386 shown in a lighter shade, a coloring scheme followed in subsequent figures. The 80386 basically extended all 16-bit registers (except the segment registers) to 32 bits, prefixing an "E" to their name to indicate the 32-bit version. The arithmetic, logical, and data-transfer instructions are two-operand instructions that allow the combinations shown in Figure D.2.

80x386, 80x486, Pentium   80x86, 80x286

	31		15	8 7	0	
GPR 0	EAX	AX	AH	AL		Accumulator
GPR 1	ECX	CX	CH	CL		Count reg: string, loop
GPR 2	EDX	DX	DH	DL		Data reg: multiply, divide
GPR 3	EBX	BX	BH	BL		Base addr. reg
GPR 4	ESP	SP				Stack ptr.
GPR 5	EBP	BP				Base ptr. (for base of stack seg.)
GPR 6	ESI	SI				Index reg, string source ptr.
GPR 7	EDI	DI				Index reg, string dest. ptr.
		CS				Code segment ptr.
		SS				Stack segment ptr. (top of stack)
		DS				Data segment ptr.
		ES				Extra data segment ptr.
		FS				Data segment ptr. 2
		GS				Data segment ptr. 3
PC	EIP	IP				Instruction ptr. (PC)
	EFLAGS	FLAGS				Condition codes

79   0

FPR 0
FPR 1
FPR 2
FPR 3
FPR 4
FPR 5
FPR 6
FPR 7

	15	0	
Status			Top of FP stack, FP condition codes

FIGURE D.1 The 80x86 has evolved over time, and so has its register set. The original set is shown in black, and the extended set in gray. The 8086 divided the first four registers in half so that they could be used either as one 16-bit register or as two 8-bit registers. Starting with the 80386, the top eight registers were extended to 32 bits and could also be used as general-purpose registers. The floating-point registers on the bottom are 80 bits wide, and although they look like regular registers they are not. They implement a stack, with the top of stack pointed to by the status register. One operand must be the top of stack, and the other can be any of the other seven registers below the top of stack.

Source/destination operand type	Second source operand
Register	Register
Register	Immediate
Register	Memory
Memory	Register
Memory	Immediate

FIGURE D.2 Instruction types for the arithmetic, logical, and data-transfer instructions. The 80x86 allows the combinations shown. The only restriction is the absence of a memory-memory mode. Immediates may be 8, 16, or 32 bits in length; a register is any one of the 14 major registers in Figure D.1 (not IP or FLAGS).

To explain the addressing modes we need to keep in mind whether we are talking about the 16-bit mode used by both the 8086 and 80286 and the 32-bit mode available on the 80386 and its successors. The seven data memory addressing modes supported are

■ absolute

■ register indirect

■ based

■ indexed

■ based indexed with displacement

■ based with scaled indexed

■ based with scaled indexed and displacement

Displacements can be 8 or 32 bits in 32-bit mode, and 8 or 16 bits in 16-bit mode. If we count the size of the address as a separate addressing mode, the total is 11 addressing modes.

Although a memory operand can use any addressing mode, there are restrictions on what registers can be used in a mode. Section D.5 on 80x86 instruction encodings gives the full set of restrictions on registers, but the following description of addressing modes gives the basic register options:

■ *Absolute*—With 16-bit or 32-bit displacement, depending on the mode.

■ *Register indirect*—BX, SI, DI in 16-bit mode and EAX, ECX, EDX, EBX, ESI, and EDI in 32-bit mode.

■ *Based mode with 8-bit or 16-bit/32-bit displacement*—BP, BX, SI, DI in 16-bit mode and EAX, ECX, EDX, EBX, ESI, and EDI in 32-bit mode. The displacement is either 8 bits or the size of the address mode: 16 or 32 bits. (Intel gives two different names to this single addressing mode, *based* and *indexed*, but they are essentially identical and we combine them. This book uses indexed addressing to mean something different and is explained next.)

- *Indexed*—Address is sum of two registers. The allowable combinations are BX+SI, BX+DI, EP+SI, and BP-DI. This mode is called *based indexed* on the 8086. (The 32-bit mode uses a different addressing mode to get the same effect.)

- *Based indexed with 8- or 16-bit displacement*—The address is sum of displacement and contents of two registers. The same restrictions on registers apply as in indexed mode.

- *Base plus scaled indexed*—This addressing mode and the next were added in the 80386, and are only available in 32-bit mode. The address calculation is

$$\text{Base register} + 2^{Scale} \times \text{Index register}$$

where *Scale* has the value 0, 1, 2, or 3, *Index register* can be any of the eight 32-bit general registers except ESP, and *Base register* can be any of the eight 32-bit general registers.

- *Base plus scaled index with 8- or 32-bit displacement*—The address is sum of the displacement and the address calculated by the scaled mode immediately above. The same restrictions on registers apply.

The 80x86 uses Little Endian addressing.

Ideally, we would refer discussion of 80x86 logical and physical addresses to Chapter 5, but the segmented address space prevents us from hiding that information. Figure D.3 shows the memory mapping options on the generations of 80x86 machines; Chapter 5 describes the segmented protection scheme in greater detail.

The assembly language programmer clearly must specify which segment register should be used with an address, no matter which address mode is used. To save space in the instructions, segment registers are selected automatically depending on which address register is used. The rules are simple: References to instructions (IP) use the code segment register (CS), references to the stack (BP or SP) use the stack segment register (SS), and the default segment register for the other registers is the data segment register (DS). The next section explains how they can be overridden.

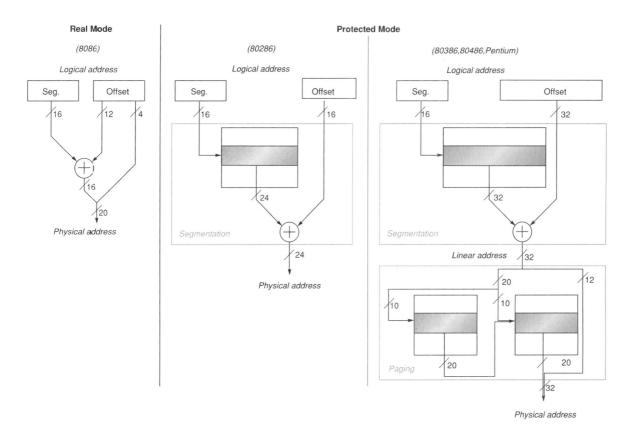

FIGURE D.3   The original segmented scheme of the 8086 is shown on the left. All 80x86 processors support this style of addressing, called *real mode*. It simply takes the contents of a segment register, shifts it left 4 bits, and adds it to the 16-bit offset, forming a 20-bit physical address. The 80286 used the contents of the segment register to select a segment descriptor, which includes a 24-bit base address among other items. It is added to the 16-bit offset to form the 24-bit physical address. The 80386 and successors expand this base address in the segment descriptor to 32 bits and also add an optional paging layer below segmentation. A 32-bit linear address is first formed from the segment and offset, and then this address is divided into two 10-bit fields and a 12-bit page offset. The first 10-bit field selects the entry in the first-level page table, and then this entry is used in combination with the second 10-bit field to access the second-level page table to select the upper 20 bits of the physical address. Prepending this 20-bit address to the final 12-bit field gives the 32-bit physical address. Paging can be turned off, redefining the 32-bit linear address as the physical address. Note that a "flat" 80x86 address space comes simply by loading the same value in all the segment registers; that is, it doesn't matter which segment register is selected.

D.3 | 80x86 Integer Operations

The 8086 provides support for both 8-bit (*byte*) and 16-bit (called *word*) data types. The data type distinctions apply to register operations as well as memory accesses. The 80386 adds 32-bit addresses and data, called double words. Almost every operation works on both 8-bit data and one longer data size. That size is determined by the mode and is either 16 or 32 bits.

Clearly some programs want to operate on data of all three sizes, so the 80x86 architects provide a convenient way to specify each version without expanding code size significantly. They decided that most programs would by dominated by either 16- or 32-bit data, and so it made sense to be able to set a default large size. This default size is set by a bit in the code segment register. To override the default size, an 8-bit *prefix* is attached to the instruction to tell the machine to use the other large size for this instruction.

The prefix solution was borrowed from the 8086, which allows multiple prefixes to modify instruction behavior. The three original prefixes override the default segment register, lock the bus so as to perform a semaphore (see Chapter 8), or repeat the following instruction until CX counts down to zero. This last prefix was intended to be paired with a byte move instruction to move a variable number of bytes. The 80386 also added a prefix to override the default address size.

The 80x86 integer operations can be divided into four major classes:

1. Data movement instructions, including move, push, and pop.

2. Arithmetic and logic instructions including logical operations, test, shifts, and integer and decimal arithmetic operations.

3. Control flow, including conditional branches and unconditional jumps, calls, and returns.

4. String instructions, including string move and string compare.

Figure D.4 shows some typical 80x86 instructions and their functions.

Instruction	Function
JE name	if equal(CC) {IP←name}; IP-128 ≤ name < IP+128
JMP name	IP←name
CALLF name, seg	SP←SP-2; M[SS:SP]←IP+5; SP← SP-2; M[SS:SP]←CS; IP←name; CS←seg;
MOVW BX,[DI+45]	BX←$_{16}$M[DS:DI+45]
PUSH SI	SP←SP-2; M[SS:SP]←SI
POP DI	DI←M[SS:SP]; SP←SP-2
ADD AX,#6765	AX←AX+6765
SHL BX,1	BX←BX$_{1..15}$ ## 0
TEST DX,#42	Set CC flags with DX & 42
MOVSB	M[ES:DI]←$_8$M[DS:SI]; DI←DI+1; SI←SI+1

FIGURE D.4 Some typical 80x86 instructions and their functions. A list of frequent operations appears in Figure D.5. We use the abbreviation SR:X to indicate the formation of an address with segment register SR and offset X. This effective address corresponding to SR:X is (SR<<4)+X. The CALLF saves the IP of the next instruction and the current CS on the stack. The hardware description language is described on the back inside cover of this book.

The data transfer, arithmetic, and logic instructions are unremarkable, except that the arithmetic and logic instructions operations allow the destination to either be a register or a memory location.

Control-flow instructions must be able to address destinations in another segment. This is handled by having two types of control-flow instructions: "near" for intrasegment (within a segment) and "far" for intersegment (between segments) transfers. In far jumps, which must be unconditional, two 16-bit quantities follow the opcode in 16-bit mode. One of these is used as the instruction pointer, while the other is loaded into CS and becomes the new code segment. In 32-bit mode the first field is expanded to 32 bits to match the 32-bit program counter (EIP).

Calls and returns work similarly—a far call pushes the return instruction pointer and return segment on the stack and loads both the instruction pointer and code segment. A far return pops both the instruction pointer and the code segment from the stack. Programmers or compiler writers must be sure to always use the same type of call *and* return for a procedure—a near return does not work with a far call, and vice versa.

String instructions are part of the 8080 ancestry of the 80x86 and are not commonly executed in most programs.

Figure D.5 lists some of the integer 80x86 instructions. Many of the instructions are available in both byte and word formats.

Instruction	Meaning
Control	**Conditional and unconditional branches**
JNZ, JZ	Jump if condition to IP + 8-bit offset; JNE (for JNZ), JE (for JZ) are alternative names
JMP, JMPF	Unconditional jump—8- or 16-bit offset intrasegment (near), and intersegment (far) versions
CALL, CALLF	Subroutine call—16-bit offset; return address pushed; near and far versions
RET, RETF	Pops return address from stack and jumps to it; near and far versions
LOOP	Loop branch—decrement CX; jump to IP + 8-bit displacement if CX $\neq$ 0
Data transfer	**Move data between registers or between register and memory**
MOV	Move between two registers or between register and memory
PUSH	Push source operand on stack
POP	Pop operand from stack top to a register
LES	Load ES and one of the GPRs from memory

Figure continued on next page

Instruction	Meaning
Arithmetic, logical	**Arithmetic and logical operations using the data registers and memory**
ADD	Add source to destination; register-memory format
SUB	Subtract source from destination; register-memory format
CMP	Compare source and destination; register-memory format
SHL	Shift left
SHR	Shift logical right
RCR	Rotate right with carry as fill
CBW	Convert byte in AL to word in AX
TEST	Logical AND of source and destination sets flags
INC	Increment destination; register-memory format
DEC	Decrement destination; register-memory format
OR	Logical OR; register-memory format
XOR	Exclusive OR; register-memory format
String instructions	**Move between string operands; length given by a repeat prefix**
MOVS	Copies from string source to destination; may be repeated
LODS	Loads a byte or word of a string into the A register

FIGURE D.5 Some typical operations on the 80x86. Many operations use register-memory format, where either the source or the destination may be memory and the other may be a register or immediate operand.

D.4 | 80x86 Floating-Point Operations

Intel provided a stack architecture with its floating-point instructions: loads push numbers onto the stack, operations find operands in the two top elements of the stacks, and stores can pop elements off the stack, just as the stack example in Figure 2.1 on page 70 suggests.

Intel supplemented this stack architecture with instructions and addressing modes that allow the architecture to have some of the benefits of a register-memory model. In addition to finding operands in the top two elements of the stack, one operand can be in memory or in one of the seven registers below the top of the stack.

This hybrid is still a restricted register-memory model, however, in that loads always move data to the top of the stack while incrementing the top of stack pointer and stores can only move the top of stack to memory. Intel uses the notation ST to indicate the top of stack, and ST(i) to represent the ith register below the top of stack.

One novel feature of this architecture is that the operands are wider in the register stack than they are stored in memory, and all operations are performed at this wide internal precision. Numbers are automatically converted to the internal

80-bit format on a load and converted back to the appropriate size on a store. Memory data can be 32-bit (single precision) or 64-bit (double precision) floating-point numbers, called *real* by Intel. The register-memory version of these instructions will then convert the memory operand to this Intel 80-bit format before performing the operation. The data transfer instructions also will automatically convert 16- and 32-bit integers to reals, and vice versa, for integer loads and stores.

The 80x86 floating-point operations can be divided into four major classes:

1. Data movement instructions, including load, load constant, and store.

2. Arithmetic instructions, including add, subtract, multiply, divide, square root, and absolute value.

3. Comparison, including instructions to send the result to the integer CPU so that it can branch.

4. Transcendental instructions, including sine, cosine, log, and exponentiation.

Figure D.6 shows some of the 60 floating-point operations. We use the curly brackets {} to show optional variations of the basic operations: {I} means there is an integer version of the instruction, {P} means this variation will pop one operand off the stack after the operation, and {R} means reverse the sense of the operands in this operation.

Data transfer	Arithmetic	Compare	Transcendental
F{I}LD mem/ST(i)	F{I}ADD{P} mem/ST(i)	F{I}COM{P}{P}	FPATAN
F{I}ST{P} mem/ST(i)	F{I}SUB{R}{P} mem/ST(i)	F{I}UCOM{P}{P}	F2XM1
FLDPI	F{I}MUL{P} mem/ST(i)	FSTSW AX/mem	FCOS
FLD1	F{I}DIV{R}{P} mem/ST(i)		FPTAN
FLDZ	FSQRT		FPREM
	FABS		FSIN
	FRNDINT		FYL2X

FIGURE D.6   The floating-point instructions of the 80x86. The first column shows the data transfer instructions, which move data to memory or to one of the registers below the top of the stack. The last three operations push constants on the stack: pi, 1.0, and 0.0. The second column contains the arithmetic operations described above. Note that the last three operate only on the top of stack. The third column is the compare instructions. Since there are no special floating-point branch instructions, the result of the compare must be transferred to the integer CPU via the FSTSW instruction, either into the AX register or into memory, followed by a SAHF instruction to set the condition codes. The floating-point comparison can then be tested using integer branch instructions. The final column gives the higher-level floating-point operations.

Not all combinations are provided. Hence

```
F{I}SUB{R}{P}
```

represents these instructions found in the 80x86:

```
FSUB
FISUB
FSUBR
FISUBR
FSUBP
FSUBRP
```

There are no pop or reverse pop versions of the integer subtract instructions.

Note that we get even more combinations when including the operand modes for these operations. The floating-point add has these options, ignoring the integer and pop versions of the instruction:

`FADD`	Both operands in stack, result replaces top of stack.
`FADD  ST(i)`	One source operand is ith register below the top of stack, and the result replaces the top of stack.
`FADD  ST(i),ST`	One source operand is the top of stack, and the result replaces ith register below the top of stack.
`FADD  mem32`	One source operand is a 32-bit location in memory, and the result replaces the top of stack.
`FADD  mem64`	One source operand is a 64-bit location in memory, and the result replaces the top of stack.

D.5 | 80x86 Instruction Encoding

Saving the worst for last, the encoding of instructions in the 8086 is complex, with many different instruction formats. Instructions may vary from one byte, when there are no operands, to up to six bytes, when the instruction contains a 16-bit immediate and uses 16-bit displacement addressing. Prefix instructions increase 8086 instruction length beyond the obvious sizes.

The 80386 additions expand the instruction size even further, as Figure D.7 shows. Both the displacement and immediate fields can be 32 bits long, two more prefixes are possible, the opcode can be 16 bits long, and the scaled index mode specifier adds another 8 bits. The maximum possible 80386 instruction is 17 bytes long.

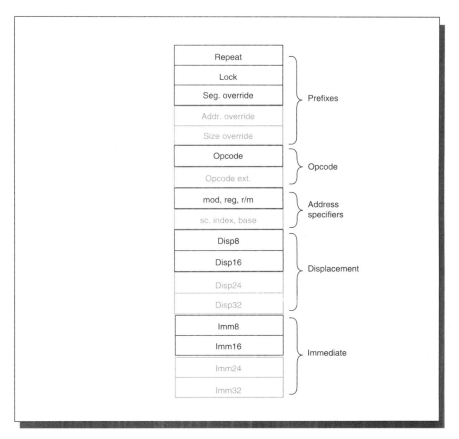

FIGURE D.7   The instruction format of the 8086 (black) and the extensions for the 80386 (shaded). Every field is optional except the opcode.

Figure D.8 shows the instruction format for several of the example instructions in Figure D.4. The opcode byte usually contains a bit saying whether the operand is a byte wide or the larger size, 16 bits or 32 bits depending on the mode. For some instructions the opcode may include the addressing mode and the register; this is true in many instructions that have the form register ←register op immediate. Other instructions use a "postbyte" or extra opcode byte, labeled "mod, reg, r/m" in Figure D.7, which contains the addressing mode information. This postbyte is used for many of the instructions that address memory. The based with scaled index uses a second postbyte, labeled "sc, index, base" in Figure D.7.

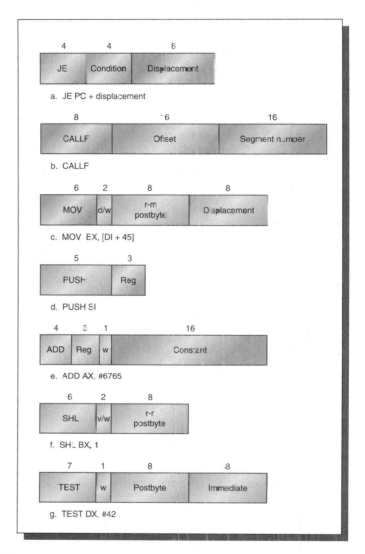

FIGURE D.8 Typical 8086 instruction formats. The encoding of the postbyte is shown in Figure D.9. Many instructions contain the 1-bit field w, which says whether the operation is a byte or word. Fields of the form v/w or d/w are a d-field or v-field followed by the w-field. The d-field in MOV is used in instructions that may move to or from memory and shows the direction of the move. The field v in the SHL instruction indicates a variable-length shift; variable-length shifts use a register to hold the shift count. The ADD instruction shows a typical optimized short encoding usable only when the first operand is AX. Overall instructions may vary from one to six bytes in length.

The floating-point instructions are encoded in the escape opcode of the 8086 and the postbyte address specifier. The memory operations reserve 2 bits to decide whether the operand is a 32- or 64-bit real or a 16- or 32-bit integer. Those same 2 bits are used in versions that do not access memory to decide whether the stack should be popped after the operation and whether the top of stack or a lower register should get the result.

Alas, you cannot separate the restrictions on registers from the encoding of the addressing modes in the 80x86. Hence Figures D.9 and D.10 show the encoding of the two postbyte address specifiers for both 16- and 32-bit mode.

reg	w = 0	w = 1 16b	w = 1 32b	r/m	mod = 0 16b	mod = 0 32b	mod = 1 16b	mod = 1 32b	mod = 2 16b	mod = 2 32b	mod = 3
0	AL	AX	EAX	0	addr=BX+SI	=EAX	*same*	*same*	*same*	*same*	*same*
1	CL	CX	ECX	1	addr=BX+DI	=ECX	*addr as*	*addr as*	*addr as*	*addr as*	*as*
2	DL	DX	EDX	2	addr=BP+SI	=EDX	*mod=0*	*mod=0*	*mod=0*	*mod=0*	*reg*
3	BL	BX	EBX	3	addr=BP+SI	=EBX	*+ disp8*	*+ disp8*	*+ disp16*	*+ disp32*	*field*
4	AH	SP	ESP	4	addr=SI	=(sib)	SI+disp16	(sib)+disp8	SI+disp8	(sib)+disp32	"
5	CH	BP	EBP	5	addr=DI	=disp32	DI+disp8	EBP+disp8	DI+disp16	EBP+disp32	"
6	DH	SI	ESI	6	addr=disp16	=ESI	BP+disp8	ESI+disp8	BP+disp16	ESI+disp32	"
7	BH	DI	EDI	7	addr=BX	=EDI	BX+disp8	EDI+disp8	BX+disp16	EDI+disp32	"

FIGURE D.9   The encoding of the first address specifier of the 80x86, "*mod, reg, r/m*". The first four columns show the encoding of the 3-bit reg field, which depends on the w bit from the opcode and whether the machine is in 16- or 32-bit mode. The remaining columns explain the mod and r/m fields. The meaning of the 3-bit r/m field depends on the value in the 2-bit mod field and the address size. Basically, the registers used in the address calculation are listed in the sixth and seventh columns, under mod = 0, with mod = 1 adding an 8-bit displacement and mod = 2 adding a 16- or 32-bit displacement, depending on the address mode. The exceptions are r/m = 6 when mod = 1 or mod = 2 in 16-bit mode selects BP plus the displacement; r/m = 5 when mod =1 or mod = 2 in 32-bit mode selects EBP plus displacement; and r/m = 4 in 32-bit mode when mod ≠3 (sib) means use the scaled index mode shown in Figure D.10. When mod = 3, the r/m field indicates a register, using the same encoding as the reg field combined with the w bit.

Index		Base
0	EAX	EAX
1	ECX	ECX
2	EDX	EDX
3	EBX	EBX
4	no index	ESP
5	EBP	if mod=0, disp32 if mod≠0, EBP
6	ESI	ESI
7	EDI	EDI

FIGURE D.10   Based plus scaled index mode address specifier found in the 80386. This mode is indicated by the *(sib)* notation in Figure D.9. Note that this mode expands the list of registers to be used in other modes: register indirect using ESP comes from Scale = 0, Index = 4, and Base = 4, and base displacement with EBP comes from Scale = 0, Index = 5, and mod = 0. The two-bit scale field is used in this formula of the effective address:

$$\text{Base register} + 2^{\text{Scale}} \times \text{Index register}$$

D.6 | Putting It All Together: Measurements of Instruction Set Usage

In this section we present detailed measurements for 80x86, and then compare the measurements to DLX for the same programs. To facilitate comparisons among dynamic instruction set measurements, we use the same subset of the SPEC92 programs used in Chapter 2. The 80x86 results were taken in 1994 using the Sun Solaris FORTRAN and C compilers V2.0 and executed in 32-bit mode. These compilers were comparable in quality to the compilers used for DLX.

Remember that these measurements depend on the benchmarks chosen and the compiler technology used. Although the authors feel that the measurements in this section are reasonably indicative of the usage of these architectures, other programs may behave differently from any of the benchmarks here, and different compilers may yield different results. In doing a real instruction set study, the architect would want to have a much larger set of benchmarks, spanning as wide an application range as possible, and consider the operating system and its usage of the instruction set. Single-user benchmarks like those measured here do not necessarily behave in the same fashion as the operating system.

We start with evaluation of the features of the 80x86 in isolation, and later compare instruction counts with those of DLX.

Measurements of 80x86 Operand Addressing

We start with addressing modes. Figure D.11 shows the distribution of the operand types in the 80x86. These measurements cover the "second" operand of the operation; for example,

```
mov EAX, [45]
```

counts as a single memory operand. If the types of the first operand were counted, the percentage of register usage would increase by about a factor of 1.5.

	Integer average	FP average
Register	45%	22%
Immediate	16%	6%
Memory	39%	72%

FIGURE D.11   Operand type distribution for the average of five SPECint92 programs (compress, eqntott, espresso, gcc, li) and the average of five SPECfp92 programs (doduc, ear, hydro2d, mdljdp2, su2cor).

The 80x86 memory operands are divided into their respective addressing modes in Figure D.12. Probably the biggest surprise is the popularity of the addressing modes added by the 80386, the last four rows of the figure. They account for about half of all the memory accesses. Another surprise is the popularity of direct addressing. On most other machines, the equivalent of the direct addressing mode is rare. Perhaps the segmented address space of the 80x86 makes direct addressing more useful, since the address is relative to a base address from the segment register.

Addressing mode	Integer average	FP average
Register indirect	13%	3%
Base + 8-bit disp.	31%	15%
Base + 32-bit disp.	9%	25%
Indexed	0%	0%
Based indexed + 8-bit disp.	0%	0%
Based indexed + 32-bit disp.	0%	1%
Base + scaled indexed	22%	7%
Base + scaled indexed + 8-bit disp.	0%	8%
Base + scaled indexed + 32-bit disp.	4%	4%
32-bit direct	20%	37%

FIGURE D.12   Operand addressing mode distribution by program. This chart does not include addressing modes used by branches or control instructions.

These addressing modes largely determine the size of the Intel instructions. Figure D.13 shows the distribution of instruction sizes. The average number of bytes per instruction for integer programs is 2.8 with a standard deviation of 1.5, and 4.1 with a standard deviation of 1.9 for floating-point programs. The difference in length arises partly from the differences in the addressing modes: Integer programs rely more on the shorter register indirect and 8-bit displacement addressing modes, while floating-point programs more frequently use the 80386 addressing modes with the longer 32-bit displacements.

Given that the floating-point instructions have aspects of both stacks and registers, how are they used? Figure D.14 shows that, at least for the compilers used in this measurement, the stack model of execution is rarely followed. (See section D.8 for a historical explanation of this observation.)

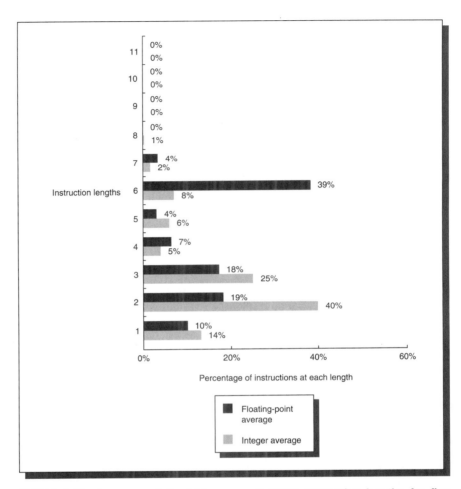

FIGURE D.13 **Averages of the histograms of 80x86 instruction lengths for five SPECint92 programs and for five SPECfp92 programs, all running in 32-bit mode.**

Option	doduc	ear	hydro2d	mdljdp2	su2cor	FP average
Stack (2nd operand ST (1))	1.1%	0.0%	0.0%	0.2%	0.6%	0.4%
Register (2nd operand ST(i), i>1)	17.3%	63.4%	14.2%	7.1%	30.7%	26.5%
Memory	81.6%	36.6%	85.8%	92.7%	68.7%	73.1%

FIGURE D.14 **The percentage of instructions for the floating-point operations (add, sub, mul, div) that use each of the three options for specifying a floating point operand on the 80x86.** The three options are 1) the strict stack model of implicit operands on the stack, 2) register version naming an explicit operand that is not one of top two elements of the stack, and 3) memory operand.

Finally, Figures D.15 and D.16 show the instruction mixes for 10 SPEC92 programs, along the same lines as Figures 2.26 and 2.27 in Chapter 2.

Instruction	compress	eqntott	espresso	gcc (cc1)	li	Int. average
load	20.8%	18.5%	21.9%	24.9%	23.3%	22%
store	13.8%	3.2%	8.3%	16.6%	18.7%	12%
add	10.3%	8.8%	8.15%	7.6%	6.1%	8%
sub	7.0%	10.6%	3.5%	2.9%	3.6%	5%
mul				0.1%		0%
div						0%
compare	8.2%	27.7%	15.3%	13.5%	7.7%	16%
mov reg-reg	7.9%	0.6%	5.0%	4.2%	7.8%	4%
load imm	0.5%	0.2%	0.6%	0.4%		0%
cond. branch	15.5%	28.6%	18.9%	17.4%	15.4%	20%
uncond. branch	1.2%	0.2%	0.9%	2.2%	2.2%	1%
call	0.5%	0.4%	0.7%	1.5%	3.2%	1%
return, jmp indirect	0.5%	0.4%	0.7%	1.5%	3.2%	1%
shift	3.8%		2.5%	1.7%		1%
and	8.4%	1.0%	8.7%	4.5%	8.4%	6%
or	0.6%		2.7%	0.4%	0.4%	1%
other (xor, not,...)	0.9%		2.2%	0.1%		1%
load FP						0%
store FP						0%
add FP						0%
sub FP						0%
mul FP						0%
div FP						0%
compare FP						0%
mov reg-reg FP						0%
other (abs, sqrt,...)						0%

FIGURE D.15   80x86 instruction mix for five SPECint92 programs.

Instruction	doduc	ear	hydro2d	mdljdp2	su2cor	FP average
load	8.9%	6.5%	18.0%	27.6%	27.6%	20%
store	12.4%	3.1%	11.5%	7.8%	7.8%	8%
add	5.4%	6.6%	14.6%	8.8%	8.8%	10%
sub	1.0%	2.4%	3.3%	2.4%	2.4%	3%
mul						0%
div						0%
compare	1.8%	5.1%	0.8%	1.0%	1.0%	2%
mov reg-reg	3.2%	0.1%	1.8%	2.3%	2.3%	2%
load imm	0.4%	1.5%				0%
cond. branch	5.4%	8.2%	5.1%	2.7%	2.7%	5%
uncond branch	0.8%	0.4%	1.3%	0.3%	0.3%	1%
call	0.5%	1.6%		0.1%	0.1%	0%
return, jmp indirect	0.5%	1.6%		0.1%	0.1%	0%
shift	1.1%		4.5%	2.5%	2.5%	2%
and	0.8%	0.8%	0.7%	1.3%	1.3%	1%
or	0.1%			0.1%	0.1%	0%
other (xor, not,…)						0%
load FP	14.1%	22.5%	9.1%	12.6%	12.6%	14%
store FP	8.6%	11.4%	4.1%	6.6%	6.6%	7%
add FP	5.8%	6.1%	1.4%	6.6%	6.6%	5%
sub FP	2.2%	2.7%	3.1%	2.9%	2.9%	3%
mul FP	8.9%	8.0%	4.1%	12.0%	12.0%	9%
div FP	2.1%		0.8%	0.2%	0.2%	0%
compare FP	9.4%	6.9%	10.8%	0.5%	0.5%	5%
mov reg-reg FP	2.5%	0.8%	0.3%	0.8%	0.8%	1%
other (abs, sqrt,...)	3.9%	3.8%	4.1%	0.8%	0.8%	2%

FIGURE D.16   80x86 instruction mix for five SPECfp92 programs.

Comparative Operation Measurements

Figures D.17 and D.18 show the number of instructions executed for each of the 10 programs on the 80x86 and the ratio of instruction execution compared with that for DLX: Numbers less than 1.0 mean the 80x86 executes fewer instructions than DLX. The instruction count is surprisingly close to DLX for many integer programs, as you would expect a load-store instruction set architecture like DLX to execute more instructions than a register-memory architecture like the 80x86.

The floating-point programs always have higher counts for 80x86, presumably due to the lack of floating-point registers and use of a stack architecture.

	compress	eqntott	espresso	gcc (cc1)	li	Int. avg.
Instructions executed on 80x86 (millions)	2226	1203	2216	3770	5020	
Instructions executed ratio to DLX	0.61	1.74	0.85	0.96	0.98	1.03
Data reads on 80x86 (millions)	589	229	622	1079	1459	
Data writes on 80x86 (millions)	311	39	191	661	981	
Data read/modify/writes on 80x86 (millions)	26	1	129	48	48	
Total data reads on 80x86 (millions)	615	230	751	1127	1507	
Data read ratio to DLX	0.85	1.09	1.38	1.25	0.94	1.10
Total data writes on 80x86 (millions)	338	40	319	709	1029	
Data write ratio to DLX	1.67	9.26	2.39	1.25	1.20	3.15
Total data accesses on 80x86 (millions)	953	269	1070	1836	2536	
Data access ratio to DLX	1.03	1.25	1.58	1.25	1.03	1.23

FIGURE D.17   Instructions executed and data accesses on 80x86 and ratios compared to DLX for five SPECint92 programs.

	doduc	ear	hydro2d	mdljdp2	su2cor	FP average
Instructions executed on 80x86 (millions)	1223	15,220	13,342	6197	6197	
Instructions executed ratio to DLX	1.19	1.19	2.53	2.09	1.62	1.73
Data reads on 80x86 (millions)	515	6007	5501	3696	3643	
Data writes on 80x86 (millions)	260	2205	2085	892	892	
Data read/modify/writes on 80x86 (millions)	1	0	139	124	124	
Total data reads on 80x86 (millions)	517	6007	5690	3820	3767	
Data read ratio to DLX	2.04	2.36	4.48	4.77	3.91	3.51
Total data writes on 80x86 (millions)	261	2205	2274	1015	1015	
Data write ratio to DLX	3.68	33.25	38.74	16.74	9.35	20.35
Total data accesses on 80x86 (millions)	778	8212	7965	4835	4782	
Data access ratio to DLX	2.40	3.14	5.99	5.73	4.47	4.35

FIGURE D.18   Instructions executed and data accesses for five SPECfp92 programs on 80x86 and ratio to DLX.

Another question is the total amount of data traffic for the 80x86 versus DLX, since the 80x86 can specify memory operands as part of operations while DLX can only access via loads and stores. Figures D.17 and D.18 also show the data reads, data writes, and data read-modify-writes for these 10 programs. The total accesses ratio to DLX of each memory access type is shown in the bottom rows, with the read-modify-write counting as one read and one write. The 80x86 performs about two to four times as many data accesses as DLX for floating-point programs, and 1.25 times as many for integer programs. Finally, Figure D.19 shows the percentage of instructions in each category for 80x86 and DLX.

Category	Integer average		FP average	
	x86	**DLX**	**x86**	**DLX**
Total data tran.	34%	36%	28%	2%
Total int. arith.	34%	31%	16%	12%
Total control	24%	20%	6%	10%
Total logical	8%	13%	3%	2%
Total FP data tran.	0%	0%	22%	33%
Total FP arith.	0%	0%	25%	41%

FIGURE D.19   Percentage of instructions executed by category for 80x86 and DLX for the averages of five SPECint92 and SPECfp92 programs of Figures D.17 and D.18.

D.7 | Concluding Remarks

Beauty is in the eye of the beholder.

Old Adage

As we have seen, "orthogonal" is not a term found in the Intel architectural dictionary. To fully understand which registers and which addressing modes are available, you need to see the encoding of all addressing modes and sometimes the encoding of the instructions.

Some argue that inelegance of the 80x86 instruction set is unavoidable, the price that must be paid for rampant success by any architecture. These authors reject that notion. Obviously no successful architecture can jettison features that were added in previous implementations, and over time some features may be seen as undesirable. The awkwardness of the 80x86 began at its core with the 8086 instruction set and was exacerbated by the architecturally inconsistent expansions of the 8087, 80286, and 80386.

A counterexample is the IBM 360/370 architecture, which is much older than the 80x86. It dominates the mainframe market just as the 80x86 dominates the PC market. Due undoubtedly to a better base and more compatible enhancements, this instruction set makes much more sense than the 80x86 more than 30 years after its first implementation.

For better or worse, Intel had a 16-bit microprocessor years before its competitors' more elegant architectures, and this head start led to the selection of the 8086 as the CPU for the IBM PC. What it lacks in style is made up in quantity, making the 80x86 beautiful from the right perspective.

The saving grace of the 80x86 is that its architectural components are not too difficult to implement, as Intel has demonstrated by rapidly improving performance of integer programs since 1978. High floating-point performance is a larger challenge in this architecture.

D.8 | Historical Perspective and References

The complexity of the x86 is not an impassable barrier. ... The biggest weakness in the x86 instruction set is the lack of registers coupled with an extremely painful addressing scheme.

Mike Johnson, Leader of 80x86 Design at AMD,
Microprocessor Report (1994)

There are numerous descriptions of the 80x86 architecture that have been published—Wakerly's [1989] is both concise and easy to understand. Crawford and Gelsinger [1988] is a thorough description of the 80386.

The ancestors of the 80x86 were the first microprocessors, produced late in the first half of the 1970s. The Intel 4004 and 8008 were extremely simple 4- and 8-bit accumulator-style machines. Morse et al. [1980] describe the evolution of the 8086 from the 8080 in the late 1970s as an attempt to provide a 16-bit machine with better throughput. At that time almost all programming for microprocessors was done in assembly language—both memory and compilers were in short supply. Intel wanted to keep its base of 8080 users, so the 8086 was designed to be "compatible" with the 8080. The 8086 was *never* object-code compatible with the 8080, but the machines were close enough that translation of assembly language programs could be done automatically.

In early 1980, IBM selected a version of the 8086 with an 8-bit external bus, called the 8088, for use in the IBM PC. They chose the 8-bit version to reduce the cost of the machine. This choice, together with the tremendous success of the IBM PC, has made the 8086 architecture ubiquitous. The success of the IBM PC was due in part because IBM opened the architecture of the PC and enabled the PC-clone industry to flourish. As discussed in the introduction of this appendix, the 80286, 80386, 80486, Pentium, and P6 have extended the architecture and provided a series of performance enhancements.

Although the 68000 was chosen for the popular Macintosh, the Macintosh was never as pervasive as the PC, partly because Apple did not allow clones until recently, and the 68000 did not acquire the same software leverage that the 8086 enjoys. The Motorola 68000 may have been more significant *technically* than the 8086, but the impact of the selection by IBM and IBM's open architecture strategy dominated the technical advantages of the 68000 in the market.

Kahan's history of the stack architecture selection for the 8086 is entertaining [1990]. The floating-point architecture of the companion 8087 had to be retrofitted into the 8086 opcode space, making it inconvenient to offer two operands per instruction as found in the rest of the 8086. Hence the decision for one operand per instruction using a stack: "The designer's task was to make a Virtue of this Necessity." Rather than the classical stack architecture, which has no provision for avoiding common subexpressions from being pushed and popped from memory into the top of the stack found in registers, Intel tried to combine a flat register file with a stack. The reasoning was the restriction of the top of stack as one operand was not so bad since it only required the execution of an FXCH instruction (which swapped registers) to get the same result as a two-operand instruction, and FXCH was much faster than the floating-point operations of the 8087.

Since floating-point expressions are not that complex, Kahan reasoned that eight registers meant that the stack would rarely overflow. Hence he urged that the 8087 use this hybrid scheme with the provision that stack overflow or stack underflow would interrupt the 8086 so that interrupt software could give the illusion to the compiler writer of an unlimited stack for floating-point data. The Intel 8087 was implemented in Israel, and 7500 miles and 10 time zones made communication difficult from California. According to Palmer and Morse [1984]:

Unfortunately, nobody tried to write a software stack manager until after the 8087 was built, and by then it was too late; what was too complicated to perform in hardware turned out to be even worse in software. One thing found lacking is the ability to conveniently determine if an invalid-operation exception is indeed due to a stack overflow. … Also lacking is the ability to restart the instruction that caused the stack overflow…

The result is that the stack exceptions are too slow to handle in software. As Kahan [1990] says:

Consequently, almost all higher-level languages' compilers emit inefficient code for the 80x87 family, degrading the chips performance by typically 50% with spurious stores and loads necessary simply to preclude stack over/underflow. …

I still regret that the 8087's stack implementation was not quite so neat as my original intention. … If the original design had been realized, compilers today would use the 80x87 and its descendents more efficiently, and Intel's competitors could more easily market faster but compatible 80x87 imitations.

The P6 renames the floating-point registers (see Chapter 4), effectively providing up to 40 floating-point registers at any given instant. The main effect of the stack organization is to force design teams to use transistors for dereferencing the stack before doing the renaming.

Hewlett Packard and Intel will announce a new, common instruction set architecture in 1997 or 1998 that will surely have much better floating-point performance. It will also be upwards compatible with both the 80x86 and PA-RISC, and thus the 80x86 instruction set will be available in some form in computers of the next century. Instruction set anthropologists will peel off layer by layer from such machines until they uncover artifacts from the first microprocessor. Given such a find, how will they judge 20th-century computer architecture?

References

CRAWFORD, J. AND P. GELSINGER [1988]. *Programming the 80386,* Sybex Books, Alameda, Calif.

KAHAN, J. [1990]. "On the advantage of the 8087's stack," unpublished course notes, Computer Science Division, University of California at Berkeley.

MORSE, S., B. RAVENAL, S. MAZOR, AND W. POHLMAN [1980]. "Intel Microprocessors—8080 to 8086," *Computer* 13:10 (October).

PALMER, J. AND S. MORSE [1984]. *The 8087 Primer,* J. Wiley, New York, p. 93.

WAKERLY, J. [1989]. *Microcomputer Architecture and Programming,* J. Wiley, New York.

E   Implementing Coherence Protocols

The devil is in the details.

Classic Proverb

E.1	Implementation Issues for the Snooping Coherence Protocol	E-1
E.2	Implementation Issues in the Distributed Directory Protocol	E-6
	Exercises	E-12

E.1 Implementation Issues for the Snooping Coherence Protocol

The major complication in actually using the snooping coherence protocol from section 8.3 is that write misses are not atomic: The operation of detecting a write miss, obtaining the bus, getting the most recent value, and updating the cache cannot be done as if it took a single cycle. In particular, two processors cannot both use the bus at the same time. Thus, we must decompose the write into several steps that may be separated in time, but will still preserve correct execution. The first step detects the miss and requests the bus. The second step acquires the bus, places the miss on the bus, gets the data, and completes the write. Each of these two steps is atomic, but the cache block does not become exclusive until the second step has begun. As long as we do not change the block to exclusive or allow the cache update to proceed before the bus is acquired, writes to the same cache block will serialize when they reach the second step of the coherence protocol. Unfortunately, this two-step process does introduce new complications in the protocol.

Figure E.1 shows the actual finite-state diagram for implementing coherence for this two-step process under the assumption that a bus transaction is atomic once the bus is acquired. This assumption simply means that the bus is not a split transaction, and once it is acquired any requests are processed before another processor can acquire the bus. We discuss the complexities of a split transaction bus shortly. In the simplest implementation, the finite-state machine in Figure E.1 is simply replicated for each block in the cache. Since there is no interaction among operations on different cache blocks, this replication of the controller works. Replicating the controller is not necessary, but before we see why, let's make sure we understand how the finite-state controller in Figure E.1 operates.

The additional states in Figure E.1 over those in Figure 8.12 on page 665 are all transient: The controller will leave those states when the bus is available. Four of the states are pending write-back states that arise because in a write-back cache when a block is replaced (or invalidated) it must be written back to the memory. Four events can cause such a write back:

1. A write miss on the bus by another processor for this exclusive block.

2. A CPU read miss that forces the exclusive block to be replaced.

3. A CPU write miss that forces the exclusive block to be replaced.

4. A read miss on the bus by another processor for this block.

In each of the cases the next state differs, hence there are four separate pending write-back states with four different successor states.

Logically replicating the controller for each cache block allows correct operation if two conditions hold (in addition to our base assumption that the processor blocks until a cache access completes):

1. An operation on the bus for a cache block and a pending operation for a different cache block are noninterfering.

2. The controller in Figure E.1 correctly deals with the cases when a pending operation and a bus operation are for the same block.

The first condition is certainly true, since operations for different blocks may proceed in any order and do not affect the state transitions for the other block. To see why the second condition is true, consider each of the pending states and what happens if a conflicting access occurs:

■ Pending write back 1—The cache is writing back the data to eliminate it anyway, so a read or write miss for the block has no new effect. Notice, however, that the pending cache *must* use the bus cycle generated by the read or write miss to complete the write back. Otherwise, there will be no response to the

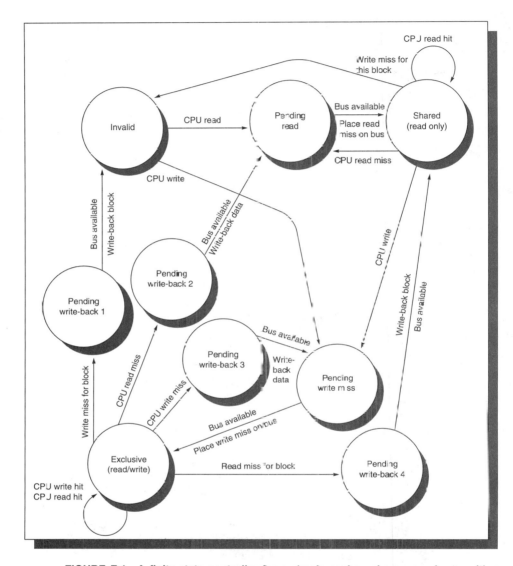

FIGURE E.1 A finite-state controller for a simple cache coherence scheme with a write-back cache. The engine that implements this controller must be reentrant, that is, it must handle multiple requests for different cache lines that are overlapped in time. The diagram assumes the processor stalls until a request is completed, but other transactions must be handled. This controller also assumes that a transition to a new state that involves a bus access does not complete until the bus access is completed. Notice that if we did not require a processor to generate a write miss when it transitioned from the shared to exclusive state, it might not obtain the latest value of a cache block, since some other processor may have updated that block. In a protocol using ownership or upgrade transitions, we will need to be able to transition out of the pending write state and restart an access if a conflicting write obtains the bus first.

miss, since the pending cache still has the only copy of the cache block. When it sees that the address of a miss matches the address of the block it is waiting to write back, it recognizes that the bus is available, writes the data, and transitions its state. This applies to all the pending write-back states.

- Pending write back 2, 3—The cache is eliminating a block in the exclusive state, so another miss for that block simply allows the write back to occur immediately. If the read or write miss on the bus is for the new block that the processor is trying to share, there is no interaction, since the processor does not yet have a copy of the block.

- Pending write back 4—In this case the processor is surrendering an exclusive block and simply completes the write back.

- Pending read, pending write miss —The processor does not yet have a copy of the block that it is waiting for, so a read or write miss for that block has no effect. Since the waiting cache still needs to place a miss on the bus and fetch the block, it is guaranteed to get a new copy.

With these additional states and our assumptions that the bus operates atomically, that misses always cause the state to be updated, and that the processor blocks until an access completes, our coherence implementation is both deadlock-free and correct. If some fairness guarantee is made for bus access, then this controller is also free of *livelock*. Livelock occurs when some portion of a computation cannot make progress, though other portions can. If one processor could be denied the bus indefinitely, then that processor could never make progress in its computation. Some guarantee of fairness on bus access prevents this.

There is still, however, one more critical implementation detail related to the bus transactions and what happens when a miss is processed. The key difference between the cache coherence case and the standard uniprocessor case occurs when the block is exclusive in some cache. Because it is a write-back cache, the memory copy is stale. In this case, the coherence unit will retrieve the block (called an *intervention*) and generate a write back. Since the memory does not know the state of the block, it will attempt to respond to the request as well. Since the data has been updated, the cache and processor will each attempt to drive the bus with different values. To prevent this, a line is added to the bus (often called the shared line) to coordinate the response. When the processor detects that it has a copy in the exclusive state, it signals the memory on this line and the memory aborts the transaction. When the write back occurs, the memory gets the data and updates its copy. Since it is difficult to bound the amount of time that it can take to snoop the local cache copy, this line is usually implemented as a wired-OR with each processor holding its input low until it knows it does not have the block in exclusive state. The memory waits for the line to go high, indicating that no cache has the copy in the exclusive state, before putting data on the bus.

If the bus had a split transaction capability then we could not assume that a response would occur immediately. In fact, implementing a split transaction with coherence is significantly more complex. One complication arises from the fact that we must number and track bus transactions, so that a controller knows when a bus action is a response to its request. Another complication is dealing with races that can arise because two operations for the same cache block could potentially be outstanding simultaneously. An example illustrates this complication best. What happens when two processors try to write a word in the same cache block? Without split transactions, one of the operations reaches the bus first and the other must change the state of the block to invalid and try the operation again. Only one of the transactions is outstanding on the bus at any point.

EXAMPLE   Suppose we have a split transaction bus and no cache has a copy of a particular block. Show how when both P1 and P2 try to write a word in that block, we can get an incorrect result using the protocol in Figure E.1 on page E-3.

ANSWER   With the protocol in Figure E.1, the following sequence of events could occur:

1.   P1 places a write miss for the block on the bus. Since P2 has the data in the invalid state, nothing occurs.

2.   P2 places its write miss on the bus; again, since no copy exists, no state changes are needed.

3.   The memory responds to P1's request. P1 places the block in the exclusive state and writes the word into the block.

4.   The memory responds to P2's request. P2 places the block in the exclusive state and writes the word into the block.

Disaster! Two caches now have the same block in the exclusive state and memory will be inconsistent.   ∎

How can this race be avoided? The simplest way is to use the broadcast capability of the bus. All coherence controllers track all bus accesses. In a split transaction bus, the transactions must be tagged with the processor identity (or a transaction number), so that a processor can identify a reply to its request. Every controller can keep track of the memory address of any outstanding bus requests, since it can see the request and the corresponding reply on the bus. When the local processor generates a miss, the controller does not place the miss request on the bus until there are no outstanding requests for the same cache block. This will force P2 in the above example to wait for P1's access to complete, allowing P1 to place the data in the exclusive state (and write the word into the block). The miss request from P2 will then cause P1 to do a write back and move the block to the invalid state. Alternatively, we could have each processor buffer only its own requests and track the responses to others. If the address of the requested block were included in the reply, then the second processor to request the block could ignore the reply and reissue its request.

These race conditions are what make implementing coherence even more tricky as the interconnection mechanism becomes more sophisticated. As we will see in the next section, such problems are slightly worse in a directory-based system that does not have a broadcast mechanism like a bus, which can be used to order all accesses.

E.2 | Implementation Issues in the Distributed Directory Protocol

One further source of complexity of a directory protocol comes from the lack of atomicity in transactions. Several of the operations that are atomic in a bus-based snoopy protocol cannot be atomic in a directory-based machine. For example, a read miss, which is atomic in the snoopy protocol, cannot be atomic, since it requires messages to be sent to remote directories and caches. In fact, if we attempt to implement these operations in an atomic fashion in a distributed memory machine, we can have deadlock. Recall from Chapter 7 that a deadlock means that the machine has reached a state from which it cannot make forward progress. This is easy to see with an example.

EXAMPLE   Show how deadlock can occur if a node treats a read miss as atomic and hence is unable to respond to other requests until the read miss is completed.

ANSWER   Assume that two nodes P1 and P2 each have exclusive copies of cache blocks X1 and X2 that have different home directories. Consider the following sequence of events shown in Figure E.2.

Events caused by P1 activity	Events caused by P2 activity
P1 read miss for X2	P2 read miss for X1
Directory for X2 receives read miss and generates a fetch that is sent to P2	Directory for X1 receives read miss and generates a fetch that is sent to P1
Fetch arrives at P1, waits for completion of atomic read miss	Fetch arrives at P2, waits for completion of atomic read miss

FIGURE E.2   Events caused by P1 and P2 leading to deadlock.

At this point the nodes are deadlocked. In this case, since the requests are for separate blocks, deadlock can be avoided by duplicating the

> controller for each block. This allows the controllers to accept a request
> for one block while a request for another block is in process. In practice,
> complications arise because requests for the same block can collide, as
> we will see shortly.   ∎

The almost complete lack of atomicity in transactions causes most of the complexities in translating these state transition diagrams into actual finite-state controllers. There are two assumptions about the interconnection network that
significantly simplify the implementation. First, we assume that the network provides point-to-point *in-order delivery* of messages. This means that two messages
sent from a single node to another node arrive in the order they were sent. No assumptions are made about messages originating from, or destined to, different
nodes. Second, we assume the network has unlimited buffering. This second assumption means that a message can always be accepted into the network. This reduces the possibility for deadlock and allows us to treat some nonatomic action,
where we would need to be able to deal with a full set of network buffers, as
atomic actions. Of course, we also assume that the network delivers all messages
within a finite time.

While the first assumption, in-order transmission, is quite reasonable and is, in
fact, true in many machines, the second assumption, unlimited buffering, is not
true. Actually, the network need only be capable of buffering a finite number of
messages, since we still assume that processors block on misses. In practice, this
number may still be large and unreasonable, so later in the section we will discuss
what has to change to eliminate the assumption that a message can always be accepted, while still preventing deadlock.

We also assume that the coherence controller is duplicated for each cache
block (to avoid having to deal with unrelated transactions) and that a state transition only completes when a message has been transmitted and a data value reply
received (when needed). This last assumption simply means that we do not allow
the CPU to continue and read or write a cache block until the read or write miss is
satisfied by a data value reply message. This simply eliminates a transition state
that waits for the block to arrive. Because we are assuming unlimited buffering,
we also assume that an outgoing message can always be transmitted before the
next incoming message is accepted.

Under these assumptions the state transition diagram of Figure 8.24 on
page 683 can be used for the coherence controller at the cache with one small addition: The controller simply throws away any incoming transactions, other than
the data value reply, while waiting for a read or write miss. Let's look at each possible case that can arise while the cache is waiting for a response from the directory. Cases where the cache is transitioning the block to invalid, either from the
shared or exclusive state, do not matter, since any incoming signals for this block
do not affect the block once it is invalid. Hence, we need only consider cases

where the processor is transitioning to the shared or exclusive state. There are two such cases:

- CPU read miss from either invalid or exclusive—The directory will not reply until the block is available. Furthermore, since any write back of an exclusive entry for this block has been done, the controller can ignore any requests.

- CPU write miss—Any required write back is done first and the processor is stalled. Since it cannot hold a block exclusive in this cache entry, it can ignore requests for this block until the write miss is satisfied from the directory.

The directory case is more complex to explain, since multiple cache controllers may send a message for the same block close to the same time. These operations must be serialized. Unlike the snoopy case where every controller sees every request on the bus at the same time, the individual caches only know what has happened when they are notified by the directory. Because the directory serializes the messages when it receives them and because all write misses for a given cache block go to the same directory, writes will be serialized by the home directory.

Thus, the directory controller's main problem is to deal with the distributed representation of the cache state. Since the directory must wait for the completion of certain operations, such as sending invalidates and fetching a cache block before transitioning state, most potential races are eliminated. Because we assume unlimited buffering, the directory can always complete a transaction before accepting the next incoming message. For this reason, the state transition diagram in Figure 8.25 can be used as an implementation. To see why, we must consider cases where the directory and the local cache do not agree on the state of a block. The cache can only have a block in a less restricted state than the directory believes the block is in, because transitioning to exclusive from invalid or shared, or to shared from invalid, requires a message to the directory and a reply. Thus, the only cases to consider are

- Local cache state is invalid, directory state is exclusive—The cache controller must have performed a data write back of the block (see Figure 8.24). Hence the directory will shortly obtain the block. Furthermore no invalidation is needed, since the block has been replaced.

- Local cache state is invalid, directory state is shared (the local cache is replacing the line)—The directory will send an invalidate, which may be ignored, since the block has been replaced. Some directory protocols send a *replacement hint* message when a shared line is replaced. Such messages are used to eliminate unnecessary invalidates and to reduce the state needed in the directory.

- Local cache state is shared, directory state is exclusive—The write back has already been done and the block has been replaced, so a fetch/invalidate, which could be sent by the directory, can be ignored.

Hence, the protocol operates correctly with infinite buffering.

Dealing with Finite Buffering

What happens when the network does not have unlimited buffering? The major implication of this limit is that a cache or directory controller may be unable to complete a message send. This could lead to deadlock. The Example on page E-6 showed such a deadlock case. Even if we assume a separate controller for each cache block, so that the requests do not interfere in the controller, the Example will deadlock if there are no buffers available to send the replies.

The occurrence of such a deadlock is based on three properties, which characterize many deadlock situations:

1. More than one resource is needed to complete a transaction: Buffers are needed to generate requests, create replies, and accept replies.

2. Resources are held until a nonatomic transaction completes: The buffer used to create the reply cannot be freed until the reply is accepted.

3. There is no global partial order on the acquisition of resources: Nodes can generate requests and replies at will.

These characteristics lead to deadlock, and avoiding deadlock requires breaking one of these properties. Imposing a global partial order, the solution used in a bus-based system, is unworkable in a larger-scale, distributed machine. Freeing up resources without completing a transaction is difficult, since the transaction must be completely backed-out and cannot be left half-finished. Hence, our approach will be to try to resolve the need for multiple resources. We cannot simply eliminate this need, but we can try to ensure that the resources will always be available.

One way to ensure that a transaction can always complete is to guarantee that there are always buffers to accept messages. Although this is possible for a small machine with processors that block on a cache miss, it may not be very practical, since a single write could generate many invalidate messages. In addition, features such as prefetch would increase the amount of buffering required. There is an alternative strategy, which most systems use, and which ensures that a transaction will not actually be initiated until we can guarantee that it has the resources to complete. The strategy has four parts:

1. A separate network (physical or virtual) is used for requests and replies, where a reply is any message that a controller waits for in transitioning between states. This ensures that new requests cannot block replies that will free up buffers.

2. Every request that expects a reply allocates space to accept the reply when the request is generated. If no space is available the request waits. This ensures that a node can always accept a reply message, which will allow the replying node to free its buffer.

3. Any controller can reject (usually with a *negative acknowledge* or *NAK*) any request, but it can never NAK a reply. This prevents a transaction from starting if the controller cannot guarantee that it has buffer space for the reply.

4. Any request that receives a NAK in response is simply retried.

To understand why this is sufficient to prevent deadlock, let's first consider our earlier example. Because a write miss is a request that requires a reply, the space to accept the reply is preallocated. Hence, both nodes will have space for the reply. Since the networks are separate, a reply can be received even if no more space is available for requests. Since the requests are for two different blocks, the separate coherence controllers handle the requests. If the accesses are for the same address, then they are serialized at the directory and no problem exists.

To see that there are no deadlocks more generally, we must ensure that all replies can be accepted, and that every request is eventually serviced. Since a cache controller or directory controller can have at most one request needing a reply outstanding, it can always accept the reply when it returns. To see that every request is eventually serviced, we need only show that any request could be completed. Since every request starts with a read or write miss at a cache, it is sufficient to show that any read or write miss is eventually serviced. Since the write miss case includes the actions for a read miss as a subset, we focus on showing the write misses are serviced. The simplest situation is when the block is uncached; since that case is subsumed by the case when the block is shared, we focus on the shared and exclusive cases. Let's consider the case where the block is shared:

■   The CPU attempts to do a write and generates a write miss that is sent to the directory. At this point the processor is stalled.

■   The write miss is sent to the directory controller for this memory block. Note that although one cache controller handles all the requests for a given cache block, regardless of its memory contents, there is a controller for every memory block. Thus the only conflict at the directory controller is when two requests arrive for the same block. This is critical to the deadlock-free operation of the controller and needs to be addressed in an implementation using a single controller.

■   Now consider what happens at the directory controller: Suppose the write miss is the next thing to arrive at the directory controller. The controller sends out the invalidates, which can always be accepted if the controller for this block is idle. If the controller is not idle, then the processor must be stalled. Since the processor is stalled, it must have generated a read or write miss. If it generated a read miss, then it has either displaced this block or does not have a copy. If it does not have a copy, then it has sent a read miss and cannot continue until the read miss is processed by the directory (the read miss will not be handled until the write miss is). If the controller has replaced the block, then we need not worry about it. If the controller is idle, then an invalidate occurs, and the copy is eliminated.

The case where the block is exclusive is somewhat trickier. Our analysis begins when the write miss arrives at the directory controller for processing. There are two cases to consider:

- The directory controller sends a fetch/invalidate message to the processor where it arrives to find the cache controller idle and the block in the exclusive state. The cache controller sends a data write back to the home directory and makes its state invalid. This reply arrives at the home directory controller, which can always accept the reply, since it preallocated the buffer. The directory controller sends back the data to the requesting processor, which can always accept the reply; after the cache is updated the requesting cache controller restarts the processor.

- The directory controller sends a fetch/invalidate message to the node indicated as owner. When the message arrives at the owner node, it finds that this cache controller has taken a read or write miss that caused the block to be replaced. In this case, the cache controller has already sent the block to the home directory with a data write back and made the data unavailable. Since this is exactly the effect of the fetch/invalidate message, the protocol operates correctly in this case as well.

We have shown that our coherence mechanism operates correctly when controllers are replicated and when responses can be NAKed and retried. Both of these assumptions generate some problems in the implementation.

Implementing the Directory Controllers

First, let's consider how these controllers, which we have assumed are replicated, can be built without actually replicating them. On the side of the cache controllers, because the processors stall, the actual implementation is quite similar to what was needed for the snoopy controller. We can simply add the transient states just as we did for the snoopy case and note that a transaction for a different cache block can be handled while the current processor-generated operation is pending. Since a processor blocks on a request, at most one pending operation need be dealt with.

On the side of the directory controller, things are more complicated. The difficulty arises from the way we handle the retrieval and return of a block. In particular, during the time a directory retrieves an exclusive block and returns it to the requesting node, the directory must accommodate other transactions. Otherwise, integrating the directory controllers for different cache blocks will lead to the possibility of deadlock. Because of this situation, the directory controller must be reentrant, that is, it must be capable of suspending its execution while waiting for a reply and accept another transaction. The only place this must occur is in response to read or write misses, while waiting for a response from the owner. This leads to three important observations:

1. The state of the controller need only be saved and restored while either a fetch or a fetch/invalidate operation is outstanding.

2. The implementation can bound the number of outstanding transactions being handled in the directory, by simply NAKing read or write miss requests that could cause the number of outstanding requests to be exceeded.

3. If instead of returning the data through the directory, the owner node forwards the data directly to the requester (as well as returning it to the directory), we can eliminate the need for the directory to handle more than one outstanding request. This motivation, in addition to the reduction of latency, is the reason for using the forwarding style of protocol. The forwarding style protocol introduces another type of problem that we discuss in the exercises.

The major remaining implementation difficulty is to handle NAKs. One alternative is for each processor to keep track of its outstanding transactions, so it knows, when the NAK is received, what the requested transaction was. The alternative is to bundle the original request into the NAK, so that the controller receiving the NAK can determine what the original request was. Because every request allocates a slot to receive a reply and a NAK is a reply, NAKs can always be received. In fact, the buffer holding the return slot for the request can also hold information about the request, allowing the processor to reissue the request if it is NAKed.

This completes the implementation of the directory scheme. In practice, great care is required to implement these protocols correctly and to avoid deadlock. The key ideas we have seen in this section—dealing with nonatomicity and finite buffering—are critical to ensuring a correct implementation. Designers have found that both formal and informal verification techniques are helpful for ensuring that implementations are correct.

EXERCISES

E.1 [20] <8.4,E.2> The Convex Exemplar is a coherent shared-memory machine organized as a ring of eight-processor clusters. Describe a protocol for this machine, assuming that the ring can be snooped and that a directory sits at the junction of the ring and can also be interrogated from inside the cluster. How much directory storage is needed? If the coherence misses are uniformly distributed and the capacity misses are all within a cluster, what is the average memory access time for Ocean running on 64 processors?

E.2 [15/20] <8.4,E.2> As we discussed in section E.2, many DSM machines use a forwarding protocol, where a write miss request to a remote dirty block is forwarded to the node that has the copy of the block. The remote node then generates both a write-back operation and a data value reply.

a.   [15] <8.4> Modify the state diagrams of Figures 8.24 and 8.25 so that the diagrams implement a forwarding protocol.

b.   [20] <8.4,E.2> Forwarding protocols introduce a race condition into the protocol. Describe this race condition. Show how NAKs can be used to resolve the race condition.

E.3 [20] <8.4,E.2> Supporting lock-up free caches can have different implications for coherence protocols. Show how, without additional changes, allowing multiple outstanding misses from a node in a DSM can lead to deadlock—even if buffering is unlimited.

References

ADVE, S. V. AND M. D. HILL [1990]. "Weak ordering—A new definition," *Proc. 17th Int'l Symposium on Computer Architecture* (June), Seattle, 2–14.

AGARWAL, A. [1987]. *Analysis of Cache Performance for Operating Systems and Multiprogramming*, Ph.D. Thesis, Stanford Univ., Tech. Rep. No. CSL-TR-87-332 (May).

AGARWAL, A. AND S. D. PUDAR [1993]. "Column-associative caches: A technique for reducing the miss rate of direct-mapped caches," 20th Annual Int'l Symposium on Computer Architecture (ISCA '20) (May 16–19), San Diego, *Computer Architecture News* 21:2, 179–90.

AGARWAL, A., R. SIMONI, J. L. HENNESSY, AND M. A. HOROWITZ [1988]. "An evaluation of directory schemes for cache coherence," *Proc. 15th Int'l Symposium on Computer Architecture* (June), 280–289.

AGERWALA, T. AND J. COCKE [1987]. "High performance reduced instruction set processors," *IBM Tech. Rep.* (March).

ALLES, A. [1993]. "ATM in private networking," *Interop '93 Tutorial.*

ALLIANT COMPUTER SYSTEMS CORP. [1987]. *Alliant FX/Series: Product Summary* (June), Acton, Mass.

ALMASI, G. S. AND A. GOTTLIEB [1989]. *Highly Parallel Computing*, Benjamin/Cummings, Redwood City, Calif.

AMDAHL, G. M. [1967]. "Validity of the single processor approach to achieving large scale computing capabilities," *Proc. AFIPS Spring Joint Computer Conf.* 30 (April), Atlantic City, N.J., 483–485.

AMDAHL, G. M., G. A. BLAAUW, AND F. P. BROOKS JR. [1964]. "Architecture of the IBM System 360," *IBM J. Research and Development* 8:2 (April) 87–101.

ANDERSON, D. W., F. J. SPARACIO, AND R. M. TOMASULO [1967]. "The IBM 360 Model 91: Processor philosophy and instruction handling," *IBM J. Research and Development* 11:1 (January), 8–24.

ANDERSON, S. F., J. G. EARLE, R. E. GOLDSCHMIDT, AND D. M. POWERS [1967]. "The IBM System/360 Model 91: Floating-point execution unit," *IBM J. Research and Development* 11, 34–53. Reprinted in Swartzlander [1990].

ANDERSON, T. E., D. E. CULLER, AND D. PATTERSON [1995]. "A case for NOW (Networks of Workstations)," *IEEE Micro* 15:1 (February), 54–64.

ANON. ET AL. [1985]. "A measure of transaction processing power," Tandem Tech. Rep. TR 85.2. Also appeared in *Datamation,* April 1, 1985.

ARCHIBALD, J. AND J.-L. BAER [1986]. "Cache coherence protocols: Evaluation using a multiprocessor simulation model," *ACM Trans. on Computer Systems* 4:4 (November), 273–298.

ARPACI, R. H., D. E. CULLER, A. KRISHNAMURTHY S. G. STEINBERG, AND K. YELICK [1995]. "Empirical evaluation of the CRAY-T3D: A compiler perspective," *Proc. 23rd Int'l Symposium on Computer Architecture* (June), Italy.

ATANASOFF, J. V. [1940]. "Computing machine for the solution of large systems of linear equations," Internal Report, Iowa State University, Ames.

ATM FORUM [1994]. *ATM User-Network Interface Specification: Version 3.1*, PTR Prentice Hall, Englewood Cliffs, N.J.

BAER, J.-L. AND W.-H. WANG [1988]. "On the inclusion property for multi-level cache hierarchies," *Proc. 15th Annual Symposium on Computer Architecture* (May–June), Honolulu, 73–80.

BAKER, M. G., J. H. HARTMAN, M. D. KUPFER, K. W. SHIRRIFF, AND J. K. OUSTERHOUT [1991]. "Measurements of a distributed file system," *Proc. 13th ACM Symposium on Operating Systems Principles* (October), 198–212.

BAKOGLU, H. B., G. F. GROHOSKI, L. E. THATCHER, J. A. KAHLE, C. R. MOORE, D. P. TUTTLE, W. E. MAULE, W. R. HARDELL, D. A. HICKS, M. NGUYEN PHU, R. K. MONTOYE, W. T. GLOVER, AND S. DHAWAN [1989]. "IBM second-generation RISC processor organization," *Proc. Int'l Conf. on Computer Design* (October), Rye, N.Y., 138–142.

BANERJEE, U. [1979]. *Speedup of Ordinary Programs,* Ph.D. Thesis, Dept. of Computer Science, Univ. of Illinois at Urbana-Champaign (October).

BARTON, R. S. [1961]. "A new approach to the functional design of a computer," *Proc. Western Joint Computer Conf.,* 393–396.

BASHE, C. J., W. BUCHHOLZ, G. V. HAWKINS, J. L. INGRAM, AND N. ROCHESTER [1981]. "The architecture of IBM's early computers," *IBM J. Research and Development* 25:5 (September), 363–375.

BASHE, C. J., L. R. JOHNSON, J. H. PALMER, AND E. W. PUGH [1986]. *IBM's Early Computers,* MIT Press, Cambridge, Mass.

BASKETT, F. AND T. W. KELLER [1977]. "An evaluation of the CRAY-1 processor," in *High Speed Computer and Algorithm Organization,* D. J. Kuck, D. H. Lawrie, and A. H. Sameh, eds., Academic Press, San Diego, 71–84.

BASKETT, F., T. JERMOLUK, AND D. SOLOMON [1988]. "The 4D-MP graphics superworkstation: Computing + graphics = 40 MIPS + 40 MFLOPS and 10,000 lighted polygons per second," *Proc. COMPCON* (spring), San Francisco, 468–471.

BBN LABORATORIES [1986]. "Butterfly parallel processor overview," Tech. Rep. 6148 (March), BBN Laboratories, Cambridge, Mass.

BELL, C. G. [1984]. "The mini and micro industries," *IEEE Computer* 17:10 (October), 14–30.

BELL, C. G. [1985]. "Multis: A new class of multiprocessor computers," *Science* 228 (April 26), 462–467.

BELL, C. G. [1989]. "The future of high performance computers in science and engineering," *Comm. ACM* 32:9 (September), 1091–1101.

BELL, C. G. AND A. NEWELL [1971]. *Computer Structures: Readings and Examples,* McGraw-Hill, New York.

BELL, C. G. AND W. D. STRECKER [1976]. "Computer structures: What have we learned from the PDP-11?," *Proc. Third Annual Symposium on Computer Architecture* (January), Pittsburgh, 1–14.

BELL, C. G., R. CADY, H. MCFARLAND, B. DELAGI, J. O'LAUGHLIN, R. NOONAN, AND W. WULF [1970]. "A new architecture for mini-computers: The DEC PDP-11," *Proc. AFIPS SJCC,* 657–675.

BELL, C. G., J. C. MUDGE, AND J. E. MCNAMARA [1978]. *A DEC View of Computer Engineering,* Digital Press, Bedford, Mass.

BHANDARKAR, D. P. [1995]. *Alpha Architecture and Implementations,* Digital Press, Newton, Mass.

BHANDARKAR, D. AND D. W. CLARK [1991]. "Performance from architecture: Comparing a RISC and a CISC with similar hardware organizations," *Proc. Fourth Conf. on Architectural Support for Programming Languages and Operating Systems* (April), Palo Alto, Calif., 310–319.

BIRMAN, M., A. SAMUELS, G. CHU, T. CHUK, L. HU, J. MCLEOD, AND J. BARNES [1990]. "Developing the WRL3170/3171 SPARC floating-point coprocessors," *IEEE Micro* 10:1, 55–64.

BLOCH, E. [1959]. "The engineering design of the Stretch computer," *Proc. Fall Joint Computer Conf.,* 48–59.

BORG, A., R. E. KESSLER, AND D. W. WALL [1990]. "Generation and analysis of very long address traces." *Proc. 17th Annual Int'l Symposium on Computer Architecture* (Cat. No. 90CH2887-8) (May 28–31), Seattle, IEEE Computer Society Press, Los Alamitos, Calif., 270–279.

BOUKNIGHT, W. J, S. A. DENEBERG, D. E. MCINTYRE. J. M. RANDALL, A. H. SAMEH, AND D. L. SLOTNICK [1972]. "The Illiac IV system," *Proc. IEEE* 60:4, 369–379. Also appears in D. P. Siewiorek, C. G. Bell, and A. Newell, *Computer Structures: Principles and Examples,* McGraw-Hill, New York (1982), 306–316.

BRADY, J. T. [1986]. "A theory of productivity in the creative process," *IEEE CG&A* (May), 25–34.

BRENT, R. P. AND H. T. KUNG [1982]. "A regular layout for parallel adders," *IEEE Trans. on Computers* C-31, 260–264.

BREWER, E. A. AND B. C. KUSZMAUL [1994]. "How to get good performance from the CM-5 data network." *Proc. Eighth Int'l Parallel Processing Symposium* (April), Cancun, Mexico, 26–29.

BUCHER, I. V. [1983]. "The computational speed of supercomputers," *Proc. SIGMETRICS Conf. on Measuring and Modeling of Computer Systems* (August), ACM New York, 151–165.

BUCHER, I. V. AND A. H. HAYES [1980]. "I/O performance measurement on Cray-1 and CDC 7000 computers," *Proc. Computer Performance Evaluation Users Group,* 15th Meeting, NBS 500-65, 245–254.

BUCHOLTZ, W. [1962]. *Planning a Computer System: Project Stretch,* McGraw-Hill, New York.

BURGESS, N. AND T. WILLIAMS [1995]. "Choices of operand truncation in the SRT division algorithm," *IEEE Trans. on Computers,* 44:7.

BURKS, A. W., H. H. GOLDSTINE, AND J. VON NEUMANN [1946]. "Preliminary discussion of the logical design of an electronic computing instrument," Report to the U.S. Army Ordnance Department, p. 1. Also appears in *Papers of John von Neumann,* W. Aspray and A. Burks, eds., MIT Press, Cambridge, Mass., and Tomash Publishers, Los Angeles, Calif. (1987), 97–146.

CALLAHAN, D., J. DONGARRA, AND D. LEVINE [1988]. "Vectorizing compilers: A test suite and results," *Supercomputing '88* (November), Orlando, Fla., ACM/IEEE, 98–105.

CASE, R. P. AND A. PADEGS [1978]. "The architecture of the IBM System/370," *Comm. ACM* 21:1, 73–96. Also appears in D. P. Siewiorek, C. G. Bell, and A. Newell, *Computer Structures: Principles and Examples,* McGraw-Hill, New York (1982), 830–855.

CENSIER, L. AND P. FEAUTRIER [1978]. "A new solution to coherence problems in multicache systems," *IEEE Trans. on Computers* C-27:12 (December), 1112–1118.

CHARLESWORTH, A. E. [1981]. "An approach to scientific array processing: The architecture design of the AP-120B/FPS-164 family," *Computer* 14:9 (September), 18–27.

CHEN, P. M. AND D. A. PATTERSON [1993]. "Storage performance-metrics and benchmarks." *Proc. IEEE* 81:8 (August), 1151–1165.

CHEN, P. M. AND D. A. PATTERSON [1994a]. "Unix I/O performance in workstations and mainframes," Tech. Rep. CSE-TR-200-94 (March), University of Michigan, Ann Arbor.

CHEN, P. M. AND D. A. PATTERSON [1994b]. "A new approach to I/O performance evaluation—Self-scaling I/O benchmarks, predicted I/O performance." *ACM Trans. on Computer Systems* 12:4 (November).

CHEN, P. M. AND E. K. LEE [1995]. "Striping in a RAID level 5 disk array." *Proc. 1995 ACM SIGMETRICS Conference on Measurement and Modeling of Computer Systems* (May), 136–145.

CHEN, P. M., G. A. GIBSON, R. H. KATZ, AND D. A. PATTERSON [1990]. "An evaluation of redundant arrays of inexpensive disks using an Amdahl 5890," *Proc. 1990 ACM SIGMETRICS Conf. on Measurement and Modeling of Computer Systems* (May), Boulder, Colo.

CHEN, P. M., E. K. LEE, G. A. GIBSON, R. H. KATZ, AND D. A. PATTERSON [1994]. "RAID: High-performance, reliable secondary storage," *ACM Computing Surveys* 26:2 (June), 145–188.

CHEN, S. [1983]. "Large-scale and high-speed multiprocessor system for scientific applications," *Proc. NATO Advanced Research Work on High Speed Computing* (June). Also in *Superprocessors: Design and Applications,* K. Hwang, ed., IEEE (August 1984).

CHEN, T. C. [1980]. "Overlap and parallel processing," in *Introduction to Computer Architecture*, H. Stone, ed., Science Research Associates, Chicago, 427–486.

Clark, D. W. [1983]. "Cache performance of the VAX-11/780," *ACM Trans. on Computer Systems* 1:1, 24–37.

CLARK, D. W. [1987]. "Pipelining and performance in the VAX 8800 processor," *Proc. Second Conf. on Architectural Support for Programming Languages and Operating Systems* (March), Palo Alto, Calif., IEEE/ACM, 173–177.

CLARK, D. AND H. LEVY [1982]. "Measurement and analysis of instruction set use in the VAX-11/780," *Proc. Ninth Symposium on Computer Architecture* (April), Austin, Tex., 9–17.

CLARK, D. AND W. D. STRECKER [1980]. "Comments on 'the case for the reduced instruction set computer'," *Computer Architecture News* 8:6 (October), 34–38.

CODY, W. J., J. T. COONEN, D. M. GAY, K. HANSON, D. HOUGH, W. KAHAN, R. KARPINSKI, J. PALMER, F. N. RIS, AND D. STEVENSON [1984]. "A proposed radix- and word-length-independent standard for floating-point arithmetic," *IEEE Micro* 4:4, 86–100.

COLWELL, R. P., R. P. NIX, J. J. O'DONNELL, D. B. PAPWORTH, AND P. K. RODMAN [1987]. "A VLIW architecture for a trace scheduling compiler," *Proc. Second Conf. on Architectural Support for Programming Languages and Operating Systems* (March), Palo Alto, Calif., IEEE/ACM, 180–192.

COMER, D. [1993]. *Internetworking with TCP/IP*, 2nd ed., Prentice Hall, Englewood Cliffs, N.J.

CONTI, C., D. H. GIBSON, AND S. H. PITKOWSKY [1968]. "Structural aspects of the System/360 Model 85, part I: General organization," *IBM Systems J.* 7:1, 2–14.

COONEN, J. [1984]. *Contributions to a Proposed Standard for Binary Floating-Point Arithmetic*, Ph.D. Thesis, Univ. of Calif., Berkeley.

CRAWFORD, J. AND P. GELSINGER [1988]. *Programming the 80386*, Sybex Books, Alameda, Calif.

CURNOW, H. J. AND B. A. WICHMANN [1976]. "A synthetic benchmark," *The Computer J.* 19:1.

DALLY, W. J. AND C. I. SEITZ [1986]. "The torus routing chip," *Distributed Computing* 1:4, 187–96.

DARLEY, H. M., ET AL. [1989]. "Floating point/integer processor with divide and square root functions," U.S. Patent 4,878,190 (October 31).

DAVIDSON, E. S. [1971]. "The design and control of pipelined function generators," *Proc. Conf. on Systems, Networks, and Computers* (January), Oaxtepec, Mexico, IEEE, 19–21.

DAVIDSON, E. S., A. T. THOMAS, L. E. SHAR, AND J. H. PATEL [1975]. "Effective control for pipelined processors," *COMPCON* (March), San Francisco, IEEE, 181–184.

DEHNERT, J. C., P. Y.-T. HSU, AND J. P. BRATT [1989]. "Overlapped loop support on the Cydra 5," *Proc. Third Conf. on Architectural Support for Programming Languages and Operating Systems* (April), Boston, IEEE/ACM, 26–39.

DEMMEL, J. W. AND X. LI [1994]. "Faster numerical algorithms via exception handling," *IEEE Trans. on Computers* 43:8, 983–992.

DESURVIRE, E. [1992]. "Lightwave communications: The fifth generation," *Scientific American* (int'l ed.) 266:1 (January), 96–103.

DIEP, T. A., C. NELSON, AND J. P. SHEN [1995]. "Performance evaluation of the PowerPC 620 microarchitecture," *Proc. 22th Symposium on Computer Architecture* (June), Santa Margherita, Italy.

DITZEL, D. R. AND H. R. MCLELLAN [1987]. "Branch folding in the CRISP microprocessor: Reducing the branch delay to zero," *Proc. 14th Symposium on Computer Architecture* (June), Pittsburgh, 2–7.

DITZEL, D. R. AND D. A. PATTERSON [1980]. "Retrospective on high-level language computer architecture," *Proc. Seventh Annual Symposium on Computer Architecture* (June), La Baule, France, 97–104.

DOHERTY, W. J. AND R. P. KELISKY [1979]. "Managing VM/CMS systems for user effectiveness," *IBM Systems J.* 18:1, 143–166.

DONGARRA, J. J. [1986]. "A survey of high performance processors," *COMPCON* (March), IEEE, 8–11.

DUBOIS, M., C. SCHEURICH, AND F. BRIGGS [1988]. "Synchronization, coherence, and event ordering," *IEEE Computer* 9:21 (February).

EARLE, J. G. [1965]. "Latched carry-save adder," *IBM Tech. Disclosure Bull.* 7 (March), 909–910.

EGGERS, S. [1989]. *Simulation Analysis of Data Sharing in Shared Memory Multiprocessors,* Ph.D. Thesis, Univ. of California, Berkeley. Computer Science Division Tech. Rep. UCB/CSD 89/501 (April).

ELDER, J., A. GOTTLIEB, C. K. KRUSKAL, K. P. MCAULIFFE, L. RANDOLPH, M. SNIR, P. TELLER, AND J. WILSON [1985]. "Issues related to MIMD shared-memory computers: The NYU Ultracomputer approach," *Proc. 12th Int'l Symposium on Computer Architecture* (June), Boston, 126–135.

ELLIS, J. R. [1986]. *Bulldog: A Compiler for VLIW Architectures.* MIT Press, Cambridge, Mass.

EMER, J. S. AND D. W. CLARK [1984]. "A characterization of processor performance in the VAX-11/780," *Proc. 11th Symposium on Computer Architecture* (June), Ann Arbor, Mich., 301–310.

FABRY, R. S. [1974]. "Capability based addressing," *Comm. ACM* 17:7 (July), 403–412.

FARKAS, K. I. AND N. P. JOUPPI [1994]. "Complexity/performance tradeoffs with non-blocking loads," *Proc. 21st Annual Int'l Symposium on Computer Architecture* (April), Chicago.

FAZIO, D. [1987]. "It's really much more fun building a supercomputer than it is simply inventing one," *COMPCON* (February), IEEE, 102–105.

FEIERBACK, G. AND D. STEVENSON [1979]. "The Illiac-IV," in *Infotech State of the Art Report on Supercomputers,* Maidenhead, England. Also appears in D. P. Siewiorek, C. G. Bell, and A. Newell, *Computer Structures: Principles and Examples,* McGraw-Hill, New York (1982), 268–269.

FISHER, J. A. [1981]. "Trace scheduling: A technique for global microcode compaction," *IEEE Trans. on Computers* 30:7 (July), 478–490.

FISHER, J. A. [1983]. "Very long instruction word architectures and ELI-512," *Proc. 10th Symposium on Computer Architecture* (June), Stockholm, Sweden, 140–150.

FISHER, J. AND S. FREUDENBERGER [1992]. "Predicting conditional branch directions from previous runs of a program," *Proc. Fifth Conf. on Architectural Support for Programming Languages and Operating Systems* (October), Boston, IEEE/ACM, 85–95.

FISHER, J. A. AND B. R. RAU [1993]. *Journal of Supercomputing,* 7:1 (January), Kluwer.

FISHER J. A., J. R. ELLIS, J. C. RUTTENBERG, AND A. NICOLAU [1984]. "Parallel processing: A smart compiler and a dumb processor," *Proc. SIGPLAN Conf. on Compiler Construction* (June), Palo Alto, Calif., 11–16.

FLEMMING, P. J. AND J. J. WALLACE [1986]. "How not to lie with statistics: The correct way to summarize benchmarks results," *Comm. ACM* 29:3 (March), 218–221.

FLYNN, M. J. [1966]. "Very high-speed computing systems," *Proc. IEEE* 54:12 (December), 1901–1909.

FOSTER, C. C. AND E. M. RISEMAN [1972]. "Percolation of code to enhance parallel dispatching and execution," *IEEE Trans. on Computers* C-21:12 (December), 1411–1415.

FRANK, S. J. [1984]. "Tightly coupled multiprocessor systems speed memory access time," *Electronics* 57:1 (January), 164–169.

FREIMAN, C. V. [1961]. "Statistical analysis of certain binary division algorithms," *Proc. IRE* 49:1, 91–103.

FRIESENBORG, S. E. AND R. J. WICKS [1985]. "DASD expectations: The 3380, 3380-23, and MVS/XA," Tech. Bull. GG22-9363-02 (July 10), Washington Systems Center.

FULLER, S. H. AND W. E. BURR [1977]. "Measurement and evaluation of alternative computer architectures," *Computer* 10:10 (October), 24–35.

GAGLIARDI, U. O. [1973]. "Report of workshop 4—Software-related advances in computer hardware," *Proc. Symposium on the High Cost of Software,* Menlo Park, Calif., 99–120.

GAJSKI, D., D. KUCK, D. LAWRIE, AND A. SAMEH [1983]. "CEDAR-A large scale multiprocessor," *Proc. Int'l Conf. on Parallel Processing* (August), 524–529.

GAO, Q. S. [1993]. "The Chinese remainder theorem and the prime memory system," 20th Annual Int'l Symposium on Computer Architecture ISCA '20 (May 16–19), San Diego, Calif., *Computer Architecture News* 21:2, 337–340.

GARNER, R., A. AGARWAL, F. BRIGGS, E. BROWN, D. HOUGH, B. JOY, S. KLEIMAN, S. MUNCHNIK, M. NAMJOO, D. PATTERSON, J. PENDLETON, AND R. TUCK [1988]. "Scalable processor architecture (SPARC)," *COMPCON* (March), San Francisco, IEEE, 278–283.

GEE, J. D., M. D. HILL, D. N. PNEVMATIKATOS, AND A. J. SMITH [1993]. "Cache performance of the SPEC92 benchmark suite," *IEEE Micro* 13:4, 17–27.

GEHRINGER, E. F., D. P. SIEWIOREK, AND Z. SEGALL [1987]. *Parallel Processing: The Cm* Experience,* Digital Press, Bedford, Mass.

GHARACHORLOO, K., D. LENOSKI, J. LAUDON, P. GIBBONS, A. GUPTA, AND J. L. HENNESSY [1990]. "Memory consistency and event ordering in scalable shared-memory multiprocessors," *Proc. 17th Int'l Symposium on Computer Architecture* (June), Seattle, 15–26.

GIBBONS, P. B. AND S. S. MUCHNIK [1986]. "Efficient instruction scheduling for a pipelined processor," *SIGPLAN '86 Symposium on Compiler Construction* (June), Palo Alto, Calif., ACM, 11–16.

GIBSON, D. H. [1967]. "Considerations in block-oriented systems design," *AFIPS Conf. Proc.* 30, SJCC, 75–80.

GIBSON, J. C. [1970]. "The Gibson mix," Rep. TR 00.2043, IBM Systems Development Division, Poughkeepsie, N.Y. (Research done in 1959.)

GOLDBERG, D. [1991]. "What every computer scientist should know about floating-point arithmetic," *Computing Surveys* 23:1, 5–48.

GOLDBERG, I. B. [1967]. "27 bits are not enough for 8-digit accuracy," *Comm. ACM* 10:2, 105–106.

GOLDSTEIN, S. [1987]. "Storage performance—An eight year outlook," Tech. Rep. TR 03.308-1 (October), Santa Teresa Laboratory, IBM, San Jose, Calif.

GOLDSTINE, H. H. [1972]. *The Computer: From Pascal to von Neumann,* Princeton University Press, Princeton, N.J.

GOODMAN, J. R. [1983]. "Using cache memory to reduce processor memory traffic," *Proc. 10th Int'l Symposium on Computer Architecture* (June), Stockholm, Sweden, 124–131.

GOSLING, J. B. [1980]. *Design of Arithmetic Units for Digital Computers,* Springer-Verlag, New York.

GRAY, J. (ED.) [1993]. *The Benchmark Handbook for Database and Transaction Processing Systems,* 2nd ed., Morgan Kaufmann, San Francisco.

GRAY, J. AND A. REUTER [1993]. *Transaction Processing: Concepts and Techniques,* Morgan Kaufmann, San Francisco.

GROSS, T. R. [1983]. *Code Optimization of Pipeline Constraints,* Ph.D. Thesis (December), Computer Systems Lab., Stanford Univ.

HAMACHER, V. C., Z. G. VRANESIC, AND S. G. ZAKY [1984]. *Computer Organization,* 2nd ed., McGraw-Hill, New York.

HANDY, J. [1993]. *The Cache Memory Book,* Academic Press, Boston.

HARTMAN J. H. AND J. K. OUSTERHOUT [1993]. "Letter to the editor," *ACM SIGOPS Operating Systems Review* 27:1 (January), 7–10.

HAUCK, E. A. AND B. A. DENT [1968]. "Burroughs' B6500/B7500 stack mechanism," *Proc. AFIPS SJCC,* 245–251.

HEINRICH, J. [1993]. *MIPS R4000 User's Manual,* Prentice Hall, Englewood Cliffs, N.J.

HENLY, M. AND B. MCNUTT [1989]. "DASD I/O characteristics: A comparison of MVS to VM," Tech. Rep. TR 02.1550 (May), IBM, General Products Division, San Jose Calif.

HENNESSY, J. [1984]. "VLSI processor architecture," *IEEE Trans. on Computers* C-33:11 (December), 1221–1246.

HENNESSY, J. [1985]. "VLSI RISC processors," *VLSI Systems Design* VI 10 (October), 22–32.

HENNESSY, J. L. AND T. R. GROSS [1983]. "Postpass code optimization of pipeline constraints," *ACM Trans. on Programming Languages and Systems* 5:3 (July), 422–448.

HENNESSY, J., N. JOUPPI, F. BASKETT, AND J GILL [1981]. "MIPS: A VLSI processor architecture," *Proc. CMU Conf. on VLSI Systems and Computations* (October), Computer Science Press, Rockville, Md.

HEWLETT PACKARD [1994]. *PA-RISC 1.1 Architecture Reference Manual* 3rd ed.

HILL, M. D. [1987]. *Aspects of Cache Memory and Instruction Buffer Performance,* Ph.D. Thesis, Univ. of California at Berkeley Computer Science Division, Tech Rep. UCB/CSD 87/381 (November).

HILL, M. D. [1988]. "A case for direct mapped caches," *Computer* 21:12 (December), 25–40.

HILLIS, W. D. [1985]. *The Connection Machine,* MIT Press, Cambridge, Mass.

HINTZ, R. G. AND D. P. TATE [1972]. "Control Data STAR-100 processor design," *COMPCON* (September), IEEE, 1–4.

HOAGLAND, A. S. [1963]. *Digital Magnetic Recording,* Wiley, New York.

HOCKNEY, R. W. AND C. R. JESSHOPE [1988]. *Parallel Computers-2, Architectures, Programming and Algorithms,* Adam Hilger Ltd., Bristol, England

HOLLAND, J. H. [1959]. "A universal computer capable of executing an arbitrary number of subprograms simultaneously," *Proc. East Joint Computer Conf.* 16, 108–113.

HORD, R. M. [1982]. *The Illiac-IV, The First Supercomputer,* Computer Science Press, Rockville, Md.

HOSPODOR, A. D. AND A. S. HOAGLAND [1993]. "The changing nature of disk controllers." *Proc. IEEE* 81:4 (April), 586–94.

HOWARD, J. H., ET AL. [1988]. "Scale and performance in a distributed file system," *ACM Trans. on Computer Systems* 6:1, 51–81.

HSU, P. Y.-T. [1994]. "Designing the TFP microprocessor," *IEEE Micro.* 14:2 23–33.

HWANG, K. [1979]. *Computer Arithmetic: Principles, Architecture, and Design,* Wiley, New York.

HWANG, K. [1993]. *Advanced Computer Architecture and Parallel Programming,* McGraw-Hill, New York.

HWU, W.-M. AND Y. PATT [1986]. "HPSm, a high performance restricted data flow architecture having minimum functionality," *Proc. 13th Symposium on Computer Architecture* (June), Tokyo, 297–307.

IBM [1982]. *The Economic Value of Rapid Response Time,* GE20-0752-0, White Plains, N.Y., 11–82.

IBM [1990]. "The IBM RISC System/6000 processor," collection of papers, *IBM J. Research and Development* 34:1 (January).

IBM [1994]. *The PowerPC Architecture.* Morgan Kaufmann, San Francisco.

IEEE [1985]. "IEEE standard for binary floating-point arithmetic," *SIGPLAN Notices* 22:2, 9–25.

IMPRIMIS [1989]. *Imprimis Product Specification, 97209 Sabre Disk Drive IPI-2 Interface 1.2 GB,* Document No. 64402302 (May).

JAIN, R. [1991]. *The Art of Computer Systems Performance Analysis: Techniques for Experimental Design, Measurement, Simulation, and Modeling,* Wiley, New York.

JOHNSON, M. [1990]. *Superscalar Microprocessor Design,* Prentice Hall, Englewood Cliffs, N.J.

JORDAN, K. E. [1987]. "Performance comparison of large-scale scientific processors: Scalar mainframes, mainframes with vector facilities, and supercomputers," *Computer* 20:3 (March), 10–23.

JOUPPI, N. P. [1990]. "Improving direct-mapped cache performance by the addition of a small fully-associative cache and prefetch buffers," *Proc. 17th Annual Int'l Symposium on Computer Architecture* (Cat. No.90CH2887-8) (May 28–31), Seattle, IEEE Computer Society Press, Los Alamitos, Calif., 364–373.

JOUPPI, N. P. AND D. W. WALL [1989]. "Available instruction level parallelism for superscalar and superpipelined processors," *Proc. Third Conf. on Architectural Support for Programming Languages and Operating Systems* (April), Boston, IEEE/ACM, 272–282.

KAHAN, J. [1990]. "On the advantage of the 8087's stack," unpublished course notes, Computer Science Division, Univ. of California at Berkeley.

KAHAN, W. [1968]. "7094-II system support for numerical analysis," SHARE Secretarial Distribution SSD-159.

KAHANER, D. K. [1988]. "Benchmarks for 'real' programs," *SIAM News* (November).

KAHN, R. E. [1972]. "Resource-sharing computer communication networks," *Proc. IEEE* 60:11 (November), 1397–1407.

KANE, G. [1986]. *MIPS R2000 RISC Architecture,* Prentice Hall, Englewood Cliffs, N.J.

KANE, G. [1988]. *MIPS RISC Architecture,* Prentice Hall, Englewood Cliffs, N.J.

KATZ, R. H., D. A. PATTERSON, AND G. A. GIBSON [1990]. "Disk system architectures for high performance computing," *Proc. IEEE* 78:2 (February).

KELLER, R. M. [1975]. "Look-ahead processors," *ACM Computing Surveys* 7:4 (December), 177–195.

KILBURN, T., D. B. G. EDWARDS, M. J. LANIGAN, F. H. SUMNER [1962]. "One-level storage system," *IRE Trans. on Electronic Computers* EC-11 (April), 223–235. Also appears in D. P. Siewiorek, C. G. Bell, and A. Newell, *Computer Structures: Principles and Examples,* McGraw-Hill, New York (1982), 135–148.

KILLIAN, E. [1991]. "MIPS R4000 technical overview—64 bits/100 MHz or bust," *Hot Chips III Symposium Record* (August), Stanford University, 1.6–1.19.

KIM, M. Y. [1986]. "Synchronized disk interleaving," *IEEE Trans. on Computers* C-35:11 (November).

KNUTH, D. [1981]. *The Art of Computer Programming,* vol. II, 2nd ed., Addison-Wesley, Reading, Mass.

KOGGE, P. M. [1981]. *The Architecture of Pipelined Computers,* McGraw-Hill, New York.

KOHN, L. AND S.-W. FU [1989]. "A 1,000,000 transistor microprocessor," *IEEE Int'l Solid-State Circuits Conf.,* 54–55.

KOREN, I. [1989]. *Computer Arithmetic Algorithms,* Prentice Hall, Englewood Cliffs, N.J.

KROFT, D. [1981]. "Lockup-free instruction fetch/prefetch cache organization," *Proc. Eighth Annual Symposium on Computer Architecture* (May 12–14), Minneapolis, 81–87.

KUCK, D., P. P. BUDNIK, S.-C. CHEN, D. H. LAWRIE, R. A. TOWLE, R. E. STREBENDT, E. W. DAVIS, JR., J. HAN, P. W. KRASKA, AND Y. MURAOKA [1974]. "Measurements of parallelism in ordinary FORTRAN programs," *Computer* 7:1 (January), 37–46.

KUNKEL, S. R. AND J. E. SMITH [1986]. "Optimal pipelining in supercomputers," *Proc. 13th Symposium on Computer Architecture* (June), Tokyo, 404–414.

LAM, M. [1988]. "Software pipelining: An effective scheduling technique for VLIW processors," *SIGPLAN Conf. on Programming Language Design and Implementation* (June), Atlanta, ACM, 318–328.

LAM, M. S. AND R. P. WILSON [1992]. "Limits of control flow on parallelism," *Proc. 19th Symposium on Computer Architecture* (May), Gold Coast, Australia, 46–57.

LAM, M. S., E. E. ROTHBERG, AND M. E. WOLF [1991]. "The cache performance and optimizations of blocked algorithms," *Fourth Int'l Conf. on Architectural Support for Programming Languages and Operating Systems* (April 8–11), Santa Clara, Calif. SIGPLAN Notices 26:4 (April), 63–74.

LAMPORT, L. [1979]. "How to make a multiprocessor computer that correctly executes multiprocess programs," *IEEE Trans. on Computers* C-28:9 (September), 241–248.

LARSON, E. R. [1973]. "Findings of fact, conclusions of law, and order for judgment," File No. 4-67, Civ. 138, *Honeywell v. Sperry Rand and Illinois Scientific Development,* U.S District Court for the State of Minnesota, Fourth Division (October 19).

LEBECK, A. R. AND D. A. WOOD [1994]. "Cache profiling and the SPEC benchmarks: A case study," *Computer* 27:10 (October), 15–26.

LEE, R. [1989]. "Precision architecture," *Computer* 22:1 (January), 78–91.

LEIGHTON, F. T. [1992]. *Introduction to Parallel Algorithms and Architectures: Arrays, Trees, Hypercubes,* Morgan Kaufmann, San Mateo. Calif.

LEINER, A. L. [1954]. "System specifications for the DYSEAC," *J. ACM* 1:2 (April), 57–81.

LEINER, A. L. AND S. N. ALEXANDER [1954]. "System organization of the DYSEAC," *IRE Trans. of Electronic Computers* EC-3:1 (March), 1–10.

LENOSKI, D., J. LAUDON, K. GHARACHORLOO, A. GUPTA, AND J. L. HENNESSY [1990]. "The Stanford DASH Multiprocessor," *Proc. 17th Int'l Symposium on Computer Architecture* (June), Seattle, 148–159.

LENOSKI, D., J. LAUDON, K. GHARACHORLOO, W.-D. WEBER, A. GUPTA, J. L. HENNESSY, M. A. HOROWITZ, AND M. LAM [1992]. "The Stanford DASH Multiprocessor," *IEEE Computer* 25:3 (March).

LEVY, H. AND R. ECKHOUSE [1989]. *Computer Programming and Architecture: The VAX,* Digital Press, Boston.

LINCOLN, N. R. [1982]. "Technology and design trade offs in the creation of a modern supercomputer," *IEEE Trans. on Computers* C-31:5 (May), 363–376.

LIPTAY, J. S. [1968]. "Structural aspects of the System/360 Model 85, part II: The cache," *IBM Systems J.* 7:1, 15–21.

LIU, L. T. AND D. E. CULLER [1994]. "Measurement of Active Message Performance on the CM-5," Tech. Rep. UCB/CSD94-807, University of California, Berkeley.

LIU, L. T. AND D. E. CULLER [1995]. "An evaluation of the Intel Paragon communication architecture," submitted to *Supercomputing '95,* San Diego, Calif.

LOVETT, T. AND S. THAKKAR [1988]. "The Symmetry multiprocessor system," *Proc. 1988 Int'l Conf. of Parallel Processing,* University Park, Penn., 303–310.

LUBECK, O., J. MOORE, AND R. MENDEZ [1985]. "A benchmark comparison of three supercomputers: Fujitsu VP-200, Hitachi S810/20, and Cray X-MP/2," *Computer* 18:12 (December), 10–24.

LUNDE, A. [1977]. "Empirical evaluation of some features of instruction set processor architecture," *Comm. ACM* 20:3 (March), 143–152.

MABERLY, N. C. [1966]. *Mastering Speed Reading,* New American Library, New York.

MAGENHEIMER, D. J., L. PETERS, K. W. PETTIS, AND D. ZURAS [1988]. "Integer multiplication and division on the HP Precision architecture," *IEEE Trans. on Computers* 37:8, 980–990.

MAHLKE, S. A., W. Y. CHEN, W.-M. HWU, B. R. RAU, AND M. S. SCHLANSKER [1992]. "Sentinel scheduling for VLIW and superscalar processors," *Proc. Fifth Conf. on Architectural Support for Programming Languages and Operating Systems* (October), Boston, IEEE/ACM, 238–247.

MAJOR, J. B. [1989]. "Are queuing models within the grasp of the unwashed?," *Proc. Int'l Conf. on Management and Performance Evaluation of Computer Systems* (December 11–15), Reno, Nev., 831–839.

MARKSTEIN, P. W. [1990]. "Computation of elementary functions on the IBM RISC System/6000 processor," *IBM J. Research and Development* 34:1, 111–119.

MCFARLING, S. [1989]. "Program optimization for instruction caches," *Proc. Third Int'l Conf. on Architectural Support for Programming Languages and Operating Systems* (April 3–6), Boston, 183–191.

MCFARLING, S. [1993]. "Combining branch predictors," WRL Tech. Note TN-36 (June), Digital Western Research Laboratory, Palo Alto, Calif.

MCFARLING, S. AND J. L. HENNESSY [1986]. "Reducing the cost of branches," *Proc. 13th Symposium on Computer Architecture* (June), Tokyo, 396–403.

MCKEEMAN, W. M. [1967]. "Language directed computer design," *Proc. 1967 Fall Joint Computer Conf.,* Washington, D.C., 413–417.

MCMAHON, F. M. [1986]. "The Livermore FORTRAN kernels: A computer test of numerical performance range," Tech. Rep. UCRL-55745 (December), Lawrence Livermore National Laboratory, Univ. of California, Livermore.

MEAD, C. AND L. CONWAY [1980]. *Introduction to VLSI Systems,* Addison-Wesley, Reading, Mass.

MELLOR-CRUMMEY, J. M. AND M. L. SCOTT [1991]. "Algorithms for scalable synchronization on shared-memory multiprocessors," *ACM Trans. on Computer Systems* 9:1 (February), 21–65.

MENABREA, L. F. [1842]. "Sketch of the analytical engine invented by Charles Babbage," Bibiothèque Universelle de Genève (October).

METCALFE, R. M. "Computer/network interface design: Lessons from Arpanet and Ethernet," *IEEE J. on Selected Areas in Communications* 11:2 (February), 173–80.

METCALFE, R. M. AND D. R. BOGGS [1976]. "Ethernet: Distributed packet switching for local computer networks," *Comm. ACM* 19:7 (July), 395–404.

MEYERS, G. J. [1978]. "The evaluation of expressions in a storage-to-storage architecture," *Computer Architecture News* 7:3 (October), 20–23.

MEYERS, G. J. [1982]. *Advances in Computer Architecture,* 2nd ed., Wiley, New York.

MIRANKER, G. S., J. RUBENSTEIN, AND J. SANGUINETTI [1988]. "Squeezing a Cray-class supercomputer into a single-user package," *COMPCON* (March), IEEE, 452–456.

MITCHELL, D. [1989]. "The Transputer: The time is now," *Computer Design* (RISC supplement), 40–41.

MIURA, K. AND K. UCHIDA [1983]. "FACOM vector processing system: VP100/200," Proc. NATO Advanced Research Work on High Speed Computing (June). Also in *Superprocessors: Design and Applications,* K. Hwang, ed., IEEE (August 1984), 59–73.

MONTOYE, R. K., E. HOKENEK, AND S. L. RUNYON [1990]. "Design of the IBM RISC System/6000 floating-point execution," *IBM J. Research and Development* 34:1, 59–70.

MOORE, B., A. PADEGS, R. SMITH, AND W. BUCHOLZ [1987]. "Concepts of the System/370 vector architecture," *Proc. 14th Symposium on Computer Architecture* (June), Pittsburgh, ACM/IEEE, 282–292.

MORSE, S., B. RAVENAL, S. MAZOR, AND W. POHLMAN [1980]. "Intel Microprocessors—8008 to 8086," *Computer* 13:10 (October).

MOUSSOURIS, J., L. CRUDELE, D. FREITAS, C. HANSEN, E. HUDSON, S. PRZYBYLSKI, T. RIORDAN, AND C. ROWEN [1986]. "A CMOS RISC processor with integrated system functions," *Proc. COMPCON* (March), San Francisco, IEEE, 191.

MOWRY, T. C., S. LAM, AND A. GUPTA [1992]. "Design and evaluation of a compiler algorithm for prefetching," Fifth Int'l Conf. on Architectural Support for Programming Languages and Operating Systems (ASPLOS-V) (October 12–15), Boston, *SIGPLAN Notices* 27:9 (September), 62–73.

MUCHNICK, S. S. [1988]. "Optimizing compilers for SPARC," *Sun Technology* 1:3 (summer), 64–77.

NGAI, T.-F. AND M. J. IRWIN [1985]. "Regular, area-time efficient carry-lookahead adders," *Proc. Seventh IEEE Symposium on Computer Arithmetic,* 9–15.

NICOLAU, A. AND J. A. FISHER [1984]. "Measuring the parallelism available for very long instruction work architectures," *IEEE Trans. on Computers* C-33:11 (November), 968–976.

OUSTERHOUT, J. K., ET AL. [1985]. "A trace-driven analysis of the UNIX 4.2 BSD file system," *Proc. 10th ACM Symposium on Operating Systems Principles* Orcas Island, Wash., 15–24.

PADUA, D. AND M. WOLFE [1986]. "Advanced compiler optimizations for supercomputers," *Comm. ACM* 29:12 (December), 1184–1201.

PALACHARLA, S. AND R. E. KESSLER [1994]. "Evaluating stream buffers as a secondary cache replacement." *Proc. 21st Annual Int'l Symposium on Computer Architecture* (April 18–21), Chicago, IEEE Computer Society Press, Los Alamitos, Calif., 24–33.

PALMER, J. AND S. MORSE [1984]. *The 8087 Primer,* J. Wiley, New York.

PAN, S.-T., K. SO, AND J. T. RAMEH [1992]. "Improving the accuracy of dynamic branch prediction using branch correlation," *Proc. Fifth Conf. on Architectural Support for Programming Languages and Operating Systems* (October), Boston, IEEE/ACM, 76–84.

PARTRIDGE, C. [1994]. *Gigabit Networking,* Addison-Wesley, Reading, Mass.

PATTERSON, D. [1985]. "Reduced instruction set computers," *Comm. ACM* 28:1 (January), 8–21.

PATTERSON, D. A. AND D. R. DITZEL [1980]. "The case for the reduced instruction set computer," *Computer Architecture News* 8:6 (October), 25–33.

PATTERSON, D. A. AND J. L. HENNESSY [1994]. *Computer Organization and Design: The Hardware/ Software Interface,* Morgan Kaufmann, San Francisco.

PATTERSON, D. A., G. A. GIBSON, AND R. H. KATZ [1987]. "A case for redundant arrays of inexpensive disks (RAID)," Tech. Rep. UCB/CSD 87/391, Univ. of Calif. Also appeared in *ACM SIGMOD Conf. Proc.* (June 1–3), Chicago (1988), 109–116.

PENG, V., S. SAMUDRALA, AND M. GAVRIELOV [1987]. "On the implementation of shifters, multipliers, and dividers in VLSI floating point units," *Proc. Eighth IEEE Symposium on Computer Arithmetic,* 95–102.

PFISTER, G. F., W. C. BRANTLEY, D. A. GEORGE, S. L. HARVEY, W. J. KLEINFEKDER, K. P. MCAULIFFE, E. A. MELTON, V. A. NORTON, AND J. WEISS [1985]. "The IBM research parallel processor prototype (RP3): Introduction and architecture," *Proc. 12th Int'l Symposium on Computer Architecture* (June), Boston, 764–771.

PRZYBYLSKI, S. A. [1990]. *Cache Design: A Performance-Directed Approach,* Morgan Kaufmann, San Mateo, Calif.

PRZYBYLSKI, S. A., M. HOROWITZ, AND J. L. HENNESSY [1988]. "Performance tradeoffs in cache design," *Proc. 15th Annual Symposium on Computer Architecture* (May–June), Honolulu, 290–298.

RADIN, G. [1982]. "The 801 minicomputer," *Proc. Symposium Architectural Support for Programming Languages and Operating Systems* (March), Palo Alto, Calif., 39–47.

RAMAMOORTHY, C. V. AND H. F. LI [1977]. "Pipeline architecture," *ACM Computing Surveys* 9:1 (March), 61–102.

RAU, B. R., C. D. GLAESER, AND R. L. PICARD [1982]. "Efficient code generation for horizontal architectures: Compiler techniques and architectural support," *Proc. Ninth Symposium on Computer Architecture* (April), 131–139.

RAU, B. R., D. W. L. YEN, W. YEN, AND R. A. TOWLE [1989]. "The Cydra 5 departmental supercomputer: Design philosophies, decisions, and trade-offs," *IEEE Computers* 22:1 (January), 12–34.

REDMOND, K. C. AND T. M. SMITH [1980]. *Project Whirlwind—The History of a Pioneer Computer,* Digital Press, Boston.

RETTBERG, R. D., W. R. CROWTHER, P. P. CARVEY, AND R. S. TOWLINSON [1990]. "The Monarch parallel processor hardware design," *IEEE Computer* 23:4 (April).

RISEMAN, E. M. AND C. C. FOSTER [1972]. "Percolation of code to enhance parallel dispatching and execution," *IEEE Trans. on Computers* C-21:12 (December), 1411–1415.

ROBINSON, B. AND L. BLOUNT [1986]. "The VM/HPO 3880-23 performance results," IBM Tech. Bull. GG66-0247-00 (April), Washington Systems Center, Gaithersburg, Md.

ROWEN, C., M. JOHNSON, AND P. RIES [1988]. "The MIPS R3010 floating-point coprocessor," *IEEE Micro* 53–62 (June).

RUSSELL, R. M. [1978]. "The CRAY-1 processor system," *Comm. ACM* 21:1 (January), 63–72.

RYMARCZYK, J. [1982]. "Coding guidelines for pipelined processors," *Proc. Symposium on Architectural Support for Programming Languages and Operating Systems* (March), Palo Alto, Calif., IEEE/ACM, 12–19.

SAAVEDRA-BARRERA, R. H. [1992]. *CPU Performance Evaluation and Execution Time Prediction Using Narrow Spectrum Benchmarking,* Ph.D. Dissertation, University of Calif., Berkeley (May).

SALEM, K. AND H. GARCIA-MOLINA [1986]. "Disk striping," *IEEE Int'l Conf. on Data Engineering.*

SALTZER, J. H., D. P. REED, AND D. D. CLARK [1984]. "End-to-end arguments in system design." *ACM Trans. on Computer Systems* 2:4 (November), 277–288.

SAMPLES, A. D. AND P. N. HILFINGER [1988]. "Code reorganization for instruction caches," Tech. Rep. UCB/CSD 88/447 (October), Univ. of Calif., Berkeley.

SANTORO, M. R., G. BEWICK, AND M. A. HOROWITZ [1989]. "Rounding algorithms for IEEE multipliers," *Proc. Ninth IEEE Symposium on Computer Arithmetic,* 176–183.

SCHNECK, P. B. [1987]. *Superprocessor Architecture,* Kluwer Academic Publishers, Norwell, Mass.

SCOTT, N. R. [1985]. *Computer Number Systems and Arithmetic,* Prentice Hall, Englewood Cliffs, N.J.

SCRANTON, R. A., D. A. THOMPSON, AND D. W. HUNTER [1983]. "The access time myth," Tech. Rep. RC 10197 (45223) (September 21), IBM, Yorktown Heights, N.Y.

SEITZ, C. [1985]. "The cosmic cube," *Comm. ACM* 28:1 (January), 22–31.

SHURKIN, J. [1984]. *Engines of the Mind: A History of the Computer,* W. W. Norton, New York.

SILICON GRAPHICS [1994]. *MIPS IV Instruction Set, Revision 2.2,* Mountain View, Calif.

SITES, R. [1979]. *Instruction Ordering for the CRAY-1 Computer,* Tech. Rep. 78-CS-023 (July), Dept. of Computer Science, Univ. of Calif., San Diego.

SITES, R. L. (ED.) [1992]. *Alpha Architecture Reference Manual,* Digital Press, Newton, Mass.

SLATER, R. [1987]. *Portraits in Silicon,* MIT Press, Cambridge, Mass.

SLOTNICK, D. L., W. C. BORCK, AND R. C. MCREYNOLDS [1962]. "The Solomon computer," *Proc. Fall Joint Computer Conf.* (December), Philadelphia, 97–107.

SMITH, A. J. [1982]. "Cache memories," *Computing Surveys* 14:3 (September), 473–530.

SMITH, A. J. [1985]. "Disk cache-miss ratio analysis and design considerations," *ACM Trans. on Computer Systems* 3:3 (August), 161–203.

SMITH, A. AND J. LEE [1984]. "Branch prediction strategies and branch target buffer design," *Computer* 17:1 (January), 6–22.

SMITH, B. J. [1981]. "Architecture and applications of the HEP multiprocessor system," *Real-Time Signal Processing* IV 298 (August), 241–248.

SMITH, J. E. [1981]. "A study of branch prediction strategies," *Proc. Eighth Symposium on Computer Architecture* (May), Minneapolis, 135–143.

SMITH, J. E. [1984]. "Decoupled access/execute computer architectures," *ACM Trans. on Computer Systems* 2:4 (November), 289–308.

SMITH, J. E. [1988]. "Characterizing computer performance with a single number," *Comm. ACM* 31:10 (October), 1202–1206.

SMITH, J. E. [1989]. "Dynamic instruction scheduling and the Astronautics ZS-1," *Computer* 22:7 (July), 21–35.

SMITH, J. E. AND A. R. PLESZKUN [1988]. "Implementing precise interrupts in pipelined processors," *IEEE Trans. on Computers* 37:5 (May), 562–573. Based on an earlier paper that appeared in *Proc. 12th Symposium on Computer Architecture*, June 1988.

SMITH, J. E., G. E. DERMER, B. D. VANDERWARN, S. D. KLINGER, C. M. ROZEWSKI, D. L. FOWLER, K. R. SCIDMORE, AND J. P. LAUDON [1987]. "The ZS-1 central processor," *Proc. Second Conf. on Architectural Support for Programming Languages and Operating Systems* (March), Palo Alto, Calif., IEEE/ACM, 199–204.

SMITH, M. D., M. HOROWITZ, AND M. S. LAM [1992]. "Efficient superscalar performance through boosting," *Proc. Fifth Conf. on Architectural Support for Programming Languages and Operating Systems* (October), Boston, IEEE/ACM, 248–259.

SMITH, M. D., M. JOHNSON, AND M. A. HOROWITZ [1989]. "Limits on multiple instruction issue," *Proc. Third Conf. on Architectural Support for Programming Languages and Operating Systems* (April), Boston, IEEE/ACM, 290–302.

SMOTHERMAN, M. [1989]. "A sequencing-based taxonomy of I/O systems and review of historical machines," *Computer Architecture News* 17:5 (September), 5–15.

SOHI, G. S. [1990]. "Instruction issue logic for high-performance, interruptible, multiple functional unit, pipelined computers," *IEEE Trans. on Computers* 39:3 (March), 349–359.

SOHI, G. S. AND S. VAJAPEYAM [1989]. "Tradeoffs in instruction format design for horizontal architectures," *Proc. Third Conf. on Architectural Support for Programming Languages and Operating Systems* (April), Boston, IEEE/ACM, 15–25.

SPEC [1989]. *SPEC Benchmark Suite Release 1.0* (October 2).

SPEC [1994]. *SPEC Newsletter* (June).

SPORER, M., F. H. MOSS, AND C. J. MATHAIS [1988]. "An introduction to the architecture of the Stellar Graphics supercomputer," *COMPCON* (March) IEEE, 464.

STERN, N. [1980]. "Who invented the first electronic digital computer?," *Annals of the History of Computing* 2:4 (October), 375–376.

STONE, H. [1991]. *High Performance Computer Architecture,* Addison-Wesley, New York.

STRECKER, W. D. [1976]. "Cache memories for the PDP-11?," *Proc. Third Annual Symposium on Computer Architecture* (January), Pittsburgh, 155–158.

STRECKER, W. D. [1978]. "VAX-11/780: A virtual address extension of the PDP-11 family," *Proc. AFIPS National Computer Conf.* 47, 967–980.

SUN MICROSYSTEMS [1989]. *The SPARC Architectural Manual,* Version 8, Part No. 800-1399-09 (August 25).

SWAN, R. J., A. BECHTOLSHEIM, K. W. LAI, AND J. K. OUSTERHOUT [1977]. "The implementation of the Cm* multi-microprocessor," *Proc. AFIPS National Computing Conf.*, 645–654.

SWAN, R. J., S. H. FULLER, AND D. P. SIEWIOREK [1977]. "Cm*—A modular, multi-microprocessor," *Proc. AFIPS National Computer Conf.* 46, 637–644.

SWARTZ, J. T. [1980]. "Ultracomputers," *ACM Trans. on Programming Languages and Systems* 4:2, 484–521.

SWARTZLANDER, E. (ED.) [1990]. *Computer Arithmetic,* IEEE Computer Society Press, Los Alamitos, Calif.

TAKAGI, N., H. YASUURA, AND S. YAJIMA [1985]. "High-speed VLSI multiplication algorithm with a redundant binary addition tree," *IEEE Trans. on Computers* C-34:9, 789–796.

TANENBAUM, A. S. [1978]. "Implications of structured programming for machine architecture," *Comm. ACM* 21:3 (March), 237–246.

TANENBAUM, A. S. [1988]. *Computer Networks,* 2nd ed., Prentice Hall, Englewood Cliffs, N.J.

TANG, C. K. [1976]. "Cache design in the tightly coupled multiprocessor system," *Proc. AFIPS National Computer Conf.* (June), New York, 749–753.

TAYLOR, G. S. [1981]. "Compatible hardware for division and square root," *Proc. Fifth IEEE Symposium on Computer Arithmetic,* 127–134.

TAYLOR, G. S. [1985]. "Radix 16 SRT dividers with overlapped quotient selection stages," *Proc. Seventh IEEE Symposium on Computer Arithmetic,* 64–71.

TAYLOR, G., P. HILFINGER, J. LARUS, D. PATTERSON, AND B. ZORN [1986]. "Evaluation of the SPUR LISP architecture," *Proc. 13th Symposium on Computer Architecture* (June), Tokyo.

THACKER, C. P., E. M. McCREIGHT, B. W. LAMPSON, R. F. SPROULL, AND D. R. BOGGS [1982]. "Alto: A personal computer," in *Computer Structures: Principles and Examples,* D. P. Siewiorek, C. G. Bell, and A. Newell, eds., McGraw-Hill, New York, 549–572.

THADHANI, A. J. [1981]. "Interactive user productivity," *IBM Systems J.* 20:4, 407–423.

Thisquen, J. [1988]. "Seek time measurements," Amdahl Peripheral Products Division Tech. Rep. (May).

THORLIN, J. F. [1967]. "Code generation for PIE (parallel instruction execution) computers," *Proc. Spring Joint Computer Conf.* 27.

THORNTON, J. E. [1964]. "Parallel operation in Control Data 6600," *Proc. AFIPS Fall Joint Computer Conf.* 26, part 2, 33–40.

THORNTON, J. E. [1970]. *Design of a Computer, the Control Data 6600,* Scott, Foresman, Glenview, Ill.

TJADEN, G. S. AND M. J. FLYNN [1970]. "Detection and parallel execution of independent instructions," *IEEE Trans. on Computers* C-19:10 (October), 889–895.

TOMASULO, R. M. [1967]. "An efficient algorithm for exploiting multiple arithmetic units," *IBM J. Research and Development* 11:1 (January), 25–33.

TORRELLAS, J., A. GUPTA, AND J. HENNESSY [1992]. "Characterizing the caching and synchronization performance of a multiprocessor operating system," Fifth Int'l Conf. on Architectural Support for Programming Languages and Operating Systems (ASPLOS-V) (October 12–15), Boston, *SIGPLAN Notices* 27:9 (September), 162–74.

TOUMA, W. R. [1993]. *The Dynamics of the Computer Industry: Modeling the Supply of Workstations and Their Components,* Kluwer Academic, Boston.

UNGAR, D., R. BLAU, P. FOLEY, D. SAMPLES, AND D. PATTERSON [1984]. "Architecture of SOAR: Smalltalk on a RISC," *Proc. 11th Symposium on Computer Architecture* (June), Ann Arbor, Mich., 188–197.

WAKERLY, J. [1989]. *Microcomputer Architecture and Programming,* J. Wiley, New York.

WALL, D. W. [1991]. "Limits of instruction-level parallelism," *Proc. Fourth Conf. on Architectural Support for Programming Languages and Operating Systems* (April), Santa Clara, Calif., IEEE/ACM, 248–259.

WALL, D. W. [1993]. *Limits of Instruction-Level Parallelism,* Research Rep. 93/6, Western Research Laboratory, Digital Equipment Corp. (November).

WALRAND, J. [1991]. *Communication Networks: A First Course,* Aksen Associations: Irwin, Homewood, Ill.

WANG, W.-H., J.-L. BAER, AND H. M. LEVY [1989]. "Organization and performance of a two-level virtual-real cache hierarchy," *Proc. 16th Annual Symposium on Computer Architecture* (May 28–June 1), Jerusalem, 140–148.

WATANABE, T. [1987]. "Architecture and performance of the NEC supercomputer SX system," *Parallel Computing 5,* 247–255.

WATERS, F. (ED.) [1986]. *IBM RT Personal Computer Technology,* IBM, Austin, Tex., SA 23-1057.

WATSON, W. J. [1972]. "The TI ASC—A highly modular and flexible super processor architecture," *Proc. AFIPS Fall Joint Computer Conf.,* 221–228.

WEAVER, D. L. AND T. GERMOND [1994]. *The SPARC Architectural Manual, Version 9,* Prentice Hall, Englewood Cliffs, N.J.

WEICKER, R. P. [1984]. "Dhrystone: A synthetic systems programming benchmark," *Comm. ACM* 27:10 (October), 1013–1030.

WEISS, S. AND J. E. SMITH [1984]. "Instruction issue logic for pipelined supercomputers," *Proc. 11th Symposium on Computer Architecture* (June), Ann Arbor, 110–118.

WEISS, S. AND J. E. SMITH [1987]. "A study of scalar compilation techniques for pipelined supercomputers," *Proc. Second Conf. on Architectural Support for Programming Languages and Operating Systems* (March), Palo Alto, Calif., IEEE/ACM, 105–109.

WEISS, S. AND J. E. SMITH [1994]. *Power and PowerPC,* Morgan Kaufmann, San Francisco.

WESTE, N. AND K. ESHRAGHIAN [1993]. *Principles of CMOS VLSI Design: A Systems Perspective,* 2nd ed., Addison-Wesley, Reading, Mass.

WIECEK, C. [1982]. "A case study of the VAX 11 instruction set usage for compiler execution," *Proc. Symposium on Architectural Support for Programming Languages and Operating Systems* (March), Palo Alto, Calif., IEEE/ACM, 177–184.

WILKES, M. [1965]. "Slave memories and dynamic storage allocation," *IEEE Trans. Electronic Computers* EC-14:2 (April), 270–271.

WILKES, M. V. [1982]. "Hardware support for memory protection: Capability implementations," *Proc. Symposium on Architectural Support for Programming Languages and Operating Systems* (March 1–3), Palo Alto, Calif., 107–116.

WILKES, M. V. [1985]. *Memoirs of a Computer Pioneer,* MIT Press, Cambridge, Mass.

WILKES, M. V. [1995]. *Computing Perspectives,* Morgan Kaufmann, San Francisco.

WILKES, M. V., D. J. WHEELER, AND S. GILL [1951]. *The Preparation of Programs for an Electronic Digital Computer,* Addison-Wesley, Cambridge, Mass.

WILLIAMS, T. E., M. HOROWITZ, R. L. ALVERSON, AND T. S. YANG [1987]. "A self-timed chip for division," *Advanced Research in VLSI, Proc. 1987 Stanford Conf.,* MIT Press, Cambridge, Mass.

WILSON, A. W., JR. [1987]. "Hierarchical cache/bus architecture for shared-memory multiprocessors," *Proc. 14th Int'l Symposium on Computer Architecture* (June), Pittsburgh, 244–252.

WOOD, D. A. AND M. D. HILL [1995]. "Cost-effective parallel computing," *IEEE Computer* 28:2 (February).

WULF, W. [1981]. "Compilers and computer architecture," *Computer* 14:7 (July), 41–47.

WULF, W. AND C. G. BELL [1972]. "C.mmp—A multi-mini-processor," *Proc. AFIPS Fall Joint Computing Conf.* 41, part 2, 765–777.

WULF, W. AND S. P. HARBISON [1978]. "Reflections in a pool of processors—An experience report on C.mmp/Hydra," *Proc. AFIPS 1978 National Computing Conf.* 48 (June), Anaheim, Calif., 939–951.

WULF, W. A., R. LEVIN, AND S. P. HARBISON [1981]. *Hydra/C.mmp: An Experimental Computer System,* McGraw-Hill, New York.

YEH, T. AND Y. N. PATT [1992]. "Alternative implementations of two-level adaptive branch prediction," *Proc. 19th Symposium on Computer Architecture* (May), Gold Coast, Australia, 124–134.

YEH, T. AND Y. N. PATT [1993]. "A comparison of dynamic branch predictors that use two levels of branch history," *Proc. 20th Symposium on Computer Architecture* (May), San Diego, 257–266.

Index

A

access bit, 454
accesses
    aligned, 73, 74 (fig.)
    distribution, 86 (fig.)
    misaligned, 74 (fig.)
    as primitives, 86
    remote, 646–647
    spin lock, 697
    unsynchronized, 713
access time
    defined, 428
    remote, 646 (fig.)
accumulator architecture, 70, 120
adaptive routing, 594
ADDD instruction, 193, 245
adders
    carry-lookahead, A-39–A-42
    carry-propagate (CPA), A-50
    carry-save (CSA), A-50–A-51
    carry-select, A-45–A-46
    carry-skip, A-43–A-44
    division with, A-57–A-61
    full, A-3
    half, A-2
    multiplication with, A-52–A-57
    ripple-carry, A-2–A-3
    single, A-49–A-52, A-57–A-61
    time and space requirements,
        A-46 (fig.)
    See also addition; arithmetic

ADD instruction, 146, 147–148, 175,
    184–185
addition
    floating-point, A-22–A-28
        algorithm steps, A-24
        complexity of, A-23
        denormalized numbers, A-28
        sign of the sum rules, A-25
            (fig.)
        speeding up, A-26–A-28
    integer, speeding up, A-38–A-46
        carry lookahead, A-39–A-43
        carry-select adder, A-45–A-46
        carry-skip adders, A-43–A-44
    multiple-precision, A-13
    ripple-carry, A-2–A-3
    unsigned, A-11
    See also adders; arithmetic
address(es)
    32-bit, 86, 111
    64-bit, 86, 111
    alias, 424
    destination, 82
    effective, 74, 232
    fault. See page fault
    fields, DLX, 105
    I/O, 460
    physical 441
    segmented, 442
    specifier 87
    target, 276
    virtual, 422–425, 441, 444 (fig.)
    See also addressing

addressing
    memory, 73–80
        interpreting, 73–74
        summary, 79
    modes, 74–79
        80x86 architecture, D-4–D-5
        autoincrement, 185
        CPI and, 75
        displacement, 76–77
        DLX, 98
        encoding, 87
        immediate, 78–79
        instruction counts and, 75
        names of, 75 (fig.)
        RISC architecture, C-3 (fig.)
        summary, 76 (fig.)
        VAX architecture and, 76
    PC-relative, 74
    See also address(es)
address space
    global, 454
    local, 454
    too small, 467
address translation, 422–425
    for accesses, 445
    defined, 441
    fast, techniques, 445–447
    time reduction, 452
    See also translation buffers
Advanced Research Project Agency
    (ARPA), 626
aggregate bandwidth, 580
Aiken, H., 55

alias analysis, 320
  effect of, 329 (fig.)
  global/stack perfect, 329
  imperfect, 328–330
  inspection, 329
  no, 329
  varying levels of, 330 (fig.)
aliases, 424
Alpha AXP 21064, 357, 380–384
  cache, reading, 381–382
  cache, writing, 382
  CPI, 350
  data cache, 380–382
  data cache organization, 381 (fig.)
  instruction cache, 382–384
  main memory width, 431
  memory hierarchy, 461–466
    illustrated, 462 (fig.)
    parameters, 452 (fig.)
    performance, 465–466
  memory management, 449–453
  PTE, 450–451
  SPEC92 benchmarks, 465 (fig.)
  TLB, 445–446, 449–453
  virtual address mapping, 451 (fig.)
  See also DEC
AMAT. *See* average memory access
  time
Amdahl's Law, 29–32, 61, 262,
  644–645
  application of, 31
  caches and, 42
  defined, 30
  design comparison and, 31–32
  diminishing returns and, 31
  parallel computers and, 734–735
  speedup and, 29–30, 644
AND instruction, 146, 152, 153
anti-aliasing, 424
antidependence, 232, 243, 251, 357
architects. *See* designers
architecture
  32-bit, 86
  1970s, C-23 (fig.)
  accumulator, 70, 120
  centralized shared-memory,
    637–638, 654–677
  decoupled, 283

defined, 4, 113
distributed memory, 639 (fig.)
distributed shared-memory
  (DSM), 640, 677–694
DLX, 96–108
extended stack, D-2
  with flaws, 110–111
general-purpose register, 70–72
instruction set, 4, 69–73
Intel 80x86, D-1–D-25
load-store, 120
memory-memory, 70, 120
register-memory, 70
register-register, 70
RISC, 2, 115, 172, 303 (fig.),
  C-1–C-25
scalable shared-memory, 640, 679
stack, 70, 120
vector processor, B-3–B-15
areal density, 490
  See also magnetic disks
arithmetic, A-1–A-69
  addition
    floating-point, A-22–A-28
    integer, speeding up, A-38–
      A-46
    multiple-precision, A-13
    ripple-carry, A-2–A-3
    unsigned, A-11
  Booth recoding, A-8, A-9 (fig.),
    A-10, A-51 (fig.), A-52 (fig.),
    A-67, A-76
  denormals, A-14–A-15
    defined, A-38
    floating-point addition, A-28
    floating-point multiplication,
      A-21
  division
    floating-point, A-28–A-32
    integer, speeding up,
      A-46–A-61
    integer examples, A-12 (fig.)
    iterative, A-28–A-32
    radix-2, A-3–A-7
    SRT, A-47–A-49, A-67
  exceptions, A-36–A-37
  floating-point, A-13–A-38
    addition, A-22–A-28

algorithms, A-1
  division, A-28–A-32
  integer conversion and, A-65
  multiplication, A-17–A-22
  number representation,
    A-15–A-17
  pre IEEE formats, A-67
  remainder, A-32–A-33
  fused multiply-add, A-34
  IEEE standard and, A-13–A-15
  integer, A-2–A-13
    addition speedup, A-38–A-46
    division speedup, A-46–A-61
    floating-point conversion and,
      A-65
    multiplication speedup,
      A-46–A-61
    radix-2 multiplication and
      division, A-3–A-7
    ripple-carry addition, A-2–A-3
    signed numbers and, A-7–A-10
    system issues, A-10–A-13
  multiplication
    floating-point, A-17–A-22
    integer, speeding up,
      A-46–A-61
    of multiple-precision integers,
      A-11
    radix-2, A-3–A-7
    two's complement, A-8
  overflow, A-7–A-8
    handling, A-11 (fig.)
    integer, A-10–A-11
    rounding and, A-21
  precisions, A-34–A-36
    double, A-34
    double extended, 34
    double rounding and, A-35
    floating-point multiplication,
      A-22
    implementations, A-34–A-35
    multiple-precision addition,
      A-13
    single, A-34
    single extended, A-34
  remainder, floating-point,
    A-32–A-33

rounding
  after rounding rule, A-38
  before rounding rule, A-38
  double, A-35
  floating-point multiplication,
    A-18–A-19
  modes, A-14
  overflow and, A-21
  rules for, A-20 (fig.)
  signed numbers, A-7–A-10
  speeding up
    floating-point addition,
      A-26–A-28
    integer addition, A-38–A-46
    integer division, A-46–A-61
    integer multiplication,
      A-46–A-61
  underflow, A-37–A-38
    gradual, A-15
    occurrences of, A-65
    signaling, A-38
arithmetic/logical instructions, 101
arithmetic logic unit (ALU), 45, 61
  bypass, MIPS R4000, 204
  in execution/effective address
    cycle (EX), 128
  forwarding data to inputs, 160
    (fig.)
  instructions, 128, 129, 131
  in pipelining, 131
  in write-back cycle (WB), 129
arithmetic mean, 25
  weighted, 26
ARPANET, 626
array indices, 290–291
  affine, 290
array multiplier, A-53 (fig.)
  multipass, A-54 (fig.)
array processors, 747
arrays
  accesses to, 410 (fig.)
  column major order storage, 408
  disk, 521–522
  even/odd, A-55 (fig.)
  loop access code and, 407
  merging, 405–406
  row major order storage, 408
  snapshot of, 408 (fig.)
asynchronous buses, 499
  See also bus(es)

asynchronous events, 181
  See also events
asynchronous transfer mode (ATM),
  604, 613–622, 627
  AAL-5 format, 616 (fig.)
  adaptation layer (AAL), 617
  cells, 617
  defining, 613
  fixed transfer size, 630
  header format, 616 (fig.)
  host interface card, 615, 617–618,
    619
  levels, 615
  packet format, 603 (fig.)
  SPARCstation performance with,
    618–622
  switches, 618
  TCP throughput, 620 (fig.)
  total time on, 622 (fig.)
  virtual circuit identifier (VCI), 615
  virtual path identifier (VPI), 615
  See also networks
Atanasoff, J. V., 54
Atlas, 472–473
atomic exchange, 694–695
attributes field, 454
availability, 521
average instruction execution time, 56
average memory access time, 384,
  385
  for associativity, 396–397
  block size vs., 395 (fig.)
  formula, 389, 395
  for four programs, 469 (fig.)
  minimizing, 387
  pseudo-associative cache,
    399–400
  two-level cache, 417
  two-way set associative, 388–389
  using miss rates, 397 (fig.)
average memory reference, 692, 693
  (fig.)
average memory stall time, 415
average residual service time,
  512–513
average rotational time, 489
average seek time, 549
average selling price (ASP), 15

B

bandwidth
  aggregate, 580
  bisection, 586, 588–590, 691
  in circuit-switched network, 595
  defined, 568
  effective, 570–572
    defined, 570
    message size vs., 572 (fig.)
  improvement techniques, 431–439
    avoiding memory bank
      conflicts, 435–437
    DRAM-specific interleaving,
      437–439
    independent memory banks,
      434–435
    interleaved memory, 431–434
    wider main memory, 431
  I/O, 504
  main memory, 428
  matching, 632
  memory system, percentage
    calculation, 479
  multiprocessor communication
    models, 641
  as network performance measure-
    ment, 622–623
  in packet-switched network, 595
  twisted pair, 577
Barnes-Hut algorithm, 650–651
  Challenge microprocessor and,
    732
  data miss rate, 668 (fig.), 669 (fig.)
  octree, 650
  parallel performance and,
    650–651
  performance, 666
  processor count increase, 667
  speedup dropoff, 732
  See also parallel applications
barrier synchronization, 700–703
  code for, 701 (fig.)
  contention and, 704
  defined, 700
  gather stage, 704
  implementation, 700–701
  performance improvement, 707

barrier synchronization *(continued)*
  release stage, 704
  sense-reversing, 701–702
    code, 708 (fig.)
  See also synchronization
base, 448
base field, 454
baseline performance, 23
  measurements, 48
  SPEC92, 57
basic block, 156
Bell, C. G., 750
benchmarks
  DebitCredit, 516–517
  disk performance, 516–521
  engineering, 48
  FP, 326
  ideal processor, 319–320
  Linpack, B-31–B-33
  parallel
    execution time components,
     733 (fig.)
    speedups for, 732 (fig.)
  Perfect Club, B-22 (fig.)
  reports of, 23
  self-scaling I/O, 518–521
  SPEC89, 48, 49, 57, 264–266
  SPEC92, 21–22, 48–49, 57, 266,
    339, 465
  SPECfp92, 48, 606
  SPECint, 606
  SPEC report, 23
  suites, 21–22
  synthetic, 20–21, 47
  system-level file server (SFS), 518
  system-oriented, 58
  toy, 20
  transaction processing, 516–517
  unfair, 476
  usefulness, 48
  validity duration of, 48–50
  See also performance
BEQZ instruction, 175
biased exponents, A-15
Big Endian byte order, 73
binary tree multiplier, A-54–A-55
bisection bandwidth, 586, 588–590,
  691

2D torus, 588–589
6-cube, 589–590
bus, 588
fully connected, 588
ring, 588
  See also bandwidth
bit-interleaved parity, 523
bit selection, 377
blocking, 408–411
  capacity misses and, 409
  defined, 584
  factor, 409
  See also block(s)
block-interleaved distribution parity,
523–525
  block interleaved parity vs.,
    524 (fig.)
block(s)
  address, 377–378
    index field, 378
    tag field, 377
  cache, 660–661
    state transition diagram, 682,
     683 (fig.)
  clean, 379–380
  data write-back, 685
  defined, 41, 375, 408
  dirty, 379, 412
  enlarging, 393–395
  file cache, 546
  finding, 377–378
    in main memory, 443
  large, 412
  least-recently used (LRU), 378,
    444
  offset, 377
  placement, 376–377
    main memory, 443
  random, 378
  read miss, 684, 685
  replacing, 378
  size
    average memory access time
     vs., 395 (fig.)
    data cache and, 672
    directory-based protocols and,
     690 (fig.)
    miss rate vs., 394 (fig.), 671
     (fig.)

multiprogrammed workload
  and, 674, 675 (fig.), 676 (fig.)
sub-blocks, 412
virtual memory misses and, 443–
  444
write miss, 685
  See also blocking; cache(s)
block transfer engine (BLT), 607
  memory access instructions vs.,
    608 (fig.)
boosting, 307–308
  creation of, 357
  defined, 307
  implementation, 308
Booth recoding, A-8, A-67, A-76
  implementing, A-10
  multiplication hardware and, A-10
  numerical example, A-9 (fig.)
  radix-4, A-51 (fig.), A-52 (fig.)
  See also arithmetic
bound, 448
branch delay, 163
  MIPS R4000 pipeline, 203 (fig.)
branch-delay slots, 168–170
  defined, 168
  scheduling, 169 (fig.)
branch(es), 80
  backward, 164
    loops and, 164–166
    probability of, 166
  behavior of, 164–166
  behavior optimization, 162
  branch targets and, 82
  cancelling, 170–172
  compare type frequency, 84 (fig.)
  conditional, 84–85, 164
  condition evaluation, 83 (fig.)
  delayed, 168–170, 172–173
  distance, 83 (fig.)
  DLX, 102
  forward, 164
    probability of, 166
  frequency, 173
  hardware, prediction, 261, 262–
    278
  history table. *See* branch-predic-
    tion buffers
  misprediction rate, 176 (fig.)

PC-relative, 82
penalties, 173–174
    DLX reduction, 271
    two-clock-cycle, 274
pipeline penalty reduction, 166–173
pipelines and. *See* control hazards
prediction accuracy, 177
predict-not-taken scheme, 167 (fig.)
predict-taken strategy, 170 (fig.), 177 (fig.)
schemes
    costs, 173 (fig.)
    penalties for, 174 (fig.)
    performance, 173–175
stalls, 161–162
    clock cycle reduction, 162
static prediction, 175–177
taken, 161
untaken, 161
See also branch prediction; jumps
branch folding, 276
branch likely, 171
branch prediction, 262–271
    accuracy, 264–265
    basic, 262–271
    correlating predictors, 267
    effectiveness, 262
    effects of, 324 (fig.), 325 (fig.)
    levels of, 324–326
    misprediction rate, 264
    no, 326
    one-bit scheme, 263
    perfect, 320, 324
    prediction bit, 263
        taken/not taken, 268 (fig.)
    schemes, 354
    selective history predictor, 324–325
    for SPEC89 benchmarks, 264–266
    static, 326
    two-bit scheme, 263–266, 325
    See also branch(es); branch-prediction buffers; branch-target buffers
branch-prediction buffers, 262–271
    (2,2), 270 (fig.)

accessing, 272
branch-target buffer and, 274
defined, 262
with global history, 270 (fig.)
implementing, 264
indexing, 269
as linear memory array, 269
two-bit, 264–266
    prediction accuracy, 265–266 (fig.)
See also branch prediction
branch-target buffers, 271–278
    accessing, 272
    branch-prediction buffer and, 274
    for CRISP, 354
    defined, 271
    illustrated, 273 (fig.)
    instruction handling steps with, 275 (fig.)
    matching entries, 273
    penalties and, 274
    procedure return prediction and, 276–277
    target address, 276
    target instructions, 276
    variation, 276
    See also branch prediction
bridges, 601
    increased bandwidth and, 605 (fig.)
    See also networks
broadcast communication, 580
bubbles, 141, 153
    in pipeline, 143 (fig.)
buckets, 511
buffers
    branch-prediction, 262–271
    branch-target, 271–278
    finite, E-9–E-11
    full, stalls, 347
    load and store, 255
    PowerPC 620, 349
    prefetch, 401
    reorder, 309
    return address, 277 (fig.)
    source operand, 260
    speed-matching, 529
    translation, 443, 445–446

write, 380, 412, 464, 470
Burroughs machines, 113
bus(es), 496–504
    asynchronous, 499
    bisection bandwidth, 588
    clock, 498
    CPU-memory, 496, 501
    defined, 496
    design, 495
        decisions, 497–500
    disadvantages of, 496
    examples, 501
    interface, 501–503
    I/O, 496, 501, 535, 573
    ISA, 573
    mapping nodes and, 590
    memory, 431
    options, 497 (fig.)
    packet-switched, 439, 498
    PCI, 573
    pipelined, 498
    preferred type, 500 (fig.)
    SCSI, 533
    snooping, 659 (fig.)
    split-transaction, 498
    standards, 500–501
    synchronous, 498–499
    transactions, 496, 497 (fig.)
        read, 496
        write, 496, 499 (fig.)
    See also input/output (I/O)
bypassing. *See* forwarding
bytes
    access, 86
    ordering, 73

C

cache coherence, 655–658, 708
    bus-based, 662
    consistency and, 656–657
    defined, 655
    directory protocol E-6–E-12
    in distributed-memory machine, 680 (fig.)
    enforcement schemes, 657–658
    finite-state controller for, E-3 (fig.)

cache coherence *(continued)*
    memory system and, 656
    processor steps, 698 (fig.)
    protocols, 657
        implementing, E-1–E-13
    read/write behavior and, 657
    requests and, 662 (fig.)
    for single memory location, 655
        (fig.)
    snooping protocols, 666–676,
        E-1–E-6
    state diagram, 665 (fig.)
    variations, 662
    write-invalidate protocol, 664
        (fig.)
    See also false sharing
cache-coherency problem, 459–461
    illustrated, 460 (fig.)
cache-coherency protocols, 461
cache(s), 375–427
    Amdahl's Law and, 42
    block placement in, 376–377
    blocks, 660–661
        state transition diagram, 682,
            683 (fig.)
    block size and, 672 (fig.)
    CPI, 333
    data, 380–382
        set-associative, 675 (fig.)
    defined, 41, 375
    direct mapped, 376, 473
        address portions, 378 (fig.)
        instruction and data miss rates,
            468 (fig.)
        tag check and, 422
    example, 376 (fig.)
    file, 375, 542–543, 544–548
    fully associative, 377
        conflict misses and, 392
    hit, 41
        steps, 380
    hit time, 384
        miss penalty and, 399 (fig.)
        pseudo-associative, 399
        read, 425
        reducing, 422–426
        write, 425
    hit time reduction techniques,
        422–426

avoiding address translation
    during cache indexing,
    422–425
small and simple caches, 422
writes for fast write hits,
    425–426
IBM 3033, 425
indexing, 422–425
    formula, 424
instruction, 382–384
I/O connected to, 526 (fig.)
lockup-free, 402, 414–416, 434
miss(es), 41
    block replacement and, 378
    capacity, 390, 409, 419
    categories, 390
    coherence, 666, 673
    collision, 390
    compulsory, 390
    conflict, 390, 410, 420, 673
    false sharing, 670
    interference, 390
    memory references and, 150
    ownership, 665–666
    penalty, 43, 333–334
    per instruction, 386
    read, 684, 685
    read priority, 411–412
    reducing, 390–411
    reduction vs. ILP, 458–459
    remote, 692
    stall reduction on, 414–416
    steps, 382
    time required for, 41
    upgrade, 665–666
    write, 685
miss penalty
    average, 413–414
    pseudo hit time and, 399 (fig.)
    reducing, 411–422
miss penalty reduction techniques,
    411–422
    early restart and critical word
        first, 412–414
    giving priority to read misses
        over writes, 411–412
    nonblocking caches to reduce
        stalls, 414–416

second-level caches, 416–422
sub-block placement for
    reduced miss penalty, 412
miss rate
    associativity and, 396
    block size vs., 394 (fig.), 674
        (fig.)
    by sizes, 391 (fig.)
    cache size vs., 418 (fig.)
    data, 384
    defined, 43
    directory-based protocols,
        687–689 (fig.)
    distribution, 392 (fig.)
    global, 417
    instruction, 384
    local, 417
    measurements, 43
    total, 392 (fig.)
    unified, 384 (fig.)
miss rate reduction techniques,
    393–411
    compiler-controlled prefetch-
        ing, 402–404
    compiler optimizations,
        405–411
    hardware prefetching of in-
        structions and data, 400–402
    higher associativity, 396–397
    larger block size, 393–395
    pseudo-associative crashes,
        398–400
    victim caches, 397–398
multilevel inclusion, 661,
    723–724
name, 375
nonblocking, 402, 414–416, 434,
    725–726
number of ports, 457–458
optimizations, 390, 426–427
    summary, 427 (fig.)
parameter ranges, 441 (fig.)
performance, 42–44, 384–390
    improving, 389–390
    predicting, 467
physical, 423
prefetch, 402
pseudo-associative, 398–400

second-level, 416–422
set associative, 377
    address portions, 378 (fig.)
    two-way, 388–389
size, changing, 393
small and simple, 422
stale data and, 525–526
victim, 397–398
virtual, 423
virtual memory vs., 441
write-back, 412, 526, 660–662
writes and, 378–380
write-through, 411, 526
See also block(s); memory;
    memory hierarchy
callee saving, 84
caller saving, 84
call gates, 456
CALLS instruction, 109–110
cancelling branches, 170–172
    advantage of, 171
    delay, 171 (fig.)
    performance, 172 (fig.)
    predicted-taken, 170 (fig.), 177
        (fig.)
    See also branch(es)
capacity misses, 390
    blocking and, 409
    second-level caches and, 419
    See also cache(s)
carry lookahead, A-39–A-43
    adder, A-39–A-42
    bits, A-43
    circuit, A-40 (fig.)
    ripple-carry adder combination,
        A-43 (fig.)
    tree, A-41–A-42 (figs.)
    See also adders; addition; arith-
        metic
carry-propagate adders (CPAs), A-50
carry-save adders (CSAs),
    A-50–A-51
carry-save multiplier, A-50 (fig.)
carry-select adder, A-45–A-46
    defined, A-45
    illustrated, A-45 (fig.), A-46 (fig.)
    See also adders; addition;
        arithmetic

carry-skip adders, A-43–A-44
    defined, A-43
    illustrated, A-44 (fig.)
    speed, A-44
    See also adders; addition;
        arithmetic
CD-ROMs, 493
cells
    defined, 617
    destination address, 617
    See also asynchronous transfer
        mode (ATM)
centralized shared-memory architec-
    tures, 637–638, 654–677
    cache-coherence protocols, 657
    defined, 637
    directory-based protocols, 657
    example protocol, 662–666
    implementation techniques,
        660–662
    private data and, 655
    shared data and, 655
    snooping protocols, 657–658, 661,
        662 (fig.), 666–676
    structure, 638 (fig.)
    write broadcast protocol, 659
    write invalidate protocol, 658,
        659–662, 664
    write update protocol, 659–660
chaining, B-23, B-24–B-25, B-30
    defined, B-19, B-24
    example, B-24
    flexible, B-24
    function of, B-24
    See also vector processors;
        vector(s)
Challenge multiprocessor, 728–733
    array machine, 742
    Barnes-Hut and, 732
    defined, 728
    DM, 738–739
    Ocean and, 732
    parallel benchmarks on, 733 (fig.)
    parallel program workload on,
        731–733
    POWERpath-2, 728–731
    system bus, 728–731
    system structure, 729 (fig.)

XL, 739
    See also Silicon Graphics
channel controllers. *See* I/O
    processors
Charlesworth, A. E., 355
chimes
    approximation, B-10
    defined, B-9
    reducing number of, B-19
    See also vector instructions; vector
        processors
Chinese Remainder Theorem, 436
choke packets, 597
circuit switched network, 592
    bandwidth in, 595
    See also networks
Clark, D., 114, 116
client/server computing
    file cache performance vs. read
        percentage, 547 (fig.)
    write policy for, 547–548
clock cycles, 37
    defined, 32
    determining, 35
    DLX, 127–129
    execution/effective address cycle
        (EX), 128–129
    instruction decode/register fetch
        cycle (ID), 127–128
    instruction fetch cycle (IF), 127
    lower limit, 137
    memory access/branch completion
        cycle (MEM), 129
    multiple instructions in, 278
    on pipelined machine, 140
    pipe stages, 132
    total number of, 33
    write-back cycle (WB), 129
    See also clock cycles per instruc-
        tion (CPI); instruction count (IC)
clock cycles per instruction (CPI)
    addressing modes and, 76
    average values, 36
    cache, 333
    DEC Alpha 21064, 350
    defined, 32
    determining for modern processor,
        36

clock cycles per instruction (CPI)
  (*continued*)
    IBM Power-2, 350
    ideal pipeline, 222
    lower, 349–350
    measuring, 36
    MIPS R4000 pipeline, 208–209
      (fig.)
    on pipelined machine, 140
    overall, 33
    penalties, 174 (fig.)
    pipeline, 36, 334
    structural hazards and, 145
    See also clock cycles; instruction
      count (IC)
clock cycle time, 37–38
    analyzing, 35
    decreasing, B-1
    estimating, 35
    on pipelined machine, 138
    See also clock cycles; clock cycles
      per instruction (CPI)
clock rate, 352–353
    increasing, 352
clock skew, 137, 210
Cm* machine, 747
CM-5, 574–575, 751
    packet format, 603 (fig.)
    wormhole routing, 594
C-mmp machine, 747
coaxial cable
    connections, 577
    defined, 577
    illustrated, 576 (fig.)
coherence misses, 666, 673
coherence protocols. *See* cache
  coherence
collision
    defined, 580
    detection, 580
    miss, 390
    See also cache(s)
column access strobe (CAS), 428
column-associative caches. *See*
  pseudo-associative caches
COMA (cache-only memory
  architecture), 752
combining barrier, 705–706

combining tree, 704–705
    defined, 704
    use example, 705
committed instructions, 185, 312
common case, 29
common data bus (CDB), 252, 370
    load and store instructions and,
      258
    performance gain and, 260
    pipeline hardware interaction, 260
    use of, 254
    widening, 316
communication
    bandwidth, 641
    broadcast, 580
    connection-oriented vs. connec-
      tionless, 592–593
    latency, 641–642
    latency hiding, 642
    message-passing, 643
    multiprocessor models, 640–644
    NEWS, 590
    point-to-point, 580
    shared-memory, 642–643
    subnets. *See* networks
compare and branch instruction, 82
compiler-based speculation, 303–308
compiler-controlled prefetching, 402–
  404
compiler(s), 89–96
    architect decisions and, 2–4
    basic block, 156
    data hazard scheduling, 155–156
    importance of, 6
    isolating, 90
    optimizations, 91–92, 405–411
      blocking, 408–411
      loop fusion, 407
      loop interchange, 406–407
      merging arrays, 405–406
    organization and consistency
      model, 726
    passes, 90 (fig.)
    phase-ordering problem, 91
    role of, 89–96
    structure of, 90–92
    support for exploiting ILP,
      289–299

    technology, 357
      improvements, 6
      vectorization, B-22–B-23
      writing, complexity of, 91
compile-time scheduler, 210–211
completion, 312
    execution, 338
    stalls, 348
compulsory misses, 390
    miss rate, 392
    See also cache(s), miss(es)
computation-to-communication
  ratio, 652
computer architecture. *See* architecture
computer designers. *See* designers
computers
    arithmetic. *See* arithmetic
    connecting. *See* networks
    SIMD, 746–747
    usage trends, 6
conditional branches. *See* branch(es),
  conditional
conditional instructions, 300–303
    annulled, 302
    concept, 300
    control flow and, 303
    defined, 300
    example, 300
    limits of, 302–303
    moving time-critical instructions
      and, 301
    in RISC architectures, 303 (fig.)
    speculation and, 300
    speed penalty, 303
    usefulness of, 302
    using, 302
    See also instructions
conditional moves, 300, 301
conflict misses, 390, 673
    divisions, 390
    fully associative and, 392
    impact of, 410
    second-level caches and, 420
    See also cache(s), miss(es)
congestion control, 595–597
connectionless communication, 592

consistency
    memory, 656, 708–721
    models. *See* multiprocessor(s),
      memory consistency models
    processor, 715
    release, 716
    sequential, 709–711
constant bit density, 488
context switch. *See* process switch
Control Data
    CDC 6600, 114, 212, A-68
      completion buses, 253
      instruction scheduler, 354
      packaging technology, 354
      scoreboard, 242, 243, 250
    CDC 7600, 145
    CYBER-205, B-36–B-37, B-39
    ETA processor, B-40
    STAR-100, B-35, B-38
control dependences, 234–238, 363
    constraints on, 234
    defined, 234
    example, 234
    limits on parallelism, 234–235
    loop unrolling and, 237
    preservation of, 236–237
control-flow instructions, 80–84
    breakdown of, 81 (fig.)
    change types, 81
    destination address, 82
    frequency of, 81
    PC-relative, 82
control hazards, 161–178
    defined, 139
    performance loss and, 161
    stall, 161–162
    See also branch(es)
control stalls, 237
    reducing, 271–278
Convex
    C1, B-40
    C2, 540 (fig.), 541, 542
    file cache size, 544
    Exemplar, 742, 752, E-12
convoys. *See* vector instructions,
    convoys
correlating predictors, 267
    defined, 267

    functioning of, 267
    one-bit, 268, 269 (fig.)
    two-bit predictor vs., 271
    types of, 271
    See also branch prediction
Cosmic Cube, 627, 751
costs, 8–17
    designs and, 8
    die, 12–13
    direct, 15
    distribution of, 14 (fig.)
    functional requirement, 5
    gross margin and, 15
    integrated circuit (IC), 10–13
    performance and, 17
    price vs., 14–17
    scoreboard, 250
    trends in, 8–17
    See also price
COWs (clusters of workstations), 743
CPU (central processing unit), 4
    execution time, 43
    internal storage type, 70
    maximum IOPS for, 531
    moving functions from, to I/O pro-
      cessor, 551–553
    performance, 19, 374 (fig.)
      measuring components of, 35–
      36
    performance equation, 32–38, 37
      advantages of using, 34
      using, 37–38
    time, 385–387, 389
    write stall, 380
    See also CPU time; processor(s)
CPU-memory buses, 498
    interfaces, 501–503
    summary, 501 (fig.)
    See also bus(es)
CPU time, 19
    characteristics, 32
    expression of, 32, 33
    system, 19
    user, 19
Cray
    C-90, B-37, B-38, B-40
    CRAY-1, 115, B-3, B-36,
      B-38–B-39

    memory pipeline, B-33
    performance, B-37, B-44
    vector execution, B-17
    CRAY-2, B-34, B-39
    CRAY-3, B-40
    floating-point format, A-67–A-68
    J90, B-40
    T3D, 607, 628, 678, 742, 751,
      B-40
    X-MP, B-36, B-39
      chaining, B-33–B-34
      instruction buffers, 481
      memory pipelines, B-33
      multiprocessor approach, B-40
      Perfect Club benchmarks,
        vectorization, B-22 (fig.)
      performance, 50 (fig.)
    Y-MP, B-40
CRISP, 354
critical path scheduling, 296–299
critical word first, 413–414
    fetch, 413
cut-through routing, 594
cycles. *See* clock cycles
cycle time, 428
Cydrome Cydra 5, 355

D

data
    distribution, 738
    integrity, 521
    nonbinding, 725
    parallelism, 746
    races, 711
    rate, 516
    switching exchanges. *See* switches
    trunks, 245
data cache, 380–382
    set-associative, 675 (fig.)
    See also cache(s)
data dependences, 229–232, 297
    defined, 229
    detecting, 232
    limitations from, 230
    removing, 231
    See also data flow; exception
      behavior

data flow, 236
  defined, 236
  execution, 308
  See also control dependences
datagrams
  defined, 611
  window, 613
data hazards, 146–161
  checking for, 194
  classification of, 150–152
  compiler scheduling for, 155–156
  defined, 139
  forwarding paths and, 149 (fig.)
  minimizing, 147–150
  overcoming with dynamic sched-
    uling, 240–262
  RAR (read after read) and, 152
  RAW (read after write), 151, 157,
    186, 197, 222, 246
  requiring stalls, 152–155
  WAR (write after read), 151–152,
    222, 245, 246, 251, 257–258
  WAW (write after write), 151, 193,
    222, 251, 257–258
  See also hazards
data-race-free programs, 711
data types, 85
  DLX, 98
deadlock, 595
  avoiding, E-9–E-10
DebitCredit, 516–517
  disk I/O, 517
  TPS, 516–517
DEC
  300 model 800, 434
  3000 model 800 workstation, 380,
    382, 463
  5000, 474
  Alpha AXP 3000, 540 (fig.), 543
  Alpha AXP 21064. *See* Alpha
    AXP 21064
  Station 3100, 58
    code size and time, 59 (fig.)
  DecStation 5000, 540 (fig.), 543
    reboot measurements, 600
    (fig.)
  PDP-11 computer family, 467,
    472–473
    Unibus, 500, 555

VAX-11/780, 56–57, 473
VAX 8600, 210
VAX 8650, 210
VAX 8700, 105–108, 210
  MIPS M2000 vs., 108
VAX 8800, 200
VAX architecture, 58, 103
  addressing modes and, 76
  floating-point format, A-67
  pipelining, 187
  summary, C-23 (fig.)
VAXCluster, 743
VAX instructions, 89
  autoincrementing, 185–186
VAXstation 3100, 58
  code size and time, 59 (fig.)
decoupled architecture, 283
delayed branch, 168–169
  behavior, 168 (fig.)
  branch-delay slot, 168, 169 (fig.)
  cancelling, 171 (fig.)
  execution cycle, 168
  hardware cost, 173
  PC and, 173
  performance, 172 (fig.)
  scheduling
    effectiveness of, 171
    limitations, 170
    schemes, 170 (fig.)
  See also branch(es)
denormals, A-14–A-15
  defined, A-38
  floating-point addition, A-28
  floating-point multiplication, A-21
  See also arithmetic
dependence distance, 290
dependences, 229–238, 362–363
  analysis of, 293
  control, 234–238, 363
  data, 229–232, 297
  detecting, 289–293
  eliminating, 289–293
  flowing through memory loca-
    tions, 231–232
  hazards and, 230
  loop-carried, 238–239, 290
  name, 232–234
  programs and, 230
  test for absence of, 291

type classification, 292
types of, 229
  See also hazards
depth of pipeline, 140, 141
descriptor table, 454
  global, 454
  local, 454
designers
  compiler technology and, 92–94
  functional requirements for, 5
    (fig.)
  task of, 3–5
designs
  Amdahl's Law and, 29–32
  common case and, 29
  cost/performance, 17
  cost-sensitive, 8
  high-performance, 17
  low-cost, 17
  quantitative principles of, 29–39
destination-based routing, 594
Dhrystone, 20
  code, optimizing compilers and,
    47
  procedure structure, 47
  See also benchmarks
dies, 10
  cost, 12–13
  yield, 12–13
  See also integrated circuits (ICs);
    wafers
Digital Equipment Corporation. *See*
  DEC
direct costs, 15
direct mapped, 376, 473
  address portions, 378 (fig.)
  instruction and data miss rates,
    468 (fig.)
  tag check and, 422
  See also cache(s)
direct memory access (DMA), 503
  sending messages and, 574
  setup, 574
  virtual, 527
  virtual memory and, 527
directory-based protocols, 657,
  679–693
  block size and, 690 (fig.)
  cache coherence in, 680

coherence protocol and, 682
exclusive, 690
home node and, 66
machine characteristics, 691 (fig.)
memory consistency, 682
miss rates, 687–689 (fig.)
optimizations, 685
performance, 686–693
remote node and, 681
shared, 679
state diagrams, 681
uncached, 679
See also distributed shared-
memory (DSM)
dirty bit, 379
disk arrays, 521
reliability, 521–522
See also arrays
disk controllers, 489
disks
average seek time, 549
performance, 541 (fig.)
subsystem performance, 540–542
See also magnetic disks; optical
disks
dispatch, 310
displacement addressing mode, 76–77
displacement field, 76–77
displacement range, 76
displacement values, 77 (fig.)
distributed directory protocol, E-6–
E-12
coherence controller, E-7
directory controller, E-8, E-11
implementing, E-11–E-12
finite buffering and, E-9–E-11
local cache state, E-8–E-9
See also protocol(s)
distributed memory architecture,
638–639
advantages, 639
structure, 639 (fig.)
distributed shared memory (DSM),
640, 677–693
data distribution in, 738
memory latency effective references, 693 (fig.)
See also directory-based protocols

distributed virtual memory (DVM),
727
division
floating-point, A-28–A-34
integer, speeding up, A-46–A-61
with one adder, 57–61
shifting over zeros, A-47–A-49
integer examples, A-12 (fig.)
iterative, A-28–A-32
advantages, A-31–A-32
Goldschmidt's algorithm,
A-30–A-31
Newton's iteration, A-29–A-30
for n-bit unsigned integers, A-4
(fig.)
nonrestoring, A-5 (fig.), A-6
radix-2, A-3–A-7
nonrestoring, A-58
quotient selection, A-58 (fig.)
radix-4, A-59 (fig.)
SRT, examples, A-61 (fig.)
SRT, quotient digits, A-60
restoring, A-5 (fig.), A-6
SRT, A-47–A-49, A-67
algorithm, A-47
analysis, A-48–A-49
compared, A-49
high-speed, A-58
radix-4, A-59, A-60–A-61
(figs.)
See also arithmetic
DLX, 96–108, C-1
address fields, 105
addressing modes, 98, C-3 (fig.)
arithmetic/logical instructions,
101 (fig.)
branches, 102
branch penalty reduction 271
compare instructions, 10_
constant extension, C-5 (fig.)
control-flow instructions, 102
(fig.)
datapath implementation, 130
(fig.)
data types for, 98
defined, 96–97
effectiveness, 103–108
emphasis, 97

exceptions in, 184–185
floating-point operations, 102, 187
floating-point unit, 103
forwarding hardware, 159
FPRs, 98
GPRs, 98
hazard detection, 159
IBM 360 vs., 252
instruction clock cycles, 127–129
instruction formats, 99, C-4 (fig.)
instruction list, 104 (fig.), C-6–C-8
(figs.)
instruction mix, 105 (fig.)
instruction set architecture, 89, 97
load and store instructions, 100
(fig.)
loops, 225
memory, 98
operations, 99–103
pipeline, 132–138
extending for multicycle operations, 187–199
FP, 197–199
simple, 132 (fig.)
with unpipelined floating-point
functional units, 188 (fig.)
pipelining, 126–138
registers for, 98
scoreboards, 243
summary, C-2 (fig.)
superscalar version of, 279–282
VAX machines vs., 105–106
DMA. See direct memory access
(DMA)
doduc, 326
DRAMs
bit refreshment, 428
capacity growth, 103
cost vs. access time, 492 (fig.)
design emphasis, 428
fast/slow times, 429 (fig.)
interleaving and, 437–439
nibble mode, 438
on disks, 492–493
optimized accesses, 438 (fig.)
page mode, 438
prices, 9 (fig.)
RAMBUS, 439

DRAMs *(continued)*
  size growth, 7–8
  static column, 438
  technology, 7
  timing signals, 437–438
  VRAM, 439
  See also main memory
DS16 (dynamic scheduled with a
  16-entry reorder buffer), 720
DS64 (dynamically scheduled with a
  64-entry reorder buffer), 720
dynamically shared libraries, 82
dynamic random access memory.
  See DRAMs
dynamic scheduling, 240–262, 370
  advantages, 241
  data moves and, 282
  defined, 241
  hardware-based speculation with,
    308
  introduction of, 354
  multiple instruction issue, 282–
    284
  PowerPC 620, 340
  scoreboarding approach, 242–251
  speculation vs., 312
  Tomasulo approach, 251–261
  See also scheduling

E

early restarts, 413–414
Eckert, J. P., 53, 54, 55
EDSAC (Electronic Delay Storage
  Automatic Calculator), 54
EDVAC (Electronic Discrete Variable
  Automatic Computer), 53, 54
effective address, 74
  of load and store instructions, 232
  See also address(es)
elapsed time, 19
El Dorado, 749
encoding
  fixed, 87–88
  hybrid, 88–89
  instruction set, 87–89
  variable, 87
  variations, 88 (fig.)

ENIAC (Electronic Numerical
  Integrator and Calculator), 53
Ethernet, 579, 601–602
  increased bandwidth and, 605
    (fig.)
  packet format, 603 (fig.)
  parallel, 601
  standards, 627
  switched, 604
  TCP throughput of ATM vs., 620
    (fig.)
  total time on, 622 (fig.)
  See also LANs; networks
European Center for Particle
  Research (CERN), 626
events
  asynchronous, 181
  coerced, 181
  resuming, 181
  synchronous, 181
  terminating, 181
  user-maskable, 181
  user-requested, 181
evolution-revolution spectrum,
  744–745
  defined, 744
  illustrated, 745 (fig.)
exception behavior, 236
  preserving, 236
  See also control dependences
exceptions, 179–184
  classes of, 179
  defined, 179
  in DLX, 184–185
  FP, 195
  inexact, A-36
  between instructions, 181
  invalid, A-36
  list of, 179
  multiple, 184
  names of, 180 (fig.)
  out-of-order completion and, 242
  precise, 183–184, 194–197
  requirements of, 179–182
  resume vs. terminate and, 181
  speculation and, 316
  synchronous vs. asynchronous
    and, 180
  terminating, 305

  types of, 179
  user maskable vs. user non-
    maskable and, 181
  user requested vs. coerced and,
    181
  within instructions, 181
execution
  beginning, 242
  checks and bookkeeping actions,
    250 (fig.)
  completing, 242, 338
  data-flow, 308
  initiated, 338
  microinstruction, 187
  out-of-order, 242
  restarting, 182–184
  speculative, 316, 458
  stage, 245
  stopping, 182–184
  unexpected sequences, 209–210
  See also execution time
execution (EX) cycle, 128–129
  latencies, 248
  Tomasulo dual-issue pipeline, 284
    (fig.)
execution stage, 338
  instruction delay, 346–347
  performance of, 346–348
execution time
  average instruction, 56, 137, 138
  CPU, 43
  decreasing, 137
  defined, 18
  distribution in multiprogrammed
    workload, 654 (fig.)
  normalized, 27–28
  for parallel benchmarks, 733 (fig.)
  performance and, 18
  ratio, 27
  second-level cache size and, 419
    (fig.), 421 (fig.)
  total, 25
  of two programs on three ma-
    chines, 24 (fig.)
  vector, B-9–B-12
  weighted, 26
  See also execution
executive process. *See* kernel process
expanded storage (ES), 492–493

exponential back-off, 704 (fig.)
exponential distribution, 515

F

fallacies
adding processor to network interface card improves performance, 623–624
Amdahl's Law doesn't apply to parallel processors, 734–735
architecture with flaws can't be successful, 110–111
average seek time is seek time of one-third of cylinders, 549–551
benchmarks remain valid indefinitely, 48–50
conversions between integer and floating point are rare, A-65
defined, 44
increasing number of pipeline stages always increases performance, 210
linear speedups are needed to make multiprocessors cost-effective, 738–739
MFLOPS is consistent and useful measure of performance, 46–47
MIPS is accurate measure for comparing computer performance, 44–46
multiprocessors are "free," 735–736
peak performance tracks observed performance, 50
predicting cache performance of one program from another, 467
processors with lower CPIs will always be faster, 349–350
scalability is almost free, 736
synthetic benchmarks predict performance for real programs, 47
there is such a thing as typical program, 110
underflows rarely occur in floating-point application code, A-65
vector performance is obtainable

without providing memory bandwidth, B-36–B-37
you can design a flawless architecture, 111
See also pitfalls
false sharing, 669–670
cause, 670
defined, 669
miss, 670
See also cache coherence
fast Fourier transform. See FFT
fat-tree interconnection
for 16 nodes, 585 (fig.)
defined, 583
faults. See exceptions
FDDI, 602–604, 627
defined, 602
uses, 604
fences
defined, 713
memory, 713
read, 713
write, 713
fetch-and-increment, 695, 707–708
atomic example, 696
sense-reverse barrier using, 708 (fig.)
using, 707
fetch on write, 380
fetch stage, 337
instruction buffers, 342
instruction loss, 342, 343 (fig.)
performance, 341–343
FFT
algorithm steps, 648–649
all-to-all communication, 690
capacity miss rate, 667
coherent miss rate, 671
data miss rate, 668 (fig.) 669 (fig.)
defined, 648
kernel, 648–649
performance, 666
fiber-distributed data interface. See FDDI
fiber optics, 577–578
cable types, 577
defined, 577
illustrated, 576 (fig.)

multimode fiber, 577
network components, 577
single-mode fiber, 577–578
T-boxes, 578
See also networks, media
file caches, 375
blocks, 546
effectiveness, 542 (fig.)
operating system policies and, 544–548
performance, 542–543, 548
vs. read percentage, 546 (fig.)
vs. read percentage for client/server computing, 547 (fig.)
policy for, 548
size of, 544, 545 (fig.)
write back, 544
for writes 546
write through, 544
See also cache(s)
files
future, 195
history, 196
register, 192–194
finite registers, 326–328
effect of, 327 (fig.)
first-in-first-out (FIFO), 511, 565
Fisher, J. A., 355
fixed-field decoding, 127
floating-point algorithms, A-1
floating point (FP), 31, 34
addition, A-22–A-28
arithmetic, A-13–A-38
benchmark (doduc), 326
code sequence, 192 (fig.)
datapath, 279
division and remainder, A-28–A-33
DLX pipeline, 197–199
enhancement speedup, 34
exceptions, 195
instructions, 193
load and stores, 190, 193
MIPS rating and, 45
multiplication, A-17–A-22
multiply, 145–146
number representation, A-15–A-17

floating point (FP) *(continued)*
    register file, 191, 192 (fig.)
    registers, 253
    stalls, 197
floating-point operations, 102, 183,
    286
    80x86, D-9–D-11
    DLX, 102, 188
    double-precision, 204
    exceptions and, 183
    independent, 190
    initiation intervals for, 205 (fig.)
    latencies for, 205 (fig.), 224 (fig.)
    multicycle, 194
    multiple outstanding, 190 (fig.)
    real vs. normalized, 66 (fig.)
    semantics of, A-13
    in Spice, 67 (fig.)
    stalls per, 198 (fig.)
    See also MFLOPS (million float-
        ing-point operations per second)
floating-point pipeline, R4000,
    204–207
    eight stages, 205 (fig.)
floating-point registers (FPRs), 98
floating-point unit, 103, 251–252
    DLX, using Tomasulo's algorithm,
        253 (fig.)
        structure, 311 (fig.)
    Tomasulo algorithm and, 252
flow control, 596
FORTRAN kernels
    compiler vectorization results,
        B-23 (fig.)
    Livermore, B-36
    performance measurements,
        B-36 (fig.)
forwarding, 147–150
    data to ALU inputs, 160 (fig.)
    defined, 147
    hardware, 148, 159
    in longer latency pipelines,
        191–194
    of operands, 150 (fig.)
    paths, 148–149
    results to ALU, 161 (fig.)
freeze, pipeline, 167
Fujisu machines, B-40
fully associative, 377
    conflict misses and, 392

See also cache(s)
functional units
    counts for, 364 (fig.)
    floating-point, 188 (fig.)
    initiation intervals for, 189 (fig.)
    latencies for, 189 (fig.), 364 (fig.)
    number and types of, 251
    PowerPC, 336 (fig.)
    scoreboard status, 246–247
    unavailable, 348
future file, 196

G

gateways. *See* routers
Gaussian elimination, 366
GE 635, 472
general-purpose register (GPR), 71
    architecture, 70–72
        characteristics, 71
        operands in, 71
    DLX, 98
    machine advantages/disadvantag-
        es, 72 (fig.)
geometric mean, 27
    of normalized execution times, 28
Gibson, D. H., 473
Gibson mix, 56
global common subexpression elimi-
    nation, 91
global data area, 93
global miss rate, 417
Goldschmidt's algorithm, A-30–A-31
    defined, A-30
    self-correction, A-31
Goldstine, H. H., 54
graduation, 312
graph coloring, 92
greatest common divisor (GCD) test,
    291, 368
gross margin, 17
    defined, 15

H

hardware
    defined, 4
    parallelism support, 299–317

smaller is faster and, 39
    See also software
hardware-based speculation, 308–317
    advantages, 308
    disadvantage, 309
    with dynamic scheduling, 308
    software-based vs., 308
hardware branch prediction, 261,
    262–278
harmonic mean, 25
    weighted, 26
Harvard architecture, 55
hazards
    branch, 161–178
    classes of, 139
    control, 139, 161–178
    data, 139, 146–161, 194
    defined, 139
    dependences and, 230
    detection, 159, 193, 194
    detection hardware, 158 (fig.)
    eliminating, 139
    in longer latency pipelines,
        191–194
    structural, 139, 141–146, 194
    See also dependences
header, 565
heap, 93
helical scan tapes, 494
Hennessy, J., 116
Hewlett-Packard
    HP 712/60, 547
    HP 730, 520, 540 (fig.), 543
    HP 7100, 279, 357
    HP 8000, 319
    HP/UX, 544, 545, 547
    PA 7100, 350
        performance, 351 (fig.)
    PA 8000, 335
    PA-RISC, A-12, C-1
        addressing modes, C-3 (fig.)
        compare and conditional
            branch, C-9
        conditional branches, C-20
        constant extension, C-5 (fig.)
        decimal operations, C-21
        DLX instruction equivalents,
            C-6–C-8 (figs.)
        features, C-22

instruction formats, C-4 (fig.)
instructions unique to,
    C-19–C-22
non-DLX instructions,
    C-10–C-11 (figs.)
nullification, C-20
summary, C-2 (fig.)
synthesized multiply and
    divide, C-20–C-21
high-level language computer archi-
    tecture (HLLCA), 115
histogram, 511
history file, 196
hit. See cache(s), hit
Hitachi S810/20, 50 (fig.)
host interface card, 617–618
    defined, 617
    illustrated, 619 (fig.)
    SBA-200, 617, 618 (fig.)
    switches, 618
    See also asynchronous transfer
        mode (ATM)
hypercube, 628
hyperexponential distribution, 512
hypoexponential distribution, 512

I

IBM
    360/85, 473
    360/91, 251–252, 309, 356, 473
        terminology, 255
    360, 114
        DLX vs., 252
        page protection, 472
    370/158, 56
    370 architecture, 472, 715, 747,
        B-41, C-23 (fig.)
        floating-point formats, A-67
    801, 115
    1311, 554
    3033 cache, 425
    3081, 751
    3090, 540 (fig.), 541, 542
    3330, 552
    7030 (Stretch), 212
    ACS, 356

PC, D-23
PC-AT Bus, 500
Power-1 architecture, 356
Power-2, B-38
    CPI, 350
    workstation, 3, 350
Powerstation 550, 48
RAMAC, 554
RP3, 751
RS/6000, 540, 543, 547, 548
    Power 2 model 900, 458
    Powerstation, 24 (fig.), 48, 49
        (fig.), 590
    RT-PC, 116
    SP-2, 628, 742
    See also PowerPC 620; PowerPC
        architecture
ideal pipeline CPI, 222
ideal processor, 318–320
    assumptions, 318
    benchmarks, 319–320
    characteristics, 320
    defined, 318
    ILP available in, 319 (fig.)
    See also processor(s)
IEEE standards
    Ethernet (802.3), 627
    floating point (754), 85, 97, A-1,
        A-13–A-14
        exceptions, A-36–A-37
        format parameters, A-16 (fig.)
        history of, A-68
        rounding modes, A-14, A-20
            (fig.)
if-conversion, 301
ILP, 221–238
    compiler support and, 289–289
    defined, 221, 222
    ideal processor, 318–320
        breakdown, 349 (fig.)
    increasing amount of, 224
    limits on, 286
    PowerPC 620, 349
    for realizable processors, 330–335
    reducing cache misses vs., 458–
        459
    scheduling, 357
    studies of, 257–258, 317–335

uncovering, 357
    See also parallelism
immediate addressing mode, 78–79
    32-bit long immediates, 79
    frequency of immediates, 78
    range of values, 78
    value distribution, 79 (fig.)
    See also addressing, modes
implementation
    barrier synchronization, 700–701
    boosting, 308
    centralized shared-memory archi-
        tectures, 660–662
    defined, 4
    DLX datapath, 130 (fig.)
    page coloring, 425
    pipeline control, 156–161
    pipelining, 178–187
    prefetching, 726
    queuing locks, 707
    relaxed model, 718–719
    release consistency, 718–719
    sequential consistency, 709–710,
        715
    speculation, 309
    synchronization, 694
    technology trends, 7–8
    write-invalidate protocol,
        660–662
inclusion
    multilevel, 723–724
    with multiple block sizes, 724
index vectors, B-27
infinite population model, 514
in-flight instructions, 319
initiation intervals
    defined, 189
    for FP operations, 205 (fig.)
    for functional units, 189 (fig.)
    implementing, 190
input/output (I/O)
    addresses, 460
    average request size, 518
    bandwidth, 504
    cached data consistency and, 459–
        461
    chain, 528
    connected to cache, 526 (fig.)

input/output (I/O) *(continued)*
  connection schemes, 528
  controllers, 525
  events, 502
  importance of, 486
  interrupt-driven, 503
  interrupts, 555
  memory-mapped, 502
  opcodes, 502
  performance, 486
    comparing, 541
    limits, 539
    measures, 504–521
    megabytes vs., 520 (fig.)
    subsystem, 540–542
  prejudice against, 485–486
  rate, 516
  responsibility, delegating,
    503–504
  screen, 48
  self-scaling benchmark, 518–521
  system, 507–508
    cost/performance goals,
      528–529
    design, 528–539
    first order performance, 518
    rules of thumb, 535
  time, 531
  See also bus(es); I/O buses; I/O
    device; I/O processors; magnetic
    disks; networks
instruction buffers, 145
instruction commit, 309
  performance of, 348
instruction completion, 338
instruction count (IC), 32
  addressing modes and, 75
  change in, 94 (fig.)
  lowering, 37
  measuring, 35
  See also clock cycles; clock cycles
    per instruction (CPI)
instruction decode (ID), 127–128
  issue stage, 242, 244–245
  read operands stage, 242, 245
instruction issue
  defined, 156
  PowerPC 620, 337–338

  See also issue stage
instruction-level parallelism. *See* ILP
instruction mix, 61
  defined, 35
  DLX, 105 (fig.)
  Gibson mix, 56
instruction register (IR), 135
instructions
  80x86, top ten, 81 (fig.)
  ALU, 128, 129, 131
  arithmetic/logical, DLX, 101 (fig.)
  average time, 144
  beginning execution, 242
  boosted, 307–308
  CALLS, 109–110
  committed, 185
  compare, DLX, 101 (fig.)
  compare and branch, 82
  completing execution, 242, 338
  conditional, 300–303
  conflicting, stalling, 193
  control dependent, 234
  control flow, 80–84
    DLX, 102 (fig.)
  data dependent, 230
  delay of, 346–347
  dependent, 229
  DLX, 104 (fig.)
  encoding, 87
  in execution, 242
  execution steps, 310–312
  fetch and decode rate, B-1–B-2
  FP, 193
  in-flight, 319
  initiated execution, 338
  load, 154–155, 157, 203
  load and store, DLX, 100 (fig.)
  pairs
    atomic, 695
    load linked, 695
    store conditional, 695
  parallel, 229
  predicated, 300–303
  prefetch, 402
  register-memory, 61
  restarting, 182
  scheduling, 155–156
  scoreboard status, 246

  scoreboard steps, 244–245
  speculative, 304, 305, 307–308
  string, 186
  target, 276
  throughput, 136
  Tomasulo's algorithm steps, 254
  too general, 109
  VAX, 89, 185–186
  vector, 223, B-2, B-7 (fig.),
    B-9–B-10
  VLIW, 285, 286 (fig.)
  See also instruction set
instruction set, 68–116
  80x86, 53
  architectures, 4, 69–70
    accumulator, 70
    address-space growth and, 6
    classifying, 70–73
    defined, 4
    DLX, 89, 97
    general-purpose register,
      70–72
    memory-memory, 70
    register-memory, 70
    register-register, 70
    stack, 70
    styles, 120
    summary, 73
  code sequence, 70 (fig.)
  encoding, 87–89
    fixed, 87–88
    hybrid, 88–89
    variable, 87
    variations, 88 (fig.)
  frequencies, 118
  "high-level," 109
  MIPS-3, 201
  operations in, 80–85
  pipelining and, 199–200
  pipelining complications,
    185–187
  properties, 95–96
  RISC, C-24 (fig.)
  simulator, 35
  See also instructions
instrumentation code, 35
  execution time increase, 36

integer arithmetic, A-1–A-13
  radix-2 multiplication and
    division, A-3–A-7
  ripple-carry addition, A-2–A-3
  signed numbers, A-7–A-10
  system issues, A-10–A-13
  See also arithmetic
integrated circuits (ICs)
  costs of, 10–13
  logic technology, 7
Intel
  80x86, D-1–D-25
    addressing modes, D-4–D-5,
      D-14
    address specifier, encoding,
      D-14 (fig.)
    awkwardness of, D-22–D-23
    comparative operation mea-
      surements, D-20–D-22
    component implementation,
      D-23
    data accesses on, D-21
    DLX data traffic vs., D-22
    double words, D-6
    extended accumulators, 111
    floating-point operations,
      D-9–D-11
    flow-control instructions, D-8
    instruction encoding, D-11–
      D-15
    instruction length histograms,
      D-18 (fig.)
    instruction mix for SPECfp92
      programs, D-19–D-20 (figs.)
    instructions, top ten, 81 (fig.)
    instruction set, 53
    instructions executed on, D-21
    instructions/functions, D-7
      (fig.)
    instruction types, D-4 (fig.)
    integer operations, D-6–D-9
    Little Endian, D-5
    measurements for instruction
      set usage, D-15–D-22
    milestones, D-1–D-2
    operand addressing measure-
      ments, D-16–D-19
    operations, D-8–D-9 (figs.)

  prefix instructions, D-11
  register set, D-3 (fig.)
  segmentation, 111
  string instructions, 186
  words, D-6
387 coprocessor, A-35
8086 architecture, C-23 (fig.), D-1
  escape opcode, D-14
  instruction formats, D-12 (fig.),
    D-13 (fig.)
  segmented scheme, D-6 (fig.)
8087 floating-point coprocessor,
  D-1–D-2
80286, 472, D-2
80386, D-2
  based plus scaled index mode
    address specifier, D-15 (fig.)
  instruction length, D-12
i860, 356
P6, 353, D-24, D-25
Paragon, 624, 751
Pentium
  8-inch wafer, 11 (fig.)
  descriptor table, 454
  protection, 453–457
  protection levels, 453
  protection structure, 449
  radix-4 division, A-59
  segment registers, 454, 455
    (fig.)
  SRT division bug, A-58–A-69,
    A-76–A-77
intelligent peripheral interface (IPI),
  500
  See also bus(es)
interarrival times, 514
interconnection networks. *See* networks
interface message processors (IMPs).
  See switches
interfaces
  bus, 501–503
  I/O, to operating system, 525–527
interference miss, 390
interleaved memory, 431–434
  bank access, 433
  defined, 432
  four-way, 432 (fig.)

  purpose of, 431–432
  See also memory
interleaving
  DRAM-specific, 437–439
  factor, 432
interlock. *See* pipeline interlock
internal fragmentation, 447
International Business Machines.
  See IBM
Internet, 609, 625, 627
internetworking, 564, 608–613
  cost of, 608
  defined, 608
  enabling technologies, 608
  protocol families, 608–609
  role of, 610 (fig.)
  TCP/IP standard, 609–613
interrupt-driven I/O, 503
interrupts. *See* exceptions
intervention, E-4
I/O. *See* input/output (I/O)
I/O buses, 496, 573
  interfaces, 501–503
  resource demands, 528
  summary, 501 (fig.)
  utilization, 535
  See also bus(es)
I/O device, 502
  CPU resource demands, 528
  physical requirements, 528
  registers, 502
I/O processors, 503–504
  defined, 503
  moving functions to, 551–553
  See also processor(s)
issue count
  maximum, 320–322
  restrictions, 331
issue stage, 242, 337–338, 343–346
  conflicts, 344
  full buffer stalls in, 347 (fig.)
  IPC throughput rate for, 345 (fig.)
  limitations, 343
  number of, 344 (fig.)
  scoreboard, 244–245
  speculative-instruction, 310
  stall reasons, 347–348
  stall sources, 346 (fig.)

Tomasulo dual-issue pipeline, 284 (fig.)
Tomasulo's algorithm, 254
See also instruction issue

J

Jouppi, N., 401
jump prediction, 323–326
jumps, 80
  indirect, 82
    predicting, 276
  register indirect, 82
  See also branch(es)

K

Kahan, J., D-24
Kendall Square Research KSR-1, 751
kernel process, 448
kernels, 20
  FFT, 648–649
  LU, 649–650
Knuth, D. E., 96
Kogge, P. M., 212

L

LANs
  defined, 554
  Ethernet, 579, 601–602
  examples, 602 (fig.)
  history of, 627
  node failures and, 598
  standards, 598, 627
  See also networks; WANs
latches
  delay from, 138
  Earle, 138
latencies, 363
  defining, 189
  EX cycle, 248
  for FP operations, 205 (fig.), 224 (fig.)
  for functional units, 189 (fig.), 364 (fig.)
  hazards/forwarding and, 191–194

memory, 428
multiprocessor communication models, 641–642
one-cycle, 364
read, hiding, 719
rotational, 488
total, 569–570
transport, 569
LD instruction, 193, 313
learning curve, 8–9
least-recently used (LRU), 378
  blocks, 444
limit field, 454
Linpack benchmark, B-31–B-33
list price, 15
Little Endian byte order, 73, D-5
Little's Law, 508–510
  to black box components, 510
  equation, 508
liveness, 237
load and store buffers, 255
load and store instructions, 100 (fig.)
  effective address of, 232
  superscalar processor and, 283
  Tomasulo's scheme and, 258, 260
  in unrolled loop, 228
load instructions, 154–155, 203
  percentage that result in stalls, 157 (fig.)
load interlock, 154 (fig.), 156, 157
  defined, 157
  detection logic, 158 (fig.)
load linked, 695–696
load locked. *See* load linked
load-store machines
  architecture, 120
  defined, 61
  measurements of, 45 (fig.)
local area networks. *See* LANs
locality
  in lock accesses, 697
  principle of, 373, 375
  of reference, 38
  spatial, 38, 41
  SPEC benchmark, 39 (fig.)
  temporal, 38, 41
local miss rate, 417
  secondary caches and, 418–419

locks
  access serialization, 700
  acquire and release time, 700 (fig.)
  implementing with coherence, 696–699
  queuing, 704
  spin, 696–708
lockup-free caches, 402, 414–416, 434
  defined, 402
  for reducing stalls, 414–416
  See also cache(s)
loop-carried dependences, 238–239
  defined, 239
  parallelism and, 239–240
  recurrence, 290
  See also dependences
loop fission, B-44
loop fusion, 407
loop interchange, 406–407
loop-level parallelism, 238–240, 333
  analysis of, 238
  converting, 223
  defined, 223
  See also parallelism
loops
  array access code and, 407
  consecutive, 227
  dependent distance, 290
  DLX, 225
  fused, 407
  loads and stores in, 228
  overhead of, 226, 260, 296
    optimizing, 230–231
  parallel, 224, 289
  reduction, B-46
  SAXPY, 365–366
  scheduling, 225
  software-pipelined, 294 (fig.)
  upper bound of, 227
  See also loop unrolling
loop unrolling, 223–228
  control dependences and, 237
  defined, 226
  example, 224
  loop overhead and, 296
  performance and, 227
  scheduling and, 226

software pipelining and, 295–296
summary, 228
superscalar, 280–281
symbolic, 293–296
uses, 226
VLIW, 285
See also loops
LU kernel, 649–650
block size increase, 671
data miss rate, 668 (fig.), 669 (fig.)
performance, 666
processor count increase, 667
LW instruction, 152, 175, 184–185

M

machine cycle, 126
McFarling, S., 354
McKeeman, W. M., 114
magnetic disks, 486–492
1993, characteristics of, 490 (fig.)
access time gap, 492
areal density, 490
average rotational time, 489
cost per disk, 491 (fig.)
cost per megabyte, 490, 491 (fig.)
cost vs. access time, 492 (fig.)
disk controller, 489
future of, 490–492
history of, 554
memory hierarchy, 487
organization, 487 (fig.)
platters, 487
read ahead, 489
read/write head, 488
roles of, 487
rotational latency, 488
sectors, 488
seek time, 488
technology, 7
tracks, 488
transfer time, 488–489
Winchester, 554
magnetic recording, 553
magnetic tapes, 493–495
disks vs., 493–494
drawbacks, 494
helical scan, 494

libraries, 494–495
capacity vs. cost, 495 (fig.)
STC PowderHorn, 494, 495
(fig.)
main memory, 427–439
bandwidth, 428, 430–439
blocks
finding, 443
placement, 443
defined, 428
maximum IOPs for, 531
performance
improvement, 430–431
measures, 428
type of, 429
wider, 431
See also memory
Mark I (Mark-II, Mark-III, Mark-IV)
computer, 55
massively parallel processor (MPP)
network, 644
CM-5, 574, 575
defined, 563
examples, 602 (fig.)
future of, 741–743
history of, 627–628
Intel Paragon, 624
interconnection characteristics,
591 (fig.)
Meiko CS-2, 624
node failures and, 598
Mauchly, J., 53, 54, 55
maximum vector length (MVL),
B-15–B-16
mean time to failure (MTTF), 522
mean time to repair (MTTR), 522
memory
access time, average, 384, 385
for associativity, 396–397
block size vs., 395 (fig.)
formula, 389, 395
for four programs, 469 (fig.)
minimizing, 387
pseudo-associative caches,
399–400
two-level cache, 417
two-way set associative,
388–389
using miss rates, 397 (fig.)

addressing, 73–80
interpreting, 73–74
summary, 79
bandwidth
increasing, 40
percentage calculation, 479
banks, 434
address within, 436
conflicts, avoiding, 435–437
defined, 435
independent, 434–435
number, 436
superbanks vs., 435 (fig.)
bus, 431
chips, 434
consistency models, 656, 708–721
DLX, 98
efficiency measurement, 120
fences, 713
interleaved, 430 (fig.), 431–434
latency, 428
main, 427–429
mapping, 441
of virtual addresses, 444 (fig.)
multiprocessor models, 640–644
order restrictions, 713
page sizes and, 447
performance of, 374 (fig.)
reference, average, 692, 693 (fig.)
remote reference, 692
shared, 540, 643–644, 726–727
smaller is faster and, 39–40
speculative execution and, 458
stall cycles, 42–43
defined, 42, 386
formula, 374
number of, 43
stall time, average, 415
virtual, 439–457, 472, 725–727
VLIW and, 287
width, 430 (fig.)
See also cache(s); memory
hierarchy; virtual memory
memory-constrained scaling, 722
memory hierarchy, 372–474
Alpha AXP 21064, 461–466
illustrated, 462 (fig.)
parameters, 452
performance, 465–466

memory hierarchy *(continued)*
    cache and, 375–427
    defined, 40
    design issues, 457–461
    example summary, 471 (fig.)
    importance of, 374
    interface vs. interconnection net-
        work, 605–606
    levels, 40 (fig.)
        questions, 375
        sizes and access times, 41 (fig.)
    magnetic disks in, 487
    main memory and, 427–439
    performance
        measures, 468–469
        operating system impact on,
            469–470
    protection schemes and, 374
    thrash, 393
    virtual memory and, 439–457
    See also memory
memory-less, 512
memory-mapped I/O, 502
memory-memory architecture, 70,
    120
memory mother boards (MMBs), 463
MFLOPS (million floating-point
    operations per second)
    defined, 46, 749
    native rating, 66
    normalized rating, 66
    performance measurement and,
        46–47
    rating, 46–47
    sustained, 750
    See also floating-point operations
microinstruction execution, 187
microprocessors
    advanced, 358
    characteristics of, 63 (fig.)
    costs, 2
    performance growth, 2 (fig.)
    See also processors
MIPS architecture, C-1
    addressing modes, C-3 (fig.)
    compare and conditional branch,
        C-9
    constant extension, C-5 (fig.)

DLX instruction equivalents,
    C-6–C-8 (figs.)
instruction formats, C-4 (fig.)
instructions for unaligned word
    reads, C-14 (fig.)
instructions unique to, C-13–C-15
nonaligned data transfers, C-13
non DLX instructions, C-10–C-11
    (figs.)
summary, C-2 (fig.)
TLB instructions, C-13
MIPS Computer Systems Inc.
    M2000, 105–108
        VAX 8700 vs., 108
    R2000, 116, 197
    R2010, 145
    R3000, 197, 200, 211, A-12
    R3010, A-61–A-64
        addition, A-62
        chip layout, A-64 (fig.)
        chip summary, A-61 (fig.)
        transistors, A-62
    R4000, 197
        ALU bypass, 204
        branch delay, 203 (fig.)
        branch stalls, 208
        double-precision add, 207
            (fig.)
        floating-point pipeline, 204–
            207
        FP divide, 207 (fig.)
        FP multiply, 206 (fig.)
        FP result stalls, 208
        FP structural stalls, 208
        integer pipeline structure, 202
            (fig.)
        load stalls, 207
        pipeline, 201–209
        pipeline CPI, 208–209 (fig.)
        pipeline performance, 207–209
        pipeline structure, 201 (fig.)
        predict-not-taken strategy, 202
    R8000, 183, B-38
    R10000, 196, 335
MIPS (million instructions per
    second), 44
    defined, 44
    performance measurement and,
        44–46

problems with using, 44
rating, 45
relative, 56–57
Stanford architecture, 213, 355
mirroring, 523
misprediction rates, 264
misses. *See* cache(s), miss(es)
miss penalty, 375
miss rate. *See* cache(s), miss rate
Motorola
    68000 architecture, C-23 (fig.),
        D-24
    68882 coprocessor, A-35
MPP. *See* massively parallel processor
    (MPP) network
multicasting, 580
multi-chip module (MCM), 741
multicomputers, 640, 750, 760
Multiflow processor, 355
multigrid methods, 651
multilevel inclusion property, 421
multimode fibers, 577
multiple context, 758
multiple-instruction issue
    with dynamic scheduling, 282–
        284
    with static scheduling, 279
multiple instruction streams, multiple
    data streams (MIMD), 637
    cost/performance advantages, 637
    flexibility, 637
multiple instruction streams, single
    data stream (MISD), 637
multiple-issue processors, 278–289
    design challenges, 287
    development of, 355–357
    hardware resources, 286–287
    improving one aspect of, 351–352
    limitations in, 285–289
    problems with, 288–289
    superscalar, 278–282
    trends in, 353
    types of, 278
    VLIW, 278, 284–285
    See also processor(s)
multiplexers, controlling, 135
multiplication
    floating-point, A-17–A-22
        algorithm cases, A-19 (fig.)

denormals and, A-21
precision, A-22
rounding and, A-18–A-19
higher-radix, A-51
integer, speeding up, A-46–A-61
with many adders, A-52–A-57
shifting over zeros, A-47–A-49
with single adder, A-49–A-52
of multiple-precision integers,
A-11
for *n*-bit unsigned integers, A-4
(fig.)
overlapping triplets and, A-51,
A-67
radix-2, A-3–A-7
two's complement, A-8
See also arithmetic
multipliers
array, A-53–A-54 (figs.)
binary tree, A-54–A-55
carry-save, A-50 (fig.)
even/odd, A-53–A-54
Wallace tree, 56 (fig.), A-67
See also arithmetic; multiplication
multiprocessor(s), 353, 634–752
application domain characteristics, 647–654
cache coherence, 655–658
clustering, 639
communication models, 640–644
advantages of, 642–644
bandwidth, 641
latency, 641–642
latency hiding, 642
performance metrics, 641–642
designs, 636
El Dorado, 749
"free," 735–736
history, 636–637
industry, 748 (fig.)
memory
architecture models, 640–644
shared, 543–544, 640
virtual shared memory, 644
memory consistency models, 656,
708–721
compiler organization and, 726
developments in, 752

examples, 717 (fig.)
orderings, 715
processor consistency, 715
PSO, 715
relaxed, 714–720, 721 (fig.)
release consistency, 716
sequential consistency,
709–711
TSO, 715
weak consistency, 715–716
multiprogrammed workloads,
652–654, 741
parallel applications, 648–652
parallel processing and, 644–647
performance measurements, 734
SGI Challenge. *See* Challenge
multiprocessor
single-chip, 743–744
small-bus, 755
software development and, 736–
738
synchronization, 694–708
workload classes, 647–648
See also multiprocessor(s)
multiprogramming, 447
block size and, 674, 675 (fig.), 676
(fig.)
execution time distribution, 654
(fig.)
kernel miss rate, 674 (fig.)
memory and I/O measurements,
653
OS workload and, 652–654
performance, 737
workload performance, 672–676
workload phases, 652
multistage interconnection networks.
See switches
multithreading, 758

N

name caches, 375
name dependences, 232–234
antidependence, 232, 243, 251,
357
defined, 232

output dependence, 232, 251, 357
See also dependences
N-body algorithms, 650
negative acknowledge (NAK), E-10,
E-12
Network File System (NFS), 571
networks 552–628
arbitration, 580
collision detection, 580
commercial issues, 597–600
congestion control, 595–597
connecting, 573–575, 579–597
defined, 563
examples, 601–605
hardware/software support for,
606–607
header, 565
hosts, 563
interconnection, 564–565
interface card, 623–624
interface hardware, 575
internetworking, 564, 608–613
local area. *See* LANs
measured, prices, 620 (fig.)
media, 576–579
coaxial cable, 576 (fig.), 577
comparison example, 579
fiber optics, 576 (fig.), 577–
578
figures of merit for, 578 (fig.)
shared vs. switched, 579–583
twisted pair, 576–577
memory hierarchy interface vs.,
605–606
message format, 565 (fig.), 566
(fig.)
messages, 566
cumulative percentage of, 573
(fig.)
delivering, 593–595
duplicate, 568
in-order-delivery, E-7
receiving, 567
sending, 566
sending with DMA, 574
size for overheads, 572 (fig.)
See also overhead, message
MPP, 563

networks *(continued)*
　node failure tolerance, 598–600
　nodes, 563
　payload, 565
　performance
　　bandwidth and, 622–623
　　parameters, 568 (fig.)
　protection of, 607
　routing, 593–595
　simple, 565–573
　standardization, 597–598
　switches. *See* switches
　system area (SANs), 628
　topologies. *See* switches, topology
　trailer, 565
　transport time, 581–582
　user access of, 607
　wide area. *See* WANs
　of workstations (NOWs), 743
　See also bridges
NEWS communication, 590
Newton's iteration, A-29
　self-correcting, A-30
nonbinding
　data, 725
　prefetch, 725–726
nonblocking caches, 402, 414–416,
　434
　defined, 402
　prefetching and, 725
　for reducing stalls, 414–416
　weak consistency and, 725
　See also cache(s)
no-write allocate, 380
NOWs (networks of workstations),
　743
nullifying branches. *See* cancelling
　branches
NUMAs (non-uniform memory
　access), 640
NYU Ultracomputer, 751

O

objects
　in global data area, 93
　in heap, 93

Ocean application, 651
　block size increase, 671
　Challenge microprocessor and,
　　732
　data miss rate, 668 (fig.), 669
　　(fig.), 720
　performance, 666
　speedup dropoff, 732
one-bit prediction, 263
opcode, 87
operands
　in accumulator architecture, 70
　addressing, 73–80
　forwarding of, 150 (fig.)
　in GPR architectures, 71
　immediate, 78
　memory, combinations, 72 (fig.)
　single-precision floating-point, 98
　size of, 85–86
　source
　　buffering, 260
　　unavailable, 346
　in stack architecture, 70
　types of, 85
operating system
　impact on memory hierarchy,
　　469–470
　policies on file cache performance,
　　544–548
operations
　atomic, 664
　DLX, 99–103
　floating-point (FP). *See* floating-
　　point operations
　in instruction set, 80–85
　invalidate, 666
　multicycle, pipelining and,
　　186–187
　in pipe stage, 134
　See also instructions
operators, categories of, 80 (fig.)
optical disks, 493
optimizations, 91–92
　global, 92
　high-level, 91
　local, 91
　machine-dependent, 92
　types of, 93 (fig.)

ordering, 714–715
　consistency model, 717 (fig.)
　partial store (PSO), 715
　total store (TSO), 715
　weak, 715–718
　See also consistency; multiproces-
　　sor(s), memory consistency
　　models
organization
　defined, 4
　See also memory hierarchy
OR instruction, 146–147, 153, 175
out-of-order completion, 195, 242
　disallowed, 346
　exception handling and, 242
out-of-order execution, 242
output dependence, 232, 251, 357
overflow, A-7–A-8
　handling, A-11 (fig.)
　integer, A-10–A-11
　rounding and, A-21
　See also arithmetic; underflow
overhead
　defined, 570
　message
　　size for, 572 (fig.)
　　software overhead and, 623
　　vs. message interarrival time
　　　for CM-5, 575 (fig.)
　receiver, 569, 606
　sender, 569
　software, 623
　See also networks
overlapping triplets, A-51, A-67
overlays, 440

P

packed decimal, 85
packets, 592
　choke, 597
　collection of, 596
　discarding, 596
　IP, 612
packet-switched bus, 439, 498
packet-switched networks, 592
　clogging in, 595

packing, 85
page coloring, 424
    implementation, 425
page defaults, 41
page faults, 314
    defined, 441
page offset, 424
pages
    defined, 441
    internal fragmentation, 447
    physical, 443
    size selection, 446–447
    See also virtual memory
page table, 443
    entry (PTE), 450–451, 461
    inverted, 443
    lock placement and, 738
    serialization, 737
    See also virtual memory
paging
    example, 442 (fig.)
    segmentation vs., 442
    virtual memory, 449–453
parallel applications, 648–652
    Barnes-Hut, 650–651, 666, 668–
        669 (fig.)
    computation/communication for,
        652
    FFT kernel, 648–649, 666, 668–
        669 (fig.)
    LU kernel, 649–650, 666, 668–
        669 (fig.)
    Ocean, 651, 666, 668–669 (fig.)
    workload performance, 666–672
parallel architectures
    Amdahl's Law and, 734–735
    performance measurement of,
        721–723
    taxonomy of, 636–639
    See also architecture
parallelism, 52, 221–240
    available, 289
        for window sizes, 331–332
            (fig.)
    data, 746
    Ethernet and, 601
    hardware support for, 299–317
    instruction-level, 221–238

insufficient, 647
loop-carried dependences and,
    239–240
loop-level, 223, 238–240, 333
parallel loops, 224, 289
parallel processors, 747–750
    high-performance, 748–749
parity, 523
    bit-interleaved, 523
    block-interleaved distribution,
        523–525
    write bottleneck, 524
partial store ordering (PSO), 715
partial sums, B-47
Patterson, D., 115
payload, 565
PC-relative addressing, 74
Pentium. *See* Intel, Pentium
percentage of vectorization, 60
performance
    Alpha AXP 21064 memory hierar-
        chy, 465–466
    baseline, 23, 48, 57
    cache, 42–44, 384–390, 467
    cancelling branches, 172 (fig.)
    comparing and summarizing,
        23–28
    computer, 1–3
    control hazards and, 161
    cost and, 17
    CPU, 19, 374 (fig.)
    delayed branches, 172 (fig.)
    directory-based coherence proto-
        cols, 686–693
    disk, 541 (fig.)
    DLX FP pipeline, 197–199
    DLX integer pipeline, 177–178
    evaluating, 20–21
    execution stage, 346–348
    execution time and, 18
    fetch stage, 341–343
    file cache, 542–543
    functional requirement, 5
    instruction commit, 348
    I/O, 486, 504–521, 520
    loop, 227
    measuring, 19, 486
        I/O, 504–521

memory hierarchy, 468–469
    MFLOPS and, 46–47
    MIPS and, 44–46
    of parallel machines, 721–723
memory, 374 (fig.)
memory hierarchy
    measures, 468–469
    operating system impact on,
        469–470
microprocessor, 2 (fig.)
MIPS R4000 pipeline, 207–209
multiprogramming and OS work-
    load, 672–676
parallel program workload
    666–672
peak
    defined, 50
    observed performance and, 50
pipeline stalls and, 139–141
pipelining and, 136–138
PowerPC 620
    overall, 348–349
    pipeline, 339–341
of relaxed models, 719–720
reporting results, 23
sequential consistency and 710
snooping coherence protocols,
    666–676
SPARCstations with ATM,
    618–622
synchronization, 699–703
synthetic benchmarks and, 47
system, 19
UNIX file system, 539–548
vector, B-23–B-29
vector processor, B-29–B-35
write update vs. write invalidate
    protocols, 659–660
See also benchmarks
phase-ordering problem, 91
physical addresses, 441
physical caches, 423
pin grid array (PGA), 63
pipeline
    bubble, 141, 153
    control implementation, 156–161
    CPI, 36, 334
    as datapaths shifted in time, 133
        (fig.)

pipeline *(continued)*
  depth, 140, 141
  designing goal, 126
  DLX, 132–138
    extending for multicycle operations, 187–199
      FP, 197–199
      with unpipelined floating-point functional units, 188 (fig.)
  floating-point, 204–207
  freeze, 167
  hazards, 139–145
  MIPS R4000, 201–209
  organization, 230
  overhead, 137
  performance, 164
  PowerPC 620
    illustrated, 339 (fig.)
    performance of, 339–341
  precise exceptions, 183
  restartable, 181
  saving state, 182–183
  scheduling, 155–156, 223–228
  self-draining, 356
  speedup, 173
  stages, 218 (fig.)
  stall cycles from branches, 173
  stalls, 139–141
    performance and, 139–141
    for structural hazard, 144 (fig.)
  superscalar, 280 (fig.)
    problems, 280
  Tomasulo, dual-issue, 284 (fig.)
  See also pipeline interlock; pipelining
pipelined bus, 498
pipelined writes, 425–426
pipeline interlock, 153–154
  defined, 153
  detecting, 157
  load, 154 (fig.), 156, 157, 158
pipeline registers, 134–135
  defined, 134
  delay, 137
  field names, 135
pipelining, 124–213
  ALUs in, 131
  branches and. *See* control hazards

clock cycle time and, 138
datapath, 133–134
defined, 125
depth of vs. speedup, 211 (fig.)
DLX, 126–138
extensive, effects, 210
hazards, 139–145
implementation, 178–187
importance of, 211
instruction set design and, 199–200
latch delay, 138
limitation of, 241
multicycle operations and, 186–187
PC in, 133–134
performance issues, 136–138
result of, 126
software, 293–296
speedup from, 137, 138
  with stalls, 140–141
superpipelining, 201
VAX, 187
See also pipeline; pipe stage(s)
pipe stage(s)
  balanced, 140
  clock cycle, 132
  defined, 125
  events on, 136 (fig.)
  increasing performance and, 210
  operations in, 134
  PowerPC 620, 337–338
pitfalls
  adding functions to interconnection systems that violate end-to-end argument, 623
  basing write buffer size on memory speed and average mix of writes, 470
  comparing price of media with price of packages system, 548–549
  concentrating on peak performance and ignoring start-up overhead, B-35–B-36
  defined, 44
  designing "high-level" instruction set oriented to high-level language structure, 109–110

evaluating compile-time scheduler on basis of unoptimized code, 210–111
extensive pipelining can impact other aspects of design, 210
ignoring operating system impact on performance of memory hierarchy, 469
ignoring software overhead when determining message overhead, 623
increasing speed of floating-point unit without increasing memory bandwidth, A-66
increasing vector performance without comparable increases in scalar performance, B-36
measuring performance of multiprocessors by linear speedup, 734
moving functions from CPU to I/O processor to improve performance, 551–553
neglecting data distribution in distributed shared-memory machine, 738
not developing software to optimize for multiprocessors, 736–738
overall performance improvement by improving one aspect of multiple-issue processor, 351–352
reduction in CPI by increasing issue rate can lead to lower performance, 350–351
simulating instructions for accurate performance measures of memory hierarchy, 468–469
too small an address space, 467
unexpected execution sequences may cause unexpected hazards, 209–210
using bandwidth as only measure of bandwidth performance, 622–623
using TCP/IP as LAN protocol, 625
$-x$ is not the same as $0 -x$, A-66
See also fallacies

plastic quad flat pack (PQFP), 63
point-to-point communication, 580
poison bits, 304
    of destination register, 306
    saving/resetting, 307
    speculation with, 306–307
polling, 503
    wasted time, 574
polycyclic scheduling, 355
position independence, 82
POWERpath-2, 728–731
    bus transactions, 730
PowerPC 620, 335–349
    branch unit (BPU), 337
    buffering, 349
    commit stage, 338
    dynamic scheduling, 340
    execution stage, 338
        instruction delay, 346–347
        performance, 346–348
    fetch stage, 337
        instruction buffers, 342
        instruction loss, 342, 343 (fig.)
        performance, 341–343
    floating-point unit (FPU), 336
    FP registers, 326
    functional units, 336 (fig.)
        limitations, 348
    instruction decode stage, 337
    instruction issue stage, 337–338
        conflicts, 344
        IPC throughput rate for, 345
            (fig.)
        limitations, 343
        number of issues, 344 (fig.)
        stall sources, 346 (fig.)
    instruction-level parallelism, 349
    instruction throughput, 340
    integer function unit (MCFXU),
        335
    integer units (XSU0, XSU1), 335
    issue stage bottlenecks, 340
    load-store unit (LSU), 335–336
    performance
        execution stage, 346–348
        fetch stage, 341–343
        instruction commit, 348
        overview, 341 (fig.)

pipeline, 339–341
    summary, 348–349
pipeline
    illustrated, 329 (fig.)
    performance of, 339–341
pipe stage losses, 348
pipe stages, 337–338
    register renaming, 337
    register set extension, 337
    reorder buffer, 337
    structure, 336 (fig.)
PowerPC architecture, C-1
    addressing modes, C-3 (fig.)
    branch registers, C-18–C-19
    compare and conditional branch,
        C-8
    constant extension, C-5 (fig.)
    count register, C-18
    DLX instruction equivalents, C-6–
        C-8 (figs.)
    instructions unique to, C-18–C-19
    link register, C-18
    non-DLX instructions, C-10–C-11
        (figs.)
    summary, C-2
    See also PowerPC 620
precise exceptions, 183–184
    defined, 183
    maintaining, 194–197
    supporting, 183
    See also exceptions
predicated instructions, 300–303
    annulled, 302
    concept, 300
    control flow and, 303
    defined, 300
    example, 300
    limits of, 302–303
    moving time-critical instructions
        and, 301
    in RISC architectures, 303 (fig.)
    speculation and, 300
    speed penalty, 303
    usefulness of, 302
    using, 302
    See also instructions
prediction. See branch prediction;
    jump prediction

predict-not-taken scheme, 167 (fig.)
    MIPS R4000, 202
predictors
    (1,1), 269
    (2,2), 269
    correlating, 267, 268, 269, 271
    one-bit, 268, 269 (fig.)
    selective history, 324–325
    two-bit, 270
predict-taken scheme, 170 (fig.)
    accuracy of, 177 (fig.)
prefetching
    binding, 725–726
    buffer, 401
    cache, 402
    compiler-controlled, 402–404
    data, 401
    faulting, 403
    hardware, 400–402
    implementation, 726
    instruction, 401, 403
    memory bandwidth and, 402
    nonbinding, 402, 725–726
    nonblocking caches and, 725
    register, 402
    stream buffer, 463
present bit, 454
price
    average selling (ASP), 15
    competition and, 17
    components, 16 (fig.)
    cost vs., 14–17
    list, 15
    See also costs
principle of locality, 373, 375
private data, 655
Privileged Architecture Library (PAL)
    code, 461
procedure returns
    branch-target buffers and,
        276–277
    SPEC benchmarks and, 276
processes
    defined, 447
    kernel, 448
    number of, 518
    operation of, 447
    protecting, 448–449

process identifier tag (PID), 424
processor(s)
    adding, to network interface card,
        623–624
    array, 747
    compute-optimized, 606
    consistency, 715
        implementation, 718
    Cydra 5, 355
    dynamically scheduled, 241
    high-performance, 359 (fig.)
    ideal, 318–320
    I/O, 503–504, 551–553
    with lower CPIs, 349–350
    Multiflow, 355
    multiple-issue, 278–289, 351–352
    pipelined, high-speed, B-2
    realizable, ILP for, 330–335
    with scoreboard, 244 (fig.)
    speculative, 316, 368–369
    superscalar, 278–282
    vector, 288, B-1–B-41
    VLIW, 278, 284–285
    See also CPU; microprocessors;
        multiprocessor(s)
process switch, 447
program counter (PC), 82
    delayed branches and, 173
    instruction frequency changing,
        165 (fig.)
    in pipelining, 133–134
programs
    benchmark. *See* benchmarks
    correctness properties, 236
    data-race-free, 711
    dependences and, 230
    kernel. *See* kernels
    locally simple, 95
    for performance evaluation, 20–21
    real, 20
    with sparse matrices, B-27–B-29
    synchronized, 710–713
    typical, 110
protection, 447–457
    Alpha AXP 21064, 449–453
    Alpha vs. Pentium, 457
    Intel Pentium, 453–457
    requested level, 456

protocol(s)
    cache-coherence, 657
    coherence. *See* cache coherence
    defined, 567
    directory-based, 657, 679–693
    families, 608–609
        goal of, 610
        key to, 610
    sliding window, 613
    snooping, 657–658, 661, 662
        (fig.), 666–676
    stacks, 611
    TCP/IP, 609–613
    UDP/IP, 567
    write broadcast, 659
    write invalidate, 658, 659–662,
        664
    write update, 659–660
pseudo-associative caches, 398–400
    average memory access time,
        399–400
    defined, 398
    hit time, 399
    See also cache(s)

Q

queue(s)
    defined, 509
    discipline, 511
queuing, 507–516
    delay, 489
    exponential distribution and, 515
    locks, 704, 706–707
        barrier performance and, 707
        defined, 706
        example, 706–707
        functioning of, 706
        implementation, 707
    model, 514
    theory, 514–516, 537

R

radix-2 multiplication and division,
    A-3–A-7
radix-4 division, A-59–A-61

RAID, 522–525
    bit-interleaved parity (RAID 3),
        523
    block-interleaved distributed pari-
        ty (RAID 5), 523–525
    block-interleaved parity (RAID 4),
        524 (fig.)
    defined, 522
    disk performance, 548
    ideas and future directions, 554
    levels, 522 (fig.)
    mirroring (RAID 1), 523
RAMAC machine, 554–555
RAMBUS, 439
randomized routing, 594
random variables, 511
Rau, B. R., 355
RAW (read after write) data hazard,
    151, 157, 186, 211
    scoreboard and, 246
    stalls for, 197, 222
    See also data hazards; hazards
read ahead, 489
read fences, 713
read latency, hiding, 719
read operands stage, 242, 245
reads
    inhibit lines and, 730
    orderings, performed by single
        processor, 714
    See also writes
receiver overhead
    compute-optimized processors vs.,
        606
    defined, 569
recurrence, 290
recursive doubling, B-46
red-black Gauss-Seidel, 651
reduced instruction set computers.
    See RISC; RISC architectures
redundant array of inexpensive disks.
    See RAID
reference bit, 444
register allocation, 92
    for stack-allocated objects, 94
register files, 192–194
    FP, 192, 193
    separate, 194

register-memory architecture, 70
register-memory instructions, 61
register prefetch, 402
register-register architecture, 70
register renaming, 232–234, 251–261, 327
    defined, 232, 252
    fewer than unbounded number of registers, 328 (fig.)
    finite registers available for, 327 (fig.)
    performance and, 327
    PowerPC 620, 337
    using, 232–234
    See also Tomasulo's scheme
registers
    allocation algorithms, 92
    count, C-18
    DLX, 98
    finite, 326–328
    floating-point, 253
    general-purpose (GPR), 70, 71
    instruction (IR), 135
    link, C-18
    number of, 71
    pipeline, 134–135
    purpose of, 71
    saving, 84
    scalar, B-5
    shift, 192
    vector, B-4
    vector-mask, B-26
    VLR, B-16
    See also register renaming; register tags
register tags, 255, 256
    illustrated, 256 (fig.)
relaxed models, 714–720
    implementation of, 718–719
    orderings, 714–715
    performance of, 719–720, 721 (fig.)
    processor consistency, 715
    PSO, 715
    release consistency, 716
    TSO, 715
    weak consistency, 715–716
    See also multiprocessor(s)

release consistency, 716–719
    defined, 716
    implementation, 718–719
    See also relaxed modes
reliability
    defined, 521
    disk arrays, 521–522
relocation, 440
remainder
    floating-point, A-32–A-33
        for argument reduction, A-33
        computing, A-32–A-33
    See also arithmetic; division
remote memory, reference cost, 692
remote procedure call (RPC), 640
renaming, 306
    register, 232–234, 251–261, 327
    speculative instructions with, 307–308
reorder buffer, 309–310
    clearing, 316
    defined, 309
    flushing, 312
    full, 348
    with in-order instruction commit, 314
    number, 310
    PowerPC 620, 337
    See also buffers
repeat intervals. See initiation intervals
reproducibility, 23
requested word first, 413
requirements, functional 4–5
    list of, 5 (fig.)
reservation stations, 252
    as extended virtual registers, 255
    fields, 255
    illustrated, 256 (fig.)
    multiple loop execution and, 259
    not initiating, 348
    Tomasulo's scheme, 254–255
resource identifiers, 728–729
response time, 19
    defined, 18, 504
    mean, 534 (fig.)
    producer-server model, 504 (fig.)
    throughput vs., 505–507

transactions vs., 508 (fig.)
    X-Y plot of, 535 (fig.)
    See also execution time; input/output (I/O)
restartable, 181
restarts, early, 413–414
resuming events, 181
return address buffer, 277 (fig.)
ring topology, 585–586
    bisection bandwidth, 588
    defined, 585
    illustrated, 586 (fig.)
    mapping nodes in, 590
    token ring, 586
    See also switches
ripple-carry adders, A-2–A-3
RISC
    defined, 115
    instruction sets, C-24 (fig.)
    machine features, C-25 (fig.)
    papers, 212
    performance advantage, 116
RISC architectures
    addressing modes, C-3 (fig.)
    compare and conditional branch, C-8–C-9
    conditional instructions in, 303 (fig.)
    constant extension, C-5 (fig.)
    delayed/nondelayed branches, 172
    development of, 2
    DLX instruction equivalents, C-6–C-8 (figs.)
    HP PA-RISC, C-1
        instructions unique to, C-19–C-22
    instruction formats, C-4 (fig.)
    non-DLX instruction, C-10–C-11 (figs.)
    PowerPC, C-1
        instructions unique to, C-18–C-19
    roots of, 115
    SGI MIPS, C-1
        instructions unique to, C-13–C-15
    SPARC, C-1
        instructions unique to, C-15–C-18

RISC architectures *(continued)*
    summary, C-2 (fig.)
    survey of, C-1–C-25
RISC-I (RISC-II), 115–116
rotational latency, 488
round digit, A-18
rounding
    after rounding rule, A-38
    before rounding rule, A-38
    double, A-35
    floating-point multiplication,
        A-18–A-19
    modes, A-14
    overflow and, A-21
    rules for, A-20 (fig.)
    See also arithmetic
routers, 601
routing, 593–595
    adaptive, 594
    arrival order and, 595
    cut-through, 594
    destination-based, 594
    randomized, 594
    source-based, 594
    See also networks
row access strobe (RAS), 428

S

SAXPY loop, 365–366
scalable shared-memory architec-
    tures, 640, 679
scalar expansion, B-46
scaling, 722–723
    cost of, 736
    "free," 736
    memory constrained, 722
    time-constrained, 722
scatter-gather, B-27–B-28
scheduling
    branch-delay slots, 169 (fig.)
    code, 237
    critical path, 296–299
    data hazard, 155–156
    delayed branch, 170–171
    dynamic, 240–262, 282–284, 308,
        312, 354, 370

global code, 297
ILP, 357
instructions, 155–156
loops, 225
loop unrolling and, 226
pipeline, 155–156, 223–228
polycyclic, 355
static, 241, 279
superscalar, 280–281
trace, 285, 293, 296–299
VLIW, 285
See also branch(es)
scoreboard, 364
    CDC 6600, 242, 243, 250
    components, 247 (fig.)
    costs, 250
    DLX, 243, 244 (fig.)
    DLX processor with, 244 (fig.)
    functional unit status, 246–247
    functioning of, 243
    goal of, 243
    hazard separation, 246
    instruction progression control,
        246
    instruction status, 246
    instruction steps, 244–245
    limitations, 250–251
    number of entries, 250–251
    operand specifier information, 249
    parts, 246–247
    register result status, 247
    responsibility, 243
    tables, 248 (fig.), 249 (fig.)
scoreboarding, 242–251
    defined, 242
    Tomasulo's algorithm vs., 252,
        257
SCSI
    buses, 533, 537–538
    controller, 537
    defined, 555
SCSI-2
    bus transfer time, 532
    maximum IOPS per controller,
        531
    minimum number of strings, 532
    number of disks per string, 536
    suggested IOPs per string, 536

second-level caches, 416–422
    capacity misses and, 419
    conflict misses and, 420
    defined, 416–417
    direct-mapped, 420
    multilevel inclusion property, 421
    relative execution time and, 419
        (fig.), 421 (fig.)
    size of, 419
    See also cache(s)
seek distances
    sample measurements, 552 (fig.)
    seek time vs., 550 (fig.), 551 (fig.)
seek time, 488, 549
    average, 549
    seek distance vs., 550 (fig.), 551
        (fig.)
segmentation
    example, 442 (fig.)
    paging vs., 442
    virtual memory, 453–457
segments
    defined, 441
    paged, 443
selective history predictor, 324–325
self-draining pipelines, 356
self-scaling benchmark, 518–521
    defined, 518
    results comparison and, 520
    See also benchmarks
semantic clash, 109
semantic gap, 109
sender overhead, 569
sense-reversing, 701–702
    code for, 702 (fig.)
    defined, 701
sequential consistency, 709–711
    defined, 709
    if statements, 709 (fig.)
    implementation, 709–710, 715
    performance and, 710
    read fences, 713
    synchronized programs and,
        710–713
    write fences, 713
    See also cache coherence
serialization, 347
    locks and, 700

page table, 737
synchronization and, 703
write, 656, 695
serpentine recording, 554
servers
average service time, 534
defined, 509
utilization, 510, 534
set associative, 377
address portions, 378 (fig.)
data cache, 675 (fig.)
two-way cache, 388–389
See also cache(s)
settle time, 549
shadowing. See mirroring
shared data
defined, 655
migration of, 657
replication of, 657
See also multiprocessor(s)
shared memory, 640
centralized, 637–638, 654–677
distributed, 640, 677–693
supporting, 643
virtual, 644
virtual memory and, 726–727
See also memory; virtual memory
shared virtual memory (SVM), 727
shifting over zeros, A-47–A-49
short-circuiting. See forwarding
signed numbers, A-7–A-10
addition table, A-56 (fig.)
biased, A-7, A-15
Booth recoding and, A-8, A-9
(fig.), A-10
one's complement, A-7
overflow, A-7–A-8, A-10–A-11
representation, A-55
sign magnitude, A-7
two's complement, A-7–A-8
See also arithmetic
Silicon Graphics
Challenge multiprocessor,
728–733
MIPS. See MIPS architecture
single instruction stream, multiple
data stream (SIMD), 637
computers, 746–747

single instruction stream, single data
stream (SISD), 637
single-mode fibers, 577–578
small computer systems interface.
See SCSI; SCSI-2
smaller-is-faster rule, 39–40
Smith, J. E., 213, 354, 356
snooping protocols, 657–658
cache miss communication, 678
cache scheme performance
summary, 676–677
coherence, 666–676
finite-state controller, E-3 (fig.)
implementation, 661, E-1–E-6
intervention, E-4
pending write-back states,
E-2–E-4
summary, 662 (fig.)
See also cache coherence;
protocol(s)
software
multiprocessor architecture and,
736–738
overhead, ignoring, 623
pipelining, 293–296
advantages, 295–296
defined, 293
loop, 368
loop unrolling algorithms,
295–296
register management and, 295
trends, 6
See also hardware
software-pipelined loop, 293–296
execution pattern, 296 (fig.)
loop iterations, 294 (fig.)
See also loops
solid state disks (SSDs), 492–493
source-based routing, 594
SPARC. See Sun Microsystems
sparse matrices, B-27–B-29
scatter-gather operations, B-27
spatial locality, 41
defined, 38
SPEC89 benchmark, 48, 49, 57
branch prediction, 254–266
SPEC92 benchmark suite, 21, 57
baseline performance, 57

eqntott, 266
gcc, 49
integer benchmarks, 48
locality, 39 (fig.)
performance report, 24 (fig.)
in PowerPC 620 performance, 339
programs, 22 (fig.)
programs running on Alpha AXP
21064, 465 (fig.)
SPECfp92 benchmark, 48, 606
80x86 instruction mix, D-19–D-20
(figs.)
operand type distribution, D-16
(fig.)
performance for, 65 (fig.)
tuning parameters, 49 (fig.)
SPECint benchmark, 606
SPEC (System Performance and
Evaluation Cooperative), 57
procedure returns and, 276
SFS benchmark, 518, 519
See also benchmarks; SPEC89
benchmark; SPEC92 benchmark
suite
speculation
compiler, with hardware support,
303–308
conditional instructions and, 300
cost of, 306
defined, 237, 300
dynamic scheduling vs., 312
exceptions and, 316
hardware-based, 308–317
hardware-software cooperation
for, 304–306
implementation, 309
instruction execution steps, 310–
312
methods, 304
with poison bits, 304, 306–307
Tomasulo's algorithm hardware
and, 309
speculative execution, 316
memory system and, 458
See also execution
speculative instructions, 304–305
with renaming, 307–308
speculative processor, 316, 368–369
speed-matching buffers, 529

speedups, 29–30
  comparing, 31
  defined, 29
  finding, 30
  linear, 738–739
  overall, 30
  for parallel benchmarks, 732 (fig.)
  relative, 734
  scaled, 723
  superlinear, 645
Spice, 20
  floating-point operations in, 67
    (fig.)
  vectorization of, B-25
spin locks, 696–699
  accesses, 697
  advantages, 700
  cache-coherent mechanisms and,
    698
  caching, 697
  defined, 696
  delay, 703–704
  with exponential back-offs, 704
    (fig.)
  implementing, 697, 703–704
  procedure modification, 697
  scaling, 699
  uses, 696
  See also locks
split-transaction bus, 439
split transactions, 498
squared coefficient of variance, 512
SRAMs
  access time, B-37
  cost vs. access time, 492 (fig.)
  defined, 428
  design emphasis, 429
  refreshing and, 428
  See also DRAMs; main memory
SSBR (statically scheduled with
  blocking reads), 719
SS (statically scheduled), 720
stack, 92
  architecture, 70, 120
  growing/shrinking, 92
  organization, 113
stale data, 525–526
  problem parts, 525

stalls, 139–141
  branch delay and, 166–173
  branches and, 161–162
  completion, 348
  control, 237, 271–278
  control hazard, 161–162
  data hazards requiring, 152–155
  for DLX FP pipeline, 199 (fig.)
  floating-point, 197
  full buffer, 347
  in issue unit, 346 (fig.)
  length of, 230
  MIPS R4000, 207–208
  percentage of instructions causing,
    178 (fig.)
  percentage of loads resulting in,
    157 (fig.)
  per FP operation, 198 (fig.)
  for structural hazard, 144 (fig.)
standards
  bus, 500–501
  IEEE, floating point (754), 85, 97
  network, 597–598
  See also IEEE standards
Stanford MIPS architecture, 213, 355
state transition diagram
  for cache block, 682, 683 (fig.)
  for directory, 684 (fig.)
static random access memory. *See*
  SRAMs
static scheduling
  defined, 241
  register-to-register code sequences
    and, 282
  superscalar processors, 279
  using, 241
  See also scheduling
STC PowderHorn, 494, 495 (fig.)
sticky bit, A-19
storage devices
  magnetic disks, 486–492
  magnetic tapes, 493–494
  optical disks, 493
  SSDs, 492–493
  types of, 486–495
storage systems, 484–555
store conditional, 695
  advantage of, 696

Strecker, W. D., 114
Stretch, IBM, 212
striping, 521
strip mining
  DAXPY loop version, B-16
  defined, B-15
  loop running time, B-17
  vector processed with, B-16 (fig.)
  See also vector processors
structural hazards, 141–146
  average instruction time and, 144
  checking for, 194
  CPI and, 145
  defined, 139, 141
  example, 144, 145
  instances of, 141
  one memory port, 142 (fig.)
  pipeline stalled for, 144 (fig.)
  stalls, 222
sub-blocks, 412
  example, 413 (fig.)
SUB instruction, 146, 147, 152, 153,
  175
subset property, 724
Sun Microsystems
  network file service (NFS), 518
  SPARC 10/50, 547
  SPARC architecture, 116, 196, C-1
    addressing modes, C-3 (fig.)
    compare and conditional
      branch, C-8
    constant extension, C-5 (fig.)
    DLX instruction equivalents,
      C-6–C-8 (figs.)
    fast traps, C-16
    instruction formats, C-4 (fig.)
    instructions unique to,
      C-15–C-18
    LISP/Smalltalk support, C-16
    multiply-step instruction, A-12
    non-DLX instructions,
      C-10–C-11 (figs.)
    overlapping integer and float-
      ing-point operations,
      C-16–C-17
    register windows, C-15–C-16
    summary, C-2 (fig.)
    two-least significant bits, C-17
      (fig.)

SPARCCenter, 737
SPARCstation-1, 540 (fig.)
SPARCstation-2, 606
SPARCstation-10, 540 (fig.), 541, 548
    organization, 614 (fig.)
SPARCstation-20, 606
SPARCstation, performance with ATM, 618–622
SuperSPARC processor, 350, 351, 614
UNIX, 424
superbanks
    banks vs., 435 (fig.)
    defined, 435
superpipelining, 201
superscalar processors, 278–282
    cache ports and, 457–458
    clock cycle instructions, 279
    DLX, 279–282
    dynamic issue capability, 279
    dynamic scheduling, 282–284
    load and store instructions, 283
    load-store units, 283
    loop unrolling, 280–281
    naming of, 356
    pipeline in operation, 280 (fig.)
    pipeline problems, 280
    problems with, 288–289
    register port problem, 280
    scheduling, 280–281
    static scheduling, 279
    two-issue, 282–284
    See also processor(s)
SuperSPARC, 350, 614
    performance, 351
    See also Sun Microsystems
supervisor process. See kernel process
switched Ethernet, 604
switches, 579–591
    ATM, 618
    multistage, 583
    names for, 580
    shared medium vs., 579–583
    single-chip, 583
    store-and-forward, 594
    topology, 583–591
        in commercial MPPs, 587 (fig.)

crossbar, 583
fat tree, 583, 585 (fig.)
illustrations, 584 (fig.)
Omega, 583
ring, 585–586
See also networks
switching
circuit, 592
packet, 592
See also switches
Synapse N+1, 750
synchronization, 694–708
    acquire operation, 711
    barrier, 700–703
    developments in, 752
    hardware primitives, 694–696
        atomic exchange, 694–695
        fetch-and-increment, 695, 707–708
        for large-scale machines, 706–708
    implementation, 694
    for large-scale machines, 703–708
    library, 713
    performance, 699–703
    contention and, 703
    program, 710–713
    release operation, 711
    serialization and, 703
    software implementations, 703–706
    user level, 694
    See also cache coherence; multiprocessor(s)
synchronous buses, 498–499
synchronous events, 181
synonyms, 424
synthetic benchmarks, 20–21
    performance for real programs and, 47
    See also benchmarks
system area networks (SANs), 628
system call, 448
system CPU time, 19
system-level file server (SFS) benchmark, 518, 519
    defined, 518
    performance, 519 (fig.)
system performance, 19

T

tags, register, 255, 256
tailgating, B-34
Tanenbaum, A. S., 114
target address, 276
target instructions, 276
TCP/IP, 609–613
    datagram, 611
    headers, 612–613 (fig.)
    using as LAN protocol, 625
technology
    cost improvements, 2–3
    implementation, 7–8
    improvements, 1–3
    integrated circuit logic, 7
    magnetic disk, 7
    performance growth rates, 1–3
temporal locality, 41
    defined, 38
terminating events, 181
Texas Instruments TI 8847, A-61–A-64
    chip layout, A-64 (fig.)
    chip summary, A-61 (fig.)
    division by iteration, A-63
Thinking Machines. See CM-5
Thornton, T. E., 354
thrashing, 393
throughput, 486
    defined, 18, 125, 568
    instruction, 136
    I/O, 504
    producer-server model, 504 (fig.)
    response time vs., 505–507
ticks. See clock cycles
time-constrained scaling, 722
time-division multiplexing, 592
time of flight, 568
timesharing, 447
timing verifiers, 35
T junction, 577
TLB. See translation buffers
token ring topology, 586
Tomasulo, R., 251
Tomasulo's scheme, 251–261, 354, 354
    advantages, 257

Tomasulo's scheme *(continued)*
  algorithm steps, 259 (fig.)
  DLX FP unit using, 253 (fig.)
  hazard detection logic distribution, 257
  ILP enhancement in, 261
  instruction steps, 254
  load and store instructions and, 258, 260
  multiple loop execution in, 259
  register tags, 255, 256
  scoreboarding vs., 252, 257
  source operand buffering, 260
  WAW/WAR hazards and, 257
  See also register renaming; reservation stations
total store ordering (TSO), 715, 720
toy benchmarks, 20
trace
  compacting, 298
  defined, 297
trace compaction, 297
trace scheduling, 285, 293, 296–299
  advantages, 297
  constraints, 298
  See also scheduling
trace selection, 296–297
traffic density, 510
trailer, 565
transaction processing (TP)
  benchmarks. 516–517
  defined, 516
transactions, 505–507
  defined, 505
  parts of, 506
  per hour, 506
  response time vs., 508 (fig.)
  user, 507 (fig.)
  See also transaction processing (TP)
transaction time, 505
transfers, 80
transfer time, 488–489
translation buffers, 445–446
  Alpha AXP 21064, 445–446, 449–453
  cache-address-tag memory and, 445

defined, 443
  misses, 447
  See also address translation
transmission control protocol/internet protocol. *See* TCP/IP
transmission time, 568
transport latency, 569
trends
  computer usage, 6
  cost, 8–17
  implementation technology, 7–8
  software, 6
Trojan horses, 453, 456
twisted pair, 577–578
  bandwidth, 577
  defined, 577
  illustrated, 577 (fig.)
  See also networks, media
2:1 cache rule of thumb, 396
two-bit prediction, 263–266
  correlating predictor vs., 271
  prediction accuracy, 265–266 (fig.)
  See also branch prediction
two-issue processor, 282–284
two-level predictors. *See* correlating predictors

U

UDP/IP protocol, 567
UMAs (uniform memory access), 638
unbiased exponents, A-15
underflow, A-37–A-38
  gradual, A-15
  occurrences of, A-65
  signaling, A-38
  See also arithmetic; overflow
underpipelined, 217
UNIVAC I computer, 55
University of Illinois Cedar project, 751
UNIX file system
  performance, 539–548
  workloads, 544
unpacked decimal, 85
unpacking, 85
use bit, 444

user CPU time, 19
user-maskable events, 181

V

vampire tap, 577
variables
  random, 511
  shared, 708
VAX. *See* DEC
vector instructions, 223
  access pattern, B-2
  convoys, B-9–B-10
    defined, B-9
    reducing number of, B-19
    starting/last result times, B-11 (fig.)
  DLXV, B-7 (fig.)
  multiple, B-10
  properties, B-2
vector-length register (VLR), B-15–B-17
vector-mask control, B-26
vector-mask register, B-26
vector processors, 288, B-1–B-41
  architecture, B-3–B-15
  DAXPY, B-7–B-8
  defined, B-2
  design trends, B-38–B-39
  DLXV, B-3–B-7, B-27
    enhanced, B-33–B-35
    peak performance, B-30–B-31
    start-up penalties, B-12 (fig.)
    stride, B-20
    sustained performance, B-31–B-33
  Linpack benchmark, B-31–B-33
  memory addresses, B-14 (fig.)
  memory banks, B-13
    conflicts, B-21
    number of, B-21
  memory-memory, B-3
  overhead, B-10–B-11
  performance, B-29–B-35
    measures of, B-29–B-30
    on enhanced DLXV, B-33–B-35

peak, B-30–B-31
start-up overhead and, B-35–B-36
sustained, on Linpack benchmark, B-31–B-33
pipelined scalar unit, B-3
SAXPY, B-7
scatter-gather, B-27–B-28
vector-register, B-3–B-9
characteristics, B-6 (fig.)
components, B-4–B-5
start-up penalties, B-12
structure, B-4 (fig.)
vector length, B-15
vector unit, B-3
See also processor(s)
vector(s)
execution time, B-9–B-12
functional units, B-5
index, B-27
initiation rate, B-9
length, B-9
control, B-15–B-19
execution time vs., B-19 (fig.)
overhead time vs., B-19 (fig.)
load-store unit, B-5, B-13–B-15
loops, B-29
memory systems, B-13–B-15
performance, B-23–B-29
memory bandwidth and, B-36–B-37
scalar performance and, B-36
registers, B-4
starting address, B-21
start-up time, B-11
stride, B-20–B-21
defined, B-20
nonunit, B-20
See also chaining; vector processors
very long instruction word processors. *See* VLIW processors
victim caches, 397–398
defined, 398
placement of, 398 (fig.)
See also cache(s)
video RAM (VRAM), 439

virtual addresses, 422–425
bits, mapping, 425
defined, 441
I/O and, 424
mapping, 444 (fig.)
Alpha, 451 (fig.)
See also address(es)
virtual caches, 423
size vs. miss rate, 423 (fig.)
See also cache(s)
virtual channel identifier (VCI), 615
virtual channels, 615
virtual circuits, 594
virtual DMA, 527
virtual functions, 82
virtual memory, 439–457, 472
caches vs., 441
defined, 439
distributed (DVM), 727
DMA and, 527
misses, block replacement and, 443–444
paged, 449–453
parameter ranges, 441 (fig.)
protection of, 447–457
purpose of, 440
segmented, 453–457
shared memory and, 726–727
shared (SVM), 727
See also cache(s); memory; pages; page table
virtual path identifier (VPI), 615
virtual paths, 615–616
VLIW processors, 278, 284–285
binary code compatibility, 288
code size, 288
five-unit, 287
functional units, 285
instruction issue hardware, 287
instructions, 285, 286 (fig.)
loop unrolling, 285
problems with, 288–289
read/write ports, 287
trace scheduling, 285
See also processor(s)
von Neumann, J., 54
von Neumann computer, 53–54

W

wafers, 10
8-inch, 11 (fig.)
number of dies and, 12
yield, 12
See also dies; integrated circuits (ICs)
waiting line. *See* queues; queuing
Wall, D. W., 358
Wallace tree, A-67
defined, A-54
multiplier, A-56 (fig.)
WANs
defined, 564
examples, 602 (fig.)
history of, 626–627
node failures and, 598
standards, 598
See also LANs; networks
WAR (write after read) data hazard, 151–152, 245, 251
eliminating, 258
scoreboard and, 246
stalls, 222
Tomasulo's scheme and, 257
See also data hazards; hazards
WAW (write after write) data hazard, 151, 193, 251
eliminating, 258
stalls, 222
Tomasulo's scheme and, 257
See also data hazards; hazards
weak ordering, 715–716
weighted arithmetic mean, 26
execution times, 26 (fig.)
weightings in, 28
weighted mean time, 511
Weitek 3364, A-61–A-65
addition algorithm, A-63
arithmetic functions on, A-62–A-63
chip layout, A-65 (fig.)
chip summary, A-61 (fig.)
Whetstone, 20
creation of, 56
floating-point loops, 47

Whetstone (continued)
    floating-point operations, 62 (fig.)
    See also benchmarks
Whirlwind project, 55
wide area networks. See WANs
Wilkes, M.V., 473
Winchester disk, 554
windows, 250–251
    defined, 250, 321, 596, 613
    packet, 596
    size of, 321
        effect, 323 (fig.)
        for FP programs, 331
        for integer programs, 331
        large, 322
        limitation, 320–323
        parallelism available for, 331
            (fig.), 332 (fig.)
        reducing, 321, 322 (fig.)
        small, 322
working set effect, 667
workstations
    clusters of (COWs), 743
    IBM Power-2, 3, 350
    networked, 760
    networks of (NOWs), 743
wormhole routing. See cut-through
    routing
wrapped fetch, 413
write allocate, 380
write around, 380
write back cache, 379, 380, 412, 526
    file cache, 544
    invalidate protocol implementa-
        tion, 660–662
    See also cache(s)
write broadcast protocol, 659
write buffer, 380, 464
    empty, 412
    size of, 470
    See also buffers
write fences, 713
write invalidate protocol, 658, 756
    cache-coherence, 664 (fig.)
    implementation, 660–662
    performance, 659–660
    write-back caches and, 660–662
    See also protocol(s)

write merging, 382
    illustrated, 383 (fig.)
write result stage
    scoreboard, 245
    speculative instruction, 311
    Tomasulo algorithm, 254
    Tomasulo dual-issue pipeline, 284
        (fig.)
writes
    back-to-back, 432
    for client/server computing,
        547–548
    file cache effectiveness for, 546
    orderings, performed by single
        processor, 714
    pipelined, 425–426
    See also reads
write serialization, 656
    simultaneous exchanges and, 695
write through cache, 379, 380, 411,
    526
    file cache, 544
write update protocol, 659, 756
    memory consistency models and,
        660
    performance, 659–660
    See also protocol(s)

                    X

XOR instruction, 146

                    Y

yield, 8
    die, 12–13
    wafer, 12

                    Z

Zuse, K., 55

---

special
a GPR

arithmetic trap on overflow

ed and unsigned

ds must be FP registers; all operations

or immediate
lf of register with immediate
variable form (S__); shifts are shift left logical,

T,GT,LE,GE,EQ,NE

jumps; PC-relative or through register

ual to zero; 16-bit offset from PC+4
the FP status register and branch; 16-bit offset fr... PC+
from PC+4 (J) or target in register (JR) ... register (JALR)
ve PC+4 in R31, target is PC-relative (JAL...
rating system at a vectored address
ser code from an exception; restore user

ations on DP and SP formats

DP, SP numbers
otract DP, SP numbers
Multiply DP, SP floating point
Divide DP, SP floating point
Convert instructions: CVTx2y converts from type x to type y, where x and y are I (integer), D (double precision), or F (single precision). Both operands are FPRs.

DP and SP compares: "__" = LT,GT,LE,GE,EQ,NE; sets bit in FP status register

DLX Instruction Set, Description Notation, and DLX Pipeline Structure

DLX Standard Instruction Set

Instruction type/opcode	Instruction meaning
Data transfers	**Move data between registers and memory, or between the integer and FP or** … **registers; only memory address mode is 16-bit displacement + contents of** …
LB, LBU, SB	Load byte, load byte unsigned, store byte
LH, LHU, SH	Load half word, load half word unsigned, store half word
LW, SW	Load word, store word (to/from integer registers)
LF, LD, SF, SD	Load SP float, load DP float, store SP float, store DP float
MOVI2S, MOVS2I	Move from/to GPR to/from a special register
MOVF, MOVD	Copy one FP register or a DP pair to another register or pair
MOVFP2I, MOVI2FP	Move 32 bits from/to FP registers to/from integer registers or pair
Arithmetic/logical	**Operations on integer or logical data in GPRs; signed** …
ADD, ADDI, ADDU, ADDUI	Add, add immediate (all immediates are 16 bits); signed and unsigned
SUB, SUBI, SUBU, SUBUI	Subtract, subtract immediate; signed and unsigned; oper…
MULT, MULTU, DIV, DIVU	Multiply and divide, signed and unsigned; operands … take and yield 32-bit values
AND, ANDI	And, and immediate
OR, ORI, XOR, XORI	Or, or immediate, exclusive or, exclusiv…
LHI	Load high immediate—loads upper h…
SLL, SRL, SRA, SLLI, SRLI, SRAI	Shifts: both immediate (S__I) an… right logical, right arithmetic
S__, S__I	Set conditional: "__" may be …
Control	**Conditional branches and** …
BEQZ, BNEZ	Branch GPR equal/not e…
BFPT, BFPF	Test comparison bit …
J, JR	Jumps: 26-bit off…
JAL, JALR	Jump and link: …
TRAP	Transfer to o…
RFE	Return to …
Floating point	**FP oper…**
ADDD, ADDF	Add …
…BD, SUBF	S…
MULTF	…

Related titles from Morgan Kaufmann

The DLX Instruction Set Architecture Handbook, by Philip M. Sailer and David R. Kaeli (ISBN 1-55860-371-9)

Solutions to Selected Exercises in Computer Architecture: A Quantitative Approach, Second Edition, by Thomas Willis and Allan Knies (ISBN 1-55860-406-5)

Computer Organization and Design: The Hardware Software Approach, by David A. Patterson and John L. Hennessy (ISBN 1-55860-428-6)

See MIPS Run, by Dominic Sweetman (ISBN 1-55860-343-3)

Readings in Computer Architecture, edited by Mark D. Hill, Norman P. Jouppi, and Gurindar S. Sohi (ISBN 1-55860-539-8)

Parallel Computer Architecture: A Hardware/Software Approach, by David E. Culler and Jaswinder Pal Singh with Anoop Gupta (ISBN 1-55860-343-3)

Scalable Shared-Memory Multiprocessing, by Daniel E. Lenoski and Wolf-Dietrich Weber (ISBN 1-55860-315-8)

Cache and Memory Hierarchy Design: A Performance Directed Approach, by Steven A. Przybylski (ISBN 1-55860-136-3)

The Student's Guide to VHDL, by Peter J. Ashenden (ISBN 1-55860-520-7)

The Designer's Guide to VHDL, by Peter J. Ashenden (ISBN 1-55860-270-4)

Logical Effort: Designing Fast CMOS Circuits. by Ivan Sutherland, Bob Sproull, and David Harris (ISBN 1-55860-557-6)

Computing Perspectives, by Maurice V. Wilkes (ISBN 1-55860-317-4)

For more computer architecture titles, please visit our catalog at http://www.mkp.com.

DLX Instruction Set, Description Notation, and DLX Pipeline Structure

DLX Standard Instruction Set

Instruction type/opcode	Instruction meaning
Data transfers	**Move data between registers and memory, or between the integer and FP or special registers; only memory address mode is 16-bit displacement + contents of a GPR**
LB, LBU, SB	Load byte, load byte unsigned, store byte
LH, LHU, SH	Load half word, load half word unsigned, store half word
LW, SW	Load word, store word (to/from integer registers)
LF, LD, SF, SD	Load SP float, load DP float, store SP float, store DP float
MOVI2S, MOVS2I	Move from/to GPR to/from a special register
MOVF, MOVD	Copy one FP register or a DP pair to another register or pair
MOVFP2I, MOVI2FP	Move 32 bits from/to FP registers to/from integer registers
Arithmetic/logical	**Operations on integer or logical data in GPRs; signed arithmetic trap on overflow**
ADD, ADDI, ADDU, ADDUI	Add, add immediate (all immediates are 16 bits); signed and unsigned
SUB, SUBI, SUBU, SUBUI	Subtract, subtract immediate; signed and unsigned
MULT, MULTU, DIV, DIVU	Multiply and divide, signed and unsigned; operands must be FP registers; all operations take and yield 32-bit values
AND, ANDI	And, and immediate
OR, ORI, XOR, XORI	Or, or immediate, exclusive or, exclusive or immediate
LHI	Load high immediate—loads upper half of register with immediate
SLL, SRL, SRA, SLLI, SRLI, SRAI	Shifts: both immediate (S__I) and variable form (S__); shifts are shift left logical, right logical, right arithmetic
S__, S__I	Set conditional: "__" may be LT, GT, LE, GE, EQ, NE
Control	**Conditional branches and jumps; PC-relative or through register**
BEQZ, BNEZ	Branch GPR equal/not equal to zero; 16-bit offset from PC+4
BFPT, BFPF	Test comparison bit in the FP status register and branch; 16-bit offset from PC+4
J, JR	Jumps: 26-bit offset from PC+4 (J) or target in register (JR)
JAL, JALR	Jump and link: save PC+4 in R31, target is PC-relative (JAL) or a register (JALR)
TRAP	Transfer to operating system at a vectored address
RFE	Return to user code from an exception; restore user mode
Floating point	**FP operations on DP and SP formats**
ADDD, ADDF	Add DP, SP numbers
SUBD, SUBF	Subtract DP, SP numbers
MULTD, MULTF	Multiply DP, SP floating point
DIVD, DIVF	Divide DP, SP floating point
CVTF2D, CVTF2I, CVTD2F, CVTD2I, CVTI2F, CVTI2D	Convert instructions: CVTx2y converts from type x to type y, where x and y are I (integer), D (double precision), or F (single precision). Both operands are FPRs.
__D, __F	DP and SP compares: "__" = LT, GT, LE, GE, EQ, NE; sets bit in FP status register